ELECTRONIC AND RADIO ENGINEERING

McGraw-Hill Electrical and Electronic Engineering Series

FREDERICK EMMONS TERMAN, *Consulting Editor*

W. W. HARMAN and J. G. TRUXAL, *Associate Consulting Editors*

Bailey and Gault · ALTERNATING-CURRENT MACHINERY

Beranek · ACOUSTICS

Bruns and Saunders · ANALYSIS OF FEEDBACK CONTROL SYSTEMS

Cage · THEORY AND APPLICATION OF INDUSTRIAL ELECTRONICS

Cauer · SYNTHESIS OF LINEAR COMMUNICATION NETWORKS, VOLS. I AND II

Cuccia · HARMONICS, SIDEBANDS, AND TRANSIENTS IN COMMUNICATION
    ENGINEERING

Cunningham · INTRODUCTION TO NONLINEAR ANALYSIS

Eastman · FUNDAMENTALS OF VACUUM TUBES

Evans · CONTROL-SYSTEM DYNAMICS

Feinstein · FOUNDATIONS OF INFORMATION THEORY

Fitzgerald and Higginbotham · BASIC ELECTRICAL ENGINEERING

Fitzgerald and Kingsley · ELECTRIC MACHINERY

Geppert · BASIC ELECTRON TUBES

Glasford · FUNDAMENTALS OF TELEVISION ENGINEERING

Happell and Hesselberth · ENGINEERING ELECTRONICS

Harman · FUNDAMENTALS OF ELECTRONIC MOTION

Harrington · INTRODUCTION TO ELECTROMAGNETIC ENGINEERING

Hayt · ENGINEERING ELECTROMAGNETICS

Hessler and Carey · FUNDAMENTALS OF ELECTRICAL ENGINEERING

Hill · ELECTRONICS IN ENGINEERING

Johnson · TRANSMISSION LINES AND NETWORKS

Kraus · ANTENNAS

Kraus · ELECTROMAGNETICS

LePage · ANALYSIS OF ALTERNATING-CURRENT CIRCUITS

LePage and Seely · GENERAL NETWORK ANALYSIS

Millman and Seely · ELECTRONICS

Millman and Taub · PULSE AND DIGITAL CIRCUITS

Rodgers · INTRODUCTION TO ELECTRIC FIELDS

Rüdenberg · TRANSIENT PERFORMANCE OF ELECTRIC POWER SYSTEMS

Ryder · ENGINEERING ELECTRONICS

Seely · ELECTRON-TUBE CIRCUITS

Seely · ELECTRONIC ENGINEERING

Seely · INTRODUCTION TO ELECTROMAGNETIC FIELDS

Seely · RADIO ELECTRONICS

Siskind · DIRECT-CURRENT MACHINERY

Skilling · ELECTRIC TRANSMISSION LINES

Skilling · TRANSIENT ELECTRIC CURRENTS

Spangenberg · FUNDAMENTALS OF ELECTRON DEVICES

Spangenberg · VACUUM TUBES

Stevenson · ELEMENTS OF POWER SYSTEM ANALYSIS

Storer · PASSIVE NETWORK SYNTHESIS

Terman · ELECTRONIC AND RADIO ENGINEERING

Terman and Pettit · ELECTRONIC MEASUREMENTS

Thaler · ELEMENTS OF SERVOMECHANISM THEORY

Thaler and Brown · SERVOMECHANISM ANALYSIS

Thompson · ALTERNATING-CURRENT AND TRANSIENT CIRCUIT ANALYSIS

Truxal · AUTOMATIC FEEDBACK CONTROL SYSTEM SYNTHESIS

ELECTRONIC AND RADIO ENGINEERING

FREDERICK EMMONS TERMAN

Professor of Electrical Engineering
Dean of the School of Engineering
Stanford University

Assisted by

ROBERT ARTHUR HELLIWELL

Associate Professor of Electrical Engineering
Stanford University

JOSEPH MAYO PETTIT

Professor of Electrical Engineering
Stanford University

DEAN ALLEN WATKINS

Associate Professor of Electrical Engineering
Stanford University

WILLIAM RALPH RAMBO

Associate Director, Applied Electronics Laboratory
Stanford University

FOURTH EDITION

McGRAW-HILL BOOK COMPANY, INC.

New York   Toronto   London

1955

PREFACE

This fourth edition has the same objective as the three prior editions, namely, to provide a text and reference book that summarizes in easily understandable terms those principles and techniques which are the basic tools of the electronic and radio engineer. In keeping with current trends, increased emphasis is placed on the general techniques of electronics, without regard to the extent of their use in radio systems. This change is reflected in the new title, "Electronic and Radio Engineering," which is more descriptive of the subject matter actually covered in the present volume than is the previous title, "Radio Engineering."

The keynote continues to be thorough coverage combined with a presentation that allows the reader to study a particular topic without having to read the entire book. The level of presentation, particularly the mathematical level, remains unchanged. Thus the present volume is designed to serve as a text and reference for the same clientele that found the previous editions so useful.

To keep pace with a rapidly advancing technology, new material has been added in practically every chapter. More than half the illustrations are new, and all have been redrawn to conform to new graphic standards. A new chapter dealing with microwave tubes makes available for the first time an explanation in simple language of the basic mechanism of operation of traveling-wave tubes and backward-wave oscillators (carcinotrons). In the treatment of wideband video and tuned amplifiers, primary emphasis is placed on the rise time, overshoot, and sag, since these characteristics are more indicative of the performance under actual conditions than is the older approach in terms of amplitude and phase behavior as a function of frequency. The material on nonlinear waveforms and pulse techniques has been greatly expanded to provide more complete coverage of this important aspect of electronics. The chapter on television has been thoroughly revised, and a compact and simple explanation is given of the system of color television now standard in the United States. Increased attention is also placed on propagation phenomena involving the troposphere.

Of particular importance is the chapter on Transistors and Related Semiconductor Devices, one of the longest in the book. Here is presented a simple, straightforward explanation of the basic phenomena occurring inside the transistor, and of how these phenomena lead to the terminal characteristics. This treatment is such that it can be understood by undergraduate students; at the same time, it is sufficiently complete and fundamental to provide a firm foundation for further study of this new and very important subject.

Special attention has been given to the needs of the teacher. Because of the growth of electronics, it is no longer possible to cover every important topic adequately in a one-year course. "Electronic and Radio Engineering" provides the instructor with an opportunity to select those topics which he himself wishes to emphasize, and at the same time provides the student with a reference book of comprehensive coverage and continuing value. It will be observed that the book breaks down into three distinct parts, namely, a group of chapters dealing with circuits (components, resonant circuits, transmission lines, waveguides, and cavity resonators); a group of chapters concerned with the fundamentals of electronic engineering (vacuum tubes, transistors, amplifiers, oscillators, modulators, detectors, nonlinear waveforms, etc.), which are the heart of the book; and a concluding group of chapters concerned with radio systems and radio engineering (antennas, propagation, transmitters, receivers, television, radar, and radio aids to navigation). Thus an instructor can, if he desires, concentrate on the material concerned with fundamental electronics and regard the remaining subject matter as available to the student, should he need to extend his knowledge at a future date. Alternatively, the instructor can choose to cover a series of selected topics, for example, waveguides, wideband systems, pulse circuits, television, etc. Another possibility is to concentrate on the material concerned primarily with radio systems. Many other combinations, are, of course, possible.

An important feature for the teacher is the more than 1250 Problems and Exercises. Many of these involve numerical calculations, but more than half of them are thought questions that will require the student to give further consideration to topics covered in the text. Such Exercises can be used to extend and solidify the student's knowledge; they are also suggestive of questions suitable for use on examinations. The number of Problems and Exercises is so large that the same problem need not be assigned to a class more often than once every two or three years.

The collaborators listed on the title page have made important contributions to the preparation of this volume. Dr. Helliwell worked on the sections dealing with ionospheric propagation, and Dr. Pettit is in large measure responsible for the general character of the chapter dealing with transistors and semiconductors. The treatment of traveling-wave tubes and backward-wave oscillators is due to Dr. Watkins. William Rambo prepared the background material used in revising the presentation on radar. In addition, acknowledgment is made to Dr. B. H. Wadia, Bruno Ludovici, and Arthur Vassilaides, graduate students at Stanford, for assistance in preparing illustrations.

FREDERICK EMMONS TERMAN

CONTENTS

CHAPTER 1

THE ELEMENTS OF A SYSTEM
OF RADIO COMMUNICATION

1-1. Radio Waves. Electrical energy that has escaped into free space exists in the form of electromagnetic waves. These waves, which are commonly called radio waves, travel with the velocity of light and consist of magnetic and electric fields that are at right angles to each other and also at right angles to the direction of travel. If these electric and magnetic fluxes could actually be seen, the wave would have the appearance indicated in Fig. 1-1. One-half of the electrical energy contained

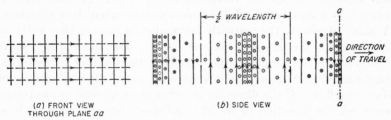

(*a*) FRONT VIEW
THROUGH PLANE *aa*

(*b*) SIDE VIEW

Fig. 1-1. Front and side views of a vertically polarized wave. The solid lines represent electric flux; the dotted lines and the circles indicate magnetic flux.

in the wave exists in the form of electrostatic energy, while the remaining half is in the form of magnetic energy.

The essential properties of a radio wave are the frequency, intensity, direction of travel, and plane of polarization. The radio waves produced by an alternating current will vary in intensity with the frequency of the current and will therefore be alternately positive and negative as shown in Fig. 1-1*b*. The distance occupied by one complete cycle of such an alternating wave is equal to the velocity of the wave divided by the number of cycles that are sent out each second and is called the wavelength. The relation between wavelength λ in meters and frequency f in cycles per second is therefore

$$\lambda = \frac{300,000,000}{f} \tag{1-1}$$

The quantity 300,000,000 is the velocity of light in meters per second. The frequency is ordinarily expressed in kilocycles, abbreviated kc, or in megacycles, abbreviated Mc. A low-frequency wave is seen from Eq.

1

(1-1) to have a long wavelength, while a high frequency corresponds to a short wavelength.

The strength of a radio wave is measured in terms of the voltage stress produced in space by the electric field of the wave, and it is usually expressed in microvolts stress per meter. Since the actual stress produced at any point by an alternating wave varies sinusoidally from instant to instant, it is customary to consider the intensity of such a wave to be the effective value of the stress, which is 0.707 times the maximum stress in the atmosphere during the cycle. The strength of the wave measured in terms of microvolts per meter of stress in space is also exactly the same voltage that the magnetic flux of the wave induces in a conductor 1 m long when sweeping across this conductor with the velocity of light.

The minimum field strength required to give satisfactory reception of a wave depends upon a number of factors, such as frequency, type of signal involved, and amount of interference present. Under some conditions radio waves having signal strengths as low as 0.1 μv per m are usable. Occasionally signal strengths exceeding 1000 μv per m are required to ensure entirely satisfactory reception at all times. In most cases the weakest useful signal strength lies somewhere between these extremes.

A plane parallel to the mutually perpendicular lines of the electric and electromagnetic flux is called the wavefront. The wave always travels in a direction at right angles to the wavefront, but whether it goes forward or backward depends upon the relative direction of the lines of magnetic and electric flux. If the direction of either the magnetic or electric flux is reversed, the direction of travel is reversed; but reversing both sets of flux has no effect.

The direction of the electric lines of flux is called the direction of polarization of the wave. If the electric flux lines are vertical, as shown in Fig. 1-1, the wave is vertically polarized; when the electric flux lines are horizontal and the electromagnetic flux lines are vertical, the wave is horizontally polarized.

Propagation of Radio Waves of Different Frequencies. As radio waves travel away from their point of origin, they become attenuated or weakened. This is due in part to the fact that the waves spread out.

In addition, however, energy may be absorbed from the waves by the ground or by the ionized regions in the upper atmosphere termed the ionosphere, and the waves may also be reflected or refracted by the ionosphere, or by conditions within the lower atmosphere, or by the ground. The resulting situation is quite complex and differs greatly for radio waves of different frequencies, as shown in Table 1-1, which summarizes the behavior of different classes of radio waves.

1-2. Radiation of Electrical Energy. Every electrical circuit carrying alternating current radiates a certain amount of electrical energy in the form of electromagnetic waves, but the amount of energy thus radiated is extremely small unless all the dimensions of the circuit approach the order of magnitude of a wavelength.   Thus, a power line carrying 60-cycle current with a 20-ft spacing between conductors will radiate practically no energy because a wavelength at 60 cycles is more than 3000 miles, and 20 ft is negligible in comparison.   On the other hand, a coil 20 ft in diameter and carrying a 2000-kc current will radiate a considerable amount of energy because 20 ft is comparable with the 150-m

TABLE 1-1
CLASSIFICATION OF RADIO WAVES

Class	Frequency range	Wavelength range	Propagation characteristics	Typical uses
Very low frequency (VLF)	10–30 kc	30,000–10,000 m	Low attenuation at all times of day and of year; characteristics very reliable	Long-distance point-to-point communication
Low frequency (LF)	30–300 kc	10,000–1000 m	Propagation at night similar to VLF but slightly less reliable; daytime absorption greater than VLF	Long-distance point-to-point service, marine, navigational aids
Medium frequency (MF)	300–3000 kc	1000–100 m	Attenuation low at night and high in daytime	Broadcasting, marine communication, navigation, harbor telephone, etc.
High frequency (HF)	3–30 Mc	100–10 m	Transmission over considerable distance depends solely on the ionosphere, and so varies greatly with time of day, season, and frequency	Moderate and long-distance communication of all types
Very high frequency (VHF)	30–300 Mc	10–1 m	Substantially straight-line propagation analogous to that of light waves; unaffected by ionosphere	Short-distance communication, television, frequency modulation, radar, airplane navigation
Ultra-high frequency (UHF)*	300–3000 Mc	100–10 cm	Same	Short-distance communication, radar, relay systems, television, etc.
Super-high frequency (SHF)*	3000–30,000 Mc	10–1 cm	Same	Radar, radio relay, navigation

* Frequencies higher than about 2000 Mc are frequently referred to as microwave frequencies.

wavelength of this radio wave.   From these considerations it is apparent that the size of radiator required is inversely proportional to the frequency.   High-frequency waves can therefore be produced by a small radiator, while low-frequency waves require a large antenna system for effective radiation.

Every radiator has directional characteristics as a result of which it sends out stronger waves in certain directions than in others.   Directional characteristics of antennas are used to concentrate the radiation toward the point to which it is desired to transmit, or to favor reception of energy arriving from a particular direction.

1-3. Generation and Control of Radio-frequency Power. The radio-frequency power required by a radio transmitter is practically always obtained from a vacuum-tube oscillator or amplifier. Vacuum tubes can convert d-c power into a-c energy for all frequencies from the very lowest up to 30,000 Mc, or even higher. Under most conditions the efficiency with which this transformation takes place is in the neighborhood of 50 per cent or higher. At frequencies up to well over 1000 Mc, the amount of

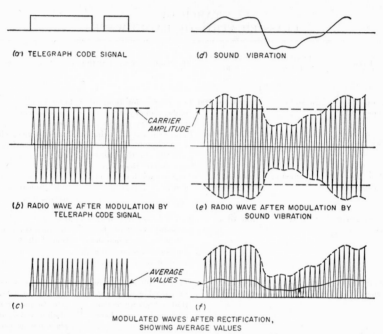

FIG. 1-2. Diagram showing how a signal may be transmitted by modulating the amplitude of a radio wave, and how the original signal may be recovered from the modulated wave by rectification. For the sake of clarity the radio frequency is shown as being much lower than would usually be the case.

power that can be generated continuously by vacuum tubes is of the order of kilowatts.

Modulation. If a radio wave is to convey a message, some feature of the wave must be varied in accordance with the information to be transmitted. One way to do this, termed *amplitude modulation*, consists in varying the amplitude of the radiated wave. In radio telegraphy, this involves turning the radio transmitter on and off in accordance with the dots and dashes of the telegraph code, as illustrated in Fig. 1-2*b*. In radio-telephone transmission by amplitude modulation the radio-frequency wave is varied in accordance with the pressure of the sound wave being transmitted, as shown in Fig. 1-2*e*. Similarly in picture transmission, the amplitude of the wave radiated at any one time is made proportional to the light intensity of the part of the picture that is being transmitted at that instant.

Intelligence may be transmitted by other means than by varying the amplitude. For example, one may maintain the amplitude constant and vary the frequency that is radiated in accordance with the intelligence, thus obtaining *frequency modulation.* This results in a wave such as shown in Fig. 1-3b, which is to be compared with the corresponding amplitude-modulated wave of Fig. 1-3a. Frequency modulation is widely used in very high-frequency communication systems.

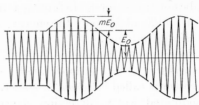

(*a*) AMPLITUDE-MODULATED WAVE

1-4. Reception of Radio Signals. In the reception of radio signals it is first necessary to abstract energy from the radio wave passing the receiving point. Any antenna capable of radiating electrical energy is also able to absorb energy from a passing radio wave. This occurs because the electromagnetic flux of the wave, in cutting across the antenna conductor, induces in the antenna a voltage that varies with time in exactly the same way as does the current flowing in

(*b*) SAME INFORMATION TRANSMITTED BY FREQUENCY-MODULATED WAVE

FIG. 1-3. Character of waves produced by amplitude modulation and by frequency modulation, where the modulation is sinusoidal in both cases. For the sake of clarity the radio frequency is shown much lower than would usually be the case.

the antenna radiating the wave. This induced voltage, in association with the current that it produces, represents energy that is absorbed from the passing wave.

Since every wave passing the receiving antenna induces its own voltage in the antenna conductor, it is necessary that the receiving equipment be capable of separating the desired signal from the unwanted signals that are also inducing voltages in the antenna. This separation is made on the basis of the difference in frequency between transmitting stations and is carried out by the use of resonant circuits which can be made to discriminate very strongly in favor of a particular frequency. The ability to discriminate between radio waves of different frequencies is called *selectivity* and the process of adjusting circuits to resonance with the frequency of a desired signal is spoken of as *tuning.*

Although intelligible radio signals have been received from radio transmitters thousands of miles distant, using only the energy abstracted from the radio wave by the receiving antenna, much more satisfactory reception can be obtained if the received energy is amplified. This amplification may be applied to the radio-frequency currents before detection, in which case it is called radio-frequency amplification; or it may be applied to the rectified currents after detection, in which case it is called audio-frequency amplification. The use of amplification makes possible the satisfactory reception of signals from waves that would otherwise be too weak to give an audible response. The only satisfactory method of amplifying radio signals that has been discovered is by the use of vacuum tubes or transistors. Before vacuum tubes were discovered, radio reception had available only the energy abstracted from the radio wave by the receiving antenna.

Detection. The process by which the message being transmitted is reproduced from the modulated radio-frequency current present in the receiver is called *detection*, or sometimes *demodulation*. With amplitude-modulated waves, detection is accomplished by rectifying the radio-frequency currents to produce a current that varies in accordance with the modulation of the received wave. Thus, when the modulated wave shown at e of Fig. 1-2 is rectified, the resulting current, shown at f, is seen to have an average value that varies in accordance with the amplitude of the original signal. In the transmission of code signals by radio, the rectified current reproduces the dots and dashes of the telegraph code, as shown at Fig. 1-2c, and could be used to operate a telegraph sounder. When it is desired to receive the telegraph signals directly on a telephone receiver, it is necessary to break up the dots and dashes at an audible rate in order to give a note that can be heard, since otherwise the telephone receiver would give forth a succession of unintelligible clicks.

The detection of a frequency-modulated wave involves two steps. First, the wave is transmitted through a circuit in which the relative response depends upon the frequency. The wave that then emerges from the circuit is amplitude-modulated, since as the frequency of the constant-amplitude input wave changes, the output amplitude will follow the variation of circuit transmission with frequency. The resulting amplitude-modulated wave is then rectified.

1-5. Nature of a Modulated Wave. A sine wave conveys very little information since it repeats over and over again. When a wave is modulated, either in amplitude or frequency, it is no longer a simple sine wave, but is instead a mixture of several waves of slightly different frequencies superimposed upon each other. The actual nature of a modulated wave can be deduced by writing down the equation of the wave and making a mathematical analysis of the result. Thus, in the case of the simple sine-wave amplitude modulation shown in Fig. 1-3a, the amplitude of the radio-frequency oscillation is given by $E = E_0 + mE_0 \sin 2\pi f_s t$, in which E_0 represents the average amplitude, f_s the frequency at which the amplitude is varied, and m the ratio of amplitude variation from the average to the average amplitude, which is called the *degree of modulation*. The equation of the amplitude-modulated wave can be hence written as

$$e = E_0(1 + m \sin 2\pi f_s t) \sin 2\pi f t \qquad (1\text{-}2)$$

in which f is the frequency of the radio oscillation.   Multiplying out the right-hand side of Eq. (1-2) gives

$$e = E_0 \sin 2\pi f t + m E_0 \sin 2\pi f_s t \sin 2\pi f t$$

By expanding the last term into functions of the sum and difference angles by the usual trigonometric formula, the equation of a wave with simple sine-wave amplitude modulation can be written in the form

$$e = E_0 \sin 2\pi f t + \frac{m E_0}{2} \cos 2\pi (f - f_s)t - \frac{m E_0}{2} \cos 2\pi (f + f_s)t \qquad (1\text{-}3)$$

Equation (1-3) shows that the wave with sine-wave modulation consists of three separate waves.   The first of these, represented by the term $E_0 \sin 2\pi f t$, is called the *carrier*.   Its amplitude is independent of the presence or absence of modulation and is equal to the average amplitude of the wave.   The two other components are alike as far as magnitude is concerned, but the frequency of one of them is less than that of the carrier frequency by an amount equal to the modulation frequency, while the frequency of the other is more than that of the carrier by the same amount.   These two components, called *sideband frequencies*, carry the intelligence that is being transmitted by the modulated wave.   The frequency of the sideband components relative to the carrier frequency is determined by the modulation frequency.   The relative amplitude of the sideband components is determined by the extent of the amplitude variations that are impressed upon the wave, i.e., by the degree of modulation.

When the modulation is more complex than the simple sine-wave amplitude variation of Fig. 1-3a, the effect is to introduce additional sideband components.   Thus, if the wave of a radio-telephone transmitter is amplitude-modulated by a complex sound wave containing pitches of 1000 and 1500 cycles, the modulated wave will contain one pair of 1000-cycle sideband components and one pair of 1500-cycle sideband components.

The analysis of a frequency-modulated wave is somewhat more complex but leads to an analogous result.   The principal difference is that the frequency-modulated wave not only contains the same sideband frequencies as does the corresponding amplitude-modulated wave, but in addition contains higher-order side bands.   Thus, if a wave has its frequency varied at a rate of 1000 times per second, the resulting modulated wave will contain not only a pair of 1000-cycle sideband components, but in addition a pair of 2000-cycle sideband components, possibly a pair of 3000-cycle sideband components, etc.   The amplitude of these various sideband pairs will depend upon the extent and upon the rate of frequency variation.

Significance of the Sidebands.   The carrier and sideband frequencies are not a mathematical fiction, but have a real existence, as is evidenced by the fact that the various frequency components of a modulated wave can be separated from each other by suitable filter circuits.   The sideband frequencies can be considered as being generated as a result of varying the wave.   They are present only when the wave is being varied, and their magnitude and frequency are determined by the character of the modulation.

It is apparent that the transmission of intelligence requires the use of a band of frequencies rather than a single frequency.   Speech and music of the quality reproduced in standard broadcasting involve frequency components from about 100 cycles up to 5000 cycles; when modulated upon a carrier wave, the total bandwidth involved is therefore 10,000 cycles.   If this entire band is not transmitted equally well through space, and by the circuits in both transmitter and receiver through which the modulated wave must pass, then the sideband frequency components that are discriminated against will not be reproduced in the receiving equipment with proper amplitude, and a loss in quality will result.   With telegraph signals, the required sideband is relatively narrow because the amplitude of the signals is varied only a few times a second, but a definite frequency band is still required.   If some of the sideband components of the code signal are not transmitted, the received dots and dashes tend to be rounded off and run together, and may become indistinguishable.

1-6. The Decibel.   The decibel (abbreviated db) is a logarithmic unit used in communication work to express power ratios.   If the powers being compared are P_1 and P_2, then

$$\text{Decibels} = 10 \log_{10} \frac{P_2}{P_1} \tag{1-4}$$

The sign associated with the number of decibels indicates which power is greater; thus a negative sign means P_2 is less than P_1.

The decibel has no other significance than that given in Eq. (1-4). Thus, if decibels are used to express amplification, this simply means that the presence of the amplification increases the power output by the number of decibels attributed to the amplification.   Again, under many conditions relative power is proportional to the square of the voltage E (or current I, or field B, etc.).   Under these conditions

$$\text{Decibels} = 20 \log_{10} \frac{E_2}{E_1} = 20 \log_{10} \frac{I_2}{I_1} = 20 \log_{10} \frac{B_2}{B_1}, \text{ etc.} \tag{1-5}$$

These relations must be used with caution, however, as they hold only when the resistance associated with E_2 (or I_2 or B_2) is the same as associated with E_1 (or I_1 or B_1).

TABLE 1-2

(a) POWER, VOLTAGE, AND CURRENT RATIOS FOR ASSIGNED
DECIBEL VALUES

Db	Current and voltage ratio		Power ratio		Db	Current and voltage ratio		Power ratio	
	Gain	Loss	Gain	Loss		Gain	Loss	Gain	Loss
0.0	1.00	1.000	1.00	1.000	10	3.16	0.316	10.00	0.100
0.2	1.02	0.977	1.05	0.955	12	3.98	0.251	15.8	0.063
0.4	1.05	0.955	1.10	0.912	14	5.01	0.200	25.1	0.040
0.6	1.07	0.933	1.15	0.871	16	6.31	0.158	39.8	0.025
0.8	1.10	0.912	1.20	0.832	18	7.94	0.126	63.1	0.016
1.0	1.12	0.891	1.26	0.794	20	10.00	0.100	100.0	0.010
1.5	1.19	0.841	1.41	0.708	25	17.8	0.056	3.16×10^2	3.16×10^{-3}
2.0	1.26	0.794	1.58	0.631	30	31.6	0.032	10^3	10^{-3}
2.5	1.33	0.750	1.78	0.562	35	56.2	0.018	3.16×10^3	3.16×10^{-4}
3.0	1.41	0.708	2.00	0.501	40	100.0	0.010	10^4	10^{-4}
3.5	1.50	0.668	2.24	0.447	45	177.8	0.006	3.16×10^4	3.16×10^{-5}
4.0	1.58	0.631	2.51	0.398	50	316	0.003	10^5	10^{-5}
4.5	1.68	0.596	2.82	0.355	60	1,000	0.001	10^6	10^{-6}
5	1.78	0.562	3.16	0.316	70	3,160	0.0003	10^7	10^{-7}
6	2.00	0.501	3.98	0.251	80	10,000	0.0001	10^8	10^{-8}
7	2.24	0.447	5.01	0.200	90	31,600	0.00003	10^9	10^{-9}
8	2.51	0.398	6.31	0.158	100	100,000	0.00001	10^{10}	10^{-10}
9	2.82	0.355	7.94	0.126	120	1,000,000	0.000001	10^{12}	10^{-12}

(b) DECIBEL EQUIVALENT OF POWER, VOLTAGE, AND
CURRENT RATIOS

Ratio	Db equivalent		Ratio	Db equivalent		Ratio	Db equivalent	
	Power	Voltage or current		Power	Voltage or current		Power	Voltage or current
10^{-6}	−60.00	−120.00	1.2	0.79	1.58	10	10.00	20.00
10^{-5}	−50.00	−100.00	1.4	1.46	2.92	12	10.79	21.58
10^{-4}	−40.00	−80.00	1.6	2.04	4.08	14	11.46	22.92
0.001	−30.00	−60.00	1.8	2.55	5.10	16	12.04	24.08
0.003	−25.23	−50.46	2.0	3.01	6.02	18	12.55	25.10
0.005	−23.01	−46.02	2.5	3.98	7.96	20	13.01	26.02
0.01	−20.00	−40.00	3.0	4.77	9.54	25	13.98	27.96
0.03	−15.23	−30.46	3.5	5.44	10.88	30	14.77	29.54
0.05	−13.01	−26.02	4.0	6.02	12.04	40	16.02	32.04
0.10	−10.00	−20.00	4.5	6.53	13.06	50	16.99	33.98
0.15	−8.24	−16.48	5.0	6.99	13.98	60	17.78	35.56
0.20	−6.99	−13.98	5.5	7.40	14.81	80	19.03	38.06
0.30	−5.23	−10.46	6.0	7.78	15.56	100	20.00	40.00
0.40	−3.98	−7.96	6.5	8.13	16.26	10^3	30.00	60.00
0.50	−3.01	−6.02	7.0	8.45	16.90	10^4	40.00	80.00
0.60	−2.22	−4.44	7.5	8.75	17.50	10^5	50.00	100.00
0.80	−0.97	−1.94	8.0	9.03	18.06	10^6	60.00	120.00
1.00	0.00	0.00	9.0	9.54	19.08	10^7	70.00	140.00

The practical value of the decibel arises from its logarithmic nature. This permits the enormous ranges of power involved in communication work to be expressed in terms of decibels without running into inconveniently large numbers, while at the same time permitting small ratios to be conveniently expressed. Thus, 1 db represents a power ratio of approximately 5:4, while 60 db represents a ratio of 1,000,000:1. The logarithmic character of the decibel also makes it possible to express the ratio of input to output powers of a complicated circuit as the sum of the decibel equivalent of the ratios of the input to output powers of the different parts of the circuit that are in cascade.

Table 1-2 gives a convenient summary of decibel values.

CHAPTER 2

CIRCUIT ELEMENTS

2-1. Inductance. A current flowing in an electrical circuit produces magnetic flux that links with (i.e., encircles) the current. The effect of this flux is expressed in terms of a property of the circuit called the *inductance*.

Inductance can be defined as the flux linkages per ampere of current producing the flux; i.e.,

$$\begin{matrix} \text{Inductance } L \\ \text{in henrys} \end{matrix} \Bigg\} = \frac{\text{flux linkages}}{\text{current (amperes) producing flux}} \times 10^{-8} \quad (2\text{-}1)$$

A flux linkage represents one flux line encircling the circuit current once. Thus in Fig. 2-1 flux line *aa* contributes eight flux linkages toward the coil inductance because it circles the current flowing in the coil eight times. On the other hand, flux line *b* of the same coil contributes only one-half a flux linkage toward the coil inductance because this particular line encircles only one-half the coil current.

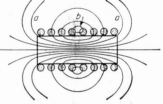

FIG. 2-1. Flux and current distribution in typical single-layer air-cored inductance coil. The current density is indicated by the density of shading.

Calculation of Inductance. The inductance of an electrical circuit is computed by assuming a convenient current flowing in the circuit. The magnetic flux produced by this current is then calculated, and the total number of flux linkages that results is counted. The inductance in henrys is this total number of flux linkages multiplied by 10^{-8} and divided by the circuit current.

Formulas have been derived by this procedure that give the inductance for all commonly used types of air-cored coils.[1] It is thus neither necessary nor desirable to guess at the number of turns and coil dimensions required to obtain a desired inductance. For example, the inductance of a single-layer solenoid, such as shown in Fig. 2-1, is given by the relation

$$\text{Inductance in microhenrys} = Fn^2d \quad (2\text{-}2)$$

[1] A comprehensive collection of such formulas is given by F. E. Terman, "Radio Engineers' Handbook," pp. 48–64, McGraw-Hill Book Company, Inc., New York, 1943.

where n = number of turns

d = diameter of coil measured to center of wire

F = constant that depends only upon the ratio of length to diameter, given in Fig. 2-2

The quantity F depends in a complicated way upon the ratio of coil length to diameter, since the geometrical distribution of the flux produced by the current in the coil does not follow a simple mathematical law. However, once the relationship represented by F has been determined,

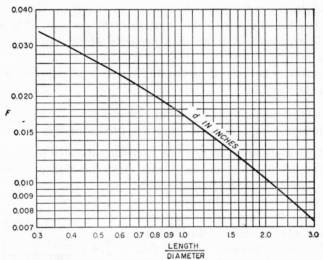

Fig. 2-2. Values of constant F for use in Eq. (2-2), to obtain the inductance of single-layer solenoids.

the value of F can be computed once for all, and presented by a curve, such as Fig. 2-2, or by a table.

The inductance of all coils with air cores is proportional to the square of the number of turns if the dimensions such as length, diameter, depth of winding, etc., are kept constant as the number of turns is altered. The reason for this behavior lies in the fact that, if the coil dimensions are kept constant, the amount of magnetic flux produced by a given coil current and the number of times each flux line links with the coil current are both proportional to the number of turns.

The inductance of all air-cored coils having the same number of turns and the same shape is always proportional to the size (i.e., to a linear dimension, such as length or radius) of the coil. Thus, if two coils have the same number of turns, but one is twice as big as the other in every dimension (such as diameter, length, width, and depth of winding), then the larger coil will have twice the inductance of the smaller one. This rule results from the fact that the cross section of the flux paths is proportional to the square of the linear dimension of the coil, while the length of these paths varies directly as the linear dimension.

In calculating the inductance of coils with magnetic cores, the flux is determined in accordance with the usual methods of making magnetic circuit calculations, taking into account air gaps, leakage and fringing flux, etc. It is also necessary to assume the proper value of permeability, as discussed below.[1] To the extent that the permeability of the core material can be considered as constant, the inductance of a coil with a magnetic core is proportional to the square of the number of turns and to the first power of the size, just as in the air-cored case.

Inductance of a Connecting Wire. The inductance associated with a connecting wire depends on the wire diameter, and can be minimized by making the diameter large. This results from the fact that when the wire diameter is small the length of the flux paths immediately outside of the wire is less than if the diameter is large. As a result the small wire is circled by more flux and hence has higher inductance.

An alternative means of achieving a low-inductance connection consists in employing a conductor comprising two or more spaced wires connected in parallel. If three wires are employed, they should be placed at the corners of an equilateral triangle; in a four-wire system the individual wires would be at the corners of a square, etc. Such arrangements give the first approximation to a solid conductor of large diameter, and will have less inductance the greater the diameter of the individual wires and the greater the spacing between the wires connected in parallel.

Initial and Incremental Permeability; Incremental Inductance. The permeability of a magnetic material is defined as the ratio B/H of the flux density to the magnetizing force, and depends upon the flux and the material. The permeability at very low flux densities, termed the *initial permeability*, is of particular importance in communication systems, where the current is commonly very weak. The initial permeability of magnetic materials is nearly always much less than the permeability at somewhat higher flux densities.

Coils having magnetic cores are frequently used in communication work under conditions where there is a large d-c magnetization upon which is superimposed a small a-c magnetization. Under these conditions, one is interested in the inductance that is offered to the superimposed alternating current. This is called the *incremental inductance,* and the corresponding permeability of the magnetic material is termed the incremental permeability.

Incremental permeability, and hence incremental inductance, depend upon the magnitude of both d-c and a-c magnetizations, and upon the previous magnetic history of the core. When a core that has been

---

[1] Such calculations are discussed in "Components Handbook" (vol. 17, Radiation Laboratory Series), chap. 4, McGraw-Hill Book Company, Inc., New York, 1949.

thoroughly demagnetized is first magnetized, the relation between current in the winding and core flux is the usual B-H curve, shown as OA in Fig. 2-3.   If the magnetizing current is then successively reduced to zero, reversed, brought back to zero, reversed to the original direction, etc., the flux goes through the familiar hysteresis loop shown in Fig. 2-3.   A direct current flowing through the magnetizing winding then brings the magnetic state of the core to some point on this hysteresis loop, such as 1 or 2 in Fig. 2-3.   When an alternating current is now superimposed on this direct current, the result is to cause the flux in the iron core to go through a minor hysteresis loop that is superimposed upon the usual hysteresis curve. Examples of such displaced hysteresis loops are shown at 1 and 2 in Fig. 2-3, corresponding to d-c magnetizations of H_1 and H_2, respectively.

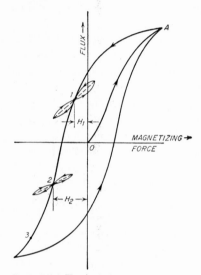

The incremental permeance of the core, and hence the incremental inductance offered to the superimposed alternating current, are proportional to the slope of the line (shown dotted in Fig. 2-3) joining the two tips of the minor hysteresis loop.   The value of permeability thus defined has two important characteristics.   First, for a given alternating current the incremental permeability (and hence the inductance) to the superimposed alternating current will be less the greater the direct current.   Second, with a given direct current the incremental permeability, and hence the inductance to the alternating current, will increase as the superimposed alternating current becomes larger.   These characteristics hold until the flux density becomes so high that the core is saturated, as shown in Fig. 2-4.

Fig. 2-3. Typical hysteresis loop, showing minor hysteresis loops 1 and 2.

In coils that are subject to considerable d-c magnetization, the incremental inductance is increased by the use of an appropriate air gap in the magnetic circuit.   In fact, there is an optimum length of air gap for which the incremental inductance will be maximum; this optimum gap increases as the d-c magnetization is increased.   The existence of an optimum air gap arises from the fact that, up to a certain point, reducing the d-c magnetization by increasing the air gap increases the incremental inductance of the magnetic portion of the circuit more than enough to counterbalance the increased reluctance of the magnetic circuit resulting from the greater air gap.

Magnetic Materials.   A wide variety of magnetic materials find use in communication and radio work. Silicon steel is used for the cores of power transformers, filter chokes, and audio-frequency transformers. When weight and size are important, there is an advantage in using a type of silicon steel in which the crystal grain orientation has been closely controlled during the manufacturing process. In this way, saturation occurs at a flux density about 30 per cent greater than in ordinary silicon steel; the permeability, including incremental permeability, is simultaneously increased, while the core losses are reduced.

A number of nickel-iron alloys have been developed which, after proper heat-treatment, are characterized by remarkably high permeability, particularly at low flux densities.[1] Thus values of initial permeability in the

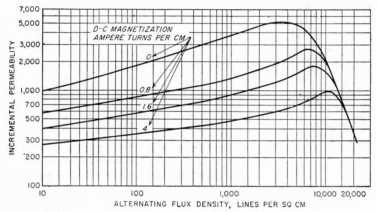

Fig. 2-4. Curve giving incremental permeability of typical silicon steel as a function of a-c magnetization for several values of superimposed direct current, showing how the inductance decreases with increased d-c and reduced a-c magnetization.

range 10,000 to 100,000 can be achieved, compared with about 300 for silicon steel. The hysteresis loss of these alloys at moderate and low flux densities is also unusually low. The flux density at which saturation takes place is moderately less than that for silicon steel, however. The incremental permeability of all of these high-permeability alloys drops very rapidly with d-c magnetization.

These nickel-iron alloys range from 45 to 80 per cent nickel and are known by such names as permalloy, hipernik, supermalloy, and mu-metal, according to the manufacturer and the exact composition. The addition of molybdenum to them increases their resistivity and hence reduces the eddy-current loss, without significant sacrifice in the low hysteresis loss or in the permeability characteristics. The resulting molybdenum permalloy is accordingly particularly well suited for use at relatively high fre-

[1] A summary of the properties of many of these alloys is given by G. W. Elmen, Magnetic Alloys of Iron, Nickel and Cobalt, *Trans. AIEE*, vol. 54, p. 1292, December, 1935.

quencies. The addition of cobalt to nickel-iron alloys introduces the possibility of obtaining substantially constant permeability up to moderate flux densities, combined with extremely low hysteresis loss at low flux densities and almost zero residual induction and coercive force (see page 17). Such alloys are termed perminvars, and also possess in large degree the high-permeability features of nickel-iron alloys such as permalloy.

Iron-cobalt alloys containing from 36 to 50 per cent cobalt are characterized by a saturation flux density appreciably higher than that of silicon steel. Such alloys also have higher incremental permeability at high d-c magnetizing forces than do other magnetic materials.

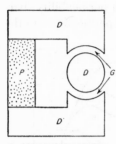

P = PERMANENT MAGNET
G = AIR GAP
D = SOFT IRON POLE PIECES

FIG. 2-5. Typical magnetic circuit involving a permanent magnet.

Magnetic cores that are nonconducting have been developed for use in radio-frequency coils.[1] They are composed of mixtures of ferrites, and have a resistivity so high that eddy-current losses are negligible in solid cores even at frequencies higher than 1 Mc. At the same time, such core material has a relatively high initial permeability, a value of 500 being typical. These nonconducting magnetic cores are not suitable for use in power transformers, however, as they saturate at low flux densities.

2-2. Permanent Magnets.[2] Permanent magnets now find many uses as a result of the development in recent years of improved permanent magnet materials. A typical system involving a permanent magnet is illustrated in Fig. 2-5. Here P is the permanent magnet, G is an air gap in which it is desired that the permanent magnet produce magnetic flux, and D denotes soft-iron pole pieces of low magnetic reluctance. In such an arrangement, the permanent magnet can be thought of as being a generator of magnetomotive force that acts on an external circuit (load) consisting of the magnetic circuit $DGDGD$ that is external to the permanent magnet.

Assume that the permanent magnet in the system of Fig. 2-5 is magnetized to saturation and that the magnetizing force is then removed. The resulting situation that exists in the magnet corresponds to a point somewhere on the part of the hysteresis loop lying in the upper left-hand quadrant of Fig. 2-3. This section of the hysteresis curve, shown enlarged in Fig. 2-6, is termed the demagnetization curve, and gives the principal characteristics of the permanent magnet. The flux density B_r

[1] See M. J. O. Strutt, Ferromagnetic Materials and Ferrites, *Wireless Eng.*, vol. 17, p. 277, December, 1950.

[2] A more detailed discussion of permanent magnets, with particular reference to design considerations, is given by Earl M. Underhill in a series of four articles in *Electronics*, beginning with the December, 1943, issue.

in the magnet for zero magnetizing force is termed the *residual induction*, while the demagnetizing force H_c which makes the flux density in the magnet zero is termed the *coercive force*.

For an operating condition of the magnet in Fig. 2-6 corresponding to point C', the flux density in the magnet is B', and the total flux generated by the permanent magnet is $B'A$ where A is the cross-sectional area of the permanent magnet. Also for the same operating point C', each unit length of the permanent magnet produces a magnetomotive force H'; hence the total magnetomotive force that is applied to the external circuit ($DGDGD$ in Fig. 2-5) by the permanent magnet is $H'l$, where l is the length of the permanent magnet. The operating point C' accordingly assumes a position on the demagnetization curve such that $H'l/B'A$ equals the reluctance of the external magnetic circuit.

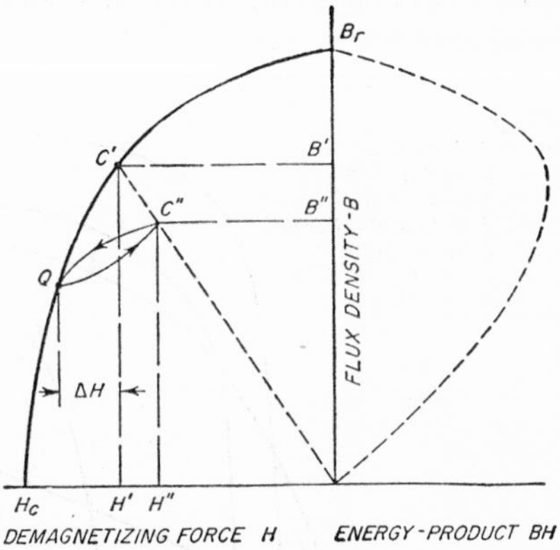

Fig. 2-6. Demagnetization and energy-product curves of a permanent magnet, showing minor hysteresis loop associated with stabilization.

Design Principles. The magnetic energy developed by the permanent magnet in the external system $DGDGD$ in Fig. 2-5 is proportional to the product $(B'A)$ $(H'l)$ of magnetic flux and magnetomotive force associated with the external circuit. Thus the magnetic energy available in the external circuit per unit volume of the permanent magnet is proportional to the product BH of the demagnetization curve, as plotted in Fig. 2-6.

It is now possible to state the principal design considerations of systems involving permanent magnets. First, the permanent magnet should be operated at a point on the demagnetization curve where the energy product BH is at or near its maximum; this operating point is a characteristic of the magnetic material involved, and defines a magnetomotive force H' per unit length and a flux density B' for the permanent magnet. Next, the cross section A of the magnet is given a value such that, when the flux density in the magnet has the value of B', the total flux $B'A$ will have the value desired for the external magnetic circuit. Finally, the length l of the permanent magnet is made such that $H'l$ will equal the magnetomotive force required to develop the required flux $B'A$ in the external magnetic circuit.

A permanent magnet operating at a point such as C' in Fig. 2-6 will have the flux density permanently changed when subjected to a transient action that momentarily reduces the flux density below B'. Thus assume that a transient demagnetizing current (or a momentary increase in reluctance) shifts the operating point from C' to Q. If this added effect is now removed, the operating point does not return to C'. Rather, it moves to a new point C'', corresponding to some new value of flux density B'' less than B', but such that the ratio $H''l/B''A$ still equals the reluctance of the external magnetic circuit; when this reluctance is linear, as when it arises from an air gap, then C'' lies on a straight line joining C' and the origin, as shown in Fig. 2-6. If the transient added force is applied a second time, the operating point will now return to Q, and upon removal of the added force will go back to C'', following the paths shown.

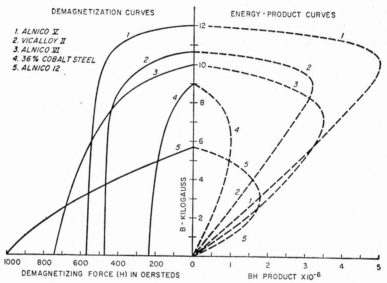

FIG. 2-7. Demagnetization and energy-product curves of typical permanent magnet materials.

Thus a permanent magnet system can be stabilized against added effects by initially subjecting the system to an added demagnetizing force ΔH; this will reduce the energy that the magnet supports in the system external to the magnet, but it prevents subsequent transient demagnetizing effects from producing a permanent change in the system provided their amplitudes do not exceed the demagnetizing force ΔH used in stabilization.[1] It will be noted that QC'' is a minor hysteresis loop analogous to the right-hand half of loop 1 in Fig. 2-3.

Permanent-magnet Materials.[2] Many different types of permanent-magnet materials have been developed; the characteristics of representative examples are illustrated in Fig. 2-7. The magnetic properties depend

[1] For further details see P. P. Cioffi, Stabilized Permanent Magnets, *Elec. Eng.*, vol. 68, p. 302, April, 1949.

[2] For further information see *Electronics Buyers' Guide*, p. M-22, June, 1949.

upon the composition and require proper cold working and heat-treatment to be fully developed.   Heat-treatment is sometimes carried out in the presence of a strong magnetizing field; in this case the material when used should be magnetized in the same direction as when heat-treated.

The choice between different materials for a particular application is determined, not only by the energy product, but also by cost, by ease of fabricating, by whether the magnet is to be used in an external system of high or low reluctance, etc.   In general, the better permanent-magnet materials are very difficult to work.   Thus the alnicos (aluminum-nickel-iron alloys) are hard, weak, and brittle, and are commonly cast to approximate shape and then finished by grinding to exact size; they cannot be machined, drilled, or tapped.

2-3. Mutual Inductance and Coefficient of Coupling.   *Mutual Inductance.*   When two inductance coils are so placed in relation to each other

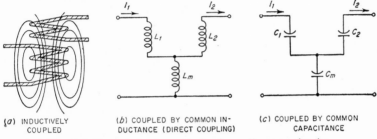

(a) INDUCTIVELY   (b) COUPLED BY COMMON IN-   (c) COUPLED BY COMMON
     COUPLED   DUCTANCE (DIRECT COUPLING)   CAPACITANCE

Fig. 2-8. Several simple methods of coupling two circuits.

that flux lines produced by current in one of the coils link with the turns of the other coil as shown in Fig. 2-8a, the two inductances are said to be inductively coupled.   The effects that this coupling produces can be expressed in terms of a property called the *mutual inductance,* which is defined by the relation

$$
\left.\begin{array}{l}\text{Mutual}\\\text{inductance}\\M \text{ in henrys}\end{array}\right\} = \frac{\left\{\begin{array}{l}\text{flux linkages in second coil}\\\text{produced by current in first coil}\end{array}\right\}}{\text{current in first coil}} \times 10^{-8} \qquad (2\text{-}3)
$$

$$
= \frac{\left\{\begin{array}{l}\text{flux linkages in first coil}\\\text{produced by current in second coil}\end{array}\right\}}{\text{current in second coil}} \times 10^{-8} \qquad (2\text{-}4)
$$

Formulas (2-3) and (2-4) are equivalent and give the same value of mutual inductance.   The flux linkages produced in the coil that has no current in it are counted just as though there were a current in this coil, so that the number of times a flux line would encircle an imaginary coil current is the number of linkages contributed by this particular line. In adding up the flux linkages it is important to note that different flux lines may conceivably link with the same coil in opposite directions, in which case the total number of linkages is the difference between the sums of positive and negative linkages. The mutual inductance may therefore be positive or negative depending upon the direction of the linkages.

The problem of calculating mutual inductance is similar in all respects to the problem of computing inductance, and formulas have been worked out by which the mutual inductance can be calculated with good accuracy in all the ordinary types of configurations.

When two coils of inductance L_1 and L_2, between which a mutual inductance M exists, are connected in series, the equivalent inductance of the combination is $L_1 + L_2 \pm 2M$. The term $2M$ takes into account the flux linkages in each coil due to the current in the other coil. These mutual linkages may add to or subtract from the self-linkages, depending upon the relative direction in which the current passes through the two coils. Thus, when all linkages are in the same direction, the total inductance of the series combination exceeds by $2M$ the sum of the individual inductances of the two coils.

Coefficient of Coupling. The maximum value of mutual inductance that can be obtained between two coils having inductances L_1 and L_2 is $\sqrt{L_1 L_2}$. The ratio of the mutual inductance M that is actually present to this maximum possible value of mutual inductance is called the *coefficient of coupling*, which can therefore be expressed by the relation

$$\text{Coefficient of coupling} = k = \frac{M}{\sqrt{L_1 L_2}} \qquad (2\text{-}5)$$

The coefficient of coupling is a convenient constant because it expresses the extent to which the two inductances are coupled, independently of the size of the inductances concerned. In air-cored coils a coupling coefficient of 0.5 is considered high and is said to represent "close" coupling, while coefficients of only a few hundredths represent "loose" coupling.

General Case of Coupled Circuits. Any two circuits so arranged that energy can be transferred from one to the other are said to be coupled, even though this transfer of energy takes place by some means such as a capacitor, resistance, or inductance common to the two circuits rather than by the aid of a mutual inductance. Examples of various methods of coupling are shown in Fig. 2-8. *Any two circuits that are coupled by a common impedance have a coefficient of coupling that is equal to the ratio of the common impedance to the square root of the product of the total impedances of the same kind as the coupling impedance that are present in the two circuits.* That is,

$$k = \frac{Z_m}{\sqrt{Z_1 Z_2}} \qquad (2\text{-}6)$$

where Z_m is the impedance common to the two circuits, and Z_1 and Z_2 are the total impedances of the *same kind* in the two circuits. When applied to case *b* in Fig. 2-8, where the coupling is furnished by the common inductance L_m, the total inductances of the two circuits are $L_1 + L_m$ and $L_2 + L_m$, respectively, and Eq. (2-6) reduces to

$$\text{Coefficient of coupling } k \text{ for Fig. 2-8}b = \frac{L_m}{\sqrt{(L_1 + L_m)(L_2 + L_m)}} \quad (2\text{-}7)$$

In Fig. 2-8c the coupling element is a common capacitance C_m, and the coefficient of coupling is[1]

$$\text{Coefficient of coupling for Fig. 2-8}c = \frac{\sqrt{C_1 C_2}}{\sqrt{(C_m + C_1)(C_m + C_2)}} \quad (2\text{-}8)$$

2-4. Skin Effect in Coils and Conductors at Radio Frequencies. The effective resistance offered by conductors to radio frequencies is considerably more than the ohmic resistance measured with direct currents. This is because of an action known as *skin effect,* which causes the current to be concentrated in certain parts of the conductor and leaves the remainder of the cross section to contribute little or nothing toward carrying the current.

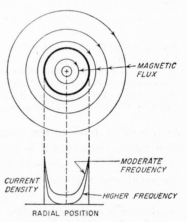

A simple example of skin effect, and one that makes its nature clear, is furnished by an isolated round wire. When a current is flowing through such a conductor, the magnetic flux that results is in the form of concentric circles, as shown in Fig. 2-9. It is to be noted that some of this flux exists within the conductor and therefore links with, i.e.,

Fig. 2-9. Isolated round conductor, showing magnetic flux paths, and also typical current distributions.

encircles, current near the center of the conductor while not linking with current flowing near the surface. The result is that the inductance of the central part of the conductor is greater than the inductance of the part of the conductor near the surface; this is because of the greater number of flux

---

[1] Equation (2-7) is derived as follows: In Fig. 2-8c, the primary circuit has C_1 and C_m in series and so has an equivalent capacitance of $C_1 C_m/(C_1 + C_m)$ while the equivalent capacitance of the secondary is similarly $C_2 C_m/(C_2 + C_m)$. The coupling reactance is $1/\omega C_m$, while the primary and secondary reactances are $(C_1 + C_m)/\omega C_1 C_m$ and $(C_2 + C_m)/\omega C_2 C_m$, respectively. The coefficient of coupling is then

$$k = \frac{1/\omega C_m}{\sqrt{\dfrac{C_1 + C_m}{\omega C_1 C_m}\dfrac{C_2 + C_m}{\omega C_2 C_m}}}$$

which reduces to Eq. (2-7).

linkages existing in the central region. At radio frequencies, the reactance of this extra inductance is sufficiently great to affect seriously the flow
of current, most of which flows along the surface of the conductor where
the impedance is low, rather than near the center where the impedance is
high. The center part of the conductor, therefore, does not carry its
share of the current and the true or effective resistance is increased, since
in effect the useful cross section of the wire is very greatly reduced. The
types of current distribution obtained in typical cases of skin effect in a
round wire are shown in Fig. 2-9.

*When skin effect is present, the current is always redistributed over the con-
ductor cross section in such a way as to make most of the current flow where it
is encircled by the smallest number of
flux lines.* This general principle
controls the distribution of current,
irrespective of the shape of the conductor involved. Thus, with a
conductor consisting of a thin flat
strip, such as shown in Fig. 2-10,
the current flows primarily along
the edges, where it is surrounded by
the smallest amount of flux, and the
true or effective resistance will be

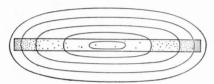

Fig. 2-10. Flux lines and current distribution in a thin strip at radio frequency, showing how skin effect causes
the current to concentrate at the edges
of the strip. The current density is indicated by the density of the shading.

high because most of the strip carries very little current. This illustration makes clear that it is not the amount of conductor surface that determines the resistance to alternating current, but rather the way in which
the conductor material is arranged.

The ratio that the effective a-c resistance bears to the d-c resistance of a
conductor is commonly called the *resistance ratio*. It increases with frequency, with conductivity of the conductor material, and with the size of
conductor. This results from the fact that a higher frequency causes the
extra inductance at the center of the conductor to have a higher reactance.
Similarly, a greater conductivity makes the reactance of the extra inductance of more importance in determining the distribution of current, while
a greater cross section provides a larger central region. It is to be noted,
however, that a larger conductor always has less radio-frequency resistance than a smaller one because, although the ratio of a-c to d-c resistance
is less favorable, this is more than made up by the greater amount of
conductor cross section present.

Skin Effect at High Frequencies.[1] When the frequency is sufficiently
high, substantially all of the current in a conductor is confined to a region
very close to the surface. The current density then falls off with depth
from the surface in accordance with the relation

---

[1] An excellent discussion of skin effect at very high frequencies is given by Harold A.
Wheeler, Formulas for the Skin Effect, *Proc. IRE*, vol. 30, p. 412, September, 1942.

$$\frac{\text{Current at depth } z}{\text{Current at the surface}} = \epsilon^{-z/\delta} \qquad (2\text{-}9)$$

Here z and δ are in the same units, and δ is a quantity called the *skin depth* that is given by the equation

$$\delta = 5033 \sqrt{\frac{\rho}{\mu f}} \qquad (2\text{-}10)$$

where δ = skin depth, cm

ρ = resistivity of conductor, ohms per centimeter cube

f = frequency, cycles

μ = magnetic permeability of core material (permeability of air equals unity), for low flux densities (that is, μ is the initial permeability)

For copper at 20°C this reduces to

$$\text{Skin depth of copper in cm} = \frac{6.62}{\sqrt{f}} \qquad (2\text{-}11)$$

At 1 Mc the skin depth in copper is thus 0.0066 cm, or 0.0026 in. The phase of the current at depth z lags the current at the surface by z/δ radians. At a depth from the surface corresponding to one skin depth, the current density has dropped to 36.8 per cent of the value at the surface, and the phase of the current lags the current at the surface by 1 radian.

Equation (2-9) is valid whenever the radius of curvature of the conductor surface is at least several times the skin depth, provided the effective thickness of the conductor is at the same time at least three or four skin depths.

The power loss associated with the current flowing under any particular portion of the conductor surface is the same as though this current were uniformly distributed down to a depth δ. Thus, in an isolated round wire, where the current is uniformly distributed over the surface, the effective resistance at high frequencies is the d-c resistance of a hollow cylindrical shell having the same outer diameter as the wire and possessing a thickness δ. The d-c resistance of a strip of surface one skin depth thick, one centimeter long, and one centimeter wide is sometimes called the *surface resistivity;* it is the resistivity that is offered to the flow of current at very high frequencies.

Proximity Effect—Skin Effect in Coils. When two or more adjacent conductors are carrying current as in a coil, the current distribution in any one conductor is affected by the magnetic flux produced by the adjacent conductor as well as by the magnetic flux produced by the current in the conductor itself. This effect, termed *proximity effect,* ordinarily causes the true or effective resistance to be greater than in the case of simple skin effect and is particularly important in radio-frequency inductance coils.

The current distribution under conditions where proximity effect is present follows the same law as for simple skin effect; i.e., the current density is greatest in those parts of the conductor encircled by the smallest number of flux lines. This is illustrated in Fig. 2-1, where the approximate current density is illustrated by relative shading.

Litz Wire. The effective a-c resistance of a conductor can be made to approach the d-c resistance at low and moderate radio frequencies by forming the conductor from a number of strands of small enameled wire connected in parallel at their ends, but insulated throughout the rest of their length and thoroughly interwoven. If the stranding is properly done, each wire will, on the average, link with the same number of flux lines as every other wire, and the current will divide evenly among the strands. If at the same time each strand is of small diameter, it will have relatively little skin effect over its cross section, so all of the material is equally effective in carrying the current. Such a stranded cable is called a *litz* conductor.

Practical litz conductors are very effective at frequencies below about 1000 kc, but as the frequency becomes higher the benefits disappear. This is because irregularities of stranding, and capacitance between the strands, cause a failure to realize the ideal condition at very high frequencies.

2-5. Capacitors and Dielectrics. A capacitor is formed wherever an insulator (i.e., dielectric) separates two conductors between which a difference of potential can exist.

Capacitor Losses and Their Representation. A perfect capacitor when discharged gives up all the electrical energy that was supplied to it in charging. Actual capacitors never realize this ideal perfectly but, rather, dissipate some of the energy delivered to them. Most of the loss in ordinary capacitors occurs in the dielectric, although at very high frequencies skin effect also causes an appreciable loss to occur in the capacitor leads and electrodes. At very high voltages corona may occur and contribute to the loss.

The merit of a capacitor from the point of view of freedom from losses is usually expressed in terms of the power factor of the capacitor.[1] The power factor represents the fraction of the input volt-amperes that is dis-

---

[1] The merit of a capacitor or of a dielectric can also be expressed in terms of the angle by which the current flowing into the capacitor fails to be 90° out of phase with the applied voltage. This angle is termed the *phase angle* of the capacitor. The power factor is the sine of the phase angle. The tangent of the phase angle is termed the *dissipation factor.* The reciprocal of the dissipation factor is termed the capacitor Q and is the ratio of the capacitor reactance to the equivalent series resistance. With ordinary dielectrics, the phase angle is so small that the power factor, the dissipation factor, and the reciprocal of capacitor Q are for all practical purposes equal to each other and to the phase angle expressed in radians. Thus a power factor of 0.01 represents a phase angle of 0.573° and a capacitor Q of 100.

sipated in the capacitor. To the extent that the losses in the capacitor are a result of dielectric losses, the power factor of the capacitor is also the power factor of the dielectric and is practically independent of the capacitor capacitance, the applied voltage, the voltage rating, or the frequency (unless polar effects are involved). Values of power factor of some typical dielectrics are given in Table 2-1.

TABLE 2-1
CHARACTERISTICS OF TYPICAL DIELECTRICS AT RADIO
FREQUENCIES WITH NORMAL ROOM TEMPERATURE

Material	Dielectric constant	Power factor
Air..	1.00	0.000
Mica (electrical)............................	5–9	0.0001–0.0007
Glass (electrical)...........................	4.5–7.00	0.002–0.016
Bakelite derivatives.........................	4.5–7.5	0.02–0.09
Wood (without special preparation)............	3–5	0.03–0.07
Mycalex.....................................	8	0.002
Steatite materials...........................	6.1	0.002–0.004
Polystyrene.................................	2.4–2.9	0.0002
Polyethelene................................	2.3	0.00015–0.0003
Rutile (titanium dioxide)....................	90–170	0.0006

Although the power factor of a capacitor is determined largely by the type of dielectric used in the capacitor, it is also affected by the conditions under which the dielectric operates. In particular, the power factor tends to become higher as the temperature is raised, and is likewise adversely affected by high humidity and by the absorption of moisture.

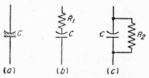

FIG. 2-11. Representation of imperfect capacitor by a perfect capacitor of same capacitance with series resistance, and by a perfect capacitor with shunt resistance.

Equivalent Series and Shunt Resistance. The action of a capacitor in an electrical circuit is taken into account by replacing the actual capacitor with a perfect capacitor associated with a resistance. This resistance may be connected in series, as in Fig. 2-11b, or in parallel, as in Fig. 2-11c. The value of the series or shunt resistance is so selected that the power factor of the perfect capacitor associated with the resistance is the same as the power factor of the actual capacitor. The value of the series resistance R_1 can be computed in terms of the power factor, capacitor capacitance C, and frequency f in the usual way, and when the power factor is low (i.e., when $R_1 < < 1/\omega C$), then R_1 is given to a high degree of accuracy by the equation

$$\text{Series resistance} = R_1 = \frac{\text{power factor}}{2\pi f C} \tag{2-12}$$

In the same way, the shunt resistance that can be used to represent the actual losses of the capacitor is related to the power factor, capacitance, and frequency to a high degree of accuracy by the equation

$$\text{Shunt resistance} = R_2 = \frac{1}{(2\pi f C)\ (\text{power factor})} \qquad (2\text{-}13)$$

Polar and Nonpolar Dielectrics. Molecules of some dielectrics are polar, while other dielectrics consist of molecules that are not polar. In the case of polar molecules, the dielectric constant under a-c conditions is increased as a result of the rotation of the polar molecules under the influence of the applied voltage. The extent to which this polar action is effective depends, however, upon the frequency and the temperature. Thus, if the frequency is made sufficiently high, the polar molecules are not able to follow the alternations of the applied field, and the dielectric constant drops. Moreover, the frequency at which this transition occurs is less the lower the temperature. As a result, temperature and frequency affect the capacitance of a capacitor possessing a polar dielectric in the manner shown in Fig. 2-12.

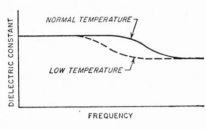

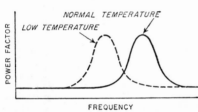

Fig. 2-12. Variation of dielectric constant and power factor of a polar dielectric as a function of frequency, for two temperatures.

The power factor of a polar dielectric shows a pronounced peak when under conditions where the dielectric constant corresponds to partial polar action, as shown in Fig. 2-12. The power factor of a polar dielectric hence becomes quite large at certain combinations of temperature and frequency.

Nonpolar molecules do not exhibit these changes in dielectric constant under temperature and frequency changes. The power factor of nonpolar dielectrics likewise does not exhibit peaks of loss such as shown in Fig. 2-12.

2-6. Capacitors for Electronics. In electronics the principal uses made of capacitors are for tuning resonant circuits, for blocking d-c voltages from parts of an electrical circuit while permitting alternating voltages to pass through, for obtaining transients with specified time constants, and for by-passing or short-circuiting alternating voltages. By-pass capacitors are frequently but not always subjected to a d-c potential.

A wide variety of dielectrics are used in capacitors designed for radio work, and new types are continually finding important applications. Among the types of importance are air; solid dielectrics such as mica, plastic films, certain ceramics, and paper; and electrolytic films.

Capacitors with Air Dielectric. Air dielectric finds its principal use in variable capacitors for tuning resonant circuits.

Although air is a perfect dielectric with zero power factor, air capacitors have losses because of the insulating material used to mount the two sets of plates, and also because of the skin-effect resistance of the leads, plates, rods, and washers, through which the capacitor current flows.

An air-dielectric capacitor can be represented by the equivalent electrical network in Fig. 2-13a. Here C is the capacitance of the capacitor

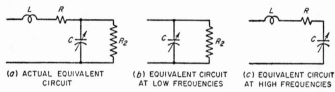

(a) ACTUAL EQUIVALENT   (b) EQUIVALENT CIRCUIT   (c) EQUIVALENT CIRCUIT
    CIRCUIT   AT LOW FREQUENCIES   AT HIGH FREQUENCIES

Fig. 2-13. Equivalent electrical circuits of a variable air condenser.

while R_2 is the equivalent shunt resistance introduced by the presence of the solid dielectric. The capacitor inductance L in Fig. 2-13a takes into account the magnetic flux associated with the current flowing in the capacitor; it is proportional to the physical dimensions of the capacitor. The resistance R represents the series resistance of the leads, washers, connecting rods, etc. It increases with frequency as a result of skin effect and is proportional to the square root of the frequency at high frequencies.

At low and moderate frequencies the effects of the inductance L and the series resistance R are negligible, and the capacitor equivalent circuit reduces to Fig. 2-13b. At very high frequencies, on the other hand, the power loss in R becomes very much larger than in R_2, and the equivalent circuit has the form shown in Fig. 2-13c.

At very high frequencies the reactance of the series inductance L is not negligible compared with the reactance of the capacitor capacitance. This causes the apparent capacitance of the capacitor as observed at the terminals to be greater than the actual capacitance according to the relation[1]

$$\text{Apparent capacitance} = \frac{C}{1 - \omega^2 L C} \qquad (2\text{-}14)$$

where $\omega = 2\pi$ times frequency, and L and C are as shown in Fig. 2-13.

[1] This results from the fact that, neglecting losses,

$$\text{Reactance at terminals} = \frac{1}{\omega C_{\text{app}}} = \left(\frac{1}{\omega C} - \omega L\right)$$

Solving for the apparent capacitance C_{app} gives Eq. (2-14).

Capacitors with Solid Dielectrics. Solid dielectrics are used in most fixed and in some adjustable capacitors. The dielectrics most commonly employed include mica, paper, plastic films, and ceramics.

Mica is characterized by low electrical losses, stability, high leakage resistance to d-c voltages, and high voltage strength. It is, however, relatively expensive. Mica capacitors find their chief use in small fixed capacitors for by-passing radio-frequency currents or blocking off d-c voltages, and in resonant circuits or in filters where a stable low-power-factor capacitor is required.

In capacitors employing paper as the dielectric the electrodes are either aluminum foil or are metal films evaporated directly on to the paper. In either case, the assembly is rolled into a bundle which is then vacuum-treated, impregnated with oil or wax, and sealed against moisture. Paper capacitors are inexpensive in proportion to capacitance, and are relatively compact in proportion to voltage rating. Such capacitors are used primarily for by-pass and blocking purposes. The power factor of paper capacitors is of the order of 0.5 per cent, and although the leakage current when subjected to direct voltages is somewhat greater than that of mica capacitors, it is not large.

Thin plastic films have been developed that are suitable for use as a capacitor dielectric in place of paper. Capacitors of this type using polystyrene dielectric have electrical qualities such as power factor, dielectric absorption, and insulation resistance superior even to mica capacitors.

Ceramics based on titanium dioxide mixtures find extensive use as dielectrics of small capacitors.[1] Dielectrics of this type are characterized by a high dielectric constant, a low to very low power factor, and a very high voltage rating. The temperature coefficient of such capacitors depends upon the actual ceramic mixture used and can be made either negative or positive as desired. Ceramic capacitors are used extensively for blocking and by-pass purposes where small mica capacitors have heretofore been employed, and have advantages of compactness and high voltage ratings. Ceramic dielectric capacitors have also found a wide field of usefulness in resonant circuits and other similar applications, where a negative temperature coefficient provided by a ceramic capacitor can be used to compensate for the positive temperature coefficient of associated coils and of capacitors of other types.

Capacitors with solid dielectric can be represented by the same equivalent electrical circuit shown in Fig. 2-13 for air-dielectric capacitors. The only difference is that all the capacitance C in this equivalent circuit is now associated with solid dielectric. As a result, at low and moderate frequencies the capacitor power factor almost exactly equals the power

[1] A survey of such ceramics is given by B. H. Marks, Ceramic Dielectric Materials, *Electronics*, vol. 21, p. 116, August, 1948.

factor of the dielectric and is independent of the capacitance of the capacitor and also of the frequency except in so far as polar molecules affect the behavior of the dielectric. At very high frequencies, the power factor increases with increasing frequency as a result of the skin-effect losses in leads and conductors. Also, the apparent capacitance at very high frequencies drops off because of the series inductance, in accordance with Eq. (2-14).

The voltage rating of capacitors with solid dielectrics is subject to two basic limitations: (1) If the applied voltage exceeds the insulation strength of the dielectric, the dielectric will spark through or at least deteriorate rapidly. (2) The temperature of the capacitor must not be permitted to rise excessively as a result of dielectric losses. This second limitation is the ruling one for all except d-c voltages and for very low frequencies. Inasmuch as the relationship between losses and temperature rise depends upon the design of the capacitor with respect to such matters as heat removal, it is not possible to give any general rules regarding voltage ratings. It is to be noted, however, that the voltage rating will drop rapidly as the frequency increases because of the increase in loss with frequency. Thus a particular low-loss air-cooled mica capacitor capable of standing 10,000 volts at low-frequencies was found by test to have a rating of 180 volts at a frequency of 10 Mc. Special cooling methods, such as the use of an air blast, will increase greatly the rating on a capacitor, and water cooling is still more effective.

Electrolytic Capacitors. The electrolytic capacitor makes use of the fact that certain metals, notably aluminum and tantalum, when placed in a suitable solution and made the positive electrodes, form a thin insulating surface film. This film is capable of withstanding considerable voltage and has a high electrostatic capacitance per unit area of film. It is the result of electrochemical action, and is formed by applying positive voltage to the electrode. The thickness of the film, and hence also the capacitance obtained per unit area of surface, depend largely upon the voltage used in this forming process. Typical voltage ratings of electrolytic capacitors range from 25 up to about 500 volts. Constructional details vary but, typically, the electrodes are of etched aluminum foil, thus giving maximum surface area. They are separated by paper or gauze, saturated with an electrolyte that is commonly a fudgelike solid, and the entire assembly is wound into a roll and mounted in a waxed cardboard tube or box.

Electrolytic capacitors are widely used for filter and by-pass purposes in situations where a superimposed d-c voltage is present. Compared with capacitors of the solid dielectric type, electrolytic capacitors have a very high power factor and appreciable leakage conductance to the superimposed d-c potential; they also vary in capacitance and loss with time, frequency, and temperature. However, for many purposes these features are unimportant and, in proportion to capacitance and voltage rating, electrolytic capacitors are the least expensive and most compact available.   They are, however, subject to progressive deterioration with time and so have limited life, and their dependability is appreciably less than that of paper capacitors designed for the corresponding applications.[1]

2-7. Coils for Resonant Circuits.   Coils intended for use in resonant circuits must have very low losses and small distributed capacitance. Both air-cored and magnetically cored coils are used for resonant circuits, with the choice depending upon circumstances.

Methods of Expressing Coil Losses—Coil Q.   The principal causes of energy loss in air-cored coils are skin effect in the conductor, proximity effect resulting from the interaction between nearby turns, dielectric losses associated with the distributed capacitance of the coil, and eddy-current losses in shields and other neighboring metallic objects present within range of the magnetic field of the coil.   In the case of coils with magnetic cores, the principal cause of energy loss is usually core loss, although factors such as skin-effect resistance of the wire and also dielectric loss are sometimes likewise of significance.

For purposes of circuit analysis the coil losses are commonly expressed in terms of an equivalent resistance, which when placed in series with the coil inductance will account for all the power losses actually observed. The most convenient way to express the merit of the coil is, however, in terms of the ratio of the reactance ωL of the coil to this equivalent series resistance R.   This ratio approximates the reciprocal of the coil power factor, and is usually referred to by the symbol Q; that is,

$$Q = \frac{\text{coil reactance}}{\text{equivalent series resistance}} = \frac{\omega L}{R} \qquad (2\text{-}15)$$

It is convenient to express the characteristics of a coil in terms of Q because the Q in the operating range of the coil usually varies only moderately with frequency; moreover, the value of Q corresponding to a good coil is substantially the same irrespective of the frequency for which the coil was designed.   The tendency for the coil Q to remain constant with frequency arises from the fact that, as the frequency increases, all the losses also increase, so that the *ratio* of coil reactance to resistance tends to be much more nearly constant with frequency than is either the reactance or the resistance of the coil.

Distributed Capacitance of Coils.   In a coil there are small capacitances between adjacent turns, between turns that are not adjacent, between terminal leads, between turns and ground, etc.   Some of the different capacitances that may exist in a typical air-cored coil are shown in Fig.

---

[1] By substituting tantalum for the less expensive aluminum foil electrodes, it is possible to increase greatly the reliability; see M. Whitehead, Tantalum Electrolytic Capacitors, *Bell Lab. Record*, vol. 28, p. 448, October, 1950.

2-14.   Each of the various capacitances associated with the coil stores a quantity of electrostatic energy that is determined by the capacitance involved and the fraction of the total coil voltage that appears across it. The total effect that the numerous small coil capacitances have can be represented to a high degree of accuracy by assuming that they can be replaced by a single capacitor of appropriate size shunted across the coil terminals.   This equivalent capacitance is called either the distributed capacitance or the self-capacitance of the coil; it causes the coil to show parallel resonance effects under some conditions (see Sec. 3-2).

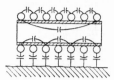

Fig. 2-14. Some of the coil capacitances that contribute to the distributed capacitance of a single-layer coil.

In multilayer coils the distributed capacitance will be high unless arrangements are used that prevent turns from different parts of the winding from being located close to each other.   Thus, in the two-layer winding shown in Fig. 2-15a, in which the turns are numbered in order, the first and last turns are adjacent; the capacitance between the turns at opposite ends of the winding then stores an undesirably large amount of electrostatic energy. This can be avoided by the use of the bank winding, shown at b.   Here the adjacent turns represent parts of the coil that are close together electrically, while the ends of the winding, which are far apart electrically, are also far apart physically.   Alternative approaches consist in using many layers with few turns per layer, as in Fig. 2-13c, or in spacing the layers, as in Fig. 2-15d.   The common "universal" multilayer coil represents a convenient mechanical method of utilizing these principles to achieve low distributed capacitance.

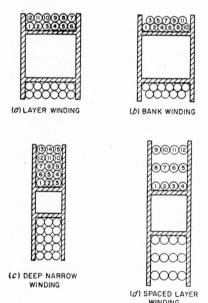

(a) LAYER WINDING

(b) BANK WINDING

(c) DEEP NARROW WINDING

(d) SPACED LAYER WINDING

Fig. 2-15. Several types of multilayer windings.

The distributed capacitance of a coil that is to be used in a resonant circuit must be small.   This is because the distributed capacitance limits the highest frequency to which the coil can be tuned, and also introduces losses that become serious at the higher frequencies.   These losses are dielectric losses occurring in the coil form, in the wire insulation, and in any other dielectric that may be in the electrostatic fields associated with the coil.

Air-cored Coils for Resonant Circuits. Air-cored coils are widely used in radio receivers and almost universally used for the resonant circuits of radio transmitters. Single-layer coils are generally employed for frequencies above 500 to 1500 kc, while at lower frequencies multilayer coils are typical, as they give the desired inductance compactly. Multilayer coils, generally of the bank-wound type, also find some use at broadcast frequencies (535 to 1600 kc).

In designing a single-layer coil, the highest Q in proportion to size is obtained when the length of the winding is somewhat less than the diameter of the coil.[1] The number of turns required is then determined by

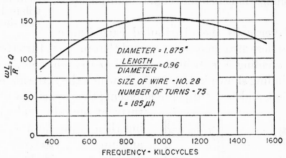

FIG. 2-16. Variation of Q with frequency for a typical air-cored coil.

the exact ratio of length to diameter that is selected, by the diameter, and by the inductance desired; when these factors are all settled, the optimum wire size corresponds to a conductor diameter that is between 0.5 and 0.75 times the distance between the centers of adjacent turns. If one compares the Q of two coils having the same inductance and the same ratio of length to diameter but different physical size, then the coil that is larger will have the highest Q provided it is wound with wire of optimum size.

The design of multilayer coils is more involved than that of single-layer coils because of the increased number of variables. In general, best results are obtained if the coil is relatively "loose," i.e., if the copper occupies only a small fraction of the actual winding cross section. Again, as in the case of single-layer coils, larger physical size will result in a higher Q associated with a given inductance value, and also requires a larger wire.

The Q of a typical air-cored coil varies with frequency in the manner illustrated in Fig. 2-16. With increasing frequency, the Q first rises slowly with frequency, then goes through a broad maximum, and finally drops at very high frequencies. The rise is due to the fact that the

[1] A discussion of coil losses under idealized conditions in which dielectric effects are neglected is given by G. W. O. Howe, The Q Factor of Single-layer Coils, *Wireless Eng.*, vol. 26, p. 179, June, 1949. An excellent discussion of coils for high frequencies is given by D. Pollack, The Design of Inductances for Frequencies between 4 and 25 Megacycles, *Trans. AIEE*, vol. 56, p. 1169, September, 1937.

inductive reactance of a coil is proportional to frequency, whereas the resistance due to skin effect cannot increase faster than the square root of the frequency; hence the ratio $Q = \omega L/R$ tends to rise with increasing frequency. If skin effect accounted for all the losses, the Q at very high frequencies would be proportional to the square root of frequency. However, dielectric losses arising from the coil form, the cotton or enamel insulation on the wire, etc., give rise to a resistance in series with the coil that is proportional to the cube of the frequency. At very high frequencies these dielectric losses become comparable to the skin-effect losses, and cause the coil Q to drop off.

The best conductor to use in an air-cored coil depends upon the frequency and coil design. In general, solid wire is used for frequencies above 1500 kc. Litz wire will give lower losses than the corresponding solid wire at frequencies below about 500 kc and will give some advantage for small multilayer coils in the frequency range 500 to 1500 kc.

A value of Q in the range 50 to 200 is typical of a good fairly small air-cored coil such as would be used for resonant circuits in a radio receiver. A Q of 10 or 20 is considered to be quite low, while Q values in excess of 300 are high and can ordinarily be achieved only by the use of coils that are physically large, such as are used in radio transmitters. These numbers are applicable for coils of all frequency ranges and inductance values.

Magnetic-cored Coils for Resonant Circuits. Coils with magnetic cores find extensive use at radio frequencies. The principal problem involved in using magnetic cores at radio frequencies is that of preventing eddy-current losses in the core material from becoming excessive. The permeability of magnetic materials does not drop off with frequency until the frequency is of the order of 10^{11} cycles. The hysteresis loss is proportional to the frequency, but since the coil reactance is likewise proportional to the frequency, the Q is not adversely affected by hysteresis loss at radio frequencies. In contrast, the eddy-current loss for a given core is proportional to the square of the frequency, whereas the reactance is proportional only to the frequency. Thus when the frequency becomes sufficiently high, eddy-current losses dominate the situation, and the coil Q drops.

The eddy-current losses can be kept low at high frequencies by arranging the magnetic material in the form of very fine particles or dust, produced either by chemical or mechanical means. These particles are coated with an insulating film, mixed with a suitable proportion of binder, pressed to the desired shape, and baked. In this way one obtains a core in which the individual magnetic particles are very finely subdivided, with resulting low eddy-current losses; such an arrangement is often called a "dust" or powder core. It is possible to make "dust" cores which have low losses at frequencies as high as 150 Mc.

The details of the magnetic core depend upon the application for which the coil is intended, and the frequency range over which the core is to operate. At audio and the lower radio frequencies, the core material is commonly made in the form of rings (toroidal core), so that a closed magnetic path may be obtained. Cores designed for use at these frequencies usually have an effective initial permeability that is quite high, such as 75 to 125, corresponding to a core involving relatively coarse particles combined with a minimum of insulating material and binder. At higher frequencies, the usual practice is to employ a single-layer winding of fine wire on a form that snugly fits an open core made in the form of a cylin-

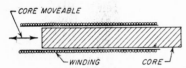

FIG. 2-17. Coil with slug-type magnetic core arranged so that the inductance can be varied by moving the core.

drical slug with a large length/diameter ratio, as in Fig. 2-17. Also, as the frequency is increased, the effective permeability that it is practical to employ in a core becomes less because the size of the particles of magnetic material in the core must be reduced, and the proportion of core material to binder and insulation becomes proportionally less. Thus cores that are suitable for use in coils operating at 100 Mc have, typically, an effective permeability of only 2 to 4, while cores for use at frequencies around 1 Mc have permeabilities from 10 to 30.

The particular magnetic material used likewise depends on frequency. For audio and the lower radio frequencies molybdenum permalloy is common; at the higher radio frequencies it is customary to use iron or magnetite, a natural iron oxide.

An alternative means of obtaining a magnetic core with low eddy-current losses is to employ a nonconducting magnetic material such as mentioned on page 16. Such material is suitable for use up to frequencies above 20 Mc; however, above some limiting frequency the dielectric and residual loss effects in the nonconducting magnetic material may adversely affect the behavior. In frequency ranges for which they are suitable, nonconducting magnetic cores result in coils having Q's as high as, or higher than, values typical of dust cores; at the same time a nonconducting core possesses considerably greater permeability than can be used in a dust core at the same frequency, and so has the advantage of compactness.[1]

Magnetic cores are particularly desirable when it is necessary to obtain a reasonable Q such as 25 to 100 in a very compact coil. They find extensive use in radio receivers. When a magnetic-cored coil is used in a resonant circuit, it is customary to employ a fixed tuning capacitance; the resonant frequency is then adjusted by varying the position of the slug

[1] A discussion of the properties obtainable in coils employing nonconducting ferrite cores is given by Strutt, *loc. cit.*

core, as indicated in Fig. 2-17. Such *permeability tuning*, as it is called, represents a means of tuning a resonant circuit that is often preferred to the alternative arrangement consisting of a fixed air-cored coil and a variable capacitance.

Radio-frequency Choke Coils. A radio-frequency choke coil is an inductance designed to offer a high impedance to alternating currents over the frequency range for which the coil is to be used. This result is obtained by making the inductance of the coil high and the distributed capacitance low, and by so proportioning that the inductance is in parallel

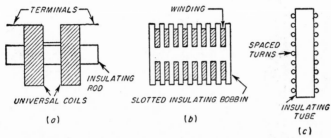

FIG. 2-18. Typical examples of radio-frequency choke coils.

resonance with the distributed capacitance somewhere in the desired operating range of frequencies.

A typical radio-frequency choke coil consists of one or more universal-wound coils mounted on an insulating rod, or of a series of "pies" wound in deep narrow slots in a slotted bobbin. A long single-layer solenoid is likewise sometimes used. Examples of radio-frequency choke coils are shown in Fig. 2-18.

The performance obtainable from a radio-frequency choke can generally be improved by the proper use of slug-type magnetic cores, which increase the inductance, and hence the impedance of the coil, without materially affecting the distributed capacitance.

2-8. Shielding of Magnetic and Electrostatic Fields. Under many conditions it is necessary to confine magnetic and electrostatic fields to a restricted space. This result is accomplished by using a shield composed of suitable material to enclose completely the space to be shielded.

The Shielding of Magnetic Flux at Radio Frequencies; Conducting Shields. The most practical shield for magnetic flux at radio frequencies is made of material having low electrical resistivity, such as copper or aluminum. Magnetic flux in attempting to pass through such a shield induces voltages in the shield which give rise to eddy currents. These eddy currents oppose the action of the flux, and in large measure prevent its penetration through the shield. In this way the flux is restricted to the interior of the shield, as illustrated in Fig. 2-19c.

To be effective a conducting shield should have a thickness *a* that is at least several times the skin depth δ as defined by Eq. (2-10). Under these conditions, and assuming that the radius of curvature of the shield is large compared with the skin depth, the ratio of the tangential components of the magnetic field intensities existing on the two sides of the shield is[1]

$$\text{Ratio of magnetic fields} = \epsilon^{a/\delta} \qquad (2\text{-}16)$$

Since the energy associated with a magnetic field is proportional to the square of the field intensity, the attenuation in decibels of the tangential component that is introduced by the conducting magnetic shield is

$$\text{Shield attenuation} = 8.69\,\frac{a}{\delta} \quad \text{db} \qquad (2\text{-}17)$$

Joints which interfere with the eddy currents by adding resistance to the eddy-current paths greatly reduce the effectiveness of a conducting shield. However, a joint parallel to the lines of current flow does not adversely affect the shielding unless it results in an open hole. This is true even if there is failure to make contact, so that the shield lacks continuity. These effects of joints are explained by the fact that the shielding is produced by the eddy currents; if the eddy currents are not disturbed, then the shielding resulting from action is not affected.

Power is dissipated in a conducting shield because the eddy currents must flow through the resistance of the shield material. When the thickness of the shield is considerably greater than the skin depth, the power loss in the shield can be determined by making use of the fact that the total magnitude I of the eddy currents in a strip of shield 1 cm wide is related to the density B in lines per square centimeter of the tangential component of flux that is adjacent to the surface of that part of the shield according to the relation

$$I = \frac{10B}{4\pi} \qquad (2\text{-}18)$$

The current I flows along the surface of the shield in a direction that is at right angles to the flux lines adjacent to the shield. For purposes of calculating power dissipation, this current can be considered as uniformly distributed to a thickness of one skin depth; it therefore encounters a resistance that is the surface resistivity of the material as calculated by skin-effect considerations (see page 23). Thus the total power loss in a shield can be obtained by first determining by some means the distribution of the tangential component of the magnetic flux adjacent to the surface of the shield. The distribution of current over the surface of the shield is next obtained with the aid of Eq. (2-18). The energy loss in each square

[1] The effect of a conducting shield on the component of magnetic field that is normal to the shield follows a different law; see B. Boston, Screening at V.H.F., *Wireless Eng.*, vol. 25, p. 221, July, 1948.

centimeter of shield surface is then determined by assuming that this current flows through a d-c resistance corresponding to a conductor that is one skin depth thick. The power consumed by a conducting shield is derived from the source of energy producing the magnetic field.

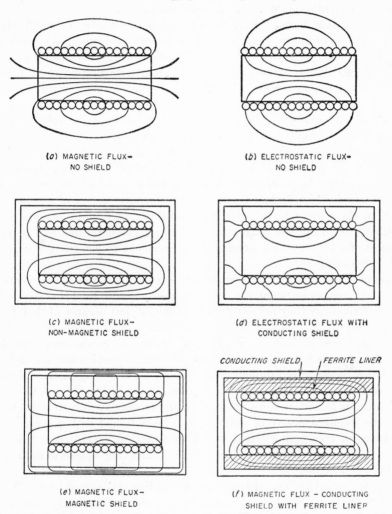

FIG. 2-19. Paths of electrostatic and magnetic-flux lines about the same coil with and without magnetic and nonmagnetic shields.

Shielding of D-C and Low-frequency Magnetic Fields; Magnetic Shields. When shielding against unidirectional magnetic fields is required, a shield composed of magnetic material is employed. Such a shield tends to short-circuit the flux lines which attempt to extend through the shield, as shown in Fig. 2-19e. The effectiveness of a magnetic shield is directly proportional to the thickness of the shield, since the reluctance that the shield offers to magnetic flux is inversely proportional to thickness. Joints or air gaps which add reluctance to the flux paths must be avoided. The degree of shielding achieved by a given total thickness of material can be increased by dividing the given thickness of magnetic material into two or more concentric shields separated by air spaces.

Magnetic shields must have high initial permeability to be effective. They are accordingly composed of high-permeability alloys such as permalloy; steel or iron is not a satisfactory material because of its low initial permeability. Since the desirable magnetic properties of perm-alloy and similar materials are adversely affected by mechanical strains, such as are introduced by drilling, punching, bending, etc., magnetic shields must be properly heat-treated *after* fabrication, to relieve these strains and develop the desirable magnetic properties.

Magnetic shields can be used for shielding alternating fields as well as d-c fields. In particular, they find extensive use at audio and power frequencies, particularly 60 cycles, where conducting shields would have to be excessively thick to be effective. The shielding action of a magnetic shield at these lower frequencies is achieved in part because of the short-circuiting action of the magnetic material on magnetic flux and in part because of eddy currents which cause the shield to act simultaneously as a conducting shield.

Magnetic shields of high-permeability material are also more effective at radio frequencies than are copper or aluminum shields. At these higher frequencies they act as conducting shields, but because of their high permeability have less skin depth. Thus the shielding obtained with a given thickness of material is greater. However, conducting material such as copper is less expensive per pound than magnetic material such as permalloy, is easier to fabricate, and requires no heat-treatment. Hence nonmagnetic conducting shields are generally used in preference to magnetic shields for alternating fields when the frequency is high enough so that the required degree of shielding can be obtained with a reasonable thickness of conducting shield; the only practical exception is when a conducting shield employs a liner of nonconducting magnetic material, as discussed below.

Electrostatic Shielding. Electrostatic shielding is obtained by enclosing the space to be shielded by a conducting surface. Accordingly, the magnetic and conducting shields for magnetic flux lines discussed above also serve as electrostatic shields. However, fairly effective electrostatic shielding can be obtained by a metal mesh made of any good to fair electrical conductor, which would be a rather poor shield for magnetic flux.

It is possible to shield electrostatic flux without simultaneously affecting the magnetic field by surrounding the space to be shielded with a conducting cage that is made in such a way as to provide no low-resistance path for the flow of eddy currents, while at the same time offering a metallic terminal upon which electrostatic flux lines can terminate. Thus, the secondary winding of a transformer may be shielded electrostatically from the primary by a shield having an insulated gap located in such a manner as to prevent the shield from becoming a short-circuited turn. This is illustrated in Fig. 2-20. Another type of electrostatic shield that does not affect the magnetic flux is illustrated below in connection with Prob. 2-45.

Energy loss is associated with electrostatic shielding as a result of the fact that the charging current induced in the shield produces currents that must flow through the surface resistance of the shield. However,

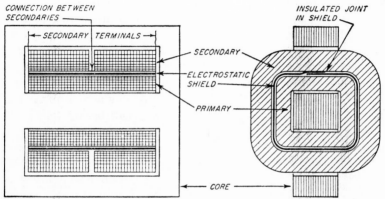

FIG. 2-20. Transformer with electrostatic shield between primary and secondary.

under most conditions these currents are quite small, so that the associated loss is generally insignificant. This is in contrast with shields for alternating magnetic flux, where the shield losses are very often substantial.

Effect of Shielding on Coils.[1] The magnetic and electric fields associated with a coil are frequently confined by placing the coil in a shield can composed of aluminum or copper. Such a shield increases the coil's distributed capacitance and effective resistance, and reduces its inductance. The distributed capacitance is increased as a result of the capacitance between the shield and various parts of the coil (see Fig. 2-19d). The inductance is decreased because the conducting shield restricts the magnetic flux lines to the space within the shield; this decreases the cross section of the magnetic circuit and thus reduces the flux linkages. The effective resistance of the coil is increased because the energy consumed by the eddy currents flowing in the shield is supplied by the coil.

The degree of shielding obtained at radio frequencies by enclosing a coil in a copper or aluminum container is very high, and if a reasonable clear-

---

[1] The quantitative relations involved are discussed by Howe, *op. cit.*; A. G. Bogle, The Effective Inductance and Resistance of Screened Coils, *J. IEE (Wireless Soc.)*, vol. 15, p. 221, September, 1940.

ance is provided between the shield and the coil, the properties of the coil are not seriously impaired.   In general, the clearance between the shield and the coil should everywhere be not less than the coil radius.   Under such conditions, the presence of the shield will not reduce the coil Q by more than 20 per cent, while the reduction in inductance will be still less.

A shielded inductance that is very compact can be achieved by making the conducting shield only slightly larger in diameter than the coil, and then using a liner of nonconducting magnetic material to fill the space between coil and shield, as shown in Fig. 2-19f.   The high permeability of the magnetic material provides a low-reluctance return path for the magnetic flux outside the coil, with the result that the inductance obtained is greater than when the coil is unshielded as in Fig. 2-19a.   This makes it practical to reduce the physical size required to obtain a given inductance at a desired value of Q.   In addition, the shielding is more effective than when only a conducting shield is used (Fig. 2-19c), because both magnetic and conducting shielding is simultaneously obtained.

PROBLEMS AND EXERCISES

2-1. If the flux shown in Fig. 2-1 is produced by a current of 0.01 amp, estimate the coil inductance.   (Assume that Fig. 2-1 gives a two-dimensional representation of the actual flux lines present in the three-dimensional coil.)

2-2. A single-layer coil is to have an inductance of 220 μh and is to be wound on a form having a diameter of 2 in.   If the ratio of length to diameter is 1.5, determine the distance between centers of adjacent turns of the winding.

2-3. A single-layer solenoidal coil having 60 turns on a winding 3 in. long and 3 in. in diameter possesses an inductance of 187 μh.   Without using Fig. 2-2, determine:

a. How many turns would be required to obtain the same inductance if the core were 2 in. in diameter and 2 in. long.

b. How many turns would be required to obtain an inductance of 400 μh with a winding 4 in. long and 4 in. in diameter.

2-4. a. On a hysteresis loop similar to that of Fig. 2-3, show a minor hysteresis loop originating at point 1 on the main loop, but corresponding to a substantially larger value of alternating magnetization.

b. Repeat for the same alternating magnetization as in (a), but with the d-c magnetization corresponding to point 3, instead of point 1.

2-5. The incremental inductance at low alternating magnetization of a particular iron-cored coil having 1000 turns is 10 henrys with no d-c saturation, and 4 henrys when carrying a d-c magnetizing current of 0.1 amp.   When the number of turns is reduced to 500, it is found that the inductance without d-c saturation is reduced to 2.5 henrys, or exactly one-fourth of the previous value, whereas with a d-c magnetizing current of 0.1 amp the incremental inductance is somewhat greater than one-fourth of 4 henrys.   Explain.

2-6. A coil uses a silicon-steel core composed of material having the characteristics given in Fig. 2-4, and the core is assembled with negligible air gap.   If the incremental inductance is 5.4 henrys with no d-c magnetization and low alternating flux density, what will be the incremental inductances with d-c magnetizations sufficient to produce 1, 2, and 3 ampere turns per cm?

2-7. *a.* A permanent magnet that is required to produce a large amount of flux in a low-reluctance magnetic circuit will be short and thick.   Explain.

b. A permanent magnet that is required to produce a small amount of flux in a high-reluctance circuit will be long and thin.   Explain.

2-8. A permanent magnet of Alnico V is required to establish a flux density of 2000 lines per sq cm in an air gap 1.2 cm long and having an effective cross section of 20 sq cm.   Determine the length and cross section of the magnet required, assuming stabilization is not necessary.

2-9. Explain why a permanent magnet stabilized as in Fig. 2-6 will have to be both larger in cross section and longer than an unstabilized magnet in order to produce the same flux in a given external circuit.

2-10. A particular permanent-magnet system employs a cylindrical magnet of Alnico V having a diameter of 1.0 in. and a length of 0.6 in.   If Alnico XII is used instead, calculate the diameter and length required to give the same result.   Assume that the permanent-magnet material is used under optimum conditions in both cases and that stabilization is not required.

2-11. A primary coil having an inductance of 100 μh is connected in series with a secondary coil of 240 μh, and the total inductance of the combination is measured as 146 μh.   Determine (*a*) the mutual inductance, (*b*) the coefficient of coupling, and (*c*) the inductance that would be observed if the terminals of one of the coils were reversed.

2-12. Two circuits are to be coupled by a common capacitor using the circuit of Fig. 2-8*c*.   If the total capacitance required in the primary circuit is 150 $\mu\mu$f, while the total capacitance required in the secondary circuit is 100 $\mu\mu$f, determine the value of the common capacitance C_m in Fig. 2-8*c* to give a coefficient of coupling of 0.02. [Note: In solving this problem do not attempt to use Eq. (2-8).]

2-13. In two circuits coupled as in Fig. 2-8*b*, $L_1 = 0.05$ henry, $L_2 = 0.08$ henry, and $k = 0.4$.   Determine (*a*) the required value of L_m, and (*b*) the total primary and total secondary inductances.

2-14. Explain why two coils that have their axes, respectively, parallel to, and at right angles to, the line joining the coil centers will have zero mutual inductance.

2-15. Two single-layer air-cored coils are located coaxially end to end, as illustrated in Fig. 2-8*a*.   It is found that, if a long cylindrical magnetic core is slipped inside of these coils so that it is common to both coils, the mutual inductance is increased more than is the self-inductance of the individual coils.   Explain.

2-16. What effect does the redistribution of current associated with skin effect have on the inductance?   Explain.

2-17. *a.* Calculate the skin depth in copper for 1 kc, 1 Mc, and 1000 Mc, and tabulate the results.

b. Repeat for aluminum.

2-18. Parts formed of brass, steel, etc., are sometimes silver- or copper-plated to reduce the effective resistance to radio frequencies.   If copper plating is employed, and the part is to be used in the frequency range 5 to 20 Mc, recommend a minimum thickness for this plating, and give the reasoning upon which this recommendation is based.

2-19. Inductances (and also shields) are sometimes plated to reduce corrosion and improve appearance.   The resistivity of the plating material suitable for this purpose is usually much higher than the resistivity of the material that is plated.   What criterion must the thickness of the plating satisfy if the effective resistance of the plated conductor is to approach closely the resistance obtained without plating?

2-20. A No. 14 copper wire (diameter 0.0641 in.) has a d-c resistance of 0.2525 ohm per 100 ft.   Calculate its resistance at 10 Mc, and at 3000 Mc, and tabulate these three values of resistance alongside of one another.

2-21. What diameter must a copper wire have if its resistance is not to exceed 3.0 ohms per 100 ft at 10 Mc?

2-22. A conductor consisting of a thin-walled tube will have much less resistance at very high frequencies than a solid wire of the same d-c resistance. Explain.

2-23. In a conductor consisting of a tube of specified outside diameter, the resistance at very high frequencies will be almost independent of wall thickness if this thickness exceeds several skin depths, but will be roughly inversely proportional to wall thickness when the thickness is small compared with the skin depth. Explain these observations.

2-24. Determine what mathematical approximation is involved in each of the following statements:

    a. The phase angle in radians is equal to the power factor.

    b. The reciprocal of capacitor Q is equal to the power factor of the capacitor.

    c. The dissipation factor is equal to the phase angle.

2-25. On the basis of the information given in Fig. 2-12 and the associated discussion, sketch curves analogous to Fig. 2-12 but showing qualitatively how the dielectric constant and power factor would vary as a function of temperature for (*a*) a low frequency, and (*b*) a high frequency.

2-26. *a.* A mica capacitor with power factor 0.0005 has a capacitance of 0.001 μf. Assuming skin-effect resistance to be negligible, what is the equivalent series resistance of the capacitor at frequencies of 1000, 100,000, and 10,000,000 cycles?

    b. What is the equivalent shunt resistance for the same conditions?

2-27. A certain air capacitor employing mycalex insulation has a power factor of 0.0003 at 1000 cycles. What will its power factor be at this same frequency and same capacitance if the mycalex insulation is replaced by polystyrene insulation of the same geometrical configuration?

2-28. The power factor of a capacitor at very high frequencies is roughly proportional to f^n where f is the frequency. What is the value of n?

2-29. Show that the power factor of a given variable air capacitor at low frequencies is independent of frequency but increases inversely with capacitance setting.

2-30. At very high frequencies, does an increase in frequency cause the power factor of a variable air capacitance for a given capacitance setting to become greater, less, or unchanged? Give an adequate justification for the answer chosen.

2-31. In a variable air capacitor the ratio of the power factor at a given high frequency to the power factor at a given low frequency becomes greater as the capacitance setting increases. Explain.

2-32. In a capacitor having a capacitance of 0.001 μf, the equivalent series inductance of the leads, etc., is 0.1 μh. At what frequency does the apparent capacitance differ from the true capacitance by 10 per cent?

2-33. A certain capacitor having air dielectric with bakelite supports obtains 10 $\mu\mu f$ of its capacitance through the bakelite dielectric having a power factor of 4 per cent, and the remainder of its capacitance from the air, which has no losses. What is the equivalent series resistance and power factor at 10,000 kc when the total capacitance is 100 $\mu\mu f$ (90 $\mu\mu f$ from air and 10 $\mu\mu f$ from bakelite)? Neglect skin-effect losses.

2-34. A particular mica capacitor having a capacitance of 0.001 μf has a power factor of 0.0005 at a frequency of 1000 cycles, while at 10 Mc the power factor has risen to 0.001. From this information deduce the values of R and R_2 applicable in Fig. 2-13 at 10 Mc.

2-35. The capacitor of Prob. 2-26 is able to stand a d-c potential of 5000 volts and is capable of dissipating safely 3 watts of heat.

    a. At what frequency will heating begin to limit the voltage rating?

    b. What is the voltage rating at frequencies of 1, 1000, and 10,000 kc?

2-36. Derive an equation giving the exact relation between the Q of a coil and the coil power factor, and from this calculate the error in the approximate relation: power factor $= 1/Q$, when $Q = 50$.

2-37. Explain why the distributed capacitance of a coil is always increased by the wax or other coating used for protection against moisture.

2-38. On the basis of proximity and skin effects, explain why it is reasonable to expect that the maximum coil Q would be obtained with a wire not so large as to leave very little clearance between adjacent turns, and not so small as to make this clearance become a large fraction of the spacing between centers of adjacent turns.

2-39. In a coil with a magnetic slug core as in Fig. 2-17, removing the core will reduce the inductance less in a system using a core designed for 100 Mc than in a system using a core designed for 1 Mc.   Explain.

2-40. A copper shield is required to reduce the magnetic flux density by 60 db. What shield thickness is required at (a) 1 kc, (b) 1 Mc, and (c) 1000 Mc?

2-41. Derive Eq. (2-17) from Eq. (2-16).

2-42. A particular magnetic shield attenuates d-c magnetic fields by 20 db.   What will the attenuation be if the shield thickness is doubled?

2-43. A conducting magnetic shield is composed of permalloy having an initial permeability of 15,000 and a resistivity of 17 μohms per cm cube.   Calculate (a) the thickness which this material must have to be 5 skin depths thick at 60 cycles, and (b) the thickness which copper must have to achieve the same degree of shielding.

2-44. Explain why magnetic material in powdered form, such as used in magnetic cores for radio frequencies, is not suitable for use as a shield of alternating magnetic fields.

2-45. A grid of wires such as shown in the accompanying figure will provide electrostatic shielding without magnetic shielding provided the structure (shown dotted in

PROB. 2-45

the illustration) supporting the sides of the shield is an insulator.   However, if the material of the supporting structure is a conductor, then magnetic as well as electrostatic fields are shielded at least to some extent.   Explain.

2-46. When a nonmagnetic shield can surrounds a solenoidal coil, it is observed that the shielding of the magnetic field is not affected appreciably by a joint in the shield provided this joint is in a plane perpendicular to the axis of the coil, but the effectiveness of the shield is very seriously reduced if the joint is in a plane that contains the axis of the coil.   Explain.

2-47. If it is necessary that a magnetic shield for d-c fields have a joint, how should this joint be oriented with respect to the direction of the magnetic flux that is being shielded?

CHAPTER 3

PROPERTIES OF CIRCUITS
WITH LUMPED CONSTANTS

3-1. Series Resonance. A circuit consisting of an inductance, capacitance, and resistance all in series, as in Fig. 3-1, is called a series resonant

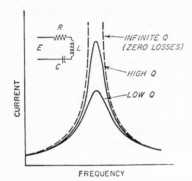

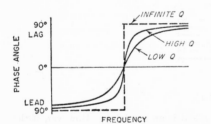

FIG. 3-1. Magnitude and phase angle of current in a series resonant circuit as a function of frequency for constant applied voltage and different circuit Q's.

or series tuned circuit. When a constant voltage of varying frequency is applied to such a circuit, the current that flows depends upon frequency in the manner shown in Fig. 3-1. At low frequencies, the capacitive reactance of the circuit is large and the inductive reactance is small. Most of the voltage drop is then across the capacitor, while the current is small and leads the applied voltage by nearly 90°. At high frequencies, the inductive reactance is large and the capacitive reactance low, resulting in a small current that lags nearly 90° behind the applied voltage, and most of the voltage drop is across the inductance. In between these two extremes there is a frequency, *called the resonant frequency*, *at which the capacitive and inductive reactances are exactly equal* and, consequently, neutralize each other; there is then only the resistance of the circuit to oppose the flow of current. The current at the resonant frequency is accordingly equal to the applied voltage divided by the circuit resistance, and is very large if the resistance is low.

A resonance curve such as illustrated in Fig. 3-1 finds extensive use in selective systems for separating a desired a-c signal from signals of other frequencies. For frequencies in the vicinity of resonance corresponding to a carrier wave and its sideband frequencies, the response is nearly uniform and is quite large. However, at frequencies differing greatly from resonance the response is relatively small, with the result that signals of such frequencies, i.e., the unwanted signals, are severely discriminated against.

The characteristics of a series resonant circuit depend primarily upon the ratio of inductive reactance ωL to *circuit* resistance R, i.e., upon $\omega L/R$. This ratio is frequently denoted by the symbol Q and is called the circuit Q.[1] Most of the loss in the usual resonant circuit is due to coil resistance because the losses in a properly constructed capacitor are small in comparison with those of a coil. The result is that the circuit Q ordinarily approximates the Q of the coil alone, which was discussed in Sec. 2-7.

The general effect of different circuit resistances, i.e., different values of Q, is shown in Fig. 3-1. It is seen that, when the frequency differs appreciably from the resonant frequency, *the actual current is practically independent of the circuit resistance and is very nearly the current that would be obtained with no losses.* On the other hand, the current at the resonant frequency is determined solely by the resistance. The effect of increasing the resistance of a series circuit is, accordingly, to flatten the resonance curve by reducing the current at resonance without significantly affecting the behavior at frequencies differing appreciably from resonance. This broadens the top of the curve, giving a more nearly uniform current over a band of frequencies near the resonant point, but does so by reducing the ability of the circuit to discriminate between voltages of different frequencies.

Analysis of Series Resonant Circuit. The elementary voltage, current, and impedance relations of series resonant circuits are discussed in every book on alternating currents. The basic quantitative relations are listed below for convenient reference.

$$\text{Resonant frequency} = f_0 = \frac{1}{2\pi \sqrt{LC}} \tag{3-2}$$

$$Z_s = R + j\left(\omega L - \frac{1}{\omega C}\right) \tag{3-3a}$$

$$|Z_s| = \sqrt{R^2 + \left(\omega L - \frac{1}{\omega C}\right)^2} \tag{3-3b}$$

---

[1] The circuit Q can also be defined as

$$Q = 2\pi \frac{\text{energy stored in circuit}}{\begin{cases} \text{energy dissipated in circuit} \\ \text{during one cycle} \end{cases}} \tag{3-1}$$

This relation follows from the fact that the energy stored in the inductance L when the current I is maximum (i.e., when all the stored energy is in the inductance) is $I^2L/2$, where I is the peak current. At the same time, the energy lost per cycle in the circuit resistance R is $I^2R/2f$, where f is the frequency.

$$\tan \theta = \frac{\omega L - (1/\omega C)}{R} \tag{3-4}$$

$$I = \frac{E}{Z_s} = \frac{E}{R + j[\omega L - (1/\omega C)]} \tag{3-5}$$

$$\text{Current at resonance} = I_0 = \frac{E}{R_0} \tag{3-6}$$

$$\text{Voltage across inductance} = j\omega L I \tag{3-7a}$$

$$\text{Voltage across capacitor} = \frac{-j}{\omega C} I \tag{3-7b}$$

where E = voltage applied to circuit

   I = current flowing in circuit, amp

   f = frequency, cycles

   $\omega = 2\pi f$

   $Q = \omega L/R$

   R = total series resistance of tuned circuit

   L = inductance, henrys

   C = capacitance, farads

   Z_s = impedance of series circuit

   θ = phase angle of impedance

   Subscript $_0$ denotes values at resonant frequency

At frequencies near resonance the voltages across the capacitor and the inductance will both be very much greater than the applied voltage. This is possible because at frequencies near resonance the voltages across the capacitor and inductance are nearly 180° out of phase with each other and so add up to a value that is much smaller than either voltage alone.

At resonance, where the circuit current is E/R, Eqs. (3-7) show that the voltage across the inductance (or capacitor) is then Q times the applied voltage; i.e., *there is a resonant rise of voltage in the circuit amounting to Q times.* Since a typical value of Q is of the order of 100, a series resonant circuit will thus develop a high voltage even with small applied potentials. At frequencies differing from resonance the voltage developed across the inductance (or capacitor) falls off. In the vicinity of resonance the resulting curve of voltage as a function of frequency has a shape that for all practical purposes can be considered to be the same as the corresponding curve of current as a function of frequency (see Fig. 3-1). The reason for this is that most of the resonance effects exist in a very narrow frequency band, typically representing a frequency variation of only a few per cent. Over this frequency range the term ωL (or $1/\omega C$) in Eqs. (3-7) is so nearly constant that to a first approximation the voltage developed across the circuit can be considered to be proportional to the circuit current.

Universal Resonance Curve. Equations (3-5) and (3-6) can also be rearranged to express the ratio of current actually flowing to the current at resonance, in terms of the circuit Q and the fractional deviation of the frequency from resonance. This leads to the universal resonance curve of Fig. 3-2.[1]

In the universal resonance curve, the frequency is expressed in terms of a parameter a that represents f_0/Q cycles, as defined in Fig. 3-2. Thus $a = 1.0$ when the cycles off resonance equal f_0/Q cycles, $a = 2$ when the number of cycles off resonance is $2f_0/Q$, etc.

The use of Fig. 3-2 in practical calculations can be illustrated by two examples.

Example 1. It is desired to know how many cycles one must be off resonance to reduce the current to one-half the value at resonance when the circuit has a Q of 125 and is resonant at 1000 kc.

Reference to Fig. 3-2 shows that the response is reduced to 0.5 when $a = 0.86$. Hence,

$$\text{Cycles off resonance} = \frac{0.86 \times 1000}{125} = 6.88 \text{ kc}$$

The phase angle of the current as obtained from the curve is 60°.

Example 2. With the same circuit as in the preceding example, it is desired to know what the response will be at a frequency 10,000 cycles below resonance.

To solve this problem it is first necessary to determine a.

$$a = \frac{10,000}{1000} \times 125 = 1.25$$

Reference to Fig. 3-2 shows that for $a = 1.25$ the response is reduced by a factor 0.37 and that the phase of the current is 68° leading.

The only assumption involved in the universal resonance curve is that Q is assumed to be the same at the frequency being considered as at the resonant frequency. *When this is true, the universal resonance curve*

---

[1] The equation of the universal resonance curve is obtained as follows: The ratio of Eq. (3-5) to Eq. (3-6) gives

$$\frac{\text{Actual current}}{\text{Current at resonance}} = \frac{R_0}{R + j[\omega L - (1/\omega C)]} = \frac{R_0}{R + j[(\omega^2 LC - 1)/\omega C]}$$

Now define the fractional deviation δ of the frequency from resonance, according to the relation

$$\omega = \omega_0(1 + \delta)$$

Substituting this expression for ω and remembering that $\omega_0 L = 1/\omega_0 C$, one obtains

$$\frac{\text{Actual current}}{\text{Current at resonance}} = \frac{R_0}{R + j\left[\dfrac{(1 + \delta)^2 - 1}{1 + \delta}\right]\omega_0 L} = \frac{1}{\dfrac{R}{R_0} + jQ\delta\left(\dfrac{2 + \delta}{1 + \delta}\right)}$$

When Q is constant, the radio-frequency resistance is proportional to frequency so that $R/R_0 = \omega/\omega_0 = (1 + \delta)$, which when substituted yields

$$\frac{\text{Actual current}}{\text{Current at resonance}} = \frac{1}{1 + \delta + jQ\delta\left(\dfrac{2 + \delta}{1 + \delta}\right)} \tag{3-8}$$

Figure 3-2 is then obtained by substituting $a = Q\delta$.

involves no approximations whatsoever. Over the limited range of frequencies near resonance represented in Fig. 3-2, the variation in Q in practical cases is so small as to introduce negligible (i.e., less than 1 per cent) error from the use of the curve, when the value of Q existing at resonance is used in determining the parameter a.

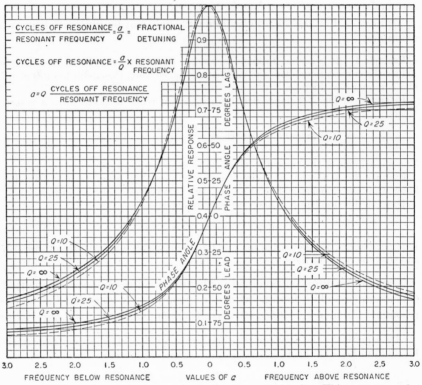

Fig. 3-2. Universal resonance curve for series resonant circuit. This curve can also be applied to the parallel resonant circuit by considering the vertical scale to represent the ratio of actual parallel impedance to the parallel impedance at resonance. When applied to parallel circuits, the angles shown in the figure as leading are lagging, and vice versa.

The universal resonance curve is useful because it is independent of the resonant frequency of the circuit and of the ratio of inductance to capacitance, and because it is substantially independent of circuit Q. It thus follows that *all resonance curves have the same relative shape irrespective of resonant frequency, Q, or ratio of inductance to capacitance of the circuit.*

Working Rules for Estimating Sharpness of Resonance. Since the curves for different values of Q are almost identical in Fig. 3-2, particularly in the neighborhood of the resonant frequency, it is possible to state several easily remembered working rules that will enable one to estimate the sharpness of any resonance curve with an error of less than 1 per cent when only the Q of the circuit is known.[1] These rules follow:

Rule 1. When the frequency of the applied voltage deviates from the resonant frequency by an amount that is $1/2Q$ of the resonant frequency, the current that flows is reduced to 70.7 per cent of the resonant current, and the current is 45° out of phase with the applied voltage. Thus the frequency band B over which the response is at least 70.7 per cent of that at resonance (i.e., within 3 db of resonance) is $B = f_0/Q$, where f_0 is the resonant frequency.

Rule 2. When the frequency of the applied voltage deviates from the resonant frequency by an amount that is $1/Q$ of the resonant frequency, the current that flows is reduced to 44.7 per cent of the resonant current, and the current is $63\frac{1}{2}°$ out of phase with the applied voltage.

Thus, in the circuit considered in the above examples, the current would be reduced to 70.7 per cent of the value at resonance when the frequency is $\frac{1}{250}$ of 1000 kc, or 4000 cycles off resonance, and to 44.7 per cent of the resonant current for a frequency deviation of $\frac{1}{125}$ of 1000 kc, or 8000 cycles. Since the resonant rise of voltage in this circuit is 125 ($=Q$) times, the rise of voltage is very nearly $0.7 \times 125 = 87.5$ times when the frequency is 4000 cycles off resonance, and is very close to $0.45 \times 125 = 56.25$ times at a frequency 8000 cycles from resonance.

Practical Calculation of Resonance Curves. The proper procedure for calculating a resonance curve is to start by determining the current at resonance, using Eq. (3-6). The working rules can then be applied to obtain the response at frequencies $1/2Q$ and $1/Q$ on either side of resonance. This gives a picture of the sharpness of resonance and is sufficient for many purposes. However, if additional points in the vicinity of resonance are needed, they can be calculated with the aid of Fig. 3-2.

At frequencies too far off resonance to come within the range of the universal resonance curve, the *magnitude* of the current can be determined with an accuracy sufficient for nearly all practical purposes by neglecting the resistance R in Eq. (3-5). The phase angle of the current under these conditions is obtained from Eq. (3-4).

The above procedure for calculating resonance curves is much superior to making calculations based directly upon Eq. (3-5). The use of the universal resonance curve in the vicinity of the resonant frequency not only reduces the amount of labor involved but also greatly improves the accuracy under ordinary conditions. This is because resonant circuit formulas such as Eq. (3-5) contain a term $\left(\omega L - \dfrac{1}{\omega C}\right)$ which involves the difference of two quantities which near resonance are nearly equal in magnitude. In order to obtain this difference without more than 1 per

---

[1] An error of 1 per cent is nearly always permissible in calculations of radio-frequency circuits. This is because the effective circuit constants at radio frequencies are very seldom known to an accuracy that involves an error of less than 1 per cent.

cent error, five-place logarithms must ordinarily be employed. Slide-rule calculations are never permissible. Neglecting the resistance at frequencies too far off resonance to come within the range covered by the universal resonance curve enormously reduces the labor involved in calculating magnitudes, and introduces an error of less than 1 per cent of the magnitude at resonance. This accuracy is ample for all ordinary purposes, and the error is undetectable when resonance curves are plotted.

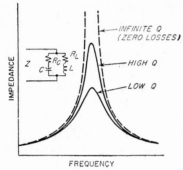

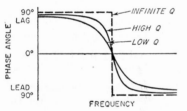

FIG. 3-3. Magnitude and phase angle of impedance of a parallel circuit as a function of frequency for different circuit Q's.

3-2. Parallel Resonance. A parallel circuit consisting of an inductance branch in parallel with a capacitance branch offers an impedance of the character shown in Fig. 3-3. Such a circuit is termed a parallel resonant or parallel tuned circuit.

When a voltage is applied to such a system, then at very low frequencies, the inductive branch draws a large lagging current while the leading current of the capacitive branch is small, resulting in a large lagging line or circuit current and a low lagging circuit impedance. At high frequencies, the inductance has a high reactance compared with the capacitance, resulting in a large leading line current and a correspondingly low circuit impedance that is leading in phase. In between these two extremes, there is a frequency at which the lagging current taken by the inductive branch and the leading current entering the capacitance branch are equal; being 180° out of phase, they then neutralize and leave only a small resultant inphase current flowing in the line. The impedance of the parallel circuit will then be a very high resistance, as is brought out in Fig. 3-3.[1]

A comparison of Figs. 3-1 and 3-3 shows that the impedance curve of a parallel circuit is similar in character to the current curve of a series circuit. In particular, increasing the resistance of a parallel resonant

[1] In obtaining a parallel resonance curve experimentally by measurements of applied voltage and line current, extreme care must be taken to ensure that the applied voltage contains no harmonics. This is necessary because at resonance the circuit impedance is extremely high to the fundamental component of the applied voltage and very low to the harmonic components, with the result that even a small harmonic-voltage component will cause line currents that mask the small fundamental component.

circuit lowers and flattens the peak of the resonance curve, just as in the analogous series resonance case.   This similarity is considered below in greater detail.

The relationship between the line and branch currents in a parallel circuit is illustrated in Fig. 3-4.   It will be noted that, unlike the line or circuit current, which shows a resonance effect, the currents in the individual branches of a parallel circuit vary only slightly in the vicinity of resonance and are relatively large.   At resonance the two branch currents have similar magnitudes, and being almost (but not quite) out of phase they add up to a very small resultant current, thus giving a high circuit impedance.   As the frequency departs from resonance the two branch currents become slightly unequal in magnitude; this causes the line current to increase as shown, which means lowered circuit impedance.   It is characteristic of parallel resonant circuits that for frequencies near resonance

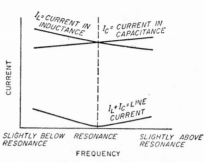

Fig. 3-4. Relationship of line and branch currents in a parallel resonant circuit in the vicinity of resonance.

the current flowing in the branches, commonly referred to as the circulating current, is much larger than the line current, i.e., than the current supplied to the circuit.

The fundamental relations of a parallel resonant circuit are derived in every introductory book on a-c circuit theory, and are listed below for convenient reference.

$$\text{Parallel impedance} = Z = \frac{Z_c Z_L}{Z_c + Z_L} = \frac{Z_c Z_L}{Z_s} \tag{3-9}$$

$$\text{Line current} = \frac{E}{Z} \tag{3-10}$$

$$\text{Inductive branch current} = \frac{E}{Z_L} = \frac{E}{R_L + j\omega L} \tag{3-11}$$

$$\text{Capacitive branch current} = \frac{E}{Z_c} = \frac{E}{R_c - (j/\omega C)} \tag{3-12}$$

where E = voltage applied to circuit
$\quad Z_c = R_c - (j/\omega C)$ = impedance of capacitive branch
$\quad Z_L = R_L + j\omega L$ = impedance of inductive branch
$\quad Z_s = Z_c + Z_L$ = series impedance of circuit
$\quad Z$ = impedance of circuit when connected in parallel
$\quad R_s = R_c + R_L$ = total series resistance of circuit
$\quad \omega = 2\pi$ times frequency
$\quad Q = \omega L/R_s$ = circuit Q

These equations are fundamental to every parallel circuit, irrespective of the circuit Q, the frequency, or the division of resistance between the branches.

Quantitative Relations in Parallel Resonant Circuits with Moderate or High Q, and the Use of Universal Resonance Curve. When the Q of a parallel resonant circuit is not too low (e.g., of the order of 10 or more), the quantitative relations become quite simple. To begin with, it is then permissible to assume that the circuit has maximum impedance and unity power factor at the same frequency, which is also the frequency at which the same circuit is in series resonance as given by Eq. (3-2). In contrast, when the circuit Q is low, this is not necessarily the case, as discussed below.

When the circuit Q is not too low, the exact expressions of Eqs. (3-9) and (3-10) can be simplified, without introducing appreciable error, by neglecting the resistance components of the impedances Z_L and Z_C in the numerator of Eq. (3-9). When this is done[1]

$$\text{Parallel impedance} = Z = \frac{(\omega_0 L)^2}{Z_s} \tag{3-13}$$

At resonance $Z_s = R_s$, and this becomes

$$\text{Parallel impedance at resonance} = \frac{(\omega_0 L)^2}{R_s} = (\omega_0 L)Q \tag{3-14}$$

In these equations ω_0 is the value of ω at resonance. It will be noted from Eq. (3-14) that *at resonance the impedance of a parallel circuit is a resistance that is Q times the reactance of one of the branches.*[2] It can, therefore, be said that the parallel arrangement of inductive and capacitive branches causes a resonant rise of impedance of Q times the impedance that would be obtained from either branch alone. It is thus apparent that very high impedances can be developed by parallel resonance. This is one of the most important properties of parallel resonance.

Under conditions where the circuit Q is not too low, the resonance curve of the parallel impedance of a circuit can be considered to have the *same shape as the resonance curve of the series current* in a circuit consisting

---

[1] This transformation is carried out as follows: If the resistance components in the numerator of Eq. (3-12) are neglected, the product $Z_L Z_C$ becomes $\omega L/\omega C = L/C$. One can now eliminate the capacitance C in this expression by multiplying both numerator and denominator by ω_0 and then noting that $1/\omega_0 C = \omega_0 L$. That is,

$$Z_L Z_C = \frac{L}{C} = \frac{\omega_0 L}{\omega_0 C} = (\omega_0 L)^2$$

[2] It also follows from Eq. (3-14) and Eqs. (3-10) to (3-12) that at resonance the branch currents are Q times as large as the line current, provided the resistance components in Eqs. (3-11) and (3-12) are small compared with the associated reactive components.

of the same inductance, capacitance, and resistances connected in a series instead of a parallel arrangement. This follows from the fact that a comparison of Eqs. (3-5) and (3-13) shows that both the parallel impedance and the series current are equal to a constant divided by Z_s. *Consequently, the universal resonance curve and the working rules that were applied for estimating the sharpness of resonance of the series circuit also apply to the case of parallel resonance when the circuit Q is moderate or high.* The only difference is that the signs of the phase angles are now reversed, the phase of the parallel impedance being leading at frequencies higher than resonance and lagging at frequencies below resonance.

The proper procedure for calculating the impedance of a parallel resonant circuit of moderate or high Q is therefore similar to that used

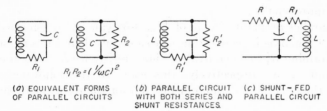

(a) EQUIVALENT FORMS OF PARALLEL CIRCUITS

(b) PARALLEL CIRCUIT WITH BOTH SERIES AND SHUNT RESISTANCES.

(c) SHUNT-FED PARALLEL CIRCUIT

FIG. 3-5. Forms of parallel resonant circuits involving a shunt resistance and shunt feed.

with a series resonant circuit. The first step is to determine the resonant frequency and the impedance at resonance, using Eqs. (3-2) and (3-14). Next, the working rules are applied to obtain the 70.7 and the 44.7 per cent points on either side of resonance. This gives the general picture of the sharpness of resonance and is sufficient for many purposes. If a more complete curve is desired in the vicinity of resonance, one may make use of the universal resonance curve of Fig. 3-2. Finally, at frequencies so far off resonance as to be outside the range of the universal resonance curve, one may determine the magnitude of the impedance by using Eq. (3-13), but neglecting the circuit resistance R when making the calculation. The power-factor angle of the impedance thus obtained is the negative of the corresponding angle for series resonance, as given by Eq. (3-4).

Parallel Resonant Circuits with Shunt Resistances and with Parallel Feed. The two types of parallel resonant circuits shown in Fig. 3-5a are equivalent to each other provided the resistances R_1 and R_2 are properly related, and provided also that the circuit Q is not too low. To determine the relationship that must exist between R_1 and R_2, one notes that R_1 can be thought of as being associated with capacitance C as its equivalent series resistance, while R_2 can be regarded as an equivalent shunt resistance of the same capacitance C. Assuming that the circuit Q is not too low [i.e., that $(1/\omega C)/R_1 >> 1$, and that $R_2/(1/\omega C) >> 1$], then from Eqs. (2-12) and (2-13) one has

$$R_1 R_2 = \left(\frac{1}{\omega C}\right)^2 \qquad (3\text{-}15)$$

Although the relationship between R_1 and R_2 is seen by Eq. (3-15) to depend on frequency, it is common practice to determine the relation between R_1 and R_2 at resonance, and then to assume that the values at resonance also hold for all frequencies in the vicinity of resonance. This approximation is equivalent to assuming that the right-hand term of Eq. (3-15) is constant at the value it has at resonance.[1] Since ω changes by only a small percentage in the limited frequency range around resonance, this assumption is not far from the truth, and the error it introduces is quite small.

The parallel resonant circuit of Fig. 3-5b can be transformed to the circuits of Fig. 3-5a by converting R_2' to an equivalent series resistance R_1 or transforming R_1' to an equivalent shunt resistance R_2. By use of Eqs. (2-12) and (2-13), respectively, this leads to the following relations between the circuits of a and b in Fig. 3-5 for the resonant frequency:

$$\left.\begin{array}{l}\text{Total effective} \\ \text{series resistance}\end{array}\right\} = R_1 = R_1' + \frac{(\omega_0 L)^2}{R_2'} \qquad (3\text{-}18a)$$

$$\left.\begin{array}{l}\text{Shunt resistance} \\ \text{equivalent to } R_1'\end{array}\right\} = R_{eq} = \frac{(\omega_0 L)^2}{R_1'} \qquad (3\text{-}18b)$$

$$\left.\begin{array}{l}\text{Total effective} \\ \text{shunt resistance} \\ \text{including } R' \text{ and } R_{eq}\end{array}\right\} = R_2 = \frac{R_{eq} R_2}{R_{eq} + R_2'} \qquad (3\text{-}18c)$$

The above analysis is of practical importance for two reasons. In the first place, it shows that to a high approximation, the effect produced by shunting a resistance across a parallel resonant circuit is merely to lower the effective Q of the circuit. The resonant frequency is unchanged, however, and the impedance curve still has the shape of a resonance curve as given by the universal resonance curve. In the second place, the analysis provides a simple means of determining the quantitative effect that a shunt resistance produces on the properties of a resonant circuit.

Still another form of parallel resonant circuit that is frequently encountered is shown in Fig. 3-5c, where a resistance R is connected in series with

---

[1] At resonance, one can write $\omega_0 L = 1/\omega_0 C$, where ω_0 is the value of ω at the resonant frequency. Under these conditions the following useful relations apply to Fig. 3-5a:

$$R_1 R_2 = (\omega_0 L)^2 \qquad (3\text{-}16)$$

$$\left.\begin{array}{l}Q \text{ of circuit} \\ \text{at resonance}\end{array}\right\} = \frac{\omega_0 L}{R_1} = \frac{R_2}{\omega_0 L} \qquad (3\text{-}17a)$$

$$\left.\begin{array}{l}\text{Parallel impedance} \\ \text{at resonance}\end{array}\right\} = \omega_0 L Q = R_2 \qquad (3\text{-}17b)$$

the parallel circuit. The behavior of arrangements of this type is analyzed in Sec. 3-7.

Parallel Circuits with Low Q. The entire discussion of parallel resonance given above except for Eqs. (3-9) to (3-12) assumes that the Q of the parallel circuit is at least reasonably high (i.e., of the order of 10 or more). In the general case when the circuit Q is low, the curve of circuit impedance as a function of frequency still has a shape that resembles a resonance curve unless the circuit Q approaches or is less than unity. However, the maximum impedance no longer necessarily occurs at the frequency of series resonance, and the condition of unity power factor does not necessarily occur either at the frequency of series resonance or when the impedance is a maximum. The actual behavior for any given Q depends upon the division of resistance between the inductive and capacitive branches, as illustrated in Fig. 3-6 for typical cases.

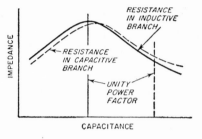

An important consideration in the use of low-Q resonant circuits occurs when such a circuit is tuned to resonance with a given frequency by varying either the inductance or capacitance of the circuit. If, for example, the tuning is accomplished by varying the capacitance, then, if all the circuit losses are in the inductive branch, the capacitance setting that makes the circuit impedance maximum also corresponds to unity power factor. If, however, part or all of the circuit resistance is in the capacitive branch, then the capacitance setting that makes the circuit impedance maximum at an assigned frequency does not correspond to the capacitance setting for which the circuit power factor is

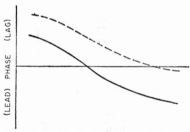

Fig. 3-6. Typical characteristics of parallel resonance circuits having low Q.

unity. This is illustrated in Fig. 3-6. Similarly, if the tuning is accomplished by varying the inductance, then the situation is reversed, and maximum impedance and unity-power-factor conditions coincide only if all the circuit losses are concentrated in the capacitive branch. These properties of parallel resonant circuits with low Q are often of considerable importance in connection with the resonant circuits of Class C amplifiers such as used in radio transmitters.

Components of Parallel Impedance. The parallel impedance as calculated by Eq. (3-9) or (3-13) can be thought of as equivalent to a resistance in series with a reactance, as shown in Fig. 3-7a. When the circuit Q is sufficiently high for Eq. (3-13) to apply, then these resistance and reactance components will be found to vary with frequency in the manner shown in Fig. 3-7b, which is a universal curve derivable directly from the universal resonance curve of the parallel circuit.   It will be noted that the resistance component has a shape superficially similar to that of a resonance curve, but differs in that it has steeper sides.   In particular,

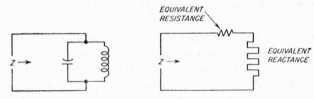

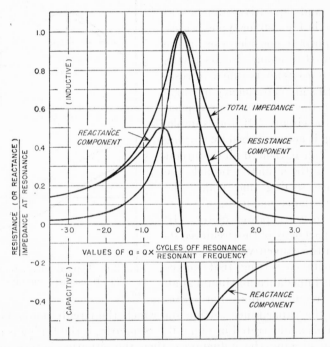

(*a*) ACTUAL CIRCUIT AND EQUIVALENT SERIES COMPONENTS

(*b*) UNIVERSAL CURVE OF IMPEDANCE COMPONENTS

Fig. 3-7. Representation of parallel impedance in terms of equivalent series resistance and reactance components, together with universal curve giving these components as a function of frequency in a parallel resonant circuit having a relatively high Q.

the resistance drops to 50 per cent of the resonant impedance at frequencies corresponding to the 70.7 per cent points of the impedance curve (i.e., when the number of cycles off resonance equals the resonant frequency divided by $2Q$).   It will also be noted that the reactance curves are characterized by maxima and minima which occur at the 70.7 per cent points of the resonance curve and which have peak amplitudes that are exactly 50 per cent of the impedance at resonance as given by Eq. (3-14).

An application of these concepts is supplied by the case of a coil having distributed capacitance. With respect to its terminals, such a coil is represented by the left-hand circuit of Fig. 3-7a, and accordingly behaves as shown in Fig. 3-7b. Below the frequency at which the distributed capacitance is resonant with the inductance, the system is equivalent to a resistance in series with an inductive reactance. The apparent inductance represented by this equivalent reactance depends on frequency, however, rising with frequency until just before resonance is reached, and then dropping rapidly. The apparent inductance becomes zero at the parallel resonant frequency, *while for higher frequencies the coil has a capacitive reactance and is therefore equivalent to a small capacitor.* The

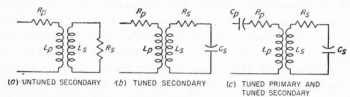

(a) UNTUNED SECONDARY   (b) TUNED SECONDARY   (c) TUNED PRIMARY AND TUNED SECONDARY

FIG. 3-8. Various types of inductively coupled circuits commonly encountered in electronics.

apparent resistance of the coil increases rapidly with the frequency until a maximum is reached at the resonant frequency, beyond which the resistance rapidly diminishes. These effects are all direct consequences of the properties of parallel resonant circuits, and can be readily deduced by an examination of Fig. 3-7 or of Eqs. (3-13) and (3-14). The behavior of an inductance coil with self-capacitance can accordingly be calculated just as one would determine the characteristics of any other parallel circuit.

3-3. Inductively Coupled Circuits; Theory. When mutual inductance exists between coils that are in separate circuits, these circuits are said to be inductively coupled. The effect of the mutual inductance is to make possible the transfer of energy from one circuit to the other by transformer action. That is, an alternating current flowing in one circuit produces magnetic flux which induces a voltage in the coupled circuit. This results in induced currents and a transfer of energy from the first or primary circuit to the coupled or secondary circuit. Several examples of inductively coupled circuits commonly encountered in electronics are shown in Fig. 3-8.

The behavior of inductively coupled circuits is somewhat complicated, but it can be readily calculated with the aid of the following rules:

Rule 1. As far as the primary circuit is concerned, the effect that the presence of the coupled secondary circuit has is exactly as though an imped-

ance $(\omega M)^2/Z_s$ *had been added in series with the primary,*[1] where $M =$ mutual inductance, $\omega = 2\pi f$, and $Z_s =$ series impedance of secondary circuit when considered by itself. The equivalent impedance $(\omega M)^2/Z_s$ which the presence of the secondary adds to the primary circuit is called the *coupled* (or reflected) *impedance* and, since Z_s is a vector quantity having both magnitude and phase, the coupled impedance is also a vector quantity, having resistance and reactance components.

Rule 2. The voltage induced in the secondary circuit by a primary current of I_p has a magnitude of $\omega M I_p$ and lags behind the current that produces it by 90°. In complex quantity notation the induced voltage is $-j\omega M I_p$.

Rule 3. The secondary current is exactly the same current that would flow if the induced voltage were applied in series with the secondary and if the primary were absent.[2] The secondary current therefore has a magnitude $\omega M I_p/Z_s$, and in complex quantity representation is given by $-j\omega M I_p/Z_s$.

These three rules hold for all frequencies and all types of primary and secondary circuits, both tuned and untuned. The procedure to follow in computing the behavior of a coupled circuit is (1) to determine the primary current with the aid of Rule 1; (2) to compute the voltage induced in the secondary, knowing the primary current and using Rule 2; and (3) to calculate the secondary current from the induced voltage by means of Rule 3. The following set of formulas will enable these operations to be carried out systematically:

[1] This can be demonstrated by writing down the circuit equations for the primary and secondary. These equations are

$$E = I_p Z_p + j\omega M I_s$$
$$\text{Induced voltage} = -j\omega M I_p = I_s Z_s$$

where Z_p is the series impedance of the primary and E is the voltage applied to the primary. Solving this pair of equations to eliminate I_s gives

$$E = I_p \left[Z_p + \frac{(\omega M)^2}{Z_s} \right] \tag{3-19}$$

This relation shows that the effective primary impedance with secondary present is $Z_p + (\omega M)^2/Z_s$, of which the second term represents the coupled impedance arising from the presence of the secondary.

[2] Some readers may wonder why it is that, although the secondary circuit couples an impedance into the primary, the primary is not considered as coupling an impedance into the secondary. The explanation for this is as follows: The effect that the secondary really has upon the primary circuit is to induce a back voltage in the primary proportional to the secondary current. This back voltage represents a voltage drop occurring in the primary circuit and is the same voltage drop that results when the primary current is assumed to flow through the hypothetical coupled impedance. The impedance that the secondary couples into the primary is hence a means of taking into account the voltage that the secondary current induces into the primary. The voltage that is induced in the secondary circuit by the primary current is taken into account by Rule 3, so that no coupled impedance need be postulated as present in the secondary to take into account the effect of the primary.

Impedance coupled into primary circuit by secondary $\left.\begin{array}{c} \\ \end{array}\right\} = \dfrac{(\omega M)^2}{Z_s}$ $\qquad$ (3-20)

Equivalent primary impedance $= Z_p + \dfrac{(\omega M)^2}{Z_s}$ $\qquad$ (3-21)

Primary current $= I_p = \dfrac{E}{Z_p + (\omega M)^2/Z_s}$ $\qquad$ (3-22)

Voltage induced in secondary $= -j\omega M I_p$ $\qquad$ (3-23)

Secondary current $= \dfrac{-j\omega M I_p}{Z_s} = \dfrac{-j\omega M E}{Z_p Z_s + (\omega M)^2}$ $\qquad$ (3-24)

In these equations Z_p is the series impedance of the primary considered as though the secondary were removed, E is the applied voltage, and the remaining notation is as previously used. The primary and secondary impedances Z_p and Z_s, respectively, are vector quantities, so that Eqs. (3-16) to (3-20) are all vector equations.

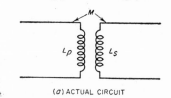

(a) ACTUAL CIRCUIT

Inductively Coupled Circuit as a Transformer. The inductively coupled circuit is a transformer, and the theory of the inductively coupled circuit that is given above is the general theory of transformers. The method commonly used to analyze the behavior of 60-cycle power transformers, which involves the use of leakage inductance, magnetizing current, and turn ratio, is a special form of the general theory that is convenient

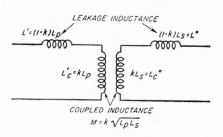

(b) SAME CIRCUIT SHOWN AS TRANSFORMER

FIG. 3-9. Inductively coupled circuit represented as a transformer with coupled and leakage inductances.

when the coupling coefficient k between the primary and secondary windings approaches unity. However, when the coupling coefficient k is small, then the use of Eqs. (3-20) to (3-24) is preferable.

The equivalent transformer circuit represented by two coils coupled together with mutual inductance M is shown in Fig. 3-9. Here the total primary inductance L_p is broken up into a leakage inductance L' and a coupled inductance L_c', while the secondary is likewise broken up into leakage inductance L'' and a coupled inductance L_c''. Each leakage inductance is considered as having no coupling whatsoever to the other winding, while the coupled inductances L_c' and L_c'' are taken as having a coefficient of coupling equal to unity. The values of these inductance components in terms of the coefficient of coupling and the primary, secondary, and mutual inductances are given in the figure. In the representation of Fig. 3-9b, turn ratio has practical significance only when the coefficient of coupling k approaches unity; when the coefficient of coupling is small, as for example, 0.01, then the primary and secondary inductances are practically entirely leakage inductances. Under these conditions the voltage induced in the secondary may be much smaller than the voltage applied to the primary terminals, even when the secondary winding has many more turns than does the primary.

3-4. Analysis of Some Simple Inductively Coupled Circuits. In this and the next section, the types of coupled circuits most commonly encountered in electronics work will be analyzed by the principles given above.

In studying the behavior of a coupled circuit the first step is always to examine the nature of the coupled impedance $(\omega M)^2/Z_s$. When the coupled impedance is small, then the primary current is very nearly the same as though no secondary were present, and the effects produced in the secondary circuit by the primary current will likewise be small. The coupled impedance will be low if the mutual inductance M is very small (i.e., if there is small coupling), or if the secondary impedance is very high, for example, if the secondary is open-circuited. In contrast, consider the case when the coupled impedance $(\omega M)^2/Z_s$ is large, either because of large M or small Z_s, or both. The voltage and current relations that exist in the primary circuit are then affected to a considerable extent by the presence of the coupled secondary, and a very considerable transfer of energy to the secondary occurs.

When determining the effect produced by the coupled impedance, it is important to note that this impedance has the same phase angle as does the secondary impedance Z_s, but with the exception that the sign of the phase angle is reversed. Thus, if the secondary impedance is inductive and has an angle of 30°, the impedance coupled in series with the primary circuit by the action of the secondary has a capacitive phase angle of 30°. The physical significance of this change in sign of the phase angle becomes apparent from the examples considered below. A particularly important case occurs when the secondary impedance Z_s is a pure resistance; under these conditions the coupled impedance will also be a resistance.

The energy consumed by the secondary circuit is the energy represented by the primary current flowing through the resistance component of the coupled impedance.

Coupled Circuit with an Untuned Secondary Consisting of a Resistance and Inductance. This arrangement is illustrated in Fig. 3-8a, and is the type of coupled circuit that results when a resistance is connected across the terminals of the secondary inductance, or, alternatively, is the case where the secondary load is a resistance and an inductance in series. Such a secondary consists of an inductance L_s in series with a resistance

R_s.   The coupled impedance is accordingly

$$\text{Coupled impedance} = \frac{(\omega M)^2}{Z_s} = \frac{(\omega M)^2}{R_s + j\omega L_s} \qquad (3\text{-}25)$$

Multiplying both numerator and denominator by $R_s - j\omega L_s$ gives

$$\text{Coupled impedance} = \frac{R_s}{R_s{}^2 + (\omega L_s)^2}(\omega M)^2 - j\frac{\omega L_s}{R_s{}^2 + (\omega L_s)^2}(\omega M)^2 \qquad (3\text{-}26)$$

Examination of Eq. (3-26) shows that the coupled impedance introduced into the primary circuit by a resistance-inductance secondary consists of a resistance in series with a capacitive reactance. The effect of the coupled resistance is to increase the effective resistance that appears between the primary terminals. The effect of the coupled capacitive reactance is to neutralize a portion of the primary inductance, thereby reducing the equivalent inductance that is observed between the terminals of the primary coil. The physical explanation of the fact that an inductive secondary produces a capacitive coupled reactance is that such a secondary causes some of the inductive reactance already possessed by the primary to be neutralized. This is done electrically by postulating a capacitive reactance of suitable magnitude in series with the primary.[1]

A special case of considerable importance is that for which the resistance R_s of the secondary circuit in Fig. 3-8a is negligible compared with the inductive reactance of the secondary. This situation will arise when the secondary coil is short-circuited, or when the secondary load is a low-loss inductance. To the extent that the resistance of the secondary circuit can be neglected, the coupled resistance introduced into the primary by the presence of such a secondary is zero; the only effect produced by the presence of the secondary is then to reduce the effective inductance that exists between the primary terminals. The percentage reduction in the equivalent primary inductance in such a situation depends only upon the coefficient of coupling between the primary and secondary circuits. If $k = 1.0$, the primary inductance is completely neutralized.[2]

A shield surrounding a coil, or a piece of metal such as a panel located in the magnetic field of a coil, represents a coupled secondary circuit that consists of an inductance in series with a resistance. Such an arrange-

---

[1] Although the coupled impedance is capacitive and so neutralizes part of the primary inductance, it is impossible to obtain a resultant capacitive reactance in the primary circuit by very large coupling since, with the maximum coupling that can possibly exist ($k = 1$), it will be found that the coupled capacitive reactance can never be greater than the value that will just neutralize all the inductive reactance of the primary.

[2] For other values of k, it can be shown by manipulating Eqs. (3-21) and (3-26) that the equivalent primary inductance is $L_p(1 - k^2)$.

ment can, accordingly, be analyzed as above. Thus the effect of a shield or metal panel on a coil is to reduce the equivalent inductance and to increase the apparent resistance observed at the coil terminals; these effects, moreover, become greater the larger the coupling, i.e., the smaller the spacing between the primary coil and the metal secondary. It is also to be noted that if the secondary resistance is low, as will be the case if the shield or metal panel is made of a good conductor such as copper or aluminum, then the principal effect produced by the presence of the metal near the coil is to reduce the equivalent inductance of the coil; under these circumstances the increase in equivalent coil resistance is only nominal. It will be noted that these conclusions derived from the viewpoint of coupled circuits are all consistent with the qualitative conclusions stated in Sec. 2-8, relative to the effect that shielding has on the properties of a coil.

Coupled Circuits with Untuned Primary and Tuned Secondary. A circuit of this type is shown in Fig. 3-8b. Here one has

$$\text{Coupled impedance} = \frac{(\omega M)^2}{Z_s} = \frac{(\omega M)^2}{R_s + j[\omega L_s - (1/\omega C_s)]} \quad (3\text{-}27)$$

An examination of this expression shows that, in the limited frequency range in which the principal resonance effects take place when the secondary Q is not too low, the numerator is substantially constant, whereas the denominator represents the series impedance of the secondary circuit. This is, therefore, an equation of the same general type as Eq. (3-13) for parallel resonance. *The coupled impedance produced by a tuned secondary circuit consequently varies with frequency according to the same general law as does the parallel impedance of the secondary circuit* (see Fig. 3-3). The absolute magnitude of the curve, however, depends upon the mutual inductance. This arrangement thus provides a means whereby the impedance of a parallel resonant circuit can be transformed in magnitude. Comparison of Eqs. (3-13) and (3-27) shows that the transformed impedance appearing in the primary circuit is $(M/L_s)^2$ times the actual parallel impedance of the resonant secondary circuit.

A special case of the circuit of Fig. 3-8b that is of particular importance occurs when the primary resistance R_p is the plate resistance of a vacuum tube. One then has the equivalent circuit of the transformer-coupled tuned radio-frequency amplifier. In this instance one is interested in the curve showing the variation of the secondary current (or of the voltage developed across the secondary capacitor C_s)[1] as the frequency is varied

---

[1] The voltage across the secondary capacitor C_s is equal to the product of the secondary current and the reactance $1/\omega C_s$ of this capacitor. In the limited frequency range represented by the vicinity around resonance ω changes very little in comparison with the variation of the secondary current. Hence, to a first approximation the voltage developed across the capacitor can be considered as being equal to

about resonances.   When $R_p >> \omega L_p$, the curve of secondary current (or of voltage across the secondary capacitor) varies with frequency according to a resonance curve having the same resonant frequency as the secondary circuit, but possessing a slightly lower Q.   When the reactance ωL_p of the primary inductance is not negligible compared with the primary resistance R_p, the curve of secondary current as a function of frequency still has the shape of a resonant curve.   However, the frequency at which the secondary current (or voltage across the secondary

capacitor) is maximum is now slightly higher than the resonant frequency of the secondary.   A typical example of this is shown by the dotted curve of Fig. 3-10.   The analysis that leads to these conclusions is presented in Sec. 3-7.

3-5. Behavior of Systems Involving Resonant Primary and Resonant Secondary Circuits. *Primary and Secondary Circuits Resonant at the Same Frequency and Having Q's That Are Equal and Not Too Low.*   When two resonant circuits having equal Q's that are not too low are tuned to the same frequency and coupled together, the resulting behavior depends very largely upon the degree of coupling, as seen from Fig. 3-11.[1]   When

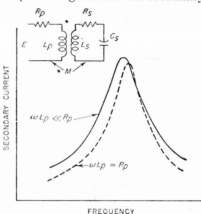

Fig. 3-10. Variation of secondary current as a function of frequency in a coupled system in which the secondary is a resonant circuit and the primary is untuned, showing that the secondary circuit follows a resonance curve, which, however, has a lower Q than that of the secondary circuit taken alone.

the coefficient of coupling is small, the curve of primary current as a function of frequency is substantially the series resonance curve of the primary circuit considered alone.   The secondary current is small and varies with frequency in such a way as to be much more peaked than the resonance curve of the secondary circuit considered as an isolated circuit. As the coefficient of coupling is increased somewhat, the curve of primary current becomes broader, as a result of a reduction in the primary current at resonance and an increase in the primary current at frequencies

---

the product of the secondary current and a constant.   In the immediate vicinity of resonance the curve of voltage across this secondary capacitor therefore has very nearly the same shape as does the curve of secondary current.

[1] The phase shift is not shown in Fig. 3-11, but varies $\pm 180°$ about the phase at the resonant frequency.   Thus the total shift in phase between input voltage and output current as the frequency varies through resonance is $360°$.   This is in contrast with systems having only one tuned circuit; the total phase shift then varies over the range $\pm 90°$, or a total of $180°$.

slightly off resonance. At the same time the secondary-current peak becomes higher and the curve of secondary current somewhat broader.

These trends continue as the coefficient of coupling is increased until the coupling is such that the resistance which the secondary circuit couples into the primary at resonance is equal to the primary resistance. This is called the *critical coupling* and causes the secondary current to

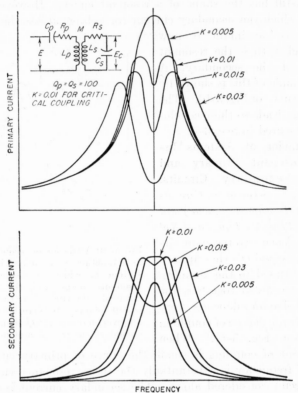

Fig. 3-11. Curves showing variation of primary and secondary currents with frequency for different coefficients of coupling when the primary and the secondary are separately tuned to the same frequency.

have the maximum value it can attain. The curve of secondary current is then somewhat broader than is the resonance curve of the secondary circuit considered alone, and has a relatively flat top. The primary current now has two peaks, being greater at frequencies just off resonance than at the resonant frequency.

As the coefficient of coupling is increased beyond the critical value, the double humps in the primary current become more prominent and the peaks spread farther apart. The curve of secondary current now also begins to display double humps, with the peaks becoming more pronounced and spreading farther apart as the coupling increases. The value of the primary current at the peaks becomes smaller the greater the coupling, but in the secondary circuit not only do the two peaks have substantially the same height, but this height is also independent of the coefficient of coupling provided only that the coupling is not less than the critical value.   The reason for the above behavior centers around the way in which the coupled impedance $(\omega M)^2/Z_s$ varies with frequency. Consider first the total primary-circuit impedance.   This consists of the actual self-impedance of the primary plus whatever impedance the secondary circuit couples into the primary.   The type of coupled impedance produced by a tuned secondary has already been discussed; it is substantially a parallel resonance curve having a shape corresponding to the Q of the secondary circuit and an amplitude determined by the mutual inductance.   The coupled impedance is hence maximum at resonance and is then a resistance.   At frequencies below resonance the coupled impedance is inductive and at frequencies above resonance it is capacitive, as shown in Fig. 3-7.

When this coupled impedance is added to the self-impedance of the primary circuit, the effect at resonance is to increase the effective primary resistance above the value that would exist in the absence of the secondary.   This causes the primary current at resonance to be reduced in all cases by the presence of the secondary.   At frequencies somewhat below resonance the coupled impedance is largely inductive whereas the primary self-impedance is largely capacitive.   The coupled inductive reactance then neutralizes some of the primary capacitive reactance, lowering the primary circuit impedance and increasing the primary current.   The situation is somewhat similar for frequencies above resonance except that now the coupled reactance is capacitive and neutralizes some of the inductive reactance which the primary circuit otherwise has at frequencies above resonance.   Consequently, the net effect of the coupled impedance is to lower the primary current at the resonant frequency and to raise the current at frequencies somewhat off resonance.   The magnitude of this effect depends upon the coefficient of coupling, being small when the coupling is small.   However, when the coupling is of the order of magnitude of the critical value or greater, the coupled impedance becomes sufficient to be the major factor in determining the impedance of the primary circuit.   In particular, at resonance the primary current tends to be relatively small because of the very large coupled resistance, while there is a frequency on each side of resonance at which the coupled reactance exactly neutralizes the primary reactance, giving zero reactance for the total primary circuit impedance and causing the flow of a large primary current.   This is the cause of the double-humped curves of primary current for high couplings, such as shown in Fig. 3-11.

The curve of secondary current is determined by the secondary impedance, and by the voltage induced in the secondary by the primary current.

The induced voltage varies with frequency in almost exactly the same way as does the primary current, since the magnitude of the induced voltage is $\omega M I_p$; and in the limited frequency range in which the resonance effects take place, ω changes very little. As a result of this, the curve of secondary current has a shape that is almost exactly the product of the shape of the curve of primary current and the shape of the resonance curve of the secondary circuit. Since the latter curve is sharply peaked, the secondary current is much more peaked than the primary current, as is clearly evident in Fig. 3-11.

At low coefficients of coupling, the curve of secondary current is particularly sharp, being substantially the product of the resonance curves of the primary and secondary circuits. As the coupling increases, the primary-current curve becomes broader, thereby making the secondary curve less sharp. At the same time, the amplitude of the secondary-current peak increases because of the increased coupling. When the coefficient of coupling reaches the critical value, the secondary current has the maximum value it can attain. Under these conditions the dip in primary current in the vicinity of resonance has a curvature that is exactly opposite from the curvature of the resonance curve of the secondary circuit. The result is that the curve of secondary current now has a very flat top in the immediate vicinity of resonance. As the coupling is increased beyond the critical value, the secondary-current peak splits into two peaks, both of which have amplitudes substantially the same as the secondary-current peak at critical coupling. The separation between these peaks increases with coupling and is substantially the same as the separation of the peaks of primary current when the peaks are pronounced.

The voltage developed across the secondary capacitor is equal to the reactance of this capacitor times the secondary current; thus it can readily be calculated once the current curve is known. For most purposes, it is sufficient to assume that the curve of voltage developed across the capacitor has the same shape as the curve of secondary current. One is interested primarily in the behavior about resonance, and the capacitor reactance changes very little in the limited frequency range consequently involved when the circuit Q's are not too low.

The exact shapes of curves such as those of Fig. 3-11 can be calculated with the aid of Eqs. (3-20) to (3-24). Such computations are, however, complicated and tedious. The usual practical procedure is accordingly to determine (1) the response at resonance, (2) the frequencies at which the peaks of secondary response occur when this response curve has double humps, (3) the heights of these two peaks, and (4) the response at one or two other frequencies so chosen as to simplify the calculations. In this way, it is possible, with a minimum of work, to obtain a good semiquantitative picture of the behavior. The following nomenclature in addition to that of Fig. 3-11 will be used in the discussion of the quantitative relations:

E_c = voltage across secondary capacitor
E = voltage applied in series with primary
k = actual coefficient of coupling
k_c = critical coefficient of coupling
Q_p = Q of primary circuit
Q_s = Q of secondary circuit

At resonance, the series impedances of the primary and secondary circuits are resistances, and the response in the secondary is given by the relation[1,2]

$$\left.\begin{array}{l}\text{Voltage across secondary}\\\text{capacitor at resonance}\\\hline\text{Voltage applied in series}\\\text{with primary}\end{array}\right\} = \frac{E_c}{E} = \sqrt{\frac{L_s}{L_p}}\,\frac{k}{k^2 + (1/Q_pQ_s)} \qquad (3\text{-}28)$$

The secondary response has its maximum value when the coefficient of coupling has a value k_c such that

$$k_c = \frac{1}{\sqrt{Q_pQ_s}} \qquad (3\text{-}29)$$

This value of coupling is called the *critical coefficient of coupling* and is the condition where the resistance that the secondary circuit couples into the primary circuit at resonance is equal to the resistance of the primary circuit, i.e., when $(\omega M)^2/R_s = R_p$.

When the coefficient of coupling equals the critical value and if $Q_p = Q_s$, then the curve of secondary current (or voltage) as a function of frequency has the maximum flatness that is possible in the vicinity of resonance. The shape of this curve is shown in Fig. 3-12, together with the resonance

---

[1] This follows from Eq. (3-24) by substituting

$$Z_s = R_s,\ Z_p = R_p,\ E_c = I_s/j\omega C_s = -j\omega L_sI_s$$

to give

$$\frac{E_c}{E} = \frac{-j\omega M}{R_pR_s + (\omega M)^2}\,(-j\omega L_s)$$

Dividing both numerator and denominator by $\omega^2 L_pL_s$ gives

$$\frac{E_c}{E} = \frac{-(M/\sqrt{L_pL_s})\,\sqrt{L_s/L_p}}{\dfrac{R_p}{\omega L_p}\dfrac{R_s}{\omega L_s} + \dfrac{M^2}{L_pL_s}}$$

Equation (3-28) is then obtained by substituting $M^2/L_pL_s = k^2$ and dropping the minus sign.

[2] It is to be noted that Eqs. (3-28) and (3-29) are not limited to the case where $Q_p = Q_s$, although the rest of the discussion in this section does assume $Q_p = Q_s$.

curve of a simple tuned circuit having the same Q as the primary or secondary. It will be noted that the coupled circuit case has a bandwidth between the 70.7 per cent response points that is $\sqrt{2}$ times as great as for the single tuned circuit. The shapes of the two curves differ greatly, the coupled system being flatter in the center and much deeper on the sides.

When the coefficient of coupling exceeds the critical value, then for $Q_p = Q_s$, double humps will always occur in the secondary response

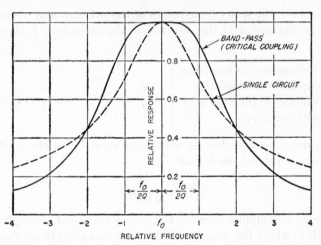

Fig. 3-12. Relative response of a bandpass system provided by two identical circuits critically coupled, together with the resonance curve of a single circuit such as used in the bandpass system.

curve. If the coefficient of coupling is at least several times the critical value these humps are quite pronounced and occur at frequencies that differ from the resonant frequency f_0 by approximately $\pm kf_0/2$ cycles.[1] When the peaks of secondary response are not pronounced, i.e., when the actual coefficient of coupling does not greatly exceed the critical value, then these peaks are somewhat closer together than indicated by this simple relation [see Eq. (3-30) and Fig. 3-16].

When the circuit Q's are equal and not too low, the peaks of the secondary current for $k > k_c$ will have almost exactly the same height as the resonant peak of secondary current at critical coupling. This relation holds irrespective of the exact location on these peaks provided only that

---

[1] An analysis that does not contain these restrictions leads to the more precise relation

$$\left. \begin{array}{l} \text{Frequency at peak of secondary} \\ \text{voltage} \\ \hline \text{Resonant frequency of tuned} \\ \text{circuits} \end{array} \right\} = \frac{1}{\sqrt{1 \pm k \left[1 - \dfrac{k_c^2}{2k^2} \left(\dfrac{Q_p}{Q_s} + \dfrac{Q_s}{Q_p} \right) \right]^{1/2}}} \qquad (3\text{-}30)$$

the coefficient of coupling involved is small compared with unity[1] and that the Q's are not too low.

When double peaks occur in the secondary response curve, additional information on the shape of the response curve can be easily obtained by taking advantage of the fact, illustrated in Fig. 3-13, that the response equals or exceeds the response at resonance over a frequency band that is $\sqrt{2}$ times the width of the frequency band between coupling peaks, as calculated from Eq. (3-30).

At frequencies that are sufficiently high or low relative to the resonant frequency to lie well on the sides of the response curve, one can neglect the resistances of the primary and secondary circuits when calculating the magnitude of the secondary response. This greatly simplifies calculations while introducing relatively little error in magnitudes.

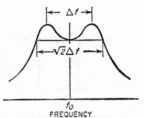

FIG. 3-13. Relationship between bandwidth and width between secondary peaks, existing when two circuits resonant at the same frequency are coupled together.

The Effects Produced by Unequal Q's. The behavior of two coupled circuits resonant at the same frequency is modified in several respects when $Q_p \neq Q_s$. The secondary response at resonance is still given by Eq. (3-28), and is maximum when the coefficient of coupling has the critical value as defined by Eq. (3-29). However, double peaks do not now appear until the coupling is somewhat greater than the critical value, and the magnitude of the response at the secondary peaks when they do appear is less than the response with critical coupling.

Coupled Resonant Circuits Tuned to Slightly Different Frequencies. Consider the case of two circuits resonant at slightly different frequencies and coupled together. When $Q_p = Q_s$, the response curve of secondary current (or voltage) has almost exactly the same shape as would be obtained if the circuits were both tuned to the same frequency and the coefficient of coupling were increased to a value k_{eq} such that

$$k_{eq} = \sqrt{k^2 + \left(\frac{\Delta}{f_0}\right)^2} \qquad (3\text{-}31)$$

where k is the actual coefficient of coupling, Δ is the difference between the resonant frequencies of the primary and secondary circuits, and f_0 is the frequency midway between the primary and secondary resonant frequencies. *Hence detuning primary and secondary circuits slightly has*

---

[1] If the coefficient of coupling is not small compared with unity, then the relative heights of the individual peaks of voltage developed across the secondary capacitor will be very nearly inversely proportional to the square of the ratio of the frequencies at which the respective peaks occur. Under these conditions the low-frequency peak will be slightly higher than the high-frequency peak, although the average height of the two peaks will still approximate the response with critical coupling.

approximately the same effect on the shape of the secondary-current curve as increasing the coefficient of coupling when there is no detuning.

In the more general case of detuning where the circuit Q's are not the same, the secondary-response curve is no longer symmetrical about the mean resonance frequency.

Shunt-fed and Shunt-loaded Coupled Circuits. In all the examples of coupled resonant circuits considered so far, the input voltage has been applied in series with the primary circuit. In many practical circumstances, however, the excitation is applied to the system as illustrated in

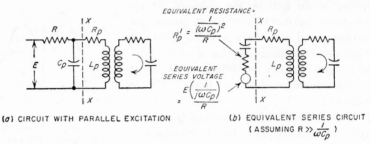

(*a*) CIRCUIT WITH PARALLEL EXCITATION

(*b*) EQUIVALENT SERIES CIRCUIT

(ASSUMING $R \gg \frac{1}{\omega C_p}$)

FIG. 3-14. Two coupled resonant circuits in which the primary circuit is excited by shunt feed.

Fig. 3-14*a*. This arrangement is analogous to the shunt-fed parallel resonant circuit discussed in connection with Fig. 3-5*c*.

The shunt-fed arrangement of Fig. 3-14*a* can be reduced to the equivalent series-fed arrangement of Fig. 3-14*b* by means of Thévenin's theorem, as explained in Sec. 3-7. Examination of the circuit of Fig. 3-14*b* shows that in a limited frequency range such as represented by the region about resonance, the equivalent voltage acting in series with the circuit is substantially constant. However, there is now an added resistance R_p' in the primary circuit that is equal to the equivalent series resistance that would be obtained by assuming that the resistance R is a shunt resistance for the primary capacitance C_p. The rest of the system is unchanged.

The principal effect of exciting a system of coupled circuits by parallel instead of series feed is accordingly to introduce some added resistance in the primary that lowers the effective value of Q_p. This effect will be slight in the usual case where the resistance R is very large compared with the reactance $1/\omega C_p$ of the capacitor C_p. Under these conditions, shunt feed and series feed accordingly give essentially the same shaped curves of secondary response as a function of frequency.

In systems involving two coupled resonant circuits, resistances are often placed in shunt with the primary and secondary resonant circuits for the purpose of adjusting the effective Q's of the primary and secondary circuits to desired values. Such resistances are sometimes placed across both primary and secondary circuits, while in other cases they are used only across the primary, or only across the secondary. An example where a resistance R is shunted across the secondary capacitor is shown in Fig. 3-15.   In each case, a resistance in shunt with a particular resonant circuit of a coupled system has the same effect on that resonant circuit as it does when this resonant circuit is isolated, instead of being part of a coupled system.   Hence a shunt resistance can be replaced by an equivalent series resistance, such as R_s' in Fig. 3-15.   The effect of a shunting resistance is accordingly to lower the effective Q of the resonant circuit with which it is associated, as discussed in connection with Fig. 3-5.

Bandpass Action in Two Coupled Resonant Circuits.   When two resonant circuits having $Q_p = Q_s$ are tuned to the same frequency and

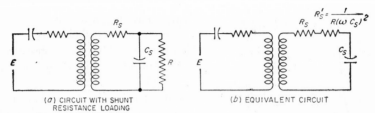

(a) CIRCUIT WITH SHUNT
RESISTANCE LOADING

(b) EQUIVALENT CIRCUIT

Fig. 3-15. Two coupled resonant circuits in which a shunt resistance loading is used to control secondary Q.

coupled together with critical coupling, the response characteristic of the secondary circuit is as shown in Fig. 3-12.   As compared with the response of a simple resonant circuit with the same 70.7 per cent points, the response of the coupled system is found to be much flatter on top, and much steeper on the sides.   Such an arrangement is often termed a *bandpass filter* because to a first approximation it responds equally well to a band of frequencies centered on the common resonant frequency, and rather sharply discriminates against frequencies outside of this band. Such bandpass characteristics are particularly desirable when handling modulated waves, because by proper adjustment of the bandwidth of the filter, the response can be made practically the same to the carrier and to all of the important sideband frequencies contained in the wave.   In contrast with this, an ordinary resonant circuit has a response that is rounded on top, as shown dotted in Fig. 3-12, and so discriminates against the higher sideband frequencies in favor of the lower sideband frequencies and the carrier.

The bandpass characteristic that is best for most purposes corresponds to a coefficient of coupling equal to the critical value.   For this case, still assuming $Q_p = Q_s$, the design equations giving the required values of k and Q to realize a given bandwidth B are[1]

$$k = k_c = \frac{B}{\sqrt{2}\,f_0} \qquad Q_p = Q_s = \frac{1}{k_c} \qquad (3\text{-}32)$$

[1] With unequal circuit Q's the formulas will be slightly different for equivalent results, since the curve with flattest top now corresponds to a coefficient of coupling greater than the critical value.

where B = the bandwidth between the 70.7 per cent response points, cycles

f_0 = center frequency of passband (i.e., resonant frequency of tuned circuits)

k_c = critical coefficient of coupling

Effect of Varying Q in Coupled Systems Tuned to the Same Frequency. (Coefficient of Coupling Constant). Additional insight into the characteristics of coupled circuits can be gained by considering what happens to the secondary response curve as the Q's of the primary and secondary circuits are changed, while keeping the coefficient of coupling constant. The effects observed are illustrated in Fig. 3-16 for a particular case. This example brings out clearly the fact that as the peaks of the response become less pronounced, they tend to move toward each other, and that at frequencies appreciably off resonance, the response differs only negligibly from the response calculated on the assumption of infinite Q (zero circuit loss).

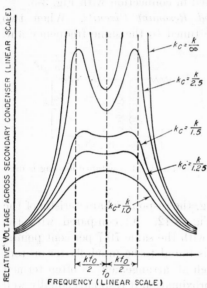

FIG. 3-16. Curves of secondary response when two circuits resonant at the same frequency are coupled together, showing the effect of varying the circuit Q's while maintaining the coefficient of coupling unchanged.

3-6. Generalized Coupled Circuits. Energy can be transferred from one circuit to another by a variety of coupling methods, in addition to the inductive coupling just considered. Thus, in Fig. 3-17a the coupling consists of an inductance L_m common to the two circuits; in Fig. 3-17b the coupling is provided by a capacitance C_m common to the two circuits, and in Fig. 3-17c by a capacitance C'_m that connects the two circuits involved. Also, an infinite variety of more complicated coupling systems can be built up from the basic elements of mutual inductance, common inductance, common capacitance, and connecting capacitance. Simple examples of such combined couplings are shown in Fig. 3-17d and e.

The behavior of all these coupled circuits follows the same general character as that discussed for inductive coupling. Thus, the secondary circuit can be considered as producing an equivalent coupled impedance in the primary circuit while the primary circuit can be considered as inducing in the secondary a voltage that gives rise to the secondary current.

The simplest method of analyzing these various forms of coupled circuits is to take advantage of the fact that all of them can be reduced to the simple coupled circuit of Fig. 3-17f, provided suitable values are assigned to Z_p, Z_s, and M. The rules that determine the values of these quantities in the simple equivalent circuit are as follows:

1. The equivalent primary impedance Z_p of the equivalent circuit is the impedance that is measured across the primary terminals of the actual circuit when the secondary circuit has been opened.

2. The secondary impedance Z_s of the equivalent circuit is the impedance that is measured by opening the secondary of the actual circuit and

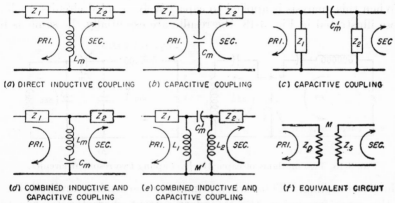

(a) DIRECT INDUCTIVE COUPLING   (b) CAPACITIVE COUPLING   (c) CAPACITIVE COUPLING

(d) COMBINED INDUCTIVE AND CAPACITIVE COUPLING   (e) COMBINED INDUCTIVE AND CAPACITIVE COUPLING   (f) EQUIVALENT CIRCUIT

Fig. 3-17. Examples of methods whereby circuits may be coupled.

determining the impedance between these open points when the primary is open-circuited.

3. The equivalent mutual inductance M is determined by assuming a current I_p flowing into the primary circuit. The voltage which then appears across an open circuit in the secondary is equal to $-j\omega M I_p$.

In making use of the equivalent circuit of Fig. 3-17f, it is to be remembered that the values of Z_p, Z_s, and M may all vary with frequency, so that it is generally necessary to determine a new equivalent circuit for each frequency at which calculations are to be made.

After the actual coupled circuit has been reduced by the above procedure to its equivalent form shown in Fig. 3-14f, one can then apply the formulas that have already been derived for inductively coupled circuits, using the appropriate values M, Z_s, Z_p as determined for the equivalent circuit. This procedure has the advantage of using the same fundamental formulas to handle all types of coupling and makes it possible to carry on the analysis in the same manner for all cases. The method is particularly convenient in the handling of complex coupling networks such as illustrated in Fig. 3-17d and e.

The quantity M that appears in the equivalent circuit represents the effective coupling that is present between the primary and secondary circuits.   It is not necessarily a real mutual inductance of the inductive type, but rather a sort of mathematical fiction that gives the equivalent effect of whatever coupling is really present.   If the actual coupling is capacitive, the numerical value of M will be found to be negative; if the coupling is of a complex type representing both resistive and reactive coupling, the numerical value of M will be found to have both real and imaginary parts.   This need introduce no uncertainty, however, since the proper procedure is to take the value of M as it comes and substitute it with its appropriate sign and phase angle whenever M appears in the expressions previously derived for inductively coupled circuits.

When this analysis is applied to capacitively coupled circuits, such as those illustrated in Fig. 3-18, the results are essentially the same as for

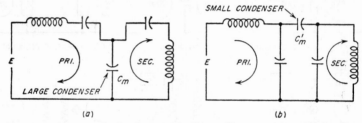

FIG. 3-18. Two methods of capacitively coupling two resonant circuits.

inductive coupling.   Thus, when primary and secondary are both tuned to the same frequency, the secondary-current characteristic has two humps if the coupling is large, i.e., if capacitor C_m is small or C'_m large, while there is only one peak of secondary current when the coupling is small, i.e., when capacitor C_m is large.

Circuits having combined electromagnetic and electrostatic coupling, such as those at d and e of Fig. 3-17, behave as ordinary coupled circuits except that the coefficient of coupling varies with frequency.   Thus, in the case of circuit d, the circuit is capacitively coupled at low frequencies and inductively coupled at high frequencies because the coupling combination of C_m in series with L_m has capacitive and inductive reactance under these respective conditions.   In between, at the resonant frequency of L_m and C_m, there is no coupling and $k = 0$.   The arrangement shown at e acts similarly as a circuit with a coefficient of coupling that varies with frequency.   Circuits having combined electrostatic and electromagnetic coupling find application where it is desired to obtain a coefficient of coupling that varies with frequency, as is commonly the case in tuned amplifiers and antenna-coupling circuits of radio receivers.

3-7. Thévenin's Theorem.   *According to Thévenin's theorem, any linear network containing one or more sources of voltage and having two terminals behaves, in so far as a load impedance connected across these terminals is concerned, as though the network and its generators were equivalent to a simple generator having an internal impedance Z and a generated voltage E, where E*

is the voltage that appears across the terminals when no load impedance is connected and Z is the impedance that is measured between the terminals when all sources of voltage in the network are short-circuited.[1,2]

This theorem means that any network and its generators, represented schematically by the block in Fig. 3-19a, can be replaced by the equivalent circuit shown in Fig. 3-19b. The only limitation to the validity of Thévenin's theorem encountered in ordinary practice is that the circuit elements of the network must be linear; i.e., the voltage developed must always be proportional to current.

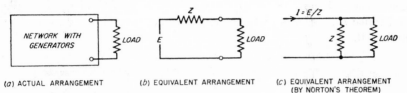

(*a*) ACTUAL ARRANGEMENT   (*b*) EQUIVALENT ARRANGEMENT   (*c*) EQUIVALENT ARRANGEMENT
                                                                                (BY NORTON'S THEOREM)

Fig. 3-19. Diagrams illustrating how Thévenin's and Norton's theorems can be used to simplify a complicated network containing generators.

Thévenin's theorem offers a very powerful means of simplifying networks, particularly when a load impedance is connected across the output terminals of a complicated network. Two examples will be used to illustrate this. First, consider the circuit of Fig. 3-10, which is redrawn in Fig. 3-20a. If one takes the secondary capacitor C_2 as the load impedance and applies Thévenin's theorem to the network to the left of C_2, the result is Fig. 3-20b, in which the equivalent generator voltage is the voltage induced in the secondary inductance L_2 when the secondary is open-circuited, and the equivalent generator impedance consists of the inductance L_2 and the resistance R_2 in series with the impedance which is coupled into L_2 by a secondary circuit consisting of L_1 shunted by the resistance R_1. The coupled impedance produced by such a secondary circuit has been previously considered; it is equivalent to adding capacitive reactance and resistance in series. The resistance causes the effective Q of the secondary-response curve to be reduced, while the series capaci-

---

[1] When the sources of energy in the network are constant-current generators instead of constant-voltage generators, the internal impedance Z is the impedance observed between the terminals when all constant-current generators are *open-circuited*. This is due to the fact that a constant-current generator is equivalent to an infinite voltage source having an infinite internal impedance, so that short-circuiting the ultimate source of voltage of the constant-current generator still leaves an infinite impedance in the circuit.

[2] An alternative circuit that is also equivalent to Fig. 3-19a is given in Fig. 3-19c. Here the network with its generators is replaced by a constant current I that is delivered to a system consisting of the source impedance Z in shunt with which is the load impedance, where I is the output current of the network when the output terminals are short-circuited, and is $I = E/Z$. The equivalence of the arrangements at *a* and *c* in Fig. 3-19 is sometimes referred to as *Norton's theorem*.

tive reactance tends to raise the apparent resonant frequency by an amount that becomes greater the higher the ratio $\omega L_1/R_1$. This accounts for the behavior of the curves of Fig. 3-10.

The second example is furnished by Fig. 3-14a. This circuit may be simplified by considering that the load is represented by the circuit to the right of the line xx, the generator being the voltage E acting in series with the resistance R and the capacitance C_p. Such a generator can be reduced immediately by Thévenin's theorem to the form shown to the left of the line xx in Fig. 3-14b. Here it is to be noted that the equivalent generator resistance R'_p is the series resistance equivalent to a shunt resistance R associated with the capacitance C_p, as given by Eqs. (2-12) and (2-13).

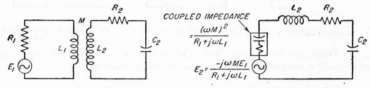

(a) ACTUAL CIRCUIT   (b) EQUIVALENT SECONDARY CIRCUIT

Fig. 3-20. Application of Thévenin's theorem to simplify and explain the behavior of the system of Fig. 3-10, consisting of a tuned secondary and untuned primary circuit coupled together.

3-8. Impedance Matching. A load connected across the output terminals of a network, such as represented schematically by Fig. 3-19a, can be matched to the source of power in either of two ways. When the load impedance has the same magnitude and phase angle as the equivalent generator impedance Z defined by Thévenin's theorem (see Fig. 3-19b), the load is said to be matched to the generator or source of power on an *image-impedance* basis. The term "image" arises from the fact that the impedances on the two sides of the output terminals are images of each other. When the load impedance is not identical with the generator impedance and it is desired to obtain impedance matching on an image basis, it is then necessary to transform the load to the correct impedance to match the generator. This transformation can be accomplished with the aid of an appropriate network of reactances or, in simple cases, by means of a transformer.

Alternatively, a load impedance may be matched to a source of power in such a way as to make the power delivered to the load a maximum.[1] This is accomplished by making the load impedance the conjugate of the generator impedance as defined by Thévenin's theorem. That is, the load impedance must have the same magnitude as the generator impedance, but the phase angle of the load is the negative of the phase angle of the generator impedance. This method of matching is shown schemat-

[1] The power delivered to the load under these conditions is termed the *available power* of the power source.

ically in Fig. 3-21. It will be noted that the reactive component of the load is then in series resonance with the reactive component of the generator impedance; i.e., the load reactance is the correct value to "tune out" the generator reactance. The resistance components of the load and generator impedances are then matched on an image-impedance basis. Such impedance matching to obtain maximum power delivered to the load is a common operation in communication circuits. It is carried out by transforming the equivalent series resistance of the load to a value equal to the resistance component of the generator impedance by the use of suitable networks and transformers, and then adding reactance to the load as required to resonate with the generator reactance.

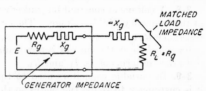

FIG. 3-21. Load impedance matched to generator in such a way as to give maximum power in the load.

It will be noted that, when the generator impedance is resistive, the conditions corresponding to matching on an image-impedance basis are identical with those corresponding to matching for maximum power output delivered to the load. Otherwise, the two conditions are not the same, and matching on an image-impedance basis then does not result in maximum possible power being delivered to the load, although it is often still used to maintain appropriate impedance relations in a system of networks.

PROBLEMS AND EXERCISES

3-1. The coil of Fig. 2-16 is tuned to resonance at 1000 kc by a capacitor having a power factor of 0.001. What is the circuit Q?

3-2. In Prob. 3-1, what tuning capacitance is required?

3-3. A variable capacitor having a maximum capacitance of 350 $\mu\mu f$ and a minimum capacitance of 20 $\mu\mu f$ is used for tuning in a broadcast receiver. The coil and associated wiring have a distributed capacitance of 20 $\mu\mu f$.

a. What size inductance coil is required to make the lowest frequency 530 kc?

b. Calculate the exact tuning range with the coil selected.

3-4. A series circuit is resonant at 800 kc and has an inductance of 160 μh and a circuit Q of 75. Calculate and plot the magnitude of the current that flows when 1 volt is applied to the circuit, carrying the curves out to 40 kc on each side of resonance. In making these calculations use the working rules and the universal resonance curve in the range near resonance and neglect the circuit resistance when calculating points too far off resonance to be within the range of the universal resonance curve.

3-5. In Prob. 3-4 calculate the exact response at 40 kc above resonance, taking into account the circuit resistance, and compare the results with those obtained when the circuit resistance is neglected.

3-6. Assume that a series resonant circuit employs the coil of Fig. 2-16, and that the tuning capacitor has negligible losses.

a. Calculate and plot from 500 to 1500 kc the width of the frequency band for which the tuned circuit response is at least 70.7 per cent of the response at resonance, as a function of resonant frequency.

b. Discuss the results obtained in (a) with respect to the reception of broadcast signals having sideband frequencies extending up to 5000 cycles on each side of the carrier frequency. Consider both the uniformity of response to the different sideband frequencies, and the ability of the circuit to discriminate against undesired signals of other frequencies.

3-7. In a series circuit that is resonant at 1150 kc it is found that when the frequency differs from resonance by 15 kc the current drops to 0.53 of the current at resonance, for the same applied voltage. From this information determine the Q of the circuit.

3-8. A voltage of constant but unknown value is applied to a series circuit resonant at the frequency of this voltage. The circuit current is observed to be I_0. A known resistance R_1 is then added to the circuit, and it is found that, with the same applied voltage as before, the current is now reduced to I_1. Derive a formula for the circuit resistance in terms of I_0, I_1, and R_1.

3-9. In variable capacitors used to tune the resonant circuits of radio receivers, it is customary to shape the plates so that the capacitance varies more slowly with angle of rotation at small capacitance settings than at high capacitance settings. Explain why this makes the resonant frequency more nearly linear with respect to the angle of rotation than if semicircular plates were employed.

3-10. What is the highest effective Q that a tuned circuit may have when it must respond to a band of frequencies 10,000 cycles wide (5000-cycle sideband frequencies) with a response always at least 70.7 per cent of the response at resonance, assuming carrier frequencies of 50, 500, 5000, and 50,000 kc?

3-11. q. A tuned circuit having an inductance of 150 μh and a Q of 70 is adjusted to resonance at 1100 kc. If the circuit is connected for parallel resonance, calculate and plot the magnitude of the parallel impedance as a function of frequency out to 60 kc on each side of resonance. Use the working rules and the universal resonance curve in the region about resonance, and neglect the circuit resistance when calculating the impedance at frequencies too far off resonance to be within range of the universal resonance curve.

b. Repeat (a) for a circuit Q of 40, and plot the results on the same axes as the results of (a).

3-12. Calculate and plot as a function of frequency the parallel impedance at resonance when the coil of Fig. 2-16 is tuned with a capacitor of negligible losses and when the resonant frequency is varied from 500 to 1500 kc.

3-13. A tuned circuit is required to have a parallel impedance of 6000 ohms and a Q of 12. If the resonant frequency is 300 kc determine the inductance, capacitance, and resistance that the circuit must have.

3-14. Using the same tuned circuit as in Prob. 3-4, but connected for parallel resonance, calculate and plot curves as a function of frequency from 760 to 840 kc for (a) magnitude and phase angle of parallel impedance; (b) line current, and current in each branch, when the applied potential is 10 volts (assume that all the circuit resistance is in the inductive branch); and (c) reactance and resistance components of the impedance of (a).

3-15. The coil of Fig. 2-16 is tuned to resonance at 1000 kc with a capacitor having negligible losses. Transform this circuit to the form shown in the right-hand part of Fig. 3-5a by determining R_2.

3-16. The circuit of Fig. 2-16 is tuned to resonance at 1000 kc with a capacitor having negligible losses, and is then shunted by a resistance R_2' of 100,000 ohms.

a. Determine the equivalent shunt resistance R_2 for such an arrangement (see Fig. 3-5).

b. Calculate the Q of this system.

3-17. If a parallel resonant circuit is shunted by a resistance R_2' and if the parallel resonant impedance of the unshunted circuit is R_0, prove that the shunt resistance R_2' reduces the equivalent Q of the circuit by the factor $R_2'/(R_2' + R_0)$.

3-18. In a low-Q parallel circuit in which the losses are all in the inductive branch, prove that, when the capacitance is varied, the capacitance that makes the parallel circuit impedance have unity power factor for a given frequency also makes this impedance have maximum magnitude at this same frequency.

3-19. A particular coil has an inductance of 180 μh at 1 kc and an apparent inductance of 200 μh at 1400 kc. Determine the distributed capacitance of the coil.

3-20. Primary and secondary coils have inductances of 75 and 300 μh, respectively, and 1 volt is applied to the primary circuit. Assuming the resistances of the coils are negligible, calculate the voltage induced in the secondary as a function of coefficient of coupling from $k = 0$ to $k = 1.0$.

3-21. Draw an equivalent transformer circuit for the coils of Prob. 3-20, for the case where the mutual inductance is 50 μh.

3-22. *a.* Explain the effect of a short-circuited turn upon the inductance and Q observed at the terminals of a coil, using coupled-circuit theory.

b. Indicate qualitatively the differences that would be expected if the short-circuited turn were the end turn of a single-layer solenoid, as in Fig. 2-1, as against being a turn near the center.

3-23. Two identical coils each having $Q = 100$ and an inductance of 200 μh are coupled together with a mutual inductance of 50 μh. If the secondary coil is short-circuited, calculate (*a*) the coupled resistance and coupled reactance at a frequency of 600 kc, (*b*) the total resistance and reactance of the primary circuit, and (*c*) the effective Q of the primary circuit including effect of the coupled impedance.

3-24. Describe a procedure for experimentally determining the coefficient of coupling between a coil and its shield can, assuming that the shield has negligible resistance.

3-25. Derive the formula in the second footnote on page 61 for the equivalent primary-circuit inductance in the presence of an inductive secondary with zero losses.

3-26. An air-cored coil is placed near a brass panel. Describe in a qualitative way the effect that copper plating this panel will have on the inductance and Q observed at the coil terminals.

3-27. The coil of Fig. 2-16 is coupled to a primary coil with a mutual inductance of 50 μh. If the secondary coil is tuned to resonance by means of a capacitor having negligible loss, calculate and plot the coupled impedance at the resonant frequency of the secondary as this resonant frequency is varied from 500 to 1500 kc.

3-28. The coil of Fig. 2-16 is coupled to a primary circuit having an inductance of 75 μh, and is tuned to resonance at 1000 kc with a capacitor having negligible losses. Calculate the impedance coupled into the primary circuit at 1000 kc as a function of coefficient of coupling from $k = 0$ to $k = 1.0$.

3-29. In the circuit of Fig. 3-8*b*, what general effect is produced on the phase and magnitude of the coupled impedance at the resonant frequency of the secondary by shunting the secondary capacitor C_s by a resistance R_2?

3-30. Explain why in Fig. 3-11 a flat-topped secondary-circuit curve (like $k = 0.01$) can be obtained only if the primary-current curve has pronounced double peaks.

3-31. Derive Eq. (3-29) from Eq. (3-28).

3-32. Two identical circuits resonant at 1000 kc, having $Q = 80$ and inductances of 140 μh, are coupled together.

a. Calculate the critical coefficient of coupling.

b. Calculate and plot the secondary current at the resonant frequency for 1 volt applied to the primary, as the mutual inductance is varied from zero to twice the critical value.

3-33. The coupling between the circuits of Prob. 3-32 is adjusted to make the coefficient of coupling have a value 0.03, and 1 volt is applied in series with the primary.

a. What will be the approximate frequencies at which the secondary-current peaks will occur?

b. What will be the approximate height of these peaks of secondary current? Assume the two peaks have equal heights.

c. What will be the secondary current at the resonant frequency?

d. Over what frequency range will the secondary response equal or exceed the secondary response at resonance?

e. With the information obtained above, sketch the approximate shape of the secondary-current curve as a function of frequency.

3-34. The circuits of Prob. 3-32 are coupled with a coefficient of coupling of 0.1. Determine the frequencies at which the secondary-current peaks occur, and give the approximate ratio of voltages across the secondary at frequencies corresponding to the low- and high-frequency peaks.

3-35. The two circuits of Prob. 3-32 are coupled with a mutual inductance of 2.8 μh ($k = 0.02$).

a. Calculate and plot the resistance and reactance components of the coupled impedance out to 40 kc on each side of resonance.

b. Calculate and plot the resistance and reactance components of the primary circuit when the secondary is removed.

c. Add (*a*) and (*b*) to obtain the curve of total primary-circuit resistance and reactance, and convert the results into curves giving the magnitude and phase of the total primary impedance in the presence of the secondary.

3-36. If, in Prob. 3-35, the mutual inductance had a value of 1 μh, then to what frequencies would it be necessary to tune the primary and secondary circuits in order to obtain the same shape of secondary-response curve as is actually obtained for the conditions given in Prob. 3-35?

3-37. In a shunt-feed circuit such as illustrated in Fig. 3-14, the tuned circuits are the same as in Prob. 3-32, and the shunt-feed resistance R is 100,000 ohms. What is the equivalent primary Q under these conditions?

3-38. The two resonant circuits in Fig. 3-15 are the same as in Prob. 3-32. What value must R have to make the effective Q of the secondary equal to 40?

3-39. A particular bandpass filter is to be used to handle a wave in which the highest modulation frequency is 4000 cycles. The carrier frequency of the wave is 456 kc. If the primary and secondary inductances are both 2 mh and if it is desired just barely to avoid double humps in the response curve, specify the proper coefficient of coupling and the proper circuit Q's, assuming equal primary and secondary Q's.

3-40. Two identical tuned circuits are used in a shunt-feed bandpass arrangement. The circuits are resonant at 450 kc, have inductances of 2.0 mh, and Q's of 80. The shunt-feed resistance has a value of 300,000 ohms. A bandwidth between 70.7 per cent response points of 30 kc is desired.

a. Calculate required values of circuit Q's, assuming $Q_p = Q_s$.

b. Determine the resistance that must be shunted across the secondary capacitor to make the effective Q of the secondary circuit have the required value.

c. Determine the resistance that must be shunted across the primary capacitor to make the effective Q of the primary have the required value when the effect of both the shunt-feed resistance and the primary-circuit resistance are taken into account.

3-41. According to Fig. 3-16 the response at resonance will increase as the Q is increased while leaving the coefficient of coupling unchanged.

a. Demonstrate that this result is predicted by Eq. (3-28).

b. Determine the ratio of response at resonance for zero circuit losses to the response for $k = 0.01$ when the circuit losses make $k = 0.01$ correspond to critical coupling.

3-42. Calculate the coefficient of coupling in the circuit of Fig. 3-18b when $C_1 = C_2 = 100 \ \mu\mu\text{f}$, and $C'_m = 1.5 \ \mu\mu\text{f}$.

3-43. Signals in the frequency range of 550 to 1500 kc are to be handled by means of a bandpass filter. If the circuits are assumed to have $Q = 100$ over this frequency range, and if the adjustment is such that $k = 0.01$ at 1000 kc, discuss how the width and shape of the passband will vary with resonant frequency when the tuning is obtained by varying the primary and secondary capacitors simultaneously and when the coupling is (a) inductive as shown at Fig. 2-8b, and (b) capacitive as shown at Fig. 2-8c. Assume that the circuit elements that provide the coupling do not change as the capacitors are varied. Illustrate the discussion with the aid of sketches showing in a general way the relative character of the response curves to be expected at 550, 1000, and 1500 kc for each type of coupling.

3-44. Explain how the magnitudes of the Thévenin-theorem equivalent voltage and impedance for a complex network can be determined experimentally from an open- and short-circuit test at the output terminals of the network, using only a voltmeter and an ammeter.

3-45. In Fig. 3-20 (also Fig. 3-10) the secondary circuit has an inductance of 150 μh, and is resonant at 1000 kc. If $R_1 = 10,000$, $L_1 = 150 \ \mu$h, and $M = 100 \ \mu$h, calculate the frequency at which the peak of secondary response occurs.

3-46. A primary circuit has an inductance of 1 mh and a resistance of 150 ohms connected in series. A secondary coil is coupled to the primary coil and delivers power to a load consisting of the secondary coil, a resistance of 50 ohms, and a tuning capacitance, all in series. If the impedance that the secondary circuit couples into the primary circuit is considered to be the load impedance of the primary circuit, determine the mutual inductance required between the two circuits and the reactance that the secondary circuit must have if the load is to match the generator on a maximum-power basis.

3-47. *a.* In order to demonstrate impedance matching for maximum-power transfer, write the equation of power P delivered to a rheostat as a function of its resistance R when connected to a d-c generator of internal resistance R_s and open-circuit voltage E_s. Show that this equation has a maximum for $R = R_s$.

b. Plot a graph of the equation of (a), showing $P/P_{\max}$ versus R/R_s, where P is the actual power when the load resistance is R, and $P_{\max}$ is the power when $R = R_s$. By how many decibels is the power reduced for the following cases of mismatch: (1) $R = 0.5R_s$ and (2) $R = 2R_s$?

CHAPTER 4

TRANSMISSION LINES

4-1. Voltage and Current Relations on Radio-frequency Transmission Lines in Terms of Traveling Waves.[1] Transmission lines find many uses in radio work. They are employed, not only to transmit energy, but also as resonant circuits at very high frequencies, as measuring devices at high frequencies, as aids to obtain impedance matching, etc.

FIG. 4-1. Transmission line, showing elementary length dl.

Basic Transmission-line Equations. Consider the voltage and current relations that exist in a very short length dl of the transmission line shown in Fig. 4-1. In this short distance the voltage between the wires changes an amount dE as a result of the voltage drop produced by the line current I flowing through the resistance $R\ dl$ and reactance $j\omega L\ dl$ of the length dl. Likewise, the current changes a small amount dI in the length as a result of the flow of current between the wires through the capacitance $C\ dl$ and conductance $G\ dl$ caused by the voltage that exists between these wires. Referring to Fig. 4-1, one can accordingly write the equations

$$dE = I \times \text{(impedance of length } dl)$$
$$= I(R + j\omega L)\ dl$$
$$dI = E \times \text{(admittance of length } dl)$$
$$= E(G + j\omega C)\ dl$$

[1] This material on transmission lines is a review and summary of those concepts and relations that are most widely used in radio work. It presupposes at least a little previous familiarity with the subject, and therefore should not be regarded as a self-supporting presentation of transmission-line theory. The reader desiring to gain a comprehensive understanding of transmission lines, or desiring the derivation of the equations made use of here, should consult one of the several excellent textbooks that are available on the subject, for example, H. H. Skilling, "Electric Transmission Lines," McGraw-Hill Book Company, Inc., New York, 1951; Walter C. Johnson, "Transmission Lines and Networks," McGraw-Hill Book Company, Inc., New York, 1950. More limited treatments of transmission lines, typically of chapter length, are to be found in most textbooks on communication engineering; these are adequate as an introduction to the material presented here.

Rearranging,

$$\frac{dE}{dl} = (R + j\omega L)I = ZI \tag{4-1a}$$

$$\frac{dI}{dl} = (G + j\omega C)E = YE \tag{4-1b}$$

where E = voltage across line at distance l from receiving end
  I = current in line at distance l from receiving end
  l = distance measured from load end of line
  R = resistance per unit length, ohms
  L = inductance per unit length, henrys
  C = capacitance per unit length, farads
  G = conductance per unit length, mhos
  $Z = (R + j\omega L)$ = line series impedance per unit length, ohms
  $Y = (G + j\omega C)$ = line shunt admittance per unit length, mhos
  $\omega/2\pi$ = frequency, cycles

Simultaneous solution of Eq. (4-1) gives[1]

$$\frac{d^2E}{dl^2} = ZYE \tag{4-2a}$$

$$\frac{d^2I}{dl^2} = ZYI \tag{4-2b}$$

Equations (4-2a) and (4-2b) are not independent of each other, since they are related through Eqs. (4-1a) or (4-1b).

Equations (4-2a) and (4-2b) are the standard differential equations of wave propagation and have solutions of the form

$$E = E_1 \epsilon^{\sqrt{ZY}\, l} + E_2 \epsilon^{-\sqrt{ZY}\, l} \tag{4-3a}$$
$$I = I_1 \epsilon^{\sqrt{ZY}\, l} + I_2 \epsilon^{-\sqrt{ZY}\, l} \tag{4-3b}$$

where E_1, E_2, I_1, and I_2 are constants of integration whose values are determined by the boundary conditions, i.e., by the load impedance and the magnitude of the voltage applied to the system. Although four constants appear in Eqs. (4-3), actually only two of them are independent since it can be readily shown that[2]

$$I_1 = \frac{E_1}{\sqrt{Z/Y}} = \frac{E_1}{Z_0} \tag{4-4a}$$

$$I_2 = \frac{-E_2}{\sqrt{Z/Y}} = \frac{-E_2}{Z_0} \tag{4-4b}$$

[1] These results are obtained by differentiating Eq. (4-1a), and then substituting Eq. (4-1b) to eliminate the resulting dI/dl. This gives

$$\frac{d^2E}{dl^2} = Z\frac{dI}{dl} = ZYE$$

Equation (4-2b) is obtained in an analogous manner.

[2] These relations are obtained by substituting Eq. (4-3a) in Eq. (4-1a), and then comparing the result with Eq. (4-3b).

Here

$$Z_0 = \sqrt{\frac{Z}{Y}} \tag{4-5}$$

The final solution of the differential Eqs. (4-1a) and (4-1b) of the transmission line can accordingly be written as

$$E = E_1 \epsilon^{\sqrt{ZY}\, l} + E_2 \epsilon^{-\sqrt{ZY}\, l} = E' + E'' \tag{4-6a}$$

$$I = \frac{E_1}{\sqrt{Z/Y}} \epsilon^{\sqrt{ZY}\, l} - \frac{E_2}{\sqrt{Z/Y}} \epsilon^{-\sqrt{ZY}\, l} = I' + I'' \tag{4-6b}$$

In these equations $Z_0 = \sqrt{Z/Y}$ is termed the *characteristic impedance* of the line. In the case of radio-frequency lines, Z_0 can nearly always be assumed to be a pure resistance, as discussed on page 88.

The quantity $\sqrt{ZY}$ is called the *propagation constant* of the line. It is a complex quantity, having a real part α called the *attenuation constant* and an imaginary part β termed the *phase constant*. That is

$$\sqrt{ZY} = \alpha + j\beta \tag{4-7}$$

4-2. Interpretation of Transmission-line Equations in Terms of Traveling Waves. The voltage and current existing on a transmission line as given by Eqs. (4-6) can be conveniently expressed as the sum of the voltages and currents of two waves. One of these waves can be regarded as traveling toward the receiving or load end of the line, and is called the *incident wave* because it is incident upon the load. The second wave can be thought of as traveling from the load toward the generator end of the line; it is termed the *reflected wave*, and is generated at the load by reflection of the incident wave. These two waves are identical in nature except for consequences arising from their different directions of travel.

The Incident Wave. The incident wave consists of the voltage component E' of Eq. (4-6a) associated with the current component I' of Eq. (4-6b). For such a wave it follows that everywhere on the line

$$\frac{E'}{I'} = Z_0 \tag{4-8}$$

The magnitude $|E'|$ of the incident wave becomes larger as the distance l from the load increases, according to the relation

$$|E'| = |E_1 \epsilon^{(\alpha + j\beta)l}| = |E_1| \epsilon^{\alpha l} \tag{4-9}$$

In this equation E_1 is the vector value of the voltage of the incident wave at the load end of the line, and α is the attenuation constant,[1] as defined

[1] The unit of α in Eq. (4-9) is the neper. In discussing attenuation of lines, values of α (or of αl) are, however, frequently described in decibels. The relation between nepers and decibels is

$$\text{Attenuation in decibels} = 8.686\alpha \tag{4-9a}$$

by Eq. (4-7). The quantity αl, the total attenuation of the line, is commonly called simply the line attenuation.

The phase of the incident wave advances β radians per unit distance from the load, where β is the phase constant as defined by Eq. (4-7). Hence the phase position of the incident wave at a distance l from the load leads the phase position at the load by βl radians.

The incident wave on the transmission line can therefore be described as a voltage accompanied by a current that is everywhere in phase with,

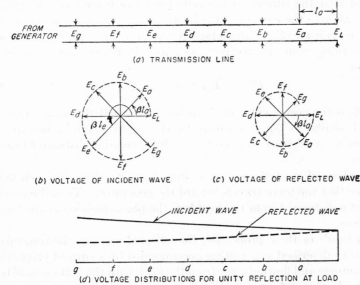

Fig. 4-2. Diagrams illustrating behavior of the voltage of the incident and reflected waves on a transmission line. The case shown assumes that the reflection coefficient at the load is unity, and that the line attenuation is only moderate. The clock diagrams show magnitude and phase of the voltage at increasing values of distance from the load.

and proportional to, the voltage, with the voltage and hence current decreasing exponentially in magnitude and dropping back uniformly in phase as the load is approached. Such a distribution is illustrated in Fig. 4-2, and can be represented by the equations

$$E' = E_1 \epsilon^{(\alpha + j\beta)l} \tag{4-10a}$$

$$I' = \frac{E'}{Z_0} = \frac{E_1}{Z_0} \epsilon^{(\alpha + j\beta)l} \tag{4-10b}$$

The incident wave is said to travel toward the load because it gets smaller as the load is approached and because its phase at a distance from the generator corresponds to the phase that existed at the generator at an earlier time proportional to distance. These are properties of a wave propagating away from a source. The velocity of propagation, called the *phase velocity*, is discussed below in connection with Eq. (4-19b).

The Reflected Wave. The reflected wave is identical with the incident wave except that it is traveling toward the generator. The reflected wave thus consists of the component voltage E'' of Eq. (4-6a) associated with a current component I'' such that everywhere on the line

$$\frac{E''}{I''} = -Z_0 \qquad (4\text{-}11)$$

This differs from Eq. (4-8) only by the negative sign, which arises from the fact that the current in the reflected wave travels toward the generator, whereas the current in the incident wave travels toward the load.

The magnitude $|E_2|$ of the reflected wave becomes smaller as the wave travels away from the receiver (i.e., as l increases) according to the relation

$$|E''| = |E_2 \epsilon^{-(\alpha+j\beta)l}| = |E_2| \epsilon^{-\alpha l} \qquad (4\text{-}12)$$

Here E_2 is the vector value of the reflected wave at the load. Equation (4-12) is similar to Eq. (4-9) except for the negative sign in the exponent; this denotes a decrease in magnitude with increasing distance l from the receiver.

The phase of the reflected wave drops back β radians for each unit of distance that the wave travels toward the generator. Thus the reflected wave at a distance l from the load lags the phase position at the load by βl radians.

As a result of these properties, the reflected wave on the transmission line can be described as a voltage accompanied by a current proportional to the voltage and flowing *away* from the load, with the voltage, and hence current, decreasing exponentially in magnitude and dropping back uniformly in phase as the distance from the load *increases*. Such a distribution is illustrated in Fig. 4-2, and can be represented by the equations

$$E'' = E_2 \epsilon^{-(\alpha+j\beta)l} \qquad (4\text{-}13a)$$

$$I'' = -\frac{E''}{Z_0} = -\frac{E_2}{Z_0} \epsilon^{-(\alpha+j\beta)l} \qquad (4\text{-}13b)$$

Relation of Incident and Reflected Waves—Reflection Coefficient. The reflected wave is generated at the load as a result of reflection of the incident wave by the load impedance. This reflection is of such a character as simultaneously to meet the following conditions: (1) The voltage and current of the incident wave at the load must satisfy Eq. (4-8); (2) the voltage and current of the reflected wave at the load must satisfy Eq. (4-11); (3) the load voltage E_L is the sum of the voltages of the incident and reflected waves at the load, that is, $E_L = E_1 + E_2$; (4) the load current I_L is the sum of the currents of the incident and reflected waves at the load, that is, $I_L = I_1 + I_2$; and (5) the vector ratio E_L/I_L must equal the load impedance Z_L.

The vector ratio E_2/E_1 of the voltage of the reflected wave to the voltage of the incident wave at the load is termed the *reflection coefficient* of the load.   Simultaneous solution of the above five relations leads to the result

$$\text{Reflection coefficient} = \rho = \frac{E_2}{E_1} = \frac{(Z_L/Z_0) - 1}{(Z_L/Z_0) + 1} \qquad (4\text{-}14)$$

The reflection coefficient has both magnitude and phase, and so is a vector quantity.   Although Eq. (4-14) is expressed in terms of the situation at the load, the ratio E''/E' of the voltages of the reflected and incident waves at a distance l from the load can be termed the reflection coefficient at the point l.   It will be noted that when $\alpha = 0$ (i.e., zero losses on the line), the reflection coefficient everywhere has the same magnitude, and equals the reflection coefficient of the load.   However, when $\alpha \neq 0$, then the reflected wave becomes smaller and the incident wave larger with increasing distance from the load, causing $|\rho|$ to decrease correspondingly. The quantitative relation is

$$|\rho_b| = |\rho_a|\epsilon^{-2\alpha(l_b - l_a)} \qquad (4\text{-}15)$$

where $|\rho_a|$ and $|\rho_b|$ are the magnitudes of the reflection coefficients at distances l_a and l_b, respectively, from the load.

The relation between the load voltage and current and the voltages of the incident and reflected waves at the load can be deduced from the above five required conditions.   It is

$$E_1 = \frac{E_L}{1 + \rho} = \left(\frac{E_L + I_L Z_0}{2}\right) \qquad (4\text{-}16a)$$

$$E_2 = \rho E_1 = \frac{\rho}{1 + \rho} E_L = \left(\frac{E_L - I_L Z_0}{2}\right) \qquad (4\text{-}16b)$$

The corresponding currents are given by Eqs. (4-8) and (4-11).

Line Voltage and Current.   The actual voltage and current existing on a transmission line are the sum of the voltages and currents, respectively, of the incident and reflected waves, as given by Eqs. (4-6), with the values for E_1 and E_2 defined as in Eqs. (4-16).[1]   Although the equations of the transmission line appear complicated, the character of the voltage and current distributions that they lead to under different conditions can be readily understood with the aid of the typical examples considered in Sec. 4-4.

4-3. Transmission-line Constants.   The electrical properties of a transmission line are determined by the inductance L, capacitance C,

---

[1] This result can also be written in an equivalent form in terms of hyperbolic functions:

$$E = E_L \cosh (\alpha + j\beta)l + I_L Z_0 \sinh (\alpha + j\beta)l \qquad (4\text{-}17a)$$

$$I = I_L \cosh (\alpha + j\beta)l + \frac{E_L}{Z_0} \sinh (\alpha + j\beta)l \qquad (4\text{-}17b)$$

series resistance R, and shunt conductance G, per unit length of line. The inductance and capacitance can be calculated by the usual formulas for transmission lines, except that at radio frequencies there are negligible magnetic-flux linkages inside the conductor as a result of skin effect; this means that one should omit the small term in the low-frequency inductance formulas that does not involve the dimensions. The series resistance of radio-frequency lines is controlled by skin effect, and so is proportional to the square root of the frequency. The shunt conductance is determined by the dielectric loss. With air insulation the shunt conductance is therefore negligible, but with solid dielectric such as used in twisted-pair and coaxial cables, the shunt conductance will be proportional to the product of frequency, power factor, and dielectric constant.

The electrical properties of the transmission line enter into the equations of the line through the characteristic impedance Z_0 and the propagation constant $\sqrt{ZY}$ as defined by Eqs. (4-5) and (4-7). At radio frequencies it is nearly always permissible to assume that $\omega L >> R$, and $\omega C >> G$. To the extent that this is true, one can rewrite Eqs. (4-5) and (4-7) as follows.

$$Z_0 = \sqrt{\frac{L}{C}} \tag{4-18a}$$

$$\alpha = \frac{R}{2Z_0} + \frac{GZ_0}{2} \tag{4-18b}$$

$$\beta = \omega \sqrt{LC} \tag{4-18c}$$

The characteristic impedance Z_0 is the ratio of voltage to current in an individual wave [see Eqs. (4-8) and (4-11)]; it is also the impedance of a line that is infinitely long or the impedance of a finite length of line when $Z_L = Z_0$. It will be noted that at radio frequencies the characteristic impedance is a resistance that is independent of frequency. Typical values for the characteristic impedance are of the order of 200 to 800 ohms for two-wire lines with air insulation, and 20 to 100 ohms for coaxial cables.

The attenuation constant of radio-frequency lines as given by Eq. (4-7) increases with frequency; this follows from Eq. (4-18b), and the fact that at high frequencies the series resistance and shunt conductance are proportional to the square root and the first power of frequency, respectively. With air insulation the conductance G is negligible, and the attenuation is due almost entirely to the skin-effect resistance of the conductors. However, in lines possessing solid dielectric, such as twisted-pair and many coaxial cables, the situation is more involved. Conductor resistance loss is then responsible for most of the attenuation at low frequencies, while the dielectric loss is the cause of most of the attenuation when the frequency is sufficiently high.

The phase constant β of a radio-frequency line is seen from Eq. (4-18c) to be proportional to frequency, and to the square root of the product LC of the line inductance and capacitance, but is independent of line resistance or conductance. The use of dielectric insulation, as is common in coaxial cables, increases the capacitance of the line, and thereby makes β larger in proportion to $\sqrt{k}$ where k is the dielectric constant of the insulation.

Wavelength and Phase Velocity. The distance λ that a wave must travel along the line in order for the total phase shift to be 2π radians is defined as the *wavelength* λ of the line. Thus, since $\beta\lambda = 2\pi$,

$$\lambda = \frac{2\pi}{\beta} \qquad (4\text{-}19a)$$

In the case of radio-frequency lines with air dielectric, λ approximates the free-space wavelength of a radio wave of the same frequency. In the case of cables with solid dielectric having a dielectric constant k, the wavelength is very closely the free-space wavelength divided by $\sqrt{k}$.

A wavelength λ at a frequency f corresponds to a velocity $v_p = f\lambda$. This is termed the *phase velocity* of the line, i.e.,

$$\text{Phase velocity} = f\lambda = \frac{2\pi f}{\beta} \qquad (4\text{-}19b)$$

In radio-frequency lines having air dielectric, the phase velocity approximates very closely the velocity of light. In lines with solid-dielectric insulation, the phase velocity is the velocity of light divided by the square root of the dielectric constant of the insulation.

4-4. Examples of Voltage and Current Distributions on Transmission Lines. The various ways in which the voltage and current may be distributed along a transmission line can be understood by considering in detail a number of special cases. In the discussion of these examples to follow, it is assumed that the attenuation constant α is small; this is done in order to simplify the phenomena involved. The modifications introduced when the attenuation constant is not small are discussed in Sec. 4-5.

Transmission Line with Open-circuited Load. When the load impedance is infinite, Eq. (4-14) shows that the coefficient of reflection will be $1/\underline{0}$. Under these conditions the incident and reflected waves will have equal magnitudes at the load, and the reflection will be such that the voltages of the incident and reflected waves have the same phase. As a result, the voltages of the two waves add arithmetically so that at the load $E_1 = E_2 = E_L/2$. Under these conditions it follows from Eqs. (4-8) and (4-11) that the currents of the two waves are equal in magnitude but opposite in phase; they thus add up to zero load current, as must be the case if the load is open-circuited.

Consider now how these two waves behave as the distance l from the load increases. The incident wave advances in phase β radians per unit length, while the reflected wave lags correspondingly; at the same time magnitudes do not change greatly when the attenuation constant α is small. The vector sum of the voltages of the two waves is then less than the arithmetic sum, as illustrated in Fig. 4-3a, for $l = \lambda/8$. This tendency continues until the distance to the load becomes exactly a quarter wavelength, i.e., until $\beta l = \pi/2$. The incident wave has then advanced 90° from its phase position at the load, while the reflected wave has dropped back a similar amount. The line voltage at this point is thus the arithmetic *difference* of the voltages of the two waves, as shown in Fig. 4-3a, for $l = \lambda/4$, and it will be quite small if the attenuation is small. The resultant voltage will not be zero, however, because some attenuation will always be present, and this causes the incident wave to be larger and the reflected wave smaller at the quarter-wave length point than at the load, where the amplitudes are exactly the same.

As the distance to the load increases to a value greater than a quarter wavelength, the phase of the incident wave continues to advance, while that of the reflected wave continues to lag. As a consequence, the voltages of the two waves depart increasingly from the condition of phase opposition existing at the quarter-wavelength point, and give a resultant value that becomes larger with increasing distance. This tendency continues until the distance from the load is a half wavelength (that is, $\beta l = \pi$); at this point the phases of the two waves have respectively advanced, and retarded, by 180°. The result is that the voltages now have the same relative phase relation with respect to each other as existed at the load, and so add arithmetically as at the load to give a large resultant line voltage. At greater distances than a half wavelength the cycle starts to repeat, as illustrated in Figs. 4-3a and 4-4a.

The voltage distribution on the open-circuited transmission line that results from this process is shown in Figs. 4-3a and 4-4a. It is characterized by voltage maxima at points that are even multiples of a quarter wavelength distant from the load, and by deep voltage minima at points that are odd multiples of a quarter wavelength from the load.

The current distribution associated with this voltage is also illustrated in Fig. 4-4a. The current distribution has minima where the voltage has maxima, and vice versa. This arises from the fact that the current of the reflected wave has the opposite phase from the reflected voltage [see Eq. (4-11)]. As a result, the currents in the two waves add where the voltages subtract, and subtract to give a minimum where the voltages add.

It will be noted that the variations in both the voltage and current distributions repeat their general character each half wavelength. This is characteristic of all distributions on transmission lines.

Transmission Line with Short-circuited Load. When the load end of the line is short-circuited, that is, $Z_L = 0$, reference to Eq. (4-14) shows that the reflection coefficient has the value $-1.0\underline{/0°} = 1.0\underline{/180°}$. As in

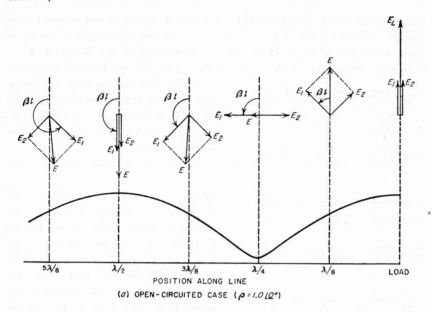

(a) OPEN-CIRCUITED CASE ($\rho = 1.0 \underline{/0°}$)

(b) RESISTIVE LOAD GREATER THAN Z_0 ($\rho = 0.5 \underline{/0°}$)

Fig. 4-3. Vector diagrams showing manner in which the incident and reflected waves combined to produce a voltage distribution on the transmission line. The cases shown correspond to a reflection in which the phase of the voltage is unchanged by reflection; it is also assumed that the attenuation of the line is quite small.

the open-circuited case, the reflected wave has an amplitude equal to the amplitude of the incident wave. However, the reflection now takes place with reversal in phase of the voltage, and without change in phase of the current. The result is that the current in each individual wave at the

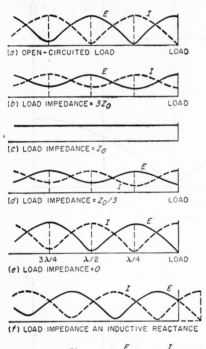

(a) OPEN-CIRCUITED LOAD   LOAD

(b) LOAD IMPEDANCE = $3Z_0$ LOAD

(c) LOAD IMPEDANCE = Z_0

(d) LOAD IMPEDANCE = $Z_0/3$ LOAD

$3\lambda/4$ $\lambda/2$ $\lambda/4$ LOAD
(e) LOAD IMPEDANCE = 0

(f) LOAD IMPEDANCE AN INDUCTIVE REACTANCE

$\frac{\lambda}{2}$
LOAD
(g) LOAD IMPEDANCE A CAPACITIVE REACTANCE

Fig. 4-4. Types of voltage and current distributions produced on a transmission line by different load impedances. It is assumed that the transmission line has low attenuation, and a characteristic impedance that is resistive.

load is half of the load current, while the voltages in the two waves add up at the load to a resultant of zero voltage, as obviously is required across a short circuit.

If one now examines the situation as the distance from the load increases, the incident wave advances in phase while the reflected wave lags correspondingly, exactly as in the case of the open-circuited load. However, since it is now the currents that add at the load end of the line and the voltages that subtract, one obtains the distribution of voltage and current illustrated in Fig. 4-4e. This differs from the corresponding distributions of the open-circuited load case only in that voltage and current are interchanged. That is, with the short-circuited load the voltage on the line goes through minima at distances from the load that are even multiples of a quarter wavelength, and through maxima at distances that are odd multiples of a quarter wavelength. As before, the positions of the current maxima correspond to the voltage minima, and vice versa.

Characteristic Impedance Load. When the load impedance is equal to the characteristic impedance, the reflection coefficient is zero; i.e., there is no reflected wave. Under these conditions the voltage and current both increase exponentially with increasing distance from the load, as illustrated in Fig. 4-4c.

The physical significance of the situation where the reflection coefficient is zero (i.e., when $Z_L = Z_0$) is that the vector ratio of the voltage to current required by the load is exactly the same as that present in the incident wave. The load is therefore able to absorb completely the incident wave. With any other value of load impedance this is not possible, and a reflected wave is then produced.

Intermediate Values of Load Impedance. When the load impedance is a resistance greater than the characteristic impedance, the reflected wave produced at the load is smaller than the incident wave, but has the same phase angle as in the open-circuited case.[1] As a result, the voltage and current distributions go through successive maxima and minima at exactly the same places as for the open-circuited load. However, since the reflected wave is smaller than the incident wave, the minima are not as deep in proportion to the load voltage; this is illustrated in Fig. 4-4b. Vector diagrams showing how the voltages of the incident and reflected waves add to give the line voltage in this case are shown in Fig. 4-3b; a comparison with the corresponding diagrams of Fig. 4-3a shows in detail why and how the situation is modified when the reflected wave is smaller than the incident wave.

When the load impedance is a resistance that is smaller in magnitude than the characteristic impedance of the line, then the reflected wave is smaller than the incident wave, and has the same phase relation with respect to the incident wave as in the short-circuited load case. Under these conditions, the voltage and current distributions possess maxima and minima at exactly the same points as for the short-circuited load, but the maxima are not as large and the minima are less deep. This is illustrated in Fig. 4-4d.

Reactive Loads. Next consider the case where the load impedance is a pure reactance. Study of Eq. (4-14) shows that if the characteristic impedance can be assumed to be a resistance, the reflection coefficient for Z_L reactive is unity irrespective of the magnitude of the load reactance; however the phase angle of the reflection coefficient will depend upon the ratio of the load reactance to characteristic impedance. The consequences of this situation are illustrated in Fig. 4-4f and g. With a reactive load impedance, the voltage and current distributions vary in the same way, and to the same extent, as with the open-circuited (or short-circuited) load case. However, a reactive load impedance causes the minima of these curves to be displaced with respect to the position of the minima for an open-circuited line.

If one takes the open-circuit distribution as a reference, then a capacitive load causes the first minimum in the voltage distribution to occur closer to the receiver than a quarter wavelength, as illustrated in Fig. 4-4g. This comes about because for capacitive loads the phase angle of the

---

[1] For the reflection coefficient to have a phase angle of exactly 0 or 180°, it is necessary that the load impedance have the same phase angle as the characteristic impedance. In the case of radio-frequency transmission lines, this means a load that for all practical purposes is resistive.

reflection coefficient is negative, i.e., the reflected wave at the load lags behind the incident wave. Thus with a capacitive load the distance from the load at which the reflected wave lags 180° behind the incident wave is less than a quarter wavelength. In contrast, an inductive load causes the first voltage minimum to occur at a distance from the load that is greater than a quarter wavelength, as illustrated in Fig. 4-4f. This

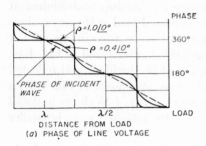

(a) PHASE OF LINE VOLTAGE

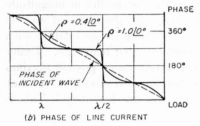

(b) PHASE OF LINE CURRENT

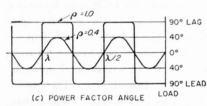

(c) POWER FACTOR ANGLE

Fig. 4-5. Phase relations on a transmission line for two typical conditions. In these curves, the voltage of the incident wave at the load is used as the reference phase, and the line attenuation is assumed to be small.

results from the fact that the phase angle of the reflection coefficient is positive in this case. With both inductive and capacitive loads, the displacement of the minima from their open-circuited position is greater the lower the load reactance. It is also to be noted that the effect of a reactive load is merely to displace the position of the minima; the distance between the adjacent minima still remains a half wavelength, just as in the open- and short-circuited cases.

Load impedances that have both resistive and reactive components will result in voltage and current distributions in which the variation in amplitude along the line is less than in the open- and short-circuited cases because the reflection coefficient is less than unity, as in Fig. 4-4b and d. However, at the same time the maxima and minima are shifted along the line in the same direction as when the load is purely reactive.

Phase Relations in Voltage and Current Distributions. The phase of the voltage and current in an individual wave drops back β radians per unit length in the direction in which the wave travels. Thus, when the load impedance equals the characteristic impedance so that only the incident wave is present, the line voltage and current advance in phase at the uniform rate of β radians per unit length as one goes from the load to the generator. The total phase shift is 2π radians per wavelength under these conditions.

When the load impedance does not equal the characteristic impedance, the phase relations are complicated by the presence of the reflected wave. The phase of the resulting line voltage (or current) then oscillates about the phase of the voltage (or current) of the incident wave, as illustrated in Fig. 4-5. The phase shift under these conditions tends to be concentrated in regions where the voltage (or current) goes through a minimum; this is increasingly the case as the reflected wave approaches equality with the incident wave. However, irrespective of the relative amplitudes of the incident and reflected waves, the phase of both voltage and current will advance exactly π radians (180°) when the distance toward the generator decreases by a half wavelength. Although in the absence of a reflected wave the variation in phase is at a uniform rate within this distance, this is not the case when a reflected wave is present.

4-5. The Effect of Attenuation on Voltage and Current Distribution—Lossless Lines. The voltage and current distributions illustrated in

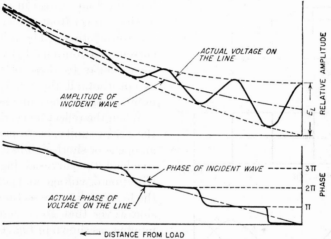

FIG. 4-6. Variation of voltage amplitude and phase with distance along a transmission line having such high attenuation that toward the generator end the reflected wave is attenuated at a very small size.

Fig. 4-4 assume that the total attenuation αl of the line is small compared with unity. Under these conditions the amplitude of the incident, and also of the reflected wave, changes only slightly in traveling the entire length of the line.

When the attenuation of the line is relatively large, the incident wave then increases rapidly in amplitude as one goes toward the generator. Similarly the reflected wave decreases rapidly in size as it recedes from the load. The resulting behavior is as illustrated in Fig. 4-6; at a considerable distance from the load the reflected wave becomes so small that the voltage and current begin to approximate the values that would exist for the case $Z_L = Z_0$, irrespective of the actual value of the load impedance. The progressive change in the ratio of reflected to incident waves that is caused by attenuation produces corresponding effects on the phase behavior. These are also illustrated in Fig. 4-6, which shows that the actual phase departs less and less from the phase of the incident wave as the reflected wave becomes smaller.

Transmission Lines with Zero Losses. The behavior of an idealized transmission line with zero losses is important because under many circumstances, and for many purposes, it is permissible to neglect the losses associated with practical radio-frequency transmission lines.

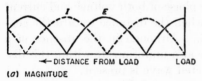

(a) MAGNITUDE

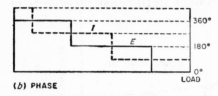

(b) PHASE

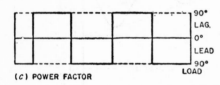

(c) POWER FACTOR

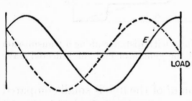

(d) MAGNITUDE AND PHASE SHOWN SIMULTANEOUSLY

Fig. 4-7. Voltage, current, and phase relations on an open-circuited transmission line having zero losses.

When the resistance and conductance of a transmission line are zero, the attenuation constant α is likewise zero, and the incident and reflected waves on the transmission line suffer no change in amplitude as they travel from one end of the line to the other. The voltage and current distributions that result are then similar to those of Fig. 4-4, except that all the maxima (and minima) are of the same height.

When the reflection coefficient of the load is unity, corresponding to an open- or short-circuited or reactive load, the curves giving the distribution of voltage and current on the loss-free line are sections of half sine waves that go to zero at the minima, as shown in Fig. 4-7a. In this case the phase of the voltage (or current) jumps 180° at each minimum, as indicated in Fig. 4-7b. The distribution curves of the lossless line are hence commonly drawn as shown in Fig. 4-7d, which simultaneously indicates both magnitude and phase by using negative amplitudes to indicate the polarity reversal associated with a 180° phase shift.

Since the waves on a lossless line do not change in amplitude as they travel along the line, the reflection coefficient in such a system is everywhere constant and equal to the reflection coefficient at the load, as given by Eq. (4-14). Similarly, the standing-wave ratio (see below) is everywhere the same on a lossless line.

4-6. Standing-wave Ratio. The character of the voltage (or current) distribution on a transmission line can be conveniently described in terms of the ratio of the maximum amplitude to minimum amplitude possessed by the distribution. This quantity is termed the *standing-wave ratio* (often abbreviated SWR); thus in Fig. 4-8,[1]

$$\text{Standing-wave ratio} = S = \frac{E_{\max}}{E_{\min}} \tag{4-20}$$

Alternatively, the standing-wave ratio may be defined in terms of maximum and minimum current; for any particular line the standing-wave ratio at a given region on the line will be the same whether defined in terms of the voltage or current distribution.

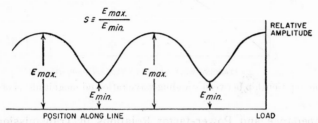

FIG. 4-8. Diagram illustrating nomenclature used in defining the standing-wave ratio.

In terms of the amplitudes $|E_1|$ and $|E_2|$ of the incident and reflected waves respectively, the standing-wave ratio can be written

$$S = \frac{|E_1| + |E_2|}{|E_1| - |E_2|} \tag{4-21}$$

The standing-wave ratio is seen from Eq. (4-21) to be a measure of the amplitude ratio of the reflected to incident waves. Thus a standing-wave ratio of unity denotes the absence of a reflected wave, while a very high standing-wave ratio indicates that the reflected wave is almost as large as the incident wave. Theoretically, for the case of zero attenuation, the standing-wave ratio will be infinite when the load is either open- or short-circuited, or is a lossless reactance.

The standing-wave ratio S is one means of expressing the magnitude of the reflection coefficient; the exact relation between the two is

$$S = \frac{1 + |\rho|}{1 - |\rho|} \tag{4-22a}$$

or

$$|\rho| = \frac{S - 1}{S + 1} \tag{4-22b}$$

This relationship is illustrated graphically in Fig. 4-9.

The importance of the standing-wave ratio arises from the fact that it can be very easily measured experimentally. Moreover, the standing-

---

[1] This definition of standing-wave ratio is sometimes called voltage standing-wave ratio (VSWR) to distinguish it from the standing-wave ratio expressed as a power ratio, which is $(E_{\max}/E_{\min})^2$.

wave ratio indicates directly the extent to which reflected waves exist on a system.   In addition, standing-wave measurements provide an important means of measuring impedance, as discussed in Sec. 4-9.

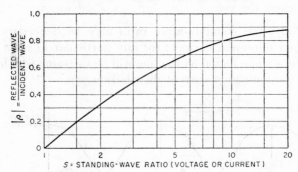

Fig. 4-9. The relationship between standing-wave ratio and magnitude $|\rho|$ of reflection coefficient.

4-7. Impedance and Power-factor Relations in Transmission Lines.
The expression "transmission-line impedance" applied to a point on a transmission line signifies the vector ratio of line voltage to line current at that particular point.   This is the impedance that would be obtained if the transmission line were cut at the point in question, and the impedance looking toward the load were measured on a bridge.

When the load impedance equals the characteristic impedance, only the incident wave is present, and the line impedance is everywhere equal to the characteristic impedance.   The line impedance is also equal to the characteristic impedance under conditions where the total attenuation αl to the load is so great that the reflected wave is of negligible amplitude compared with the incident wave.   Under these conditions the impedance of the transmission line is independent of conditions at the load.

When a reflected wave is present, the impedance will be alternately greater and lower than the characteristic impedance, as illustrated in Fig. 4-10.   Since the line current is always a minimum when the voltage is maximum, and vice versa, the impedance maxima and minima coincide with the voltage maxima and minima, respectively.   The magnitude of the line impedance therefore varies cyclically with a periodicity of a half wavelength.   If the line losses are low and the reflection coefficient of the load is not too close to unity, the line impedance repeats almost exactly in successive half-wave intervals, as illustrated in Fig. 4-10a.   However, when the reflection coefficient at the load approaches unity (large standing-wave ratio), then the line attenuation, even if small, will cause the peaks of impedance to diminish in amplitude at progressively larger distances to the load, as in Fig. 4-10b.

The power factor of the line impedance varies according to the standing-wave situation.   When the load impedance equals the characteristic impedance, there is no reflected wave and the power-factor angle of the line is zero, corresponding to a resistive impedance. However, when a reflected wave is present, the power-factor angle is zero only at the points on the line where the voltage goes through a maximum or a minimum. At other points the power-factor angle will alternate between leading and lagging at intervals of a quarter wavelength, as shown in Figs. 4-10 and 4-5c. When the line is short-circuited at the receiver (Fig. 4-10b), or if

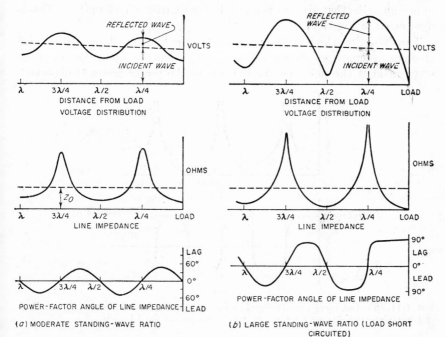

Fig. 4-10. Magnitude and power factor of line impedance with increasing distance from the load, for load impedances that are, respectively, a resistance less than the characteristic impedance, and a short circuit. These diagrams assume that the attenuation of the line is small.

the load is a resistance less than the characteristic impedance so that the voltage distribution is of the short-circuit type (Fig. 4-10a), the power factor is inductive (lagging) for lengths corresponding to less than the distance to the first voltage maximum, and thereafter alternates between capacitive and inductive at intervals of a quarter wavelength. Similarly, with an open-circuited receiver, or with a resistance load greater than the characteristic impedance so that the voltage distribution is of the open-circuit type (Fig. 4-5), the power factor is capacitive for lengths less than the distance to the first voltage minimum. Thereafter, the power factor alternates between capacitive and inductive at intervals of a quarter wavelength, exactly as in the short-circuited case.

If one considers the impedance at the generator end of a transmission line of fixed length under conditions where the frequency of measurement is progressively increased, the impedance will vary in magnitude with frequency in much the same manner as with increasing length. Thus, with a short-circuited load, the line impedance will go through successive maxima at frequencies that make the line length correspond to one-quarter, three-quarters, five-quarters, etc., of a wavelength, and will go through minima at frequencies that correspond to line lengths measured in wavelengths that are an even number of quarter wavelengths. This is illustrated in Fig. 4-11.

The extent to which the power factor of the line impedance varies with changes in length, or changes in frequency, depends upon the standing-wave ratio at the point on the line where the power factor is observed.

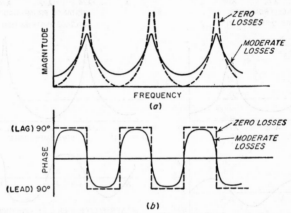

Fig. 4-11. Effect of variation in frequency on the magnitude and phase of the sending-end impedance of a short-circuited transmission line of fixed length.

If the standing-wave ratio is large, and the line losses low (solid curve in Fig. 4-11), the power-factor angle will approach 90° except in the immediate vicinity of the voltage maxima and minima. Then the power-factor angle suddenly shifts between nearly +90° and nearly −90°, as illustrated in Fig. 4-11b and Fig. 4-5c. In fact, in the case of a short-circuited or open-circuited ideal line of zero losses, the power-factor angle is exactly 90° everywhere except at the voltage maxima and minima, as illustrated in Fig. 4-7c, and by the dotted line in Fig. 4-11a. On the other hand, if the standing-wave ratio is small or moderate, the maximum range over which the power-factor angle varies about unity power factor will be correspondingly less than 90° (see Figs. 4-5c and 4-10a).

4-8. Transmission-line Charts—the Smith Chart. The various properties of a transmission line can be presented graphically in an almost endless variety of charts. The most useful graphical representations, however, are those which give the impedance relations that exist along a lossless line for different load conditions.

The Smith chart shown in Fig. 4-12 is the most widely used transmission-line chart of this class.[1] This diagram is based on two sets of orthogonal circles. One set represents the ratio R/Z_0, where R is the resistance component of the line impedance, and Z_0 is the characteristic impedance (which for a lossless line is a resistance). The second set of circles represents the ratio jX/Z_0, where X is the reactive component of the line impedance. These coordinates are so chosen by means of a conformal transformation that conditions on the lossless line corresponding to a given standing-wave ratio (or what is the same thing, a given magnitude of the load reflection coefficient) lie on a circle having its origin at the center of the chart.

The standing-wave ratio S corresponding to any particular circle is equal to the value of R/Z_0 at which the circle crosses the horizontal axis on the right-hand side of the chart center (see Prob. 4-25). This same circle intersects the horizontal axis to the left of the center at a value of R/Z_0 such that $1/S = R/Z_0$. Intersections with the horizontal axis that are on the left of the chart center represent voltage minima; intersections with the horizontal axis on the right of the center correspond to voltage maxima.

Moving around a given standing-wave circle is equivalent to traveling along a lossless transmission line on which the standing-wave ratio corresponds to the circle involved; thus the successive values of impedance indicated by a given circle correspond to the line impedances at successive points along the lossless line. Distance on the actual transmission line is directly proportional to the angle of rotation around the standing-wave circle, with one complete revolution corresponding to exactly a half wavelength on the transmission line. Thus in Fig. 4-12 the distance between points on the line where the impedance conditions are represented by P and Q on the chart is 0.05 wavelength, because P and Q lie on the same circle, and radial lines OPA and OQB drawn from the center of the chart are displaced by 0.05λ on the outer scale; this corresponds to 36° angular displacement, or $36/720 = 0.05$ wavelength.[2] Travel around the circle in a clockwise direction is toward the generator, whereas travel in a counterclockwise direction is toward the load; this fact is marked on the periphery of the chart.

The impedance at any point on a transmission line for a given load

[1] P. H. Smith, Transmission Line Calculator, *Electronics*, vol. 12, p. 29, January, 1939; P. H. Smith, An Improved Transmission Line Calculator, *Electronics*, vol. 17, p. 130, January, 1944. Graph paper and a plastic calculator are commercially available. A paper covering the theoretical foundations of the Smith chart, and its relation to the so-called rectangular chart, is H. L. Krauss, Transmission Line Charts, *Elec. Eng.*, vol. 68, p. 767, September, 1949.

[2] Distances greater than a half wavelength are handled by going around the standing-wave circle as many times as required. Thus the distance OA to OB actually represents $0.05\lambda + n\lambda/2$, where n can be any interger, including zero.

condition, including the load impedance, is represented by a point properly located on the Smith chart. Thus P in Fig. 4-12 corresponds to the impedance $Z_0(0.98 + j0.7)$, and lies on the circle centered at O that corresponds to a standing-wave ratio of 2 (because the circle through P intersects the R/Z_0 axis on the right of the chart at $R/Z_0 = 2$). If the line were terminated with a load having an impedance corresponding to

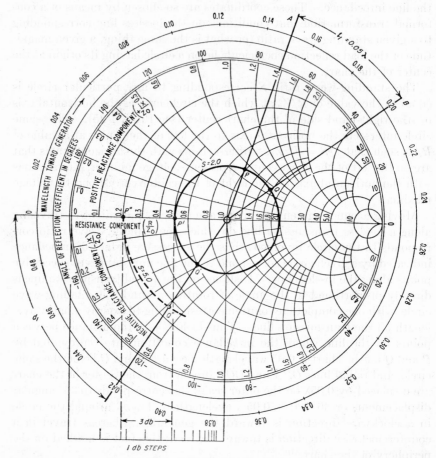

Fig. 4-12. The Smith chart.

P, then the standing-wave ratio that would exist on the line would be 2.0; the impedance at other points along the line could be obtained by traveling clockwise around the circle passing through P by an amount indicated by the calibration on the periphery of the chart. For example, at a distance 0.05λ toward the generator from P, the line impedance is $Z_0(1.56 + j0.7)$, corresponding to point Q, while 0.27λ distant from P, the impedance corresponds to Q' and is $Z_0(0.6 - j0.38)$. Again, if the load impedance corresponded to the value Q, the standing-wave ratio would still be 2, but the impedance at Q' would now be the line impedance at a distance 0.22λ from the receiver, since Q' is 0.22λ around the circle in a clockwise direction from Q.

The Smith chart thus shows very simply and directly the standing-wave ratio corresponding to a given load impedance. It also shows the line impedance at any desired point, given the standing-wave ratio and the impedance at any other point on the line, for example, the load imped-ance. From the standing-wave ratio, one can obtain the magnitude of

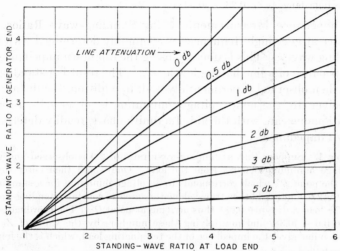

Fig. 4-13. Relationship between standing-wave ratios at two points on a trans-mission line, for different values of line attenuation between these points.

the reflection coefficient from Eq. (4-22b) or Fig. 4-9. The phase angle of the reflection coefficient is given on the chart periphery. Thus for point P one has $\rho = 0.33\underline{/72°}$. The Smith chart can also be used to determine impedance from data obtained from standing-wave measure-ments; this is discussed in Sec. 4-9.

Effect of Line Attenuation. The Smith chart assumes that the line attenuation is zero. Under these conditions the standing-wave ratio is everywhere constant, and the chart implies that this is the case. When attenuation is present it is, however, still possible to use the Smith chart by using Fig. 4-13 to correct for the change in standing-wave ratio with position.[1] The method ot doing this is made clear by the following example.

Example. Assume that the conditions existing at some point on the line correspond to P in Fig. 4-12; this may be the generator end of the line although it is not so limited. It is then desired to know the line impedance at a point 0.23λ closer to the load when

[1] The curves in Fig. 4-13 are obtained by combining Eqs. (4-15), (4-22a), (4-22b), and (4-9a).

the total attenuation for the line length of 0.23λ is known to be 3.0 db rather than zero. The first step is to ignore the line attenuation and travel *counterclockwise* around the circle passing through P for a distance corresponding to 0.23λ. This brings one to point Q', which corresponds to the line impedance that would exist at the desired point if the line had no attenuation. However, Fig. 4-13 shows that a line attenuation of 3 db causes a standing-wave ratio of 2.0 at the generator end of the section of line to correspond to a standing-wave ratio of 5.0 at the load end. A circle, shown dotted in Fig. 4-12, is then drawn corresponding to this standing-wave ratio. The intersection of this circle with the radial line OQ' then defines a point Q'' on the chart that corresponds to the desired impedance, taking into account the line attenuation;[1] this impedance is Z_0 (0.26 − j0.52).

4-9. Impedance Measurements Using Standing-wave Ratios.[2] The impedance at very high frequencies is commonly determined with the aid of standing waves. This is done by using the unknown impedance as the load impedance of a line having low losses. The resulting standing-wave ratio is then observed experimentally and, in addition, the distance from the receiver to the first voltage minimum is observed. From this information one can, with the aid of a Smith chart, readily determine the unknown impedance.

Example 1. Suppose that a standing-wave ratio of 2.0 is observed and that the first voltage minimum is 0.08λ from the load. One would then enter the Smith chart at the point P', which corresponds to a voltage minimum for a standing-wave ratio that is 2.0, and would then travel along this circle of constant standing-wave ratio toward the load a distance 0.08λ thus arriving at point Q'. The coordinates of this point are 0.6 − j0.38, and multiplying these numbers by the value of Z_0 for the transmission line gives the impedance of the terminating load, which is the impedance to be determined.

Example 2. Assume that once again the standing-wave ratio is observed to be 2.0, but that it is now inconvenient to measure the actual distance from the load to the first voltage minimum. The procedure then consists in first connecting the unknown impedance across the end of the line and observing the position of some convenient voltage minimum. Next, the unknown impedance is replaced by a short circuit, and the position of the first voltage minimum *on the load side* of the original minimum is observed. Assume that this minimum is 0.35λ toward the load from the original minimum. It is then permissible to regard this new minimum as the equivalent position of the load. This follows from the fact that on a lossless line impedances repeat exactly each half wavelength. Therefore one enters the Smith chart at point P', which corresponds to the voltage minimum with the load connected, and travels 0.35λ *toward the load* along the circle for S = 2.0. This leads to point P, which has the coordinates 0.98 + j0.7; these numbers multiplied by Z_0 then give the unknown

---

[1] Smith charts are sometimes provided with an auxiliary decibel scale that can be used to determine the effect of the attenuation on the radius of the standing-wave circle. Such a scale is shown in Fig. 4-12, and is calibrated so that each unit on the auxiliary scale represents the change in circle radius associated with 1 db attenuation. Thus starting with a standing-wave circle of radius OQ' in Fig. 4-12, the circle passing through Q'' is drawn with a radius that is 3.0 units different on the decibel scale than OQ' as shown, because the line attenuation is 3.0 db.

[2] An extensive summarizing discussion of this subject is given by F. E. Terman and J. M. Pettit, "Electronic Measurements," pp. 135–152, McGraw-Hill Book Company, Inc., New York, 1952.

impedance.   An alternative procedure would be to note that if the reference point is taken as the minimum with the unknown connected at the load, then when the line is short circuited, the first minimum on the generator side of this reference point is $0.5 - 0.35 = 0.15\lambda$ *toward the generator.*   Entering the chart at P' as before, one could therefore proceed 0.15λ toward the generator (i.e., a distance -0.15λ toward the load).   This also brings one to point P.

Equipment for Experimental Determination of Standing-wave Ratio for Impedance Measurements.   The standing-wave ratio on a transmission

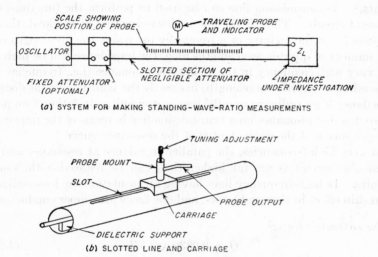

(*a*) SYSTEM FOR MAKING STANDING-WAVE-RATIO MEASUREMENTS

(*b*) SLOTTED LINE AND CARRIAGE

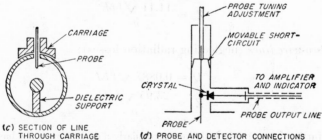

(*c*) SECTION OF LINE THROUGH CARRIAGE   (*d*) PROBE AND DETECTOR CONNECTIONS

FIG. 4-14. Details of a slotted-line type of standing-wave detector for a coaxial line.

line can be observed by exploring along the length of the line with a pickup arrangement that will indicate the strength of either the electric field (line voltage) or the magnetic field (line current), in the vicinity of the line.   A typical example of such a *standing-wave detector* that is suitable for coaxial systems is illustrated in Fig. 4-14.   This arrangement consists of a section of coaxial line having air insulation and a longitudinal slot in the outer conductor, as shown.   Mounted on this slotted section is a traveling carriage carrying a probe that projects through the slot toward the center conductor, as shown.   To this probe there is connected some form of power- or voltage-indicating device, often a simple detector. An oscillator is connected to one end of the slotted line, while the other end is connected to the unknown impedance or, alternatively, to the input of the transmission line that is to have its standing-wave ratio observed. The standing-wave pattern is then obtained by moving the carriage (and hence the probe position) and observing the resulting variations in the probe output.

4-10. Transmission Lines as Resonant Circuits and as Circuit Elements.[1] A transmission line can be used to perform the functions of a resonant circuit. Thus, if the line is short-circuited at the load, then at frequencies in the vicinity of a frequency for which the line length is an odd number of quarter wavelengths long, the impedance will be high and will vary with frequency in the vicinity of resonance (i.e., frequency corresponding to quarter wavelength) in exactly the same manner as does the impedance of an ordinary parallel resonant circuit. It is therefore possible to describe resonance on a transmission line in terms of the impedance at resonance and the equivalent Q of the resonance curve.[2]

At very high frequencies, the parallel impedance at resonance and the obtainable circuit Q are far higher than can be realized with lumped circuits. In high-frequency lines having air insulation the losses all arise from skin effect in the conductors, and one has with copper conductors

For concentric lines:[3]

$$Q = 0.0839 \sqrt{f}\, bH \qquad (4\text{-}23a)$$

$$Z_s = \frac{11.11 \sqrt{f}\, bF}{n} \qquad (4\text{-}23b)$$

For two-wire lines (neglecting radiation losses):

$$Q = 0.0887 \sqrt{f}\, bJ \qquad (4\text{-}24a)$$

$$Z_s = \frac{23.95 \sqrt{f}\, bG}{n} \qquad (4\text{-}24b)$$

[1] For further information, including particularly a derivation of the basic relations, see F. E. Terman, Resonant Lines in Radio Circuits, *Elec. Eng.*, vol. 53, p. 1046, July, 1934. In this paper it was demonstrated for the first time that the resonance curve of a transmission line has the same shape as the resonance curve of a circuit with coil and capacitor, and so can be described by specifying a Q.

[2] The Q in such a situation can be defined in terms of the detuning required to reduce the response to 70.7 per cent of the response at resonance, in accordance with Rule 1 on p. 49; alternatively, one may employ Eq. (3-1).

[3] Examination of Fig. 4-15 shows that in an air-insulated coaxial line of given outer radius b, Q will be maximum when the inner conductor has a size such that $b/a = 3.6$, corresponding to $Z_0 = 77$ ohms. These are also the proportions for minimum power loss in a transmission line operated with $Z_L = Z_0$. However, the maximum power that can be transmitted without exceeding a given voltage gradient occurs when $b/a = 1.65$, giving $Z_0 = 30$ ohms.

where Q = circuit Q defined from the resonance curve so that Q = $f_0/2\Delta f$, where f_0 is the resonant frequency and Δf is the number of cycles off resonance at which the response is 70.7 per cent of the response at resonance

Z_s = sending end or input impedance

f = frequency, cycles

b = inner radius of outer conductor of a concentric line, or spacing of wire centers in two-wire line, cm

a = outer radius of inner conductor in concentric line, or wire radius in two-wire line, cm

n = number of quarter wavelengths in the line

F, G, H, J = constants determined by b/a and given in Fig. 4-15.

Substitution of reasonable values in these equations leads to surprising results. Thus, at a wavelength of 150 cm (200 Mc), a concentric line with copper conductors and air insulation in which $b/a = 3.6$ and with a diameter of outer conductor of 5 cm (2 in.) possesses a Q of approximately 3000; when the line length is a quarter wavelength long (approximately 15 in.), the resonant impedance is over 250,000 ohms. Because of favorable properties such as these, together with the fact that the physical size of a resonant line is relatively large in proportion to wavelength as com-

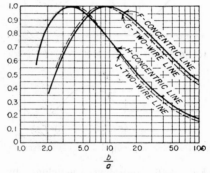

FIG. 4-15. Factors F, G, H, and J for use in Eqs. (4-23) and (4-24).

pared with a coil-and-capacitor combination, resonant transmission lines find extensive use as resonant circuits at the higher radio frequencies, particularly at frequencies of the order of 100 Mc and greater.

A behavior corresponding to that of a series resonant circuit can be obtained from a transmission line that is an odd number of quarter wavelengths long and open-circuited at the receiver. Under these conditions, the voltage at the load is much higher than the applied voltage, as is apparent from Fig. 4-4. Furthermore, at frequencies near resonance the voltage step-up varies with frequency in exactly the same manner as does a resonance curve, and has an equivalent Q given by Eq. (4-23a) or (4-24a) as the case may be. The voltage step-up ratio is, however, $Q \times 4/\pi n$, instead of Q as in the case of the ordinary series resonant circuit.

Transmission lines can be used to provide low-loss inductances or capacitances by employing the proper combination of length, frequency, and termination. Thus a line short-circuited at the load will offer an inductive reactance when less than a quarter wavelength long, and a capacitive reactance when between a quarter and a half wavelength long. With an open-circuited load, conditions for inductive and capacitive reactances are interchanged.

4-11. Impedance Matching in Transmission Lines.[1] Energy is transmitted most efficiently by a transmission line when no reflected wave is present.[2] However, only under exceptional cases will the load impedance be a resistance that is exactly equal to the characteristic impedance of the line. Thus, to obtain transmission of energy with maximum efficiency, it is necessary to provide means for matching the actual load impedance to the characteristic impedance of the line. Again, it is often desired that the line impedance be independent of the distance to the load. Likewise in making many types of measurements in systems involving transmission lines, it is frequently desirable, and in some cases very necessary, that there be no reflected wave present.

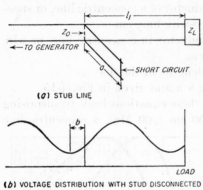

(a) STUB LINE

(b) VOLTAGE DISTRIBUTION WITH STUD DISCONNECTED

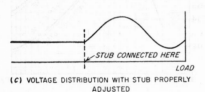

(c) VOLTAGE DISTRIBUTION WITH STUB PROPERLY ADJUSTED

Fig. 4-16. Impedance matching by means of a short-circuited stub line. Although the arrangement shown is a two-wire system, coaxial lines may be employed.

At the lower radio frequencies a load can be matched to the characteristic impedance of a line by associating with the load a network of reactances that tunes out the load reactance and simultaneously transforms the resulting resistance to a value equal to the characteristic impedance of the line. This is discussed further in Sec. 4-12.

At very high and microwave frequencies, impedance matching is normally achieved with the aid of transmission-line techniques. The *stub* line arrangement of Fig. 4-16 is a common example. Here a short

[1] For additional information of a design character see T. E. Moreno, "Microwave Transmission Data," pp. 103–110, McGraw-Hill Book Company, Inc., New York, 1948.

[2] When the characteristic impedance is a resistance, as is always the case at high frequencies, one can consider that the incident wave delivers energy to the load and that the reflected wave carries energy from the load back toward the generator. If the load impedance does not equal the characteristic impedance, i.e., if the load is not matched to the line, then some of the incident energy is reflected by the load and travels a round trip over the line, dissipating power in the line without delivering energy to the load. Thus the ratio of energy lost in the line to power dissipated in the load is increased by reflection.

section of short-circuited transmission line is connected in shunt with the transmission line.   The distance l_1 from the load, and the length a of the stub, are so chosen that the reflected wave produced by the shunting impedance of the shunt line is equal in magnitude and opposite in phase to the reflected wave existing on the line at this point as a result of the reflection from the load imped-ance Z_L.   Thus, although a re-flected wave is present in the length l_1 because of reflection from Z_L, there is no reflected wave on the generator side of the stub line as a result of the cancellation of the two reflected waves.[1]

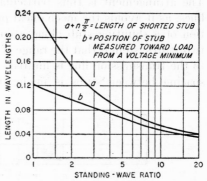

The practical design of a stub-line system of this type can be readily carried out with the aid of Fig. 4-17, which gives the length a of the stub[2] and its position b with

FIG. 4-17. Design information giving the length and position required for a short-circuited stub in order to obtain imped-ance matching.   If desired, the stub line may be made any convenient multiple of a half wavelength greater than a.

respect to a voltage minimum of the standing-wave pattern existing in the absence of the stub.   A stub line used in this way will enable any load im-pedance to be matched to the characteristic impedance of a transmission line provided only that the load is not an open-circuit, short-circuit, or pure reactance.

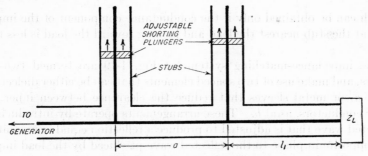

FIG. 4-18. Double-stub impedance-matching system.

Another arrangement often used to match a load to a transmission line is the two-stub system of Fig. 4-18.   Here two spaced stubs whose lengths are individually controllable are shunted across the line near the load as

---

[1] Another way of expressing this situation is to say that the stub position and length are so selected that the input impedance of line l_1 shunted by the input impedance of stub line a will equal the characteristic impedance Z_0.

[2] The stub length can actually be made any convenient number of half wavelengths plus the value a given by Fig. 4-17.

shown. This arrangement has the advantage that trial-and-error adjustment of the impedance-matching system can be made without the necessity of providing a connection that can be slid along the transmission line.
The arrangement is thus particularly suitable for coaxial transmission
lines, as it avoids the mechanical problems involved in moving the position of a shunting stub along a coaxial line. The disadvantage of the
two-stub system is that the range of load impedances that can be matched
to the transmission line is limited. Thus, in the typical case where the
spacing between stubs is made an eighth wavelength, an impedance

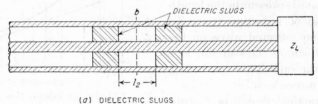

(a) DIELECTRIC SLUGS

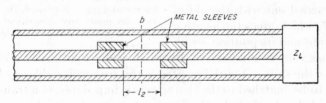

(b) METAL SLEEVE SLUGS

Fig. 4-19. Double-slug system for impedance matching in a concentric-line system.

match can be obtained only if the conductance component of the impedance at the stub nearest the load and looking toward the load is less than
$2/Z_0$.[*]

The impedance-matching systems of Fig. 4-19 are termed two-slug
tuners, and make use of two spaced elements that can be either dielectrics,
as at a, or metal sleeves that reduce the clearance between inner and
outer conductors, as at b. These arrangements operate by introducing a
reflected wave that is adjusted to produce a reflection equal in magnitude
and opposite in phase to the reflected wave produced by the load impedance. The phase of the reflection introduced in this way is controlled by
moving the slugs along the line while maintaining the spacing l_2 between
them constant. The magnitude of the reflected wave can be controlled
with little effect on the phase by moving the two slugs equal amounts in
opposite directions (i.e., by changing l_2 while keeping the slugs symmetrical with respect to reference line b). Like the two-stub arrange-

[*] When this requirement is not satisfied, an impedance match can still be obtained
by increasing the distance l_1 from the double-stub tuner to the load by a quarter
wavelength. This is because of the impedance-transforming action of a quarter-
wave line, as discussed in connection with Eq. (4-31).

ment, slug tuners are limited in the range of load impedances that can be matched to a given line.

When the load impedance is resistive, or when it can easily be made resistive by tuning, the impedance-matching problem is considerably simplified. It is then merely necessary to transform the resistance actually present to a resistance that is equal to the characteristic impedance of the line. Transmission-line techniques that can be used to achieve this result, in addition to those discussed above, include the use of a quarter-wave transformer and a tapered section, as discussed in connection with Figs. 4-27 and 4-28, respectively.

Nonreflecting Terminations for Ultra-high-frequency and Microwave Transmission Lines.[1,2] In some circumstances, particularly in measurement work, it is necessary to terminate a transmission line so that the reflected wave is as small as possible. In many cases this condition must be realized for a substantial band of frequencies. The problem of achieving a nonreflecting load contrasts with the case where one starts with an assigned load impedance that is to absorb the power and desires to match this load as well as possible to the transmission line.

A simple and effective means of obtaining a nonreflecting load impedance is to connect the end of the transmission line involved to a length of transmission line having high loss but the same characteristic impedance as the line being terminated. This arrangement is illustrated in Fig. 4-20a. An incident wave reaching such a termination will proceed into the lossy line and will be completely absorbed if the attenuation of the lossy line is sufficient. For example, if the attenuation of this line is 20 db, then even if the reflection coefficient at the end of the lossy line is unity, the reflected wave emerging from the junction of the two lines will be 40 db weaker than the incident wave, corresponding to a reflection coefficient of 0.01, or a standing-wave ratio of 1.02.

Lossy lines must be especially designed so that the total attenuation required can be achieved in a reasonable length. Flexible cable is commercially available for these applications in which the attenuation has been intentionally made very high by the use of insulation having high radio-frequency losses, and by employing resistance wire for the center conductor of the cable. In lines having air insulation, high attenuation can be obtained in coaxial systems by plating a high-resistivity coating on the center conductor of the coaxial line to give high skin-effect losses; in the case of two-wire open-air lines it is customary to obtain a high attenuation by using resistance wire or iron wire for the conductors.

---

[1] For further information on this subject see F. E. Terman and J. M. Pettit, "Electronic Measurements," sec. 14-7, McGraw-Hill Book Company, Inc., New York, 1952.

[2] Emphasis is placed here on the higher frequencies. At short-wave and lower frequencies lumped resistance terminations are entirely satisfactory.

An alternative type of nonreflecting termination that is particularly suitable for coaxial systems with air insulation makes use of a tapered section of lossy dielectric arranged as illustrated in Fig. 4-20b. The taper provides a gradual transition between the nonattenuating and the attenuating regions, so that no reflection is produced in spite of the fact that the dielectric changes the characteristics of the line. The lossy dielectric can be some type of plastic loaded with conducting material. Nonreflecting terminations of this type have the advantage that the total length of the termination is relatively small compared with the length of

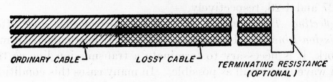

ORDINARY CABLE   LOSSY CABLE   TERMINATING RESISTANCE
                                              (OPTIONAL)

(a) TERMINATION BY LOSSY CABLE.

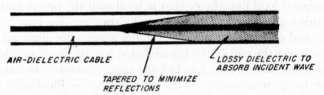

AIR-DIELECTRIC CABLE   LOSSY DIELECTRIC TO
                           ABSORB INCIDENT WAVE

TAPERED TO MINIMIZE
REFLECTIONS

(b) TERMINATION BY TAPERED LOSSY SECTION

FIG. 4-20. Nonreflecting terminations for coaxial transmission lines, suitable for use at very high frequencies.

a lossy cable required to achieve a similar result. This difference arises from the fact that the taper makes it possible to work up to a very much higher attenuation per unit length without reflection than can be obtained in a uniform structure such as a lossy cable.

4-12. Artificial Lines. An artificial line is a four-terminal network composed of resistance, inductance, and capacitance elements. In so far as the terminals are concerned, such a network can be considered as being the equivalent of some transmission line when symmetrical about the mid-point, or a combination of a transmission line and a transformer when unsymmetrical.[1]

It can be demonstrated that any four-terminal network can have its properties at any one frequency represented, in so far as the terminals are concerned, by three independent constants. From this it follows that the most general artificial lines possible can be represented at any one frequency by three independent impedances. These can be arranged either in the form of a T or a π, as in Figs. 4-21a and 4-21b.[2] The L network

---

[1] The unsymmetrical case is also equivalent to a tapered transmission line.

[2] It will be noted that the T and π can be drawn as Y and Δ arrangements of impedances, respectively.

shown in Fig. 4-22 is a special case of the more general three-element network in which one of the impedance arms has become either zero or infinity.

The characteristics of a four-terminal artificial line can be expressed, from the transmission-line point of view, in terms of a propagation

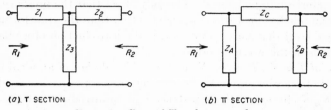

(a) T SECTION   (b) π SECTION

FIG. 4-21. General T and π networks.

constant $\alpha + j\beta$ that has exactly the same significance as in ordinary transmission-line theory (see Secs. 4-1 and 4-2), together with two characteristic impedances (or resistances), one associated with one pair of terminals and the other with the other set of terminals. When the network is symmetrical about its mid-point, i.e., when $Z_A = Z_B$ for the π network, or $Z_1 = Z_2$ for the T network, these two characteristic impedances are identical.[1] However, when the network is unsymmetrical, the two characteristic impedances differ, and the transmission line, in addition to introduc-

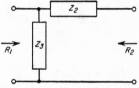

FIG. 4-22. General L network.

ing a certain attenuation and phase shift, also introduces a transformation of the characteristic impedance. The artificial line is then equivalent to a line plus a transformer or, what is the same thing, to a tapered line, as discussed below in connection with Fig. 4-27.

Artificial lines find extensive use in radio work for impedance matching

---

[1] The relations between the impedances of such a symmetrical artificial line and the constants Z_0 and $\alpha + j\beta$ of the equivalent transmission line are:

For symmetrical T section of Fig. 4-21a ($Z_1 = Z_2$):

$$Z_0 = \sqrt{Z_1{}^2 + 2Z_1Z_3} \tag{4-25a}$$

$$\cosh(\alpha + j\beta) = 1 + \frac{Z_1}{Z_3} \tag{4-25b}$$

For symmetrical π section of Fig. 4-21b ($Z_A = Z_B$):

$$Z_0 = \frac{Z_AZ_C}{\sqrt{Z_C{}^2 + 2Z_AZ_C}} \tag{4-26a}$$

$$\cosh(\alpha + j\beta) = 1 + \frac{Z_C}{Z_A} \tag{4-26b}$$

Corresponding formulas for unsymmetrical artificial lines (that is, $Z_1 \neq Z_2$ and $Z_A \neq Z_B$) are given by F. E. Terman, "Radio Engineers' Handbook," p. 208, McGraw-Hill Book Company, Inc., New York, 1943.

and for introducing phase shifts. Networks for these purposes are composed of reactive elements having the smallest possible resistance and conductance in order that the artificial line will consume little or no energy. In this way it is possible to realize an artificial line which has almost zero attenuation and which simultaneously has resistive values for the characteristic impedances. The only effect that the presence of such an artificial line has on a traveling wave, other than the transformation in impedance level that may be present, is the introduction of a phase shift of β radians in the wave involved.[1]

Design of T and π Reactive Networks.[2] The design of an ideal network composed of reactive impedances with zero losses to give assigned values R_1 and R_2 of characteristic impedance and to introduce a desired phase shift β can be carried out with the aid of the following relations:

For T section:

$$Z_1 = -j \frac{R_1 \cos \beta - \sqrt{R_1 R_2}}{\sin \beta}$$

$$Z_2 = -j \frac{R_2 \cos \beta - \sqrt{R_1 R_2}}{\sin \beta} \qquad (4\text{-}27)$$

$$Z_3 = -j \frac{\sqrt{R_1 R_2}}{\sin \beta}$$

For π section:

$$Z_A = j \frac{R_1 R_2 \sin \beta}{R_2 \cos \beta - \sqrt{R_1 R_2}}$$

$$Z_B = j \frac{R_1 R_2 \sin \beta}{R_1 \cos \beta - \sqrt{R_1 R_2}} \qquad (4\text{-}28)$$

$$Z_C = j \sqrt{R_1 R_2} \sin \beta$$

The reactances obtained from these equations are inductive or capacitive according to whether their sign is $+$ or $-$, respectively. R_1 and R_2 are the two values of characteristic impedance associated with the network. The angle β in Eqs. (4-27) and (4-28) is the angle by which the phase of the wave reaching the output terminals of the network lags behind the phase that the corresponding wave had at the input terminals; a negative value of β is possible and indicates that passage of the wave through the network advances the phase. It is to be noted that this phase shift is the same irrespective of the direction in which the wave travels through the network. A single reactive T or π section is capable of transforming the impedance level from any assigned resistance R_1 to any other resistance

---

[1] It is customary to discuss the behavior of an artificial line in terms of the incident and reflected waves that would exist on the equivalent transmission line. Although these wave trains cannot exist physically on the artificial line, the behavior, in so far as the terminals are concerned, is exactly as though they were present.

[2] For further information on design details see F. E. Terman, "Radio Engineers' Handbook," pp. 210–215, McGraw-Hill Book Company, Inc., New York, 1943.

R_2, without restriction on the values of these resistances, and is capable of introducing phase shifts of any desired value between 0 and $\pm 180°$.

In case the load (or for that matter the generator) has a reactive impedance component, this reactance can be used to supply part of the reactance required by the network. For example, if a load impedance $R_L + jX_L$ is connected to the right-hand terminals of the T network of Fig. 4-21a, then one would consider X_L to be part of the impedance Z_2 of the impedance-matching network. In the same way, if the load is regarded as a resistance shunted by a reactance, then the shunting reactance can be used to supply part of the shunt impedance Z_B of the π section of Fig. 4-21b.

L Reactive Networks. An L network composed of reactive impedances is able to transform from one arbitrarily assigned characteristic impedance to a second arbitrarily assigned characteristic impedance. However, since the L network contains only two circuit elements, the phase shift β introduced by the L section is determined by the ratio of these two impedances. The design equations of a reactive L network in terms of the characteristic impedances R_1 and R_2 at the two pairs of terminals are, assuming the configuration of Fig. 4-22, and that $R_1 > R_2$,

$$Z_2 = \pm j \sqrt{R_2(R_1 - R_2)}$$
$$Z_3 = \mp jR_1 \sqrt{\frac{R_2}{R_1 - R_2}} \tag{4-29}$$

One may employ either the two top signs, or the two bottom signs. The phase shift β corresponding to the characteristic impedances R_1 and R_2 is

$$\cos \beta = \sqrt{\frac{R_2}{R_1}} \tag{4-30}$$

4-13. Directional Couplers.[1] A directional coupler is a device that couples a secondary system only to a wave traveling in a particular direction on a primary line, and ignores entirely the wave traveling in the opposite direction.

Loop-type Directional Coupler. A number of types of directional couplers have been devised. One example is illustrated in Fig. 4-23a. This is a coaxial arrangement in which the secondary system consists of lines A and B interconnected by coupling loop D that projects into the primary line in such a manner as to be subjected to the simultaneous influence of the electric and magnetic fields produced by the waves traveling on the primary line.

The operation of this arrangement will now be explained. Assume that a wave is traveling on the primary line toward the right. The

---

[1] For a further discussion, together with an extensive list of references on the subject, see Terman and Pettit, *op. cit.*, p. 57.

electric field of this wave induces a charge on the loop D that produces a wave in part A of the secondary system, and also a wave in part B. The equivalent circuit that describes this action is illustrated in Fig. 4-23b; it consists of a voltage E_1 that is applied to coaxial systems A and B in parallel through series capacitance C_1, producing currents as indicated by the arrows. At the same time loop D links with the magnetic flux from the wave in the primary line, and therefore has a voltage E_2 induced in series with it, as illustrated by the equivalent circuit of Fig.

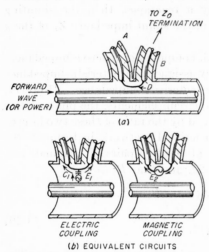

4-23b. This series voltage gives rise to an additional wave in A and likewise a second wave in part B. These magnetically induced waves are characterized by currents that flow in the directions indicated by the arrows.

The two waves in section A produced by magnetic and electrostatic coupling, respectively, are of the same polarity and so add, while the two waves produced in section B are of opposite polarity and so tend to cancel each other. It is accordingly apparent that if the electric and magnetic couplings are so proportioned that the waves induced by the magnetic effect have the same amplitudes as the waves induced by the electric coupling,

FIG. 4-23. Loop type of directional coupler for coaxial line, together with equivalent circuits that take into account the effects produced by the electric and magnetic fields on the primary line.

then complete cancellation takes place in section B. When this is the case, then a wave traveling to the right in the primary line will induce only one resultant wave in the secondary system, namely, a wave that travels in the direction of A. No wave is induced that travels in direction B.

The relative magnitude of electric and magnetic couplings in Fig. 2-23a can be readily controlled by the design of the coupling loop D. The electric coupling depends on the amount of electric field that terminates on the loop, and so is determined by the length of the loop and by the width (or diameter) of its conductor. Similarly, the magnetic coupling is determined by the amount of magnetic flux that links with the loop, and so is determined by the area enclosed between the loop and the outer conductor and by the orientation of the plane of the loop with respect to the axis of the line.

Assuming that the coupling arrangement in Fig. 4-23 has been designed so that a wave traveling to the right on the primary system produces no induced wave in part B, then consider the effect of a wave traveling to the left in the primary system. The component waves induced in A and B by the electric and magnetic fields in the primary coaxial line will again be equal to each other, since their relative magnitudes are not affected by the direction of travel of the primary wave. However, the polarity of the waves produced by magnetic coupling will now be reversed with respect to the polarity of the induced waves resulting from electric coupling. Accordingly, the two waves induced in A now cancel each other, while the two waves induced in B add. Consequently, a wave traveling to the left in the primary line produces no effect in section A, but does produce an induced wave traveling to the right in section B. By terminating B of the secondary system in its characteristic impedance, this induced wave is absorbed. The final result is that any wave traveling to the left in section A is determined only by the wave traveling to the right in the primary system, and is independent of the presence or absence of a wave traveling to the left in the primary system. Thus one has achieved a directional coupling system.

It is to be noted that to obtain the directional action it is absolutely necessary that B be terminated in its characteristic impedance. If the impedance terminating B produces a reflection, the resulting reflected wave will return along line B, pass through

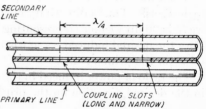

FIG. 4-24. Example of two-hole directional coupler for coaxial line.

the coupling loop, and enter A. The actual wave traveling to the left in A will then be the resultant of the desired effect produced by the wave traveling to the right in the primary line and an undesired effect proportional to the product of the amplitude of the wave traveling to the left in the primary system and the reflection coefficient at the termination of B.

Two-hole Coupler. A quite different type of directional coupling system is shown in Fig. 4-24. This is known as a two-hole coupler, and consists of primary and secondary systems which are coupled *either* electrically or magnetically at two points separated by an odd multiple of a quarter wavelength. It is essential that the coupling at each of these two points be either primarily electric or primarily magnetic. This result can be achieved by using probes (for electric coupling), loops (for magnetic coupling), or suitably shaped and oriented slots that favor either one or the other type of coupling.[1] In the two-hole coupler a wave traveling to the right in the primary system gives rise to a wave that also

[1] Details relating to the use of slots as a means of coupling are discussed on p. 133. The narrow axially oriented slots in Fig. 4-24 provide coupling that is predominately electrostatic.

travels to the right in the secondary system, but not to a wave traveling to the left; similarly, a wave traveling to the left in the primary system gives rise to a wave traveling to the left in the secondary system, but not to a wave traveling to the right. This result comes about because although each hole induces waves that travel in the secondary system in both directions away from the coupling point, the induced waves traveling in the favored direction away from the two holes add in phase, while those in the reverse direction cancel exactly if they are of equal amplitude, provided the holes are an odd multiple of a quarter wavelength apart.

Directivity and Coupling in Directional Couplers. In an ideal directional coupler, the secondary system will respond only to a wave traveling in the favored direction on the primary line. In actual directional couplers, mechanical imperfections, frequency differing from the design value, second-order effects, etc., will ordinarily result in a small output being produced by a wave traveling in the backward direction. The ratio of the responses to waves traveling in the two directions on the primary is called the *directivity* of the coupling system, and is commonly expressed in decibels. Thus a directivity of 30 db means that the undesired induced wave is 30 db weaker (representing only one-thousandth as much power) than the desired induced wave when equal waves travel in opposite directions on the primary line.

The ratio of power induced in the secondary system by a wave traveling in the desired direction on the primary line to the power of this wave on the primary line is called the *coupling* of the directional coupler. The coupling is ordinarily expressed in decibels, and represents the attenuation introduced by the coupling system.

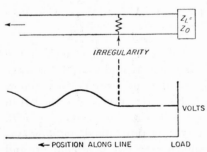

4-14. Miscellaneous Aspects of Transmission Lines. *Transmission-line Irregularities—Discontinuity Capacitance.* When a wave traveling along a transmission line encounters an isolated discontinuity, it is partially reflected; i.e., while a portion of the wave continues to travel down the line, another portion

Fig. 4-25. Diagram illustrating standing waves produced on the generator side of an irregularity in the case of a transmission line terminated with a load impedance equal to the characteristic of the line.

of the wave is reflected backwards. Thus, in a transmission line terminated with a load equal to the characteristic impedance, an irregularity at some point on the line as shown in Fig. 4-25 will cause standing waves to exist on the generator side of the irregularity, as indicated.

Irregularities may be introduced in many ways. Typical causes are sharp bends, insulating supports, joints possessing resistance, coupled circuits, and extraneous objects that affect the electric or magnetic field, such as probes, dielectric or metal bodies, etc.

A type of irregularity that is particularly important at very high frequencies results from the distortion of the electric and magnetic fields associated with a change in line geometry. Consider, for example, a coaxial line in which the characteristic impedance changes abruptly as a result of a change in diameter of the outer conductor, as illustrated in Fig. 4-26a. It can be shown[1] that the distortion of the electric and magnetic fields in the vicinity of the junction is equivalent to shunting a capacitance across the junction, as shown in Fig. 4-26b, in addition to whatever effects are caused by the change in characteristic impedance. This "discontinuity capacitance" is ordinarily only a few tenths of a micromicrofarad; however, at ultrahigh frequencies and higher frequencies its reactance becomes low enough to affect the behavior significantly.

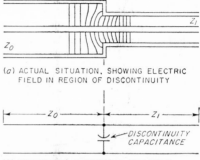

(a) ACTUAL SITUATION, SHOWING ELECTRIC FIELD IN REGION OF DISCONTINUITY

(b) EQUIVALENT ELECTRICAL SITUATION, SHOWING DISCONTINUITY CAPACITANCE THAT TAKES INTO ACCOUNT DISTORTION OF ELECTRIC FIELD

FIG. 4-26. Transmission line with discontinuity in the characteristic impedance, showing distortion of the electric field that results, and how this is taken into account by postulating a discontinuity capacitance at the point of irregularity in addition to the discontinuity in characteristic impedance.

A discontinuity capacitance is ordinarily present whenever a geometrical change occurs. Thus, in Figs. 4-16 and 4-18, the change in geometry at the points where the stubs are connected to the lines has an effect equivalent to a small capacitance connected in shunt across the coaxial line at the junction point. This shunting capacitance is in addition to the shunting action of the stub.

Tapered Transmission Lines.[2] A length of transmission line in which the characteristic impedance varies gradually and continuously from one value to another is said to be tapered. A traveling wave passing through such a section will have its ratio of voltage to current transformed in accordance with the ratio of the characteristic impedances involved.

The requirement for a satisfactory taper is that the change in characteristic impedance per wavelength must not be too large; otherwise the

[1] See J. R. Whinnery, H. W. Jamieson, and T. E. Robbins, Coaxial Line Discontinuities, *Proc. IRE*, vol. 32, p. 695, November, 1944.

[2] For further information see Wilbur N. Christensen, The Exponential Transmission Line Employing Straight Conductors, *Proc. IRE*, vol. 35, p. 576, June, 1947; Charles E. Burrows, Exponential Transmission Line, *Bell System Tech. J.*, vol. 17, p. 555, October, 1938; Harold A. Wheeler, Transmission Line with Exponential Taper, *Proc. IRE*, vol. 27, p. 65, January, 1939; Moreno, *op. cit.*, pp. 53–55.

tapered section will introduce a reflection. That is, if the change in characteristic impedance per wavelength is excessive, then the tapered section acts as a lumped irregularity rather than producing merely a gradual transformation.

From these considerations it follows that a tapered section of transmission line acts as a perfect impedance transformer at the higher frequencies. However, as the frequency is lowered, such a section finally fails to be satisfactory as an impedance transformer, because the distance represented by a wavelength, and hence the change in characteristic impedance per wavelength, becomes greater. Thus as the frequency is reduced the taper introduces an increasingly large reflection. The practical lower-frequency limit of usefulness of a tapered section that thereby results corresponds to the frequency for which the characteristic impedance changes by a factor between about 1.3 and 4.0 per wavelength, with the exact value depending upon the standing-wave ratio that can be tolerated.

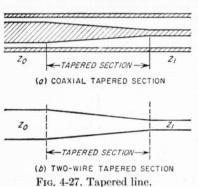

(a) COAXIAL TAPERED SECTION

(b) TWO-WIRE TAPERED SECTION

FIG. 4-27. Tapered line.

A line can be tapered by varying the spacing of the conductors in the case of a two-wire line, or by varying the diameter of the inner (or outer) conductor in the case of a concentric line. The ideal type of taper is one in which the characteristic impedance changes uniformly with length, so that the higher derivatives of the rate of change of characteristic impedance with length are minimized. However, nearly as satisfactory results are obtained by the much more practical arrangement shown in Fig. 4-27, in which the spacing varies linearly with distance. Such straight-line tapers are accordingly used in ordinary practice.

Quarter- and Half-wave Transformers. Sections of transmission lines that are exactly a quarter wavelength or a half wavelength long have unique impedance-transforming properties that are frequently made use of in radio work. Thus consider the situation illustrated in Fig. 4-28. When the length l of the line is exactly an odd number of quarter wavelengths, then to the extent that the losses in l can be neglected, the impedance looking into the system is

$$Z_s = \frac{Z_0{}^2}{Z_L} \qquad (4\text{-}31)$$

where Z_0 is the characteristic impedance of the line l. When the load impedance Z_L is a resistance, the effect of the line is thus to transform this resistance into another resistance Z_s that is inversely proportional to the resistance Z_L. Again, when Z_L is a capacitive reactance, then the impedance-transforming action of the line causes Z_s to be an inductive reactance having a magnitude inversely proportional to the capacitive reactance of Z_L.

In an arrangement such as illustrated in Fig. 4-28, the ratio of impedance transformation obtained can be varied by adjusting the characteristic impedance Z_0 of the connecting transmission line l. In the case of a two-wire line, this is readily accomplished by varying the spacing between the conductors that form the line. With coaxial lines, one can change the diameter of the inner conductor, or can move the inner conductor so that it is eccentric with respect to the outer conductor.

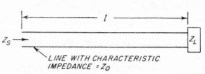

Fig. 4-28. Transmission line as an impedance transformer.

When the transmission line of Fig. 4-28 is exactly a whole number of half wavelengths long, then

$$Z_s = Z_L \tag{4-32}$$

This relation holds irrespective of the characteristic impedance of the line provided only that the line losses can be neglected. The half-wave line is thus a one-to-one impedance transformer. A typical practical application of such an arrangement is to provide a short circuit across an inaccessible pair of terminals. This can be achieved by connecting a transmission line to these terminals and then placing a short circuit across the line at an accessible point that is exactly a whole number of half wavelengths away from the terminals across which it is desired that a short circuit exist.

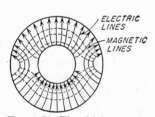

Fig. 4-29. First higher mode in a coaxial transmission line.

Higher-order Modes. When the spacing between the two wires of a transmission line exceeds a half wavelength, or when the circumference of a coaxial line exceeds a wavelength, it is possible for energy to propagate down the transmission line by using configurations of electric and magnetic fields that differ from the field arrangements ordinarily associated with transmission lines. These special configurations are termed *higher-order modes*. The first such higher-order mode that can exist on a coaxial transmission line is illustrated in Fig. 4-29. Fields of this particular type will propagate freely provided that the arithmetic mean circumference exceeds the wavelength λ' in the cable, i.e., when

$$\lambda' < 2\pi \frac{b + a}{2} \tag{4-33}$$

where a and b are the radii of the inner and outer conductors, respectively. Modes of still higher order are also possible on two-wire lines.

The amplitude of the higher mode (or modes), compared with the amplitude of the normal mode, is determined by the extent to which the method of applying voltage to the cable produces a field configuration corresponding to the higher mode (or modes). However, even if a higher mode is produced at the terminals of a transmission line, the mode will not propagate along the line unless the wavelength is less than the cutoff value given by relations such as Eq. (4-33). This can happen in ordinary cables and lines only at the higher microwave frequencies.

Loaded Lines. A loaded line is an ordinary transmission line to which lumped elements, usually capacitances or inductances, are added at

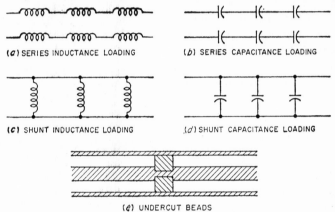

(a) SERIES INDUCTANCE LOADING   (b) SERIES CAPACITANCE LOADING

(c) SHUNT INDUCTANCE LOADING   (d) SHUNT CAPACITANCE LOADING

(e) UNDERCUT BEADS

Fig. 4-30. Examples of loaded transmission lines.

regular intervals, as illustrated in Fig. 4-30. When these lumped loading impedances are spaced uniformly at distances that do not appreciably exceed a quarter wavelength, they act almost exactly as though their impedances were uniformly distributed. However, if the frequency is so high that the spacing appreciably exceeds a quarter wavelength, then the loading impedances act as irregularities that tend to prevent transmission.

The most common use of loading is in connection with telephone cables where inductance coils are commonly added at regular intervals, as in Fig. 4-30a. Such inductance loading makes the equivalent inductance per unit length of the transmission line greater than the actual inductance of the unloaded line, thereby increasing the characteristic impedance and lowering the velocity of propagation. Also, if most of the line losses result from the series resistance of the line, the attenuation constant is reduced by inductive loading. Loading by means of series capacitances, as in Fig. 4-30b, reduces the characteristic impedance and increases the phase velocity to a value greater than that of light, while shunt inductances as in Fig. 4-30c increase both characteristic impedance and the phase velocity. These results follow from Eqs. (4-18a) and (4-18c), by noting that series inductive loading increases the equivalent line inductance, and series capacitive loading reduces it, while shunt loading similarly increases the equivalent line capacitance if capacitive, and reduces it if inductive.

An important case of loading is provided by the beads sometimes used to support the center conductor of a concentric cable having air insulation. These beads introduce localized additions to the line capacitance and so represent shunt capacitive loading, as illustrated in Fig. 4-30d. This has the effect of increasing the effective line capacitance and thereby lowering the characteristic impedance and the velocity of phase propagation, as well as fixing an upper frequency beyond which the line does not behave properly. In order to overcome these effects, the beads are sometimes undercut, as in Fig. 4-30e. Here the reduction in diameter of the center conductor is so chosen as to make up for the increased dielectric constant of the space occupied by the bead, as well as the discontinuity capacitance introduced by the bead. In this way the characteristic impedance of the section containing the bead can be made the same as that of the portion of the line having only air insulation.

PROBLEMS AND EXERCISES

4-1. Assume that Fig. 4-1 is modified so that the length l is measured from the generator or sending end of the line instead of from the load end as in Fig. 4-1. Set up the differential equations of the line in terms of this notation, and obtain a solution to the transmission line analogous to Eqs. (4-6), but in terms of the amplitudes E_1', E_2', I_1', and I_2' of the individual waves at the generator end of the line.

4-2. Redraw Fig. 4-2b, c, and d for (a) an attenuation that is considerably greater than in Fig. 4-2, and (b) zero attenuation.

4-3. In a transmission line 100 ft long terminated so that only the incident wave is present, the power at the load end of the line is 1.2 db less than at the generator end. What is the value of α per foot?

4-4. Derive Eq. (4-14).

4-5. In a transmission line in which $Z_0 = 50$ ohms, calculate and plot the reflection coefficient as a function of load resistance for load resistances ranging from 0 to 250 ohms.

4-6. In a transmission line in which $Z_0 = 50$ ohms and which has a reactive load, calculate and plot the magnitude and phase angle of the reflection coefficient as a function of load reactance in the range from $-j100$ ohms to $+j100$ ohms.

4-7. Derive Eq. (4-15). In doing this, start by assuming that the incident wave at point a is E_a, and then express the magnitudes of the various waves at a and b in terms of E_a and $|\rho_a|$.

4-8. Derive Eq. (4-16a).

4-9. a. The line conductance will be negligible in a transmission line with air dielectric. Under these conditions the attenuation constant α of a radio-frequency line is proportional to the square root of the frequency. Explain.

b. In a coaxial transmission line with solid dielectric, the dielectric losses at extremely high frequencies will be very much greater than the losses resulting from the line resistance. Under these conditions, how does the attenuation constant α vary with frequency?

4-10. A transmission line with air dielectric is 20 m long. What is the line length, measured in wavelengths, and what is the value of β at frequencies of 10 and 100 Mc?

4-11. Show vector diagrams and curves for the current distributions that go with the voltage distributions in Fig. 4-3a and b. On the resulting curves show the voltage distributions of Fig. 4-3 by dotted lines.

4-12. Draw curves and vector diagrams similar to those of Fig. 4-3b, except for the case $\rho = 0.5/\underline{180°}$.

4-13. Calculate the exact distance from the load in wavelengths at which the first voltage maximum occurs in Fig. 4-4f when $Z_L/Z_0 = j0.5$.

4-14. Sketch the voltage distribution on a low-loss transmission line in the manner shown in Fig. 4-4, but for the case where $Z_L/Z_0 = 2.0/\underline{45°}$.

4-15. Sketch curves of voltage and current distribution on a low-loss transmission line analogous to the curves of Fig. 4-4, but for the following load impedance conditions. (Note: In each case calculate location and relative amplitude of minima and maxima accurately, and show these minima and maxima in correct positions and in correct magnitudes in the sketch, carrying the curves for a distance of slightly more than one wavelength from the load end of the line.)

    a. Reflection coefficient at load = $0.2/\underline{0°}$.

    b. Reflection coefficient at load = $0.8/\underline{0°}$.

    c. Reflection coefficient at load = $0.8/\underline{45°}$.

    d. Reflection coefficient at load = $1.0/\underline{-45°}$.

4-16. Derive a formula giving the distance from the load to the first minimum of voltage in terms of the phase shift β per unit length of line and the phase angle δ of the coefficient of reflection of the load.

4-17. Sketch curves analogous to those of Fig. 4-5, except applying to a short-circuited load.

4-18. Sketch curves analogous to those of Fig. 4-6, except assume that the attenuation of the line is approximately twice as great as in Fig. 4-6. For purposes of comparison, sketch the solid curves from Fig. 4-6 on the same axes.

4-19. Derive Eq. (4-22a) starting with Eq. (4-21).

4-20. Calculate and plot the standing-wave ratio as a function of Z_L/Z_0 for resistive loads, for values of this ratio ranging from 0.1 to 10.0.

4-21. Prove that resistive loads of R_1 and R_2 will produce the same standing-wave ratio provided $R_1R_2 = Z_0^2$.

4-22. Sketch curves similar to those of Fig. 4-10a and b, except applying to cases where the load is (a) a resistance greater than the characteristic impedance, and (b) an open circuit, respectively.

4-23. In a transmission line having negligible losses, derive formulas giving, respectively, the maximum impedance and the minimum impedance that can occur anywhere on the transmission line in terms of magnitude of the reflection coefficient of the load and the characteristic impedance of the line.

4-24. Sketch curves similar to those of Fig. 4-10b except applying to a transmission line having considerably greater attenuation.

4-25. When the load impedance of a transmission line is a resistance R_L, prove that $S = R_L/Z_0$ when $R_L > Z_0$, and likewise that $S = Z_0/R_L$ when $R_L < Z_0$.

    Note that this proof shows that the standing-wave ratio corresponding to any particular circle on the Smith chart is given by the intersection of this circle with the horizontal axis, as stated in the second paragraph on page 101.

4-26. In a particular transmission line the load impedance is such that

$$Z_L = (0.8 - j0.6)Z_0$$

With the aid of the Smith chart, determine the standing-wave ratio on the line, and the magnitude and phase angle of the reflection coefficient.

4-27. Assuming that the line of Prob. 4-26 has negligible losses, plot the magnitude and phase of the line impedance as a function of distance from the load up to a distance slightly greater than one wavelength. Make use of the Smith chart to determine the resistive and reactive components of the impedance.

4-28. An impedance of $35 + j75$ ohms is connected across the load end of a transmission line having a characteristic impedance of 60 ohms.

a. With the aid of the Smith chart, and assuming that the line has negligible losses, determine the standing-wave ratio produced on the line, and also the input impedance of the line when the line length is 1.8λ.

b. If the total attenuation of the line is 1.4 db, determine the standing-wave ratio and the line impedance at the generator end of the line.

c. Tabulate the results from (*a*) and (*b*) side by side, and explain in physical terms how attenuation accounts for the differences observed.

4-29. With the aid of the Smith chart determine the magnitude and the phase angle of an impedance which, when placed at the receiving end of a transmission line having the characteristic impedance $R_0 = 75$ ohms, would account for an observed standing-wave ratio of 1.65 with a voltage distribution such that the voltage minima with a short-circuited load are 0.2λ closer to the load than the voltage minima produced by the impedance to be measured.

4-30. Same as Prob. 4-29, except that $S = 2.10$, and the minima with a short-circuited load are 0.10λ closer to the *generator* than the minima produced by the impedance to be determined.

4-31. A concentric transmission line having copper conductors and air insulation is short-circuited at the receiving end and is to be in quarter-wavelength resonance at a frequency of 100 Mc. Determine (*a*) the smallest diameter of the outer concentric line for which a Q of 5000 can be obtained, and (*b*) the sending-end impedance of the line in *a*.

4-32. A resonant quarter-wave coaxial transmission line 25 cm long has $b = 1$ cm and $b/a = 3.6$. Determine the resonant frequency, Q, and standing-end impedance.

4-33. A load impedance is connected to a transmission line and is found to produce a standing-wave ratio of 2.0. The first voltage minimum occurs at a distance of 0.4 wavelength from the load. Design a stub-line impedance-matching system for this situation.

4-34. A load impedance of $70/\underline{30°}$ is connected to a concentric transmission line having a characteristic impedance of 50 ohms. Calculate the resulting standing-wave ratio and the location of the voltage minima. From this information specify the length and position of a stub line that will match the load to the transmission line.

4-35. Assume that the double-slug tuner of Fig. 4-19*b* is adjusted to give an impedance match. Will this impedance match be destroyed if the right-hand slug is then displaced a half wavelength to the right, while leaving the position of the other slug unchanged? Explain.

4-36. A short-circuited lossy line is used to terminate a transmission line. How much total attenuation must the lossy line have if the standing-wave ratio on the terminated line is not to exceed $S = 1.10$? Assume the lossy line is open-circuited.

4-37. Design a reactive T network that at 1000 kc will match a load impedance of 100 ohms to a line having a characteristic impedance of 50 ohms, and introduce a phase shift of 30° leading in the load current.

4-38. Design a reactive T network that will match a load impedance of $100 + j50$ ohms to a 50-ohm line, and introduce a phase shift of 30° leading in the load current.

4-39. Explain how the directional coupler of Fig. 4-23 can be arranged so that the wave in the secondary section B is proportional to the wave traveling to the left on the primary line and is not affected by the primary wave traveling to the right.

4-40. Explain how one could measure the magnitude of the reflection coefficient on a line by apparatus including (a) a directional coupler of the type illustrated in Fig. 4-23, and (b) two instruments suitable for measuring voltage on transmission lines.

4-41. In the directional coupler system of Fig. 4-23, assume that the left-hand side of the secondary system (i.e., line A) is terminated by a load equal to the characteristic impedance but that the right-hand is not. Under these conditions prove that the intensity of the secondary wave traveling to the right in B is proportional to the strength of the primary wave traveling to the left, irrespective of the presence or absence of a primary wave traveling toward the right, but that the secondary wave traveling to the left in A is dependent on *both* the primary wave traveling to the left and the primary wave traveling to the right.

4-42. Give a detailed explanation of why the two-hole directional coupler of Fig. 4-24 theoretically can give ideal directional coupler action only when the hole spacing is exactly $n\lambda/4$, where n is odd. Include a justification for the fact that increasing the spacing by a half wavelength makes no difference.

4-43. A two-hole coupler such as illustrated in Fig. 4-24 is operated at a frequency 5 per cent higher than the value that makes the hole spacing exactly $\lambda/4$. What is the directivity in decibels caused by this incorrect operating frequency?

4-44. Sketch a curve similar to that of Fig. 4-25, except for an irregularity that is a series resistance equal in magnitude to the characteristic impedance. Be careful to show the correct standing-wave ratio on the generator side of the irregularity, as well as the correct location of the minima with respect to the irregularity, and also show the voltage drop in the series resistance.

4-45. In Fig. 4-25, the irregularity consists of a shunt discontinuity capacitance of 0.2 $\mu\mu f$. Determine the standing-wave ratio on the generator side of the irregularity at 100 and 10,000 Mc, assuming that the characteristic impedance of the line is 50 ohms.

4-46. Two coaxial lines having characteristic impedances of 50 and 100 ohms, respectively, are to be joined by a tapered section. If it is desired that the reflections introduced by the tapered section be kept very small in the frequency range 2000 to 11,000 Mc, determine the minimum length of tapered section that can be used.

4-47. A load resistance of 300 ohms is to be matched to a two-wire transmission line having a characteristic impedance of 600 ohms by means of a quarter-wave matching line. What characteristic impedance must the matching line have?

4-48. From the behavior of incident and reflected waves, demonstrate the correctness of Eq. (4-32).

4-49. In a particular coaxial transmission line, $b/a = 3.6$ and $b = 1$ cm. What is the shortest wavelength that can be transmitted on the line without danger of a higher-order mode being generated?

4-50. Explain with the aid of Eq. (4-18c) why the different types of loading illustrated in Fig. 4-30a to d have the effects on phase velocity summarized on page 122.

CHAPTER 5

WAVEGUIDES AND CAVITY RESONATORS

5-1. Waveguides—General Considerations.[1,2] A hollow conducting tube used to transmit electromagnetic waves is termed a waveguide. At ultra-high and microwave frequencies, waveguides provide a practical alternative to transmission lines for the transmission of electrical energy.

Any configuration of electric and magnetic fields that exists inside a waveguide must be a solution of Maxwell's equations. In addition, these fields must satisfy the boundary conditions imposed by the walls of the guide. To the extent that the walls are perfect conductors there can therefore be no tangential component of electric field at the walls. Many different field configurations can be found that meet these requirements. Each such configuration is termed a *mode*.

A critical examination of the various possible field configurations or modes that can exist in a waveguide reveals that they all belong to one or the other of two fundamental types. In one type, the electric field is everywhere transverse to the axis of the guide, and has no component

---

[1] The practical possibilities of waveguides as transmission systems for very high-frequency waves was discovered independently and almost simultaneously by W. L. Barrow and G. C. Southworth. Fundamental papers on the subject include: W. L. Barrow, Transmission of Electromagnetic Waves in Hollow Tubes of Metal, *Proc. IRE*, vol. 24, p. 1298, October, 1936; G. C. Southworth, Hyper-frequency Wave Guides—General Considerations and Experimental Results, *Bell System Tech. J.*, vol. 15, p. 284, April, 1936; L. J. Chu and W. L. Barrow, Electromagnetic Waves of Hollow Metal Tubes of Rectangular Cross Section, *Proc. IRE*, vol. 26, p. 1520, December, 1938.

[2] The discussion given here of waveguides is intended to provide a description of their more important characteristics, together with formulas for calculating quantitatively their principal characteristics. The rigorous derivation of the quantitative relations existing in waveguides is a specialized subject that would take more space than is available in a book of this type. The reader who wishes to study the techniques by which waveguide equations are derived is referred to Ramo and Whinnery, "Field and Waves of Modern Radio," John Wiley & Sons, Inc., New York, 1944; H. H. Skilling, "Fundamentals of Electric Waves," John Wiley & Sons, Inc., New York, 1948. An excellent discussion of the physical phenomena involved in waveguides is given by H. G. Booker, The Elements of Wave Propagation Using the Impedance Concept, *J. IEE*, vol. 94, part III, p. 171, May, 1947. Useful summary information on waveguide techniques is given by M. H. L. Prece, Waveguides, *J. IEE*, vol. 93, part IIIA, no. 1, p. 33, 1946; T. E. Moreno, "Microwave Transmission Data," McGraw-Hill Book Company, Inc., New York, 1948.

anywhere in the direction of the guide axis; the associated magnetic field does, however, have a component in the direction of the axis. Modes of this type are termed *transverse electric* or *TE modes* (also sometimes called *H* modes). In the other type of distribution, the situation with respect to the fields is reversed, the magnetic field being everywhere transverse to the guide axis while at some places the electric field has components in the axial direction. Modes of this type are termed *transverse magnetic* or *TM modes* (also sometimes called *E* modes).[1] The different modes of each class are designated by double subscripts, such as TE_{10}, as explained below.

The behavior of a waveguide is similar in many respects to the behavior of a transmission line. Thus waves traveling along a guide have a phase velocity, and are attenuated. When a wave reaches the end of a guide it is reflected unless the load impedance is carefully adjusted to absorb the wave; also an irregularity in a waveguide produces reflection just as does an irregularity in a transmission line. Again, reflected waves can be eliminated by the use of an impedance-matching system, exactly as with a transmission line. Finally, when both incident and reflected waves are simultaneously present in a waveguide, the result is a standing-wave pattern, such as illustrated in Fig. 4-4, that can be characterized by defining a standing-wave ratio.

In some other respects waveguides and transmission lines are unlike in their behavior. The most striking difference is that a particular mode will propagate down a waveguide with low attenuation only if the wavelength of the waves is less than some critical value determined by the dimensions and the geometry of the guide. If the wavelength is greater than this critical *cutoff* value, the waves in the waveguide die out very rapidly in amplitude even when the walls of the guide are of material having infinite conductivity. Different modes have different values of cutoff wavelength; the particular mode for which the cutoff wavelength is greatest is termed the *dominant* mode.

5-2. Rectangular Waveguides. The most frequently used type of waveguide has a rectangular cross section, as illustrated in Fig. 5-1. In such a guide, the preferred mode of operation is the dominant mode.

Field Configuration of the Dominant Mode in a Rectangular Waveguide. At wavelengths less than the cutoff value, the electric and magnetic fields representing the dominant mode in a rectangular waveguide have the character illustrated in Fig. 5-2. Here the electric field is transverse to the guide axis, and extends between the two walls that are closest together, i.e., between the top and bottom of Fig. 5-1. The intensity of this elec-

---

[1] Following this system of designation, the field configuration normally associated with a coaxial line is sometimes called the TEM mode, because both the electric and magnetic fields are transverse to the axis of the line. The higher-order coaxial mode illustrated in Fig. 4-29 is a TE mode, since the electric field is everywhere transverse to the line.

tric field is maximum at the center of the guide, and drops off sinusoidally to zero intensity at the edges, as shown. The magnetic field is in the form of loops which lie in planes that are at right angles to the electric field, i.e., planes parallel to the top and bottom of the guide in Fig. 5-1. The magnetic field is the same in all of these planes, irrespective of the position of the plane along the y axis.

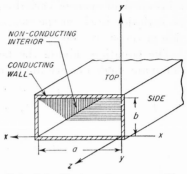

This field configuration travels along the waveguide axis (in the z direction in Fig. 5-1).[1] As it travels a distance l down the guide, the amplitude will be reduced by the factor $\epsilon^{-\alpha l}$ as a result of energy losses in the walls of the guide, and the wave will drop back in phase βl radians, just as in the analogous

FIG. 5-1. Rectangular waveguide, illustrating notation.

transmission-line case, where α and β are termed the *attenuation constant* and *phase constant* respectively.

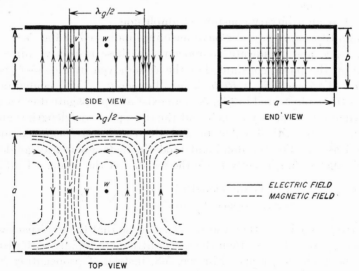

FIG. 5-2. Field configuration of the dominant or TE$_{10}$ mode in a rectangular waveguide.

The field configuration representing the dominant mode illustrated in Fig. 5-2 is seen to be a transverse electric mode and is designated as the

---

[1] Thus Fig. 5-2 can be regarded as representing a snapshot of the fields as they exist at some particular moment. As this field configuration travels down the guide, the fields at any given point vary sinusoidally in amplitude. Thus, although the fields at position w in Fig. 5-2 have zero intensity, a quarter cycle later the fields will have moved a distance $\lambda_g/4$, and the amplitude at w will then be the same as the amplitude shown for position v in Fig. 5-2.

TE$_{10}$ mode.   The subscript 1 means that the field distribution in the direction of the long side of the waveguide (x direction in Fig. 5-1) contains one-half cycle of variation.   The subscript 0 indicates that there is no variation in either the electric or magnetic field strength in the direction of the short side (y axis) of the guide.

The equations giving the fields at frequencies above cutoff for the dominant mode in a rectangular waveguide filled with air are as follows:

$$E_z = E_x = B_y = 0$$

$$E_y = A \frac{\omega a}{\pi} \sin \frac{\pi x}{a} \sin (\omega t - \beta z)$$

$$B_z = -A \cos \frac{\pi x}{a} \cos (\omega t - \beta z) \tag{5-1}$$

$$B_x = \frac{\beta}{\omega} E_y$$

where E = electric field intensity, abvolts per cm
$\quad\quad B$ = magnetic field intensity, gauss
$\quad \omega/2\pi$ = frequency
$\quad\quad t$ = time
$\quad\quad A$ = an arbitrary constant of amplitude

The quantities a, x, y, and z have meanings indicated in Fig. 5-1.   Subscripts x, y, and z indicate components in these respective directions. Finally β, the phase constant, has the value given by Eq. (5-4) below.

Cutoff Wavelength in a Rectangular Waveguide.   Field configurations such as those illustrated in Fig. 5-2 can exist and propagate down a guide only when the frequency is such that the free-space wavelength is greater than a certain critical value termed the *cutoff wavelength*, commonly denoted as λ_c.   For the dominant mode in rectangular waveguide, the cutoff wavelength is exactly twice the width a of the guide.   That is

$$\left. \begin{array}{l} \text{Cutoff wavelength based} \\ \text{on free-space conditions} \end{array} \right\} = \lambda_c = 2a \tag{5-2}$$

If the frequency is less than the cutoff value, so that the free-space wavelength is greater than λ_c, then the waves attenuate rapidly with distance down the guide, as discussed in Sec. 5-8, instead of propagating freely.

The fact that a waveguide must have a dimension approaching a wavelength in order for the fields to propagate limits the practical use of waveguides to extremely high frequencies.   For example, to transmit 300 Mc the guide width must exceed 20 in.

Each mode that can exist in a waveguide has its own cutoff wavelength The dominant mode is by definition the particular mode having the largest possible cutoff wavelength (lowest cutoff frequency).   Accordingly, there is usually a frequency range between the dominant and the next higher mode in which only the dominant mode will propagate freely.   By so proportioning a waveguide that the frequency to be transmitted lies in this range, all higher modes are suppressed after traveling a short distance down the guide; thereafter the only fields present in the guide will be those of a single pure mode, the dominant mode.   In the case of a rectangular guide so proportioned that $a = 2b$, such single-mode operation occurs for free-space wavelengths lying between $2a$ and a. This matter is discussed further on page 138.

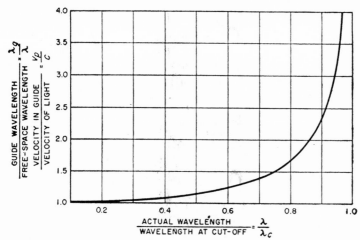

Fig. 5-3. Variation of phase velocity and wavelength in waveguides as a function of ratio of actual wavelength to the cutoff wavelength.

Guide Wavelength, Phase Constant, Group and Phase Velocity.   The axial length λ_g corresponding to one cycle of variation of the field configuration in the axial direction (see Fig. 5-2) is termed the *guide wavelength*.   It is related to the free-space wavelength λ and the cutoff wavelength λ_c according to the equation

$$\text{Guide wavelength} = \lambda_g = \frac{\lambda}{\sqrt{1 - (\lambda/\lambda_c)^2}} \tag{5-3}$$

Results calculated from Eq. (5-3) are plotted in Fig. 5-3.   It will be noted that the guide wavelength exceeds the wavelength in free space, with the ratio of the two becoming increasingly large as the cutoff wavelength is approached.

The guide wavelength λ_g also represents the distance that a wave travels down the guide when undergoing a phase shift of 2π radians. Accordingly, the phase constant β, representing the phase shift per unit distance traveled by the wave, has the value

$$\beta = \frac{2\pi}{\lambda_g} = \frac{2\pi}{\lambda}\sqrt{1 - \left(\frac{\lambda}{\lambda_c}\right)^2} = \sqrt{\frac{\omega^2}{c^2} - \frac{\pi^2}{a^2}} \tag{5-4}$$

where c is the velocity of light.   It will be noted that the phase constant β has the same significance in waveguides as in transmission lines.

The quantity $v_p = f\lambda_g$ is the distance the wave travels in f cycles (i.e., one second) and so has the dimension of a velocity.   Termed the *phase velocity*,[1] it is related to the velocity of light c by the equation

$$\frac{\text{Phase velocity}}{\text{Velocity of light}} = \frac{v_p}{c} = \frac{\lambda_g}{\lambda} = \frac{1}{\sqrt{1 - (\lambda/\lambda_c)^2}} \tag{5-5}$$

This relation is plotted in Fig. 5-3.   It is seen from Eq. (5-5) that the velocity of phase propagation always exceeds the velocity of light.   In

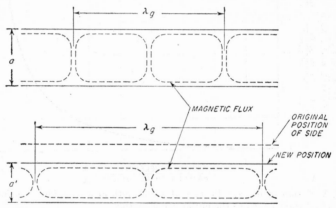

FIG. 5-4. Top view of TE_{10} field in a rectangular waveguide, showing the effect upon the guide wavelength λ_g of reducing the guide dimension a.

particular, as the frequency is lowered so that it approaches the cutoff value, the phase velocity increases and becomes indefinite at cutoff. Similarly, as the guide width is reduced so that the cutoff wavelength is made to approach the free-space wavelength, the phase velocity and λ_g increase and β decreases.   This behavior arises from the fact that, as the width of the guide is reduced while keeping the frequency constant, the field configuration required to satisfy Maxwell's equations is affected in the manner shown in Fig. 5-4; specifically, compressing the flux sidewise by narrowing the guide is compensated for by an axial expansion that increases the guide wavelength and hence the phase velocity.

Currents in Waveguide Walls.   The fields inside a waveguide induce currents that flow on the inner surface of the walls and that can be considered to be associated with the magnetic flux adjacent to the wall.   The

[1] The phase velocity is an apparent velocity deduced from the rate of phase change with position along the axis.   The actual velocity with which a pulse of energy travels is termed the group velocity v_{gr}, and is related to v_p and c by the equation $v_p v_{gr} = c^2$. Thus the group velocity is less than the velocity of light to the extent that the phase velocity is greater.   This matter is discussed further on p. 142.

relationship between flux density at the surface of the wall and the current flowing in the wall is given by Eq. (2-18). The direction in which the current flows at any point in the wall is at right angles to the direction of the adjacent magnetic flux. The resulting lines of instantaneous current flow in the walls of a rectangular guide for the dominant mode are illustrated in Fig. 5-5. In the sides of the guide the current everywhere flows vertically, since the magnetic flux in contact with the side walls lies in planes parallel to the top and bottom sides of the guide. In the top and bottom of the guide there are a transverse component of current proportional to the axial component B_z of magnetic field, and an axially flowing current component proportional at any point to the transverse magnetic field B_x.

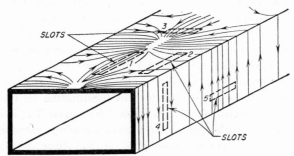

FIG. 5-5. Paths of current flow in the walls of a rectangular waveguide when propagating the dominant mode, showing slots transverse and parallel to the lines of current flow.

The current in the guide walls penetrates in accordance with the laws of skin effect, as given in Eq. (2-9). The depth of penetration is accordingly inversely proportional to the square root of the frequency. At the very high frequencies at which waveguides are used, this penetration is very small, and the walls provide practically perfect shielding.

Coupling and Leakage through Slots and Holes in Waveguide Walls. A hole or joint or slot in the waveguide wall introduces the possibility that energy will leak from the guide to outer space. When this happens, the fields inside the guide are affected, thereby introducing an irregularity with resulting reflection. The coupling thus introduced by a hole in the guide wall may be either to the electric or magnetic fields inside the guide. Electric coupling occurs when electrostatic flux lines that would normally terminate on the guide wall are able to pass through the hole into outside space. Magnetic coupling results when the hole or slot interferes with the current flowing in the guide wall. With either type of coupling, both electric and magnetic fields will be present outside the guide. Thus electric flux leaking through the hole will induce currents on the outer surface of the guide that produce a magnetic field. Again, when magnetic flux leaks through a hole, the associated interference with the flow of currents in the wall produces a voltage across the hole that gives rise to an electric field that will extend outside of the guide.

The nature and magnitude of the coupling in any particular case depend upon the size, shape, and orientation of the coupling hole, and upon the thickness of the guide wall. The factors involved can be understood by considering the effects produced by long narrow slots oriented in various ways, as illustrated in Fig. 5-5. Thus slot 1, which is transverse to the magnetic field inside the guide and so produces a minimum of interference with currents in the guide wall, introduces little or no magnetic coupling. It will, however, permit electric coupling if the slot width is great enough in proportion to the wall thickness to permit a reasonable number of electric flux lines to pass through the slot. However, if the slot is in the nature of a joint representing two surfaces fitted together, or is very narrow, then the electric coupling will be negligible. Similarly, long, narrow slot 4 produces little magnetic coupling because it is transverse to the magnetic flux and therefore interferes only negligibly with the flow of current in the guide wall; neither does it produce electric coupling because there is no electric field terminating on the side wall. Such a slot will therefore have negligible effect even if it is quite long. In contrast, slot 5, while causing no electric coupling, introduces a substantial amount of magnetic coupling to outside space through the fact that its long dimension is parallel to the magnetic field in the guide; this slot is hence oriented in such a manner as to permit easy escape of magnetic flux lines and to interfere to a maximum extent with the wall currents. This coupling is fully effective even if the slot is quite narrow, since it is necessary only that the slot interrupt the flow of current in the wall. Slots 2 and 3 in Fig. 5-5 also give rise to magnetic coupling, because they interfere with the flow of current in the guide wall. In the case of slot 2, the amount of magnetic coupling will be greater the farther the slot is to the side of the center line of the guide. Slots 3 and 2 will also simultaneously introduce electric coupling to the extent that the slot is wide enough in relation to the wall thickness to permit the passage of electric flux. In the case of slot 2, the electric coupling becomes less the farther the slot is from the center line, because the intensity of the electric field terminating on the top and bottom sides of the guide becomes less as the side walls are approached.

Attenuation. The propagation of energy down a waveguide is accompanied by a certain amount of attenuation as a result of the energy dissipated by the current induced in the walls of the guide. The magnitude of this current at any point is determined by the intensity of the magnetic field adjacent to the wall at that point, as explained above. The resistivity that the induced currents encounter is determined by the skin effect of the wall as discussed in Sec. 2-4, and is proportional to the square root of the frequency and the square root of the resistivity of the material of which the wall is composed.

The total energy loss in a waveguide can be calculated by summing up the I^2R loss in the top, bottom, and two sides of the guide for each unit area over a length corresponding to a half wavelength. This is done for the magnetic field distribution actually present, as calculated by Eqs. (5-1), assuming the field at any one point varies sinusoidally with time; under these circumstances the rms value of the field (and current) determines the time average of the power loss occurring at the point.[1]

The energy loss is conveniently expressed in decibels attenuation per unit length. With rectangular guides the loss has the general behavior illustrated in Fig. 5-6. It will be noted that for each mode there is a particular frequency for which the attenuation is a minimum. This is a result of two opposing tendencies. Thus as the frequency is lowered the skin depth becomes greater, causing the effective resistivity of the walls to decrease. At the same time, as the

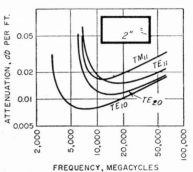

Fig. 5-6. Attenuation of different modes in a particular rectangular copper waveguide as a function of frequency.

frequency approaches the cutoff value for the mode in question, the group velocity decreases. This causes the magnetic fields adjacent to the walls to become rapidly stronger for a given rate of energy flow down the guide.

5-3. Higher Modes in Rectangular Waveguides. The dominant mode is only one of an infinite series of field configurations that can exist in a waveguide. Fields for several of the higher-order modes that are possible in a rectangular waveguide are illustrated in Fig. 5-7.[2] In addition to TE modes, these include TM types, in which the magnetic flux lines lie in planes that are at right angles to the axis of the guide.

These various modes are designated by double subscripts, such as TE_{10}, TE_{20}, TE_{11}, TE_{mn}, TM_{11}, TM_{21}, and TM_{mn}. In this system of nomenclature the first subscript denotes the number of half-period variations of the electric (or magnetic) field in the transverse plane in the direction of the long side of the rectangle (along the x axis in Fig. 5-1); the second subscript denotes the number of half-period variations of the same field in the direction of the short side of the rectangle (along the y axis in Fig. 5-1).

[1] Formulas for the attenuation of different modes in rectangular waveguides are given by Moreno, *op. cit.*, chap. 8; they are also to be found in most handbooks.

[2] Equations for the fields of the various higher modes are to be found in many reference books; for example, see Moreno, *op. cit.*, p. 115.

Each mode has its own cutoff wavelength, guide wavelength, phase constant, and phase and group velocities. Equations (5-3) to (5-5) giving relations between these quantities apply to the higher-order modes as well as to the dominant mode [except for the right-hand form of Eq. (5-4)].

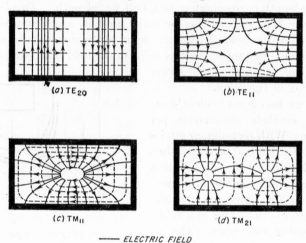

——— ELECTRIC FIELD
----- MAGNETIC FIELD

Fig. 5-7. Field configurations in the transverse plane for the first four higher modes in a rectangular waveguide.

The cutoff wavelength in the general case is given by the relation

$$\lambda_c = \frac{2a}{\sqrt{(m^2) + (na/b)^2}} \tag{5-6}$$

Here a and b have the significance shown in Fig. 5-1, and m and n are, respectively, the first and second subscripts describing the mode. Equation (5-1), giving the cutoff wavelength of the dominant mode, is a special case of Eq. (5-5), in which $m = 1$ and $n = 0$. Results from Eq. (5-6) are tabulated in Table 5-1 for a few of the lowest-order modes for rectangular

TABLE 5-1
CUTOFF WAVELENGTHS IN WAVEGUIDES

Rectangular guide $a = 2b$		Square guide $a = b$		Circular guide radius $= r$	
Mode	Cutoff wavelength	Mode	Cutoff wavelength	Mode	Cutoff wavelength
TE_{10}	$2a$	TE_{10}	$2a$	TE_{11}	$3.42r$
TE_{01}	a	TE_{01}	$2a$	TM_{01}	$2.61r$
TE_{20}	a	TE_{11}	$1.4a$	TE_{21}	$2.06r$
TE_{11}	$0.89a$	TM_{11}	$1.4a$	TE_{01}	$1.64r$
TM_{11}	$0.89a$	TE_{20}	a	TM_{11}	$1.64r$

guides that are square ($a/b = 1$), and for the shape $a/b = 2$ that is customarily used.

Generation of Different Waveguide Modes.   Any actual configuration of
electric and magnetic fields existing in a waveguide can be regarded as
being the result of a series of modes that are superimposed upon one
another.   If the magnitude, phase, and position along the axis of each
individual mode is properly chosen, then the sum of the fields of the
individual modes can be made to equal any actual electric and magnetic
fields that can be present.   Modes in waveguides are thus analogous to
the harmonics of a periodic wave, since a periodic wave of arbitrary shape

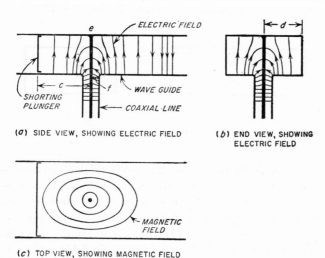

(*a*) SIDE VIEW, SHOWING ELECTRIC FIELD   (*b*) END VIEW, SHOWING
                                                       ELECTRIC FIELD

(*c*) TOP VIEW, SHOWING MAGNETIC FIELD

FIG. 5-8. Launching of TE_{10} wave in a waveguide excited by a coaxial line.

can always be considered as being represented by the sum of a series of
properly chosen harmonic components.

The magnitude of each component mode associated with a given configuration of fields is determined by the character of the field distribution
involved.   For example, consider the arrangement illustrated in Fig. 5-8,
where a concentric line delivers energy to a waveguide as a result of the
electric and magnetic fields produced in the waveguide by the extension
ef of the center coaxial conductor that extends from the bottom to the
top of the guide.   Current in *ef* generates a magnetic field in the guide,
which lies in planes parallel to the top and bottom sides of the guide.   At
the same time, the voltage drop along *ef*, and the consequent difference in
voltage thereby produced between the top and bottom of the guide, result
in electric fields being produced as shown.   This configuration suggests
the TE_{10} mode, in that the magnetic field lies in planes parallel to the top
and bottom of the guide, while the electric field is vertical and is maximum
midway between the sides of the guide.   Thus the TE_{10} is the largest

single component in the field configuration of Fig. 5-8. The difference between the field configuration of this mode and the actual field present is then accounted for by the presence of a succession of higher-order modes, each of which is of smaller amplitude than the TE_{10} component. These higher-order modes will be primarily TE types, since examination of Fig. 5-8 indicates that, except to a very minor extent, the electric field is everywhere almost exactly transverse to the guide axis. Again, since the coupling element *ef* is located midway between the sides, the system is symmetrical with respect to the center of the guide; this means that, for this particular situation, no mode can be present that is unsymmetrical about the guide center; i.e., modes such as the TE_{20} or TE_{40} cannot exist.

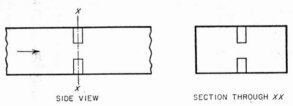

SIDE VIEW   SECTION THROUGH *XX*

Fig. 5-9. Rectangular waveguide with vertical stub posts extending into the guide from the top and bottom sides.

While the modes initially present in a waveguide are determined by the field configuration used to excite the guide, new modes are generated whenever the field is distorted. For example, consider the situation in Fig. 5-9, where an obstacle in the form of a pair of metal posts is present in the guide, and assume that a TE_{10} mode is traveling down the guide. The posts distort both the electric and magnetic fields, which, therefore, in the vicinity of the posts can no longer have the configuration corresponding to a pure TE_{10} mode. The resulting distorted configuration can, however, be represented by a TE_{10} mode of different amplitude from that which would be present in the absence of the posts, plus superimposed higher-order modes.

It is thus seen that an irregularity transforms a portion of an original mode into new modes. This is true irrespective of the exact nature of the irregularity, which, for example, can be a bend, a twist, a constructional irregularity, etc., instead of a post. Also any arrangement for absorbing energy from the waveguide (i.e., a load termination) can in general be expected to distort the field and generate new modes unless special care is taken to avoid this result.

Suppression of Unwanted Modes. An attempt is usually made to operate waveguides so that only a single pure mode is present. In this way coupling systems and terminations can be designed on the basis of a definitely known type of field pattern. In most cases, the dominant mode is preferred because the guide then has the smallest possible dimensions, and the undesired modes can be very simply eliminated.

A dominant mode, free of higher-order modes, can be obtained by taking advantage of the fact that the dominant mode has the lowest cut-off frequency of all possible modes. Thus, by proportioning the guide so that it is large enough to transmit the dominant mode while too small to permit propagation of any other mode, the higher-order modes do not travel down the guide, but rather are confined to the region where they are generated.

In rectangular guides, mode suppression of this character is most effective when the guide is so proportioned that $a/b = 2$ in Fig. 5-1. With these proportions, there is a two-to-one frequency range over which only the dominant mode propagates (see Table 5-1, page 136). In contrast, if the guide were made square, the TE_{01} mode would have the same cutoff wavelength as the TE_{10} mode, and there would be no frequency range over which only a single mode could propagate. Because of considerations such as this, rectangular guides are practically always proportioned so that $a/b = 2$, as this ratio gives the best mode separation of all possible proportions.

Modes which are beyond cutoff, and so cannot propagate, are sometimes termed *evanescent* modes. They represent localized field distributions, i.e., induction fields, that introduce reactive effects but do not carry energy away from the point of origin as does the dominant mode. For example, if the waveguide in Fig. 5-9 is so proportioned that only the dominant mode can propagate, the end result of the field distortion introduced by the post will be equivalent to introducing an irregularity in the waveguide that causes a portion of the dominant wave to be reflected as though from a reactive load. In addition, there will be induction fields in the immediate vicinity of the irregularity that represent reactive energy obtained from the incident dominant mode. However, if in Fig. 5-9 the waveguide were made sufficiently large to permit some of the higher-order modes produced by the post to propagate in the guide, these modes would then travel away from the post, carrying energy with them that was derived from the incident dominant mode. The remaining modes, of such high order as to be unable to propagate, would still be evanescent modes, and would give rise to reactive effects.

Another method of suppressing undesired modes consists in modifying the guide in such a manner that fields of undesired modes are interfered with, while fields of the desired mode are not affected. An example of such a *mode filter* is illustrated in Fig. 5-10. Here the metal vanes do not affect the fields of the TE_{mo} modes, but do interfere with both the electric and magnetic fields of any TM or TE_{on} mode that might be present. Thus such an arrangement is an effective means of suppressing the transverse magnetic mode in a rectangular waveguide.

An obvious means of mode suppression is to arrange matters so that as far as possible the undesired modes are never generated. This means exciting the waveguide in such a manner that the initial field configuration resembles the desired mode as much as possible, and then avoiding irregularities, including terminations, that introduce distortions in the field pattern. For example, a means of launching the waves in the guide that produces only transverse vertical electric fields that do not vary in strength in the vertical direction will not generate any TM mode, or any of the TE$_{on}$ series of modes. Further, if the launching system is also symmetrical with respect to the center of the long side of the rectangular guide, the only modes present will be of the TE$_{mo}$ type, where m is odd.

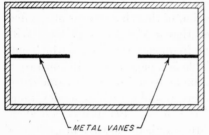

FIG. 5-10. Simple mode filter.

5-4. Physical Picture of Propagation in Rectangular Waveguides.

It is possible to explain many of the properties of waveguide propagation by means of a simple physical picture. To do so, start by considering two parallel conducting planes; these planes will later define the top and bottom walls of a rectangular waveguide. A plane radio wave such as illustrated in Fig. 1-1 will propagate freely in the space between these surfaces provided the electric field is vertical. Such a wave travels with the velocity of light, and its electric and magnetic fields are everywhere in time phase. Some of the details involved are portrayed in Fig. 5-11. This wave can

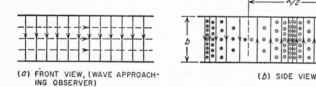

(*a*) FRONT VIEW, (WAVE APPROACH-
ING OBSERVER)

(*b*) SIDE VIEW

FIG. 5-11. Electric and magnetic fields of a plane radio wave that is propagating between two parallel conducting planes.

also be represented by successive crests spaced a wavelength apart, as illustrated in Fig. 5-12*a*, where θ is the direction of travel of the wave with respect to some reference axis. A second similar wave, differing in that the direction of travel with respect to the same reference axis is $-\theta$, is illustrated in Fig. 5-12*b*.

If now both waves are simultaneously present in the space between the conducting planes, one obtains the situation pictured in Fig. 5-12*c*. A close examination of Fig. 5-12*c* shows that if the two waves have equal amplitudes, then in vertical planes indicated by the heavy dotted lines, *cc* and *dd*, the electric fields of the two waves are equal and opposite and so cancel. The transverse components of the magnetic fields likewise cancel at *cc* and *dd*, causing the resultant magnetic field at these planes to be parallel to lines cc and dd. Vertical conducting sheets can accordingly be placed along bb and cc without affecting either magnetic or electric fields in any respect. These vertical conducting surfaces, together with the conducting horizontal planes, define a rectangular waveguide with conducting walls. The fields inside this guide satisfy the boundary conditions imposed by the walls, and also satisfy Maxwell's equations in the space inside the guide. The resultant field configuration obtained by adding the fields of these two plane waves that travel at angles θ and $-\theta$, respectively, is the TE$_{10}$ mode; this is illustrated by the dotted lines in Fig. 5-12c, which show the resultant magnetic flux and are seen to correspond to the magnetic-flux distribution given in Fig. 5-2.

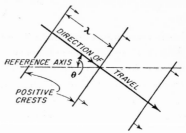

(a) FIRST PLANE WAVE

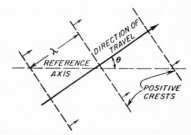

(b) SECOND PLANE WAVE

Study of Fig. 5-12c shows that it is now possible to consider that the fields inside the waveguide are the result of a pair of electromagnetic waves that travel back and forth between the sides of the guide, following a zigzag path as illustrated in Fig. 5-12d. Each time such a wave strikes the conducting side wall, it is reflected with reversal of the electric field, with an angle of reflection equal to the angle of incidence, as illustrated.

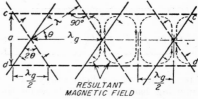

(c) WAVES OF (a) AND (b) SUPERIMPOSED, SHOWING PLANES cc AND dd OF ZERO RESULTANT ELECTRIC FIELD

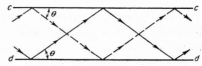

(d) ZIG-ZAG WAVE PATHS THAT REPRESENT SITUATION ILLUSTRATED IN (c)

Fig. 5-12. Steps involved in building up a physical picture of propagation in a rectangular waveguide.

The guide wavelength λ_g for the situation in Fig. 5-12c is the distance along the axis between points in the guide where the positive crests coincide. It will be noted that the guide wavelength λ_g exceeds the free-space wavelength λ of the plane wave by an amount that will increase as θ becomes larger. Various relations follow from the geometry of Fig. 4-42c; thus

$$\cos \theta = \frac{\lambda}{\lambda_g} \tag{5-7a}$$

$$\tan \theta = \frac{\lambda_g/4}{a/2} = \frac{\lambda_g}{2a} \tag{5-7b}$$

Combining to eliminate θ gives

$$\lambda_g = \frac{\lambda}{\sqrt{1 - (\lambda/2a)^2}} \qquad (5\text{-}8)$$

This is equivalent to Eq. (5-3) when it is noted that $\lambda_c = 2a$.

Examination of the geometry of Fig. 5-12c reveals that, if the distance between successive crests is increased (i.e., free-space wavelength λ increased), then if the electric fields are to cancel along planes cc and dd, it is necessary that θ be increased. As the free-space wavelength approaches closer and closer to the cutoff wavelength, θ thus becomes increasingly large, and the zigzag path of the waves becomes increasingly transverse, as illustrated in Fig. 5-13.

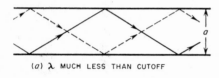

(a) λ MUCH LESS THAN CUTOFF

(b) λ MODERATELY LESS THAN CUTOFF

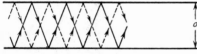

(c) λ CLOSE TO CUTOFF

FIG. 5-13. Paths followed by a wave traveling back and forth between the sides of a waveguide for values of free-space wavelengths differing from the cutoff wavelength by various amounts.

The fact that the guide wavelength λ_g in Fig. 5-12c exceeds the free-space wavelength causes the phase velocity in the rectangular guide to exceed the velocity of light. At the same time, the individual waves themselves advance more slowly down the guide than the velocity of light, since the individual waves travel by a zigzag path. This rate at which the waves progress down the guide is the *group* velocity and corresponds to the rate at which a pulse of energy would travel. As the free-space wavelength approaches more closely the cutoff wavelength of the guide (i.e., as $\lambda \to 2a$), the phase velocity becomes progressively larger and the group velocity progressively less. In the limit, at the cutoff wavelength, the waves travel back and forth between the sides of the guide at right angles to the axis ($\theta = 90°$). Under these conditions nothing at all travels down the guide, so the group velocity is zero, while the phase velocity is infinite.[1]

This picture that has been developed of wave propagation in a rectangular guide can be readily extended to take into account the higher-order modes. For example, in Fig. 5-12c, it is apparent that there are also other vertical planes in which the electric fields of the two component waves cancel exactly; one such plane is indicated by ee in Fig. 5-14a. If

[1] An excellent discussion of the significance of group and phase velocities is given by J. A. Stratton, "Electromagnetic Theory," pp. 330–340, McGraw-Hill Book Company, Inc., New York, 1941; also see H. H. Skilling, "Electric Transmission Lines," pp. 369–373, McGraw-Hill Book Company, Inc., New York, 1951.

now vertical conducting sheets are placed at *cc* and *ee* instead of *cc* and *dd*, one again has formed a rectangular waveguide inside of which are fields (illustrated in Fig. 5-14*b* and *c*) that satisfy all of the required conditions; this particular configuration is the TE_{20} mode.

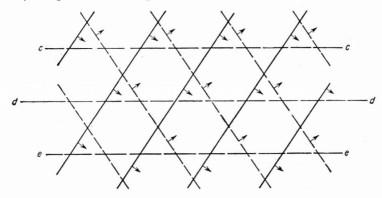

(*a*) COMPONENT WAVES SUPERIMPOSED, SHOWING THREE PLANES WHERE THE ELECTRIC FIELDS CANCEL

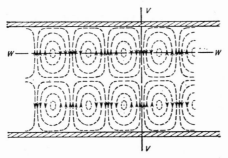

(*b*) RESULTANT MAGNETIC FIELD CORRESPONDING TO (*a*); PLAN VIEW

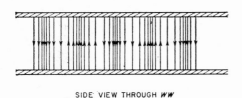
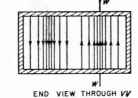

SIDE VIEW THROUGH *WW*   END VIEW THROUGH *VV*

(*c*) RESULTANT ELECTRIC FIELD CORRESPONDING TO (*a*), IN VERTICAL PLANES

FIG. 5-14. Physical picture showing how the TE_{20} mode arises in a rectangular waveguide.

5-5. Circular Waveguides.

It might be thought that waveguides with circular cross sections would be preferred to guides with rectangular cross sections, just as circular pipes are commonly used for carrying water and fluids in preference to rectangular pipes. However, circular waveguides have the disadvantage that there is only a very narrow range

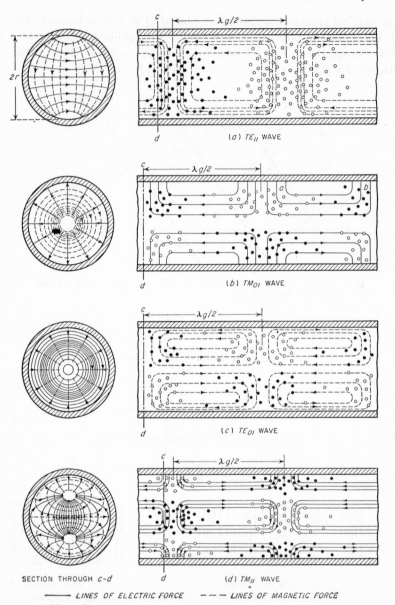

SECTION THROUGH *c-d*

——— LINES OF ELECTRIC FORCE   — — — LINES OF MAGNETIC FORCE

Fig. 5-15. Field configuration of the dominant TE_{11} mode, and of the first few higher-order modes in a circular waveguide.

between the cutoff wavelength of the dominant mode and the cutoff wavelength of the next higher mode. Thus the frequency range over which pure mode operation is assured is relatively limited. Also, because of its circular symmetry, the circular guide possesses no characteristic that positively prevents the plane of polarization of the wave from rotating about the guide axis as the wave travels. As a result, circular waveguides are used only under special circumstances, for example, where it is necessary to introduce a rotating joint into a waveguide system.

Field configurations for the more important circular modes are illustrated in Fig. 5-15. As with rectangular guides, these modes may be classified as transverse electric (TE) or transverse magnetic (TM), according to whether it is the electric or magnetic lines of force that lie in planes perpendicular to the axis of the guide. The different modes are designated by a double subscript system analogous to that for rectangular guides.[1]

The wavelength corresponding to cutoff for a particular mode in a circular guide is proportional to the diameter of the waveguide, with the exact relationship being given by the equation

$$\text{Cutoff wavelength} = \lambda_c = \frac{2\pi r}{\mu}$$

(5-9)

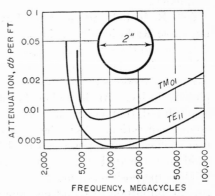

Fig. 5-16. Attenuation as a function of frequency of the dominant and first higher-order mode in a particular circular waveguide with copper walls.

where r is the guide radius and μ is a constant that depends on the order of the mode.[2] Results of Eq. (5-9) for the first few modes are tabulated in Table 5-1.

The TE_{11} circular mode (see Fig. 5-15) has the longest cutoff wavelength, and is accordingly the dominant circular mode. The next higher circular mode is the TM_{01} mode, for which the cutoff wavelength is 0.76 times that of the dominant mode. The corresponding ratio is 0.5 for the first two modes in a rectangular guide with $a/b = 2$. Thus the ratio of frequencies over which only the dominant mode will propagate is over 50 per cent greater for the rectangular guide than for the circular guide.

The guide wavelength λ_g in a circular guide is greater than the wavelength λ in free space, just as in the rectangular guide. In fact, Eq. (5-3) applies to circular as well as to rectangular guides. The velocity of phase propagation is λ_g/λ times the velocity of light in all cases.

A wave traveling down a circular guide is attenuated as a result of

---

[1] For example, in the TM_{om} mode, the magnetic field is circular, and m is the number of cylinders, including the boundary of the guide, to which the electric vector is normal. Rules for determining the subscripts for the various possible cases are given in "Standards on Radio Wave Propagation—Definitions of Terms Related to Guided Waves," Institute of Radio Engineers, New York, 1945.

[2] For TE_{nm} waves, μ is the mth root of the equation $J'_n(x) = 0$, and for TM_{nm} waves, it is the mth root of the relation $J_n(x) = 0$.

power dissipated in the walls by the induced wall currents, exactly as in the case of a rectangular guide. Curves of attenuation as a function of frequency are given in Fig. 5-16 for the first two modes in a particular guide. These are similar in character to the corresponding curves of Fig. 5-6 for the rectangular guide, in that the attenuation passes through a minimum at a frequency that is moderately greater than the cutoff frequency.[1]

5-6. Reflected and Incident Waves, Field Distributions, and Standing-wave Ratio in Waveguides. As indicated previously, the field configuration in the waveguide behaves in the same way as a wave on a transmission line. That is, the electric and magnetic fields associated with a particular mode, such as the TE_{10} mode, travel down the guide at the phase velocity. At the end of the guide, or at an irregularity, a reflection is produced that creates a similar field configuration traveling in the opposite direction. As in the analogous transmission line case, the reflection coefficient at a point can be defined as the ratio of the reflected to incident wave at that point in the guide.

The superposition of incident and reflected waves in a waveguide gives rise to amplitude distributions along the guide that are of exactly the same character as the voltage and current distributions encountered in transmission lines (illustrated in Fig. 4-4) provided one interprets the electric and magnetic fields of the guide as being equivalent, respectively, to the voltage and current of the transmission line. Thus a short-circuited receiver (zero voltage or zero electric field at the receiving end of the system) gives a distribution in which the resultant electric field is maximum at distances from the load corresponding to an odd number of quarter wavelengths based on λ_g, the guide wavelength. At the same time, the resultant magnetic field is maximum at the load, and at distances from the receiver corresponding to an even number of quarter wavelengths. Resistive loads of the incorrect value to absorb the incident wave completely will give partial reflections, but with the maxima and minima in the distribution occurring at the same places as in the corresponding open- and short-circuited cases. On the other hand, load impedances that have a reactive component will have the minima displaced, exactly as in the case of the transmission line.

The extent to which a reflected wave is present in a waveguide can be conveniently expressed in terms of a standing-wave ratio. As applied to a waveguide, the standing-wave ratio has the same significance and

[1] An exception to this otherwise general behavior is the TE_{01} mode, sometimes called the "smoke ring" mode, in which the attenuation decreases steadily with increasing frequency and becomes zero at infinite frequency. This result comes about through the fact that in this mode the magnetic field adjacent to the walls of the guide becomes progressively weaker as the ratio of free-space to cutoff wavelengths becomes less. In the limit, at infinite frequency, this magnetic field becomes zero, resulting in zero current induced in the walls.

usefulness as in the analogous transmission-line situation, provided that one remembers that the magnetic and electric fields in the guide correspond respectively to current and voltage in the transmission line.

Any irregularity in a waveguide will give rise to reflections and hence will establish standing waves, just as does a load impedance that is not matched to the waveguide. Thus bends, twists, joints, probes, mechanical imperfections, pieces of dielectric, etc., all give rise to reflections, the magnitude of which can be expressed in terms of the resulting standing-wave ratio.[1]

Transmission-line Equivalent of a Waveguide System. In dealing with a waveguide system possessing an irregularity, it is commonly convenient to regard the arrangement as though it were a transmission line possessing a corresponding irregularity. The characteristic impedance of this equivalent transmission line can be taken as the waveguide impedance defined in whatever manner is most convenient (see below). The impedance of the transmission-line irregularity[2] (and also the load impedance) is then assigned the value such that in relation to the characteristic impedance the resulting reflection coefficient associated with the transmission-line irregularity will be the same as the reflection coefficient actually produced in the waveguide by the irregularity. The standing-wave situation existing on the equivalent transmission line is then the same in every respect as is actually present on the waveguide; an example is given on page 149.

5-7. Impedance Relations in Waveguides. *Waveguide Impedance.* In a transmission line, one can define a characteristic impedance that is determined by the geometry of the line and which holds for all frequencies. In contrast, there are several different ways in which a "characteristic impedance" can be defined for a waveguide, and each of these definitions gives a different numerical result. In addition, the waveguide impedance for a given guide will be a function of frequency irrespective of how defined.

One commonly used approach is to define the impedance associated with a waveguide as the ratio of the transverse components of the electric to magnetic field strength. This is termed the *wave impedance;* for a guide with air dielectric it is given by the formulas

For TE waves:

$$\text{Wave impedance} = 377 \frac{\lambda_g}{\lambda} \quad \text{ohms} \quad (5\text{-}10)$$

---

[1] The quantitative effects produced by bends, twists, etc., are summarized by N. Elson, Rectangular Waveguide Systems, *Wireless Eng.*, vol. 24, p. 44, February, 1947; also see Moreno, *op. cit.*, pp. 162–169.

[2] In many cases an irregularity is more satisfactorily represented by a simple T or π network, or a simple resonant circuit, than by a single circuit element. Examples of such cases are given in Figs. 5-19c and 5-28.

For TM waves:

$$\text{Wave impedance} = 377 \frac{\lambda}{\lambda_g} \quad \text{ohms} \quad (5\text{-}11)$$

Here λ and λ_g are the free-space and guide wavelengths, respectively. The wave impedance has the desirable feature that it is independent of the physical proportions or shape of the guide, or of the transmission mode, except in so far as these affect the guide wavelength λ_g. The concept of wave impedance is particularly useful in the study of waveguide discontinuities and loads.

Another approach is to define the impedance of a waveguide as the ratio of the *maximum* value of the transverse voltage developed across the guide to the total longitudinal current flowing in the guide walls for a traveling wave when no reflected wave is present. On this basis, the waveguide impedance Z_0 for the TE_{10} mode in an air-filled rectangular guide is

$$Z_0 = 377 \frac{\lambda_g}{\lambda} \frac{\pi}{2} \frac{b}{a} \quad (5\text{-}12)$$

This definition of waveguide impedance is useful in the design of systems for coupling waveguides to coaxial lines, such as illustrated in Fig. 5-8. It must be used with some caution, however, because in contrast with transmission lines, the fields of a guide are not uniformly distributed over the cross section.

Impedance Matching in Waveguides. Reflected waves are generally to be avoided in waveguides for exactly the same reasons that they are avoided in transmission lines. One method of achieving this result in a waveguide is to arrange matters so that the load impedance that is used will completely absorb the incident fields exactly as they arrive, so that there is nothing left over to be reflected; this corresponds to characteristic impedance termination in a transmission line. A second approach to the problem is to create a reflected wave near the load that is equal in magnitude but opposite in phase from the wave reflected by the load; in this way the two reflected waves cancel each other. Most commonly both methods of impedance matching are used simultaneously. That is, the system is initially so arranged that the load provides as good an impedance match as is possible to obtain with reasonable effort, and then what reflected wave still remains is eliminated by the use of an impedance-matching system that introduces a neutralizing reflection.

Numerous waveguide arrangements have been devised for introducing a controllable reflection. Some of these are analogous to the impedance-matching arrangements employed in transmission lines (described in Sec. 4-11), while others are unique to waveguides.

The waveguide analogue of the stub line of Fig. 4-16 is the stub guide or T section illustrated in Fig. 5-17. Two possibilities are to be distinguished.[1] At a the reactance at the input of the stub guide is effectively in series with the equivalent transmission line of the guide, while with the stub as in b, the reactance introduced by the stub is in shunt in the equivalent transmission line circuit of the guide. This is shown schematically at c and d, respectively. The magnitude of the reflection introduced by such a stub guide is controlled by the position of the short-circuiting plunger in the stub guide. The phase of the reflected wave produced by the stub is determined by the position of the stub in relation

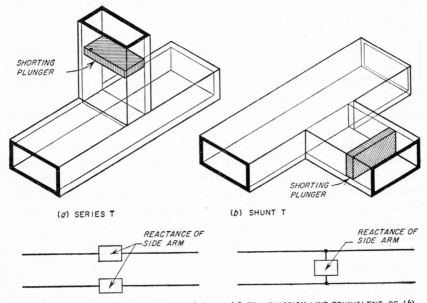

FIG. 5-17. Waveguides provided with tuning stubs in arrangements analogous to that of Fig. 4-18, together with equivalent transmission-line circuits.

to a minimum of the standing-wave pattern existing in the absence of the stub. Thus, to eliminate a reflected wave using a single stub, it is necessary to be able to vary not only the effective length of the stub, but also its distance to the load. This latter requirement makes a single stub arrangement unsatisfactory in systems that must be adjusted by trial and error, since there is no simple way that the position of the stub can be continuously varied. When trial-and-error adjustment is required, one can, however, employ two waveguide stubs spaced approximately $n\lambda_g/8$, where n is odd, to give the waveguide equivalent of the two-stub tuner of Fig. 4-18.

An alternative to the waveguide stub is an adjustable screw or probe

[1] The arrangements at a and b are often referred to as E and H stubs, respectively, because the axis of the stub is parallel to the E lines and H plane, respectively, in the main guide.

that projects into the waveguide in a direction parallel to the electric field, as illustrated in Fig. 5-18. Such an arrangement has the same effect as shunting a capacitive load across the equivalent transmission line of the waveguide, with the susceptance of this capacitive load increasing with penetration into the guide up to the point where the equivalent penetration is a quarter of a wavelength.[1] Thus the extent to which such

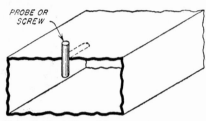

a probe (or screw) projects into the waveguide determines the magnitude of the compensating reflection, while the position of the probe with respect to the standing-wave pattern that is to be eliminated determines the phasing of the reflected wave. When it is necessary that the axial position of the probe or screw be adjustable experimentally, this can be achieved by providing

FIG. 5-18. Adjustable screw (or probe) for producing an adjustable reflection for impedance-matching purposes.

the guide with a longitudinal slot located in the middle of the broad side, as shown dotted in Fig. 5-18. As pointed out in connection with Fig. 5-5, such a slot (labeled 1 in this figure) produces a minimum of interference with the fields inside the guide, and has little tendency to radiate energy. Where it is desirable to avoid the use of a slot, one can instead employ two spaced probes in an arrangement analogous to that of Fig. 4-18.

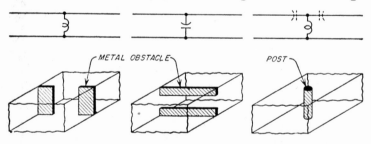

(*a*) INDUCTIVE WINDOW   (*b*) CAPACITIVE WINDOW   (*c*) POST (INDUCTIVE)

FIG. 5-19. Examples of obstacles used in waveguides to introduce reflection, together with equivalent transmission-line systems.

Another impedance-matching system consists of a thin metallic barrier, or "window," placed at right angles to the axis of the guide, as illustrated in Fig. 5-19. The arrangements at *a* and *b* introduce, respectively, inductive and capacitive shunts in the equivalent transmission-line circuit of the waveguide as shown, the magnitudes of which depend upon the size

---

[1] When the equivalent penetration is exactly a quarter wavelength, the probe becomes resonant. The system then acts as though a series resonant circuit of low resistance was connected in shunt with the waveguide; thus at exact resonance the probe acts as a shunt of very low resistance.

of the opening.   A conducting cylindrical post going from top to bottom of a rectangular waveguide, as at *c*, produces an inductive shunt susceptance[1] having a magnitude determined by the size of the waveguide, the diameter of the post, and the post position in the transverse plane.   Still another type of obstacle is illustrated in Fig. 5-9.   Reflections introduced by obstacles such as illustrated in Fig. 5-19 cannot be conveniently adjusted experimentally.   These arrangements are of practical use, however, in systems where a reflected wave of known and unvarying character is to be neutralized.[2]

Impedance Matching with Resistive Loads.   There is the theoretical possibility of matching a resistance load directly to the waveguide in such a manner as to avoid a reflected wave; this eliminates the need of introducing a compensating reflection.   Thus consider the situation illustrated in Fig. 5-20, *case a*, where the load consists of a resistance R_L connected between the top

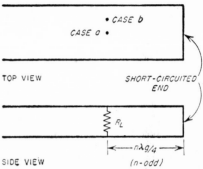

Fig. 5-20. Resistance load connected between top and bottom sides of waveguide.

and bottom planes of the guide midway between the sides, and an odd multiple of a quarter of a guide wavelength away from a short circuit.[3] If the load resistance R_L is now equal to the waveguide impedance Z_0 as defined by Eq. (5-12), then the incident wave will be absorbed without reflection.   If the resistance R_L that is to be used differs from the value called for by Eq. (5-12), one can change the guide impedance as required

[1] Actually the equivalent circuit will be a simple shunt inductance only when the diameter of the post is not more than a few per cent of the guide width.   With thicker posts, the equivalent circuit includes series capacitances in addition to the shunt inductance, as shown dotted in Fig. 5-19c.   These capacitances become larger (i.e., have lower reactance) the smaller the post diameter and have negligible reactance in the case of very thin posts.   The T network shown in Fig. 5-19c will accurately represent the behavior of even a very thick post over a wide range of frequencies when the inductance and capacitances of the equivalent section are properly chosen. Similarly, if the strips forming the windows at *a* and *b* are not thin, the obstacle is represented more accurately by a T network than by a single shunting reactance.

[2] Quantitative analysis of the structures shown in Fig. 5-19, and also of other forms of obstacles, is given in "Waveguide Handbook" (vol. 10, Radiation Laboratory Series, chap. 5, McGraw-Hill Book Company, Inc., New York, 1951; also see Moreno, *op. cit.*, chap. 9.

[3] The short circuit placed an odd multiple of a quarter of a guide wavelength distant from the load is necessary because if the guide is continued indefinitely beyond the resistance, then R_L would act merely as a shunt irregularity in the guide.   Alternatively, if the guide simply ended at the point where the resistance was connected, then part of the energy of the incident wave would be radiated from the open end of the guide rather than being dissipated in the resistance.

by varying the height b of the guide, using a gradual taper as illustrated in Fig. 5-21a to avoid introducing a reflection. A variation consists in tapering only the center portion of the guide to form a ridge, as in Fig. 5-21b.

An alternative arrangement, suitable for use when the load resistance is less than the guide impedance, consists in placing R_L off center as indicated by *case b* of Fig. 5-20. This subjects R_L to less voltage than case a, and so gives an impedance-transforming action.[1] A similar effect is also obtained by making the distance from R_L to the short circuit differ from an odd multiple of a quarter wavelength.

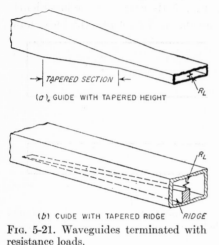

(a) GUIDE WITH TAPERED HEIGHT

(b) CUIDE WITH TAPERED RIDGE

Fig. 5-21. Waveguides terminated with resistance loads.

In actual practice, arrangements of the type illustrated in Fig. 5-20 usually introduce a discontinuity capacitance. When this is the case, no adjustment of the resistance match will eliminate completely the reflected wave; to achieve such a result some additional impedance-matching adjustment, such as obtainable with a probe or a stub guide, must also be used.

Nonreflecting Loads. In systems involving waveguides it is often necessary, particularly in measurement work, to provide a termination that

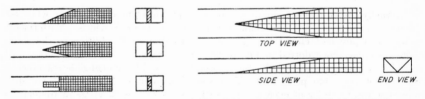

(a) LOSSY VANES   (b) LOSSY WEDGE OF DIELECTRIC OR POLYIRON

Fig. 5-22. Examples of nonreflecting terminations for waveguides.

will completely absorb any wave going down the guide, irrespective of the exact frequency of this wave, and without any adjustment being required.

This result is most conveniently achieved by absorbing the wave in a lossy section tapered so gradually as to introduce no reflection. Examples of such sections are illustrated in Fig. 5-22; these involve lossy vanes, or wedges of lossy dielectric or iron dust core material, tapered on the enter-

[1] The off-center connection causes the resistive impedance that the guide presents to the coaxial line to be less than Eq. (5-12) by the factor $\cos^2 (\pi x/a)$, where x is the distance off center and a is the guide width.

ing edge, and having a sufficient length to absorb an entering wave almost completely.[1]

5-8. Waveguide Behavior at Wavelengths Greater than Cutoff.[2] When a waveguide is excited at a wavelength greater than cutoff, the behavior is entirely different from the behavior at wavelengths less than cutoff. In particular, the electric and magnetic fields now decay exponentially with distance at a very much more rapid rate than is accounted for by energy losses in the walls. The rate of this attenuation, moreover, depends only on the ratio λ/λ_c of the free-space wavelength to the cutoff wavelength; unlike waves shorter than the cutoff wavelength the attenuation is independent of the material of the guide walls. The exact law of attenuation can be derived by application of the fundamental field equations, and is

$$\left.\begin{array}{c}\text{Attenuation in}\\ \text{db per unit length}\end{array}\right\} = \alpha = \frac{54.6}{\lambda_c}\sqrt{1 - \left(\frac{\lambda_c}{\lambda}\right)^2} \qquad (5\text{-}13a)$$

When the actual wavelength is much greater than cutoff ($\lambda \gg \lambda_c$), then

$$\alpha \approx \frac{54.6}{\lambda_c} \qquad (5\text{-}13b)$$

TABLE 5-2
ATTENUATION FORMULAS FOR CUTOFF ATTENUATORS

Mode	Attenuation, db per unit length	Value of λ_c
Circular waveguides of radius r		
TE_{11}	$\dfrac{16.0}{r}$	$3.42r$
TM_{01}	$\dfrac{20.9}{r}$	$2.61r$
TE_{01}	$\dfrac{33.3}{r}$	$1.64r$
Rectangular guide of width a and height b		
TE_{10}	$\dfrac{27.3}{a}$	$2a$
TE_{11} and TM_{11}	$\dfrac{27.3}{a}\sqrt{1 + \left(\dfrac{a}{b}\right)^2}$	$\dfrac{2a}{\sqrt{1 + \left(\dfrac{a}{b}\right)^2}}$

[1] For further discussion of nonreflecting terminations for waveguides see F. E. Terman and J. M. Pettit, "Electronic Measurements," p. 639, McGraw-Hill Book Company, Inc., New York, 1952.

[2] The original paper on this subject was by Daniel E. Harnett and Nelson P. Case, The Design and Testing of Multirange Receivers, *Proc. IRE*, vol. 23, p. 578, June, 1935.

Here λ is the free-space wavelength and λ_c is the cutoff wavelength, measured in the same units of length used in expressing the attenuation. Equations (5-13) apply to all modes of propagation in all types of waveguides. The resulting relation between the rate of attenuation and the guide dimensions is given in Table 5-2 for cases of particular interest.

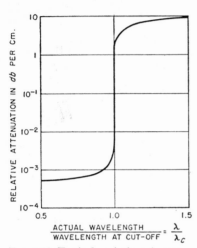

FIG. 5-23. Typical variation of attenuation in a waveguide with frequency in the vicinity of cutoff.

Frequency enters into the expression for attenuation only through the term λ_c/λ in Eq. (5-13a). When this is small, the attenuation is substantially independent of frequency.[1] As the wavelength approaches the cutoff value, the rate of attenuation will diminish in accordance with Eq. (5-13a). This is illustrated in Fig. 5-23. As cutoff is very closely approached, a rapid transition takes place, as shown, and when the wavelength is less than cutoff, the attenuation assumes the comparatively low value associated with wall losses.

Waveguides operated at wavelengths greater than cutoff, termed *waveguide attenuators*, are often used as attenuators in signal generators. The usual arrangement for this purpose, illustrated in Fig. 5-24, involves exciting the guide, which may be either circular or rectangular, with a coil, the axis of which is at right angles to the axis of the guide. The pickup system then consists of a similar coil with its axis parallel to the

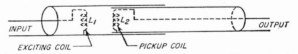

FIG. 5-24. Schematic diagram of typical waveguide attenuator.

axis of the exciting coil. Such an arrangement uses the TE_{10} mode in the rectangular case, and the TE_{11} mode when the guide is circular.[2] The

---

[1] This neglects the variation with frequency of the depth of current penetration into the wall. To obtain maximum accuracy when using Eqs. (5-13), the effective internal dimensions of the waveguide should be taken as extending into the walls a distance equal to one-fourth the skin depth as given by Eq. (2-10). Since this skin depth varies with frequency, the value to be assigned λ_c will likewise vary with frequency, increasing slightly as the frequency is reduced, and hence introducing a small additional cause of variation of attenuation per unit length.

[2] These are the dominant modes and are employed because they attenuate more slowly with distance than do higher-order modes. Hence when the dominant mode is initially mixed to some extent with higher-order modes, then the mode becomes increasingly pure as one goes down the guide away from the exciting coil.

output of such an attenuator is varied by adjusting the distance between the pickup coil and the exciting coil. The change in output produced by a known displacement of the pickup coil can be calculated from the waveguide dimensions, using Table 5-2 or Eqs. (5-13). The waveguide operated at wavelengths greater than cutoff hence provides a simple and reliable way of introducing known changes in the output.[1]

5-9. Miscellaneous Aspects and Properties of Waveguides. *Coupling between Coaxial Lines and Waveguides.* Numerous arrangements have been devised for coupling a coaxial transmission line to a waveguide so that power may flow from one transmission system into the other. A typical example[2] is illustrated in Fig. 5-8. As viewed by the coaxial transmission line, the waveguide in this arrangement behaves like a resistance equal to the waveguide impedance as defined by Eq. (5-12). In addition, there is a reactive effect associated with the coupling as a result of the induct- ance of the length of conductor extending across the waveguide, and also as a result of evanescent modes present at the junction. In order to obtain an im- pedance match between a coaxial line and waveguide such that power will pass from one system to the other without producing a reflected wave, it is therefore

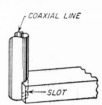

Fig. 5-25. Wave- guide-to-coaxial- line coupling sys- tem based upon a slot in the outer conductor of the coaxial line.

necessary not only to match the characteristic impedance of the coaxial line properly to the waveguide impedance, but in addition a compensat- ing reactance must be introduced at the coupling point. A simple method of producing the required neutralizing effect consists in adjusting the dis- tance c in Fig. 5-8a so that the shunt reactance observed by the coaxial line, when looking toward the short-circuited end of the waveguide, is equal and opposite to the shunt reactance associated with the coupling system.[3]

A very different approach to the problem of coupling a waveguide to a coaxial line is illustrated in Fig. 5-25. Here a transverse slot in the outer conductor of the coaxial line allows magnetic flux to leak from the line into the waveguide. At the same time, the slot interrupts the flow of current in the outer conductor of the coaxial line, thereby creating a voltage difference across the slot that produces an electric field between the top and bottom sides of the waveguide. In this way a wave on the

---

[1] A more extensive discussion of waveguide attenuators is given by Terman and Pettit, *op. cit.*, p. 656.

[2] The detailed design of systems of this type is given by Seymour B. Cohn, The Design of Simple Broad-band Waveguide-to-coaxial-line Junctions, *Proc. IRE*, vol. 35, p. 920, September, 1947.

[3] The resistance that the waveguide offers the coaxial line can, when desired, be reduced by placing the coupling point off center, i.e., by making distance d in **Fig. 5-8b** less than half the guide width.

coaxial line introduces electric and magnetic fields into the waveguide that correspond roughly to the fields of the dominant mode. Conversely, a dominant mode traveling down the waveguide will excite a wave on the coaxial system.

Waveguide Directional Couplers. It is possible to devise directional-coupling systems involving waveguides that are analogous to the transmission-line directional-coupling arrangements discussed on page 115. The waveguide equivalent of the two-hole directional coupler of Fig. 4-24 is illustrated in Fig. 5-26. Directional coupling between a waveguide and a coaxial system is also possible. Thus, if the primary line in Fig. 4-23 is replaced by a waveguide, one obtains directional coupling between a waveguide primary and a coaxial secondary system.

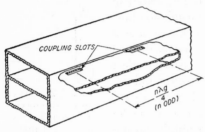

FIG. 5-26. Two-hole directional coupler for waveguide analogous to the two-hole coaxial line coupler of Fig. 4-24. The narrow slot parallel to the guide axis provides coupling that is predominantly electrostatic.

Magic T. The waveguide arrangement illustrated in Fig. 5-27a, termed a *magic T*, possesses many of the qualities of a bridge. Thus if the two side outlets C and D have the same length and are terminated identically, then power delivered to the system at A divides at the junction and flows equally to C and D, with no output whatsoever being obtained at B; similarly, power supplied at B divides between C and D and none of it appears at A. On the other hand, if power is delivered to the system at A and the terminations at C and D are not identical, then there will be an output at B proportional to the difference between the waves reflected at C and D.

This behavior can be explained as follows: A wave of the dominant mode traveling down A cannot turn the corner into B, because the orientation of the electric field in A is such that in turning into B the electric field would necessarily have to be parallel to the long dimension of the guide. For this field configuration, guide B will have a cutoff wavelength less than the wavelength of the wave arriving from A, provided the proportions and absolute dimensions of the system are properly chosen. The waves arriving from A can, however, divide and travel in directions C and D, it merely being necessary for the electric flux to turn corners into similar guides. Equal reflections from C and D, upon reaching the junction of the magic T, will divide between A and B. The portions entering A from C and D are in phase and so combine to give standing waves in A. However, the portions of these reflected waves that attempt to enter B do so as a result of the electric vector turning a corner as illustrated in Fig. 5-27b, and it will be noted that the reflections from C and D when entering B are of opposite polarity and so tend to cancel. This cancellation is complete if the reflected waves from C and D are identical upon arrival at the junction, in which case there is no transmission to B.   However, if the reflected waves produced at C and D are not identical in magnitude and phase as they arrive at the junction, then there will be a resulting component entering B that is proportional to the vector difference of the two waves.[1,2]

The Resonant Obstacles in Waveguides.[3]   When certain types of obstructions are placed in waveguides, a resonant effect is introduced that is equivalent to shunting the equivalent transmission line of the guide with either a series or shunt resonant circuit, as the case may be.   The quarter-

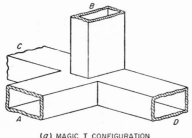
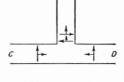

(*a*) MAGIC T CONFIGURATION

(*b*) BEHAVIOR OF REFLECTIONS FROM *C* AND *D*

FIG. 5-27. Magic-T arrangement.

wave resonant post discussed in connection with Fig. 5-18 is an example, and is equivalent to a series resonant system connected across the guide. Another example is provided by a rectangular window in a rectangular waveguide, illustrated in Fig. 5-28a, which acts as a parallel resonant shunt.   In contrast, an obstacle having the configuration shown in Fig. 5-28b acts as a series resonant shunt, the resonance occurring at a frequency determined largely by the peripheral length of the obstructing rectangular ring.   Many other forms of resonant obstacles are also possible.

Obstructions that behave as shunting series-resonant systems will transmit energy rather freely at all frequencies except those in the immediate vicinity of the series resonant frequency, where the shunting impedance is so low as to reflect nearly all of the energy.   In contrast,

---

[1] This explanation assumes that the discontinuity capacitances existing at the common junction of the magic-T configuration have been neutralized by the introduction of appropriate inductive irregularities, such as a window of the type illustrated in Fig. 5-19a.

[2] Another waveguide arrangement, known as the *hybrid ring*, has properties similar to those of the magic T, and can be regarded as an alternative arrangement.   Various forms of the hybrid ring are described by W. A. Tyrell, Hybrid Circuits for Microwaves, *Proc. IRE*, vol. 35, p. 1294, November, 1947.

[3] Further material on this subject, particularly design information, is given by Moreno, *op. cit.*, pp. 150–157; also see "Waveguide Handbook," *op. cit.*, chap. 5.

an obstacle that acts as a parallel resonant shunt will have no effect on the transmission at the resonant frequency of the obstacle, but at all frequencies differing appreciably from the resonant frequency it will introduce a low shunting reactance that permits very little energy to be transmitted past the obstacle.

Ridged Waveguides.[1]   Under some circumstances there is an advantage in providing a rectangular waveguide with a ridge analogous to the ridge shown in Fig. 5-21b except not tapered.   This increases the cutoff wavelength, and widens the frequency range over which only the dominant mode will propagate.   Thus a ridged structure has advantages when physical compactness is important, and when the guide is to be used over

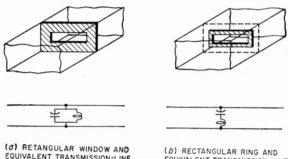

(a) RETANGULAR WINDOW AND EQUIVALENT TRANSMISSION-LINE CIRCUIT

(b) RECTANGULAR RING AND EQUIVALENT TRANSMISSION-LINE CIRCUIT

Fig. 5-28. Typical resonant obstacles, together with their equivalent transmission-line circuits.

an unusually wide frequency range.   At the same time, the attenuation of the ridged structure per unit length is greater than for the corresponding rectangular guide.   The impedance of the ridged structure analogous to the impedance defined in Eq. (5-12) is less than in a rectangular guide; this is sometimes an advantage when matching impedances (see Fig. 5-21b), or when coupling a coaxial line to a waveguide.

Comparison of Waveguides and Coaxial Transmission Lines.   Waveguides find their principal use in the transmission of power at wavelengths of the order of 10 cm or less, under conditions where low attenuation or high power-carrying capacity is important.   The power losses in a waveguide will be of the order of one-third as great as in a comparable coaxial line having air dielectric with supporting insulators, and the superiority is many times greater as compared with the best flexible cable.   The power-carrying capacity of a waveguide as limited by flashover is likewise from three to ten times as great as that of a standard coaxial line having air dielectric with supporting insulators, and may be of the order of thousands of times as great as that of a flexible cable with solid dielectric.

[1] For further details see Seymour B. Cohn, Properties of Ridge Wave Guide, *Proc. IRE*, vol. 35, p. 783, August, 1947.

A waveguide must have a size that is a reasonable fraction of a wavelength. This is an advantage at very short wavelengths, such as 1 cm, where coaxial lines with proportions that avoid higher modes are prohibitively small. However, at wavelengths much greater than 10 cm, the waveguide becomes undesirably large and so then finds use only in special applications. Other things being equal, waveguides also have the advantage in mechanical simplicity over coaxial lines with air insulation and dielectric support.

5-10. Cavity Resonators.[1] Any space enclosed by conducting walls possesses a resonant frequency for each particular type of field configuration that can exist in the space. Resonators of this type, commonly called *cavity resonators*, find extensive use as resonant circuits at extremely high frequencies. Their behavior is analogous to that of coil-and-capacitor combinations, but for microwave frequencies cavity resonators have the advantages of reasonable dimensions, simplicity, remarkably high Q, and very high shunt impedance.

Cavity resonators can take many forms, since any enclosed surface, irrespective of how irregular its outline, forms a cavity resonator. The simplest cavity resonator is a length of circular or rectangular waveguide short-circuited at each end to form a cylinder or rectangular prism, respectively. A spherical cavity is also of interest from a theoretical point of view, although not very useful in a practical way. Cavities such as illustrated in the lower half of Fig. 5-29, in which the opposite sides are brought close together to form a reentrant structure, are of importance when an electron beam is passed through the cavity, as in klystron tubes.[2] In such arrangements, the electric field is very strong in the gap formed by the reentrant sections, thus permitting effective interaction with electrons passing across this gap.

Cavity resonators can also be derived from coaxial lines. For example, a line short-circuited at each end, as in Fig. 5-30a, is resonant whenever the length is a multiple of a half wavelength. Alternatively, it is possible to arrange a coaxial transmission line, as illustrated in Fig. 5-30b; this can be regarded as a line short-circuited at one end and open at the other end except for the localized capacitance between the center conductor and

---

[1] Resonant cavities were introduced to radio by W. W. Hansen, A Type of Electrical Resonator, *J. Appl. Phys.*, vol. 9, p. 654, October, 1938. Useful information on properties of cavities is given by Moreno, *op. cit.*, pp. 210–241; Terman and Pettit, *op. cit.*, pp. 204–210; I. G. Wilson, C. W. Schramm, and J. P. Kinzer, High Q Resonant Cavities for Microwave Testing, *Bell System Tech. J.*, vol. 25, p. 408, July, 1946; J. P. Kinzer and I. G. Wilson, Some Results on Cylindrical Cavity Resonators, *Bell System Tech. J.*, vol. 26, p. 410, July, 1947; End Plate and Side Wall Currents in Circular Cylinder Cavity Resonator, *ibid.*, vol. 26, p. 31, January, 1947.

[2] Properties of such resonators are given by T. E. Moreno, *op. cit.*; also see W. W. Hansen and R. D. Richtmyer, On Resonators Suitable for Klystron Oscillators, *J. Appl Phys.* vol. 10, p. 189, March, 1939.

the conducting surface that closes the end of the line.   It is also possible
to regard the cavity of Fig. 5-30*b* as a reentrant cavity analogous to that
of Fig. 5-29*f*.[1]

Modes in Cavities.   As in waveguides, it is possible for many different
types of field configurations, or modes, to exist in a cavity.   Associated
with each such mode is a resonant frequency that is determined by the
particular field configuration involved and by the cavity dimensions.

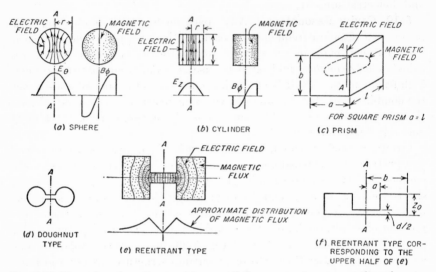

Fig. 5-29. Examples of cavity resonators.   All these resonators except the prism are
shown as cross sections of figures of revolution.   The field distributions shown for
certain of the resonators correspond to the distributions with the dominant mode of
operation.

Thus each cavity resonator possesses an infinite number of resonant frequencies.   As in the case of the waveguide, the lowest resonant frequency
associated with a particular cavity is termed the *dominant mode*, while
the remaining resonant frequencies are referred to as higher-order modes.

The cavity modes can in many cases be associated with waveguide
modes.   Thus in the case of the rectangular prism of Fig. 5-29*c*, a TE or
TM wave traveling in the *l* direction will be in resonance whenever the
frequency is such as to make the cavity length *l* a multiple of half of a
guide wavelength for the mode in question.   An analogous situation also

[1] Resonant lines of this type are sometimes termed hybrid lines, since as the center
conductor is shortened in length compared with the length of the outer conductor
(*see c* and *d* of Fig. 5-30), the behavior, including field configurations, is intermediate
between that of a resonant line and that of a cylindrical cavity.   The properties of
coaxial cavity resonators are discussed by W. L. Barrow and W. W. Mieher, Natural
Oscillations of Electrical Cavity Resonators, *Proc. IRE*, vol. 28, p. 184, April, 1940;
also see W. W. Hansen, On the Resonant Frequency of Closed Concentric Lines,
J. Appl. Phys., vol. 10, p. 38, January, 1939.

exists with cylindrical cavities.　However, in the case of the cylindrical cavity, it happens that the dominant mode corresponds to the field configuration illustrated in Fig. 5-29*b*, for which there is no waveguide counterpart.　In contrast, the dominant mode for the rectangular prism corresponds to the TE_{10} waveguide mode traveling along the axis that is longest when measured in guide wavelengths.　In reentrant cavities, the dominant mode corresponds to a field configuration of the type illustrated in Fig. 5-29*e*; here the electric field is most intense in the gap.

Modes in a cavity are classified as transverse electric (TE) or transverse magnetic (TM) modes, corresponding as far as possible to the analogous waveguide modes.　The particular mode of any such class is then commonly designated by three subscripts.　Thus the field configuration

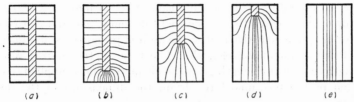

FIG. 5-30. Transition from concentric line to cylindrical cavity, showing electric fields for various intermediate or hybrid cases.

shown in Fig. 5-29*b* is the TM_{010} mode.　Here TM denotes that the magnetic field lies in planes transverse to the axis of the cylinder, while the first and third subscripts denote, respectively, that the variation of the magnetic field is zero with radial direction and with position along the axis, and the second subscript indicates that there is one-half cycle of variation in the field along a radial line passing from one edge of the cylinder to the other edge.　Again, the field configuration indicated in Fig. 5-29*c* is the TE_{101} mode, meaning that the electric field is transverse to an axis in the *l* direction and that the variation of the electric field is one-half cycle, zero, and one-half cycle in the *a*, *b*, and *l* directions, respectively.

A cavity resonator possesses many more modes than does the corresponding waveguide.　For example, in the rectangular prism of Fig. 5-29*c*, there are an infinite number of TE_{10n} modes for each of the three axes of the prism.　Thus a triple infinity of modes exists in the rectangular prism corresponding to the single infinity of TE_{no} waveguide modes. As a result, at frequencies appreciably greater than that corresponding to resonance at the dominant mode, it is found that the resonant frequencies of cavities will be extremely closely spaced.　This results in an impossible situation if one wishes to obtain pure mode operation; at the same time, it is an advantage if one desires to make it as easy as possible for the cavity to resonate with an arbitrary exciting frequency.

Resonant Frequency of Cavity Resonators. A resonant frequency of a cavity resonator corresponds to a possible solution of Maxwell's equations for the electric and magnetic fields within the resonator. The resonant frequencies (or wavelengths) can be calculated mathematically for geometrical shapes such as spheres, cylinders, and rectangular prisms and some idealized forms of reentrant sections. Formulas for the resonant wavelength of the dominant mode are given in Table 5-3 for spheres, cylinders, and square prisms. In the case of prisms it will be noted that the length l corresponds to $\lambda_g/2$ for the corresponding TE_{10} waveguide mode.[1]

The resonant wavelength is proportional in all cases to the size of the resonator; i.e., if all dimensions are doubled, the wavelength corresponding to resonance will likewise be doubled. This fact simplifies the construction of resonators of shapes that cannot be calculated. To obtain a resonator operating exactly at a desired frequency, one first constructs a resonator of convenient size and of the desired proportions and measures the resulting resonant wavelength. The ratio of the desired resonant wavelength to this wavelength gives a scale factor that is applied to every dimension of the test model to obtain the dimensions of the desired resonator.

The resonant frequency of a cavity resonator can be changed by altering the mechanical dimensions, by coupling reactance into the resonator, or by means of a copper paddle. Small changes in mechanical dimensions can be achieved by flexing walls, while large changes require some type of sliding member. Reactance can be coupled into the resonator through a coupling loop in the manner discussed below, thus affecting the resonant frequency. A copper paddle placed inside the resonator will affect the normal distribution of flux and tend to alter the resonant frequency by an amount that can be controlled by the orientation of the paddle.

Q of Cavity Resonators. The Q of a cavity resonator has the same significance as for an ordinary resonant circuit. It can be defined on the basis that when the response has dropped to 70.7 per cent of the response at resonance, the cycles off resonance are the resonant frequency divided by $2Q$ (see Rule 1, page 49). In the case of cavity resonators, it is also sometimes convenient to base the definition of Q upon Eq. (3-1), namely,

$$Q = 2\pi \frac{\text{energy stored}}{\text{energy lost per cycle}} \tag{5-14}$$

The energy stored is proportional to the square of the magnetic flux density integrated throughout the volume of the resonator, while the energy lost per cycle in the walls is proportional to the skin depth and to the square of the magnetic flux density integrated over the surface of the

[1] Design data for reentrant cavities of the type illustrated in Fig. 5-29d and e are given by Moreno, *op. cit.*, pp. 230–238.

cavity.   Thus, to obtain high Q, the resonator should have a large ratio of volume to surface area, since it is the volume that stores energy and it is the surface area that dissipates energy.   As a consequence, resonators such as spheres, cylinders, and prisms can in general be expected to have higher Q's than corresponding resonators with pronounced reentrant sections.

TABLE 5-3

PROPERTIES OF CAVITY RESONATORS FOR DOMINANT MODE

Type of cavity	Sphere	Cylinder	Square prism
Figure illustrating notation....	5-29a	5-29b	5-29c
Wavelength λ_0 at resonance....	2.28r	2.61r	1.414a
Q..........................	$0.318\dfrac{\lambda_0}{\delta}$	$0.383\dfrac{1}{1+(r/h)}\dfrac{\lambda_0}{\delta}$	$0.353\dfrac{1}{1+(a/2b)}\dfrac{\lambda_0}{\delta}$
Shunt impedance across AA at resonance................	$104.4\dfrac{\lambda_0}{\delta}$	$72\dfrac{h}{r}\dfrac{1}{1+(r/h)}\dfrac{\lambda_0}{\delta}$	$120\dfrac{b}{a}\dfrac{1}{1+(a/2b)}\dfrac{\lambda_0}{\delta}$

All dimensions are in centimeters.

δ = skin depth as defined by Eq. (2-10)

   = $6.62/\sqrt{f}$ cm for copper, where f is in cycles

Quantitative analysis leads to the formulas given in Table 5-3 for the Q of the dominant mode of spheres, cylinders, and square prisms.   Some typical values of Q obtainable in practical cavity resonators are given in Table 5-4.   It will be noted that the values are extremely high compared with those encountered in ordinary resonant circuits (e.g., Fig. 2-16). This is true even in the case of the reentrant cavity.

TABLE 5-4

PROPERTIES OF TYPICAL CAVITY RESONATORS
WHEN OPERATING IN THE DOMINANT MODE

Resonator	Dimensions, cm	Resonant wave-length λ_0, cm	Q (copper walls)	Shunt resistance, ohms (copper walls)
Sphere.................	$r = 5$	11.4	28,000	9.7×10^6
Cylinder................	$r = h/2 = 5$	13.0	24,000	9.1×10^6
Square prism (cube).......	$a = b = l = 10$	14.1	23,000	7.8×10^6
Reentrant (Fig. 5-29f).....	$a = 0.81$	12.8	4,000	0.17×10^6
	$b = 1.69$	(approx.)	(approx.)	(approx.)
	$z_0 = 1.82$			
	$d/2 = 0.20$			

The Q of resonators of the same proportions but of different size will be proportional to the square root of the resonant wavelength.   This arises from the fact that, whereas the ratio of volume to wall surface is proportional to a resonant wavelength, the skin depth (and hence the energy dissipation per unit of surface) is proportional to the square root of the wavelength.

Shunt Impedance of Cavity Resonators. The shunt impedance of a cavity resonator between two surfaces, such as those intersected by the axis AA in Fig. 5-29, can be defined as the square of the line integral of voltage along a path such as AA divided by the power loss in the resonator when excited to give the voltage used in the line integration. This impedance corresponds to the parallel resonant impedance of a tuned circuit, and at resonance becomes a resistance termed the shunt resistance of the resonator.

The shunt resistance obtained with spheres, cylinders, and square prisms operating in the dominant mode can be calculated from the formulas given in Table 5-3. Values of shunt resistance for the dominant mode in several typical cases are given in Table 5-4, and are seen to be very large compared with the shunt resistances obtainable with ordinary resonant circuits. It is further to be noted that although the shunt resistance of the reentrant cavity is much less than that of the other cavities, this impedance is developed across such a short distance that the impedance per unit length is of the same order of magnitude as the maximum value obtainable with other geometries.

5-11. Coupling to Cavity Resonators. To make use of a cavity resonator it must be coupled in some manner to a transmission line or

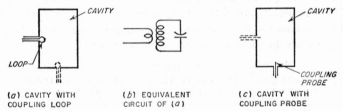

(a) CAVITY WITH   (b) EQUIVALENT   (c) CAVITY WITH
COUPLING LOOP   CIRCUIT OF (a)   COUPLING PROBE

Fig. 5-31. Loop and probe coupling to cavity resonator.

waveguide. One means of accomplishing this is to employ a small loop so oriented as to link with magnetic flux lines existing in the desired mode of operation, as illustrated in Fig. 5-31a. A current passed through such a loop will then excite oscillations of this mode· conversely, oscillations existing in the resonator will induce a voltage in the coupling loop. The combination of the coupling loop and cavity resonator is equivalent to the inductively coupled system of Fig. 5-31b. In such a system, the ratio of the impedance that the cavity couples into the loop to the shunt resistance of the cavity resonator is equal to the square of the ratio of the coupled flux to the total magnetic flux lying to one side of the cylinder axis.[1] The

[1] When the plane of the coupling loop is at right angles to the direction of the flux lines, the loop area is in the most favorable position for enclosing magnetic flux; then if the loop is located at a position where the magnetic flux density approximates the

magnitude of the magnetic coupling can be readily controlled by the orientation of the loop, and its location with respect to the magnetic field. Thus the coupling is reduced to zero when the plane of the loop is rotated so that it is parallel to the magnetic flux. Also the coupling will be low if the loop is placed at a point of low magnetic flux density; thus a loop near the vertical axis, as shown dotted in Fig. 5-31a, will have little coupling to the dominant mode.

Coupling to a cavity can also be achieved by means of a probe as illustrated in Fig. 5-31c. Here the electric flux of the desired mode terminates on the probe, inducing a current in it; conversely a voltage applied to the probe produces electric fields inside the cavity that excite oscillations. This is thus a form of capacitive coupling, the magnitude of which is determined (1) by the surface that the probe exposes to the electric field of oscillations of the desired mode and (2) by the intensity of the electric field at the position of the probe. Thus maximum coupling is obtained in a cylindrical cavity operating in the TM_{010} mode when the probe is located on the axis as shown; the coupling to this mode will be zero if the probe projects into the cavity from the side wall instead of the end (dotted probe in Fig. 5-31c).

Still another method of coupling to a cavity is by means of a hole or slot. The principles involved in this situation are the same as in the corresponding waveguide case, and are discussed in detail on page 133.

PROBLEMS AND EXERCISES

5-1. Sketch fields corresponding to the side view in Fig. 5-2, for three successive values of time each differing by one-quarter of a cycle. Show the three cases one above the other.

5-2. Sketch field distributions similar to those of Fig. 5-2, for $\lambda = 1.5a$, being careful to show λ_g and a to scale.

5-3. A particular rectangular waveguide has a width of 2 in. and a height of 1 in. What is the lowest frequency wave that will be transmitted by this waveguide?

5-4. Calculate and plot the ratio of phase shift per unit length in a rectangular waveguide (dominant mode) to the phase shift per unit length in a coaxial transmission line having air dielectric, as the dimension a of the waveguide is varied from 0.55λ to λ.

5-5. A wave having a frequency of 10,000 Mc travels down a rectangular guide for which dimension $a = 2$ cm. Calculate the value of β per cm, and compare the result with the value of β that would be obtained at the same frequency on an air-filled coaxial line.

5-6. What is the ratio v_p/c at a frequency such that the guide width a is exactly $\lambda_g/2$?

---

average flux density in the cavity, one has to a rough approximation:

$$\left.\begin{array}{l}\text{Impedance coupled} \\ \text{into loop}\end{array}\right\} = \left(\frac{\text{area of loop}}{\text{half of cross-sectional}}\atop{\text{area of cavity}}\right)\left(\text{shunt impedance}\atop\text{of cavity}\right) \quad (5\text{-}15)$$

5-7. Draw curves similar to those of Fig. 5-4, but for $a = 0.55\lambda$ and $a = 0.7\lambda$. Be careful to show a and λ_g to scale.

5-8. In a waveguide operating at a wavelength of 3 cm, calculate the depth in the copper walls at which the current density is reduced to 0.0001 of the density at the inner surface of the walls.

5-9. In the waveguide of Fig. 5-5, discuss how the distribution of the current flowing in the walls will change at times differing by (a) one-half cycle, and (b) one-quarter cycle.

5-10. In Fig. 5-5, what would be the consequences of making holes 1 and 4 round instead of rectangular, assuming that the area of the hole is the same in each case?

5-11. In Fig. 5-5, what effects are produced on the electric coupling by making slot 1 half as long and twice as wide, thus keeping the area of the opening unchanged?

5-12. An incident TE_{10} wave of 5000 Mc travels down the guide of Fig. 5-6. How far must it go before the amplitude is reduced to 70.7 per cent of the initial amplitude?

5-13. A rectangular waveguide has dimensions 2.5 by 5 cm. Determine λ_g, β, and phase velocity at a wavelength of 4.5 cm for the dominant mode and the first higher-order mode, and tabulate results side by side.

5-14. What are the lowest frequencies for which the waveguide of Prob. 5-13 will transmit (a) the dominant mode, and (b) the first higher-order mode?

5-15. A rectangular waveguide is 2 by 3 cm. What are the cutoff wavelengths for the dominant and the first two higher-order modes?

5-16. What higher-order modes will tend to be excited in a waveguide by the coaxial line exciting systems illustrated in the attached figure?

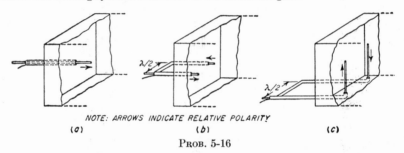

NOTE: ARROWS INDICATE RELATIVE POLARITY

(a)   (b)   (c)

PROB. 5-16

5-17. Suggest an arrangement involving a coaxial line terminating in a loop for exciting the TM_{11} mode in a rectangular waveguide.

5-18. In a rectangular guide in which $a = 4$ cm, calculate and plot cutoff wavelength as a function of b/a for $b/a = 0$ to $b/a = 1$, for TE_{10}, TE_{01}, TE_{20}, TE_{11}, and TM_{11} modes.

5-19. Which of the following modes will be unaffected by the posts of Fig. 5-9 (assuming the posts are located midway between the vertical sides): TE_{10}, TE_{01}, TE_{20}, TM_{11}, TM_{21}?

5-20. Draw a diagram similar to Fig. 5-12, but assume $\theta = 70°$. Be sure to mark the distances representing λ and λ_g. Compare the ratio λ_g/λ_c with the ratio for Fig. 5-12, and show that the result is consistent with Fig. 5-3.

5-21. Explain how Fig. 5-14 is consistent with the fact, deduced from Eq. (5-6), that with a given guide, the cutoff wavelength for the TE_{20} mode will always be exactly twice the cutoff wavelength for the TE_{10} mode.

5-22. Sketch curves for the TE_{11} mode, analogous to those given in the right-hand part of Fig. 5-15a, for a frequency of 3000 Mc in a circular waveguide when the *diameter* of the guide is (a) 6.3 cm, and (b) 8 cm. Draw the curves to full-scale size, and be careful to show λ_g correctly.

5-23. In a circular waveguide in which the radius is 1.5 in. ($r = 3.8$ cm) calculate the value of β and the phase velocity for the dominant mode at a wavelength of 10 cm.

5-24. One has available in a wall a circular hole of 2 in. *diameter* through which a waveguide is to be passed. If it is desired to obtain the longest possible cutoff wavelength, what are the relative merits of the following guides: (a) circular; (b) rectangular, $a = b$; (c) rectangular, $b/a = 0.5$; and (d) rectangular, $b/a \rightarrow 0$?

5-25. A long, narrow longitudinal slot is to be cut in the wall of a circular waveguide. Assuming the fields in the guide are as shown in Fig. 5-15a, where should this slot be located on the circumference of the guide if it is desired that the slot provide (a) coupling to the electric field, but not to the magnetic field inside the guide, and (b) magnetic coupling but no electric coupling?

5-26. Plot the voltage (i.e., electric field) distribution of the standing-wave pattern as a function of position from 0 to 20 cm from the receiver for a rectangular waveguide carrying a wave having a free-space wavelength of 10 cm, when the receiving end of the waveguide is short-circuited and the waveguide dimensions are 6 by 3 cm. Show the position of the minima and maxima accurately. Neglect attenuation.

5-27. The rectangular waveguide illustrated in Fig. 5-6 carries a TE_{10} wave of 5000 Mc. If the standing-wave ratio produced at the load end of the waveguide is 2, what will be the standing-wave ratio 100 ft from the load end of the line?

5-28. In a 6 by 3 cm rectangular guide, calculate and plot the waveguide impedance Z_0, as a function of frequency, from cutoff to twice the cutoff frequency.

5-29. How should a longitudinal vane projecting radially inward from the side of a circular waveguide carrying the TE_{11} mode be arranged to serve as (a) a mode filter, and (b) as an impedance-matching device?

5-30. Explain why in Fig. 5-18 a probe projecting into the guide from the side, with its axis horizontal, will be of no assistance in impedance matching for the TE_{10} mode, but would be useful in the case of TE_{01}, TE_{11}, and TM_{11} modes.

5-31. The power transmitted down a rectangular waveguide is to be delivered to a 50 ohm load resistance that is connected between the top and bottom sides of the guide, and matched by a tapered section, as in Fig. 5-21a. If the guide on the input side of the taper is 2.5 by 1.25 in. and the frequency is 3000 Mc, then what is the required height on the load side of the taper?

5-32. The 50-ohm load in Prob. 5-31 is matched to the guide by being placed off center, as in case b in Fig. 5-20, instead of by tapering the guide. How far to the side of the center line should the load resistance be placed?

5-33. In a particular rectangular waveguide attenuator based upon the TE_{10} mode, it is desired that the attenuation be exactly 10 db per in. Determine the width that the waveguide must have, assuming that the wavelength is many times the waveguide width.

5-34. In a circular waveguide attenuator, it is found that at a particular distance from the source of excitation there is an undesired TE_{01} mode present which is 30 db weaker than the desired TE_{11} mode. If the fields are now examined at a position where the attenuation to the TE_{11} mode is increased by 48 db, how strong is the undesired TE_{01} mode output compared with the TE_{11} output?

5-35. *a.* Repeat Prob. 5-34, but assume that the modes are interchanged; i.e., assume that initially the TE_{01} mode (which is now the desired mode) is 30 db stronger than the TE_{11} mode.

b. Explain why in this case the attentuation in decibels per inch will be different for large values of attenuation as compared with small values of attenuation.

5-36. In a circular waveguide attenuator using the TE_{11} mode, what will be the effect of rotating the pickup coil 90° about the axis of the guide?

5-37. A coaxial line is to be coupled to a waveguide in the manner illustrated in Fig. 5-8. If a good impedance match is desired, show that the guide cannot have the proportion $a/b = 2.0$ if the characteristic impedance of the coaxial line is in the range 50 to 100 ohms.

5-38. If the slot in Fig. 5-25 were replaced by a round hole aligned with the center axis of the guide, what mode would be excited in the waveguide by energy in the coaxial line?

5-39. Suggest a means by which a coaxial line could be coupled to a circular waveguide in such a manner as to excite the TE_{11} mode.

5-40. Describe an experimental means which could be used to measure the terminating impedance actually existing on a waveguide without removing this unknown terminating impedance from its guide, and involving a magic-T junction and a calibrated adjustable terminating impedance.

5-41. A waveguide system possesses an obstacle, the exact nature of which is not known, although the position of the obstacle is. Explain how, by the aid of standing-wave measurements, one can determine whether the obstacle is inductive, capacitive, series resonant, or shunt resonant.

5-42. Sketch curves showing qualitatively how the electric and magnetic fields are distributed in a cylindrical cavity resonator operating in the TE_{11} waveguide mode, under conditions where the cavity is a half guide-wavelength long.

5-43. Derive the formula given in Table 5-3 for the wavelength of a square prism type of cavity from the properties of the TE_{10} mode in a rectangular waveguide.

5-44. In a cavity that is a rectangular prism operating in the TE_{10} waveguide mode, it is found that the resonant frequency is independent of the dimension b in Fig. 5-29c. Explain how this is consistent with waveguide theory.

5-45. Derive a formula for the resonant frequency of a cylindrical cavity formed by a section of length h of the guide shown in Fig. 5-15a, short-circuited at both ends, and operating in the TE_{11} waveguide mode in such a manner that one-half cycle of field variation occurs in the h direction.

5-46. Show that, when a cylindrical cavity is operated in the waveguide TE_{11} mode, the resonant frequency depends on both the radius and length of the cavity.

5-47. A particular cavity with copper walls is found to have a Q of 10,000. The walls are then plated with a material having a resistivity seven times that of copper. What value will the Q then have, assuming that the plating is relatively thick?

5-48. A cylindrical cavity has a radius of 2 in. and is 6 in. long. Calculate the resonant frequency for the mode illustrated in Fig. 5-29b (the dominant mode), the circuit Q, and the shunt impedance, assuming copper walls. Tabulate the results.

5-49. A sphere, cylinder, and square prism (cube) are all so proportioned as to have the same resonant wavelength of 12.8 cm. Calculate Q, shunt impedance, and shunt impedance per unit length of shunt path, for each case. Tabulate the results, and include in the table the corresponding results from Table 5-4 for the reentrant cavity of Fig. 5-29f. Also give in the tabulation the largest linear dimension (i.e., diameter, or length of side) for each resonator.

5-50. A coupling loop 1 cm in diameter is inserted in the cylindrical cavity resonator of Table 5-4, as in Fig. 5-31a. Calculate the approximate value of the impedance that the resonator will couple into this loop at resonance, considering the resonator as a secondary, and the loop as a primary.

5-51. *a.* Describe how to locate a probe so as to couple to the TE_{101} cavity mode illustrated in Fig. 5-29c.

b. How could a loop be arranged to couple to the same mode? Give both the location of the loop and the required orientation of its plane.

CHAPTER 6

FUNDAMENTAL PROPERTIES OF ELECTRON TUBES

6-1. Electron Tubes. Devices that utilize the flow of free electrons in a vacuum or a partial vacuum are referred to as electron tubes. Such tubes are used to generate the radio-frequency power required by radio and radar transmitters, to control the energy thus generated, to amplify the weak radio-frequency signals present at the receiver, to rectify or "detect" the signal, to amplify this rectified signal, and so on. The electron tube has made possible the long-distance telephone, talking pictures, public-address systems, modern broadcasting, television, high-frequency and microwave radio, radar, guided missiles etc. Altogether, it may be said that the electron tube is one of the most important devices that has resulted from modern science.

6-2. Electrons, Ions, and Their Motions. *Free Electrons and Ions.* Free electrons can be produced in a number of ways. The method normally employed in electron tubes is *thermionic emission,* in which advantage is taken of the fact that, if a solid body is heated sufficiently, some of the electrons that it contains will escape from its surface into the surrounding space. Radiation represented by ultraviolet light, X rays, and visible light falling on appropriate surfaces will cause electrons to be emitted even at normal temperatures. Electrons obtained in this way from the action of visible light are said to result from the *photoelectric* effect. Electrons are also ejected from solid materials as a result of the impact of rapidly moving electrons or ions. This is referred to as *secondary electron emission,* because it is necessary to have a primary source of electrons (or ions) before the secondary emission can be obtained. Finally, it is possible to pull electrons directly out of solid substances by an intense electrostatic field at the surface; this action is termed *field emission.*

Positive ions represent atoms or molecules that have lost one or more electrons. They are hence charged bodies having a weight approximating that of the atom or molecule concerned, and a positive charge equal to the negative charge of the lost electrons. Unlike electrons, positive ions are not all alike and may differ in charge or weight, or both. They are much heavier than electrons and resemble the molecule or atom from which derived. Ions are designated according to their origin, such as mercury ions or hydrogen ions.

Positive ions are produced when a rapidly moving electron (or previously produced ion) strikes a gas molecule with sufficient velocity to dislodge an electron from the gas molecule.   This process is referred to as *ionization by collision.*

Negative ions represent atoms or molecules that have one or more excess electrons attached.   Negative ions occur much less commonly than positive ions.

Motions of Electrons and Ions in an Electrostatic Field.[1]   Electrons and ions are charged particles and so have forces exerted upon them by an electrostatic field in the same way that other charged bodies do.   The electrons, being negatively charged, travel toward the positive or anode electrode, while the positively charged ions travel in the other direction toward the negative or cathode electrode.   The force exerted upon a charged particle by an electrostatic field is proportional to the product of the charge e of the particle and the voltage gradient G of the electrostatic field.   Expressed in the form of an equation this relation is

$$\text{Force in dynes} = \begin{pmatrix} \text{gradient } G \text{ in} \\ \text{volts per cm} \end{pmatrix} (\text{charge } e \text{ in coulombs}) \times 10^7 \quad (6\text{-}1)$$
$$= Ge \times 10^7$$

This force upon the ion or electron is in the direction of the electrostatic-flux lines at the point where the charge is located and acts toward or away from the positive terminal, depending on whether a negative or positive charge, respectively, is involved.

The energy that a charged particle acquires in traveling (i.e., falling) between two points having a difference of potential of V volts is

$$\text{Energy in joules} = Ve \quad (6\text{-}2)$$

where e is the particle charge in coulombs.   This relation follows from the fact that the energy is equal to the product of force and distance.   It will be noted that the energy which a charged body acquires in falling through a given potential difference is independent of the mass of the particle.

The force that the field exerts on the charged particle causes an acceleration in the direction of the field at a rate that can be calculated by the ordinary laws of mechanics when the velocity does not approach that of light.   That is,

$$\begin{matrix} \text{Acceleration in cm} \\ \text{per sec per sec} \end{matrix} \Big\} = \frac{\text{force in dynes}}{\text{mass in grams}} \quad (6\text{-}3)$$

The velocity an electron or ion acquires in being acted upon by an electrostatic field can be conveniently expressed in terms of the voltage through which the electron (or ion) has fallen in acquiring the velocity.

[1] For more details see K. R. Spangenberg, "Vacuum Tubes," chap. 6, McGraw-Hill Book Company, Inc., New York, 1948.

The relationship between velocity v and the accelerating voltage V is, for velocities well below the velocity[1] of light,

$$v = \left\{ \begin{array}{l} \text{velocity in cm per sec} \\ \text{corresponding to } V \end{array} \right. = \sqrt{\frac{2Ve \times 10^7}{m}} \qquad (6\text{-}4)$$

where e is in coulombs and m is the mass of the particle in grams. In the case where e and m correspond to values appropriate for an electron, Eq. (6-4) becomes

$$\left. \begin{array}{l} \text{Electron velocity} \\ \text{corresponding to } V \end{array} \right\} = 59.3 \sqrt{V} \times 10^6 \text{ cm per sec} \qquad (6\text{-}5)$$

The velocity with which electrons and ions move in fields of even moderate strength is very great. Thus an electron dropping through a potential difference of 10 volts will attain a velocity of 1160 miles per sec; at 2500 volts it has a velocity approximately one-tenth the velocity of light.

When the velocity is expressed in volts, it is to be noted that the resulting actual velocity corresponding to a given voltage is inversely proportional to the square root of the mass of the particle. Thus a mercury ion having a charge equal to that of an electron will move less than $\frac{1}{600}$ as fast as an electron in the same electrostatic field.

Effect of a Magnetic Field on a Moving Electron. An electron (or ion) in motion represents an electric current of magnitude ev, where e is the magnitude of the charge on the electron, and v is its velocity. A magnetic field accordingly exerts a force on a moving electron exactly as it exerts a force on an electric current in a wire. The magnitude of the

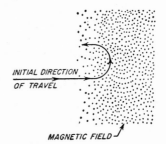

INITIAL DIRECTION
OF TRAVEL

MAGNETIC FIELD

FIG. 6-1. Path of moving electron entering a magnetic field.

force is proportional to the product of the equivalent current ev represented by the moving electron, and the strength of the *component* of the magnetic field in the plane at *right angles* to the motion of the electron. The resulting force is then in a direction at right angles both to the direction of motion of the electron and to the component of the magnetic field that is producing the force. As a result, an electron entering a magnetic field with high velocity will follow a curved path similar to that shown in Fig. 6-1. The radius of curvature of this path is smaller the greater the

[1] This follows from the fact that the energy acquired by the particle, as given by Eq. (6-2), is all converted to kinetic energy of motion. Thus the velocity in Eq. (6-4) is obtained from the relation:

$$Ve = (mv^2/2) \times 10^{-7}$$

strength of the magnetic field, and the more slowly the electron is moving through the field.[1]

Effect of Combined Electric and Magnetic Fields on Electrons. When an electron is subjected to the simultaneous action of both electric and magnetic fields, the resulting force acting on the electron is the vector sum of the force due to the electric field and that due to the magnetic field, each considered separately. The electron motion that results depends on the magnitude and direction of the initial velocity of the electron, and upon the magnitude and direction of the magnetic field, and of the electric field, all considered as vectors in space. A variety of effects can be obtained depending on the relative orientation of these three vectors. Particular cases of importance in electronics work where electrons are acted on simultaneously by electric and magnetic fields occur in the magnetron tube (see Sec. 19-6) and in the propagation of radio waves through the ionosphere (see Sec. 22-8).

6-3. Thermionic Emission of Electrons. The electrical conductivity of metals is the result of electrons within the material which at the moment are not definitely attached to any particular molecule. For these free electrons to escape from the surface, they must perform a certain amount of work to overcome gravitational-like forces of attraction present at the surface. Hence, unless the available kinetic energy of a free electron within the material exceeds the work that the electron must perform to overcome the surface forces of the conductor, the electron cannot escape. For all known substances this energy which an electron must expend in escaping is so related to the kinetic energy possessed by the electrons in the material that practically none escape at room temperature unless aided by additional energy obtained from incident radiation (light, X rays, etc.), or high-velocity particles, striking the surface. However, as the temperature of the conductor is increased, the kinetic energy of the free electrons in the material is increased. At sufficiently high temperatures an appreciable number of electrons will have the kinetic energy required to escape through the surface of the material. This results in *thermionic emission of electrons.*

---

[1] The radius R of the curvature of the path followed by the electron is

$$R = 3.37 \ \sqrt{\bar{V}}/B \text{ cm} \tag{6-6}$$

where V is the velocity of the electron in volts and B is the component of magnetic flux density at right angles to the velocity in gauss. When the magnetic field is uniform, the path traversed by the electrons is a circle. The frequency of rotation is the number of times the electron would travel around such a circle in 1 sec, and is

$$\left. \begin{array}{c} \text{Frequency of rotation} \\ \text{in cycles} \end{array} \right\} = 2.80 \times 10^6 B \tag{6-7}$$

It is to be noted that this frequency, which is sometimes called the *cyclotron frequency,* is independent of the velocity V of the electron.

The process of thermionic emission from a solid substance is very similar to the evaporation of vapor from the surface of a liquid.   In the case of the vapor the evaporated molecules are molecules that have obtained sufficient kinetic energy to overcome the restraining forces at the surface of the liquid, and the number of such molecules increases rapidly as the temperature is raised.   The thermionic emission of electrons from hot bodies is seen to represent the same process.   It can be considered as an evaporation of electrons in which the energy the electron must give up in escaping corresponds to the latent heat of vaporization of the liquid.

The number of electrons evaporated per unit area of emitting surface is related to the absolute temperature T of the emitting material and a quantity b that is a measure of the work an electron must perform in escaping through the surface, according-ing to the equation

$$I = AT^2\epsilon^{-b/T}   \qquad (6\text{-}8)$$

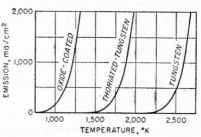

FIG. 6-2. Variation of electron emission with absolute temperature of typical emitters.

where I is the electron current in amperes per square centimeter and A is a constant, the value of which may vary with the type of emitter. The type of relationship represented by Eq. (6-8) is shown in Fig. 6-2.   It is characterized by a very rapid rate of increase of emission with increase in temperature, once the temperature is sufficient to cause significant emission.

Practical Emitters.[1]   The properties of matter are such that thermionic emission of electrons does not become appreciable until temperatures of the order of 900°K or higher are reached.   This fact, together with considerations relating to life, limits the number of substances available for use as practical thermionic emitters to a very few, of which tungsten, thoriated tungsten, and oxide-coated emitters are the only ones used commercially in vacuum tubes.

Tungsten is superior to other emitters in ability to operate under adverse conditions, particularly conditions associated with very high anode voltages.   However, tungsten is not used when thoriated-tungsten or oxide-coated emitters can be employed, as the emission efficiency of tungsten expressed in amperes emission per watt of heating power is not very high, even when the tungsten is operated at the highest temperature that will give reasonable life, i.e., about 2550°K.

Thoriated-tungsten emitters consist of tungsten containing a reducing

---

[1] For further information see Spangenberg, *op. cit.* chap. 4; Millman and Seely, "Electronics," chap. 6, McGraw-Hill Book Company, Inc., New York, 1951.

agent (ordinarily carbon) and a small quantity (1 or 2 per cent) of thorium oxide. Such cathodes when properly activated[1] give electron emission at temperatures of 500 to 600°K lower than does pure tungsten. This increased electron emission is the result of a layer of thorium one molecule deep that forms on the surface of the tungsten and reduces the work an electron must do to escape. During operation of a thoriated-tungsten emitter, thorium is being continuously evaporated from the surface layer, but is replenished by diffusion of additional thorium from the interior of the tungsten. Thoriated-tungsten emitters are always carbonized by converting the surface to tungsten carbide (W_2C). Since the thorium adheres much more firmly to a tungsten carbide surface than it does to tungsten, the result is that carbonizing reduces the rate of evaporation of the thorium.

The thorium layer on the surface of the thoriated-tungsten emitter tends to be stripped off when bombarded by positive ions. Carbonizing reduces this tendency to some extent, but in general, tubes employing thoriated-tungsten emitters must have a very high degree of vacuum. Otherwise, positive ions produced as a result of ionization by collision will seriously affect the electron emission.

Thoriated-tungsten emitters are more efficient than tungsten emitters in terms of the thermionically emitted current obtainable per watt of heating power. Practical thoriated-tungsten emitters also have a greater emission per unit surface than do other types of emitters. Thus thoriated tungsten has a definite field of usefulness, even though less efficient than the oxide-coated emitter; in particular, thoriated-tungsten emitters find extensive use in medium to large power tubes.

The oxide-coated emitter consists of a mixture of barium and strontium oxides coated on the surface of a suitable metal, commonly nickel or nickel alloy. When properly prepared and activated, such a surface will emit electrons profusely at a temperature of the order of 1150°K, as compared with an operating temperature of approximately 1900°K for thoriated tungsten.[2] Although the mechanism of operation of the oxide-coated emitter is only partially understood, it appears that the increased

---

[1] A typical activation procedure consists in heating the emitter to approximately 2600 to 2800°K for one or two minutes (called flashing) and then glowing for some minutes at an activating temperature of 2100 to 2200°K. The flashing raises the temperature to the point where the impregnated carbon reduces some of the thorium oxide to metallic thorium; the subsequent treatment at the activating temperature allows this thorium to diffuse to the surface to build up and maintain the mono-molecular surface layer of thorium.

[2] The details involved in producing and activating the oxide coating vary greatly from manufacturer to manufacturer. The coating is commonly applied to the core in the form of barium and strontium carbonates. These are reduced to the oxide by heating while the tube is on the pump. The emitter is then put through an activating cycle, the nature of which varies from one laboratory to the next.

emission arises as a result of free electrons in the semiconductor represented by the oxide coating.[1]

Oxide-coated emitters are used whenever possible, since they give more emission per watt of heating power than any other type of emitter. At the same time, the emitting surface is readily "poisoned" by impurities, and also deteriorates more rapidly than does thoriated tungsten when subjected to bombardment by high energy positive ions. Oxide-coated emitters are universally used in small tubes, and also in power tubes up to anode voltages of several thousands. Still higher operating voltages can be employed under carefully controlled conditions, but here tungsten and thoriated tungsten are commonly preferred.

Oxide-coated emitters have the unique and very valuable property of being able to give very high instantaneous electron emission for brief periods. This high transient emission, however, drops off in a comparatively few microseconds, and then is not fully restored until after a rest of at least a few hundred microseconds. This effect is utilized to advantage in tubes designed to generate short pulses of high power, such as radar transmitting tubes.

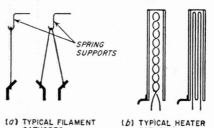

(a) TYPICAL FILAMENT CATHODES (b) TYPICAL HEATER CATHODES

FIG. 6-3. Typical filament and heater structures.

Practical Emitting Structures. A practical form of thermionic emitter consists of a filament of emitting material which is heated to the desired operating temperature by a current passing through the filament. Alternatively, the emitting structure may consist of an indirectly heated cathode comprising a cylinder of thin metal, usually nickel, covered with an oxide coating. The cylinder is heated by an internal insulated tungsten ftlament or "heater." Typical filament and heater structures are shown in Fig. 6-3. In the case of filaments, a spring suspension is usually employed to keep the filament taut as it expands with heating.

Velocity of Emission. An electron emitted from a hot cathode comes out with a velocity that represents the difference between the kinetic energy possessed by the electron just before emission and the energy that must be given up to escape. Since the energy of the different electrons within the emitter is not the same, the velocity of emission will be different for different electrons and will commonly range from zero up to over 1 volt.

Experiment shows that the velocities of emission are distributed very

[1] An extremely readable discussion of various viewpoints regarding the source of the emission in an oxide-coated cathode is given by J. R. Pierce, The Cathode Art, *Phys. Today*, vol. 2, p. 18, October, 1949.

nearly according to Maxwell's law for the distribution of velocities in a gas composed of electrons and having the temperature of the emitting cathode. The average velocity of emission accordingly increases with the cathode temperature, just as does the average velocity of gas molecules.

6-4. Secondary Emission.[1] Both metals and insulators will emit secondary electrons when bombarded by electrons. The number of secondary electrons emitted per primary electron depends upon the velocity of the primary bombarding electrons and upon the nature and condition of the material composing the surface being bombarded. Typical behavior is shown in Fig. 6-4. Few secondary electrons are produced when the primary velocity is very low. With increasing potential of the primary bombarding electrons, the ratio of secondary to primary electrons first increases, then goes through a maximum at a potential that is commonly between 200 and 500 volts, and finally decreases. With pure metal surfaces, the maximum ratio of secondary to primary electrons typically ranges from somewhat less than one to about three, while some of the more complex surfaces yield ratios of secondary to primary electrons as high as ten.

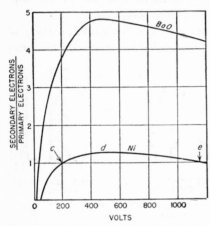

Fig. 6-4. Secondary-emission characteristics of two typical surfaces.

About 90 per cent of the secondary electrons emitted from a conducting surface have velocities less than 20 volts when the primary potential is 50 volts or more, and the greatest number of secondaries have velocities of about 10 volts. However, a few secondary electrons are emitted with higher velocities, and several per cent have a velocity practically equal to the velocity of the bombarding primary electrons.

Insulators, as well as conductors, may emit secondary electrons. The ratio of secondary to primary electrons as a function of primary electron potential is of the same character for insulators as for metals. The ratio of secondary to primary electrons usually exceeds unity over a considerable range of potential, with the maximum commonly occurring at primary electron velocities between 300 and 800 volts.

Potential Assumed by an Insulated Secondary Emitting Target Bombarded

[1] An excellent summary of the characteristics of secondary electron emission is given by James S. Allen, Recent Applications of Electron Multiplier Tubes, *Proc. IRE*, vol. 38, p. 346, April, 1950; also see Spangenberg, *op. cit.*, pp. 48–57.

by an Electron Beam. Consider the situation illustrated in Fig. 6-5. Here S is a secondary emitting surface which is insulated from ground, but will be assumed to be initially at ground potential. This target is bombarded by an electron beam which strikes the target with velocity V_1 when the target is at ground potential. Electrode A is a ringlike anode at a positive potential with respect to ground that collects secondary electrons emitted from the surface of S.

The factors involved in the behavior of this system can be understood by assuming that the target is nickel with the secondary emitting characteristics illustrated in Fig. 6-4. Three cases are then to be distinguished: (1) the velocity V_1 of the bombarding beam is less than the potential corresponding to point c on the target characteristic; (2) the velocity of the bombarding beam is greater than the potential corresponding to point e; and (3) the velocity V_1 of the bombarding beam corresponds to a potential between c and e.

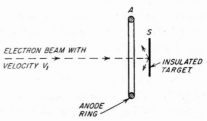

In case 1 target S loses on the average less than one secondary electron for each primary electron that arrives. When the electron beam is initially turned on, target

FIG. 6-5. System consisting of an insulated target bombarded by an electron beam, and associated with an anode electrode that collects the secondary electrons.

S accordingly starts to accumulate a negative charge; the potential of S thus becomes increasingly negative with respect to ground. This process continues until S is so negative with respect to ground that the electrons of the bombarding beam are all repelled, and no further primary electrons are received. This behavior is referred to as "blocking."

In case 2 the target similarly starts accumulating negative charge. However, when the potential of S has thereby become sufficiently negative with respect to ground so that the velocity with which the primary electrons strike the target is reduced to the potential corresponding to point e in Fig. 6-4, then one secondary electron is lost on the average for each arriving primary electron. This results in an equilibrium being established. The target potential thus "sticks" at a value such that the velocity of the bombarding primary electrons corresponds to e. It will be observed that as long as the initial velocity V_1 of the primary beam is greater than the potential corresponding to e, the target will assume the same equilibrium potential e, irrespective of the exact value of V_1.

Finally, when the initial beam velocity V_1 corresponds to a condition between c and e, such as d, each primary electron will on the average produce more than one secondary electron. The target then loses more secondary electrons to the anode A than it gains primary electrons from the beam, and so starts accumulating a positive charge. The target potential therefore rises until it reaches a positive potential above ground such that either (1) the electrons in the primary beam strike the target with a voltage corresponding to e, or (2) the target becomes as positive[1] as the collecting electrode A; whichever limit is first reached determines the end result. The target S can never acquire a potential appreciably more positive than the collecting electrode A because the secondary electrons will then have no place to go other than returning to the target; also the potential of the target will not rise above a potential such that the velocity of the impinging electrons exceeds e.

Although the discussion above has implied that the target S is a conductor, the same situation exists when it is an insulator. The target potential then represents the potential of the part of the insulator surface that is being bombarded by primary electrons. In the case of an insulated surface bombarded by a beam of very high velocity it will be noted from case 2, above, that the maximum velocity with which the electrons can be made to hit the surface under equilibrium conditions is determined only by the secondary-emission characteristics of the surface. The velocity of impact is not affected by the velocity V_1 initially given the primary beam, provided only that this velocity is greater than that corresponding to point e on the secondary-emission characteristic. This fact is very important in connection with the operation of cathode-ray fluorescent screens.

6-5. Diodes—Space-charge Effects. A diode is a two-electrode vacuum tube containing a cathode that emits electrons by thermionic emission, surrounded by an anode (or plate). Such a tube is a rectifier, since when the plate is positive with respect to the cathode it attracts electrons and current passes through the tube, while when the plate is negative with respect to the cathode it repels the electrons and no current flows.

Voltage and Current Relations. The relation between plate voltage and the current flowing to the positive plate is shown in Fig. 6-6 in a typical case. When the plate voltage is sufficiently high, electrons are drawn away from the cathode as rapidly as emitted. The plate current is then limited by the electron emission of the cathode and so depends upon cathode temperature rather than upon plate voltage.[2]

At low or moderate plate voltages, however, the plate current is less than the emission of which the cathode is capable. This is because the

---

[1] Actually the target will become slightly positive with respect to the anode as a result of the velocity of emission of the secondary electrons.

[2] Actually, the completeness of this voltage saturation effect depends upon the type of emitter. With oxide-coated emitters, the electron emission from the cathode is appreciably affected by the electrostatic field at the surface of the cathode. As a result, saturation is less pronounced in oxide-coated cathodes, as shown by the dotted curves in Fig. 6-6.

electrons traveling in the space from cathode to plate produce a negative space charge that reduces the attraction that the positive plate has upon the electrons just leaving the cathode. As a consequence, the total number of electrons in transit at any one instant cannot exceed the number that will provide a negative space charge that completely neutralizes the electrostatic field that the positive plate produces at the surface of the cathode. All electrons in excess of the number necessary for such complete neutralization are repelled back into the cathode by the negative space charge of the electrons in the plate-cathode space. This is true irrespective of how many excess electrons the cathode emits. When the plate current is limited in this way by *space charge*, the plate current is determined by the plate

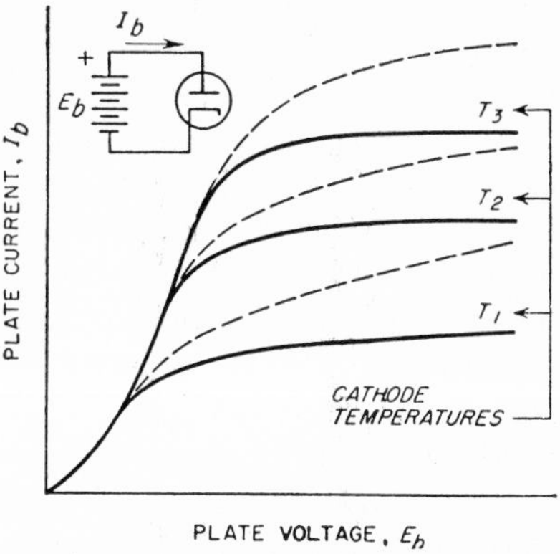

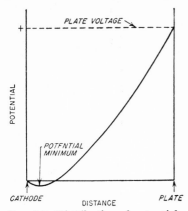

Fig. 6-6. Plate current as a function of plate voltage in a two-electrode tube for three cathode temperatures, all sufficiently low to show voltage saturation. The solid lines are the characteristics actually obtained with a tungsten cathode, whereas the dotted lines show the type of characteristic that would be obtained with an oxide-coated emitter.

potential and is substantially independent of the electron emission of the cathode.

If the space-charge situation is examined in detail, it will be found that the negative charge of the electrons in transit between cathode and plate will be sufficient to give the space in the immediate vicinity of the cathode a slight negative potential with respect to the cathode, as illustrated in Fig. 6-7. The electrons emitted from the cathode are projected out into this negative field with an emission velocity that will vary with different electrons. The negative field causes the emitted electrons to slow down as they move away from the cathode. Those electrons having the highest velocities of emission will be sent out with sufficient force to penetrate the most negative part of the field and reach the region where they are drawn toward the positive plate. The remainder, i.e., those electrons having low emission velocities, will be brought to a stop by the

Fig. 6-7. Distribution of potential in the cathode-plate space of a diode when the current flow is limited by space charge, showing the potential minimum adjacent to the cathode caused by velocity of emission.

negative field adjacent to the cathode and will fall back into the cathode. The potential minimum thus assumes a value such that only enough electrons to supply a plate current appropriate to the plate voltage will have emission velocities greater than this minimum.

The energy that is delivered to the tube by the plate voltage is first expended in accelerating the electrons traveling from cathode to plate, and so is converted into kinetic energy. When these swiftly moving electrons strike the plate, this kinetic energy is then transformed into heat as a result of the impact, and appears at the plate in the form of heat.

Plate Current When Limited by Space Charge. When limited by space charge, the plate current received from any portion of the cathode is proportional to the $\frac{3}{2}$ power of the voltage between the plate and that part of the cathode contributing the current. In heater-type cathodes where the cathode is an equipotential surface, the total plate current for positive plate voltages is hence given by the equation[1]

$$\text{Plate current} = I_b = K E_b^{\frac{3}{2}} \tag{6-9}$$

where K is a constant, called the *perveance*, that is determined by the geometry of the tube and E_b is the anode (plate) voltage with respect to the cathode.[2]

A justification for the $\frac{3}{2}$-power law in Eq. (6-9) can be obtained directly without mathematical analysis. Thus it will be noted that the number of electrons that must be in the interelectrode space at any instant in order to neutralize the plate potential will be proportional to E_b; i.e., if the plate voltage is increased by a factor of 4, then four times as many electrons must be in transit at a particular instant to neutralize the field of the plate. Furthermore, the velocity with which these electrons travel will be proportional to $\sqrt{E_b}$ so that, if the plate voltage is increased by a factor of 4, each electron will stay in this space only half as long. The rate at which electrons arrive at the plate is the product of the number in the space at any instant and the velocity with which they travel, and so

---

[1] This relation was first worked out by C. D. Child, and its derivation is found in many textbooks; thus see K. Spangenberg, *op. cit.*, pp. 170–183.

[2] When the plate voltage is low and when very precise results are to be obtained, the voltage E_b appearing in Eq. (6-9) must be interpreted to mean the actual plate voltage plus a correction to take into account the contact potential existing between plate and cathode and also the effective velocity of emission of the electrons. Each of these corrections ordinarily amounts to less than 1 volt and can be neglected where the plate voltage is moderately high unless precision results are desired.

In filament-type tubes the voltage drop produced in the cathode by the heating current causes different parts of the filament to have different potentials with respect to the plate. If the plate voltage is referred to the negative end of the filament, the result is to cause the total plate current to vary at a power of the plate voltage as measured with respect to the negative side of the filament, which is greater than the $\frac{3}{2}$ power but which approaches the $\frac{3}{2}$ power when the plate voltage is large compared with the voltage drop in the cathode.

is proportional to $E_b \sqrt{E_b} = E_b^{3/2}$, i.e., four times the plate voltage gives $4 \times \sqrt{4} = 8 = 4^{3/2}$ times as much current.

Practical Diodes. Diode tubes of the high-vacuum type, such as discussed above, find extensive use as rectifiers for small and moderate powers. In particular, very small diodes are used as detectors in receivers where the applied potential is only a few volts and the rectified power is a very small fraction of a watt. Diodes are also used as rectifiers for supplying the anode power required in radio receivers, public-address amplifiers, etc.; here the rectified power is tens of watts and the applied voltage is typically a few hundred volts. High-vacuum diodes can be built for higher voltages and higher power ratings, but other forms of rectifiers are generally preferred for such applications (see Sec. 20-2).

6-6. Triodes—Action of the Control Grid. A triode tube can be thought of as a diode to which there has been added a third electrode,

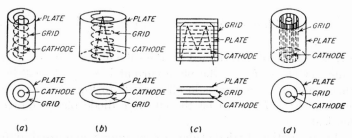

(a) (b) (c) (d)

Fig. 6-8. Grid, plate, and cathode structures of a number of typical triode tubes. It will be observed that in every case the grid is a screenlike electrode that affects the electrostatic field near the cathode while permitting the electrons to flow to the plate.

located between the cathode and plate, for the purpose of controlling the flow of electrons to the plate. This third electrode is in the form of a screen or grid that serves as an imperfect electrostatic shield, allowing some but not all of the electrostatic flux from the plate to leak to the cathode. This *control grid* is commonly operated at a negative potential with respect to the cathode, and so controls the number of electrons that pass between the grid wires and go on to the plate. Several typical grid structures used in commercial triode tubes are illustrated in Fig. 6-8.

Voltage and Current Relations in Triode Tubes. The number of electrons that reach the anode in a triode tube under space-charge-limited conditions is determined almost solely by the electrostatic field in the cathode-grid space; once the electrons have passed the grid, they travel so rapidly to the plate that space-charge effects in the grid-plate space can, to a first approximation, be neglected. The action that takes place in the cathode-grid space is analogous to that occurring in a diode tube. The only essential difference is that the electrostatic field in this space is determined by the potentials of both the grid and the plate. The theory of electrostatic shielding produced by imperfect shields shows that if the grid structure has no dissymmetries, the electrostatic field in the vicinity of the cathode is proportional to the quantity $(E_c + E_b/\mu)$, where E_c and E_b are the grid and plate voltages, respectively, with respect to the cathode, and where μ is a constant that is determined by the geometry of the tube and is independent of the grid and plate voltages.[1]

The constant μ is known as the *amplification factor* of the tube. It is a measure of the relative effectiveness of grid and plate voltages in producing electrostatic fields at the surface of the cathode, and so is a measure of the screening effect of the control grid.

The space current, i.e., the total number of electrons drawn from the cathode in a three-electrode tube, accordingly varies with $(E_c + E_b/\mu)$ in exactly the same way that the plate current of a diode tube varies with the plate voltage. Assuming that the grid is negative, so that all of this current goes to the plate, then one has for positive values of $(E_c + E_b/\mu)$

$$\text{Plate current} = I_b = K \left(E_c + \frac{E_b}{\mu} \right)^{3/2} \qquad (6\text{-}10)$$

where K is a constant determined by the tube dimensions.[2,3] For negative values of $(E_c + E_b/\mu)$, the plate current is zero. It will be noted that this equation is analogous in all respects to Eq. (6-9) and that, by interpreting $(E_c + E_b/\mu)$ to be the effective diode plate voltage, they are identical.

The characteristics of triode tubes are commonly expressed by families of curves showing the relationship between (1) plate current and plate voltage with constant grid voltage, and (2) plate current and grid voltage with constant plate voltage. Examples of such curves are shown in Figs. 6-9 and 6-10.

The various curves in Fig. 6-9 corresponding to different values of plate voltage all have approximately the same shape and differ primarily in being displaced with respect to each other. This results from the fact that the plate current is determined by $(E_c + E_b/\mu)$, and not by the particular combination of grid and plate voltages involved. Thus a curve for a particular voltage is like the curve for a lower plate voltage except that it is displaced toward a more negative grid potential. Similarly, and for the same reason, the various curves in Fig. 6-10 are similar to each other in that an increase in the negativeness of the grid merely displaces the curve toward a higher plate voltage without appreciably

---

[1] The subscripts c and b originate from the fact that the sources of the grid and plate voltages were once referred to as the C and B batteries, respectively.

[2] For highest accuracy, the quantity in the parentheses on the right-hand side of the equation must be corrected to take into account contact potential and velocity of emission, as discussed in connection with Eq. (6-9).

[3] Equation (6-10) assumes that the cathode is an equipotential surface. If this is not the case the relationship is modified to some extent.

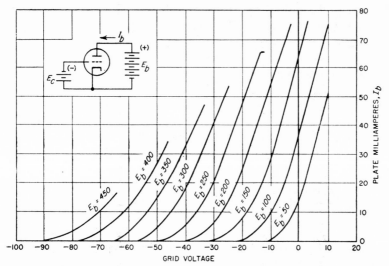

Fig. 6-9. Relationship between grid voltage and plate current for several values of plate voltage in a typical triode tube. Note that the principal effect of changing the plate voltage is to displace the curves along the grid-voltage axis without changing their shape.

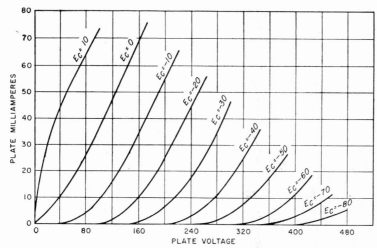

Fig. 6-10. Relationship between the plate voltage and plate current for several values of grid voltage for the same tube as in Fig. 6-9. Note that the principal effect of changing the grid voltage is to displace the curves along the plate-voltage axis without changing the shape, and that the curves have the same general shape as those of Fig. 6-9.

changing its character. Furthermore, the curves of Fig. 6-10 have the same general shape as the curves in Fig. 6-9; this is because varying the grid voltage has the same effect on $(E_c + E_b/\mu)$ as is produced by a variation in the plate voltage.

The range covered by Figs. 6-9 and 6-10 lies in the region where the plate current is limited by the space charge.   Figure 6-11 shows the situation that exists when the electron emission is sufficiently low to bring in the beginning of voltage saturation at large plate currents.   It is seen that the plate current is still a function of $(E_c + E_b/\mu)$, exactly as in Fig. 6-9, but the shape of the curves is now different as the result of voltage saturation.   However, the

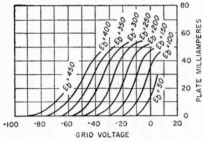

Fig. 6-11. Grid-voltage–plate-current curves differing from those of Fig. 6-9 only in that the cathode temperature has been lowered to the point where voltage saturation begins to appear at large plate currents, causing the tops of the curves to bend over.

various curves of the family still all have approximately the same shape, differing principally in being displaced with respect to control grid voltage.   The curves of Figs. 6-9 and 6-10 would show saturation effects similar to those of Fig. 6-11 if extended to sufficiently high values of plate current.

The plate current of a three-electrode tube becomes zero when $(E_c + E_b/\mu)$ is zero or negative.   The condition $(E_c + E_b/\mu) = 0$ exists when the grid is just sufficiently negative to neutralize the positive field produced at the cathode by the plate voltage.   This condition is known as *cutoff* and corresponds to

$$\text{Cutoff grid voltage (or bias)} = -\frac{E_b}{\mu} \qquad (6\text{-}11)$$

Grid Current.   If the grid potential is allowed to become slightly positive, it will collect a portion of the space current attracted from the cathode, although most of the electrons will still go through the spaces between the grid wires and pass on to the plate.   When the grid is positive, Eq. (6-10) can be rewritten as

$$\text{Total space current} = I_b + I_c = K\left(E_c + \frac{E_b}{\mu}\right)^{3/2} \qquad (6\text{-}12)$$

where I_b and I_c are the plate (anode) and grid currents, respectively.

The division of the total space current between the grid and the plate depends upon the electrode potentials.[1]   Typical behavior is shown in Fig. 6-12 for the usual case where the grid is less positive than the plate.   Under these conditions the grid current is a relatively small fraction of the total space current.   The grid current is, moreover, reduced by increasing the plate voltage, because a high plate voltage tends to attract the electrons away from the grid.

Practical Triode Tubes.   Commercially produced triode tubes are

---

[1] An extensive analysis of this subject is given by Spangenberg, *op. cit.*, pp. 218–237.

available from subminiature types up to tubes capable of developing several hundred kilowatts of output.   The smaller types, such as used in radio receivers, public-address systems, etc., are air-cooled, employ either glass or metal envelopes, and use oxide-coated cathodes.   Both heater and filament types are available.   Larger tubes capable of dissipating plate powers up to about one kilowatt usually have glass envelopes and employ either oxide-coated or thoriated-tungsten filament emitters. Still larger tubes use tungsten or thoriated-tungsten filament emitters and have copper anodes (plates) which serve as part of the envelope to permit cooling of the plate by water or forced air draft.

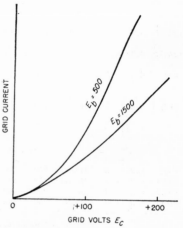

FIG. 6-12. Typical relationship between grid current and grid voltage in a triode tube, for two values of anode voltage, both of which are higher than the grid voltage.

Characteristics of some typical triode tubes are tabulated in Tables 6-1 (page 186) and 13-1 (page 455).

6-7. Coefficients of Triode Tubes.[1] Although the complete characteristics of a triode tube can be specified only by a set of characteristic curves, the behavior of the tube in the vicinity of a particular operating point can be expressed in terms of three coefficients or constants, termed the *amplification factor* μ, the *plate resistance* r_p (sometimes called the dynamic plate resistance), and the *transconductance* g_m. With the aid of these coefficients, it is possible to make quantitative calculations of tube performance under many conditions without resort to the complete characteristic curves.

Amplification Factor.   The amplification factor μ has already been defined in Sec. 6-6 as the ratio of the effectiveness of the grid and plate voltages in producing electrostatic fields at the cathode surface.   The amplification factor depends primarily upon the grid structure and will be increased by anything that causes the grid to shield the cathode more completely from the plate.   Thus larger grid wires or a closer spacing of the grid wires will increase the amplification factor, as does increasing the distance between the grid and plate.   Commercially available triode tubes have amplification factors ranging from about two as a minimum to about one hundred as a maximum.   The most desirable value of amplification factor varies with the purpose for which the tube is to be used.

[1] Methods of measuring triode coefficients are described by F. E. Terman and J. M. Pettit, "Electronic Measurements," Sec. 7-3, McGraw-Hill Book Company, Inc., New York, 1951.

TABLE 6-1
TYPICAL SMALL VACUUM TUBES

Tube	Filament voltage	Filament current, amp	Cathode type	Typical characteristics								Comments
				Plate voltage	Screen-grid voltage	Control-grid voltage	Plate current, ma	Screen-grid current, ma	μ	Plate resistance	Trans-conductance, μmhos	
Small general-purpose triodes												
12AX7	6.3	0.3	Heater	250	...	− 2	1.2	...	100	62,500	1,600	Twin triode
12AU7	6.3	0.3	Heater	250	...	− 8.5	10.5	...	17	7,700	2,200	Twin triode
6AU6	6.3	0.3	Heater	250	...	− 4	12.2	...	36	7,500		Triode connected
6SJ7	6.3	0.3	Heater	180	...	− 6	6.0	...	19	8,250	2,300	Triode connected
Small general-purpose pentodes												
6SJ7	6.3	0.3	Heater	250	100	− 3	3	0.8	.....	> 1meg	1,650	} Sharp cutoff
6AU6	6.3	0.3	Heater	250	125	− 1	7.6	3.0	.....	> 1meg	4,450	
6SK7	6.3	0.3	Heater	250	100	− 3	9.2	2.6	1,600	800,000	2,000	} Variable mu
6BA6	6.3	0.3	Heater	250	100	− 1	11.0	4.2	.....	1.5 meg	4,400	
Small high-performance pentodes												
6AC7	6.3	0.45	Heater	300	150	− 1.6	10	2.5	.....	1 meg	9,000	
6AG7	6.3	0.65	Heater	300	125	− 2	28	7	.....	130,000	11,000	
6AK5	6.3	0.175	Heater	180	120	− 1.5	7.7	2.4	.....	690,000	5,100	Miniature type
Small power triodes												
6B4G	6.3	1.0	Filament	250	...	−45	60	...	4.2	800	5,250	Similar to 2A3
6F6	6.3	0.7	Heater	250	...	−20	31	...	6.8	2,600	2,600	} Triode connected
6Y6	6.3	1.25	Heater	135	...	−13.5	61.5	...	5.2	700	7,400	
6AS7	6.3	2.5	Heater	135	...	−31	125	...	2.0	280	7,000	Twin triode
Small power pentodes												
6F6	6.3	0.7	Heater	285	285	−20	38	7	199	78,000	2,550	} Pentode connected
6Y6	6.3	1.25	Heater	135	135	−13.5	58	3.5	65	9,300	7,000	
6AK6	6.3	0.15	Heater	180	180	− 9	15	2.5	460	200,000	2,300	Miniature type
Small power beam tubes												
6V6	6.3	0.45	Heater	315	225	−13	34	2.2	289	77,000	3,750	
6L6	6.3	0.9	Heater	350	250	−18	54	2.5	171	33,000	5,200	
6Y6	6.3	1.25	Heater	200	135	−14	61	2.2	130	18,300	7,100	

When the relative effectiveness of the grid and plate voltages in producing electrostatic field at the cathode is the same for all parts of the cathode, then the amplification factor μ is absolutely independent of plate, grid, and filament voltages. This situation would occur if the grid were a perfectly symmetrical uniform electrostatic shield. Under such circumstances the amplification factor is determined solely by the geometry of the system comprising the grid, plate, and cathode electrodes; the amplification factor can then be calculated in terms of the

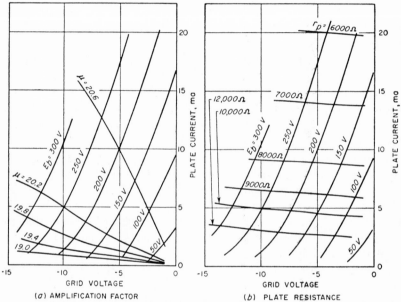

FIG. 6-13. Curves showing variations in amplification factor and plate resistance in a typical triode tube.

dimensions of the tube by using the theory of electrostatic shielding.[1] However, in practical tubes, dissymmetries introduced by support wires, etc., cause the amplification factor to be different for different parts of the tube. The effective amplification factor of such a combination will then vary somewhat with plate and grid voltages. In particular, the amplification factor will tend to become lower as cutoff is approached, as shown in Fig. 6-13; this is because as the grid becomes more negative those parts of the tube having the highest value of μ will reach cutoff first, leaving only the low μ parts of the tube contributing to the plate current.

In the practical case where dissymmetries prevent the amplification factor from being a purely geometrical constant, it is defined as the rela-

[1] Thus see Spangenberg, *op. cit.*, chap. 7.

tive effectiveness of grid and plate voltages in controlling the plate current. This leads to the following mathematical relation:

$$\text{Amplification factor} = \mu = \frac{\partial I_b / \partial E_c}{\partial I_b / \partial E_b} = -\frac{dE_b}{dE_c}\bigg|_{I_b \text{ constant}} \quad (6\text{-}13)$$

where E_c and E_b are the control-grid and plate potentials, and I_b is the plate current.

Plate Resistance. The plate resistance (short for dynamic plate resistance) of a vacuum tube represents the resistance that the plate circuit offers to a *small increment* of plate voltage. Thus, when an increment of plate voltage ΔE_b produces an increment in the plate current of ΔI_b, the plate resistance is given by the relation

$$\text{Plate resistance} = r_p = \frac{\Delta E_b}{\Delta I_b} = \frac{\partial E_b}{\partial I_b} \quad (6\text{-}14)$$

The plate resistance is therefore the *reciprocal of the slope* of the plate-current–plate-voltage characteristic shown in Fig. 6-10. It is important to remember that the plate resistance *is not the ratio of total plate voltage to total plate current.*

In any particular tube, the plate resistance depends primarily upon the plate current and only to a small extent upon the combination of grid and plate voltages used to produce this current. Furthermore, the plate resistance becomes progressively lower as the plate current is increased. This behavior is shown in Fig. 6-13b. It is a result of the fact that to a good approximation the different plate-voltage–plate-current curves in Fig. 6-10 differ only in being displaced along the plate-voltage axis, and that the slope of each curve increases as the plate current becomes greater.[1]

The plate resistance of a triode tube depends upon the dimensions and relative positions of the cathode, plate, and grid. It becomes less as the cathode surface area is increased and as the distance between the cathode and the other electrodes is reduced. Also, tubes differing only in grid structure will have a plate resistance that increases with the amplification factor of the tube. This is because a high amplification factor means that the plate voltage has very little effect on the electrostatic field near the cathode; consequently, when the amplification factor is high the plate voltage has very little effect on the plate current.

---

[1] To the extent that μ is constant and that Eq. (6-10) is true, the plate resistance depends only on the plate current I_b, and is inversely proportional to $\sqrt[3]{I_b}$. This can be demonstrated by substituting Eq. (6-10) into Eq. (6-14) and noting that

$$(E_c + E_b/\mu)^{1/2} = \sqrt[3]{I_b/K}$$

This enables one to write

$$r_p = \frac{\partial E_b}{\partial I_b} = \frac{1}{\partial I_b / \partial E_b} = \frac{2\mu}{3K[E_c + (E_b/\mu)]^{1/2}} = \frac{2\mu}{3K^{2/3}\sqrt[3]{I_b}} \quad (6\text{-}15)$$

Transconductance (*or Mutual Conductance*).   The transconductance g_m (sometimes called mutual conductance) is defined as the rate of change of plate current with respect to a change in grid voltage.   Thus, if the grid voltage is changed by ΔE_c, the resulting plate-current change ΔI_b is related to the transconductance by the equation

$$\Delta I_b = \Delta E_c g_m$$

Hence

$$g_m = \frac{\Delta I_b}{\Delta E_c} = \frac{\partial I_b}{\partial E_c} = \frac{dI_b}{dE_c}\bigg|_{E_b \text{ constant}} \tag{6-16}$$

Dividing Eq. (6-13) by (6-14) shows that the transconductance is also the ratio of amplification factor to plate resistance.   That is,

$$g_m = \frac{\partial I_b}{\partial E_c} = \frac{\mu}{r_p} \tag{6-17}$$

It will be noted that the transconductance corresponds to the slope of the E_c-I_b curves of Fig. 6-9.

The transconductance is a rough indication of the design merit of a tube.   This is because a low plate resistance and a high amplification factor are desired, and the transconductance measures the extent to which this feature is attained.   Tubes of equal design merit, but with different values of amplification factor, will have substantially the same value of transconductance under normal operating conditions.

In a particular triode tube, the transconductance depends primarily upon the plate current, and only to a small extent upon the combination of grid and plate voltages used to produce this current.   This follows from the fact that since the amplification factor is approximately constant, the transconductance will vary inversely with the plate resistance. The transconductance of a given tube accordingly increases approximately as the cube root of the plate current.

6-8. Pentodes.   A pentode is a five-electrode tube consisting of cathode, plate, and three grids, which are concentrically arranged between cathode and plate as in Fig. 6-14.   The inner grid is called the control grid and corresponds to the grid of a triode tube.   The next grid is termed the screen, while the outer grid is called the suppressor.   In normal operation, the control grid is commonly maintained negative with respect to the cathode as in the triode.   The screen grid is operated at a fixed positive potential, while the suppressor is usually connected directly to the cathode.   The plate is operated at a positive potential.

The additional grids operated in this way modify the voltage and current relations within the tube in a way that is desirable for many purposes.   The extra grids also provide electrostatic shielding between the anode (plate) and the control grid.   This eliminates coupling between electrical circuits associated with the control grid and circuits associated with the plate. Such shielding is particularly important when the tube is used to amplify radio frequencies. Capacitive coupling between the control-grid and plate leads can be largely prevented by the arrangement shown in Fig. 6-14, in which the control-grid lead is brought out through the top of the tube envelope. Alternatively, the control-grid and plate connections can both be brought out through the base by using diagonally opposite pins for these two leads and, in addition, providing shielding inside the tube that minimizes electrostatic coupling between the leads and pins involved.

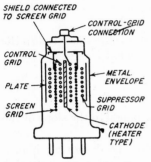

SHIELD CONNECTED TO SCREEN GRID

CONTROL-GRID CONNECTION

CONTROL GRID

PLATE

SCREEN GRID

METAL ENVELOPE

SUPPRESSOR GRID

CATHODE (HEATER TYPE)

FIG. 6-14. Schematic diagram of typical pentode tube, showing electrode arrangement that provides effective electrostatic shielding between control grid and plate electrodes and their connecting leads.

Voltage and Current Relations in Pentode Tubes. The voltage and current relations existing in a pentode tube are somewhat more complicated than those of a triode as a result of the action of the additional grids.

The number of electrons drawn from the cathode of a pentode under conditions of space-charge limitation is determined by the electrostatic field at the surface of the cathode, exactly as in the case of the triode. This field in pentodes depends upon the potential of the control and screen grids and upon the geometry of the tube. It is not affected by the plate potential because the screen and suppressor grids effectively shield the cathode from the electrostatic effects produced by the plate. The result is that the *number of electrons drawn from the space charge is substantially independent of the plate voltage.*

Following the analogy with the triode tube, the electrostatic field at the surface of the cathode is proportional to the quantity $E_{c1} + (E_{c2}/\mu_s)$, where E_{c1} and E_{c2} are the control- and screen-grid potentials, respectively, and μ_s is a constant analogous to the amplification factor μ of the triode. The constant μ_s is determined by the tube construction and is a measure of the relative effectiveness of control- and screen-grid voltages in producing electrostatic field at the surface of the cathode. The total space current, i.e., the sum $I_b + I_{c2}$ of plate and screen currents, drawn from the space charge by this electrostatic field has the same form as Eq. (6-10) for the triode[1]

$$\text{Total space current} = I_b + I_{c2} = K_1\left(E_{c1} + \frac{E_{c2}}{\mu_s}\right)^{3/2} \quad (6\text{-}18)$$

[1] For highest accuracy, the quantity inside the parentheses on the right-hand side of the equation must be corrected to take into account contact potential and velocity of emission, exactly as discussed in connection with Eq. (6-9) for the case of diodes.

When the control grid is positive, the total space current becomes $I_b + I_{c2} + I_{c1}$, in analogy with Eq. (6-12).

where K_1 is a constant. It will be noted that the total space current becomes zero when $E_{c1} = -E_{c2}/\mu_s$, so that μ_s can be termed the *cutoff amplification factor*.

The electrons drawn from the space charge in accordance with Eq. (6-18) pass between the control-grid wires and are accelerated to a high velocity as the screen grid is approached. At this high velocity, the electrons travel in substantially straight lines, so only those which happen to be going directly toward the screen-grid wires are intercepted by this screen. The remaining electrons pass through the screen grid and travel on toward the suppressor. As the suppressor is approached, the electrons slow down because of the retarding field between the suppressor and the screen; however, if the plate is reasonably positive, they will pass on through the spaces between the suppressor-grid wires and reach the plate without stopping. This is because the suppressor, being only an imperfect electrostatic shield, does not prevent the plate from attracting the electrons in the screen-suppressor space.

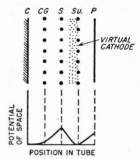

Fig. 6-15. Schematic representation of potential distribution in a pentode tube when a virtual cathode is present in the suppressor region.

When the plate voltage is very low, and particularly when the total space current is large at the same time, the above behavior is modified. Under these conditions the plate is not capable of producing sufficient electrostatic field on the screen side of the suppressor to draw away the electrons as rapidly as they arrive at the suppressor. Some of the electrons that approach the suppressor then come to rest just before reaching the suppressor, and return toward the screen. Other electrons, mainly those emitted from the cathode with particularly high initial velocities, slow down almost to a stop, but go on to the plate. The result is that the space-charge conditions on the cathode side of the suppressor are similar to those present in the vicinity of the cathode, as illustrated in Fig. 6-15. This space charge is called a *virtual cathode*, since it has many of the properties of an actual cathode.

The actual voltage and current relations existing in a pentode tube can be shown by means of characteristic curves, of which those of Figs. 6-16 and 6-17 are typical. The total space current varies with screen-grid and control-grid potential in exactly the same way as the plate current of a triode varies with control-grid and plate voltages, as to be expected from Eq. (6-18). The division of this total space current between plate and screen is also to a first approximation independent of plate potential, provided the plate potential is not too low.[1] As a consequence the plate

---

[1] The only effects that can alter the division of space current between plate and screen, when the plate voltage is adequate to prevent the formation of a virtual cathode

current and the screen-grid current both vary with control-grid and screen-grid voltages in the same way as does the total space current (except when the plate potential is so low that a virtual cathode is present).

At plate voltages so low that a virtual cathode is formed on the cathode side of the suppressor, the plate current drops as a result of electrons turned back by the virtual cathode. At the same time, the screen current increases because the screen captures some of the returning electrons (the rest go to the emitting cathode). Likewise, the total space

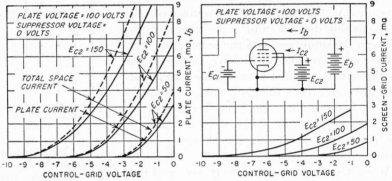

Fig. 6-16. Curves showing total space current, plate current, and screen current of a pentode tube as a function of control-grid voltage for several values of screen potential E_{c2}. Note that all of these curves have the same general shape as those of the plate current of a triode (Fig. 6-9).

current drops below the value given by Eq. (6-18) because of the contribution made to the space charge near the emitting cathode by those returned electrons that pass between the screen-grid wires and approach the cathode. These effects are all apparent in Fig. 6-17.

In most applications the pentode must be operated so that the plate current is substantially independent of plate voltage. This requires that the plate voltage always be kept sufficiently high to prevent the formation of a virtual cathode. Under these conditions, the plate current will depend only upon the voltages applied to the control and screen

---

in the vicinity of the suppressor grid, are the facts (1) that an increased plate potential may divert a few of the small number of electrons that would otherwise go to the suppressor; (2) that an increased plate potential will modify the electrostatic fields existing at the screen grid and hence may divert to the plate a few electrons that would otherwise be intercepted by the screen; and (3) that the positive screen-grid wires deflect slightly the paths of the approaching electrons, causing the screen potential to have a small influence on the fraction of electrons that the screen intercepts. All these effects are relatively small, however, so that to a first approximation the division of current between plate and screen is roughly independent of the control-grid, screen, and plate potentials, provided the plate potential is not low enough to cause a virtual cathode to form.

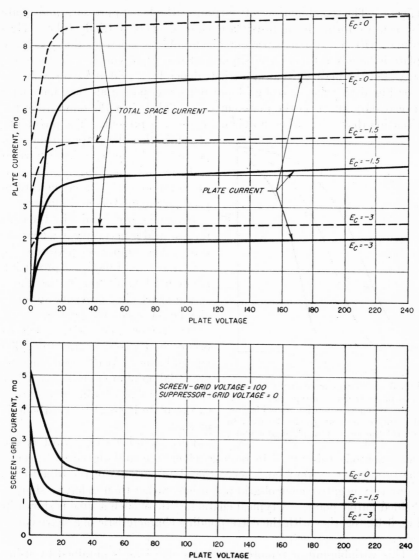

Fig. 6-17. Curves showing plate and screen current and total space current of a pentode as a function of plate voltage for various control-grid potentials. Note that, when the plate potential is not too low, plate voltage has relatively little effect on the currents.

grids, and can be varied by varying the control-grid potential, just as in a triode.

The plate potential at which a virtual cathode forms depends upon the suppressor-grid potential. If the suppressor grid is biased negatively, the result is to increase the plate potential required to avoid virtual cathode effects. The combination of virtual cathode, suppressor, and plate is seen to form the approximate equivalent of a triode tube. Thus when a virtual cathode is present, the number of electrons that reach the plate is largely a function of suppressor and plate voltages, in the same way that the plate current of a triode depends on grid and plate voltages (see Fig. 6-18); the control-grid and the screen potentials then have only a secondary effect on the plate current. This is just the opposite of the situation that exists when no virtual cathode is present. The possibility of controlling the plate current of a pentode tube by creating a virtual cathode and then varying the suppressor potential is used in certain types of modulators and mixers.

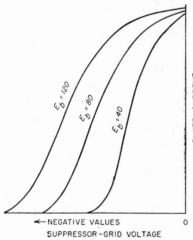

It may be wondered why the suppressor grid is necessary in a pentode tube. The suppressor performs the very important function of producing a potential minimum in the plate-screen space that prevents an interchange of secondary electrons between screen and plate, such as occurs in the screen-grid tube discussed below. At the same time the potential minimum does not affect the desired flow of primary electrons to the plate if no virtual cathode is present.

Fig. 6-18. Plate current as a function of suppressor-grid voltage for several values of plate potential, showing how the suppressor voltage can be used to control the current reaching the plate.

Variable-mu Tubes. Most of the small pentode tubes used in radio receivers are so designed as to cause the total space current (and hence the plate current) of the tube to tail off at very negative control-grid potentials, rather than to have a sharply defined cutoff point. A typical characteristic of such a tube is shown in Fig. 6-19, together with the corresponding characteristic of a sharp cutoff tube.

This variable-mu or remote cutoff characteristic is obtained by using a nonuniform control-grid structure such that the amplification factor μ_s is different for different parts of the tube. Those parts of the tube having the lowest value of μ_s will hence require an extremely negative grid bias to cut off all plate current. It will be noted that this effect is an intentional exaggeration of the factors that cause the amplification factor μ of the triode to become less as cutoff is approached, as discussed in connection with Fig. 6-13a. The usual method of obtaining the variable μ_s consists in varying the pitch of the control-grid wires.

Variable-mu tubes are used where it is desired to control transconductance by varying the control-grid potential of the tube. Compared with sharp cutoff tubes, the variable-mu characteristic gives more gradual control and also greatly reduces cross-talk effects (see Sec. 12-4) by reducing the rate of change of curvature of the characteristics in the vicinity of cutoff.

Practical Pentodes. Commercial pentode tubes are available from subminiature types up to tubes capable of developing 1 or 2 kw of output. The most important use of pentodes is in audio-frequency and tuned radio-frequency voltage amplifiers. In addition, they are extensively used for the development of audio-frequency power for radio receivers and small public-address systems.

Characteristics of some typical pentodes are tabulated in Tables 6-1 (page 186) and 13-1 (page 455).

6-9. Screen-grid (Tetrode) Tubes.

The screen-grid tube is a four-electrode (tetrode) tube which can be thought of as a pentode with the suppressor grid removed.   The omission of the suppressor grid permits secondary electrons to flow between screen and plate.   When the plate

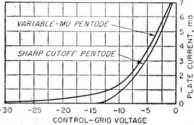

Fig. 6-19. Characteristic curve of a typical variable-mu tube compared with the corresponding characteristic curve of a sharp cutoff tube.

is at a lower potential than the screen grid, secondary electrons produced at the surface of the plate by the impact of the primary electrons from the cathode will be drawn to the screen.   Similarly, when the plate is at a higher potential than the screen, the secondary electrons produced at the screen will be attracted to the plate, particularly if they are ejected on the plate side of the screen.

This interchange of secondary electrons between plate and screen is superimposed upon the flow of primary electrons from the cathode to these electrodes, and so makes the voltage and current relations for the screen-grid tube differ from those existing in a pentode. No such interchange of secondary electrons occurs in pentode tubes; this is because the suppressor grid of the pentode lowers the potential of the space between the screen and plate, producing a potential minimum in this space that is less positive than the potential of either screen or plate.   The result is that the secondary electrons produced in pentode tubes at the screen and plate are attracted back to the electrode of their origin, whereas this is not necessarily the case in the screen-grid tube.

The number of secondary electrons produced at an electrode is proportional to the number of arriving primary electrons and is affected by the voltage of the electrode and the surface condition, as discussed in Sec. 6-4.   Secondary emission is commonly appreciable at potentials of 25 to 75 volts, and it is not unusual for each primary electron to produce, on the average, one to two secondary electrons. On the other hand, when the electrode surfaces have been specially treated to resist secondary emission, the ratio of secondary to primary electrons is much less than unity, commonly 0.2 to 0.1.

Voltage and Current Relations in Screen-grid Tubes. The voltage and current relations existing in a screen-grid tube can be expressed in terms of characteristic curves, such as those given in Figs. 6-20 and 6-21. These curves are seen to be similar in many respects to those of pentodes, given in Figs. 6-16 and 6-17. Thus the total space current of the screen-grid tube is determined by Eq. (6-18), exactly as in the pentode and for the same reasons. The only essential differences between the characteristic curves of pentode and screen-grid tubes occur when the plate potential is less than the screen voltage. Under these conditions, secondary electrons produced in the screen-grid tube as a result of primary electrons striking the surface of the plate are attracted to the screen in large numbers. The net plate current is thereby reduced in value, while the screen current is correspondingly increased.

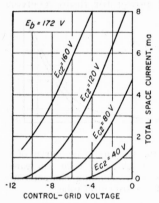

Fig. 6-20. Typical curves showing the effect of electrode voltages on the total space current $(I_b + I_{c_2})$ in a screen-grid tube. Note the similarity to the corresponding curves of the pentode given in Fig. 6-16.

The effects produced by secondary electron emission in the screen-grid tube can be understood by studying the way in which the plate and screen currents vary with plate potential, assuming that the screen and control-grid voltages are constant. Such characteristics are shown in Fig. 6-21. When the plate is more positive than the screen, the plate receives, in addition to the primary electrons emitted from the cathode, secondary electrons produced at the screen grid. The number of such secondary electrons received by the plate is relatively small, however, since the screen intercepts only a small fraction of the primary electrons; furthermore, the secondaries produced at the screen are usually on the cathode side of the screen and therefore are not under the direct influence of the plate. When the plate is more positive than the screen, the plate current is hence very nearly independent of plate voltage, as in the pentode.

When the plate potential is reduced until it is less positive than the screen voltage, the situation changes suddenly. Secondary electrons produced at the surface of the plate are now attracted to the more positive screen, so that the actual plate current represents the difference between the number of primary electrons arriving and the number of secondary electrons lost. Commonly, each primary produces, on the average, more than one secondary electron; when this is the case the plate current reverses and becomes negative. A still further lowering of the plate potential does not change the number of primary electrons that strike the plate but, since the velocity of impact is determined by the plate voltage, the number of secondaries is reduced, and the net plate current is increased accordingly. This increase in plate current with reduction in plate voltage continues until the plate potential becomes so low that a virtual cathode forms adjacent to the plate. Beyond this point, the plate current decreases with further reduction in the plate potential.

During these variations of plate potential, the total space current remains constant except at plate potentials so low that a virtual cathode forms; some of the electrons then return to the vicinity of the cathode and reduce the total space current by adding to the space charge adjacent to the emitting cathode. The variations in screen current are consequently the inverse of the variations in plate current, because to the extent that the total current remains constant, the screen receives the current that does not go to the plate.

The actual shape of the plate-current–plate-voltage characteristic of a screen-grid tube for plate potentials less than the screen voltage is thus

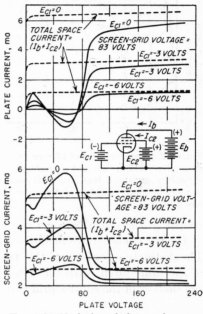

FIG. 6-21. Variation of plate and screen-grid currents, and of total space current, with plate voltage (screen-grid voltage) constant. Note that changing the control-grid voltage alters the magnitude of the curves without changing their shape.

dependent upon the extent to which secondary electrons are produced at the plate. This is illustrated in Fig. 6-22, which shows characteristics for two screen-grid tubes with different amounts of secondary emission at the plate.[1] The corresponding characteristic of a pentode tube is also shown for comparison. It is seen that the addition of a suppressor grid as in the pentode gives the same characteristic as would be obtained with a screen-grid tube having no secondary emission at the plate.

Practical Screen-grid Tubes. Historically, screen-grid tubes came after

---

[1] It will be noted from an examination of Figs. 6-21 and 6-22 that, with appreciable secondary emission at the plate, there is a region where the plate current *increases* as the plate voltage is *reduced*. This gives a negative resistance, and the screen-grid tube when operated in this region as a negative resistance device is termed a *dynatron*.

the triode tube was developed and before practical pentode tubes were available. Screen-grid tubes at present have limited practical application, however, because of the undesirable effects that result from the interchange of secondary electrons between plate and screen. In particular, the practical operating region, corresponding to a plate current that is substantially independent of plate voltage, is limited in the screen-grid tube to plate potentials greater than the screen voltage. In contrast, the useful operating range of pentodes and beam tubes extends to much lower values of plate voltage (see Fig. 6-22).

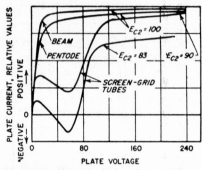

FIG. 6-22. Characteristics of two screen-grid tubes having different amounts of secondary emission, together with corresponding characteristics of a pentode and a beam tube.

6-10. Beam Tubes. The beam tube can be considered to be a special type of screen-grid tube in which the design has been so modified that the action of a suppressor grid is obtained by accentuating the space-charge effects of the electrons in transit in the space between the screen and the plate.

The electrode arrangements of a beam tube are illustrated in Fig. 6-23. The distinctive features of this tube are control- and screen-grid helixes of the same pitch, with the wires so aligned that the screen wires lie in the shadow of the control-grid wires, a flat cathode, side deflecting plates,

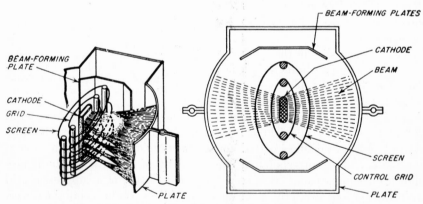

FIG. 6-23. Constructional features of a beam power tube.

and a relatively large screen-plate distance. The side deflecting plates are connected to the cathode and, in conjunction with the flat cathode, form the electrons into a beam with small lateral spread, as shown. Furthermore, the alignment of the grids produces a focusing action that causes this beam to exist in sheets of relatively high current density. The grid alignment combined with the focusing action present also results in relatively low screen current (see discussion in connection with Fig. 7-4).

Characteristic curves giving the variation of plate current with plate voltage in a typical beam tube are given in Fig. 6-24. Comparison with the corresponding curves of Fig. 6-17 for a pentode shows great similarity. The only significant difference is that with the larger values of plate current in the beam tube the plate current is substantially independent of plate voltage down to a somewhat lower plate voltage than in the pentode tube. This, brought out by Fig. 6-22, means that the useful operating

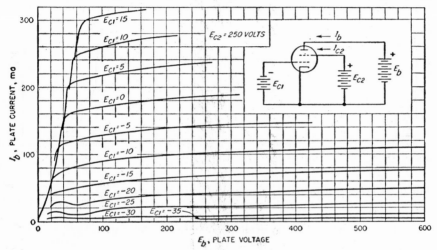

Fig. 6-24. Plate current as a function of plate voltage in a typical beam tube.

range of the beam tube is a little greater than that of a corresponding pentode.

The suppressor-grid effect achieved in the beam tube results from the action of the space charge in the screen-plate space. By concentrating the electrons in a beam and in sheets, as illustrated in Fig. 6-23, and by making the screen-plate distance large so that many electrons are in transit at any one time, the negative space charge in the screen-plate region is sufficient to lower the potential of this space to a value less than either the plate or screen voltage. This gives an action similar to that of a suppressor grid. In fact, since the electrons are distributed, whereas the suppressor grid is a nonuniform structure, the suppressor action of the space charge approximates the action of an ideal suppressor more closely than does an actual suppressor grid.

Space-charge Effects in Screen-plate Space.[1] The details of the action

[1] Comprehensive discussions of this subject are given by C. S. Bull, Space-charge Effects in Beam Tetrodes and Other Valves, *J. IEE*, vol. 95, part III, p. 17, January, 1948; B. O. Salzberg and A. V. Haeff, Effects of Space Charge in the Grid-anode Region of Vacuum Tubes, *RCA Rev.*, vol. 2, p. 336, January, 1938; O. H. Schade, Beam Power Tubes, *Proc. IRE*, vol. 26, p. 137, February, 1938.

taking place in the screen-plate space of a beam tube can be quite complicated. Four basic situations are to be distinguished, corresponding to the four potential distributions in the interelectrode space shown in Fig. 6-25.

The distribution (type A) shown in Fig. 6-25a is characterized by possessing no minimum and no point of zero potential. This is the situation that exists when the space-charge effects in the interelectrode space are small. It occurs when the plate current is small, since this means small space charge. A large screen voltage also tends to favor condition A as against B by increasing the electron velocity, and hence reducing space-charge effects in the screen-plate space. With the type A distribution,

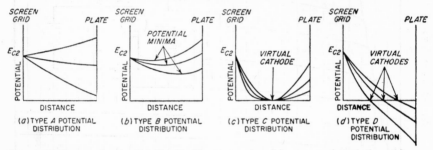

Fig. 6-25. Types of potential distribution encountered in screen-plate region of beam tubes, showing conditions existing for several values of anode voltage in each case.

secondary electrons will be exchanged between the screen grid and the plate, the action being exactly as in the screen-grid tube. As a consequence, beam tubes at low plate current (for example, relatively negative control-grid voltages) tend to show typical screen-grid behavior in the plate-current–plate-voltage characteristic; this is apparent in Fig. 6-24.

The type B distribution shown in Fig. 6-25b is characterized by a minimum in potential in the screen-plate space. This type of distribution occurs when the current density in the interelectrode space is greater than that corresponding to the type A distribution, and under conditions where the plate is still able to attract all the electrons that pass the screen grid. The potential minimum occurring in the type B distribution prevents the exchange of secondary electrons between plate and screen and accordingly causes the beam tube to behave as though it were a pentode tube. The type B distribution corresponds to the normal operation of the beam tube over all of the useful operating range, except at very low current or low plate voltage, as shown in Fig. 6-24.

The type C distribution of potential in the interelectrode space is obtained when the space-charge effects are great enough to neutralize all of the field of the plate. This distribution is characterized by a region where a virtual cathode forms and reduces the potential at some point in the space to zero. This virtual cathode returns toward the screen the excess electrons that the plate is not able to attract.   The type C distribution occurs in beam tubes when the space current is large and the plate voltage low.   Low screen potentials are also favorable for the formation of the type C condition by reducing electron velocity and hence increasing the space-charge effects.   This case corresponds to the portion of the plate-current–plate-voltage characteristic in Fig. 6-24 where the plate current is dependent on plate voltage, instead of being substantially independent of plate potential.   The transition between the type B and the type C distribution takes place very abruptly, giving rise to a sharp knee in the characteristic curves at low plate voltage, as shown in Fig. 6-24.[1]

The type D distribution occurs when the plate is negative, and is characterized by a region of zero potential where all of the electrons arriving from the cathode are returned toward the screen, with the formation of a virtual cathode.

Practical Beam Tubes.   The beam tube finds use as a power tube for small to moderately high power ratings.   It is used for both audio-frequency and radio-frequency power amplification, and has tended to supersede pentode and screen-grid tubes for such applications.

Characteristics of typical beam tubes are given in Tables 6-1 (page 186) and 13-1 (page 455).

6-11. Coefficients of Pentode, Screen-grid, and Beam Tubes.[2]   In tubes having four or more electrodes, the number of coefficients or constants required to define completely all the characteristics of the tube in the vicinity of a particular operating point becomes very large.   These constants naturally divide into three types: the dynamic resistances of the various electrodes, particularly of the screen and plate; the amplification factors (or mu factors); and various transconductances.

Mu Factor (Amplification Factor) of Pentode, Beam, and Screen-grid Tubes.   The mu factor is a generalized amplification factor, being defined as the relative effect that changes in potentials on some two electrodes have on some current in the tube.   In the case of pentode and similar tubes, one can accordingly define mu factors for the relative effectiveness of control-grid and screen voltages on plate current, or on the total space current, and also for the relative effectiveness of control-grid and plate potentials on each of these currents, etc.   In general terms, the mu factor of electrode 1 relative to electrode 2 with respect to current 3 in a given tube is given by the relation

$$\text{Mu factor} = \frac{dE_2}{dE_1}\bigg|_{I_3 \text{ constant}} \qquad (6\text{-}19)$$

---

[1] Some investigators have indicated that a hysteresis effect is to be expected in the vicinity of this knee.   However, recent studies indicate that such an action does not exist in the tube characteristic, and that where observed it is a result of the measuring circuit introducing oscillations; thus see Bull, *op. cit.*

[2] Methods for measuring these coefficients are described by Terman and Pettit, *op. cit.*

where E_1 and E_2 are potentials on electrodes 1 and 2, respectively, and I_3 is the current of electrode 3.

With pentode, beam, and screen-grid tubes there are two mu factors of importance. The first is the relative effectiveness of control-grid and plate voltages on the plate current. This corresponds to the amplification factor of a triode; it is usually simply called the *amplification factor* and is represented by the symbol μ. Under conditions where the plate current tends to be independent of plate voltage, this amplification factor is very high, since then the plate potential has almost no effect on the plate current, whereas the control-grid potential is very effective. Values of amplification factor in excess of 1000 are not unusual for pentodes.

The second mu factor of importance in pentodes and similar tubes is μ_s of Eq. (6-18), the relative effectiveness of control grid and screen on the total space current. This can be termed the *cutoff amplification factor*, since it determines the relative screen and control-grid potentials giving plate current cutoff. Values of μ_s of the order of 5 to 25 are typical.

Dynamic Resistance. The dynamic resistance of an electrode is the resistance that it offers to a small *increment* in applied voltage; the dynamic resistance corresponds to the plate resistance of the triode tube. In the case of pentode, beam, and screen-grid tubes, the resistances of the plate and screen circuits are of importance. They can be defined as follows:

$$\text{Plate resistance} = r_p = \frac{dE_b}{dI_b}\bigg|_{E_{c2} \text{ and } E_{c1} \text{ constant}} \tag{6-20a}$$

$$\text{Screen resistance} = r_s = \frac{dE_{c2}}{dI_{c2}}\bigg|_{E_b \text{ and } E_{c1} \text{ constant}} \tag{6-20b}$$

where E_{c1}, E_b, and E_{c2} are the control-grid, plate, and screen-grid potentials, respectively, and I_b and I_{c2} are the plate and screen currents.

The plate resistance of pentode, beam, and screen-grid tubes is very high under the usual operating conditions, i.e., when the plate voltage is sufficiently high to make the plate current substantially independent of plate voltage. Values of hundreds of thousands of ohms to megohms are typical.

In contrast, the screen resistance of these tubes is moderate, corresponding to values encountered with triodes having an amplification factor about the same as μ_s, and operated at an anode current corresponding to the screen current.

Transconductance. The transconductance can be defined in the general case in terms of the change of current at electrode 2 as a result of a voltage increment applied to electrode 1; i.e.,

$$\text{Transconductance} = \frac{\partial I_2}{\partial E_1} \tag{6-21}$$

In the case of pentodes and similar tubes, one is primarily interested in the transconductance from control-grid voltage to plate current, and occasionally in the transconductance from control-grid voltage to screen current. The former corresponds to the transconductance of a triode and has about the same numerical value as in the corresponding triode. The transconductance with respect to the screen-grid current is smaller than that with respect to the plate current in proportion to the ratio of screen current to plate current. The transconductance from the control-grid voltage to the plate current is the most important single coefficient of a pentode tube. In analogy with Eq. (6-17), it is related to μ and r_p by the equation

$$g_m = \frac{\mu}{r_p} \qquad (6\text{-}22)$$

Relation between Coefficients of Pentode and Similar Tubes and Triode Coefficients. Tubes possessing a screen grid are often employed as triodes by connecting the screen grid and suppressor electrodes to the plate as discussed in Sec. 6-14. Data on the triode performance under these conditions is commonly available in tube data books. By combining such data with information on operation as a pentode (or beam) tube it is possible to infer the numerical values of coefficients on which tube books ordinarily give no information. Some of the more useful relations of this type are:

Amplification factor μ_s of screen:

$$\mu_s \approx \mu \text{ (triode)} \qquad (6\text{-}23a)$$

Transconductance of screen electrode:

$$g_m \text{ (screen)} \approx \frac{I_{c2}}{I_b} g_m \text{ (pentode or beam)} \qquad (6\text{-}23b)$$

Screen resistance:

$$r_s = \frac{I_b + I_{c2}}{I_{c2}} r_p \text{ (triode)} \qquad (6\text{-}23c)$$

Here I_{c2} and I_b are the screen and plate currents respectively. In Eq. (6-23c) the triode plate resistance is that obtained when the triode grid and plate voltages correspond to the control-grid and screen-grid voltages, respectively, for the pentode (or beam) connections. Under these conditions[1] the triode plate current is $I_b + I_{c2}$. In Eq. (6-23b), g_m

---

[1] In attempting to use Eq. (6-23c), it is normally found that the values of I_{c2} and I_b given in the tube books for pentode (or beam) operation are not for the same electrode voltages and total space current $I_b + I_{c2}$ that apply to the triode operating conditions. However, if the triode plate current $I_b + I_{c2}$ is known, the corresponding value of I_{c2} can be obtained from the pentode data by taking advantage of the fact that the ratio I_{c2}/I_b is very closely independent of electrode voltages, total space current, or type of connection, provided only that a virtual cathode does not exist in the tube. After thus obtaining the screen resistance for a screen current corresponding to that flowing to the screen for the triode connected situation, the screen resistance for other screen currents is roughly inversely proportional to the cube root of the screen current [see Eq. (6-15)] unless the tube is of the variable-mu type.

(pentode or beam) denotes the ordinary pentode or beam-tube transconductance that expresses the effect of the control grid on the plate current.

6-12. Mathematical Representation of Characteristic Curves of Tubes. In carrying out the analysis of circuits involving vacuum tubes, it is sometimes desirable to be able to express the characteristic curves of the tubes by means of mathematical expressions. The principal means that have been employed to do this are the power-law method and the power-series method.

Power-law Method of Expressing Tube Characteristics. This method of representing tube characteristics has already been made use of in Eqs. (6-9), (6-10), and (6-18), which for the sake of convenience will be rewritten below in slightly modified form.

For diodes:

$$I_b = K_1 E_b{}^\alpha \tag{6-24}$$

For triodes:

$$I_b + I_c = K_2 \left(E_c + \frac{E_b}{\mu} \right)^\alpha \tag{6-25}$$

For pentode, screen-grid, and beam tubes:

$$I_b + I_{c2} + I_{c1} = K_3 \left(E_{c1} + \frac{E_{c2}}{\mu_s} \right)^\alpha \tag{6-26a}$$

When pentodes, beam tubes, and screen-grid tubes are operated with a plate potential sufficiently high to make the plate current substantially independent of plate voltage, then the plate current is almost exactly proportional to the total space current. For these conditions one accordingly has

$$I_b = K_4 \left(E_{c1} + \frac{E_{c2}}{\mu_s} \right)^\alpha \tag{6-26b}$$

The notation in Eqs. (6-23) to (6-26) is the same as that previously employed, with the addition that α is a constant which in Eqs. (6-9), (6-10), and (6-18) was assumed to be $3/2$. However, when there are dissymmetries in the tube, i.e., when μ and μ_s are not true geometrical constants, it is sometimes possible to approximate the actual characteristic more accurately by employing a slightly different value of α.

It is assumed in Eqs. (6-23) to (6-26) that the velocity with which the electrons are emitted from the cathode, and also the contact potential of the grid and plate electrodes with respect to the cathode, can be neglected. These effects can, however, be taken into account by adding suitable corrections inside the parentheses on the right-hand side of the equations. These equations also assume that the cathode is either an equipotential surface, or that the effect of voltage drop in a filamentary cathode due to heating current can be taken into account by appropriately adjusting the value of the exponent α. Finally, these equations assume that a full space charge exists about the cathode, and that an electron once drawn out of the space charge will not return to it. Hence the equations do not hold when a virtual cathode is present somewhere within the tube.

The power-law method of representing tube characteristics will be applied in Secs. 13-2 and 13-5 to the analysis of class C amplifiers and harmonic generators.

Power-series Method of Representing Characteristic Curves of Tubes. In the power-series method, the tube characteristics in the vicinity of an operating point are expressed in terms of a Taylor series, or power series. The details of this method can be understood by applying it to the case of a triode with equipotential (heater) cathode and assuming that over the limited range to be represented, the amplification factor μ can be considered constant. In such a triode the plate current I_b is some function of the quantity $E_c + (E_b/\mu)$; that is,

$$I_b = f\left(E_c + \frac{E_b}{\mu}\right) \tag{6-27}$$

where E_c and E_b are the actual potentials applied to the grid and plate, respectively. This equation can be corrected for contact potential and velocity of emission in the usual manner, if desired.

In obtaining results based upon Eq. (6-27), one is normally interested, not in the total plate and grid voltages and total plate current, but rather in variations of the plate current which result from variations of the electrode voltages about an operating point. Assume that this point corresponds to a plate voltage E_b, grid voltage E_c, and a plate current I_b. Then one can write

$$\begin{aligned}
\text{Actual plate current} &= i_b = I_b + i_p \\
\text{Actual plate voltage} &= e_b = E_b + e_p \\
\text{Actual grid voltage} &= e_c = E_c + e_g
\end{aligned} \tag{6-28}$$

The letters i_p, e_p, and e_g represent the variations about the operating point, such as might result when a small signal voltage is applied to the grid of the vacuum tube and produces changes in the plate current and plate voltage. Substituting Eqs. (6-28) into Eq. (6-27), and then expanding the latter into a Taylor series,[1] gives

[1] According to Taylor's series one can write

$$f(v + x) = f(v) + f'(v)x + (1/2!)f''(v)x^2 + \cdots$$

or

$$f(v + x) - f(v) = f'(v)x + (1/2!)f''(v)x^2 + \cdots$$

In the case at hand $x = e_g + (e_p/\mu)$, $v = E_c + (E_b/\mu)$, and $f(v) = I_b$. **Therefore** $f(v + x) - f(v) = i_b - I_b = i_p$, $f'(v) = \partial I_b/\partial E_c$, and $f''(v) = \partial^2 I_b/\partial E_c{}^2$.

$$i_p = a_1 \left(e_g + \frac{e_p}{\mu} \right) + a_2 \left(e_g + \frac{e_p}{\mu} \right)^2 + a_3 \left(e_g + \frac{e_p}{\mu} \right)^3$$

$$+ \cdots + a_k \left(e_g + \frac{e_p}{\mu} \right)^k + \cdots \quad (6\text{-}29a)$$

where

$$a_1 = \frac{\partial I_b}{\partial E_c} = g_m = \frac{\mu}{r_p}$$

$$a_2 = \frac{1}{2!} \frac{\partial^2 I_b}{\partial E_c{}^2} = \frac{1}{2!} \frac{\partial g_m}{\partial E_c} = \frac{-\mu \partial r_p}{2! \, r_p{}^2 \partial E_c}$$

$$a_3 = \frac{1}{3!} \frac{\partial^3 I}{\partial E_c{}^3} = \frac{1}{3!} \frac{\partial^2 g_m}{\partial E_c{}^2} = \frac{2\mu}{3! r_p{}^3} \left(\frac{\partial r_p}{\partial E_c} \right)^2 - \frac{1}{3!} \frac{\mu}{r_p{}^2} \frac{\partial^2 r_p}{\partial E_c{}^2}$$

$$a_k = \frac{1}{k!} \frac{\partial^k I_b}{\partial E_c{}^k} = \frac{1}{k!} \frac{\partial^{k-1} g_m}{\partial E_c{}^{k-1}}$$

$$(6\text{-}29b)$$

Here r_p is the plate resistance, g_m is the transconductance, and all derivatives are evaluated at the point E_b, E_c, I_b.

Equation (6-29a) expresses the characteristics of the vacuum tube in the vicinity of the operating point E_b, E_c, and I_b at which the tube coefficients a_1, a_2, etc., are evaluated. This equation is exact provided a sufficient number of terms are included in the series, and provided the instantaneous plate current i_b is greater than zero and is less than the saturation value, and does not possess a discontinuity. In actual practice, the series converges very rapidly so that two or at most three terms are sufficient to explain many important aspects of tube behavior.

The power-series method of representing tube characteristics finds use in the analysis of the factors causing amplitude distortion and cross-talk in amplifiers, in the analysis of detection, and in certain other phenomena such as automatic synchronization. Applications of the method to these specific problems are taken up in later chapters.

6-13. Residual Gas and Its Effect on the Characteristics of High-vacuum Tubes. There are always some gas molecules present in a vacuum tube, even though the number may be small. Electrons collide with these gas molecules, and in many instances the result of such collisions is the production of positive ions. These positive ions are then attracted toward electrodes of low or negative potential, particularly the control grid and the cathode.

Effect of Positive-ion Bombardment on Cathodes. A positive ion that ends its existence by falling into the cathode strikes the cathode surface with a velocity corresponding to the difference in potential between the point in space at which the positive ion was produced and the potential of the cathode. Unless this velocity is low, damage to the cathode may result. In the case of thoriated-tungsten cathodes, bombardment by positive ions tends to strip off the monomolecular surface layer of thorium that causes the enhanced emission. If there are a large number of positive ions, or if their velocity is very high, the rate at which thorium is thereby lost from the surface layer may be greater than the rate of replenishment by diffusion of thorium from the interior of the cathode. In this case the effect of the residual gas present in the tube is to cause the thermionic emission from the cathode to drop off with time to a low value.

With oxide-coated cathodes, ion bombardment causes mechanical disintegration of the emitting surface. This effect begins to appear when the velocity of the ions exceeds about twenty volts, and increases with the voltage and the number of ions.

Ions (and gas molecules) may also damage the cathode by reacting chemically with the cathode material in such a manner as to destroy the emitting properties. This result occurs only for certain combinations of gases and emitting materials; however, it takes only a small trace of an undesirable gas to have a serious adverse effect on the emission. Oxide-coated cathodes are particularly susceptible to "poisoning" of this type.

As a result of positive-ion bombardment of the cathode, the life of vacuum tubes, particularly those using thoriated-tungsten and oxide-coated cathodes, is greatly affected by the anode voltage and the space current at which the tube is operated. A high anode voltage increases the likelihood of a gas molecule being ionized upon collision and, in addition, causes the resulting ions to bombard the cathode with correspondingly high velocity. A large space current increases the number of collisions with gas molecules, thereby increasing the number of ions that are produced. In general, oxide-coated cathodes are most susceptible to positive-ion damage; thoriated-tungsten cathodes are somewhat less susceptible; while tungsten cathodes are the most immune.

Because of the adverse effect of positive ions, the life of a cathode will be greater the better the vacuum that is maintained in the tube during operation.

Evacuation of Tubes—"Getters." In order to minimize positive-ion effects, vacuum tubes are ordinarily evacuated in a manner calculated to achieve the best possible vacuum during their entire life. This requires not only that the gas initially within the tube be removed, but also that the gas absorbed (or adsorbed) by the glass and metal parts of the tube likewise be removed as completely as possible during the evacuation process. Since gas absorbed and adsorbed by solid bodies tends to be given up when heated, it is customary to heat the glass and metal parts of tubes during the exhaust process. If this heating is carried to a considerably higher temperature during exhaust than is ever reached during normal operation, then little or no gas will be subsequently liberated during operation. It is necessary to choose carefully the materials used in a vacuum tube, since different substances vary greatly in the amount of gas they contain and in the ease with which they give it up. In the case of high-power vacuum tubes, the problem of removing all of the gas is often a delicate and tedious procedure, since the normal operating temperature of some parts of the tube may be very close to the maximum permissible temperature to which these parts may be heated with safety during exhaust.

One means of obtaining a high degree of vacuum in a tube consists in introducing into the tube a material that is capable of readily absorbing gas. Such a substance is termed a *getter;* examples are magnesium and barium. Getters are useful not only in obtaining a high initial vacuum, but also because they will combine with any gas that may subsequently be liberated through accidental overheating, etc.

Getters are used in most receiving tubes, and are also frequently employed in medium-sized power tubes.

Grid Current Due to Ions—Maximum Permissible Grid Resistance. Some of the positive ions produced by ionization of residual gas will be attracted to a negative control grid, and will thus cause a small grid current to flow even when the control grid is negative. This ion current has a polarity that is opposite from the grid current that flows when the grid is positive and attracts electrons. Because of its reverse polarity, the presence of ion current sets a limit to the maximum d-c resistance that it is desirable to place in series with the control-grid electrode. This is because the voltage drop that the ion current produces across such a resistance has a polarity that makes the grid less negative than the grid bias. Thus, if the resistance placed in series with the grid circuit is excessively high, the actual potential of the control grid will not only differ appreciably from the bias applied to this electrode, but will be determined by the gas conditions within the tube.

The reduction in negative grid bias resulting from the voltage drop of the ion current in the grid-circuit resistance produces an increase in the total space current of the tube. This increases the number of positive ions that are produced, causing the grid current to increase still further, with consequent further loss in negative bias. If the resistance in the grid circuit is sufficiently high, and if the tube at the same time has a tendency to become increasingly gassy as it warms up due to increased plate current, this process can become cumulative. The control-grid potential then suddenly approaches zero (or even becomes positive); with many tube types the result is destruction caused by overheating due to excessive plate current.

The pressure of the gas inside a tube can be estimated from the amount of grid current present when the grid is negative. This current is proportional to the number of positive ions, which in turn is proportional to the total space current and to the gas pressure. Thus the ion current produced by a given tube structure with an arbitrarily chosen plate voltage and total space current is a direct measure of the gas pressure within the tube.   This is the basis of the ionization gauge used to measure very low gas pressures.

6-14. Special Connections for Conventional Tubes.   It is possible to rearrange the connections and potentials of the various electrodes of ordinary tubes, and thereby modify the characteristics.   Thus a pentode tube can be connected as a triode having a moderate amplification factor μ approximately equal to μ_s by connecting the screen and suppressor grids to the plate, as shown in Fig. 6-26a.   Alternatively, a pentode will func-

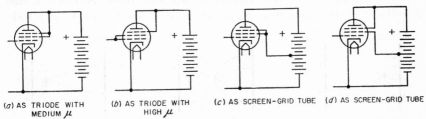

(a) AS TRIODE WITH   (b) AS TRIODE WITH   (c) AS SCREEN-GRID TUBE   (d) AS SCREEN-GRID TUBE
    MEDIUM μ HIGH μ

Fig. 6-26. Pentode tube connected in various ways.

tion as a triode with high amplification factor if the control and screen grids are connected together to provide the grid, and the suppressor is connected to the plate, as in Fig. 6-26b.   Again, a pentode tube may be connected as a screen-grid tube, as shown in Fig. 6-26c and d, by connecting the suppressor grid either to the plate or to the screen.

In an ordinary triode tube, the functions of the grid and plate can be interchanged by making the grid the anode, and by using the plate as the negative control electrode, as shown in Fig. 6-27.   In such an *inverted* tube the negative plate affects the electrostatic field in the vicinity of the cathode and hence controls the anode (grid) current.   However, since this control electrode is relatively well shielded from the cathode, the amplification factor is

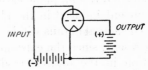

Fig. 6-27. Circuit of inverted tube.

low, being approximately $1/\mu$, where μ is the amplification factor of the tube operated as a triode in the normal manner.   The inverted tube is a useful laboratory tool where it is necessary to control a current by a very high voltage without at the same time consuming energy from the high potential source.[1]

6-15. Transit-time Effects in Diodes, Triodes, and Pentode Tubes. At ordinary radio frequencies, such as 1 Mc, the time it takes an electron to travel from cathode to plate is negligibly small compared with the length of time represented by a cycle.[2]   Under these conditions one can

---

[1] See F. E. Terman, The Inverted Vacuum Tube, A Voltage Reducing Power Amplifier, *Proc. IRE*, vol. 16, p. 447, April, 1928.

[2] In the case of a diode with parallel plane electrodes spaced d centimeters apart,

assume that the electron traverses the tube instantaneously, and that the plate current is due to the electrons striking the plate. However, at frequencies so high that the transit time is not a negligibly small fraction of a cycle, it is necessary to inquire into the details of what goes on while the electron is in transit.

Electrode Current Resulting from Electron Motion.[1] The current flowing to an electrode is the rate of change of charge on the electrode with respect to time. The charge produced on the electrode by an electron in flight is determined by the number of flux lines from the electron that terminate on the electrode. As the electron moves toward an electrode,

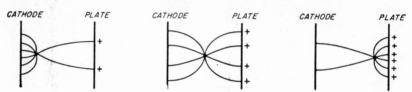

Fig. 6-28. Diagram illustrating flux lines associated with an electron in successive stages of flight between cathode and plate, showing how the charge induced on the plate increases as the electron approaches the plate.

the number of flux lines terminating on the electrode will increase progressively, as illustrated in Fig. 6-28; at the same time there is a corresponding decrease in the number of flux lines terminating on the electrode from which the electron is receding. In addition, as the electron approaches the positive electrode its velocity rises. As a result, the rate of change of charge increases steadily; thus, in the case of an electron emitted from a plane cathode and attracted to a parallel plate anode, the current induced in the plate will vary with time, as shown in Fig. 6-29. The actual details will be affected by whether or not a full space charge is present, since the existence of space charge affects the potential distribution in the interelectrode space, and thereby influences the way the velocity of the electron varies with position.

It follows from Fig. 6-29 that a single electron traveling to the plate produces a triangular-shaped pulse of anode current that begins when the electron is emitted, rises steadily until the electron arrives at the plate, and then drops instantly to zero. The total current flowing to the plate will be the sum of many such pulses, one for each emitted electron that is attracted to the plate.

The anode current of Fig. 6-29 acting in conjunction with the plate

and with full space charge present, one has

$$\text{Transit time in microseconds} = 0.051d/\sqrt{E} \qquad (6\text{-}30)$$

where E is the anode voltage. Thus, if $d = 0.2$ cm and $E = 10$ volts, the transit time at 1 Mc is 0.003 cycle.

[1] This presentation follows B. J. Thompson, Review of Ultra-high-frequency Vacuum-tube Problems, *RCA Rev.*, vol. 3, p. 146, October, 1938.

voltage represents energy that is delivered to the electron and becomes kinetic energy of motion. Since the cumulative total of the energy received by the electron in this way increases as the electron approaches the plate, the velocity of the electron likewise increases as it approaches the plate; this result is consistent with other considerations. Thus the action of the induced current provides the means by which electrons in motion interact with electric fields and exchange energy with the electrodes that produce these fields.

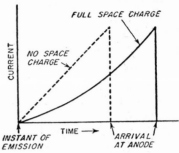

Fig. 6-29. Diagrams indicating the variation of current induced on the plate in Fig. 6-28 as a function of time.

An electron in flight will induce current on any electrode in the vicinity, irrespective of whether or not this electrode ultimately captures the electron. For example, in the case of the control grid of a tube as illustrated in Fig. 6-30, an electron emitted from the cathode and approaching the grid will induce a current pulse *abc* on the grid, where *c* represents the instant at which the electron passes between the grid wires. As the electron recedes from the grid, the induced current is negative according to some curve such as *cdef*, and finally becomes zero at *f* when the electron reaches the plate and is collected. Since no charge is col-

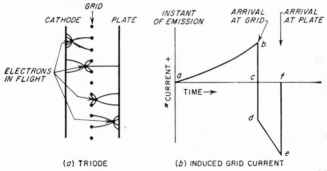

(a) TRIODE   (b) INDUCED GRID CURRENT

Fig. 6-30. Mechanism by which an electron in flight induces a charge, and hence current, on the control-grid structure, together with curve showing variation of this induced current with time for a single electron in flight.

lected by the grid in this case, the positive area *abc* must equal the negative area *cdef*.

Transit-time Effects in Diodes—Small-signal Case.[1] This case is illustrated in Fig. 6-31a; here the voltage applied to the diode consists of a d-c potential upon which is superimposed a much smaller radio-frequency

[1] See Spangenberg, *op. cit.*, pp. 495–504.

voltage. The situation of practical importance is when a full space charge exists.

In so far as the alternating voltage applied to the plate is concerned, the diode can be considered as consisting of a resistance (or conductance) shunted by a capacitance, as shown in Fig. 6-31b. At low frequencies the diode resistance equals the dynamic plate resistance as defined according to Eq. (6-20a). However, as the frequency increases, the transit time introduces a phase difference between the alternating component of the plate current and the alternating component of the plate voltage. The

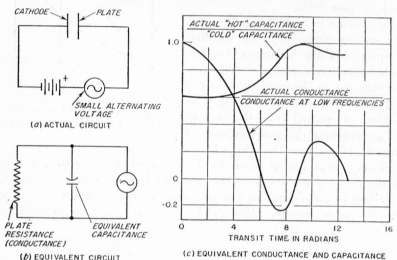

FIG. 6-31. Small-signal transit-time effects in a diode.

resulting behavior is shown in Fig. 6-31c, where the transit time is expressed as the time measured in radians at the applied frequency required for the electron to travel from cathode to plate. It will be noted that the equivalent plate conductance of the tube decreases with increasing transit time, becomes zero (infinite plate resistance) at a transit time of one cycle ($= 2\pi$ radians), and then oscillates alternately between negative and positive values.

The small values of conductance at large transit angles come about as follows: When the transit angle is large, electrons emitted on successive half cycles of the applied signal voltage will commonly be in the inter-electrode space at the same time. The velocities of the electrons emitted during the positive and negative half cycles of the applied voltage will be respectively greater than and less than the velocity produced by the d-c plate potential alone. As a result the alternating currents induced in the plate by these two classes of electrons will be, respectively, positive and negative, and so will tend to cancel. This causes the resultant induced current, and hence the electrode conductance, to be less than at low frequencies when all the electrons in flight at any one time are emitted during the same half cycle.

With certain values of transit time, for example, slightly over one cycle of transit time, the distribution of the velocities of the different groups of electrons in the interelectrode space is such that the net induced current at the plate is of opposite polarity from the alternating component of the voltage applied to the plate. This accounts for the negative conductance shown in Fig. 6-31c.

The equivalent capacitance between plate and cathode of the diode tube is also affected by the transit time of the electrons that are in flight. If one considers only the active portion of the interelectrode capacitance, i.e., the capacitance due to the interelectrode space that is carrying electrons, then the electrons that are in transit reduce the equivalent dielectric constant of this active space, and hence reduce the equivalent interelectrode capacitance.[1] At low frequencies, the capacitance of the interelectrode space with the electrons present (tube "hot") is 0.6 times the capacitance of the same space in the absence of electrons (tube "cold"). At higher frequencies, the capacitance oscillates between the hot and the cold values, as shown in Fig. 6-31c.

Transit-time Effects in Diodes—Large-signal Condition.[2] This case is illustrated in Fig. 6-32a. Here

[1] The mechanism that leads to this result is discussed in detail in Sec. 22-8.

[2] Spangenberg, *op. cit.*, p. 516.

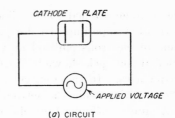

(a) CIRCUIT

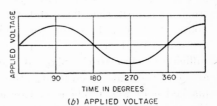

(b) APPLIED VOLTAGE

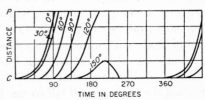

(c) LOWEST FREQUENCY (SMALL TRANSIT TIME)

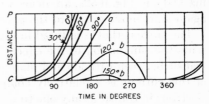

(d) HIGHER FREQUENCY (MEDIUM TRANSIT TIME)

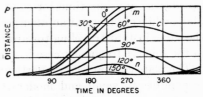

(e) VERY HIGH FREQUENCY (LARGE TRANSIT TIME)

Fig. 6-32. Behavior of diode under influence of a large applied signal, showing the position, as a function of time, of the electrons emitted at various portions of the cycle of applied voltage, for frequencies corresponding to small, medium, and large transit times. The effects of space charge have been neglected to simplify the situation.

the voltage applied to the diode plate is a large alternating potential without a superimposed d-c potential. The variation of position with time of electrons emitted at various parts of the positive half cycle of applied voltage is shown in Fig. 6-32 when the applied voltage has different frequencies. In these curves the top of the distance axis represents the plate position, while the bottom is the cathode position.

A number of important phenomena are illustrated in Fig. 6-32. Thus at the end of the positive half cycle of applied voltage there will be electrons in transit that have not yet reached the plate. As the applied voltage reverses, these electrons are subjected to forces that slow them down and tend to return them to the cathode. Some, however, will be sufficiently close to the plate at the time of reversal that they will still arrive at the plate, even though the voltage has been reversed. The case marked *a* in Fig. 6-32*d* is in this class. Other electrons (marked *b* in Fig. 6-32*d*), which were farther away from the plate at the time of reversal of the plate voltage, will be slowed down to zero velocity and returned to the cathode. These returning electrons will in general strike the cathode with appreciable velocity and so will deliver energy to the cathode, an effect termed *back heating*. If the frequency is very high, some of the electrons that slowed down to zero velocity and started back toward the cathode will fail to reach the cathode by the time the applied voltage has reversed and become positive again. These electrons, marked *c* in Fig. 6-32*e*, are hence brought to rest a second time and then again start moving toward the plate.

The current that is induced in the plate electrode at any instant represents the summation of the effects of the motions of all the electrons in transit between cathode and plate at that moment. The determination of this current is a relatively complicated process because the different electrons in transit at any one time left the cathode at different times and so are distributed not only in position but in velocity as well. Thus it is possible at any one time for some electrons to be traveling toward the plate, while electrons at another position in the interelectrode space are at the same instant traveling toward the cathode, as illustrated by *m* and *n* in the highest frequency case in Fig. 6-32.

The plate current for two particular examples is shown in Fig. 6-33, corresponding to small and moderate transit-time effects. In both cases, positive current continues to flow to the plate after the plate voltage has reversed. This is a result of the fact that, immediately after the plate voltage reverses in polarity, the electrons in the interelectrode space that were traveling toward the plate continue to do so and therefore continue to induce positive current on the plate electrode. However, with time, some of these electrons reach the plate and so are removed from the scene, while others are finally brought to rest and started back toward the cathode. When the majority of the electrons in the space are returning toward the cathode, a negative current is induced in the plate and continues to flow either until all the returning electrons have reached the cathode, as in the low-frequency case in Fig. 6-33, or until the next positive half cycle has lasted long enough to make the preponderance of electron motion in the interelectrode space a movement toward the plate (high-frequency case in Fig. 6-33). With small transit time, the current wave is characterized by an initial peak caused by a bunching action occurring at the beginning of the cycle. This is similar to the action existing in a klystron tube (see Sec. 19-2).

The net result of these various transit-time effects on the plate current is accordingly to distort the shape of the plate-current wave, to delay the current wave with respect to the voltage wave, and to produce a negative current at the plate during certain portions of the cycle. It will also be noted that the length of time during which positive current flows to the plate is, in general, greater than a half cycle.

Transit-time Effects in Triode and Pentode Tubes. Consider a tube in which a small alternating voltage is applied to the control grid superimposed upon the normal d-c grid-bias voltage. As the frequency of this alternating voltage is increased to a very high value, transit-time effects appear, which affect in an important way the behavior of the tube.

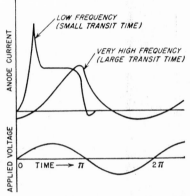

Fig. 6-33. Induced plate current for small and large transit times for a diode tube under conditions illustrated in Fig. 6-32.

The first and most obvious effect of transit time is that the alternating component of the plate current lags behind the alternating component of the control-grid voltage. This is equivalent to stating that transit time causes the transconductance of the tube to have a lagging phase angle.

An even more important consequent of transit time is that the grid absorbs power just as though a conductance proportional to the square of the frequency were connected between grid and cathode. This loss, which is present even when the grid is sufficiently negative so that it draws no electrons, is caused by the current induced in the grid by the passing electrons (see Fig. 6-30).

The mechanism whereby power is absorbed from a small alternating voltage of very high frequency applied to a negatively biased control grid can be understood by the following qualitative reasoning:[1] Consider a triode with a negatively biased grid, upon which is superimposed a small

[1] This line of reasoning is due to W. R. Ferris, Input Resistance of Vacuum Tubes as Ultra-high Frequency Amplifiers, *Proc. IRE*, vol. 24, p. 82, January, 1936.

alternating voltage, as shown in Fig. 6-34. During the portion of the cycle when the instantaneous grid potential is becoming less negative, the number of electrons flowing to the plate is increasing, but the electron density is proportionately greater on the cathode side of the grid than on the plate side since the finite transit time delays the arrival of the electrons at the plate. Under such conditions a current flows into the grid as a result of the positive charge induced on the grid structure by the excess of approaching over receding electrons.

Somewhat later in the cycle, when the instantaneous grid voltage is decreasing, the opposite situation exists, as there is now a disproportionately small number of electrons approaching the grid from the cathode in relation to the number receding from the grid toward the plate. The net result of this excess of receding electrons is to cause an induced current that represents a current flowing out of the grid.

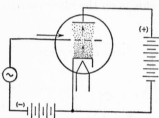

Fig. 6-34. Diagram illustrating the effect of transit time on grid losses. At the instant shown, the grid potential is increasing and there is a consequent disproportionate number of electrons between grid and cathode (shown by density of dots) so that a current flows into the grid.

The magnitude of this current flowing first in and then out of the grid as a result of the finite transit time is proportional to the number of electrons involved (i.e., to the transconductance), to the signal voltage applied to the grid, to the transit time τ from cathode to grid plane measured in seconds, and to the frequency f.

From the above discussion it might be thought that the effect of transit time would be to produce a grid current 90° out of phase with the voltage applied to the grid, i.e., a reactive current. This is only partly true, however, because a closer examination reveals that the alternating current induced in the grid is not exactly in quadrature with the signal voltage applied to the grid. Consider the instant when the grid potential is at its least negative value (maximum positive value of applied voltage). Because of the finite transit time, there is still a disproportionately large number of electrons on the cathode side of the grid as compared with those on the plate side. There is hence still positive current induced on the grid at the crest of the cycle, thereby giving the grid current a component that represents power loss. The phase of displacement between the maximum signal voltage and the moment of zero grid current is proportional to the product of frequency f and transit time τ (measured in seconds), i.e., to the time measured in cycles (or electrical degrees) it takes an electron to travel from the cathode to the grid plane. Since this number of electrical degrees is small, and since both the phase angle and magnitude of the grid current are proportional to $f\tau$, the grid-cathode conductance that can be regarded as accounting for the power loss is proportional to $g_m f^2 \tau^2$.   That is,

$$\left.\begin{array}{l} \text{Grid conductance resulting} \\ \text{from finite transit time} \end{array}\right\} = \text{constant} \times g_m f^2 \tau^2 \qquad (6\text{-}31)$$

The energy absorbed by the grid electrode in this manner is transferred to the electron stream and alters slightly the velocity of the electrons. Small dimensions are of great help in raising the input resistance that a tube offers to very high frequencies.   In particular, close spacing between cathode and control grid is particularly helpful, as the transit time is directly proportional to the spacing.

6-16. Tubes for Very High Frequencies.[1]   Tubes intended for operation at extremely high radio frequencies must have small transit time in order to minimize grid loss, as discussed above.   It is also necessary that both the inductance of the leads and the capacitance between electrodes be as small as possible; this is because at very high frequencies such reactances become very important circuit elements.   Finally, tubes intended for operation at the highest frequencies should have lead arrangements that make them suitable for use with resonant lines (coaxial or two-wire, as the case may be) or resonant cavities, since these are the resonant systems commonly used at very high radio frequencies.

Transit time can be minimized by using closely spaced electrodes, and is helped by employing relatively high electrode voltages.   Lead inductance can be minimized by the use of short leads of large diameter, or by multiple leads (see page 13).   The capacitance between electrodes is proportional to the ratio of electrode area to interelectrode spacing; thus if the linear dimension of the electrodes is made proportional to the spacing, the interelectrode capacitance will be directly proportional to the spacing.

The result of these considerations is that tubes intended for operation at the very highest frequencies are characterized by extremely close spacing of the electrodes, by small electrode areas, and by special lead arrangements.   If the power to be handled by the plate is at all appreciable, it is necessary that the tube, because of its small size, operate at high cathode current densities and with a high power loss per unit area of plate.

Examples of commercial high-frequency tubes incorporating these features are illustrated in Fig. 6-35.   The "acorn" tube of Fig. 6-35a, is characterized by very small size, close spacing of the electrodes, and leads that come out through a ring seal instead of a base, thereby minimizing length.   The type 227A tube of *b* is characterized by closely spaced electrodes, and multiple grid and plate leads that go directly through the glass envelope rather than through a base.

[1] The discussion here is concerned only with triode, pentode, and beam types. Microwave tubes operating on different principles, such as magnetrons and traveling-wave tubes, are discussed in Chap. 19.

The tube of Fig. 6-35c, which goes by such names as the disk-seal, parallel-plane, and "lighthouse" tube, represents a quite different approach to the problem.[1]   Here the active parts of the cathode, grid, and plate are parallel planes as illustrated, and the leads are metal disks. Such a structure can be fitted in to a system of concentric lines as shown,

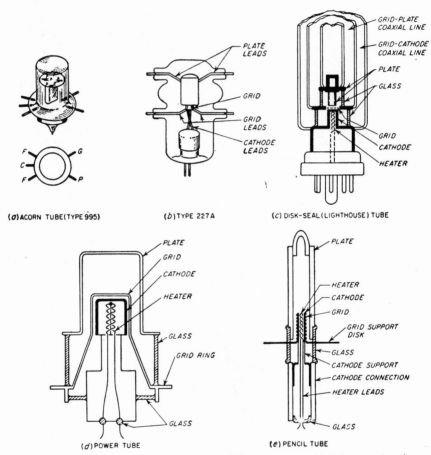

(a) ACORN TUBE (TYPE 995)   (b) TYPE 227A   (c) DISK-SEAL (LIGHTHOUSE) TUBE

(d) POWER TUBE   (e) PENCIL TUBE

Fig. 6-35. Examples of tubes designed for use at very high frequencies.

and for all practical purposes represents an uninterrupted continuation of the line, with the minimum possible lead inductance effects.   In addition, extremely close spacings of the electrodes can be achieved practically with the parallel-plane construction; thus tubes of this type have been built with grid-cathode spacings as small as 1 mil.

Closely spaced cylindrical structures arranged for operation with

[1] E. D. McArthur, Disk-seal Tubes, *Electronics*, vol. 18, p. 98, February, 1945; J. A. Morton, A Microwave Triode for Radio Relay, *Bell Lab. Record*, vol. 27, p. 166, May, 1949.

coaxial and cavity resonators are illustrated in Fig. 6-35d and e.[1] Although mechanical considerations prevent the minimum spacings of these structures from being as small as obtainable with the parallel-plane arrangement, the cylindrical system of d has advantages, particularly for high-power tubes.

6-17. Hot-cathode Gas Tubes. *Gas Diodes.* The hot-cathode gas diode can be thought of as an ordinary diode containing gas, such as mercury vapor in equilibrium with liquid mercury, or helium, argon, neon, etc., at a pressure of the order of 1 to 30×10^{-3} mm of mercury.

As the anode voltage is increased from zero, the plate current of a hot-cathode gas diode starts to increase in the same manner as in a high-vacuum tube. However, when the ionization potential of the gas is reached (commonly 10 to 15 volts), ionization by collision sets in. If external circuit conditions permit, the plate current will then increase to the full electron emission of the cathode

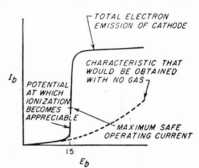

Fig. 6-36. Current-voltage characteristic of a typical gas diode.

without perceptible further increase in plate voltage, as illustrated in Fig. 6-36. This behavior is a result of the fact that the positive ions produced by the ionization by collision neutralize completely the space charge of the negative electrons, thus removing this limitation to the flow of current through the tube.

It has been found that, with oxide-coated and thoriated-tungsten emitters, positive ions that strike the cathode in a gas-filled tube with velocities less than about 22 volts do not adversely affect the cathode behavior. If the velocity of the ions appreciably exceeds this value, however, progressive disintegration of the emitting surface occurs as the result of the positive-ion bombardment. As a consequence, it is important that the circuit external to a gas tube be so arranged that the anode current in the tube is limited by the external circuit to a value that is safely below the cathode emission.

The space-charge neutralization that occurs in the gas tube permits the use of electrode structures that would not be practical in high-vacuum tubes. Thus anode plates can be quite small in proportion to current rating because the low voltage drop of the tube makes the power dissipa-

[1] Typical tubes using closely spaced cylindrical structures are described by W. P. Bennett, E. A. Eshbach, C. E. Haller, and W. R. Keye, A New 100-watt Triode for 1000 Megacycles, *Proc. IRE*, vol. 36, p. 1296, October, 1948; S. Frankel, J. J. Glauber, and J. P. Wallensteen, A Medium-power Triode for 600 Megacycles, *Proc. IRE*, vol. 34, p. 986, December, 1946; and G. M. Rose, D. W. Power, and W. A. Harris, Pencil-type UHF Triodes, *RCA Rev.*, vol. 10, p. 321, September, 1949.

tion at the plate small.   Relatively large spacings between plate and cathode are also permissible.   Emitting surfaces can be enclosed or shielded from the direct influence of the plate because the space-charge neutralizing positive ions are able to penetrate into remote corners. Thus, for a filament, it is possible to use a wide ribbon that is crimped and folded to give a large emitting surface in a small volume and hence have low heat radiation, as shown in Fig. 6-37a.   Indirectly heated cathodes having high current ratings are commonly constructed, as shown in Fig. 6-37b, in the form of a cup containing vanes or disks that are coated with emitting oxide.   This provides a large emitting surface in proportion to heat-radiating area and is permissible because the space-charge neutralizing action of the positive ions penetrates even into the deep pockets of the cathode.   Such a cathode is heated from a central heater, and the entire cathode is ordinarily surrounded by one or more shields that are polished to reduce the radiation of heat.

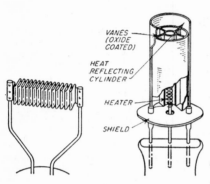

(a) FILAMENT TYPE   (b) HEATER TYPE

FIG. 6-37. Hot-cathode emitting structures suitable for use in gas diodes and triodes.

Hot-cathode gas diodes are widely used for the rectification of alternating current to produce anode power for radio transmitters, public-address systems, etc., where the power requirements are appreciably greater than those of a home radio receiver.   Typical characteristics of tubes for this purpose are given in Table 20-1.

Grid-controlled Gas Triodes (Thyratrons).   The grid-controlled gas triode tube can be considered to be a hot-cathode gas rectifier tube in which there has been inserted a control electrode between cathode and plate. This control electrode serves a function analogous to that of the control grid of an ordinary vacuum tube.   The nature of the resulting control action is, however, strikingly different in some respects from the action of the control grid in a high-vacuum triode.   Thus, if one starts with a grid potential considerably more negative than the cutoff value and then gradually reduces this negative bias, it is found that, at the point where the plate current would just start to flow if the tube contained no gas, the plate current suddenly jumps from zero to a very high value, which, if external circuit conditions permit, readily reaches the full emission of the cathode with plate voltages as low as 15 to 20 volts.   After the flow of plate current has once been started, the control grid has no further effect, and the grid can be made much more negative than cutoff without altering the plate current appreciably.   To stop the plate current, one must reduce the plate voltage below the ionizing potential of the gas in the tube.

The above behavior is caused by the fact that, as soon as the plate current starts to flow, positive ions are produced as a result of ionization by collision. Some of these are attracted toward the negative grid, surrounding it with a sheath of positive ions that neutralize the electrostatic effect of the grid and so destroy the normal control action of the grid. At the same time, other positive ions are attracted toward the cathode and neutralize the space charge. Hence, once ionization has started, there is no space charge to limit the current flow, and the control action of the grid has been lost.

The result is a relay or trigger device that has numerous important practical uses, particularly in control work. It takes little energy at the negative grid to initiate the discharge, and at the same time the resulting energy turned on may be many kilowatts.

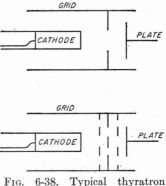

Practical thyratron tubes differ greatly in structure from high-vacuum triodes. The "grid" is typically a cylinder having a diaphragm with one or more holes in it, which separates the cathode from the plate and which is extended to enclose the cathode and plate relatively completely, as illustrated in Fig. 6-38.

FIG. 6-38. Typical thyratron electrode structures.

Mercury vapor in equilibrium with liquid mercury is commonly used in thyratrons to provide gas of the correct pressure. Argon and hydrogen are also used and have the advantage over mercury of not being sensitive to ambient temperature. In addition, hydrogen, because of the great mobility of its positive ions, deionizes very rapidly. Hydrogen thyratrons, therefore, find application where rapid action is required, as in the formation of pulses for radar systems.

PROBLEMS AND EXERCISES

6-1. An electron falls through an accelerating electrostatic field of 200 volts.

a. Calculate the velocity acquired by the electron in centimeters per second and miles per hour.

b. After the electron has been fully accelerated, how long would it require to travel a distance of 1 mm?

c. Determine the energy that the electron acquires from the electrostatic field, expressing the result in both joules and ergs.

6-2. Answer the questions of Prob. 6-1 for the case of a hydrogen ion.

6-3. An electron with a velocity acquired by falling through 100 volts is injected into a region in which the retarding potential gradient is 25 volts per cm. How far will the electron travel into this region before its direction is reversed, and what velocity will the electron have when it returns to the point of injection?

6-4. An electron is injected into a magnetic field with an initial velocity V that is at right angles to the magnetic flux. It is desired that the electrons have a circular path with a radius of 10 cm and that the frequency of rotation around this circular path be 15 Mc. Determine the value of V and the strength of the magnetic field that is required.

6-5. Derive Eq. (6-7) from Eqs. (6-5) and (6-6).

6-6. An electron with an initial velocity is injected into a magnetic field that is parallel to the direction of the velocity. What effect does the magnetic field have on the electron?

6-7. For a tungsten emitter having the emission constants A and b in Eq. (6-8) of 60.2 and 52,400, respectively, calculate the percentage increase in electron emission that results from raising the operating temperature of the emitter from 2500 to 2550°K.

6-8. In tubes employing thoriated-tungsten emitters it is found that accidental overloading of the tube may cause the filament emission to drop to a low value. The emission lost in this way can often be restored by operating the filament for a short time at slightly above normal temperature. Explain what is happening in the cathode under these circumstances.

6-9. What would be the principal difficulty of attempting to employ a thoriated-tungsten emitting surface in the heater-type structures of Fig. 6-3b?

6-10. *a.* A filament emitter is placed in a magnetic field in which the flux lines are parallel to the axis of the filament. If there is no electrostatic field present to attract the emitted electrons, describe the path that these electrons will follow as a result of their velocity of emission. Neglect effects of space charge, and assume that the electrons under discussion are emitted in a direction that is radial with respect to the filament surface.

b. What would be the effect of increasing the strength of the magnetic field?

6-11. When it is desirable that the velocity of emission of the electrons be as low as possible, what type of emitter should be used?

6-12. A secondary-emission curve similar to that of Fig. 6-4, except applying to an insulator, shows unity ratio of secondary to primary electrons at electron velocities of 275 and 950 volts. A target of this material is bombarded by an electron beam which has a velocity such as to strike a grounded target with a velocity of 600 volts.

a. What potential will the insulated surface assume with respect to ground if the auxiliary anode A in Fig. 6-5 that collects the secondary electron has a potential of +600 volts with respect to ground?

b. What difference, if any, would result from making the potential of the anode A with respect to ground (1) +100 volts, (2) −200 volts, and (3) −400 volts?

6-13. In a system such as illustrated in Fig. 6-5, the target is nickel and has the secondary-emitting characteristics illustrated in Fig. 6-4. Assume that the target is initially at ground potential and that under these conditions the electrons strike it with a velocity $V_1 = 1200$ volts. What potential does the nickel target then assume with respect to ground under equilibrium conditions when the potential of electrode A with respect to ground is (*a*) 0, (*b*) −400, and (*c*) −1100?

6-14. In Fig. 6-7, the minimum of potential near the cathode will be less negative if the plate potential is increased. Describe the mechanism that causes this to be the case.

6-15. In a two-electrode tube it is found that at a plate potential of +100 volts, the plate current with full space charge is 90 ma. What plate voltage will be required to produce a plate current of 45 ma?

6-16. In a two-electrode tube it is found that at a plate potential of $+100$ volts, the plate current with full space charge is 90 ma. What will be the plate current when the plate potential is 30 volts?

6-17. In a two-electrode tube a sine-wave alternating voltage, instead of d-c voltage, is applied to the plate.

a. Sketch the resulting wave of plate current as a function of time, assuming that the plate current is space-charge limited at all times.

b. Repeat (*a*), but assume that the plate current is limited by electron emission to half the peak value obtained when the plate current is space-charge limited.

6-18. In a particular triode tube having an amplification factor of 8, the plate current is 10 ma when $E_b = 250$ volts and $E_c = -15$ volts. Estimate the current when $E_b = 200$ volts and $E_c = -5$ volts, assuming that full space charge is maintained at all times.

6-19. In a particular tube having an amplification factor of 8, the plate current is 10 ma when $E_b = 250$ volts and $E_c = -15.0$ volts. Estimate the grid bias required to make the plate current 20 ma.

6-20. A triode tube has an amplification factor of 13 and is operated at a plate potential of 275 volts. What grid potential is required to reduce the plate current to zero?

6-21. Explain the procedure that one would follow in order to plot an entire family of grid-voltage–plate-current curves such as shown in Fig. 6-9, knowing the amplification factor of the tube and having available only one curve of the family.

6-22. Explain the procedure that one would follow in order to plot an entire family of plate-voltage–plate-current curves such as shown in Fig. 6-10, knowing the amplification factor of the tube, and having available only one curve of the family.

6-23. Two tubes are identical except that one has a grid structure that gives a higher amplification factor than the other. If the grids are made positive, and the grid and plate voltages are the same for the two tubes, then the tube with the higher amplification factor will have more grid current and less total space current than the other tube. Explain why this is so.

6-24. In Fig. 6-13 explain why for a given grid voltage the amplification factor becomes less the smaller the plate potential.

6-25. It is desired to operate a d-c relay in the plate circuit of a triode by superimposing a small d-c voltage on the grid bias, thereby changing the plate current. Two tubes are available. One has an amplification factor of 3 and a plate resistance of 2100 ohms, the other has an amplification factor of 12 and a plate resistance of 5000 ohms. Which is preferable from the standpoint of sensitivity (i.e., current change in the relay) if the resistance of the relay is negligible?

6-26. If the tube of Figs. 6-9 and 6-10 is operated in the region $E_c = -20$, $E_b = 200$, determine the approximate values of μ, r_p, and g_m applying to this condition.

6-27. Fill in the blanks in the following table:

	μ	r_p, ohms	g_m, μmhos	$E_b = 250$ volts		$E_b = 180$ volts	
				E_c, volts	I_b, ma	E_c, volts	I_b, ma
Triode 1	3.5		2125	-50		-31.5	31
Triode 2	35	11,300		-5.0	6.0	-6.5	
Triode 3		9,500	1450	-13.5	5.0		3.3
Triode 4			1600	-22	12.6	-16.5	12.6

6-28. If the suppressor and control grids of a pentode were made positive so that both drew current, how would it be necessary to modify Eq. (6-18)?

6-29. Why is it that the suppressor-grid potential does not appear in Eq. (6-18)?

6-30. What would be the qualitative effect on the curves of Figs. 6-16 and 6-17 if the cathode temperature were reduced to the point where saturation occurred at about 5-ma total space current? In answering this question include a sketch indicating the behavior when saturation exists.

6-31. In the usual pentode tube the suppressor grid has a rather coarse mesh. If a suppressor grid with a fine mesh were to be employed instead, what effect would this have upon the lowest plate voltage at which the plate current was substantially independent of plate voltage?

6-32. In a pentode tube in which the control grid is operated at a moderate positive potential so that there is control-grid current, it is observed that the control-grid current is independent of plate potential except when the plate potential is very small. However, when the plate potential is small, decreasing the plate voltage causes the control-grid current to increase. Explain.

6-33. A careful examination of Fig. 6-17 reveals that the plate current and also the total space current are substantially independent of plate voltage down to a lower plate voltage when the plate current is small than is the case when the plate current is large. Explain why this is the case.

6-34. Suggest at least one method of construction that will give a variable-mu characteristic, other than the variable-pitch control-grid structure mentioned in the text.

6-35. *a.* In a screen-grid tube, what would be the effect on the tube characteristics of treating the screen-grid surfaces in such a manner as to enhance greatly the secondary emission at the screen? Illustrate by sketches.

b. What would be the effect if the screen grid of a pentode were treated to enhance the secondary emission?

6-36. If you were given a tube that might be either a pentode with a suppressor internally connected to the cathode, or a screen-grid tube, but you did not know which, what electrical tests could be made to determine which kind of tube it was?

6-37. What happens to the secondary electrons produced at the plate of diode and triode tubes by the impact of the arriving primary electrons?

6-38. It is sometimes found that the current drawn by a positive control grid is negative. Explain how this can happen in a high-vacuum tube.

6-39. A screen-grid tube has the characteristic illustrated in the accompanying figure. Sketch the characteristic that would be obtained if the screen-grid potential were reduced to 50 volts and the control-grid bias simultaneously reduced so that the total space current was unchanged from the conditions shown.

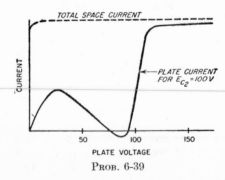

PROB. 6-39

6-40. The curves of total space current for a beam tube will show a slight drop as the plate voltage approaches zero.   Give the cause of this behavior.

6-41. In a beam power tube, the spacing between screen grid and plate required to obtain suppression of secondary-electron effects is less for tubes designed to operate with large plate current than it is for tubes designed for operation with small plate current.   Explain.

6-42. It is stated on page 200 that when the plate current of a beam tube is small, the plate-current–plate-voltage characteristic shows typical screen-grid behavior. Point out the exact feature of Fig. 6-24 that verifies this statement.

6-43. In a beam tube with operating conditions corresponding to a type B potential distribution (see Fig. 6-25), the fraction of the total space current intercepted by the screen grid tends to be independent of plate voltage and is also a small fraction of total space current.   In contrast, the type C distribution is characterized by a screen current which is a high proportion of the total space current, and which, moreover, increases as the plate voltage decreases.   Explain.

6-44. Describe the effect that varying the plate voltage has on the screen current of a beam tube when a type A potential distribution (see Fig. 6-25) exists.

6-45. When a type D potential distribution exists in a beam tube (Fig. 6-25d), is the screen current appreciably affected by the exact value of the plate potential? Explain the reasons for your answer.

6-46. What effect, if any, does a virtual cathode in a pentode tube have on the amplification factor μ?

6-47. In a pentode tube operated so that the total space current is substantially independent of plate voltage, the mu factor μ_s of the control-grid and plate voltages relative to the plate current is substantially the same as the mu factor μ_{sg} of the control-grid and plate voltages relative to the *screen* current.   Explain why this would be expected to be the case provided there is no virtual cathode present in the tube.

6-48. In a pentode, what would be the qualitative effect on μ_s of (a) employing a control-grid structure of finer mesh so that it is a more nearly perfect electrostatic shield; and (b) making the screen grid structure with closer mesh so that it is a more perfect electrostatic shield?

6-49. Evaluate the plate resistance of the tube of Fig. 6-21 when $E_c = 0$, and (a) $E_b = 160$, (b) $E_b = 40$.   Only approximate values are expected.

6-50. a. Estimate the value of the coefficients μ_s, r_p, r_s, and g_m for the pentode tube of Figs. 6-16 and 6-17 in the vicinity of the operating point $E_c = -1.5$, $E_{c2} = 100$, $E_b = 100$.

b. From these values of r_p and g_m calculate μ.

6-51. In a pentode or beam tube operated under conditions where no virtual cathode exists, the transconductance from the control-grid voltage to plate current is approximately μ_s times as great as the transconductance from screen-grid voltage to plate current.   Give the reason for this behavior.

6-52. From the data given in Table 6-1, determine the following constants for the 6AU6 tube when connected as a pentode:

a. μ_s.

b. Transconductance of control-grid with respect to screen current for $I_{c2} = 3.0$ ma.

c. Dynamic resistance of screen electrode, for $E_{c1} = 4.0$ volts, and $E_{c2} = 250$ volts.

d. Dynamic resistance of the screen electrode when the plate current is 0.8 ma.

6-53. Under what conditions could a virtual cathode be formed in a triode tube?

6-54. What limitation is involved in using Eq. (6-25) to represent the characteristics of a variable-mu tube?

6-55. a. If electrons on the average are emitted from the cathode with a velocity v, how should Eq. (6-24) be modified to take this fact into account?

b. The contact potentials of the grid and plate of a triode tube with respect to the cathode are v_g and v_p, respectively. How should Eq. (6-24) be modified to take these contact potentials into account?

6-56. Carry out the steps involved in deriving Eq. (6-29*a*) from Eqs. (6-27) and (6-28).

6-57. In a triode tube, ions produced by collisions of electrons with gas molecules adjacent to the anode will cause more damage to the cathode than ions produced by collisions with gas molecules in the vicinity of the control grid. Explain.

6-58. *a*. Is it possible for the control grid of a vacuum tube to attract positive ions when it is positive?

b. In the case of a triode tube, is the answer to (*a*) affected by whether the control grid is more or less positive than the plate?

6-59. A vacuum tube is operated under conditions such that $g_m = 2000$ micromhos and $I_b = 8$ ma. If the grid current due to ions under these conditions is 10^{-8} amp, then what will be the plate current when a resistance of 50 megohms is inserted in series with the grid? Assume for the purposes of simplicity that the positive ion current flowing to the grid does not change significantly when the resistance is inserted in the grid circuit.

6-60. There are no variable-mu triodes manufactured commercially. Explain how to connect the electrodes of a variable-mu pentode to obtain a tube having the characteristics of a variable-mu triode.

6-61. Describe how a screen-grid tube could be connected to function as (*a*) a high-mu triode, (*b*) a low-mu triode, (*c*) an inverted tube.

6-62. Draw a curve analogous to Fig. 6-30*b* but representing (qualitatively) the current induced by an electron in the suppressor grid of a pentode tube. Show the time axis extending from the time the electron leaves the cathode until it arrives at the plate.

6-63. In a parallel-plane diode the electrodes are 0.1 cm apart. What is the percentage reduction in conductance caused by transit time effects when a small 500 Mc voltage is applied superimposed upon a plate potential of (*a*) 10 volts, and (*b*) 100 volts? Assume full space charge.

6-64. Justify the statement that the transit angle measures in radians of the electrons in a tube is proportional to $fd/\sqrt{E}$, where f is the frequency, d is proportional to the linear dimension of the tube, and E is proportional to the electrode voltages.

6-65. Describe in detail the motion of the electron corresponding to the curve marked 90° in Fig. 6-32*e*, considering in particular where the electron is, and in what direction it is moving, at different parts of the cycle.

6-66. In Fig. 6-32*d* electrons corresponding to the case marked 120° produce a different amount of back heating from the electrons for the case marked 150°. Explain why this is so, indicating which group of electrons causes the most back heating.

6-67. In a particular pentode tube designed with close spacing for ultra-high-frequency applications, the input resistance due to transit time effects is 5000 ohms at 250 Mc with normal operating voltages. What would be the input resistance at 25 Mc if the negative control-grid bias voltage were at the same time reduced sufficiently to double the tube transconductance? Neglect the effect that the change in control-grid voltage might have on transit time.

6-68. Explain how Eq. (6-31) shows that the input resistance is directly proportional to the electrode voltages if one neglects the effect of electrode voltages on the transconductance, but will be proportional to something less than the first power of the voltages when one takes into account the effect of the voltage on the transconductance.

6-69. Explain why reducing all tube dimensions by the factor k reduces both interelectrode capacitance and lead inductance by the factor k.

6-70. Sketch diagrams showing how the grid and plate electrodes of the tubes of Fig. 6-35d and e might be connected across the end of a coaxial transmission line.

6-71. In a hot-cathode gas-rectifier tube the current that flows to the anode is represented almost entirely by electrons emitted from the cathode, the additional electrons produced by ionization being so few in number as to have only insignificant effect.   However, even though only one positive ion is produced for each electron created by the ionization, nevertheless the positive ions are able almost completely to neutralize the space charge of the numerous emitted electrons.   Explain why this is possible.

6-72. In a thyratron tube, a potential of 200 volts is applied to the plate electrode through a resistance of 800 ohms.   Estimate the plate current that will flow when the tube is conducting.

6-73. With a given plate voltage, the grid bias required to prevent conduction from taking place is a more negative voltage for the grid-controlled gas triode in the upper part of Fig. 6-38 than for the electrode structure in the lower part of this figure. Explain.

CHAPTER 7

ELECTRON OPTICS AND CATHODE-RAY TUBES

7-1. Electron Optics—Electrostatic Lenses.[1] Electric and magnetic fields can be arranged to control the flow of electrons in the same way that optical lenses control the travel of light. Thus it is possible by the use of suitable fields to concentrate electrons into a fine spot, or to produce cylindrical or fan-shaped beams of electrons, etc.

Focusing Action of Electrostatic Fields. An electron traveling through a localized distortion in an electrostatic field is subjected to transverse deflecting forces that produce a focusing or lens action. Thus consider the system illustrated in Fig. 7-1. When a potential difference exists between the cylinders, an electrostatic field such as shown in Fig. 7-1a is produced in the vicinity of the junction between cylinders. Now assume that electrons such as a, b, c, and d are traveling in cylinder A along paths parallel to the axis as in Fig. 7-1b; for convenience one may assume that these electrons have a velocity equal to the potential E_1 of cylinder A, although this assumption is not necessary. The electrostatic field in the vicinity of the junction between A and B then causes this parallel beam of electrons to converge to a spot at a point that is some distance along the axis inside cylinder B. This action of the electrostatic field is analogous to that of the optical lens shown in Fig. 7-1d.

The mechanism whereby this focusing action occurs can be understood by a study of the forces produced on the electrons by the electrostatic field in Fig. 7-1. Thus consider an electron following a path such as a that is off the axis. As this electron approaches the junction of the cylinders, it enters the electrostatic field created by the difference in potential between the cylinders. This field exerts a force on the electron that is in a direction opposite to that of the flux lines. The flux lines to the left of the junction accordingly produce a force component directed *toward* the axis, and the electron is accelerated toward the axis. At the same time, the axial component of the flux increases the axial velocity of the electron, since in Fig. 7-1 $E_1 < E_2$. Thus, as the electron emerges from cylinder A and enters B, it has been deflected toward the axis, as illustrated; at the same time, this electron in passing from electrode A to electrode B has undergone an increase in axial velocity as a result of the axial component of the electric field.

[1] A comprehensive treatment of this subject is given by K. R. Spangenberg, "Vacuum Tubes," chap. 13, McGraw-Hill Book Company, Inc., New York, 1948.

Upon entering cylinder B, the electron encounters flux lines that are curved oppositely from the field existing inside cylinder A. The electron is now subjected to a radial force directed away from the axis. However, since the electron travels in cylinder B with a velocity greater than the velocity it had while in electrode A, it is under the influence of this diverging field for a smaller time than it was under the influence of the converging field inside of A. The net over-all effect of the passage of the electron through the electrostatic field created by the difference in potential between the cylinders is hence to bend the path of the electron toward the axis, and to cause the path ultimately to cross the axis as shown.

The radial component of the focusing field in Fig. 7-1 increases with distance off the axis. As a result, an electron path is bent through a greater angle, the farther the original path is off the axis; this causes electrons traveling parallel to each other in cylinder A, but at different distances from the axis (as a and b in Fig. 7-1b), to cross the axis at approximately the same point.

The above discussion has assumed that the incident electrons all travel in paths parallel to the axis. The analogy with physical optics still holds, however, when this is not the

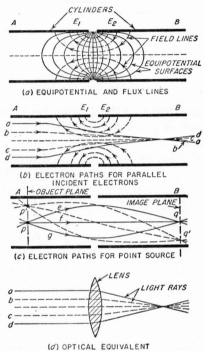

(a) EQUIPOTENTIAL AND FLUX LINES

(b) ELECTRON PATHS FOR PARALLEL INCIDENT ELECTRONS

(c) ELECTRON PATHS FOR POINT SOURCE

(d) OPTICAL EQUIVALENT

Fig. 7-1. Electrostatic electron lens consisting of two cylinders at different potentials, together with electron paths for various circumstances for $E_2 > E_1$. The electrodes and fields shown are cross sections of a figure of revolution.

case. For example, consider the electrons e, f, and g in Fig. 7-1c, which are traveling in slightly different directions, but along paths that intersect at a common point p lying on the axis. The action of the electrostatic lens in such a case is to focus these electrons to a common point q in cylinder B as shown. However, the divergence of the incident electrons now causes the distance from the junction of the cylinders to the point of focusing q to be greater than for the parallel incident beam of electrons in Fig. 7-1b. In analogy with physical optics, the points p and q can be referred to as image and object distances with respect to the center of the lens.

Further, in Fig. 7-1c, if the point at which the paths of the incident electrons intersect is off the axis, as at p', then the point of focus will be similarly off the axis, as shown by q'. Moreover, if p and p' lie in the same plane perpendicular to the axis, then similarly q and q' will lie in the same plane; i.e., for a given image distance the object distance is not affected by whether or not the object is on or off the axis. It is thus

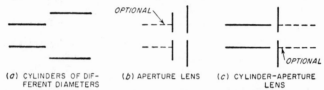

(a) CYLINDERS OF DIF-
FERENT DIAMETERS   (b) APERTURE LENS   (c) CYLINDER-APERTURE
LENS

Fig. 7-2. Typical types of electrostatic electron lenses.

apparent that the distribution of electrons in a plane perpendicular to the axis at p will be reproduced or imaged on a corresponding plane perpendicular to the axis at q. The position of the image plane for a given position on the object will depend upon the geometry of the lens and the magnitude of the voltage difference between the sections of the lens. The greater the difference in voltage, the stronger will be the lens, i.e., the closer will be the image to the center of the lens for a given object position.

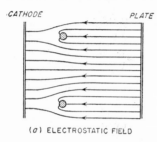

(a) ELECTROSTATIC FIELD

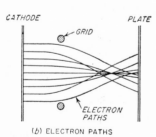

(b) ELECTRON PATHS

Fig. 7-3. Electrostatic field and electron paths for a typical triode situation, showing tendency for electrons to focus in the grid-plate space.

In Fig. 7-1c the ratio qq'/pp' can be thought of as representing magnification. The numerical value of magnification will depend upon the position of the object plane and upon the relative voltages of the two electrodes; it may be either greater or less than unity, according to circumstances.

Examples of Electron Lens Systems— Focusing Action in Triode and Beam Tubes. Any arrangement that produces a locally distorted electrostatic field gives rise to focusing action. Thus the lens arrangement of Fig. 7-1 is only one of an infinite number of possible electrostatic lens systems. A few additional possibilities involving combinations of cylinders and apertures arranged in various ways are illustrated in Fig. 7-2. Furthermore, it is not required that the configurations of Figs. 7-1 and 7-2 be cross sections of figures of revolution (i.e., spherical lenses); they may be regarded as cross sections of cylindrical lenses.

The control grid of a triode tube has a focusing effect on the electrons traveling to the plate. For example, when the potential of the control grid is zero, the electrostatic field has the character shown in Fig. 7-3a.

Electrons passing near the grid experience forces that deflect them away from the grid, with the result that the electron paths have the general character shown in Fig. 7-3b.   The resulting focusing of the electrons on small areas of the plate is a disadvantage in high-power tubes, as it causes uneven heating of the plate with consequent trouble from hot spots.

In the beam tube, the control-grid and screen-grid wires are aligned in a manner that produces a lens system that focuses the electrons into sheets, as shown in Figs. 6-23 and 7-4.   One result of this action is that the screen grid intercepts very little current even though it is at a high positive voltage.   Another consequence is that regions of high electron density are produced on the plate side of the screen grid, which give an action similar to that of the suppressor grid of the pentode tube.

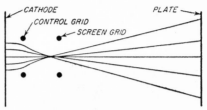

FIG. 7-4. Electron paths in a beam tube under typical conditions, showing focusing action that causes electrons to travel in a fan-shaped beam.

Aberrations.   Electron lenses suffer from the same types of distortions that occur in the lenses of physical optics.   Spherical aberration is one of the most serious of these defects of electron lenses.   It causes electrons entering the lens parallel to the axis to have a focal length that depends on the distance of the initial path from the axis, as shown in Fig. 7-5a. In electron lenses the focal length always tends to become less as the radial distance from the axis increases, and so cannot be corrected for as in

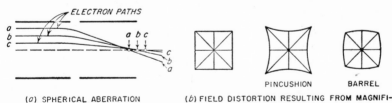

(a) SPHERICAL ABERRATION   (b) FIELD DISTORTION RESULTING FROM MAGNIFICATION DEPENDING ON RADIAL DISTANCE

FIG. 7-5. Diagrams illustrating spherical aberration and field distortion in an electron lens system.

physical lenses, where it is possible to combine elements with equal positive and negative spherical aberrations.

Another typical defect of electron lenses is distortion of the field as a result of magnification depending upon radial distance in the lens.   Thus, if the object is a small checkerboard, then the image with field distortion will have either a pincushion or barrel look, as shown in Fig. 7-5b, according to whether the magnification increases or decreases with radial distance.

Other distortions of physical lenses, such as astigmatism, coma, and curvature of the field, also can be found in electrostatic lenses.   In addition, electrostatic lenses have defects of their own for which there is no counterpart in physical lenses.   In particular, the mutual repulsion between the electrons within a beam makes it impossible to obtain a perfect point focus.

7-2. Magnetic Lenses.[1]   Electrons can be focused by the use of magnetic fields as well as by electrostatic fields.   One way of doing this is illustrated in Fig. 7-6, which represents a system analogous to the electrostatic arrangement of Fig. 7-1.   Here a concentrated magnetic field acts on the electrons, changing their direction of travel in such a way as to focus all electrons passing through a point p on the object plane to a corresponding point q on an image plane.

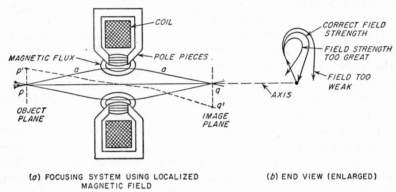

(*a*) FOCUSING SYSTEM USING LOCALIZED   (*b*) END VIEW (ENLARGED)
MAGNETIC FIELD

FIG. 7-6. Magnetic focusing system using localized magnetic field, showing electron paths corresponding to proper adjustment for focusing, and effect of incorrect field strength.

The mechanism whereby this result is achieved is as follows: An electron entering the magnetic field after having traveled a path such as a, is seen to possess a component of velocity that is in a direction which is at right angles to the direction of the magnetic flux lines.   This results in a force being applied to the electron that causes it to rotate about the axis as explained in connection with Fig. 6-1.   This rotational effect, combined with the axial velocity of the electron, bends the path through an arc such that, as the electron emerges from the magnetic field, it is traveling in a different direction than upon entrance into the field When the strength of the magnetic field is properly adjusted, all of the electrons associated with a particular point on the image plane will be deflected in such a way that they are returned to a common point on an object plane, as illustrated in Fig. 7-6.   The strength of the magnetic field required to give this focusing action is quite critical.   If the field is too strong, the electron paths are bent too much when under the influence

---

[1] For further information, see Spangenberg, *op. cit.*, chap. 14.

of the magnetic field; if the field is too weak, they do not bend sufficiently, as shown in Fig. 7-6b.

In a magnetic lens, electrons originating at a point p' off the axis will focus at a point q' that is similarly off the axis, continuing the analogy with physical and electrostatic lenses.   However, in the case of the magnetic lens, the point q' is rotated about the axis with respect to p' as a result of the spiraling effect produced by the magnetic field.

Magnetic lenses of the type illustrated in Fig. 7-6 are subject to all the defects encountered in electrostatic lenses.   In addition, they can suffer distortion resulting from the fact that it is possible for the rotation of different parts of the image to be a function of radial position. This results in the spiral type of distortion illustrated in Fig. 7-7.

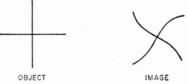

OBJECT   IMAGE

Fig. 7-7. Spiral distortion produced by magnetic lens of Fig. 7-6, in which the rotation of different parts of the image is a function of the radial distance.

Magnetic Lenses Using Longitudinal Field. Instead of employing a concentrated magnetic field for focusing electrons, an alternative possibility is to use a magnetic field uniformly distributed along the entire path of the electrons.   Such an arrangement is illustrated in Fig. 7-8, where the coil is assumed to produce a uniform axial magnetic field.   Here electrons such as a, b, c, and d, passing through a common point on an object plane, possess components of velocity that are radial with respect to the axis.   As a result the electrons acquire a velocity component corresponding to travel in a circular orbit that is in a plane at right angles to the axis of the field, in accordance with Eq. (6-6), where V is to be interpreted as the radial component of velocity.   The combination of axial velocity with this circular rotation in the transverse plane causes each electron in Fig. 7-8 to follow a helical or corkscrew path.   The side of every turn of the helix is tangent to the axis; i.e., at the end of each revolution the electrons all return to a position corresponding to their position on the object plane.   Since the pitch of the helix associated with any particular electron is independent of the radial component of velocity possessed by the electron at the object plane,[1] all electrons passing through a common point on the object plane, such as p, will therefore return to a common point q on an image plane at the end of a complete

---

[1] This results from the fact that the time required for an electron to complete one turn of the helical path is seen by Eq. (6-7) to be determined only by the magnetic flux intensity; the radial velocity has no effect.   The pitch of the helical path represents the axial distance that the electron travels in a time represented by one turn of the helix (i.e., the time it takes an electron to make one revolution).   The pitch is therefore determined only by the axial velocity and the strength of the magnetic field, and is independent of radial velocity.

revolution.   A succession of image planes is possible, each one corresponding to an integral number of revolutions of the helical path.

The radius of the helical path is given by Eq. (6-6); it increases with the radial component V of velocity, and decreases as the magnetic field strength is made greater.   Thus individual electrons a, b, c, and d with different radial components of velocity will travel along different paths,

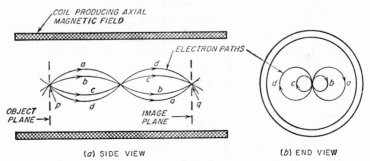

(a) SIDE VIEW   (b) END VIEW

Fig. 7-8. Magnetic focusing of electrons passing through a common point on an object plane, showing how the electrons focus at an image plane.   The particular electron paths shown are for electrons lying in the plane of the paper when in the vicinity of the object and image planes.

as shown in Fig. 7-8b; however, at the end of each revolution all of these paths cross to produce an image, provided these electrons initially all have the same axial velocity.

In this discussion of Fig. 7-8, it has been assumed that the magnetic field was aligned so that its axis coincided with the axis of the electron stream passing the object plane.   If this is not the case, or if the magnetic field subsequently curves, *then the electrons will tend to follow the lines*

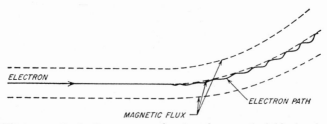

Fig. 7-9. Electron paths in the presence of a curved magnetic field, showing how the electrons tend to follow the lines of magnetic flux.

of magnetic flux.   This can be understood by considering the situation in Fig. 7-9.   Where the magnetic flux lines curve, the electrons can be considered as possessing components of velocity that are parallel to, and at right angles to, the direction of the magnetic field.   The latter component causes the electrons to spiral tangent to an axis defined by the magnetic flux line, as discussed above; at the same time the velocity in the direction of the magnetic field is not affected by the presence of the field.   Thus, as the magnetic field curves away from the initial direction of travel of the electrons, each electron follows a helical (i.e., corkscrew) path of such a character that once each revolution of the helix, the electron becomes tangent to the same flux line.   If the strength of the magnetic field is appreciable, and if the magnetic field does not change its direction too rapidly, the radii of the helical paths will be small.   *Under these conditions the electrons will follow very closely the lines of magnetic flux.*

7-3. Electron Beams of Uniform Cross Section and High Current Density.   In some electronic devices, notably klystron and traveling-wave tubes, it is necessary to produce a beam that consists of electrons

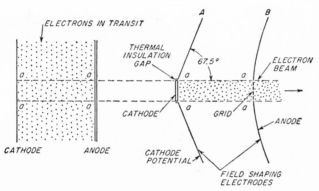

FIG. 7-10. Pierce gun for producing a beam of electrons characterized by rectangular (rectilinear) flow of the electrons.

traveling along parallel paths and representing a relatively high current density.   The production of such a beam requires (1) an electron gun that forms the electrons in parallel paths with a suitable density, and (2) means for preventing the mutual repulsion of the electrons from causing the beam to spread as it travels.

The Pierce Gun.[1]   A beam consisting of electrons traveling in parallel paths can be formed with the aid of an electrostatic field by the following procedure: First, consider a cathode and anode consisting of infinite plane electrodes, as illustrated in Fig. 7-10a.   In such an arrangement, the electrons obviously flow in parallel paths from cathode to anode.   Assume now that one cuts away all except a small finite section of this system and then introduces electrodes that produce the same potential distribution at the edges *aa* of the finite section of electrons still flowing that would exist if these electrons were a part of the infinite system.   Then the electrons of the finite section will flow along parallel paths, just as they would do if part of the infinite system of Fig. 7-10a.   An electrode arrangement

[1] See J. R. Pierce, Rectilinear Electron Flow in Beams, *J. Appl. Phys.*, vol. 11, p. 548, August, 1940; A. L. Samuel, Some Notes on the Design of Electron Guns, *Proc. IRE*, vol. 33, p. 233, April, 1945.

that accomplishes these results is illustrated in Fig. 7-10*b*, where *A* is operated at cathode potential and *B* is at anode potential.[1] The resulting arrangement, commonly referred to as a *Pierce electron gun*, not only produces a beam consisting of electrons that flow in parallel paths;[2] in addition, the only electrons drawn from the cathode are those contained in the beam.

The maximum current density in the beam of Fig. 7-10*b* is limited by the maximum density of emission that can be obtained from the cathode surface. Still greater beam densities can, however, be otained by applying the principles of the Pierce gun to electron flow between concentric spheres. Thus, in Fig. 7-11*a*, all electrons flow in radial paths, and the current density at the anode is greater than at the cathode in accordance

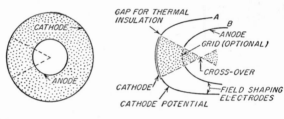

(*a*) SPHERICAL SYSTEM OF   (*b*) PIERCE GUN FOR RADIAL FLOW
ELECTRODES

Fig. 7-11. Pierce gun for producing an electron beam characterized by radial flow.

with the ratio of the squares of the radii.   In Fig. 7-11*b*, which is analogous to Fig. 7-10*b*, all parts of the spherical system have been cut away except the conical section shown, and the electrical effects that the missing parts of the electron flow produce on the rest of the system are simulated by suitably shaped electrodes *A* and *B* at cathode and anode potential, respectively.   The electrons in the conical section accordingly flow along radial lines, exactly as though this section were part of the spherical system of Fig. 7-11*a*.

The electron beam entering the anode aperture of Fig. 7-11*b* consists of converging electron paths. If left alone, the beam will behave as shown, converging to a very small cross section with correspondingly high current density at a point termed the "crossover," beyond which the beam diverges. A parallel beam having high current density can, however, be obtained by the use of a suitable electron optical system that focuses the diverging beam beyond the cross over into a parallel stream

---

[1] Although there is only one configuration of electrodes that gives exactly the desired results, there are many different arrangements that will approximate the required behavior satisfactorily.

[2] The grid shown incorporated in electrode *B* prevents distortion of the electrostatic at the surface of the anode.   If the grid is omitted, the field distortion caused by the resulting hole in the anode gives a diverging lens that causes the beam emerging from the anode to spread slightly.   This matter is considered in Prob. 7-10.

of electrons; alternatively, the converging beam between the crossover and the anode can be converted into a parallel beam by an electron lens system having a diverging characteristic.[1,2]

Control of Mutual Repulsion Effects.   Even after a beam has been formed in which all the electrons are initially traveling along parallel paths, the diameter of the beam will tend to increase with distance as a result of the mutual repulsion of the electrons.   This effect is more pronounced the higher the current density of the beam, and is quite serious in beams of appreciable length.

The spreading of an electron beam can be minimized, or even eliminated entirely, by the use of a magnetic field.   For example, if the combination of gun and beam of Fig. 7-10b is placed in a uniform axial magnetic field, as illustrated in Fig. 7-12a, the electrons will tend to follow the magnetic flux lines, as explained in connection with Fig. 7-9.   In such an arrangement, the radial component of velocity that the electrons acquire as a result of mutual repulsion is converted to rotational velocity.   The spreading of the beam will then be small if the magnetic field is strong, although the spreading can never be made zero.

A modification of this arrangement, illustrated in Fig. 7-12b, is capable of preventing all spread of the beam from mutual repulsion effects.[3,4] Here the beam emerging from the anode aperture encounters a magnetic field produced in the manner shown; the magnetic material serves both as a return path for the magnetic flux and as a shield that excludes magnetic field from the beam-forming gun.   The magnetic field is in an axial direction along most of the path of the beam; however, in the region immediately adjacent to the aperture in the anode the magnetic flux lines converge toward the axis as indicated.   Therefore in this region the field possesses a radial component which in conjunction with the axial component tends to make the electrons spiral inward toward the axis. At the same time the repulsive effect tends to cause the electrons to spiral outward; when the magnetic field strength is suitably adjusted, the two actions can be made to balance exactly, and the electron beam may be as long as desired without any change in cross section taking place.   Under

[1] If the aperture in the anode through which the beam passes is not covered by a grid, then the distortion in the electrostatic field caused by the aperture gives a diverging lens action, which reduces the rate of convergence with which the beam approaches the crossover.

[2] Instead of a parallel beam of high current density, a spot having extremely high current density can be obtained by using a lens system, such as that of Fig. 7-1, that produces an image of the crossover with a magnification less than unity.

[3] This method of preventing the spreading of a beam is often termed *Brillouin flow*, after L. N. Brillouin, who first proposed it.

[4] The theory of guns of this type is given by A. L. Samuel, On the Theory of Axially Symmetric Electron Beams in an Axial Magnetic Field, *Proc. IRE*, vol. 37, p. 1252, November, 1949; C. C. Wang, Electron Beams in Axially Symmetrical Electric and Magnetic Fields, *Proc. IRE*, vol. 38, p. 135, February, 1950.

these conditions, as the electrons travel down the beam they maintain constant distance from the beam axis while spiraling about the axis, and there is no tendency whatsoever for the beam to spread, even when it travels a long distance. The strength of the magnetic field required to achieve this result is appreciably less than the strength of the simple axial magnetic field required to hold a beam reasonably well together.

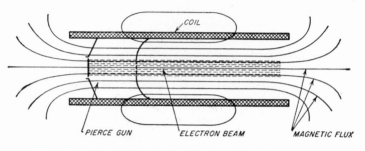

(*a*) PIERCE GUN IN AXIAL MAGNETIC FIELD

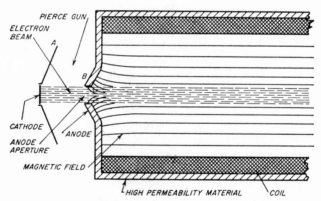

(*b*) COUNTERACTION OF REPULSIVE EFFECTS BY MAGNETIC FIELD
("BRILLOUIN FLOW")

Fig. 7-12. Two methods of employing a magnetic field to minimize beam spread caused by the mutual repulsion of the electrons.

Positive ions produced by collision of electrons in the beam with residual gas are also helpful in minimizing the spread due to mutual repulsion. Such ions are drawn to the center of the beam by the attraction of the negative electrons, and thereby neutralize, at least in part, the space charge of the electrons in the beam. This effect is of considerable magnitude, for even through ions are not produced in large numbers when the vacuum is high, nevertheless, once an ion has been captured by the electron beam, the only way it can disappear is to travel down the beam toward the cathode. In the part of the beam that has passed through the anode aperture (see Fig. 7-10), the axial gradient available to drive the positive ions toward the cathode is very small. This, combined with the large mass of the ions, causes each ion to stay in the beam for a long time.[1]

7-4. Fundamental Features of Cathode-ray Tubes.   The cathode-ray tube provides a visual representation of electrical effects.   Its usefulness arises from the fact that it does so directly and with a speed limited only by the velocity with which electrons travel.   Cathode-ray tubes consist of three fundamental components: (1) an arrangement for producing and focusing an electron beam, termed the electron gun; (2) means for deflecting this beam either electrostatically or magnetically, in accordance with the phenomena to be displayed; and (3) a fluorescent screen upon which

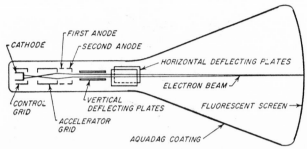

FIG. 7-13. Diagram showing the arrangement of various parts of a cathode-ray tube with electrostatic focusing and deflection.

the electron beam is focused to form a fine spot and which gives forth light when bombarded by electrons.   These essential parts of a typical cathode-ray tube are shown in Fig. 7-13, where the gun consists of the group of electrodes to the left of the vertical deflecting plates.

The Electron Gun.   Beams used in cathode-ray tubes are usually formed and focused by means of electrostatic fields.   A typical electron gun of the electrostatic type consists of a heater-type cathode and four cylinders, as illustrated in Fig. 7-13.

The first two electrodes following the cathode perform the same function as do the control grid and screen grid in beam and pentode tubes, and so are termed control and screen (or accelerating) grids, respectively, even though these electrodes are not gridlike in their physical construction. The first, or control, grid is normally operated at a moderate negative potential with respect to the cathode.   The second, or accelerating, grid is at a moderate or high positive potential with respect to the cathode; in many cases the accelerating grid is operated at the same potential as the second anode.   The number of electrons drawn from the space charge about the cathode is determined by the potentials of these two grids. Control of the number of electrons in the beam in actual practice is

---

[1] A theory of this action is given by L. M. Field, K. R. Spangenberg, and R. Helm, Control of Electron-beam Dispersion at High Vacuum by Ions, *Elec. Commun.*, vol. 24, p. 108, March, 1947.   This paper also describes a means of trapping the ions so they cannot leak out the cathode end of the beam.

achieved by varying the negative bias on the first grid. The apertures in the second grid limit the angle of divergence of those electrons in the beam that succeed in passing through the two grids to the remainder of the electron gun.

The final two electrodes of the gun, termed anodes, provide an electron lens system for focusing the beam into a spot on the fluorescent screen. The glass walls of the tube between the second anode and the fluorescent screen are usually coated with Aquadag, a conducting layer of carbon particles, which is connected to the second anode. In tubes of the metal cone type, the metal walls are connected to the second anode.

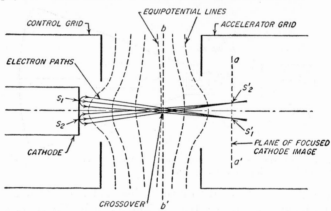

Fig. 7-14. Details of the focusing action that takes place in the region between the cathode, control grid, and accelerator grid.

Both of the anodes are operated at positive voltages with respect to the cathode. The potential of the second anode is sometimes the same as that of the second grid and sometimes higher; the potential of the first anode is always considerably less than that of the second anode. The second anode is connected to ground, while the cathode and other electrodes are made negative with respect to ground. The second anode is provided with an aperture which ensures that the beam emerging from the second anode will be well defined. The first anode either has no aperture, or its aperture is larger in diameter than the beam; in this way the first anode draws little or no current. The velocity with which the electrons travel toward the screen is determined by the potential of the second anode with respect to the cathode.

The electron gun illustrated in Fig. 7-13 is really a multiple lens system. The first lens results from the configuration of electrostatic fields produced by the control and accelerator grids in conjunction with the cathode, and is illustrated in greater detail in Fig. 7-14. Those electrons emitted from the cathode which succeed in passing through the aperture in the control grid are focused in a plane aa at which there is accordingly an image of the electron emission from the cathode. That is, the electrons emitted in different directions from a common point such as S_1 will all converge again at S_1' in plane aa as shown; the same is true for electrons emitted from some other point, such as S_2. In traveling from the cathode to this image, it will be noted that the electrons cross the axis, and at bb the bundle of electrons has a minimum diameter. This is termed the *crossover* and, since its diameter is considerably less than that of the cathode image, it is the crossover that is focused on the fluorescent screen to form the cathode-ray spot.

The combinations of accelerator grid and first anode, and first and second anodes, provide additional lenses, each of which has a converging action on the beam. The focusing action of these lenses is adjusted by varying the potential of the first anode while maintaining the second anode and the accelerating grid at a fixed potential. The optimum adjustment is that which produces the smallest spot on the fluorescent screen, corresponding to the situation that exists when the crossover is brought into focus at the screen.

The size of the spot appearing on the cathode-ray screen is determined by the size of the crossover and by the magnification of the lens system associated with the anodes; this magnification can be appreciably less than unity. The minimum spot size that can be obtained is reduced as the apertures in the gun are made smaller, since in this way the more diverging electrons are discarded. The smallest possible spot size is, however, limited by the mutual repulsion of the electrons within the cathode-ray beam and by the fact that since different electrons are emitted from the cathode with different velocities of emission, there is a randomness in the beam behavior.[1]

In a few types of cathode-ray tubes the final focusing of the electron beam into a spot is accomplished with the aid of a magnetic field. Such a tube, shown in Fig. 7-15, uses a magnetic lens system of the type illustrated in Fig. 7-6. When magnetic focusing is employed, only a single anode is required.

Deflection Systems. The beam emerging from the electron gun may be deflected either electrostatically or magnetically.

In electrostatic deflection, two pairs of deflecting plates at right angles to each other are provided, as in Fig. 7-13; the position on the fluorescent screen which the beam strikes can then be controlled by voltages applied between these plates. The deflection obtained in this way is proportional to the deflecting voltage and inversely proportional to the beam voltage, according to the relation

$$\text{Deflection on screen} = \frac{Lb}{2a}\frac{E_d}{E_a} \tag{7-1}$$

[1] A good introductory discussion on minimum spot size is given by J. R. Pierce, Physical Limitations in Electron Ballistics, *Bell System Tech. J.*, vol. 24, p. 305, July–October, 1945.

where L = length of beam from center of deflecting plates to fluorescent screen

b = effective length of deflecting plates in direction of beam[1]

a = spacing of deflecting plates at right angles to the beam

E_d = deflecting voltage between plates

E_a = beam voltage, i.e., voltage between cathode and final anode

Any units of length may be used. With typical tubes, the deflection sensitivity is usually between 50 and 200 volts per in. at moderately high beam voltages.

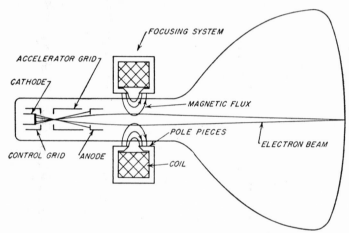

Fig. 7-15. Cathode-ray tube employing magnetic focusing.

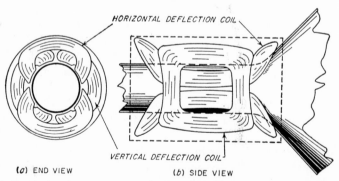

(a) END VIEW   (b) SIDE VIEW

Fig. 7-16. Typical coil system for producing magnetic deflection. The arrangement shown provides one pair of coils for vertical deflection, and a second set for horizontal deflection.

Magnetic deflection is obtained by applying a magnetic field in such a way that the flux lines are perpendicular to the beam for a short distance along its length and also at right angles to the direction of the desired deflection (see Fig. 7-16). Electrons passing through this magnetic field

[1] When fringing flux is taken into account, the effective length of the deflecting plates exceeds the actual length by approximately the spacing between the plates.

will then have a force exerted on them that is at right angles to the direction of motion of the electrons and to the direction of the field, as explained in Sec. 6-2, and so will move along a section of an arc which, if the field is constant, will be a section of a circle. This causes the electrons emerging from the magnetic field to be traveling at an angle with respect to their original direction. In the idealized case, where the magnetic field is of uniform strength B gauss over a limited distance l, and is zero outside of this region, then the deflection is

$$\text{Deflection at screen in centimeters} = \frac{0.296lLB}{\sqrt{E_a}} \qquad (7\text{-}2)$$

where L is the distance from the center of the deflecting field to the fluorescent screen, and E_a is the voltage of the beam, i.e., the voltage between cathode and final anode. All dimensions in Eq. (7-2) are in centimeters.

Magnetic and electrostatic deflecting systems possess different properties, and as a result each has its own special field of usefulness. Electrostatic deflection requires little or no power for deflection, whereas coils have losses and require a large current as well. Also, electrostatic deflection can be used at frequencies far above those for which practical deflecting coils will produce the required magnetic field. As a result, electrostatic deflection is preferred for instrument use, and at the higher frequencies. At the same time, the deflection sensitivity of an electrostatic arrangement decreases more rapidly with increased anode voltage than is the case with magnetic deflection; also, electrostatic deflection suffers greater deflection defocusing (see below) than does magnetic deflection when the beam is bent through a large angle. Thus magnetic deflection is preferred in cathode-ray tubes used in television, because the larger permissible angle of deflection reduces the tube length for a given diameter.

Examination of Eqs. (7-1) and (7-2) shows that the deflection sensitivity decreases as the beam voltage is increased. At the same time, the brightness of the spot produced at the fluorescent screen increases with beam voltage. Thus in general it is necessary to sacrifice deflection sensitivity to achieve visual sensitivity, or vice versa.

When an electron beam is deflected from the axial direction, there is a tendency for the shape of the spot that appears on the fluorescent screen to be distorted and for the size of the spot to be enlarged. This phenomenon is termed *deflection defocusing*. It is less with magnetic deflection; hence when a large deflection angle is desired, magnetic deflection is preferred to electrostatic deflection.

Cathode-ray tubes are available which possess a radial deflecting electrode in addition to the normal electrostatic deflection system shown in Fig. 7-13. An arrangement of this type is illustrated in Fig. 7-17a. The usual method of using such a tube consists in applying to the two pairs of electrostatic deflecting plates, sinusoidal deflecting voltages that are equal in magnitude but 90° out of phase. This produces a circular path on the fluorescent screen, as illustrated in Fig. 7-17b. Voltage applied between the radial deflecting electrode and the second anode (which is connected to the Aquadag coating on the walls of the tube) then produces a radial deflection of this circular trace. Thus the effect of applying a short negative pulse to the radial electrode once each cycle is illustrated in Fig. 7-17b.

The Cathode-ray Screen. The cathode-ray screen is composed of material, termed a phosphor, that will emit light when bombarded by electrons.

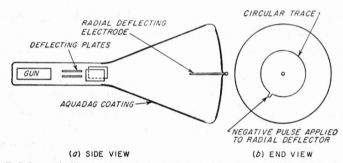

FIG. 7-17. Schematic illustration of a cathode-ray tube with radial reflecting electrode, together with a typical screen pattern such as would result from using the deflecting plates to produce a circular trace while applying a synchronized pulse to the radial electrode.

There are innumerable possible phosphors which differ in color, persistence, efficiency, etc. One of the commonest is willemite (zinc orthosilicate, $ZnO + SiO_2$, with traces of manganese as an activator), which produces the familiar greenish trace of small general-purpose cathode-ray tubes. Other useful screen materials include compounds of zinc, cadmium, magnesium, and silicon.[1] The presence, in proportions as small as 1 part in 100,000, of certain metals, such as silver, manganese, copper, and chromium, may increase the light output of the screen by a factor of 10 to 100 and will also affect the color. Such materials are termed "activators." Phosphors are prepared by grinding, crystallizing, regrinding, etc., and are then deposited on the end of the cathode-ray tube by settling out of a liquid suspension.

The light output of a fluorescent screen is proportional to the number of bombarding electrons, i.e., to the beam current, and increases approximately as the square of the anode voltage. The spectral distribution of the light depends upon the base material and upon the activator, and a great variety of colors is available.

[1] A useful tabulation of phospors is Fluorescent Compounds, *Electronics Buyers Guide*, p. M-11, June, 1949.

The light produced by the screen does not disappear immediately when bombardment by electrons ceases; likewise, it takes the light a brief time to reach its maximum.   Typical build-up times range from a few microseconds to a few milliseconds, depending upon the screen material.   Likewise, the persistence may be as short as a few microseconds, or as long as tens of seconds or even minutes.

A long persistence time is achieved by the use of double-layer screens. Here the fluorescent material adjacent to the glass is of a type having very long persistence, and is excited by the light generated by a second layer of different composition having a very short persistence.   This second layer is bombarded by the electron beam, and is sufficiently thick so that the electrons do not penetrate it.   The colors emitted by the two layers are typically different, the short-persistence layer usually being bluish, while the long-persistence screen gives yellowish phosphorescence.

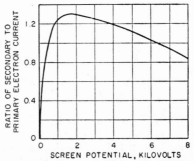

FIG. 7-18. Secondary-emission characteristic of a typical cathode-ray screen.

The return circuit to the cathode for the electrons striking the screen of a cathode-ray tube is usually completed by the secondary electrons emitted from the screen.   This comes about through the fact that most screen materials have such low conductivity that they act as insulators in the manner discussed on page 177.   Stable operation is accordingly possibly only when at least one secondary electron is produced per primary electron; in this case the potential of the fluorescent screen will approximate either the anode potential or the "sticking" potential of the screen, whichever is lower.   The secondary-emission characteristic of a typical cathode-ray screen is given in Fig. 7-18.

7-5. Cathode-ray Tubes—Special Considerations.   *Transit-time Effects with Electrostatic Deflection.*   The deflection sensitivity with electrostatic deflection as calculated by Eq. (7-1) assumes that the time required by an electron in the beam to travel a distance corresponding to the length of the deflecting plate is negligible compared with the length of time represented by a cycle of the deflecting voltage.   When the frequency of the deflecting voltage is so high that this is not true, then the magnitude of the deflection is reduced, and there is a phase difference in the deflections produced by the vertical and by the horizontal plates as a result of the time required by the electrons to travel between the two sets of plates.

The effect of transit time on the deflection sensitivity is given by the equation[1]

$$\frac{\text{Deflection at high frequency}}{\text{Deflection at low frequency}} = \frac{\sin (\omega T/2)}{\omega T/2} \qquad (7\text{-}3)$$

where T is the time in seconds, required for the electron to travel a distance that is equal to the effective length of the deflecting plates, and ω is 2π times the frequency of the deflecting voltage in cycles per second. It will be noted that ωT is the transit time in radians. The results of Eq. (7-3) are plotted in Fig. 7-19. The deflection sensitivity is seen to be 0.9 times the static sensitivity when the transit angle along the deflecting plate is $\pi/2$ radians (i.e., 90°), i.e., when the time required to travel the length of the deflecting plate is one-fourth of a cycle.

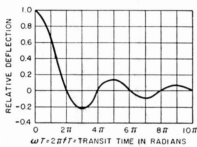

FIG. 7-19. Relative deflection of cathode-ray tube spot as a function of the time required by the electron to travel the length of the deflecting plate measured in radians at the frequency of the deflecting voltage.

Typical cathode-ray tubes with moderately high anode voltages do not suffer seriously from transit-time effects until the frequency of the deflecting voltage is well in excess of 100 Mc.

Cathode-ray Tubes with Post-deflection Acceleration. The desirability of combining high deflection sensitivity with high visual sensitivity has lead to the development of cathode-ray tubes employing postdeflection acceleration. Such tubes can be considered as consisting of an ordinary electrostatically deflected cathode-ray tube with a moderate anode voltage, to which there has been added an "intensifier" electrode that accelerates the electrons after deflection, and just before they strike the screen. In this way, good deflection sensitivity is obtained because it is a relatively low velocity beam that is being deflected; at the same time the visual sensitivity is high because of the subsequent acceleration of the electrons. The intensifier electrode consists of a ring of conducting material inside the tube near the fluorescent screen, as illustrated in Fig. 7-20, which is operated at a potential with respect to the cathode that is several times as great as the potential of the second anode.[2]

---

[1] This is an idealized formula; practical results will be modified by fringing flux, and the displacement of the emerging beam from the axis. An excellent discussion of transit-time effects is given by Hans E. Hollmann, The Dynamic Sensitivity and Calibration of Cathode-ray Oscilloscopes at Very-high Frequencies, *Proc. IRE*, vol. 38, p. 32, January, 1950.

[2] For further information on postdeflection acceleration, see I. E. Lempert and R. Feldt, "The 5RP Multiband Tube; an Intensifier Type Cathode-ray Tube for High-voltage Operation," *Proc. IRE*, vol. 34, p. 432, July, 1946.

Postdeflection acceleration has the disadvantage that it increases deflection defocusing. Also, the method is useful only with electrostatic deflecting systems; no useful benefit being obtained with magnetic deflection when one also takes into account the minimum possible spot size obtainable.[1]

Ion Spot ("Burning") and Ion Trap. Thermionic cathodes emit a small number of negative ions, which, if allowed to strike the same part of the fluorescent screen over long periods of time, produce a darkening of the screen, termed "burning." These ions follow the same path through the electrostatic focusing and deflecting fields of a cathode-ray

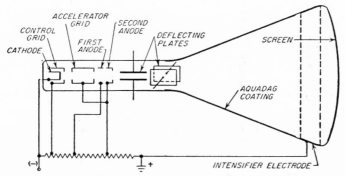

FIG. 7-20. Cathode-ray tube with postdeflection acceleration.

tube as do electrons, but having very low velocity they are substantially unaffected by magnetic fields used for either focusing or deflecting.

Ions are particularly troublesome in cathode-ray tubes employing electrostatic focusing and magnetic deflection. Here the focusing system concentrates the ions into a sharply defined beam, while the fact that the magnetic deflecting field has negligible effect upon the ions causes the ions always to strike the same spot on the screen. The result then is that as the tube is used, a dark spot gradually appears at a point on the screen corresponding to zero deflection.

This ion blemish can be prevented by the use of a trap that removes the ions without affecting the electrons. While many forms of traps are possible, the most commonly employed arrangement is illustrated in Fig. 7-21. Here, the electrostatic field between the second (accelerator) grid and the first anode is given a transverse component by arranging the geometry so that the slot between these electrodes is at an angle with respect to the axis of the gun. This transverse component produces a transverse deflecting action that affects the electrons and the ions equally. However, the tendency for the path of the electrons to bend is then counteracted by a magnetic field of suitable strength that is applied to

[1] See J. R. Pierce, After-acceleration and Deflection, *Proc. IRE*, vol. 29, p. 28, January, 1941.

the beam in the region of the transverse electric field. This magnetic field has negligible effect on the ions, however, which accordingly strike the sides of the gun and are thereby removed.[1]

"Burning" from negative ions can be greatly reduced by the use of an aluminized screen (see below) which will intercept most of the ions. The use of a high anode voltage is also helpful, the burning effect tending to disappear when the anode voltage is in excess of 10 kc.

Aluminized Screens.[2] In some cathode-ray tubes, the side of the fluorescent screen toward the gun is covered with an extremely thin film of aluminum deposited by evapora-

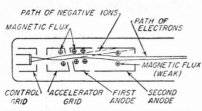

FIG. 7-21. Schematic diagram of ion trap.

tion. Such a film is almost completely transparent to high voltage electrons, and has a number of advantages when the anode voltage is in the order of 10 kv or more. Thus the aluminized screen removes the "sticking" action at high anode voltages by providing a means for removing the primary electrons without depending upon secondary emission. It also eliminates ion-spot trouble, gives improved contrast between the light and dark areas, and increases the light output by reflecting forward the light that would otherwise be radiated backward toward the gun.

Photography of Cathode-ray Traces.[3] In photographing cathode-ray traces, it is desired to obtain a dense negative trace with high contrast. The photographic effect will naturally be greater as the beam power for a given spot size is increased, as this increases the brightness of the spot. The effectiveness will also depend upon the type of screen, being for example much greater with the phosphor designated as P1 than for the phosphor P5. In photographing recurrent traces, the exposure time is limited only by the fogging due to stray light and can be determined experimentally. In the case of transient phenomena, the film trace density is determined by the speed of the trace, the beam power of the cathode-ray tube, the lens stop, and the image magnification. Again, suitable combinations can be determined experimentally. Potentials of the order of 2.5 kv on the anode permit writing speeds of the order of 10

[1] R. M. Bowie, The Negative Ion Blemish in a Cathode-ray Tube and Its Elimination, *Proc. IRE*, vol. 36, p. 1482, December, 1948.

[2] D. W. Epstein and L. Pensak, Improved Cathode-ray Tubes with Metal-backed Luminescent Screws, *RCA Rev.*, vol. 7, p. 5, March, 1946.

[3] R. Feldt, Photographic Patterns on Cathode Ray Tubes, *Electronics*, vol. 17, p. 130, February, 1944; "Photographic Materials Available for Use with Oscillograph, Cathode-ray Tubes, and Similar Recording Instruments," a booklet available from Eastman Kodak Company; R. G. Hopkinson, The Photography of Cathode-ray-tube Traces, *J. IEE (Radiolocation Conven.)*, vol. 93, pt. IIIA, p. 808, 1946.

to 100 km per sec to be recorded, and it has been found possible to photograph traces with writing speeds as high as 1000 km per sec with standard tubes at an anode potential of 10 kv.

PROBLEMS AND EXERCISES

7-1. Describe qualitatively the lens action that occurs in Fig. 7-1*b* when the potential of cylinder *B* is less than the potential of cylinder *A*, so that the direction of the electric lines of flux is reversed from that shown.

7-2. In the electron lens system of Fig. 7-1, explain why it is reasonable to expect that the electrons will come to a focus at a point that is closer to the junction of the cylinders if the difference in voltage between the cylinders is increased.

7-3. The electrode arrangement of the accompanying figure produces lines of electric flux as shown when the inner electrode is more positive than the outer electrode.

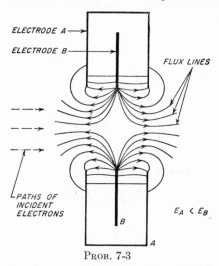

PROB. 7-3

a. Determine the type of lens action that occurs when a beam of electrons approaches the aperture in the manner indicated.

b. Will the focusing action obtained be changed in general character if the potential of the inner electrode is less than that of the outer electrode, so that the directions of the flux lines in the figure are reversed? If so, what type of action is obtained? Give reasons for the conclusions drawn.

7-4. Deduce the type of focusing action produced by the electrode configuration of Fig. 7-2*c* for electrons traveling parallel to the axis of the cylinder, from left to right, and assuming that the plane electrode is more positive than the cylinder. In the discussion make use of a sketch that shows qualitatively the flux configuration and equipotential lines associated with the lens system. Assume that the dotted cylinder is present.

7-5. Deduce that a converging lens action would be expected from the electric field configuration of Fig. 7-3*a* in so far as electrons originating at the cathode and traveling toward the grid are concerned.

7-6. In a lens possessing pincushion distortion, as in Fig. 7-5, assume the object is a series of concentric circles. Then show the nature of the distortion that the lens introduces by making a rough sketch of the image that would result, showing a sketch of the object alongside for comparison.

7-7. In a system such as illustrated in Fig. 7-6, the velocity of the electron beam, as measured in volts, is increased by a factor of 4. What change in strength must the focusing field have in order to maintain the same electron paths with the same radius of curvature, so that the beam will be brought to focus at the same point as before?

7-8. In an arrangement such as illustrated in Fig. 7-8, calculate the distance between the object and the first image plane, and between successive image planes, when the electron beam possesses an axial velocity of 1000 volts and the strength of the magnetic field is 100 gauss.

7-9. In Prob. 7-8, determine the *diameter* of the helical path for an electron having a radial component of velocity of 1.6 volts. Neglect space-charge repulsion effects.

7-10. In the Pierce gun of Fig. 7-10b, omission of the grid in the anode will cause the electric field in the vicinity of the anode aperture to have the character shown in the accompanying figure. For this situation, show that the electron beam emerging from the anode will not consist of electrons flowing in parallel paths, but rather will be a diverging beam.

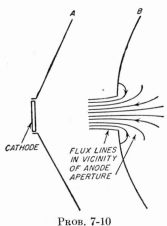

PROB. 7-10

7-11. In an electron gun of the type illustrated in Fig. 7-11b, it is desired that a beam of 1.2 amp enter an anode aperture that has an area of 1 sq cm. If the maximum current density that it is desired to draw from the cathode is limited to 0.2 amp per sq cm, determine the cathode area and the radius of curvature of the cathode surface when the spacing between the anode and the cathode along the axis of the beam is 3 cm.

7-12. In a beam of the type illustrated in Fig. 7-10, positive ions resulting from ionization by collision are attracted to the center of the beam by the negative space charge; however, the density of the ions in the portion of the beam between cathode and anode is very much less than the density of the ions in the portion of the beam to the right of the anode aperture. Explain.

7-13. For the electron gun of Fig. 7-13, make a qualitative sketch of the electric flux lines which the beam encounters in the region between the accelerator grid, first anode, and second anode, for the case where the accelerator grid and second anode are at the same potential, while the first anode is at a much lower potential. From these fields, deduce that the gap between the accelerator grid and first anode and the gap between the first and second anodes both produce a converging action on the electron beam.

7-14. In a cathode-ray tube, an image of the cathode appears in plane *aa* of Fig. 7-14.

Would it be possible to form a spot at the screen by proper focusing of this cathode image? Even if this were possible, explain why it would not be done in practical tubes.

7-15. In Fig. 7-15 the crossover of the electron beam is focused into a spot at the fluorescent screen by a combination of a magnetic and an electrostatic lens. What electrodes form the electrostatic lens involved?

7-16. It will be noted from Eq. (7-1) that electrostatic deflection is not affected by the mass of the changed particle being deflected provided that the velocity in *volts* is independent of the mass. Explain how this can be true in view of the fact that, as the mass increases, a given deflecting force produces a smaller acceleration in the sidewise direction.

7-17. In an electrostatic deflecting system, explain by geometrical means why the deflection produced by a given voltage with a particular set of deflecting plates is proportional to the distance between the plates and the fluorescent screen.

7-18. Compare the relative deflection sensitivities of two cathode-ray tubes which differ in that all physical dimensions of one tube are half those of the other, while the anode voltage of the smaller tube is also reduced to one-half that of the larger tube. Consider both electrostatic deflection sensitivity (centimeters per volt) and magnetic deflection sensitivity (centimeters per gauss).

7-19. Explain why a badly focused electron beam produces the same total light output when striking a fluorescent screen as does the same beam well focused, even though the brightness of the properly focused spot is much greater.

7-20. In a cathode-ray tube the velocity of the electron beam passing the deflecting plates is 2000 volts, and the effective length of the deflecting plates in an axial direction is 2 cm. What is the highest frequency for which the deflection sensitivity is at least 0.9 times the static sensitivity of deflection?

7-21. In a system of postdeflection acceleration, explain why an intensifier electrode should be placed very close to the fluorescent screen, as in Fig. 7-19, rather than midway between screen and deflector plates.

7-22. Explain why with magnetic focusing the ion spot has a diameter somewhat larger than the diameter of the aperture in the anode (see Fig. 7-15), whereas with electrostatic focusing the ion spot has a diameter less than the diameter of the anode aperture.

7-23. *a.* In a cathode-ray tube using a fluorescent screen having the properties illustrated in Fig. 7-18, it is found that the light output is no greater when the anode voltage is 8 kv than when the anode voltage is 6.3 kv. Explain, assuming that the screen material is a good insulator.

b. Would aluminizing the screen make any difference? Explain.

CHAPTER 8

VOLTAGE AMPLIFIERS FOR AUDIO FREQUENCIES

8-1. Vacuum-tube Amplifiers. A vacuum tube is able to amplify energy as a result of the fact that the control grid draws no electrons when maintained at a negative potential, while at the same time variations in the negativeness of the grid potential can cause corresponding variations in the plate current of the tube. In this way a small signal voltage representing a small amount of energy can control a much larger quantity of electrical energy in a plate circuit.

In some circumstances the control-grid potential of an amplifier is allowed to go moderately positive at the positive crests of the signal voltage to be amplified. This causes the grid to attract some electrons and means that the signal to be amplified must supply some energy to the tube. However, if the grid is not allowed to go too far positive, the number of electrons attracted by the control grid is relatively small, and the energy that the signal voltage delivers to the control grid is still much less than the energy developed in the plate circuit. Hence, there is still amplification of energy, although to a lesser extent than when the control grid is always negative.

Because its operation is based on electrons, a vacuum-tube amplifier is capable of operating up to frequencies well over a billion cycles. By employing a number of amplifying tubes in cascade, almost any desired amount of amplification can be obtained.

The vacuum-tube amplifier is one of the most important devices of electrical engineering. It has made possible modern radio as we know it today, the long-distance telephone, talking pictures, television, public-address systems, guided missiles, radar, etc. A surprisingly large part of modern technology is built around the fact that a vacuum tube is capable of acting as an amplifier up to very high frequencies.

Basic Circuit of Vacuum-tube Amplifier. The basis circuit of a vacuum-tube amplifier is shown in various forms in Fig. 8-1. Consider first Fig. 8-1a. Here the grid of a triode tube is maintained negative with respect to the cathode by means of the grid-bias voltage E_{cc} (also sometimes called the C voltage), upon which is superimposed the signal voltage e_g that is to be amplified. A positive potential[1] E_{bb} is applied to the plate

---

[1] This voltage applied to the plate circuit is variously called the plate, plate-supply, plate-battery, and B voltage.

through a load impedance Z_L. Variations in the plate current resulting
from the action of the signal voltage e_g applied to the control grid flow
through the load impedance Z_L and develop the amplified energy in this
load impedance.

In practical amplifiers it is often desirable to obtain the grid-bias voltage from the plate-supply potential, rather than from a separate source of
voltage. This can be accomplished, as shown in Fig. 8-1b, by connecting
a resistance R_k (called cathode or bias resistance) in series with the
cathode as shown and by-passing this resistance with a capacitor C_k large
enough to be an effective short circuit to alternating currents of the
lowest frequencies to be amplified. Such an arrangement places the

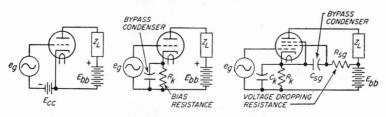

(a) TRIODE WITH SEPARATE   (b) TRIODE WITH SELF BIAS   (c) PENTODE WITH SELF BIAS
          BIAS

Fig. 8-1. Basic circuits of vacuum-tube amplifiers employing triode and pentode tubes.

cathode at a positive potential with respect to the control grid; the magnitude of this potential is equal to the voltage drop produced by the
space current when flowing through the bias resistance. This arrangement is the equivalent of a negative bias for the grid, since it makes the
grid negative with respect to the cathode just as does the separate grid-
bias potential E_{cc} in Fig. 8-1a.

A typical circuit of a pentode amplifier is shown in Fig. 8-1c. This is
similar to the corresponding circuit of Fig. 8-1b for the triode tube, but
with the addition that the suppressor grid is connected to the cathode, and
a resistance R_{sg} is employed to reduce the plate-supply voltage to a value
appropriate for operating the screen grid. This resistance is always by-
passed to the cathode by a capacitor C_{sg} as shown, which is ordinarily
large enough to be an effective short circuit to the alternating currents
being amplified.

Voltage and Current Relations in an Amplifier Tube. The voltage and
current relations existing in a simple amplifier are illustrated in Fig. 8-2,
where it is assumed that the applied signal e_g is a sine wave of small amplitude and that the load impedance Z_L is resistive. The voltage applied to
the grid of the amplifier tube is the signal e_g superimposed upon the negative bias voltage E_{cc}, as shown in Fig. 8-2b. The plate current that
results, shown at c, consists of an alternating component i_p produced
by the signal voltage e_g, superimposed upon the d-c plate current I_b that
is present in the absence of a signal. The current flowing to the plate of

the tube is seen to be maximum when the signal e_g is most positive, as is to be expected.

The voltage conditions existing in the plate circuit of this amplifier are illustrated in Fig. 8-2d.   In the absence of a signal, the voltage applied to the plate electrode of the tube is E_b; this voltage will be less than the plate-supply voltage E_{bb} to the extent that there is a d-c voltage drop in

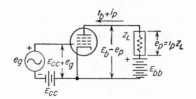

(a) SCHEMATIC CIRCUIT AND NOMENCLATURE

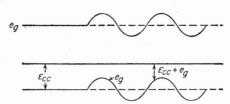

(b) VOLTAGE RELATIONS IN CONTROL-GRID CIRCUIT

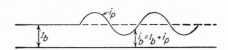

(c) CURRENT RELATIONS IN PLATE CIRCUIT

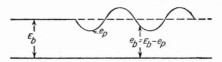

(d) VOLTAGE RELATIONS IN PLATE CIRCUIT

FIG. 8-2. Voltage and current relations in a simple amplifier in which the load impedance Z_L is resistive.

the load impedance Z_L as a result of the plate current I_b flowing through Z_L.   When a signal voltage e_g is applied to the amplifier, the resulting alternating variations in plate current i_p produce an alternating voltage drop e_p in the load impedance Z_L.   The actual voltage applied to the plate electrode of the tube then becomes E_b minus this voltage drop, and so is as shown by e_b.   The ratio e_p/e_g of the voltage e_p developed across Z_L to the signal voltage e_g is the *voltage amplification* or voltage gain of the amplifier.

It is to be noted that the polarities in Fig. 8-2 are such that the instantaneous plate voltage e_b is least positive when the instantaneous value of the signal e_g is most positive. This must necessarily be the case, since the voltage drop in the load impedance is greatest when the plate current is largest, i.e., when the signal is most positive. The result is that a *one-stage amplifier introduces a reversal in polarity.*

Methods of Classifying Amplifiers. Amplifiers are classified in ways descriptive of their character and properties. One approach is to describe amplifiers according to the nature of the load impedance; this leads to such terms as tuned, untuned, resistance-coupled, and transformer-coupled amplifiers. Another basis of classification is according to the frequencies to be amplified. Thus an audio amplifier is suitable for frequencies that are audible to the ear; while a video amplifier is designed to handle frequencies such as those contained in a television signal.

Amplifiers can also be divided into voltage and power amplifiers according to whether the object is to produce as much voltage or as much power as possible in the load impedance. The reason that it is necessary to distinguish between these objectives can be understood by considering the problem of obtaining a large quantity of power from a signal voltage that is so small as to require more amplification than can be obtained from a single tube. Under such circumstances, it is customary to use a number of amplifiers in cascade, each one of which amplifies the output of the preceding tube and delivers its output to another tube for additional amplification. In arranging such an amplifier, the best results are obtained by making all the amplifying tubes except the last one operate as voltage amplifiers, while the last tube functions as a power amplifier. The power tube then has the maximum possible signal voltage applied to its grid and is therefore able to deliver the greatest amount of power. There is no object in making the other tubes function as power amplifiers, since the purpose of these tubes is to increase the signal voltage delivered to the last tube, the power output of which represents the output of the amplifier.

Amplifiers are also designated as Class A, Class AB, Class B, Class C, or linear amplifiers according to the operating conditions. The term Class A is applied to an amplifier adjusted so that the plate current flows continuously throughout the cycle of the applied signal voltage. The subscript 1 is sometimes used to indicate that no grid current flows, while subscript 2 can be used to denote that the grid is driven positive at some part of the cycle of applied voltage. Thus a Class A_2 amplifier is one in which grid current does flow. In the Class B and linear amplifiers the tube is biased approximately to cutoff so that the plate current in an individual tube flows in pulses lasting approximately a half cycle, while the Class C amplifier is adjusted so the plate current flows in pulses that last less than a half cycle. The Class AB is intermediate between the

Class A and Class B adjustments. The linear amplifier and Class B amplifier differ only in that the former employs a tuned load circuit.

The type of amplifier is fixed primarily by the constants of the associated electrical circuits and by the grid-bias and plate voltages employed. It is possible to make any particular tube function as any kind of amplifier, although the tube characteristics best suited for each type of amplifier are somewhat different.

8-2. Distortion in Amplifiers. An ideal amplifier produces an output that exactly duplicates the input in all respects except magnitude. An actual amplifier can fall short of this ideal by failing to amplify the different frequency components of the input voltage equally well, by giving an output that is not exactly proportional to the amplitude of the input, or by making the relative phases of the different frequency components in the output differ from the relative phase existing in the input. These effects are commonly referred to as *frequency, amplitude* (or *nonlinear*), and *phase* (or *time-delay*) *distortion*, respectively.

Frequency distortion is caused by the circuits associated with the amplifier tube, and sets a limit to the range of frequencies that will be satisfactorily amplified in any particular case.

Amplitude distortion arises from nonlinear relations between voltage and current occurring in the amplifier tube, and limits the amount of voltage or power output that an amplifier can develop. Amplitude or nonlinear distortion results in the production of frequencies in the amplifier output that are not present in the input voltage applied to the grid, such as harmonics of the frequencies contained in the input signal.

Phase Distortion and Time Delay. Phase shift between the output and input of an amplifier is related to the time of transmission through the amplifier in accordance with the relation

$$\text{Phase shift (lag) in radians} = \omega\tau + n\pi \qquad (8\text{-}1)$$

where τ is called the *time delay in seconds*, ω is 2π times the frequency, and n is an integer which will be odd if the amplifier has an inherent tendency to reverse the phase of all components of the applied voltage, and will be even if there is no tendency for phase reversal (a value $n = 0$ is considered as an even value). Equation (8-1) comes about since a phase shift at a particular frequency may be directly expressed in time. Thus a 90° phase shift of a 1000-cycle wave corresponds to a quarter of a cycle, or 0.00025 sec, since each cycle represents 0.001 sec.

It will be noted that the phase shift corresponding to a given time delay increases with the frequency, since the higher the frequency the greater the phase angle corresponding to a given time interval. *In order to avoid distortion, the time delay τ must be the same for all frequencies* or, what is equivalent, the curve of phase shift plotted as a function of frequency on a linear frequency scale must be a straight line passing through an integral multiple of π at zero frequency. A simple example illustrating time delay, and phase or time-delay distortion, is given in Fig. 8-3.

Time-delay distortion is important in all circumstances where wave shapes must be accurately maintained during amplification, as when reproducing pulses. It is not important in amplifying and reproducing sound, since the ear is not able to detect relative phase angles of the components of a sound wave.

8-3. Equivalent Circuit of the Vacuum-tube Amplifier. The variations i_p produced in the plate current of a vacuum tube by the application of a small signal voltage e_g to the control grid (see Fig. 8-2) are to a first approximation the same variations that would be produced in the plate current by a generator developing a voltage $-\mu e_g$ and acting inside the tube from cathode toward the plate, where μ is the amplification factor of the tube as defined in Eq. (6-13) or (6-19).[1] This leads to the equivalent plate circuit of the vacuum-tube amplifier shown in Fig. 8-4b, which also applies to pentode, beam, and screen-grid tubes as well as to the

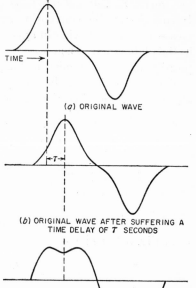

(a) ORIGINAL WAVE

(b) ORIGINAL WAVE AFTER SUFFERING A
TIME DELAY OF T SECONDS

(c) ORIGINAL WAVE AFTER SUFFERING
TIME-DELAY DISTORTION

Fig. 8-3. Oscillograms showing the effect of time delay and time-delay distortion on a complex wave consisting of a fundamental and third harmonic. In the wave suffering time-delay distortion, the relative phase of the third harmonic component differs by 180° from its relative phase in the original wave.

triode illustrated. According to this equivalent circuit, *the effect on the plate current of applying a signal voltage e_g to the grid is exactly as though the*

---

[1] This can be demonstrated as follows: The plate current which a grid-voltage increment e_g produces causes a voltage drop $Z_L i_p$ in the plate load impedance Z_L. Hence, the application of e_g to the grid reduces the voltage actually applied to the plate of the tube by an amount $-Z_L i_p$; the minus sign arises because i_p is taken as positive when flowing from cathode toward the plate, i.e., when flowing in the opposite direction to the d-c plate current. The plate current increment i_p that flows in the system is the result of the joint action of the voltage increment $+e_g$ applied to the grid and the *reduction* $-Z_L i_p$ in the plate voltage. Since by definition of μ, the voltage e_g produces the same effect on the plate current as an increase of μe_g in the plate voltage, then the *increase* in plate current $-i_p$ *flowing from plate to cathode* is the same current that would flow if the voltage actually applied to the plate was increased by $[\mu e_g - (-Z_L i_p)]$ volts. From the definition of plate resistance as given by Eqs. (6-14) and (6-20a), one can then write $i_p = -(\mu e_g + Z_L i_p)/r_p$. Solving this for i_p yields Eq. (8-2a), which is a mathematical statement of the equivalent circuit.

plate-cathode circuit of the tube were a generator developing a voltage $-\mu e_g$ *and having an internal resistance equal to the plate resistance* r_p *of the tube.* In this circuit, the convention as to signs is such that a positive current means a current flowing in *opposition to* the steady direct current present in the plate circuit when no signal is applied. This is not the same as the positive direction implied in Fig. 8-2a.

The current i_p, and the voltage e_p produced across the load impedance Z_L by the application of a signal potential e_g to the control grid, are seen

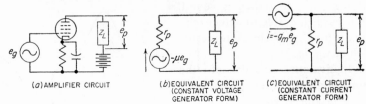

(a) AMPLIFIER CIRCUIT   (b) EQUIVALENT CIRCUIT (CONSTANT VOLTAGE GENERATOR FORM)   (c) EQUIVALENT CIRCUIT (CONSTANT CURRENT GENERATOR FORM)

Fig. 8-4. Actual and equivalent plate circuits of a vacuum-tube amplifier.

from Fig. 8-4b to be

$$i_p = \frac{-\mu e_g}{r_p + Z_L} \tag{8-2a}$$

Voltage e_p across load $= i_p Z_L = \dfrac{-\mu e_g Z_L}{r_p + Z_L} \tag{8-2b}$

It is sometimes convenient to rearrange Eqs. (8-2a) and (8-2b) by dividing both numerator and denominator of the right-hand side by r_p. Doing this gives

$$i_p = \frac{-\mu e_g}{r_p[1 + (Z_L/r_p)]} = -g_m e_g \frac{r_p}{r_p + Z_L} \tag{8-3a}$$

Voltage across load $= e_p = -g_m e_g \dfrac{r_p Z_L}{r_p + Z_L} \tag{8-3b}$

Here $g_m = \mu/r_p$ is the transconductance of the tube. This method of expressing the relations existing in an amplifier tube shows that the effect of applying a signal voltage e_g to the control grid can also be interpreted as assuming that the tube generates a current $-e_g g_m$ flowing through an impedance formed by the plate resistance in parallel with the load impedance, as shown in Fig. 8-4c. This alternative form of the equivalent plate circuit of a vacuum-tube amplifier can be called the *constant-current generator form*, as contrasted with the *constant-voltage generator form* of Fig. 8-4b. The two are exactly equivalent, being simply different ways of expressing the same relationship. It is, however, generally found that the constant-voltage generator form of the equivalent circuit is most convenient to use when dealing with triode tubes, while the constant-current generator form is usually most convenient in dealing with pentode, beam, and screen-grid tubes, where the plate resistance is extremely high.

The equivalent circuits of the amplifier give only those currents and voltage drops that are produced as a result of the application of a signal voltage upon the amplifier grid. The actual currents and potentials existing in the plate circuit are the sum of the currents and potentials developed in the equivalent circuit and those existing in the amplifier when no signal is applied. Since the steady values that are present when no signal is applied are of no particular interest so far as the amplifier performance is concerned, it is usually unnecessary to superimpose them upon the results calculated on the basis of the equivalent circuit. In particular, when the signal applied to the grid is an alternating voltage, as is usually the case, the equivalent circuit gives directly the a-c currents and voltages produced in the plate circuit by the signal voltage.

Either form of the equivalent circuit of the vacuum-tube amplifier gives the exact performance to the extent that the plate resistance r_p and the amplification factor μ (or the transconductance g_m), which are used in setting up the equivalent circuit, are constant over the range of variations of control-grid and plate voltages produced by the signal voltage. Hence, when the signal is small, the equivalent circuit is almost exactly correct, and even with rather large signal voltages, the equivalent circuits are still relatively accurate. The exact behavior with large applied signal voltages can be obtained by the method discussed in Sec. 10-3.

8-4. Resistance-coupled Amplifiers. The simplest and most widely used form of untuned voltage amplifier employs a load impedance consisting of the resistance-capacitance combination illustrated in Fig. 8-5a. Here R_c and R_{gl} are relatively high resistances, termed the coupling and grid-leak resistances, respectively, and are so proportioned that $R_{gl} \geqslant R_c$. The capacitance C_c, termed the coupling capacitor, is of such size as to have a relatively low reactance at the frequencies being amplified, as compared with the associated resistances. The purpose of the grid-leak resistance and the coupling capacitor is to isolate the d-c potential of the plate-supply voltage from the output terminals where the amplified alternating voltage e_p is obtained. The combination $R_c R_{gl} C_c$ represents the load impedance of the amplifier.

Resistance coupling is the most widely used method of obtaining voltage amplification at audio frequencies. In such amplifiers, pentode tubes are practically always employed.

Variation of Amplification with Frequency When Screen and Cathode By-passing Are Fully Effective. An important property of the resistance-coupled amplifier is the way in which the amplification (i.e., gain) varies with frequency. Such a characteristic is shown by the solid line in Fig. 8-6 for the case where the screen and cathode by-pass capacitors C_{sg} and C_k in Fig. 8-5a are fully effective to the lowest frequencies of interest.[1]

---

[1] Amplification can be expressed either as a voltage ratio, as is done in Fig. 8-6, or by the decibel equivalent of the voltage ratio. Thus when the voltage drops to 70.7 per cent, the power is reduced by the factor $(0.707)^2 = 0.5$, or 3 db.

The distinguishing feature of this characteristic is an amplification that is substantially constant over a wide range of frequencies but drops off at both very low and very high frequencies.

The falling off in amplification at very low frequencies is a result of the fact that the high reactance which the coupling capacitor C_c offers to low frequencies consumes some of the low-frequency voltage that would

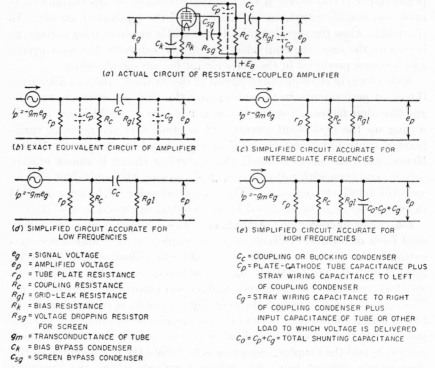

(*a*) ACTUAL CIRCUIT OF RESISTANCE-COUPLED AMPLIFIER

(*b*) EXACT EQUIVALENT CIRCUIT OF AMPLIFIER

(*c*) SIMPLIFIED CIRCUIT ACCURATE FOR INTERMEDIATE FREQUENCIES

(*d*) SIMPLIFIED CIRCUIT ACCURATE FOR LOW FREQUENCIES

(*e*) SIMPLIFIED CIRCUIT ACCURATE FOR HIGH FREQUENCIES

e_g = SIGNAL VOLTAGE
e_p = AMPLIFIED VOLTAGE
r_p = TUBE PLATE RESISTANCE
R_c = COUPLING RESISTANCE
R_{gl} = GRID-LEAK RESISTANCE
R_k = BIAS RESISTANCE
R_{sg} = VOLTAGE DROPPING RESISTOR FOR SCREEN
g_m = TRANSCONDUCTANCE OF TUBE
C_k = BIAS BYPASS CONDENSER
C_{sg} = SCREEN BYPASS CONDENSER

C_c = COUPLING OR BLOCKING CONDENSER
C_p = PLATE-CATHODE TUBE CAPACITANCE PLUS STRAY WIRING CAPACITANCE TO LEFT OF COUPLING CONDENSER
C_g = STRAY WIRING CAPACITANCE TO RIGHT OF COUPLING CONDENSER PLUS INPUT CAPACITANCE OF TUBE OR OTHER LOAD TO WHICH VOLTAGE IS DELIVERED
$C_0 = C_p + C_g$ = TOTAL SHUNTING CAPACITANCE

Fig. 8-5. Circuit of resistance-coupled amplifier employing a pentode tube, together with equivalent plate circuits useful in making amplifier calculations. Screen and bias by-pass capacitors are assumed to have negligible effect.

otherwise be developed across the grid leak. The reduction in amplification at high frequencies is caused by the various capacitances which shunt the coupling and grid-leak resistances. When the frequency is sufficiently high, these shunt reactances become low enough to decrease significantly the effective load impedance, with corresponding reduction in the voltage developed at the amplifier output.

The amplification characteristic can be calculated by replacing the tube by its equivalent circuit, thereby reducing the problem to the analysis of an ordinary electric circuit. Either form of the equivalent circuit of the vacuum-tube amplifier can be employed, but in the usual case where a pentode tube is involved, the constant-current generator form is the most convenient to use.

The exact equivalent circuit of the resistance-coupled amplifier obtained in this way is shown in Fig. 8-5b.   This exact equivalent circuit is quite complicated, but can be simplified by considering only a limited range of frequencies at a time.   Thus, in the middle range of frequencies, the reactance of the coupling capacitor C_c in the usual design of amplifier will be so small as to be the practical equivalent of a short circuit as compared with the grid-leak resistance, whereas the reactance of the shunting capacitances will be so high as to be the practical equivalent of an open

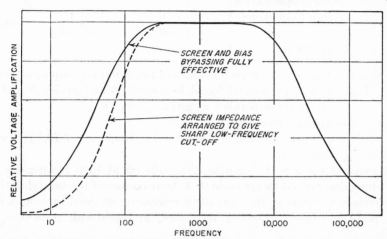

Fig. 8-6. Variation of amplification with frequency in a typical resistance-coupled amplifier.   The solid curve corresponds to large screen and bias by-pass capacitors, while the dotted curve shows the increased sharpness of low-frequency cutoff that can be produced by an impedance in the screen circuit.   Note particularly the great reduction in the amplification of very low frequencies that arises from the presence of the screen impedance.

circuit.   Under these conditions the equivalent circuit takes the form shown in Fig. 8-5c.   Ignoring the reversal in polarity introduced by the amplifier tube, the voltage amplification as calculated from the circuit is readily found to be

$$\left. \begin{array}{l} \text{Amplification in middle} \\ \text{range of frequencies} \end{array} \right\} = \left| \frac{e_p}{e_g} \right| = g_m R_{\text{eq}} \qquad (8\text{-}4)$$

Here g_m is the transconductance of the amplifier tube, and R_{eq} is the equivalent resistance formed by the tube plate resistance r_p, the grid-leak resistance R_{gl}, and the coupling resistance R_c, all in parallel.   That is,

$$R_{\text{eq}} = \frac{R_c r_p R_{gl}}{R_c R_{gl} + R_c r_p + R_{gl} r_p} = \frac{R_c}{1 + (R_c/R_{gl}) + (R_c/r_p)} \qquad (8\text{-}5)$$

At high frequencies it is not permissible to neglect the effect of the capacitance shunting the coupling and grid-leak resistances.   This shunting capacitance is made up of the plate-to-ground capacitance of the amplifier tube, the capacitance-to-ground of C_c and the wiring in the plate circuit, and the capacitance of the load to which the output voltage e_p is applied (commonly the input capacitance of another amplifier stage, as discussed in Secs. 12-10 and 12-12). The equivalent circuit of a resistance-coupled amplifier at very high frequencies accordingly takes the form shown in Fig. 8-5e. An analysis of this comparatively simple circuit gives the result[1]

$$\left.\begin{array}{l}\text{Actual amplification}\\ \text{at high frequencies}\\ \hline \text{Amplification in}\\ \text{middle range}\end{array}\right\} = \frac{1}{1 + j(R_{eq}/X_0)} = \frac{1}{1 + j(f/f_2)} \qquad (8\text{-}6)$$

where $X_0 = 1/2\pi f C_0$ = actual reactance of total shunting capacitance C_0

   R_{eq} = resistance formed by plate, coupling, and grid-leak resistances, all in parallel, as given by Eq. (8-5)

   f = actual frequency

   f_2 = frequency at which $X_0 = R_{eq}$ (i.e., frequency of 70.7 per cent response)

The extent to which the amplification falls off at high frequencies is, therefore, determined by the ratio that the reactance of the total shunting capacitance C_0 bears to the equivalent resistance obtained by combining the plate resistance, coupling resistance, and grid-leak resistance in

---

[1] Equation (8-6) is derived by applying Thévenin's theorem to the network to the left of the shunting capacitance C_0 in Fig. 8-5e. According to Thévenin's theorem, this network can be replaced by an equivalent generator in series with a resistance, as shown in Fig. 8-7b. The voltage of the generator in this circuit is the voltage

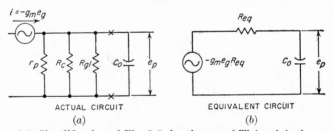

ACTUAL CIRCUIT   EQUIVALENT CIRCUIT
(a)   (b)

Fig. 8-7. Simplification of Fig. 8-5e by the use of Thévenin's theorem.

appearing across the capacitor terminals when the capacitor is open-circuited, and so is the output voltage in the middle range of frequencies as given by Eq. (8-4). The internal resistance of the generator is the resistance R_{eq} formed by plate, coupling, and grid-leak resistances, all in parallel, and so is given by Eq. (8-5). Referring to Fig. 8-7b, it is apparent that when the polarity reversal introduced by the tube is ignored, the amplification at high frequencies is given by the relation

$$\text{High-frequency amplification} = \left|\frac{e_p}{e_g}\right| = g_m R_{eq}\frac{-jX_0}{R_{eq} - jX_0} = g_m R_{eq}\frac{1}{1 + j(R_{eq}/X_0)}$$

Dividing this by Eq. (8-4) gives Eq. (8-6).

parallel. This loss of amplification at high frequencies can be estimated by the fact that, *at the frequency that makes the reactance of the shunting capacitor C_0 equal the equivalent resistance formed by r_p, R_c, and R_{gl} in parallel, the amplification drops to 70.7 per cent $(-3\ db)$ of its middle frequency range value.*

At low frequencies, the shunting capacitance C_0 has such a high reactance as to be equivalent to an open circuit. However, the reactance of the coupling capacitor C_c now becomes sufficient to cause a falling off in output voltage. Hence the equivalent circuit under these conditions has the form shown in Fig. 8-5d. An analysis of this circuit shows that[1]

$$\left.\begin{array}{l}\text{Amplification at}\\ \text{low frequencies}\\ \hline \text{Amplification in}\\ \text{middle range}\end{array}\right\} = \frac{1}{1 - (jX_c/R)} = \frac{1}{1 - (jf_1/f)} \qquad (8\text{-}7)$$

where $X_c = 1/2\pi f C_c$ = actual reactance of coupling capacitor C_c

$R = R_{gl} + \dfrac{R_c r_p}{R_c + r_p} = R_{gl} + \dfrac{R_c}{1 + (R_c/r_p)}$ = resistance formed by the grid leak R_{gl} in series with the combination of plate and coupling resistances in parallel

f = actual frequency

f_1 = frequency at which $X_c = R$ (i.e., frequency of 70.7 per cent response)

The extent to which the amplification falls off at low frequencies is therefore determined by the ratio of the reactance of the coupling condenser to the equivalent resistance R obtained by combining the grid-leak resistance in series with the parallel combination of coupling resistance and

[1] Equation (8-7) can be derived as follows: By applying Thévenin's theorem to the network to the left of C_c in Fig. 8-5d (to the left of xx in Fig. 8-8a), one obtains the

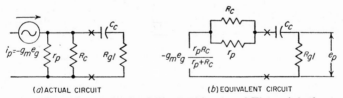

(a) ACTUAL CIRCUIT   (b) EQUIVALENT CIRCUIT

FIG. 8-8. Simplification of circuit of Fig. 8-5d by use of Thévenin's theorem.

equivalent circuit of Fig. 8-8b. In this circuit, ignoring the phase reversal introduced by the tube,

$$|e_p| = g_m e_g \frac{r_p R_c}{r_p + R_c} \frac{R_{gl}}{R - jX_c} \qquad (8\text{-}7a)$$

Equation (8-7) is then obtained by solving this relation to give the amplification e_p/e_g, dividing by Eq. (8-4), and rearranging.

plate resistance. This loss of amplification at low frequencies can be estimated by the fact that, *at the frequency that makes the reactance of the coupling capacitor equal the equivalent resistance R, the amplification falls to 70.7 per cent (-3 db) of its value in the middle range of frequencies.*

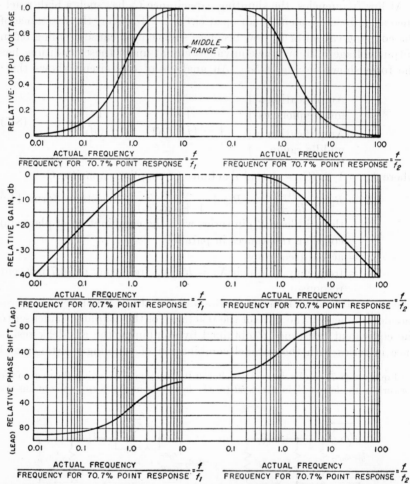

FIG. 8-9. Universal amplification curve, showing the falling off in amplification and the phase shift that occurs in a resistance-coupled amplifier at high and low frequencies when the screen and bias by-pass capacitors have negligible effect.

Universal Amplification Curve of Resistance-coupled Amplifier. The simplicity of Eqs. (8-6) and (8-7) makes it possible to express the way in which the amplification of a resistance-coupled amplifier varies with frequency by means of the universal amplification curve of Fig. 8-9. This gives the actual amplification relative to the amplification in the middle range of frequencies, and also gives the relative phase shift.[1]   It is a universal curve that applies to all ordinary resistance-coupled amplifiers in which the screen and cathode by-passing are fully effective.

The procedure for obtaining the amplification characteristic by using the universal amplification curve is: (1) Calculate the amplification in the middle-frequency range using Eq. (8-4).   (2) Calculate the frequency f_1 at which the reactance of the coupling capacitance C_c equals the resistance R in Eq. (8-7), and then use the universal amplification curve to get the low-frequency falling off in amplification.   (3) The total shunting capacitance C_0 is estimated; the frequency f_2 is determined at which this capacitance has a reactance equal to the resistance R_{eq} in Eq. (8-5); and then the high-frequency response is obtained with the aid of the universal amplification curve.

8-5. Resistance-coupled Amplifiers with Incomplete Screen and Bias By-passing.   *Effect of Screen Impedance.*[2]   A signal voltage applied to the control grid of a pentode tube produces variations in the screen current as well as in the plate current.   If there is an impedance Z_{sg} in the screen circuit between screen and cathode, this amplified screen current will develop a voltage e_{sg} across the screen-circuit impedance, and hence between screen and cathode.   This voltage affects the plate current and alters the amplification in such a manner as to reduce the gain.   Thus if Z_{sg} is resistive, a positive signal applied to the control grid increases the screen and plate currents, causing a voltage drop in Z_{sg} that reduces the screen voltage.   This in turn tends to reduce the plate current, preventing the full increase in plate current that would otherwise result from the positive signal, and thereby lowering the amplification.   Quantitative analysis shows that[3]

[1] Phase-shift curves of this type are always plotted with the convention that a leading phase angle for the voltage amplification (or transmission) is negative; i.e., a negative (lagging) angle in Eq. (8-6) is plotted as positive while a positive (leading) angle in Eq. (8-7) is plotted as a negative value.

[2] This analysis was first given by F. E. Terman, W. R. Hewlett, C. W. Palmer, and W. Y. Pan, Calculation and Design of Resistance-coupled Amplifiers Using Pentode Tubes, *Trans. AIEE*, vol. 59, p. 879, 1940.

[3] This can be derived with the aid of the equivalent screen-grid circuit of Fig. 8-10, where μ_s is the mu factor of the screen grid relative to the control grid.   This equivalent circuit is exactly analogous to the equivalent plate circuit of the vacuum-tube

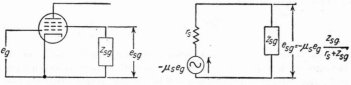

(*a*) ACTUAL SCREEN CIRCUIT   (*b*) EQUIVALENT SCREEN CIRCUIT

FIG. 8-10. Equivalent screen circuit used in determining the effect of impedance in the screen circuit. For the sake of simplicity the source of d-c screen potential is not shown in this circuit.

$$\frac{\text{Actual amplification}}{\text{Amplification with } Z_{sg} = 0} = \beta = \frac{r_s}{r_s + Z_{sg}} = \frac{1}{1 + (Z_{sg}/r_s)} \quad (8\text{-}8)$$

Here r_s is the dynamic resistance of the screen-grid circuit of the tube and is analogous to r_p. Approximate numerical values for r_s can be derived from information given in tube manuals with the aid of Eq. (6-23c) and the fact that the dynamic resistance of the screen (and also of the plate of the equivalent triode) is roughly proportional to the cube root of the current flowing to the electrode.

The value of the factor β in Eq. (8-8) is plotted in Fig. 8-11 for the case where the screen-circuit impedance Z_{sg} consists of a voltage dropping resistance R_{sg} by-passed to the cathode by a capacitor C_{sg} (see Fig. 8-5a). A study of this figure, or of Eq. (8-8), shows that *for the by-passing in the screen circuit to be fully effective, i.e., for β to approach unity, the by-pass capacitor C_{sg} must have a reactance that is appreciably less than the equivalent resistance formed by the voltage-dropping resistance R_{sg} in parallel with the dynamic screen-grid tube resistance r_s.* Furthermore, it should be noted that in practical situations r_s is commonly much smaller than R_{sg}, so that the resistance of the two in parallel is usually only slightly less than r_s. When the by-passing is very inadequate the reduction in amplification is greater the higher the ratio R_{sg}/r_s of dropping resistance to tube resistance.

Effect of Bias Impedance. A bias impedance such as represented by $R_k C_k$ in Fig. 8-5a affects the amplification as the result of the fact that amplified signal currents flow through this impedance. Such currents cause a voltage drop in the bias impedance that represents a voltage acting in the circuit between control grid and cathode in opposition to the

---

amplifier, discussed in Sec. 8-3, and is justified in the same way, since the screen grid is an anode just as is the plate. It will be noted, however, that whereas what happens in the screen circuit is independent of the plate circuit provided only that the plate voltage is sufficient to make the plate current independent of plate voltage, the reverse is not the case. From Fig. 8-10b, the voltage e_{sg} developed across Z_{sg} by the signal e_g is $e_{sg} = -\mu_s e_g Z_{sg}/(Z_{sg} + r_s)$. By definition of μ_s, this voltage acting on the screen-grid electrode can be regarded as having the same effect on the space current as a voltage $1/\mu_s$ times as great acting on the control grid. As a result the presence of impedance in the screen circuit can be taken into account by considering the effective signal voltage acting on the control grid to be $(e_g + e_{sg}/\mu_s)$, instead of the actual value e_g. Hence one can write

$$\beta = \frac{e_g + e_{sg}/\mu_s}{e_g} = 1 - \frac{Z_{sg}}{r_s + Z_{sg}} = \frac{r_s}{r_s + Z_{sg}} \quad (8\text{-}8a)$$

This derivation assumes that the mu factor of the screen grid relative to the control grid is the same with respect to plate current as with respect to screen current (and hence total space current); in the case of self-bias it also assumes that the bias impedance Z_k is very much smaller than the dynamic screen resistance r_s at medium frequencies and that $(r_s + R_{sg}) >> R_k$. These assumptions are all closely met in practice.

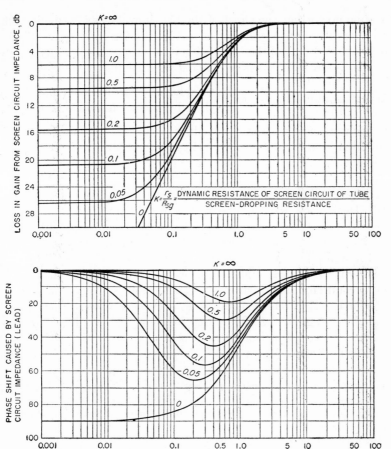

Fig. 8-11. Curves giving falling off and phase shift in output voltage at low frequencies in a resistance-coupled amplifier as a result of a finite by-pass capacitor from screen to cathode.

applied signal e_g. This reduces the amplification and also introduces an additional phase shift in accordance with the relation[1]

$$\frac{\text{Actual output voltage}}{\text{Output voltage with zero bias impedance}} = \gamma = \frac{1}{1 + \beta g_m Z_k} \qquad (8\text{-}9)$$

where β = factor given by Eq. (8-8)

g_m = transconductance of amplifier tube in mhos

Z_k = bias impedance, i.e., impedance of R_k and C_k in parallel (see Fig. 8-5a)

[1] This equation assumes that the a-c current flowing in the screen circuit all flows directly to the cathode through by-pass capacitor C_{sg}, and that the coupling resistance

It will be noted that the effect of the bias impedance in reducing amplification is influenced by the impedance in the screen circuit. This is in addition to the effect of the screen-circuit impedance as given by Eq. (8-8). When both screen and bias by-passing are incomplete, one has

$$\text{Actual amplification} = \beta\gamma \times \begin{pmatrix} \text{amplification with screen and} \\ \text{bias by-passing fully effective} \end{pmatrix} \quad (8\text{-}10)$$

In the usual case where the impedance in the bias circuit is a resistance R_k shunted by a capacitance C_k, as in Fig. 8-5a, then if the screen-circuit impedance has negligible effect, the value of the factor γ in Eq. (8-9) is given in Fig. 8-12. Equation (8-9) or Fig. 8-12 can be used to determine the adequacy of the cathode by-pass capacitor C_k for any given situation.

8-6. Design of Resistance-coupled Amplifiers. Resistance-coupled amplifiers for audio-frequency applications are commonly proportioned according to tabulated data supplied by tube manufacturers. However, it is still desirable to understand the considerations involved in the design of a resistance-coupled amplifier, particularly as special circumstances are often encountered for which the tabulated designs are not suitable.

The first design requirement is that the resistance-coupled amplifier be capable of amplifying the desired frequency range;[1] in particular the grid-leak and coupling resistances must be so chosen in relation to the expected shunt capacitance so that the response will be satisfactory up to the highest frequency of interest. A second objective is to obtain as much amplification as practical over the desired band of frequencies,

---

is considerably less than the plate resistance of the tube. These assumptions seldom introduce appreciable error.

The derivation of Eq. (8-9) follows. The voltage present between cathode and grid is $e_g - e_k$, where e_g is the applied signal voltage and e_k is the voltage $-i_p Z_k$ developed by the amplified plate current i_p flowing through the bias impedance Z_k. The negative sign arises from the fact that a positive amplified current is assumed to be a current flowing in the opposite direction from the d-c plate current. The presence of the bias impedance can hence be taken into account by considering the effective signal voltage acting on the control grid to be $e_g - e_k$ instead of e_g. Thus

$$\gamma = (e_g - e_k)/e_g = (e_g + i_p Z_k)/e_g$$

Equation (8-9) then follows by substituting for i_p the relation

$$i_p = -\beta g_m (e_g - e_k) = -\beta g_m (e_g + i_p Z_k)$$

or

$$i_p = -\beta g_m e_g / (1 + \beta g_m Z_k)$$

---

[1] In this connection it is to be noted that when several amplifier stages are connected in cascade, the over-all amplification falls off more sharply at high and low frequencies than does the amplification of a single stage; in addition the frequency range over which the response is relatively constant is simultaneously reduced. Thus in a resistance-coupled amplifier with three identical stages, the over-all response at high frequencies falls to 70.7 per cent (-3 db) of the mid-frequency value at a frequency that is $0.51f_2$, where f_2 is the frequency at which the response of a single stage falls to 70.7 per cent of the mid-frequency value.

starting with a given plate-supply voltage. Finally, it is general practice to arrange the design so that the amplified output voltage obtainable without undue amplitude distortion is as large as possible without excessive sacrifice in the gain of the amplifier.

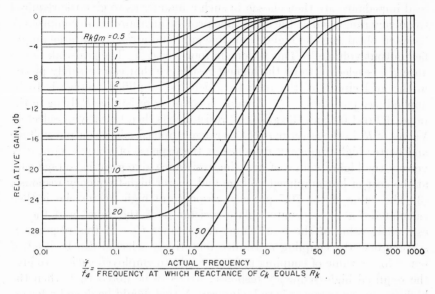

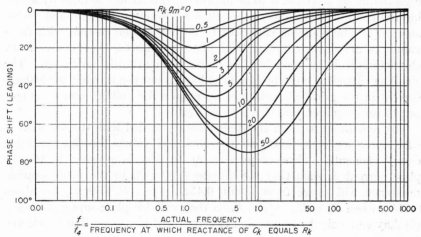

FIG. 8-12. Curves giving the reduction in magnitude and the added phase shift of output voltage occurring at low frequencies in a resistance-coupled amplifier as a result of a resistance-capacitor bias impedance R_kC_k, for various values of R_kg_m, for the case where the screen-circuit impedance has negligible effect on the amplification.

The design naturally starts with a tube; this is normally a small sharp-cutoff, general-purpose pentode.[1] The exact type number is not critical,

[1] Variable-mu pentodes are used when it is necessary to be able to control the amplification by varying a voltage; this is discussed further on p. 364.

and is ordinarily determined by such considerations as cost, desired physical size, available heater voltage, presence of other similar tubes in the same equipment, etc.

Having selected a tube, the circuit elements R_c, R_{gl}, and C_c of the plate load impedance are then chosen in such a manner as to give the required frequency range and at the same time provide an appropriate compromise between obtaining the highest possible gain and a relatively large amplified output voltage.[1] This is done in four steps: (1) The grid-leak resistance R_{gl} is selected to be the highest resistance that can be safely placed in the grid circuit of the tube to which the amplified voltage is to be applied (see page 208). (2) A value of coupling resistance R_c lying in the range 0.2 to 1.0 times the grid-leak resistance is then tentatively selected. Values of R_c in the lower part of this range emphasize large output voltage and better high-frequency response at the expense of voltage gain; conversely the higher values of coupling resistance give greater voltage gain at the cost of less amplified voltage and poorer high-frequency response. (3) The value of the 70.7 per cent response at high frequencies is then calculated for an estimated plate resistance of the tube[2] and for an estimated value of the total shunt capacitance C_0. If this response is satisfactory, the coupling resistance tentatively selected can be used; if not, a lower value of coupling resistance is then employed such as to give the required high-frequency response. It is to be noted that when the high-frequency response is to be improved, this should be done by lowering the coupling resistance rather than by lowering the grid-leak resistance. (4) The coupling capacitor C_c is then chosen so that with these values of grid-leak, coupling, and plate resistances, the low-frequency characteristic is as good but no better than actually necessary. The coupling capacitor must be of a type having low d-c leakage, for leakage current in the grid-leak resistance develops a d-c voltage across the output of the amplifier, and this is to be avoided.

The remaining steps in the design are concerned with the selection of tube operating conditions and the choice of values for the remaining circuit elements. These steps are: (5) A value is assigned to the d-c plate current I_b such that the voltage drop $I_b R_c$ in the plate-coupling resistance will range from about $0.45E_{bb}$ when $R_c = 0.2R_{gl}$ to about $0.55E_{bb}$ when $R_c = R_{gl}$, where E_{bb} is the available plate-supply voltage.[3] (6) Any convenient combination of screen and bias potentials is selected

---

[1] The design procedure from this point on is that outlined by Terman, Hewlett, Palmer, and Pan, *loc. cit.* The reader desiring justification of any of the design steps should consult this paper.

[2] The plate resistance of small general-purpose pentodes is ordinarily so high that it is common practice to assume that the plate resistance is infinite when making this calculation.

[3] This assumes that the plate current required does not exceed the rated plate current of the tube. Otherwise the rated plate current should be chosen.

that will give this desired plate current.   (7) The screen-dropping resistance R_{sg} is then given a value such that the voltage drop in this resistance produced by a screen current corresponding to the bias and screen voltages already chosen will give the correct screen potential.   (8) If self-bias is to be employed, the bias resistance R_k is selected[1] so that the desired bias will be obtained when the space current corresponding to the design condition flows through R_k.

The final step in the design of the amplifier consists in determining appropriate values for C_{sg} and C_k.   If a gradual low-frequency cutoff is desired, these capacitors are selected to give adequate by-passing on the basis of Eqs. (8-8) and (8-9) and Figs. 8-11 and 8-12.   However, for reasons discussed on page 362, it is often desirable that the low-frequency amplification fall off as sharply as possible.   This result can be achieved by employing a screen by-pass capacitor C_{sg} of such size[2] that the frequency f_3 in Fig. 8-11 coincides with the 70.7 per cent point in Fig. 8-9 (that is, $f_3 = f_1$).   The dotted curve in Fig. 8-6 gives a typical example of how the sharpness of low-frequency cutoff can be increased by employing the proper value of C_{sg}.

A resistance-coupled amplifier designed in the manner indicated above will develop without excessive distortion an output voltage on the order of 0.25 to 0.4 times the plate-supply potential.[3]   The exact value will depend upon the amount of distortion that is permissible and upon the design details.   In particular, the amount of output voltage obtainable will tend to drop as the coupling resistance R_c approaches R_{gl}.

When a given tube is associated with a given set of circuit constants, variation in plate-supply voltage will cause the undistorted output voltage that can be obtained to be proportional to the plate-supply voltage. However, the voltage amplification that is obtained will be proportional to something between the square root and the cube root of the plate-supply voltage up to the point where the plate-supply voltage cannot be further increased without causing the d-c plate current called for by the design procedure to exceed the rated value.   Because of this behavior the loss in amplification resulting from using relatively low supply voltages is not great.

Under circumstances where the signal to be amplified is always so

---

[1] In practice the exact values of R_{sg} and R_k are often most easily determined by trial and error.   That is, one starts with a convenient value for one of these resistances, and then by trial and error arrives at a resistance that, when used as the other, will result in the desired d-c plate current.

[2] In actual practice it is necessary to determine C_{sg} experimentally, since tube manufacturers do not ordinarily publish values of screen resistance, and C_{sg} is determined largely by the screen resistance.

[3] When the amplified output voltage is to exceed a few volts, the plate-supply voltage must accordingly be not less than 2.5 to 4 times the peak value of amplified voltage that is desired.

small that the amplified output never exceeds a few volts, the above design procedure can be modified to advantage. Specifically, the plate current I_b can be increased until the voltage drop I_bR_c in the coupling resistance is from 80 to 90 per cent of the plate-supply voltage; this will result in an increase in the voltage amplification by about 20 per cent, obtained at the expense of ability to develop an appreciable output voltage without distortion. In addition, under these conditions it is desirable that the coupling resistance be as nearly equal to the grid-leak resistance as considerations relating to the high-frequency response will permit.

The design procedure outlined above for resistance-coupled amplifiers will result in circuit proportions that are reasonably satisfactory for any requirements that may be specified. The absolute optimum design for any particular set of requirements can be obtained only by a trial-and-error process using the above design as the starting point. However, the performance of the resistance-coupled amplifier is not critically dependent upon the exact details of the design; for example, the penalty arising from using a resistance in the system that differs moderately from the design value is not great.

When building a resistance-coupled amplifier, care must be taken to arrange matters so that the elements R_c, R_{gl}, and C_c, together with the associated leads, contribute as little shunt capacitance as possible to C_0. This requires that the leads be short and that the placement of the various components be such as to minimize the capacitance of leads and circuit elements to ground.

The coupling resistance R_c used in an amplifier stage operating at low signal level must be of a type that generates relatively little "noise" voltage when carrying the d-c plate current. Wire-wound resistors and certain composition and film types are suitable, while ordinary carbon-rod resistors are not.

Resistance-coupled Amplifiers Using Triode Tubes. Triode tubes are occasionally used in resistance-coupled amplifiers. They have the advantage of less amplitude distortion when large output voltages are being developed, but develop appreciably less amplification per stage than do resistance-coupled amplifiers employing pentode tubes and likewise tend to have poorer high-frequency characteristics for a given gain because of the high input capacitance of the triode amplifier (see page 424).

In designing triode resistance-coupled amplifiers, a tube having a high amplification factor is ordinarily used. The coupling resistance is then chosen to be of the order of three to six times the plate resistance of the tube, and the plate current is so selected that the d-c drop in the coupling resistance is from one-third to one-half of the plate-supply potential.

Sample Design Calculations. The procedures involved in designing a resistance-coupled amplifier and the nature of the design decisions required are made tangible by the following examples.

Example 1.   A resistance-coupled amplifier is required to amplify the frequency range 30 to 10,000 cycles with at least 70.7 per cent of mid-range response, and must develop an amplified output of 75 volts peak that is to be applied to the deflecting plates of a cathode-ray tube.   The capacitance of the deflecting system is 11 $\mu\mu$f, and it is estimated that the circuit and wiring capacitance will be 4 $\mu\mu$f.   It is planned to use a 6SJ7 tube because this same tube is also used in other parts of the apparatus. The tube data book shows the 6SJ7 has the voltage-current characteristics given in Fig. 8-13; the plate-to-ground (output) capacitance of this tube is likewise given as 7 $\mu\mu$f and the control-grid-to-ground (input) capacitance as 6 $\mu\mu$f (see Table 9-1, page 292).   Auxiliary considerations make it undesirable to connect more than 1 megohm between the deflecting plates of the cathode-ray tube.

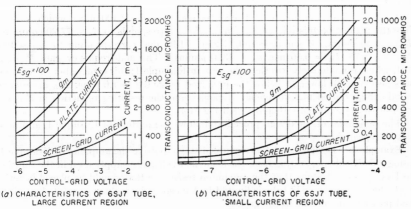

(a) CHARACTERISTICS OF 6SJ7 TUBE,   (b) CHARACTERISTICS OF 6SJ7 TUBE,
    LARGE CURRENT REGION   SMALL CURRENT REGION

Fig. 8-13. Characteristics of 6SJ7 tube.

Design a suitable plate-coupling network; specify suitable plate-supply, screen, and bias voltage; choose screen and bias resistors; and determine the amplification to be expected.

Solution.   Since a large output voltage is desired, a coupling resistance $0.25R_{gl}$ or 250,000 ohms is tentatively chosen as reasonable to go with $R_{gl} = 1$ megohm.   Neglecting the plate resistance of the tube, which at the small plate current to be used will be many megohms, Eq. (8-5) gives $R_{eq} = 200,000$ ohms.   The total shunting capacitance is $7 + 4 + 11 = 22$ $\mu\mu$f, which has a reactance of 724,000 ohms at 10,000 cycles. As this exceeds R_{eq} the tentative value for R_c is satisfactory.   For 70.7 per cent response down to 30 cycles, the coupling capacitor must have a reactance of not more than $R_{gl} + R_c = 1.25$ megohms at 30 cycles; this corresponds to a value of 0.0042 μf.

Next it is noted that in a system designed to develop a large output voltage and having R_c considerably less than R_{gl}, the peak output voltage will be of the order of one-third the plate-supply voltage.   Thus to obtain an amplified output of 75 volts, it is necessary that E_{bb} be at least 225 volts; to be safe 250 volts is selected.   The plate current I_b must then be such that the drop I_bR_c in the coupling resistance is approximately $0.5E_{bb}$; hence $I_b = 125/250,000 = 0.5$ ma.   From Fig. 8-13 a suitable combination for screen and bias voltages is 100 and -5.3 volts, respectively; this corresponds to $I_{c2} = 0.16$ ma and $g_m = 610$ μmhos.

The mid-range amplification is $g_mR_{eq} = 610 \times 10^{-6} \times 200,000 = 122$.   The required screen-dropping resistance $R_{sg} = (250 - 100)/0.16 \times 10^{-3} = 940,000$ ohms. The bias resistance is $E_{c1}/(I_b + I_{sg}) = 5.3/(0.5 + 0.16)10^{-3} = 8030$ ohms.

The by-pass capacitor for the bias resistance should be made large enough so that its reactance X_k will make $g_m X_k$ appreciably less than unity at 30 cycles.   For

$$g_m = 610 \ \mu\text{mhos}$$

this requirement will be met by a capacitor of the order of 5 to 10 μf.

The by-pass capacitor C_{sg} for the screen circuit would normally be chosen on a cut-and-try basis, since the tube data books do not give the resistance r_{sg} of the screen circuit of the tube.[1]   The experimental procedure would be to apply a 30-cycle signal to the amplifier input and by trial arrive at a value of C_{sg} that is: (1) the smallest value at which the loss of gain is negligible, if gradual low-frequency cutoff is desired; or (2) the value at which the gain is about 70.7 per cent of the value when a very large capacitor is used, if a sharp low-frequency cutoff is desired.

Example 2.   The situation is the same as in Example 1, except the frequency range is to be extended to 100,000 cycles.

Solution.   The shunting reactance at 100,000 cycles is 72,400 ohms, which is therefore the highest permissible value of R_{eq}.   This corresponds to $R_c = 77,200$ ohms for $R_{gl} = 1$ megohm.   Then $I_b = 150/77,200 = 1.94$ ma, corresponding to $E_{c2} = 100$, $E_{c1} = -3.75$, $I_{sg} = 0.50$ ma, $g_m = 1310 \ \mu$mhos.   The mid-frequency gain $R_{eq}g_m$ is 101, which is moderately less than the gain in Example 1; this comes about because it was necessary to lower R_c below the preferred range 0.2 to 1.0 times R_{gl}, in order to obtain the required high-frequency response, and the resulting reduction in R_{eq} was greater than the increase thereby resulting in g_m.

The remainder of the design procedure follows the pattern of Example 1, and need not be repeated.

Example 3.   Design a resistance-coupled stage to drive the amplifier of Example 1, using a 6SJ7 tube, operating from the same 250-volt plate supply used in the solution to Example 1.   Assume that the maximum resistance that should be placed in series with the grid of the 6SJ7 tube is limited to 1 megohm by leakage current through C_c and positive-ion current to the grid.

Solution.   In this case one can design for maximum amplification, since the amplifier of Example 1 will develop full output when the signal applied to its control grid has a peak value of less than 1 volt.   Consequently R_c is chosen as 1.0 megohm, corresponding to $R_{eq} = 0.5$ megohm.   A check shows that this gives an acceptable high-frequency characteristic for a total shunting capacitance of $7 + 6 + 4 = 17 \ \mu\mu$f, which are, respectively, the plate-ground and grid-ground capacitances of the 6SJ7 tube and an assumed stray-circuit capacitance to ground.

The plate current is chosen so $I_b R_c = 0.85 E_{bb}$.   This corresponds to $I_b = 0.21$ ma, which, according to Fig. 8-13, can be obtained with $E_{sg} = 100$, $E_c = -6.2$, and $I_{sg} = 0.08$.   For this condition $g_m = 380 \ \mu$mhos.   The mid-frequency voltage gain $R_{eq}g_m$ is 190, which is to be compared with 122 for Example 1.   This increase of about 50 per cent is due to the fact that, with only a very small output voltage

[1] It is possible, however, to estimate roughly the dynamic screen-grid resistance with the aid of Eq. (6-23c) from the data given for triode connected operation of the 6SJ7 tube.   From Table 6-1, page 186, the triode plate resistance is 8250 when triode plate current (sum of screen and actual plate currents) is 6.0 ma, while the ratio of screen to screen plus plate currents for this tube is approximately 0.21.   Hence by Eq. (6-23c), $r_s = 8250/0.21 = 39,000$ ohms for $I_{c2} = 0.21 \times 6 = 1.26$ ma.   To the extent that r_s is inversely proportional to the cube root of I_{c2}, then for $I_{c2} = 0.16$, $r_s = 37,500 \times \sqrt[3]{1.26/0.16} = 75,000$ ohms.   The resistance formed by r_s and R_{sg} in parallel is then $(75,000 \times 940,000)/(75,000 + 940,000) = 69,000$ ohms.   If the screen by-passing is to be effective, then the reactance of C_{sg} at 30 cycles must be small compared with 69,000; i.e., the capacitance should be at least 0.2 μf.   On the other hand, if sharp low-frequency cutoff is desired, the reactance of C_{sg} at 30 cycles should be of the order of 69,000 ohms, corresponding to C_{sg} about 0.08 μf.

required, it was possible (1) to use a higher value of R_c, and (2) to use a plate current that consumed a larger fraction of the plate-supply voltage E_{bb} as voltage drop in R_c.

The remainder of the design follows the pattern of Example 1, and need not be repeated.

8-7. Transformer-coupled Voltage Amplifiers and Input Transformers.

In the transformer-coupled voltage amplifier, the load impedance in the

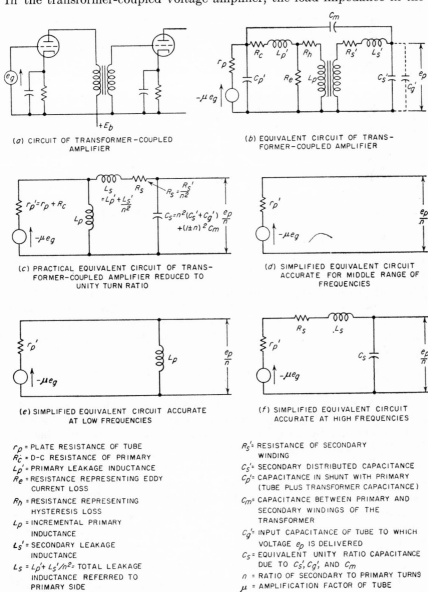

(a) CIRCUIT OF TRANSFORMER-COUPLED AMPLIFIER

(b) EQUIVALENT CIRCUIT OF TRANSFORMER-COUPLED AMPLIFIER

(c) PRACTICAL EQUIVALENT CIRCUIT OF TRANSFORMER-COUPLED AMPLIFIER REDUCED TO UNITY TURN RATIO

(d) SIMPLIFIED EQUIVALENT CIRCUIT ACCURATE FOR MIDDLE RANGE OF FREQUENCIES

(e) SIMPLIFIED EQUIVALENT CIRCUIT ACCURATE AT LOW FREQUENCIES

(f) SIMPLIFIED EQUIVALENT CIRCUIT ACCURATE AT HIGH FREQUENCIES

r_p = PLATE RESISTANCE OF TUBE
R_c' = D-C RESISTANCE OF PRIMARY
L_p' = PRIMARY LEAKAGE INDUCTANCE
R_e = RESISTANCE REPRESENTING EDDY CURRENT LOSS
R_h = RESISTANCE REPRESENTING HYSTERESIS LOSS
L_p = INCREMENTAL PRIMARY INDUCTANCE
L_s' = SECONDARY LEAKAGE INDUCTANCE
$L_s = L_p' + L_s'/n^2$ = TOTAL LEAKAGE INDUCTANCE REFERRED TO PRIMARY SIDE

R_s' = RESISTANCE OF SECONDARY WINDING
C_s' = SECONDARY DISTRIBUTED CAPACITANCE
C_p' = CAPACITANCE IN SHUNT WITH PRIMARY (TUBE PLUS TRANSFORMER CAPACITANCE)
C_m = CAPACITANCE BETWEEN PRIMARY AND SECONDARY WINDINGS OF THE TRANSFORMER
C_g' = INPUT CAPACITANCE OF TUBE TO WHICH VOLTAGE e_p IS DELIVERED
C_s = EQUIVALENT UNITY RATIO CAPACITANCE DUE TO C_s', C_g', AND C_m
n = RATIO OF SECONDARY TO PRIMARY TURNS
μ = AMPLIFICATION FACTOR OF TUBE

FIG. 8-14. Circuit of a transformer-coupled amplifier, together with exact and approximate equivalent circuits.

plate circuit of the tube is supplied by a step-up transformer (often called an *interstage* transformer) that commonly applies its secondary voltage to the grid of another tube, as shown in Fig. 8-14a. The amplifier tube employed in association with the transformer is ordinarily a triode having a plate resistance on the order of 5000 to 10,000 ohms, and a rated d-c plate current in the range 5 to 10 ma.

The most important characteristics of such a transformer-coupled voltage amplifier are the amount of amplification obtained and the way in which the amplification varies with frequency. A typical amplification curve is shown in Fig. 8-15. The distinguishing features of this curve are the relatively constant amplification in the middle range of frequencies, a falling off at low frequencies similar to that encountered in resistance-coupled amplifiers, and a falling off at high frequencies that is considerably more rapid than for the resistance-coupled amplifier.

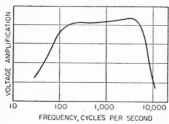

Fig. 8-15. Variation of amplification with frequency in a typical transformer-coupled amplifier.

Transformer-coupled voltage amplifiers have less voltage gain, poorer frequency response, and are more expensive than resistance-coupled amplifiers; they are therefore used only when the latter are not suitable. The usual situation calling for a transformer-coupled rather than a resistance-coupled amplifier is when the control grid of the tube to which the amplified voltage is to be applied is to be driven positive at the peak of each cycle.[1] Under these circumstances the d-c resistance in series with the control grid of the output tube must be kept small in order that the grid current will not develop an appreciable voltage drop in series with the grid; this means that a grid-leak resistance is not permissible if the grid current exceeds a few microamperes.

Analysis of Transformer-coupled Amplifiers. The behavior of a transformer-coupled voltage amplifier can be determined by replacing the tube and transformer by an equivalent electrical circuit and analyzing the resulting network. The transformer itself is a complicated combination of inductances, capacitances, and resistances, but can be represented fairly accurately by the equivalent circuit of Fig. 8-14b. For practical amplifier analysis, it is convenient to replace this circuit by the corresponding unity-turn-ratio network of Fig. 8-14c.[2] Here the essential

---

[1] Transformer coupling was formerly widely used to drive push-pull amplifiers, but has been displaced in this application by phase-inverter arrangements (see Fig. 10-19) except where grid-current flow in the driven stage prevents the use of arrangements based on resistance coupling.

[2] This circuit is approximate in that it neglects eddy-current and hysteresis loss in the transformer core, and the distributed capacitance of the primary winding. However, the errors thereby introduced are small, and consist principally in a slight reduc-

circuit elements are the primary inductance, the total leakage inductance, the turn ratio, the d-c resistances of the two windings, and the total capacitance that is effectively in shunt with the secondary.   This second-ary shunting capacitance includes not only the distributed capacitance of the secondary winding, but also the input capacitance of the tube or other load connected to the secondary winding, and a component result-ing from the presence of the secondary-to-primary capacitance C_m.

In the middle range of frequencies, the reactances of the primary inductance and of the secondary capacitance are so high as to be sub-stantially open circuits, while the reactance of the leakage inductance is low.   The equivalent circuit then reduces to the simplified form of Fig. 8-14d.   Ignoring the minus sign introduced by the phase reversal caused by the tube, this circuit gives

$$\left.\begin{array}{l}\text{Amplification in middle}\\ \text{range of frequencies}\end{array}\right\} = \frac{e_p}{e_g} = \mu n \qquad (8\text{-}11)$$

Here μ is the amplification factor of the tube, and n is the turn ratio of the transformer.   Somewhere in this middle range of frequencies, the primary inductance L_p is in parallel resonance with the capacitances shunting the primary winding, causing the impedance across the primary terminals of the transformer to be extremely high.

At low frequencies, the reactance of the primary incremental induct-ance falls off so that this circuit element can no longer be neglected.   This leads to the equivalent circuit of Fig. 8-14e, which is applicable to low fre-quencies, and from which a simple analysis shows

$$\frac{\text{Amplification at low frequencies}}{\text{Amplification in middle range}} = \frac{e_p}{e_g} = \frac{1}{1 + (r'_p/j\omega L_p)} = \frac{1}{1 - (j f_1/f)}$$

$$(8\text{-}12)$$

The notation is as in Fig. 8-14 with the addition that $\omega = 2\pi f$, where f is the actual frequency; also f_1 is the frequency at which the reactance ωL_p of the primary inductance equals the effective plate-circuit resistance r'_p.   It is important to note that the inductance L_p of the primary is the *incremental* inductance since the d-c plate current that passes through this winding superimposes a d-c magnetization on the core.   The falling off in response at low frequencies is shown by Eq. (8-12) to be determined only by the ratio of primary reactance to effective plate resistance, and by comparing Eqs. (8-7) and (8-12) is seen to follow the same law as for resistance coupling provided f_1 is appropriately interpreted in each case. *The low-frequency response thus falls off to 70.7 per cent of its mid-range*

---

tion in mid-range amplification as a result of eddy-current losses; this is discussed further by F. E. Terman, "Radio Engineers' Handbook," p. 367, McGraw-Hill Book Company, Inc., New York, 1943.

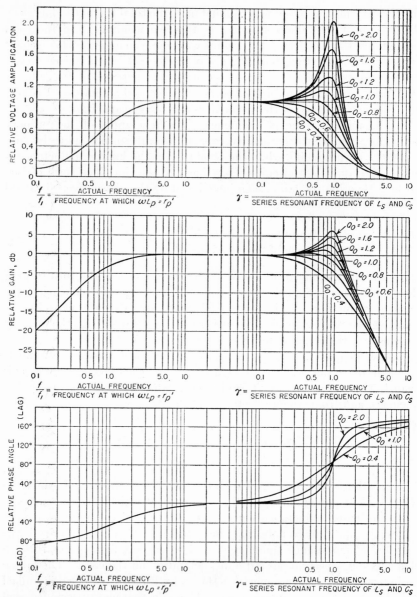

Fig. 8-16. Universal amplification curve of transformer-coupled amplifier, giving the relative amplification and the phase-shift characteristics.

value μn at the frequency for which the reactance of the primary incremental inductance equals the effective plate resistance r_p'. This low-frequency characteristic is represented by the universal amplification curve of Fig. 8-16.

At high frequencies, the reactance L_p of the primary inductance is so high that this circuit element can be regarded as an open circuit. However, the reactance of the capacitance C_s in shunt with the secondary can no longer be neglected, and the effect of the leakage inductance on the current drawn by this capacitance must also be considered. This leads to the equivalent circuit of Fig. 8-14f, which is applicable to high frequencies, and is a series resonant circuit having a high series resistance (i.e., low Q). The behavior of the transformer-coupled amplifier at high frequencies depends on the resonant frequency of this series circuit and the Q at resonance ($= Q_0$), as shown in Fig. 8-16.[1] In general, it can be said that the response will fall off rapidly at frequencies appreciably higher than the series resonance frequency, and that the response is most nearly uniform at the higher frequencies when Q_0 approximates 0.9.

Transformer and Tube Characteristics. Characteristics desired in the transformer of a transformer-coupled stage are high primary inductance, high series resonant frequency, and large turn ratio.[2] Desirable tube characteristics include low plate resistance and a high amplification factor. Since these various requirements are mutually conflicting, compromises must be made. For example, high amplification factor goes with high plate resistance. Again, a high primary inductance requires that a large fraction of the total winding space be allocated to the primary, which means a low turn ratio. Finally, a high series resonant frequency is most easily obtained when the physical size of the transformer is small, but small size means small primary inductance. The result of this situation is that it takes considerable experience and some experimentation to produce a good transformer design.

It is important to note that a given transformer should be used in association with the particular values of plate resistance and output load capacitance for which it was designed. Otherwise the performance will be degraded. For example, it might be thought advantageous to use a transformer with a plate resistance lower than the design value, as this improves the low-frequency response; however, the lower plate resistance raises Q_0 and thus introduces a peak in the high-frequency response.

---

[1] The equation for the amplification at high frequencies is obtained by writing down the voltage relations existing in the circuit of Fig. 8-14f and is

$$\frac{\text{Amplification at high frequencies}}{\text{Amplification in middle range}} = \frac{e_p/e_g}{\mu n} = \frac{1/j\omega C_s}{r_p' + j[\omega L_s - (1/\omega C_s)]} \qquad (8\text{-}13)$$

Here ω is 2π times the actual frequency f. By introducing the relations

$$2\pi f_0 = 1/\sqrt{L_s C_s} \qquad \text{and} \qquad Q_0 = 2\pi f_0 L_s/r_p'$$

Eq. (8-13) can be converted to the universal form presented in Fig. (8-16).

[2] These properties of the transformer can be measured experimentally by methods described by Terman, *op. cit.*, p. 971.

Input Transformers.   Transformers are often employed to couple a low-impedance source of energy, such as a microphone or a transmission line, to the control grid of an amplifier tube, as shown in Fig. 8-17.   A transformer used in this way is referred to as an *input transformer.*   Such an arrangement corresponds to an ordinary transformer-coupled voltage amplifier provided the source impedance associated with the primary of the transformer is regarded as analogous to the plate resistance of the tube in the transformer-coupled voltage amplifier.   The only differences are: (1) The source impedance of the input transformer is usually much lower than the plate resistance of a tube, so that the primary inductance

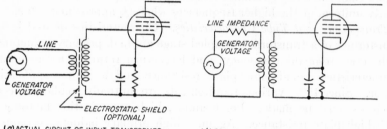

(*a*) ACTUAL CIRCUIT OF INPUT TRANSFORMER   (*b*) EQUIVALENT CIRCUIT IN WHICH LINE HAS BEEN REPLACED BY EQUIVALENT GENERATOR USING THÉVENIN'S THEOREM

FIG. 8-17. Circuit of input transformer.

can be proportionately reduced; this permits fewer primary turns and results in a step-up ratio that is inversely proportional to the square root of the source impedance.   (2) The primary circuit of the input transformer ordinarily is not called upon to carry direct current.   This last fact permits the core of the input transformer to be composed of high permeability material that has high initial permeability but poor incremental permeability characteristics.   Moreover, the core can be assembled in such a way as to give the minimum possible air gap.   As a result, it is possible to obtain a performance in input transformers much superior to that obtainable with an interstage transformer in which the primary winding carries a direct current that subjects the core to a d-c magnetization.

8-8. D-C (Direct-coupled) Amplifiers.   D-c voltages (and also voltages of extremely low frequency) can be amplified with resistance-coupled circuits by omitting blocking capacitors and employing direct coupling. Such amplifiers find extensive use in computers, in d-c voltmeters of the vacuum-tube type, as oscilloscope deflection amplifiers, and in many applications involving electronic instrumentation.

An elementary form of direct-coupled amplifier is shown in Fig. 8-18a, where the plate of tube T_1 is directly coupled to the grid of T_2 through a bias battery E_c.   This arrangement has serious disadvantages, however. First, it requires a source of voltage E_c that is ungrounded.   Second, the load impedance R_L must carry the d-c plate current of tube T_2. Third, neither terminal of output load impedance R_L is at ground potential. Fourth, any change in plate, heater, or grid-bias voltage, or any aging of the tube, will produce changes (commonly termed "drift") in the d-c output that will be indistinguishable from a d-c signal being amplified.

Numerous circuits have been devised to overcome these limitations and provide stable d-c amplification in useful form. While it is not possible in the space available here to review the subject exhaustively, some of the more important concepts are summarized below.[1]

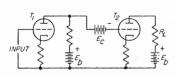 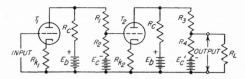

(*a*) ELEMENTARY D-C AMPLIFIER   (*b*) D-C AMPLIFIER WITH GROUNDED BATTERIES AND GROUNDED OUTPUT

Fig. 8-18. Simple forms of d-c amplifiers.

The undergrounded battery E_c and the direct current flowing through the output in the circuit of Fig. 8-18*a* can be eliminated by the use of a second grounded power supply E_c, arranged as shown in Fig. 8-18*b*. By using suitable values for resistances R_1 and R_2, tube T_2 will have the correct bias, while by appropriately selecting R_3 and R_4, the output voltage (and hence current) in load resistance R_L can be made zero in the absence of an applied signal.

When a d-c amplifier is used to operate a meter for the measurement of d-c voltages, it is necessary that no direct current flow through the output meter in the absence of an applied signal, but it makes no difference whether or not the output load, i.e., meter, is at a d-c potential above ground. These requirements are satisfied by the circuit illustrated in Fig. 8-19*a*; here resistances R_1, R_2, and R_3 are so proportioned as to make points *a* and *b* have the same potential in the absence of an applied signal.

Drift in D-C Amplifiers. The most serious problems involved in the design and use of d-c amplifiers center around the drift in the output arising from changes in the various voltages applied to the amplifier tubes. Drift presents an especially difficult problem in amplifiers having high gain, since drift occurring in the input stage then undergoes a large amount of amplification before appearing in the output.

---

[1] For further information, the reader is referred to the extensive literature that is available on d-c amplifiers. References that are particularly helpful include Maurice Artzt, Survey of D-C Amplifiers, *Electronics*, vol. 18, p. 112, August, 1945; Edward L. Ginzton, D-C Amplifier Design Technique, *Electronics*, vol. 17, p. 98, March, 1944; D. B. Penick, Direct-current Amplifier Circuits for Use with the Electrometer Tube, *Rev. Sci. Instr.*, vol. 6, p. 115, April, 1935; G. and T. Korn, "Electronic Analog Computers," chap. 5, McGraw-Hill Book Company, Inc., New York, 1952; "Vacuum Tube Amplifiers" (Vol. 18, Radiation Laboratory Series), chap. 11, McGraw-Hill Book Company, Inc., New York, 1948.

An obvious way of minimizing drift is to regulate very closely the voltages applied to the amplifier. Regulated power supplies of the type described in Sec. 20-8 are therefore very commonly used for producing the plate and bias voltages required by a d-c amplifier. However, no means of comparable simplicity and economy is available for regulating the heater voltage.

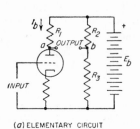 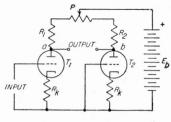

(a) ELEMENTARY CIRCUIT   (b) BALANCED CIRCUIT

Fig. 8-19. Direct-current amplifiers in which zero signal d-c voltage is eliminated from the output by a bridge arrangement.

A useful way of reducing drift is to balance identical tubes against each other in such a manner that the consequences of supply voltage changes cancel in so far as the amplifier output is concerned, whereas the amplified signal does not. A simple arrangement of this type is illustrated in Fig. 8-19b; this is a modification of Fig. 8-19a, in which R_3 has been replaced

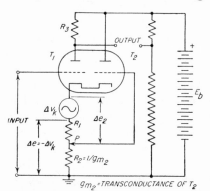

Fig. 8-20. Direct-current amplifier in which compensation is used to prevent variations in heater voltage from affecting the amplifier output.

by a second tube similar to T_1. To the extent that T_1 and T_2 are actually identical, then, changes in plate or heater voltage will produce no voltage difference between the terminals ab.

In addition to regulated voltage sources and balancing circuits, drift may also be minimized by compensation. That is, the same influence that causes drift is also used to produce an equal and opposite effect in the amplifier output. A compensating arrangement for eliminating the effect of heater voltage changes is illustrated in Fig. 8-20.[1] Here the effect of a variation in heater voltage is represented by the voltage ΔV_k, which represents the change in velocity of emission of the electrons. In the circuit of Fig. 8-20, the tendency for ΔV_k to alter the potential

[1] This particular method of compensating for heater-voltage variation is due to Stewart D. Miller, Sensitive D-C Amplifier with A-C Operation, *Electronics*, vol. 14, p. 27, November, 1941. Other means of accomplishing the same result are described by Artzt, *loc. cit.*, and in "Vacuum Tube Amplifiers," *op. cit.*, pp. 458–467.

between cathode and ground, and hence the plate current of T_1, is exactly neutralized[1] by an equal and opposite voltage Δe developed in $R_1 + R_2$ by amplified plate current from T_2 produced by voltage Δe_2 acting between cathode and grid of T_2.

Since it is never possible completely to eliminate all sources of drift it is always necessary to provide d-c amplifiers with means whereby in the absence of an input signal the output voltage can be adjusted either to zero or to a predetermined d-c value. Such a "zero balance" or "zero set" can be obtained in a number of ways; typical examples are provided by the potentiometers P in Figs. 8-19b and 8-20. In the latter figure it might be thought that adjustment of the zero balance would upset the compensation. However, the variations in R_2 required to accommodate the maximum drift that can be expected in a well-designed d-c amplifier will be so small as to have negligible effect on the effectiveness of the compensation.

Tubes for D-C Amplifiers. D-c amplifiers usually employ triode tubes with relatively high amplification factors. In cases where the tubes are used in pairs, as in Figs. 8-19b and 8-20, it is customary to employ twin tubes, i.e., tubes having two complete sets of electrodes in the same vacuum envelope. While a pentode can give more gain per stage for d-c signals, and is capable of amplifying to higher frequencies, the screen represents another electrode that must be supplied with anode voltage. This is commonly a serious disadvantage and can be an additional source of drift; however, d-c amplifier circuits using pentodes and other multi-grid tubes have been devised that utilize the additional grids to achieve compensation for changes in anode and heater voltages.[2]

PROBLEMS AND EXERCISES

8-1. A 6SK7 pentode tube is to be used as an amplifier under the operating conditions given in Table 6-1, page 186. Determine (a) the bias resistance required, and (b) the screen resistor R_{sg} for a plate-supply voltage $E_{bb} = 250$ volts.

8-2. By means of sketches, show the consequences in Fig. 8-2 of doubling the load resistance. For purposes of comparison, repeat the oscillograms of Fig. 8-2b to d as dotted lines.

8-3. Add a curve to Fig. 8-2 showing screen current when the impedance in the screen circuit is zero (that is, $R_{sg} = 0$ in Fig. 8-1c).

[1] This situation can be analyzed as follows; If the application of voltage ΔV_k is to have no effect on the plate current of T_1, then the plate current of T_2 must decrease an amount ΔI_2 such that the voltage drop $\Delta e = \Delta I_2 (R_1 + R_2)$ of this current flowing through $R_1 + R_2$ will be equal and opposite to ΔV_k. Now $\Delta I_2 = -\Delta e_2 g_{m2}$; however, since $\Delta e = -\Delta V_k$, then $\Delta e_2 = \Delta V_k[1 - R_1/(R_1 + R_2)] = \Delta V_k R_2/(R_1 + R_2)$. Hence $\Delta I_2 = -g_{m2} \Delta V_k R_2/(R_1 + R_2)$ and $\Delta e = \Delta I_2 (R_1 + R_2) = -g_{m2}R_2 \Delta V_k$. When $R_2 = 1/g_{m2}$, then $\Delta e = -\Delta V_k$, and perfect compensation is achieved.

[2] For examples, see Penick, *loc. cit.*

8-4. Draw curves similar to those of Fig. 8-2 but showing voltage and current relations in screen and plate circuits when an alternating voltage is superimposed on the d-c screen-grid voltage and $R_{sg} = 0$.

8-5. A 1000-cycle wave is accompanied by a second-harmonic component that is half as large. In the original wave, the second-harmonic component is so phased that both fundamental and second harmonic pass through zero, becoming positive, at the same instant. Sketch this original complex wave. Then sketch this same wave after it has passed through an electrical system such that the fundamental component suffers a time delay of 0.0005 sec, while the second-harmonic component suffers a time delay of 0.00075 sec.

8-6. Calculate the time delays represented by a phase shift of 45° at 60 cycles and at 4 Mc.

8-7. *a.* An alternating potential of 2 volts effective of a frequency of 1000 cycles is applied to the grid of a triode having $\mu = 14$, $r_p = 10,000$, and a resistance load of 12,000 ohms. Calculate (1) the alternating current in the load, (2) the alternating voltage across the load, (3) the alternating power dissipated in the load, and (4) the ratio of voltage across the load to the voltage applied to the grid.

b. Repeat the above for a load consisting of 2 henrys inductance.

8-8. Calculate the amplitudes of the alternating waves in Fig. 8-2c and d when $E_b = 250$ volts, $I_b = 12$ ma, $Z_L = 25,000$ ohms, $e_g = 2$ volts, and $g_m = 2000$ μmhos.

8-9. In a particular resistance-coupled amplifier of the type illustrated in Fig. 8-5, $R_c = 500,000$ ohms, $R_{gl} = 500,000$ ohms, $C_c = 0.0025$ μf, and $C_0 = 20$ μμf. The transconductance of the tube at the operating point is 644 μmhos. Assuming that the plate resistance is infinite, calculate and plot on a logarithmic frequency scale the curve of amplification and phase shift for the frequency range 10 to 200,000 cycles, using the universal amplification curves, and assuming that the screen and bias by-passing are fully effective.

8-10. In the amplifier of Prob. 8-9, it is desired to limit the frequency range so that the response is within 3 db of the mid-frequency value only from 100 cycles to 6000 cycles, in order that interference outside of this frequency band will be discriminated against. Determine the proper size of coupling-capacitor capacitance, and determine how much capacitance must be present in shunt with the coupling resistance R_c in order to achieve the desired result.

8-11. In the amplifier of Prob. 8-9, plot the time delay in seconds as a function of frequency on a *linear* frequency scale [assume $n = 0$ in Eq. (8-1)].

8-12. In the amplifier of Prob. 8-9 indicate qualitatively the effect on the mid-frequency amplification and on the frequency characteristic of (*a*) making the grid bias more negative, (*b*) increasing the plate and screen voltages simultaneously, (*c*) decreasing the coupling resistance, and (*d*) increasing the grid-leak resistance.

8-13. In the amplifier of Prob. 8-9, the screen-dropping resistance R_{sg} is 2.4 megohms, the dynamic resistance r_s of the screen-grid electrode is 125,000 ohms at the operating point, and the screen by-pass capacitor C_{sg} is 0.04 μf. Assuming that the bias resistance is fully by-passed, plot as a function of frequency the magnitude and phase of the factor β by which the amplification obtained in Prob. 8-9 must be multiplied in order to take into account the effects of this impedance in the screen circuit.

8-14. Explain where in the derivation of Eq. (8-8) it is necessary to assume that the mu factor of the screen grid relative to control grid is the same with respect to plate current as it is with respect to screen current.

8-15. In the amplifier of Probs. 8-9 and 8-13, determine the magnitude of the screen by-pass capacitor C_{sg} required to give sufficient by-passing so that the effect upon the amplification will be less than 1 db at all frequencies above 10 cycles.

8-16. In a particular pentode tube, $\mu = 2000$, $\mu_s = 20$, and $g_m = 2000$ μmhos. What plate current flows as a result of simultaneously applying 1 volt to the control grid and -12 volts to the screen grid? Assume both voltages are of the same frequency (but of opposite polarity as indicated by the negative sign).

8-17. In a resistance-coupled amplifier, a parallel resonant circuit is connected in series between the screen grid and its d-c voltage source. Describe qualitatively the effects produced on the frequency response characteristic, using sketches, and show the difference in the behavior when the resonant circuit has low Q and high Q for a given inductance and capacitance.

8-18. Follow through a line of reasoning that demonstrates that, when a signal voltage is applied between control grid and ground and when there is a resistive impedance between cathode and ground, the alternating voltage drop across the cathode impedance is of such polarity as to reduce the net voltage between control grid and cathode to a value less than the signal voltage.

8-19. In the amplifier of Prob. 8-9, the bias impedance consists of a resistance of 3000 ohms, shunted by a capacitance of 3.0 μf. Plot the magnitude and phase of the gain reduction factor γ as a function of frequency down to 10 cycles.

8-20. In the analysis given on page 267 of the effects produced by a bias impedance, it was assumed that the screen grid was by-passed by C_{sg} directly to the cathode. How would Eq. (8-9) have to be modified if the screen-grid by-pass capacitor was connected to ground instead of the cathode? To make the discussion specific, assume that the screen current is 0.25 times the plate current. Also assume that at the frequencies of interest, the bias impedance and the impedance in the screen circuit are small compared with the dynamic screen resistance.

8-21. Assume that the bias impedance system of Fig. 8-5 is modified by inserting an inductance in series with C_k of such value as to give series resonance in the middle of the frequency range. Describe qualitatively the effect this will have on the curve of amplification as a function of frequency.

8-22. Design a resistance-coupled amplifier using a 6SJ7 tube to give as much output voltage as possible when the available plate supply voltage is limited to 100 volts. The amplification is to be within 3 db of the mid-frequency value for the frequency range 40 to 15,000 cycles. The amplified output is to be applied to a power tube having an input capacitance of 10 $\mu\mu$f, and the stray wiring capacitance is estimated as 5 $\mu\mu$f. The maximum resistance that can be placed in series with the grid of the power tube is 0.2 megohm.

The design consists in specification of all circuit constants (except C_{sg}) and also specification of plate and screen voltages and currents.

8-23. Estimate r_{sg} and the resulting value of C_{sg} in Prob. 8-22 from the fact that when a 6SJ7 tube is connected as a triode it has characteristics such as given in Table 6-1, page 186. Assume that r_{sg} is inversely proportional to the cube root of the screen current, and that sharp low-frequency cutoff is desired.

8-24. Design a resistance-coupled amplifier for the same conditions as Prob. 8-22, except that the available supply voltage is 300 volts, and the grid-leak resistance can have any value up to 2.0 megohms.

8-25. With the aid of the design procedure outlined on page 270, compute the mid-frequency gain of resistance-coupled amplifiers under the following conditions when a 6SJ7 tube is used. Assume that the high-frequency response is not a limiting factor.

a. Supply voltage = 400 volts. Maximum permissible $R_{gl} = 2.0$ megohms. Objective is good gain with a large output voltage.

b. Same as (a) except supply voltage = 50 volts.

c. Same as (a) except maximum permissible $R_{gl} = 0.1$ megohm.

d. Same as (a) except objective is maximum possible gain.

Tabulate the results.

8-26. *a.* For the design arrived at in Example 1, p. 273, determine the highest frequency for which the response will be not less than 3 db below the mid-frequency value.

b. Determine suitable values of R_c and I_b for top frequencies of 50, 200, and 1000 kc, calculate the mid-frequency gain in each case, and tabulate the results [including the data from (*a*)].

8-27. Repeat Example 1, page 273, using the following modifications in specifications:

Maximum permissible R_{gl} = 2.0 megohms.

Desired peak output voltage = 150 volts.

Required frequency range = 20 to 30,000 cycles.

8-28. Complete the remaining details of Example 2, page 274.

8-29. Complete the remaining details of Example 3, page 274.

8-30. A fundamental restriction on the low-frequency limit of a resistance-coupled amplifier arises from the fact that d-c leakage current in the coupling capacitor causes a positive bias voltage to be developed across the grid-leak resistance. If the bias developed in this way cannot be allowed to exceed some specified value, then the lowest frequency obtainable is determined by the leakage conductance per microfarad of the type of coupling capacitor used, and is independent of the size of the capacitor provided that there is no limit to the magnitude of the grid-leak resistance that it is permissible to use. Explain.

8-31. A tube handbook put out by a manufacturer proposes the following circuit constants as being satisfactory for the design of a resistance-coupled amplifier employing a particular pentode tube: E_b = 300 volts; R_c = 250,000 ohms; R_{gl} = ½ megohm; I_b = 0.6 ma; maximum undistorted output voltage = 88 volts; and voltage amplification at mid-frequency = 167.

a. Demonstrate from this information that this amplifier is proportioned to provide a large output voltage, and compare the maximum undistorted output voltage actually obtainable with the rough rule stated on page 271.

b. Redesign this amplifier for maximum voltage amplification, by specifying a new coupling resistance and a new plate current. On the assumption that the transconductance of the tube is proportional to the cube root of the plate current, calculate the increase in amplification obtained for the modified design as compared with the design proposed in the tube handbook.

8-32. Derive Eq. (8-12).

8-33. Derive Eq. (8-13).

8-34. A certain interstage coupling transformer has the following characteristics:

Primary incremental inductance at rated primary current............ 20 henrys
Primary inductance with secondary shorted........................ 0.15 henry
Turn ratio of transformer.. 4.0
Series resonant frequency of secondary (with no tube shunted across the
secondary)... 13,000 cycles
R_e so large as to be of no consequence
Primary d-c resistance... 300 ohms
R'_s (actual value before reducing to unity-turn ratio)............... 10,000 ohms

This transformer is to be used with a 12AU7 triode operated under conditions given in Table 6-1, page 186. The input capacitance of the following tube is estimated as 50 $\mu\mu$f. Calculate and plot the way in which the amplification would be expected to vary with frequency, making use of the universal amplification curve of Fig. 8-16 in this calculation.

8-35. What would be the best value of plate resistance to use with the transformer of Prob. 8-34?

8-36. A resistance shunted across the primary terminals of the transformer in a transformer-coupled amplifier tends to make the high-frequency response peaked, extends the low-frequency end of the amplification curve, and reduces the mid-frequency amplification. Explain, using Thévenin's theorem to simplify the network consisting of tube and shunting resistance that is associated with the primary terminals.

8-37. A transformer-coupled amplifier is to cover the frequency range 80 to 8,000 cycles with a response at least 70.7 per cent, and not more than 110 per cent, of the mid-frequency value.

a. If the tube to be used has a plate resistance of 10,000 ohms, specify required values of primary inductance, leakage inductance reduced to unity-turn ratio, and frequency of series resonance (when the load capacitance is connected across the secondary).

b. Assuming that the turn ratio will be 3.5 and that the input capacitance of the tube to which the amplified voltage is delivered is 25 $\mu\mu f$, how much distributed capacitance should the secondary of the transformer have, and what is the series resonance frequency desired in the transformer when the secondary is not connected to the next tube?

8-38. A transformer is to couple a 500-ohm line to the grid of a tube. Specify the minimum allowable primary inductance if the response is not to fall to less than 70.7 per cent of the mid-frequency response at 60 cycles.

8-39. In a transformer-coupled amplifier, what will be the effect upon the shape of the amplification characteristic of (*a*) increasing the capacitance of the load connected across the secondary terminals of the transformer, and (*b*) increasing the d-c current flowing through the transformer primary?

8-40. *a.* Determine the voltage gain between the grids of T_1 and T_2 in Fig. 8-18*b* when the tube and circuit constants involved are $\mu = 70$, $r_p = 80,000$ ohms, $R_c = \frac{1}{4}$ megohm, $R_1 = \frac{1}{2}$ megohm, $R_2 = 1$ megohm, and $R_k = 0$.

b. What is the effect on gain if $R_k = 1000$ ohms?

8-41. In Fig. 8-18*b*, assume that E_b, R_c, R_3, and R_{k2} are specified for T_2. Then prove that the value of R_4 which causes the d-c output in the absence of an applied signal to be zero, depends only on E_c. Also show that if the output voltage for $R_L = \infty$ is to be a large fraction of the amplified voltage developed across R_c, E_c must then be considerably larger than the d-c voltage actually acting on the plate of T_2.

8-42. In Fig. 8-19*a*, $I_b = 0.8$ ma, $R_1 = 250,000$ ohms, and $E_b = 300$ volts. Specify R_1 and R_2 if the current drain in the voltage divider R_1 and R_2 is 1 ma.

8-43. What is the equivalent output impedance as seen by the load in Fig. 8-19*b*, if $R_1 = R_2 = 200,000$ ohms and the tubes each have a plate resistance of 80,000 ohms? Assume that $R_k = 0$ and that the resistance of P can be neglected.

8-44. Modify the amplifier circuit of Fig. 8-18*b* in such a manner as to incorporate the same type of compensation against heater-voltage changes that is illustrated in Fig. 8-20.

CHAPTER 9

VOLTAGE AMPLIFIERS FOR VIDEO FREQUENCIES

9-1. Video-frequency (Wideband) Voltage Amplifiers. An amplifier having a frequency range extending from a low value up to the order of a megacycle or higher is termed a *video amplifier*, or *wideband amplifier*. Television signals, short pulses, etc., involve frequency ranges of this character. The term video is applied to such amplifiers because they were first developed to handle the picture signals of television systems.

The requirements which video-frequency amplifiers must meet are often very rigorous. Thus in order to reproduce the complicated wave shapes of television signals with reasonable fidelity, it is necessary that the total amplification of the whole system involving many stages of video amplification be constant to within a few decibels from 60 cycles to about 4 Mc. At the same time the total time-delay distortion of the system of many stages must not exceed approximately 0.06 μsec at the high frequency end of the range, or about 250 μsec at 60 cycles; this corresponds to phase errors of about 90° and 5°, respectively.

Response of Video Amplifiers to Pulses. An important characteristic of a video amplifier is its ability to reproduce abrupt changes in wave shape. For example, if an ideal rectangular pulse (or step wave) having vertical sides and a flat top, such as illustrated in Fig. 9-1, is applied to a video amplifier, the limited frequency range and the phase distortion of the amplifier will prevent the output wave from being an exact replica of the input wave. The principal modifications introduced by the amplifier to the shape of such an ideal pulse are: (1) the amplitude rises (and falls) at a finite rate rather than instantaneously; (2) in some cases the initial amplitude rise will *overshoot*[1] the correct value; when this occurs there is a corresponding *undershoot* when the amplitude suddenly falls; (3) the top of the reproduced pulse will tend to fall off or *sag* with time, instead of being flat. These defects are illustrated in Fig. 9-1.

The rate at which the output voltage rises when an input voltage is suddenly applied is commonly expressed in terms of the time it takes the output voltage to rise from 10 to 90 per cent of its full amplitude. This *rise time* is inversely proportional to the bandwidth of the amplifier, and

---

[1] The initial overshoot is sometimes followed by a damped oscillation, as illustrated Fig. 9-9. When this happens the initial undershoot is also followed by decaying oscillations.

when the overshoot is zero or small it is given with good accuracy by the relation[1]

$$\text{Rise time in seconds} = \frac{0.35 \text{ to } 0.45}{B} \qquad (9\text{-}1)$$

Here bandwidth B is defined as the highest frequency in cycles for which the over-all response of the amplifier, irrespective of the number of stages, does not fall below 70.7 per cent (3 db) of the mid-frequency response. The value 0.35 should be used for overshoots less than 5 per cent.

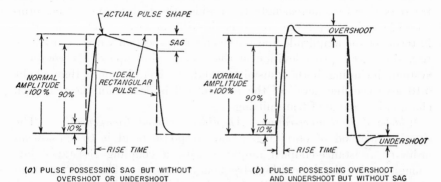

(*a*) PULSE POSSESSING SAG BUT WITHOUT OVERSHOOT OR UNDERSHOOT

(*b*) PULSE POSSESSING OVERSHOOT AND UNDERSHOOT BUT WITHOUT SAG

Fig. 9-1. Modifications in pulse shape introduced by an amplifier, together with definition of terms used to describe these modifications.

The presence of overshoot, and its amount when present, depends upon the time-delay characteristic of the amplifier, and the way in which the amplification falls off with increasing frequency near the high-frequency limit of the amplifier. An overshoot that is small or zero goes with a response curve that falls off moderately at the higher frequencies together with a time delay that is at least reasonably constant.

Sag is a consequence of low-frequency deficiencies in the response characteristic of the amplifier. Time-delay distortion at low frequencies is particularly important in this connection.

The portion of the response to a pulse or suddenly applied voltage, represented by the initial rise and the subsequent overshoot (if any) in Fig. 9-1, is often termed the *transient response* of the amplifier. It represents the ability of the amplifier to reproduce sudden changes in amplitude of the applied signal.

The fact that the maximum possible speed of rise and fall is determined by the bandwidth of the video amplifier sets a limit to the shortest pulse that a given amplifier can produce at its output. This minimum pulse length is approximately $1/2B$ seconds. If the length of the applied pulse

---

[1] This is an empirical law based on observations of individual cases; see "Vacuum-tube Amplifiers" (Vol. 18, Radiation Laboratory Series), p. 80, McGraw-Hill Book Company, Inc., New York, 1948.

is shorter than this, the output pulse will still have a length of about $1/2B$ seconds.

In most applications the transient response of a video amplifier is of more practical importance than the variation of amplification and time delay with frequency at the higher frequencies. This is because the transient response gives directly the property that is usually of prime importance in video amplifiers, namely the ability to reproduce sudden changes in wave shape. In contrast, the amplification and phase-shift characteristic gives this essential information only indirectly.[1] The trend is therefore increasingly to consider the high-frequency performance of a video amplifier in terms of rise time and overshoot, rather than in terms of the amplitude and phase effects associated with the response to a sine wave. In television, if the over-all rise time of the complete system, including both transmitter and receiver, is more than about 0.10 μsec the fine detail of the picture will be less than the television channel is capable of transmitting.

Wideband Resistance-coupled Amplifiers without Compensation. The simplest method of obtaining a wide response band is to employ an ordinary resistance-coupled amplifier with a coupling resistance low enough to give the desired high-frequency response. The gain per stage of such an arrangement will be low when the required top frequency is high; thus the wider the bandwidth, the greater the number of stages that must be employed to obtain a given total amplification.

The amplification in the mid-frequency range of such an arrangement can be taken as

$$\text{Mid-frequency amplification} = g_m R_c \qquad (9\text{-}2)$$

where g_m is the transconductance of the amplifier tube, and R_c is the coupling resistance. The result is a degenerated form of Eq. (8-4) which makes use of the fact that to achieve a wideband, R_c must be made so low that R_{eq} as given by Eq. (8-5) does not differ significantly from R_c. The amplification and phase characteristic of this type of wideband amplifier are given by Eq. (8-6) and the universal amplification curve of Fig. 8-9. The transient response is given by curve 1 of Fig. 9-2;[2] it is characterized by the absence of overshoot, and a 10 to 90 per cent rise time having the value

$$\text{Rise time in seconds} = 2.2 R_c C_0 \qquad (9\text{-}3)$$

The notation here is the same as in Fig. 8-5e.

While a simple resistance-coupled wideband amplifier is satisfactory

---

[1] The transient response can, however, be determined from the steady-state properties with the aid of the Laplace Transform; see for example, H. H. Skilling, "Transient Electric Currents," chap. 10, McGraw-Hill Book Company, Inc., New York, 1952.

[2] The transient response is a simple exponential curve having the time constant $R_c C_0 = T_0$.

where the frequency and time-delay distortion requirements are analogous to those of ordinary audio-frequency amplifiers, it does not, however, satisfactorily meet the requirements of television and of pulsed systems. For this reason it is found desirable in nearly all video amplifiers to compensate the simple resistance-coupled amplifier by introducing additional reactive elements in the coupling network to improve the amplifier behavior at both the high and low ends of the frequency range being amplified. Methods of doing this are discussed in Secs. 9-2 and 9-4.

Tubes for Video Voltage Amplification—The Gain-bandwidth Concept. The merit of a tube as a video voltage amplifier is measured in terms of the amount of amplification that can be obtained for a given bandwidth. In the case of a simple resistance-coupled video amplifier the top frequency can be taken as the value f_2 in Eq. (8-6). If the shunting capacitance C_0 is then taken to be the sum C_p of the plate-ground output capacitance of the amplifier tube plus the capacitance C_g between control grid and ground (input capacitance) of the next tube of the amplifier system, and if it is assumed $R_{eq} \approx R_c$, then from the definition of f_2 one can write

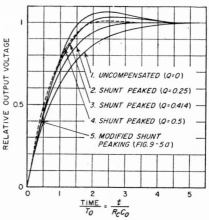

FIG. 9-2. Transient response of video amplifiers with two-terminal plate-coupling networks.

$$R_c = \frac{1}{2\pi f_2 (C_p + C_g)}$$

Solving this relation for the bandwidth f_2, and combining with Eq. (9-2) to eliminate R_c, yields the result

$$\text{Gain} \times \text{bandwidth} = \frac{g_m}{2\pi(C_g + C_p)} \tag{9-4}$$

This equation shows that what is desired in a video amplifier tube is large transconductance in proportion to electrode capacitances. In order to achieve this, the spacing between control grid and cathode must be small; this is a result of the fact that reducing the spacing increases the transconductance faster than it increases the capacitance. Typical tubes suitable for video voltage amplifiers are listed in Table 6-1, page 186, under the heading "Small high-performance pentodes." Data pertinent to video amplification on these and other pentode[1] tubes are given in Table 9-1.

[1] Triodes can be used as video amplifiers by employing triodes that have a high transconductance and moderate value of μ. The gain per stage obtainable in this

The significance of the gain-bandwidth product of Eq. (9-4) can be understood by an example. Thus, if a stage bandwidth of 10 Mc is required, then by using the 6AK5 tube of Table 9-1, a voltage gain of $120/10 = 12$ per stage could be obtained in the ideal case of zero circuit capacitance. Again, for a stage bandwidth of 2 Mc, the voltage gain would be 60 per stage in the ideal case. In actual practice the gains obtainable for a given bandwidth will be somewhat less than these values

TABLE 9-1

CHARACTERISTICS OF TUBES OF INTEREST
IN VIDEO AMPLIFICATION

Type	g_m,* μmhos	i_p,* ma	C_1 (output), $\mu\mu$f	C_2 (input), $\mu\mu$f	C_0 (total), $\mu\mu$f	Gain-band-width factor*	Remarks
6AC7	9,000	10	5	11	16	89	
6AG7	11,000	28	7.5	13	20.5	85	
6AK5	5,100	7.7	2.8	4	6.8	120	Miniature type
6SJ7	1,650	3	7	6	13	20	General-purpose pentode
6AU6	5,200	10.8	5	5.5	10.5	79	Miniature type
6L6	5,200	54	12	10	22	38	Beam power tube

* Values are for typical operating conditions, with bandwidth in megacycles.

as a result of the additional capacitance introduced by the circuit elements and the wiring of the coupling network. Also, greater bandwidths are obtainable by using a coupling impedance more complicated than a simple resistance R_c. In any case, however, the *merit* of the tube as a wideband amplifier is expressed by the gain-bandwidth product.

9-2. High-frequency Compensation of Video Amplifiers. *Shunt-peaking and Other Two-terminal Compensating Systems.*[1] The simplest

way for a given speed of rise (or bandwidth) is lower than for the corresponding pentode, however, because of the high input capacitance of triodes (see Sec. 12-10). At the same time, by employing a low coupling resistance, it is possible to obtain more gain for a given bandwidth from a two-stage video amplifier employing a twin triode than from a single pentode stage.

[1] The literature on this subject is very extensive. A few of the articles that would be useful supplementary reading are: "Vacuum-tube Amplifiers," *op. cit.*, particularly pp. 64–83; H. E. Kallman, R. E. Spencer, and C. P. Singer, Transient Response, *Proc. IRE*, vol. 33, p. 169, March, 1945 (and correction, vol. 33, p. 482, July, 1945); D. G. Tucker, Bandwidth and Speed of Build-up as Performance Criteria for Pulse and Television Amplifiers, *J. IEE* (Radio Section), vol. 94, pt. III, p. 218, May, 1947; A. V. Bedford and G. L. Fredenall, Transient Response of Multistage Video-frequency Amplifiers, *Proc. IRE*, vol. 27, pp. 277, April, 1939; H. A. Wheeler, Wide Band Amplifiers for Television, *Proc. IRE*, vol. 27, p. 429, July, 1939; P. M. Seal, Square-wave Analysis of Compensated Amplifier, *Proc. IRE*, vol. 37, p. 48, January, 1949; W. E. Thompson, Transient Response of V-F Couplings, *Wireless Eng.*, vol. 24, p. 20,

means of improving the high-frequency response of a resistance-coupled amplifier is by the addition of a small inductance in series with the coupling resistance, as illustrated in Fig. 9-3a.   This arrangement, which is known as *shunt peaking*, introduces an increase in the plate load impedance at high frequencies that tends to correct for the falling off in amplification that otherwise occurs at high frequencies.   It also modifies the phase-shift characteristic in such a manner as to reduce the time-delay distortion.   As a result, the speed of rise is increased.

The behavior of a shunt-peaking system depends upon the parameter $Q_2 = 2\pi f_2 L/R_c = L/R_c^2 C_0$, where f_2 is the frequency at which the response

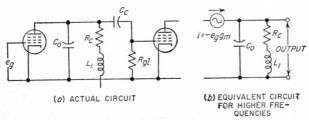

(a) ACTUAL CIRCUIT   (b) EQUIVALENT CIRCUIT FOR HIGHER FRE-QUENCIES

Fig. 9-3. Shunt-peaking circuit for compensating the high-frequency response of a resistance-coupled amplifier, together with the equivalent plate circuit applicable for moderate and high frequencies.

of the uncompensated amplifier has dropped to 70.7 per cent of the mid-frequency value.   That is, f_2 is the frequency at which the reactance of C_0 is equal to the coupling resistance R_c.   The quantitative relations involved can be derived with the aid of the equivalent circuit of Fig. 9-3b, which is applicable to moderate and high frequencies.[1]

The transient response of the shunt-peaking circuit to a suddenly applied voltage[2] is given by curves 2, 3, and 4 of Fig. 9-2 for typical circuit proportions.   The largest amount of compensation that can be employed without overshoot corresponds to $Q_2 = 0.25$; the overshoot is 3.1 per cent for $Q_2 = 0.414$ and becomes 6.7 per cent for $Q_2 = 0.50$.   The rise time decreases as the amount of compensation is increased; the speed of rise (i.e., the reciprocal of the 10 to 90 per cent rise time) for $Q_2 = 0.25$ and $Q_2 = 0.414$ is, respectively, 1.4 and 1.7 times as great as for the uncompensated amplifier having the same values of R_c and C_0.

January, 1947; A. B. Bereskin, Cathode-compensated Video Amplification, *Electronics*, vol. 22, p. 98, June, 1949; *ibid.*, p. 104, July, 1949; J. M. Miller, Jr., Cathode Neutralization of Video Amplifiers, *Proc. IRE*, vol. 37, p. 1070, September, 1949.

[1] In this equivalent circuit it is assumed that the grid-leak and plate resistance are so high compared with R_c that $R_{eq} = R_c$ in Eq. (8-5).   This approximation is permissible in view of the small value of coupling resistance that must be used to obtain a wideband response.

[2] The transient response is obtained by assuming that a d-c voltage e_g is suddenly applied in Fig. 9-3a, and then calculating the behavior of the equivalent circuit of Fig. 9-3b by the usual methods of transient analysis.

Universal curves giving the amplification and phase-shift characteristics of the shunt-peaking amplifier for different values of Q_2 are given in Fig. 9-4. These are obtained by calculating the performance of the

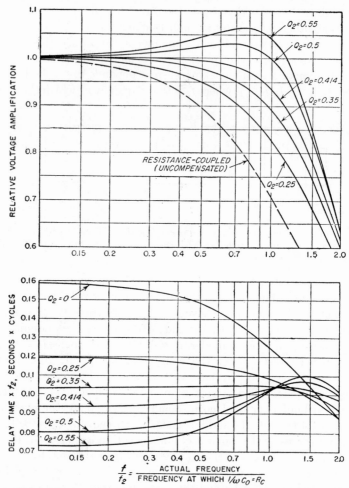

Fig. 9-4. Universal curve showing the amplification and phase-shift characteristics of a shunt-peaking amplifier for different circuit proportions.

equivalent circuit of Fig. 9-3b when e_g is assumed to be a sine-wave voltage.[1]

In examining Fig. 9-4, several critical cases are to be noted. Thus the best time-delay characteristic is obtained when the shunt-peaking

[1] The formula that results is

$$\text{Amplification} = -g_m R_e \frac{1 + jQ_2(f/f_2)}{1 - Q_2(f/f_2)^2 + j(f/f_2)} \tag{9-5}$$

inductance has a value such that $Q_2 = 0.34$. This corresponds to a response that drops off moderately at high frequencies. The largest amount of compensation (largest Q_2) that can be employed without causing the amplification to go through a peak as the frequency increases from the mid-range value corresponds to $Q_2 = 0.414$, and is sometimes referred to as the *maximum flatness* case. Another curve of interest is that for $Q_2 = 0.5$, which gives nearly constant amplification up to the frequency f_2; for this case the amplification rises to a maximum of about 3 per cent ($= 0.3$ db) above the mid-range value, as shown.

Correlation between the transient response and the amplitude and phase characteristic at high frequencies is obtained by considering curves 2, 3, and 4 of Fig. 9-2 in relation to the amplitude and phase characteristics given in Fig. 9-4 for the same values of Q_2. It will be noted that a good transient characteristic, i.e., a rapid rise and a small overshoot, corresponds to the combination of an amplification that falls off moderately at the high frequencies and a time delay that is substantially constant until the amplification has fallen considerably. An amplification characteristic that tends to be more nearly constant up to the top frequency, such as $Q_2 = 0.50$, has a less desirable transient characteristic in that, although the speed of rise is good, the overshoot is relatively large. This is a result of the poorer time-delay characteristic that is associated with this amplification curve, and illustrates

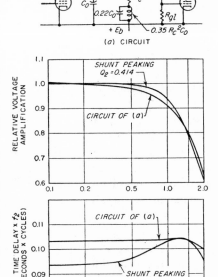

Fig. 9-5. Circuit of a two-terminal coupling system having one more reactive element than the shunt-peaking system of Fig. 9-3, together with amplitude and time-delay characteristics. The circuit proportions indicated are such as to give the lowest possible rise time with low overshoot.

the fact that the amplitude and phase (or time-delay) characteristics only indirectly indicate the transient behavior that can be expected.

The shunt-peaking circuit of Fig. 9-3a is the simplest of a family of compensating arrangements termed two-terminal systems. The next step in complexity, shown in Fig. 9-5a, consists in adding a small capacitance in shunt with the peaking inductance. The characteristics of this circuit depend upon the exact values chosen for the various circuit ele-

ments.   A desirable combination is illustrated in Fig. 9-5a;[1] for a given
R_c and hence a given gain, this particular arrangement has a speed of rise
that is 1.77 times that of the uncompensated resistance-coupled amplifier
and possesses only 1 per cent overshoot, as shown by dotted curve 5 in
Fig. 9-2.   The amplitude and time-delay characteristics of this circuit
are given in Fig. 9-5b, compared with a shunt-peaking circuit that is also
designed to give the same gain with a small overshoot.

The possible improvement in transient behavior obtainable by going to
more complicated networks than the shunt-peaking circuit is quite small.
As a result, one usually either uses shunt peaking or goes to four-terminal
systems.

Four-terminal Compensating Networks.   The high-frequency performance of a video amplifier can be further improved by employing a four-
terminal coupling network that separates the plate-ground capacitance of
the amplifier tube from the grid-ground capacitance of the next stage of
amplification.   In this way, each of these two capacitances acts separately instead of their combining to form a single large capacitance, as in
two-terminal coupling systems.   Examples of four-terminal coupling systems are illustrated in Fig. 9-6, where a is commonly referred to as a series-
peaked arrangement, while b and c are called series-shunt-peaked systems.

The design of a four-terminal coupling network depends upon the
capacitance ratio[2] C_2/C_1, and upon whether it is desired to emphasize
small rise time, constant gain to the highest possible frequency, or constant delay time, in the performance of the system.   Typical proportions
are given in Fig. 9-6; these emphasize constant gain in circuits a and b,
and rapid rise combined with small overshoot in circuit c.

The transient response obtained by using the four-terminal coupling
network of Fig. 9-6c is shown in Fig. 9-7.   The speed of rise is 2.48 times
as great as in an uncompensated amplifier having the same mid-frequency
gain and the same total capacitance $C_0 = C_1 + C_2$; the overshoot is less
than 1 per cent.   The corresponding figure for a shunt-peaked circuit
with a little greater overshoot is 1.7.   If C_3 in this circuit is omitted, but
everything else left unchanged, the relative speed of rise drops to 2.43 and
the overshoot increases to only 2 per cent; thus the exact value of capacitance C_3 in this circuit is not critical if C_3 does not exceed the size specified
in Fig. 9-6c.

[1] It will be noted that this is the shunt-peaking circuit for $Q_2 = 0.35$ with a capacitance $0.22C_2$ added in shunt with the inductance.   It is thus apparent that the distributed capacitance of the inductance of a shunt-peaking system has no adverse
effect as long as it does not exceed $0.22C_2$.

[2] The ratio C_2/C_1 is determined by the plate-cathode and plate-grid tube capacitances, but can be controlled somewhat by placement of circuit elements, and by an
auxiliary padding capacitor in shunt with C_1, which is usually the smaller.   Tube
properties are such that, as far as the tube capacitances alone are concerned, C_2/C_1
in a typical case has a value of about 2 when the tube in the stage under consideration
and the following tube are identical.

The transient response of the networks shown in Fig. 9-6a and b is less satisfactory in that it is characterized by large overshoot. This arises from the fact, shown in Fig. 9-8, that, although these particular networks have substantially constant amplification to a higher frequency than does

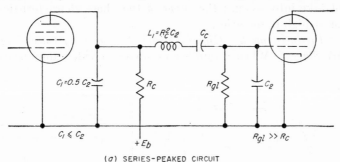

(a) SERIES-PEAKED CIRCUIT

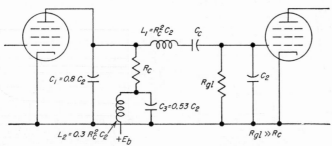

(b) SERIES-SHUNT PEAKED CIRCUIT PROPORTIONED
FOR CONSTANT AMPLIFICATION

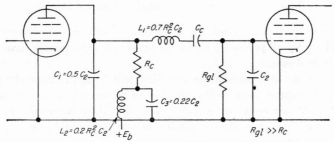

(c) SERIES-SHUNT PEAKED CIRCUIT PROPORTIONED FOR
BEST TRANSIENT CHARACTERISTIC

Fig. 9-6. Examples of four-terminal compensating networks.

the circuit of Fig. 9-6c for the same value of coupling resistance, the time-delay characteristic of the latter arrangement is very much superior. By reproportioning the relative sizes of the reactive elements in the networks of Fig. 9-6a and b, it is possible to obtain a transient response with small overshoot; thus c is the same circuit as b with different proportions. However, when this is done the amplification characteristic will now drop off at high frequencies as shown in Fig. 9-8 for the circuit of Fig. 9-6c, and the bandwidth becomes less. It is considerations such as these that cause the top frequency of the video amplifier to be of less practical significance than the transient response, since the frequency range alone does not take into account the effect of the phase characteristic on the behavior at high frequencies.

Effects Produced on the High-frequency Response by Cascading Video Amplifier Stages. When a number of stages of video amplification are

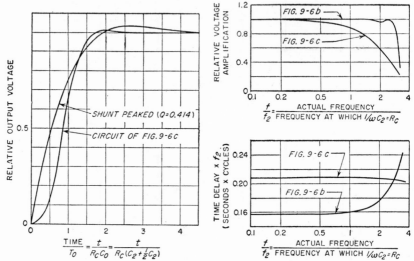

FIG. 9-7. Transient response of coupling network of Fig. 9-6c, together with corresponding curve for a shunt-peaked circuit of similar overshoot.

FIG. 9-8. Amplitude and time-delay characteristics of typical four-terminal compensating networks designed for constant amplification and constant time delay.

connected in cascade, the defects of the individual stages become cumulative. The over-all performance of the system is thus poorer than that of the individual stages.

The rise time of a multistage amplifier will be approximately proportional to the square root of the number of stages when the overshoot is small (1 to 2 per cent) or zero.[1,2] The rise time increases much less rapidly than this when the overshoot of the individual stages is of the order of 5 to 10 per cent, or greater.

The overshoot of a multistage system increases very slowly or not at

---

[1] To the extent that Eq. (9-1) is true, this implies that the 3-db bandwidth of a multistage amplifier is inversely proportional to the square root of the number of stages.

[2] If the rise times of the successive stages are t_1, t_2, t_3, etc., then the total rise time t_0 of the system for zero or small overshoot is

$$t_0 = \sqrt{t_1{}^2 + t_2{}^2 + t_3{}^2 + \cdots} \tag{9-6}$$

all as the number of stages increases, when the overshoot of each individual stage does not exceed 1 or 2 per cent. However, when the overshoot of the individual stages is of the order of 5 to 10 per cent, the overshoot of the over-all system is approximately proportional to the square root of the number of stages.

Connecting video amplifier stages in cascade introduces a general delay in the time when the response occurs that is closely proportional to the number of stages. This effect is illustrated in Fig. 9-9, which also shows the reduction in speed of rise and the increased overshoot that go with an increasing number of stages.

The cascading of stages also modifies the shape of the amplification curve in distinctive ways. Thus the 0.3-db peak in amplification of the

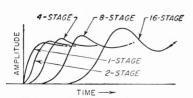

FIG. 9-9. Effect upon the transient response of increasing the number of stages, where each individual stage is of the shunt-peaked type possessing a moderate overshoot.

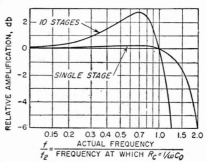

FIG. 9-10. Example showing how a small peak in the amplification curve of a single stage becomes a large peak when many similar stages are involved.

shunt-peaked stage for $Q_2 = 0.50$ will become a 3-db peak in the case of an amplifier composed of 10 such stages. This is illustrated in Fig. 9-10. Alternatively, if the amplification of the individual stages falls off at the higher frequencies without passing through a peak, then connecting a number of such stages in cascade *will cause the bandwidth of the over-all system to be less than the bandwidth of the individual stages.* This bandwidth narrowing is illustrated in Fig. 9-11 for the case of shunt peaking designed to give maximum flatness ($Q_2 = 0.414$). It will be noted that the reduction in bandwidth is considerable; for example if the over-all amplification of a 10-stage amplifier is to be constant within 1 db up to 4 Mc, then the amplification of each individual stage, in this case, must be constant to within 1 db up to a frequency of $4 \times (1.18/0.62) = 7.6$ Mc.

The bandwidth narrowing is much less with shunt-peaked stages designed for maximum flatness than it is for uncompensated resistance-coupled stages. Similarly, when still more complicated coupling systems, such as the four-terminal configurations of Fig. 9-6b and c, are proportioned to give maximum flatness, the bandwidth narrowing that occurs with increasing number of stages will then be less than in the case where the individual stages are of the maximum flatness shunt-peaked type.

Practical Construction of High-frequency Compensating Networks. The circuit constants called for in a particular high-frequency compensating system may be obtained by measuring the individual circuit components separately and then combining; alternatively, a purely experimental process may be used to obtain the desired circuit proportions. Measurement is recommended where possible; however, the small capacitances

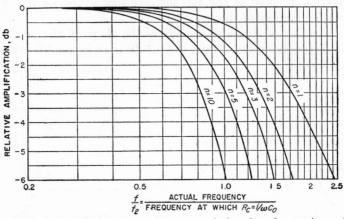

Fig. 9-11. Effect of cascading shunt-peaking stages designed to give maximum flatness, showing the bandwidth narrowing that occurs as the number of stages increases.

involved can be determined accurately only if special apparatus is available, and even then considerable care is required in carrying out the measurement.

The exact details of the experimental method of adjusting the circuit constants will vary with the type of compensating network involved, but the general principles can be illustrated by considering the shunt-peaking circuit of Fig. 9-3a. Here the proper coupling resistance R_c is obtained by short-circuiting the shunt-peaking inductance L_1 and adjusting R_c until the amplification at the frequency f_2, as measured experimentally, is 70.7 per cent of the mid-frequency value defined on page 290. The short circuit is next placed across the coupling resistance and the shunt-peaking inductance varied by adding or subtracting turns (or changing turn spacing) until the resulting tuned amplifier shows a peak of amplification at the frequency $f_2/\sqrt{Q_2}$, where Q_2 corresponds to the desired characteristic. Upon removal of the short circuit, one then has the desired compensated coupling system, even though not a single resistance, inductance, or capacitance was measured in obtaining this result.

After a high-frequency compensating system has been constructed, its performance should, if possible, be checked experimentally by applying a pulse or square wave having extremely rapid rise time to the amplifier input, and observing the resulting amplified output wave on a suitable oscilloscope.[1]

General Summarizing Comments on High-frequency Characteristics of Video Amplifiers.   As already stated, the ability of a video amplifier to reproduce abrupt changes in wave shape, such as represented by pulses and television signals, is determined directly by the rise time that can be obtained with only small or zero overshoot.   It is therefore preferred practice to design the high-frequency compensation of a video amplifier on the basis of rise-time considerations, rather than in terms of an upper-frequency limit.

For most purposes, the individual stages should be designed to give a small overshoot such as 1 to 3 per cent.   The required rise time per stage will then, by Eq. (9-1), be the rise time that is to be associated with the over-all amplifier system, divided by the square root of the number of amplifier stages involved.   The required bandwidth per stage will be inversely proportional to the rise time per stage.   For any given type of high-frequency compensation the gain per stage will be directly proportional to this rise time; for stages of different types of compensation having the same rise time, the stage gain will be proportional to the relative speed of rise listed in Table 9-2.

The comparative transient behavior of different high-frequency compensating arrangements[2] designed to have low overshoot is summarized in Table 9-2.   It is assumed in this table that the total shunting capacitance C_0 and the mid-frequency amplification are the same in each case.

A definite relation does exist between the transient response on the one hand and the amplification and phase characteristic on the other hand. Thus the best transient response in a video amplifier system, irrespective of whether one or many stages are involved, is obtained when the over-all amplification drops off gradually at high frequencies; the curve for $Q_2 = 0.35$ in Fig. 9-4 is an example of such a characteristic.   The proper amount of rounding off to be used in any particular case is a compromise between the desire to obtain the smallest possible rise time, corresponding to little or no dropping off, and the desire to keep the overshoot either zero or small, which corresponds to a very substantial falling off in the high-frequency response.   The best compromise always goes with a high-frequency amplification characteristic that falls off at a rate that approxi-

---

[1] Details involved in such tests are discussed by F. E. Terman and J. M. Pettit, "Electronic Measurements," p. 331, McGraw-Hill Book Company, Inc., New York, 1952.   In such experimental work it is essential that the rise time of the test wave, and also of the oscilloscope, either be small compared with the rise time of the amplifier under test, or at least be known and then corrected for with the aid of Eq. (9-6).

[2] An excellent series of curves giving the transient behavior of these and other circuit arrangements is given by R. C. Palmer and L. Mautner, A New Figure of Merit for the Transient Response of Video Amplifiers, *Proc. IRE*, vol. 37, p. 1073, September, 1949.

mates the shape of the Gaussian error curve,[1] combined with a substantially constant time delay up to the frequency for which the response is still not so low as 3 db below the mid-frequency amplification.

TABLE 9-2

COMPARATIVE TRANSIENT PERFORMANCE OF
DIFFERENT HIGH-FREQUENCY COMPENSATING ARRANGEMENTS

Circuit	Overshoot, %	Relative speed of rise*,†	Relative bandwidth for drop in gain of	
			1 db	3 db
Uncompensated resistance-coupled.....	0	1.00	0.53	1.00
Shunt-peaking:				
$Q_2 = 0.25$........................	0	1.4	0.76	1.41
$Q_2 = 0.414$.......................	3	1.7	1.18	1.72
$Q_2 = 0.50$........................	7	1.9	1.36	1.80
Two-terminal (Fig. 9-5a).............	1	1.77	1.08	1.77
Series-shunt-peaked (Fig. 9-6c)........	0.4	2.48	1.1	2.45
Series-shunt-peaked (Fig. 9-6c with C_3 omitted)........................	2	2.43	1.1	2.45

* All data are for same mid-frequency amplification, and also for same total shunt capacitance $C_0 = C_1 + C_2$.

† The rise time for the uncompensated resistance-coupled stage is 2.2 $R_c C_0$ [see Eq. (9-3)]; for other cases the rise time is inversely proportional to the speed of rise.

9-3. Low-frequency Defects of Video Amplifiers. In the above paragraphs it has been shown how the high-frequency characteristics of a video amplifier determine the speed of rise and the overshoot of the amplifier when reproducing an abrupt change in amplitude of the applied signal. In a similar manner, the low-frequency characteristic of the video amplifier determines the ability to reproduce the flat top of a square wave or a pulse. That is, deficiencies in the low-frequency characteristic of the amplifier cause *sag*, such as illustrated and defined in Fig. 9-12b (also see Fig. 9-1a). The low-frequency deficiencies of a video amplifier can also be expressed in terms of the amplification and phase-shift characteristics at low frequencies. Thus an amplifier without sag would also have constant amplification to very low frequencies, and zero phase shift at the low-frequency end of the response range.

The amount of sag that can be tolerated in an individual amplifier stage depends on the application involved. In video amplifiers for television systems, it is typically necessary that the sag of an individual stage not exceed 5 per cent in the time of one picture field, that is, $\frac{1}{60}$ sec.

[1] In this connection, it is to be noted that if the amplification characteristic of each individual stage follows a Gaussian curve, then the amplification characteristic obtained by placing several such stages in cascade will also be a Gaussian curve.

This corresponds to a phase shift of about 1° at a frequency of 60 cycles. When dealing with pulses, it is often desired that the amount of sag occurring in a time interval corresponding to the length of the pulse be of the order of 1 per cent or less. In order to meet requirements such as these, great care must be taken in designing the portions of the amplifier that affect the low-frequency response, and, generally, it is further necessary to compensate in some manner for the low-frequency deficiencies that still exist.

Analysis of the Low-frequency Performance of Video Amplifiers in Terms of Transient Behavior.[1] The output wave of a video amplifier can exhibit sag as a result of the action of the grid leak–capacitor combination, the impedance of the by-pass capacitor in the screen-grid circuit, and the impedance of the cathode-biasing system.

The action of the grid-leak capacitor can be determined by applying a sudden voltage, i.e., a step voltage[2] such as shown in Fig. 9-12a, to the control grid under conditions where the screen impedance Z_{sg} and cathode impedance Z_k in Fig. 9-13a are zero. So far as the equivalent plate circuit is concerned, this is the same as closing the switch shown in

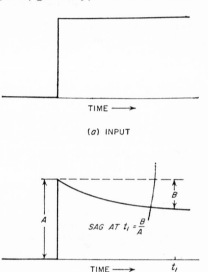

TIME ⟶

(a) INPUT

SAG AT $t_i = \dfrac{B}{A}$

TIME ⟶ t_i

(b) OUTPUT

FIG. 9-12. Oscillograms showing sag introduced by an amplifier when a step (or square) wave is applied.

the system in Fig. 9-13b. Neglecting the reversal in polarity introduced by the amplifier tube, the output voltage e_p developed across the grid-leak resistance R_{gl} is then by ordinary circuit theory found to be

$$e_p = e_g g_m R_c \epsilon^{-t/R_{gl}C_c} \tag{9-7}$$

Here e_g is the amplitude of the applied step, g_m is the transconductance of the tube, and t is time after the step voltage is applied; it is also assumed that $R_{gl} >> R_c$. Equation (9-7) is an ordinary exponential curve of the character shown in Fig. 9-13c. By definition the sag at time t is accordingly

$$\left.\begin{array}{l}\text{Sag caused by}\\ \text{coupling capacitor } C_c\end{array}\right\} = S_c = \frac{e_g g_m R_c - e_p}{e_g g_m R_c} = 1 - \epsilon^{-t/R_{gl}C_c} \tag{9-8a}$$

[1] Useful supplementary information is given by Seal, *loc. cit.*; also "Vacuum-tube Amplifiers," *op. cit.*, pp. 84–90, 114–138.

[2] In experimental work this step voltage is ordinarily supplied by a half cycle of a square wave, or by a pulse with rapid rise followed by a flat top.

It will be noted that $e_g g_m R_c$ is the magnitude of the output voltage at $t = 0$. Equation (9-7) assumes $R_{gl} >> R_c$.

When t is small compared with the time constant $R_{gl}C_c$, the sag is small, and Eq. (9-8a) takes the simple form

$$\left.\begin{array}{c}\text{Sag caused by}\\ \text{coupling capacitor}\end{array}\right\} = S_c = \frac{t}{R_{gl}C_c} \tag{9-8b}$$

Examination of Eq. (9-8b) shows that if the sag introduced by the grid leak–capacitor combination is to be kept small, the grid-leak resistance and coupling-capacitor capacitance should both be made as large as possible.

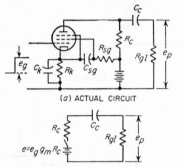

(a) ACTUAL CIRCUIT

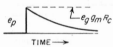

(b) EQUIVALENT PLATE CIRCUIT WHEN $Z_k = 0$ AND $Z_{sg} = 0$ (NEGLECTING PHASE REVERSAL INTRODUCED BY TUBE)

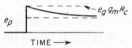

(c) VOLTAGE RELATIONS FOR EQUIVALENT CIRCUIT OF (b)

(d) SAG CAUSED BY SCREEN-GRID (OR BIAS) IMPEDANCE —OTHER SAGS ASSUMED NEGLIGIBLE

Fig. 9-13. Video amplifier showing circuit elements that introduce sag, and oscillograms showing the nature of the sag introduced by the coupling capacitor, and by bias and screen impedances.

A screen-grid impedance composed of a resistance-capacitance combination such as shown in Fig. 9-13a causes the amplified plate voltage e_p to have a transient response of the character illustrated in Fig. 9-13d. At the first instant after a sudden voltage is applied, the output has the same amplitude as though the screen-grid impedance were zero. However, with the passage of time, the amplitude decays exponentially to a value corresponding to the value that would be obtained if the screen impedance consisted of the resistor R_{sg} shunted by a zero by-pass capacitance.

A quantitative analysis for this case can be obtained by going through the transient analogue of the procedure followed in obtaining Eq. (8-8), taking advantage of the fact that the equivalent circuits of the tube apply to transient as well as to sinusoidal voltages. Such a procedure applied to determining the effect of a resistance-capacitance impedance in the screen circuit under conditions where there is zero bias impedance and negligible sag produced by the grid leak–capacitor combination yields the following result when the phase reversal introduced by the tube is neglected:

$$e_p = e_g g_m R_c \left(\frac{r_s}{r_s + R_{sg}}\right)\left(1 + \frac{R_{sg}}{r_s} e^{-t/C_{sg}R_1}\right) \tag{9-9}$$

The notation is as in Fig. 9-13a and as used above, with the addition that r_s is the dynamic screen resistance of the tube and $R_1 = r_s R_{sg}/(r_s + R_{sg})$ is the equivalent resistance formed by the screen resistance r_s in parallel with the screen voltage dropping resistance R_{sg}. The sag at time t corresponding to Eq. (9-9) is

$$\left.\begin{array}{l} \text{Sag caused by} \\ \text{screen impedance} \end{array}\right\} = S_{sg} = \frac{1}{1 + (r_s/R_{sg})}\left(1 - \epsilon^{-t/C_{sg}R_1}\right) \quad (9\text{-}10a)$$

When $t << C_{sg}R_1$ the sag is small, and this reduces to

$$\left.\begin{array}{l} \text{Sag caused by} \\ \text{screen impedance} \end{array}\right\} = S_{sg} = \frac{t}{C_{sg}R_1[1 + (r_s/R_{sg})]} = \frac{t}{C_{sg}r_s} \quad (9\text{-}10b)$$

A resistance-capacitance bias impedance produces the same kind of effect as a resistance-capacitance screen-grid impedance. As shown in Fig. 9-13d, the first instant after the application of a sudden voltage the amplified plate voltage e_p is just as though the cathode impedance were zero, but subsequently decays exponentially to the value that would be obtained if the bias impedance consisted of the bias resistor R_k without shunting capacitance. Under conditions where there is zero screen-grid impedance and negligible sag introduced by the grid leak–capacitor combination, a transient analogue of the analysis used to obtain Eq. (8-9) gives

$$e_p = \frac{e_g g_m R_c}{1 + g_m R_k}\left(1 + g_m R_k \epsilon^{-\frac{1 + g_m R_k}{R_k C_k}t}\right) \quad (9\text{-}11)$$

Here e_p is the output voltage obtained when a step voltage of amplitude e_g is applied to the input, and the remaining notation is the same as illustrated in Fig. 9-13 or as used in Eq. (9-8); also, the reversal in phase introduced by the tube is neglected for purposes of convenience. The sag corresponding to Eq. (9-11) is

$$\left.\begin{array}{l} \text{Sag caused by} \\ \text{bias impedance} \end{array}\right\} = S_k = \frac{g_m R_k}{1 + g_m R_k}\left(1 - \epsilon^{-\frac{1 + g_m R_k}{R_k C_k}t}\right) \quad (9\text{-}12a)$$

When $t << R_k C_k/(1 + g_m R_k)$, the sag is small and becomes

$$\left.\begin{array}{l} \text{Sag caused by} \\ \text{bias impedance} \end{array}\right\} = S_k = \frac{g_m}{C_k}t \quad (9\text{-}12b)$$

Practical Considerations Relating to Transient Behavior at Low Frequencies. It is instructive to introduce reasonable numbers into Eqs. (9-8b), (9-10b), and (9-12b), and determine the size of capacitor that is required in each case to keep the sag within tolerable limits for a video amplifier that is to handle television signals.[1]   Assume that the maximum permissible sag is 0.05 in a time corresponding to one picture field, that is, $\frac{1}{60}$ = 0.0167 sec.   Assume a 6AC7 tube is used, with R_{gl} = 0.5 megohm, R_{sg} = 60,000 ohms, r_s = 20,000, R_k = 160 ohms, g_m = 9000 μmhos, R_c = 3000 ohms.   Then for S_c = 0.05, one has

$$C_c = \frac{0.0167}{0.5 \times 10^{-6} \times 0.05} = 0.667 \ \mu f \tag{9-13}$$

$$C_{sg} = \frac{0.0167}{0.05 \times 15,000(1 + 0.333)} = 16.7 \ \mu f \tag{9-14}$$

$$C_k = \frac{9000 \times 10^{-6} \times 0.0167}{0.05} = 3000 \ \mu f \tag{9-15}$$

The capacitor called for in Eq. (9-13) is a practical size, although a little bulkier than would be preferred.   On the other hand, the size of screen by-pass capacitor indicated by Eq. (9-14) is unreasonably large, and can be achieved practically only by the use of a relatively large electrolytic capacitance.   Finally the capacitor required to by-pass the cathode impedance is even more unreasonable.   This situation is typical and makes it desirable to avoid the use of resistance-capacitance combinations in the bias impedance and screen circuit of video amplifiers for television.   Instead, the screen voltage is preferably obtained either directly from a source of suitable voltage or, alternatively, is derived from a resistance voltage divider so proportioned as to represent a source of voltage having an internal resistance that is low compared with the dynamic screen resistance of the tube.   Similarly, the bias is preferably obtained either by some means other than a bias impedance or, alternatively, by means of a bias resistance R_k that is un-by-passed.   In this latter case, the mid-frequency amplification is reduced by the factor $1/(1 + g_mR_k)$.   However, this loss can be gained back by making the coupling resistance have a value $1 + g_mR_k$ times as great as would otherwise be used.   While this larger value of R_c will tend to make the high-frequency response poorer and so increase the rise time, this tendency can be entirely or at least largely eliminated by shunting R_k with a small by-pass capacitor of such size that the cathode by-passing begins to be effective in the frequency range where the high-frequency output begins to drop off seriously.   In this way, the tendency to obtain a poorer response at high frequencies can be almost if not completely counteracted by the reduction in bias impedance at the higher frequencies.[2]   The per-

---

[1] The capacitor sizes required to give satisfactory performance with short pulses will be much smaller.   In this case C_k is the only capacitance that is likely to be excessively large.

[2] It is in fact possible to employ compensation of this type as a substitute for shunt peaking or other two-terminal compensation; thus see Bereskin, *loc. cit.*; J. M. Miller, Jr , *loc. cit.*

formance that results is, however, never any better than that given by the same amplifier with zero bias impedance, but it may be about as good.

It is apparent that the total sag of a single stage of video amplification may be the result of effects existing in several parts of the amplifier. When the sag is small to moderate, one can calculate the sag introduced by each individual part of the amplifier as though no other sources of sag existed, and can then add these individual sags arithmetically to obtain the total sag. For example, if the grid leak–capacitor combination causes 1 per cent sag, the screen impedance 3 per cent sag, and the bias impedance 7 per cent sag, then the total sag of the output will be approximately 11 per cent. This procedure gives erroneous results, however, if the total sag is large.

In a similar manner, when several amplifier stages are connected in cascade, then one may add the sags of the individual stages, provided these sags are not excessively large. Thus two stages of the amplifier mentioned above would introduce a total sag of 22 per cent.

Analysis of Low-frequency Performance of Video Amplifiers in Terms of Amplification and Phase Characteristics. The low-frequency deficiencies of a video amplifier are often expressed in terms of the phase shift and variation in amplification at low frequencies. This is preferable in some applications; however, from the point of view of pulses and television signals the sag is a direct expression of the low-frequency deficiencies. When the low-frequency deficiencies are small, there is a direct relationship between the sag and the phase at low frequencies that is given by Eq. (9-17) below. A sag characteristic that is satisfactory for television signals corresponds to a phase shift at 60 cycles that does not exceed a few degrees.[1]

The effect on amplification and phase shift of the coupling capacitor, screen impedance, and bias impedance can be calculated with the aid of Eqs. (8-7), (8-8), and (8-9), respectively. When typical numbers are substituted in these relations it is found that the phase shift at low frequencies presents much more of a problem than does variation in amplification. Thus assuming $R_{gl} >> R_c$, one can rewrite Eq. (8-7) to give

$$\text{Phase shift (lead)} = \phi_c = \tan^{-1} \frac{1/\omega C_c}{R_{gl}} \tag{9-16a}$$

$$\text{Falling off in gain at low frequencies} = \cos \phi_c \tag{9-16b}$$

[1] In the ideal video amplifier, the amplification is constant at the mid-frequency value down to the lowest frequency of interest, and the phase-shift characteristic is such that when *extrapolated to zero frequency the phase shift is zero at zero frequency.* However, the lowest frequency of interest in video amplifiers used in television, namely 60 cycles, is so close to zero frequency as compared with the top frequency limit of the amplifier that the practical objective in television is to make the phase shift of the video amplifier as low as possible at 60 cycles. A similar situation also ordinarily exists in the case of video amplifiers intended for other applications.

It follows from these relations that when the phase shift is 2°, often an excessively large value in television applications, the amplification is still 0.9994 times the mid-frequency amplification.

When several sources of phase shift are present simultaneously in an amplifier, for example a screen impedance in addition to the inevitable coupling capacitor, the individual phase shifts can be calculated separately and then added to give the total phase shift of the amplifier.[1] In the case of a multistage amplifier, the over-all phase shift of the system is obtained by adding the phase shifts of the individual stages.

Relation of Phase Shift to Sag.   When the phase shift at low frequencies is small, the sag at the end of a time interval t_1 is directly proportional to the phase shift at the frequency $f_1 = 1/t_1$. The exact quantitative relation between sag and phase shift can be obtained by substituting the value of $R_{gl}C_c$ defined by Eq. (9-16a) into Eq. (9-8b), while noting that for small values of ϕ_a in Eq. (9-16) one can write $\tan \phi_a = \phi_a$. This gives

$$\text{Sag at } t_1 = \frac{t_1}{R_{gl}C_c} = 2\pi f_1 t_1 \phi_1 = 2\pi \phi_1 \qquad (9\text{-}17)$$

where ϕ_1 is the phase shift in radians at a frequency of f_1 cycles per second. Although Eq. (9-17) was derived by making use of the phase shift introduced by the coupling capacitor capacitance, it holds equally well for phase shifts introduced by screen or bias impedances provided the resulting sag is small enough for Eqs. (9-10b) and (9-12b) to apply. The accuracy of Eq. (9-17) is good when the sag is less than 10 per cent, and is fair up to values of the order of 20 per cent. Substitution in Eq. (9-17) shows that a phase shift of 1° at 60 cycles will cause a sag of 0.10 in $\frac{1}{60} = 0.0167$ sec, which corresponds to the time of one field of a television signal.

9-4. Compensation for Low-frequency Deficiencies of Video Amplifiers.   The low-frequency deficiencies of video amplifiers can be minimized[2] by inserting a properly designed resistance-capacitance network R_1C_1 in series with the coupling resistance R_c as shown in Fig. 9-14a.

---

[1] The only exception to this is that the phase shift introduced by the bias impedance will also depend somewhat upon the phase shift introduced by the screen impedance. However, when the latter is small to moderate, the interaction is a second-order effect. When calculating the bias impedance effects by Eq. (8-9), it is hence permissible in most cases to assume that $\beta = 1$.

[2] Alternative methods of obtaining low-frequency compensation are described by K. Schlesinger, Low-frequency Compensation for Amplifiers, *Electronics*, vol. 21, p. 103, February, 1948; M. J. Larsen, Low-frequency Compensation of Video-frequency Amplifiers, *Proc. IRE*, vol. 33, p. 666, October, 1945; D. E. Norgaard and J. L. Jones, Versatile Multichannel Control Equipment, *Proc. IRE*, vol. 29, p. 250, May, 1941; G. W. Edwards, Amplifier Characteristics at Low Frequencies, *J. IEE* (Wireless Sec.), vol. 15, p. 204, September, 1940; *ibid.*, vol. 87, p. 178, 1940; Thompson *loc. cit.*

The behavior of such a compensating system can be readily analyzed by Thévenin's theorem by considering everything to the left of the point xx in Fig. 9-14a to be a generator.   On this basis, the equivalent generator voltage e acting in the equivalent circuit of Fig. 9-14b when a current $i_p = -g_m e_g$ suddenly starts flowing in the plate circuit is found by

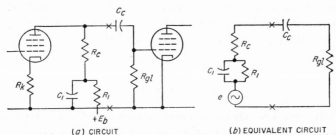

(a) CIRCUIT   (b) EQUIVALENT CIRCUIT

Fig. 9-14. Actual and equivalent circuit for obtaining low-frequency compensation in a video amplifier.

transient theory to be

$$e = i_p R_c + i_p R_1 (1 - \epsilon^{-t/R_1 C_1}) \tag{9-18a}$$

or

$$\left. \begin{array}{l} \text{Actual voltage} \\ \overline{\text{Voltage with no com-}} \\ \text{pensation } (R_1 = 0) \end{array} \right\} = 1 + \frac{R_1}{R_c} (1 - \epsilon^{-t/R_1 C_1}) \tag{9-18b}$$

The resulting sag is by definition

$$\text{Sag introduced by } R_1 C_1 = -\frac{R_1}{R_c} (1 - \epsilon^{-t/R_1 C_1}) \tag{9-19a}$$

When the sag is small this becomes

$$\left. \begin{array}{l} \text{Sag introduced by} \\ R_1 C_1 \text{ at time } t \end{array} \right\} = -\frac{t}{R_c C_1} \tag{9-19b}$$

A negative sag in these equations denotes a voltage whose absolute amplitude *increases* with time.   Note that in this case (i.e., small sag), the sag is independent of R_1.   Similarly for sinusoidal voltages one has[1]

$$\left. \begin{array}{l} \text{Actual voltage} \\ \overline{\text{Voltage with no}} \\ \text{compensation } (R_1 = 0) \end{array} \right\} = 1 + \frac{Z_1}{R_c} \tag{9-20}$$

Here Z_1 is the vector impedance of the compensating network $R_1 C_1$.

[1] In the usual case one has $R_1^2 >> (1/\omega C_1)^2$ for the frequencies of interest, and Eq. (9-20) simplifies to

$$\frac{\text{Amplitude of actual output voltage}}{\text{Output voltage with no compensation}} = 1 + \frac{(1/\omega C_1)^2 / R_1}{R_c} \tag{9-20a}$$

$$\left. \begin{array}{l} \text{Phase angle (lag) introduced} \\ \text{by compensation} \end{array} \right\} = \delta = \tan^{-1} \frac{1/\omega C_1}{R_c \left[1 + \frac{(1/\omega C_1)^2 / R_1}{R_c} \right]} \tag{9-20b}$$

Examination of these equations shows that the compensating network R_1C_1 introduces a *negative* sag and a lagging phase shift. These are just the characteristics required to compensate for deficiencies resulting from the coupling capacitor, the screen-grid capacitor, and the bias by-pass capacitor.

The sag, phase shift, and variations in amplification introduced by the grid capacitor C_c can be completely eliminated at all frequencies provided the compensating network is so proportioned that[1]

$$R_1 >> \frac{(1/\omega C_1)^2}{R_c} \tag{9-21a}$$

$$R_cC_1 = R_{gl}C_c \tag{9-21b}$$

Effects introduced by the screen-grid capacitance C_{sg} will be completely neutralized when the compensating network R_1C_1 is so proportioned that[2]

$$R_1 = \frac{R_cR_{sg}}{r_s} \tag{9-22a}$$

$$R_1C_1 = R_{sg}C_{sg} \tag{9-22b}$$

By similar reasoning, it is found that the deficiencies introduced by bias impedance will be completely compensated when

$$R_1 = R_kg_mR_c \tag{9-23a}$$

$$R_1C_1 = R_kC_k \tag{9-23b}$$

Design Considerations. In the actual compensation of low-frequency defects, various practical considerations must be taken into account. In the first place, it is generally found difficult to obtain a very good low-frequency performance when it is necessary to compensate for a large

---

[1] This is shown as follows: The relative voltage with no compensation is given by Eq. (8-7), while the effect of compensation is given by Eq. (9-20). Hence for perfect compensation

$$\left(1 + \frac{Z_1}{R_c}\right) \frac{1}{1 + j(X_c/R_{gl})} = 1$$

This can be true only if Z_1 is reactive, that is, R_1 is very large, and if, further,

$$\frac{X_1}{R_c} = \frac{X_c}{R_{gl}}$$

which corresponds to Eq. (9-21b).

[2] As above, this is obtained by combining Eqs. (8-8) and (9-20) as follows:

$$\frac{1}{1 + (Z_{sg}/r_s)}\left(1 + \frac{Z_1}{R_c}\right) = 1$$

If this relation is to be true it is necessary that $Z_1/R_c = Z_{sg}/r_s$, or $Z_1/Z_{sg} = R_c/r_s$. Now the vector ratio Z_1/Z_{sg} will be equal to a real number only if the phase angle of Z_1 equals the phase angle of Z_{sg}, which gives Eq. (9-22b). Equation (9-22a) follows from the fact that when the phase angles are the same the magnitude of the ratio Z_1/Z_{sg} will be $R_c/r_s = R_1/R_{sg}$.

deficiency.   This is because of the close tolerances and freedom from aging which the circuit constants must have if a large effect is to be precisely balanced out.   In particular, arrangements involving electrolytic capacitances present difficulties because of the variation in capacitance with age.   In the second place, it is not possible in video amplifiers for television applications to satisfy Eq. (9-21a) without R_1 introducing an excessive d-c voltage drop; this means that compensation for the effect of the coupling capacitance can be only approximate rather than exact.   A third consideration is that a simple resistance-capacitance compensating network R_1C_1 such as illustrated in Fig. 9-14a can provide only approximate compensation when several sources of sag are simultaneously present.

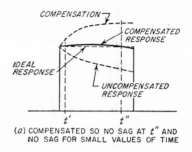

(a) COMPENSATED SO NO SAG AT *t″* AND NO SAG FOR SMALL VALUES OF TIME

As a result of these last two factors, the design of the low-frequency compensating network R_1C_1 is normally a compromise.   A common practice is to select a value of C_1 such that the compensating sag at some very small time t' as calculated by Eq. (9-19b) is equal in magnitude to the total sag from Eqs. (9-8b), (9-10b), and (9-12b) for the same value of t'.   When this is done the resultant sag for small values of time is zero.   The resistor R_1 is then chosen so that at some later time t'' the compensating sag is again equal in magnitude to the total sag of

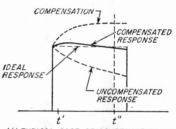

(b) TYPICAL CASE OF COMPENSATION WHEN R_1 CAN NOT BE LARGE ENOUGH TO GIVE BEHAVIOR SHOWN AT *(a)*

Fig. 9-15. Typical sag characteristics of compensated amplifiers under conditions where perfect compensation is not possible with a simple R_1C_1 network.

the amplifier at time t'' from all sources.[1]   The net sag is then zero for small values of time, and again at t''.   For values of time between t' and t'' the net sag, though not zero, will normally be small; this is illustrated in Fig. 9-15a.   In the case of television signals, t'' would be taken as a little less than $\frac{1}{60} = 0.0167$ sec.

An alternative approach to the practical design problem consists in proportioning[2] the compensating network R_1C_1 with the aid of Eqs. (9-20a)

[1] When the value of R_1 required to realize this result is so high as to introduce an excessive d-c voltage drop, R_1 should be made as large as permissible.   Capacitor C_1 is then given a value such that for very small values of time the system is overcompensated, while at time t'' the system is correspondingly undercompensated.   This case, which corresponds to C_1 less than the value that would be used with optimum R_1, is illustrated in Fig. 9-15b.

[2] This is done by first calculating the value of $(\omega C_1)^2 R_1$ required in Eq. (9-20a)

and (9-20b) so that the phase angle it introduces at some chosen frequency is the negative of the total phase shift from all other sources, while simultaneously the increase in magnitude of the output voltage introduced at this frequency is just enough to correct for the falling off in amplification produced by the low-frequency deficiencies.[1]

In constructing low-frequency compensating networks, the usual procedure is to calculate the required circuit proportions and connect these design values into the circuit. The resulting behavior actually obtained is then checked experimentally by applying a square-wave voltage to the amplifier input, and observing the sag of the amplified output waves. A tilt such as shown at b in Fig. 9-16 indicates undercompensation, while a tilt with negative slope as at c denotes overcompensation. It is to be noted that the total sag in a half cycle of the square wave occurs in a time $1/2f_1$, where f_1 is the frequency of the wave.

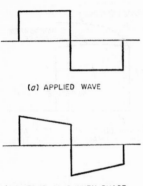

(a) APPLIED WAVE

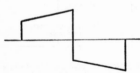

(b) OUTPUT WAVE WHEN PHASE
LEADS AT LOW FREQUENCY

(c) OUTPUT WAVE WHEN PHASE LAGS
AT LOW FREQUENCY

Fig. 9-16. Effects produced upon a square wave by low-frequency deficiencies of an amplifier.

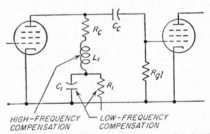

HIGH-FREQUENCY   LOW-FREQUENCY
COMPENSATION   COMPENSATION

Fig. 9-17. Typical arrangement for combining high-frequency and low-frequency compensation.

Thus the sag occurring in one field of a television signal is the sag observed during one-half cycle of a 30-cycle square wave. In such tests it is important that the sag of the square wave used in making the tests, and of the oscilloscope used in observing the results, be small. When this is not the case, the true sag of the amplifier can be obtained by subtracting the sag of the test equipment from the observed sag.

Low-frequency compensation can be combined with high-frequency compensation, as shown in Fig. 9-17, by placing the low-frequency equal-

---

to give the increase in amplitude needed to compensate for the amplitude deficiencies. This value, when substituted in Eq. (9-20b) enables $1/\omega C_1$ to be calculated in terms of the compensating angle that is desired.

[1] The resulting compensation will thus be perfect for this chosen frequency; in the case of television systems this frequency would be typically a little higher than 60 cycles.

izing circuit on the low-potential side of the high-frequency network. In this way the presence of the high-frequency network has no effect upon the low-frequency equalization because at very low frequencies the high-frequency network simply reduces to the coupling resistance R_c. Similarly, at high frequencies, the low-frequency compensating capacitance C_1 acts as a short circuit that causes the low-frequency compensating system to become inactive.

9-5. Distributed Amplifiers.[1] The maximum bandwidth, and hence the maximum speed of rise, that can be obtained with ordinary video amplifiers is limited by the fact that the voltage gain obtained from a

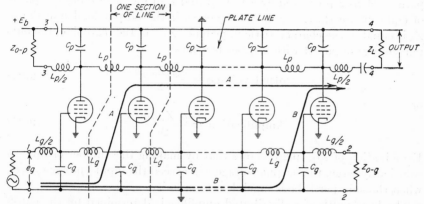

FIG. 9-18. Distributed amplifier with elementary form of artificial line.

single tube must exceed unity if the amplifier is to be useful. In the distributed amplifier this restriction is removed by an expedient that enables a number of tubes to act in parallel in so far as plate currents are concerned while their capacitances do not add in parallel.

A simple form of distributed amplifier is illustrated in Fig. 9-18. Here the grid and plates of tubes are connected at regular intervals to artificial lines, as shown, with the tube capacitances supplying the line capacitances. The grid and plate lines are furthermore so proportioned as to have the same phase shift between adjacent tubes, and characteristic impedance terminations Z_{o-g} and Z_{o-p} are provided at terminals 2-2 and 3-3.

The operation of this distributed amplifier can be explained as follows: The signal voltage e_g at the terminals 1-1 produces a wave that travels along the grid line, and applies voltages of e_g to control grids of the succes-

[1] For further information see E. L. Ginzton, W. R. Hewlett, J. H. Jasberg, and J. D. Noe, Distributed Amplification, *Proc. IRE*, vol. 36, p. 956, August, 1948; William H. Horton, J. H. Jasberg, and J. D. Noe, Distributed Amplifiers: Practical Considerations and Experimental Results, *Proc. IRE*, vol. 38, p. 748, July, 1950; F. Kennedy and H. G. Rudenberg, 200-Mc Traveling Wave Chain Amplifier, *Electronics*, vol. 22, p. 106, December, 1949.

sive tubes with a progressive phase difference determined by the phase shift per section of line. The resulting plate current $e_g g_m$ thereby produced in each tube divides, half flowing toward the terminating resistance Z_{o-p} and half toward the load impedance Z_L. Because of phase differences, the currents flowing to the left from the various tubes cancel each other to a large extent, and whatever is not canceled is absorbed by the impedance Z_{o-p}. However, the currents flowing toward the output terminals 4-4 from the various tubes produce waves that all add together at the load. This is because the phase difference in each section of plate line is the same as in each section of the grid line, with the result that paths such as represented by arrows A and B in Fig. 9-18 represent paths of equal phase shift. As a consequence, if the output load impedance Z_L is equal to the characteristic impedance Z_{o-p} of the plate line, the output voltage obtained with n tubes becomes[1]

$$\text{Output voltage} = \frac{e_g g_m Z_{o-p} n}{2} \tag{9-24}$$

or

$$\text{Amplification} = \frac{g_m Z_{o-p} n}{2} \tag{9-25}$$

Examination of Eq. (9-25) shows that by making the number of tubes n sufficiently large, the output voltage will exceed the input voltage e_g even when the gain per tube is much less than unity.

The bandwidth of a distributed amplifier is determined by the cutoff frequency of the artificial line. In general, the higher this cutoff frequency the lower will be the characteristic impedance of the line, and hence the less the voltage gain. The constancy of the amplification with frequency below the cutoff value will depend on the extent to which the characteristic impedance of the artificial line is constant with variation in frequency, and upon the exactness of the impedance matches that exist at the line terminals.[2] The time-delay characteristic is controlled primarily by the way in which the phase shift of each section of the artificial line changes with frequency, but is also influenced by impedance mismatching at the terminals of each line.

In practical distributed amplifiers it is necessary to employ a type of artificial line more complex than that of Fig. 9-18 if satisfactory amplification and time-delay characteristics are to be obtained. An arrangement that has found extensive practical use for both plate and grid lines is the bridged-T network shown in Fig. 9-19.[3] Here each section of line

[1] If terminals 4-4 are open-circuited, reflection of the wave traveling to the right will cause the output voltage to be twice that given by Eq. (9-24).

[2] At very high frequencies the amplification is also affected by the variation of the tube input conductance with frequency (see Sec. 12-12).

[3] Many other forms of artificial sections can also be used; thus see Ginzton, Hewlett, Jasberg, and Noe, *op. cit.*

includes coils L_1L_1 bridged by capacitance C_1 and coupled together with negative mutual inductance M. The shunt capacitance to ground is supplied by the tube as before. By adjusting the inductance of the coils, the coupling between them, and the bridging capacitance, it is possible to achieve a wide range of characteristics. Thus the amplification can be made substantially constant up to some specified high frequency, above which it falls off rapidly. Alternatively, one can obtain a substantially linear time delay; or again, the curve of amplification as a function of frequency can be made to follow the Gaussian characteristic, thereby giving a transient response that is free of overshoot.

Any desired amount of amplification can be obtained in a distributed amplifier by using an appropriate number n of tubes, as called for by Eq. (9-25). Alternatively, two or more distributed amplifiers may be used, with the output of the first amplifier supplying the voltage that is applied to the grid line of the next distributed amplifier, and so on. Analysis shows that a given total amplification will be obtained with a minimum number of tubes when the number of tubes in each distributed amplifier is such as to make the voltage gain of the individual distributed amplifier have the value 2.72 $(=\epsilon)$.

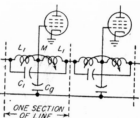

FIG. 9-19. Bridged-T artificial line sections suitable for use in practical distributed amplifiers; although the sections are shown as being used in the grid line they may be also employed in the plate line.

Distributed amplifiers provide a practical means of achieving a five- to tenfold improvement in speed of rise and bandwidth, as compared with video amplifiers of the type described in Table 9-2, page 302. They find extensive use in nuclear instrumentation, and as amplifiers for cathode-ray tubes to make possible the accurate reproduction of very short pulses. The possibilities of the distributed amplifier are illustrated by a commercial design that uses five 6AK5 tubes, has a gain of 10 db, and has a rise time of 0.0018 μsec with no overshoot.[1]

PROBLEMS AND EXERCISES

9-1. The United States television standards make it possible to transmit video signals up to 4 Mc. What is the minimum rise time that can be hoped for in a well-designed television system?

9-2. An uncompensated resistance-capacitance amplifier is to have a rise time of 0.03 μsec.

a. At what frequency must the 70.7 per cent response point occur?

b. What is the maximum possible voltage gain that can be expected using (1) 6AK5 and (2) 6AC7 tubes?

[1] N. B. Schrock, A New Amplifier for Milli-microsecond Pulses, *Hewlett-Packard Journal*, vol. 1, p. 1, September, 1949.

9-3. *a.* Demonstrate that Eqs. (9-1) and (9-3) are consistent with each other.

b. Check the correctness of the value of the coefficient 2.2 in Eq. (9-3).

9-4. Derive Eq. (9-5).

9-5. Check the value of gain-bandwidth factor given in Table 9-1 for the 6AK5 and 6AU6 tubes operating under the conditions given in Table 6-1, page 186.

9-6. The output of a video amplifier is to be applied to a cathode-ray tube having a capacitance of 15 $\mu\mu$f. Recalculate the gain-bandwidth factors in Table 9-1, assuming this capacitance replaces the tube capacitance C_2. Tabulate the results alongside those of the last column of Table 9-1, and then discuss the factors that cause a capacitance load to alter the relative merits of tubes for video amplification.

9-7. *a.* Will the gain-bandwidth factors in Table 9-1 be affected favorably or unfavorably by using a system consisting of two tubes connected in parallel?

b. Will connecting four tubes in parallel alter the conclusions in Prob. 9-6? For purposes of discussion, confine the consideration to the 6AK5 and 6AC7 tubes.

9-8. Is there such a thing as a gain–rise-time factor for an uncompensated resistance-coupled amplifier that is a property of the tube independent of the actual gain, in the same way as the gain-bandwidth factor? If so, calculate this factor for the tubes of Table 9-1 and tabulate results.

9-9. A video amplifier employs a 6AC7 tube in a shunt-peaking circuit under the conditions listed in Tables 6-1, page 186, and 9-1, page 292. It is estimated that the shunting capacitance introduced by the wiring and circuit elements will be 5 $\mu\mu$f. Specify the coupling resistance and shunt-peaking inductance required to give a rise time of 0.05 μsec with an overshoot not to exceed about 3 per cent. For the circuit constants chosen, also determine the mid-frequency amplification, and the frequency at which the response drops to 70.7 per cent of the mid-range value. Make use of Fig. 9-4 to the extent that this is helpful.

9-10. Among the tubes of Table 9-1, what is the fastest possible rise time that can be obtained from a shunt-peaking system with an overshoot that does not exceed 3 per cent if the gain of the stage is to be not less than 5, and it can be assumed that the shunt capacitance introduced by the wiring and circuit elements of the coupling network is 3 $\mu\mu$f? This will involve selecting a tube and determining the resulting rise time.

9-11. A video amplifier employs a 6AC7 tube in a shunt-peaking circuit under the conditions listed in Tables 6-1, page 186, and 9-1, page 292. The stray shunting capacitances of the circuit are 5 $\mu\mu$f.

a. If it is necessary to maintain a maximal flatness type of characteristic with a falling off in amplification that is not to exceed 0.5 db per stage up to 4 Mc, specify the coupling resistance and shunt-peaking inductance required, calculate the amplification in the middle-frequency range, state the rise time of the amplifier, and plot relative amplification as a function of frequency from 0.5 Mc up to about 6 Mc on a logarithmic scale.

b. Repeat (*a*) for the case in which $Q_2 = 0.50$.

9-12. With the aid of Fig. 9-4, demonstrate that the relative rise times of shunt-peaking circuits for $Q_2 = 0.25$ and 0.414 as given in Table 9-2 are consistent with Eq. (9-1).

9-13. *a.* Determine the circuit constants of a four-terminal coupling network of the type illustrated in Fig. 9-6c to give a rise time of 0.03 μsec. Use a 6AK5 tube and assume that the wiring and circuit elements of the coupling network cause the input capacitance C_1 and output capacitance C_2 to have values of 4 and 8 $\mu\mu$f, respectively. Also calculate the mid-frequency gain, and with the aid of Fig. 9-8 state the 70.7 frequency of the amplifier stage.

b. Compare this result with the gain of a shunt-peaking stage employing the same tube, having the same rise time, and having the same total shunt capacitance $C_0 = C_1 + C_2$.

9-14. The first three tubes in Table 9-1, page 292, are to be considered for use in the circuit of Fig. 9-6c. Assume that in order to make $C_2/C_1 = 2$, the particular tube capacitance that is too small to satisfy this relation is built out by an auxiliary capacitance (thus C_2 for the 6AK5 tube would be increased from 4.0 to 5.6 $\mu\mu$f). Determine an equivalent gain-bandwidth factor for this situation with the aid of Fig. 9-8, and tabulate the results alongside the corresponding values from Table 9-1.

9-15. *a.* With the aid of the amplification characteristic of the circuit of Fig. 9-6c as given in Fig. 9-8, demonstrate that the rise time as given in Table 9-2 is consistent with Eq. (9-1).

b. Explain why the amplifier circuit of Fig. 9-6b, which has the amplification characteristic shown in Fig. 9-8, will have a rise time different from that given by Eq. (9-1).

9-16. A television system containing 10 identical amplifier stages is to have a total rise time not to exceed 0.1 μsec. Determine the maximum rise time that an individual stage can have, assuming all stages are identical and that the overshoot is small.

9-17. A four-stage amplifier that is shunt-peaked for maximum flatness is to have an over-all 3-db bandwidth of 4 Mc. What is the required 3 db bandwitdh of the individual stages?

9-18. Prove that the procedure outlined on page 300 for experimentally adjusting a shunt-peaking circuit actually leads to the proper value of coupling resistance R_c, and the proper shunt-peaking inductance.

9-19. Describe a procedure analogous to that on page 300 for experimentally adjusting the circuit of Fig. 9-5a to give the indicated circuit proportions.

9-20. A stage of amplification employing a 6AK5 tube is required to have a rise time of 0.03 microsec. If the effective input and output capacitances C_1 and C_2 are assumed to be 4 $\mu\mu$f and 8 $\mu\mu$f, respectively, when the shunt capacitance of wiring and circuit elements is taken into account, tabulate the mid-frequency voltage gains for the different circuit arrangements included in Table 9-2.

9-21. Derive Eq. (9-7).

9-22. Derive Eq. (9-8b) from Eq. (9-8a).

9-23. Derive Eqs. (9-10a) and (9-10b) from Eq. (9-9).

9-24. Demonstrate that at large values of time t the amplified output in Eq. (9-9) has a value corresponding to that given by an amplifier with an un-by-passed screen resistance.

9-25. Derive Eqs. (9-12a) and (9-12b) from Eq. (9-11).

9-26. In a video amplifier in which $R_{gl} = 0.25$ megohm, and $C_c = 0.50$ μf, calculate the sag that occurs in a time corresponding to $\frac{1}{60}$ sec. Assume that no other source of sag is present.

9-27. *a.* The video amplifier using a 6AC7 tube that is described on page 306 is required to reproduce pulses having a length of 20 μsec with a sag that does not exceed 1 per cent. Calculate the minimum permissible values of C_c, C_{sg}, and C_k, assuming that the total sag is equally divided among the three causes.

b. What values of capacitances would be required if a five-stage amplifier were involved in which the over-all sag of the system was limited to 0.01?

9-28. The total permissible sag in a particular video amplifier handling television signals is 20 per cent. If three stages are involved, and the grid-leak resistance in each case is 0.75 megohm, what is the smallest permissible value of coupling capacitance C_c, if the only source of sag in each stage is the coupling capacitor?

9-29. In the video amplifier described on page 306, it is desired to operate without a cathode by-pass capacitor.

a. What reduction in voltage gain will result?

b. To prevent this loss in gain take the following steps: Increase R_c to a value R_c' such as to restore the mid-frequency gain to the value obtained with complete cathode by-passing and $R_c = 3000$. Next, shunt R_k with a capacitance C_k such that $C_k R_k = C_0 R_c'$, where C_0 is the total shunting capacitance in the plate circuit. Then compare this case with the fully by-passed case by calculating and plotting curves giving amplification as a function of frequency up to 6 Mc for the two situations, taking into account the effect of C_k by means of Fig. 8-12. Assume that an uncompensated amplifier is employed and that $C_0 = 22 \ \mu\mu\text{f}$.

9-30. Derive Eqs. (9-16) from Eq. (8-7).

9-31. A video amplifier is found experimentally to have a sag of 3 per cent in a time corresponding to one field of a television picture. What will be the phase shift of this amplifier at 30 cycles, 60 cycles, and 120 cycles?

9-32. The measured phase shift of a video amplifier intended for television work is 1.25° at 60 cycles. What will be the sag in a time corresponding to one picture field of a television picture?

9-33. Derive Eq. (9-19*b*), starting with Eq. (9-18*a*) and showing all the intermediate steps and reasoning.

9-34. *a.* The video amplifier referred to on page 306 employs capacitances having the values given in Eqs. (9-13), (9-14), and (9-15) (corresponding to a total sag of $3 \times 0.05 = 0.15$). It is desired to compensate for the low-frequency deficiencies of this system in such a manner that the sag is zero for very small values of time, and is again zero when the time is 0.014 seconds. Determine the proper value of compensating capacitance C_1 and compensating resistance R_1 to be used in Fig. 9-15*a*.

b. Calculate the phase shift of the uncompensated amplifier, and the phase shift introduced by the compensating network, at 30 and 60 cycles. From these results, discuss the extent to which the design that minimizes sag corresponds to very low phase shift at low frequencies.

9-35. Derive Eq. (9-23*a* and *b*).

9-36. It is possible with the aid of a good cathode-ray oscilloscope to observe values of sag as small as 1 or 2 per cent. Explain on this basis how one could employ a square wave to determine values of phase shift that would be so small as to be difficult to obtain by direct measurement.

9-37. In testing a video amplifier for television by means of a square wave, the observed sag during the half cycle of a 30-cycle square wave is 0.04. If, however, the amplifier is removed from the system and the square-wave generator applied directly to the oscilloscope, the sag observed is 0.015. From this information, determine the actual sag of the amplifier in $\frac{1}{60}$ and 0.01 sec, and the phase shift at 30 and 60 cycles.

9-38. In the distributed amplifier of Fig. 9-18, explain the mechanism which causes the amplification to vary with frequency when the terminating resistance at 3-3 fails to equal the characteristic impedance of the plate line.

9-39. Convert Eq. (9-25) into a formula giving power gain in decibels when the characteristic impedances of the grid and plate lines are Z_{o-g} and Z_{o-p}, respectively.

9-40. A distributed amplifier employs 6AK5 tubes (Table 9-2, page 302), with plate and grid lines each having a characteristic impedance of 250 ohms. How many tubes are required to give a total voltage gain of 20, and how should they be arranged?

CHAPTER 10

AMPLIFIER DISTORTION, POWER AMPLIFIERS, AND AMPLIFIER SYSTEMS

10-1. Causes of Amplitude Distortion in Amplifiers. Amplitude distortion arises in amplifiers when large signal voltages are applied. Under these conditions, the amplifier output will contain frequency components, such as harmonics, not present in the applied signal. It is amplitude distortion that limits the output voltage that it is practical to obtain from a resistance-coupled or video amplifier, and that limits the power that can be obtained from a power amplifier.

The various types of distortion that may occur in an amplifier can be understood by studying oscillograms giving the voltage and current relations in the tube under different conditions. For purposes of reference, consider first a sine-wave signal of moderate amplitude applied to the control grid of a triode having a simple resistance load. The resulting wave shapes are as illustrated by the solid wave in Fig. 10-1a (also see Fig. 8-2); here the plate current flows continuously (Class A operation), and the output plate current and voltage waves are rather good replicas of the signal applied to the control grid. The little distortion that does occur is a result of variations in the plate resistance and amplification factor of the tube with changes in the voltages applied to the electrodes. However, if the amplitude of the applied signal is now increased until the plate current is cut off at the negative peaks of the signal, the output voltage and current wave shapes are flattened on the negative peaks, as shown by the dashed curve of Fig. 10-1a.

Next, if the amplitude of the applied signal exceeds the grid bias, grid current flows at the positive peaks. If there is then an impedance in series with the grid circuit, or, what is the same thing, if the source of signal voltage exciting the grid has a substantial internal impedance, a voltage drop is produced by the grid current. This drop flattens the positive peaks of the signal voltage actual acting on the grid, causing corresponding distortion of the output wave, as shown by the dotted curves in Fig. 10-1a. This effect is in addition to whatever other sources of distortion exist; thus the combination of plate-current cutoff and grid current can cause flattening of both positive and negative peaks of the output voltage, as shown in Fig. 10-1a.

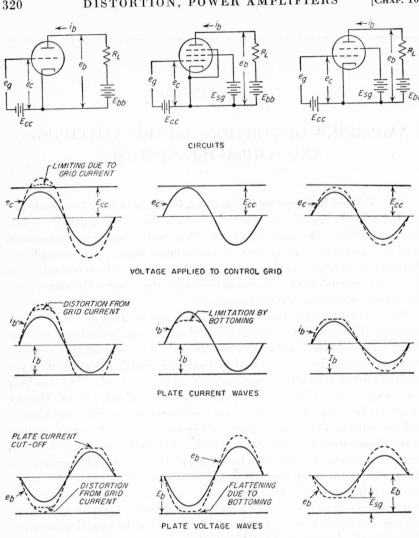

Fig. 10-1. Wave shapes in amplifiers under various conditions, illustrating how amplitude distortion of output wave shapes can arise. Here E_b and I_b represent the d-c plate voltage and current, respectively, in the absence of an applied signal.

With tubes possessing a screen grid, it is possible for the output wave to be flattened at the positive peaks of the applied signal even when no grid current flows. Thus, in the case of beam and pentode tubes, flattening occurs whenever the instantaneous plate voltage becomes low enough to cause a virtual cathode to form in the space between screen grid and plate. This is illustrated in Fig. 10-1b. Here the solid line shows what might be regarded as typical operating conditions for large output without severe distortion, while the dashed curves show the result of increasing the load resistance (while simultaneously increasing E_{bb} to keep E_b unchanged in spite of the larger load resistance). It is seen that the formation of a virtual cathode limits the plate current, and hence the output voltage, at the positive peaks of the applied signal. This effect is sometimes termed *bottoming*.[1]

In the screen-grid tube, a similar flattening of the output wave occurs on the positive peaks of the applied signal if the voltage drop in the load impedance is great enough to make the instantaneous plate voltage slightly less than the screen voltage. This effect, illustrated in Fig. 10-1c, arises from the fact that in the screen-grid tube the plate loses secondary electrons to the screen whenever the plate is less positive than the screen.[2] The fact that the minimum instantaneous plate voltage that can be obtained in a screen-grid tube approximates the screen voltage, rather than being much less as in beam and pentode tubes, is one of the principal reasons that the latter tubes have largely superseded the screen-grid tube.

By way of summary, it is seen that serious distortion can be caused in all types of tubes by flattening of the output wave at the negative peaks of the applied signal due to plate-current cutoff, and at the positive peaks because of grid current. In pentode and beam tubes (but not triodes) flattening of the output wave on the positive peaks of the applied signal can also occur as a result of the formation of a virtual cathode, and in screen-grid tubes as a result of secondary electrons produced at the plate. When none of these effects exist, the distortion of the output wave shape will be small to moderate, and what distortion is present is caused by variations of the tube coefficients with changes in the instantaneous voltages acting on the tube electrodes.

10-2. Graphic Method of Determining Amplifier Wave Shapes and Distortion with Resistance Loads. The relationship between the various waveforms of Fig. 10-1 can be determined quantitatively with the aid of a *load line* plotted on the plate-voltage–plate-current characteristic of the tube, as illustrated in Fig. 10-2. This is a straight line intersecting the plate-voltage axis at E_{bb} and the plate current axis at E_{bb}/R_L; its slope is $1/R_L$. Each point on such a line corresponds to a possible combination of control-grid voltage, plate current, and plate voltage that is consistent with the plate-supply voltage E_{bb} and the load resistance R_L. The intersection of the load line with the grid-voltage curve corresponding to the

[1] Bottoming occurs whenever the plate current is limited by a virtual cathode, irrespective of the cause of the virtual cathode. Thus, in Fig. 10-1b, increasing the amplitude of the applied voltage e_g without changing R_L will also cause bottoming if the resulting voltage drop in R_L at the positive peak of e_g makes the minimum voltage actually at the plate low enough to cause the formation of a virtual cathode. This is in addition to any limiting produced when grid current flows.

[2] This effect is reduced to the extent that the screen grid is treated in such a manner as to minimize the emission of secondary electrons.

operating grid bias E_{cc} gives the plate current and plate voltage in the absence of an applied signal; this is called the *quiescent point*, or *operating point*.

When a signal is applied to the control grid, the instantaneous grid voltage varies about the quiescent point, causing the actual operating conditions to move along the load line. Thus, if the quiescent point in Fig. 10-2 is Q, applying a signal $e_g = +1$ volt causes the operating conditions to shift to point P. By repeating this operation for different values of e_g it is possible to determine the wave shapes of the plate current and voltage caused by applying a signal voltage to the control grid.

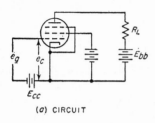

(a) CIRCUIT

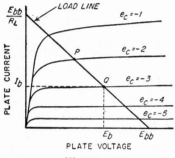

PLATE VOLTAGE

(b) LOAD LINE

Fig. 10-2. A typical load line.

In Fig. 10-1, the load resistance is in series with the plate-supply voltage. In actual practice the load is more likely to include a resistance-capacitance shunt, a transformer, or a shunt-feed system, as illustrated in Fig. 10-3. In all of these arrangements the effective load resistance to alternating current will then differ from the load resistance offered to direct current or to very slow changes. The behavior under dynamic (alternating) conditions accordingly will then differ from the behavior under static (d-c) conditions.

Consider now the load line for the system illustrated in Fig. 10-3a. Here the quiescent point Q is determined by a load line drawn for a load

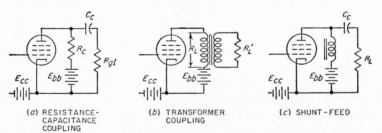

(a) RESISTANCE-
CAPACITANCE
COUPLING

(b) TRANSFORMER
COUPLING

(c) SHUNT-FEED

Fig. 10-3. Examples of amplifier circuits in which the load impedance to direct currents differs from the load impedance to alternating currents.

resistance equal to the coupling resistance R_c, as shown by the solid line in Fig. 10-4. However, for a signal in the mid-frequency range, the effective load resistance R_{eq} corresponds to the coupling resistance R_c shunted by the grid-leak resistance R_{gl}; variations produced by such a signal accordingly occur along a new load line[1] passing through the quiescent point Q and having a slope $1/R_{eq}$. Such a line, shown dotted in Fig. 10-4, is called a *dynamic* load line, in contrast with the *static* load line corresponding to R_c.

When a resistance load is introduced into the plate circuit of the amplifier by a transformer or by shunt feed, as in Figs. 10-3b and c, the d-c resistance thereby added in series with the plate circuit is very small. Under these conditions, the static load line is essentially vertical, and the quiescent point corresponds to a potential E_b at the plate of the tube equal to the plate-supply potential E_{bb}. The dynamic load line then passes through this operating point, and intercepts the zero plate current axis as shown in Fig. 10-5. Here the dynamic load line has the slope $1/R_L$,

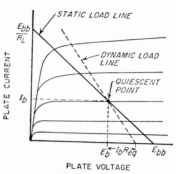

Fig. 10-4. Relation of dynamic and static load lines.

where R_L is the equivalent load resistance that is effectively in series with the plate circuit for alternating currents. Examination of Fig. 10-5 shows that during the negative half cycle of the applied signal, the

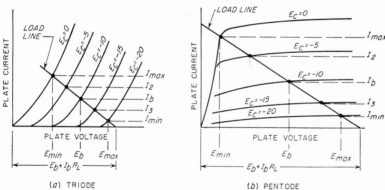

(a) TRIODE   (b) PENTODE

Fig. 10-5. Typical load lines for transformer coupling or shunt feed, showing operating points on the load line that have particular significance.

voltage at the plate of the tube rises to a value greater than the plate-supply voltage $E_{bb} = E_b$. This possibility arises because the inductance in these particular coupling systems stores magnetic energy that gen-

[1] A dynamic load line drawn in this way implies that the rectified component of the amplified plate current (see p. 326) encounters the same load resistance as do the alternating components of the amplified signal. Actually this is not true in any of the circuits of Fig. 10-3. However, the error involved is small, and, moreover, can be removed if necessary by shifting the operating point under dynamic conditions in such a manner as to give d-c conditions consistent with those obtained from the mathematical analysis described in Sec. 10-3.

erates a voltage that adds to E_b during the parts of the cycle when the instantaneous plate current is less than the plate current I_b at the operating (or quiescent) point.

Dynamic Characteristic. In attempting to visualize the wave shapes developed in an amplifier, it is sometimes helpful to plot the points corresponding to the dynamic load line on the grid-voltage–plate-current

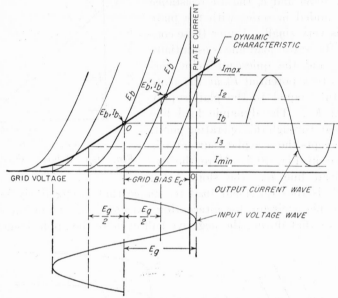

Fig. 10-6. Typical dynamic characteristic of a triode tube, together with oscillograms showing relationship of input and output waves.

characteristic curves of the tube. A dynamic load line plotted in this way is shown in Fig. 10-6 and is often called a *dynamic characteristic.*

The dynamic characteristic of a triode does not follow the characteristic curve of the tube because the voltage drop produced in the load resistance alters the voltage at the plate of the tube. The dynamic characteristic can be drawn directly on the tube characteristics of Fig. 10-6 by making use of the fact that when the quiescent point is E_b, I_b, the dynamic characteristic crosses the plate voltage curve E'_b at a plate current I'_b such that

$$E_b - E'_b = -R_L(I_b - I'_b) \qquad (10\text{-}1)$$

With triode tubes, the slope of the dynamic characteristic at any point is given by the relation

$$\text{Slope} = \frac{\mu}{r_p + R_L} \qquad (10\text{-}2)$$

Here μ is the amplification factor of the tube, and r_p and R_L are the plate and load resistances, respectively. Thus the higher the load resistance, the less will be the slope of the dynamic characteristic; at the same time a high load resistance reduces the curvature of the dynamic characteristic by making the slope less sensitive to variations[1] in r_p.

With pentode and beam tubes operated under conditions where the plate current is substantially independent of plate voltage, i.e., no virtual cathode present, the grid-voltage–plate-current curves for different values of plate voltage very nearly coincide with each other and the dynamic characteristic then follows the tube characteristic, as shown by the dashed

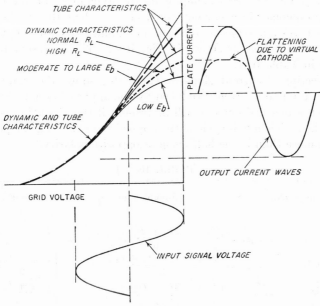

FIG. 10-7. Typical dynamic characteristics of a pentode tube, showing the relation of input and output waveforms under different conditions.

line in Fig. 10-7. However, when the voltage actually applied to the plate becomes sufficiently low to permit the formation of a virtual cathode, as will occur at high plate currents when the load resistance is sufficiently high, then the dynamic characteristic will depart from the static characteristic in the manner illustrated by the dotted line in Fig. 10-7.

It is apparent from Figs. 10-6 and 10-7 that the output wave will be a faithful reproduction of the signal voltage applied to the control grid to the extent that the dynamic characteristic is linear over the range of voltages involved. However, if the dynamic characteristic is curved, or if the operating range extends beyond the end of the dynamic characteristic into the cutoff region, then the shape of the output wave will differ from the wave shape of the signal. In particular, the dynamic character-

---

[1] It is to be noted that when $R_L \gg r_p$, the dynamic characteristic will be linear to the extent that μ is constant.

istic of a triode tube tends to be more nearly linear than that of a beam (or pentode) tube, because the latter more closely follows the characteristic curves of the tube. As a result, triode amplifiers tend to produce less distortion of wave shapes under Class A conditions than do pentode and beam tubes.

Quantitative Evaluation of Distortion from Load Lines. Under conditions where the wave shapes in an amplifier with resistance load suffer only small or moderate distortion, the harmonic components of the output wave can be determined by employing the dynamic load line to obtain the instantaneous plate current (or voltage) when the applied signal voltage is at zero, maximum, and minimum, and at 0.50 of the maximum and minimum values, as shown in Fig. 10-5. The necessary formulas[1] are given in Table 10-1.

The "rectified" current given in Table 10-1 shows the change in the average or d-c plate current produced by the application of a signal voltage. Such a rectified current will be present if the distortion is unsymmetrical, i.e., when a half cycle of the applied signal having one polarity is amplified more than is the half cycle of opposite polarity.

TABLE 10-1

Component	5-point analysis	3-point analysis
Rectified..................	$\dfrac{I_{max} + 2I_2 + 2I_3 + I_{min}}{6} - I_b$	$\dfrac{I_{max} + I_{min} - 2I_b}{4}$
Fundamental..............	$\dfrac{I_{max} + I_2 - I_3 - I_{min}}{3}$	$\dfrac{I_{max} - I_{min}}{2}$
2d harmonic..............	$\dfrac{I_{max} - 2I_b + I_{min}}{4}$	$\dfrac{I_{max} + I_{min} - 2I_b}{4}$
3d harmonic..............	$\dfrac{I_{max} - 2I_2 + 2I_3 - I_{min}}{6}$	
4th harmonic..............	$\dfrac{I_{max} - 4I_2 + 6I_b - 4I_3 + I_{min}}{12}$	

NOTE: Voltages may be used in place of currents in these formulas, if desired.

Evaluation of Wave-shape Distortion Resulting from Grid Current. The load line (or dynamic characteristic) gives the relationship that exists between the voltage actually applied to the control grid of the tube and the plate current that results. If, however, the control grid of the tube is driven positive at the positive peaks of the applied signal, then there

[1] When the distortion of the wave shapes is of a type that slightly flattens a peak of one polarity and slightly accentuates the other (see Fig. 10-6), rather than flattening both peaks of the output wave, then the principal distortion components of the output wave will be a second harmonic and a rectified component, and one can use the third column of the table. In the more general case, third harmonics will also be present, and the formulas of the second column should be used.

is distortion of the signal voltage that is applied to the control grid of the tube; this results in distortion of the output wave, even when the dynamic characteristic is a straight line.

The details involved are illustrated further in Fig. 10-8. Here the solid line in b gives the output voltage in the absence of distortion; this corresponds to zero impedance in series with the control-grid electrode. The dotted curves show the change in the amplitude of the positive peaks of the signal voltage acting on the grid that results for two different values of equivalent resource resistance R_s.   The maximum flattening that occurs is given by the relation

$$\frac{\text{Reduction in peak amplitude}}{\text{Undistorted peak amplitude}} = \frac{i_{gm}R_s}{E_g} \quad (10\text{-}3)$$

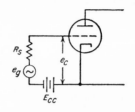

(a) CIRCUIT

Here i_{gm} is the grid current that flows when the grid is most positive.   It is apparent that if wave-shape distortion from grid current is to be minimized, it is necessary that either the source impedance R_s be low, or that the grid current be small or zero, or both.

10-3. Mathematical Analysis of Amplitude Distortion and Cross Modulation in Amplifiers. The graphic method of analyzing amplifier performance using a load line or dynamic characteristic gives a direct picture of what causes the distortion.   At the same time this method possesses three fundamental limitations: (1) it is applicable only to resist-

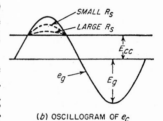

(b) OSCILLOGRAM OF e_C

Fig. 10-8. Effect of driving the grid positive on the wave shape of the voltage actually applied to the control grid.

ance loads;[1] (2) it assumes that the load impedance is the same to the harmonics and other distortion components generated by the amplifier (including the "rectified" component) as to the fundamental frequency that is being amplified; and (3) it is difficult to apply when the applied signal is more complex than a sine wave.   An analysis of amplifier behavior that avoids these limitations can be obtained by utilizing Eq. (6-29a) to provide a mathematical relation between the signal voltage applied to the control grid and the resulting amplified plate current and voltage.

Power-series Analysis of Amplifier Behavior.   It is convenient to begin by rewriting Eq. (6-29a):

$$i_p = g_m\left(e_g + \frac{e_p}{\mu}\right) + \frac{1}{2!}\frac{\partial g_m}{\partial E_c}\left(e_g + \frac{e_p}{\mu}\right)^2 + \frac{1}{3!}\frac{\partial^2 g_m}{\partial E_c{}^2}\left(e_g + \frac{e_p}{\mu}\right)^3 + \cdots$$

$$(10\text{-}4)$$

[1] Thus, when the load impedance has a reactive component, the load line and dynamic characteristic both open up into ellipses which are deformed by distortion.

where e_g = instantaneous signal voltage applied to grid

$\qquad e_p$ = instantaneous voltage acting on plate as result of voltage drop of i_p in load impedance

$\qquad g_m = \mu/r_p$ = transconductance at operating point

$\qquad \mu$ = amplification factor

$\qquad r_p$ = plate resistance

$\qquad i_p$ = instantaneous plate current caused by the action of e_g and e_p

The tube constants and the derivatives appearing in Eq. (10-4) are evaluated at the control-grid and plate voltages E_c and E_b, respectively, corresponding to the operating point upon which the signal voltage is superimposed. The convention with respect to sign made in deriving Eq. (10-4) is such that a positive current is a current flowing in the *same direction* as the normal d-c plate current. Equation (10-4) assumes either that the amplification factor μ is constant or that the load impedance is so low compared with the plate resistance that e_p/μ is negligible compared with e_g. The equation therefore holds reasonably well for triodes in the normal operating range, where the amplification factor is substantially constant, and is highly accurate for pentode amplifier tubes, since pentodes normally have a very high plate resistance compared with the load resistance.

Since the voltage e_p appearing in Eq. (10-4) represents the voltage arising from the current i_p in flowing through the load impedance Z, one can substitute the relation $e_p = -i_p Z$ in Eq. (10-4). Doing this gives

$$i_p = g_m \left(e_g - \frac{i_p Z}{\mu} \right) + \frac{1}{2!} \frac{\partial g_m}{\partial E_c} \left(e_g - \frac{i_p Z}{\mu} \right)^2 + \cdots \qquad (10\text{-}5)$$

Equation (10-5) as it stands is of limited usefulness, as it gives i_p as an implicit function of e_g. What is really wanted is an explicit relation that gives i_p and hence $e_p = -i_p Z$ in terms of the applied signal voltage e_g. This can be obtained by first postulating that the desired relation is of the form

$$i_p = b_1 e_g + b_2 e_g{}^2 + b_3 e_g{}^3 + \cdots \qquad (10\text{-}6)$$

where b_1, b_2, b_3, etc., are coefficients that are assumed to be independent of e_g. When these b's are evaluated in such a manner as to make Eq. (10-6) equivalent to Eq. (10-5), one obtains[1]

---

[1] To carry out this evaluation of the b's, one first substitutes the value of i_p from Eq. (10-6) for i_p wherever it appears in Eq. (10-5), and expands each parenthesis to the appropriate power. This gives an equation in terms of e_g, Z, the b's, and the tube coefficients μ, g_m, $\partial g_m/\partial E_c$, etc. The values of the b's can then be obtained by equating the coefficients of like powers of e_g on the two sides of the equation. Such relations between the coefficients must be identities if the equation in terms of e_g, Z, the b's, and the tube coefficients is to be true for every possible value of e_g. When these steps

$$i_p = \frac{\mu e_g}{r_p + Z_1} + \frac{1}{2!\mu g_m}\frac{\partial g_m}{\partial E_c}\frac{e_1{}^2}{r_p + Z_2}$$

$$+ \frac{\dfrac{1}{3!\mu^2 g_m}\dfrac{\partial^2 g_m}{\partial E_c{}^2}e_1{}^3 - \dfrac{1}{\mu g_m}\dfrac{\partial g_m}{\partial E_c}e_1 e_2}{r_p + Z_3} + \cdots \quad (10\text{-}8)$$

where r_p = plate resistance at the operating point

Z = load impedance. The subscripts 1, 2, and 3 denote the impedance offered to the first-, second-, and third-order components of the plate current. When any one order plate current contains components of several frequencies, the appropriate value of Z must be used for each component.

$e_1 = \mu e_g\dfrac{r_p}{r_p + Z_1}$ = voltage drop produced in plate resistance by the first-order component of current

$e_2 = \dfrac{Z_2}{r_p + Z_2}\dfrac{1}{2!\mu g_m}\dfrac{\partial g_m}{\partial E_c}e_1{}^2$ = voltage drop produced across the load impedance Z_2 by the second-order component of current

The remaining notation is as used previously.

When $Z/r_p \ll 1$, as is nearly always the case with pentode, beam, and similar tubes, and also in triodes when the load impedance is negligible, one has $r_p + Z \approx r_p$, $e_1 \approx \mu e_g$, $e_2 \approx 0$. Under these conditions Eq. (10-8) simplifies to

$$i_p \text{ (for pentodes)} = g_m e_g + \frac{1}{2!}\frac{\partial g_m}{\partial E_c}e_g{}^2 + \frac{1}{3!}\frac{\partial^2 g_m}{\partial E_c{}^2}e_g{}^3 + \cdots \quad (10\text{-}9)$$

Examination of Eq. (10-8) or Eq. (10-9) shows that the actual current that flows in the plate circuit as a result of the signal voltage e_g consists of a series of components proportional, respectively, to the first, second, third, etc., powers of the signal voltage involved.[1] The total plate current is the sum of these various components plus the steady d-c plate current present at the operating point when no signal is applied to the grid.

---

are carried out, one obtains

$$b_1 = \frac{\mu}{r_p + Z_1}$$

$$b_2 = \frac{1}{2!\mu g_m}\frac{\partial g_m}{\partial E_c}\frac{\left(\dfrac{\mu r_p}{r_p + Z_1}\right)^2}{r_p + Z_2} \qquad (10\text{-}7)$$

$$b_3 = \frac{\dfrac{1}{3!\mu^2 g_m}\dfrac{\partial^2 g_m}{\partial E_c{}^2}\left(\dfrac{\mu r_p}{r_p + Z_1}\right)^3 - \dfrac{1}{\mu g_m}\dfrac{\partial g_m}{\partial E_c}\dfrac{\mu r_p}{r_p + Z_1}b_2 Z_2}{r_p + Z_3}$$

Equation (10-8) then results when these values for the b's are substituted in Eq. (10-6).

[1] This is true in Eq. (10-8) as well as in Eq. (10-9) since e_1 and e_2 are proportional to e_g and $e_g{}^2$, respectively.

Generalized Equivalent Circuit of Vacuum-tube Amplifier. Equations (10-8) and (10-9) can be interpreted in terms of the equivalent circuits of Fig. 10-9a, which is a generalized form of the equivalent vacuum-tube amplifier circuit of Fig. 8-4b. Here the various components of the plate current can be considered as being produced by a number of equivalent voltages acting in a circuit consisting of the plate resistance r_p of the tube in series with the load impedance Z. If the positive direction is taken as from cathode toward plate [the opposite of the positive direction in Eq.

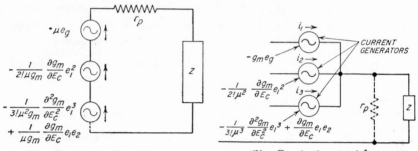

(a)   Constant-voltage form   (b)   Constant-current form

FIG. 10-9. Generalized form of constant-current generator circuit, taking into account higher-order effects.

(10-8)], the equivalent voltage represented in the first term on the right-hand side of Eq. (10-8) is

$$\begin{rcases} \text{Equivalent voltage producing first-} \\ \text{order components of plate current} \end{rcases} = -\mu e_g \qquad (10\text{-}10)$$

This voltage is that used in Sec. 8-2 in setting up the equivalent circuit of the vacuum-tube amplifier, which now by a rigorous analysis is shown to be the first-order approximation that results when the characteristics of the tube are expressed in terms of a power series.

The equivalent voltage represented by the second term on the right-hand side of Eq. (10-8) is proportional to e_g^2 and so can be termed a second-order effect. Assuming the positive direction is from cathode toward the plate [which is opposite from Eq. (10-8)], one has

$$\begin{rcases} \text{Equivalent voltage producing} \\ \text{second-order component of} \\ \text{plate current} \end{rcases} = -\frac{1}{2!\mu g_m} \frac{\partial g_m}{\partial E_c} \left(\mu e_g \frac{r_p}{r_p + Z_1} \right)^2$$

$$= -\frac{1}{2!\mu g_m} \frac{\partial g_m}{\partial E_c} e_1^2 \qquad (10\text{-}11)$$

These second-order effects represent to a first approximation the error involved when all components except the first are neglected.

The third term on the right-hand side of Eq. (10-8) represents an equivalent voltage proportional to e_g^3, and so can be termed a third-order effect. Assuming the positive direction is again from cathode to plate, it is given by the relation

$$\left.\begin{array}{l}\text{Equivalent voltage produc-}\\\text{ing third-order component}\\\text{of plate current}\end{array}\right\} = -\frac{1}{3!\mu^2 g_m}\frac{\partial^2 g_m}{\partial E_c^2}e_1{}^3 + \frac{1}{\mu g_m}\frac{\partial g_m}{\partial E_c}e_1 e_2 \quad (10\text{-}12)$$

The third-order component represents to a first approximation the error involved when all components except the first and second are neglected.

The analysis could be continued to higher order components with similar results, but this will not be done since terms higher than the third order are not particularly important.

The constant-current generator form of the circuit of Fig. 10-9a is shown at Fig. 10-9b, and is analogous to the equivalent vacuum-tube amplifier circuit of Fig. 8-4c. Here, each order effect is represented by a constant-current generator that delivers a current component, equal to the corresponding voltage in a divided by r_p, to a circuit consisting of the load impedance Z shunted by the plate resistance r_p.

To summarize the above, it is seen that the behavior of the amplifier tube, including the distortion effects produced when large signal voltages are applied, can be determined by postulating a series of constant-voltage generators acting in a circuit consisting of the plate resistance of the tube in series with the load impedance as shown at Fig. 10-9a, or by a corresponding set of constant-current generators supplying current to the load shunted by the plate resistance, as shown in Fig. 10-9b. There is one such generator for each order effect, with the values of the generator voltages given by the expressions indicated in Fig. 10-9. The only assumptions involved in the equivalent circuits of Fig. 10-9 and the analysis given above are (1) that the plate current does not reach either zero or the full saturation value, (2) that the amplification factor is constant (or that the load impedance is small compared with the plate resistance), and (3) that the tube characteristic has no discontinuities.

Analysis of Distortion in Typical Cases. The first-order generator in the equivalent circuit of Fig. 10-9 needs no discussion. It represents the part of the output wave that is free of amplitude distortion, and which was used throughout Chap. 8.

The distortion components of the amplified plate current are produced by the second-, third-, and still higher-order equivalent generators. The nature of these distortion currents can be investigated by writing down e_g as a function of time, and inserting the results in Eq. (10-8) or (10-9), or Fig. 10-9. Such expressions for $e_g{}^2$ and $e_g{}^3$ are given in Table 10-2 for typical cases.

Examination of Table 10-2 shows that the second-order action introduces a rectified or direct current, second harmonics of the frequencies contained in the signal, and frequencies that are the sums and differences of frequencies contained in the signal. It is to be noted, however, that even when second-order effects are present, the part of the amplified signal that is of fundamental frequency is still given by the first-order effect. The harmonic and sum and difference frequencies arising from second-order action are the principal sources of amplitude distortion in untuned amplifiers when operated to give only moderate distortion. The second-order effects are proportional to the curvature of the characteristic curves of the tube at the operating point; thus they can be minimized by operating where the characteristic curves of the tube are most nearly linear.

Study of Eq. (10-8) shows that the third-order equivalent generator has two parts. These are both proportional to $e_g{}^3$ since e_1 and e_2 are by definition proportional to e_g and $e_g{}^2$, respectively. As a result, both parts of the third-order generator produce the same types of distortion currents. The magnitude of the first part depends upon the rate of change of curvature of the tube characteristic. In contrast, the second part, which

TABLE 10-2

Signal	Second-order components	Third-order components
$e_g = E \sin \omega t$	$e_g{}^2 = \dfrac{E^2}{2} - \dfrac{E^2}{2} \cos 2\omega t$	$e_g{}^3 = \dfrac{3E^3}{4} \sin \omega t - \dfrac{E^3}{4} \sin 3\omega t$
$e_g = E_a \sin \omega_a t$ $+ E_b \sin \omega_b t$	$e_g{}^2 = \dfrac{E_a{}^2 + E_b{}^2}{2}$ $- \dfrac{E_a{}^2}{2} \cos 2\omega_a t$ $- \dfrac{E_b{}^2}{2} \cos 2\omega_b t$ $+ E_a E_b \cos (\omega_a + \omega_b)t$ $+ E_a E_b \cos (\omega_a - \omega_b)t$	$e_g{}^3 = \left(\dfrac{3E_a{}^3}{4} + \dfrac{3E_a E_b{}^2}{2}\right) \sin \omega_a t$ $+ \left(\dfrac{3E_b{}^3}{4} + \dfrac{3E_a{}^2 E_b}{2}\right) \sin \omega_b t$ $- \dfrac{E_a{}^3}{4} \sin 3\omega_a t - \dfrac{E_b{}^3}{4} \sin \omega_b t$ $- \dfrac{3E_a{}^2 E_b}{4} \sin (2\omega_a + \omega_b)t$ $- \dfrac{3E_a{}^2 E_b}{4} \sin (-2\omega_a + \omega_b)t$ $- \dfrac{3E_a E_b{}^2}{4} \sin (\omega_a + 2\omega_b)t$ $- \dfrac{3E_a E_b{}^2}{4} \sin (\omega_a - 2\omega_b)t$

is present only when the load impedance is not negligible compared with the plate resistance, is the result of interaction of the first-order and second-order components, and depends upon the curvature of the tube characteristics in the same way as does the second-order action.

Third-order action in the case of a simple sine-wave signal is seen from Table 10-2 to generate a third harmonic of the signal frequency, together with a component of signal frequency that is proportional to the cube of the amplitude of the applied signal. This latter component, when combined with the first-order action, makes the total signal-frequency current flowing in the plate circuit fail to be proportional to the signal voltage. Thus the component of the amplified signal that is of fundamental frequency is affected by the third-order action as well as by the first-order effect. Again, Table 10-2 shows that when the applied signal consists of two sinusoidal voltages of different frequencies f_a and f_b, the third-order distortion contains third harmonics of each signal frequency, third-order combination frequencies such as $f_a \pm 2f_b$ and $2f_a \pm f_b$, and terms having the same frequencies as are contained in the signal, but which are not proportional to the signal amplitude. A particularly important feature of the behavior is that the output obtained at frequency f_a is dependent to some extent upon the amplitude of the signal component of frequency f_b, and vice versa.[1] This effect is termed *cross modulation*, since it causes the amplitude of the amplified current of one frequency to be dependent upon (i.e., modulated by) the amplitude of a signal component having a different frequency.

Fourth- and higher even-order effects are similar in their consequences to the second-order action, giving rise to even harmonics, even-order combination frequencies, and d-c terms. In like manner, fifth- and higher odd-order actions produce consequences similar to the third-order equivalent generators, causing odd harmonics, odd-order combination frequencies, cross modulation, and lack of proportionality between input and output. These higher-order terms are, however, much smaller in magnitude than the second- and third-order terms. They can hence be neglected except under special circumstances.

It is to be noted that the distortion produced by even-order action is quite different in character from the distortion arising from odd-order behavior. Thus even-order distortion is characterized by even harmonics, sum and difference frequency components, and a rectified current. In contrast, odd-order distortion gives rise to odd harmonics, odd-order combination frequencies, cross modulation, and lack of proportionality between the signal-frequency components of the input and output, but does not introduce a rectified current, even harmonics, or sum and difference frequencies.

An examination of Eqs. (10-11) and (10-12) shows that the higher-order effects can be reduced by making the load impedance Z high compared with the plate resistance r_p, since by the definitions associated with Eq. (10-8), it is seen that doing so reduces e_1 and thereby e_2. This condition of high Z/r_p can be readily realized in the case of triode tubes, and makes it possible to reduce the second- and higher-order distortion of triodes to a much lower value than is possible with pentode and beam

[1] Thus in the second line of Table 10-2, there is a component of frequency f_a having an amplitude proportional to $E_b{}^2$, and in the third line another component of frequency f_b proportional in amplitude to $E_a{}^2$.

tubes. The distortion is also less in a triode with a high load impedance than in a triode with a low load impedance. Another way of describing these results in triodes is to say that increasing the ratio Z/r_p reduces the curvature of the dynamic characteristic, as discussed on pages 324 and 325.

10-4. Resistance-coupled and Video Amplifiers Designed for Large Output Voltages. *Resistance-coupled Amplifiers.* When the coupling resistance, grid-leak resistance, and plate-supply voltage of the resistance-coupled amplifier of Fig. 10-3a are specified, the output voltage obtainable without excessive distortion will be maximum when the quiescent point so locates the *dynamic* load line that (1) the minimum instantaneous signal current I_{min} approaches zero at the negative peaks of the applied signal, and (2) the minimum instantaneous plate voltage E_{min} at the positive peaks of the applied signal is barely enough to avoid the formation of a virtual cathode. Examples of load lines meeting these requirements are given by the solid lines in Fig. 10-10. The fact that the minimum current I_{min} approaches zero means

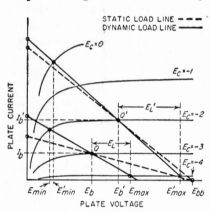

FIG. 10-10. Static and dynamic load lines for typical resistance-coupled amplifiers designed to give maximum output voltage when the coupling resistance equals the grid-leak resistance (quiescent point Q), and when the coupling resistance is much less than the grid-leak resistance (quiescent point Q').

that the peak amplitude I_L of the amplified plate current approximates I_b, the quiescent plate current. As a result

$$\left.\begin{array}{l}\text{Maximum obtainable} \\ \text{amplified voltage}\end{array}\right\} = E_L = I_L R_{eq} \approx I_b R_{eq} \tag{10-13}$$

$$\left.\begin{array}{l}\text{Minimum instantaneous} \\ \text{plate voltage}\end{array}\right\} = E_{min} = E_b - E_L \approx E_b - I_b R_{eq} \tag{10-14}$$

Here R_{eq} is the equivalent load resistance formed by R_c and R_{gl} in parallel.

In practical resistance-coupled amplifiers, the grid-leak resistance is generally made as high as circumstances will permit. If the designer wishes to emphasize large gain, the coupling resistance R_c will then be given a value approximating R_{gl}, as discussed on page 270. With these circuit proportions, the adjustment to obtain a large amplified voltage without excessive distortion leads to static and dynamic load lines, such as associated with the quiescent point Q in Fig. 10-10. Here the grid bias is so adjusted that the quiescent point Q corresponds to a d-c voltage drop $I_b R_c$ in the coupling resistance that is of the order of 0.55 to 0.65

times the plate-supply voltage E_{bb}.   The amplified output voltage obtainable without severe distortion under these circumstances is shown as E_L in Fig. 10-10, and is in the range 0.25 to 0.35 times the plate-supply voltage, with the exact value depending largely upon the amount of amplitude distortion that can be tolerated.

Increased output voltage can be obtained with a given value of grid-leak resistance R_{gl} and plate-supply voltage E_{bb} by reducing the coupling resistance R_c and appropriately readjusting the grid bias.   Load lines for this situation correspond to those associated with quiescent point Q' in Fig. 10-10.   Here the static load line has a much greater slope than before because of the lower value of R_c; also the dynamic load line now differs only very slightly from the static load line, since if $R_c << R_{gl}$, then R_{eq} differs only slightly from R_c.   The quiescent point that will give maximum possible output voltage without severe distortion for this condition corresponds to a d-c voltage drop in the coupling resistance R_c that approximates $0.45E_{bb}$, as shown by Q' in Fig. 10-10.   The maximum amplified voltage then obtainable will be of the order of 0.35 to 0.4 times E_{bb}, as shown by E'_L in Fig. 10-10, which is significantly greater than for the case where $R_c = R_{gl}$.   The voltage gain, however, will be somewhat less when R_c is much less than R_{gl}.

Video Amplifiers.   From the point of view of output voltage obtainable without severe amplitude distortion, the video amplifier can be regarded as a resistance-coupled amplifier in which R_c is low and also much less than R_{gl}, and which is so adjusted that the plate current at the quiescent point is the rated value for the tube.   Under these conditions Eq. (10-13) becomes

$$\left. \begin{array}{l} \text{Peak alternating} \\ \text{output voltage} \end{array} \right\} = E_L = I_b R_c \tag{10-15}$$

Here I_b is the rated plate current of the tube.   In order to avoid the formation of a virtual cathode at the positive peaks of the applied signal, it is necessary that the plate-supply voltage E_{bb} be at least slightly more than twice the d-c voltage drop $I_b R_c$ in the coupling resistance with rated plate current.

The output voltage represented by Eq. (10-15) will be inversely proportional to the capacitance shunting the coupling resistance.   This is because to achieve a particular bandwidth, the highest value of R_c that can be used is inversely proportional to the shunt capacitance.   The merit of a particular tube from the point of view of developing a large output voltage in a video amplifier can be determined by assuming that the tube supplies all of the shunting capacitance.   One then has

$$\text{Merit of tube} = \frac{I_b}{C_p} \tag{10-16}$$

Here C_p is the output capacitance of the tube (plate-cathode plus plate-suppressor or plate-screen capacitance), and I_b is the rated d-c plate current.

When the required output voltage is greater than is obtainable from a particular tube type, as given by Eq. (10-15), it might be thought helpful to increase I_b by placing tubes in parallel. However, to the extent that all of the output capacitance is supplied by the tubes, placing several tubes in parallel makes it necessary to use proportionately lower coupling resistance R_c if the high-frequency response is to be unchanged. Thus, under these conditions, paralleling tubes will not increase the output voltage available, and to obtain more voltage it is necessary to change the type of tube to one having a higher value of I_b/C_p. The direct paralleling of tubes will increase the output voltage obtainable only when a substantial part of the capacitance associated with the output of the amplifier is supplied by the load to which the output voltage is applied, for example, when the load is the capacitance between the electrodes of a cathode-ray tube.[1]

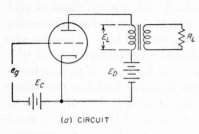

(a) CIRCUIT

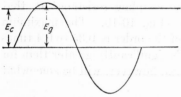

(b) TYPICAL GRID VOLTAGE WAVE

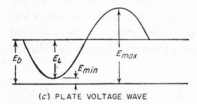

(c) PLATE VOLTAGE WAVE

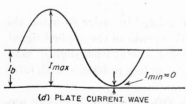

(d) PLATE CURRENT WAVE

FIG. 10-11. Oscillograms showing typical Class A operation of a triode amplifier.

10-5. Class A Power Amplifiers. In the Class A power amplifier, the objective is to convert as much of the d-c plate power as possible into amplified signal power delivered to a load impedance, while operating under Class A conditions. This result is achieved by (1) coupling the load resistance into the plate circuit of the tube by means of a transformer or shunt-feed system, so that there will be no d-c power dissipated in the load resistance (see Fig. 10-3b and c); (2) selecting operating conditions so that at the negative peak of the signal the instantaneous plate current

---

[1] However, the distributed amplifier principle described in Sec. 9-5 provides a means whereby tubes can be paralleled in such a way as to increase the output voltage obtainable, irrespective of the load capacitance.

I_{min} approaches zero; and (3) operating so that at the positive peaks of the applied signal, the instantaneous plate voltage E_{min} is small compared with the plate-supply voltage E_b. These conditions are illustrated by the oscillograms of Fig. 10-11, and also correspond to the operating conditions depicted in Fig. 10-1a and b (solid waves).

Basic Power Relations. An understanding of the fundamental power relations existing in a Class A amplifier can be obtained by ignoring distortion, which is the same as assuming that the waves of plate voltage and current in Fig. 10-11 are sinusoidal, and that the dynamic characteristic of Fig. 10-6 (or Fig. 10-7) is a straight line. In terms of the notation given in Fig. 10-11 one can then write[1]

$$\left.\begin{array}{l}\text{Peak alternating volt-}\\ \text{age developed across}\\ \text{load resistance}\end{array}\right\} = E_L = E_b - E_{min} = E_b\left(1 - \frac{E_{min}}{E_b}\right) \qquad (10\text{-}17)$$

$$\left.\begin{array}{l}\text{Peak alternating cur-}\\ \text{rent flowing through}\\ \text{load resistance}\end{array}\right\} = I_L = I_b - I_{min} = I_b\left(1 - \frac{I_{min}}{I_b}\right) \qquad (10\text{-}18)$$

$$\left.\begin{array}{l}\text{Output power devel-}\\ \text{oped in load resistance}\end{array}\right\} = \frac{E_L I_L}{2} = \frac{E_b I_b}{2}\left(1 - \frac{E_{min}}{E_b}\right)\left(1 - \frac{I_{min}}{I_b}\right) \qquad (10\text{-}19)$$

$$\text{Plate efficiency} = \frac{\text{power in load}}{E_b I_b} = 0.5\left(1 - \frac{E_{min}}{E_b}\right)\left(1 - \frac{I_{min}}{I_b}\right) \qquad (10\text{-}20)$$

$$\text{Load resistance} = R_L = \frac{E_L}{I_L} = \frac{E_b\,[1 - (E_{min}/E_b)]}{I_b\,[1 - (I_{min}/I_b)]} \qquad (10\text{-}21)$$

Plate Efficiency. The plate efficiency represents the efficiency with which the d-c power supplied by the plate supply E_b is converted into amplified a-c energy. Its value in an ideal Class A amplifier can never exceed 50 per cent, and will approach this limiting value only to the extent that E_{min}/E_b and I_{min}/I_b are both small. While it is quite practical to operate the tube so that the minimum plate current I_{min} approaches zero provided a moderate amount of distortion can be tolerated, the minimum permissible plate voltage E_{min} is determined in practice by the fact that this voltage must be sufficient to draw to the plate the maximum plate current $I_{max} = I_l + I_L \approx 2I_b$.

With pentode and beam tubes it is necessary that E_{min} be sufficient to avoid the formation of a virtual cathode when the plate current is I_{max}; otherwise bottoming will occur.[2] Values of E_{min}/E_b as low as 0.1 to 0.25 are typical for tubes of this class.

---

[1] The exact quantitative relations, taking into account distortion, can be obtained with the aid of Table 10-1 and data obtained from a load line (see Sec. 10-2).

[2] With screen-grid tubes, the minimum permissible plate voltage is limited to a value that approximates the screen voltage.

In triodes, the value of E_{min} required for a given I_{max} tends to be larger than with pentode and beam tubes as there is no screen grid at relatively high potential to aid in drawing electrons from the cathode space charge. Hence when the control grid is not driven positive, E_{min}/E_b is likely to be relatively high in triodes. However, driving the control grid positive at the positive peaks of the cycle will reduce the value of E_{min} necessary to draw the required peak plate current I_{max}, and will thereby improve the efficiency at the expense of making it necessary to cope with grid current and the resulting amplitude distortion that grid current tends to introduce.

Practical efficiencies obtainable in typical Class A power amplifiers without severe distortion are in the range 35 to 45 per cent with pentode and beam tubes, and 20 to 40 per cent with triodes.[1] The smaller values in these ranges tend to be associated with operation at low d-c plate voltages, since it is then difficult to keep E_{min}/E_b small.

Distortion in Class A Power Amplifiers. Amplitude distortion in a Class A amplifier will be small if care is taken to avoid the causes of excessive distortion listed on page 321. In particular, when low distortion is important, it is desirable that the minimum plate current I_{min} not approach zero too closely, since the dynamic characteristic is always much more curved very close to cutoff than elsewhere. Distortion is also minimized by operating without driving the grid positive, or at least by operating so that the grid current is small; likewise it is necessary to avoid the formation of a virtual cathode with resulting distortion due to bottoming. When these conditions are realized the distortion will be largely second harmonic, and the percentage of second harmonic occurring in the output wave will be very closely proportional to the amplitude of the output voltage.

When flattening also occurs at the positive peaks of the applied signal, third-harmonic distortions appear in the output along with second-harmonic effects. The possible causes of positive peak flattening are grid current and bottoming.

Triode tubes usually give less distortion than do amplifiers employing pentode and beam tubes. This is because in the general region of the quiescent point the dynamic characteristic of a triode tube is always straighter than the characteristic curves of the tube, as explained on page 326. In contrast, the dynamic characteristic of pentode and beam tubes in the vicinity of the operating point has the same amount of curvature as do the characteristic curves of the tube.

Tubes for Class A Power Amplification. Triode, beam, and pentode

---

[1] These are the efficiencies when the output power has the maximum value that can be obtained without severe amplitude distortion. With smaller output powers, the plate efficiency will be proportional to the output power (i.e., to the square of the signal voltage).

tubes all find use as Class A power amplifiers.[1] Triodes have the advantage of less distortion,[2] but generally give lower plate efficiency, and require a greater driving voltage than do beam and pentode tubes.

A distinguishing feature of tubes for Class A power amplification is that the d-c power which the plate of the tube must be able to dissipate without overheating is necessarily proportional to the amplified output power to be obtained. As compared with the small tubes used for voltage amplification, tubes for Class A power amplification therefore have a higher rated plate current, a larger anode, a larger cathode, a larger plate-dissipation rating, and usually a higher rated plate voltage. Characteristics of typical Class A power amplifier tubes such as used to operate loudspeakers are tabulated in Table 6-1, page 186. It will be noted that all of these tubes have higher plate current and hence higher rated plate dissipation than the small general-purpose tubes intended for voltage amplification.

Triode tubes intended for power amplification also differ from triode tubes for other purposes in that the amplification factor of the power amplifier types is usually small. This makes it easier to obtain the required maximum plate current with a relatively small value of minimum instantaneous plate voltage E_{min}; this is particularly important in triode power tubes operating at plate potentials below about 500 volts.

Selection of Operating Conditions and Load Resistances for Class A Amplifiers. The proper operating conditions for Class A operation of the commonly used power tubes are given in tube manuals, together with the amount of output power that can be obtained without excessive distortion. It is accordingly necessary to determine operating conditions only in the case of tubes for which complete data are not available, new tubes, or tubes operated under special conditions.

Beam and pentode tubes used in Class A power amplifiers are usually operated at a screen voltage such that when the grid bias is zero, the plate current will approximate twice the rated value. The grid bias is then chosen to give the rated plate current at this screen voltage. Finally, the load resistance is selected with the aid of Eq. (10-21) to be consistent with these electrode voltages; the proper load resistance will normally be slightly less than E_b/I_b.

In triode Class A power amplifiers, one ordinarily starts by operating the tube at the rated plate voltage and current, and selecting a load resistance that will be appropriate for these conditions.[3] This selection

---

[1] There is, however, a tendency for beam tubes to displace pentodes in this application.

[2] However, by the use of negative feedback (see p. 376), the resultant distortion can be made very small, even with pentode and beam tubes.

[3] An exception is sometimes encountered with tubes operating at low plate voltages (such as 250 volts) when the grid is not permitted to go appreciably positive at the

is carried out by determining the plate voltage $E_{\min}$ required to draw a plate current approximately twice the rated current at zero grid voltage when operation without grid current is desired, or at an appropriately positive grid voltage if the grid is to be driven positive. The load resistance for this operating situation is then calculated by Eq. (10-21), assuming $I_{\min}/E_b$ is small, such as 0.05 to 0.15.

These procedures can be regarded as giving a good first approximation to the optimum conditions. To refine the results thus obtained, one draws the corresponding load line, and accurately calculates power output, distortion, and plate efficiency. It is then possible to revise the load line slightly and calculate new results to see if they are better; by a succession of such trials the most favorable combination can be arrived at.

It is to be noted that the load resistance in a Class A amplifier is a dependent design variable that is chosen to give a result consistent with the desired values of $E_{\min}$, $I_{\min}$, etc.; one does not start with an arbitrarily chosen load resistance, and then select electrode voltages to match. It is also to be noted that the proper load resistance to use will be greater when the grid is driven positive (low $E_{\min}$) than when operation is without grid current; also the load resistance will be greater the higher the ratio E_b/I_b at the operating point.

When the bias is obtained by means of a cathode resistor, any rectified current produced by distortion in the amplifier will alter the grid bias. Best results are then obtained when the value of the bias resistor is so chosen as to give the proper grid bias for full signal conditions.

10-6. Output Transformers in Class A Amplifiers. The load impedance is usually coupled to the tube of a Class A power amplifier by means of a transformer, termed an *output transformer*, as shown in Fig. 10-12a. This arrangement avoids passing the d-c plate current through the load impedance and also makes it possible, by the use of the proper turn ratio, for any arbitrarily assigned load to present the proper impedance to the tube.

The use of an output transformer causes the output voltage of the amplifier to fall off at high and low frequencies in the manner shown in Fig. 10-13. The falling off at low frequencies is determined by the inductance of the transformer primary, while the falling off at high frequencies is caused by the leakage inductance in the case of triode tubes, and by the combination of leakage inductance and capacitance shunting the primary in the case of pentodes and beam tubes.

---

positive peaks of the exciting voltage. If under these conditions, the load resistance called for by the above procedure is less than twice the plate resistance of the tube at the operating point, then it will be found desirable to increase the negative bias of the grid until the load resistance called for is twice the plate resistance. This results in operation at less than rated plate current, but because of the increase in load resistance, will actually give greater power output than operation at rated current.

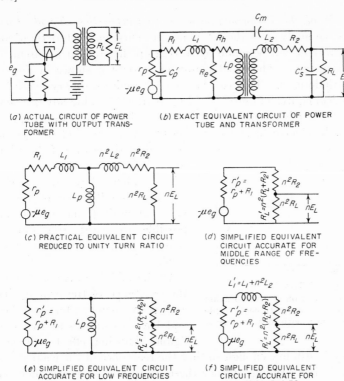

FIG. 10-12. Equivalent circuits for triode power amplifier using output transformer.

Notation

μ = amplification factor of tube

r_p = plate resistance of tube (in a push-pull amplifier r_p is twice the plate resistance of one tube)

R_1 = d-c resistance of primary winding

$r_p' = r_p + R_1$ = effective plate resistance

R_2 = d-c resistance of secondary winding

R_L = load resistance

$R_L' = n^2(R_L + R_2)$ = effective load resistance reduced to unity turn ratio

$R = R_L' r_p' / (R_L' + r_p')$ = resistance formed by r_p' and R_L' in parallel

$R' = R_L' + r_p'$ = sum of effective load and effective plate resistances

R_h = resistance representing hysteresis loss of transformer core

R_e = resistance representing eddy-current loss of transformer core

n = step-down voltage ratio = ratio of primary to secondary turns

L_p = incremental primary inductance with appropriate d-c saturation

L_1 = leakage inductance of primary winding

L_2 = leakage inductance of secondary winding

$L_1' = L_1 + n^2 L_2$ = total leakage inductance reduced to unity turn ratio

$X = \omega L_p$ = reactance of transformer primary inductance

$X' = \omega L_1'$ = reactance of transformer leakage inductance reduced to unity turn ratio

e_g = input voltage

E_L = output voltage

Analysis of the Frequency-response Characteristics—Triode Case. A quantitative analysis of the frequency-response characteristic of an output transformer can be made by setting up the equivalent circuit of the amplifier system. The exact equivalent circuit is shown in Fig. 10-12b for the triode case. This can be reduced under ordinary conditions to the practical equivalent circuit of Fig. 10-12c by taking advantage of the facts that the eddy-current and hysteresis losses are usually quite low, and that the electrostatic capacitances C'_p, C_m, and C'_s of the system can be neglected because of the relatively low triode plate and load resistances with which they are associated. Further simplification of the equivalent circuit of the transformer is possible by considering only a restricted range of frequencies at one time.

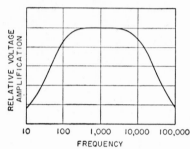

FIG. 10-13. Variation of amplification with frequency in a typical triode power amplifier with output transformer.

In the middle range of frequencies, the reactance of the primary inductance is so much greater than the plate and load resistances as to have negligible shunting effect, whereas the frequency is still low enough so that the reactance of the leakage inductance is relatively small. Under these conditions, the equivalent circuit reduces to the network of resistances shown in Fig. 10-12d. Analysis of the voltage and current relations of this circuit gives

$$\text{Mid-frequency response} = E_L = e_g \frac{\mu n R_L}{r'_p + R'_L} \qquad (10\text{-}22)$$

The notation is shown in Fig. 10-12.

At low frequencies the shunting effect of the primary inductance must be considered, so that the equivalent circuit takes the form given in Fig. 10-12e. Analysis of the voltage and current relations of this circuit shows that at low frequencies[1]

$$\frac{\text{Low-frequency response}}{\text{Mid-frequency response}} = \frac{1}{1 - j(R/X)} = \frac{1}{1 - j(f_1/f)} \qquad (10\text{-}23)$$

where X and R have the meaning given in Fig. 10-12, while f is the actual frequency and f_1 is the frequency at which $X = R$ (i.e., frequency of 70.7 per cent response).

It is to be noted that the falling off in response at low frequencies depends only upon the ratio X/R, where X is the reactance of the *incre-*

---

[1] In Eqs. (10-23) and (10-24) a positive angle denotes a leading output voltage. However, when amplifier phase shifts are plotted, it is customary to plot leading angles as negative, as shown in Fig. 10-14.

mental primary inductance and R is the resistance formed by the effective plate resistance shunted by the effective load resistance. The way in which the relative amplification depends upon f/f_1 is plotted in Fig. 10-14, which can be used to determine the low-frequency response. *It will be observed that the output voltage falls off to* **70.7** *per cent of its mid-frequency*

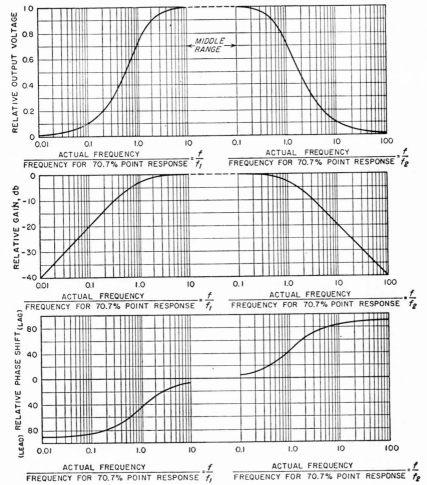

FIG. 10-14. Universal amplification curve of transformer-coupled power amplifier employing triode tube.

range value when the frequency is such that the reactance of the primary incremental inductance equals the resistance R formed by the effective plate resistance r_p' in parallel with the effective load resistance R_L'.

At high frequencies, the shunting effect of the primary inductance can be neglected, but the leakage reactance must be considered; the equivalent circuit then takes the form shown at Fig. 10-12f. Analysis of this circuit shows that at high frequencies

$$\frac{\text{Response at high frequencies}}{\text{Mid-frequency response}} = \frac{1}{1 + j(X'/R')} = \frac{1}{1 + j(f/f_2)} \quad (10\text{-}24)$$

where X' and R' have the meaning given in Fig. 10-12, while f is the actual frequency, and f_2 is the frequency at which $X' = R'$ (i.e., frequency of 70.7 per cent response).

From Eq. (10-24) it is seen that the falling off in response at high frequencies is determined by X'/R', where X' is the reactance of the leakage inductance, and R' is the sum of the effective load and plate resistances. The relation between the relative high-frequency response and X'/R' is plotted in Fig. 10-14, which can be used to determine the way in which the response falls off at high frequencies. *It will be observed that the output voltage at high frequencies falls to 70.7 per cent of its value in the middle range of frequencies when the frequency is such that the reactance of the leakage inductance is equal to the resistance R' formed by the effective plate resistance r'_p and the effective load resistance R'_L in series.*

A consideration of the above equations and of Fig. 10-14 shows that, in order to obtain good reproduction at low frequencies, the transformer should have a high primary inductance, while, in order to maintain the response to high frequencies, the transformer should at the same time have a low leakage inductance. With any given load and plate resistances, the ratio of highest to lowest frequency satisfactorily reproduced is thus determined by the ratio of leakage to primary inductance. On the other hand, with a given triode plate resistance and a given transformer, increasing the load resistance will greatly improve the high-frequency response while adversely affecting to a slight extent the response at low frequencies.

Analysis of the Frequency-response Characteristics—Pentode- and Beam-tube Case. The practical equivalent circuit, reduced to unity turn ratio, of a Class A power amplifier with transformer coupling and using a beam or pentode tube, differs from the circuit of Fig. 10-12c for the triode case in that the equivalent eddy-current resistance R_e and primary shunting capacitance C'_p cannot be neglected in view of the relatively large plate resistance of pentode and beam tubes. While these circuit elements produce little effect at low and intermediate frequencies, they cause the circuit of Fig. 10-15a to represent more accurately the behavior of beam and pentode amplifiers at high frequencies than does Fig. 10-12f. Here R_e frequently has a magnitude comparable with the plate resistance r_p; also with many transformers, the reactance of C_{eq} will equal the leakage reactance $\omega L'_1$ somewhere in the useful range of frequencies. In such cases, the frequency response characteristic of the pentode or beam-tube power amplifier has the form shown in Fig. 10-15b at high frequencies.

At intermediate and low frequencies, Figs. 10-12*b* to *e* and 10-14 still apply.

Transformation Ratio and Transformer Efficiency. It is well known that placing a load impedance Z_L on the secondary side of a transformer is equivalent to placing another impedance $n^2 Z_L$ across the primary terminals, where n is the ratio of primary to secondary turns.[1] When transformer coupling is employed with a power amplifier, the usual practice is to make the turn ratio such that $n^2 R_L$ is equal to the load resistance that should be presented to the power amplifier. This procedure neglects the resistance of the transformer windings, but is sufficiently accurate for ordinary requirements.

Losses in the output transformer cause the power delivered to the load to be less than the power that the tube delivers to the transformer primary. Most of the transformer loss is caused by the resistance of the windings since flux densities are usually so low that the core losses are negligible. To the extent that the wire resistance accounts for all the transformer dissipation, reference to Fig. 10-12*d* gives

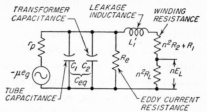

(*a*) EQUIVALENT CIRCUIT AT HIGH FREQUENCIES

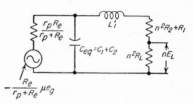

(*b*) EQUIVALENT CIRCUIT OF (*a*) SIMPLIFIED BY THÉVENIN'S THEOREM

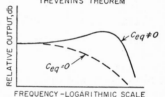

(*c*) TYPICAL HIGH-FREQUENCY RESPONSE

FIG. 10-15. Output-transformer behavior at high frequencies with pentode and beam tubes.

$$\text{Efficiency} = \frac{\text{power delivered to load}}{\text{power delivered to primary}} = \frac{1}{1 + [(R_1 + n^2 R_2)/n^2 R_L]}$$

(10-25)

Practical efficiencies are of the order of 80 per cent.

Measurement of Transformer Characteristics. The essential characteristics of an output transformer are the primary inductance, the leakage inductance reduced to unity turn ratio, the turn ratio, and the copper-loss resistances also reduced to unity turn ratio. In transformers to be used with pentode and beam tubes, the distributed capacitance of the primary winding (or the frequency at which this capacitance is resonant with the leakage inductance) may also be of importance.

The primary inductance that is effective is the incremental inductance

---

[1] Note that this definition of n is the reciprocal of the definition used in Fig. 8-14.

discussed in Sec. 2-1; this is the value obtained with the appropriate d-c saturation in the core and with relatively low alternating flux density. The leakage inductance reduced to unity turn ratio can be determined by short-circuiting the secondary of the transformer and measuring the equivalent inductance appearing across the primary terminals. This inductance depends upon flux paths that are largely in air and so is unaffected by d-c saturation, alternating flux density, etc. The resistances of the windings can be measured on a Wheatstone bridge and the turn ratio can be obtained either from the manufacturer or by applying a known voltage to the primary and reading the resulting open-circuit secondary voltage with a vacuum-tube voltmeter.

The frequency at which the distributed capacitance of the primary winding is resonant with the leakage inductance of the transformer is

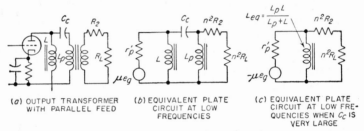

(a) OUTPUT TRANSFORMER WITH PARALLEL FEED   (b) EQUIVALENT PLATE CIRCUIT AT LOW FREQUENCIES   (c) EQUIVALENT PLATE CIRCUIT AT LOW FREQUENCIES WHEN C_c IS VERY LARGE

FIG. 10-16. Actual and equivalent circuits of power amplifier employing shunt feed.

obtained by short-circuiting the secondary terminals of the transformer and observing from the transformer primary terminals the frequency of parallel resonance that results. From this frequency and the leakage inductance, one may determine the equivalent distributed capacitance of the transformer primary. The capacitance C_{eq} in Fig. 10-15 is then the sum of this capacitance and of the plate-to-ground capacitance of the tube with which the transformer is to be associated.

Transformers with Shunt Feed. The shunt-feed (also called parallel-feed) arrangement illustrated in Fig. 10-16a is often used in order to avoid passing the d-c plate current through the primary winding of the transformer. This eliminates d-c saturation of the core, thereby increasing the incremental inductance of the primary.

The equivalent circuit for the shunt-feed system for low frequencies is shown in Fig. 10-16b in the constant-voltage form. When the blocking capacitor C_c is large enough to be a virtual short circuit, as is often the case, this circuit reduces to that of Fig. 10-16c. This latter is the same as the equivalent circuit of the ordinary transformer-coupled amplifier if the effective primary inductance is taken as the inductance formed by the actual inductance of the transformer primary in parallel with the shunt-feed choke, and Eq. (10-23) applies, provided X is interpreted on this basis. In the mid-frequency and high-frequency ranges, the equivalent circuits of Fig. 10-12d and f, respectively, also apply for shunt-feed systems.

The use of shunt feed makes possible considerable improvement in the performance obtainable with a given transformer or, alternatively, makes it possible to obtain a given result with a less expensive transformer. This follows from the fact that, by removing the direct current from the primary of the transformer, it is possible to reduce the air gap in the transformer core and also to use high-permeability core materials if desired. This increases the primary inductance without changing the leakage inductance, or alternatively makes it possible to obtain a given primary inductance with less leakage inductance; it also makes possible a given frequency-response characteristic with a physically smaller transformer having higher power efficiency, etc.

Shunt feed must be employed with output transformers having high-permeability alloy cores, since the incremental permeability of all such alloys is greatly reduced with even small d-c magnetization.

Power Rating of Output Transformers. The maximum current that an output transformer can carry is determined by the heating of the windings, while the maximum voltage that can be applied is limited by the permissible flux density in the core. These two factors operating together determine the power rating of the output transformer.

If the alternating flux density in the core is high, the inductance varies during the cycle because of the nonlinear character of the magnetization curve. This limits the maximum permissible flux density. The relationship between the applied voltage and the flux density depends on the frequency and core cross section according to the well-known equation

$$\left.\begin{matrix}\text{Effective value of} \\ \text{applied voltage}\end{matrix}\right\} = 4.44 f N B A \times 10^{-8} \qquad (10\text{-}26)$$

where N = number of turns

f = frequency

B = flux density in the core, lines per unit area

A = net area of the core

It is apparent that the maximum voltage that can be applied for a given permissible flux density is proportional to the frequency. Hence the voltage limit occurs at the lowest frequencies to be amplified.

The permissible flux density depends upon the amount of distortion that can be tolerated, the characteristics of the iron, whether or not d-c saturation is present, and upon the circuits associated with the transformer. It is commonly found that, with commercial output transformers operated within their power ratings, appreciable distortion will occur at frequencies for which the amplification has not yet fallen to 70.7 per cent of the mid-frequency value. Thus the low-frequency limit of power transformers is commonly determined by distortion arising from saturation of the core rather than from insufficient primary inductance.[1]

Because the maximum flux density in the core must be kept low to avoid distortion, an output transformer tends to be appreciably larger than a 60-cycle power transformer of corresponding power rating. This is particularly so when the output transformer must respond to relatively low frequencies.

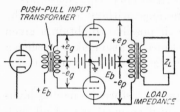

(*a*) PUSH-PULL CIRCUIT

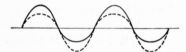

(*b*) OUTPUT WAVEFORMS OF INDIVIDUAL TUBES

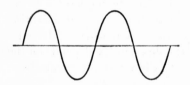

(*c*) WAVEFORM IN LOAD IMPEDANCE AFTER COMBINING OUTPUT OF THE TWO TUBES

FIG. 10-17. Circuit diagram of push-pull amplifier, together with output waveforms for the individual tubes and for the load impedance.

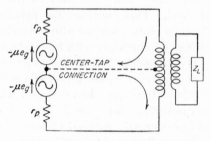

(*a*) EQUIVALENT CIRCUIT FOR FIRST-ORDER EFFECTS (SIMILAR CIRCUIT APPLIES FOR ALL ODD ORDERS)

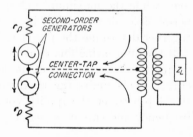

(*b*) EQUIVALENT CIRCUIT FOR SECOND AND ALL OTHER EVEN-ORDER EFFECTS

FIG. 10-18. Equivalent circuits of the push-pull amplifier, showing the difference in behavior with respect to odd-order and even-order effects.

10-7. Push-Pull Class A Amplifiers. In the push-pull amplifier, two identical tubes are so arranged that their grids are excited with equal voltages 180° out of phase, and the outputs of the two tubes are combined by means of an output transformer having a center tap. A typical push-pull circuit arrangement is shown in Fig. 10-17*a*. The corresponding first-order equivalent plate circuit that results is shown in Fig. 10-18*a*. It is seen that the two tubes together are equivalent to a single tube hav-

[1] Discussions of harmonic distortion in audio-frequency transformers resulting from core saturation and its relation to transformer design are given by Norman Partridge, Harmonic Distortion in Audio-frequency Transformers, *Wireless Eng.*, vol. 19, p. 394, September, 1942; *ibid.*, p. 451, October, 1942; *ibid.*, p. 503, November, 1942; K. A. MacFadyen, The Calculation of Wave-form Distortion in Iron-cored Audio-frequency Transformers, *Proc. IEE*, vol. 98, pt. III, p. 153, March, 1951.

ing a plate resistance $2r_p$ and an amplification factor 2μ, where r_p and μ are the plate resistance and amplification factor of an individual tube.

The advantages of the push-pull connection, *assuming identical tubes*, are:

1. There is no d-c saturation in the core of the output transformer. (The direct currents in the two halves of the primary magnetize the core in opposite directions, and so produce zero resultant magnetization.)

2. There is no current of signal frequency flowing through the source of plate power. This means the push-pull power amplifier produces no regeneration, even when there is an impedance common to the power and other stages (see Sec. 10-10); it also means that no by-pass capacitor is required across a cathode-biasing resistor that is common to the two tubes.

3. Alternating-current hum voltages present in the source of d-c plate power produce no hum in the output because the hum currents flowing in the two halves of the primary balance each other.

4. There is less distortion for a given power output per tube, or more power output per tube for a given distortion, as a result of cancellation of all even harmonics and even-order combination frequencies.

The reason for the elimination of the even harmonics in the push-pull amplifier can be understood by reference to Fig. 10-17. Assuming that the amplifier is sufficiently overloaded so that some second-order distortion occurs, the individual tubes develop output waves as shown by the dotted and solid lines of Fig. 10-17*b*. The sum of these waves, which represents the amplified output, is shown in Fig. 10-17*c*. When the two tubes have identical characteristics, the positive and negative half cycles of this resultant output wave differ in sign but not in shape, and therefore contain only odd harmonics. This similarity in the shapes of the positive and negative half cycles in the combined output results from the fact that at time intervals that are exactly one-half cycle apart the tubes have merely interchanged functions; i.e., at the later time tube 2 is operating under exactly the same conditions as was tube 1 a half cycle earlier, and vice versa.

A quantitative analysis of the behavior of a push-pull power amplifier can be obtained by a modification of the load-line technique described on page 321.[1] Alternatively, one can extend the equivalent circuit of Fig. 10-18*a* to include second- and higher-order generators in accordance with the principles discussed in Sec. 10-3. When this is done it is found that the second- and higher even-order generators act as shown in Fig. 10-18*b*,

[1] The use of load lines in push-pull systems was originated by B. J. Thompson, Graphical Determination of Performance of Push-pull Audio Amplifiers, *Proc. IRE*, vol. 21, p. 591, April, 1933; a description of the method is also given by F. E. Terman, "Radio Engineers' Handbook," p. 384, McGraw-Hill Book Company, Inc., New York, 1943. The use of load lines in situations where unbalance exists between the two sides of the push-pull system is described by K. R. Sturley, Push-pull AF Amplifier, *Wireless Eng.*, vol. 26, p. 338, October, 1949.

and so oppose each other in so far as the secondary of the output transformer is concerned. In contrast, all odd-order generators (including the first) have the same relative polarities as the first-order effect in Fig. 10-18a, and so appear in the secondary of the push-pull output transformer without alteration.

It is characteristic of the push-pull connection that the even-order effects, which do not appear in the secondary of the output transformer, do appear in the circuit between the center tap of the output-transformer primary and the cathode, whereas currents resulting from the first- and the third-order action do not appear in this part of the circuit. This behavior of the even-order distortion components of current can be understood from the schematic equivalent circuit of Fig. 10-18b, which shows that the even-order distortion generated in the individual tubes gives rise to currents that flow through the two halves of the output-transformer primary in opposition, and return to the cathode through the plate-supply system. In contrast to this situation, the cathode and the center tap of the output-transformer primary are at a neutral point with respect to all odd-order effects, both first and third, and no currents of these types flow through the power supply.

Exciting Systems for Push-Pull Amplifiers. The two tubes of a push-pull system should be excited by voltages of equal magnitude but opposite phase. Since it is customary to use push-pull amplification only in power stages, this presents the problem of obtaining an exciting voltage balanced to ground from an amplifier that normally develops an output voltage unsymmetrical with respect to ground.

One method of exciting a push-pull system is to use an interstage coupling transformer having a symmetrical center-tapped secondary. Such an arrangement, shown in Fig. 10-17a, is normally employed whenever it is necessary that the d-c resistance in the grid circuits of the push-pull stage be low, for example, when the grids of the push-pull tubes are to be driven positive.

Transformer coupling has the disadvantage, however, that transformers are expensive and possess a limited frequency range. As a result, a number of push-pull exciting arrangements based on the resistance-coupled amplifier have been devised. Typical circuits of this type are illustrated in Fig. 10-19;[1] such systems are often termed *phase inverters.* They are widely employed in small push-pull power amplifiers, such as those used in radio receivers and public-address systems; another important application is to provide a voltage symmetrical with respect to ground for application to the deflecting plates of a cathode-ray tube.

In the circuit of Fig. 10-19a, tube B_1 is driven by A_1 acting as an

---

[1] A detailed analysis of the properties of the circuits of Fig. 10-19b, c, and d is given by M. S. Wheeler, An Analysis of Three Self-balancing Phase Inverters, *Proc. IRE,* vol. 34, p. 67, February, 1946.

ordinary resistance-coupled stage; at the same time tube A_2 is excited by a voltage developed across part of the grid-leak resistance of B_1. Tube A_2 accordingly drives B_2 with a voltage e_2 that is opposite in phase to the voltage e_1 applied to B_1, since tube A_2 introduces a phase reversal; in addition, e_2 will be equal in magnitude to e_1 provided the tap P is properly located on the grid-leak resistance. Comparison of e_{g_1} and e_1 shows that the phase inverter of Fig. 10-19a gives an amplification corresponding to one stage of resistance coupling. Thus the second exciting voltage e_2 for the push-pull system is obtained at the cost of one extra tube.

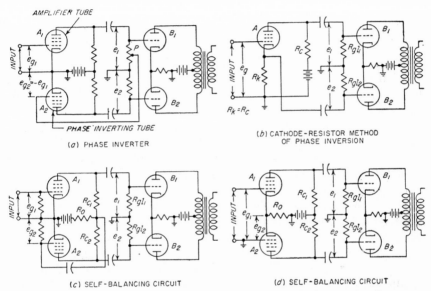

Fig. 10-19. Circuits for exciting a push-pull amplifier without the use of an interstage transformer. For the sake of simplicity, methods of developing the grid bias are not shown in all cases.

In the push-pull exciting circuit of Fig. 10-19b, resistors R_k and R_c are made large and equal; when this is done the voltages e_1 and e_2 applied to tubes B_1 and B_2 will be equal in magnitude and opposite in phase. Although this arrangement requires only one tube, the voltages e_1 and e_2 will be slightly smaller than the input voltage e_{g_1} as a result of cathode-follower action (see Sec. 10-9); thus again the price paid to obtain push-pull excitation is one extra tube in the system.

The operation of the circuit of Fig. 10-19c can be explained as follows: When voltages of opposite phase act on the grids of tubes A_1 and A_2, the current in R_0 is the difference between the amplified plate currents of the individual tubes. The resulting voltage developed across R_0 by this current difference is then used to provide the excitation e_{g_2} for A_2. Under operating conditions, e_{g_2} will be just enough less than e_{g_1} to provide the difference current required to develop a voltage drop e_{g_2} in R_0. If R_0 is large, of the same order of magnitude as R_{c_1}, then the difference between e_{g_1} and e_{g_2} will be very small; however, e_{g_2} will always be less than e_{g_1}. Hence if it is important that the push-pull exciting voltages e_1 and e_2 be absolutely identical, one can make R_{c_2} enough larger than R_{c_1} to correct for this difference; ordinarily it is satisfactory to have $R_{c_1} = R_{c_2}$, and $R_{g l_1} = R_{g l_2}$.

The circuit of Fig. 10-19d is analogous to that at c, except that here the common resistor R_0 is placed between cathode and ground. As before, R_0 should be of the same order of magnitude as R_{c_1}.

Transformers for Push-Pull Class A Amplifiers. The same considerations apply to the push-pull output transformer as to the output transformer of the ordinary Class A power amplifier. The only special features are that (1) there is a d-c saturation of the core only to the extent that the d-c currents of the two tubes differ; (2) the alternating flux density in the core, as calculated from Eq. (10-26), corresponds to a peak voltage from plate to plate that is twice the voltage developed in the plate circuit of the corresponding Class A amplifier; and (3) the frequency-response characteristic of the push-pull output transformer is calculated on the basis of an equivalent plate resistance that is twice the plate resistance of the individual tubes (see Fig. 10-18a).

In the push-pull Class A power amplifier, the load impedance that should be presented from plate to plate by the primary of the output transformer is twice the load resistance that would be used with the same tube in a Class A power amplifier as calculated by Eq. (10-21). The turn ratio of the output transformer must be selected accordingly.

The same tubes used in the simple Class A power amplifier are also equally suitable for use in Class A push-pull systems. Thus, although Figs. 10-17 and 10-19 show triodes, beam and pentode tubes can be employed equally satisfactorily.

10-8. Class B and Class AB Power Amplifiers. The Class B amplifier[1] is a push-pull amplifier in which the tubes are biased approximately to cutoff. When operated in this manner, one of the tubes amplifies the positive half cycles of the signal voltage, while the other amplifies the negative half cycles. The output transformer then combines these half cycles in such a manner as to give an amplified reproduction of the applied signal. The Class B amplifier is characterized by high plate efficiency, and large output power for a given tube type.

Analysis of Class B Operation. The voltage and current relations of an individual tube in a Class B amplifier are illustrated in Fig. 10-20. These oscillograms are analogous to those of Fig. 8-2 (and 10-1) for the Class A amplifier, except that the plate current flows in pulses having a duration

---

[1] The Class B amplifier originated with L. E. Barton, High Audio Output from Relatively Small Tubes, *Proc. IRE*, vol. 19, p. 1131, July, 1931.

of approximately a half cycle, instead of flowing continuously as in the Class A amplifier.

The pulses of plate current in the two tubes of a typical Class B amplifier are related as illustrated in Fig. 10-21a. The push-pull output transformer combines these pulses in such a way that the resulting output wave in the transformer secondary reproduces the signal, as illustrated in Fig. 10-21b.

The output power, plate efficiency,

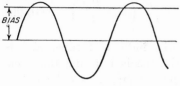

(a) GRID VOLTAGE WAVE

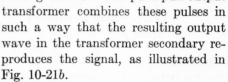

CURRENT IN UPPER HALF OF PRIMARY

CURRENT IN LOWER HALF OF PRIMARY

(a) CURRENT FLOWING IN TRANSFORMER PRIMARY

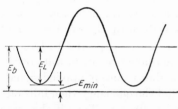

(b) PLATE VOLTAGE WAVE

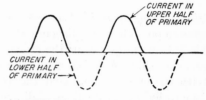

(c) PLATE CURRENT WAVE

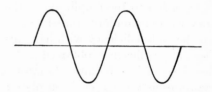

(b) CURRENT IN TRANSFORMER SECONDARY

FIG. 10-20. Oscillograms applying to a typical Class B amplifier.

FIG. 10-21. Current waves flowing in the primary and secondary of the output transformer of a Class B amplifier.

and proper load resistance in a Class B amplifier can be determined with an accuracy sufficient for ordinary purposes by assuming that the pulses of plate current illustrated in Figs. 10-20 and 10-21 are half sine waves. On this basis[1]

[1] These equations are derived as follows: Since the plate-current pulse of each individual tube flows through only half the transformer primary, the combined output of the two tubes is equivalent to an alternating current having a crest value I_{max} flowing through half of the transformer primary, or to a current $I_{max}/2$ flowing through the entire primary. If R_L is the equivalent plate-to-plate load resistance between primary plate-to-plate terminals of the output transformer, the alternating drop produced between plate and cathode of a single tube is one-half the voltage drop of the current $I_{max}/2$ in the resistance R_L or $R_L I_{max}/4$. The minimum instantaneous plate potential is hence

$$E_{min} = E_b - E_L = E_b - (R_L I_{max}/4)$$

Solving this for R_L results in Eq. (10-29). The power output is one-half the square

$$\left.\begin{array}{c}\text{Power output from}\\ \text{two tubes}\end{array}\right\} = \frac{I_{\max}E_b}{2}\left(1 - \frac{E_{\min}}{E_b}\right) \qquad (10\text{-}27)$$

$$\text{Plate efficiency} = \frac{\pi}{4}\left(1 - \frac{E_{\min}}{E_b}\right) \qquad (10\text{-}28)$$

$$\left.\begin{array}{c}\text{Proper load resistance}\\ \text{from plate to plate}\end{array}\right\} = R_L = \frac{4E_b}{I_{\max}}\left(1 - \frac{E_{\min}}{E_b}\right) \qquad (10\text{-}29)$$

Here $I_{\max}$ is the peak plate current of the individual tube, $E_{\min}$ is the minimum instantaneous plate potential reached during the cycle ($E_{\min} = E_b - E_L$), and E_b is the plate-supply voltage, as indicated in Fig. 10-20.

Discussion of Operating Features of Class B Amplifiers. The theoretical maximum possible plate efficiency that can be realized in a Class B amplifier is $\pi/4$ or 78.5 per cent; the closeness with which the actual efficiency approaches this theoretical maximum is determined by the ratio $E_{\min}/E_b$.

With the largest signal that the amplifier can be expected to handle satisfactorily, $E_{\min}/E_b$ will be small, and the actual efficiency at full power is commonly of the order of 60 per cent. Smaller values of applied signal cause $E_{\min}/E_b$ to be correspondingly larger, and the efficiency then falls off in proportion to the amplitude of the signal voltage.[1] Thus if the efficiency with maximum permissible signal (i.e., full output) is 60 per cent, then the plate efficiency with half this signal applied will be 30 per cent.

The plate efficiency obtained in Class B operation is higher than for Class A conditions because (1) most of the plate current flows when the instantaneous voltage between plate and cathode is quite small, as seen from Fig. 10-20, and (2) no current flows at all when the plate-cathode voltage equals or exceeds the plate-supply voltage. These features keep the power dissipated at the plate of the tube to a minimum.

An important feature of Class B operation is that the average power dissipation at the plates of the tubes is much less than for Class A operation giving the same output power. This is in part because at full output, the Class B plate efficiency is greater, and in part because in Class B operation, the power input to the plates becomes less as the signal is reduced. In the limit, when no signal is applied, the plate loss of the Class B amplifier is zero, whereas in the Class A case the power dissipation at the plates

---

of the peak load current times the load resistance, or

$$\text{Power output} = R_L I^2{}_{\max}/8$$

Equation (10-27) results when R_L is eliminated by the use of Eq. (10-29). The d-c plate current drawn by the individual tube, assuming a sine-wave half cycle of current, is $I_{\max}/\pi$, so that the total d-c plate current of the two tubes is $2I_{\max}/\pi$ and the power input is $2I_{\max}E_b/\pi$. Dividing the output by this input gives the plate efficiency, as in Eq. (20-28).

[1] In contrast, the efficiency of a Class A amplifier is proportional to the square of the signal voltage, as pointed out in the footnote on p. 338.

of the tubes is even greater than when delivering full output. This is very important when amplifying speech signals, where the average amplitude is quite small compared with the peak amplitude.

The power output obtainable from Class B operation at a given plate voltage is determined by the peak plate current I_{max}; this in turn is determined by the minimum plate voltage E_{min}, and the maximum grid voltage at the positive peak of the applied signal. One desires a large I_{max} in order to obtain large output, and a small E_{min} in order to have good efficiency. This is normally achieved by driving the control grid of the tube somewhat positive at the peak of each cycle.

With I_{max} and E_{min} determined by considerations of power output and plate efficiency, respectively, it is required that R_L have the value given by Eq. (10-29). If R_L is smaller than it should be, then E_{min} is thereby increased, and both efficiency and output power suffer. On the other hand, if R_L is made too large, E_{min} becomes very small. With triodes this causes I_{max}, and hence the output power, to decrease; with pentode and beam tubes, a virtual cathode forms if E_{min} is too small, and flattens off the plate current peaks.

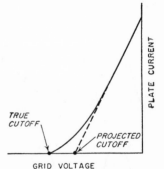

Fig. 10-22. Curve illustrating the meaning of projected cutoff.

The frequency-response characteristics of Class B amplifiers depend upon the output transformer in much the same way as for Class A amplifiers. Thus there is a falling off in amplification at low frequencies that is determined by the primary inductance of the output transformer, while the falling off in gain at high frequencies is determined by the leakage inductance of the transformer. The exact relationships existing in Class B operation are, however, much more complicated than in Class A amplifiers, because of the intermittent character of the plate currents of the individual tubes. This fact also makes it desirable that the leakage inductance between the two halves of the primary winding be as small as possible.

The amplitude distortion generated in a Class B amplifier tends to be somewhat greater than with the corresponding Class A amplifier. However, making the grid-bias voltage that is used in the Class B amplifier correspond to the bias that would be obtained if the main part of the plate-current–grid-voltage curve of the tube for the operating plate-supply potential were projected to cutoff as a straight line, as shown in Fig. 10-22, keeps the distortion quite small.[1] The use of *projected cutoff*

[1] A quantitative analysis can be made of the distortion in a Class B amplifier by means of load lines drawn on a set of composite characteristic curves, as discussed in in the references given in the footnote on p. 349.

bias causes the plate efficiency to be slightly less than that calculated by Eq. (10-28), but otherwise does not greatly change the behavior.

The same power triode, pentode, and beam tubes that are suitable for Class A amplifiers can be used in Class B systems.

Since the d-c plate current a Class B amplifier draws from the power supply depends upon the amplitude of the signal voltage applied to the Class B system, it is very important that the power-supply system used with a Class B arrangement have good voltage regulation. Otherwise the grid bias voltage corresponding to projected cutoff will vary with the amplitude of the signal voltage applied to the amplifier. To the extent that d-c grid current affects the bias voltage applied to the Class B amplifier system, it is also necessary that the grid-bias voltage have good inherent voltage regulation if, as is usually the case, the grids of the tubes are driven positive to obtain the full rated output.

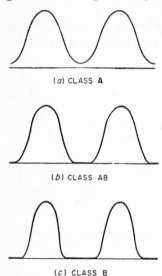

(*a*) CLASS A

(*b*) CLASS AB

(*c*) CLASS B

Fig. 10-23. Plate-current waves illustrating differences between Class A, Class AB, and Class B operation.

Compared with Class A power amplifiers, the Class B arrangement has the advantage of higher plate efficiency, negligible power loss when no signal voltage is applied, and greater output power available from a given tube and given plate-supply system. The disadvantages of Class B operation are a tendency toward somewhat higher amplitude distortion, more critical operating conditions, and the necessity that the plate-supply and bias voltages have good regulation. Class B amplifiers find their chief use where the amount of power to be developed is large, as is the case in large public-address systems and in the modulation of radio transmitters.

Class AB Amplifiers. The Class AB amplifier is a push-pull system in which the grid bias is adjusted to a value intermediate between that which would be used for Class A power amplification and that which would be appropriate for Class B power amplification. Under these conditions, the instantaneous plate current of each individual tube flows for more than half of each cycle, but becomes zero for a small part of each cycle, as shown in Fig. 10-23b. This causes the wave of current in the plate circuit of an individual tube to be considerably distorted. However, the push-pull connection removes much of this distortion, and if negative feedback (see Sec. 11-1) is then added, the results are quite acceptable for most requirements.

The Class AB power amplifier has operating characteristics such as plate efficiency, variation of d-c plate current with signal amplitude, average plate loss, etc., intermediate between Class A and Class B behavior.

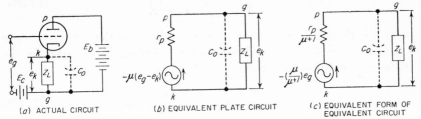

(a) ACTUAL CIRCUIT   (b) EQUIVALENT PLATE CIRCUIT   (c) EQUIVALENT FORM OF EQUIVALENT CIRCUIT

Fig. 10-24. A cathode-follower amplifier, together with equivalent circuits. Although separate grid bias is shown, self-bias is often used.

Class AB amplifiers are widely used for generating small and moderate quantities of audio-frequency power, such as required in small public-address systems. For such applications, they have displaced the true Class A push-pull amplifier to a considerable extent. Compared with Class B amplifiers, the Class AB arrangement has the advantage of being less critical with respect to bias adjustment, but has the disadvantage of somewhat lower plate efficiency and less available output power from a given plate-supply system and given tubes.

10-9. Cathode-follower Amplifiers. The load impedance of an amplifier is sometimes placed between the cathode and ground, as illustrated in Fig. 10-24a. Such an arrangement is termed a *cathode-follower* circuit, and possesses properties that are useful in many applications.

Analysis of Cathode-follower Circuit. Oscillograms showing the voltage and current relations in a cathode-follower system are shown in Fig. 10-25. It is to be noted that the amplified output voltage e_k that is developed across the load impedance

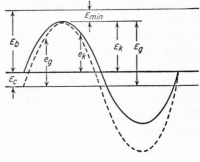

(a) VOLTAGE WAVES

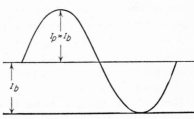

(b) PLATE CURRENT WAVE

Fig. 10-25. Voltage and current relations in the cathode-follower amplifier of Fig. 10-24a. The particular conditions shown correspond to maximum load power for a given value of d-c plate current I_b, and for the minimum valve of plate voltage E_b that can be used without driving the grid positive.

Z_L is in series between the cathode and grid, and has a polarity such as to oppose the applied signal e_g. Hence the net voltage acting between the control grid and cathode of the tube is $e_g - e_k$, which then acts in the equivalent amplifier plate circuit of Fig. 10-24b.[1] This leads to the relation

$$e_k = \mu(e_g - e_k) \frac{Z_L}{r_p + Z_L} \qquad (10\text{-}30a)$$

where μ is the amplification factor of the tube, r_p is the plate resistance of the tube, and Z_L is the load impedance. Solving this equation for the voltage e_k across the load gives

$$e_k = \frac{\mu}{\mu + 1} e_g \frac{Z_L}{[r_p/(\mu + 1)] + Z_L} \qquad (10\text{-}30b)$$

Examination of Eq. (10-30a) shows that the behavior of the cathode-coupled amplifier is as though it were an ordinary amplifier in which the signal voltage e_g was applied to the grid of a tube having an amplification factor $\mu/(\mu + 1)$ and a plate resistance $r_p/(\mu + 1)$. This corresponds to the equivalent circuit of Fig. 10-24c. When the actual amplification factor μ is considerably greater than unity, as is normally the case, the cathode-follower system then acts, in so far as the load is concerned, as though the equivalent amplification factor of the tube was slightly less than unity, and as though the effective plate resistance of the tube was approximately $r_p/\mu = 1/g_m$, a relatively low resistance.

Operating Characteristics of Cathode-follower Amplifiers. The cathode-follower circuit gives power amplification rather than voltage amplification. In fact, examination of Fig. 10-24c makes it clear that the voltage e_k developed across the load impedance must necessarily always be less than the signal voltage e_g. However, the signal voltage e_g can be developed across a very high impedance, whereas the output voltage e_k exists across a load impedance that can be relatively small. Under these conditions, the cathode follower acts as an impedance transformer, which takes a voltage developed across a relatively high impedance and applies it, reduced somewhat in amplitude, to a much lower output impedance. Thus amplification of power is obtained while at the same time the impedance level is reduced.

The cathode-follower circuit has an excellent high-frequency response characteristic; this is because of the very low equivalent plate resistance in the circuit of Fig. 10-24c. For example, assume a triode-connected 6AG7 tube with $g_m = 13,500$ μmhos and $Z_L = R_L = 100$ ohms. According to Eq. (8-6) the response is 70.7 per cent of the midrange value when the reactance of the capacitance C_0 shunting the load has a value equal to 100 ohms in parallel with the equivalent plate resistance

[1] In order to make clear the relations between the actual circuit of Fig. 10-24a and the equivalent circuits of b and c, points representing the plate, cathode, and ground are labeled with the same letters p, k, and g, respectively, in the three parts of Fig. 10-24.

$r_p/(1 + \mu) \approx 1/g_m = 78$ ohms. This reactance is 41 ohms, and for $C_0 = 20$ $\mu\mu f$, it occurs at 194 Mc, a very large value indeed. The performance at low frequencies can likewise be made very good by permitting the d-c cathode current to flow through the load impedance as shown in Fig. 10-24a, so that blocking capacitors with resulting phase shift and loss in voltage are avoided.

The maximum power that a cathode-follower stage is capable of developing in the load impedance is the power delivered to the load resistance when the plate current swings from the operating value down to virtually zero at the negative peaks of the signal. Thus, to a first approximation

$$\left.\begin{matrix}\text{Maximum power output with-}\\ \text{out excessive distortion}\end{matrix}\right\} = \frac{I_b{}^2 R_L}{2} \qquad (10\text{-}31a)$$

where I_b is the d-c plate current at the operating point (which in this case approximates the peak value I_p of the amplified plate current as shown in Fig. 10-25b), and R_L is the resistance component of the load impedance. For a resistive load, the corresponding peak voltage E_k that is then developed across the load is[1]

$$E_k = I_b R_L \qquad (10\text{-}31b)$$

In order to realize the power and voltage given in Eqs. (10-31a) and (10-31b), it is necessary that the peak value E_g of the applied signal be larger than E_k, as calculated from Eq. (10-30b) and shown in the oscillograms of Fig. 10-25. If this signal voltage is not to drive the grid positive, it is then necessary that the grid bias E_c satisfy the relation

$$|E_c| \gtrless E_g - E_k \qquad (10\text{-}32)$$

It will be noted that this bias can be considerably less than the peak amplitude of the applied signal. The proper plate-supply voltage E_b is the value that gives the desired d-c plate current I_b when the bias has the chosen value; E_b is necessarily somewhat larger than E_k (see Fig. 10-25a).

The amplitude distortion introduced by a cathode-follower amplifier will be very small as long as operation is kept within the limits imposed by zero grid potential at the positive peaks, and cutoff at the negative peaks, of the applied signal. This is because the cathode-follower circuit inherently possesses negative feedback of the type discussed in Sec. 11-1 and in connection with Fig. 11-11c.

---

[1] However, when the applied signal consists of pulses having very rapid rates of rise (or fall), the transient effects that are present introduce complications, such as increased possibility of grid current when the applied voltage wave has a positive slope, together with wave-shape distortion on the negative slopes. For further discussion of transient effects in cathode-follower systems, see B. Y. Mills, Transient Response of Cathode Followers in Video Circuits, *Proc. IRE*, vol. 37, p. 631, June, 1949; A. J. Shimmins, Cathode-follower Performance, *Wireless Eng.*, vol. 17, p. 289, December, 1950.

The equivalent generator impedance that the load impedance Z_L sees when looking back toward the tube in a cathode-follower stage is so low as to make it possible to obtain an impedance match between the tube and a low impedance load such as a cable or other transmission line. Such matching between generator impedance and load impedance is often desired in television systems to eliminate reflections at the sending end of the cable, and thereby to reduce echoes. When an impedance match is desired between a tube and a transmission line, a triode tube is selected such that with normal operation the equivalent tube impedance $r_p/(1 + \mu) \approx 1/g_m$ will approximate the characteristic impedance of the transmission line. A final adjustment can then be made either by varying the grid bias of the cathode-follower stage, or by adding trimming resistances in shunt with the input of the line if the tube resistance is too high, or in series with the load if the tube resistance is too low.

Cathode-follower systems normally employ heater-type triode tubes, or heater-type pentode tubes connected to operate as triode tubes. In most cases, tubes with high transconductance are required, since this causes the effective plate resistance (i.e., the equivalent output impedance) of the tube to be small.

The chief use of the cathode-follower amplifier is as a wideband power amplifier for delivering power to loads of relatively low impedance, for example, a coaxial cable. For such applications, the cathode-follower amplifier has excellent frequency response and low distortion, and also enables an impedance match to be achieved between the tube and a low impedance load when this is desired.[1]

10-10. Regeneration in Multistage Audio- and Video-frequency Amplifiers. Under ideal conditions the gain of a multistage amplifier is the product of the amplifications of the individual stages, and the frequency response is therefore the product of the frequency-response curves of the individual stages. Actually this is true only when none of the amplified energy gets inadvertently transferred back to the input stages of the amplifier. Such transfer, termed *regeneration*, is a form of uncontrolled feedback that will distort the amplification curve and may cause the amplifier to break into oscillation in addition.

The tendency toward regeneration is more pronounced the higher the gain of the amplifier, for then a smaller fraction of the output energy will have a significant effect when transferred to the input. Thus, if the total voltage amplification is 100,000, the ratio of powers at input and output points of the amplifier, assuming the same load resistances, is 10^{10}. In this situation it is obvious that even an extremely small portion of the output energy transferred back to the input will not be negligible in compari-

---

[1] In addition, the cathode-follower amplifier offers a higher input (grid-ground) impedance than does the corresponding grounded-cathode amplifier. The reasons for this are discussed in connection with Eq. (12-35).

son with the input signal power that is being amplified, and so will introduce feedback (or regeneration) that greatly modifies the amplifier behavior.

Regeneration at Low Frequencies—Motorboating. The most troublesome form of regeneration in audio- and video-frequency amplifiers occurs when several stages of amplification operate from a common source of

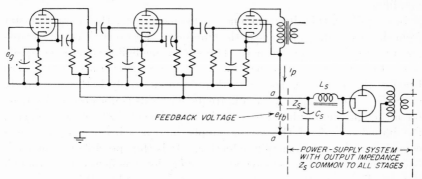

(*a*) MULTISTAGE AMPLIFIER WITHOUT DECOUPLING FILTERS

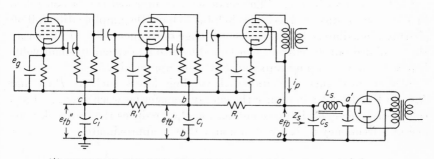

(*b*) MULTISTAGE AMPLIFIER WITH DECOUPLING FILTERS $R_i C_i$ AND $R_i' C_i'$

FIG. 10-26. Multistage amplifier having common power-supply system for all stages, showing how decoupling filters are used to minimize the regeneration resulting from the internal impedance Z_c of the power supply.

plate power, as shown in Fig. 10-26a. Here amplified current i_p in flowing through the source impedance Z_s develops a voltage e_{fb} across the output terminals aa of the power supply, which acts directly in the plate circuits of all of the stages. This corresponds to a form of feedback analogous to the feedback discussed in Chap. 11.

Although power sources are ordinarily by-passed with a large capacitor (indicated by C_s in Fig. 10-26a), this by-passing becomes ineffective at quite low frequencies. The internal impedance of the power-supply system for such frequencies therefore approaches the equivalent internal resistance determined on the basis of the regulation of the d-c output voltage. Although the coupling between amplifier stages introduced by the internal impedance of the power-supply system is negligibly small except at frequencies so low as normally to be outside of the useful range of frequencies, this coupling is often the cause of oscillations that have a frequency of only a few cycles per second. Such oscillations are commonly referred to as *motorboating* because they produce a "put-put" sound in a loudspeaker. Their presence destroys the usefulness of an amplifier.

In evaluating this situation, one need consider only the energy transfer from the last to the first stage of the amplifier. Feedback involving transfer of energy between other pairs of stages has negligible effect in comparison. In the normal frequency range, e_{fb} in Fig. 10-26a approaches zero because the by-pass capacitor C_s of the power supply is then extremely effective. However, at very low frequencies this is not necessarily true, for although the amplified current i_p drops in value at low frequencies, the impedance Z_s of the power supply increases because the by-pass capacitor C_s is no longer fully effective. It is thus possible for the feedback voltage e_{fb} to be excessive at some very low frequency, even though it is negligible in the useful frequency range. When this is the case motorboating usually occurs.

Control of Motorboating. The tendency to motorboat can be controlled in a number of ways. First, it is helpful to have the amplification fall off sharply immediately below the useful range of frequencies.[1] In this way the amplified output current can be reduced to an extremely small value before the power-supply impedance Z_s rises appreciably.

Second, resistance-capacitance decoupling filters such as R_1C_1 and $R_1'C_1'$ in Fig. 10-26b will reduce the energy transfer between stages. Each such resistance-capacitance combination R_1C_1 reduces the feedback voltage at a frequency $\omega/2\pi$ by an amount that is approximately[2]

$$\frac{\text{Voltage fed back with filter}}{\text{Voltage fed back without filter}} = \frac{1/\omega C_1}{R_1} \qquad (10\text{-}33)$$

When two or more filter sections are connected in cascade, as between a and c in Fig. 10-26b, the total voltage reduction in feedback voltage between filter input and filter output is very closely the product of the

---

[1] A sharp low-frequency cutoff can be obtained by employing a properly designed impedance in the screen circuit, as discussed in Sec. 8-5 and on page 271.

[2] This assumes that $1/\omega C_1$ and Z_s are both much less than R_1. These conditions are normally satisfied except at extremely low frequencies. Equation (10-33) is then simply derived as follows: The voltage e_{fb} in Fig. 10-26b produced by the amplified current i_p flowing through the impedance Z_s of the power-supply system causes a current e_{fb}/R_1 to flow in R_1 (because $R_1 >> 1/\omega C_1$). This current then develops a voltage $e_{fb}' = (e_{fb}/R_1)(1/\omega C_1)$ across C_1, since if $R_1' >> 1/\omega C_1$ practically all of the current in R_1 flows through C_1. The reduction in voltage introduced by the filter section R_1C_1 is then e_{fb}'/e_{fb}, which is expressed by Eq. (10-33).

voltage reductions of the individual stages.[1]   Decoupling filters are very helpful in resistance-coupled amplifiers for audio frequencies, since R_1 can be of the order of 100,000 ohms or more without consuming excessive d-c voltage, while C_1 can be an electrolytic capacitor of 5 to 10 μf.[*]

Third, a source of d-c potential having low internal low-frequency impedance, i.e., good regulation, is very effective in reducing regeneration at low frequencies, since this reduces the coupling impedance Z_s between input and output stages.   A voltage-regulated power supply, such as described in Sec. 20-8, has an effective internal impedance that is very close to zero, and is therefore advisable in difficult situations.

Fourth, the use of push-pull amplification, particularly in the final or power stage, is very helpful since in this way the amplified current that flows through the impedance Z_s of the power supply is merely the unbalanced current due to dissymmetries between the two sides of the push-pull system, and is therefore ordinarily small.   Finally, it is always possible to use separate power supplies for the input and output portions of the amplifier, thereby eliminating all possibility of common coupling arising through the power-supply system.[2]

High-frequency Regeneration.   Regeneration at the higher frequencies is occasionally encountered in audio- and video-frequency amplifiers. Such regeneration is almost always the result of unshielded electrostatic couplings between the input and output stages of the amplifier.   These couplings result from failure to shield glass envelope tubes, or from wiring so arranged that there is appreciable electrostatic coupling directly between the input and output portions of the system, particularly portions that have a high impedance to ground.   The remedies are obvious, and are easily applied.

10-11. Volume Control in Audio- and Video-frequency Amplifiers.   It is always necessary to provide means of controlling the gain of an amplifier so that the output can be kept at the desired level, irrespective of the magnitude of the signal voltage being amplified.

---

[1] In a multistage amplifier it is customary to use one decoupling filter between each amplifier stage, as illustrated in Fig. 10-26b.   This arrangement provides some degree of decoupling between adjacent stages, together with maximum possible decoupling between input and output stages, i.e., between points a and c.

[*] Decoupling filters are not very helpful in video amplifier systems, however.   This is because the plate current of a typical video stage is so large that if R_1 is not to consume excessive d-c voltage, it must be too small to be very effective as a filter element. As a result, a regulated power supply is commonly the principal means used to suppress motorboating in video systems, while decoupling filters plus sharp low-frequency cutoff are usually depended upon to handle the situation in most audio amplifier systems.

[2] A compromise in this regard consists in using separate filter systems, as by connecting the right-hand end of R_1 in Fig. 10-26b to point a' instead of to a, but leaving the final tube connected at a.   This reduces the common impedance, and in addition causes L_sC_s to serve as a one-stage decoupling filter instead of as a common impedance.

The standard method of controlling volume manually in audio-frequency amplifiers, shown in Fig. 10-27a, makes use of a grid leak in the form of a high-resistance potentiometer. In such an arrangement, the changes in the frequency-response characteristic that occur with volume setting are small and in the nature of a slight improvement in the high-frequency response at low-volume settings as a result of the reduced resistance across which the input capacitance of the output tube is connected. This arrangement also avoids direct current in the volume-control potentiometer, a requirement that must be met by any volume-control arrangement that is not to be noisy when adjusted.

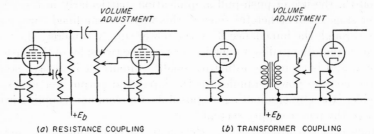

(a) RESISTANCE COUPLING   (b) TRANSFORMER COUPLING

Fig. 10-27. Common methods of controlling volume in resistance- and transformer-coupled amplifiers.

An alternative means of controlling volume is to vary the transconductance g_m of a resistance-coupled amplifier tube by varying the control-grid bias or the screen-grid potential. In such an arrangement, it is customary to employ a variable-mu type of pentode, as in this way the change in gain is less critical with changes in grid bias (or screen voltage).

It is possible to control the volume of a transformer-coupled amplifier stage by means of a potentiometer connected across the transformer secondary as in Fig. 10-27b. Such an arrangement has the disadvantage, however, of causing the frequency-response characteristic to vary considerably with gain setting. As a result, it is customary to control the gain of an audio-frequency amplifier in a resistance-coupled stage whenever possible.

The volume control in an amplifier system must always be placed at a relatively low-power-level point in the system. Otherwise, the first stages of amplification can become overloaded when large signals are present, because the volume control is then not effective for such stages

Automatic Volume Control—Volume Expansion and Contraction. In some applications using audio amplifiers it is desired that the output power of the amplifier be substantially independent of the amplitude of the input signal. Thus, in an electric dictaphone, best recording will be obtained when the output of the audio amplifier is not greatly affected by the loudness with which the dictator speaks. This result can be achieved by the use of automatic volume control (AVC), shown schematically in

Fig. 10-28. Here a small portion of the amplifier output is applied to a
rectifier associated with circuits such that the d-c output of the rectifier
corresponds to an averaged intensity of the amplifier output. This rectified voltage is then applied with negative polarity to the control grids of
one or more stages of the amplifier. A change in the average amplitude
of the output signal thereby alters the bias of the amplifiers and hence
the amplification in a manner that tends to minimize changes in the
amplifier output. When dealing with voice-frequency currents, the time
constants of the electrical circuits in the rectifier output are very important, since they determine the particular characteristics of the speech
that control the amplifier gain.

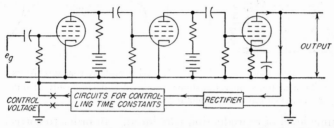

Fig. 10-28. A schematic diagram of circuit arrangements suitable for either automatic
volume control, or volume compression. The type of action obtained is determined by
the time constant of the circuits in the rectifier output.

Under many circumstances it is desirable or necessary to restrict the
volume range in audio-frequency circuits. Thus in recording sound on
phonograph records, the loudest passages must be reduced in intensity to
prevent the needle from cutting into adjacent grooves, while the weaker
passages must have their intensity increased in order that they will not be
lost in the background of hiss. This process is termed *volume compression;* the inverse action in which the load passages are emphasized and the
weak passages deemphasized is termed *volume expansion.*

Volume compression can be achieved automatically by employing the
same system as shown in Fig. 10-28 but using small time constants in the
output circuits of the rectifier output. In this way the amplification will
follow rapid fluctuations in the output intensity. In contrast, in the
automatic-volume-control case, the time constants are made so large that
the gain depends upon the output intensity as averaged over a much
longer time interval. Volume expansion can be obtained by reversing
the polarity of the control voltage in Fig. 10-28, for example, by introducing one stage of d-c amplification at xx; an increase in the rectified output
will then cause an increase in the amplification, and vice versa.

Tone Controls and Tone-compensated Volume Controls. Audio-frequency amplifiers are frequently provided with controls for altering the
response at high and at low frequencies. Termed *tone controls,* these
modify the aesthetic effects of the reproduced sound; they can also be

used to compensate for room acoustics, reduce hum, reduce hiss or scratch, etc. A typical tone-control circuit providing means for independently varying the frequency response at both high and low frequencies is shown in Fig. 10-29.

The characteristics of the ear are such that the apparent loudness of low-frequency tones relative to middle- and high-frequency tones is less as

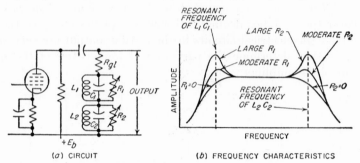

(a) CIRCUIT   (b) FREQUENCY CHARACTERISTICS

Fig. 10-29. Typical tone-control system; if control is desired only at one end of the frequency range, then only one resonant circuit is required.

the volume level of reproduction is reduced. In order to correct for this effect, volume controls are sometimes arranged so that, as the volume control reduces the gain, the reduction is less for low frequencies than for middle- and high-frequency components. Such an arrangement is termed a *tone-compensated volume control*. A typical example is shown in Fig. 10-30.

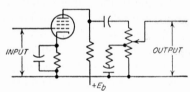

Fig. 10-30. Tone-compensated volume control.

10-12. Hum and Microphonic Effects in Audio and Video Amplifiers.

Hum. The term *hum* refers to alternating voltages appearing in the output of an amplifier as a result of the effect of power-frequency voltages, currents, and fields. In audio- and video-frequency amplifiers, hum results from the introduction into the amplifier circuits of currents of the power frequency and its harmonics, which are amplified directly by the amplifier. Such hum is particularly troublesome in high-gain systems, since then effects introduced in low-level stages are subjected to large amounts of amplification.

The possible sources of hum are stray magnetic fields, stray electrostatic fields, alternating currents in the heaters or filaments of the tubes, and incompletely filtered power-supply systems. The problem of avoiding hum while using alternating current to heat the cathodes of the amplifier tubes is discussed in Sec. 20-1 and can be handled by a suitable choice of tubes. Hum from the power-supply system is a design problem, the solution of which presents no particular difficulty. The hum that is most difficult to handle arises from stray magnetic and electrostatic fields.

Magnetic fields induce voltages in coils, or in loops that can exist if the wiring is improperly arranged, and may even affect the flow of electrons between the cathode and the plate of a tube.   The principal sources of magnetic fields in the vicinity of an amplifier are the power transformer and the leads carrying the filament or heater currents of the tubes.   Such leads should hence be arranged in the form of a twisted pair to minimize their magnetic effects.   Power transformers should be placed as far as possible from portions of the system sensitive to magnetic fields, particularly input transformers and associated tubes.   The stray magnetic field can be minimized by designing the power transformer to have low leakage flux (achieved by using low flux densities and the smallest possible air gap in the core).   It is also helpful to employ a nonmagnetic chassis or, at least, to isolate the input and power transformers from a sheet-iron chassis by mounting either or both upon a nonmagnetic base that is then fastened to the chassis.

Input transformers present a particularly difficult problem in high-gain audio-frequency amplifiers because they operate at the point in the system where the power level is the lowest.   The input transformer of a high-gain audio-frequency amplifier must be magnetically shielded and should be placed as far as possible from the power transformer, with an orientation that experiment indicates will minimize hum pickup.   In many cases, the input transformer and one or two stages of resistance-coupled amplification are built in a separate unit termed a preamplifier, which can be located some distance from the main amplifier chassis and transformer and is energized through cables.   Lines connecting the microphone or other source of power to an input transformer, and lines connecting the output of the preamplifier system to the main amplifier, should preferably be of low impedance, i.e., 600 ohms or less, and should consist of a twisted pair of wires electrostatically shielded.   The input transformer should always be provided with an electrostatic shield between primary and secondary.

Electrostatic fields cause trouble with parts of the amplifier having a high impedance to ground, since any electrostatically induced current in flowing to ground will produce a hum voltage that is proportional to the impedance between this part of the circuit and the ground.   In particular, when the grid of an audio-frequency amplifier tube is left disconnected, or is grounded through a very high resistance, the impedance between grid and ground is so high that an especially large hum voltage will be developed between grid and ground by the electrostatic fields of nearby lighting circuits.   To eliminate trouble from electrostatic pickup, the tubes should be shielded, and the grid leads should be either shielded or made very short.   In audio-frequency amplifiers having very high over-all gain, it is usually necessary to enclose the first one or two stages in a metal box, not leaving even a fraction of an inch of the input circuit (including wires, plugs, etc.) without electrostatic shielding. Filament wires carrying alternating current to the first stages of a high-gain amplifier should be enclosed in grounded metal braid. It is also essential that the chassis of high-gain amplifiers be grounded to water pipes or to a stake driven into moist earth unless all power, filament, input, and output transformers have electrostatic shields.[1]

Microphonic Effects. When a tube is jarred, the electrodes tend to vibrate mechanically, giving rise to effects characterized by the term *microphonic action.* Thus vibrations cause changes in the plate current which are usually in the audible frequency range and which are, therefore, amplified in audio- and video-frequency amplifiers.

Vibrations may be transmitted to the tube either mechanically through the tube socket, or acoustically through the action of sound waves. Microphonic effects are most troublesome when tubes are operated in the vicinity of loudspeakers, or when equipment is subjected to vibration, as on airplanes, automobiles, etc. Microphonic effects can be minimized by preventing vibrations from reaching the tubes, by selection of individual tubes for low microphonic action, and by the use of special tubes of unusually rigid construction. Individual tubes of the same type often vary greatly in their tendency to microphonic action, so there is much to be gained by selecting the least microphonic tube from a large number for use in the low-power-level stages of an amplifier. When microphonic action is troublesome, it is also helpful to mount the tubes that are at the lowest power level on a support that does not transmit vibrations readily, and then, in addition, to protect these tubes from direct contact with sound waves.

PROBLEMS AND EXERCISES

10-1. For reference purposes, draw a set of waves corresponding to the solid curves in Fig. 10-1*a*. Then superimpose a set of waves (to be drawn dotted) for the case where e_g, E_{cc}, and E_{bb} are unchanged, but where R_L is substantially increased.

10-2. For reference purposes, draw a set of curves corresponding to the solid curves in Fig. 10-1*b*. Then superimpose a set of waves (to be drawn dotted) for everything unchanged except that the suppressor grid potential is made sufficiently negative to cause a virtual cathode to form at the positive peaks of the applied signal.

10-3. For reference purposes draw a set of curves corresponding to the solid curves of Fig. 10-1*b*. Then superimpose a set of waves (to be drawn dotted) for a substantially lower screen-grid voltage, everything else being left unchanged.

10-4. Assume that the tube in Fig. 10-2 has the characteristics given in Fig. 6-17.

a. Determine the d-c potential E_b at the plate of the tube corresponding to the quiescent point when $E_{bb} = 200$, $E_c = 1.5$, and $R_L = 25,000$ ohms.

[1] An amplifier system should, however, never be grounded at more than one point. Otherwise stray 60-cycle power-line currents that commonly circulate in the earth will get mixed up with the amplifier by flowing through the low resistance path that goes from one ground through the amplifier system and back to the other ground, instead of confining themselves to the higher resistance earth.

b. Specify the instantaneous values of plate current and voltage at the positive and negative peaks of an applied signal having a peak amplitude of 1.5 volts.

c. Determine the percentage of second harmonic with respect to the fundamental component of the amplified plate current when the applied signal has a peak amplitude of 1.5 volts, and also the magnitude of the rectified current.

d. Repeat (a), (b), and (c) for $R_L = 40,000$ ohms; tabulate results for the two values of R_L side by side, and discuss the differences.

10-5. Referring to Fig. 10-4 (which applies to the circuit of Fig. 10-3a) show by a succession of sketches the effect of (a) increasing E_{bb} but leaving everything else unchanged, (b) decreasing R_{gl} but leaving everything else unchanged, and (c) increasing R_c but leaving everything else unchanged.

10-6. Assume that the tube in Fig. 10-3a has the characteristics given in Fig. 6-17.

a. Draw the dynamic load line for $E_{bb} = 240$, $E_c = -1.5$, $R_c = R_{gl} = 40,000$.

b. Specify the instantaneous values of plate current at the positive and negative peaks of an applied signal having a peak amplitude of 1.5 volts.

c. Determine the percentage of second harmonic, and of rectified current, with respect to the fundamental component of the amplified plate current, when the signal has a peak amplitude of 1.5 volts.

10-7. The triode tube of Figs. 6-9 and 6-10 is employed in the shunt-feed circuit of Fig. 10-3c with $E_{bb} = 250$ volts, $E_c = -30$ volts, and $R_L = 7000$ ohms.

a. At what value of instantaneous plate voltage will the instantaneous plate current be zero?

b. What will be the instantaneous plate voltage and current when the instantaneous grid voltage is zero?

c. Determine the power output on the fundamental frequency, and the percentage of second harmonic in the output voltage, when a signal having a peak amplitude of 30 volts is applied to the control grid.

10-8. a. Draw the dynamic characteristic corresponding to the conditions specified in Prob. 10-7.

b. Using this dynamic characteristic, sketch the output wave shapes obtained when alternating signal voltages having peak amplitudes of 20 and 40 volts are applied to the control grid. Ignore distortion resulting from grid current.

10-9. Prove the correctness of Eq. (10-2) and justify the related footnote on page 325.

10-10. a. The beam tube of Fig. 6-24 is employed in the shunt-feed circuit of Fig. 10-3c, with $E_{bb} = 300$, $E_{c2} = 250$, $E_{cc} = -15$, and $R_L = 4200$ ohms. Determine the output power and voltage at the fundamental frequency and the percentage of second-, third-, and fourth-harmonic voltages relative to the fundamental voltage appearing across the load impedance, for alternating signal voltages having peak values of 20 and 10 volts applied to the control grid. Tabulate all results. Assume that conditions are such that grid current produces negligible distortion.

b. Repeat (a) for load resistances of 2600 ohms and 6300 ohms, and tabulate the results along with those of (a).

10-11. A signal source that develops 40 volts peak amplitude on open circuit is applied to the control grid of a tube biased to -30 volts. It is desired that the flattening of the positive peaks resulting from grid current not exceed 5 volts. What is the highest value of internal impedance that the source of exciting voltage may have if a grid current of 0.05 ma flows when the grid is 5 volts positive?

10-12. Carry out the steps by which the relations of Eq. (10-7) are derived from Eqs. (10-5) and (10-6).

10-13. Carry out the details of the transformation by which Eq. (10-9) is obtained from Eq. (10-8).

10-14. Make substitutions in Eq. (10-12) that show that each term on the right-hand side is proportional to $e_g{}^3$.

10-15. Prove that the current that flows in the load impedance Z_L in Fig. 10-9b is the same as the current in the impedance Z_L of Fig. 10-9a.

10-16. In Fig. 10-9b determine the correctness of the formulas giving the values of i_1, i_2, etc., by starting with the formulas shown for the values of the voltage generators in Fig. 10-9a.

10-17. Verify the correctness of the entries in Table 10-2 for the case $e_g = E \sin \omega t$.

10-18. Prove that it is possible to obtain third-order effects in triode amplifiers even when the curvature of the tube characteristic does not change (i.e., when $\partial^2 g_m/\partial E_c{}^2 = 0$), whereas with pentodes or beam tubes in which the plate resistance is very high, third-order effects are obtained only when the curvature of the tube characteristic changes.

10-19. The amount of second-harmonic distortion produced in an amplifier when the applied signal is a sine wave is often estimated roughly by noting the change in d-c plate current produced by the presence of the signal. Demonstrate that this rectified plate current is proportional to the amount of second harmonic present even when all effects up to and including the third order are taken into account.

10-20. The signal voltage applied to the control grid of an amplifier consists of a 200-cycle wave and its sixth harmonic, 1200 cycles. List the frequency components present in the output of the amplifier when (a) only first- and second-order distortion effects are important, and (b) distortion effects up to and including the third order are important.

10-21. In a particular pentode tube in which an alternating voltage having a peak value of 2.4 volts is applied to the control grid, it is found that the peak value of the alternating component of plate current of fundamental frequency is 4 ma, while the plate current contains 5 per cent second harmonic and 1 per cent third harmonic. With this information determine g_m, $\partial g_m/\partial E_c$, and $\partial^2 g_m/\partial E_c{}^2$.

10-22. Starting with the value of load resistance corresponding to quiescent point Q' in Fig. 10-10, show qualitatively the effect that reducing the grid-leak resistance has on the dynamic load line, and also on the maximum value of amplified voltage that can be obtained without excessive distortion.

10-23. Compare the voltage amplification obtainable from two resistance-coupled amplifiers employing the same tube, the same plate-supply voltage, and the same grid-leak resistance, but with the coupling resistances respectively $0.2R_{gl}$ and $1.0R_{gl}$. Both amplifiers are adjusted to produce large output voltage, a result achieved by making the d-c voltage drop in the coupling resistances in the two cases $0.45E_{bb}$ and $0.60E_{bb}$, respectively. Assume that the transconductance is proportional to the cube root of the d-c plate current.

10-24. Determine the relative merits of the different tubes of Table 9-1, page 292, with respect to ability to develop a large output voltage without severe amplitude distortion when used as video amplifiers.

10-25. Determine the maximum output voltage obtainable when the 6L6 tube of Table 9-1, page 292, is used in a video amplifier shunt-peaked for maximum flatness, and designed so that the amplification falls off 3 db at 4.5 Mc. Assume that the load impedance introduces a shunting capacitance of 9 $\mu\mu$f in addition to the output capacitance of the tube.

10-26. The power output calculated from Eq. (10-19) will in general differ from that obtained with the aid of Table 10-1, page 326. Explain the reason for the difference.

10-27. If the plate-supply voltage is increased, but the plate dissipation at the operating point is kept constant, show that the proper load resistance for Class A amplifier operation with no grid current increases, and that the plate efficiency increases.

10-28. In a Class A amplifier, compare the power dissipated at the plate of the tube when a signal is applied to the grid with the power dissipated when there is no signal.

10-29. Two Class A power amplifiers using, respectively, triode and beam tubes have the same d-c plate voltages and currents. Both amplifiers are to be operated without driving the control grid positive. Explain why a beam amplifier requires a slightly lower load resistance and gives a higher plate efficiency and power output.

10-30. Prove the correctness of the statement made on page 338 that when the distortion is largely second order, the percentage of second harmonic present in the output will be closely proportional to the output voltage.

10-31. The tube of Fig. 6-10 is to be used as a Class A power amplifier with $E_b = 250$ and $E_c = -30$. If the grid is not to be driven positive, determine to a first approximation the proper load resistance, the power output, and the plate efficiency.

10-32. *a.* Using a set of plate-current–plate-voltage characteristics of an actual tube as assigned, draw a load line for an operating condition recommended for Class A power amplification, and from the resulting information, calculate maximum power output, second-harmonic distortion, and the actual plate efficiency. When calculating the d-c power supplied to the amplifier take into account the rectified plate current. Tabulate these results alongside those specified by the tube manufacturer for the recommended operating conditions.

b. Calculate approximate values of power output, plate efficiency, and load resistance according to Eqs. (10-19), (10-20), and (10-21) and tabulate along with results from (*a*).

Note: The curves can be a full-page blueprinted reproduction of characteristics of an actual tube in the tube handbook; alternatively, one can use the beam tube of Fig. 6-24 operated under the following conditions listed in the RCA Tube Handbook: $E_b = 250$, $E_{c2} = 250$, $E_c = -14$, peak signal amplitude = 14 volts, $R_L = 2500$, second-harmonic distortion = 10 per cent, power output = 6.5 watts, and rectified current = 7 ma.

10-33. Derive Eqs. (10-22), (10-23), and (10-24).

10-34. A particular output transformer is to be used to couple the plate circuit of a tube having $r_p = 800$ ohms to a load of 50 ohms. The transformer must offer a load impedance of 2500 ohms to the tube and give a response that does not drop to less than 70.7 per cent of the midrange value between 80 and 6000 cycles. Specify the required turn ratio, the largest permissible leakage inductance referred to the primary, and the lowest permissible primary inductance. Neglect resistance of windings.

10-35. An output transformer with the following constants is to be used with a type 6F6 tube operated as a Class A triode power amplifier (see Table 6-1, page 186):

Primary incremental inductance	9 henrys
Leakage inductance (referred to primary)	0.20 henry
Step-down ratio	30
Resistance, primary winding	300 ohms
Resistance, secondary winding	0.6 ohm
Load resistance	4 ohms

Determine the resistance that the transformer primary presents to the tube in the mid-frequency range, including the effect of winding resistance, and calculate and plot on a logarithmic frequency scale the frequency response that can be expected with this load resistance.

10-36. What will be the effect on the frequency response of a Class A transformer-coupled power amplifier if the load resistance is made (*a*) appreciably less than the design value, and (*b*) appreciably greater than the design value?

10-37. Derive Eq. (10-25).

10-38. Calculate the efficiency of the transformer of Prob. 10-35.

10-39. Explain why the shunt-feed inductance L in Fig. 10-16 can be designed to carry a very large d-c plate current and to have a very high incremental inductance, without adversely affecting the high-frequency response of the system.

10-40. In a particular Class A power output transformer which must meet quite severe requirements with respect to distortion and low-frequency falling off, it is found that the lowest frequency at which the transformer will be satisfactory is different for large-power output than for medium-power output, but is the same when the output power ranges from a very small value up to a medium value. Explain.

10-41. List the undesirable consequences that result in a push-pull connection when the individual tubes do not have identical characteristics.

10-42. *a.* Discuss the relative falling off at high frequencies of voltages e_1 and e_2 in Fig. 10-19*a*, assuming that these voltages are identical in the mid-frequency range.

b. Discuss the factors determining the relative high-frequency response of e_1 and e_2 in Fig. 10-19*b*, assuming $R_k = R_c$ and $R_{gl_1} = R_{gl_2}$.

10-43. Explain in detail the operation of the circuit of Fig. 10-19*d*.

10-44. In the circuit of Fig. 10-19*a*, the relative values of the two output voltages e_1 and e_2 will depend very greatly on the relative transconductances of tubes A_1 and A_2, whereas in the circuit of Fig. 10-19*c*, this is not true provided R_0 is large. Explain the reason for the difference.

10-45. An output transformer, designed for a push-pull Class A amplifier, will not give a correct impedance match to the load with a single output tube when one-half the center-tapped winding is used as a primary. Explain, and state where the tap should be placed.

10-46. *a.* Two tubes having the characteristics shown in Figs. 6-9 and 6-10 are to be used in a Class B amplifier with $E_b = 400$ volts. If the peak plate current is to be 75 ma, and is to be obtained by driving the control grid 10 volts positive, determine the total power output developed by the two tubes, the plate efficiency, the plate loss per tube, and the proper load resistance from plate to plate.

b. Repeat (*a*) for the restriction that the control grid is not to be driven positive, and tabulate the results alongside those of (*a*).

10-47. The beam tube of Fig. 6-24 is used in a Class B amplifier with a plate potential $E_b = 400$ volts and $E_{c2} = 250$. Determine the maximum power output obtainable from two tubes, the plate efficiency, the power loss per tube, and the proper load resistance from plate to plate (*a*) if the control grid is not to be driven positive, and (*b*) if the control grid can be driven 10 volts positive.

10-48. Prove that the plate efficiency and the power loss at the plate of each tube in an ideal Class B amplifier are both proportional to the amplitude of the exciting voltage when the exciting voltage is smaller than the value giving full power output.

10-49. Sketch plate-voltage and plate-current waves similar to those of Fig. 10-20, but applying to a Class B amplifier employing a beam tube, and having a load resistance so high that a virtual cathode forms within the tube.

10-50. Determine an appropriate grid bias for Class B operation of the tube of Fig. 6-9 when the plate-supply voltage is $E_b = 400$.

10-51. A Class AB amplifier operates as a Class A amplifier for small signal voltages. Explain.

10-52. Determine the equivalent values of plate resistance and amplification factor that are effective in the equivalent circuit of Fig. 10-24*c* when 6F6 and 6Y6 tubes of Table 6-1, page 186, are used as triode-connected cathode-follower amplifiers.

10-53. In a cathode-follower system, what effect does increasing the load impedance Z_L in Fig. 10-24 have on the minimum grid bias that will prevent the grid from being driven positive at full-power output?

10-54. In order to increase the power output that a cathode-follower system delivers to the load impedance Z_L, n tubes are connected in parallel.   How do the following properties of the resulting system vary with n: (a) output voltage, (b) output power, (c) equivalent amplification factor and plate resistance in Fig. 10-24c, (d) proper value of grid bias, (e) signal voltage for full output, and (f) high-frequency response? Give quantitative answers to (a), (b), and (c) and qualitative answers to (d), (e), and (f).

10-55. A cathode-follower amplifier employs a triode connected 6Y6 tube operated at a plate current of 61.5 ma (see Table 6-1, page 186).   The load impedance is 200 ohms supplied by the input of a transmission line.

  a. Determine the peak voltage that can be developed across the load, and the maximum power output that can be delivered to the load without excessive distortion.

  b. Calculate the signal voltage that must be applied to the control grid to develop the full output power.

  c. Specify the minimum value of grid bias that can be used without driving the control grid positive.

  d. From the data given in Table 6-1, determine the plate voltage that is required to give a plate current of 61.5 ma when the bias in c is used instead of the bias specified in the table.

  e. If the tube capacitance between cathode and ground together with other capacitances shunting the load totals 20 $\mu\mu$f, calculate the highest frequency for which the response will be not more than 3.0 db below the mid-frequency output.

10-56. In Fig. 10-26b calculate the reduction in energy transfer in decibels resulting from a two-stage resistance-capacitance filter in which $R_1 = 100,000$ ohms, and $C_1 = 2$ μf, for frequencies of 3, 10, and 60 cycles.

10-57. In decoupling filters intended to operate at the higher audio frequencies and at radio frequencies, it is common practice to replace the resistance R_1 in Fig. 10-26b with audio-frequency or radio-frequency choke coils.   Explain the advantages of such an arrangement for the higher frequencies.   Likewise explain why such an arrangement is less desirable than the use of resistances when the filter is to be effective at the lower audio frequencies.

10-58. Explain why the effectiveness of push-pull amplification in avoiding motorboating is greatly reduced if there is an appreciable dissymmetry between the two sides of the push-pull system.

10-59. a. What would be the objections to varying the amplification of a resistance-coupled amplifier by varying the grid-leak resistance?

  b. What would be the disadvantage of controlling the amplification of a transformer-coupled amplifier by varying a resistance shunted across the secondary.

  c. Would it be satisfactory to control the amplification of a transformer-coupled amplifier by varying the grid bias in order to change the transconductance of the amplifier tube?

10-60. Sketch the amplitude-modulated wave of Fig. 1-3, and then show qualitatively how the envelope would be modified by passage of this wave through (a) a volume compressor, and (b) a volume expander.

10-61. Explain how the tone-compensated volume control in Fig. 10-30 operates.

10-62. Explain why a transformer in a permalloy case has less hum pickup than the same transformer in a cast-iron case.

10-63. In a stage of resistance-coupled amplification in which shielding against electrostatic hum fields is very important, explain why the shielding of the leads and circuit elements associated with the control grid of the tube is much more important than the shielding of the leads and circuit elements associated with the plate of the same tube.

10-64. When microphonic troubles are encountered in a multistage audio-frequency system, it is ordinarily necessary to give special attention only to the input stage of the amplifier in order to minimize these effects.   Explain.

CHAPTER 11

NEGATIVE FEEDBACK IN AMPLIFIERS

11-1. Feedback Amplifiers—Fundamental Considerations Relating to Amplification and Distortion.[1] In the feedback amplifier, a voltage derived from the amplifier output is superimposed upon the amplifier input in such a way as to oppose the applied signal in the normal frequency range. By properly carrying out this operation, it is possible to reduce the distortion generated by the amplifier, to make the amplification substantially independent of the electrode voltages and tube constants, and to reduce greatly the phase and frequency distortion.

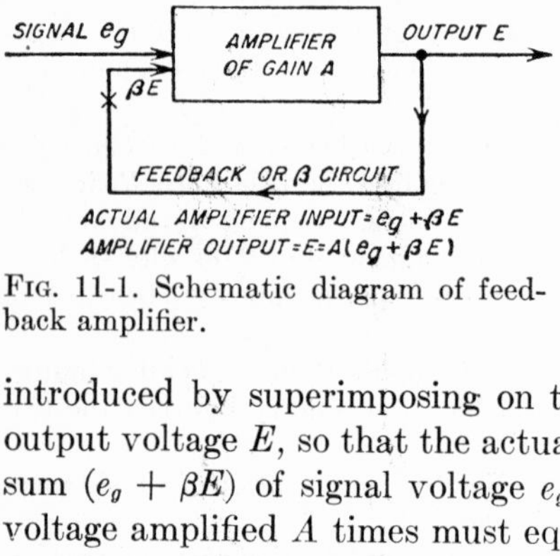

SIGNAL e_g → AMPLIFIER OF GAIN A → OUTPUT E

βE

FEEDBACK OR β CIRCUIT

ACTUAL AMPLIFIER INPUT=$e_g + \beta E$
AMPLIFIER OUTPUT=$E = A(e_g + \beta E)$

Fig. 11-1. Schematic diagram of feedback amplifier.

Effect of Negative Feedback on Voltage Amplification. The operation of a feedback amplifier can be understood by reference to the schematic diagram of Fig. 11-1. Here the amplifier gain in the absence of feedback is A. Feedback is then introduced by superimposing on the amplifier input a fraction β of the output voltage E, so that the actual input to the amplifier consists of the sum $(e_g + \beta E)$ of signal voltage e_g plus the feedback voltage βE. This voltage amplified A times must equal E, i.e.,

$$(e_g + \beta E)A = E \tag{11-1}$$

The voltage gain is by definition the ratio E/e_g of output to signal voltage. Hence solving Eq. (11-1) for E/e_g gives the gain in the presence of feedback, which is found to be

$$\left. \begin{array}{l} \text{Voltage gain, taking} \\ \text{into account feedback} \end{array} \right\} = \frac{A}{1 - A\beta} \tag{11-2}$$

The assumption as to signs in Eqs. (11-1) and (11-2) is such that $A\beta$ is negative for negative feedback, i.e., for feedback that opposes the applied signal.

The quantity $|A\beta|$ can be termed the *feedback factor*, and represents the amplitude of the feedback voltage superimposed upon e_g compared with

[1] Amplifiers employing negative feedback originated with H. S. Black of the Bell Telephone Laboratories; see his classic paper, Stabilized Feedback Amplifiers, *Elec. Eng.*, vol. 53, p. 114, January, 1934.

the actual voltage applied to the input terminals.[1] Thus, if $A\beta = -50$, then for each millivolt existing between the input terminals, the feedback voltage will be 50 mv, and if the phase is such as to give negative feedback, a signal of 51 mv will be required to produce 1 mv at the amplifier input terminals.

It is often helpful to regard the feedback factor $A\beta$ as the transmission around the circuit consisting of the amplifier plus the feedback (or β) circuit. This complete circuit is often termed the *feedback loop;* its transmission can be measured experimentally by opening the loop at some convenient point such as $\times$ in Fig. 11-1, applying a voltage to the amplifier side of $\times$, and observing the voltage that appears on the feedback side of $\times$. The vector ratio of these two voltages is then $A\beta$. Thus $A\beta = 12\underline{/160°}$ means that the voltage amplification around the feedback loop is 12, and that the phase shift is such that the feedback is within 20° of being exactly negative. When this particular value of feedback is present, then, from Eq. (11-2), the voltage gain is

$$A/(1 - 12\underline{/160°}) = (0.077\underline{/19°}) \times A$$

as compared with the gain A in the absence of feedback.

Examination of Eq. (11-2) shows that, if the feedback factor $A\beta$ is negative, the amplification is reduced by the presence of feedback. Furthermore, when $|A\beta| >> 1$, Eq. (11-2) reduces to

$$\text{Amplification with large feedback} = -\frac{1}{\beta} \qquad (11\text{-}3)$$

Expressed in words, Eq. (11-3) states that, when the feedback factor $|A\beta|$ is large, the effective amplification depends only upon the fraction β of the output voltage that is superimposed upon the amplifier input, and *is substantially independent of the gain A actually produced by the amplifier itself.*

This remarkable behavior is a result of the fact that, when the feedback factor $|A\beta|$ is large, the voltage actually applied to the amplifier input terminals represents a small difference between relatively large signal and feedback voltages. A moderate change in the amplification A therefore produces a large change in the difference between signal and feedback voltages, thereby altering the actual input voltage in a manner that tends to correct for the alteration in amplification.[2] Thus, in the amplifier

---

[1] The amount of feedback is commonly expressed in terms of the resulting reduction in amplification. Thus 20 db feedback means that the actual gain as calculated by Eq. (11-2) is 20 db less than A, or a voltage gain of $A/10$. This corresponds to $A\beta = -9$.

[2] The consequences of this action, when generalized, lead to the rule that, when the feedback factor $|A\beta|$ is large, the output voltage E assumes whatever magnitude, phase position, wave shape, etc., are required to make the feedback voltage βE opposite in polarity and almost, but not quite, equal in magnitude to the signal voltage applied to the feedback amplifier.

considered above where $A\beta = -50$, if the amplification A were halved by a change in design, it would then take 2 mv across the input terminals to deliver the same output as before. With β unchanged, the feedback voltage would still be 50 mv, so it would require a signal of $50 + 2 = 52$ mv, instead of the previous 51 mv, to produce the same output. Thus a 2 per cent loss in effective over-all amplification results when the gain A is reduced by 50 per cent.

Inasmuch as the quantity β depends upon circuit elements, such as resistances, that are permanent, the amplification with large feedback is substantially independent of the tube characteristics and electrode voltages. Furthermore, Eq. (11-3) shows that the amplification with large feedback is inversely proportional to β, so that, if the fraction β of the output voltage that is superimposed upon the input is obtained by a resistance network, the amplification will be substantially independent of frequency and will have negligible phase shift. On the other hand, if it is desired to have the amplification vary with frequency in some particular way, this can be readily accomplished by making the β (or feedback) circuit have the same transmission-loss characteristic as the desired gain characteristic. It is to be kept in mind, however, that this dependence of the effective amplification on β, to the exclusion of all other considerations, occurs only when the amount of feedback is large, i.e., only when $|A\beta| >> 1$.

Effect of Negative Feedback on Distortion and Hum. The presence of negative feedback also greatly reduces the amplitude distortion appearing at the output terminals of an amplifier. Assuming that d represents the amount of distortion present in the output of a given amplifier in the absence of feedback, the distortion *with sufficient excitation to produce the same output voltage E* will then be less than d. This is because some of the distortion is fed back to the amplifier input through the feedback circuit and reamplified in such a way as to tend to cancel out the distortion originally generated.

To analyze this situation, let D represent the distortion voltage actually appearing in the output in the presence of feedback. The distortion voltage applied to the amplifier input by the feedback circuit is then βD, and this is amplified A times by the amplifier. The total distortion output is therefore the distortion d actually generated in the amplifier plus the amplified feedback distortion βDA. That is, $D = d + \beta DA$, or

$$\left.\begin{array}{r}\text{Distortion with} \\ \text{feedback}\end{array}\right\} = D = \frac{d}{1 - A\beta}$$
$$= \frac{\text{distortion in absence of feedback}}{1 - A\beta} \quad (11\text{-}4)$$

This shows that the amplitude distortion appearing in the output is reduced by the factor $(1 - A\beta)$. If $|A\beta|$ is made large by employing a large amount of feedback, the result is a very great reduction in the ratio of distortion to desired output.

Comparison of Eqs. (11-2) and (11-4) shows that feedback reduces the distortion for a given output voltage by the same factor that it reduces the amplification. Hence to reduce the distortion 20 db requires that the signal voltage driving the amplifier be 20 db larger than required with no feedback; alternatively, the amplifier must be so designed that the gain with the feedback disconnected is 20 db greater than the gain actually required.

Hum and other extraneous noise introduced into a given amplifier from an external source is treated by negative feedback just as though it were distortion generated within the amplifier. Negative feedback thus reduces such effects, with the amount of reduction being given by Eq. (11-4). An important consequence of this action is that d-c plate voltage for the power tube of an amplifier employing feedback can be obtained from a poorly filtered (and hence inexpensive) power-supply system; in such a case the feedback is depended upon to reduce the power-line hum in the amplifier output to a reasonable value.[1,2]

11-2. Conditions for Avoiding Oscillations in Feedback Amplifiers.[3] In order to realize the advantages of negative feedback, the amplifier and its feedback must be so arranged that oscillations do not occur. In the normal range of frequencies this presents no problem, because here the circuit arrangements are such that the feedback is negative. However, at both very low and very high frequencies, the amplifier stages produce phase shifts that cause the phase of the feedback factor $A\beta$ to differ from the phase corresponding to negative feedback. This introduces the possibility of $A\beta$ reversing its polarity and thereby introducing positive feedback that directly assists in the production of oscillations. To be unconditionally stable, i.e., free of oscillations under all conditions, it is necessary that the circuit arrangements be such that the feedback factor $A\beta$ have a magnitude less than unity under conditions where the phase

---

[1] This is true only when the system is so arranged that the hum voltage fed back is a fraction of the hum voltage actually associated with the load; for further discussion of this point see Geoffrey Builder, The Effect of Negative Feedback on Power-supply Hum in Audio-frequency Amplifiers, *Proc. IRE* (*Waves and Electrons Sec.*), vol. 34, p. 140W, March, 1946.

[2] Negative feedback will not, however, improve the *signal-to-noise ratio* of an amplifier when the noise is introduced into the system at the amplifier input, as by a hum voltage induced in the input transformer by stray 60-cycle magnetic fields. This is because the feedback reduces the amplification of the signal by exactly the same amount that it reduces the noise, thus leaving the ratio unchanged in these circumstances.

[3] An excellent tutorial discussion of this subject from the point of view of modern network theory is given by William A. Lynch, The Stability Problem in Feedback Amplifiers, *Proc. IRE*, vol. 39, p. 1000, September, 1951.

shift of the feedback factor $A\beta$ differs by 180° from the negative value applying to the mid-frequency range.

The situation existing with respect to oscillations in a feedback amplifier is often shown by plotting a curve, called a Nyquist diagram, showing on the complex plane the variation in the transmission $A\beta$ around the feedback loop as the frequency is varied from zero to infinity. Typical diagrams of this type are shown in Fig. 11-2. At a the amplifier is unconditionally stable because when the phase angle of $A\beta$ is zero (positive feedback), the magnitude of $A\beta$ is less than unity. The diagram at b is the same as a except that the amplification has been increased until $|A\beta| > 1$ when the phase angle is zero; in this case oscillations occur.

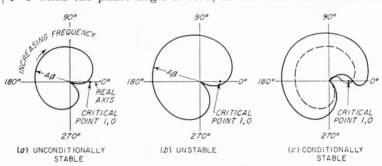

(a) UNCONDITIONALLY STABLE

(b) UNSTABLE

(c) CONDITIONALLY STABLE

Fig. 11-2. Typical Nyquist diagrams.

The case shown by the solid curve in c represents *conditional stability*. Here oscillations do not occur because the curve does not enclose the point 1,0; however, if the gain A is now reduced so that conditions correspond to the dotted line, then oscillations will start, because the point 1,0 is now enclosed by the $A\beta$ curve.[1]

The phase-shift and amplification characteristics of the individual stages of the amplifier are, therefore, of particular importance in connection with feedback systems since they affect the feedback factor through their relation to A. It is characteristic of all amplifier stages that the falling off in amplification at both low and high frequencies is accompanied by a phase shift with respect to the phase relation existing in the middle range of frequencies where the amplification is substantially constant with frequency. Also, in all amplifiers except the direct-coupled amplifier, the amplification drops off to zero at extremely low and extremely high frequencies. In the case of a single stage of resistance coupling with adequate screen and bias by-passing, the phase shift reaches a maximum value of ±90° at the extreme frequencies where the amplification drops to zero. When screen- or bias-impedance effects are

[1] The mathematical theory of this behavior is given by H. Nyquist, Regeneration Theory, *Bell System Tech. J.*, vol. 11, p. 126, January, 1932; also see J. G. Kreer and L. A. Ware, Regeneration Theory and Experiment, *Proc. IRE*, vol. 22, p. 1191, October, 1934.

present, the maximum phase shift may be greater than 90° at low frequencies but will always be less than 180°. Similarly, with transformer-coupled voltage amplifiers, the maximum phase shift at low frequencies is 90° not including bias- and screen-impedance effects, while at very high frequencies it will reach 180°, as is apparent in Fig. 8-16. A power-amplifier stage employing an output transformer will have phase shift of $\pm 90°$ if shunt feed is not employed, while with shunt feed, the phase shift can reach 180° at low frequencies. If, in addition, screen- or bias-impedance effects are present, the maximum phase shift at low frequencies will be increased and can theoretically even exceed 180° for a single shunt-feed power stage, although this very seldom happens in practice.

The tendency of a feedback amplifier to oscillate becomes greater as the number of amplifier stages involved is increased. Thus when the feedback loop includes only a single stage of amplification, the phase shift introduced in $A\beta$ by this stage will ordinarily be less than $\pm 180°$ for all frequencies, and oscillation troubles are not encountered. However, when a two-stage amplifier is involved, it frequently happens that the total phase shift will reach 180° under conditions where the amplification is small but not zero. Hence two-stage amplifiers will often oscillate when the feedback factor $|A\beta|$ is very large, but will be stable when $|A\beta|$ is small or moderate. When feedback is applied to amplifiers having more than two stages, oscillation troubles can always be expected, even with moderately small feedback, unless special design procedures have been employed to keep the maximum phase shift of $A\beta$ below $\pm 180°$ until the frequency is so low (or so high) that the magnitude of the transmission $|A\beta|$ around the feedback loop has dropped to less than unity.

11-3. Design of Feedback Systems as Influenced by Oscillation Considerations. *Relation of Phase Shift to Transmission Characteristics.* Oscillation problems in feedback amplifiers can be minimized by design procedures that make use of the relation that exists between the phase shift and the transmission characteristics of an electrical system.

In networks of the type encountered in feedback amplifiers, it can be shown that a definite relation exists between the *variation* of the amplitude of $A\beta$ with frequency and the phase angle of $A\beta$ as a function of frequency.[1] Thus, if the amplitude variations of $A\beta$ are completely speci-

---

[1] The exceptions to this are where circuit elements with distributed constants are involved, such as transmission lines, or where the system contains an all-pass filter. The relation between amplitude variations and phase shift was first developed by H. W. Bode, Relations Between Attenuation and Phase in Feedback Amplifier Design, *Bell System Tech. J.*, vol. 19, p. 421, July, 1940; also see U.S. Patent 2,123,178. The subject is further developed in H. W. Bode, "Network Analysis and Feedback Amplifier Design," D. Van Nostrand Company, Inc., New York, 1945.

The relation existing between amplitude and phase of transmission is of course not limited to feedback or vacuum-tube systems, but applies to any transmission system (even mechanical or electromechanical) that does not have distributed con-

fied as a function of frequency, then the phase shift of $A\beta$ is thereby determined, and vice versa. Alternatively, one may specify the variation in relative amplitude of $A\beta$ over a portion of the frequency range, and the phase shift over the remainder of the frequency range, and in doing so actually be specifying both amplitude variation and phase shift of the transmission $A\beta$ of the feedback loop over the entire frequency range.

The derivation of the actual relation between amplitude variation and phase shift of transmission as a function of frequency is a complicated mathematical operation; however, the result is not at all difficult to understand. The general rule is that phase shift depends upon the variation in the amplitude α of transmission with frequency,[1] and has a polarity depending upon the sign of the slope of the transmission characteristic. If the transmission is constant with frequency, then the phase shift will be zero. However, if the amplitude of transmission α varies at a constant rate from zero to infinite frequency, then the phase shift will have a value exactly proportional to the slope of the amplitude characteristic such that

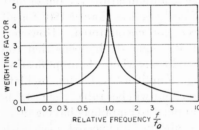

Fig. 11-3. Weighting factor giving relative influence of the slope of the transmission characteristic on the phase shift, as the frequency differs increasingly from the frequency f_0 at which the phase shift occurs.

$$\left.\begin{array}{c}\text{Phase shift}\\\text{in radians}\end{array}\right\} = \frac{\pi}{12}\frac{d\alpha}{du} \quad (11\text{-}5)$$

Here $d\alpha/du$ is the variation in the amplitude of transmission (i.e., change in amplitude of $A\beta$) expressed in decibels change in transmission per octave change in frequency.[2] Thus a slope of 12 db per octave corresponds to a phase shift of 180°. Finally, if the slope of the curve giving the amplitude of transmission is not constant, then the slope at a frequency f influences the phase shift at f_0 in accordance with the weighting factor[3] given in Fig. 11-3. It is apparent from this curve that the slope of α at frequencies near f_0 has more effect on the phase shift at f_0 than does slope at more remote frequencies, but that some influence is exercised on the phase shift by the slope of the amplitude characteristic α at frequencies that differ from f_0 by as much as several octaves.

Examples of the relation between phase shift and the variation of

---

stants or contain an all-pass filter. Systems for which the relation does apply are sometimes termed *minimum phase-shift circuits.*

[1] In the case of feedback systems $\alpha = |AB|$.

[2] This method of expressing slope means the change in amplitude of transmission, expressed in decibels, for a change in frequency corresponding to a doubling or halving of the frequency.

[3] From Bode, *loc. cit.* (either reference).

amplitude of transmission are shown in Fig. 11-4 for a number of simple cases. Case *a* will be recognized as the series resonance curve plotted in decibels. Similarly, *b* corresponds to the effects introduced by a screen or bias impedance (see Figs. 8-11 and 8-12), while *e* and *f* correspond, respectively, to the low-frequency and high-frequency behavior of the resistance-coupled amplifier shown in Fig. 8-9. It will be noted that in each case the phase shift is directly related to the slope of the amplitude characteristic as weighted in accordance with Fig. 11-3. Thus in Fig.

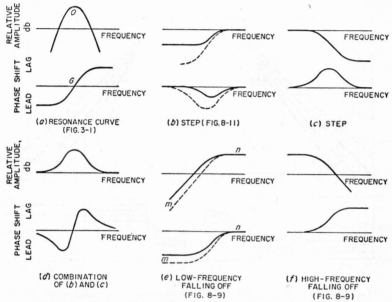

Fig. 11-4. Examples of the relationship that exists between phase shift and the variation in transmission.

11-4*e*, the phase shift at low frequencies approaches a constant value because the slope of the amplitude characteristic in the region *m* is a constant; at the same time the phase shift at high frequencies approaches zero because the slope in region *n* is zero. Again in Fig. 11-4*a* the phase shift at low and high frequencies approaches constant values of opposite sign because the slopes of the amplitude characteristics in these regions are constant but of opposite sign. However, the phase shift at *O* is zero because (1) at this frequency the slope of the amplitude characteristic is zero, and (2) the slopes at other frequencies symmetrically above and below *O* are equal but of opposite sign, so their influences cancel out when weighted according to Fig. 11-3. Similar lines of reasoning can be used to relate the phase shift and amplitude variations in the other cases shown in Fig. 11-4.

Idealized Feedback Characteristics. The relation that exists between phase shift and variation in amplitude of transmission makes it possible to formulate a general method of designing feedback amplifiers that will ensure the absence of oscillations. This involves appropriately shaping the curve giving the *magnitude* of $A\beta$ as a function of frequency. It is not necessary to pay any attention to the phase shift of $A\beta$ in carrying out the design, since the phase shift of $A\beta$ is determined by the amplitude variations of $A\beta$. It is therefore possible to guarantee that the phase shift will be less than 180° at all frequencies for which $|A\beta| \geqslant 1$, merely by properly controlling the variation of $|A\beta|$ with frequency.

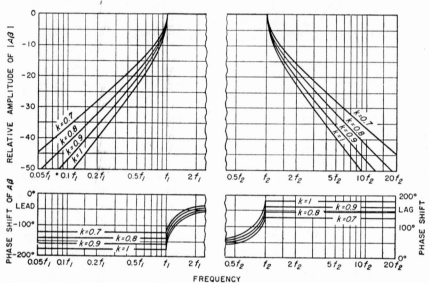

FREQUENCY

Fig. 11-5. Universal curves giving ideal low-frequency and high-frequency cutoff characteristics for feedback factor $|A\beta|$. Here k is a factor such that the phase shift at low and high frequencies is 180k (i.e., for $k = 0.8$ the phase shift is 144°).

An ideal feedback system can be regarded as one in which the magnitude of the feedback factor $A\beta$ is constant in the band of frequencies to be amplified, and then at higher and lower frequencies diminishes in magnitude as rapidly as possible, while still keeping the phase shift less than 180° by a safe margin. Idealized feedback-loop transmission characteristics based on this principle are shown in Fig. 11-5.[1] Here k is the factor by which the actual phase shift at frequencies above f_2 and below f_1 is less than 180°, and represents a safety factor. Thus the curve for $k = 0.8$ corresponds to a maximum phase shift of $0.8 \times 180° = 144°$; this is 36° less than the value that makes oscillations possible. For frequencies between f_1 and f_2 the phase shift will then be less than $\pm 144°$.

By designing a feedback amplifier so that for frequencies below f_1 and above f_2, the slope of the $A\beta$ characteristic is less than the slope of the

[1] Taken from Bode, *loc. cit.* (either reference).

ideal curve for $k = 1$ in Fig. 11-5, one can be assured that oscillations will not occur. An $A\beta$ characteristic that meets this requirement is indicated by the dotted curve of Fig. 11-6, which applies to a two-stage resistance-coupled amplifier that is free of screen- and bias-impedance effects, and which obtains feedback by means of a resistance network.[1]

The ideal characteristic of Fig. 11-5, while showing one way to avoid oscillations, has serious practical disadvantages when used as a guide in the design of practical feedback systems, particularly those involving three or more stages of amplification. This arises from the fact that this ideal characteristic calls for a slope of $12k$ db per octave at very high and very low frequencies, and *requires that this slope be continued to zero frequency and infinite frequency.* However, in all actual amplifiers having three or more stages (and in some two-stage amplifiers as well) the amplification falls off more rapidly than 12 db per octave at very low and very high frequencies. Thus what is really desired is a design procedure whereby the curve

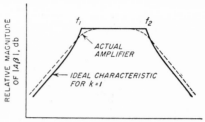

Fig. 11-6. Ideal characteristic of Fig. 11-5 for $k = 1.0$, together with the characteristic of an actual two-stage resistance-coupled amplifier that is free of screen- and bias-impedance effects.

of loop transmission $|A\beta|$ can be shaped over a limited range of frequencies in such a way that the phase shift will be safely less than 180° until $|A\beta|$ is less than unity, while outside of this range of frequencies $|A\beta|$ is allowed to fall at a more rapid rate that is dictated by the amplifier characteristics.

Practical Form of Ideal Feedback Characteristic. A practical way of meeting these requirements consists in modifying the ideal characteristic of Fig. 11-5 as illustrated in Fig. 11-7a. Here region $3'34566'$ is identical with the ideal characteristic of Fig. 11-5; however, at the points 3 and 4, where the transmission $A\beta$ around the feedback loop has dropped to a value of unity, the ideal curve is discontinued and flat steps 23 and 67 are introduced as shown. At frequencies below f_2 and above f_7, the magnitude of $|A\beta|$ is allowed to fall off in accordance with the normal variation in amplifier amplification that occurs at very very high and very very low frequencies. The slope of the $|A\beta|$ curve at these extreme frequencies is termed the *asymptotic* slope, and will in general be higher than 12 db per octave. The purpose of the steps 23 and 67 is to prevent the phase shift in the region 3456 from being adversely affected by the excessive slope of the $A\beta$ characteristic in the regions 12 and 78. The steps achieve this

---

[1] When the feedback is introduced by a resistance network, which is usually the case, then β is independent of frequency, and all variations that occur in the magnitude of the transmission $|A\beta|$ of the feedback loop are a result of variations in the amplification A with frequency.

result when their length satisfies the relation

$$f_2 = \frac{12k}{\text{slope below } f_2 \text{ in db per octave}} f_3 \qquad (11\text{-}6a)$$

$$f_7 = \frac{\text{slope above } f_7 \text{ in db per octave}}{12k} f_6 \qquad (11\text{-}6b)$$

The notation is illustrated in Fig. 11-7, with the addition that k has the same meaning as in Fig. 11-5.

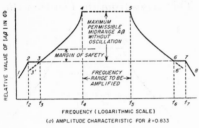

(a) AMPLITUDE CHARACTERISTIC FOR $k = 0.833$

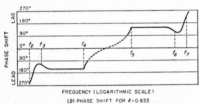

(b) PHASE SHIFT FOR $k = 0.833$

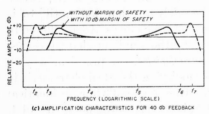

(c) AMPLIFICATION CHARACTERISTICS FOR 40 db FEEDBACK

FIG. 11-7. Modified form of ideal $A\beta$ characteristic that permits $A\beta$ to drop off rapidly below 2 and above 7 without introducing excessive phase shift in the frequency range 234567.

The phase shift associated with the amplitude characteristic of Fig. 11-7a is shown in Fig. 11-7b. It is seen that in the frequency range between f_2 and f_7 the phase shift is everywhere less than 180°. This system will accordingly be free of oscillations as long as the feedback factor $|A\beta|$ in the useful frequency range 45 does not exceed the "maximum permissible" value marked on the figure; only when the mid-frequency feedback factor is greater than this value is it possible for the magnitude $|A\beta|$ of the transmission around the feedback loop to exceed unity at a frequency for which the phase shift is 180°.

The amplification characteristic corresponding to Fig. 11-7a and b as calculated by Eq. (11-2) for 40 db feedback[1] is shown in Fig. 11-7c for resistive feedback such that β is independent of frequency. It is to be noted that the feedback causes the amplification to be substantially constant to frequencies much lower than f_4 and much higher than f_5. However, outside the range $f_4 f_5$ the feedback is progressively less than 40 db,

[1] The relation between $A\beta$ and the reduction in voltage gain, assuming that the feedback is exactly negative (i.e., $\beta = 180°$), is from Eq. (11-2)

$$\text{Reduction in gain in db} = F_0 = 20 \log_{10} (1 + A\beta) \qquad (11\text{-}7)$$

Thus for 40 db feedback (e.g., a gain reduction of 40 db), $(1 + A\beta) = 100$, and $A\beta = 99$. On the curve of Fig. 11-7a, which gives relative values, this means that for 40 db feedback, steps 23 and 67 would occur where $A\beta$ was $\frac{1}{99}$ of the midrange value, or 39.91 db below the midrange value.

with consequent reduction in the suppression of distortion, in the stability of amplification, etc.

Asymptotic Slope of Amplifiers. The asymptotic slope of the $A\beta$ characteristic of the actual amplifier system can be estimated by inspecting the circuits. Each resistance- or impedance-coupled stage will contribute 6 db per octave to the asymptotic slope at high frequencies, as will each output transformer fed from a tube and having a resistance load. An interstage coupling transformer will add 12 db per octave to the slope at high frequencies. Similarly at low frequencies each grid leak–condenser combination will contribute 6 db per octave to the slope, as will each transformer (output, input, or interstage) excited from a resistance source, such as a tube or line. Transformers with resonated primaries, or shunt-feed systems, can contribute 12 db per octave at low frequencies.

Frequency Range over Which Control of $|A\beta|$ Is Required. The frequency range, represented by f_2f_4 and f_5f_7 in Fig. 11-7a, over which the transmission characteristics $|A\beta|$ of the feedback loop must be controlled if oscillations are to be avoided is surprisingly great, and, together with the loss in gain resulting from the use of negative feedback, represents the price paid in order to obtain the benefits of negative feedback. The control must exist over approximately one octave for each 10 db of usable feedback, plus about one or two octaves extra as a margin of safety to take care of failure to realize exactly the practical ideal characteristic of Fig. 11-7a. Thus in the example described below, where 30 db of feedback is required in an amplifier having a useful frequency range of 100 to 10,000 cycles, it is necessary to control the $|A\beta|$ curve outside of this range down to 4.4 cycles and up to 220,000 cycles; this is between four and five octaves beyond the range 100 to 10,000 cycles.

11-4. Practical Application of Design Principles. The practical design of a feedback system based on the idealized characteristic of Fig. 11-7 can best be understood by considering an actual example.

Example. A resistance-coupled amplifier consisting of four identical stages is to amplify frequencies in the range 100 to 10,000 cycles. The amplifier is so designed that the 70.7 per cent response points of the individual stages in the absence of feedback are 25 and 40,000 cycles; the amplifier circuit arrangements are such that no screen-grid or bias-impedance effects are present. It is planned to use 30 db of negative feedback in the mid-frequency range. In order to be certain that this amount of feedback can always be achieved without danger of oscillation, the system is to be designed with a 10-db factor of safety; i.e., the design must permit the feedback to be raised to 40 db before the onset of oscillations. The circuit for introducing the negative feedback is to be an electrical network consisting of resistors, so β is a constant independent of frequency; all variations in $|A\beta|$ are hence due to changes in the amplification A.

Solution. (1) First, calculate and draw the curve of relative amplifier amplification $|A|$ in decibels as a function of frequency; this is shown by the dotted curve in Fig. 11-8a; since β is resistive, this curve also gives relative $|A\beta|$. (2) Next, draw a theoretical ideal $|A\beta|$ characteristic corresponding to a maximum phase shift less than 180° by an appropriate factor of safety using data obtained from Fig. 11-5. Such a curve is given by 3'34566' in Fig. 11-8a for a maximum phase shift of 144° (k = 0.8); this corresponds to a safety factor of 36°. This curve is plotted so that its midrange amplitude is the same as that of the curve giving the amplification $|A|$ of the actual amplifier. (3) Steps 23 and 67 are now introduced into this theoretically ideal characteristic at both high and low frequencies to convert the theoretically ideal characteristic to the practical ideal of Fig. 11-7. These steps are placed at points 3 and 6 on the theoretical ideal curve such that the distance F_0 as defined in Eq. (11-7) is 39.9 db (corresponding to 40 db feedback); from Fig. 11-5 the frequencies corresponding to 3 and 6 are 0.11 × 100 = 11 cycles, and 8.8 × 10,000 = 88,000 cycles, respectively. The length of the steps is now calculated with the aid of Eq. (11-6).

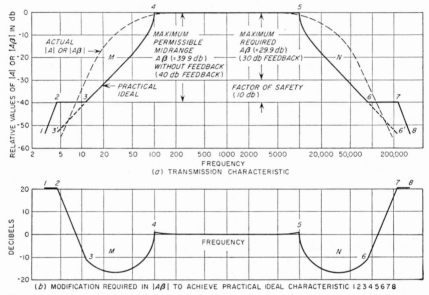

FIG. 11-8. Example of an amplifier designed to provide 30 db of useful feedback with margins of safety for amplitude and phase of 10 db and 36°, respectively.

Since the asymptotic slope of a simple resistance-coupled stage is 6 db per octave, the asymptotic slope for the four-stage system is 24 db per octave. Hence

$$f_d = 11 \times 12 \times 0.8/24 = 4.4 \text{ cycles}$$
$$f_i = 88,000 \times 24/(12 \times 0.8) = 220,000 \text{ cycles}$$

(4) These steps are drawn in as shown in Fig. 11-8a, and the practical ideal curve is completed by adding the asymptotic sections 12 and 78 with slopes of 24 db per octave. (5) The final step in the design procedure consists in introducing correcting networks in the feedback loop (i.e., in either A or β) for the purpose of modifying the actual $|A\beta|$ characteristic to give the desired shape 12345678. Methods of introducing the equalization are discussed below. Examination of Fig. 11-8b, giving the difference between the actual and the desired characteristic, shows that in this particular case, the required modification of the original $|A\beta|$ curve consists primarily in decreasing the gain in regions M and N in such a way as to increase the slope of the $|A\beta|$ charac-teristic in these regions, and at the same time introducing the flat step and raising the

gain in regions 23 and 67.   (6) As a check to ensure that the actual design characteristic has been obtained, the $|A\beta|$ characteristic of the final equalized system is sometimes measured experimentally.   This is particularly helpful in diagnosing difficulties when the amplifier is found to oscillate with substantially smaller values of feedback than should be the case.[1,2]

It is to be noted that in this particular amplifier it has been necessary to control the $|A\beta|$ characteristic quite rigidly over frequencies from 4.4 to 220,000 cycles in order to achieve 30 db of useful feedback over a frequency range 100 to 10,000 cycles with an adequate factor of safety. The design effort thereby involved, together with the 30-db gain reduction, is the price paid for realizing the benefits associated with 30 db of negative feedback.

Methods of Modifying $|A\beta|$ Characteristic to Satisfy Requirements of Feedback Systems.   The shape of the curve giving the magnitude of $A\beta$ as a function of frequency can be controlled by (1) obtaining the feedback by means of a resistance network so that β is independent of frequency, and then adding correcting networks to the amplifier stages so that A varies in the required manner; (2) allowing the amplification A to remain unchanged, and designing the feedback network so that β varies with frequency in such a way that the magnitude of the feedback factor $|A\beta|$ has the required characteristics; (3) combining these two methods so that part of the correction is carried out in the amplifier, and part in the feedback circuit.

The most sophisticated method of obtaining the required $|A\beta|$ characteristic is to use modern network theory to synthesize a system having the prescribed variation of amplitude with frequency.   It is possible in this way to approximate the practical ideal characteristic to any desired extent, although the electrical circuits called for become more complex the closer the approximation desired.   This represents the best approach when the design situation is difficult, or when optimum performance is important, but has the disadvantage of requiring a high level of competence in network theory.

Most feedback amplifiers are, however, designed without benefit of any specialized knowledge of network theory, by combining some degree of ingenuity with generous safety factors to make up for the lack of close design.   A typical procedure consists in modifying the amplification by inserting in the amplifier correcting networks designed on a cut-and-try basis so that the $|A\beta|$ curve acquires a shape having a general resemblance to the practical ideal curve.

[1] Such measurements are discussed by F. E. Terman and J. M. Pettit "Electronic Measurements," p. 353, McGraw-Hill Book Company, Inc., New York, 1952.

[2] When a feedback amplifier oscillates under these conditions, one can assume that the actual curve giving $|A\beta|$ has an excessive slope in the vicinity of the frequency of oscillation.   By taking advantage of this fact it is often possible to diagnose and cure the difficulty without making any measurements except of the oscillation frequency.

Examples of simple correcting networks useful in modifying the shape of the $|A|$ characteristic are illustrated in Fig. 11-9.[1,2]   Introduction into the amplifier of a correcting network having a step characteristic (as at Fig. 11-9a and b) will change the slope of the $|A|$ characteristic in the

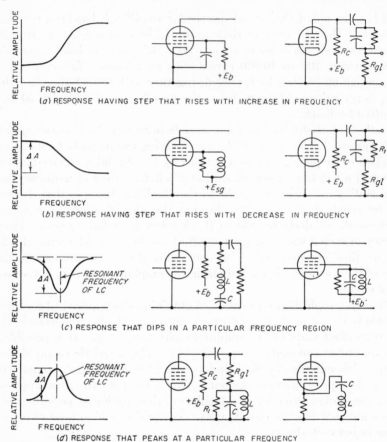

(a) RESPONSE HAVING STEP THAT RISES WITH INCREASE IN FREQUENCY

(b) RESPONSE HAVING STEP THAT RISES WITH DECREASE IN FREQUENCY

(c) RESPONSE THAT DIPS IN A PARTICULAR FREQUENCY REGION

(d) RESPONSE THAT PEAKS AT A PARTICULAR FREQUENCY

FIG. 11-9. Typical arrangements for modifying the amplification characteristic $|A|$ of an amplifier in order to shape the $|A\beta|$ characteristic.

range of frequencies in which the step occurs; a succession of such networks appropriately staggered in frequency can be used to change the slope in a controlled way over an extended range of frequencies.

A step in the $|A\beta|$ curve can be introduced in the manner illustrated in Fig. 11-10.   Assume that 5678 is the desired idealized characteristic.

[1] A comprehensive discussion of such network elements, including their use in controlling the $|A\beta|$ characteristic of a feedback amplifier system and the necessary design formulas, is given by Vincent Learned, Corrective Networks for Feedback Circuits, *Proc. IRE*, vol. 32, p. 403, July, 1944.

[2] It will be noted that correcting network a is a resistance-capacitance screen impedance and so can be designed with the aid of Fig. 8-11.

The first stage in approximating this curve is to correct the actual characteristic so that it becomes the smoothly falling curve 569. This is then combined with a correcting characteristic of the type illustrated in Fig. 11-9d, and indicated by *EFGH* in Fig. 11-10b. The resultant curve 5'6'7'8' is thereby obtained as the sum of 5678 and *EFGH*. In order for

the step in 5'6'7'8' to be flat at the frequency f_{67} midway between f_6 and f_7 and to be of the proper width, it is necessary (1) that the resonant frequency f_r of the resonant correcting system be slightly greater than f_7, and (2) that the Q and L/C ratio for the correcting network in Fig. 11-9d be such as to make $\Delta A = \Delta A'$ in Fig. 11-10, and at the same time cause the slope of *EFGH* at f_{67} to be equal and opposite to the slope of 569 at f_{67}.

It is also possible to modify the shape of the $|A\beta|$ characteristic by staggering the 70.7 per cent points of the individual stages. This expedient is particularly useful when the maximum value of feedback required is small to moderate, such as 10 to 20 db. In such circumstances, oscillations can generally be avoided by so proportioning the individual stages that the falling off in amplification of one of the stages equals the desired midrange feedback before any one of the remaining stages undergoes more than 1 or 2 db falling off in its response. In this way the

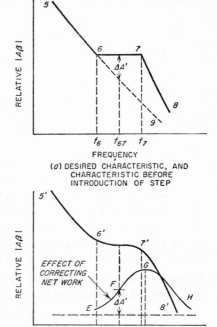

(a) DESIRED CHARACTERISTIC, AND CHARACTERISTIC BEFORE INTRODUCTION OF STEP

(b) STEP CHARACTERISTIC INTRODUCED BY COMBINING CORRECTING NETWORK WITH CURVE 569

Fig. 11-10. Example showing how a flat step can be introduced in the $|A\beta|$ characteristic by the use of a correcting network of the type illustrated in Fig. 11-9d.

slope of the over-all $|A\beta|$ characteristic will not be appreciably more than the slope of $|A|$ for the narrow-band amplifier stage until the over-all $|A\beta|$ has dropped to a value less than the desired midrange feedback. This avoids oscillations for values of feedback of interest, since the slope in $|A\beta|$ introduced by a single stage corresponds to a phase shift that is less than 180°.

The extent to which the actual $|A\beta|$ characteristic of the system must approximate the practical ideal characteristic in order to avoid oscillations depends upon the factor of safety that the design provides for the phase shift and in the total amount of feedback. If these safety margins are reasonably large, it is only necessary that the actual slope everywhere in the frequency range 3456 in Fig. 11-7 be less than 12 db per octave, and that steps 23 and 67 be supplied in approximate form as illustrated in Fig. 11-10.

11-5. Feedback Amplifiers—Miscellaneous Aspects. *Practical Circuit Arrangements for Producing Negative Feedback.* Typical feedback amplifier circuits are shown in Figs. 11-11 to 11-13. In order to simplify these

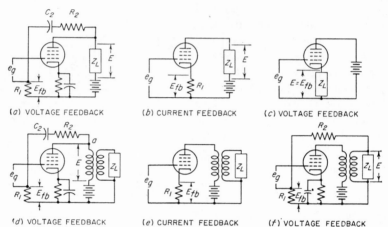

(a) VOLTAGE FEEDBACK   *(b)* CURRENT FEEDBACK   *(c)* VOLTAGE FEEDBACK

(d) VOLTAGE FEEDBACK   *(e)* CURRENT FEEDBACK   *(f)* VOLTAGE FEEDBACK

FIG. 11-11. Typical feedback circuits involving a single stage of amplification. Note that circuit *c* is the cathode follower of Fig. 10-12.

diagrams, means for obtaining bias and screen-grid voltages, etc., have been omitted. A uniform notation is employed as follows:

R_1 = resistance across which feedback voltage E_{fb} is developed

R_2 = resistance that, in conjunction with R_1, forms a voltage divider for making the feedback voltage the desired fraction of the output voltage

C_2 = by-pass or blocking capacitor, the reactance of which does not affect feedback

E = output voltage

I = output current

E_{fb} = feedback voltage developed across R_1

In some of the circuits designated as "voltage feedback," the feedback voltage E_{fb} is introduced in series between control grid and ground; in the other circuits it is introduced between cathode and ground. These two types of arrangements differ in that with the former the feedback voltage applied to the control grid has the same polarity as the output voltage of the amplifier, whereas when cathode injection is employed, the feedback voltage that is effectively applied to the control grid has a polarity opposite to the output voltage. Since each stage of amplification possessing plate coupling reverses the polarity, the type of injection that must be used to achieve negative feedback depends upon the number of stages unless there is somewhere in the system a transformer that can have its polarity reversed at will.   Thus in the voltage-feedback cases, when the feedback is derived from the output voltage, as in Figs. 11-11a and d and 11-13a, then in the absence of transformers grid injection must be used when the number of stages with plate coupling is odd, and cathode injection when it is even.[1]

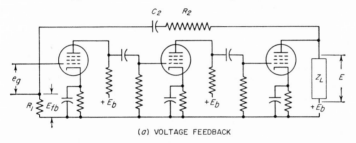

(*a*) VOLTAGE FEEDBACK   (*b*) CURRENT FEEDBACK

Fig. 11-12. Typical feedback circuits involving two stages of amplification.

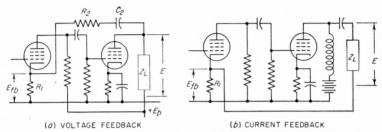

(*a*) VOLTAGE FEEDBACK

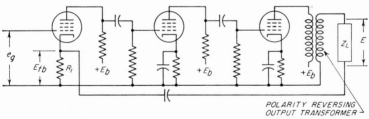

POLARITY REVERSING
OUTPUT TRANSFORMER

(*b*) CURRENT FEEDBACK

Fig. 11-13. Typical feedback circuits involving three stages of amplification.

Voltage Feedback and Current Feedback.   The circuits of Figs. 11-11 to 11-13 can also be divided into two types from another point of view.   In certain of these circuits, the feedback voltage superimposed upon the input is derived from the current flowing through the output of the amplifier, thus giving *current feedback*.   In other cases the feedback voltage is derived from the output voltage, giving *voltage feedback*.

Voltage feedback causes the *output voltage* from which the feedback is

---

[1] Cathode-coupled stages are not counted, as they do not reverse the polarity.

derived to reproduce accurately the signal voltage with respect to amplitude, wave shape, phase, freedom from hum, etc.   On the other hand, current feedback acts in such a way as to cause the *output current* to reproduce accurately the signal voltage with respect to amplitude, wave shape, phase, and freedom from hum.

These two effects are not synonymous.   Thus voltage feedback used in connection with an output transformer in the manner illustrated in Fig. 11-11d makes the voltage E across the transformer *primary* accurately reproduce the signal voltage.   This improves the frequency response at low frequencies and reduces amplitude distortion produced by nonlinearities in the tube and by core saturation.   The arrangement does not, however, improve the response at high frequencies, because the high-frequency falling off is a result of leakage reactance that is present on the load side of primary terminal a.   On the other hand, when current feedback is used with the same output transformer, as in Fig. 11-11e, the action of the feedback is to make the current that flows through the transformer primary reproduce the wave shape of the applied signal, and be independent of the applied frequency.   This causes the frequency response to be better at high frequencies and worse at low frequencies than in the absence of feedback.   Also, the amplitude distortion due to core saturation of the transformer will be increased, since the effect of feedback is to force the magnetizing current of the transformer to be a sine wave, whereas with a sinusoidal voltage across the transformer primary, the magnetizing current is a distorted sine wave.   In contrast, the arrangement at f improves the response at both high and low frequencies and reduces distortion of the output voltage E because in this case the feedback voltage E_{fb} is here derived directly from the output voltage E.

Effect of Negative Feedback on Effective Output Impedance of Amplifiers.
The output impedance of an amplifier can be defined as the equivalent impedance that the load observes when looking back toward the plate circuit of the final amplifier tube.   The effective value of this impedance is influenced to an important degree by the use of negative feedback. Thus voltage feedback tends to make the output voltage constant irrespective of load impedance; this is equivalent to decreasing the output impedance of the amplifier.   In a similar manner, current feedback tends to make the output current constant irrespective of load impedance, and this is equivalent to increasing the effective output impedance of the amplifier.

The quantitative effect of negative feedback on the output impedance of an amplifier can be derived as follows:[1] Assume that a voltage E is applied to the output terminals of the amplifier in the absence of an

[1] See H. F. Mayer, Control of the Effective Internal Impedance of Amplifiers by Feedback, *Proc. IRE*, vol. 27, p. 213, March, 1939.

external input signal, as in Fig. 11-14a. Then the output impedance is defined as E/I, where I is the current flowing into the plate electrode of the output tube as a result of E. The presence of voltage and current feedback in such a system causes voltages βE and $-\alpha I$ to be applied simultaneously to the amplifier input terminals even when no external signal is applied to the control grid.[1] Here β has the same meaning as in Fig. 11-1, while α is the corresponding factor by which one multiplies the amplified output current to obtain the feedback voltage due to current

feedback. The feedback voltage $(\beta E - \alpha I)$ applied to the control grid of the input tube produces a voltage A_0 times as great acting in the equivalent plate circuit of the output tube of Fig. 11-14a, in opposition to E. Hence

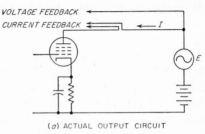

$$I = \frac{E - A_0(\beta E - \alpha I)}{r_p} \quad (11\text{-}8)$$

Rearranging gives

$$\text{Output impedance} = \frac{E}{I}$$

$$= \frac{r_p - \alpha A_0}{1 - \beta A_0} \quad (11\text{-}9)$$

(a) ACTUAL OUTPUT CIRCUIT

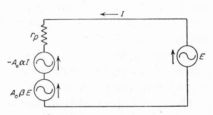

(b) EQUIVALENT OUTPUT CIRCUIT

Fig. 11-14. Equivalent output circuit of an amplifier having both voltage and current feedback.

Here r_p is the actual plate resistance of the output tube, and the convention as to signs is such that α and β are negative for negative feedback. A_0 can be regarded as the voltage gain of the amplifier from the control grid of the input tube to the output terminals, when the output is an open circuit. Equation (11-9) also applies when either or both feedbacks are positive, instead of negative. For pure negative voltage feedback $\alpha = 0$, and β is negative; for pure negative current feedback $\beta = 0$ and α is negative.

The effect of negative feedback on the output impedance has important practical consequences. For example, if a moderately large amount of negative voltage feedback is employed in an amplifier system having a pentode or beam power-output tube, the output impedance (i.e., the equivalent plate resistance) becomes a resistance of the same order of magnitude as the plate resistance of a triode power tube. Now it happens that loudspeakers tend to vibrate with excessive amplitude at their natural resonant frequency if operated from a source of power having a

[1] The negative sign associated with I arises because the current I in Fig. 11-14a flows in the opposite direction from an amplified current.

relatively high output impedance. Thus, before negative feedback became available, pentode and beam power tubes could not be used satisfactorily to operate loudspeakers because of their high plate resistance; however, with voltage feedback, pentode and beam tubes are generally preferred to triodes for this application because they are easier to drive and have greater plate efficiency.

Practical Use of the Feedback Principle in Amplifiers. The most important practical application of negative feedback is to reduce the amplitude distortion that would otherwise occur in audio-frequency power amplifiers. Thus negative feedback makes it possible to operate a given Class A power amplifier with such a large power output that the distortion would be excessive if negative feedback was not used. This increases both the output power and plate efficiency obtainable from a given tube and power supply. Again, negative feedback makes it possible to use high-efficiency–high-output Class B and Class AB amplifiers for applications requiring very low distortion, even though in the absence of negative feedback the distortion would be excessive. The use of negative feedback also makes it permissible to operate the power stage of an amplifier system with relatively little filtering in the power-supply system and still obtain negligible hum in the amplifier output, thus greatly reducing the cost of the power-supply system. Negative feedback will likewise make up, to a limited extent, for deficiencies in the amplifier with respect to the frequency-response characteristic.

These are important economic considerations. They lead to cost savings in the tube complement, power-supply system, and circuit components that in most cases are much greater than the cost of the additional amplification required to make up for the gain lost from the feedback action. Thus in audio power amplifiers, negative feedback makes it possible to obtain *better* performance at *lower* cost.

While negative feedback is a very valuable tool, it is not a substitute for poor engineering. For example, if a power amplifier is designed so that to obtain full output, the grid must be driven beyond cutoff, then no amount of negative feedback will remove the resulting distortion; to do this would require that the plate current of the tube reverse in polarity! Again, when negative feedback is used to improve the frequency-response characteristic of a power-amplifier stage, then the power output obtainable without excessive distortion will be less than the full value at those frequencies where the response would otherwise fall off.

Negative feedback finds very important uses in laboratory equipment. By arranging so that β is determined solely by resistances, then from Eq. (11-3) it is apparent that the frequency-response characteristic can be made almost ideally flat over the useful range of frequencies for which the amplifier already has a reasonably good characteristic, and the phase shift is reduced to negligible value. This gives a performance that is ideal for measurement purposes or for oscillograph amplifiers. The stability of the amplification that can be obtained from the use of negative feedback is particularly useful in laboratory measuring equipment, since with large values of $A\beta$ the amplification will stay constant with changes in electrode voltages, tube replacements, etc., to about the same extent that an ordinary d-c voltmeter will maintain its calibration.

A modified form of negative feedback is used in radio transmitters. This is described in Sec. 24-1.

11-6. Servomechanisms. It was shown in Sec. 11-1 that negative feedback tends to make the output of a system reproduce the input. The concepts of negative feedback can thus be applied to the analysis and

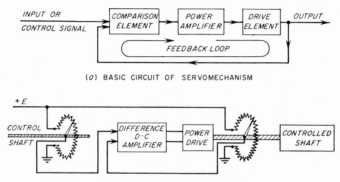

(*a*) BASIC CIRCUIT OF SERVOMECHANISM

(*b*) EXAMPLE OF A SERVOMECHANISM

Fig. 11-15. Schematic diagrams of servomechanism, showing basic elements, and a particular example.

synthesis of control systems of the closed-loop type, such as shown in Fig. 11-15*a*. Here the output of the control system is compared with the input in such a manner that any failure of the output to have the desired relationship to the input produces a difference or error signal. This error signal is then used to modify the output in a way that reduces the error. The output correction is commonly achieved by energy representing the amplified error signal, in which case the closed-loop system is said to be a *servomechanism*. Such amplification reduces the error, which can be made as small as desired by employing sufficient amplification.

The control system of Fig. 11-15*a* need not be purely electrical; in fact, it commonly involves hydraulic, pneumatic, and mechanical components. Thus the output of the system may represent the position of a shaft that controls the rudder of a ship, or the position of a gun turret, and which requires a large torque, while the input signal is the position of another shaft, but one which requires negligible torque. The purpose of the servo system is then to drive the output shaft so that its position follows that of the control shaft. One possible method of achieving this result is shown schematically in Fig. 11-15*b*. Here the shaft positions are translated into d-c voltages by using each shaft to control the position of a potenti-ometer slider.   The difference between the d-c voltages developed by the two potentiometers is hence a measure of the error in position of the out-put shaft, with the polarity of the difference denoting the sense of the error.   This difference or error signal is amplified, and used to control some device that applies power to the output shaft in such a way as to correct its position.   The power-drive device may be a reversible d-c motor run from the amplifier output; or the amplifier output can control valves of a hydraulic or pneumatic system for supplying the torque needed to correct the position of the output shaft, etc.

It is apparent that servomechanisms are a generalized form of the negative-feedback amplifiers discussed in the earlier part of this chapter. Thus, if the phase shift around the closed loop from input to output and back to input reaches 180° before the amplification around this loop has dropped to unity, the system will oscillate.   The design technique for pre-venting this condition from arising is the same as in feedback amplifiers. As discussed in Sec. 11-3, it consists in keeping the rate of change in trans-mission around the closed loop from exceeding approximately 10 db per octave; this is true irrespective of whether electrical, mechanical, pneu-matic, hydraulic, or other components are involved.   At the same time, the attention in servomechanisms is often centered on aspects of the system that are not given much consideration in feedback amplifiers. For example, in servomechanisms, the control signal often varies quite irregularly, causing one to be very much interested in the ability of the system output to follow the input under transient conditions.   Again, the effect that random extraneous disturbances (such as noise) have on the faithfulness with which the output follows the input is often of great importance.

There are an enormous number of variations that can be employed in carrying out the basic operations of the servomechanism illustrated schematically in Fig. 11-15.[1]   However, irrespective of these details, every servomechanism is based upon the same concepts as the feedback amplifier.

PROBLEMS AND EXERCISES

11-1. Calculate the value of $|A\beta|$ corresponding to a gain reduction of 15 db assum-ing $A\beta$ is negative.

11-2. In a particular amplifier it is found by measurement (or calculation) that $A\beta = 7\underline{/-150°}$, at a particular frequency.   Calculate the effect that negative feed-back has on the gain at this frequency.

[1] The literature on servomechanisms has become quite extensive since 1946, and is growing rapidly.   A useful textbook treatment of the subject is given by Thaler and Brown, "Servomechanisms Analysis," McGraw-Hill Book Company, Inc., New York, 1953.

11-3. A two-stage amplifier employs two identical resistance-coupled stages in which no screen- and bias-impedance effects of significance are present.   Each individual stage of the amplifier has a mid-frequency voltage gain of 100, and is so proportioned that the 70.7 per cent points are 100 and 10,000 cycles at the low- and high-frequency ends of the range, respectively.   Sufficient negative feedback is then introduced by means of a resistance network to reduce the mid-frequency amplification to 200.   Calculate and plot the relative amplification as a function of frequency over the frequency range 50 to 20,000 cycles when feedback is absent and when feedback is present, using a decibel scale with the amplification in the mid-frequency range taken as 0 db.   Also show curves of phase shift of the amplified voltage as a function of frequency for the same conditions.

11-4. A certain three-stage amplifier used in a measuring instrument obtains a high degree of stability of amplification with respect to variation in plate-supply voltage by introducing 30 db of negative feedback.   In the absence of negative feedback the voltage amplification is 4×10^6 under normal conditions.   Without feedback a 10 per cent plate-supply voltage change causes the total voltage gain to vary by 25 per cent.   What will be the change in amplification in decibels with 30 db feedback?

11-5. A particular power amplifier develops 6 per cent second-harmonic distortion in the absence of negative feedback.   It is desired that the same power output be obtained with only 1 per cent second-harmonic distortion.   Determine the number of decibels of feedback required to achieve this result, the corresponding value of $|A\beta|$, and the factor by which the amplitude of the exciting voltage must be increased.

11-6. A resistance-coupled amplifier contains three identical stages that are free of bias- and screen-impedance effects.   Calculate the maximum permissible value that $|A\beta|$ may have in the mid-frequency range if oscillations are to be avoided, and if the only cause of variations in $|A\beta|$ with frequency is the falling off in amplification of the resistance-coupled stages at high and low frequencies.

11-7. *a.* Sketch Nyquist diagrams for two- and three-stage resistance-coupled amplifiers.   Assume identical stages free of bias- and screen-impedance effects, and assume that $A\beta = -10$ in the mid-frequency range.

b. On the basis of these results, discuss the difference in tendency for oscillations to occur in the two cases.

11-8. *a.* Sketch the Nyquist diagram of a two-stage resistance-coupled amplifier having identical stages that are free of screen- and bias-impedance effects.   Assume $A\beta = -10$ in the mid-frequency range.

b. Next assume that each stage has a resistance-capacitance impedance in the screen such that $K = 0.05$ and $f_3 = f_1$, in accordance with the notation in Figs. 8-9 and 8-11.   Superimpose the Nyquist diagram corresponding to these conditions on the diagram of (*a*).

c. Discuss the effect of the screen impedance on the tendency to oscillate at high and low frequencies.

11-9. Justify qualitatively the shape of the phase-shift curves of *c*, *d*, and *f* of Fig. 11-4 from the shapes of the corresponding curves of relative amplitude.

11-10. Give qualitative justification for the shapes of the phase-shift curves shown in Fig. 8-16 for different values of Q_0, on the basis of the shapes of the corresponding curves giving relative amplification of the transformer-coupled amplifier at high frequencies.

11-11. Explain why it is not possible in a video amplifier to obtain an amplification that is exactly constant up to some top frequency f_2, combined with a phase shift that is exactly proportional to frequency up to this same top frequency, unless the amplifier includes an all-pass filter.

11-12. Describe in qualitative terms the effect that would be produced on the phase-shift characteristic in Fig. 11-4*c* if the change in transmission from one amplitude to the second amplitude took place in a smaller frequency range than illustrated. Illustrate the discussion with sketches, and give reasons for the comparative behavior that is shown.

11-13. In Fig. 11-5, the slope of $|A\beta|$ at a frequency just less than f_1 is exactly twice the slope at frequencies very much less than f_1, yet the phase shift is the same. Explain how this is consistent with Fig. 11-3 and not inconsistent with Eq. (11-5).

11-14. Explain why the phase shift associated with the actual amplifier in Fig. 11-6 at very low and very high frequencies will be almost, but never quite, as great as the phase shift corresponding to the ideal characteristic. Also explain why the phase shift of the actual amplifier in the vicinity of f_1 and f_2 will be appreciably less than that represented by the ideal characteristic at the same frequencies.

11-15. Discuss in qualitative terms the effect on the minimum permissible length of step 2-3 in Fig. 11-7 if this step, instead of being level, (a) slopes upward to the left, and (b) slopes downward to the left.

11-16. On the basis of the circuit elements involved, explain why the asymptotic slope of a resistance-coupled amplifier stage at high frequencies is 6 db per octave, while the asymptotic slope that results when interstage transformer coupling is used (Fig. 8-14) is 12 db per octave at high frequencies. It is suggested that in arriving at an answer, one start in each case with a high frequency, and then determine the effect on the output voltage of doubling the frequency.

11-17. Determine the lowest and highest frequencies between which the $|A\beta|$ characteristic must be controlled in a feedback amplifier when the frequency range to be amplified is 50 to 15,000 cycles, and the useful feedback desired in the middle frequencies is (a) 10 db, and (b) 40 db. Allow factors of safety of 5 and 10 db, respectively; also a phase margin of 36°. Assume the asymptotic slopes are 24 db per octave.

11-18. Recalculate the example on page 385 to provide 18 db useful negative feedback with a factor of safety of 6 db and 30°.

11-19. A four-stage amplifier consists of three identical resistance-coupled stages, together with a Class A power amplifier employing an output transformer as in Fig. 10-12a. The resistance-coupled stages are so proportioned that $f_1 = 50$ cycles and $f_2 = 20,000$ cycles, while the characteristics of the output transformer are such that $f_1 = 100$ cycles and $f_2 = 8000$ cycles. In order to reduce distortion and improve the response characteristic generally, it is desired to introduce 20 db of useful feedback, with a margin of safety of 10 db. Further, to minimize the possibility of oscillations, a factor of safety of 30° is desired for the phase shift. The frequency band of interest is 50 to 8000 cycles. Screen-grid- and bias-impedance effects are assumed to be absent. For this situation:

a. Plot the actual $|A\beta|$ transmission characteristic in decibels in the manner shown in Fig. 11-8a, taking $A\beta$ in the mid-frequency range as zero db.

b. Calculate and plot the idealized characteristic corresponding to a 150° phase shift at very high and at very low frequencies for the regions below 50 cycles and above 8000 cycles.

c. Introduce the ideal step characteristic in the manner illustrated in Fig. 11-8a.

d. Determine the difference between the idealized step characteristic and the actual characteristic, and plot the difference as shown in Fig. 11-8b.

e. From the results in (d) discuss qualitatively the manner in which the characteristics of the original amplifier system must be modified in order to avoid oscillations.

11-20. *a.* Explain qualitatively how the right-hand circuit in Fig. 11-9a and the two circuits in Fig. 11-9b introduce the steps in the amplification curve that are indicated in the figure.

b. Explain qualitatively how the circuits of Fig. 11-9*c* produce the indicated dip in the amplification curve.

c. Explain qualitatively how the circuits of Fig. 11-9*d* produce the indicated peak in amplification.

11-21. Derive a formula giving ΔA in decibels for the right-hand circuit in Fig. 11-9*d*.

11-22. Derive a formula for ΔA in decibels for the left-hand circuit of Fig. 11-9*d*. Assume that the plate resistance of the pentode tube is extremely high, and that the principal losses in the resonant system LC are supplied by the resistance R_1.

11-23. In a three-stage resistance-coupled amplifier, the phase shift at high frequencies is minimized by staggering the 70.7 per cent points of the individual stages.

a. If the 70.7 per cent point of the first stage is 10,000 cycles, and of the second stage is 20,000 cycles, what is the lowest value it can be for the third stage if the phase shift is not to exceed 180° until the frequency is greater than 25,000 cycles?

b. What will be the value of $|A\beta|$ in decibels at 25,000 cycles relative to the mid-frequency value, if the only cause of reduction in $|A\beta|$ is the falling off in amplification of the individual stages?

11-24. Verify the fact that the circuits of Figs. 11-11*a*, *b*, and *c*, 11-12*a* and *b*, and 11-13*a* all give negative feedback.

11-25. Sketch the circuit of a three-stage amplifier consisting of two resistance-coupled stages and a cathode-follower output stage, and possessing negative voltage feedback.

11-26. Assume that the load impedance in Fig. 11-11*a* consists of a coupling resistance and grid leak–capacitor combination, corresponding to resistance coupling. Discuss the differences, if any, produced in the high-frequency and the low-frequency response characteristics that result from connecting the feedback resistance R_2 to the coupling-resistance side of the coupling capacitor, as compared to the grid-leak side.

11-27. Assume that the tube in Fig. 11-11*a* is a 6L6 beam tube operated as a Class A amplifier under conditions specified in Table 6-1, page 186. Calculate the equivalent output impedance of the tube when R_1 and R_2 are so chosen that $E_{fb}/E = 0.1$.

11-28. Assume that the tube in Fig. 11-11*b* is the 6L6 tube of Table 6-1, page 186. Determine the equivalent output impedance when $R_1 = 3200$ ohms.

11-29. It is possible, by suitably combining negative current feedback and negative voltage feedback, to obtain negative feedback without affecting the output impedance. What relationship must exist between α and β in Eq. (11-9) to achieve this result?

11-30. Justify the statement on page 394 that the power output obtainable without excessive distortion in the presence of feedback will be less than the full rated value at those frequencies where the response would fall off if it were not for the negative feedback.

11-31. Explain why there is no inconsistency between the fact demonstrated in Sec. 11-3 that to avoid low-frequency oscillations in a feedback amplifier, the low-frequency response should fall off slowly and the statement on page 362 that it is helpful to have the amplification at low frequencies fall off rapidly when it is desired to prevent motorboating oscillations as a result of feedback introduced by a power supply that is common to several stages of amplification.

11-32. In Fig. 11-15*b*, what effect is produced by changes in voltage E?

CHAPTER 12

TUNED VOLTAGE AMPLIFIERS

12-1. Tuned Voltage Amplifiers. In a tuned amplifier, the load impedance is supplied by a resonant circuit, with parallel resonance used to obtain the necessary high load impedance. The tube and stray circuit capacitances that limit the ability of untuned amplifiers to amplify at high frequencies then assist in tuning, and therefore are not necessarily detrimental. Tuned amplifiers in which the objective is voltage amplification are used to amplify signal-frequency voltages in radio receivers, in which case they are referred to as tuned radio-frequency amplifiers. They are also used to amplify intermediate-frequency voltages in superheterodyne receivers.

The utilization of the resonance phenomenon to obtain a high load impedance makes a tuned amplifier selective with respect to frequency. Thus only frequencies in the vicinity of the resonant frequency of the tuned load impedance are amplified, while frequencies differing appreciably from resonance are strongly discriminated against.

Tuned amplifiers can be classified as narrow-band or broad-band according to the width of the frequency band that is amplified. Thus a radio-frequency wave modulated by voice-frequency currents would be handled by a narrow-band amplifier, because the frequency band occupied by such a wave, including the sideband frequencies, would be relatively small. In contrast, a radio-frequency wave modulated by a television video signal, or by a short pulse, would involve sidebands extending over such a very wide frequency band as to require a wideband amplifier.[1]

Tuned voltage amplifiers always employ pentode tubes of the same types used with resistance-coupled and video amplifiers (see Table 6-1). Narrow-band tuned voltage amplifiers customarily employ the same pentode tubes used with ordinary resistance-coupled amplifiers, while wideband tuned amplifiers employ the same types of pentodes used in video-frequency amplifiers.

The important characteristics of a tuned voltage amplifier are the

---

[1] The term "wideband" is also sometimes used to designate a system in which the bandwidth is a large percentage of the center frequency. On this basis a bandwidth of 10 Mc centered at 20 Mc would be wideband, while if centered at 3000 Mc it would be narrow band, whereas according to the definition given above both cases would be wideband.

amplification at resonance, the variation of amplification with frequency in the immediate vicinity of resonance, and the discrimination against frequencies differing appreciably from resonance.

12-2. The Single-tuned Amplifier. *Direct Coupling.* The simplest form of tuned amplifier is the direct-coupled arrangement of Fig. 12-1a,

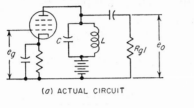
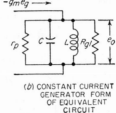

(a) ACTUAL CIRCUIT

(b) CONSTANT CURRENT GENERATOR FORM OF EQUIVALENT CIRCUIT

FIG. 12-1. Actual and equivalent circuits of direct-coupled single-tuned amplifier.

the equivalent circuit for which is shown in Fig. 12-1b. The voltage amplification can be written down by inspection as

$$\text{Voltage amplification} = g_m Z_L \qquad (12\text{-}1)$$

Here g_m is the transconductance of the amplifier tube, and Z_L is the impedance of the resonant circuit LC when shunted by grid-leak resistance R_{gl} and the plate resistance r_p of the tube, as shown.

It follows from Eq. (12-1) that the amplification varies with frequency in the same manner as does the parallel resonant impedance Z_L. The amplification characteristic accordingly has the shape illustrated in Fig. 12-2. The quantitative relations involved are obtainable from the universal resonance curve of Fig. 3-2, in terms of the amplitude at resonance, the effective Q of the resonant system, and the resonant frequency. By substituting Eq. (3-14) into Eq. (12-1) the amplification at resonance is found to be

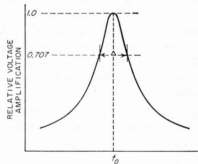

FIG. 12-2. Variation of amplification with frequency in a single-tuned amplifier.

$$\text{Amplification at resonance} = g_m \omega_0 L Q_{\text{eff}} \qquad (12\text{-}2)$$

Here Q_{eff} is the effective Q of the resonant circuit and $\omega_0/2\pi$ is the resonant frequency. In most practical narrow-band amplifiers, r_p and R_{gl} are so high that Q_{eff} approximates very closely the actual Q of the resonant circuit LC.[1]

[1] The plate resistance r_p is so large in the case of pentodes that its presence in the equivalent circuit of Fig. 12-1b can always be safely neglected. However, to the

The bandwidth of a tuned amplifier is commonly defined as the width of the band of frequencies over which the power amplification does not drop to less than one-half, or -3 db of the power amplification at resonance (i.e., voltage amplification at least 0.707 of maximum). The properties of parallel resonant circuits are such (see page 52) that the frequency band between these 3-db or half-power points is

$$\begin{matrix} \text{Bandwidth between} \\ \text{half-power points} \end{matrix} \Big\} = \Delta = \frac{f_0}{Q_{\text{eff}}} \qquad (12\text{-}4)$$

where f_0 is the resonant frequency, and Q_{eff} is the effective Q of the amplification curve.

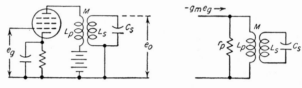

(b) CONSTANT-CURRENT-GENERATOR FORM OF EQUIVALENT CIRCUIT

Fig. 12-3. Actual and equivalent circuits of transformer-coupled single-tuned amplifier.

Transformer or Inductive Coupling. The necessity of using a grid-leak and coupling capacitor in a single-tuned amplifier can be eliminated by the use of inductive coupling as indicated in Fig. 12-3a. The equivalent circuit of this arrangement is illustrated in Fig. 12-3b.[1] This is the constant-current form of the circuit discussed in connection with Figs. 3-10 and 3-20, and, as there shown, results in an output voltage and hence amplification that varies with frequency in accordance with a resonance curve. On the easily justifiable assumption that the plate resistance of the tube is very much greater than the impedance that the tuned secondary couples into the primary coil L_p, one has

$$\text{Amplification at resonance} = g_m \omega_0 M Q_{\text{eff}} \qquad (12\text{-}5)$$
$$Q_{\text{eff}} = Q_s \qquad (12\text{-}6)$$

Here M is the mutual inductance between L_p and L_s in Fig. 12-3a, and Q_s is the actual Q of the secondary circuit.

Comparison of Eq. (12-5) and (12-2) shows that they are identical

---

extent that the shunting effect of the grid-leak resistance is not negligible, then Q_{eff} is found with the aid of Eq. (3-18a) to have the value

$$Q_{\text{eff}} = \frac{Q_0}{1 + (\omega_0 L Q_0 / R_{gl})} \qquad (12\text{-}3)$$

Here Q_0 is the actual Q of the resonant circuit LC with R_{gl} and r_p removed.

[1] This circuit assumes that the capacitance across the primary terminals, and any capacitance existing between primary and secondary, are equivalent to an appropriate capacitance connected across the tuned secondary. This assumption is permissible unless the primary inductance is so large that these capacitances cause pronounced resonance effects in the primary, in which case one no longer has a single-tuned circuit.

except that M in the inductively coupled case has replaced L in the formula applying to direct coupling.   Thus when the same tuned circuit is involved, the only difference in behavior between transformer coupling and direct coupling is that the amplification is modified in accordance with the ratio M/L.   The half-power bandwidth is unchanged, however.

Complex Coupling.   In tuned radio-frequency amplifiers, the resonant frequency of the tuned load impedance is varied to accommodate signals of different frequencies.   In such a situation it is desirable that the amplification be approximately the same, irrespective of the resonant frequency.   Inasmuch as resonant circuits ordinarily have a value of Q that changes only moderately with frequency, the amplification tends to increase with frequency when tuning is accomplished by varying the capacitance (L constant), and to decrease with frequency if the tuning is done by varying the inductance.

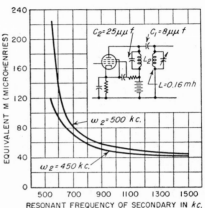

Fig. 12-4. Variation of equivalent mutual inductance with frequency in typical complex coupling systems.

This difficulty can be overcome by coupling the amplifier tube to the tuned circuit by a complex coupling system such that the equivalent mutual inductance M of the coupling network varies with frequency.   Such circuits were discussed in Sec. 3-6, and a typical example used in tuned amplifiers is illustrated in Fig. 12-4.   As this circuit is commonly encountered, the primary L_2 has a high inductance compared with the secondary inductance L, and is hence so large that when associated with capacitance C_2, representing the distributed capacitance of L_2 plus the plate-cathode capacitance of the amplifier tube, the combination L_2C_2 resonates at a frequency slightly below the lowest frequency to be amplified.   The primary inductance L_2 normally possesses no inductive coupling whatsoever to the secondary inductance L, the entire coupling being provided by the capacitance C_1 which is very small, often only 2 or 3 $\mu\mu f$ provided by stray capacitances.   The equivalent mutual inductance as determined by the method outlined in Sec. 3-6 is (assuming $1/\omega C_1 >> L$)

$$\text{Equivalent } M = \frac{LC_1}{C_1 + C_2}\left[1 + \frac{1}{(\omega/\omega_2)^2 - 1}\right] \qquad (12\text{-}7)$$

where $\omega/2\pi$ is the actual frequency, and $\omega_2/2\pi$ is the frequency at which the primary inductance L_2 resonates with the capacitance $C_2 + C_1$.   By making ω_2 less than the lowest frequency to be amplified, the equivalent M will decrease with increasing frequency at a rate determined by the choice of ω_2. The behavior in typical cases is illustrated in Fig. 12-4 for two values of ω_2. It is apparent that, by suitable choice of this resonant frequency, it is possible to counteract in a large measure the tendency for the amplification to increase with increase in the resonant frequency of the tuned secondary.

Multistage Single-tuned Amplifiers. In an amplifier system consisting of more than one stage of amplification the over-all characteristic is the product of the amplification curves of the individual stages. As a result, the 3-db or half-power band-width of a multistage amplifier composed of identical single-tuned stages is less than the bandwidth of a single stage, as illustrated in Fig. 12-5. Thus in order to maintain a given bandwidth, it is necessary that Q_{eff} of the individual stages be decreased as more stages are incorporated in the amplifier system. It is also to be noted that as the number of stages increases, the response curve becomes flatter on top and steeper on the sides.

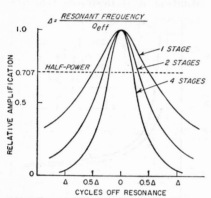

Fig. 12-5. Curve showing effect on the bandwidth of cascading a number of identical single-tuned stages.

The quantitative relationship between the 3-db or half-power band-width B of a multistage amplifier, consisting of identical single-tuned stages, and the 3-db bandwidth Δ of an individual stage is[1]

$$\left. \begin{array}{r} \text{Half-power bandwidth} \\ \text{of } n\text{-stage amplifier} \end{array} \right\} = B = \Delta \sqrt{2^{1/n} - 1} \qquad (12\text{-}8)$$

[1] An analysis of this situation in general terms can be carried out as follows:

Let B = bandwidth of multistage system for reduction in power by factor m^2

$$m = \frac{\text{actual multistage output voltage at } B/2 \text{ cycles off resonance}}{\text{output multistage voltage at resonance}}$$

    n = number of stages, assumed all alike

    Δ = half-power bandwidth of single stage

Then for a single stage it follows from the shape of a resonance curve as given by Eq. (3-8), where $\delta = B/2f_0$, that when $\delta \ll 1$, one has

$$m = \frac{1}{\sqrt{1 + (B/\Delta)^2}}$$

For n similar stages

$$m = \frac{1}{[1 + (B/\Delta)^2]^{n/2}} \qquad (12\text{-}8a)$$

Solving for B/Δ gives

$$B/\Delta = \sqrt{(1/m^2)^{1/n} - 1}$$

This equation gives the relationship between the multistage bandwidth B for a loss in power amplification of m^2 in an n-stage amplifier, and the half-power bandwidth Δ of a single stage. Equation (12-8) is the special case of Eq. (12-8a) for $m = 0.707$.

Results calculated from Eq. (12-8) are shown in Table 12-1; it is apparent that the bandwidth narrowing in a multistage single-tuned amplifier is very considerable.

TABLE 12-1

RELATIVE VALUES OF HALF-POWER BANDWIDTH OF
MULTISTAGE TUNED AMPLIFIER COMPOSED OF IDENTICAL STAGES

Number of stages	Relative values of half-power bandwidth	
	Single-tuned	Double-tuned*
1	$1.00\Delta_1$	$1.00\Delta_2$
2	0.64	0.80
3	0.51	0.71
4	0.44	0.66
6	0.35	0.59
8	0.30	0.55
10	0.27	0.52

* Assumes identical primary and secondary circuits critically coupled.

12-3. The Double-tuned Amplifier. The double-tuned amplifier employs a load impedance consisting of two circuits resonant at the same frequency and coupled together, as illustrated schematically in Fig. 12-6. When the tube in such an arrangement is replaced by the constant-current form of its equivalent plate circuit, the double-tuned amplifier has the equivalent circuit shown in Fig. 12-6b. This can be simplified by applying Thévenin's theorem to the portion of the system to the left of point xx, giving the results shown in Fig. 12-6c. The circuit at c is the same as the bandpass circuit considered at length in Sec. 3-5. As a result, this earlier discussion of the properties and analysis of coupled resonant circuits can be applied without change to the double-tuned amplifier. Thus the amplification of the double-tuned amplifier at the common resonant frequency can be calculated by applying Eq. (3-28) to Fig. 12-6c. This gives

$$\left.\begin{array}{l}\text{Amplification at} \\ \text{resonant frequency}\end{array}\right\} = g_m k \frac{\omega_0 \sqrt{L_s L_p}}{k^2 + (1/Q_p Q_s)} \tag{12-9}$$

where g_m = transconductance of tube

k = coefficient of coupling between primary and secondary inductances

$\omega_0 = 2\pi$ times resonant frequency

$Q_p = \omega L_p/R_p$ for primary circuit, taking into account any equivalent resistance that may be added by the plate resistance of the tube

$Q_s = \omega L_s/R_s$ for secondary circuit

L_p, L_s = primary and secondary inductances, respectively

For critically coupled systems with identical primary and secondary circuits Eq. (12-9) becomes[1]

$$\text{Amplification at resonance } = g_m\omega_0 LQ/2 \qquad (12\text{-}10)$$

The exact shape of the amplification curve of a double-tuned system depends upon the ratio k/k_c of actual to critical coefficient of coupling, as

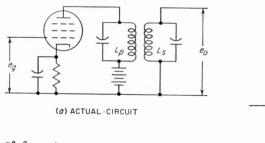

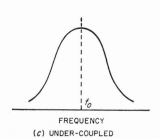

(a) ACTUAL CIRCUIT

(a) OVER-COUPLED

FREQUENCY

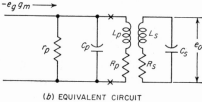

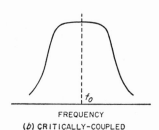

(b) EQUIVALENT CIRCUIT

FREQUENCY

(b) CRITICALLY-COUPLED

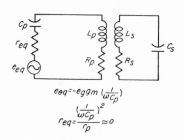

$$e_{eq} = -e_g g_m \left(\frac{1}{\omega C_p}\right)$$

$$r_{eq} = \frac{\left(\frac{1}{\omega C_p}\right)^2}{r_p} \approx 0$$

(c) EQUIVALENT CIRCUIT SIMPLIFIED
BY THEVENIN'S THEOREM

FREQUENCY

(c) UNDER-COUPLED

FIG. 12-6. Actual and equivalent circuits of a double-tuned amplifier.

FIG. 12-7. The effect of coefficient of coupling upon the shape of the amplification curve of a double-tuned amplifier.

illustrated in Fig. 12-7 (also see Fig. 3-11). The response curve will have maximum possible flatness in the vicinity of resonance when the coupling equals the critical value,[2] assuming the primary and secondary circuits have equal values of Q; this is shown at b, and corresponds to maximum flatness in video amplifiers as discussed on page 295. When the coupling

[1] The critical coefficient of coupling is defined by Eq. (3-29) and is

$$k_c = 1/\sqrt{Q_pQ_s} \qquad (12\text{-}11)$$

[2] This case is sometimes referred to as *transitional coupling*.

exceeds the critical value (termed *overcoupling*), double humps result as at *a*, while a coefficient of coupling less than the critical value (termed *undercoupling*) causes the top of the amplification curve to be rounded off as at *c*.

The bandwidth in the case of an amplifier system employing double-tuned circuits is defined in the same manner as for a system employing single-tuned circuits; i.e., it is the bandwidth over which the power amplification does not drop to less than one-half, or -3 db, of the power amplification at resonance; this corresponds to the voltage amplification dropping to 70.7 per cent of its maximum value.   When the Q's of the two circuits are the same and the coefficient of coupling equals the critical value, the half-power bandwidth Δ_2 of the double-tuned stage is $\sqrt{2}$ times the half-power bandwidth Δ_1 of the single-tuned stage using the same tuned circuit, as given by Eq. (12-4); that is

$$\left.\begin{array}{l}\text{Half-power bandwidth}\\ \text{with critical coupling}\end{array}\right\} = \Delta_2 = \sqrt{2}\,\Delta_1 \qquad (12\text{-}12)$$

Compared with a single-tuned amplifier having the same half-power bandwidth, the double-tuned stage possesses a response that is flatter near the resonant frequency and has steeper sides, as illustrated in Fig. 3-12.   This property of double-tuned systems represents one of the important characteristics of the double-tuned amplifier.

When a number of identical double-tuned stages of amplification are connected in cascade, the over-all bandwidth of the system is thereby narrowed, and the steepness of the sides of the amplification characteristic is increased, just as when single-tuned stages are connected in cascade. The quantitative relation between the half-power or 3-db bandwidth B of n identical double-tuned critically coupled stages compared with the bandwidth Δ_2 of a single stage of such a system can be shown to be[1]

$$\left.\begin{array}{l}\text{Half-power bandwidth}\\ \text{of } n \text{ identical stages}\end{array}\right\} = B = \Delta_2 \sqrt[4]{2^{1/n} - 1} \qquad (12\text{-}13)$$

Results calculated from Eq. (12-12) are presented in Table 12-1.   It is seen that the percentage narrowing of the bandwidth that occurs with increasing number of stages is much less in the double-tuned amplifier than when single-tuned stages are employed.   This is a result of the flatter top and steeper sides that are characteristic of the individual double-tuned stage.

It is instructive to compare a single-tuned amplifier with a double-tuned stage using the same resonant circuit and the same amplifier tube. Comparison of Eqs. (12-2) and (12-10) shows that the amplification at

---

[1] This assumes that the bandwidth Δ_2 is small compared with the resonant frequency f_0.

resonance of a direct-coupled stage is twice the amplification at resonance of the double-turned stage composed of the same resonant circuits critically coupled ($k = 1/Q$). From Eq. (12-12) the half-power bandwidth of the double-tuned system is, however, $\sqrt{2}$ times as great as that of the corresponding single-tuned stage having the same resonant circuits. If the circuit Q's of the double-tuned stage are increased so that the half-power bandwidth is the same as for the corresponding single-tuned stage (circuit L and C unchanged, however), then the amplification at resonance of a critically coupled double-tuned amplifier is 0.707 times the amplification of a single-tuned amplifier stage having the same half-power bandwidth. However, as the number of amplifier stages is increased, the superiority of the single-tuned system rapidly disappears because of the greater bandwidth narrowing in single-tuned systems. Thus in two-stage systems in which the Q's are adjusted to give the same half-power over-all bandwidth (while keeping the circuit L's and C's unchanged), the single-tuned system has only very slightly more gain per stage, while in a three-stage system there is no difference at all, and in a four-stage amplifier the double-tuned arrangement gives higher voltage amplification per stage than does the corresponding single-tuned system of the same over-all bandwidth. In addition, a given number of stages of double-tuning always gives more off-channel selectivity than does the corresponding single-tuned amplifier, as discussed below.

Double-tuned amplifiers find extensive use as intermediate-frequency amplifiers in radio receivers. In such applications it is customary to make the stage slightly undercoupled, i.e., to make the coefficient of coupling slightly less than the critical value. This gives slightly better off-channel selectivity, and by causing the response curve to have a slight peak makes it easier to adjust the individual circuits to resonance at a common frequency.

12-4. Miscellaneous Aspects of Tuned Amplifiers. *Off-channel Selectivity.* An important consideration in tuned voltage amplifiers is the amount of discrimination that is obtained against signals of frequencies differing moderately from the frequency of the signals to be amplified. This characteristic is termed the *off-channel selectivity*, and is commonly expressed quantitatively in terms of the ratio of the bandwidth of the amplifier system, when the amplification is 60 db less than at resonance, to the bandwidth of the system when the amplification is 6 db less than at resonance. This ratio is termed either the 6–60 *db bandwidth ratio*, or the 6–60 *db selectivity ratio*, and is illustrated in Fig. 12-8. In a typical intermediate-frequency amplifier system involving several double-tuned stages, this bandwidth ratio will have a numerical value in the range 2.5 to 5. The bandwidth ratio of a multistage system is determined primarily by the total number of tuned circuits involved. Thus an amplifier with double-tuned stages will have much greater off-channel selectivity than a single-tuned amplifier of the same bandwidth and number of stages.

Phase and Time-delay Characteristics of Tuned Amplifiers—Envelope Delay. Tuned amplifiers introduce a phase shift that varies with frequency and so give rise to time-delay effects and time-delay distortion analogous to those occurring in audio- and video-frequency amplifiers. The characteristic of importance in the case of tuned amplifiers is the phase shift of the sidebands of a modulated wave, compared with the phase shift suffered by the carrier frequency, since this *relative* phase shift appears as a time delay in the output wave after demodulation. Thus, in the case of an amplitude-modulated wave, if the upper and lower side-bands suffer equal phase shifts of 45° of opposite polarity with respect to the carrier, this causes the *envelope* of the wave likewise to be shifted in phase by 45°. The modulation-frequency output after detection then possesses the 45° phase shift at the modulation frequency, even though the phase shift as introduced in the tuned amplifier was a shift in phase at radio frequency.

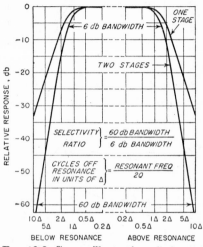

Fig. 12-8. Curves illustrating off-channel selectivity, and the 6–60 db bandwidth ratio of a two-stage tuned amplifier employing double-tuned circuits.

The envelope delay that results in this way for an amplitude-modulated wave is

$$\left.\begin{array}{c}\text{Envelope delay}\\\text{in seconds}\end{array}\right\} = \frac{\Delta\phi}{\omega_m} \tag{12-14}$$

where $\Delta\phi$ = phase shift of the sideband frequencies relative to the phase of the carrier, in radians, and $\omega_m/2\pi$ = modulation frequency. In this equation it is assumed that the upper and lower sideband frequencies have phase shifts $\Delta\phi$ with respect to the carrier frequency, which are of equal magnitude but are opposite in sign, and that $\Delta\phi$ is positive if the higher-frequency sideband suffers a lagging phase shift while the lower-frequency sideband undergoes a leading phase shift.

The envelope delay will be constant with variations in the modulation frequency only to the extent that the phase shift of the tuned amplifier is a linear function of frequency over the range of sideband frequencies involved. The magnitude of the time delay depends upon the slope of the curve of phase shift plotted as a function of frequency on a *linear* frequency scale.

Envelope-delay characteristics for a single-tuned amplifier, and for typical cases of double-tuned amplifiers, are shown in Fig. 12-9; these curves assume an amplitude-modulated wave with the carrier centered at the resonant frequency. Examination of Fig. 12-9 reveals that the envelope delay of the single-tuned circuit behaves exactly the same as the time delay of a resistance-coupled amplifier (see curve for $Q_2 = 0$ in Fig. 9-4). In the case of the double-tuned amplifier, the envelope-delay characteristic depends upon the ratio of the actual coupling relative to the critical coupling. The envelope delay will be most nearly constant within the half-power bandwidth of the amplifier when the actual coupling is moderately less than the critical value. This situation corresponds to an amplification curve that is somewhat rounded off in the vicinity of resonance rather than a curve of maximum flatness; it is analogous to the behavior of video amplifiers illustrated in Fig. 9-4, where the most nearly constant time delay $(Q_2 = 0.34)$ is associated with an amplitude curve that drops off moderately at the higher frequencies.

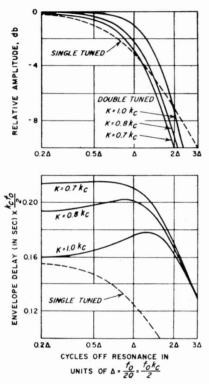

Fig. 12-9. Amplitude and envelope-delay characteristics of single-tuned and typical double-tuned amplifiers. Here k_c is the critical coupling corresponding to the value of Q applicable to the resonant circuits, and f_0 is the resonant or center frequency.

Amplitude Distortion and Cross-talk in Tuned Amplifiers. Amplitude distortion occurs in tuned amplifiers when the output wave contains frequency components not present in the wave being amplified. These spurious frequencies also normally cause the modulation envelope of the wave being amplified to possess spurious frequency components not present in the original modulation envelope.

The most important type of amplitude distortion that can occur in tuned amplifiers is *cross-talk* (or *cross modulation*) produced when the signal being amplified consists of two modulated waves having carrier frequencies not too greatly different. In such a situation it is possible under certain conditions for the modulation of one carrier frequency to get transferred to some extent to the other carrier frequency. This happens when third-order effects such as discussed in Sec. 10-3 are present. The amplified output of one of the modulated waves then depends to some extent on the amplitude of the other wave that makes up part of the signal. Hence if the latter is an amplitude-modulated wave the amplification of the first wave will vary with the modulation of the second wave.

In addition to cross-talk, third-order action also causes the amplification to depend upon the amplitude of the wave being amplified. When the signal involved is a modulated wave, the shape of the modulation envelope will then be distorted, since the modulation peaks and troughs will undergo slightly different amounts of amplification. However, under practical conditions this type of distortion is not of great practical significance, since it is ordinarily still quite moderate when the cross-talk is intolerable.

Unlike the situation existing with audio- and video-frequency amplifiers, harmonics produced by nonlinear action of the tube do not in themselves introduce amplitude distortion in tuned amplifiers. This is because harmonics and similar combination frequency components are discriminated against by the tuned load impedance, and so do not appear in the amplifier output.

Volume Control in Tuned Amplifiers. The amplification of tuned amplifiers is normally controlled by varying the control-grid voltage. In this way the transconductance g_m, and hence the voltage gain, can be varied without appreciably affecting the resonant frequency or shape of the response curve.[1] This arrangement also permits the amplification of several stages to be controlled simultaneously, thus giving more effective control.

Variable-mu pentodes are always employed in preference to sharp cutoff pentodes in stages where the amplification is controlled by varying the transconductance. This is because in sharp-cutoff pentodes the transconductance does not become small until cutoff is approached. This introduces two undesirable effects: (1) Since the third-order curvature is relatively large in sharp-cutoff tubes operated close to cutoff, the cross-talk tends to become excessive with strong signals (i.e., when the required gain is low). (2) The transconductance changes very greatly with small variations in grid bias around cutoff in this type of pentode, so that the volume-control adjustment is very critical at low volume levels. Both of these disadvantages are eliminated by the use of the variable-mu tube, which stretches out what would otherwise be the region close to cutoff; this reduces the third-order action, and at the same time causes the

[1] There is a small effect on the resonance frequency, as discussed in Sec. 12-12.

transconductance to vary much less rapidly with changes in control-grid potential.

12-5. Wideband Tuned Amplifiers.[1] Tuned amplifiers designed to reproduce abrupt changes in amplitude of a modulation envelope, such as encountered when handling carrier waves modulated by short pulses or by a television video signal, are termed *wideband amplifiers*. Such amplifiers must meet requirements as to transient response, bandwidth, and envelope-delay characteristics that are analogous to those of the corresponding video amplifier that would be used to handle signals having wave shapes corresponding to the modulation envelope. There is, in fact, a one-to-one correspondence between a tuned amplifier and the corresponding video or low-pass amplifier. Thus the effect on the modulation envelope that is produced by a single-tuned stage possessing the amplitude and envelope-delay characteristics given in Fig. 12-9 is exactly the same as the effect that is produced on a modulation-frequency wave by the uncompensated video stage of Fig. 9-4.

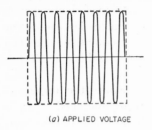

(a) APPLIED VOLTAGE

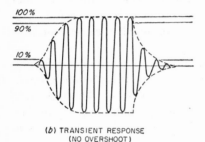

(b) TRANSIENT RESPONSE (NO OVERSHOOT)

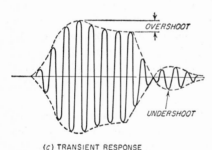

(c) TRANSIENT RESPONSE (WITH OVERSHOOT)

FIG. 12-10. Typical transient responses of tuned amplifier to a pulse-modulated wave, showing cases with and without overshoot.

Transient Response of Tuned Amplifiers.[2] When a pulse-modulated radio-frequency wave of carrier frequency equal to the center frequency of the amplification curve is suddenly applied to a tuned amplifier, the amplifier output voltage builds up to its final value in the manner illustrated in Fig. 12-10. The *envelope* of this curve is exactly the same as the transient response of the analogous

---

[1] An extensive treatment of this subject is given in "Vacuum Tube Amplifiers" (Vol. 18, Radiation Laboratory Series), chaps. 4, 5, 6, and 7, McGraw-Hill Book Company, Inc., New York, 1948.

[2] For more detailed information on the transient behavior of tuned amplifiers see *ibid.*, chap. 7; also D. G. Tucker, Transient Response of Tuned Circuit Cascades, *Wirelsss Eng.*, vol. 23, p. 250, September, 1946.

video amplifier to a pulse corresponding to the envelope of the applied signal.[1]

The transient characteristics of tuned amplifiers are therefore described in terms of rise time and overshoot of the envelope defined in exactly the same way as in a video amplifier.[2] It is merely necessary to remember that in the tuned amplifier one deals with envelope shape instead of actual wave shape, envelope delay instead of time delay, and instantaneous envelope amplitude instead of instantaneous amplitude of the actual wave.

When the overshoot is zero to moderate, the rise time of a tuned amplifier, i.e., the time it takes the envelope in Fig. 12-10 to increase from 10 to 90 per cent of its final value, is given with good accuracy by the semiempirical relation[3]

$$\text{Rise time in seconds} = \frac{0.70 \text{ to } 0.90}{B} \tag{12-15}$$

Here B is the half-power or 3-db bandwidth of the tuned amplifier in cycles. The value 0.70 should be used for overshoots of less than 5 per cent.

A comparison of Eq. (12-15) with Eq. (9-1) shows that for a given rise time, the bandwidth of the tuned amplifier must be twice the bandwidth of the corresponding video amplifier. This is associated with the fact that the two sidebands of a modulated wave occupy a frequency band that is twice the modulating frequency.

The overshoot in a tuned amplifier will be small or zero if the response curve is moderately rounded off, and if at the same time the envelope delay is reasonably constant to somewhat beyond the half-power bandwidth. This is analogous to the behavior of a video amplifier as discussed on pages 301 and 302.

When a number of stages of tuned amplification are connected in cascade, the overshoot and rise time behave in the same manner as in video amplifiers (see page 298). Thus, if the overshoot of the individual stage does not exceed 1 or 2 per cent, then the overshoot of the multistage system composed of identical stages is approximately that of an individual stage and the rise time is proportional to the square root of the number of stages. On the other hand, if the overshoot of the individual

---

[1] The only special consideration in Fig. 12-10 is that passage of the modulation envelope of the output wave through zero amplitude during undershoot is to be interpreted as a reversal in sign of the corresponding video wave, as shown in Fig. 12-10c.

[2] It will be noted that the phenomenon of sag occurring in a video amplifier has no counterpart in the ordinary tuned amplifier. This is because a tuned amplifier possesses no deficiencies for low modulation frequencies such as are present in video amplifiers at low frequencies.

[3] This equation also gives the 90 to 10 per cent decay time.

stage is of the order of 5 to 10 per cent, then the overshoot of the over-all system is approximately proportional to the square root of the number of stages, while the rise time increases much less rapidly than the number of stages.

The fact that the maximum possible speed of rise and fall is determined by the bandwidth of the tuned amplifier sets a limit to the shortest pulse that a given tuned amplifier can produce at its output. This minimum pulse length is approximately $1/B$ seconds. If the length of the applied pulse is shorter than this, the output pulse will still have a length of about $1/B$ seconds.

12-6. Single-tuned Wideband Amplifiers. The bandwidth of a single-tuned amplifier can be made large by using a resonant system having a

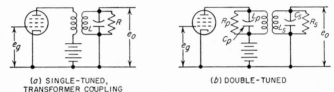

(a) SINGLE-TUNED, TRANSFORMER COUPLING   (b) DOUBLE-TUNED

Fig. 12-11. Single-tuned and double-tuned amplifiers in which the bandwidth has been made large by shunting each resonant circuit with a resistance.

low effective Q, as seen from Eq. (12-4). The usual method of achieving a desired low value of Q_{eff} consists in shunting the resonant circuit with a resistance of appropriate value. In the circuit of Fig. 12-1a this can be achieved by a grid leak of low resistance; with transformer coupling an auxiliary resistance is required, indicated as R in Fig. 12-11a. When the bandwidth thus achieved is made large, the coil and capacitor losses of the resonant circuit are small compared with the loss introduced by the resistance R shunting the resonant circuit. When this is the case, Eqs. (12-2), (12-5), and (12-4) can be written, respectively,[1]

$$\left.\begin{array}{l}\text{Voltage amplification at}\\\text{resonance for direct coupling}\end{array}\right\} = g_m R = g_m \omega_0 L \frac{f_0}{\Delta} \qquad (12\text{-}16)$$

$$\left.\begin{array}{l}\text{Voltage amplification at resonance}\\\text{for transformer coupling}\end{array}\right\} = g_m R \frac{M}{L} = g_m \omega_0 M \frac{f_0}{\Delta} \quad (12\text{-}17)$$

$$R = \frac{f_0}{\Delta} \omega_0 L = \frac{f_0}{\Delta} \frac{1}{\omega_0 C} \qquad (12\text{-}18)$$

[1] The fact that the amplification of a direct-coupled circuit is $g_m R$ follows from Eq. (12-1) when it is noted that the parallel impedance at resonance is R when the Q of the resonant system is determined primarily by R. The right-hand side of Eq. (12-16) is obtained by substituting $Q_{\text{eff}} = f_0/\Delta$ in Eq. (12-2). Equation (12-17) is derived in the same manner, starting with Eq. (12-5).

Equation (12-18) follows from Eq. (12-4) by making use of the fact that when R supplies practically all the circuit losses, then

$$Q_{\text{eff}} = R/\omega_0 L = R\omega_0 C \qquad (12\text{-}19)$$

where f_0 = resonant frequency

$\omega_0 = 2\pi f_0$

g_m = transconductance of tube

R = resistance shunting resonant circuit

Δ = half-power bandwidth

L, M, C = circuit elements as shown in Figs. 12-1 and 12-3

Analogy with Uncompensated Video Amplifier. The single-tuned wideband amplifier is analogous in every respect to the uncompensated resistance-coupled video amplifier discussed on page 290, provided one remembers that the half-power bandwidth of the tuned amplifier is twice as great as the half-power bandwidth of the corresponding video amplifier. Thus the single-tuned wideband amplifier is free of overshoot, and the relationship between rise time and the half-power bandwidth in an individual stage is given by Eq. (12-15), using a value of 0.7 for the numerical constant. In analogy with Eq. (9-3), the 10 to 90 per cent rise time can also be written as

$$\text{Rise time in seconds} = 4.4RC \qquad (12\text{-}20)$$

where R is the resistance shunting the resonant circuit, while C is the tuning capacitance of the circuit. The envelope delay of a single-tuned amplifier stage varies with modulation frequency in exactly the same manner as the time delay of the corresponding video amplifier varies with video frequency; this is apparent from a comparison of Figs. 9-4 and 12-9.

Because of these similarities with the uncompensated video amplifier, the single-tuned amplifier has the same defects as the uncompensated video amplifier, namely, low gain for a given rise time, and excessive bandwidth narrowing when a number of stages are connected in cascade. As a result, double-tuned or stagger-tuned stages are ordinarily used in preference to single-tuned stages in wideband systems.

The Gain-bandwidth Concept with Special Reference to Single-tuned Stages, and Tubes for Wideband Tuned Amplifiers. Since the bandwidth that an individual stage must have is determined by the required rise time in accordance with Eq. (12-15), the greater the speed of rise the larger must be the bandwidth. For a given bandwidth (or rise time) it is apparent from Eqs. (12-16) and (12-17) that the amplification will be greater the larger the inductance of the resonant circuit, i.e., the smaller the tuning capacitance. However, the minimum tuning capacitance that can possibly be present is the plate-cathode (output) capacitance C_{pk} of the amplifier stage, plus the grid-cathode (input) capacitance C_{gk} of the succeeding amplifier stage to which the amplified voltage is applied. This sets a limit to the amount of amplification obtainable from a single-tuned stage required to have a specified bandwidth Δ. With the direct-coupled circuit of Fig. 12-1a, the minimum tuning capacitance is $C_{gk} + C_{pk}$.

It is instructive for this case to combine Eqs. (12-16) and (12-18), and then rearrange as follows:

$$\text{Gain} \times \text{half-power bandwidth} = \frac{g_m}{2\pi(C_{gk} + C_{pk})} \qquad (12\text{-}21)$$

This result is identical with Eq. (9-4), and the gain-bandwidth product it defines has the same meaning as discussed on page 291 for the corresponding video case. Thus the product of voltage gain and bandwidth of a single-tuned stage is independent of resonant frequency or of bandwidth, and is dependent only upon the transconductance of the tube and upon the total tuning capacitance C. To the extent that this tuning capacitance is supplied solely by the tube capacitances $C_{gk} + C_{pk}$, the gain-bandwidth product of a direct-coupled single-tuned amplifier is a property of the tube that indicates tube merit. The significance of this gain-bandwidth product can be understood by considering a numerical case. Thus assume that the tube transconductance is 5000 μmhos and the tube capacitances total 10 $\mu\mu$f; then the gain-bandwidth product is 80×10^6. This means that, if the half-power bandwidth corresponding to the desired rise time is 1 Mc, a voltage gain of 80 can be obtained; whereas, if the required bandwidth is 5 Mc, the voltage gain is $80/5 = 16$, etc.

It follows from the similarity of Eqs. (12-21) and (9-4) that the qualities desired in a tube for a wideband tuned amplifier are large transconductance and small electrode capacitances, just as for video amplification. Thus the same pentode tubes that are desirable for video amplification (such as those listed in Table 9-1, page 292) are likewise desirable for wideband tuned amplifiers. In addition, if the frequency band to be amplified is a very high or ultra-high frequency, as is commonly the case, the tube must also be a type having low input conductance at such frequencies.[1] This is discussed in Sec. 12-12.

12-7. Double-tuned Wideband Amplifiers.[2] A double-tuned amplifier can be given wideband characteristics by shunting the primary and secondary resonant circuits by resistances, as shown in Fig. 12-11b, in order to achieve low circuit Q's, and by changing the coefficient of coupling correspondingly. Ordinarily the primary and secondary circuits are made identical, with equal shunt resistances, so that the primary and secondary Q's are the same.[3] When this is the case, and the coupling has the critical value, the bandwidth is then given by Eq. (12-12).

---

[1] Such a tube (the 6AK5) is described in detail by G. T. Ford, Characteristics of Vacuum Tubes for Radar Intermediate-frequency Amplifiers, *Bell System Tech. J.*, vol. 25, p. 385, July, 1946.

[2] For further details on this subject, see "Vacuum Tube Amplifiers," *op. cit.*, chap. 5.

[3] It is possible, however, to obtain a wideband characteristic with a resistance shunted across only one of the circuits. This gives somewhat higher amplification for a given bandwidth, but has the disadvantage that a slight error in tuning will result in an asymmetrical amplification curve.

The relationship existing between the amplification and the half-power bandwidth Δ_2 in a critically coupled double-tuned amplifier with identical primary and secondary circuits can be expressed by rewriting Eq. (12-10) as follows:[1]

$$\text{Amplification at resonance} = g_m \frac{R}{2} = \frac{1}{\sqrt{2}} g_m \omega_0 L \frac{f_0}{\Delta_2} \quad (12\text{-}22)$$

Also

$$R = \sqrt{2} \frac{f_0}{\Delta_2} \omega_0 L = 2 \sqrt{2} \frac{f_0}{\Delta_2} \frac{1}{\omega_0 (C_p + C_s)} \quad (12\text{-}23)$$

The notation in these relations is the same as previously used, with the addition that with reference to Fig. 12-11b, it is assumed $R = R_p = R_s$, $L = L_p = L_s$, and $C_p = C_s$.

Transient Response of Double-tuned Amplifiers. The transient response of double-tuned amplifiers, irrespective of whether the circuits are over-coupled or undercoupled, is always characterized by overshoot. The amount of overshoot increases with the coefficient of coupling; with systems having equal primary and secondary Q's, it is 4.3 per cent with critical coupling, and 2 per cent when the coupling is 80 per cent of the critical value.[2]

The rise time of a double-tuned amplifier is given by Eq. (12-15), which is generally applicable to all tuned amplifiers. When the coefficient of coupling does not exceed the critical value, the rise time of a single stage of double-tuned amplification is obtained by assuming the numerical constant in the equation is 0.7.

In a multistage double-tuned amplifier with equal primary and secondary Q's, and possessing critical coupling, the overshoot will be almost, but not quite, proportional to the square root of the number of stages. The rise time under these conditions will increase only very slowly with the number of stages. However, when the coefficient of coupling is reduced to 0.80 or less, the overshoot will not increase significantly with the number of stages, while the rise time will then be proportional to the square root of the number of stages connected in cascade.

Comparison of Double-tuned and Single-tuned Wideband Amplifiers. Study of Eq. (12-22) shows that for a given bandwidth Δ_2 of the individual stage, the amplification of a double-tuned amplifier will be greater

---

[1] Equation (12-22) is obtained by combining Eqs. (12-10), (12-12), and (12-4) in such a manner as to eliminate Q and Δ. Equation (12-23) is Eq. (12-18) rewritten to replace Δ by Δ_2 with the aid of Eq. (12-12).

[2] The exact expression for overshoot when the primary and secondary Q's are the same is

$$\text{Overshoot} = \epsilon^{-\pi(k_c/k)} \quad (12\text{-}24)$$

where k_c/k is the ratio of the critical to the actual coefficient of coupling. This is from "Vacuum Tube Amplifiers," *op. cit.*, p. 278.

the larger the coil inductance, i.e., the smaller the tuning capacitance. The minimum capacitances that can be used to tune the primary and secondary circuits are respectively the plate-cathode or output capacitance C_{pk} of the amplifier stage in question, and the grid-cathode or input capacitance C_{gk} of the following stage to which the amplified voltage is applied. When these two capacitances are equal, an expression for the product of voltage amplification and bandwidth can be obtained by rearranging Eq. (12-22), and noting that the $\omega_0 L = 2/\omega_0(C_{pk} + C_{gk})$. This leads to the result

$$\left.\begin{array}{l}\text{Gain-bandwidth product} \\ \text{of double-tuned stage} \\ \text{for } C_{gk} = C_{pk}\end{array}\right\} = \frac{\sqrt{2}\, g_m}{2\pi(C_{gk} + C_{pk})} \qquad (12\text{-}25)$$

A comparison of Eq. (12-25) with Eq. (12-21) shows that the gain-bandwidth product of the double-tuned amplifier with $C_{gk} = C_{pk}$ is $\sqrt{2}$ times the gain-bandwidth product of the corresponding single-tuned amplifier having the same capacitances. In addition, the bandwidth narrowing in a multistage system is less with double-tuned circuits than when single-tuned circuits are used. Hence the initial advantage of double tuning becomes progressively still greater as the number of stages increases. Double-tuned stages are therefore greatly superior to single-tuned stages for wideband amplification. This applies equally to the transient response, since it follows from Eq. (12-15) that the speed of rise is directly proportional to the bandwidth.

12-8. Stagger-tuned Amplifiers.[1] A curve of amplification as a function of frequency such as obtained with double tuning can also be achieved by using two single-tuned stages in which the individual resonant circuits are symmetrically detuned about the center frequency of the band to be amplified. Specifically, if δ is the frequency difference between the resonant frequencies of the individual circuits, i.e., if each circuit is detuned symmetrically $\delta/2$ cycles from the center frequency f_0, then the shape of the over-all amplification curve of the staggered-tuned pair is identical with the shape of the amplification curve of a single-stage double-tuned amplifier in which the coefficient of coupling is δ/f_0.* The transient response and envelope delay of such a staggered-tuned pair are also identical with the characteristics of the corresponding double-tuned stage.

Basic Relationships in Stagger-tuned Pair, and Comparison with Single-tuned and Double-tuned Systems. The relationship between detuning, half-power bandwidth, and gain in a stagger-tuned pair can be understood by considering the case where two amplifier stages initially identical are

---

[1] For further information, see Henry Wallman, Stagger-tuned Amplifier Design, *Electronics,* vol. 21, p. 100, May, 1948; also "Vacuum Tube Amplifiers," *op. cit.,* p. 176.

* This is in accordance with the discussion on p. 69.

detuned sufficiently to give an amplification curve corresponding to critical coupling (that is, $k = k_c = \delta/f_0$). This is termed the *maximum flatness* or *transitional* case. The amount of detuning required to achieve this result is[1]

$$\text{Detuning } \delta/2 \text{ from center frequency} = \frac{f_0}{2Q} = \frac{\Delta_1}{2} = \frac{\Delta_2}{2\sqrt{2}} \quad (12\text{-}26)$$

where Q is the value applicable to the individual resonant circuits of the amplifier, Δ_1 is the half-power band-width of a single tuned circuit, and Δ_2 is the half-power bandwidth of the stagger-tuned pair. The amplification characteristics of the individual detuned circuits are then related to each other as shown in Fig. 12-12. It will be noted that the center frequency f_0 is now at the 70.7 per cent point of the individual amplification curves, since by Eq. (12-26) the difference $\delta/2$ between the resonant frequency and the center frequency is $f_0/2Q = \Delta_1/2$.

The over-all response of the two-stage stagger-tuned pair is compared in Fig. 12-13 with the corresponding two-stage nonstaggered pair having the same resonant circuits. It is seen that staggering reduces the total amplification of the center frequency to 0.5 of the value obtained before detuning, since at the center frequency each detuned stage has an amplification that is 0.707 of the peak amplification of the individual stage. Thus the equivalent voltage amplification *per stage* of the staggered pair is 0.707 times as great as when the same two stages are used without staggering. However, since the amplification curve of the stagger-tuned pair has a bandwidth corresponding to that of a critically coupled double-tuned stage, the half-power bandwidth Δ_2 of the staggered pair is $\sqrt{2}$ times as great as the half-power bandwidth $\Delta_1 = f_0/Q$ of an individual single-tuned stage as given by Eq. (12-4). Hence the equivalent gain-bandwidth product per stage of a stagger-tuned pair is $0.707 \times \sqrt{2} = 1.00$ times that of the individual single-tuned stages.

By readjusting circuit Q's and the detuning to give the staggered pair the same bandwidth Δ_1 previously possessed by an individual single-tuned

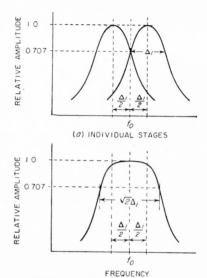

(a) INDIVIDUAL STAGES

(b) OVERALL CHARACTERISTIC OF PAIR

FIG. 12-12. Relation of amplification characteristics of individual stages in a staggered pair to the over-all amplification of the two stages.

[1] The right-hand term of Eq. (12-26) results from the fact that with critical coupling $k = 1/Q = \delta/f_0$, so that $\delta = f_0/Q$.

stage, one obtains a staggered pair that has the same equivalent voltage amplification *per stage* as does the single-tuned stage; thus two-stage staggered systems will have the characteristics shown by the dotted curve in Fig. 12-13. In comparison the two-stage identically tuned system with the same gain per stage as this staggered pair will have a bandwidth only 0.644 times as great as does the staggered pair; this is because of the bandwidth narrowing that results when two identically tuned single-tuned stages are cascaded.

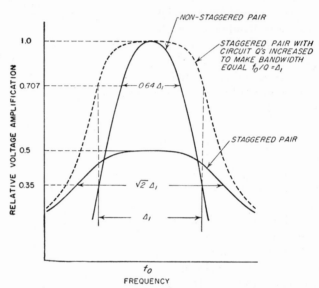

FIG. 12-13. Curves showing relative amplitudes and bandwidths of the over-all response of a two-stage amplifier with the stages identically tuned and stagger-tuned, and also for a two-stage staggered pair with the Q's modified to give the same equivalent gain per stage as the actual gain per stage of the original identically tuned system.

The behavior of stagger-tuned systems compared with single- and double-tuned arrangements is summarized in Table 12-2, which gives the relative over-all bandwidth obtainable for the same gain per stage. In addition to being greatly superior to the two-stage identically tuned single-tuned system, as noted above, the staggered pair has a performance almost as good as two double-tuned stages, and is both simpler and less expensive than using double tuning.

The voltage gain *per stage* will also be proportional to the factors in Table 12-2 if the over-all bandwidth is kept constant at a specified value. Thus in a four-stage system, staggering in pairs gives a relative voltage gain per stage of 0.8, whereas the relative voltage gain per stage in a four-stage identically tuned system of the same bandwidth is 0.44. As a result, when these two four-stage systems are so proportioned as to have the same over-all half-power bandwidth, their relative voltage gain is

$(0.80/0.44)^4 = 10.9$. This is a very large difference, and emphasizes the great advantage to be obtained in wideband systems by arranging single-tuned stages in staggered pairs instead of adjusting them all to be resonant at the same frequency.

The staggering of single-tuned stages introduces very little in the way of practical complications. To align the staggered system, one first applies to the amplifier input a test voltage corresponding to one of the detuned resonant frequencies, and then successively adjusts every other stage of the system separately to give maximum amplified output; the

TABLE 12-2

Number of amplifier stages (tubes) in system	Relative 3-db bandwidth *of over-all system* for same gain per stage, or relative gain *per stage* for same over-all 3-db bandwidth of system		
	Single-tuned stages	Double-tuned stages*	Stagger-tuned stages
1	1.00	1.414	
2	0.64	1.13	1.00
4	0.44	0.93	0.80

* Adjusted for maximum flatness (or critical coupling).

test signal is then reset to the other resonant frequency, and each of the remaining stages then is similarly adjusted for maximum output.

Staggered Systems of Higher Order. The stagger-tuning idea can be readily extended to more complicated arrangements. Thus in a multistage single-tuned system, the stages may be arranged in groups of three or four, or even more; in such arrangements each stage in the group is tuned to a different frequency, and in addition some stages will have different Q's. In a similar manner, stagger tuning may be applied to double-tuned systems; thus one can stagger double-tuned stages in pairs by using different values of coupling coefficients and different Q's for the individual stages.

In general, when staggering is properly carried out, the more complicated the staggering pattern, and the more complicated the individual stages, the greater will be the gain per stage obtainable for a given half-power bandwidth. However, systems more complicated than staggered pairs ordinarily find use only when special requirements are to be met, for example, when the bandwidth required is so large that the gain per stage becomes very small unless a system more complicated than staggering in pairs is employed.

12-9. Regeneration in Multistage Tuned Amplifiers. Regeneration will occur in tuned amplifiers when there is a transfer of energy between stages, exactly as in the case of audio- and video-frequency amplifiers (see

Sec. 10-10).   It is a form of uncontrolled feedback that seriously distorts the shape of the curve of amplification, particularly within the half-power bandwidth.   This distortion comes about through the fact that the feedback will commonly vary so rapidly with frequency that it will change from positive to negative within the frequency range encompassed by the half-power bandwidth.   At those frequencies for which the feedback is negative, the gain is reduced by the regeneration.   At frequencies that make the feedback positive, the gain is increased, and if the regeneration is great enough oscillations will result.

This makes it important to eliminate regeneration almost completely from a multistage tuned amplifier.   It is not sufficient merely to prevent oscillations, since an amount of feedback that is much less than the value required to cause oscillations will still distort greatly the shape of the amplification curve, adversely affect the envelope-delay characteristic, and spoil an otherwise good transient response.

The problem of eliminating regeneration in tuned amplifiers is made especially difficult by the fact that at the high frequencies involved in such amplifiers, a very small amount of capacitive coupling will transfer appreciable current because the reactance of a capacitance is inversely proportional to frequency.   Likewise, a very small amount of inductance common to various parts of the amplifier is particularly serious at high frequencies because the reactance of this coupling inductance is proportional to frequency.

Control of Regeneration.   Impedances common to two or more stages are particularly troublesome causes of regeneration in tuned amplifiers, because at the high frequencies involved a wire only a few inches long and common to two circuits will have sufficient reactance to provide an effective means of transferring energy.   Common couplings of this type can be eliminated by care in the location of grounds so that the chassis is not used as a common return circuit, and by the proper use of by-pass capacitors.   The important factors involved in locating grounds are illustrated in Fig. 12-14.   Thus, if the coils of the two resonant circuits are returned to ground as shown by b_3 and b_4, instead of directly to the tuning capacitors, as shown by a_3 and a_4, then the chassis will carry tuned-circuit currents from b_3 to c_3 and from b_4 to c_4.   Since these currents will spread out through the entire chassis, their paths will inevitably overlap each other to some extent, resulting in energy transfer between stages, *i.e.*, regeneration.   A similar situation exists with respect to the by-pass capacitor connections to ground.   The proper arrangements are indicated in Fig. 12-14 by a_1 and a_2 the improper ones by b_1 and b_2.

By-pass capacitors as illustrated by C in Fig. 12-14, particularly when combined with small series resistances as indicated by R in Fig. 12-14, are a very effective means of preventing coupling through common power-supply connections.   In order to be fully effective, however, the capacitors must be of a type having low inherent inductance, and if the by-passing is to be fully effective at the ultra-high frequencies, they must be arranged with relatively short leads. Otherwise the lead and capacitor inductance will prevent the capacitor from being fully effective as a by-pass. It is also desirable when a considerable number of stages of amplification are involved that these resistance-capacitor decoupling sections be arranged in the form of a ladder, as shown in Fig. 12-14, rather than having a separate resistance-capacitance decoupling network leading from the power supply to each stage. The advantage of the ladder arrangement is that it places the maximum possible number of decoupling

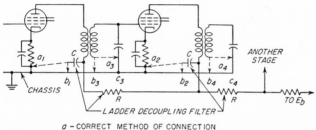

a – CORRECT METHOD OF CONNECTION
b – INCORRECT METHOD OF CONNECTION

Fig. 12-14. Methods of locating ground connections in a multistage tuned amplifier to minimize common couplings introduced by the chassis, together with decoupling filters RC for isolating individual stages.

sections between input and output stages of the amplifier, and uses a minimum amount of material in doing so (compare with Fig. 10-26b and Sec. 10-10).

Regeneration arising as a result of stray inductive and capacitive couplings that exist between different parts of the amplifier can be reduced by properly placing and orienting different parts of the amplifier, supplemented in many cases by shielding. Coils of resonant circuits are ordinarily either enclosed in a shield, or made physically small with axes carefully oriented to minimize coupling between adjacent coils.

When the amplifier consists of many stages, as is often the case in wideband systems where the large bandwidth results in low gain per stage, direct capacitive and inductive coupling between different parts of the amplifier, including coupling between unshielded coils, can be minimized by arranging the stages in a line so that the different parts of the amplifier are spaced in proportion to the difference in their power levels. A ladder decoupling system is then used as shown in Fig. 12-14, and filament wires are provided with grounded shields or otherwise arranged so they do not act as exposed transmission lines that can carry energy freely between input and output ends of the amplifier chain. If the system of coils, capacitors, filters, tubes, etc., in such a system is now enclosed by a conducting container of size such that the largest transverse dimension of the enclosed space is considerably less than a half wavelength at the frequency being amplified, the amplifier can be regarded as being located within a waveguide attenuator such as discussed in Sec. 5-8. If the proportions of the enclosing walls or waveguide are such that the attenuation for the dominant mode in a distance equal to the spacing between amplifier stages exceeds the stage gain, then the stray electric and magnetic fields from coils, high potential leads, etc., will attenuate more rapidly with distance than the amplifier gain increases with distance. Under these conditions no further shielding, and no particular care in the detailed arrangement of circuit components, is required.

12-10. Input Admittance of Triode Amplifiers. The input admittance of a vacuum-tube amplifier is defined as the current flowing into the control-grid electrode divided by the voltage that is applied between this

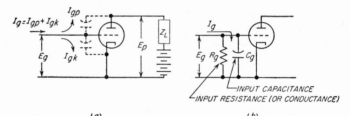

(*a*)   (*b*)

Fig. 12-15. Diagrams illustrating input admittance effects in a vacuum-tube amplifier.

electrode and the cathode. Thus, the input admittance is the admittance that is observed between the grid and cathode terminals when looking toward the tube. The input admittance takes into account the capacitance between the control grid and other electrodes, the transfer of energy between grid and plate circuits through couplings within the tube, and interaction between the potential applied to the control-grid electrode and the electron stream. Furthermore, if the grid is driven positive and so collects electrons, the input admittance is thereby altered, although this action is generally considered as a separate effect.

The input admittance of a vacuum-tube amplifier is normally represented as an equivalent capacitance shunted by an equivalent resistance, as illustrated in Fig. 12-15b. This capacitance is called the *input capacitance*, and the resistance is termed either the *input resistance* or *input conductance*. The parallel combination of input capacitance and conductance forms the input admittance.

Analysis of Input Admittance of Triodes. The input admittance of a triode is determined by the currents I_{gk} and I_{gp} that flow through the grid-cathode and grid-plate capacitances, respectively, when a voltage is applied to the control grid, as illustrated in Fig. 12-15a. Here I_{gk} represents the current flowing through capacitance C_{gk} as a result of the applied voltage E_g, and requires no discussion. However, the current component I_{gp} representing the current flowing from grid to plate through the grid-plate capacitance C_{gp} depends upon the voltage difference $E_g - E_p$ existing across C_{gp}. This voltage difference in turn depends upon the amplification E_p/E_g, and will commonly be much larger than the applied signal voltage E_g. As a result, the input admittance of a triode amplifier will be greater than the admittance of $C_{gk} + C_{pk}$; moreover, the input admittance will have a magnitude and phase that depend upon the vector value of the amplification, and hence upon the load impedance in the plate circuit of the tube.

A quantitative analysis of the relations involved in Fig. 12-15a leads to the following expression for the input capacitance and input resistance as shown in Fig. 12-15b:[1]

$$\text{Input resistance} = R_g = -\frac{1/\omega C_{gp}}{A \sin \theta} \tag{12-27}$$

$$\text{Input capacitance} = C_g = C_{gk} + C_{gp}(1 + A \cos \theta) \tag{12-28}$$

The notation is the same as in Fig. 12-15a with the following additions:

$A = |E_p/E_g| = $ magnitude of amplification, not including any voltage transformation that may exist in the load impedance

$\theta = $ angle by which the voltage E_p across the load impedance will lead the equivalent voltage $-\mu E_g$ that acts in the plate circuit (θ positive for inductive load impedances)

Examination of Eq. (12-28) shows that the input capacitance of the triode amplifier depends only on the amplification A, the phase shift θ, and the tube capacitances.[2] The input capacitance is independent of the frequency except as frequency affects the magnitude A and phase angle θ

---

[1] In deriving these relations, one starts by using the voltage E_g as a phase reference and regards the symbols E_g and E_p as representing magnitude only. Then if the angle by which E_p leads $-\mu E_g$ is θ, E_p leads E_g by the angle $(\theta + 180°)$. With these definitions the vector value of the voltage across the grid-plate tube capacitance C_{gp} is $(E_g - E_p/\underline{\theta + 180°})$, and the current flowing from grid to plate as a result of this voltage across C_{gp} is $j\omega C_{gp}(E_g - E_p/\underline{\theta + 180°})$. The current flowing from grid to cathode through the grid capacitance C_{gk} is $j\omega C_{gk}E_g$, so that the total grid current, which is the sum of these, is

$$\begin{aligned}\text{Total grid current} &= j\omega C_{gk}E_g + j\omega C_{gp}(E_g - E_p/\underline{\theta + 180°}) \\ &= \omega C_{gk}E_g/\underline{90°} + \omega C_{gp}(E_g/\underline{90°} - E_p/\underline{\theta + 270°})\end{aligned}$$

This total current divided by the voltage E_g gives the admittance of the grid, which is therefore

$$\text{Admittance of grid} = \omega C_{gk}/\underline{90°} + \omega C_{gp}[1/\underline{90°} - (E_p/E_g)/\underline{\theta + 270°}]$$

The real part of this admittance represents the input conductance (i.e., the reciprocal of the input resistance), while the quadrature part is the input susceptance, which when divided by ω gives the input capacitance. Equations (12-27) and (12-28) are merely these two components of the input admittance with $|E_p/E_g|$ denoted by the symbol A.

[2] The influence of amplification on the input capacitance of a triode is sometimes termed the Miller effect, after John M. Miller, who first recognized and studied this phenomenon.

of the amplification.   The maximum possible input capacitance is

$$\left.\begin{array}{l}\text{Maximum possible triode}\\ \text{input capacitance}\end{array}\right\} = C_{gk} + (1 + \mu)C_{gp} \qquad (12\text{-}29)$$

Here μ is the amplification factor of the tube.   This situation results when the load impedance is very much greater than the plate resistance; one then has $A \approx \mu$, and $\theta \approx 0$.   The minimum possible input capacitance occurs when the load impedance is zero ($A = 0$), and is

$$\left.\begin{array}{l}\text{Minimum possible triode}\\ \text{input capacitance}\end{array}\right\} = C_{gk} + C_{gp} \qquad (12\text{-}30)$$

The actual input capacitance will be much larger than this minimum value if the amplification is appreciable.

The input resistance of the vacuum tube may be either positive or negative, as seen from Eq. (12-27).   A positive input resistance results when the load impedance in the plate circuit is a capacitive reactance, while a negative resistance is obtained with an inductive load in the plate circuit. *A positive input resistance means that energy is transferred from the grid to the plate through the grid-plate capacitance, while a negative input resistance indicates that the phase relations are such that energy is transferred from the output or plate circuit of the tube to the grid circuit.*   The value of input resistance for a given amplification A and phase shift θ varies inversely as the frequency, and may be very low at high frequencies.

Practical Importance of the Input Admittance in Triode Audio and Video Amplifiers.   The principal reason that pentode tubes are preferred to high-mu triodes for resistance-coupled amplification and as video amplifiers is that triodes have high input capacitance when the amplification is at all appreciable.   In contrast, the input capacitance of pentodes always has a value equivalent to the minimum specified by Eq. (12-30), as discussed below in Sec. 12-12.   This high input capacitance of the triode voltage amplifier adversely affects the high-frequency response of the preceding amplifier stage, and so is a serious disadvantage in video voltage amplifiers, and in most resistance-coupled audio-frequency voltage amplifiers as well.

Input capacitance effects do not, however, place triode audio-frequency power amplifiers at an especially serious disadvantage with respect to beam and pentode powes tubes.   This is because triode tubes with low to moderate amplification factors are used in power amplification in order to achieve a large plate current with small voltage drop in the tube without driving the grid appreciably positive.   Under these conditions the amplification A is not large, and the input capacitance does not exceed the minimum value to anything like the extent that it does in triode voltage amplifiers.

Input Impedance of Tuned Amplifiers.   In a tuned amplifier the magnitude A and the phase shift θ of the amplification will vary greatly with frequency. This causes the input conductance and the input capacitance of the triode tuned amplifier to go through corresponding changes, as illustrated in Fig. 12-16 for the case of single tuning. It is to be noted that the input conductance is negative at frequencies below resonance where the plate load impedance is inductive, is zero at resonance where the plate load impedance is resistive, and is positive above resonance where the plate load impedance is capacitive.

The maximum value of input capacitance in Fig. 12-16 is the value given by Eq. (12-28) for resonance, i.e., when $A = A_0$ and $\theta = 0$; thus the "resonant rise" above the base line $C_{gk} + C_{pg}$ is $A_0 C_{gp}$. The peaks of the conductance curve in Fig. 12-16 occur at the 70.7 per cent response points of the amplification curve, and correspond to values of input resistance given by the relation

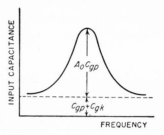

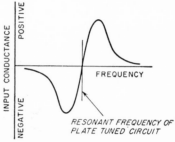

FIG. 12-16. Variation of input capacitance and input conductance of a triode amplifier having a load impedance that is a single resonant circuit.

$$\left.\begin{array}{c}\text{Minimum input}\\\text{resistance}\end{array}\right\} = \pm \frac{1/\omega C_{gp}}{A_0/2} \quad (12\text{-}31)$$

where A_0 is the amplification of resonance, not including any voltage transformation that may exist in the plate load impedance.[1] The resistance given by Eq. (12-31) can have quite low values at radio frequencies. For example, if $C_{gp} = 2\ \mu\mu\text{f}$ and $A_0 = 15$, then at 1500 kc the minimum input resistance is 7070 ohms. This is a low value compared with the parallel impedance of a resonant circuit that it might shunt.

If a tuned circuit is connected between the grid and cathode of an amplifier tube having an input admittance such as shown in Fig. 12-16, the resonance curve of this tuned circuit is considerably distorted if its resonance frequency is the same (taking into account the input capacitance at resonance) as that of the tuned load impedance in the plate circuit of the amplifier. Alternatively, if the grid tuned circuit is resonant at a slightly lower frequency, then the negative input resistance shunting the grid resonant circuit at its resonant frequency will ordinarily cause the system to break into oscillation. These effects of input admit-

---

[1] When the tuned load circuit is coupled to the plate circuit of the tube, as with transformer coupling, the value of A_0 is less than the actual voltage amplification of the stage by the factor $(M/L_s)^2$, where M is the mutual inductance between primary and secondary, and L_s is the inductance of the secondary.

tance in tuned amplifiers are so serious that pentode, beam, or screen-grid tubes are employed in tuned amplifiers in preference to triodes whenever possible.   If circumstances require the use of triode tubes in tuned amplifiers, it is then necessary either to neutralize the energy transfer taking place between grid and plate circuits of the tuned triode amplifier, or to employ a grounded-grid circuit.

12-11. Neutralization of Input Admittance of Vacuum-tube Amplifiers —Grounded-grid Systems.   The effects produced by the transfer of energy between the grid and plate circuits of a vacuum-tube amplifier

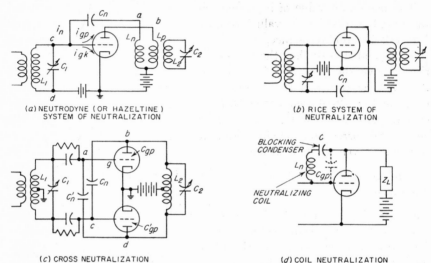

(a) NEUTRODYNE (OR HAZELTINE)
SYSTEM OF NEUTRALIZATION

(b) RICE SYSTEM OF
NEUTRALIZATION

(c) CROSS NEUTRALIZATION

(d) COIL NEUTRALIZATION

Fig. 12-17. Typical circuits for neutralizing the coupling between the input and output circuits of a triode amplifier arising from the grid-plate capacitance effects.

through the grid-plate tube capacitance can be neutralized by an electrical network that transfers an equal amount of energy in the opposite direction.   Examples of such circuits are given in Fig. 12-17a, b, and c.

In each of these a neutralizing capacitor C_n connects the input (i.e., grid) circuit to the output (i.e., plate) circuit in such a way that the current passing through C_n is of the proper amplitude and phase to neutralize exactly the transfer of energy between the input and output circuits of the amplifier *via* the grid-plate tube capacitance.   Thus consider Fig. 12-17a. This is an ordinary transformer-coupled single-tuned radio-frequency amplifier to which there has been added a neutralizing inductance L_n closely coupled to L_p and connected with a polarity such that the voltage at the end a of this coil is in phase opposition to the voltage at the corresponding end b of the primary inductance L_p.   By making C_n the proper size, the currents i_n and i_{gp} that flow through C_n and the grid-plate capacitance, respectively, are then oppositely affected by the voltages developed in L_n and L_p.   The result is complete neutralization of the energy transfer that would otherwise take place between the input and output tuned circuits, through the tube capacitance. The input capacitance of such an amplifier with perfect neutralization is $C_{gk} + C_{gp} + C_n$, and the input resistance is infinite. If the coupling between L_n and L_p is very close, the value of C_n required to give complete neutralization is nearly independent of frequency.

In the circuit of Fig. 12-17b, the inductance of the input resonant circuit is provided with a center tap and arranged as shown. If $C_n = C_{gp}$, the current flowing through the neutralizing capacitor C_n from the input circuit to the plate circuit will then be equal and opposite to the corresponding current through C_{gp}. In push-pull amplifiers, neutralization can be accomplished as illustrated in Fig. 12-17c. Here the fact that all

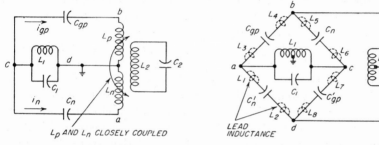

(a) EQUIVALENT BRIDGE CIRCUIT APPLYING TO FIG 12-17 a

(b) EQUIVALENT BRIDGE CIRCUIT APPLYING TO FIG.12-17 c

FIG. 12-18. Equivalent bridge circuits of neutralized amplifiers of Fig. 12-17a and c.

circuits are symmetrical with respect to ground makes neutralization particularly simple and effective.

Each of the systems a, b, and c of Fig. 12-17 can be considered as a bridge in which the output and input circuits are connected across the opposite diagonals. Thus Fig. 12-18a and b shows bridge equivalents of Fig. 12-17a and c, respectively. When the neutralization is so adjusted as to balance the bridge, the input tuned circuit receives no energy from the output tuned circuit because the two are in electrically neutral locations with respect to each other.

If a system is adjusted to give perfect neutralization at a particular frequency, it is found that the neutralization becomes less effective for frequencies that depart increasingly from the frequency at which the adjustment was made. This is because the inductances of the leads in series with the neutralizing capacitors, shown dotted in Fig. 12-18b,[1] cause the equivalent bridge represented by the neutralizing system to be frequency sensitive, particularly at high frequencies. Wideband neutralization can be obtained by adjusting lead lengths and connecting the input

[1] Thus L_1 is the inductance of the lead from junction a to C'_n, L_2 the inductance of the lead from C'_n to junction d, L_3 the inductance from a to the grid electrode, L_4 the inductance from the plate electrode to junction b, and so on.

and output leads to points on the system such that these various lead inductances are so distributed in the equivalent bridge circuit that $(L_1 + L_2)/(L_3 + L_4) = (L_7 + L_8)/(L_5 + L_6) = C_{gp}/C_n' = C_n/C_{gp}'$. In this case the bridge balance in Fig. 12-18c is not affected by frequency, and the neutralization is hence maintained over a wide frequency band.

Coil Neutralization. When neutralization need be achieved only at a single frequency, the coil neutralizing system of Fig. 12-17d is useful. Here the neutralizing inductance L_n is of such size as to resonate with the grid-plate capacitance C_{gp} at the frequency for which neutralization is to be effective. In this way, the current flowing from control grid to plate is reduced practically to zero, thus eliminating the grid-plate capacitance as far as input admittance effects are concerned. In order that the neutralizing coil will not ground the plate-supply potential, it is necessary to place a blocking capacitor C in series with the inductance. Coil neutralization is used extensively in broadcast transmitters.

Grounded-grid Circuits. The necessity of neutralizing a triode amplifier can be avoided by using the grounded-grid circuit of Fig. 12-19a. Here the control grid acts as a grounded shield between the output terminals (plate to ground) and the input terminals (cathode to ground). As a result, energy transfer between input and output circuits through the tube capacitances is avoided to the extent that the plate and cathode electrodes and associated leads are so arranged that there is no direct capacitance between them.[1]

The equivalent plate circuit of the grounded-grid amplifier is shown in Fig. 12-19b,[2] where the arrows are drawn on the basis that a positive value of input voltage E_g makes the cathode negative with respect to ground, corresponding to the grid positive with respect to the cathode. Study of the relations in this circuit shows that since the signal voltage E_g acts between cathode and ground, it is also in series with the plate circuit of the tube. As a result, the amplified output E_L is the same as though the grid of the tube were excited in the normal manner with a voltage E_g, and the amplification factor had the value $(\mu + 1)$ instead of μ, as shown in Fig. 12-19c.

The input resistance of the grounded-grid amplifier is relatively low. This is because the input voltage E_g, in addition to producing a voltage difference between the cathode and grid, also acts directly in the plate circuit and thereby supplies energy that is in part delivered to the plate tuned circuit, and in part dissipated in the plate resistance of the tube.

---

[1] The effect of any residual plate-cathode capacitance that is present can be eliminated by employing a neutralizing system; see J. J. Muller, Cathode-excited Linear Amplifiers, *Electrical Commun.*, vol. 23, p. 297, September, 1946.

[2] For the sake of simplicity these equivalent circuits neglect the effects of transit time, lead inductance, etc., such as discussed in Sec. 12-12, which can be important at the very high frequencies where grounded-grid amplifiers are of practical importance.

The equivalent load impedance presented by the tube to the input voltage E_g and circuit L_1C_1 is shown in Fig. 12-19d,[1] where Z_L is the impedance of the plate tuned circuit L_2C_2. It is apparent that the impedance offered to E_g is relatively low; this fact limits the power amplification that can be obtained from the grounded-grid circuit to a value much less than that obtainable with a neutralized grounded-cathode amplifier.[2]

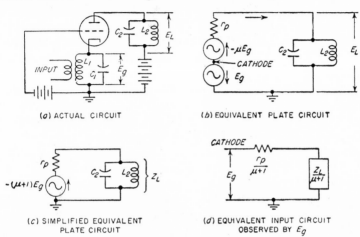

(*a*) ACTUAL CIRCUIT   (*b*) EQUIVALENT PLATE CIRCUIT

(*c*) SIMPLIFIED EQUIVALENT PLATE CIRCUIT   (*d*) EQUIVALENT INPUT CIRCUIT OBSERVED BY E_g

FIG. 12-19. Circuit of grounded-grid amplifier, together with equivalent plate and input circuits.

The grounded-grid triode amplifier finds use as a tuned voltage amplifier at frequencies too high to permit the use of pentode or beam tubes.[3] In these circumstances disk-seal, pencil, or similar closely spaced triodes (see Fig. 6-35) are employed in a grounded-grid circuit using coaxial transmission lines to supply the resonant circuits. Grounded-grid systems using ordinary high-frequency triodes are also often used as Class C and

---

[1] This equivalent circuit results from the fact that the radio-frequency current flowing through the input circuit L_1C_1 is seen from Fig. 12-19c to be $\mu + 1$ times as great as the current that would be produced by the voltage E_g acting in a circuit consisting of r_p and Z_L in series.

[2] The ratio of amplified to input power, i.e., the power amplification of the grounded-grid circuit, for the case of a resistive load ($Z_L = R_L$) can be readily shown to be

$$\left.\begin{array}{c}\text{Power amplification of}\\ \text{grounded-grid amplifier}\end{array}\right\} = (\mu + 1)\frac{R_L}{R_L + r_p} \qquad (12\text{-}32)$$

[3] Further information on grounded-grid amplifiers in such applications is given by Milton Dishal, Theoretical Gain and Signal-to-noise Ratio Obtained with the Grounded-grid Amplifier at Ultra-high Frequencies, *Proc. IRE*, vol. 32, p. 276, May, 1944; M. C. Jones, Grounded-grid Radio-frequency Voltage Amplifiers, *Proc. IRE*, vol. 32, p. 423, July, 1944; J. Foster, Grounded-grid Amplifier Valves for Very Short Waves, *J. IEE* (*Radiolocation Conv.*), vol. 93, pt. IIIA, p. 868, March–May, 1946; A. E. Bowen and W. W. Mumford, a New Microwave Triode: Its Preformance as a Modulator and as an Amplifier, *Bell System Tech. J.*, vol. 29, p. 531, October, 1950.

linear power amplifiers at high frequencies in preference to neutralized arrangements employing the same tube type.[1]   The use of grounded-grid systems at high frequencies is in part because neutralizing systems are increasingly critical of adjustment as the frequency is increased, and in part because the elimination of the neutralizing capacitors reduces the effective input and output capacitances of the tube.   This last feature is of particular importance in wideband systems such as linear amplifiers for television transmitters, as it increases the output power and efficiency obtainable from a particular tube for a given bandwidth.[2]

12-12. Input Admittance of Pentode, Beam, and Screen-grid Tubes. *Input Capacitance.*   In analogy with Eq. (12-28), the input capacitance of pentode and similar tubes is

$$\text{Input capacitance} = C_{gk} + C_{gs} + C_{gp}(1 + A \cos \theta) \qquad (12\text{-}33)$$

where C_{gs} is the grid-screen capacitance, and the remaining notation is as in Eq. (12-28).   It is to be noted, however, that because of the shielding action of the screen grid, the grid-plate capacitance C_{gp} is now a residual stray capacitance much smaller in magnitude than C_{gp} in triodes.

The input capacitance of a tube with a screen grid varies slightly with grid bias.   This is in part due to the change in $C_{gp}(1 + A \cos \theta)$ as the grid bias varies the amplification A, and in part due to the fact that the variation in the plate current by grid bias alters the effective position of the space charge surrounding the cathode, and thereby affects C_{gk}.   The total variation in input capacitance that can be produced in this way may reach as much as 1 to 3 $\mu\mu$f in some tubes, which is sufficient to produce a noticeable detuning of many tuned amplifiers.[3]

Input Conductance of Pentodes and Similar Tubes.   The input conductance of a negative-grid pentode at low and moderate radio frequencies is practically zero, but at very high frequencies cannot be ignored.   Coupling between the plate and control-grid circuits through the stray grid-plate capacitance C_{gp} can contribute to the input conductance in accordance with Eq. (12-27).   However, the inductance of the cathode lead[4]

[1] For detailed discussions of grounded-grid amplifiers for such purposes, see E. E. Spitzer, Grounded-grid Amplifier, *Electronics*, vol. 19, p. 138, April, 1946; C. E. Strong, The Inverted Amplifier, *Electronics*, vol. 13, p. 14, July, 1940; J. J. Muller, *loc. cit.*

[2] A discussion of the use of grounded-grid power amplifiers for television is given by P. A. T. Bevan, Earthed-grid Power Amplifiers, *Wireless Eng.*, vol. 26, p. 182, June, 1949.

[3] This effect can be neutralized if desired by placing a suitable small resistance, not by-passed, between cathode and ground; see R. L. Freeman, The Use of Feedback to Compensate for Vacuum-tube Input-capacitance Variations, *Proc. IRE*, vol. 26, p. 1360, November, 1938.

[4] The transit-time and cathode-lead inductance effects are also present in triode tubes.   However, in such tubes they are so overshadowed by the input admittance effects introduced by the grid-plate capacitance as to be of comparatively little practical importance.

and the transit time of the electron stream are ordinarily the most important causes of input conductance in pentode tubes and also in other tubes having screen grids.

The inductance L_k of the cathode return lead must carry the amplified plate current in a pentode tube, and so has a voltage E_k developed across it. This voltage acts in the input circuit between cathode and control grid as shown in Fig. 12-20, and so makes the voltage difference acting across the grid-cathode capacitance differ from the applied signal voltage E_g by the amount of the voltage drop E_k in the cathode inductance. Since E_k is 90° out of phase with E_g, the result is to produce a component of current flowing through the grid-cathode capacitance

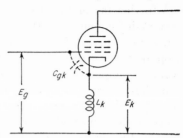

FIG. 12-20. The input circuit of a pentode tube taking into account the inductance of the cathode lead and the capacitance between control grid and cathode.

that is in phase with the applied voltage E_g, and accordingly causes the input admittance of the tube to have a conductance component. The magnitude of this conductance is[1]

$$\left.\begin{array}{l}\text{Input conductance resulting} \\ \text{from inductance of cathode lead}\end{array}\right\} = \omega^2 g_m L_k C_{gk} \qquad (12\text{-}34)$$

At very high frequencies the fact that the extremely small length of time it takes an electron to travel from cathode to screen is not negligible compared with the time represented by a cycle of an extremely high-frequency wave causes power to be consumed by the grid of the tube even when the grid is biased negatively and attracts no electrons. Discussed on page 215, this produces an effect equivalent to shunting a conductance [in addition to that of Eq. (12-34)] between control grid and cathode. This transit-time conductance is given by Eq. (6-31) and, like the conductance due to cathode-lead inductance, is proportional to the transconductance and the square of the frequency.

In practical tubes these two effects are commonly of the same order of magnitude. At broadcast frequencies they are negligible but become

---

[1] Equation (12-34) assumes that the reactance of the lead inductance L_k is small compared with the reactance of the grid-cathode capacitance C_{gk}, and that voltage E_k across L_k is small compared with the applied signal E_g. The derivation is as follows: The voltage E_k developed across L_k by the amplified plate current has a magnitude $g_m \omega L_k E_g$, where g_m is the transconductance of the tube. The voltage E_k acting on the capacitance C_{gk} produces a current $g_m \omega L_k E_g (\omega C_{gk})$. This current is in phase with the applied voltage E_g because the voltage across L_k is 90° out of phase, and there is another 90° phase shift arising from the capacitive reactance of C_{gk}. The resulting input conductance associated with this effect is the current in phase with E_g divided by the grid voltage E_g; Eq. (12-34) is a mathematical expression of this ratio.

increasingly important at higher frequencies, since the conductance varies with the square of the frequency. Thus, a typical general-purpose pentode at 1 Mc may have an input resistance of 20 megohms, but at 100 Mc this becomes only 2000 ohms.[1]

A further factor that can affect the input conductance of pentodes at very high frequencies is the inductance of the screen-grid lead. Amplified screen current flowing through this inductance develops a voltage drop between screen and ground. This voltage in turn introduces a negative component to the input conductance in the same way as does the grid-plate current in a triode possessing an inductive plate load impedance, as discussed above. The resulting negative conductance is proportional to the square of the frequency. By properly adjusting the inductance in the screen circuit it is hence possible to neutralize the positive input conductance arising from cathode-lead inductance and transit time as long as the inductance required to achieve this result is not so large as to resonate with the tube capacitances.

Input Admittance of Amplifier Tubes Subjected to Negative Feedback. When a negative feedback voltage is superimposed upon the signal applied to an amplifier, the equivalent input admittance offered by the system to the applied voltage is less than in the absence of negative feedback according to the factor[2]

$$\left.\begin{array}{l}\text{Input admittance with} \\ \text{negative feedback} \\ \hline \text{Input admittance} \\ \text{without negative feedback}\end{array}\right\} = \frac{1}{1 - A\beta} \qquad (12\text{-}35)$$

where $A\beta$ is the feedback factor, as discussed on page 374. The reduction in input admittance is considerable when $A\beta$ has a large negative value, and arises from the fact that most of the signal voltage is used to overcome the feedback voltage, and only a small fraction is applied across the grid-cathode terminals of the tube to produce current flowing to the grid electrode.

12-13. Circuit and Tube Noise. The weakest signal that can be usefully amplified is limited by randomly varying voltages and currents existing in the circuits and tubes of the amplifier.

Resistance Noise. Every electrical conductor produces an irregularly varying voltage across its terminal as a result of the random motion of the free electrons in the conductor caused by thermal action. This effect

---

[1] When the combined effects of transit time and cathode-lead inductance are not too great, it is possible to neutralize them by methods given by R. L. Freeman, Input Conductance Neutralization, *Electronics*, vol. 12, p. 22, October, 1939; or see F. E. Terman, "Radio Engineers' Handbook," p. 472, McGraw-Hill Book Company, Inc., New York, 1943.

[2] This relation applies to triode amplifiers, as well as those employing pentode and similar tubes.

is referred to by such names as *circuit noise, thermal noise, resistance noise,* and *Johnson noise.* The magnitude of this noise voltage associated with a resistance is

$$\text{Square of rms value of voltage components lying between frequencies } f_1 \text{ and } f_2 \bigg\} = e_n^2 = 4kT \int_{f_1}^{f_2} R \, df \quad (12\text{-}36)$$

where k = Boltzmann's constant = 1.374×10^{-23} joule per °K

T = absolute temperature, °K

R = resistance component of impedance across which the thermal agitation is produced (a function of frequency)

f = frequency

In the special case where the resistance component of the impedance is constant over the range of frequencies from f_1 to f_2, Eq. (12-36) reduces to the much simpler form

$$e_n^2 = 4kTR(f_2 - f_1) = 4kTRB \quad (12\text{-}37)$$

Here $B = f_2 - f_1$ is the bandwidth of the noise.

It is important to note that Eq. (12-37) shows that the mean-square noise voltage e_n^2 developed across a resistance is proportional to the bandwidth B, and is independent of the center frequency of the band. This means that the mean-square noise voltage developed across a given resistance in a frequency band from 1000 to 2000 cycles is exactly the same as the mean-square noise voltage developed in any other band of the same width, as, for example, from 1,001,000 to 1,002,000 cycles. The effective value of the noise voltage e_n observed across a resistance is proportional to the *square root* of the bandwidth of the noise being observed.

The magnitude of the noise voltage generated by a resistance is indicated by the fact that the rms noise e_n developed across a resistance of 100,000 ohms for a frequency band 5000 cycles wide is 2.8 μv at room temperature. Since the noise voltage varies randomly, the peak noise will be larger than this. However, the peaks only rarely exceed four times the rms value, and practically never at all reach ten times the rms amplitude.

When the impedance generating the noise has a reactive component, then R in the above equations is the resistance component of the impedance, considering this impedance as an equivalent resistance R in series with an equivalent reactance.

A resistance R and its associated noise voltage e_n may be represented by the equivalent circuit given in Fig. 12-21a. Here the noise voltage is supplied by an equivalent generator e_n, and the resistance R is regarded as being noise-free. It follows from this equivalent circuit that if a resistance is short-circuited, the mean-square noise current i_n^2 that flows through the short circuit has the value $i_n^2 = e_n^2/R^2$.

Tube Noise. Random noise similar in character to that produced in a resistance is generated in tubes as a result of irregularities in electron flow. Tube noise can be divided into (1) shot effect, representing random variations in the rate of emission of electrons from the cathode; (2) partition noise, arising from chance variations in the division of current between two or more positive electrodes; (3) induced grid noise, produced as a result of variations in the electron stream passing adjacent to a grid; (4) gas noise, generated by random variations in the rate of production of ions by collision; (5) secondary-emission noise, arising from random variations in the rate of production of secondary electrons; and (6) flicker

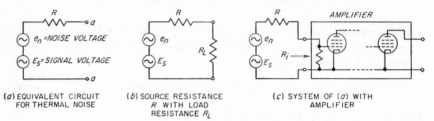

(a) EQUIVALENT CIRCUIT FOR THERMAL NOISE

(b) SOURCE RESISTANCE R WITH LOAD RESISTANCE R_L

(c) SYSTEM OF (a) WITH AMPLIFIER

Fig. 12-21. Equivalent circuits showing thermal noise voltage e_n associated with a resistance R, together with a signal voltage.

effect, a low-frequency variation in emission that occurs with oxide-coated cathodes.

Shot effect in the presence of space charge, partition noise, and induced grid noise are the principal sources of tube noise that must be considered in most practical cases.

Shot-effect Noise in Diodes. The anode current of a diode contains a noise component as a result of random variations in the rate of emission of electrons from the cathode. When the current flow is limited *by the cathode temperature,* i.e., when all electrons emitted are attracted to the anode, the noise component of the anode current, i.e., the shot-effect noise, is

$$i_n{}^2 = 2eI_b(f_2 - f_1) = 2eI_bB \qquad (12\text{-}38)$$

where i_n = rms value of noise current, amp, having frequency components lying in the band $(f_2 - f_1) = B$

e = charge on an electron, coulombs ($= 1.59 \times 10^{-19}$ coulomb)

I_b = d-c anode current, amp

$B = (f_2 - f_1)$ = frequency band over which noise current i_n is desired, cycles

When the anode current of a diode is limited *by space charge,* the consequences of irregularities in emission are greatly smoothed out, and the noise component of the plate current becomes only a small fraction of the noise associated with the same plate current under temperature-limited conditions. This smoothing action arises from the fact that a random increase in emission instantaneously increases the negative space charge. This in turn causes some electrons that would otherwise just barely be able to go to the plate to return to the cathode instead, thus minimizing the consequences of the increase in emission.

Triode Noise. The noise component of the plate current, i.e., the shot-effect noise, of a space-charge-limited triode operated with negative grid is the same as for the equivalent diode that has an anode potential equal to the effective potential of the grid plane of the triode.

It is convenient to express the plate-current noise of a triode tube in terms of an equivalent resistance R_{eq}. This resistance is assigned a value

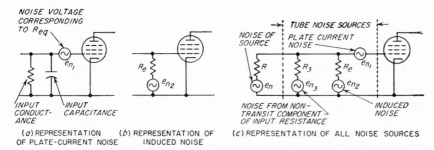

Fig. 12-22. Equivalent circuits involving representation of tube noise.

such that the noise voltage generated by it at room temperature in accordance with Eq. (12-36), when applied to the grid of a noiseless tube, will produce the same noise current in the plate circuit as is actually present. The use of an equivalent resistance to express tube noise has the advantage that it is then not necessary to specify the frequency band involved. This is because the distribution of the noise with frequency is the same in a resistance as it is in shot effect, or with other sources of random noise.

In applying the equivalent noise resistance concept to amplifier tubes, the noise voltage e_{n_1} generated by the resistance R_{eq} is applied directly in series with the grid, as illustrated by the equivalent circuit of Fig. 12-22a. Any electrode capacitance or grid-cathode input conductance that may exist is assumed to be on the left-hand side of this equivalent noise voltage, as shown.

For triode tubes with oxide-coated cathodes, the equivalent noise resistance due to shot-effect noise when the plate current is space-charge-limited is given approximately by the relation

$$R_{eq} = \frac{2.5}{g_m} \tag{12-39}$$

where g_m is the tube transconductance in mhos.

Values of R_{eq} for typical triodes are given in Table 12-3.

Pentode Noise. The noise component of the plate current of a pentode tube is greater than for a triode tube with the same plate current, because in a pentode one has partition noise in addition to shot-effect noise. The

TABLE 12-3
TUBE NOISE VALUES*

Type	Application	Plate, ma	Screen, ma	Transcon-ductance, μmhos	R_{eq} Noise-equivalent resistance	
					Calcu-lated, ohms	Measured, ohms
6J5	Triode amplifier	9	....	2,600	960	1,250
955	Triode amplifier	4.5	....	2,000	1,250	
6AC7/1852	Triode amplifier	....	....	11,200	220	200
6SK7	Pentode amplifier	9.2	2.4	2,000	10,500	9,400–11,500
6SJ7	Pentode amplifier	3	0.8	1,650	5,800	5,800
6SG7	Pentode amplifier	11.8	4.4	4,700	3,300	
6AC7/1852	Pentode amplifier	10	2.5	9,000	720	600–760
956	Pentode amplifier	5.5	1.8	1,800	9,400	
1T4	Pentode amplifier	2	0.65	750	20,000	
6J5	Triode mixer	2.1	....	620†	6,500	
6AC7/1852	Triode mixer	....	....	4,200†	950	
955	Triode mixer	2.8	....	660†	6,100	
6AC7/1852	Pentode mixer	5.2	1.3	3,400†	2,750	3,000
6SG7	Pentode mixer	3	1.1	1,180†	13,000	
956	Pentode mixer	2.3	0.8	650†	33,000	
6SA7	Pentagrid converter	3.4	8	450†	240,000	210,000
6K8	Triode-hexode con-verter	2.5	6	350†	290,000	
6L7	Pentagrid mixer	2.4	7.1	375†	255,000	210,000

* From W. A. Harris, Fluctuations in Vacuum-tube Amplifiers and Input Systems, *RCA Rev.*, vol. 5, p. 505, April, 1941.

† Conversion transconductance value.

equivalent grid resistance R_{eq} representing the noise of a negative-grid pentode amplifier is given approximately by the relation

$$R_{eq} = \frac{I_b}{I_b + I_{c2}}\left(\frac{2.5}{g_m} + \frac{20I_{c2}}{g_m{}^2}\right) \tag{12-40}$$

where I_b = d-c plate current, amp

I_{c2} = d-c screen current, amp

g_m = transconductance, mhos

Representative values of equivalent grid resistance R_{eq} of pentode tubes, given in Table 12-3, are typically of the order of three to ten times as great as for comparable negative grid triodes.

Induced Input-circuit Noise.   At very high frequencies, random variations in the number of electrons passing a negative control grid will induce noise currents of significant amplitude.   Analysis shows that the magnitude of the noise thus introduced into the control-grid circuit of a triode or a pentode tube is the same as the noise generated by a resistance equal to that part of the input grid-cathode conductance of the tube that results from the transit time, provided that this input conductance (or resistance) is considered to be at a temperature 1.4 times the cathode temperature, or approximately five times room temperature in the case of oxide-coated cathodes.[1]

The equivalent circuit taking into account this induced noise is illustrated in Fig. 12-22b, where R_e is the input resistance due to transit time, and e_{n_2} is the associated noise voltage for 1.4 times the cathode temperature.   To a first approximation, the induced grid noise is in random phase relation to the plate-current noise, so that the two can be added together as though they were independent.   This leads to the equivalent circuit of Fig. 12-22c that takes into account both plate-current noise and induced noise, and also shows the noise generators e_n and e_{n_2} that are, respectively, for the equivalent source resistance R, and for the part R_3 of the input conductance that does not arise from transit time.   To obtain the total rms noise voltage acting between grid and cathode in Fig. 12-22c, the grid-cathode voltage produced by each component of noise voltage is calculated separately.[2]   The total rms noise is then the square root of the sum of the squares of the component noise voltages.

Since the equivalent electronic grid-cathode input resistance R_e of the tube is inversely proportional to the square of the frequency, the noise introduced into the input circuits by the electronic conductance depends upon the frequency.   This is in contrast with the other noise effects which are independent of frequency.   At very high frequencies, the low value of R_e causes the signal-to-noise ratio in the input circuit of the tube to deteriorate, resulting in a poorer noise figure (see Sec. 12-14) at very high frequencies than at low or moderate frequencies.

12-14. Signal-to-noise Ratio and Noise Figure.   *Signal-to-noise of an Ideal System.*   The ratio of signal to noise describes the extent to which noise is associated with the signal.   This ratio can be expressed either as a voltage or power ratio, or by the decibel equivalent of the power ratio.

The maximum possible signal-to-noise ratio that can be associated with a signal source having an internal resistance R occurs when the only noise

---

[1] It is necessary here to distinguish between input conductance resulting from transit time and input conductance resulting from inductance in the cathode lead. Although for all other purposes these two factors contribute to the input-conductance act in exactly the same way, as discussed in Sec. 12-12, they are quite different in so far as noise is concerned.

[2] Thus the shunting effect of R and R_3 on the noise generated in R_e must be taken into account, etc.

present is that resulting from the resistance noise of R, and an open-circuit condition exists. In this case, the equivalent circuit of Fig. 12-21a applies, and one has, using Eq. (12-37),

$$\left.\begin{array}{l}\text{Maximum possible}\\\text{signal-to-noise}\\\text{power ratio}\end{array}\right\} = \frac{E_s^2}{e_n^2} = \frac{E_s^2}{4kTRB} \qquad (12\text{-}41)$$

It is important to note that the maximum possible signal-to-noise ratio as given by Eq. (12-41) is obtained only when the load is an open circuit. If a load resistance R_L is connected across R as in Fig. 12-21b, then the signal-to-noise ratio is reduced. For example, if $R_L = R$, the signal voltage across terminals aa is exactly half the open-circuit voltage. However, the noise voltage across these same terminals as given by Eq. (12-37) is now $1/\sqrt{2}$ times the open-circuit noise voltage across R, since the equivalent resistance between terminals aa that produces the noise is R in parallel with R_L or $R/2$. The signal-to-noise power ratio is hence $0.707^2 = 0.5$ times the open-circuit signal-to-noise ratio. Thus the addition of the matching load resistance R_L degrades the signal-to-noise ratio by 3 db.*

Noise Figure. Assume now that terminals aa in Fig. 12-21a are connected to the input of an amplifier, as at Fig. 12-21c. The signal-to-noise ratio at the amplifier output will then be less than the value given by Eq. (12-41) for an ideal system; this is a result of noise generated by the amplifier tubes.[1] The relation between the signal-to-noise ratio in an actual system and in the corresponding ideal system is given by the *noise figure* of the actual system, which is defined as

$$\text{Noise figure} = F = \frac{\left\{\begin{array}{l}\text{signal-to-noise power}\\\text{ratio of ideal system}\end{array}\right.}{\left\{\begin{array}{l}\text{actual signal-to-noise}\\\text{power ratio of output}\end{array}\right.} \qquad (12\text{-}43)$$

The noise figure can be expressed either as a power ratio, as in Eq. (12-43), or in decibels. Thus a noise figure of 4 means that the actual signal-to-noise ratio is one-fourth of the value in the ideal system, or 6 db less.

In Eq. (12-43) it is implied that the equivalent bandwidth B of the noise (see below) is the same for the ideal and actual systems at both the input and output. Equation (12-43) also assumes that the system is linear. This means that the amplifier does not clip noise peaks, or compress the signal, etc.

---

* The general formula for reduction in signal-to-noise ratio due to the load resistance R_L in Fig. 12-21b is

$$\frac{\text{Actual signal-to-noise power ratio}}{\text{Maximum possible signal-to-noise power ratio}} = \frac{R_L}{R_L + R} \qquad (12\text{-}42)$$

[1] If the input resistance of the amplifier is not infinite this also lowers the signal-to-noise ratio, as given by Eq. (12-42).

In practice, the noise figure of an amplifier is usually determined by the first tube and its input circuit. This is because noise introduced by other tubes and circuits of the system will undergo less amplification, and so will be relatively unimportant in the system as long as the amplification of the first stage is at least moderate. As a result the noise figure can often be estimated with good accuracy by relatively simple methods. Thus in Fig. 12-21c, if $R_i >> R$, and R_{eq} is the equivalent noise resistance of the first amplifier tube, then one has

$$\text{Noise figure} = 1 + \frac{R_{eq}}{R} \qquad (12\text{-}44)$$

The noise figure in practical amplifiers can be kept below a few decibels up to frequencies of the order of 100 Mc, by suitable choice of the first tube, combined with proper circuit design. However, as one goes to frequencies so high that the electronic component of the tube input conductance is low enough to be an important component of the input circuit system of the tube, the lowest noise figure that can be realized will be greater than at lower frequencies.

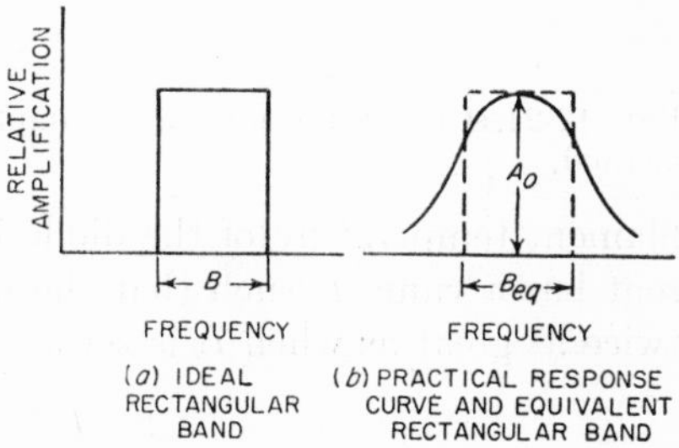

(a) IDEAL RECTANGULAR BAND   (b) PRACTICAL RESPONSE CURVE AND EQUIVALENT RECTANGULAR BAND

FIG. 12-23. Ideal and actual response bands.

Equivalent Noise Bandwidth of an Amplifier. In defining the signal-to-noise ratio of an amplifier it is necessary to define an equivalent bandwidth for the noise. This would be simple if the amplifier had an ideal rectangular response band as in Fig. 12-23a. Actually, the response always drops off near the edges of the band, as indicated in Fig. 12-23b. One can, however, define an equivalent bandwidth B_{eq} that has the same noise power as is actually developed by the amplifier output. This equivalent noise bandwidth, shown dotted in Fig. 12-23b, is given by the relation

$$B_{eq} = \frac{\int_0^\infty A^2 \, df}{A_0{}^2} \qquad (12\text{-}45)$$

Here A is the amplification at frequency f, and A_0 is the maximum amplification.

Measurement of Noise Figure.[1] Although an approximate indication of the noise figure may sometimes be obtained by calculation, as in Eq. (12-44), a value that is certain to be accurate can be obtained only by an actual measurement.

[1] For further information see F. E. Terman and J. M. Pettit, "Electronic Measurements," p. 363, McGraw-Hill Book Company, Inc., New York, 1952.

Perhaps the simplest method of determining the noise figures of an amplifier consists in comparing the actual noise with the noise generated by a diode in which the plate current is temperature limited and which accordingly generates noise in accordance with Eq. (12-38). A suitable circuit arrangement is shown in Fig. 12-24. To make a measurement, the

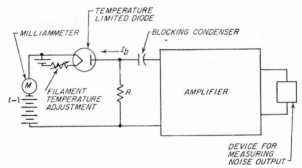

Fig. 12-24. Circuit for measuring amplifier noise factor by diode noise generator method.

filament temperature of the diode is increased until the diode plate current has a value I_b such that the noise output power of the amplifier is twice as great as when I_b is zero. The noise figure is then[1]

$$F = 20 I_b R \qquad (12\text{-}46)$$

PROBLEMS AND EXERCISES

12-1. A direct-coupled single-tuned amplifier uses the coil of Fig. 2-16. Assuming that the losses in the tuning capacitance are negligible, calculate and plot the amplification as a function of frequency up to 30 kc on each side of resonance for a resonant frequency of 1000 kc, when a 6SJ7 tube is used under conditions given in Table 6-1, page 186, and (a) the grid-leak resistance is 2 megohms, and (b) the existence of the grid leak is ignored. In both cases assume that the plate resistance is so high that its shunting effect on the tube circuit can be ignored.

[1] This relation is derived as follows: The noise voltage developed when the noise current from the diode passes through R can be regarded as a signal e_s'. Hence when the diode current doubles the output noise power, the actual signal-to-noise power ratio is unity. From Eq. (12-43) the noise figure is then the ideal signal-to-noise ratio for this value of signal e_s'. From Eq. (12-38) one has

$$e_s'^2 = 2eI_b B_{eq} R^2 \qquad (12\text{-}47)$$

At the same time the noise voltage e_n resulting from thermal noise in R is, from Eq. (12-37),

$$e_n^2 = 4kTRB_{eq} \qquad (12\text{-}48)$$

Hence

$$(e_s'/e_n)^2 = F = eI_b R/2kT \qquad (12\text{-}49)$$

Equation (12-46) then follows by substituting appropriate values for e and k and assuming room temperature ($T = 290°k$).

12-2. *a.* Calculate and plot the amplification at resonance as a function of resonant frequency over the range 550 to 1500 kc for the amplifier of Prob. 12-1, neglecting the grid-leak resistance.

b. Calculate and plot the bandwidth, i.e., the frequency band for which the response is at least 70.7 per cent of the response at resonance, as a function of resonant frequency for the range 550 to 1500 kc.

12-3. Derive Eq. (12-3) from Eq. (3-18a).

12-4. Justify Eq. (12-4).

12-5. *a.* Derive Eq. (12-5).

b. Justify the relation represented by Eq. (12-6).

12-6. The amplifier of Prob. 12-1 is changed to transformer coupling in which $L_p = L_s$. The coefficient of couplings between these coils is 0.8. Calculate the amplification and the half-power bandwidth at a frequency of 800 kc.

12-7. Derive Eq. (12-7).

12-8. Calculate a curve similar to those in Fig. 12-4 but for the case $\omega_2 = 425$ kc.

12-9. Go through the detailed steps of deriving Eq. (12-8a) from Eq. (3-8).

12-10. A two-stage single-tuned amplifier is required to have an over-all half-power bandwidth of 8 kc at a center frequency of 700 kc. Determine the value of Q required for the individual resonant circuits assuming that the stages are identical.

12-11. Derive Eqs. (12-9) and (12-10).

12-12. A single-stage double-tuned amplifier is required to have a half-power bandwidth of 7.5 kc centered on 450 kc. If critical coupling is employed, calculate the circuit Q and the coefficient of coupling that are necessary, assuming identical primary and secondary circuits.

12-13. A three-stage double-tuned amplifier system is to have a half-power bandwidth of 20 kc centered on a center frequency of 450 kc. Assuming that all the stages are identical and that the primary and secondary circuit Q's are the same, determine the half-power bandwidth of a single stage, the coefficient of coupling required between the two tuned circuits associated with each amplifier stage, and the circuit Q's, assuming coupling for maximal flatness.

12-14. With the aid of Table 12-1, calculate the ratio of the voltage gain *per stage* of a critically coupled double-tuned system to the gain per stage of the corresponding single-tuned system for the same over-all half-power bandwidth and the same values of L and C in the resonant circuits for (*a*) a two-stage system, and (*b*) a four-stage system.

12-15. A three-stage amplifier consisting of identical single-tuned stages is adjusted so that the over-all half-power bandwidth is 8 kc at a center frequency of 450 kc. From this information determine the 6- to 60-db bandwidth ratio of the system.

12-16. Calculate and plot the envelope delay in microseconds as a function of frequency up to 15 kc off resonance for a single-tuned stage of amplification in which the half-power bandwidth is a 10 kc centered at 800 kc. Use the universal resonance curve of Fig. 3-2 to obtain the phase shift of this amplifier.

12-17. Identify in Table 10-2 the particular term that represents cross-talk in which the modulation of signal *a* becomes transferred to the carrier wave of signal *b* when the applied signal consists of two sine waves $E_a(1 + m \sin v_a t) \sin \omega_a t + E_b \sin \omega_b t$.

12-18. Why would it be unsatisfactory to vary the output voltage e_0 in Fig. 12-1a by obtaining the output from a sliding contact operating on the grid-leak resistance R_{gl}? Assume that the output voltage e_0 is to be applied to another stage of amplification.

12-19. Assume that in a particular application, a radio-frequency pulse will have satisfactory fidelity if it is reproduced with a rise time that does not exceed 20 per cent of the pulse length. What bandwidth must a tuned amplifier have in order to meet this requirement when the pulse length is (*a*) 1.5 μsec, and (*b*) 0.25 μsec?

12-20. Go through the details of deriving Eqs. (12-16), (12-17), and (12-18).

12-21. A three-stage single-tuned amplifier is required to have a rise time of 0.8 μsec. What half-power bandwidth must the individual stages have if the individual stages are identical?

12-22. In a particular wideband single-tuned amplifier employing the circuit of Fig. 12-1a and using a 6AK5 tube (see Table 9-1, page 292), the total tuning capacitance is 10 μμf. The required half-power bandwidth of a single stage is 2 Mc centered on 30 Mc. What gain per stage can be expected and what value of L and R_{gl} must be used?

12-23. Show in detail the steps involved in deriving Eqs. (12-22) and (12-23).

12-24. A double-tuned critically coupled amplifier stage is required to have a half-power bandwidth of 4 Mc centered at 60 Mc. If a 6AK5 tube (see Table 9-1, page 292) is to be used, determine L_p, L_s, R_p, R_s, in Fig. 12-11b, and the amplification at the center frequency, if the total capacitance of each tuned circuit, including tube capacitance and miscellaneous stray capacitances, is 7 μμf.

12-25. Show in detail the steps involved in obtaining Eq. (12-25) from Eq. (12-22).

12-26. A three-stage double-tuned critically coupled amplifier is required to have a rise time of 0.8 μsec. What half-power bandwidth must the individual stages have assuming they are all identical?

12-27. With the aid of Table 12-1 fill in an additional line in Table 12-2 for six-stage systems.

12-28. *a.* A two-stage stagger-tuned system is to have an over-all half-power bandwidth of 4 Mc, centered at 60 Mc. Assume that 6AK5 tubes are employed (see Table 9-1, page 292) and that the total capacitance per stage including tube and miscellaneous stray capacitances can be taken as 14 μμf. Determine the required detuning of the individual stages, the effective Q that each stage must have, and the total amplification that can be obtained from the two-stage system.

b. If the stages are identically tuned and the over-all bandwidth is to remain unchanged, determine the effective Q of the individual stages and the total amplification of the two-stage identically tuned system.

12-29. A wideband tuned amplifier employs the 6AK5 tube of Table 9-1, page 292. When tube, wiring, and trimmer capacitor capacitances are taken into account in a particular case, the total capacitance shunting the tuning inductance of a single-tuned circuit can be taken as 14 μμf, while in the case of a double-tuned circuit the tuning capacitance to be associated with each individual tuned circuit can be taken as half this value. A sufficient number of amplifier stages are required to give a total voltage amplification of 100,000. The 3-db bandwidth required for the over-all characteristic is 5 Mc, and the carrier frequency is centered at 30 Mc.

a. If the amplifier consists of identical single-tuned stages, determine the minimum number of stages required, and specify the 3-db bandwidth and effective circuit Q required for the individual stages.

b. Determine the minimum number of stages of amplification required when identical double-tuned circuits of maximum flatness are employed, and specify the 3-db bandwidth for the individual stages and the Q's of the individual circuits.

c. Determine the minimum number of stages required when stagger-tuned pairs with maximum flatness are employed, and specify the amount of detuning required from the center frequency for each circuit, the proper circuit Q for each individual resonant circuit, and the 3-db bandwidth of an individual pair.

d. Tabulate the number of stages required in (*a*), (*b*), and (*c*) and discuss the practical significance of the differences.

12-30. A four-stage wideband amplifier employs 6AK5 tubes with tube and circuit capacitances as in Prob. 12-29. It is necessary to obtain a rise time of 0.2 μsec. Determine the half-power bandwidth of the individual stages, and also the total amplification of the system, when the individual stages are (a) single-tuned with identical tuning, (b) stagger-tuned in pairs for maximum flatness, and (c) double-tuned with critical coupling. Summarize final results in a single table.

12-31. Explain in words the reason for the fact that in a two-stage system, stagger-tuning has less advantage over identical tuning than when a larger number of stages are involved.

12-32. In a tuned radio-frequency amplifier in which the resonant frequency is adjustable over a wide range of frequencies, it is normally found that regeneration is most pronounced at the high-frequency end of the tuning range. Explain.

12-33. In an amplifier the coupling between stages is to be minimized by arranging the various stages in a line and then surrounding them by an enclosure equivalent to a square waveguide that is 1.75 in. on a side. Estimate with the aid of Table 5-2, page 153, the minimum spacing between stages having a voltage gain per stage of 20, if the stray coupling fields between stages in the waveguide are to be attenuated more than enough to counteract the gain per stage.

12-34. Two resistance-coupled amplifiers employing triode and pentode tubes, respectively, each give a voltage gain of 60. For the triode tube

$$C_{gk} = 3.0 \ \mu\mu f \quad \text{and} \quad C_{gp} = 2.8 \ \mu\mu f$$

For the pentode tube $C_{gk} = 3.0 \ \mu\mu f$, $C_{gs} = 3.0 \ \mu\mu f$ (grid-screen capacitance), and $C_{gp} = 0.005 \ \mu\mu f$. With this information, calculate the input capacitances of the two amplifiers in the mid-frequency range, and discuss in a qualitative way the differences from the point of view of the best high-frequency response that it would be possible to obtain in a multistage amplifier in each case.

12-35. Assume that the load impedance in an amplifier is a negative resistance such as might be supplied by dynatron action in a screen-grid tube, as explained in the footnote on page 197. If this negative resistance is less in absolute magnitude than the plate resistance of the tube, will the input capacitance be greater or less than the value given by Eq. (12-30)? Explain the reasoning that leads to your answer.

12-36. Prove that the positive and negative peaks of the input conductance curve of Fig. 12-16 occur at the 70.7 per cent response points of the amplification curve, and that the corresponding minimum values of the input resistance are as given by Eq. (12-31).

12-37. Show that the value of peak input capacitance indicated in Fig. 12-16 is consistent with Eq. (12-28).

12-38. Prove that in Fig. 12-17a the input capacitance of the tube with perfect neutralization is $C_{gk} + C_{gp} + C_n$ in the idealized situation where $L_n = L_p$ and the coefficient of coupling between these coils is unity. Start by noting that the total input current is the sum of the currents $i_{gk} + i_{gp} + i_n$, and that the component current i_n can be determined in a manner analogous to that used to determine I_{gp}, by noting that the voltage between a and ground is equal in magnitude but opposite in phase from the amplified voltage between b and ground.

12-39. Draw a bridge circuit analogous to those in Fig. 12-18, but applying to the neutralizing system of Fig. 12-17b.

12-40. Identify the particular lengths of wire in the circuit of Fig. 12-17c that give rise to the inductances $L_1, L_2, L_3,$ and L_4 in Fig. 12-18b. Then explain why the effectiveness of the neutralization over a wide frequency band is not affected by the point along lead ad at which the neutralizing capacitor C'_n is inserted, while it is very greatly influenced by the place that junction a is located on the lead from grid C_g to a to C'_n.

12-41. Neutralization is normally used only in tuned amplifiers. What benefit, if any, would result from neutralizing a push-pull audio-frequency power amplifier that employs triode tubes?

12-42. A Class A grounded-grid tuned amplifier uses a type 2C40 lighthouse tube for which $\mu = 48$ and $r_p = 6000$. The load impedance Z_L at resonance is 10,000 ohms. Calculate voltage amplification, and also the impedance that the amplifier presents to the input tuned circuit.

12-43. In a particular grounded-grid power amplifier the power developed in the load is 10 kw. The voltage E_L in Fig. 12-19a across the load is 3500 volts crest value, while the exciting voltage E_g that is required is 850 volts crest value. From this information determine the exciting power required, neglecting circuit losses in the tuned input circuit.

12-44. Referring to Fig. 12-19, and denoting the parallel impedance of L_1C_1 as Z_1, what is the equivalent output impedance of the tube, i.e., the impedance that the tuned circuit L_2C_2 observes when looking toward the plate of the tube? Hint: Note the technique used on page 392 to determine the output impedance of a feedback amplifier.

12-45. Derive Eq. (12-32).

12-46. The pentode tube of Prob. 12-34 is used in a direct-coupled single-tuned amplifier having a resonant frequency of 1.4 Mc. The equivalent circuit Q is 80 and the voltage amplification at resonance is 120.

    a. Determine the minimum negative input resistance that will result from energy transferred through the grid-plate capacitance, and specify the frequency at which this minimum negative resistance occurs.

    b. Determine the change in input capacitance at the resonant frequency that results from the action of the grid-plate capacitance if the transconductance of the tube is reduced to 10 per cent of its original value.

12-47. In a particular pentode tube, the input resistance at 6 Mc due to transit-time and cathode-inductance effects is 500,000 ohms with normal electrode voltages. Cathode-lead inductance and transit-time effects contribute equally to the conductance represented by the input resistance.

    a. What would be the input resistance at 60 Mc if the negative control-grid bias voltage were reduced sufficiently to double the tube transconductance? Neglect the effect that the change in control-grid voltage might have on transit time.

    b. What would be the input resistance at 60 Mc if the electrode voltages were arranged to reduce the transit time to 0.7 of its value with the combination of voltages used at 6 Mc? Assume that the transconductance of the tube is left unchanged.

12-48. Derive a formula giving the input conductance that arises from an inductance L_s in series with the screen. Assume that ωL_s is small compared with the screen resistance r_s. Express the result in terms of the reactance of the capacitance between the control and screen grids, the transconductance g_s from control to screen grid, and reactance ωL_s of the screen inductance. Be sure to indicate whether the input conductance is positive or negative.

12-49. Justify Eq. (12-35).

12-50. The available noise power that a resistance develops is defined as the noise power that the resistance generating the noise would be able to deliver to a matched load resistance that did not generate noise itself. Derive a formula for the available noise power in watts per megacycle bandwidth in a resistance R at 291°K, and calculate the numerical value of available power for $R = 1000$ ohms and $R = 10,000$ ohms.

12-51. A 100,000-ohm resistance is shunted by a capacitance of 500 $\mu\mu f$. Calculate the variation of relative noise voltage across the resistance-capacitor combination as a function of frequency, for the range 0 to 10,000 cycles, taking the noise voltage at zero frequency as 100 per cent.

12-52. The plate current of a particular diode tube is limited to 10 ma by the cathode temperature. Calculate the noise component of the diode current for the frequency band 0 to 10,000 cycles. Is this noise current affected by doubling the anode voltage?

12-53. Calculate the equivalent noise resistance R_{eq} of the small general-purpose triodes and pentodes, and the small high-performance pentodes, of Table 6-1, page 186, and tabulate all results.

12-54. In the case of the pentode amplifier tubes appearing in Table 12-3, calculate the percentage of the total noise that is due to partition effect.

12-55. Is the noise component of triode plate current affected by whether or not the control grid draws current?

12-56. *a.* In Fig. 12-22*c*, assume that at a particular frequency

$$R = R_3 = R_e = 10,000 \text{ ohms}$$

and that the equivalent resistance R_{eq} representing the plate circuit noise is 500 ohms. Calculate the actual noise voltage appearing on the control grid of the tube for an equivalent bandwidth of 50 kc, assuming an oxide-coated cathode. Assume tube capacitances are tuned out.

b. Repeat calculations of (*a*) except for a frequency three times as great.

12-57. Go through the actual steps of deriving Eqs. (12-41), (12-42), and (12-44).

12-58. It is desired to amplify an audio-frequency voltage developed across a 100,000 ohm resistance. What is the minimum signal voltage for which the signal-to-noise ratio will be 20 db, when the amplifier tube (see Table 12-3) is (*a*) a 6J5 triode, and (*b*) a 6SJ7 pentode? Assume the frequency band of interest is 60 to 8000 cycles, and that the resistance is at a temperature of 291°K.

12-59. A resonant circuit having a resistive impedance of 20,000 ohms provides the source that applies a signal to the input of an amplifier. The bandwidth of interest is 500 kc.

a. Calculate the noise figure when the first amplifier tube (Table 12-3) is (*a*) a 6SK7 (pentode), and (*b*) a 6AC7 (neutralized triode). Make these calculations when the input impedance of the amplifier is much greater than 20,000 ohms and also when the amplifier input impedance is a resistance of 10,000 ohms. Assume that none of the latter input resistance arises from transit time effects.

b. Calculate the signal-to-noise ratio for the various conditions in (*a*) when an input signal of 10 μv is developed across the input resonant circuit on open circuit.

12-60. Prove that the noise generated by a rectangular band of width B_{eq} as given by Eq. (12-45) will have the same noise power as the actual amplifier.

12-61. Prove that the circuit of Fig. 12-24 and the relation expressed by Eq. (12-46) will give correctly the noise figure, irrespective of whether the amplifier input presents an open circuit R or a finite input resistance R_i.

CHAPTER 13

TUNED POWER AMPLIFIERS

13-1. Class C Tuned Amplifiers. The Class C tuned amplifier differs from the tuned voltage amplifiers of Sec. 12-1 in that the bias is made greater than the cutoff value corresponding to the plate-supply voltage. When a signal is applied under these conditions, the plate current flows in pulses that last for less than half a cycle. The Class C amplifier is characterized by high plate efficiency, and is used to develop radio-frequency power when a proportionality between input and output voltages is not required.

Voltage, Current, and Impedance Relations in Class C Amplifiers. The voltage and current relations of a Class C amplifier can be understood by considering oscillograms such as those of Fig. 13-1. The voltage actually applied to the grid electrode of the tube consists of the grid bias E_c plus the exciting voltage E_g. The relations are normally such that at the crest of the cycle the grid is driven appreciably positive and consequently draws some grid current. The voltage actually appearing at the plate of the tube consists of the battery voltage E_b minus the alternating voltage drop E_L in the plate load impedance; thus it has the wave shape shown in Fig. 13-1b. The phase relations are such that the minimum instantaneous plate potential $E_{\min}$ and the maximum grid potential $E_{\max}$ occur simultaneously. The alternating components of the plate and grid voltages are also always sinusoidal since they are developed across resonant circuits.

The plate and grid currents i_p and i_g, respectively, that flow at any instant are the result of the combined action of the plate and grid potentials e_p and e_g, respectively, at that instant, and so can be determined from these potentials with the aid of a set of characteristic curves of the tube that extend into the positive grid region. The plate current is in the form of a pulse flowing for an electrical angle θ_p that is something less than half a cycle. The grid current flows only when the grid is positive. The sum $(i_p + i_g)$ of instantaneous plate and grid currents represents the total instantaneous space current flowing away from the cathode, and always has its peak value I_m at the instant when the grid and plate potentials are $E_{\max}$ and $E_{\min}$, respectively, as shown at Fig. 13-1d. The average value of the plate-current pulse over a complete cycle represents the direct current I_b that will be drawn from the source E_b of plate power. The average value of the grid-current pulse over a complete cycle is likewise the d-c grid current I_g which will be observed if a d-c milliammeter is placed in the grid circuit.

The impedance that the load should supply in order to obtain proper operation is whatever impedance must be placed in series with the plate electrode of the tube to develop the desired alternating plate voltage when excited by the plate current pulses. The magnitude of this impedance can be controlled by varying the coupling of the load to the plate tuned circuit.

Power and Efficiency. The power delivered to the amplifier by the plate-supply voltage at any instant is the product of instantaneous plate current and the d-c plate-supply voltage E_b, and so varies in the same way as does the instantaneous plate current (see Fig. 13-1g). Part of this plate-input power is delivered to the plate tuned circuit and represents useful output, while the remainder is dissipated at the plate electrode of the tube. At any instant, the division of the total energy between tuned circuit and tube is in proportion to the voltage drops across these parts of the circuit. Thus, the plate loss at any instant is equal to the product of instantaneous plate current and instantaneous plate voltage, and so is given by the shaded area of Fig. 13-1g. The unshaded area under the total power curve of this same figure represents the energy delivered to the tuned circuit and available for producing useful output. The average input, output, and plate loss are obtained by averaging the instantaneous values of Fig. 13-1g over a full cycle.

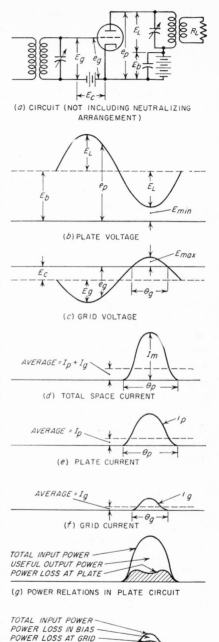

(a) CIRCUIT (NOT INCLUDING NEUTRALIZING ARRANGEMENT)

(b) PLATE VOLTAGE

(c) GRID VOLTAGE

(d) TOTAL SPACE CURRENT

(e) PLATE CURRENT

(f) GRID CURRENT

(g) POWER RELATIONS IN PLATE CIRCUIT

(h) POWER RELATIONS IN GRID CIRCUIT

FIG. 13-1. Voltage, current, and power relations in a typical Class C amplifier.

The high efficiency of the Class C amplifier is a result of the fact that plate current is not allowed to flow except when the instantaneous voltage drop across the tube is low; i.e., E_b supplies energy to the amplifier only when the largest portion of this energy will be absorbed by the tuned circuit. Because of the way in which the instantaneous plate-cathode voltage varies during the cycle (see Fig. 13-1b) the plate efficiency is greater the smaller the fraction of the cycle during which the plate current flows. If the duration of current flow is very small, plate current will flow only when the voltage drop between plate and cathode of the tube is at its lowest value, and the efficiency is then high and will approach 100 per cent if E_{min} approaches zero. However, making the duration of current flow very small reduces the plate input power and thus the power output, even though the output that is obtained is developed at a high efficiency. Hence, in practical work, it is necessary to compromise between high efficiency and high output. Under usual conditions the balance occurs for current pulses lasting for 120 to 150°, corresponding to practical efficiencies in the range 60 to 80 per cent.[1]

The power required to drive the grid positive in a Class C amplifier comes from the alternating voltage applied to the grid of the tube. At a particular instant the exciting power is equal to the product of instantaneous exciting voltage and instantaneous grid current; thus it varies during the cycle as shown in Fig. 13-1h. Part of this exciting power represents energy dissipated at the grid electrode in the form of heat, while the remainder is power delivered to the bias battery (or dissipated in the grid-leak resistance in the case of grid-leak bias).

Factors Involved in the Operation of Class C Amplifiers with Particular Reference to Triode Tubes. The fundamental factors controlling the behavior of a Class C amplifier are the maximum space current I_m reached during the cycle (or what is very nearly the same thing, the peak plate current), the minimum instantaneous plate potential E_{min}, the maximum instantaneous grid potential E_{max}, the number of electrical degrees θ_p during which the plate current flows, the number of electrical degrees θ_g during which the grid is positive, and the plate-supply voltage E_b. These are illustrated in Fig. 13-1. The load impedance is not a fundamental factor since it is dependent upon the above quantities.

The maximum permissible value of peak space current I_m is determined by the electron emission that the cathode can be depended upon to supply throughout the useful life of the tube.

In the case of a triode tube, the values of maximum instantaneous grid potential E_{max} and minimum instantaneous plate potential E_{min} must be such that with these potentials applied to the grid and plate electrodes,

---

[1] Another consideration in determining a suitable angle of plate-current flow is driving power. This favors the larger angles and makes it impractical in most cases for θ_p to be less than about 120°. See p. 451 for further discussion of this point.

respectively, the resulting space current I_m will be the desired value. Possible combinations of voltage values that will draw any particular peak space current can be determined from complete characteristic curves of the tube.[1]

While there are many combinations of grid and plate voltages that will draw the same space current in a triode tube, it is desired to make E_{min} as low as practicable in order to reduce the plate losses. At the same time the minimum plate voltage E_{min} must equal or exceed the maximum grid potential E_{max}, or the grid electrode will draw an excessive current; this is largely because then the grid will collect secondary electrons produced at the plate. Excessive grid current is to be avoided because it reduces the output power and increases the exciting power. When low exciting power is important, it is desirable to make E_{min} appreciably greater than E_{max}; in this way the grid current and hence the exciting power are considerably reduced, although at the expense of lowered plate efficiency because of the higher E_{min} then required in the triode to draw the desired value of I_m.

With a given peak space current I_m, maximum grid potential E_{max}, and minimum plate potential E_{min}, the angle θ_p of plate current flow determines the plate efficiency, the d-c input power to the plate circuit, and the alternating output power. Making θ_p larger increases both the input and the output power, makes the plate dissipation greater, and lowers the efficiency. This is because the additional power input obtained by increasing θ_p represents current flowing during portions of the cycle when the instantaneous voltage at the plate is relatively high, and so is converted to alternating output with lower efficiency.

The signal voltage required to excite a Class C amplifier has a crest value equal to $E_c + E_{max}$ and depends upon the angle of plate-current flow, being greater as θ_p is decreased. This increase in signal required as the angle of flow is reduced causes the driving power that the exciting voltage must supply to increase as the angle of flow is reduced and to become excessive at angles less than about 120°.

The plate-supply voltage E_b is of considerable importance in determining the output power and plate efficiency. This is because increasing the plate-supply voltage increases the voltage drop across the load in proportion to the voltage drop across the plate of the tube for the same minimum plate voltage E_{min}. Hence, with given values of θ_p and E_{min}, increasing the plate-supply voltage will increase the power output almost propor-

---

[1] If complete characteristic curves of the tube are not available, it is possible to make an approximate determination of suitable combinations of E_{min} and E_{max} by extrapolating characteristic curves covering only the negative grid region. This is accomplished by plotting $(i_p + i_g)$ as a function of $[e_g + (e_p/\mu)]$ upon logarithmic paper. A nearly straight line will be obtained, as seen from Eq. (6-25), and this can be extrapolated to the desired total space current I_m.

tionately, while increasing the plate dissipation only slightly.   The grid-driving power will also be increased somewhat as the plate voltage is made higher, since the grid bias and hence exciting voltage required for a given angle of flow are somewhat dependent upon the plate voltage.

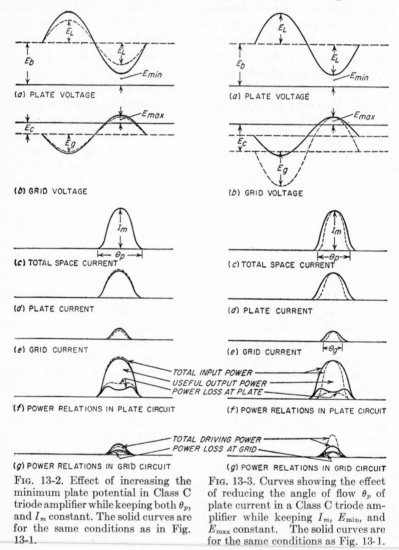

Fig. 13-2. Effect of increasing the minimum plate potential in Class C triode amplifier while keeping both θ_p, and I_m constant. The solid curves are for the same conditions as in Fig. 13-1.

Fig. 13-3. Curves showing the effect of reducing the angle of flow θ_p of plate current in a Class C triode amplifier while keeping I_m, E_{min}, and E_{max} constant.   The solid curves are for the same conditions as Fig. 13-1.

Oscillograms showing how the above factors affect a Class C amplifier are illustrated in Figs. 13-2 to 13-5.   Thus Fig. 13-2 brings out the effect of increasing the minimum plate potential and simultaneously readjusting E_{max} and E_c so that the value of I_m, angle of flow of plate current, and bias remain unchanged; this increases the plate power loss and so lowers efficiency, but at the same time reduces the grid driving power.   Likewise, Fig. 13-3 shows the effect of changing the angle θ_p of plate current flow on the output power, driving power, and plate loss, assuming E_b, E_{min}, E_{max}, and I_m are kept constant.   Again Fig. 13-4 illustrates the great increase

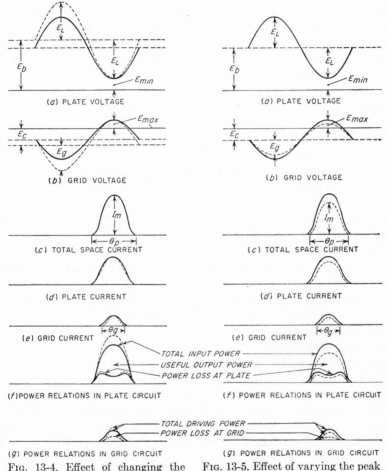

FIG. 13-4. Effect of changing the plate-supply voltage in a Class C triode amplifier while keeping I_m, E_{min}, E_{max}, and θ_p constant. The solid curves are for the same conditions as Fig. 13-1.

FIG. 13-5. Effect of varying the peak space current I_m in a Class C triode amplifier while keeping E_{min} constant. The solid curves are for the same conditions as Fig. 13-1.

in output power with only a small increase in plate dissipation that results from increasing the plate-supply voltage, while readjusting E_c as required to keep θ_p, E_{min}, E_{max}, and I_m unchanged.   Finally, Fig. 13-5 shows what happens when the peak space current I_m is reduced by lowering E_{max} while keeping E_c, E_b, and E_{min} unchanged; it is seen that there is a substantial loss in output with little improvement in efficiency when the full electron emission of the cathode is not utilized.

Class C Amplifiers Employing Beam, Pentode, and Screen-grid Tubes. Beam and related tetrode tubes, and to a lesser extent pentode and screen-grid tubes, find extensive use as low-power and medium-power Class C amplifiers. Class C operation is achieved by biasing the control grid more negative than the cutoff value corresponding to the d-c screen-grid potential that is employed. The oscillograms giving the voltage, current, and power relations existing in the control-grid and plate circuits are the same with beam and similar tubes as with triodes, as shown in Fig. 13-12, below. A discussion of the special considerations involved in the use of beam and similar tubes as Class C amplifiers is given in Sec. 13-4.

Tubes Suitable for Class C Amplifiers. The same triode, beam, and pentode tubes[1] used for Class A and Class B amplification are also equally suitable for Class C operation. The only special considerations involved in Class C amplifier tubes is that in some cases the output power required from a single tube is very great, and that the frequency of operation is sometimes quite high.

The power that a tube can handle is determined by the voltage that may be safely applied to the plate of the tube, by the electron emission of the cathode, and by the amount of power that can be dissipated within the tube without overheating, particularly at the plate. Glass-envelope tubes are commonly used to develop output powers up to about 1 kw, while tubes with copper anodes, cooled either by water or by forced air draft, are used when higher powers are required. Plate voltages as great as 10,000 to 20,000 volts are employed in the highest powered tubes. The cathodes are usually thoriated-tungsten filaments, although oxide-coated filaments and heater-type emitters find use in tubes that operate at the lower anode potentials, i.e., of the order of 1000 volts or less.

Operation at the higher radio-frequencies with high output powers presents a number of problems. Lead inductances and interelectrode capacitances must be minimized, and transit times of the electrons kept small. These factors all introduce serious design problems, particularly when large powers are involved. In order to keep the inductances, capaci-

---

[1] The pentode tube is largely obsolete for Class C applications, as is likewise the case for Class A and Class B power amplification. Beam tubes used for Class C amplification are of two types. The first is the true beam tube with aligned grids and beam forming plates, as shown in Fig. 6-23. The second type, commonly termed a tetrode, has the wires of the control and screen grids aligned as in Fig. 6-23, but omits the beam-forming plates. The plate of such a tetrode is normally treated to reduce secondary emission and the screen-plate distance may be such that with very large plate currents there is sufficient space change to produce a potential minimum in the screen-plate space when the plate voltage is low. Such a tetrode thus behaves very much, but not necessarily exactly, like a true beam tube; it is, however, much more like a beam tube than it is like a screen-grid tube.

tances, and the transit time of the tube small, the tube should likewise be physically small. However, if the tube is physically small, the power that it can dissipate is limited accordingly.

As a result of these various conflicting factors, tubes used for generating moderate to large powers at the higher frequencies are characterized by relatively small physical size, close spacing of electrodes, and relatively high operating voltage (to minimize transit time and cathode-current densities). In addition, special arrangements of leads such as illustrated

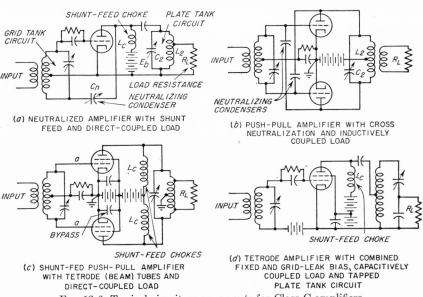

(a) NEUTRALIZED AMPLIFIER WITH SHUNT FEED AND DIRECT-COUPLED LOAD

(b) PUSH-PULL AMPLIFIER WITH CROSS NEUTRALIZATION AND INDUCTIVELY COUPLED LOAD

(c) SHUNT-FED PUSH-PULL AMPLIFIER WITH TETRODE (BEAM) TUBES AND DIRECT-COUPLED LOAD

(d) TETRODE AMPLIFIER WITH COMBINED FIXED AND GRID-LEAK BIAS, CAPACITIVELY COUPLED LOAD AND TAPPED PLATE TANK CIRCUIT

Fig. 13-6. Typical circuit arrangements for Class C amplifiers.

in Fig. 6-35 are commonly used. These various expedients all have their limitations, however, with the result that the highest output power that it is practical to design a tube to deliver decreases with increasing frequency when the frequency is in excess of about 10 or 20 Mc.

Examples of typical tubes used as Class C amplifiers, together with representative performance data, are given in Table 13-1.

Circuit Arrangements and Considerations in Class C Amplifiers. The basic circuit[1] of the Class C amplifier is shown schematically in Fig. 13-1a. The detailed arrangements may vary considerably, however. Thus, shunt feed is commonly used in the plate circuit as illustrated in Fig. 13-6a; this has the advantage that one side of the plate tuned circuit L_2C_2 can be at ground potential with respect to both d-c and radio-frequency voltages. The shunt-feed inductance L_c in such an arrangement is supplied by a radio-frequency choke (see Sec. 2-7) and is preferably rela-

[1] At very high frequencies the grounded-grid version of this circuit is often used, as discussed on p. 430.

tively large compared with L_2 so that L_c carries only a small part of the radio-frequency current circulating in the plate resonant circuit.

Push-pull arrangements are very common with Class C amplifiers. An example is shown in Fig. 13-6b.

The load impedance to which the output power of the Class C amplifier is delivered can be associated with the plate resonant circuit in a variety of ways. Arrangements illustrating direct, inductive, and capacitive coupling are illustrated at *a*, *b*, and *d*, respectively, in Fig. 13-6, where for convenience the load has been indicated as a resistance R_L.

TABLE 13-1

CHARACTERISTICS OF REPRESENTATIVE CLASS C AMPLIFIER TUBES

(a) Characteristics of Tubes

Tube		Cathode			Max allowable dissipation (continuous operation), watts			Class C ratings for continuous operation					μ	μ_s	Notes
								Max d-c volts			Max d-c ma				
Type	Kind	E	I	Type	Plate	Screen	Control grid	E_b	E_{c1}	E_{c2}	I_b	I_{c1}			
812A	Tri.	6	4	Thor.	45	..	..	1,250	−200	....	175	35	29		
5588	Tri.	6	2.5	Heat.	200	..	..	1,000	−200	....	300	100	16	..	*,†
833A	Tri.	10	10	Thor.	400	..	..	4,000	−500	....	500	100	35		
5762	Tri.	12	29	Thor.	2,500	..	..	5,250	−1000	....	1400	300	29	..	†
5671	Tri.	11½	285	Thor.	25,000	..	..	15,000	−2000	....	8000	1000	39		
6146	Beam	6	1.2	Heat.	20	..	..	600	−150	250	140	4	..	4	‡
4-65A	Tetr.	6	3.5	Thor.	65	10	5	1,000	−500	400	150	....	..	5	‡
813	Beam	10	5	Thor.	100	..	..	2,000	−300	400	180	25	..	8	
4-125A/-4D21	Tetr.	5	6.5	Thor.	125	20	5	3,000	−500	400	225	....	..	6	‡
4X-150A	Tetr.	6	2.6	Heat.	150	15	2	1,250	−250	300	250	....	..	5	‡
4-250A/-5D22	Tetr.	5	14.5	Thor.	250	35	5	4,000	−500	600	350	....	..	5	
6166	Tetr.	5	175	Thor.	10,000	..	..	6,600	−1000	2000	2750	600	..	10	‡

* Lighthouse type.

† Grounded-grid type.

‡ VHF or UHF type.

Class C amplifiers using triodes must either be neutralized or must employ the grounded-grid circuit (see page 430). Neutralization using circuits such as illustrated in Fig. 12-17 is customary in most cases. The grounded-grid circuit, however, finds use as an alternative to neutralization at very high frequencies, where effective neutralization is hard to achieve, particularly if a considerable range of frequencies is involved. In wideband systems, such as Class C amplifiers for television signals, grounded-grid systems also have the advantage over neutralized arrangements of possessing lower effective input and output capacitances, since the capacitance of the neutralizing capacitor is avoided.

Class C amplifiers employing pentode, beam, or screen-grid tubes do not require neutralization. However, it is necessary in such tubes that the screen be effectively by-passed to the cathode, since impedance in series with the screen produces effects in pentode and similar tubes that correspond to the consequences of a plate load impedance in an unneutralized triode. At very high frequencies the inductance of the leads in the

TABLE 13-1 (Continued)

(b) Typical Operating Conditions as Class C Amplifier

Tube type	E_b	E_{c2}	E_{c1}	Peak excit. volts	D-c currents, ma			Excit. power watts	Screen dissipation, watts	Output power watts	Plate eff., %	Max freq.,* Mc
					I_b	I_{c1}	I_{c2}					
812A	1,500	....	-120	240	173	30	...	6.5	...	190	73	60
5588	835	....	-70†	.....	300†	40†	...	32†	...	100†	40†	1350
833A	3,000	....	-200	360	415	55	...	20	...	1,000	80	40
5762	5,000	....	-750	1075	1100	250	...	240	...	4,100	75	>110
	5,000†	....	-1000†	1350†	1100†	245†	...	1680†	...	5,500†		
5671	15,000	....	-1500	2270	6000	1000	...	2040	...	70,000	77	17
6146	600	150	-85	100	113	3	11	0.3	2	52	74	90
4-65A	3,000	250	-90	170	115	10	20	1.7	5	280	81	>100
813	2,000	400	-120	205	180	10	45	1.9	18	275	76	40
4-125A/-4D21	3,000	350	-150	280	167	9	30	2.5	10	375	75	135
4X-150A	1,250	250	-90	106	200	11	20	1.2	5	195	78	>500
4-250A/-5D22	4,000	500	-225	303	312	9	45	2.5	22	1,000	80	85
6166	5,800	1200	-175	370	2600	222	267	750	320	9,000	60	220

* For 90% rated output.
† Grounded-grid operation.

screen-grid circuit provides a load impedance in the screen circuit that may affect the behavior (see page 434).

The grid bias of Class C amplifiers is commonly obtained by a grid leak–capacitor combination, such as illustrated in Fig. 13-6a, instead of from a battery, as illustrated in Fig. 13-1a. A cathode resistor can also be employed, while in other instances combinations of several methods are used. The grid-leak arrangement makes use of the fact that when the grid of the tube is driven positive, the resulting d-c component of the grid current will produce a negative bias when passed through a resistance in series with the grid circuit. The magnitude of the bias thus obtained is equal to the product of the grid-leak resistance and the d-c grid current. For a given value of grid drive E_{max}, the bias is determined primarily by the grid-leak resistance. Thus when the leak resistance is high the bias will be correspondingly large, and it takes a large exciting voltage to realize a given value of E_{max}; conversely when the leak resistance is small the bias for a given E_{max} is small, and the exciting voltage required to realize this value of E_{max} is likewise small.   The grid leak is by-passed to radio-frequency voltages by a capacitance, called the grid capacitor. The grid capacitor must be large enough to act as an effective by-pass for the grid-leak resistance at the frequencies involved, and at the same time must also be appreciably larger than the input capacitance of the tube.

The grid-leak arrangement has the advantage of simplicity, and the fact that it tends to be self-adjusting with respect to maximum grid potential E_{max}.   Thus, small changes in exciting voltage, which would produce large changes in E_{max} with a fixed bias, do not do so with the grid leak. This is because any tendency to change E_{max} produces a large effect on the grid current, which tends to change the grid bias in such a way as to maintain E_{max} nearly constant.   The only disadvantage of the grid-leak arrangement is that when the exciting voltage is removed, the grid bias is lost.   If the resulting high plate current will damage the tube, it is necessary to use either a fixed bias or a combination of grid-leak and fixed bias, as shown in Fig. 13-6d, or a combination of grid-leak bias and cathode resistor.

Considerations Relating to the Plate Tank Circuit.   The plate resonant circuit, commonly called the *plate tank circuit*, simultaneously performs several functions.   First, it must introduce in the plate circuit of the tube the particular value of load impedance required for proper operation of the Class C amplifier.   Second, most of the alternating power delivered to the plate tank circuit by the tube should be transferred to the load impedance, and only a small fraction dissipated in the tank circuit itself. Third, the effective Q of the plate tank circuit, taking into account the presence of the load, should be high enough to provide reasonable discrimination against the harmonic components contained in the pulses of plate current.

In dealing with tank circuits, it is convenient to distinguish between the value of Q possessed by the resonant system when the load is disconnected and the effective Q of the resonant system when the load is connected.   These are commonly referred to as the unloaded and loaded Q's and can be designated as Q_u and Q_L, respectively.

The proportion of the total power delivered by the tube to the tank circuit that is actually transferred to the load can be termed the *tank circuit efficiency*.   It is a simple matter to show that

$$\text{Tank circuit efficiency} = 1 - \frac{Q_L}{Q_u} \qquad (13\text{-}1)$$

From the point of view of efficiency, it is thus desirable that the loaded Q_L of the tank circuit be much smaller than the unloaded value Q_u.

The proper value of Q_L to use in a Class C amplifier, assuming that Q_L/Q_u is low enough to ensure reasonable tank-circuit efficiency, is a design compromise. A low value of Q_L reduces the reactive energy that must be stored in the resonant circuit, and so permits the use of inductances and capacitances with smaller voltampere ratings; this is an important consideration in very high-power amplifiers. At the same time, a high value of Q_L results in better discrimination against the harmonics contained in the plate-current pulses, and therefore reduces the amount of harmonic power that reaches the load impedance. A value $Q_L = 10$ represents a typical compromise. However, in some very high-power Class C amplifiers, values of Q_L as low as 2 or 3 are employed.[1]

The required value of ωL (and hence of $1/\omega C$) for the tank circuit can be expressed in terms of the desired value of Q_L, the power P that is to be delivered to the tank circuit by the tube, and the peak voltage E_L developed across the circuit. The quantitative relation follows directly from the properties of parallel resonant circuits and is[2]

$$\omega L = \frac{E_L{}^2}{2PQ_L} \tag{13-2}$$

In circuit arrangements such as Fig. 13-6a where the full tank circuit is in series between plate and cathode, the peak voltage across the tank circuit will, under normal operating conditions, be $E_L = E_b - E_{min}$, or a little less than supply potential E_b. In push-pull systems of the type illustrated in Fig. 13-6c, the peak voltage developed across the entire tank circuit will be $2(E_b - E_{min})$, or slightly less than $2E_b$. When the plate is connected to a tap on the tank circuit, as in Fig. 13-6d, the voltage E_L across the tank circuit will exceed the plate-supply voltage E_b.

13-2. Class C Amplifier Calculations and Design. *Calculation of Triode Class C Amplifier Performance.* The instantaneous plate and grid potentials at various points on the oscillograms such as those of Fig. 13-1b and c are given by the relations

Instantaneous plate voltage $= e_p = E_b - (E_b - E_{min}) \cos \beta$ (13-3)
Instantaneous grid voltage $= e_g = (E_c + E_{max}) \cos \beta - E_c$ (13-4)

Here β is the number of electrical degrees at which e_p and e_g are to be evaluated, measured with reference to the crest of the cycle, and the remaining notation is as shown in Fig. 13-1. Since the value of β that makes the instantaneous grid potential zero is $\theta_g/2$ in the notation used in Fig. 13-1c and f, it follows from Eq. (13-4) that

$$\cos \frac{\theta_g}{2} = \frac{E_c}{E_c + E_{max}} = \frac{E_c}{E_g} \tag{13-5}$$

[1] With such low values of Q_L, it is necessary to use a tuning procedure that causes the tank circuit to offer a resistance impedance to the tube, even though this impedance may not be the maximum impedance obtainable from the load (see p. 55).

[2] It follows from Eq. (13-2) that for a given value of power and of plate-supply voltage (which means E_L fixed), a tank circuit having a large tuning capacitance (small L) corresponds to a high value of Q_L. Thus a "high-C" tank circuit is synonymous with high Q_L.

In the case of triodes, plate-current cutoff occurs when $e_g + e_p/\mu = 0$; the corresponding value of β is $\theta_p/2$. It therefore follows from Eqs. (13-3) and (13-4) that

$$\cos \frac{\theta_p}{2} = \frac{1}{1 + [(\mu E_{max} + E_{min})/(\mu E_c - E_b)]} \quad (13\text{-}6a)$$

$$\text{Grid bias} = E_c = \frac{E_b}{\mu} + \left(E_{max} + \frac{E_{min}}{\mu}\right)\frac{\cos (\theta_p/2)}{1 - \cos (\theta_p/2)} \quad (13\text{-}6b)$$

The exact performance of a Class C amplifier can be obtained by plotting curves such as those of Fig. 13-1. This is done by determining the instantaneous plate and grid voltage for different values of β with the aid of Eqs. (13-3) and (13-4). For each combination of instantaneous grid and plate potentials, the corresponding instantaneous grid and plate currents can be obtained from characteristic curves of the tube. In this way, the plate- and grid-current pulses can be plotted point by point. Curves of instantaneous power input to the plate circuit of the tube, and of power dissipated at the plate electrode, can be obtained by multiplying the instantaneous plate current curve by the plate-supply voltage E_b and by the instantaneous plate voltage e_p, respectively. Similarly, the instantaneous power supplied by the exciting voltage E_g is equal to the instantaneous value of exciting voltage $E_g \cos \beta$ multiplied by the grid current at that instant. The part of this power that is dissipated at the grid is the product of the instantaneous grid current and the grid-cathode voltage e_g at that instant. The d-c plate and grid currents represent the average of the current pulses over the full cycle, while the input, output, and other powers are obtained in the same way by an averaging process. These averages can be obtained by planimetering the areas under the pulses, by plotting the curves on cross-section paper and counting the number of squares under the pulses, or by averaging the values calculated for regular steps in β.

The exact method of calculating Class C amplifier performance, as outlined above, results in an accuracy limited only by the extent that the tube characteristics used apply to the particular tube involved under the operating conditions actually existing. The method has the disadvantage of being very laborious; accordingly, it is generally preferable to use the much simpler, and nearly as accurate, approximate method now to be described.

Calculation of Triode Class C Amplifier Performance—Approximate Method. The performance of a Class C amplifier can be determined,[1] with an accuracy sufficient for ordinary design purposes, without point-by-point calculations, by taking advantage of the fact that the total instantaneous space current $(i_p + i_g)$ can be expressed rather accurately

[1] This procedure is from F. E. Terman and Wilber C. Roake, Calculation and Design of Class C Amplifiers, *Proc. IRE*, vol. 24, p. 620, April, 1936.

by the relation [see (Eq. 6-25)]

$$\text{Total instantaneous space current} = i_p + i_g = K \left(\frac{e_p}{\mu} + e_g \right)^{\alpha} \quad (13\text{-}7)$$

Here e_p and e_g are the instantaneous plate and grid potentials, respectively, μ is the amplification factor of the tube (assumed constant), K is a

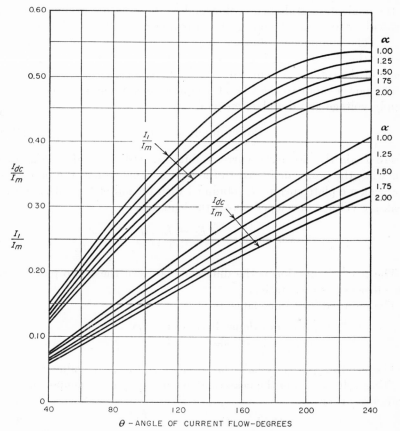

FIG. 13-7. Curves giving the d-c and fundamental-frequency components of the space current pulse as a function of angle of flow θ, and the peak amplitude I_m of the pulse.

constant, and α is another constant normally having a value very close to $\frac{3}{2}$. To the extent that Eq. (13-7) holds, the pulses of space current in a Class C amplifier have a definite form in which the d-c and fundamental-frequency components are functions only of the angle of flow θ, the peak value I_m of the space current, and the exponent α. This relationship has been worked out[1] and is presented in Fig. 13-7 for values of α between 1 and 2.

The d-c and fundamental-frequency components of the total space

[1] *Ibid.*

current divide between the grid and plate electrodes. The portion going to the grid electrode can be calculated from the fact that, with normal amplifier adjustment, the pulses of grid current usually have a shape that approximates the square of a section of a sine wave. Accordingly, by assuming that $\alpha = 2$, Fig. 13-7 can be used to determine the d-c and fundamental-frequency components of the grid current from a knowledge of the angle θ_g of grid-current flow and of the peak d-c grid current corresponding to instantaneous grid and plate electrode potentials E_{max} and E_{min}. The components flowing to the plate electrode are obtained by subtracting the parts going to the grid from the corresponding components of the total space current.

The power input to the Class C amplifier is now the product of plate-supply voltage and d-c plate current, or

$$\text{Power input} = E_b I_{dc} \qquad (13\text{-}8)$$

where I_{dc} is the d-c plate current obtained with the aid of Fig. 13-7. Likewise, the power delivered to the load is equal to half the product of the peak a-c plate current I_1, obtained with the aid of Fig. 13-7, and the peak a-c voltage developed across the load, or

$$\text{Power output} = \frac{(E_b - E_{min})I_1}{2} \qquad (13\text{-}9)$$

The plate dissipation is the difference between these two powers and the efficiency is their ratio.

The required load impedance is

$$\left.\begin{array}{l}\text{Load impedance between} \\ \text{plate and cathode}\end{array}\right\} = \frac{E_b - E_{min}}{I_1} \qquad (13\text{-}10)$$

The exciting power is half the product of the peak value E_g of the exciting voltage and of the peak fundamental-frequency component I_{g_1} of grid current, or[1]

$$\text{Grid exciting power} = \frac{E_g I_{g_1}}{2} \qquad (13\text{-}11)$$

The portion of this power delivered to the bias is equal to the product of bias voltage and d-c grid current. The difference between the exciting power and the bias power is dissipated at the grid electrode of the tube.

The only approximations involved in this method of analyzing Class C amplifiers are the assumptions that μ and the exponent α in Eq. (13-7) are

---

[1] The grid exciting power is also given with good accuracy by the approximate relation

$$\text{Grid exciting power} = E_g I_{g_{dc}} \qquad (13\text{-}11a)$$

where $I_{g_{dc}}$ is the d-c grid current. This relation follows from the fact that for the values of θ_g ordinarily encountered $I_{g_{dc}} \approx I_{g_1}/2$.

constant, and that the grid-current pulse follows a square law.   Under ordinary conditions, the results are accurate to within better than 5 per cent, which is usually better than the accuracy with which one knows the actual characteristics of the particular tube being used.

An example showing the details involved in calculating Class C amplifier performance by this method is given on page 464.

Design Considerations in Triode Class C Amplifiers.   In designing a Class C amplifier, the customary objectives are high efficiency, large power output, and low exciting power.   Efficiency can be made high by using a small angle of plate-current flow θ_p and a minimum instantaneous plate potential E_{min} that is small compared with the plate-supply voltage. Low exciting power is obtained by (1) keeping the grid current low by making E_{max} small and E_{min} large, and (2) using a small exciting voltage, achieved by a bias only slightly greater than cutoff, corresponding to a large value of θ_p.   A large output power is obtained by making θ_p large (which makes I_1/I_m large), combined with values of E_{max} and E_{min} great enough so that the maximum space current I_m is large.

The best compromise between these various conflicting factors involved in the design is obtained when the angle of plate-current flow θ_p is of the order of 120 to 150 electrical degrees, as mentioned above.   The exciting voltage should then drive the grid sufficiently positive so that the plate-current pulse will give an average plate current equal to the rated value when θ_p has the desired value.   The load impedance should be adjusted so that the voltage drop in the load with this plate-current pulse gives a minimum plate potential moderately greater than the maximum grid potential.

The maximum allowable peak amplitude I_m of the pulse of space current is the maximum electron emission that the filament can be depended upon to produce throughout its useful life.   With tungsten filaments, it is permissible to make I_m equal very nearly the full emission obtainable from the filament, while in the case of thoriated-tungsten and oxide-coated filaments, the deterioration during life is such that I_m must be made much less than the emission initially obtainable from the cathode.   When no information is available that gives directly the allowable peak space current, I_m can be taken as being four to five times the sum of the d-c plate and grid currents specified by the manufacturer as being permissible in normal Class C amplifier operation.   Alternatively, one may assume that for Class C operation the allowable peak milliamperes per watt of heating power is typically 2 to 4 for tungsten (or 0.65 of this value for linear and modulated amplifiers), 20 to 40 for thoriated-tungsten filaments, and of the order of 75 to 125 for oxide-coated emitters.

Design Procedure for Class C Amplifiers Employing Triode Tubes.   The design of a triode Class C amplifier can be systematically worked out on paper with the aid of the following procedure:

1. Select the peak space current I_m on the basis of the electron emission of which the filament is capable, as discussed above.

2. Select a suitable combination of maximum grid potential E_{max} and minimum plate potential E_{min} that will draw this total space current. The minimum plate voltage must not be less than the maximum grid potential and, if low exciting power is important, the minimum plate potential should be appreciably larger than the maximum grid potential, although still relatively small compared with the plate-supply voltage.

3. Decide upon a suitable angle of plate-current flow θ_p, making a reasonable compromise between the high efficiency, small output, and large driving power obtained with small angles of flow, and the large output, small driving power, and low efficiency with large angles. Under most circumstances, the angle of flow will lie between 120 and 150°.

4. Calculate the grid bias by the use of Eq. (13-6b). This also determines the exciting voltage required, since the peak value of the exciting voltage is $E_c + E_{max}$.

5. Determine the d-c plate current, d-c grid current, plate dissipation, power output, efficiency, grid exciting power, etc.

6. Examine the results obtained to see if they are satisfactory. If not, revise the design, and recalculate the performance.

7. Design the tank circuit in accordance with the principles discussed on page 458.

This design procedure and the details involved in calculating the performance by the approximate method are illustrated by the following example:

Example. A Class C amplifier is to be designed employing the type 812A tube of Table 13-1 and Fig. 13-8, for a plate-supply potential of 1000 volts.

The peak space current will be arbitrarily chosen as four times the maximum rated value of $(I_b + I_g)$, or $4(175 + 35) = 840$ ma. This corresponds to 33.5 ma/watt of filament heating power. Reference to Fig. 13-8 shows that a suitable combination of E_{max} and E_{min} for drawing this current without excessive grid current while at the same time keeping E_{min} low is $E_{min} = 150$, and $E_{max} = 115$. The corresponding peak grid current is 175 ma. The next step is the selection of a suitable angle of plate-current flow, which will be taken as 140° as a reasonable compromise between efficiency and output. On the assumption that $\alpha = \frac{3}{2}$, Fig. 13-7 gives the d-c and fundamental-frequency components of the total space current as 0.22 and 0.39, respectively, of the peak space current I_m. The d-c component of the total space current is hence $840 \times 0.22 = 185$ ma, and the crest fundamental-frequency component of the total space current is $840 \times 0.39 = 328$ ma crest value. It is now necessary to make allowance for the part of the total space current diverted to the grid. With the use of Eq. (13-5), and the grid bias as calculated below, θ_g is found to be 126°; so from Fig. 13-7, assuming $\alpha = 2$, the d-c and fundamental-frequency components of the grid current are 0.18 and 0.34 times the peak value, or 32 and 59 ma, respectively. The d-c plate current is then $185 - 32 = 153$ ma, and the fundamental-frequency component is $328 - 59 = 269$ ma crest value. The power input to the plate is found from Eq. (13-8) to be $1000 \times 0.153 = 153$ watts. The power delivered to the load is obtained from Eq. (13-9) and is

$$(1000 - 150) \times 0.269/2 = 114 \text{ watts}$$

The plate loss is 153 $-$ 114 = 39 watts, and the plate efficiency is found to be

$$100 \times 114/153 = 75 \text{ per cent}$$

The grid bias calculated by Eq. (13-6b) is 97 volts, and can be developed by a grid-leak resistance 97/0.032 = 3030 ohms.   The peak exciting voltage is 97 + 115 = 212 volts,

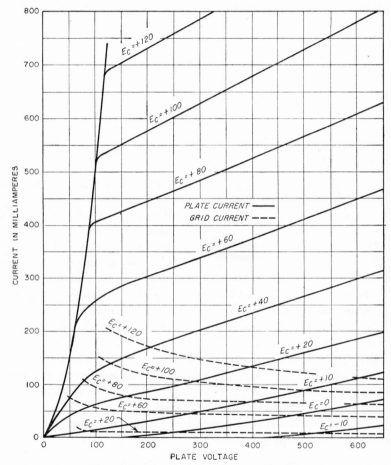

FIG. 13-8. Characteristics of type 812A tube.

and Eq. (13-11) shows the exciting power to be 212 $\times$ 0.059/2 = 6.3 watts, of which 97 $\times$ 0.032 = 3.1 watts is dissipated in the bias, and 6.3 $-$ 3.1 = 3.2 watts at the grid of the tube.   The proper load impedance is given by Eq. (13-10) as

$$(1000 - 150)/0.269 = 3160 \text{ ohms}$$

A check against the rated values of d-c plate and grid currents and maximum allowable plate and grid losses, as given by Table 13-1 for the type 812A tube, shows that this design results in a set of operating conditions that are quite satisfactory.

The tank-circuit inductance and capacitance can now be determined, with the aid of the above data and Eq. (13-2), for any desired value of Q_L and any desired frequency.

13-3. Practical Adjustment of Triode Class C Amplifiers.

The adjustment of Class C amplifiers to realize the design conditions is ordinarily carried out by a cut-and-try process. The usual starting point is either a design worked out as above, or data for Class C amplifier operation supplied by the tube manufacturer. In both cases one knows the proper grid bias, desired d-c plate current, proper tank-circuit inductance and capacitance, and the expected power output.

Saturation in Class C Amplifiers. The experimental adjustment of a triode Class C amplifier is greatly aided by an understanding of the relation that exists between the exciting voltage and the output voltage of the amplifier, and the effect of the load impedance upon this relation and the associated output power. With fixed grid bias, the output voltage of a Class C amplifier operating under normal conditions can be expected to vary with exciting voltage in the manner illustrated in Fig. 13-9. There is no output voltage until the exciting voltage has sufficient amplitude to drive the grid above cutoff at the positive peaks. With further increase in exciting voltage the output voltage first increases approximately linearly, but then rather sharply levels off as the peak output voltage approaches the plate-supply voltage;[1] thereafter, the output increases very little with additional exciting voltage. A Class C amplifier driven with sufficient exciting voltage to place it in this last operating range is said to be *saturated,* since further increase in the driving voltage does not produce any significant effect on the output voltage.

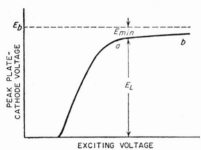

FIG. 13-9. Saturation characteristic of typical Class C amplifier having fixed bias.

The saturation condition corresponds to an output voltage only slightly less than the plate-supply voltage; i.e., to a small value of E_{min}. *Thus an*

---

[1] This implies that the load is coupled to the plate tank circuit with sufficient closeness so that with the recommended exciting voltage the load power approximates the rated value. However, if the load resistance is so loosely coupled to the plate tank circuit that very little power is delivered to the load with normal excitation, then the peak alternating voltage E_L developed between plate and cathode may be greater than the plate-supply voltage E_b, and the minimum instantaneous plate voltage will be negative. Under these conditions saturation effects will be absent, at least in part, and Fig. 13-9 does not apply. This situation in Class C amplifiers is discussed by Leo E. Dwork, Maximum Tank Voltage in Class C Amplifiers, *Proc. IRE,* vol. 38, p. 637, June, 1950; also see Prob. 13-4.

amplifier that is saturated is operating at high plate efficiency. Conversely, if the exciting voltage is appreciably less than the value corresponding to the onset of saturation, E_{min} is large and the plate efficiency is low.

The effect on the saturation characteristic of the impedance of the plate tank circuit is shown in Fig. 13-10. With a low loaded impedance, such as results by closely coupling the load resistance to the resonant circuit (low Q_L), the amplifier requires more exciting voltage to give saturation. This is because it takes larger pulses of plate current to develop the saturation voltage when the impedance of the plate tank circuit is low than when the impedance is high, and increased excitation is required to make the pulses larger.

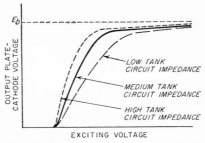

Fig. 13-10. Effect of plate tank-circuit impedance on the saturation characteristics of a Class C amplifier having fixed bias.

When a Class C amplifier is saturated, the peak voltage across the tank-circuit impedance is very nearly the same, irrespective of the tank-circuit impedance, or the exact value of exciting voltage (see Fig. 13-10). This causes both the output power and the d-c plate current of the saturated amplifier to be approximately inversely proportional to the impedance of the loaded tank circuit. Thus reducing the load impedance while maintaining saturation results in larger plate current pulses, higher d-c plate current, and higher output power, but causes little change in the output voltage.

When grid-leak bias is used, the relationship between exciting voltage and output voltage is as shown in Fig. 13-11. These curves differ from those of Figs. 13-9 and 13-10 in that some output voltage is obtained even when the excitation is quite small, since under these conditions the tube has little or no

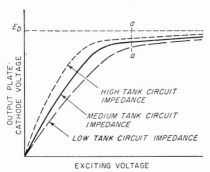

Fig. 13-11. Saturation characteristic of Class C amplifier employing grid-leak bias.

bias. However, the Class C amplifier with grid-leak bias saturates as before when the alternating plate-cathode voltage is only slightly less than the plate-supply voltage. The impedance offered by the loaded plate tank circuit affects the d-c plate current and output power at saturation, and also the exciting voltage at which saturation occurs, in the same manner as in the case of fixed bias. Thus if the tank-circuit impedance is increased in a Class C amplifier employing grid-leak bias, saturation occurs with a smaller exciting voltage, corresponding to less d-c plate current, less output power delivered to the load impedance, less E_{max}, and less bias.

Adjustment Procedures. With an understanding of Figs. 13-9 and 13-10, it is possible to define a straightforward procedure for adjusting a Class C amplifier that is operated with a fixed bias. One starts with the proper bias and a value of plate tank-circuit inductance having the size determined by Eq. (13-2) on the basis of the expected power output and the desired loaded tank circuit Q_L. The load impedance is coupled only moderately to the plate tank circuit, exciting voltage is applied to the system, and the plate tank circuit is adjusted to resonance in the manner described below. The exciting voltage is then increased until the amplifier is moderately saturated. Next, the corresponding value of d-c plate current I_{dc} (or power delivered to the load) is noted, and readjustments made in the loaded tank-circuit impedance and the exciting voltage as required to realize the desired value of I_{dc} (or load power) under saturation conditions. Thus if the value of I_{dc} initially obtained under saturation conditions is less than the expected value, then the coupling between the load resistance and the tank circuit is increased to reduce the loaded impedance of the tank circuit; and the exciting voltage is also increased as required to maintain saturation.

After a suitable value of loaded tank-circuit impedance has been achieved in this way, consideration must be given to the exciting power. The d-c grid current, and hence the exciting power, will increase rather rapidly with increase in excitation beyond that corresponding to the beginning of saturation. Hence the exciting power will depend largely on whether operation corresponds to the start of saturation, designated as a in Fig. 13-9, or to a highly saturated condition as at b in Fig. 13-9. A suitable combination can be readily realized experimentally by small cut-and-try variations in exciting voltage and coupling of the load to the plate tank circuit.

This experimental procedure for adjusting a Class C amplifier is modified slightly when the Class C amplifier employs grid-leak bias. One now starts with an estimated or calculated value of grid-leak resistance, and proceeds to find a combination of exciting voltage and loaded tank-circuit impedance that will give the rated d-c plate current when the amplifier is only moderately saturated. The resulting d-c grid current is then noted, and the grid bias is calculated to determine how it agrees with the design value. If the bias is too great, it can be reduced by using a smaller value of grid-leak resistance, or by readjusting operating conditions to reduce the grid current by operating so that the amplifier is somewhat less saturated. Conversely, if the bias initially obtained is not adequate to give proper Class C operation, it can be increased by employing a higher-resistance grid leak.

It is necessary that the plate tank circuit of the Class C amplifier be kept tuned to resonance at all times during the experimental adjustment of the system. This is usually accomplished by exciting the amplifier and adjusting the tuning of the plate tank circuit while observing the d-c plate current of the Class C amplifier; tank-circuit resonance corresponds to minimum plate current.[1] This behavior results from the fact that the d-c plate current of the amplifier will be minimum when the impedance in the plate circuit is maximum, corresponding to resonance.

The possibility of parasitic oscillations being present (see Sec. 14-9) must always be considered when placing in operation and adjusting a Class C amplifier.

13-4. Special Considerations Involved in Class C Amplifiers Using Beam, Tetrode, and Similar Tubes. The analysis of a Class C amplifier using a tube having a screen grid is the same as in the triode case except for minor modifications introduced by the screen grid. Thus the peak space current I_m is now determined by the screen potential E_{c2} and the maximum control-grid potential E_{max}, instead of by E_{min} and E_{max}, respectively, as in the triode case. Part of this space current goes to the control grid when the latter is positive, exactly as in the triode case. However, the remainder, representing what would be the plate current in the corresponding triode, now divides between the screen and plate, with most, but by no means all, going to the plate electrode. Oscillograms showing the voltage, current, and power relations for a typical case are given by the solid lines in Fig. 13-12. The similarity to the triode case is seen by comparison with Fig. 13-1.

Considerable latitude is permissible in choosing the combination of E_{max} and E_{c2} to give a desired total space current I_m. However, it is customary to choose a pair of values such that the d-c screen voltage is considerably larger than the maximum grid potential E_{max}. In this way it is possible to obtain a given value of I_m with a relatively small value of control-grid current and hence with low exciting power. At the same time E_{c2} is normally made much less than E_b, in order to minimize screen dissipation.

In a properly operating Class C amplifier using a beam, tetrode, or pentode tube, the minimum instantaneous plate voltage E_{min} is just large enough to prevent the formation of a virtual cathode when the plate current has its maximum instantaneous value. If E_{min} is larger than this the power dissipated at the plate is unnecessarily increased. On the

---

[1] This assumes that the value of Q_L that is applicable to the loaded tank circuit is of the order of 10 or more, so that the conditions for maximum tank-circuit impedance and unity power factor are essentially identical. If the effective Q of the loaded tank circuit is so low that this assumption is not permissible, then the tank circuit should be adjusted to provide an impedance having unity power factor at the frequency of operation, in accordance with the discussion on p. 55.

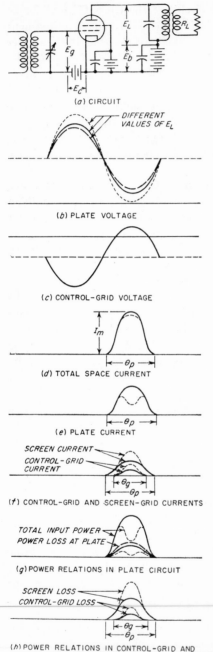

(a) CIRCUIT

(b) PLATE VOLTAGE

DIFFERENT VALUES OF E_L

(c) CONTROL-GRID VOLTAGE

(d) TOTAL SPACE CURRENT

(e) PLATE CURRENT

(f) CONTROL-GRID AND SCREEN-GRID CURRENTS

SCREEN CURRENT
CONTROL-GRID CURRENT

(g) POWER RELATIONS IN PLATE CIRCUIT

TOTAL INPUT POWER
POWER LOSS AT PLATE

(h) POWER RELATIONS IN CONTROL-GRID AND SCREEN-GRID CIRCUITS

SCREEN LOSS
CONTROL-GRID LOSS

other hand, if $E_{\min}$ is so small that a virtual cathode forms, then electrons that should go to the plate are returned to the screen and control grids, reducing the power output and increasing the screen dissipation and exciting power. This is illustrated by the dotted oscillograms of Fig. 13-12. Values of $E_{\min}/E_b$ in the range 0.05 to 0.20 are representative of typical operating conditions with the larger values corresponding to operation at relatively low values of plate-supply voltage E_b.

In the case of screen-grid tubes and likewise in some other tetrodes, the minimum instantaneous plate potential $E_{\min}$ must not be less than the screen-grid potential. Otherwise the plate will lose secondary electrons to the screen, causing loss in power output and increased screen dissipation.

Calculation of Performance. The d-c and fundamental-frequency components of total space current of a Class C amplifier employing a tube with a screen grid are determined with the aid of Fig. 13-7, exactly as in the triode case, in terms of the angle θ_p of plate-current flow and the peak space current I_m, assuming $\alpha = \frac{3}{2}$. The components of this current that are intercepted by the control grid are likewise calculated exactly as in the triode case, in terms of the angle θ_g of grid-current flow, as given by Eq. (13-5), and the peak grid current, assuming that for the grid-current pulse $\alpha = 2.0$. Similarly the d-c and fundamental-fre-

Fig. 13-12. Effect of different values of E_L on the voltage, current, and power relations in typical Class C amplifier employing a beam tube; it is to be observed that in many of the oscillograms, the solid and dashed curves coincide. Note the similarity of the solid curves to the oscillograms of Fig. 13-1.

quency components of the screen current are obtained with the aid of Fig. 13-7 in terms of the peak screen current and the angle θ_p of screen-current flow, assuming $\alpha = 2$. The d-c and fundamental-frequency components of the plate current are then the corresponding components of the total space current less the amounts going to control and screen grids.[1]

In designing a Class C amplifier that uses a tube having a screen grid, the control-grid bias required to achieve a desired angle θ_p of plate-current (and also screen current) flow is determined by μ_s and the screen voltage E_{c2}. The quantitative relation, analogous to Eq. (13-6b), is

$$\text{Grid bias} = E_c = \frac{(E_{c2}/\mu_s) + E_{\max} \cos{(\theta_p/2)}}{1 - \cos{(\theta_p/2)}} \tag{13-12}$$

The special considerations involved in calculating the performance of Class C amplifiers employing beam and similar tubes are illustrated by the following example:

Example. It is desired to design a Class C amplifier using the type 4-65A tetrode (see Table 13-1) which is to operate with $E_b = 1250$ volts and $E_{c2} = 250$ volts.

Assuming that the maximum permissible peak space current is four times the rated d-c value, then I_m should not exceed about $4 \times (150 + 40 + 15) = 820$ ma. Reference to a tube manual suggests that a suitable operating condition would be $E_{\max} = 100$ and $E_{\min} = 250$; the peak values of plate, screen, and control-grid currents are then 515, 175, and 69 ma, respectively; this corresponds to $I_m = 759$ ma, which does not exceed the allowable value. An appropriate angle θ_p of plate-current flow is next selected; a value of 140° is a reasonable compromise when power output, efficiency, and exciting power are all taken into account. The corresponding value of grid bias as given by Eq. (13-12) for $\mu_s = 5$, as given in Table 13-1, is then 128 volts, so that the peak exciting voltage is $128 + 100 = 228$ volts. The angle θ_g of control-grid current flow is given by Eq. (13-5) as 112°. With this information one now has, with the aid of Fig. 13-7,

D-c space current for $\theta = 140°$ and $\alpha = \frac{3}{2}$	$= 759 \times 0.22 = 167$ ma
D-c screen current for $\theta = 140°$ and $\alpha = 2$	$= 175 \times 0.20 = 35$ ma
D-c control-grid current for $\theta = 112°$ and $\alpha = 2$	$= 69 \times 0.16 = 11$ ma
D-c plate current	$= 167 - 35 - 11 = 121$ ma
Peak a-c space current for $\theta = 140°$ and $\alpha = \frac{3}{2}$	$= 759 \times 0.39 = 296$ ma
Peak a-c screen current for $\theta = 140°$ and $\alpha = 2$	$= 175 \times 0.36 = 63$ ma
Peak a-c control-grid current for $\theta = 112°$ and $\alpha = 2 = 69 \times 0.30 = 20$ ma	
Peak a-c plate current	$= 296 - 63 - 20 = 213$ ma
Output power delivered to tank circuit	$= (1250 - 250) \times 0.213/2 = 106.5$ watts
D-c input power to plate	$= 1250 \times 0.121 = 151$ watts
Plate efficiency	$= 100 \times 106.5/151 = 77$ per cent
Plate dissipation	$= 151 - 106.5 = 44.5$ watts

---

[1] A simpler but slightly less accurate procedure for determining the d-c and fundamental frequency component of the plate current is to start with the peak plate current and the angle θ_p of plate-current flow, and apply Fig. 13-7. The results obtained in this way will be most accurate if it is assumed that α is slightly less than $\frac{3}{2}$, ordinarily about 1.40. This is a consequence of the fact that since the pulses of current flowing to the control and screen grids are more peaked than is the wave of space current, the plate-current wave is less peaked.

Screen dissipation	$= 250 \times 0.035 = 8.75$ watts
Exciting power	$= 228 \times 0.020/2 = 2.3$ watts
Power lost in bias	$= 128 \times 0.011 = 1.4$ watts
Power dissipated at control grid	$= 2.3 - 1.4 = 0.9$ watts
Grid-leak resistance	$= 128/0.011 = 11,600$ ohms
Required tank-circuit loaded impedance	$= (1250 - 250)/0.213 = 4700$ ohms

These results are all safely within the tube ratings, and so represent a satisfactory combination of operating conditions. However, since the rated plate and screen dissipations are 65 and 10 watts, respectively, it is possible to obtain greater power output by increasing the input plate power until the rated dissipations are reached. One way to accomplish this is to drive the control grid more positive; this increases I_m at the expense of greater exciting power. Alternatively, one can make θ_p larger, thereby increasing the power associated with a given peak current, but at the cost of lowered plate efficiency. If circumstances permit the use of a higher plate voltage, this is an even better solution.

Experimental Adjustment. The procedure for adjusting Class C amplifiers employing tubes possessing screen grids is essentially the same as when triode tubes are used. The only difference is that with beam and pentode tubes, saturation of the output voltage corresponds to the formation of a virtual cathode in the tube, and is accompanied by a sudden rise in the control-grid and screen-grid currents.[1] The adjustment procedure accordingly can be carried out by starting with the load resistance moderately coupled to the plate tank circuit. The exciting voltage is then increased until saturation starts to appear, and the corresponding d-c plate current is observed. The exciting voltage and the coupling to the load are then readjusted as required so that the d-c plate current is the rated value when the output is almost, but not quite, ready to saturate.[2] If grid-leak bias is employed, some cut-and-try readjustment of the bias resistance may be called for as well.

In adjusting the amplifier it is to be noted that for a given screen voltage the total space current is determined by the amount E_{max} that the control grid is driven positive at the peak of the cycle, but unlike the triode case is independent of the tank-circuit loading. Since saturation in a beam, tetrode, or pentode Class C amplifier corresponds to the formation of a virtual cathode, then with a given screen voltage, control-grid bias, and E_{max}, saturation will occur when the tank-circuit impedance is excessive, corresponding to insufficient coupling to the load. This condition is illustrated by the dotted curves of Fig. 13-12. On the other hand, if the load coupling is greater than necessary to avoid saturation, the conditions shown by the dashed oscillogram in Fig. 13-12 exist.

---

[1] In the case of screen-grid tubes, saturation ordinarily occurs when the minimum plate voltage E_{min} approximates the screen voltage.

[2] If the d-c plate current has the rated value in the absence of a virtual cathode (i.e., no saturation) then the d-c screen current will ordinarily likewise have the rated d-c value as a result of the proportionality that can be expected between instantaneous screen and plate currents in the absence of a virtual cathode.

Here E_{min} is greater than necessary, and the power loss at the plate of the tube is needlessly large.

In adjusting Class C amplifiers that employ tubes possessing screen grids, it is commonly found that if no trace of saturation is present, the plate potential has so little effect on the plate current that tank-circuit resonance with the exciting voltage cannot be detected by watching for a minimum in the d-c plate current. If the tank circuit must be tuned to resonance under these conditions, one adjusts the resonant circuit so that the alternating current in the load is a maximum.

Comparison of Triodes with Beam and Similar Tubes as Class C Amplifiers. Beam tubes or related tetrodes are nearly always used in preference to triodes for Class C amplification when possible. This is because such tubes require no neutralization, and generally require much less exciting power than a triode giving the same output power. However, there is little or nothing available in tubes with screen grids for power ratings corresponding to a plate dissipation much greater than 250 watts. As a result, triode Class C amplifiers are necessarily used for generating the higher powers where no alternative is available, while beam and tetrode types are generally preferred for small to medium powers, where one has the opportunity to choose between a triode and a tube with a screen grid.

13-5. Harmonic Generators. By taking advantage of the fact that the pulses of plate current have appreciable harmonic content, a Class C amplifier can be used to generate output power that is a harmonic of the exciting voltage applied to the control grid. It is merely necessary to tune the plate tank circuit to the desired harmonic of the exciting voltage, and adjust the angle of flow of plate current to a value such that the plate current pulses contain a substantial component at the harmonic frequency involved. Harmonic generators of this character are frequently used in radio transmitters and for other communication purposes.

Oscillograms showing voltage, current, and power relations in a typical harmonic generator are shown in Fig. 13-13; they are seen to be almost identical with the corresponding oscillograms of Figs. 13-1 and 13-12 for a Class C amplifier using triode and beam (or tetrode) tubes, respectively. The significant factors are still the maximum grid potential E_{max}, the minimum plate potential E_{min}, and the angle θ_p of plate-current flow. The considerations involved in the design and adjustment are essentially the same as in the case of a Class C amplifier except for the fact that, since the harmonic content of the plate-current pulses depends upon the angle of flow of the plate current, it is necessary to choose this angle rather carefully in relation to the harmonic to be generated.

The same tube types are used for harmonic generators as for Class C amplifiers. Thus triodes, beam, and tetrode tubes all find use in this application. Beam and tetrode tubes, however, have the advantage of lower exciting power, which is a particularly important consideration in

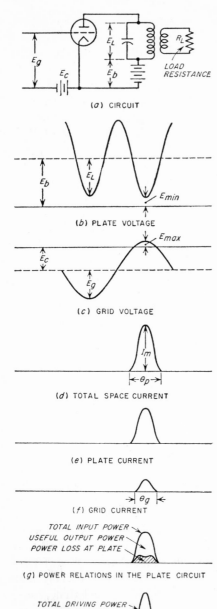

(a) CIRCUIT

(b) PLATE VOLTAGE

(c) GRID VOLTAGE

(d) TOTAL SPACE CURRENT

(e) PLATE CURRENT

(f) GRID CURRENT

(g) POWER RELATIONS IN THE PLATE CIRCUIT

(h) POWER RELATIONS IN THE GRID CIRCUIT
[SCALE DIFFERENT FROM (g)]

Fig. 13-13. Voltage, current, and power relations in a typical Class C triode harmonic generator; note the similarity to the oscillograms of Fig. 13-1.

harmonic generators, where the exciting power is always higher than in the corresponding Class C case.

Factors Governing Harmonic-generator Performance. The most desirable angle θ_p of plate-current flow in a Class C harmonic generator is a compromise between conflicting factors. The shorter the length of the current pulses, the higher will be the plate efficiency when generating a particular harmonic; however, the bias, exciting voltage, and exciting power are increased as θ_p is reduced. Also, if the pulse is too long or too short, the output power drops off appreciably. Values for θ_p representing a practical compromise between these conflicting factors are given in Table 13-2. Since these angles represent a half cycle or more at the harmonic frequency, the plate efficiencies obtained in harmonic generation are typically somewhat less than those commonly achieved in Class C amplifiers.

The harmonic power output that is obtained for a given peak space current $I_{\max}$ decreases with the order of the harmonic. The relative harmonic output obtainable from a given tube compared with the Class C output on the fundamental frequency with the same peak space current is approximately inversely proportional to the order of the harmonic, as shown by Table 13-2. The required value of loaded tank-circuit impedance increases with the order of the harmonic, as shown in Table 13-2; this results from the fact that the tank-circuit impedance required to develop a given voltage E_L is inversely proportional to the power delivered to the tank circuit [see Eq.

(13-2)]. The exciting power required by a harmonic generator is greater than with corresponding Class C amplifier operation because of the smaller angle of plate-current flow, and increases rapidly with the order of the harmonic.

Design and Analysis of Harmonic-generator Performance.[1] The maximum instantaneous grid voltage E_{max} and the peak space current I_m have the same significance and are determined by the same considerations in harmonic generators as in Class C amplifiers. The angle of plate-current flow θ_p is selected in accordance with Table 13-2. With tubes

TABLE 13-2
PLATE-CURRENT PULSE LENGTH AND POWER OUTPUT
OF HARMONIC GENERATORS

Harmonic	Optimum length of pulse, electrical degrees at the fundamental frequency	Approximate power output, assuming that normal Class C output is 1.0	Relative load impedance, assuming that Class C case is 1.0 (approx)
2	90–120	0.50–0.65	1.5–2.0
3	80–120	0.30–0.40	2.5–3.3
4	70–90	0.25–0.30	3.3–4.0
5	60–72	0.20–0.25	4.0–5.0

having a screen grid, the control-grid bias required to produce a given angle θ_p of plate-current flow is given by Eq. (13-12), where θ_p is in electrical degrees at the *fundamental* frequency. In the case of triodes the grid bias is

Grid bias $= E_c$

$$= \frac{E_b[1 - \cos{(n\theta_p/2)}] + E_{min} \cos{(n\theta_p/2)} + \mu E_{max} \cos{(\theta_p/2)}}{\mu[1 - \cos{(\theta_p/2)}]} \quad (13\text{-}13)$$

The notation is the same as in Eq. (13-6b), with the addition that n is the order of harmonic involved and θ_p is in fundamental-frequency degrees.

With E_{min}, E_{max}, E_b, θ_p, grid bias, and the signal voltage determined, oscillograms of plate and grid currents, instantaneous grid and plate losses, power input, etc., can be drawn from characteristic curves of the tube exactly as in the case of a Class C amplifier. Averaging these curves over a full cycle of fundamental frequency then gives exact values of power output, plate losses, d-c plate current, etc.

An approximate analysis of harmonic-generator behavior can be made by noting that *the pulse of total space current in a harmonic generator for a given E_{max}, E_{min}, E_b, and θ_p has practically the same shape as in the case of a*

---

[1] This treatment is discussed in greater detail by F. E. Terman, Analysis and Design of Harmonic Generators, *Trans. AIEE*, vol. 57, p. 640, November, 1938; also see R. H. Brown, Harmonic Amplifier Design, *Proc. IRE*, vol. 35, p. 771, August, 1947.

Class C amplifier. To the extent that the shape is exactly the same in these two cases, the harmonic content of the space-current pulse is given by Fig. 13-14. The details involved are illustrated by the following example:

Example. It is desired to design and calculate the performance of a third-harmonic generator employing the same type 812A tube used in the Class C amplifier example on page 464, operating at a plate potential of 1000 volts.

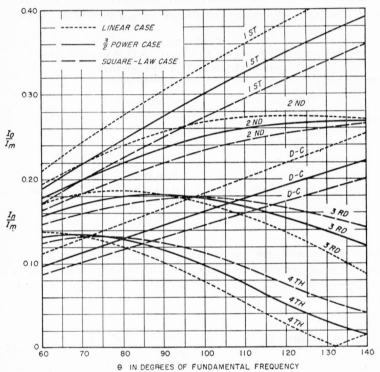

FIG. 13-14. Curves giving the d-c and harmonic components of a current pulse as a function of angle of flow θ and the peak amplitude I_m of the current pulse.

Since the plate efficiency that can be expected is less for harmonic operation than as a Class C amplifier, smaller currents must be used. A peak plate current of 500 ma with $E_{min} = 125$ volts is tentatively chosen. By reference to Fig. 13-8 this is seen to correspond to $E_{max} = 94$ volts, a peak grid current 124 ma, and $I_m = 624$ ma.

The next step is the selection of a value for θ_p. From the discussion given above, combined with an examination of Fig. 13-14, it appears that $\theta_p = 100°$ would be reasonable. With this value of θ_p and assuming a $\frac{3}{2}$ power law, Fig. 13-14 then gives $I_{dc}/I_m = 0.161$, and $I_3/I_m = 0.177$. The d-c and third-harmonic components of the total space current are then $624 \times 0.161 = 100$ ma, and $624 \times 0.177 = 110.5$ ma, respectively. From Eq. (13-13) the grid bias is found to be 340 volts, which makes the peak signal voltage 434 volts. The angle θ_g of grid-current flow is then given by Eq. (13-5) as 77°. Assuming a square-law grid-current pulse, reference to Fig. 13-14 shows that $I_{dc}/I_m = 0.110$, $I_1/I_m = 0.215$, and $I_3/I_m = 0.167$, so for a peak grid current of 124 ma, the d-c, fundamental-frequency, and third-harmonic components of the grid current are 14, 27, and 21 ma, respectively. Since the peak signal voltage is 434 volts, the grid exciting power is $(434 \times 0.027)/2 = 5.9$ watts. If grid-leak bias is used, the leak resistance is $340/0.014 = 24,300$ ohms. Next, subtracting the d-c and third-harmonic components of the grid current from the total space current gives 86 and 89.5 ma, respectively, as the d-c and third-harmonic components of the plate current. This calls for a tank-circuit impedance of $875/0.0895 = 9800$ ohms. The power input to the plate is $1000 \times 0.086 = 86$ watts, while the third-harmonic power delivered to the tank circuit is $0.0895 \times 875/2 = 39$ watts. The plate efficiency is hence calculated as $(39/86) \times 100 = 46$ per cent, and the plate dissipation is $86 - 39 = 47$ watts.

This value of plate loss approximates the permissible plate dissipation of the type 812A tube, which is given in Table 13-1 as being 45 watts. It is therefore unnecessary to revise the design.

The practical procedure for adjusting a Class C harmonic generator is identical with that for the Class C amplifier except that the plate tank circuit is tuned to a harmonic of the exciting voltage. In particular, saturation effects are similar in character and significance in the two cases, and are made use of in the same way to aid in adjusting the harmonic generator to realize proper operating conditions.

13-6. Linear (or Tuned Class B) Amplifiers. A linear amplifier is a Class C amplifier so adjusted that the amplified output voltage that is developed is proportional to the exciting voltage applied to the amplifier. This is accomplished by making the bias of the tube correspond to "projected cutoff" as explained in connection with Fig. 10-22. The linear amplifier is the tuned equivalent of the Class B audio amplifier discussed in Sec. 10-8, but differs in that it need not be push-pull because the tuned circuit eliminates the harmonics.

The same tubes and circuits suitable for Class C amplification are also suitable for linear amplifiers. Thus triode, beam, and pentode tubes all find use. In the case of triode linear amplifiers neutralization of the grid-plate tube capacitance is required unless the grounded-grid circuit is employed.

The linear amplifier finds an important use as a power amplifier of amplitude-modulated waves. It is the most efficient means available of increasing the power of an amplitude-modulated wave without distorting the modulation.

The relationship between output and exciting voltages in a typical linear amplifier is shown in Fig. 13-15. It is almost exactly linear up to a critical amplitude of exciting voltage; while for greater amplitudes the output saturates just as in the Class C amplifier.

The linear amplifier can be analyzed and designed as a Class C amplifier in which the angle θ_p of plate-current flow is slightly greater than 180°, corresponding to projected cutoff. The only special consideration is that the design value of the minimum plate potential E_{min} is chosen perhaps slightly higher than in the case of Class C amplifier operation.

The exciting voltage appropriate for this condition then corresponds to the voltage that when applied to the linear amplifier (and corresponding to the peak of the modulation cycle) will give conditions just beginning to approach saturation.

The power that the exciting voltage of a linear amplifier is called upon to supply varies with the amplitude of the exciting voltage. Thus when the exciting voltage is small, the linear amplifier grid will be negative even at the positive peak of the cycle, and the required exciting power will be negligible. On the other hand, when the exciting voltage has the maximum permissible value, the grid of the linear amplifier will be driven positive and the exciting power required will be considerable. It is accordingly necessary to employ an exciter of relatively large power capacity in order that its voltage regulation under load will be good, or alternatively to use negative feedback (see Sec. 24-1) or some equivalent system of distortion correction.

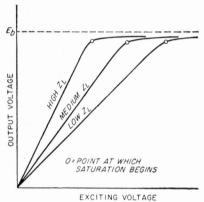

Fig. 13-15. Typical linearity or saturation curves of linear amplifier for different load impedances introduced between the plate and cathode by the plate tank circuit.

When a linear amplifier is excited by a modulated wave, the d-c component of the plate current should not vary with the degree of modulation. Any change in the d-c current with modulation indicates either envelope distortion or a carrier shift (i.e., change in carrier amplitude), although the absence of variation does not give an absolute guarantee that there is no envelope distortion.

The grid bias corresponding to "projected cutoff" must be maintained constant, irrespective of the amplitude of the exciting voltage and of the grid current, and so must be obtained from a fixed voltage. A cathode resistor can be used to develop the bias when the exciting voltage is an amplitude-modulated wave, since then the d-c plate current will be constant irrespective of the degree of modulation, as noted above. Grid-leak arrangements are not permissible under any circumstances.

Efficiency and Power. The plate efficiency of an ideal linear amplifier, assuming that the tube characteristic is linear and that the plate current flows exactly 180° during each cycle, is

$$\left.\begin{array}{r}\text{Idealized plate}\\ \text{efficiency}\end{array}\right\} = \frac{\pi}{4}\left(1 - \frac{E_{min}}{E_b}\right) \times 100 \text{ per cent} \qquad (13\text{-}14)$$

Here E_b is the plate-supply voltage, and E_{min} is the minimum instantaneous plate voltage during the cycle. Equation (13-14) is identical with

Eq. (10-28) applying to the Class B amplifier, and can be derived in exactly the same way. Under practical conditions, where the tube characteristics are curved and operation is at "projected cutoff," the efficiency is slightly less than indicated by Eq. (13-14).

The plate efficiency of a linear amplifier at full output under practical conditions is usually of the order of 50 to 65 per cent. With less than the full output, the efficiency is proportional to the exciting voltage. This is a result of the fact that with linear operation the amplitude of the plate-current pulses, and hence the d-c plate current and plate input power, will be proportional to the exciting voltage, whereas with linear operation the output power is necessarily proportional to the square of the exciting voltage.

When the signal to be amplified is a carrier wave modulated 100 per cent, the carrier amplitude is half the peak amplitude to be handled. The plate efficiency for the unmodulated wave then cannot exceed half the maximum efficiency, or 25 to about 32 per cent under ordinary conditions. The average efficiency of a linear amplifier used with amplitude-modulated waves is hence relatively low, because ordinarily the wave is fully modulated only a small part of the time. Moreover, even when fully modulated, such a wave is at or near the crest of the modulation cycle for only a small fraction of the modulation cycle.[1] The power dissipated at the plate will be maximum when the exciting wave is unmodulated. This is because the d-c plate current, and hence the plate input power, are constant, irrespective of modulation. However, when the wave is modulated the output power is increased by the amount of the power in the sidebands, so that correspondingly less of the input power is lost at the plate of the tube.

The peak output power that can be developed by a tube operating as a linear amplifier is approximately the same as the power developed by the same tube in Class C amplifier operation, or it may even be slightly greater because the linear amplifier does not operate at peak level continuously. Since the peak power of a completely modulated wave is four times the carrier power, a tube used as a linear amplifier of an amplitude-modulated wave is hence ordinarily capable of developing a little more than one-fourth as much carrier power as the output obtainable from the same tube operated as a Class C amplifier.

---

[1] Systems have been devised that give linear amplification of an amplitude-modulated wave with average efficiencies in excess of 50 per cent. However, these arrangements are complicated and difficult to maintain in proper adjustment, so are suitable for operation only where changes in frequency are not required. They are thus seldom used in equipment of current design. For further information, see W. H. Doherty, A New High-efficiency Amplifier for Modulated Waves, *Proc. IRE*, vol. 24, p. 1163, September, 1936; Sidney T. Fisher, A New Method of Amplifying with High Efficiency a Carrier Wave Modulated in Amplitude by a Voice Wave, *Proc. IRE*, vol. 34, p. 3, January, 1946.

13-7. Linear Amplification of Wideband Signals. Linear amplifiers are sometimes called upon to amplify signals having frequency components distributed over a wide band of frequencies. The most common example is the case of a television signal; here the bandwidths are about 9 Mc in a double-sideband situation, and about 5.75 Mc when the signal is of the vestigal-sideband type.

If a linear amplifier is to respond uniformly to a signal containing different frequencies, its plate tank circuit must offer substantially the same impedance to all frequency components contained in the signal. It is therefore necessary that the loaded Q_L be inversely proportional to the desired bandwidth.

When very wide frequency bands are involved, as in the case of television signals, it is found that Q_L must be so low that the maximum tank circuit impedance obtainable is often less than the value required to develop full output power from the tube. This can be understood by the following simple analysis. First, from the properties of parallel resonant circuits, the resonant impedance Z_L of a direct-coupled tank circuit of inductance L and capacitance C will be

$$Z_L = \omega_0 L Q_L = \frac{1}{\omega_0 C} Q_L \tag{13-15}$$

where $\omega_0/2\pi = f_0$ is the resonant frequency. For a given Q_L, the circuit impedance will obviously be greatest when the tuning capacitance is minimum, i.e., when the only capacitance present is the output capacitance C_p of the tube. From this, and the fact that Q_L can be expressed in terms of the resonant frequency f_0 and the half-power bandwidth Δ by means of Eq. (12-4), one can rewrite Eq. (13-15) to give

$$\text{Maximum possible } Z_L = Z_{L\text{max}} = \frac{1}{2\pi C_p \Delta} \tag{13-16}$$

It is thus apparent that the maximum possible tank-circuit impedance that can be obtained in a wideband linear amplifier is inversely proportional to the bandwidth Δ and the tube output capacitance C_p.

When the maximum tank-circuit impedance obtainable as given in Eq. (13-16) is less than the value that would be used in a narrow-band system, as calculated from Eq. (13-10) for the peak of the modulation cycle, then the output voltage that can be developed across the tank circuit by plate-current pulses corresponding to the rated d-c plate current is less than desirable for narrow-band operation, with corresponding reduction in the output power. Under these conditions the tube is preferably operated at reduced d-c plate voltage in order to avoid unnecessary plate losses.[1]

---

[1] The quantitative relations are as follows: From Eqs. (13-2) and (13-16) one can

It is now apparent that when bandwidth is the limiting factor in a linear amplifier, the power output obtainable from a given tube will be inversely proportional to the bandwidth.   Also, when different tubes are compared from the point of view of their behavior under wideband conditions, the best results are obtained with a tube that has a small output capacitance and which requires a low load impedance (i.e., has a high rated d-c plate current in proportion to rated d-c plate voltage).   It is to be noted that the ability of a particular tube to handle a wide frequency band is not affected by the carrier frequency at which this band is centered, provided that the carrier frequency is not so high that transit time and lead inductance effects cause serious deterioration in the performance of the tube.

It follows from these considerations that beam (or tetrode) and pentode tubes that are suitable for wideband video power amplification, as discussed on page 335, also possess the characteristics that are desirable for wideband linear amplification.   Such tubes are generally preferred when available.   However, when the amount of power that must be generated is too large, or the frequency of operation is too high, to permit the use of beam or similar tubes, then triodes in a grounded-grid circuit are employed.   In wideband operation it is generally preferable to use a triode in a grounded-grid circuit instead of in a neutralized system because the output capacitance is then less.[1]   Thus it is possible to realize greater load impedance, and hence more output power under wideband condi-

---

write

$$E_L = I_1 Z_{L\max} = \sqrt{2P_c\omega LQ_L} = \sqrt{2P_c Z_{L\max}} \tag{13-17}$$

Here E_L is the peak plate-cathode voltage under carrier conditions when the fundamental-frequency component of the plate current pulses is I_1, and P_c is the corresponding *carrier* power.   The proper value of E_b for linear amplification of a fully modulated wave is then slightly more than twice the value of E_L given by Eq. (13-17). A larger value of E_b makes $E_{\min}$ greater than necessary at all times, even at the peak of the modulation cycle, and so causes needless power loss; a smaller value will not be adequate to provide for the modulation peaks.

[1] The higher output capacitance of a neutralized arrangement results from the fact that the neutralizing capacitor acts effectively in parallel with the output capacitance of the tube, in so far as the output system is concerned.   Thus in Fig. 12-18b, if $C_n = C_{gp} = C'_n = C'_{gp}$, the capacitance that the plate tank circuit sees when looking back toward the terminals bd is $C_{gp} + C_{pk}$.   In contrast, the capacitance observed by the plate tank circuit of a push-pull grounded-grid arrangement is the output capacitance of the two tubes in series, or $(C_{gp} + C_{pk})/2$.   In actual practice, stray circuit capacitances prevent the theoretical advantage of the grounded-grid circuit from being fully realized; nevertheless the grounded-grid circuit in practice gives an output impedance for a given bandwidth that is about 50 per cent greater than that obtainable from the same triode tube in a neutralized system.   This subject is discussed in further detail by P. A. T. Bevan, Earthed-grid Power Amplifiers, *Wireless Eng.*, vol. 26, p. 182, June, 1949; E. E. Spitzer, Grounded-grid Amplifier, *Electronics*, vol. 19, p. 138, April, 1946.

tions, from a given tube in a grounded-grid circuit than from the same tube in a grounded-cathode circuit.

13-8. Special Considerations Involved in the Operation of Class C and Similar Amplifiers at Ultra-high Frequencies. *Transit-time Effects.* The behavior of a Class C or a linear amplifier, or of a harmonic generator, is modified when the frequency is so very high that the transit time of the electrons is not a negligible fraction of a cycle.   The most important of these consequences of transit time are (1) the pulses of plate current are distorted and lengthened, causing lowered plate efficiency and reduced output power; (2) the cathode is subjected to "back heating"; (3) the control grid absorbs additional driving power as a result of energy transferred from the control grid to the passing electrons.

When the transit time is not a negligible fraction of a cycle, the electrons leaving the cathode at different parts of the plate-current pulse will take different amounts of time to travel from cathode to plate. This is illustrated in Fig. 13-16b for a triode[1] where the transit time is a relatively large fraction of the cycle. Here electrons, such as c and d, that leave the cathode after the peak of exciting voltage is reached will be subjected to weaker fields while in transit in the grid-cathode space than are the electrons leaving the cathode earlier, such as a and b, and so have longer transit times. As a result, the pulses of plate current are distorted and develop a "tail," as illustrated in Fig. 13-16c. The resulting increase in the angle of plate-current flow causes the plate efficiency and the power output to drop at high frequencies.

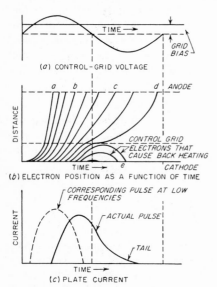

(a) CONTROL-GRID VOLTAGE

(b) ELECTRON POSITION AS A FUNCTION OF TIME

(c) PLATE CURRENT

Fig. 13-16. Behavior of electrons in a typical Class C triode amplifier when the cathode-grid transit time is not a negligible faction of a cycle.

It is also apparent from Fig. 13-16 that transit time causes the pulse of current at the plate to lag somewhat behind the peak of the exciting voltage.

Back heating of the cathode occurs when the transit time in the grid-cathode space is sufficient to cause an appreciable number of electrons to be in transit at the point in the cycle the plate current would be cut off in the case of low-frequency operation.   A considerable fraction of the

---

[1] A similar situation exists in the case of a beam, or other tube type employing a screen grid.

electrons thus caught in the interelectrode space are returned to the cathode by the negative field that exists in the grid-cathode space during the cutoff portion of the cycle. These returning electrons, illustrated by e in Fig. 13-16b, will heat the cathode exactly as in the corresponding diode case discussed in connection with Fig. 6-32. At very high frequencies this back heating may represent a significant part of the total cathode heating power required to maintain the cathode at normal operating temperature. When this is the case, the filament or heater current required to develop a given cathode temperature depends on the operating conditions within the tube. In addition, the bombardment of the emitting surface by the returning electrons may damage the cathode and thereby shorten its life.

Transit-time effects in Class C and similar amplifiers produce an input loading analogous to that existing in the small-signal amplifier discussed in connection with Fig. 6-34. The energy thus absorbed by the control grid is transferred directly to the electron stream of the tube. Part of it is then used by the electrons to cause back heating of the cathode, while the remainder modifies the velocity that the electrons possess when they reach the plate of the tube.

Transit-time effects under Class C and similar operating conditions can be minimized by the use of small spacings between the electrodes of the tube, particularly between cathode and control grid, and by the use of high voltages on the electrodes to increase the electron velocities. It is also important that no electrons be permitted to follow stray paths that have unusually large transit times, since such electrons extend and enlarge the tail of the plate-current pulse.

Circuits for Ultra-high-frequency Class C and Similar Power Amplifiers.
When Class C and similar power amplifiers are operated at very-high and ultra-high frequencies, special attention must be given (1) to obtaining adequate tank-circuit impedance, (2) to the effects of lead inductances and interelectrode capacitances, and (3) to the avoidance of feedback between plate and grid tank circuits.

Interelectrode capacitance and lead inductance combine to limit the highest resonant frequency that can be realized in the grid and plate tank circuits. Together with lead losses, they also lower the highest tank-circuit impedance that can be realized with reasonable tank-circuit efficiency.

At the higher frequencies, it is customary to use resonant-line tank circuits. Not only do such circuits have a higher shunt impedance for a given loaded Q than do tank circuits using lumped constants (i.e., coils and capacitors), but in addition, the lead inductance and electrode capacitances introduce less limitation when acting as extensions of a transmission line than when associated with lumped circuits. Tank circuits with distributed constants can frequently be operated to advantage on a harmonic mode, as for example by making the line three-quarters of a wavelength long. In this way, the first voltage minimum quarter wavelength point) can actually be located within the tube envelope in some cases.

Coupling between plate and grid tank circuits must be entirely eliminated if satisfactory amplifier operation is to be obtained (except of course in the case of harmonic generators). Coupling external to the tube can be prevented by proper shielding of leads and circuit elements. Energy transfer through the tube can be eliminated by the use of neutralization, by the use of tubes with screen grids, or by the use of triodes in the grounded-grid circuit of Fig. 12-19. Grounded-grid triode systems find especial favor at the very highest frequencies. In this case the triode tube used is often especially designed for use with concentric-line circuits; the disk-seal (lighthouse) type of structure illustrated in Figs. 6-35c and 14-8 is an example of this.

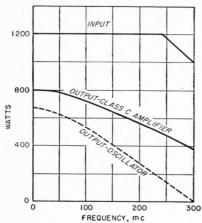

FIG. 13-17. Performance of a typical tube when operated as a Class C amplifier or oscillator at increasing frequency.

Tubes and Tube Performance at Ultra-high Frequencies. Tubes used as ultra-high-frequency amplifiers are characterized by having close spacing between electrodes and are physically small in proportion to power rating. They are frequently water-cooled or cooled by forced air draft, even when of relatively low power rating, in order to permit a high plate dissipation per unit area and thereby keep down the size for a given power-handling capacity. Great care is taken in arranging the leads to minimize lead inductance and capacitance, as discussed in Sec. 6-16.

The performance of a typical tube designed for very high-frequency operation is given in Fig. 13-17. The essential features are a falling off in plate efficiency, and hence of output power, as the frequency is increased. At the highest frequencies, it is necessary to reduce the d-c power supplied to the plate circuit, as shown, to prevent the plate dissipation from becoming excessive when the efficiency falls off. Theoretical studies show that, at the frequency at which the output has dropped to half the low-frequency value in a Class C amplifier, the transit time in the grid-cathode space at the peak of the cycle is of the order of 60°.

Different tubes have different high-frequency limits, with the frequency limit being higher the smaller the physical dimensions of the tube and the closer the spacing of the electrodes. Small triode disk-seal tubes are available that will operate at frequencies above 4000 Mc.

PROBLEMS AND EXERCISES

13-1. *a.* Draw a series of oscillograms similar to those of Fig. 13-1 except that $\theta_p = 225°$.

b. Show that during a portion of each cycle, the plate resonant circuit supplies energy that is dissipated at the plate of the tube, instead of always receiving energy from the plate voltage E_b, as in Fig. 13-1.

13-2. Draw a series of oscillograms similar to those of Fig. 13-1 except that the maximum grid potential E_{max} is slightly greater than E_{min}. For purposes of comparison show dotted oscillograms corresponding to the same E_{min} and θ_p but with $E_{max} < E_{min}$ as in Fig. 13-1.

13-3. *a.* Sketch a series of oscillograms similar to those of Fig. 13-1 except applying to the case where the tank circuit of the Class C amplifier is slightly detuned so that its impedance has a phase angle of 45° lagging at the frequency of the exciting voltage.

b. With the aid of these oscillograms discuss qualitatively the effect that detuning would be expected to produce on power output, plate losses, plate efficiency, and grid current as compared with the same tank circuit tuned to resonance with the exciting voltage.

13-4. Draw a series of oscillograms similar to those of Fig. 13-1, but assume that E_L is slightly greater than E_b so that E_{min} is negative (corresponding to a negative value of e_p). Discuss qualitatively the resulting d-c plate current, power output, efficiency, grid current, and exciting power as compared with the type of operation illustrated in Fig. 13-1, and draw conclusions as to whether operation in which E_{min} is allowed to be negative is desirable, undesirable, or a matter of indifference.

13-5. The permissible d-c plate current is less for a given tube when the angle θ_p of the plate current is small than when θ_p is large. Explain.

13-6. In designing a tube to operate at extremely high frequencies it is helpful to employ cathodes of a type permitting the highest possible electron emission per unit area of cathode surface. Explain why high cathode emission density is more important in tubes intended for very high radio frequencies than for tubes to be used only at the medium to low radio frequencies.

13-7. In Fig. 13-6*a*, derive a formula for the power that will be dissipated in the shunt-feed choke L_c in terms of the reactance X_c and the associated value of Q_c of the choke, and the peak alternating voltage E_L developed across the plate tank circuit.

13-8. In Fig. 13-6*b* and *c*, would there be any objection to employing a separate grid leak–capacitor combination in each of the leads *aa* instead of employing a grid leak–capacitor combination that is common to the two tubes as shown?

13-9. Derive Eq. (13-1).

13-10. Derive Eq. (13-2).

13-11. Demonstrate from the properties of parallel resonant circuits that when the tank circuit of a Class C amplifier using a given tube at a given plate voltage and output power is proportioned to have a low loaded Q_L, (*a*) the impedance to the second harmonic of the fundamental frequency will be higher than when the tank circuit is proportioned to give high Q_L, and (*b*) the reactive volt-amperes stored in the capacitor and in the inductance of the parallel resonant circuit will be less when the tank circuit has a low Q_L.

13-12. Justify Eqs. (13-6*a*) and (13-6*b*).

13-13. The components I_{dc} and I_1 of the plate current can be determined with the aid of Fig. 13-7 from the peak value of the plate-current pulse and the angle θ_p by assuming that α has a value slightly less than $\frac{2}{3}$. Explain why the value of α that should be used is progressively smaller as the ratio of grid to plate current increases.

13-14. With numerical values obtained from Fig. 13-7, justify the approximate correctness of Eq. (13-11*a*).

13-15. With numerical values obtained from Fig. 13-7, verify the correctness of the statement contained on page 463 that one can assume I_m is four to five times the sum of the rated d-c grid and plate currents.

13-16. Recalculate the example on page 464 for a plate potential of 1500 volts, but keeping I_m, E_{max}, E_{min}, and θ_p the same as in the example. Tabulate results of the new calculation alongside the results given in the example, and on the basis of this tabulation discuss the principal effects produced on Class C amplifier operation by increasing the plate-supply voltage. Ignore the fact that $E_b = 1500$ exceeds the recommended maximum value for continuous operation.

13-17. Recalculate the example on page 464 for $\theta_p = 110°$, while keeping I_m, E_{max}, E_{min}, and E_b the same as in the example. Tabulate the results alongside those of the example and discuss the principal effects produced on Class C amplifier operation by decreasing the angle θ_p of plate current flow.

13-18. Recalculate the example on page 464 for a value E_{max} of 90 volts, while keeping E_{min}, θ_p, and E_b the same as in the example. Tabulate the results alongside those from the example in the text, and on the basis of this tabulation discuss the principal effects produced on Class C amplifier operation by reducing the value of I_m.

13-19. Plot a curve showing the peak value of exciting voltage as a function of angle of plate-current flow for the type 812A tube in the example on page 464, keeping E_{max} and E_{min} at the same value as in the example. Cover the range θ_p from 60 to 220°.

13-20. Assume that two Class C amplifier tubes are connected in push-pull as in Fig. 13-6b. Assuming that the tubes operate under the same conditions as the tube in the example on page 464, determine the inductance L_2 and capacitance C_2 of the plate tank circuit if it is desired that $Q_L = 10$, and the frequency of operation is 1000 kc.

13-21. Derive a formula for the peak exciting voltage in Fig. 13-9 at which output first appears, in terms of E_c, E_b, and μ.

13-22. *a.* In Fig. 13-9 explain what goes on in a Class C amplifier that prevents the output voltage from increasing appreciably when the exciting voltage is increased from *a* to *b*.

b. How would this mechanism differ in the case of grid-leak bias?

13-23. Draw oscillograms corresponding to those of Fig. 13-1b to *g*, inclusive, for exciting voltages corresponding to *aa* in Fig. 13-11, and for tank circuit impedances that are respectively high and low. Show the two cases, by means of dotted and solid curves, in their proper qualitative relationship to each other. Assume fixed bias.

13-24. At a certain point in the process of adjusting a particular Class C triode amplifier, assume that it is found the d-c plate current and output power are less than the desired value even though the grid bias is a suitable value, and the plate efficiency is satisfactory. What readjustments should be made to remedy this situation? Assume fixed bias.

13-25. In a Class C triode amplifier it is found that the output power and plate efficiency are satisfactory, but the driving power required is excessive. What adjustments should be made to remedy this situation? Assume fixed bias

13-26. If the coupling of the load to the tank circuit in a properly adjusted Class C triode amplifier using grid-leak bias is removed, the d-c plate current will decrease to a small fraction of its original value, while the d-c grid current will increase somewhat. Explain the reasons for this.

13-27. A Class C triode amplifier is operating under satisfactory conditions, using grid-leak bias. If the value of the grid-leak resistance is increased very considerably but no other adjustments are made, what will be the effect on the grid bias, the d-c plate current, the grid driving power, and the alternating voltage across the load? In each case state the reasons for the answers given.

13-28. Explain the mechanism that causes the plate current in a triode Class C amplifier to pass through a minimum when the plate tank circuit is tuned to resonance (i.e., maximum impedance).

13-29. Derive Eq. (13-12).

13-30. *a.* Recalculate the example on page 471 for $E_b = 2000$, but leaving θ_p, E_{min}, and E_{max} the same as in the text.

b. Tabulate the results from (*a*) alongside of those from the example in the text, and discuss the effect of operating at a higher plate voltage.

13-31. In a triode Class C amplifier the exciting power becomes excessive if the maximum control-grid voltage appreciably exceeds the minimum plate voltage. Is this also true in a Class C amplifier employing a beam tube? Explain.

13-32. In a Class C amplifier employing a tetrode tube, discuss the relative merits of the following situations with respect to minimizing the screen current: (*a*) beam tube with aligned grids and beam-forming plate, as illustrated in Fig. 6-23; (*b*) aligned grids, but no beam-forming plate, surface of plate electrode treated to minimize secondary emission; (*c*) same as (*b*) except grids not aligned; (*d*) same as (*b*) except surface of plate not specially treated to minimize secondary electron emission.

13-33. A Class C amplifier employing a tetrode tube is operating satisfactorily with respect to power output, plate efficiency, and everything else except that the dissipation at the screen is slightly above the rated value. How could this difficulty be remedied without sacrifice of output power or efficiency?

13-34. Explain the mechanism taking place in the tube that accounts for the behavior of the plate, screen, and control-grid currents given by the dotted curves in Fig. 13-12*e* and *f* relative to the behavior shown by the solid curves.

13-35. Explain why the curves of current for the conditions corresponding to the dashed curve in Fig. 13-12*b* coincide with the solid curves in Fig. 13-12*d*, *e*, and *f*.

13-36. In a Class C amplifier employing a tube with a screen grid as in Fig. 13-12, it is found that when a fixed bias is used, exciting the tube with much more driving voltage than necessary to cause the beginning of saturation results in excessive power dissipation at the screen grid. However, if grid-leak bias is employed, the screen dissipation with excessive saturation is only moderately greater than when the exciting voltage corresponds only to the beginning of saturation. Explain.

13-37. Draw a set of oscillograms corresponding to those of Fig. 13-13 but applying to a tetrode tube arranged to generate the third harmonic.

13-38. Derive Eq. (13-13).

13-39. *a.* Design and calculate the performance of a harmonic generator employing a type 812A tube operating with the same E_{min} and E_b as in the example on page 476, but generating the second harmonic. (For the sake of uniformity it is suggested that all students in the class assume $\theta_p = 105°$.)

b. Tabulate the results of (*a*) alongside the results for fundamental operation, as given on page 464, and for third-harmonic generation, as given on page 476, and compare the relative power outputs and load impedances with the approximate values predicted in Table 13-2. Also tabulate and discuss the exciting voltages and powers for these cases.

13-40. The tetrode of the example on page 471 is used to generate the third harmonic. Design the system and calculate its performance, assuming E_b, E_{c2}, E_{min}, and E_{max} are the same as in the example.

13-41. Calculate the exciting voltage and grid bias required when the type 4-65A tetrode tube in the example on page 471 is used to generate the second, third, fourth, and fifth harmonics. Assume $E_{max} = 100$ volts, $E_{c2} = 250$ volts, and $\mu_s = 5$, and select an appropriate angle of plate-current flow for each case. Tabulate the results and discuss qualitatively the significance of these results with respect to exciting power as a function of the order of the harmonic.

13-42. A triode harmonic generator does not need to be neutralized as does a triode Class C amplifier. Explain.

13-43. Derive Eq. (13-14).

13-44. *a.* The type 812A tube used in the example on page 464 is readjusted to operate as a linear amplifier with a grid bias corresponding to projected cutoff (i.e. with an angle of flow of plate current slightly greater than 180°, such as 200°). Design the system and calculate the performance by the approximate method on the basis of exciting conditions corresponding to the peak of the modulation cycle. Tabulate the results alongside those of the Class C amplifier on page 464, and discuss the significant differences.

b. Estimate the power output and plate dissipation under carrier conditions, and indicate whether it appears that the average plate dissipation would exceed the rated value if the linear amplifier were handling a wave that was fully modulated.

13-45. Assume that the type 4-65A tube in the example on page 471 is readjusted to operate as a linear amplifier with a control-grid bias such that θ_p is 200°. Carry out the same design and calculations as called for in Problem 13-45, and compare the results with those applying to Class C operation as discussed on page 471.

13-46. Derive Eq. (13-16) from Eq. (13-15).

13-47. A type 4-65A tube is to be operated as a wideband linear amplifier using a plate-supply potential of 2000 volts. This tube possesses an output capacitance of 2.6 $\mu\mu$f. Assume that the additional capacitance introduced by the leads and circuit elements associated with the plate tank circuit is 6.4 $\mu\mu$f.

a. Estimate roughly the maximum bandwidth that can be realized without loss in efficiency while obtaining a power output of 200 watts at the modulation peaks.

b. Estimate roughly the output obtainable at the modulation peaks if the required bandwidth is 5 Mc, and specify an approximate value of d-c plate potential that would be suitable for operation with this bandwidth.

13-48. Demonstrate that to the extent that the entire tuning capacitance of the plate tank circuit is supplied by the tube output capacitances, bandwidth is neither gained nor lost by connecting tubes in parallel or in push-pull.

13-49. Two tubes have the same output capacitance and the same rated output power, but are designed to operate at different d-c plate voltages. Explain why the tube operating at the lower plate voltage will be superior as a wideband linear amplifier.

13-50. The type 5762 triode (see Table 13-1) has capacitances as follows: $C_{gp} = 19.5$ $\mu\mu$f, $C_{gk} = 19$ $\mu\mu$f, and $C_{pk} = 0.5$ $\mu\mu$f. The capacitance added by the leads and circuit components associated with the plate tank circuit is estimated as 15 $\mu\mu$f. Assuming that the rated carrier output power as a linear amplifier is one-fourth of the output under Class C conditions as given in Table 13-1, estimate the maximum bandwidth obtainable with rated output (*a*) for grounded-grid operation, and (*b*) as a neutralized triode in which the neutralizing capacitance adds 19.5 $\mu\mu$f to the output capacitance.

13-51. Show a series of oscillograms analogous to those of Fig. 13-1 but applying to the case of high-frequency operation where transit-time effects exist that correspond to those shown in Fig. 13-16c. On the basis of these oscillograms explain the mechanism whereby transit-time effects adversely affect the plate loss and hence the efficiency.

13-52. In a given tube it will be found that when the frequency is increased 20 per cent the transit-time effects will be unchanged provided the voltages applied to all the electrodes are simultaneously increased $(1.2)^2$ times, or 44 per cent. Explain.

13-53. Sketch a suitable geometrical arrangement for associating concentric line input and output tank circuits with the tubes of Fig. 6-35d and e.

CHAPTER 14

VACUUM-TUBE OSCILLATORS

14-1. Oscillator-circuit Arrangements. Since the power required by the input of an amplifier tube is necessarily less than the amplified output, it is possible to make an amplifier supply its own input. When this is done the result is an oscillator.

The typical oscillator is a tuned amplifier so arranged as to provide an exciting voltage between the grid and cathode of the tube that is approximately 180° out of phase with respect to the alternating voltage developed

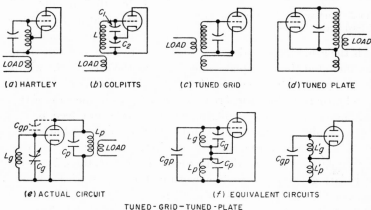

(a) HARTLEY   (b) COLPITTS   (c) TUNED GRID   (d) TUNED PLATE

(e) ACTUAL CIRCUIT   (f) EQUIVALENT CIRCUITS

TUNED-GRID-TUNED-PLATE

Fig. 14-1. Schematic circuits of common types of power oscillators. To simplify the circuit diagrams the methods of introducing the plate-supply voltage and of developing the grid bias are not shown.

between plate and cathode. This phase relation counteracts the phase reversal produced by the amplifying operation, and so enables the exciting voltage to have the polarity required to generate the amplifier output.

Schematic diagrams of commonly used oscillator circuits are shown in Fig. 14-1. In the Hartley and Colpitts circuits the necessary phase relation is obtained by connecting the grid and plate electrodes to the opposite ends of the tuned or tank circuit; in the tuned-grid and the tuned-plate circuits the mutual inductance must have the appropriate polarity. In the tuned-grid–tuned-plate circuit, oscillations are obtained only when the grid tuned circuit L_gC_g and the plate tuned circuit L_pC_p are both adjusted to offer an inductive reactance at the frequency to be generated. This arrangement can accordingly be redrawn as shown in Fig. 14-1f, and is equivalent to a Hartley circuit in which the tuning capacitance is supplied by the grid-plate capacitance of the tube.

In the oscillator circuits of Fig. 14-1 the ratio of grid-cathode exciting voltage to the plate-cathode voltage developed by the amplifier output is determined by the circuit proportions. In the Hartley circuit this ratio is determined by the point on the tank-circuit inductance at which the cathode connection is made, the ratio being less the closer the cathode connection is to the grid end of the coil. In the tuned-grid and tuned-

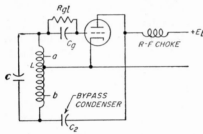

FIG. 14-2. Hartley oscillator circuit with shunt feed and grid-leak bias.

plate circuits, the ratio depends on the mutual inductance of the coupled coils. For the tuned-grid–tuned-plate arrangement the ratio of exciting to output voltage is equal to the ratio L_g'/L_p' of the equivalent inductances in Fig. 14-1f; these inductances are in turn determined by the amount the corresponding grid and plate resonant circuits are detuned from resonance.

Thus if the grid circuit is detuned considerably more from the frequency being generated than the plate tuned circuit, the ratio L_g'/L_p' will be low.

The d-c plate voltage can be introduced into the oscillator circuits of Fig. 14-1 either by shunt or series feed, exactly as in the case of the Class C amplifier. A Hartley oscillator circuit with shunt feed is shown in Fig. 14-2; similar arrangements can be applied to the Colpitts and other circuits. In general, the shunt-feed circuits involve (1) a radio-frequency choke that permits the direct current to reach the plate of the tube while isolating the radio frequency from the source of d-c power, and (2) a capacitor that by-passes radio-frequency currents while blocking off direct current from portions of the circuit other than the plate.

The bias in oscillators that operate as Class C amplifiers is practically always obtained by means of a grid-leak–grid-capacitor arrangement such as illustrated in Fig. 14-2. This is exactly analogous to grid-leak bias in Class C amplifiers, and has the merit of causing the oscillator to adjust itself automatically to conditions corresponding to good efficiency when such parameters as the frequency of oscillation, load impedance, tube characteristics, and plate-supply voltage change in value.

Oscillators in which the tube operates as a Class A amplifier commonly employ a fixed bias. This may be obtained by means of a separate voltage source, or alternatively with the aid of a by-passed resistance between cathode and ground.

14-2. Operating Conditions in Vacuum-tube Oscillators. *Starting of Oscillations.* Oscillations will start up spontaneously when the oscillator tube is first turned on provided the amplification of the system is such that a small voltage e applied to the grid will, when amplified, cause a voltage e' larger than e to be applied to the grid. When this situation exists, the voltage e' after amplification causes a still larger voltage e'' to be applied to the grid, and so on, with the result that there is a progressive building up in the amplitude of the oscillations present in the system.

The initial voltage e required to start the building up process is ordinarily supplied by the noise voltage always present in the circuits associated with the tube. Since a noise voltage contains energy at all frequencies, it always possesses a component at a frequency that is correct for oscillator operation.

Amplitude of Oscillations—Amplitude Limiting. Once oscillations are initiated they rapidly grow in size until their amplitude becomes great enough to introduce nonlinear effects that reduce the amplification of the system. An equilibrium then becomes established at an amplitude where the amplification of the loop from grid to plate and back to grid has dropped to exactly unity. If it were not for this *limiting*, as the nonlinear action is often called, the oscillation amplitude would build up to infinity.

The nonlinear action that establishes the equilibrium amplitude in an oscillator may take a variety of forms. Thus when grid-leak bias is employed the grid bias increases with amplitude; this reduces the amplification by causing both the transconductance of the tube and the angle of plate-current flow to become less. Again, when the oscillator tube operates as a Class A amplifier, grid current will flow when the amplitude is great enough to make the exciting voltage applied to the grid exceed the bias. Still other forms of limiting are illustrated below in Figs. 14-12 and 14-29.

Class A and Class C Oscillators. The oscillator tube may be operated either as a Class A or a Class C amplifier. Class C operation is generally employed as it gives high plate efficiency and maximum power output for a given tube. Class A operation is used only when special requirements are to be met, for example, in laboratory oscillators where great purity of waveform is essential. In Class A systems, the limiting action must be introduced in such a manner as not to destroy the linearity that is characteristic of Class A operation; one method of doing this is discussed below in connection with Fig. 14-12.

Intermittent Operation of Oscillators Employing Grid-leak Bias. When the grid-bias voltage is obtained by means of a grid leak, it is sometimes found that the generated oscillations are periodically interrupted. These interruptions may be at audible rate, or at a low radio frequency.

Such intermittent operation arises from the fact that in an oscillator operated as a Class C amplifier, the oscillations will ordinarily die out spontaneously if the bias has a fixed value independent of the amplitude of the oscillations. This is because any effect that produces a small reduction in amplitude will normally cause the amplification of the tube to become less, thus leading to further reduction in amplitude that causes still greater lowering of amplification, etc.   In the case of grid-leak bias, the time constant $R_{gl}C_c$ of the leak-capacitor combination determines the speed with which the bias voltage developed across the leak can adjust itself to changes in amplitude of the oscillations.   When this rate of change is slow in comparison with the rate at which the oscillations can die out in the oscillator circuits (large time constant), the situation begins to resemble fixed bias conditions, and there is a tendency toward instability.

When the time constant $R_{gl}C_c$ is large enough to cause intermittent operation, the sequence of events is as follows: The oscillations first build up in amplitude to the equilibrium condition.   Any slight irregularity tending to reduce the amplitude of oscillations will then cause the oscillations to die out.   After cessation of oscillations, the grid capacitor gradually discharges through the grid leak, reducing the bias until the tube will again amplify.   The oscillations thereupon build up again to the equilibrium value to repeat the process.

The tendency for intermittent oscillations to occur is proportional to the ratio τ_1/τ_2, where $\tau_1 = R_{gl}C_g$ is the time constant of the leak-capacitor combination, and $\tau_2 = Q_L/\pi f_0$ is the time constant governing the rate at which oscillations can die out in the resonant circuit.   Here Q_L represents the loaded Q of the oscillator tank circuit, and f_0 is the resonant frequency. It is seen that trouble from intermittent oscillation is more likely to occur the higher the frequency.

When intermittent oscillations are encountered in a particular oscillator, the remedies available consist in (1) decreasing the time constant of the leak-capacitor combination either by reducing the grid-leak resistance or the grid-capacitor capacitance, or both; (2) readjusting the oscillator circuits to increase the loaded Q and thereby decrease the rate at which the oscillations die out in the tank circuit; and (3) reducing the ratio of grid-cathode to plate-cathode voltage, so that a given percentage change in oscillation amplitude will produce less change in volts of the grid-cathode voltage.

Noise Modulation in Oscillators.   The oscillations generated by a vacuum tube always possess minute random irregularities that can be thought of as representing a combination of amplitude and frequency modulation.   Most of this noise energy is in the form of sideband frequencies that are very close to the carrier, and which decrease rapidly in amplitude as the frequency differs increasingly from the carrier value.

In general, the energy in the noise sidebands is greater the higher the frequency, and the lower the loaded Q of the oscillator system.[1]   Noise

[1] The theory that leads to these results is presented by W. A. Edson, "Vacuum-tube Oscillators," pp. 374–383, John Wiley & Sons, Inc., New York, 1953.

sidebands are particularly troublesome in low-power microwave oscillators using magnetron and klystron tubes.

14-3. Design and Adjustment of Power Oscillators. Oscillators in which the object is to produce appreciable power output are adjusted so that the tube operates as a Class C amplifier. The voltage and current relations that then exist in the tube are exactly the same as in the corresponding Class C amplifier. The power relations are likewise identical, except for the fact that the output power of the oscillator is less than that of the Class C amplifier by the amount of the grid-driving power. The procedure for design and analysis of a power oscillator is accordingly the same as that of a Class C amplifier, except for modifications that are made clear by the following example:

Example. An oscillator is to be designed to operate under the same conditions as the Class C amplifier of page 464, using the Hartley circuit of Fig. 14-2 with a loaded tank-circuit Q of 50.

The total alternating voltage across the tank circuit will be the sum of the exciting and alternating plate voltages, or $212 + 850 = 1062$ peak volts. The filament tap is located so that the ratio between grid and plate voltages is 212/850. The tank-circuit inductive reactance ωL required is found by Eq. (13-2) to be

$$(1062)^2/(2 \times 114 \times 50) = 99 \text{ ohms}$$

for a tank-circuit power of 114 watts. From this the required tank-circuit inductance and capacitance for any frequency can be calculated. The power output (neglecting tank-circuit losses) is the Class C output minus the exciting power, or

$$114 - 6 = 108 \text{ watts}$$

The plate loss, grid-leak resistance, d-c grid and plate currents, etc., are the same as in the corresponding Class C amplifier. The grid-capacitor capacitance should be large enough to be an effective short circuit to the grid-leak resistance at the operating frequency, but not so large as to cause intermittent oscillations.

If the grid and plate connections are not made to the ends of the coil, the voltage across the tank circuit must be increased accordingly and a higher tank-circuit inductance is required to obtain the required conditions with the same value of loaded Q (see Prob. 14-9).

When an oscillator has been completely laid out as in the above example, it will require only minor readjustments to realize exactly the desired behavior in actual operation. In most practical cases, however, except where the power involved is very large, the paper design is carried only to the point where the tank-circuit inductance and capacitance, the expected power output, operating grid bias, d-c plate current, etc., are known. Such things as the coupling to the load, the grid-leak resistance, and the point at which the cathode connects with the tank circuit in the Colpitts and Hartley circuit are then determined by trial and error. It is desirable to start such adjustments with little or no coupling between the load and tank circuit. After oscillations are obtained, the load coupling is then increased until the power output approximates the rated value, and the input power, efficiency, grid bias, etc., are noted. Readjustments are then made of grid-leak resistance, exciting voltage, load coupling, etc., as required to realize optimum conditions. The principles involved in adjusting a Class C amplifier that are outlined in Sec. 13-3 are also applicable in the adjustment of a power oscillator. The only difference is that the grid exciting voltage is now determined by the coupling between the grid-cathode and the plate-cathode parts of the circuit, taking into account that in a Class C amplifier operating with good efficiency the peak voltage between plate and cathode is always only a little less than the d-c plate voltage. Thus in the Hartley circuit of Fig. 14-2 the exciting voltage can be varied by adjusting the point on the tank circuit to which the cathode is connected. In the Colpitts circuit of Fig. 14-1b, increase of the exciting voltage is obtained by decreasing C_1, and then simultaneously increasing either C_2 or L to restore the original frequency.

14-4. Frequency and Frequency Stability of Oscillators. An oscillator operates at the frequency that makes the grid-cathode voltage have exactly the phase required to generate the plate-cathode voltage present in the oscillator and which in turn produces the grid-cathode voltage. This frequency approximates the resonant frequency of the tuned circuit but often differs slightly therefrom. Such frequency deviation occurs when an unwanted phase shift is introduced by some aspect of the system, for example, the fact that the plate current flows through only part of the resonant tank circuit. In order to achieve the required phase relation between grid and plate voltages, it then becomes necessary for the oscillator to operate slightly off resonance so that the tank circuit can introduce a compensating phase shift.

Factors Contributing to High Stability of Frequency. For many requirements it is essential that the generated frequency be as nearly constant as possible over both short and long time intervals. The first requirement for frequency stability is that the resonant frequency of the tank circuit be independent of changes in temperature. Tube capacitances present a particular difficulty in this regard, since they are a part of the resonant system and tend to vary as the tube warms up. For this reason the frequency stability is generally improved by arranging matters so that the tube capacitances represent only a small part of the total capacitance of the tank circuit (see Prob. 14-10).

The frequency stability of an oscillator with respect to changes in tank-circuit resistance and changes in tube voltages is minimized by employing a tank circuit having a very high effective Q. This is because the frequency deviation required to develop a given phase correction is inversely proportional to the loaded Q of the resonant system. As a result, an oscillator is ordinarily designed to operate with a tank circuit having a much higher value of loaded Q than is the corresponding Class C amplifier.[1]

Variations of frequency resulting from changes in the plate-supply voltage are ordinarily associated with the factors that cause the frequency to differ from the resonant frequency of the tank circuit. As a result, the dependence of the frequency upon the plate-supply voltage can be largely eliminated by inserting a suitable reactance in series with either the grid or plate lead in order to introduce the compensating phase shift that would otherwise have to be introduced by off-resonance operation of the oscillator.[2] Such a reactance can be supplied by a grid capacitor or plate-blocking capacitor of appropriate size.

When a load impedance is coupled directly to the oscillator resonant circuit, any variation in the reactive component of the coupled impedance will alter the resonant frequency of the tank circuit and hence produce corresponding changes in the generated frequency. Therefore, when frequency stability is important it is customary to isolate the load from the oscillator by obtaining the load power from an amplifier that is excited by the oscillator. Such an arrangement is termed a master-oscillator–power-amplifier system (abbreviated MOPA). The electron-coupled oscillator described below in Sec. 14-5 is a variation of the same idea.

Oscillators with Multiply Resonant Circuits. Consider an oscillator which has two resonant frequencies, and in which the coupling from plate to grid is sufficient to sustain oscillation at each of these frequencies. When the two resonant frequencies are quite different, oscillations at both frequencies will exist simultaneously, with the high-frequency oscillation being modulated by the low-frequency oscillation. High-frequency parasitic oscillations (see Sec. 14-9) in a Class C oscillator are an example of this situation.

When the two possible frequencies of oscillation are quite close together and there is approximately an equal tendency to oscillate in the two modes, it is generally found that whichever frequency happens to get started first will suppress oscillation at the other frequency. However, even a momentary stoppage of the oscillations, or even a transient, may cause the frequency to jump to the other possible value. In other circumstances, however, oscillations will occur simultaneously on both frequencies. The behavior in any particular case depends upon the type of nonlinear characteristic possessed by the oscillating system.

A particularly important case of multiple resonance arises when there is coupled to the tank circuit a resonant load that is tuned to the same

---

[1] It is often stated that for good frequency stability the tank circuit of an oscillator would have high capacitance (i.e., low L/C ratio). This is because as explained on p. 459, a large tuning capacitance corresponds to a high value of Q_L.

[2] For details see F. B. Llewellyn, Constant Frequency Oscillators, *Proc. IRE*, vol. 19, p. 2063, December, 1931.

resonant frequency as the oscillator.   If the coupling between the tank circuit and such a secondary is sufficiently close, two possible frequencies of oscillation are introduced as a result of the two humps in the coupling curve discussed in Sec. 3-5.   In this case it is a matter of chance which of these two frequencies predominates, as discussed above.   However, when the coupling is small enough so that the system has only a single peak, then the only effect of the coupled secondary is to absorb power from the system and reduce the loaded Q.   This is a desirable result when the coupled secondary is the load circuit.   However, when the coupled secondary is a parasitic circuit, the energy it absorbs is diverted away from the useful load.   This can cause the useful output to be seriously reduced, and in some cases will even stop the oscillations.

Synchronization of Vacuum-tube Oscillators.   Vacuum-tube oscillators have an inherent tendency to synchronize with any other oscillation of approximately the same frequency that may be present.   The behavior of two oscillators loosely coupled together and generating frequencies not widely different illustrates what can be expected.   If the two frequencies initially differ by only a very small percentage, they are shifted from their normal values in such a way as to reduce the difference.   As the difference between the normal oscillating frequencies is made less, this attraction of the two frequencies toward each other increases, until finally the oscillators pull into synchronism even though they would operate at slightly different frequencies if isolated from each other.   The extent to which the frequency of an oscillator can be shifted from its normal value by coupling to a slightly different frequency will increase as the coupling is increased, and as the frequency stability of the oscillator is lowered.

It has been shown that the tendency for oscillators to synchronize can be accounted for by the same third-order action in the tube system that causes cross modulation (see Sec. 10-3).[1]

14-5. Electron-coupled Oscillators.[2]   The electron-coupled oscillator is a single-tube arrangement that provides isolation between output and oscillator circuits equivalent to that achieved by a master-oscillator–power-amplifier system.

Typical electron-coupled oscillator arrangements are illustrated in Fig. 14-3.   In the arrangement at (a), cathode, control grid, and screen grid form a Hartley triode oscillator in which the screen serves as the anode or plate.   The electrons that are intercepted by the screen represent the oscillator anode current that produces the oscillations.   The remaining electrons, which represent most of the space current, pass through the screen and go on to the plate, where they produce output power by flow-

[1] Balth. van der Pol, The Non-linear Theory of Electric Oscillations, *Proc. IRE*, vol. 22, p. 1051, September, 1934.

[2] J. B. Dow, A Recent Development in Vacuum-tube Oscillator Circuits, *Proc. IRE*, vol. 19, p. 2095, December, 1931.

ing through the load impedance that is connected in series with the plate electrode.   This plate current is controlled by the oscillator part of the tube; thus in Class C operation of the oscillator section there is a pulse of plate current once each cycle.   The load impedance has no effect on the frequency because the plate current of a pentode or beam tube is independent of the plate potential (and hence of the load impedance in the plate circuit) if the minimum plate potential is not so low as to cause the formation of a virtual cathode.   Under these conditions the load impedance and the oscillator section of the tube are coupled only by the electron stream.

Another form of the electron-coupled circuit that finds common use is illustrated in Fig. 14-3b.   Here the screen grid is by-passed to ground and serves as an electrostatic shield between the oscillator and output sections

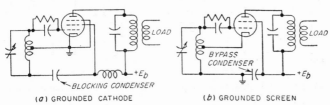

(a) GROUNDED CATHODE   (b) GROUNDED SCREEN
Fig. 14-3. Electron-coupled oscillator circuits.

of the system, while the heater cathode is ungrounded, as shown.   This arrangement has the advantage that the entire space current of the tube flows through the cathode-to-ground section of the oscillator resonant circuit, and is therefore available to aid in the generation of oscillations. Even though most of this space current also flows through the output load impedance, this fact does not cause the load to react on the oscillator section since the plate current of the system is substantially independent of impedance in the plate circuit as long as a virtual cathode is not formed within the tube.   The circuit of Fig. 14-3b is particularly well adapted to use with beam tubes; if a pentode tube is used, then the suppressor grid must be tied to the screen or the plate electrodes.   Connection of the suppressor to the cathode is not permissible in this circuit since a radio-frequency voltage exists between cathode and ground, and thus capacitative coupling between the oscillator and output sections would be introduced by a cathode-connected suppressor.

14-6. Oscillators for Very High Frequencies.   The operation of oscillators at very high frequencies is complicated by transit-time effects, the inductance of the leads to the tube electrodes, and the capacitance of leads and electrodes.   As a result, oscillators for the higher frequencies typically employ tubes especially designed for high-frequency operation, and make use of circuits that often differ in some details from the circuit arrangements in common use at the lower frequencies.

A circuit widely used for ultra-high frequency oscillators is shown in Fig. 14-4a.   When stray capacitances to ground and interelectrode tube capacitances are taken into account, this reduces to the equivalent of Fig. 14-4b.   This is a Colpitts circuit in which the ratio of grid-cathode to plate-cathode alternating voltages is $(C_{pk} + C_2)/(C_{gk} + C_1)$, where C_1 and C_2 are stray capacitances and C_{pk} and C_{gk} are tube capacitances.   The principal advantage of this circuit is that only one tuning adjustment is required, and that there are only two leads from the tube to the associated resonant circuit.

The circuit of Fig. 14-4b is frequently modified by the insertion of a radio-frequency choke between the cathode and ground, as illustrated in

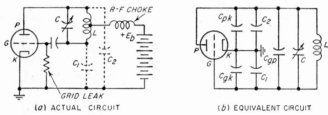

(a) ACTUAL CIRCUIT   (b) EQUIVALENT CIRCUIT

Fig. 14-4. Widely used ultra-high-frequency oscillator arrangement, showing actual and equivalent circuits.

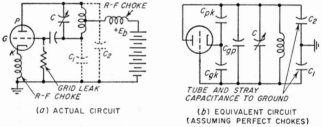

(a) ACTUAL CIRCUIT   (b) EQUIVALENT CIRCUIT
(ASSUMING PERFECT CHOKES)

Fig. 14-5. Modification of Fig. 14-4.

Fig. 14-5a.   The equivalent circuit of this arrangement is illustrated in Fig. 14-5b.   The choke is normally so proportioned that at the resonant frequency of the tank circuit the choke is in parallel resonance with its own stray capacitance, and so introduces an extremely high impedance between the cathode and ground.   The ratio of grid-cathode to plate-cathode voltage is then determined primarily by the ratio C_{pk}/C_{gk} of the interelectrode capacitances of the tube, and is relatively independent of the stray capacitances C_1 and C_2 to the ground.   Thus the feedback action in this case is determined by the tube, not by the proximity to ground of the tube and various parts of the circuit.   However, the ratio of grid-cathode to plate-cathode voltage may be controlled, where necessary, by detuning the cathode choke from resonance.

Push-pull arrangements, such as the tuned-grid–tuned-plate system of Fig. 14-6, are often used in ultra-high-frequency oscillators.   They have the advantage of being symmetrical with respect to ground; also since the interelectrode capacitances of the two tubes are in series, the total effective tube capacitance seen by the external tank circuit is half as great as when a single tube is employed.

Resonant-line Arrangements.   The resonant circuits illustrated in Figs. 14-5a and 14-6 are commonly supplied by resonant lines.   The parallel-line equivalents of these circuits are shown in Fig. 14-7.   In other cases, coaxial lines are employed; they have the advantage of higher Q, absence of radiation, and ability to integrate with certain tube types. An example of a coaxial-line oscillator using a parallel-plane (lighthouse) tube in a grounded-grid amplifier circuit is shown in Fig. 14-8.

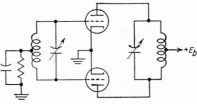

Fig. 14-6. Push-pull form of tuned-grid–tuned-plate oscillator.

It will be noted that the structure of this particular type of tube is especially adapted for use with coaxial lines, since the tube electrodes function for all practical purposes as an uninterrupted continuation of the resonant line, rather than introducing lumped capacitances and inductances that load the line.

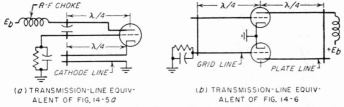

(a) TRANSMISSION-LINE EQUIV-
ALENT OF FIG. 14-5a

(b) TRANSMISSION-LINE EQUIV-
ALENT OF FIG. 14-6

Fig. 14-7. Typical oscillator circuits employing parallel lines as resonators.

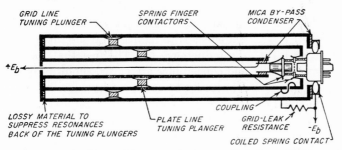

Fig. 14-8. Coaxial-line oscillator employing parallel-plane (lighthouse) tube.

Butterfly Oscillators.[1]   Tunable low-power oscillators operating in the range 100 to 1000 Mc commonly employ a form of resonant system termed a "butterfly."

[1] E. Karplus, Wide-range Tuned Circuits and Oscillators for High Frequencies, *Proc. IRE*, vol. 33, p. 426, July, 1945.

A typical butterfly is illustrated in Fig. 14-9. It consists of a system of stationary and rotating plates, typically shaped as shown, that mesh in the same manner as do the stationary and rotating plates of a variable air-dielectric capacitor. Viewed from the points *aa*, this arrangement has the equivalent circuit shown in Fig. 14-10, which is seen to be a parallel resonant circuit with *aa* the points of high impedance. Comparing Fig.

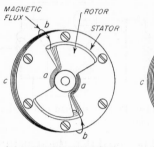
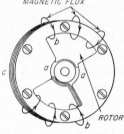
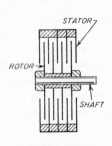

(*a*) BUTTERFLY RESONATOR   (*b*) BUTTERFLY RESONATOR   (*c*) CROSS SECTION
(HIGH-FREQUENCY POSITION)   (LOW-FREQUENCY POSITION)

Fig. 14-9. Butterfly resonator and rotor positions when resonant at high and low frequencies.

14-10 with Fig. 14-9, *C* is seen to be the capacitance between one side of the stator and the corresponding meshed portion of the rotor; two such capacitances are in series between points *aa*. Similarly each inductance *L* in the equivalent circuit of Fig. 14-10 is supplied by the inductance represented by the one-turn loop *aba* of Fig. 14-9; two such inductances are in parallel between the points *aa*.

A variation in the position of the butterfly rotor changes both the inductance and the capacitance of this equivalent resonant system. Thus when the rotor is changed from the low-frequency position of Fig. 14-9*b* to the high-frequency position shown in Fig. 14-9*a*, the effect is to reduce both the capacitance *C* and the inductance *L*. The fact that the inductance and capacitance are varied simultaneously enables a butterfly to cover a very wide frequency range; frequency ratios as great as 5:1 are obtainable with an appropriate design. The circuit has reasonably

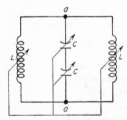

Fig. 14-10. Equivalent circuit of butterfly resonator.

high *Q*, excellent mechanical stability, and no sliding contacts.

Butterfly oscillator circuits are usually based on Fig. 14-5, with the butterfly supplying the resonant circuit. The grid and plate electrodes of the tube are connected to the butterfly at points *aa* in Fig. 14-9, while the radio-frequency choke in the plate lead goes to a point on the butterfly stator such as *c*. Output may be obtained from the system by placing a coupling loop near point *b*, oriented to link with the magnetic field produced by the current flowing in arm *b*.

Holes and Discontinuities in High-frequency Oscillators Having a Wide Tuning Range.   Ultra-high-frequency oscillators that are tunable over a wide frequency range often cease to oscillate, or oscillate only very weakly, at certain frequency settings.   When this behavior occurs the oscillator is said to possess a "hole."   In other cases, even when no hole is present, the tuning curve of the oscillator may possess a discontinuity, with the actual frequency at certain settings of the oscillator tuning control being different when the setting is approached from the low-frequency side from what it is when the setting is approached from the high-frequency side.

These anomalies commonly arise either from parasitic resonant circuits coupled with the oscillator tuned circuit, or from undesired resonances in some portion of the oscillator itself.   Holes may also be caused by inadequate feedback coupling at certain frequencies, either as a result of undesired resonances in the oscillator, or because of a change of voltage and current distribution and hence of coupling associated with a change in frequency.   Radio-frequency chokes are also an important source of holes in oscillators having a wide tuning range.

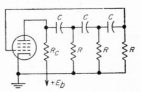

Fig. 14-11.   Elementary phase-shift oscillator circuit.

14-7. Oscillators with Resistance-Capacitance Tuning ("R-C Oscillators").   It is not necessary that an oscillator employ a resonant circuit; any circuit that provides the necessary phase relation between plate-cathode and grid-cathode voltage can be used.   Thus the arrangement shown in Fig. 14-11, commonly termed a phase-shift oscillator,[1] will oscillate at the frequency that causes the resistance-capacitance network to introduce a phase-shift of 180°, provided of course that the gain of the amplifier from grid to plate electrodes is greater than the attenuation of the resistance-capacitance network.

A *resistance-capacitance tuned oscillator* that finds wide use as a laboratory test oscillator at audio and the lower radio frequencies is illustrated in Fig. 14-12a.[2]   Here the necessary phase reversal is obtained by employing a two-stage resistance-coupled amplifier in which the exciting voltage for the grid of the first stage is derived from the output of the second stage by the resistance-capacitance network $R_1C_1R_2C_2$.

This arrangement will oscillate at a frequency such that the input voltage from *b* to ground has the same phase as the voltage from *a* to ground.

---

[1] See E. L. Ginzton and L. M. Hollingsworth, Phase-shift Oscillators, *Proc. IRE*, vol. 29, p. 43, February, 1941.

[2] This type of oscillator was developed by W. R. Hewlett at Stanford University; see F. E. Terman, R. R. Buss, W. R. Hewlett, and F. C. Cahill, Some Applications of Negative Feedback with Particular Reference to Laboratory Equipment, *Proc. IRE*, vol. 27, p. 649, October, 1939.

This occurs when the phase angles of the two resistance-capacitance impedances R_1C_1 and R_2C_2 are the same. In the usual case where $R_1 = R_2 = R$ and $C_1 = C_2 = C$, the oscillator frequency is

$$\text{Frequency} = \frac{1}{2\pi RC} \qquad (14\text{-}1)$$

The frequency is normally controlled by varying the capacitances, which can be conveniently supplied by a gang variable air-dielectric capacitor. It will be noted that unlike oscillators with resonant circuits, the frequency is inversely proportional to capacitance, instead of to the square root of capacitance. Hence when the ratio of maximum to minimum capacitor capacitance is 10:1, a single half turn of the tuning capacitance

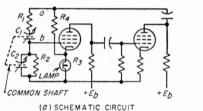
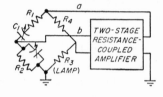

(a) SCHEMATIC CIRCUIT   (b) CIRCUIT DRAWN AS WIEN BRIDGE

Fig. 14-12. Resistance-capacitance tuned oscillator.

shaft will sweep the frequency through a complete decade. The frequency range can then be changed in decimal increments by varying the resistances R by factors of 10.

The oscillations in Fig. 14-12a are limited to the linear part of the tube characteristic by introducing negative feedback with the aid of a voltage divider R_3R_4, in which resistance R_3 is supplied by the filament of an incandescent lamp. When the oscillations are infinitesimally small, the current through R_3 consists only of the d-c space current. The system is so arranged that under these conditions the resulting resistance R_3 is low enough to reduce the negative feedback sufficiently to enable the system to generate oscillations. However, as the oscillations build up in amplitude, an alternating current flows through R_3 superimposed upon the d-c space current, and raises the temperature of the filament. This increases the resistance of the lamp filament, increasing the negative feedback, and thereby lowering the amplifier gain. In this way the amplitude can be made to stabilize at a value that does not overload the tube. This fact, combined with the large amount of negative feedback present in the amplifier, makes it possible to keep the wave-shape distortion of the oscillations very small indeed.

Examination of the circuit $R_1C_1R_2C_2R_3R_4$ shows it to be equivalent to a Wien bridge (see Fig. 14-12b), with the amplifier output applied across one pair of diagonally opposite corners of the bridge, while the amplifier input is obtained from the other diagonally opposite corners. The regenerative coupling between the amplifier output and its input terminals can accordingly be regarded as arising from unbalance of the bridge. When the oscillations are just starting up, the resistance R_3 is smaller than the value required to balance the bridge, so that a very considerable transmission takes place from amplifier output to input. However, as the oscillations grow in amplitude the resistance R_3 increases, as explained above. This brings the bridge closer to balance, reducing the coupling between the amplifier output and input, and thereby reducing the tendency to oscillate. The result is a stabilization of the oscillations at an amplitude such that the bridge is almost, but not quite, balanced.

14-8. Negative-resistance Oscillators. When a parallel resonant circuit is shunted by a negative resistance that has an absolute magnitude less than the parallel resonant impedance of the circuit, oscillations start

(a) SCHEMATIC ARRANGEMENT   (b) DYNATRON OSCILLATOR

Fig. 14-13. Negative-resistance oscillators.

up and increase in amplitude until limited by curvature of the tube characteristic, or by some other form of amplitude control. Such an arrangement, illustrated schematically in Fig. 14-13a, is sometimes referred to as a *two-terminal oscillator* because only two connections are required to the resonant system of the oscillator.

A variety of negative-resistance devices is available for use with two-terminal oscillators.[1] One possibility is the negative plate-cathode resistance of a screen-grid tube operated with the plate voltages less than the screen voltage (see page 197); this leads to the circuit illustrated in Fig. 14-13b, which is commonly called a *dynatron* oscillator. The magnetron (see Sec. 19-6) is also an oscillator of the negative-resistance type.

14-9. Parasitic Oscillations. The term *parasitic* is applied to any undesired oscillation occurring in an oscillator or power amplifier. Such oscillations are commonly encountered when large tubes are employed. They are to be avoided because they absorb power that would otherwise go to generating useful output and because they also often produce excessive voltage stresses in portions of the circuit. In addition, the presence of parasitic oscillations will normally cause distortion in linear amplifiers, modulators, and Class A and Class B audio amplifiers. Low-frequency parasitic oscillations will also modulate a carrier wave either at an audio or at a low radio frequency.

[1] See E. W. Herold, Negative Resistance and Devices for Obtaining It, *Proc. IRE,* vol. 23, p. 1201, October, 1935.

Examples of Parasitic Oscillations. Parasitic oscillations result from the fact that, when the tube capacitances, lead inductances, shunt-feed chokes, etc., are all taken into account, it is usually found that several possible modes of oscillation can exist in addition to the desired type of operation. The nature of these parasitic circuits and the means for preventing them from giving rise to oscillations can be understood by considering several typical examples.[1,2]

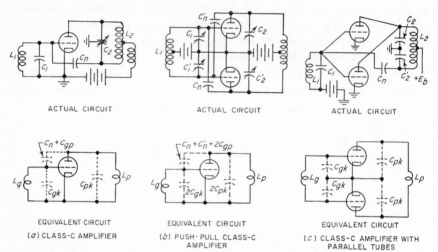

Fig. 14-14. Some actual amplifier circuits, and the equivalent circuits involved in high-frequency parasitic oscillation.

Consider, first, the simple Class C amplifier circuit of Fig. 14-14a. At frequencies very much above the normal frequency of operation, the tank-circuit capacitances C_1 and C_2 can be considered to be short circuits, while the tank-circuit inductances L_1 and L_2 can be approximated by open circuits. Under these conditions the oscillator circuit reduces to that shown, which is a tuned-grid–tuned-plate oscillator circuit, with the grid and plate tuning capacitances supplied by the grid-cathode and plate-cathode tube capacitances, respectively. The inductances L_g and L_p are supplied by the inductances of the leads between the tube electrodes and ground through the tuning capacitances C_1 and C_2. It will be noted that the neutralization is not effective because the coil L_2 does not participate in the parasitic oscillation. Instead, the neutralizing capacitor C_n simply adds to the grid-plate capacitance C_{gp} and helps provide coupling between the grid and plate tuned circuits.

[1] Additional examples are described by G. W. Fyler, Parasites and Instability in Radio Transmitters, *Proc. IRE*, vol. 23, p. 985, September, 1935.

[2] The examples given here are all of the type requiring coupling between the control-grid and the plate circuits. It is, however, also possible to obtain parasitic oscillations of the negative-resistance type, for example, when dynatron action exists at the control grid.

Next, consider the neutralized push-pull amplifier circuit of Fig. 14-14*b*. This arrangement is commonly troubled with high-frequency parasitic oscillations of the type just discussed, having the equivalent circuit shown in Fig. 14-14*b*, with the two tubes acting in parallel.

Similarly, when two tubes are operated in parallel as in Fig. 14-14*c* instead of in push-pull, one finds there is the possibility of a very high-frequency parasitic oscillation of the tuned-grid–tuned-plate type based on the equivalent circuit of Fig. 14-14*c*, in which the two tubes operate in push-pull. Here the tuning inductances consist of the inductances L_g and L_p of the leads from grid to grid and from plate to plate, while tuning capacitances are the interelectrode capacitances of the tubes in series. The neutralization has no effect on this parasitic because, as

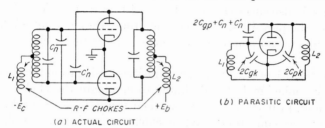

(*a*) ACTUAL CIRCUIT

(*b*) PARASITIC CIRCUIT

Fig. 14-15. Amplifier circuit with radio-frequency chokes, together with low-frequency parasitic circuit that can exist as a result of these chokes.

far as the parasitic oscillation is concerned, the neutralizing condenser is between points that are effectively at ground potential.

Parasitic oscillations at frequencies lower than the normal operating frequency can arise from radio-frequency chokes, as illustrated in Fig. 14-15. At frequencies much lower than the operating frequency, the tank-circuit inductances can be considered as short circuits, so that the equivalent circuit for parasitic action is a tuned-grid–tuned-plate circuit, as shown, in which the inductances of the tank circuits are supplied by the chokes, while the tuning capacitances are supplied by the interelectrode capacitances of the tubes. It will be noted that the neutralizing capacitors are not effective in preventing coupling between the plate and grid circuits, because, for the parasitic action, the tubes operate in parallel instead of push-pull, exactly as in Fig. 14-14*b*.

Screen-grid, beam, and pentode power-amplifier tubes are practically immune from most types of parasitic oscillations, provided the screen grid is really at ground potential, since then no energy transfer through the tube is possible. However, if the circuit from the screen-grid electrode through the screen by-pass capacitor to the cathode has appreciable inductance, it is possible for parasitic oscillations of the tuned-grid–tuned-plate type to exist, with the screen serving the same function as the plate in the ordinary triode circuit.

Although the examples of Figs. 14-14 and 14-15 relate to parasitic oscillations in tuned amplifiers, exactly the same types of parasitics can occur in untuned audio power amplifiers and in power oscillators. In fact, parasitic oscillations can be expected as a matter of course in any new design of amplifier, either radio- or audio-frequency, or of power oscillator, involving large tubes.

Various expedients are available for eliminating parasitics. In the case of high-frequency parasitics of the tuned-grid–tuned-plate type, the use of short grid leads and long plate leads, or the insertion of a small choke in the plate lead next to the tube, will cure the trouble. In this way, the parasitic plate circuit is tuned to a much lower resonant frequency than is the parasitic grid circuit, which prevents parasitic oscillations from occurring. The use of resistors connected in the grid and plate leads next to the tube is also effective, since these resistors are in series with the tank circuits of the parasitics. At the same time, they are not a part of the tank circuits for normal operation and so have little effect on the desired oscillations.

The possibility of low-frequency parasitics arising from the use of radio-frequency chokes makes it desirable to eliminate the chokes wherever possible and, in particular, to avoid their use in both the grid and plate circuits of the same tube. When chokes must be employed, low-frequency parasitics of the tuned-grid–tuned-plate type can be avoided by using chokes of such relative size that the resonant frequency produced in the plate circuit by the plate choke is much less than the corresponding resonant frequency resulting from the grid choke.

The simplest method of investigating the presence of parasitic oscillations in a Class C or other power amplifier is to remove the exciting voltage, make the grid bias small or even zero, and operate with a plate voltage lowered sufficiently to keep within the rated dissipation of the tube. This ensures a high transconductance and gives conditions favorable for the excitation of most types of parasites. These oscillations can then be searched for by some simple means, for example, a neon lamp at the end of a wooden rod. When the lamp is brought near a point of high voltage it will glow, thus making it possible to determine what parts of the circuit are involved in the parasitic oscillation. After a parasitic oscillation has been thus located and its frequency determined, the equivalent circuit can be deduced and remedial means devised. It is often found that, upon the elimination of one parasitic oscillation, another oscillation of a different type will appear and that, upon the elimination of this, still other parasitic oscillations may start up.

14-10. Piezoelectric Quartz Crystals.[1] An unusually high degree of frequency stability, particularly over long periods of time, can be obtained

---

[1] This subject, particularly the aspects having to do with the properties of quartz crystals, has become a highly technical specialty. An excellent discussion of the properties, production, and use of quartz crystals for radio and other similar applica-

by replacing the usual resonant circuit of an oscillator with a mechanically vibrating piezoelectric quartz crystal, and utilizing the piezoelectric effect to establish a connection between the electrical circuits and the mechanical vibrations. Such crystal oscillators are the standard means of maintaining the frequency of radio transmitting stations at the assigned value, and also find extensive use in the reception of signals from transmitter stations of specified frequencies, for example, in connection with aircraft-to-ground radio communication.

Piezoelectricity.[1] Piezoelectric quartz crystals when complete have a hexagonal cross section with pointed ends as shown in Figs. 14-16 and 14-17. The properties of such a crystal can be expressed in terms of three sets of axes. The axis joining the points at the ends of the crystal is known as the optical axis. Electrical stresses applied in this direction produce no piezoelectric effect. The three axes X', X'', and X''' passing through the corners of the hexagon that forms the section perpendicular to the optical axis are known as the electrical axes. The three axes Y', Y'', and Y''', which are perpendicular to the faces of the crystal, are the mechanical axes.

If a flat section is cut from a quartz crystal in such a way that the flat sides are perpendicular to

Fig. 14-16. Illustration showing the natural quartz crystal and the relation of the electrical, mechanical, and optical axes, the X, Y, and Z axes, respectively, to the crystal structure. The upper section shows a Y cut plate, while the plate in the center section is an X cut. The third Y axis $Y''Y''$ is not shown because the perspective of the drawing makes it coincide with the Z axis.

tions is to be found in the book edited by R. A. Heising, "Quartz Crystals for Electrical Circuits—Their Design and Manufacture," D. Van Nostrand Company, Inc., New York, 1946.

[1] Piezoelectric properties are exhibited by a number of natural crystal substances, of which the most important are quartz, Rochelle salt, and tourmaline. The effect is exhibited to the greatest degree by Rochelle salt, which is used in crystal microphones and loudspeakers. Quartz, though exhibiting the piezoelectric effect to a smaller degree than Rochelle salt, is employed for frequency control in oscillators because of its permanence, low temperature coefficient, and high mechanical Q. Tourmaline is similar in these respects to quartz but is more expensive.

In recent years a number of synthetic piezoelectric crystals have been discovered, such as ADP (ammonium dihydrogen phosphate), EDT (ethylene diamine tartrate), and DKT (dipotassium tartrate). These find use in filter circuits and as electromechanical transducers, but have less inherent stability than quartz and so do not compete seriously with the latter in oscillator applications. For further information see W. P. Mason, New Low-coefficient Synthetic Piezoelectric Crystals for Use in Filters and Oscillators, *Proc. IRE*, vol. 35, p. 1005, October, 1947.

an electrical axis, as indicated in Fig. 14-17b (X cut), it is found that mechanical stresses along the Y axis of such a section produce electrical charges on the flat sides of the crystal section. If the direction of these stresses is changed from tension to compression, or vice versa, the polarity of the charges on the crystal surfaces is reversed. Conversely, if electrical charges are placed on the flat sides of the crystal by applying a voltage across these faces, a mechanical stress is produced in the direction of the Y axis.

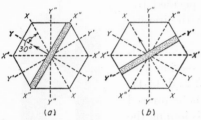

This property by which mechanical and electrical properties are interconnected in a crystal is known as the *piezoelectric effect* and is exhibited by nearly all sections cut from a piezoelectric crystal. Thus, if mechanical forces are applied across the faces of a crystal section having its flat sides perpendicular to a Y axis, as in Fig. 14-17a

Fig. 14-17. Cross section of the quartz crystal shown in Fig. 14-16, taken in a plane perpendicular to the optical axis ZZ. The plates shown at a and b are, respectively, the Y and X cuts of Fig. 14-16.

(which is known as the Y or 30° cut), piezoelectric charges will be developed because forces and potentials developed in such a crystal have components across at least one of the Y and X axes, respectively.

An alternating voltage applied across a quartz crystal will cause the crystal to vibrate and, if the frequency of the applied alternating voltage approximates a frequency at which mechanical resonance can exist in the crystal, the vibrations will be intense. Any quartz plate (or bar) has a

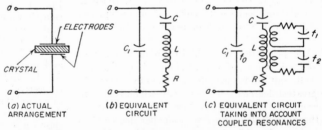

(a) ACTUAL ARRANGEMENT   (b) EQUIVALENT CIRCUIT   (c) EQUIVALENT CIRCUIT TAKING INTO ACCOUNT COUPLED RESONANCES

Fig. 14-18. Equivalent electrical networks representing the effect that a vibrating quartz crystal has on the electrical circuits associated with it.

number of such resonant frequencies that depend upon the crystal dimensions, the type of mechanical oscillation involved, and the orientation of the plate cut from the natural crystal.

Equivalent Electrical Circuit of Vibrating Quartz Crystal. As far as the electrical circuits associated with a vibrating quartz crystal are concerned, the crystal can be replaced by the resonant circuit LCC_1R of Fig. 14-18b. Here C_1 represents the electrostatic capacitance between the crystal electrodes when the crystal is not vibrating, and the series combination L, C, and R represents the electrical equivalent of the vibrational characteristics of the material. The inductance L is the electrical equivalent of the crystal mass that is effective in the vibration, C is the electrical equivalent of the effective mechanical compliance, while R represents the electrical equivalent of the mechanical friction. Electrical

TABLE 14-1
CHARACTERISTICS OF A TYPICAL QUARTZ CRYSTAL

Mechanical characteristics	Electrical characteristics
Length............................ 2.75 cm	$L = 3.3$ henrys
Width............................. 3.33 cm	$C = 0.042$ $\mu\mu$f
Thickness........................ 0.636 cm	$C_1 = 5.8$ $\mu\mu$f
Resonant frequency (thickness vibration):	$Q = 23,000$ (approx)
Series resonance................. 427.4 kc	
Parallel resonance............... 430.1 kc	

circuits involving piezoelectric crystals can therefore be analyzed by replacing the crystal with its equivalent electrical network and then determining the behavior of the resulting circuit.

The magnitudes of L, C, R, and C_1 that enter into the equivalent electrical network of the vibrating quartz crystal depend upon the way in which the crystal is cut, its size, and the type of vibrations involved. Numerical values can be calculated when these factors are known, and have values of which those in Table 14-1 are typical.

The equivalent resonant circuit LCC_1R of a vibrating crystal is characterized by a remarkably high Q. Values in excess of 20,000 are always to be expected, and values well over 1,000,000 have been observed under special circumstances. The quartz crystal resonator also has a remarkably high ratio of inductance to capacitance, as is apparent from Table 14-1. Further, the capacitance ratio C/C_1 is always very small; this causes the coupling between the crystal resonator and the external circuit in Fig. 14-18a to be inherently small.

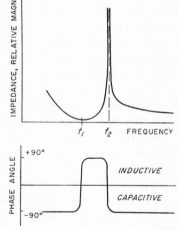

Fig. 14-19. Variation of impedance with frequency of a quartz crystal in the immediate vicinity of the series and parallel resonant frequencies f_1 and f_2, respectively.

The circuit of Fig. 14-18b has the impedance characteristic illustrated in Fig. 14-19. At the frequency $f_1 = \omega_1/2\pi$ which makes $\omega_1 L = 1/\omega_1 C$, the branch LCR is in series resonance, and so offers an impedance at the external terminals that is low and resistive. At a slightly higher frequency $f_2 = \omega_2/2\pi$, branch LCR has an inductive reactance equal to the capacitative reactance $1/\omega_2 C_1$ of C_1.

The crystal system is then in parallel resonance, and so at this frequency offers a very high impedance at the external terminals. The difference $f_2 - f_1$ between the frequencies of series and parallel resonance is quite small, typically less than one per cent.

Crystal Activity. The term "activity" applied to a quartz crystal denotes the magnitude of the piezoelectric effect for the particular crystal plate, electrode arrangements, and vibrational mode under consideration. A crystal operating at the series resonant frequency will be more active the lower the resistance R in the equivalent circuit of Fig. 14-18b. Similarly, the activity of a crystal that is operating at its parallel resonant frequency is proportional to the parallel resonant impedance that is developed between the crystal electrodes, i.e., the impedance across the capacitance C_1 in Fig. 14-18b. This impedance, and hence the activity, are again inversely proportional to the crystal resistance R, but in addition they are also inversely proportional to the square of the capacitance C_1. Thus when a crystal is used at its parallel resonant frequency, care should be taken to minimize the contributions made to C_1 by circuit and tube capacitances that may shunt the crystal electrodes.

Crystal Electrodes and Mounting. The crystal electrodes are commonly thin metal films formed directly on the surface of the crystal by spraying and firing a silver solution, or by evaporation of gold, silver, or aluminum. The crystal is then ordinarily supported by flexible wires fastened with low-melting-point solder to the film electrode at a nodal region, or at an edge of the plate where inhibiting the vibrations will do no harm and may even help suppress undesired vibrational modes.

When a crystal that is provided with plated electrodes is too heavy or unwieldy to be supported by a flexible wire, as is the case with long thick rods, the crystal can be rigidly clamped at a nodal point.

It is also possible to use metal plates to supply the crystal electrodes. The surfaces of such plate electrodes are preferably slightly concave, so that when the crystal is pressed between top and bottom plates it is clamped only at the corners. However, when the system is not subject to mechanical shock, for example, in broadcast-station applications, the plate electrodes can be flat. In this case the crystal simply rests on the lower plate, while the upper plate is mounted so that it is parallel to the upper surface of the crystal but with a very slight air gap.

The mounted crystal is ordinarily enclosed in a sealed container to protect the crystal from moisture, etc. In some cases the crystal container is evacuated to eliminate the damping effect of the air and thereby increase the crystal Q. The crystal holder is also sometimes provided with a heater and thermostat for the purpose of maintaining the crystal at a specified temperature.

14-11. Resonant Frequencies in Crystals. *Vibrational Modes and Actual Equivalent Electrical Circuit.* The resonant frequency of a crystal depends upon the mechanical dimensions, the mode of vibration involved, and the elastic constants of the crystal for this mode. The actual situation is very complicated because the crystal has different elastic constants in different directions, and there are three mechanical dimensions to consider in a simple rectangular plate. Also, the crystal plate may have any one of an infinite number of orientations with respect to the crystal axes. Finally, several types of vibrations are possible, and each type of vibration can exist in a fundamental and in overtone (or harmonic) modes.

The various types of vibrations that are possible in a crystal are conveniently classified as longitudinal (extensional), flexural, and shear. Longitudinal vibrations produce a displacement in the direction of the

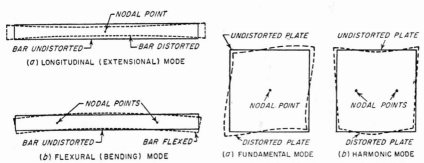

Fig. 14-20. Quartz plate vibrating in the longitudinal and flexural modes. For the sake of clarity the magnitude of the motion is greatly exaggerated.

Fig. 14-21. Motion associated with a low-frequency face-shear type of vibration. For the sake of clarity the magnitude of the motion is greatly exaggerated.

length, as illustrated in Fig. 14-20a. Flexural vibrations result in the kind of motion shown in Fig. 14-20b. Shear vibrations are of two types: a low-frequency or face-shear motion along the diagonal of a square plate, as shown in Fig. 14-21a, and a high-frequency shear vibration (Fig. 14-22b) where the resonant frequency is determined by the thickness of a thin plate.

Associated with each of these fundamental modes are overtone[1] modes that represent additional resonant frequencies. Examples of the motions associated with such overtone modes are given in Figs. 14-21b and 14-22c and d. The Q of the overtone modes of a crystal is of the same order of magnitude as for the fundamental; however, the activity of the crystal is always progressively less the higher the overtone.

It is thus apparent that an individual quartz plate can be expected to

---

[1] The term *overtone* is used in place of harmonic because the overtone (harmonic) frequencies are ordinarily not in exact integral ratios to the fundamental. Thus the third overtone illustrated in Fig. 14-22c occurs at approximately, but not exactly, three times the resonant frequency of the corresponding fundamental mode of Fig. 14-22b.

have many different resonant frequencies.[1] Although a few of these are
of no interest from a piezoelectric point of view because they are of such a
nature as to produce little or no piezoelectric effect, most of them are
sufficiently piezoelectrically active to be of significance.   To make things
still more complicated, elastic (i.e., mechanical) couplings exist between
many of the different vibrational modes.   Thus it is possible for mechanical vibrations of a thickness mode to excite an overtone of a width mode
if there is such an overtone that is resonant at approximately the same
frequency as the thickness vibration.

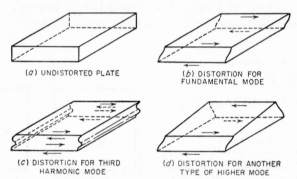

(a) UNDISTORTED PLATE

(b) DISTORTION FOR
FUNDAMENTAL MODE

(c) DISTORTION FOR THIRD
HARMONIC MODE

(d) DISTORTION FOR ANOTHER
TYPE OF HIGHER MODE

Fig. 14-22. Motions associated with fundamental and higher modes of vibration of the
high-frequency shear type. For the sake of clarity the amplitude of the motion is
greatly exaggerated.   The arrows indicate the direction of motion.

The actual equivalent electrical circuit for a particular vibration is
therefore not exactly as shown in Fig. 14-18b, but rather more typically
resembles the arrangement shown schematically in Fig. 14-18c.   This is a
multiple resonant system such as discussed on page 495, in which f_1, f_2,
etc., represent schematically other mechanical resonances of the crystal
that are coupled to the resonance f_0 which is of primary interest.   The
reactance and resistance that these secondary circuits couple into the
resonant circuit $LRCC_1$ depend upon the elastic couplings existing
between the particular types of resonances involved, and upon the relative
frequencies of the resonances involved.   The effect that these coupled
systems have on the resonant frequency of circuit f_0 can be appreciable.
Thus when a particular secondary resonant frequency approximates the
desired resonant frequency f_0, this secondary circuit couples sufficient
resistance into the primary to lower appreciably the crystal activity;
when the elastic couplings are large this reduction may be so great that
the crystal will not oscillate when placed in the usual crystal oscillator
circuit.   Again, if the coupling is sufficiently great, and if at the same

[1] It will be observed that each of the vibrational modes illustrated in Figs. 14-20 to
14-22 possesses nodal points where the crystal plate is at rest.   These are indicated
in the various figures, and are sometimes taken advantage of when mounting the
crystal.

time the secondary resonant frequency coincides exactly with that of the primary circuit, then the resonant frequency f_0 will be split into two resonant frequencies corresponding to the two peaks of response that arise when two circuits resonant to the same frequency are closely coupled together (see Fig. 3-11).

Troubles from secondary resonances are particularly severe when the desired vibration is a high-frequency vibration corresponding to a thickness mode of a relatively thin plate.   Under these conditions, overtones of various resonances determined by other and larger dimensions of the crystal result in numerous coupled resonances, some of which often approximate the resonant frequency of the desired thickness vibration.

As a result, crystals operating in a thickness mode commonly exhibit, in so far as the electrical terminals are concerned, a series of resonances distributed relatively closely in the frequency spectrum, as illustrated in Fig. 14-23. Such undesirable behavior can be avoided by properly proportioning the crystal plate so that the resonant frequencies of the undesired modes differ appreciably from that of the desired mode, by orienting the plate with respect to

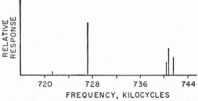

Fig. 14-23. Frequency spectrum of a thin quartz plate, showing several closely spaced resonant frequencies. The lengths of the vertical lines indicate in a rough way the relative tendency to oscillate at the different resonant frequencies.

the crystal axes in such a manner as to reduce the elastic couplings between the most troublesome spurious modes and the desired oscillation, and by mounting the crystal in such a way as to suppress the undesired modes of resonance whose overtones create the trouble.   Such expedients must always be employed in the case of crystals to be used at high frequencies and are an essential part of the design of such crystals.

Temperature Coefficient of Resonant Frequency. The resonant frequency of a particular mode of vibration in a quartz crystal has a temperature coefficient that depends upon the type of vibration involved, the crystal dimensions, and the way in which the crystal plate is oriented with respect to the axes of the crystal.   Certain types of resonances have a positive temperature coefficient, while others have a negative coefficient.

By judiciously arranging matters so that the desired vibration is mechanically coupled to the appropriate degree with some other mode of vibration having a temperature coefficient of opposite sign, it is possible to balance positive and negative effects and obtain zero temperature coefficient. A number of ways have been discovered for applying this principle to give crystals that have a low temperature coefficient of frequency for some particular mode of vibration that is piezoelectrically active. Some, but by no means all, of these are tabulated in Table 14-2;

TABLE 14-2
TYPICAL CRYSTAL CUTS WITH LOW-TEMPERATURE COEFFICIENTS

Cut name	Frequency range for which most useful, kc	Type of vibration
AT	500–10,000*	High-frequency shear (Fig. 14-22b)
BT	500–10,000*	High-frequency shear (Fig. 14-22b)
CT	100–500	Low-frequency shear (Fig. 14-21a)
DT	100–500	Low-frequency shear (Fig. 14-21a)
GT	100–500	Longitudinal (Fig. 14-20a)
−18°	60–300	Longitudinal (Fig. 14-20a)
MT	50–100	Longitudinal (Fig. 14-20a)
NT	4–50	Flexural (Fig. 14-20b)

    * By means of overtone operation the upper frequency limit can be extended to between 50 and 100 Mc.

the corresponding orientation of the crystal plates and bars with respect to the crystal axes is shown in Fig. 14-24.

    The temperature coefficient of typical low-temperature cuts varies with temperature as shown by the examples in Fig. 14-25. The coefficient is ordinarily zero only over a limited temperature range; an exception is the

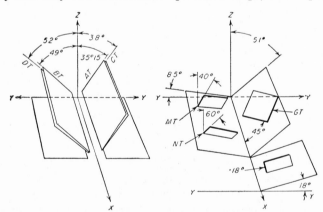

FIG. 14-24. Relation of different types of low-temperature coefficient crystals to the crystal axes.

GT cut which has negligible temperature coefficient over the entire range 0 to 100°C. In general, the region of low temperature coefficient is reasonably broad, however, and can be centered on any temperature desired by properly controlling the orientation of the crystal plate with respect to the crystal axes.

    Frequency Range of Crystal Oscillators. Resonant frequencies ranging from a few hundred cycles to above 100 Mc can be obtained from crystals of practical size. Over most of this range Table 14-2 shows that it is possible to achieve a very low temperature coefficient of resonant frequency.

Resonant frequencies as low as a few hundred cycles can be obtained by a crystal that is cut in the form of a ring with a gap, as illustrated in Fig. 14-26, and vibrating in a mode that causes the gap length to vary. The lowest frequency that can be realized in this way is limited by the maximum value of diameter d and the minimum value of thickness t that it is practical to achieve.[1]

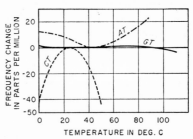

Fig. 14-25. Variation of resonant frequency with temperature with several types of crystals.

The highest resonant frequency obtainable for practical operation from a crystal vibrating in the fundamental mode is about 30 Mc. This figure is set by the minimum thickness that it is feasible to employ in a crystal plate. However, by means of overtone operation it is practical to extend this upper frequency limit to above 100 Mc.

Variation of Resonant Frequency with Time—Aging. A crystal can be expected to experience variations in its resonant frequency and in its activity during its initial months of use. Known as *aging,* this is in large measure due to a disturbed layer at the surface of the crystal involving fractured particles of quartz and imbedded fragments of grinding compound arising from the process of grinding the crystal.

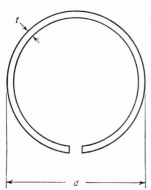

Fig. 14-26. Ring crystal with gap for generating very low frequencies.

Aging can be reduced by thoroughly scrubbing the finished crystal to remove imbedded particles. It can be further minimized by chemically etching the crystal with concentrated hydrofluoric acid that removes a surface layer, or by optically polishing the crystal plate to the point where optical means indicate negligible surface imperfections. It is also helpful to mount the finished crystal in a vacuum or in an inert gas in order to eliminate the possibility of chemical reactions that would change the crystal surface in any respect.

14-12. Crystal Oscillator Circuits. A quartz crystal can be used to control the frequency of an oscillator by so locating the crystal in the oscillator circuit that the equivalent electrical network of the crystal

---

[1] J. E. Thwaites, Quartz Vibrations for Audio Frequencies, *Proc. IRE*, vol. 99, pt. IV, p. 83, April, 1952.

becomes a part of the resonant circuit that would normally control the frequency. Typical crystal oscillator circuits are illustrated in Figs. 14-27 to 14-29.

Miller Circuit. The circuit arrangement of 14-27a is often termed the Miller circuit. When the crystal is replaced by its equivalent electrical network, the resulting circuit of Fig. 14-27b is seen to be a conventional tuned-grid–tuned-plate arrangement in which the grid tuned circuit is supplied by the crystal operating just below the parallel resonant frequency (but above the series resonant frequency) in such a manner as to produce the inductive reactance required by the tuned-grid–tuned-plate circuit. Oscillations then occur when the plate resonant circuit is tuned

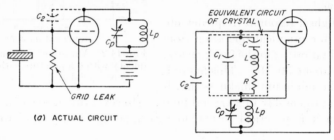

FIG. 14-27. Crystal oscillator employing the Miller circuit, showing actual and equivalent circuits. It will be noted that this is a tuned-grid–tuned-plate arrangement.

to a frequency slightly higher than the resonant frequency of the crystal mode that is to be excited; this gives the inductive reactance required between plate and cathode in the tuned-grid–tuned-plate circuit. The amplitude of the generated oscillations is determined by the amount of inductive reactance in the plate circuit.[1]

Pierce Circuit. The crystal oscillator circuit shown in Fig. 14-28a is commonly termed the Pierce circuit, after its originator G. W. Pierce. When the crystal is replaced by its equivalent electrical network, the resulting circuit (Fig. 14-28b) is seen to be a Colpitts circuit analogous to Fig. 14-1b, in which the crystal operates at a frequency just sufficiently below parallel resonance to give an inductive reactance that will resonate with the tube capacitances C_p and C_g.

The Pierce circuit will oscillate at whatever frequency is necessary to place the operation slightly on the inductive side of parallel resonance in

---

[1] When the crystal in the Miller circuit has several possible resonant modes, it will vibrate at the frequency which is favored by the tuning of the plate resonant circuit. Thus an *AT* cut crystal can be made to operate at an overtone instead of at the fundamental by adjusting the plate tuned circuit so that it is resonant at a frequency slightly higher than the desired overtone frequency instead of slightly higher than the fundamental. Oscillations at the overtone frequency will then occur provided the tube amplification is sufficient to give an oscillatory system in spite of the lowered activity of the crystal for overtone operation.

the crystal.   Hence unlike the Miller circuit, the Pierce circuit does not require any circuit adjustment when a crystal of one resonant frequency is replaced by a crystal having a different resonant frequency.   This is a very considerable advantage in multichannel equipment in which different crystals must be employed at different times.   However, the Pierce circuit possesses the disadvantage that the crystal will operate on what-

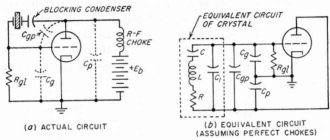

(*a*) ACTUAL CIRCUIT   (*b*) EQUIVALENT CIRCUIT
(ASSUMING PERFECT CHOKES)

Fig. 14-28. Crystal oscillator employing Pierce circuit, showing actual and equivalent circuits.   This circuit is a Colpitts oscillator.

ever mode has the highest activity.   Thus if there is an undesired mode of high activity at a frequency differing significantly from the desired resonant frequency, the Pierce circuit may very likely excite the undesired rather than the desired mode.   In contrast, the Miller circuit will not do so because its plate tuned circuit can be adjusted to favor the desired resonant frequency.

Bridge-stabilized Oscillator Circuit.[1]   In the bridge circuit of Fig. 14-29 the series resistance of the crystal supplies one arm R_4 of a bridge, and the other three arms are resistances R_1, R_2, and R_3.   Resistance R_2 is supplied by the filament of a lamp, and the circuit proportions are such that when the lamp filament is cold R_2 is a little less than R_1R_3/R_4, that is, the bridge is moderately unbalanced.   The input terminals of a

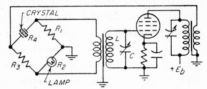

FIG. 14-29. Bridge-stabilized crystal oscillator.

tuned amplifier are connected across one diagonal of the bridge as shown, while the amplifier output is applied to the other diagonal.

This arrangement is analogous to the bridge circuit of Fig. 14-12*b*.   In the absence of oscillations the bridge is unbalanced, and a regenerative coupling exists between the amplifier input and output terminals as a result of the unbalance of the bridge.   Oscillations then build up at the frequency that causes the crystal to act as a series resistance R_4.   However, as the oscillation amplitude increases, the filament of the lamp warms up, increasing R_2 and bringing the bridge nearer into balance.

[1] L. A. Meacham, The Bridge-stabilized Oscillator, *Proc. IRE*, vol. 26, p. 1278, October, 1938.

If the amplification is large, an equilibrium becomes established at an amplitude such that the bridge is almost, but not quite, in balance, and at a frequency that is very nearly equal to the series resonant frequency of the crystal. The frequency is then almost solely dependent upon the crystal, and is substantially independent of tube characteristics and of circuit adjustments.

Adjustment of Exact Frequency. The accuracy with which a crystal will realize a desired resonant frequency is determined in the first place by the accuracy with which the crystal is ground to the proper dimensions. When the crystal electrodes are metal films on the surface of the crystal, it is possible to correct for slight errors in the resonant frequency by taking

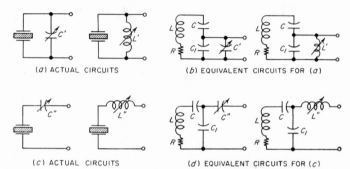

(a) ACTUAL CIRCUITS   (b) EQUIVALENT CIRCUITS FOR (a)

(c) ACTUAL CIRCUITS   (d) EQUIVALENT CIRCUITS FOR (c)

Fig. 14-30. Methods of modifying the equivalent parallel and series resonant frequencies of a crystal by the addition of reactances external to the crystal.

advantage of the fact that the metal film lowers the resonant frequency slightly by an amount that increases with thickness. Thus by controlling the thickness of the electrodes deposited on the crystal surfaces it is possible to realize a desired frequency with an extremely small tolerance.

It is also possible to use the etching process to achieve a desired frequency more closely than is possible by grinding, since etching slowly dissolves material from the surface and so causes the resonant frequencies to increase. Thus a fine control over the final frequency can be realized by means of the time the crystal is allowed to remain in the etching fluid.

In some applications it is necessary that the actual frequency of the oscillations be adjustable exactly to a prescribed value. This situation exists for example in oscillators that are employed as frequency standards. Frequency changes up to a few parts in a million can be produced by means of an adjustable d-c voltage applied to the crystal electrodes.[1]

Somewhat larger changes in the resonant frequency of a crystal can be produced in the case of parallel resonant operation by shunting the crystal electrodes with a variable capacitance or a variable inductance as illustrated by C' and L' in Fig. 14-30a and b. Such a reactance external to

[1] See John M. Shaull, High Precision Frequency and Time Standards, *Proc. IRE*, vol. 38, p. 6, January, 1950.

the crystal alters slightly the parallel resonant frequency of the system involving the crystal.   When the crystal is operated at series resonance, a similar control of the series resonant frequency can be realized by placing a variable capacitive or inductive reactance in series with the crystal as illustrated by C'' and L'' in Fig. 14-30c and d.

The quantitative effect of the external reactances in Fig. 14-30 can be determined by replacing the crystal by its equivalent electrical circuit and then calculating the change in resonant frequency of the system that is caused by the added reactance.   The maximum possible percentage change that it is practical to realize is very small, but the use of an adjustable external reactance does provide a means whereby it is possible to exercise a little control over the oscillator frequency without having to regrind the crystal.

Power Output and Frequency Stability of Crystal Oscillators.   The power that can be generated by a crystal oscillator is limited at the lower frequencies by the maximum amplitude of vibration that is possible without cracking the crystal from the resulting mechanical stress.   At high frequencies the output power is limited by the heating of the crystal. Although a crystal can be made to generate appreciable power, it is in general preferable to operate with relatively small output power, and to obtain the desired power by the use of a tuned amplifier excited by the crystal oscillator.   In some cases an electron-coupled form of Miller or Pierce circuit is used in order to separate the crystal as much as possible from the generation of power.

The frequency stability of the oscillations obtained from a crystal is very high.   Stabilities of a few parts in a million can be readily realized over long periods of time.   When the utmost care is taken to hold constant all of the factors that affect the frequency, it is possible to maintain the frequency constant to approximately 1 part in 100,000,000 over indefinitely long periods of time.   The extent of such precision is indicated by the fact that 1 part in 100,000,000 of the distance from the Atlantic to the Pacific Ocean across the United States is about 1.5 in.

PROBLEMS AND EXERCISES

14-1. In the Hartley and Colpitts oscillator circuits of Fig. 14-1, follow through the phase relation in detail and show that the phase relations necessary for oscillation are realized in both of these circuits.

14-2. Draw a Colpitts circuit with shunt feed and grid leak–capacitor bias.   Be sure to arrange the grid-leak resistance so that the d-c grid current can return to the cathode.

14-3. Explain why an oscillator with grid bias developed by a source of fixed voltage will not be self-starting if it is to be operated as a Class C amplifier, whereas it will be self-starting if the equilibrium conditions correspond to Class AB amplifier operation. Explain.

14-4. In an oscillator that is generating intermittent oscillations, explain why the frequency of interruption of the oscillations is decreased by increasing the capacitance of the grid capacitor.

14-5. The oscillator in the example of Sec. 14-3 is to employ the Colpitts circuit of Fig. 14-1b. Determine the reactances of capacitances C_1 and C_2 and of inductance L.

14-6. Calculate the current that circulates in the tank circuit (i.e., the branch current of the resonant circuit) of the oscillator described in the example of Sec. 14-3.

14-7. In a properly adjusted oscillator, increasing the resistance that the load couples into the tank circuit will increase the d-c plate current, while causing the d-c grid current and the a-c current in the tank circuit to decrease slightly. Explain the mechanism that causes this behavior.

14-8. A tuned circuit that has its resonant frequency varied by means of a variable capacitor is loosely coupled to the tank circuit of an oscillator. The capacitor adjustment that makes the resonant frequency of the tuned circuit the same as the frequency of oscillations is indicated by a slight jump in the d-c plate current of the oscillator and a drop in the d-c current. Explain.

14-9. In a particular Hartley oscillator, the grid and plate connections to the tank-circuit coil are made at points a and b, respectively, in Fig. 14-2, instead of to the ends of the coil. Demonstrate that with a given loaded Q this "tapping down" on the tank circuit calls for a higher value of L/C than when the grid and plate connections are made to the ends of the tank circuit.

14-10. Demonstrate that when the Hartley circuit of Fig. 14-2 is modified in accordance with Prob. 14-9, the variation of the tube capacitances with temperature will have less effect on the frequency than in Fig. 14-2.

14-11. Demonstrate that when the loaded Q of the tank circuit is increased, the coupling required between the load and the tank circuit to transfer a given amount of power to the load is reduced, and that this in turn reduces the effect of changes in the load reactance upon the frequency of oscillation.

14-12. Devise a circuit arrangement for a vacuum-tube oscillator that includes two tank circuits tunable to different frequencies, and with couplings between plate and grid electrodes sufficient to sustain oscillations at each of these tank-circuit frequencies.

14-13. In an electron-coupled oscillator, explain the mechanism that causes the load impedance in the plate circuit to affect the frequency when a virtual cathode is present in the tube.

14-14. Draw a series of oscillograms analogous to those on Fig. 13-12 but applying to the electron-coupled oscillator of Fig. 14-3b when the oscillator section is operated as a Class C amplifier. The oscillograms should show the voltage to ground that acts on the screen, control-grid, cathode, and plate electrodes, and also the screen, plate, and cathode currents.

14-15. Will the ratio of grid-cathode to plate-cathode alternating voltages in Fig. 14-4a be increased or decreased by bringing a grounded object close to the lower end of the inductance L?

14-16. Redraw the oscillator circuit of Fig. 14-8 with the resonant lines replaced by lumped coils and capacitors. Be careful to show correctly the point at which the circuit is grounded, and also the method by which coupling is achieved between the grid and plate resonant circuits.

14-17. Doubling the number of stator and rotor plates of the butterfly of Fig. 14-9 will double the equivalent capacitance of the resonant system. Will this change cause the inductance for the rotor position of Fig. 14-9b to be increased, decreased, or left unchanged?

14-18. Verify the fact that when Eq. (14-1) is satisfied, the voltage from a to ground in Fig. 14-12a has the same phase as the voltage from b to ground.

14-19. Derive a formula for the frequency of the resistance-capacitance tuned oscillator that is analogous to Eq. 14-1, but which does not require that $R_1 = R_2$ and $C_1 = C_2$, but only that $R_1C_1 = R_2C_2$..

14-20. In the resistance-capacitance tuned oscillator of Fig. 14-12, will a phase shift in the amplifier that causes the amplified output voltage at a to lead the amplifier input voltage at b cause the frequency of oscillation to be increased, decreased, or left unchanged?

14-21. Will adding an inductance in series with the lamp in Fig. 14-12 cause the frequency of oscillation to be increased, decreased, or left unchanged?

14-22. Demonstrate mathematically that when the absolute magnitude of the negative resistance in Fig. 14-13a is equal to the parallel resonant impedance of the tuned circuit LC, the negative resistance $-R_n$ exactly neutralizes the actual series resistance R so that the system becomes equivalent to a coil-and-capacitor combination with zero losses.

14-23. Discuss various types of parasitic oscillations that could arise in an amplifier comprising four tubes arranged to provide a push-pull system in which the amplifier on each side of the push-pull connection consists of two tubes in parallel.

14-24. Explain in detail the mechanism whereby parasitic oscillations can arise in an amplifier employing a beam tube when the inductive reactance of the lead between screen and cathode is not negligible at very high frequencies.

14-25. On page 506 it is stated that parasitic oscillations of the tuned-grid–tuned-plate type will not arise when the parasitic plate circuit is resonant at a frequency much lower than the parasitic tuned circuit associated with the grid. Justify this statement in terms of the equivalent circuit of the tuned-grid–tuned-plate oscillator shown in Fig. 14-1f.

14-26. Is it possible for parasitic oscillations to exist in a tuned-grid–tuned-plate oscillator? Explain.

14-27. Explain why resistances connected in series with the grid and plate leads are attractive as a means of suppressing parasitic oscillation only when the interelectrode capacitances of the tube represent a very small part of the tank-circuit capacitance required for normal operation.

14-28. Calculate the series resistance of the crystal of Table 14-1.

14-29. Check the values of series and parallel resonant frequencies given in Table 14-1. Use four-place logarithms in order to achieve adequate accuracy.

14-30. Calculate the coefficient of coupling between the external terminals aa and the crystal resonant circuit LCC_1 of Fig. 14-18b for the crystal of Table 14-1.

14-31. Prove that when the capacitance ratio C/C_1 in the equivalent circuit of Fig. 14-18b is small, $(f_2 - f_1)/f_1 = C/2C_1$, where f_1 and f_2 are, respectively, the series and parallel resonant frequencies of the crystal system (see Fig. 14-19).

14-32. Derive a formula giving the parallel resonant impedance appearing across the crystal electrodes (i.e., the activity) in terms of the crystal Q, the frequency, and the capacitances C and C_1 of the equivalent circuit. Make whatever assumptions are appropriate in view of the fact that the ratio C/C_1 is quite small compared with unity.

14-33. Sketch the distortions that are produced when the crystal bars of Fig. 14-20 are vibrating at overtones corresponding to resonant frequencies that are approximately twice and three times the fundamental frequency.

14-34. Demonstrate that when the resonant frequency of the coupled vibration f_1 in Fig. 14-18c is greater than the resonant frequency f_0 of the resonant system LCC_1R, the resultant resonant frequency as viewed from the crystal electrodes aa is decreased, but that when $f_1 < f_0$, the frequency at which parallel resonance occurs is more than f_0.

14-35. In the case of a long bar operating in an extensional mode, no trouble is ordinarily encountered from secondary resonances represented by thickness and shear modes coupled to the desired mode. Explain why this would be expected to be the case.

14-36. Demonstrate that when the resonant frequency of a coupled secondary resonant circuit in a crystal oscillator (such as f_1 in Fig. 14-18c) decreases with increasing temperature, the reactance which this secondary circuit couples into the primary circuit LCC_1R will change with decreased temperature in such a way as to tend to raise the equivalent resonant frequency as viewed from the external terminals aa, irrespective of whether the secondary circuit is resonant at a frequency that is less than or greater than the primary circuit.

14-37. The Miller circuit (Fig. 14-27) will not operate when a pentode tube is employed unless an external capacitance is shunted between plate and control grid. Explain why this is the case, and state whether or not such a capacitance would be required in the Pierce circuit of Fig. 14-28 if the triode tube is replaced by a pentode.

14-38. a. In a particular Pierce-type crystal oscillator, it is desired to decrease the ratio of grid exciting voltage to alternating plate-cathode voltage. How can this result be achieved?

b. How would the same result be achieved in the Miller circuit?

14-39. The resonant circuit LC in Fig. 14-29 is detuned so that it introduces a phase shift of 45° leading. Will this cause the frequency of oscillation of the system to increase or decrease? Justify the answer given.

14-40. Calculate the maximum change in the parallel resonant frequency that can be produced in the crystal of Table 14-1 by shunting the crystal electrodes with a variable capacitance having a maximum value of 40 $\mu\mu f$.

14-41. A crystal operated in a Miller or Pierce circuit under conditions where the crystal activity is not quite sufficient to enable oscillations to be generated will oscillate when the crystal electrodes are shunted by an inductance that has a reactance slightly greater than the capacitive reactance C_1 of the crystal equivalent circuit. Explain.

14-42. State whether the frequency of series resonance of a crystal will be lowered or raised when there is connected in series with the crystal (a) a capacitance C'', and (b) an inductance L'', as in Fig. 14-30c.

CHAPTER 15

AMPLITUDE MODULATION

15-1. Waves with Amplitude Modulation. In an amplitude-modulated wave, the amplitude of the radio-frequency oscillations is varied in accordance with the intelligence being transmitted, as discussed in Sec. 1-3. Examples of amplitude-modulated waves are illustrated in Figs. 1-2 and 15-1.

The extent of the amplitude variations in the envelope of a modulated wave is expressed as the *degree of modulation m,* which is defined in accordance with the relations

$$\text{Positive peak modulation} = m_+ = \frac{E_{\max} - E_0}{E_0} \qquad (15\text{-}1a)$$

$$\text{Negative peak modulation} = m_- = \frac{E_0 - E_{\min}}{E_0} \qquad (15\text{-}1b)$$

Here $E_{\max}$, $E_{\min}$, and E_0 are the maximum, minimum, and average amplitudes of the modulation envelope, as illustrated in Fig. 15-1. When the

modulation is symmetrical, as is the case with sinusoidal envelope variations, then $m_+ = m_- = m$.

A wave is said to be fully modulated when the envelope amplitude goes to zero during the negative peaks of the envelope variation; this corresponds to $m_- = 1.0$, or 100 per cent, for the negative peaks.

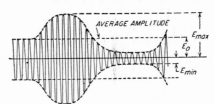

Fig. 15-1. Amplitude-modulated wave, showing notation for Eq. (15-1).

Analysis of Amplitude-modulated Waves. The nature of an amplitude-modulated wave was analyzed in Sec. 1-5. It was there shown that such a wave consists of a carrier wave plus sideband frequencies. The carrier corresponds to the oscillations that are present when the amplitude is not being varied; it accordingly represents the average amplitude of the modulation envelope (E_0 in Fig. 15-1), and is the same in amplitude and frequency irrespective of the presence or absence of modulation.[1] A

[1] This implies that the modulation impressed on the carrier wave is alternating with no unidirectional component. If this is not true, the average amplitude of the wave will change when modulation is applied, causing the carrier amplitude to change in the presence of modulation; such action is termed "carrier shift." In television, "carrier shift" is intentionally introduced for the purpose of indicating average brightness.

carrier wave transmits no information, since it is not affected by the modulation; the intelligence is carried by the sideband frequencies which can be thought of as being generated by the process of varying the amplitude of the radio-frequency wave.

Each frequency component contained in the equation of the modulation envelope produces a pair of sideband frequencies symmetrically disposed on each side of the carrier frequency and differing from the carrier frequency by the corresponding envelope frequency. Thus if the amplitude of a 1000 kc wave is varied at 1.2 kc, then sidebands having frequencies of 1001.2 and 998.8 kc are produced.

It is apparent that the width of the frequency spectrum occupied by an amplitude-modulated wave is twice the highest frequency contained in the modulation, and so will be greater the more rapidly the amplitude is varied. The bandwidth that must be transmitted to obtain satisfactory communication therefore depends on the type of intelligence involved; it is quite narrow for the transmission of telegraph signals, and very large for television. Modulation frequencies involved in representative cases are given in Table 15-1.

TABLE 15-1

MODULATION FREQUENCIES CORRESPONDING TO TYPICAL SIGNALS

Type of signal	Minimum frequency range that must be transmitted, cycles
Telegraph—Morse code at 500 letters (100 words) per minute	0–120*
Speech:	
Highest fidelity	40–15,000
Typical broadcast program	100–5000
Long-distance telephone quality	250–3500
Intelligible but poor quality	500–2000
Television—standard, 525-line picture, interlaced, 30-cycle repetition rate	60–4,500,000
Pulse—1 μsec long	0–1,000,000

* This assumes that in order to preserve the wave shapes of ,the dots and dashes it is necessary to transmit all frequencies up to three times the dot frequency.

The energy contained in a modulated wave is the sum of the energies of the separate frequency components, and is therefore increased during the modulation because of the energy added by the sidebands. Thus when the carrier wave is completely modulated by a sinusoidal variation of the envelope amplitude, i.e., when $m = 1.0$ in Eqs. (1-2) and (15-1), there are two sideband components, each having an amplitude one-half that of the carrier wave. Each of these hence contains one-fourth as much power as does the carrier, so that the two sidebands together make the power of the completely modulated wave 50 per cent greater than the carrier power. In this case, only one-third of the total energy is in the sidebands, while two-thirds is in the carrier. When the degree of modulation is less than 1.0, the sideband power will be proportionate to m^2. As a result, the fraction of the total energy that is contained in the intelligence bearing sidebands decreases rapidly as the degree of modulation is reduced. For this reason a high degree of modulation is generally sought.

Distortion in Amplitude-modulated Waves. An amplitude-modulated wave possesses distortion to the extent that the modulation envelope fails to reproduce exactly the modulating signal. This distortion can be classified as frequency, amplitude (nonlinear), or phase (time-delay) distortion. Frequency distortion arises when the degree of modulation produced by a modulating signal of given amplitude varies with the frequency of this signal; when it is present the sideband components of different frequencies do not have the correct relative amplitude. Time-delay distortion occurs when the phase relations between different frequency components of the modulation envelope differ from the relations that exist in the modulating signal. Amplitude distortion exists when the modulation envelope contains frequency components not present in the modulating signal. Thus if the modulating signal is a sine wave, then amplitude distortion will cause the envelope to contain harmonics of the modulating signal, which in turn denotes the presence of higher-order sideband components that differ from the carrier frequency by harmonics of the modulating frequency.

Distortion in an amplitude-modulated wave can arise either from imperfections in the modulating system that produce the wave, or from the action of circuits that transmit the wave. Thus when an amplitude-modulated wave is applied to a tuned circuit resonant at the carrier frequency, the upper and lower sideband frequencies are reduced in amplitude symmetrically by an amount that increases the higher the modulation frequency. At the same time, the sideband frequencies undergo symmetrical phase shifts which introduce a time delay, as discussed in connection with Eq. (12-14). Again, if the carrier frequency does not coincide with the resonant frequency of the tuned circuit, then the upper and lower sidebands undergo unequal transmission and suffer unsymmetrical phase shifts with respect to the carrier. This introduces quite severe amplitude distortion of the modulation envelope, as discussed in Sec. 16-7.

15-2. Plate-modulated Class C Amplifiers. The most widely used method of obtaining an amplitude-modulated wave in radio work consists in plate-modulating a Class C amplifier. Here a voltage corresponding to the signal is superimposed upon the d-c plate-supply voltage of an ordinary Class C amplifier. In this way the total effective plate-supply voltage of the amplifier is caused to vary in accordance with the desired modulation envelope.

Plate-modulated Class C Amplifiers Employing Triode Tubes. A typical circuit arrangement for a plate-modulated Class C amplifier employing a triode tube is shown in Fig. 15-2a.   Here the equivalent plate supply voltage is varied in accordance with the modulating signal by the output from a power amplifier that is usually, but not necessarily, of the Class B type.   The output of this amplifier is normally introduced by means of a transformer into the plate circuit of the Class C stage, which serves as the load impedance of the power amplifier.   A power amplifier used in

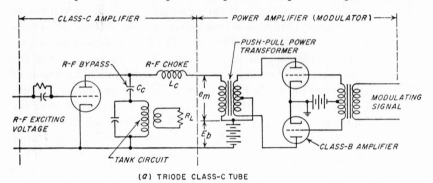

(a) TRIODE CLASS-C TUBE

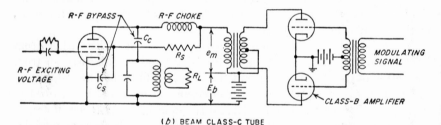

(b) BEAM CLASS-C TUBE

Fig. 15-2. Circuit diagrams of typical plate-modulated Class C amplifiers.   For the sake of simplicity the neutralizing arrangement for the triode case is omitted.

this way is often termed a *modulator*, and its output transformer is similarly called a *modulating transformer*.   The radio-frequency choke L_c must offer a high impedance to radio-frequency voltages, but a low impedance to modulating frequencies.   Conversely, the coupling capacitor must be large enough to be a radio-frequency by-pass and small enough to be a high impedance at modulating frequencies.

The action of the modulator is to cause the equivalent value of the plate-supply voltage that is applied to the plate of the Class C tube to vary in accordance with the signal, as shown in Fig. 15-3a for the case of a sinusoidal signal of such amplitude as to modulate the plate voltage completely.   It is then desired that the radio-frequency oscillations generated by the Class C amplifier output have an amplitude proportional to this equivalent supply voltage applied to the plate.   Such a result is achieved by employing a combination of radio-frequency exciting voltage, grid bias, and load impedance in the Class C amplifier such that at the peak of the modulation cycle, when the equivalent plate-supply voltage in Fig. 15-3a is $2E_b$, the amplifier is operating under moderately saturated Class C conditions, i.e., develops a peak radio-frequency output voltage between plate and cathode that is only slightly less than the effective plate voltage and has an angle of plate-current flow[1] that is less than 180°. When this is the case the Class C amplifier will necessarily be operating under saturated conditions throughout the modulation cycle; this ensures that the output amplitude will faithfully reproduce the modulating voltage, as illustrated in Fig. 15-4.

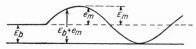

(a) EQUIVALENT PLATE-SUPPLY VOLTAGE

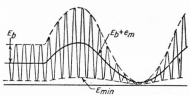

(b) TOTAL VOLTAGE ACTUALLY APPLIED TO PLATE

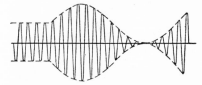

(c) RADIO-FREQUENCY PLATE-CATHODE VOLTAGE

The fact that a properly adjusted plate-modulated Class C amplifier operates with sufficient exciting voltage to produce saturation at the peak of the modulation cycle when the equivalent plate-supply voltage of the tube is $2E_b$ means that the excitation is very much greater than is necessary to produce saturation during the remainder of the modulation cycle. This tends to cause the grid current, and hence the associated power loss at the grid electrode, to become excessively large at the trough of modulation, where the saturation is extreme, as shown by the oscillograms given in Fig. 15-3. Such a result can in large measure be avoided, however, by arranging matters so that the source of radio-frequency oscillations that excites the control grid of the Class C amplifier has very poor regulation, i.e., possesses barely sufficient power to cause

(d) VOLTAGE ACTING ON CONTROL GRID—FIXED BIAS AND PERFECT REGULATION OF R-F VOLTAGE

(e) GRID CURRENT FOR FIXED BIAS AND PERFECT REGULATION OF R-F VOLTAGE

(f) VOLTAGE ACTUALLY APPLIED TO GRID WITH GRID-LEAK BIAS AND PERFECT REGULATION OF R-F VOLTAGE

FIG. 15-3. Oscillograms illustrating the operation of plate-modulated Class C amplifier with fixed bias and with grid-leak bias.

[1] To achieve an angle of flow less than 180° at the peak of the modulation cycle when the effective plate voltage is $2E_b$, the bias voltage must exceed $2E_b/\mu$.

saturation at the peak of the modulation cycle when the grid current (and hence driving power) is at a minimum.   Then when the grid current tends to increase during the parts of the modulation cycle when the Class C amplifier is oversaturated, the exciting voltage is unable to supply the additional power that is involved, and so decreases in amplitude just when less exciting voltage would be desirable.

The same end result can also be reached by obtaining the bias of the modulated Class C tube from a grid leak–condenser combination.   This

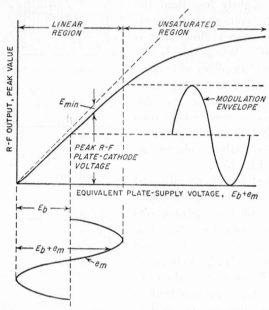

Fig. 15-4. Relationship between radio-frequency output voltage and modulating voltage in a typical plate-modulated Class C amplifier.

causes the bias to increase when the grid current is large, and thereby reduces the tendency of the grid current to become excessive at the troughs of the cycle.   Likewise the bias will also become less at the peak of the modulation cycle when the grid current tends to be small, thus increasing the extent to which the grid is driven positive just at the time when such action is helpful in carrying the peak of the modulation.   This action is illustrated in Fig. 15-3f.   However, in order to make use of a grid leak–capacitor combination in this way, it is necessary that the grid capacitor shunting the grid-leak resistance have a reactance that is at least twice the resistance of the grid leak at the highest modulating frequency to be employed.   Otherwise the bias will not be able to follow the amplitude fluctuations of the modulation cycle, and the benefit of grid-leak bias will be lost at the higher modulation frequencies.

A properly adjusted plate-modulated Class C amplifier produces an output wave having an envelope that follows the modulation very closely. If any amplitude distortion does exist, it is usually in the form of a flattening of the positive peaks of the modulation envelope caused by a lack of saturation at the positive peak of the modulation cycle.

Special Considerations in Plate-modulated Class C Amplifiers Employing Beam or Tetrode Tubes. The same considerations that are important in plate-modulated Class C amplifiers using triodes also apply in the case where the tube has a screen grid. In particular, the modulated wave that is produced will have an envelope that follows very faithfully the modulating voltage provided the tetrode or beam Class C amplifier is operated so that at the positive peak of the modulation cycle the minimum plate voltage is just barely enough to avoid the formation of a virtual cathode.

The only matter of special concern in the plate modulation of tubes having a screen grid is that the screen voltage must be modulated simultaneously with the plate voltage. This increases the total space current at the positive peak of the modulation cycle when the plate current must be large, and reduces the total space current at the trough of modulation when the plate current is small. By thus varying the total space current in accordance with the current requirements of the plate, the screen current, and hence the power loss at the screen, is kept at a minimum. If the screen voltage is not modulated, then the space current is constant throughout the modulation cycle, and when the plate current is less than its value at the peak of the modulation cycle, the screen current is correspondingly increased, resulting in high average screen current and dissipation.

Modulating voltages may be conveniently obtained by applying the output voltage of the plate modulation transformer to the screen through a series resistance R_s, as illustrated in Fig. 15-2b. In such an arrangement by-pass capacitor C_s must be small enough so that it does not form an effective by-pass for the highest modulation frequency involved; otherwise the screen voltage will not be modulated at the higher modulation frequencies. At the same time C_s must be large enough to be an effective by-pass to the carrier frequency. By-pass capacitor C_c must meet similar requirements.

Power Requirements of the Modulator. The modulator must provide sufficient power at the modulating frequency to vary the effective plate-supply voltage from zero to twice the d-c plate potential, assuming that complete modulation is desired. The modulator is usually, though not necessarily, a Class B amplifier such as described in Sec. 10-8.

When a plate-modulated Class C amplifier is properly adjusted, the impedance that the plate circuit of the Class C tube offers to the modulator is a resistance equal to the ratio E_b/I_b, where E_b is the d-c plate-supply voltage and I_b is the d-c plate current of the Class C tube in the absence of modulation. The degree of modulation is then determined by the alternating voltage developed by the modulator across this load impedance. For 100 per cent modulation, the crest alternating signal voltage E_m must equal the plate-supply voltage E_b, and the alternating signal-frequency current has a peak value that is equal to I_b. This makes the modulator power $E_bI_b/2$, or exactly one-half of the d-c power that the plate supply is called upon to deliver.[1] For lesser degrees of modulation, the modulator power will be proportional to the square of the degree of modulation. *The power relations that exist in a plate-modulated Class C amplifier can hence be summarized by stating that the power required to generate the carrier wave is supplied from the d-c plate-supply voltage, while the power required to generate the sideband components of the modulated wave must be supplied from the output of the modulator.*

The power that the modulator must deliver becomes large in the case of high-power Class C amplifiers. Thus if a 10-kw carrier is to be modulated 100 per cent and the plate efficiency is 75 per cent, the d-c plate power required is 13.33 kw and the modulator power output is half of this, or 6.67 kw. If the degree of modulation is less than 100 per cent, the demand made upon the modulator is correspondingly less, but so is the sideband energy generated.

Miscellaneous Aspects of Plate-modulated Class C Amplifier. The loaded Q_L of the plate tank circuit of a plate-modulated Class C amplifier, in addition to satisfying the requirements for proper Class C operation, as discussed on page 458, must likewise have a value low enough so that it will offer substantially the same impedance to the higher sideband frequencies as to the carrier frequency. In other words, the half-power bandwidth of the loaded tank circuit must be at least equal to, and preferably somewhat greater than, twice the highest modulation frequency of importance.

The plate efficiency of a plate-modulated Class C amplifier approximates that of a simple Class C amplifier. This efficiency is normally at least 60 per cent and in many cases will range as high as 70 to 80 per cent.

Plate-modulated Class C amplifiers normally employ the same triode, beam, and pentode tubes that are used for ordinary Class C amplifiers. However, the rated d-c plate voltage and carrier power of a tube used for plate modulation are less than the corresponding ratings of the same tube when used as an unmodulated Class C amplifier. This is because at the peak of a completely modulated wave the equivalent plate-supply voltage applied to the tube is twice the d-c value, and the power output

---

[1] In the case of beam and tetrode tubes, the modulator must likewise supply the power required to modulate the screen grid. In the circuit of Fig. 15-2b, where most of the screen modulating power is dissipated in the resistance R_s, the ratio of screen modulating power to plate modulating power is the ratio of screen to plate current. This is commonly of the order of 0.05 to 0.15.

at modulation peaks is four times the carrier power.   However, the tube operates at these peak values for only a small fraction of the time, and the average power output generated under fully modulated conditions is 1.5 times the carrier power.   The power rating for plate modulation therefore ordinarily corresponds to a carrier power that is roughly about two-thirds of the rated Class C amplifier output, and a plate voltage that is about 80 per cent of the maximum value allowable for unmodulated operation.

15-3. Grid-modulated Class C Amplifiers.   In the grid-modulated Class C amplifier, modulation is accomplished by superimposing on a fixed bias a modulating voltage corresponding to the signal that is to be modulated on the radio-frequency wave, as shown in Fig. 15-5a.   The relation existing between output and the effective bias in a typical Class C amplifier is illustrated in Fig. 15-6.   It is apparent that by properly choosing the bias E_c and superimposing upon it a modulation voltage having an appropriate peak amplitude E_m it is possible to obtain a completely modulated wave having a carrier amplitude corresponding to E_0, as shown.

Oscillograms showing the details of operation of a typical grid-modulating Class C amplifier are given in Fig. 15-5.   At the positive peaks of the modulation cycle, corresponding to x in Figs. 15-5 and 15-6, conditions are such that the tube

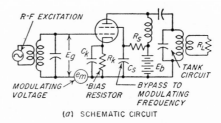

(a) SCHEMATIC CIRCUIT

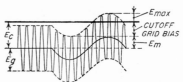

(b) VOLTAGE APPLIED TO CONTROL GRID

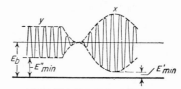

(c) PLATE-CATHODE VOLTAGE

Fig. 15-5. Circuit of tetrode grid-modulated Class C amplifier, together with oscillograms showing details of operation

operates as a very slightly saturated Class C amplifier with rated output, low minimum plate voltage E'_{min}, and good plate efficiency.   The equivalent grid bias is then $E_c - E_m$.   During unmodulated intervals, corresponding to y in Figs. 15-5 and 15-6, the plate-current pulses are then reduced to approximately half amplitude because of the greater negative bias, with resulting reduction in the amplitude of the output voltage to half the peak value, as shown.   Under these conditions the minimum plate potential E''_{min} will be slightly greater than $E_b/2$ as shown.

The carrier power obtainable from a grid-modulated Class C amplifier is approximately one-quarter of the rated power that the same tube can deliver as an ordinary Class C amplifier.   This follows from the fact that the peak power of the modulated output wave corresponds to the Class C rating, and is four times the carrier power of the wave.

The plate efficiency during unmodulated intervals is much lower than at the crest of the cycle, since the minimum plate voltage E''_{min} under these conditions is quite large, as discussed above. If the modulation is reasonably linear, it is a simple matter to show that the plate efficiency

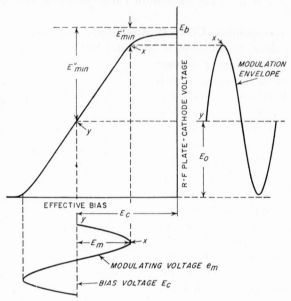

FIG. 15-6. Relationship between output voltage and modulating voltage in a typical grid-modulated amplifier.

when generating an unmodulated carrier is very closely half that obtainable in Class C operation.[1,2]

The power dissipated at the plate of a grid-modulated Class C amplifier is always greater during unmodulated conditions than when the system is fully modulated. This is because the d-c component of the plate current, and hence the input power to the plate circuit, are the same irrespec-

[1] This arises from the fact that if the plate current pulses are reduced in amplitude so that their fundamental-frequency component is halved, then the d-c component of these pulses, and hence the d-c input power to the plate of the grid-modulated amplifier, will also be almost precisely half as big as at the crest of the modulation cycle. The output power is, however, only one-quarter as great at carrier level, so the efficiency is halved.

[2] Special circuit arrangements have been devised in which, by dividing the modulator system into two parts, it is possible to obtain grid modulation with an average efficiency that is only slightly less than with plate modulation. For details, see F. E. Terman and John R. Woodyard, A High-efficiency Grid-modulated Amplifier, *Proc. IRE*, vol. 26, p. 929, August, 1938.

tive of the presence or absence of modulation,[1] whereas the part of this power converted into useful output during modulation is increased by the sideband power.

In designing and analyzing a grid-modulated Class C amplifier, the first step is to determine the radio-frequency exciting voltage, the load impedance, and the equivalent grid bias, that will give satisfactory Class C conditions corresponding to the peak of the modulation cycle. The bias arrived at in this way corresponds to $-E_c + E_m$, where $-E_c$ is the bias that will be used in the grid-modulated amplifier, and E_m is the peak amplitude of the modulating signal, as illustrated in Figs. 15-5 and 15-6. The amplitude of E_m required for complete modulation is[2]

$$E_m = \frac{1}{2}\left(\frac{E_b}{\mu} + E_{max}\right) \tag{15-2}$$

where E_b is the plate-supply voltage, E_{max} is the amount the grid is driven positive at the positive peak of the modulation cycle (see Fig. 15-5b), and μ is the amplification factor in the case of triodes, or is taken to mean μ_s in the case of tubes possessing a screen grid.

The grid-modulated Class C amplifier is normally operated so that at the positive peak of the modulation cycle the control grid is driven somewhat positive, as shown in Fig. 15-5b. This presents something of a problem both to the modulating voltage and with respect to the source of radio-frequency exciting voltage, since it places a load on both of these voltages at the positive peaks of the modulation cycle that is not present during the remainder of the cycle. At the same time, if flattening of the positive peaks of the modulation envelope is to be avoided, it is necessary that neither of these voltages applied to the control grid drop off in amplitude as a result of the grid current that flows at the modulation peaks. Both exciting and modulating voltages must therefore be derived from sources having good regulation, i.e., relatively large power capacity;[3] at

---

[1] The fact that the d-c current is constant makes it convenient to obtain the bias by means of a cathode resistor, as shown in Fig. 11-5a. The bias by-pass capacitor C_k must then be large enough to be an effective by-pass to currents of the modulating frequency as well as to the radio frequency.

[2] This relation follows from the fact that at the positive peak of the modulation cycle the control-grid voltage is $E_b/\mu + E_{max}$ greater than the grid voltage for which the output current is just zero. However, since the peak-to-peak variation in bias produced by E_m is $2E_m$, then at the negative peaks of a fully modulated wave one must have

$$2E_m = (E_b/\mu) + E_{max}$$

Equation (15-2) follows at once from this.

[3] It is also necessary that the fixed grid-bias voltage have good regulation since there is a power drain on the bias voltage source at the positive peaks of the modulation cycle, but not during the remainder of the cycle. A convenient way of handling this situation is to obtain the bias by means of a cathode resistor by-passed at modula-

the same time the Class C amplifier should require as little exciting power as is practical. As a result beam and tetrode tubes are often favored for grid-modulated amplifiers.

As compared with plate modulation, the grid-modulated Class C amplifier has the advantage of requiring relatively little modulating power, but the disadvantage of much lower plate efficiency. In addition, the grid-modulated amplifier tends to be less linear in its modulation characteristic (i.e., has higher amplitude distortion) and is somewhat more critical in adjustment than is the plate-modulated Class C amplifier. For most applications, the balance is slightly in favor of plate modulation. However, in wideband applications, notably in television transmitters, the difficulties of generating the large amount of video modulating power needed for plate modulation are such as to make grid modulation standard practice.

15-4. Miscellaneous Systems of Modulation. Although the amplitude-modulated waves used in radio systems are most commonly produced by either plate or grid modulation of a Class C amplifier, many other systems of modulation have been devised. Several of the more important of these are described below.

Suppressor-grid-modulated Class C Amplifier. In a pentode Class C amplifier, amplitude modulation can be obtained by applying to the suppressor grid a modulating voltage superimposed upon a suitable negative bias, as illustrated in Fig. 15-7a. As the suppressor grid in such an arrangement becomes more negative, the minimum plate potential at which current can be drawn to the plate is increased as explained in connection with Fig. 6-18. The result is a relationship between radio-frequency output voltage and suppressor-grid potential of the type shown in Fig. 15-7b. This is similar to the relation illustrated in Fig. 15-6 between radio-frequency output and control-grid voltage, and results in suppressor-grid modulation being similar in many respects to control-grid modulation. Thus the power output at the peaks of the modulation cycle corresponds approximately in both cases to the output obtained under ordinary Class C amplifier operation. Likewise the plate efficiency is about the same for control-grid and suppressor-grid modulation, and the modulating power required in suppressor modulation is relatively small just as in control-grid modulation.

There is a tendency in suppressor-grid modulators for the average screen current to be excessively high as a result of the fact that a virtual cathode exists in the tube throughout the modulation cycle except at the modulation peaks. This can be largely overcome, however, by obtaining

---

tion frequencies, as illustrated in Fig. 15-5a. This takes advantage of the fact that the average value of the total space current is substantially independent of the degree of modulation, and is not significantly changed by diversion of space current to the control grid at the peaks of the fully modulated wave.

the screen voltage from the plate supply through a series resistance R_s as shown in Fig. 15-7a; in this way the screen voltage drops as the screen current increases, thereby limiting the screen losses by simultaneously lowering the screen voltage and the screen current.   The capacitor C_s in Fig. 15-7a should be large enough to give effective by-passing of the carrier frequency, but should be small enough to have little or no by-passing effect at the highest modulation frequencies of interest.

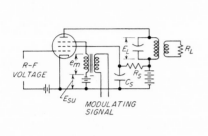

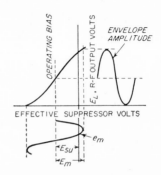

(a) CIRCUIT OF SUPPRESSOR-GRID
    MODULATED CLASS-C AMPLIFIER

(b) RELATION BETWEEN SUPPRESSOR-
    GRID VOLTAGE AND AMPLIFIER OUTPUT

Fig. 15-7. Circuit of suppressor-grid-modulated amplifier, together with curve showing typical relationship between output voltage and suppressor-grid voltage.

Screen-grid-modulated Class C Amplifiers.   Class C amplifiers employing tubes having screen grids can be modulated by varying the screen-grid voltage in accordance with the desired modulation envelope, as illustrated in Fig. 15-8.   Such a screen-grid-modulated amplifier should be so adjusted that at the peak of the modulation cycle the operating conditions correspond to those for ordinary Class C operation under rated conditions.   The d-c screen-grid voltage E_{sg} used in the modulated amplifier should then be half the screen voltage required for rated Class C output.   Complete modulation is obtained when the peak modulating voltage E_m equals E_{sg}; the effective screen voltage then varies from zero to $2E_{sg}$.

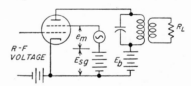

Fig. 15-8. Schematic circuit of a screen-grid-modulated Class C amplifier.

Screen-grid modulation is an alternative to control-grid and suppressor-grid modulation.   The plate efficiencies of the three methods of modulation are essentially the same, and the carrier powers that can be generated by a given tube are likewise approximately identical.   Screen-grid modulation has the disadvantage, however, of ordinarily requiring slightly more modulating power than either control- or suppressor-grid modulation.   However, it has the advantage of presenting to the modulating voltage a load that is substantially independent of the amplitude of this voltage; this avoids the problem of waveform distortion at the positive peaks of modulation that is encountered in control-grid and suppressor-grid modulation.   The linearity of modulation in a screen-grid-modulated system is about the same as in the corresponding suppressor-grid- or control-grid-modulated systems.

Modulated Class A Amplifier.   This type of modulator takes advantage of the fact that the transconductance, and hence amplification, of an ordinary Class A amplifier depend upon the grid bias.   Thus by super-imposing a modulating voltage upon a fixed bias voltage, so that the effective grid bias varies in accordance with the modulation, the amplification

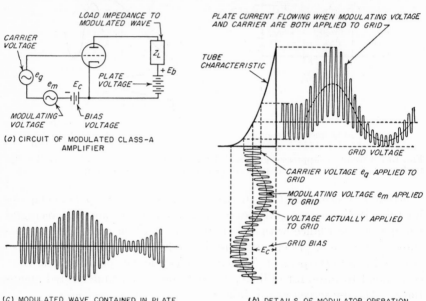

(a) CIRCUIT OF MODULATED CLASS-A AMPLIFIER

(c) MODULATED WAVE CONTAINED IN PLATE CURRENT

(b) DETAILS OF MODULATOR OPERATION

Fig. 15-9. Circuit of modulated Class A amplifier, together with oscillograms showing details of operation.

to a small superimposed carrier voltage will vary in accordance with the modulating voltage.   The schematic circuit, and the waveforms involved, are illustrated in Fig. 15-9.   The degree of modulation obtained depends upon the amplitude of the modulating voltage that is applied to the control grid and also upon the curvature of the tube characteristics, i.e., upon the variation of the amplification with grid bias.

An analysis of the grid-modulated Class A modulator can be readily made by means of the power-series analyses of the vacuum-tube amplifier discussed in Sec. 10-3, and the resulting equivalent circuit illustrated in Fig. 10-9.   The sidebands of the modulated output are the sum- and difference-frequency terms produced by the second-order action when the input consists of two sine waves (see Table 10-2), while the carrier is the carrier-frequency output produced by first-order action. The power-series analysis further shows that the grid-modulated Class A modulator will give distortionless modulation provided the tube characteristic over the operating range employed can be expressed by the first two terms in Eq. (10-5), i.e., provided the third- and higher-order terms in Eq. (10-8) are negligible.[1]

The importance of the modulated Class A amplifier arises from the fact that it is extensively used in carrier-suppression systems such as discussed in Sec. 15-5. This method of modulation finds very little use, otherwise, since it is not well adapted to generating a wave having a high degree of modulation. Also, this type of modulation is suitable for generating only very small amounts of modulated power because its plate efficiency is very low.

Plate-modulated Oscillator. In a modulated oscillator, the modulating voltage is used to vary the amplitude of the generated oscillations. This is in contrast with modulated amplifiers, where the modulation is accomplished by varying the amplification of a constant radio-frequency exciting voltage.

The most common type of modulated oscillator is that in which plate modulation is used in the same manner as in the plate-modulated Class C amplifier. Here if the oscillator obtains its bias from a grid leak–capacitor arrangement and is then adjusted to operate at high efficiency, the amplitude of oscillation will always assume a value such that the crest value of the alternating plate-cathode voltage is only slightly less than the plate-supply voltage, as discussed on page 490. Accordingly, if the effective plate-supply voltage is varied by a modulating signal, the amplitude of the generated oscillations will faithfully follow the modulation.

A typical circuit of a plate-modulated oscillator is shown in Fig. 15-10. This is analogous in every respect to the circuit of Fig. 15-2a for the corresponding plate-modulated Class C amplifier. The power relations and the efficiency obtained with this type of modulation are also similar to those for the corresponding plate-modulated Class C amplifier.

The distortion in a properly adjusted plate-modulated oscillator is as low as, or lower than, that of any other modulating system. The only

---

[1] This can be shown by assuming that the load impedance in Fig. 10-9 is Z_L for frequencies in the vicinity of the carrier frequency, and is negligible for other frequencies (including particularly the modulation frequency), and by considering that the applied signal consists of the sum of two sine waves that are of carrier and modulating frequencies, respectively. By applying Eq. (10-8) to this situation with the aid of Table 10-2, it is found that the only components of the plate current having a frequency near the carrier frequency are the sum- and difference-frequency terms (i.e., the desired sidebands), and the carrier. Thus no spurious sidebands are present. In addition, the analysis shows that the amplitude of the sideband components, and hence the degree of modulation, are proportional to the amplitude of the modulating voltage.

special precaution required to obtain substantially distortion-free modulation, other than arranging for the tube to operate at high plate efficiency and to have an effective tank circuit Q that is not too high, is to employ a small enough grid capacitor so that the grid bias is capable of following the modulation at the higher modulation frequencies. This requires that the grid-capacitor reactance at the highest modulation frequency be at least twice the grid-leak resistance if 100 per cent modulation is to be employed.

The modulated oscillator has the great disadvantage that the frequency generated by an oscillator ordinarily depends somewhat upon the plate-supply voltage.[1]   The carrier frequency generated by a plate-modulated

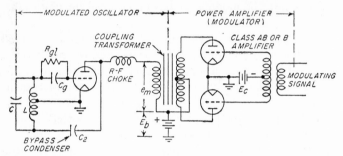

Fig. 15-10. Circuit diagram of plate-modulated oscillator analogous to plate-modulated Class C amplifier of Fig. 15-2a.

oscillator therefore tends to vary with the modulation envelope, introducing incidental frequency modulation (see Chap. 17).   As a result, modulated oscillators find only occasional use.

Modulation by Means of Nonlinear Circuit Elements.   Amplitude modulation results whenever a carrier and a modulating voltage are simultaneously applied to a nonlinear circuit element.   A simple modulator based on this principle is illustrated in Fig. 15-11a in which the nonlinear element is a rectifier, typically a crystal or a copper-oxide rectifier.   By choosing the modulating, carrier, and bias voltages E_m, E_{rf}, and E_c, respectively, so that $E_m = E_c = E_{rf}/2$, the current passing through the rectifier will be in the form of pulses having an amplitude that varies with the modulating voltage E_m as shown in Fig. 15-11b.   These pulses excite the resonant circuit LC that is tuned to the carrier frequency, and develop across it and across R_L a voltage that is modulated in the desired manner.

In nonlinear modulators of the type illustrated in Fig. 15-11, the modulating and carrier voltages are required to supply all of the power represented by the modulated output wave.   This is in contrast with

[1] An exception is the crystal oscillator; here the plate-supply voltage has very little effect on frequency.   However, the crystal oscillator cannot be modulated satisfactorily, as the crystal Q is so high as to prevent the amplitude from changing rapidly enough to follow the modulation; i.e., the sidebands are severely discriminated against because of the high Q of the crystal.

modulated amplifiers and oscillators, where either all or at least a considerable part of the power of the modulated wave that is produced is derived from the d-c plate power through the amplifying action of the tube. As a result, such nonlinear modulators are normally used only at low power levels, such as milliwatts or at most a few watts.

Although Fig. 15-11a shows one possible form of nonlinear modulator, many variations of this principle are possible. Thus the bias E_c in Fig. 15-11a may be omitted. In other cases a small carrier voltage is superimposed on a much larger modulating voltage, and the system is biased so that operation is centered on a voltage-current characteristic that is curved, but with some conduction always possible; the modulated Class A amplifier of Fig. 15-9 makes use of nonlinear action of this type.

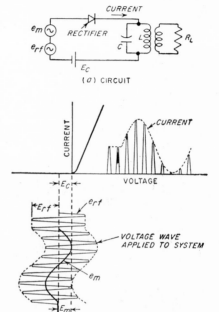

15-5. Carrier Suppression, Single-sideband, and Vestigial-sideband Systems. The frequency, amplitude, and phase of the carrier component of an amplitude-modulated wave are unaffected by the presence or absence of modulation. The carrier accordingly contains none of the intelligences represented by the modulation, and therefore need not be transmitted. Moreover each sideband considered separately contains all of the information present in the modulated wave.

Fig. 15-11. Circuit of elementary form of nonlinear modulator, together with oscillograms showing details of operation.

It is therefore possible to convey all the information represented by a modulating signal by transmitting only a single sideband, while suppressing both the carrier and the other sideband. Such a *single-sideband system* requires a frequency band only half as wide as that occupied by a modulated wave consisting of two sidebands and the carrier. Furthermore, the single-sideband system saves over two-thirds of the power because of the suppression of the carrier. For these reasons, single-sideband transmission is used extensively in carrier communication over wire lines, and also finds some application in radio-telephone communication.

The effect on the wave shapes of suppressing the carrier of a sinusoidally modulated wave is illustrated in Fig. 15-12c. The resulting envelope varies at twice the modulation frequency, and possesses an apparent phase that reverses each time the modulating signal goes through zero.

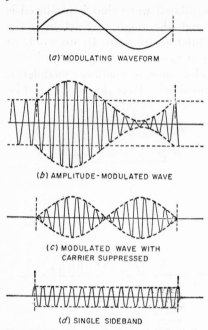

(a) MODULATING WAVEFORM

(b) AMPLITUDE-MODULATED WAVE

(c) MODULATED WAVE WITH CARRIER SUPPRESSED

(d) SINGLE SIDEBAND

Fig. 15-12. Waves that result when the carrier is removed from an amplitude-modulated wave, and also when only one sideband is present.

When one of these sidebands as well as the carrier is suppressed, the resulting single sideband is represented by the oscillation shown in Fig. 15-12d. This particular case corresponds to the upper sideband, since there is one more cycle of oscillation in the period corresponding to one cycle of modulation than is possessed by the amplitude-modulated wave of Fig. 15-12b.

Carrier Suppression by Means of Balanced Modulators. The usual method of suppressing the carrier component of an amplitude-modulated wave is to employ a balanced modulator, two forms of which are illustrated in Fig. 15-13. The particular arrangement of Fig. 15-13a consists of two identical modulated Class A amplifiers[1] arranged as shown. Carrier voltage is applied to the grids of the two tubes in the same phase, while the modulating signal is applied in opposite phase to the two tubes by means of the center-tapped transformer. The outputs of the two tubes are combined through

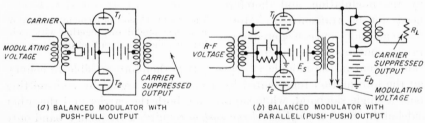

(a) BALANCED MODULATOR WITH PUSH-PULL OUTPUT

(b) BALANCED MODULATOR WITH PARALLEL (PUSH-PUSH) OUTPUT

Fig. 15-13. Balanced-modulator arrangements for generating double-sideband wave with carrier suppressed.

a transformer with a center-tapped primary. When such a system is symmetrical, it is apparent that carrier voltage does not appear in the

[1] If desired the two modulated Class A amplifiers could be replaced by plate- or grid-modulated Class C amplifiers. Nonlinear modulators of the rectifier type may also be used, with a variety of circuit arrangements possible; for further information see R. S. Caruthers, Copper Oxide Modulators in Carrier Telephone Systems, *Trans. AIEE*, vol. 58, p. 253, June, 1939.

output because the carrier is applied in the same phase to the two tubes and hence cancels out in the primary of the output transformer.   On the other hand, the sideband components generated in the two tubes are of opposite phase because the modulating signal voltage is applied in opposite phase to the two tubes.   The sidebands thus do appear in the output.[1]

In Fig. 15-13b both the modulating and radio-frequency voltages are applied in push-pull to the two modulated amplifiers, which in this case are shown as screen-grid-modulated Class C amplifiers.   The carrier suppressed output then appears in the plate lead that is common to the two tubes.

Single-sideband Generation.   A single sideband can be obtained by passing the output of a carrier-suppression system through filter circuits that are sufficiently selective to transmit one sideband while suppressing the other.   The requirements that the filter must meet are rather severe; thus if the lowest modulating frequency is 100 cycles, the filter characteristic must change from full transmission to very effective rejection in a frequency range of $2 \times 100 = 200$ cycles.   Even with well-designed filters such sharpness of discrimination is possible only if the carrier frequency involved is low enough so that 200 cycles is not too small a percentage of the carrier frequency.   As a result, the filter method is suitable only for obtaining single sidebands corresponding to low or moderate carrier frequencies.   If the sideband must be located in a high-frequency part of the spectrum, then it must be produced at a low carrier frequency and subsequently translated in frequency by heterodyne action, as discussed in connection with Fig. 24-18a.

A second means that is used to obtain a single sideband eliminates the unwanted sideband by phase cancellation.   A system of this type is illustrated schematically in Fig. 15-14.   It consists of two balanced modulators arranged with radio-frequency inputs that differ in phase by 90°, and with modulating inputs that are likewise identical except that each frequency component of the modulating voltage applied to the second balanced modulator differs in phase by 90° from the phase of the corresponding component of the modulating voltage applied to the first balanced modulator.   It can then be shown that when the outputs of

[1] This can be shown as follows.   The equation of the modulated wave produced by T_1 in Fig. 15-13a can be written

$$e_1 = E_0(1 + m \sin \omega_m t) \sin \omega_c t = E_0 \sin \omega_c t + mE_0 \sin \omega_m t \sin \omega_c t \qquad (15\text{-}3a)$$

The wave produced by T_2 is the same except that the phase of the modulating voltage is reversed; hence

$$e_2 = E_0(1 - m \sin \omega_m t) \sin \omega_c t = E_0 \sin \omega_c t - mE_0 \sin \omega_m t \sin \omega_c t \qquad (15\text{-}3b)$$

Subtracting voltages e_1 and e_2, as is accomplished by the push-pull output connection, results in cancellation of the carrier and simultaneous addition of the terms in $\sin \omega_m t \times \sin \omega_c t$ which represent the sidebands.

these two balanced modulators are added one of the sidebands is canceled out; this, together with the fact that the carrier is suppressed by the balanced modulators, results in an output that contains only a single sideband.[1]

A method of applying these principles is illustrated in Fig. 15-15.[2] Here each tube pair 1-2 and 3-4 represents a balanced-modulator system

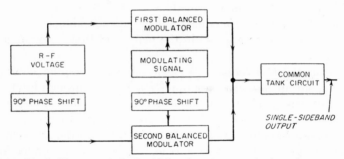

FIG. 15-14. Block diagram of single-sideband system employing phase cancellation.

using screen-grid-modulated Class C amplifiers.[3]   They are excited by radio-frequency voltages obtained from a pair of critically coupled resonant circuits tuned to the same frequency.   Critical coupling is required

---

[1] This can be shown as follows: The equation of a wave with the carrier removed is simply Eq. (15-3a) with the term $E \sin \omega_c t$ omitted.   This gives

$$e_1 = mE \sin \omega_m t \sin \omega_c t \tag{15-4a}$$

where $\omega_m/2\pi$ and $\omega_c/2\pi$ are the modulating and carrier frequencies, respectively, while mE is an amplitude factor.   When both modulating and carrier frequencies are shifted 90° in phase, Eq. (15-4a) can be rewritten as

$$e_2 = mE \sin (\omega_m t + 90°) \sin (\omega_c t + 90°) = mE \cos \omega_m t \cos \omega_c t \tag{15-4b}$$

Adding Eqs. (15-4a) and (15-4b) then gives

$$
\begin{aligned}
e_1 + e_2 &= mE \sin \omega_m t \sin \omega_c t + mE \cos \omega_m t \cos \omega_c t \\
&= \frac{mE}{2} [\cos (\omega_c - \omega_m)t - \cos (\omega_c + \omega_m)t] \\
&\qquad\qquad + \frac{mE}{2} [\cos (\omega_c - \omega_m)t + \cos (\omega_c + \omega_m)t] \\
&= mE \cos (\omega_c - \omega_m)t \tag{15-5}
\end{aligned}
$$

Equation (15-5) corresponds to the equation of the lower or difference-frequency sideband.   If the polarity of one of the modulating or one of the radio-frequency voltages is reversed, the other sideband would appear at the output terminals.

[2] The practical development of this system is due to O. G. Villard, Jr., "A High Level Single Sideband Transmitter," Proc. IRE, vol. 36, p. 1419, November, 1948.

[3] Beam, tetrode, or pentode tubes must be used, since for proper addition of the output currents of the two balanced modulators, it is necessary that the plate current of an individual tube be determined only by the screen- and control-grid voltages of that tube without being affected by the instantaneous voltage existing across the load impedance.

in order that the voltages applied to the two balanced modulators will be the same, while the resonant circuits must be tuned to the same frequency in order to obtain a phase shift between primary and secondary voltages

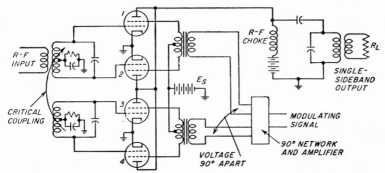

Fig. 15-15. Schematic circuit diagram of modulating system for generating a single sideband by means of phase cancellation in accordance with Fig. 15-14.

that is exactly 90°. Modulating voltages for the two balanced modulator systems are obtained by means of a special network that develops two voltages that have equal magnitude but are 90° apart in phase.[1]

Practical plate efficiencies obtained in an arrangement of this type are about 50 per cent for conditions corresponding to full output, while the modulating power required approximates the d-c screen power of a single tube when operated as an ordinary Class C amplifier.

Vestigial-sideband Systems. Under some circumstances it is desirable to obtain a wave consisting of a carrier plus one sideband, with the other sideband suppressed. Such a result can be approximated by transmitting an ordinary amplitude-modulated wave through a filter that is so designed that the edge of the transmission band of the filter accurately coincides with the carrier frequency as shown in Fig. 15-16b. The resulting wave then has the frequency spectrum illustrated in Fig. 15-16c, which is characterized by a residual second sideband. This is termed a *vestigial-* or *asymmetric*-sideband system, and has the advantage of requiring less

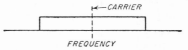

(*a*) MODULATED WAVE WITH DOUBLE SIDEBANDS

(*b*) TRANSMISSION CHARACTERISTIC OF FILTER

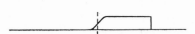

(*c*) FREQUENCY SPECTRUM OBTAINED BY PASSING WAVE (*a*) THROUGH FILTER (*b*)

Fig. 15-16. Schematic diagram illustrating generation of vestigial-sideband signal.

[1] Simple networks of this type are described by R. B. Dome, Wideband Phase-shift Networks, *Electronics*, vol. 19, p. 112, December, 1946; the design of more precise networks is discussed by H. J. Orchard, Synthesis of Wide-band Two-phase Networks, *Wireless Eng.*, vol. 27, p. 72, March, 1950; *ibid.*, vol. 28, p. 30, January, 1951.

total bandwidth than does the amplitude-modulated wave with its two full sidebands. It is the standard type of signal used in television transmitters.

PROBLEMS AND EXERCISES

15-1. The equation of an amplitude-modulated wave is

$$e = 25(1 + 0.7 \cos 5000t - 0.3 \cos 10,000t) \sin 5 \times 10^6 t$$

a. What frequency components are contained in the modulated wave, and what is the amplitude of each?

b. Sketch the modulation envelope, and evaluate the degree of modulation for the peaks and troughs.

15-2. Determine the number of amplitude-modulated broadcast stations that could theoretically be operated in the frequency band occupied by one sideband of a television station.

15-3. Derive an expression for the effective value of a sinusoidally modulated wave in terms of the carrier amplitude and the degree of modulation.

15-4. A 1000-kc carrier wave modulated 40 per cent at 4000 cycles is applied to a resonant circuit tuned to the carrier frequency and having $Q = 140$. What will be the degree of modulation of the wave after transmission through this circuit?

15-5. In the plate-modulated amplifier of Fig. 15-2a, enumerate the circuit elements in the modulator and in the modulated amplifier that are likely to cause the degree of modulation that is obtained at low frequencies and at high frequencies to differ from the degree of modulation in the mid-frequency range, when the modulating signal indicated in Fig. 15-2a has the same amplitude irrespective of frequency.

15-6. Draw oscillograms similar to those of Fig. 15-3a, b, and c, except applying to the case where the exciting voltage is not sufficient to cause saturation at the positive peak of the modulating cycle.

15-7. Redraw the oscillograms of Fig. 12-3a to e so as to apply to the case in which the exciting voltage has extremely poor regulation.

15-8. In a properly adjusted plate-modulated Class C amplifier it is found that the d-c component of the plate current of the modulated amplifier is substantially unaffected by the application of modulation.

a. Explain the reasons for this behavior.

b. If the bias of the Class C tube is obtained by means of a resistance between cathode and ground, explain why the by-pass capacitor associated with this bias resistor must be an effective by-pass not only to radio-frequency currents, but to modulation-frequency currents as well.

15-9. *a.* The Class C amplifier in the example on page 464 is to be employed as a Class C plate-modulated amplifier with a d-c plate potential of 1000 volts. Explain why the modulation will be distorted unless the grid excitation is greater than the value employed in the example.

b. Estimate the approximate audio-frequency modulating power required for complete modulation assuming that the d-c plate current has the same value as in the example on page 464.

15-10. Assume that the oscillograms of Fig. 15-3a and b apply to a plate-modulated Class C amplifier employing a beam tube.

a. Add a series of three more oscillograms showing, respectively, (1) voltage acting on the screen grid when the circuit of Fig. 15-2b is used, (2) pulses of total space current, and (3) pulses of screen current.

b. Repeat (a) for the case where the screen voltage is a fixed d-c voltage that is unmodulated.

15-11. A type 4-65A tetrode tube is employed in the circuit of Fig. 12-2b under operating conditions that in the absence of modulation correspond to the example on page 471. Specify (a) power required to modulate the plate voltage, (b) power required to modulate the screen voltage, (c) load impedance offered by the system to the secondary of the modulation transformer, and (d) approximate plate power dissipation with 100 per cent modulation by a sinusoidal modulating voltage.

15-12. Draw oscillograms similar to those of Fig. 15-5b and c, but applying to conditions that would be represented in Fig. 15-5 by a modulating voltage about 50 per cent greater than the value shown. Assume no change in load impedance.

15-13. Explain why it is not sufficient that the by-pass capacitor C_k in Fig. 15-5 merely be large enough to provide an adequate by-pass to radio-frequency currents, but rather must be large enough also to be an effective by-pass for modulation-frequency currents.

15-14. A type 4-65A tetrode tube is to be used as a grid-modulated Class C amplifier with conditions at the peak of the modulation cycle corresponding to those worked out in the example on page 471. What values of grid-bias and peak modulating voltage are required, what carrier power will be obtained, and what will be the plate loss during unmodulated conditions?

15-15. Repeat Prob. 15-14 for the type 812-A tube in the example on page 464.

15-16. In a particular grid-modulated Class C amplifier the plate efficiency during unmodulated conditions is 36 per cent. What will be the plate efficiency when the amplifier is fully modulated?

15-17. Assuming plate efficiencies of 75, 60, and 40 per cent for typical Class C, B, and A operation, respectively, estimate the sum of the d-c input power required by modulator and modulated tubes when the carrier power is 1000 watts and the modulation is 0 and 100 per cent for (a) plate-modulated Class C amplifier, Class A modulator; (b) plate-modulated Class C amplifier, Class B modulator; and (c) grid-modulated amplifier. In (c) assume that the modulator power is negligible.

15-18. In a grid-modulated Class C amplifier employing a tube having a screen grid, it is permissible to obtain the screen potential from a source of fixed voltage, as in Fig. 15-5a, whereas in the plate-modulated Class C amplifier this is not the case. Explain the reasons for the difference.

15-19. a. Draw oscillograms analogous to those of Fig. 15-3 but for the suppressor-grid-modulated amplifier of Fig. 15-7, showing the voltages acting on the control grid, suppressor grid, screen grid, and plate, and also the total space current, screen current, and the plate current.

b. Repeat (a) when the screen potential in Fig. 15-7 is obtained directly from a voltage source such that the screen voltage is constant irrespective of screen current. Discuss the differences between the resulting oscillograms and those obtained in (a).

15-20. Assume that the screen-grid-modulated amplifier of Fig. 15-8 is so proportioned that it gives satisfactory performance with 100 per cent modulation when $E_m = E_{sg}$. Sketch the shape of the envelope of the output wave that would result if E_m were moderately greater than E_{sg}, and explain the reasons for the envelope distortions that are present.

15-21. Demonstrate that if in the modulated Class A amplifier it is necessary to include third-order effects in Eq. (10-8) to express the tube behavior, then the modulation envelope will contain a second harmonic of the modulating frequency.

15-22. Sketch oscillograms applying to the plate-modulated oscillator of Fig. 15-10, showing the actual voltage acting between the plate and cathode (in analogy with Fig. 15-3b), and also the actual voltage acting between the grid and cathode.

15-23. Would it be practical to obtain an amplitude-modulated wave by grid-modulating the oscillator of Fig. 15-10 instead of plate-modulating it? Give reasons for the conclusion presented.

15-24. Explain with the aid of oscillograms analogous to those of Fig. 15-11b that an amplitude-modulated wave will be produced even when the bias voltage in Fig. 15-11a is omitted.

15-25. The oscillogram in Fig. 15-12d corresponds to the upper sideband. How would the corresponding oscillogram for the lower sideband differ?

15-26. By means of an analysis analogous to that involving Eqs. (15-3), verify the fact that the output in Fig. 15-13b is a carrier-suppressed wave.

15-27. What kind of output would be obtained in Fig. 15-13a if the modulating voltage and the carrier voltages were interchanged, so that the latter was applied in push-pull and the former in parallel to the two grids?

15-28. Repeat the analysis beginning with Eq. (15-4) but applying to the case where the polarity of the modulating voltage applied to balanced modulator 3-4 is reversed. Interpret the resulting output in relation to the output represented by Eq. (15-5).

15-29. In the generation of a single sideband by phase cancellation, as in Figs. 15-14 and 15-15, determine the amplitude of the undesired sideband expressed in decibels relative to the amplitude of the desired sideband when imperfections in the phase-shifting system for the modulating signal are such that (a) the modulating voltages applied to the two balanced modulators differ in phase by 90°, but one voltage is 5 per cent less in amplitude than the other; and (b) the modulating voltages applied to the two balanced modulators have the same amplitudes, but their phase difference is 85° instead of the desired 90°. Assume that the system is balanced so that when the modulating voltages applied to the two balanced modulators have the same amplitude and differ in phase by 90°, complete cancellation of the undesired sideband will occur.

CHAPTER 16

DETECTORS AND MIXERS

16-1. Detection of Amplitude-modulated Waves. Detection, also sometimes called *demodulation*, is the process of recovering from a modulated wave a voltage or current that varies in accordance with the modulation present on the wave. In the case of amplitude-modulated waves, detection is accomplished by rectifying the wave, thereby obtaining a pulsating direct current varying in amplitude in accordance with the modulation envelope of the wave.

The output of an ideal detector reproduces exactly the modulation existing on the wave. If the detector fails to do this, distortion results. This may be of several types. Thus the detector output may include frequencies that are not contained in the modulation envelope, thereby giving rise to amplitude distortion. The detector may also discriminate between modulation frequencies, giving an output that depends upon the modulation frequency, and may thus introduce frequency distortion. Finally a detector may reproduce the different frequency components of the modulation envelope with altered phase relations, resulting in phase distortion.

16-2. Diode Detectors.[1] Detection of amplitude-modulated waves is ordinarily accomplished by means of a diode rectifier.[2] A simple circuit for such a diode detector is shown in Fig. 16-1a, where C is a small capacitor, R a relatively high resistance, and the combination RC is the load impedance across which the rectified output voltage E_L of the diode is developed. At each positive peak of the radio-frequency cycle of

---

[1] The discussion given here for diode detectors was worked out by the author with the aid of C. K. Chang. It originated with and represented an extension of the principles presented by H. A. Wheeler, Design Formulas for Diode Detectors, *Proc. IRE*, vol. 26, p. 745, June, 1938.

[2] In the past, diode vacuum tubes have ordinarily been used for this purpose. However, crystal rectifiers, often called crystal diodes, such as described in Sec. 16-14, are finding increasing use, and it is possible that within a few years crystal diodes will have replaced vacuum diodes in most applications. Vacuum and crystal diodes behave similarly in the circuits of Figs. 16-1 and 16-2. Thus wherever a vacuum diode is shown in this chapter, it can be replaced by a crystal diode without significantly altering the behavior. Similarly, a vacuum diode can always be used in place of a crystal diode except at extremely high frequencies, where transit-time effects have a much greater adverse influence on the behavior of a vacuum diode than a crystal diode.

exciting voltage, the capacitance C charges up to a potential that is almost, but not quite, equal to the peak of the applied voltage; it fails by a small amount to reach the peak voltage because of the voltage drop produced in the diode tube by the charging current that flows through the tube. Between peaks, some of the charge on capacitor C leaks off through the resistance R, to be replenished by an appropriate new charge at the peak of the next radio-frequency cycle. The result of this situa-

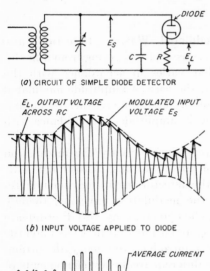

(a) CIRCUIT OF SIMPLE DIODE DETECTOR

(b) INPUT VOLTAGE APPLIED TO DIODE

(c) CURRENT THROUGH DIODE

Fig. 16-1. Circuit of simple diode detector, with oscillograms illustrating mechanism of operation.

tion is that the voltage E_L developed across the load impedance RC varies as shown in Fig. 16-1b. Neglecting the radio-frequency ripple, the voltage E_L is seen from Fig. 16-1b to reproduce the modulation envelope of the applied signal. The only special requirement is that the time constant of the resistance-capacitance combination RC must be small enough so that during those parts of the modulation cycle when the envelope is decreasing in amplitude, the voltage across C will decrease as fast as the envelope diminishes in amplitude.

The current that flows through the diode tube is in the form of pulses occurring at the peak of each radio-frequency cycle as shown in Fig. 16-1c. The pulses assume whatever amplitude is necessary to charge capacitor C up to a voltage that is almost, but not quite, equal to the peak of the applied radio-frequency voltage. The average value of the pulses of current flowing through the diode tube, i.e., the rectified current, is a pulsating direct current, as shown in Fig. 16-1c. The output voltage E_L, neglecting the radio-frequency ripple, is then the voltage that this rectified current produces across the load impedance RC when flowing through the impedance formed by R and C in parallel.

The ratio E_L/E_s of output voltage to peak radio-frequency voltage applied to the diode is termed the *efficiency of rectification*. The rectification efficiency will be high, typically in excess of 80 per cent, in the usual case where the diode load resistance R is very large compared with the plate resistance possessed by the diode when conducting.

The power that a diode detector absorbs from the applied voltage can be represented by a resistance shunted across the diode input circuit.

When the rectification efficiency η is high, this equivalent input resistance is almost exactly $R/2\eta$, and so is slightly greater than one-half the load resistance R.* A high load resistance R, therefore, reduces the power absorbed by the detector. This is to be expected, since with a high load resistance the energy that is dissipated in the load is less for a given voltage across it.

16-3. Practical Diode Detectors. The simple diode detector of Fig. 16-1a has the disadvantage that the voltage E_L at the output terminal is the sum of a d-c voltage representing the average envelope amplitude, an alternating voltage of modulation frequency, and a small radio-frequency ripple voltage.

This situation is avoided in practical diode-detector systems by employing circuit arrangements of the type illustrated in Fig. 16-2. Here R_1C_1 functions as a resistance-capacitance filter that prevents the radio-frequency ripple voltage developed across C from reaching the output terminals. Capacitor C_2 is for the purpose of preventing the d-c component of the rectified output from reaching volume-control potentiometer R_4, and must be large enough so that its reactance at modulation frequencies is small compared with the resistance R_4.

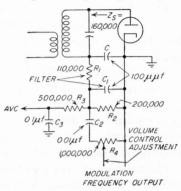

FIG. 16-2. Typical diode detector such as used in broadcast receivers, with provisions for automatic volume control and for obtaining modulation-frequency output free of d-c voltage.

The combination R_3C_3 is a resistance-capacitance filter proportioned to remove modulation frequency components. It provides a d-c voltage proportional to the rectified carrier, and free of modulation-frequency components, for purposes of automatic volume control, as discussed in Sec. 24-6.

In this practical diode-detector circuit, the load resistance that is offered to the d-c component of the rectified current is $R_1 + R_2$. However, to modulation frequencies the diode load impedance will be less than $R_1 + R_2$. Thus at low- and middle-range modulation frequencies such

---

* This is shown as follows: The diode current flows only when the signal voltage is at or near its crest value, as is clearly shown in Fig. 16-1c. The power absorbed by the detector input is accordingly only slightly less than the product of the crest signal voltage and the average diode current. Since the average current is equal to $\eta E_s/R$ where the output voltage across R is ηE_s, and E_s is the crest value of signal voltage, one can write

$$\text{Power loss} = \eta E_s^2/R = (\text{effective signal})^2/(R/2\eta)$$

The denominator of this last term represents the equivalent input resistance to the signal, which is, accordingly, $R/2\eta$.

that by-pass capacitors C_2 and C_3 are fully effective, while capacitors C and C_1 have such high reactances that they can be considered to be open circuits, the diode load impedance is resistive and consists of R_1 in series with an equivalent resistance formed by R_2, R_3, and R_4, all in parallel. Further, at high modulation frequencies the shunting effect of capacitors C and C_1 can no longer be neglected. The diode load impedance at high modulation frequencies is therefore still lower than that offered to moderate modulation frequencies, and in addition possesses a reactive component.

This situation causes the behavior of the practical diode detector of Fig. 16-2 to be more complicated than that of the simple diode circuit of Fig. 16-1a in which the load impedance offered to low and moderate modulation frequencies is the same as the resistance offered to the rectified direct current. Like the simple diode, the detector of Fig. 16-2 operates so that at the positive peak of each radio-frequency cycle capacitor C is charged to a voltage almost, but not quite, equal to the envelope of the amplitude-modulated wave. Thus the voltage developed across C reproduces the modulation envelope of the wave both as to shape and amplitude; this is shown in Fig. 16-3b.

The rectified current that flows through the diode is then whatever current must flow through the load impedance of the diode to develop this voltage. It is in this connection that the circuit of Fig. 16-2 behaves differently from the simple diode of Fig. 16-1a. Thus the d-c component I_0 of the rectified current must be such as to satisfy the relation

$$I_0 R_0 = \eta E_0 \qquad (16\text{-}1)$$

Similarly the peak value I_m of the modulation-frequency component of the rectified current must have a value such that

$$I_m Z_m = \eta m E_0 \qquad (16\text{-}2)$$

In these equations E_0 is the carrier amplitude of the applied wave, m is the degree of modulation of this wave, R_0 and Z_m are, respectively, the d-c and modulation-frequency impedance offered by the load, while η is the rectification efficiency.[1] It now follows from Eqs. (16-1) and (16-2) that when $Z_m < R_0$, the ratio of the modulation-frequency component of the

---

[1] Strictly speaking, the rectification efficiency will be slightly different for the modulation-frequency component of the rectified current than for the d-c component when Z_m and R_0 differ. Thus when $Z_m < R_0$, the increase in the modulation-frequency component of the rectified current which results from the fact that the load impedance to the modulation frequency is less than to direct current increases the voltage drop in the diode to modulation-frequency variations in the rectified current; this lowers the modulation-frequency output correspondingly. However, this difference between the efficiency of rectification for the carrier and for the modulation is usually so small as to be of little practical significance.

rectified current to the d-c component is larger than the degree of modulation of the original wave.   Also when Z_m is reactive, there is, in addition, a phase shift of the modulation-frequency component of the rectified current relative to the modulation envelope of the applied wave.   These effects are illustrated in Fig. 16-3c and d, respectively.

Peak Clipping in Diode Detectors.   The modulation of the rectified current is by definition the ratio of the peak modulation-frequency current to the average current; hence from Eqs. (16-1) and (16-2) one has

Modulation of rectified current

$$= \frac{I_m}{I_0} = m \frac{R_0}{|Z_m|} \quad (16\text{-}3)$$

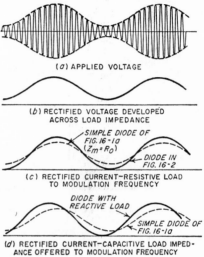

(a) APPLIED VOLTAGE

(b) RECTIFIED VOLTAGE DEVELOPED ACROSS LOAD IMPEDANCE

SIMPLE DIODE OF FIG. 16-1a ($Z_m = R_0$)

DIODE IN FIG. 16-2

(c) RECTIFIED CURRENT—RESISTIVE LOAD TO MODULATION FREQUENCY

DIODE WITH REACTIVE LOAD

SIMPLE DIODE OF FIG. 16-1a

(d) RECTIFIED CURRENT—CAPACITIVE LOAD IMPEDANCE OFFERED TO MODULATION FREQUENCY

FIG. 16-3. Effects of various types of load impedances on the rectified diode current.

The modulation of the rectified current in an actual diode can never exceed unity at the negative peaks. This is because if $I_m > I_0$ then at the negative peaks the resultant rectified current $I_0 - I_m$ would reverse in polarity, an obvious impossibility when the current must pass through a rectifier.   If the wave shape of the output voltage of the diode is to follow faithfully the envelope of the applied wave, it is thus necessary that the degree of modulation of the applied wave not exceed the value of m in Eq. (16-3) that makes $I_m = I_0$.   Hence

$$\left.\begin{array}{l}\text{Maximum permissible} \\ \text{value of } m \text{ without distortion}\end{array}\right\} = m_{\max} = \frac{|Z_m|}{R_0} \quad (16\text{-}4)$$

When the degree of modulation of the radio-frequency wave applied to the input terminals of the diode exceeds the value specified by Eq. (16-4), then the rectified current is zero during those parts of the modulation cycle that the rectified current would have to be negative if the diode output voltage were to follow the modulation envelope.   This is illustrated by the second line of Fig. 16-4b and c.   The resulting wave-shape distortion of the rectified current then causes a corresponding distortion in the wave shape of the output voltage, which no longer follows the modulation envelope at the negative peaks.   This is illustrated in the third line of Fig. 16-4b and c.

At low and moderate modulation frequencies in Fig. 16-2, when the diode load impedance to the modulation frequency is resistive and less than the d-c resistance R_0, the situation is as shown in Fig. 16-4a and b.

Here the distortion of the wave of rectified current that occurs when $m > m_{max}$ causes the negative peaks of the output voltage wave to be clipped during the interval the rectified current is zero. This clipping is perfectly flat to the extent that the blocking capacitor C_2 and the by-pass capacitor C_3 in Fig. 16-2 are large enough so that the voltages across them do not decrease appreciably during the period that the diode delivers no rectified current to the load.

At high modulation frequencies, where Z_m is not only smaller in magnitude than R_0 but also has a reactive component that is capacitive, the

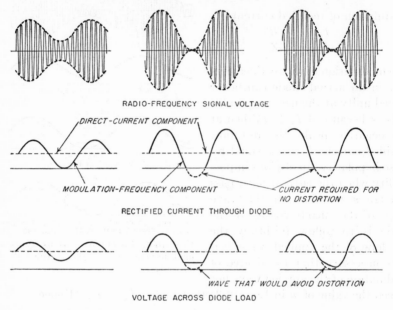

RADIO-FREQUENCY SIGNAL VOLTAGE

RECTIFIED CURRENT THROUGH DIODE

VOLTAGE ACROSS DIODE LOAD

(*a*) RESISTANCE LOAD
$m = R_m/R_0$

(*b*) RESISTANCE LOAD
$m > R_m/R_0$

(*c*) LOAD WITH PHASE ANGLE
$m > Z_m/R_0$

FIG. 16-4. Behavior of a practical diode detector such as shown in Fig. 16-2, showing negative peak and diagonal clipping.

conditions existing when $m > m_{max}$ are as shown in Fig. 16-4c. Here the distortion of the rectified current when $m > m_{max}$ no longer occurs exactly at the negative peak of the modulation cycle; this is because of the phase shift resulting from the capacitive load impedance. The result is a *diagonal* clipping of the output wave, such as illustrated in the bottom line of Fig. 16-4c. The exact shape of the output voltage wave during this distortion interval, when there is no rectified current flowing through the diode, will be determined by the discharge of capacitors C and C_1 through the resistances of the diode load impedance.

Input Impedance of Practical Diodes, and Demodulation of the Applied Signal. When the diode load circuit offers different impedances to the modulation-frequency and to the d-c components of the rectified current, the input impedance that the diode presents to the applied radio-frequency voltage is not the same for the sideband frequencies contained in the amplitude-modulated wave as it is for the carrier component. The input resistance to the carrier is very nearly $R_0/2\eta$, where R_0 is the load resistance offered by the diode load impedance to the d-c component of rectified current, and η is the efficiency of rectification. Likewise it can be shown that the magnitude of the input impedance that the diode offers to the sideband components of the applied radio-frequency signal approximates the value

$$\left.\begin{array}{l}\text{Input impedance of diode} \\ \text{to sideband frequencies}\end{array}\right\} = \left|\frac{Z_m}{2\eta}\right| \qquad (16\text{-}5)$$

The phase angle of the input impedance to the upper (or sum-frequency) sideband has the same magnitude and sign as does the phase angle of Z_m to the modulation frequency. The phase angle of the input impedance to the lower (or difference-frequency) sideband has the same magnitude as the phase angle of Z_m, but is of opposite sign.

In applying Eq. (16-5) to a practical situation, it is to be noted that in the practical diode of Fig. 16-2 the impedance Z_m is resistive but less than the load impedance to direct current at low and midrange modulation frequencies, while at high modulation frequencies it is even smaller and also has a capacitive component. Thus the input impedance to the sidebands corresponding to low- and midrange modulation frequencies is resistive and less than the input resistance to the carrier. At the same time the input resistance to the sideband frequencies corresponding to the higher modulation frequencies of the applied radio-frequency wave is less than that to lower frequency sidebands, and, in addition, has a reactive component.

The fact that the diode detector has a finite input impedance makes the radio-frequency voltage appearing at the input terminals of the diode less than if the diode system drew no current from the applied radio-frequency voltage. The amount of this reduction is determined by the input impedance of the diode in relation to the equivalent generator impedance of the source of applied voltage. For values of Z_m/R_0 less than unity, the sidebands will be reduced in amplitude proportionately more than the carrier because the diode input impedance is less to the sidebands than to the carrier. The result is that the *degree of modulation of the radio-frequency voltage actually present at the input terminals of the diode is less than the degree of modulation of the original radio-frequency signal.* The extent of this reduction in the degree of modulation, or "demodulation," is[1]

---

[1] This is derived as follows: To the carrier, the diode offers a load resistance $R_0/2\eta$, so that the presence of the diode reduces the carrier voltage across the tuned input circuit by the factor $|(R_0/2\eta)/(Z_s + R_0/2\eta)|$. Since the input impedance to the sidebands is

Degree of modulation of diode input voltage

$$\frac{\text{Degree of modulation of diode input voltage}}{\text{Actual degree of modulation of original signal}} = \frac{|Z_m| \times |Z_s + (R_0/2\eta)|}{R_0 \times |Z_s' + (Z_m/2\eta)|} \quad (16\text{-}6)$$

Here Z_s and Z_s' are the output impedances to carrier and sidebands, respectively, of the source of applied radio-frequency voltage as viewed from the diode terminals. In Eq. (16-6) the "original signal" is the signal that would be present if the diode were disconnected, but includes any discrimination against sidebands ("sideband trimming") that may exist as a result of selectivity of the tuned input circuit.

The lowering of the degree of modulation of the applied radio-frequency signal that results when $|Z_m/R_0|$ is less than unity produces a reduction in, and may even eliminate, the distortion that would otherwise occur when the degree of modulation of the original signal is high. That is, the reduction in the degree of modulation of the applied radio-frequency signal that occurs when $Z_m < R_0$ makes it easier to satisfy Eq. (16-4). Also, even in the worst possible case of a wave that was originally completely modulated, the amount of distortion of the output waveform arising from peak clipping will be reduced.

The extent to which the degree of modulation is reduced by the loading effect of the diode depends primarily on the ratio of the source impedance of the radio-frequency voltage to the diode load impedance. When the source impedance is much smaller than either Z_m or R_0, then Eq. (16-6) shows that there is negligible reduction in the degree of modulation. Under these conditions, Eq. (16-4) gives the maximum modulation that the original signal may have if clipping is to be avoided. However, when the source impedance of the radio-frequency voltage acting on the diode is very much greater than either the modulation-frequency or d-c impedance of the diode load, then Eq. (16-6) shows that when[1] $Z_s = Z_s'$, the loading effect of the diode reduces the modulation of the applied signal by the

---

$Z_m/2\eta$, the presence of the diode reduces these by the factor $|(Z_m/2\eta)/(Z_s' + Z_m/2\eta)|$. The ratio of these two reduction factors gives the factor by which the modulation is altered, and leads at once to Eq. (16-6). This result assumes that the impedance Z_s' of the source to the sidebands has the same magnitude for the lower as for the upper sideband, but that the phase angles are conjugates in the two cases. It also assumes that the rectification efficiency is the same for the carrier and the sidebands.

[1] When $Z_s' < Z_s$, as typically occurs for sideband frequencies high enough to suffer sideband trimming due to the selectivity of the tuned circuit associated with the diode, the "demodulation" factor is larger than Z_m/R_0. However, even here clipping of the output wave still normally will not occur if R_0 and Z_m are small compared with Z_s and Z_s'. This is because the selectivity of the input tuned circuit that causes Z_s' to be less than Z_s also reduces the amplitude of the sidebands relative to the carrier by the ratio Z_s'/Z_s. When R_0 and Z_m are both small compared with Z_s' and Z_s, this additional reduction in modulation just makes up for the increase in the factor giving the reduction in modulation that occurs when Z_s' is less than Z_s.

factor Z_m/R_0.   In this case no clipping can occur because the action of the diode load is to reduce the modulation of a completely modulated wave to the value m_{max} defined by Eq. (16-4).

16-4. Amplitude, Frequency, and Phase Distortion in Practical Diode Detectors. The only important cause of amplitude distortion in a diode detector is the clipping of the negative peaks that occurs when the degree of modulation of the signal actually applied to the diode input exceeds the value specified by Eq. (16-4). When such clipping is avoided, the output voltage of the diode will ordinarily follow the modulation envelope quite faithfully. In the absence of peak clipping the only distortion that can occur is variation in the efficiency of rectification with envelope amplitude arising as a result of curvature of the tube characteristic. If the signal amplitude is not too small this distortion will normally be less than 1 or 2 per cent. For very small signals square-law behavior is obtained and the distortion is $m/4$, as explained below.

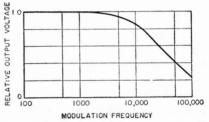

Fig. 16-5. Variation of output voltage with increasing modulation frequency for a typical diode detector.

When a radio-frequency wave of a given degree of modulation m that is less than the value that will cause peak clipping is applied to a diode-detector system such as that of Fig. 16-2, it is found that when the modulation frequency is increased while keeping m constant, the diode output voltage will drop off at high frequencies in the manner illustrated in Fig. 16-5. This frequency distortion arises from the fact that the degree of modulation of the voltage at the actual input terminals of the diode drops off at high modulation frequencies. Two factors working together cause this result. The first is the tendency of the inherent selectivity of the tuned input circuit of the diode to discriminate against the higher side-band frequencies, thus reducing the degree of modulation of the signal applied to the input terminal. The second is the falling off of the input impedance of the diode detector at very high frequencies because of the shunting effect of the capacitance of the diode load at the higher modulation frequencies.

The first factor, i.e., the selectivity of the tuned input circuit, controls the situation when the input impedance of the diode is much higher than the source impedance of the radio-frequency voltage applied to the input terminals of the diode. To obtain a good high-frequency characteristic under these conditions, it is necessary that the Q of the tuned input circuit be correspondingly low.

The second factor, i.e., the dropping off in the impedance of the diode load at high frequencies, controls the situation when the input impedance of the diode is much lower than the radio-frequency source impedance.

Under these conditions the discrimination that occurs against the higher-frequency sidebands is determined by the relative loading of the input resonant circuit by the diode at high modulation frequencies, as compared with the loading at moderate modulation frequencies.   The output voltage will then vary with modulation frequency in the same way that Z_m/R_0 varies with modulation frequency, and is very little affected by the inherent selectivity possessed by the tuned input circuit when the diode is disconnected.   In this case a good response characteristic at high modulation frequencies requires that the diode load impedance be so proportioned that its shunting capacitance does not lower the load impedance significantly at the highest modulation frequencies of interest.   In order to achieve this result it is necessary that the resistances R_1, R_2, etc., used in the output system of the diode (see Fig. 16-2) be inversely proportional to the highest modulation frequency of importance.

It is apparent that where the response is to be extended to very high modulation frequencies, as in television, the resistances in the diode load circuit must be quite small.   Values of the same order of magnitude as the coupling resistance that would be used in the corresponding video amplifier are called for.   At the same time the Q of the tuned input circuit must be reduced in proportion to the bandwidth involved.

The same factors that cause the degree of the modulation to drop off at the higher modulation frequencies will also simultaneously shift the phase of the higher modulation frequencies relative to the phase at the lower modulation frequencies.   This hence introduces the possibility of phase distortion at the higher modulation frequencies.

Performance of Practical Diode Detectors.   Typical circuit proportions for a diode detector intended for use in broadcast receivers are shown in Fig. 16-2.   Here R_3 and R_4 are made large compared with R_2 to minimize the difference between the impedance to the d-c and the modulation-frequency components of the rectified current, and R_1 is made larger than actually needed from the point of view of radio-frequency filtering for the same reason.   The behavior of this detector can be analyzed as follows:

Performance Calculations.   With the circuit proportions shown in Fig. 16-2, the load impedance R_0 to direct currents is $110,000 + 200,000 = 310,000$ ohms.   To low and moderate modulation frequencies it is 110,000 ohms in series with the combination of 500,000, 200,000, and 1,000,000 ohms all in parallel, or

$$Z_m = 110,000 + 125,000 = 235,000 \text{ ohms}$$

From Eq. (16-4) it then follows that at moderate modulation frequencies peak clipping will occur when the degree of modulation of the radio-frequency wave at the diode input terminal exceeds $m_{max} = 235,000/310,000 = 0.76$.

Assuming a rectification efficiency of 0.9, the input impedance of the diode to carrier and sideband frequencies is respectively $310,000/2 \times 0.9 = 172,000$ ohms, and $235,000/2 \times 0.9 = 130,000$ ohms.   If it is assumed that the source impedance of the tuned input circuit is 160,000 ohms to both carrier and sideband frequencies, then by

Eq. (16-6) the action is such that the actual modulation existing at diode input terminals is (235,000/310,000) × (160,000 + 172,000)/(160,000 + 130,000) = 0.87 times
the modulation of the "original signal." Thus there will be no peak clipping at low
and moderate modulation frequencies unless the degree of modulation of the incoming signal exceeds 0.76/0.87 = 0.875.

Further investigation of the circuit of Fig. 16-2 shows that shunting reactance of
capacitance C lowers the diode load impedance significantly, i.e., to less than roughly
70 per cent of its mid-frequency value when the modulation frequency is above about
10,000 cycles. If the Q of the input resonant circuit with the diode disconnected is
such that the 70.7 per cent response of this circuit also occurs at a frequency of 10,000
cycles or more off resonance, then the detector system of Fig. 16-2 will have a satisfactory frequency response for all modulation frequencies below about 10,000 cycles.

16-5. Plate Detectors. Although detection is normally carried out
with the aid of a diode rectifier, it is also possible to achieve detection by
using the nonlinear relation that
exists between grid bias and plate
current of a triode or pentode amplifier tube. Such plate detectors
were once widely used, and they
still find application in the measurement of voltage (see Sec. 16-6).
Two main types of plate detectors
are to be distinguished. These can
be termed Class B and Class A,
from their analogy with the corresponding types of amplifiers.
Either triode or pentode tubes may
be employed.

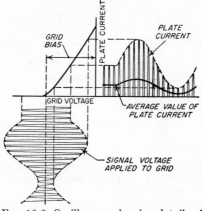

Fig. 16-6. Oscillogram showing details of
operation of a Class B plate detector.

In the Class B plate detector, the
tube is biased approximately to cut-
off, as in the Class B amplifier, and the modulated radio-frequency voltage
is applied to the control grid. The resulting plate current is shown in
Fig. 16-6. Each positive half cycle of applied voltage produces a half-
cycle pulse of plate current having an amplitude determined by the peak
amplitude of the applied voltage, while during the negative half cycles, no
plate current flows. Thus when the applied voltage is a modulated wave,
the average value of the plate current will vary in accordance with the
modulation envelope. Modulation-frequency output is then obtained by
coupling to the plate circuit as in an ordinary audio-frequency amplifier,
using resistance or transformer coupling, as is appropriate for the circumstances involved.[1]

As compared with a diode detector, the Class B plate detector has the
advantage that no power is consumed by the input circuit provided the

[1] The design of the audio-frequency coupling system can be carried out most satisfactorily by the equivalent circuit discussed in F. E. Terman, "Radio Engineers'
Handbook," p. 562, McGraw-Hill Book Company, Inc., New York, 1943.

control grid is not allowed to go positive; also peak clipping troubles are ordinarily not encountered.   However, if the peak value of the applied radio-frequency voltage at the positive crest of the modulation cycle exceeds the grid bias, then grid current flows and the modulation envelope is distorted.   This introduces amplitude distortion and therefore limits the amplitude of the signal voltage that may be applied to the plate detector.   Also there is no simple way of obtaining from a plate detector a negative voltage proportional to the average amplitude of the wave, and hence suitable for automatic volume control.   For these reasons plate detection is no longer used for radio receivers.

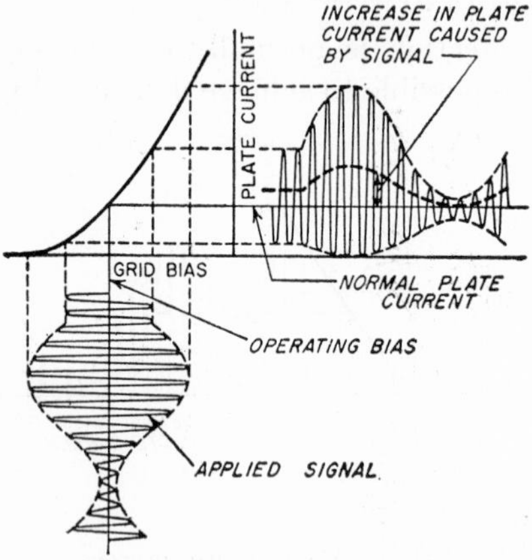

Fig. 16-7. Oscillogram showing details of operation of a typical Class A or square-law plate detector.

Class A Detector and Square-law Action.   In the Class A plate detector, the tube is operated as a Class A amplifier[1] biased to operate on a curved part of the tube characteristic.   The detecting action obtained under these conditions is illustrated in Fig. 16-7.   Because of the curvature of the tube characteristic, the positive half cycles of the wave are amplified more than the negative half cycles, causing the average plate current to be increased by the presence of the applied signal.   The amount of this increase will be greater the larger the applied voltage, so that if the latter is a modulated wave the plate current will vary with the modulation.

The behavior of the Class A plate detector can be analyzed by the power-series method discussed in Sec. 10-3.   Under ordinary conditions, the useful detector output consists of the d-c component of output current that is produced by even-order action.   An exception to this may occur when the signal consists of two sine waves of different frequencies; in this case the desired detector output is sometimes the difference-frequency component of the output likewise generated by even-order action.

When the applied signal is not too large, only the first- and second-order generators in the equivalent circuit of Fig. 10-9 need be considered in the power-series analysis of the Class A plate detector.   Under these conditions the rectified output current is proportional to the square of the effective value of the applied signal voltage, giving a *square-law* detector.

Square-law detectors are of importance for several reasons.   Thus, every rectifier becomes a square-law device when the applied signal is

[1] It will be recalled that the distinguishing feature of Class A operation is that the plate current flows continuously throughout the cycle.

sufficiently small. This is because, no matter what the rectification characteristic is for large signals, a very limited portion of this characteristic can always be approximated by a section of a parabola. Also square-law detectors are useful in measurement work because they have a simple and exact law of behavior, and because the d-c component of the rectified current that they develop is exactly proportional to the power of the applied wave.

Square-law detectors are not particularly satisfactory for the detection of signals that are modulated waves. This arises from the fact that since the output of the square-law detector is proportional to the square of the amplitude of the applied signal, then when this signal varies in amplitude the resulting rectified current will represent a distorted reproduction of the modulation envelope of the applied signal.[1]

16-6. Vacuum-tube Detectors as Vacuum-tube Voltmeters.[2] A detector can serve as a voltmeter by using the rectified current (or the d-c output voltage) as a measure of the voltage applied to the detector input. The resulting vacuum-tube voltmeter is one of the most useful measuring devices available for audio and radio frequencies. It need consume little or no power from the voltage being measured, and when properly designed a calibration made at low frequency, such as 60 cycles, will apply without correction up to a very high radio frequencies.

Vacuum-tube voltmeters in common use are either of the diode-or plate-detection types. The diode-type vacuum-tube voltmeter, illustrated[3] in Fig. 16-8a, consists essentially of a simple diode detector with a high load resistance R such that the efficiency of rectification and the input resistance are both high. The voltage across R is then applied to a simple d-c amplifier, shown here as the type illustrated in Fig. 8-19a. The output of this amplifier operates an ordinary d'Arsonval type of d-c meter that requires a current of the order of 0.1 to 1.0 ma to produce full-scale deflection. Vacuum-tube voltmeters of this type are in extensive use, and a number of models are commercially available.

[1] In the case of square-law detection of a wave with sinusoidal modulation it is a simple matter to show that the distortion is entirely second harmonic and is $m/4$, where m is the degree of modulation. Thus the distortion will be 25 per cent for a completely modulated wave.

[2] For a more comprehensive survey of this subject see F. E. Terman and J. M. Pettit, "Electronic Measurements," pp. 15–36, McGraw-Hill Book Company, Inc., New York, 1952.

[3] The circuit of the diode-detector type of voltmeter is commonly arranged as in Fig. 16-8b. Here the capacitor C charges up to a voltage ηE_s, just as in Figs. 16-1b and 16-8a, where η is the efficiency of rectification and E_s is the positive peak input voltage. Likewise between peaks when the diode is nonconducting, charge from C leaks off through the circuit formed by R and whatever is connected between the input terminals. The only difference in behavior between a and b is that in the latter, the resistance R is in shunt with the input terminals, so that the load impedance to the applied signal is the diode input resistance $R/2\eta$ in parallel with R, instead of being $R/2\eta$.

Plate-detection Types.   Plate-detection vacuum-tube voltmeters may be either of the Class B or Class A type.   In Class B operation the tube, normally a triode, is biased approximately to cutoff.   The rectified d-c output current produced by a large applied voltage will thus be very nearly proportional to the average amplitude of the positive half cycles of the applied wave (see Fig. 16-6); this results in what can be called a *linear half-wave voltmeter.*   However, assuming the applied signal is moderately small, so that operation during the positive half cycles is largely on the curved portion of the tube characteristic in Fig. 16-6, then the rectified d-c output is more nearly proportional to the square of the peak amplitude of the positive half cycles of the applied voltage.   This

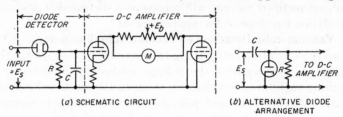

(*a*) SCHEMATIC CIRCUIT   (*b*) ALTERNATIVE DIODE ARRANGEMENT

Fig. 16-8. A schematic diagram of diode type vacuum-tube voltmeter provided with d-c amplifier.

type of operation is sometimes called *square-law half-wave detection.*   Thus in practice, the curve giving the relation between the applied signal and the rectified d-c output current of a Class B plate-detection vacuum-tube voltmeter is a square-law curve for small and moderate amplitudes, but tends to become linear when the applied signal is large.

Vacuum-tube detectors of the Class A type are useful as vacuum-tube voltmeters because when the applied signal is not too large they function as true square-law devices, as discussed above.   The rectified current is then exactly proportional to the power of the applied wave irrespective of wave shape.

In Class A detectors, a large residual d-c plate current is present in the absence of an applied signal.   This current is often much larger than the change in plate current produced by the application of a signal voltage. It is therefore customary to arrange the circuits of vacuum-tube voltmeters employing Class A detection, and sometimes those using Class B detection as well, so that the meter indicating the rectified current will read zero in the absence of an applied signal.   In this way the full-scale range is available to present the change in d-c plate current produced by the applied voltage.   A simple circuit arrangement for accomplishing this result is shown in Fig. 16-9.[1]   Here resistance R is adjusted so that in the

---

[1] More sophisticated arrangements are represented by circuits analogous to Figs. 8-19*b* and 8-20 for d-c amplification, in which a balancing tube is used in order to provide compensation against supply-voltage changes.   In such circuits, the plate and cathode of the active tube must be effectively by-passed to ground at the frequency of the applied wave.

absence of an applied signal, the current I' flowing through R is equal to the residual plate current I_b flowing through M. When this is the case the resultant current in the meter M is zero in the absence of a signal. At the same time, practically all of the increase in plate current resulting from the application of a signal passes through M if R is large compared with the meter resistance.

Vacuum-tube voltmeters of the plate-detection type are occasionally operated under conditions intermediate between Class A and Class B. In this case the system acts as a square-law Class A system for small signals but is more like a Class B system when the amplitude is large. Again, occasionally a plate-detection type of vacuum-tube voltmeter is biased beyond cutoff. This can be described as Class C operation, in that rectified current flows only near the positive peaks of the cycles of applied voltage, and no current at all flows in the plate circuit when the applied signal is small.

Waveform Effects in Vacuum-tube Voltmeters. In the case of square-law operation, the output indication of a vacuum-tube voltmeter is always proportional to the square of the effective value of the applied wave, but is otherwise independent of the details of wave shape. In contrast a vacuum-tube voltmeter that employs linear Class B plate detection will give an output that is proportional to the area under the positive half cycles of the applied wave when this wave is of large amplitude, but is not affected by the details of the wave shape that produce this area. Finally the diode voltmeters of Fig. 16-8 measure the amplitude of the positive peaks of the applied signal, but are not otherwise affected by wave shape, and are not affected by the amplitude of the negative peaks.[1]

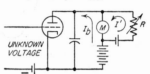

Fig. 16-9. Circuit of a triode plate-detection vacuum-tube voltmeter, showing method of balancing residual direct current out of the indicating meter.

An understanding of the effect of wave shape can be gained by considering the response of different types of vacuum-tube voltmeters to the waves illustrated in Fig. 16-10. The first three of these waves all have positive peaks of the same amplitude; the fourth wave differs from the third only in that the phase of the third harmonic has been shifted 180° at the harmonic frequency. A diode vacuum-tube voltmeter will accordingly give the same indication for waves a, b, and c, but will give a lower value for wave d. If now the applied voltage is reversed in polarity, then the waves at a and d give the same reading as before, but now b gives a lower indication. This change in indication produced by reversal of polarity of the applied signal is called *turnover*.

[1] However, special problems are encountered in interpreting the readings of diode voltmeters when the applied voltage consists of pulses of short duration, or when it is a modulated wave. These and related waveform problems are discussed by Terman and Pettit, *op. cit.*, pp. 19–24.

If the voltmeter is a linear half-wave Class B plate-detection type, then the rectified current will be less in b, c, and d than in a. Moreover the reading for wave shape d will be larger than for wave shape c, which is just the opposite from the way the diode voltmeter responded. Turnover effects will be absent with the half-wave linear detector because the area under the positive and negative half cycles of an alternating wave is the same.

With a true square-law vacuum-tube voltmeter, the indication will depend only on the effective value of the wave shape involved. For this reason the waves at b, c, and d will give the same reading, which, however,

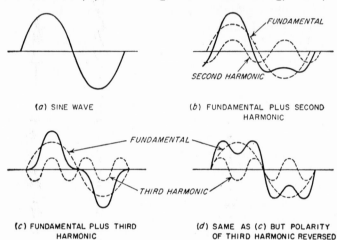

(a) SINE WAVE

(b) FUNDAMENTAL PLUS SECOND HARMONIC

(c) FUNDAMENTAL PLUS THIRD HARMONIC

(d) SAME AS (c) BUT POLARITY OF THIRD HARMONIC REVERSED

Fig. 16-10. Various wave shapes that might be encountered by a vacuum-tube voltmeter.

is less than for the wave at a. Turnover is absent in voltmeters based on true square-law detectors, since such devices indicate the effective value of the entire wave, taking into account both positive and negative portions, and so are not affected by polarity.

It is apparent from these considerations that the reading of a vacuum-tube voltmeter must be very carefully interpreted when the wave shape is not sinusoidal. The situation can be summarized by stating that the indication obtained from a complex wave will always depend upon the harmonics that are present, and in some cases will be affected as well by the phase relations of these harmonics.

Crystal-diode Voltmeters. Diode detectors using crystal diodes instead of vacuum-tube diodes are often used at microwave frequencies where ordinary vacuum diodes do not function satisfactorily because of transit-time problems. In this case the load impedance for the crystal is very commonly a microammeter shunted by an appropriate by-pass capacitor. The microammeter is then used as a direct indication of the applied voltage, and the d-c amplifier illustrated in Fig. 16-8 is not used.

Crystal diodes are, however, generally avoided for vacuum-tube-volt-meter applications at the lower frequencies where vacuum diodes are satisfactory.   This is because crystal diodes will be damaged and their calibration changed if overloaded even momentarily, whereas vacuum diodes are both more rugged and more stable.

16-7. The Use of Rotating Vectors to Determine Envelope Properties and Phase Variations of Modulated Waves.   Rotating vectors provide a simple means of determining the way in which the carrier and sideband frequencies of a modulated wave combine to produce amplitude and phase variations of the resulting oscillation.   Thus in Fig. 16-11, vectors C, U, and L represent the carrier, upper sideband, and lower sideband, respectively, of an amplitude-modulated wave.   If the carrier vector C is

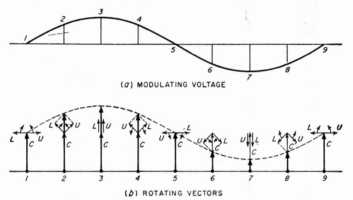

(a) MODULATING VOLTAGE

(b) ROTATING VECTORS

Fig. 16-11. Vector diagrams showing relations between carrier and sidebands in amplitude-modulated wave with sinusoidal modulation.

used as a reference it can be considered as stationary.   The sideband vectors then rotate as indicated by the arrows, the vector L steadily dropping back in phase because it has a lower frequency than the carrier, while U steadily gains in phase because it is higher in frequency than the carrier.   The envelope amplitude represents the sum of these three vectors, as indicated by the heavy-line vector.   This resultant vector is seen to vary in amplitude with time in such a way as to produce the envelope variations characteristic of an amplitude-modulated wave, but does not change its phase position.

Consider next the more complicated situation illustrated in Fig. 16-12a, where an amplitude-modulated voltage wave such as represented by Fig. 16-11 is applied to a tuned amplifier which is detuned with respect to the carrier frequency.   The detuning alters the relative amplitudes and phases of the carrier and sidebands C', U', and L', appearing at the ampli-fier output, and also destroys the symmetry of the sidebands, as seen by comparing Fig. 16-12b and c.   If one now takes the carrier vector C' as the reference, and uses the rotating-vector technique to determine the character of the resultant voltage developed across the tuned amplifier by the vectors of Fig. 16-12c, the result is as illustrated in Fig. 16-13. It is apparent that the modulation envelope is now a substantially distorted replica of the original modulation and so no longer represents

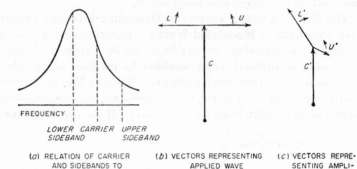

(a) RELATION OF CARRIER   (b) VECTORS REPRESENTING   (c) VECTORS REPRE-
    AND SIDEBANDS TO   APPLIED WAVE   SENTING AMPLI-
    RESPONSE CURVE   FIED WAVE

Fig. 16-12. Effect of a detuned resonant circuit on the carrier and sideband components of a modulated wave.

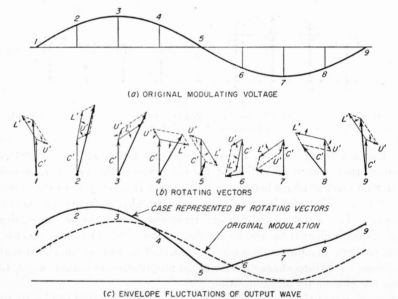

(a) ORIGINAL MODULATING VOLTAGE

(b) ROTATING VECTORS

(c) ENVELOPE FLUCTUATIONS OF OUTPUT WAVE

Fig. 16-13. The use of rotating vectors to determine the envelope of the amplified wave corresponding to Fig. 16-12c.

exactly the intelligence modulated upon the wave. In addition, the phase of the resultant voltage is seen to vary about the reference-phase position. This means that the amplified output is now also phase (or frequency) modulated (see Chap. 17) along with the distorted amplitude modulation.

16-8. Behavior of Detectors When the Applied Signal Consists of Two Amplitude-modulated Waves.   Circumstances sometimes arise, particularly in the reception of broadcast signals, where in addition to the desired signal, there is simultaneously applied to the detector input an interfering signal that is weaker, but still of more than negligible amplitude.   The behavior under these conditions depends upon the difference in the carrier frequencies of the desired and undesired signals.

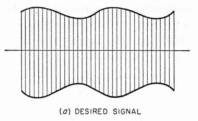

(a) DESIRED SIGNAL

When the difference between the two carrier frequencies is in the audible range, the most important interfering component in the output of the rectifier is a continuous whistle corresponding to the difference frequency between the two carriers.   If, however, this difference frequency is too low to be audible, the most disturbing audible components in the detector output arising from the presence of the undesired signal are then the difference frequencies formed by the carrier of the desired signal and the sideband frequencies of the weaker or undesired signal.   The resulting effect is termed sideband noise.   When the carrier frequencies differ only by a few cycles per second, this sideband noise gives rise to the characteristic flutter often heard when two broadcast stations are simultaneously transmitting on approximately the same frequency.

(b) UNDESIRED WEAKER SIGNAL

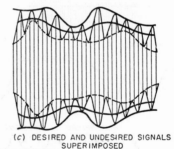

(c) DESIRED AND UNDESIRED SIGNALS
SUPERIMPOSED

SUPERSONIC BEAT FREQUENCY
AUDIO-FREQUENCY COMPONENT

(d) WAVE (c) AFTER LINEAR RECTIFICATION

FIG. 16-14. Waveforms obtained in the linear detection of a signal consisting of a weak modulated wave superimposed upon a strong modulated wave.

When two modulated signals of unequal amplitudes and of carrier frequencies that are so different as to produce an inaudible difference frequency are simultaneously applied to the input of a distortionless (linear) detector, it is found that the weaker of the two is not rectified.   This is because the envelope of the combined wave possesses a principal modulation representing the desired modulation and a minor variation corresponding to the inaudible difference frequency between the two carriers. This minor variation pulsates in amplitude in accordance with the modulation of the undesired carrier.   However, since the output of a distortionless rectifier follows the modulation envelope, the detector output contains no component that follows the modulation of the undesired weaker signal.   This is shown in Fig. 16-14.

This suppression of a weak signal in the presence of a strong signal is equivalent to an increase in the effective selectivity of the system, and represents an important property of a distortionless (linear) detector.   In order that the suppression of the weaker signal may be complete, it is

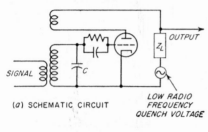

(a) SCHEMATIC CIRCUIT

(b) HYPOTHETICAL SIGNAL

(c) VOLTAGE ON THE PLATE

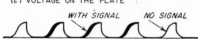

(d) AMPLITUDE OF OSCILLATIONS ACROSS C

FIG. 16-15. Simple superregenerative circuit, together with details showing the mechanism by which the superregenerative action is obtained.

necessary that the strong signal be considerably larger than the weaker, and that the detector be exactly linear.   With ordinary rectifiers the suppression becomes very pronounced when the ratio of signal amplitudes exceeds 2:1.

16-9. Superregenerative Detectors.[1]   A superregenerative detector is essentially an ordinary oscillator which is alternated between an oscillating and a nonoscillating condition at a low radio-frequency rate.   A typical superregenerative detector circuit is shown schematically in Fig. 16-15a.   This is identical with the tuned-grid oscillator circuit which is shown in Fig. 14-1c. except that the plate-supply potential is an alternating voltage derived from a separate oscillator (not shown) operating at a low radio frequency.   With proper adjustment, oscillations will build up in such a system near the positive peaks of each cycle of the low-frequency "quench" voltage, and will die out when the voltage is negative or too low to provide oscillating conditions.   The signal voltage that is to be detected is coupled into the tuned grid circuit of the detector.

The operation of this superregenerative detector for the usual method of operation[2] can be explained as follows: In the absence of an applied signal, the oscillations that build up during each cycle of the quench

[1] A helpful discussion of present-day concepts of this subject is given by A. Hazeltine, D. Richman, and B. D. Loughlin, Superregenerator Design, *Electronics*, vol. 2, p. 99, September, 1948.

[2] The type of operation described here is known as the logarithmic mode.   In an alternative method of operation, known as the linear mode, the oscillations are quenched before they reach equilibrium value.

voltage start with an initial amplitude determined by the noise voltages in the input circuit and reach a final value corresponding to the equilibrium value for the oscillator. These oscillations then die out as the "quench" voltage becomes small and then goes negative. For proper operation the oscillations must decay to an amplitude less than the circuit noise before the oscillating condition is again restored.

Assume now that a signal voltage is superimposed upon the system and is larger in magnitude than the thermal agitation noises in the tuned input circuit. Then, when the oscillations start to build up, their initial amplitude corresponds to the amplitude of the superimposed signal rather than the smaller amplitude of the noise voltages in the circuit. The oscillations, therefore, reach their equilibrium value more quickly than before because of the larger initial amplitude. This is illustrated in an exaggerated way in Fig. 16-15d, and is seen to increase the area under the envelope of the oscillations during the build-up period to the extent of the shaded area in Fig. 16-15d. The equilibrium value that is reached by the oscillations, and the decay of the oscillations during the quench period, are not significantly affected by the presence of the signal, however. The action of the signal is accordingly to increase the average area under the envelope of the oscillations by an amount that becomes greater the larger the amplitude of the signal. The d-c plate current of the tube is proportional to the area under the curves in Fig. 16-15c, and so varies with the amplitude of the applied signal.

A quantitative study of the details involved in this mode of operation reveals that the change in d-c plate current caused by the signal is proportional to the logarithm of the signal intensity. When the signal is a modulated wave, the variations in the output or plate current therefore represent a highly distorted reproduction of the modulation envelope. At the same time, the logarithmic characteristic results in a pronounced limiting action that is helpful in minimizing the effect of noise pulses of large amplitude but small duration.[1]

Superregeneration provides a simple means of obtaining a very large amount of radio-frequency amplification at frequencies that are difficult to amplify by conventional means. Also, as a result of the logarithmic characteristic, when two signals are present the stronger one controls the initiation of the build-up period and so suppresses almost completely the weaker signal that is also present. This behavior, and the ability to suppress noise pulses, are sometimes very useful. At the same time, superregeneration has the disadvantage of providing poor selectivity, of

[1] Suppression of noise pulses of short duration is also aided by the fact that in superregeneration the system is sensitive to the incoming signal for only a small fraction of the total time. Thus only those noise pulses which happen to coincide in time with these sensitive moments produce any effect on the detector output. The system is completely unresponsive to the remaining noise pulses arriving at other values of time, which represent most of the noise.

developing a characteristic hiss in the absence of a signal as a result of amplified thermal agitation noise, and of reproducing a distorted replica of the modulation envelope. Because of these limitations and the fact that the adjustments required for proper operation are relatively critical, superregeneration is used only in special circumstances.

16-10. Frequency Translation. Many circumstances arise in which it is desired to translate a signal to another place in the frequency spectrum without disturbing the relation of the sidebands to the carrier. Thus in standard broadcast receivers, a signal having a carrier frequency anywhere in the broadcast band 535 to 1605 kc, and voice-modulated at frequencies up to 5000 cycles, is ordinarily transformed to a carrier frequency of approximately 455 kc with the same voice modulation. In this way it is possible to employ a fixed amplifier (commonly termed the *intermediate-frequency amplifier*) operating at 455 kc for the amplification of all incoming signals, irrespective of their particular frequency.

The translation of the frequency of a signal from one place in the spectrum to another is accomplished with the aid of a locally generated oscillation that interacts with the signal in such a manner as to produce a new frequency, ordinarily a simple difference frequency. Thus in the case of the standard broadcast receiver referred to above, an incoming signal of frequency 1120 kc could be converted to an intermediate frequency of 455 kc by appropriate interaction with a locally generated oscillation of 1575 kc. This process of frequency translation is also referred to by such names as frequency conversion, heterodyne action, mixing, and beating.

There are two principal types of interaction that can be employed to achieve frequency translation: (1) The locally generated oscillations may be used to modulate the incoming signal, or, vice versa, the incoming signal may be used to modulate the local oscillations. The resulting lower sideband then represents the difference between the frequencies of the signal and of the local oscillation, and can be used as the new frequency.[1] (2) The local oscillation may be superimposed upon the signal, and the combined wave then rectified. As shown below, this gives a difference-frequency wave.

Analysis of Heterodyne Action Resulting from Superimposing Two Waves of Different Frequencies. When two alternating waves of different frequencies are superimposed, the result is as shown in Fig. 16-16. The higher-frequency wave continuously gains in phase position relative to the lower frequency wave because of its greater angular velocity. As a result, the envelope of the combined wave fluctuates in amplitude as the variation in relative phase causes the two waves successively to add and then subtract. The frequency of the envelope pulsation is the difference

---

[1] Alternatively, it is possible to employ the upper sideband, thereby obtaining a new frequency that is the sum of the signal and locally generated frequencies.

between the frequencies of the two alternating waves involved, since each cycle that the higher-frequency wave gains with respect to the lower-frequency wave causes one cycle of envelope fluctuation.

The equation of the envelope in Fig. 16-16c can be derived with the aid of the rotating vectors illustrated in Fig. 16-16d. Here vector E_0, representing the larger of the two waves in Fig. 16-16 (the superimposed

(a) FIRST WAVE (SIGNAL)

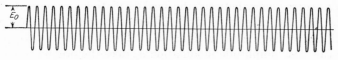

(b) SECOND WAVE (SUPERIMPOSED OSCILLATION)

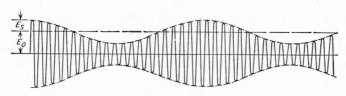

(c) SUM OF (a) AND (b)

(d) ROTATING VECTORS

Fig. 16-16. Diagrams illustrating how superimposing two waves of different frequencies results in a wave that pulsates in amplitude at the difference frequency of the component waves. The associated rotating vectors are also shown.

local oscillation), is taken as a fixed reference, while E_s, representing the smaller of the waves (i.e., the signal), rotates with respect to E_0 at the angular velocity $(\omega_s - \omega_0)$ radians per sec, where $\omega_s/2\pi$ and $\omega_0/2\pi$ are the frequencies of E_s and E_0, respectively. The envelope amplitude in Fig. 16-16c at any instant is then the vector sum E of these two vectors at the corresponding value of time; this is shown in Fig. 16-16d for different parts of the beat-frequency cycle of the wave of Fig. 16-16c. The vector sum is seen to be the third side of a triangle having sides E_s and E_0 and an included angle of $(\omega_s - \omega_0)t + \alpha$, where α is the phase difference between E_0 and E_s at the instant $t = 0$. This gives

$$\left.\begin{array}{c}\text{Envelope} \\ \text{amplitude}\end{array}\right\} = \sqrt{E_s{}^2 + E_0{}^2 + 2E_sE_0 \cos\left[(\omega_s - \omega_0)t + \alpha\right]} \quad (16\text{-}7)$$

When one wave is much smaller than the other, i.e., when $E_s << E_0$, then Eq. (16-7) can be written

$$\left.\begin{array}{c}\text{Envelope} \\ \text{amplitude}\end{array}\right\} = E_0 \left\{1 + \frac{E_s}{E_0} \cos\left[(\omega_s - \omega_0)t + \alpha\right]\right\} \quad (16\text{-}8)$$

It is apparent from Eq. (16-8) that when the superimposed oscillation E_0 is much larger than the signal E_s, the envelope amplitude varies exactly in accordance with the amplitude of the signal E_s. When such a combined wave is rectified, the resulting rectified wave not only varies at the difference frequency between the local oscillation and the signal, but at the same time the amplitude of the difference-frequency wave is exactly proportional to the incoming signal E_s. Thus the new wave possesses exactly the same amplitude modulation as does the original wave. It is to be noted that even phase relations are maintained, a certain phase difference α existing before frequency conversion still being present as the same phase shift α at the new carrier frequency after the frequency change.[1]

16-11. Mixer and Converter Tubes for Frequency Translation. The vacuum tube used to provide the interaction between local oscillation and signal required in a frequency-translation system is commonly termed a *mixer*.[2] If the tube that carries out the mixing operation also simultaneously generates the local oscillation, it is referred to as a *converter* tube.

A variety of vacuum-tube arrangements finds practical use as mixers. These can be classified as follows: (1) triode and pentode plate detectors; (2) suppressor-grid-modulated arrangements, including pentagrid mixers; (3) converter tubes which provide separate oscillator and mixer in a common envelope; (4) pentagrid converters; and (5) crystal diodes. In all of these arrangements it is customary to apply local oscillations of relatively large amplitude to the mixer. The incoming signal that is to have its frequency translated is then normally quite small in comparison.

In the triode and pentode plate-detector types of mixer, the signal and the local oscillator voltages are simultaneously applied between control grid and cathode of a Class B plate detector (see Sec. 16-5). Coupling between signal and oscillator circuits can be minimized by applying these voltages between control grid and ground and cathode and ground, respectively.[3]

---

[1] It is also noted that any frequency modulation possessed by E_s likewise appears as identical frequency modulation of the new carrier frequency, since variations in the frequency of E_s produce corresponding variations in the difference frequency $(\omega_s - \omega_0)/2\pi$.

[2] In the case of radio receivers, the term *first detector* is also employed.

[3] Coupling between signal and oscillator circuits is generally to be avoided because it

In a pentode tube, mixing can also be obtained by applying the signal to the control grid, and the local oscillator voltage to the suppressor grid, or vice versa.   Such an arrangement represents a suppressor-grid-modulated amplifier, such as discussed in connection with Fig. 15-4, and generates the desired difference frequency in the form of the lower sideband. This method of using a pentode as a mixer gives greater isolation between the local oscillator and the signal than when plate detection is used.   It has the disadvantage, however, that the plate resistance resembles that of a triode tube rather than having the high value of a pentode.

This limitation of the pentode suppressor-grid-modulated mixer can be avoided by introducing two additional grids between the suppressor and the plate.   The result is the *pentagrid mixer* tube, exemplified by the 6L7, which is illustrated in Fig. 16-17.   Here grids G_1, G_2, and G_3 correspond to the control, screen, and suppressor grids of an ordinary pentode.   Grid G_4 is a screen grid operated at the same potential as G_2, while G_5 is a suppressor grid that is connected to the cathode.   This arrangement is accordingly a suppressor-grid-modulated amplifier, in which grids G_4 and G_5 provide an output characteristic corresponding to that of a pentode tube.   That is, the plate resistance is very high, and the plate current is substantially independent of plate voltage until the plate voltage becomes very small.   The pentagrid mixer also has the advantage of eliminating coupling between the signal and the local oscillator even more completely than does the suppressor-grid-modulated pentode, since the tube can be specifically designed to minimize second-order couplings.

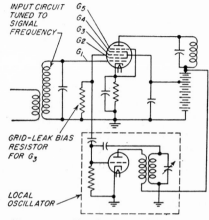

FIG. 16-17.   Circuit of pentagrid mixer.

The pentagrid mixer tube of Fig. 16-17 requires a separate local oscillator.   This may be an entirely separate tube, but often the triode oscillator and pentagrid mixer are combined in some manner in a common envelope.   In such a *converter* tube, the oscillator and mixer sections are sometimes entirely independent, merely sharing a common vacuum envelope.   However, in other cases some elements of the oscillator and mixer are related; for example, in one tube type a flat cathode is employed, one side of which supplies electrons for a triode oscillator, while the other side

introduces a tendency for the local oscillator to synchronize with a strong incoming signal, and also causes the local oscillator frequency to be somewhat dependent upon the tuning of the signal circuit.

of the same cathode provides electrons for the mixer portion of the converter tube. All such arrangements are, however, equivalent electrically to a separate oscillator plus a pentagrid or other form of mixer tube.

The Pentagrid Converter. A typical pentagrid-converter arrangement is illustrated in Fig. 16-18. Here G_1 and G_2 function as the control grid and anode, respectively, of an electron-coupled oscillator of the type illustrated in Fig. 14-3*b*. This oscillator causes the flow of electrons from the cathode to be in the form of pulses that occur at the positive peak of each cycle of the oscillator. Most of the electrons in these pulses of current drawn from the cathode pass through the spaces between the wires of G_2 and come to rest on the cathode side of the grid G_3, where a virtual cathode is formed. The signal voltage is applied to G_3 and so affects the number of electrons that are drawn from this virtual cathode toward the plate instead of being returned to the cathode. Grids G_4 and G_5 are screen and suppressor grids, respectively, that serve to give the plate circuit of the tube a pentode characteristic. The action occurring in the pentagrid converter is seen to be the same as would occur in the pentagrid mixer of Fig. 16-17 if the local oscillator voltage were applied to the first grid and the signal voltage to the third grid.

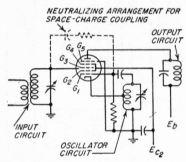

FIG. 16-18. Typical pentagrid converter arrangement.

The pentagrid converter has the advantage of simplicity and economy. It thus finds extensive use, particularly in standard-broadcast receivers.

The pentagrid converter is not particularly satisfactory at very high frequencies, however. The fact that there is a virtual cathode in the vicinity of the signal grid (G_3 in Fig. 16-18) that pulsates at the oscillator frequency causes a form of capacitive coupling to exist between the pulsating space charge and the signal grid which induces a current in the signal-grid circuit that is proportional to the frequency. The result is that at very high frequencies a considerable oscillator voltage may be developed across the load impedance in the circuit of the signal grid. This affects the converter output, which then becomes dependent upon the signal-circuit impedance, and hence upon the tuning of the signal circuit.[1,2] Still another factor making the pentagrid converter unsatis-

---

[1] This space-charge coupling can be neutralized to a first approximation by connecting a small capacitance between the signal and oscillator grids, or better still a capacitance in series with a small resistance. Such a neutralizing arrangement, shown dotted in Fig. 16-18, is usually desirable if circumstances make it necessary to employ a pentagrid converter at very high frequencies.

[2] The pentagrid mixer of Fig. 16-17 avoids space-charge coupling by applying the signal to the first or inner grid, which is not associated with a pulsating virtual cathode.

factory at very high frequencies is its very high inherent noise level (see Sec. 16-13).

16-12. Quantitative Analysis of Mixer-tube Operation—Conversion Transconductance. The operation of all types of mixers discussed in Sec 16-11 can be analyzed by assuming that when the local oscillator amplitude is large and the signal small, the signal-grid-to-plate transconductance of the tube is at any instant determined only by the instantaneous amplitude of the local oscillator, and is independent of the signal voltage.[1]

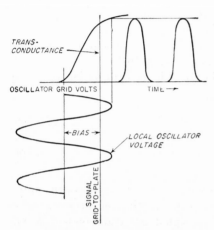

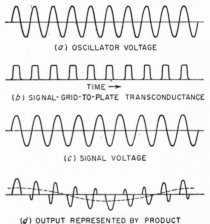

(a) OSCILLATOR VOLTAGE

TIME →
(b) SIGNAL-GRID-TO-PLATE TRANSCONDUCTANCE

(c) SIGNAL VOLTAGE

(d) OUTPUT REPRESENTED BY PRODUCT OF (b) AND (c)

Fig. 16-19. Signal-grid-to-plate transconductance as a function of instantaneous voltage applied to the oscillator grid of mixer tube, together with curves showing variation of the transconductance with time during a cycle of oscillator voltage.

Fig. 16-20. Oscillograms illustrating action of mixer tubes.

In accordance with this assumption, the transconductance of the tube from signal grid to output will vary during the oscillator frequency in the manner illustrated in Fig. 16-19, which shows a typical situation in which the circuit adjustments are such that the transconductance is zero during the negative half cycles of the oscillator voltage and is relatively large during most of each positive half cycle. A signal voltage such as at Fig. 16-20c applied to the mixer tube operated under these conditions will then produce a plate current that fluctuates in accordance with the product of the signal voltage and the transconductance curve of Fig. 16-20b. This

[1] Signal-grid transconductance is not to be confused with conversion transconductance defined in connection with Eq. (16-13), below. The signal-grid transconductance represents the ordinary transconductance for amplifier action, as defined by Eq. (6-21) for the change in plate current produced by a change in voltage applied to the grid electrode to which the signal voltage is applied. It is to be noted that the signal grid in mixer operation is not necessarily the inner grid, i.e., the grid adjacent to the cathode.

causes the resulting output to be modulated in accordance with the local oscillator frequency, as shown in Fig. 16-20d. The lower sideband of this modulated signal voltage is shown by the dotted curve, and represents the desired difference frequency, i.e., the translated signal.[1]

Quantitative Analysis.[2] The quantitative relations represented in Figs. 16-19 and 16-20 will now be developed. The curve of signal-grid-to-plate transconductance represented by Fig. 16-19 or 16-20b can be represented by the Fourier series

$$g_m = a_0 + a_1 \cos \omega_0 t + a_2 \cos 2\omega_0 t + \cdots \qquad (16\text{-}9)$$

where g_m = instantaneous signal-grid transconductance
   $\omega_0/2\pi$ = frequency of local oscillator
a_0, a_1, etc. = coefficients determined by shape of the curve of g_m as a
   function of time, according to Eq. (16-10)
By the usual method of determining the coefficients of a Fourier series, one has

$$a_0 = \frac{1}{2\pi} \int_0^{\omega_0 t = 2\pi} g_m \, d(\omega_0 t) \qquad (16\text{-}10a)$$

$$a_n = \frac{1}{\pi} \int_0^{\omega_0 t = 2\pi} g_m \cos n\omega_0 t \, d(\omega_0 t) \qquad (16\text{-}10b)$$

The plate current i_p that flows at any instant as the result of the application of a small signal voltage $E_s \sin \omega_s t$ is the product of this instantaneous signal voltage and the instantaneous signal-grid transconductance as given by Eq. (16-9) and so can be written

$$i_p = a_0 E_s \sin \omega_s t + a_1 E_s \sin \omega_s t \cos \omega_0 t$$
$$+ a_2 E_s \sin \omega_s t \cos 2\omega_0 t + \cdots \qquad (16\text{-}11)$$

Expanding terms of the type $\sin \omega_s t \cos \omega_0 t$ in terms of the sum and difference of two angles gives

$$i_p = a_0 E_s \sin \omega_s t + \frac{a_1}{2} E_s [\sin (\omega_s - \omega_0)t + \sin (\omega_s + \omega_0 t)]$$

$$+ \frac{a_2}{2} E_s [\sin (\omega_s - 2\omega_0)t + \sin (\omega_s + 2\omega_0)t] + \cdots \qquad (16\text{-}12)$$

Examination of Eq. (16-12) shows that the plate current contains a component having a difference frequency $(\omega_s - \omega_0)/2\pi$ and a magnitude $a_1 E_s/2$. The term $a_1/2$ is termed the *conversion transconductance* g_c. It

---

[1] Mixer tubes are normally designed so that the signal-grid electrode has a variable-mu characteristic. This is so that the amplitude of the translated output signal can be controlled over a wide range by varying the bias on the signal grid, just as in a tuned amplifier (see p. 411).

[2] The method of analysis presented here was first described by E. W. Herold, The Operation of Frequency Converters and Mixers for Superheterodyne Reception, *Proc. IRE*, vol. 30, p. 8, February, 1942.

is analogous to the transconductance g_m of an amplifier and represents the factor which, when multiplied by the amplitude of the applied signal, will give the amplitude of the difference-frequency component of the plate current. The conversion transconductance g_c for the difference frequency is seen from Eq. (16-10b) to have the value

$$g_c = \frac{1}{2\pi} \int_0^{2\pi} g_m \cos \omega_0 t \, d(\omega_0 t) \qquad (16\text{-}13)$$

The conversion transconductance will normally be greatest when the oscillator grid bias approximates cutoff and the local oscillator voltage has sufficient amplitude to make the instantaneous transconductance as high as possible during most of each positive half cycle of the local oscillator voltage (see Fig. 16-19). Under these conditions, the conversion transconductance will typically lie between 25 and 30 per cent of the maximum signal-grid-to-plate transconductance reached during the oscillator cycle.

Harmonic and Sum-frequency Operation of Mixers. Examination of Eq. (16-12) shows that, in addition to the difference frequency, the mixer output also contains components of the type $(\omega_s - n\omega_0)/2\pi$, where n can be 2, 3, etc. Thus, instead of operating the local oscillator at a frequency such that $(\omega_s - \omega_0)/2\pi$ is the desired difference frequency, one can instead operate the oscillator at one-half, one-third, etc., of this frequency. Such harmonic operation is sometimes used where practical considerations make it inconvenient to operate the oscillator at the high frequency otherwise required. The conversion transconductance for operation of the nth harmonic is $a_n/2$, where a_n is defined as in Eq. (16-10b). Optimum harmonic operation is obtained when the bias on the oscillator electrode is somewhat greater than the bias for fundamental operation, and correspondingly larger peak oscillator voltages are then required. With optimum adjustment, the numerical value of the conversion transconductance for second-harmonic operation is approximately half that for fundamental operation; for third-harmonic operation it is about one-third the value for the fundamental mode.

Equation (16-12) also shows that the output of the mixer contains components of the type $(\omega_s + n\omega_0)2\pi$, where n is an integer that can have values 1, 2, 3, etc. These sum-frequency components, usually the one for $n = 1$, find use where the frequency to which the signal is to be transformed is greater than the signal frequency. The numerical values of conversion transconductance for sum-frequency operation are the same as the numerical values for the corresponding difference-frequency operation; i.e., the fundamental modes will have the same conversion transconductance in both cases; likewise the second-harmonic modes will be about half the numerical value for the fundamental mode, etc.

Equivalent Plate Circuit of Mixer Tubes. With respect to currents and voltages of the translated frequency, the mixer tubes discussed above have the equivalent plate circuits of Fig. 16-21. These are analogous to the corresponding equivalent circuits of the amplifier given in Fig. 8-4, but with the difference that g_c now replaces the transconductance g_m, while the plate resistance r_p is replaced by an equivalent mixer plate resistance $r_p'' = \mu/g_c$, where μ is the ordinary amplification factor of the signal grid relative to the plate with respect to plate current.[1]

The application of the equivalent circuit of Fig. 16-21a to a typical situation where the mixer output has a pentode characteristic (that is, $r_p'' >> Z_L$) shows that the amplification of the mixer, i.e., the ratio of output voltage E_{if} at the translated or intermediate frequency, to the applied voltage E_s at signal fre-

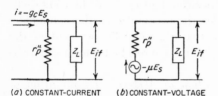

$i = -g_c E_s$

(a) CONSTANT-CURRENT GENERATOR FORM   (b) CONSTANT-VOLTAGE GENERATOR FORM

Fig. 16-21. Constant-current and constant-voltage forms of the equivalent plate circuit of a mixer tube.

quency is

Mixer amplification $= g_c Z_L$

$$(16\text{-}14)$$

where Z_L is the load impedance that the plate circuit offers to the translated frequency. Equation (16-14) is analogous to the corresponding Eq. (12-1) of the pentode amplifier, and shows that the amplification of a mixer is less by the factor g_c/g_m than the amplification of the same tube when used as an intermediate-frequency amplifier with the same load impedance at intermediate frequencies. Thus a converter stage will typically give from one-third to one-fourth of the voltage amplification of a corresponding stage of intermediate-frequency amplification using a tube of approximately the same transconductance.

16-13. Noise in Mixer Tubes. The smallest signal that may be usefully handled in a mixer is limited by the noise generated by the mixer tube. The magnitude of this tube noise can be obtained by considering the mixer to be an amplifier at the output (i.e., intermediate) frequency, and then averaging the intermediate-frequency noise power over the plate-current variations occurring during one local oscillator cycle. The result can be conveniently expressed in terms of an equivalent grid resistance R_{eq}, as discussed in Sec. 12-13. However, as applied to the mixer situation, R_{eq} is the resistance that when placed in series with the signal grid circuit of a noiseless tube will generate just enough signal-frequency

[1] In the case of mixers having a pentode or screen grid output characteristic, r_p'' is so very large that it can be neglected in Fig. 16-21a. However, in the case of a triode mixer the equivalent mixer plate resistance can by no means be neglected, even though it is typically three or four times the ordinary plate resistance of the same triode used as an amplifier. While the equivalent circuit of Fig. 16-21a still applies to triode mixers, it is often more convenient to convert this circuit to the equivalent constant-voltage form of Fig. 16-21b.

noise, so that after conversion to the intermediate frequency, this noise will exactly equal the amount of intermediate-frequency noise actually present. Formulas analogous to those of Eqs. (12-39) and (12-40), which give the approximate value of equivalent mixer noise resistance R_{eq}, are as follows:[1]

Triode plate detection mixers:

$$R_{eq} = \frac{4}{g_c} \tag{16-15}$$

Pentode plate detection mixers:

$$R_{eq} = \frac{I_b}{I_b + I_{c2}} \left(\frac{4}{g_c} + \frac{20 I_{c2}}{g_c{}^2} \right) \tag{16-16}$$

Pentagrid converters and pentagrid mixers:

$$R_{eq} = \frac{20 I_b}{g_c{}^2 I_{sp}} (I_{sp} - I_b) \tag{16-17}$$

In these equations g_c is the conversion transconductance, while I_{sp}, I_b, and I_{c2} are the total space current, plate current, and screen current, respectively, averaged over the oscillator cycle.

Values of the equivalent noise resistance of representative mixer tubes are given in Table 12-3. It will be noted that the equivalent resistance of triode and pentode mixers is of the order of four times the equivalent noise resistance of the corresponding amplifier, the difference being accounted for primarily by the fact that the conversion transconductance of the mixer tube is about one-fourth the transconductance for amplifier operation. The equivalent noise resistance of pentagrid mixer and converter tubes may be from twenty to a hundred times the noise resistance of the pentode mixer. This difference arises from the fact that in such tubes the plate current is only a small, rather than a large, fraction of the total space current, causing the partition noise to be excessive.

Relative Merits of Different Mixer Types with Respect to Noise. Examination of Eqs. (16-15) to (16-17) and of Table 12-3 shows that the triode plate mixer has the lowest equivalent noise resistance, while the pentagrid mixer and pentagrid converter are by far the worst with respect to noise. Thus under conditions where low mixer noise is important, as is commonly the case in ultra-high-frequency television, etc., triode mixers are generally preferred. Conversely in applications where mixer noise is unimportant, as is ordinarily the case in the standard broadcast receiver and in many short-wave and high-frequency applications, pentagrid converters are used because of their simplicity and economy.

---

[1] These formulas originated with W. A. Harris, Fluctuations in Vacuum-tube Amplifiers and Input Systems, *RCA Rev.*, vol. 5, p. 505, April, 1941. They do not take into account induced grid noise (see p. 439), which should be treated as part of the applied signal and added to the noise arising from R_{eq}.

16-14. Crystal Diode Mixers.[1]   At frequencies above about 1000 Mc, the most satisfactory mixer available is a silicon crystal diode rectifier. Vacuum-tube types of mixers, even including vacuum diodes, are found to be inferior to crystal mixers at these higher frequencies as a result of transit-time and noise effects.   Germanium diodes are an alternative to the silicon type, but at microwave frequencies the latter generally have an over-all superiority when the desirability of low conversion loss, low noise, ability to stand momentary overloads, and the maintenance of response to very high frequencies are all taken into account.

The schematic circuit of a crystal mixer system is illustrated in Fig. 16-22.   Signal and local oscillator voltages are superimposed to form a heterodyne signal, such as illus-

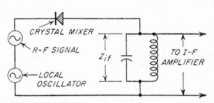

FIG. 16-22. Schematic circuit of a crystal mixer.

trated in Fig. 16-16c.   This combined wave is then rectified by the crystal mixer, thereby producing a difference-frequency current that develops the output voltage across the impedance Z_{if} provided by a tuned circuit resonant at the difference frequency.

A typical silicon crystal diode is illustrated schematically in Fig. 16-23a. It consists essentially of a pointed tungsten wire made in the form of a spring that presses against the surface of a silicon wafer suitably "doped" with impurities.   Rectification occurs at the point contact in accordance with the principles discussed in Sec. 21-16; a typical voltage-current characteristic is shown in Fig. 21-23c.

For purposes of design, the crystal diode can be regarded as having the equivalent electrical circuit illustrated in Fig. 16-23b.   Here R, termed the "spreading resistance," represents the resistance that the body of the crystal offers to the current flowing away from the region of the point contact.   The nonlinear resistance that gives rise to the rectification is represented by r; this resistance will be small to voltages in the conducting direction and large to voltages in the nonconducting direction.   Capacitance C represents the capacitance of the barrier layer that is the seat of the rectification.   The inductance L_0 of the tungsten wire and the capacitance C_0 of the crystal holder can be used as part of the resonant

[1] Useful summary papers on this subject include J. H. Scaff and R. S. Ohl, The Development of Silicon Crystal Rectifiers for Microwave Radar Receivers, *Bell System Tech. J.*, vol. 26, p. 1, January, 1947; R. Bleaney, J. W. Ryde, and T. H. Kinman, Crystal Valves, *J. IEE*, vol. 93, pt. IIIA (*Radiolocation Conv.*), p. 847, 1946; C. F. Edwards, Microwave Mixers, *Proc. IRE*, vol. 35, p. 1181, November, 1944; W. W. Stephens, Crystal Rectifiers, *Electronics*, vol. 19, p. 112, July, 1946. More detailed treatments are to be found in the books "Crystal Rectifiers" and "Microwave Mixers" (Vols., 15 and 16, Radiation Laboratory Series), McGraw-Hill Book Company, Inc., New York, 1948.

system associated with the crystal, and thus their only effect is to modify slightly the conditions giving resonance. In contrast, r, R, and C are related to the rectifying action, and so affect the ability of the crystal mixer to operate satisfactorily at very high frequencies. In a mixer designed to operate at a wavelength of the order of 10 cm, typical values of R and C are 30 ohms and 0.3 $\mu\mu f$, respectively.

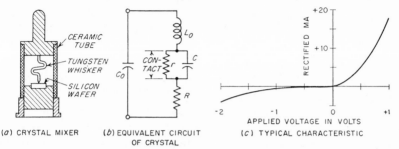

(a) CRYSTAL MIXER   (b) EQUIVALENT CIRCUIT   (c) TYPICAL CHARACTERISTIC
OF CRYSTAL

FIG. 16-23. Crystal-mixer unit, its equivalent circuit, and a voltage-current characteristic of a typical silicon crystal mixer.

Practical Operating Considerations—Conversion Loss and Noise Temperature. Figure 16-24 shows a typical arrangement for carrying out at microwave frequencies the functions illustrated schematically in Fig. 16-22. Here A is a resonant transmission line three-quarters of a wavelength long, with a silicon crystal mounted at the open end as shown. The signal is fed through transmission line B, which is coupled to the resonant line A by probe D in such a manner as to provide an impedance match between transmission line B and the resonant system consisting of the line A and its associated crystal. Local oscillator power is introduced into transmission line B through branch line C that is loosely coupled to B by means of probe E, as indicated. The intermediate-frequency output developed by the mixer is brought out through transmission line A'', which is an extension of A but isolated by by-pass capacitance F. The output of this line is coupled to the tuned input circuit of the intermediate-frequency amplifier.

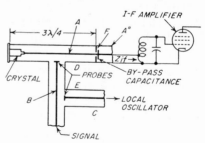

FIG. 16-24. Typical crystal-mixer system for microwaves.

A crystal mixer will possess a good performance only when operated under proper conditions. A reasonably good impedance match should exist between the crystal unit and the source of signal power, so that the crystal will absorb as much as possible of the available signal power. The local oscillator energy should be so injected that as little as possible of the signal power finds its way into the circuits of the local oscillator; in Fig. 16-24 this is achieved by making the coupling between probe E and the transmission line B quite small. It is also important that the tuned input circuit of the intermediate-frequency amplifier be so coupled as to provide a load impedance Z_{if} at the intermediate frequency that will match the output impedance of the crystal. In this way as much as possible of the available intermediate-frequency power will be usefully employed. Since the effective input and output impedances of a crystal diode are of the order of a few hundred ohms or less, the impedance-matching problems encountered with crystal mixers differ greatly from those that arise when using vacuum-tube mixers, for example, a pentagrid converter. Also the input and output impedances will depend upon the amplitude of the local oscillations.

The ratio of the available intermediate-frequency output power to the signal input power available to be supplied to the crystal is termed the *conversion loss*, and is ordinarily expressed in decibels. Values of conversion loss of 6 to 10 db are typical in a microwave mixer, corresponding to a ratio of intermediate-frequency output power to signal-frequency input power of from 0.25 to 0.10. The part of the input power supplied to the crystal by the signal that does not reappear as intermediate-frequency output power is dissipated as resistance loss within the crystal. The conversion loss in crystal mixers ordinarily decreases with increasing amplitude of the local oscillations.

The intermediate-frequency noise developed by the output circuit of a crystal rectifier is in excess of the thermal-agitation noise of the crystal output resistance as calculated by Eq. (12-37), assuming room temperature. This situation can be taken into account by assuming that the crystal acts as though its output resistance were at an absolute temperature higher than the absolute room temperature. The ratio t of the equivalent noise temperature to the actual room temperature is typically of the order of 1.5 to 3.0.

The "noisiness" of a crystal mixer is defined quantitatively in terms of the noise figure F of the crystal, analogous to the noise figure of an amplifier as defined in Sec. 12-14. If F is expressed as a power ratio (not in decibels), then

$$F = Lt \tag{16-18}$$

Here L is the conversion loss expressed as a power ratio greater than unity (i.e., $L = 6$ db corresponds to a power ratio of 4, and a power gain of 0.25). Equation (16-18) follows from the fact that the available output noise power of the mixer is t times that of an ideal system of the same output resistance, while the available output signal power is $1/L$ times the available signal input power. Thus the signal-to-noise ratio of the crystal output is Lt times worse than in an ideal system having no excess noise and no loss of signal power.

The equivalent noise temperature will increase as the rectified current produced by the local oscillator becomes greater. For this reason the best amplitude for the local oscillator is a compromise between a large value that gives low conversion loss and a small value that gives minimum noise. Optimum operating conditions typically correspond to an oscillator amplitude that will produce a rectified direct current in the range 0.3 to 1.0 ma. This represents a power of the order of 1 mw absorbed by the crystal from the local oscillator.

A bias voltage applied to a crystal in such a direction as to oppose the flow of the rectified direct current will always increase the noise. For this reason, the d-c load resistance offered to the rectified current must be low, since the d-c voltage drop produced across such a resistance in the circuit represents a bias that increases the noise generated by the crystal.

The intermediate-frequency load impedance Z_{if} associated with a crystal mixer has some influence on the input impedance that the crystal offers to the radio-frequency signal. Similarly the source impedance of the radio-frequency signal will likewise have some influence on the equivalent output impedance that the crystal presents to the intermediate-frequency load. The magnitude of these interaction effects depends upon the conversion loss, and will be considerable when nearly all of the input power is delivered to the output terminals in the form of rectified power, i.e., when the conversion loss is low. However, with silicon crystal mixers operated under conditions giving a low noise figure, the conversion loss is sufficiently high so that the interaction between input and output systems is too small to be of much importance in practical design.[1]

Silicon crystal mixers can be designed to operate satisfactorily up to frequencies in excess of 25,000 Mc, and are superior to all types of vacuum-tube mixers at frequencies above about 1000 to 2000 Mc. At still lower frequencies either silicon or germanium crystals can be used as mixers, but vacuum-tube triodes become competitive, and in most cases are superior.[2]

PROBLEMS AND EXERCISES

16-1. Show by sketches how the oscillograms of Fig. 16-1b and c would be changed if (a) R were increased, and (b) C were decreased but R kept unchanged.

---

[1] The actual behavior can be represented by means of an equivalent π network; for further information either consult "Radio Engineering," 3d ed., pp. 535–538, or see E. W. Herold, Some Aspects of Radio Reception at Ultra-high Frequency— Frequency Mixing in Diodes, *Proc. IRE*, vol. 31, p. 575, October, 1943. This subject is also discussed in "Microwave Mixers," *op. cit.*, pp. 68–75.

[2] Vacuum-tube diodes can also be employed as mixers, but do not find much practical use. This is because at the microwave frequencies crystals have lower noise figures, while at frequencies of the order of 1000 Mc and less, triode mixers are at least equal to diodes with respect to noise, and at the same time introduce amplification instead of a conversion loss.

16-2. Explain the detailed mechanism accounting for the fact that the efficiency of rectification of a diode detector is increased by (a) increasing the load resistance R, and (b) decreasing the plate resistance of the diode.

16-3. An unmodulated voltage of 10 volts effective is applied to a diode detector in which the load resistance is 500,000 ohms. A microammeter shows that the rectified d-c current in this resistance is 26 μa.

a. What is the efficiency of rectification?

b. What is the input resistance of the detector?

16-4. a. In the circuit of Fig. 16-2a what requirements must C_3 satisfy?

b. Discuss the consequences of making R_1 (1) appreciably smaller, and (2) appreciably larger, than the value indicated.

c. What are the consequences of making C_1 (1) appreciably smaller, and (2) appreciably larger, than the value indicated?

16-5. Assume that a wave modulated 50 per cent and having a carrier amplitude of 15 volts effective is applied to the input terminals of the diode detector of Fig. 16-2, and assume that the efficiency of rectification is 0.90. Calculate the d-c voltage developed for automatic-volume-control purposes, and the modulation-frequency voltage developed across R_4 at moderate modulation frequencies such that the by-passing of capacitors C_2 and C_3 is fully effective.

16-6. Determine the degree of modulation of the rectified current flowing through the diode under the conditions of Prob. 16-5.

16-7. In a diode detector, the indication of a d-c microammeter located in series with the load resistance will not be affected by the presence or absence of modulation, provided there is no clipping of the negative peaks. However, the microammeter reading will increase whenever there is either diagonal or negative peak clipping. Explain why this is the case.

16-8. If the voltage applied to the input terminals of the diode of Fig. 16-2 is completely modulated, calculate the percentage of the negative peak amplitude that is clipped off. Assume that $\eta = 0.90$, and that the modulation frequency is low enough so that capacitances C and C_1 produce negligible shunting action.

16-9. In the diode detector of Fig. 16-1, $R = 250,000$ ohms, $C = 100$ $\mu\mu$f, and $\eta = 0.85$. Calculate and plot, as a function of modulation frequency up to 20,000 cycles, (a) the highest degree of modulation that the applied modulated wave can have without introducing clipping distortion, and (b) the magnitude and phase angle of the input impedance to the upper sideband.

16-10. a. Prove that the input impedance the diode detector in Fig. 16-1 offers to the sidebands varies with modulation frequency in the same way as does the impedance of a resonant curve, with the resonant frequency corresponding to the carrier frequency.

b. Derive formulas for the impedance at resonance, the half-power bandwidth, and the equivalent Q of the impedance curve representing the input impedance.

16-11. Prove the statement made in the last sentence of the footnote on page 554.

16-12. a. Assume that in the diode detector circuit of Fig. 16-2 the resistance R_1 is shunted by an inductance large enough to have a reactance that considerably exceeds R_1 at all modulation frequencies of importance. If the inductance has a low d-c resistance, what is the maximum degree of modulation that the voltage at the diode input terminals may have without negative peak clipping occurring?

b. Discuss the effect that this shunting inductance has upon the tendency for the modulation of the applied signal to be reduced by the diode.

16-13. Discuss in qualitative terms the variation of magnitude and phase of the ratio Z_m/R_0 in Fig. 16-2 as the modulation frequency is reduced from a moderate value to a value approaching zero.

16-14. It is observed experimentally that for a given value of $|Z_m/R_0|$, the harmonic distortion of the output voltage wave, and the change in d-c rectified current associated with peak clipping, will be less when the clipping is of the diagonal type than when it is negative peak clipping. Explain how this observation is consistent with the oscillograms of Fig. 16-4*b* and *c*.

16-15. Justify the fact that the variation of diode output voltage with modulation frequency is (*a*) largely unaffected by the diode input impedance when this impedance is large compared with the radio-frequency source impedance, and (*b*) proportional to the diode load impedance when the diode input impedance is small compared with the source impedance.

16-16. Recalculate the example on page 556 on the assumption that the source impedance of the tuned input circuit is (*a*) 80,000 ohms, and (*b*) 320,000 ohms. From the results thus obtained, together with those given in the example in the text, discuss the effect of source impedance upon the amplitude distortion that a completely modulated original signal could be expected to experience from negative peak clipping.

16-17. Explain why in a Class B plate detector employing a pentode tube, it is generally inadvisable to operate the screen at a lower voltage than the plate if doing so requires deriving the screen voltage from a series resistance associated with a screen by-passing capacitor, such as R_{sg} and C_{sg} in the corresponding amplifier circuit of Fig. 8-1*c*.

16-18. Is there any difference between a square-law plate detector and an amplifier that possesses second-order distortion?

16-19. It is desired to operate a tube as a square-law detector over a certain range of voltages. It is found, however, that over this range the tube characteristic possesses a considerable third-order component, although the fourth- and higher-order components are very small. Will the tube under these conditions develop a rectified d-c current that is proportional to the square of the effective value of the applied voltage? Give reasons for your answer.

16-20. Prove the statements made in the footnote on page 559 regarding the distortion resulting from square-law detection of a sinusoidally modulated wave.

16-21. In the diode vacuum-tube voltmeter of Fig. 16-8*a* it would be possible to indicate the output voltage directly by means of a portable microammeter inserted in series with resistance *R* if this resistance were made moderately low such as 10,000 ohms. What would be the chief disadvantage of such an arrangement?

16-22. *a.* The situation illustrated in Fig. 16-6 approximates linear half-wave rectification. Sketch the shape of tube characteristic that would give square-law half-wave detection of the same signal, and draw oscillograms analogous to those of Fig. 16-6, but applying to this case.

b. Does the average value of the rectified current now reproduce the modulation envelope as faithfully as for the case illustrated in Fig. 16-6?

16-23. Derive a formula giving the effect of the resistance *R* and the meter resistance R_m on the sensitivity of the indication in Fig. 16-9.

16-24. Justify the correctness of the statements made on page 562 relative to the behavior of a linear half-wave Class B plate-detector voltmeter with respect to the various wave shapes of Fig. 16-10.

16-25. Compare the response of different types of vacuum-tube voltmeters to a square wave such as illustrated in Fig. 9-16*a* with the response to a sine wave of the same peak amplitude.

16-26. Demonstrate, with the aid of sketches similar to those of Fig. 16-10, that when a second harmonic is present in the wave being measured with a diode voltmeter, the magnitude of the indication, and also the amount of turnover present, will vary as the phase of the harmonic changes. Also show that when a third instead of second harmonic is involved, the phase of the harmonic affects the magnitude of the voltage indication, but does not alter the situation with respect to turnover.

16-27. Draw a series of rotating vectors analogous to the series in Fig. 16-11, but applying to the case where the wave consists of two sidebands with carrier removed. Show that the results obtained are consistent with Fig. 15-12c.

16-28. Demonstrate with the aid of rotating vectors that when a wave with sinusoidal amplitude modulation is applied to a tuned circuit in which the resonant frequency coincides with the carrier frequency, that the discrimination against the sideband frequencies resulting from the selectivity of the circuit does not distort the shape of the envelope of the wave, but rather only reduces the degree of modulation and shifts the phase of the modulation.

16-29. Explain why the ability to suppress weaker modulations discussed on page 565 is fully effective only when the strong desired signal is not completely modulated.

16-30. In a superregenerative detector, what effect would be produced by operating conditions which did not permit the oscillations to die out to a smaller amplitude than the circuit noise during the nonoscillating period?

16-31. Identify in Fig. 16-15d those time intervals during which a superregenerative system will be sensitive to incoming noise, and also those time intervals during which incoming noise will have no effect on the output.

16-32. Draw two sets of oscillograms similar to those of Fig. 16-16a and b, except that in one case the signal oscillations lag 90° in phase with respect to their phase for the other case. Then in each case add the signal and local oscillations to obtain a result analogous to Fig. 16-16c. Note the difference in phase of the resulting envelopes in the two cases, and show that this phase difference is consistent with the results that would be obtained from the rotating vector method.

16-33. Go through the steps of deriving Eq. (16-8) from Eq. (16-7). Call attention explicitly to the point at which the approximation involved in this transformation is made.

16-34. Would it be possible to obtain mixer action in a triode by applying the signal to the control grid and using power developed from the local oscillator to provide the plate-supply voltage of the tube? Give adequate justification of the answer made.

16-35. In a triode or pentode mixer, application of the signal and local oscillator voltages to the control grid and cathode, respectively, will not eliminate all coupling between these circuits. Explain why some coupling will still exist in this situation.

16-36. In a pentagrid mixer it is found that there is some signal-frequency current flowing in the local oscillator circuit associated with grid G_3 even when this grid is so operated that it is negative at all times throughout the oscillator cycle. This effect is observed to be proportional to frequency. Explain.

16-37. In the pentagrid converter of Fig. 16-18 it is found that difference-frequency output current flows in the circuit of G_2 as well as in the plate circuit. Explain, and discuss the phase relations of the difference-frequency currents flowing in these two circuits.

16-38. Explain how a very small capacitance between G_1 and G_3, as in Fig. 16-18, will deliver a current to the input circuit in approximately the correct phase to neutralize the current induced by space-charge coupling, and explain why this neutralizing action is independent of frequency even though the current through the neutralizing capacitance is proportional to frequency.

16-39. What would be the disadvantage in a pentagrid mixer of applying the signal voltage to grid G_3 and the local oscillator voltage to G_1?

16-40. In mixer operation, such as illustrated in Figs. 16-19 and 16-20, what would be the disadvantages, if any, of readjusting the bias voltage in Fig. 16-19 to be (a) considerably greater than cutoff, and (b) appreciably less than cutoff? Assume in each case that the amplitude of the local oscillator voltage is readjusted so that the oscillator grid is driven the same amount positive.

16-41. What is the penalty of operating the mixer tube of Fig. 16-19 with appreciably less oscillator voltage applied to the oscillator grid than is shown in **Fig. 16-19**? Assume no change in oscillator-grid bias.

16-42. A pentagrid converter will give best mixer performance when the oscillator section of the tube operates under conditions that approximate Class B action. Explain why this is more desirable than Class C action in the oscillator.

16-43. Explain with the aid of Eq. (16-10b) why the conversion transconductance obtainable for harmonic operation will be higher when the signal-grid-to-plate transconductance in Fig. 16-19 is zero for more than half the time, instead of being zero for half the time as illustrated in Fig. 16-19.

16-44. A 6SJ7 pentode tube, such as appears in Table 6-1, page 186, is used as a plate-detection mixer. The plate-coupling system is such that for amplifier operation at the operating conditions given in Table 6-1, page 186, the voltage amplification at the difference frequency would be 140. Estimate the ratio of intermediate-frequency voltage obtained from the output of the mixer to the signal voltage that is applied to the control grid.

16-45. When a particular pentagrid mixer is operated as a triode by connecting all grids except the first to the plate it has $g_m = 6500$ μmhos and $I_b = 10$ ma. When this tube is reconnected to act as a pentode mixer it has $I_b = 8$ ma and $I_{c2} = 2$ ma, and when used as a pentagrid mixer it has $I_{sp} = 10$ ma and $I_b = 2.5$ ma. Estimate the values of equivalent noise resistance R_{eq} for these three arrangements, assuming that the signal-grid-to-plate transconductance, and hence the conversion transconductance, will be proportional to plate current.

16-46. *a.* A 6SA7 mixer operated under the conditions given in Table 12-3, page 438, has applied to it a signal voltage developed across a circuit with a parallel resonant impedance of 50,000 ohms. Calculate the signal voltage that must be developed across this circuit in order to achieve a 20-db signal-to-noise ratio in the mixer output for a bandwidth of 10 kc. Assume that the room temperature is 291°K. Be sure to take into account circuit as well as tube noise.

b. Repeat the calculations when the 6SA7 tube is replaced by a 6AC7 pentode mixer.

c. Would there be any substantial further improvement in the behavior if a triode mixer were used in place of the pentode mixer?

16-47. Note that in the equivalent circuit of Fig. 16-22 no source impedance is shown for either the local oscillator or the signal voltages. Sketch these in. Since signal power is inevitably lost in the local-oscillator impedance, state whether the circuit shown is better adapted to high- or low-impedance local-oscillator sources. Show an alternative circuit for the opposite type of local-oscillator impedance.

16-48. With the aid of the equivalent circuit of Fig. 16-23b, discuss the reason that the signal-frequency voltage that is developed across the rectifying contact of a crystal by a given amount of signal-power input to the crystal drops off at very high frequencies.

16-49. *a.* Derive a formula in terms of r, R, C, and ω, giving the total *power* that must be supplied to the equivalent circuit of Fig. 16-23b, i.e., the power that will be dissipated in r and R, to develop a given voltage E across the contact.

b. On the basis of this formula, explain why the output power of a given crystal mixer is found to fall off very rapidly when the frequency increases above a critical value, and why best operation at high frequencies is obtained with crystal units characterized by inherently low barrier layer capacitance in proportion to r and R.

16-50. From experiments with a particular crystal, it is found that the ratio of intermediate-frequency output power to signal-frequency input power is 0.18, and that replacing the crystal by a resistance equal to the crystal output resistance reduces the noise power at the intermediate frequency to 0.60 times the value for the crystal. What is the noise figure of the crystal?

16-51. A crystal mixer has a noise figure of 8 db and a noise temperature ratio of 1.6. What is the noise figure (expressed in decibels) of the crystal mixer?

CHAPTER 17

FREQUENCY MODULATION

17-1. Frequency-modulated Waves.[1] In frequency modulation, the *instantaneous* frequency of the radio-frequency wave is varied in accordance with the signal to be modulated on the wave, while the amplitude of the radio-frequency wave is kept constant. This results in oscillations of the character illustrated in Fig. 17-1. Here the number of times per second that the instantaneous frequency is varied about the average (or carrier frequency) is the modulating frequency, while the *amount* that the frequency varies away from the average, often called the *frequency deviation*, is proportional to the amplitude of the modulating signal. Thus, if

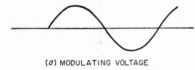

(*a*) MODULATING VOLTAGE

(*b*) FREQUENCY-MODULATED VOLTAGE

Fig. 17-1. Frequency-modulated wave in which instantaneous frequency varies in accordance with the modulating voltage.

a 500-cycle sound wave is to be transmitted by frequency modulation of a 1,000,000-cycle carrier wave, this could be done by varying the instantaneous frequency between 1,000,010 and 999,990 cycles, 500 times a second. If the pitch of the sound wave is increased to 1000 cycles, the instantaneous frequency would be varied between the same two limits 1000 times a second, while a sound wave of twice the intensity will be transmitted by varying the instantaneous carrier frequency through twice the frequency range, i.e., from 1,000,020 to 999,980 cycles in the above case, and a sound wave 1000 times as strong would correspond to a frequency deviation of 10,000 cycles.

Analysis of Frequency-modulated Waves. In order to understand the quantitative relations existing in a frequency-modulated wave, it is necessary first to have a clear understanding of the meaning of instantaneous frequency f_i and the associated instantaneous angular velocity $\omega_i = 2\pi f_i$. To do this one first writes the equation of an a-c wave in the generalized form

$$e = A \sin \phi(t) \tag{17-1}$$

[1] An excellent survey paper on this subject is W. L. Everitt, Frequency Modulation, *Trans. AIEE*, vol. 59, p. 613, November, 1940.

Here e = instantaneous amplitude

A = peak amplitude

$\phi(t)$ = total angular displacement at the time t

The instantaneous angular velocity ω_i is then by definition the instantaneous rate of increase $d\phi(t)/dt$ of angular displacement $\phi(t)$. One can therefore write

$$\text{Instantaneous angular velocity} = \omega_i = 2\pi f_i = \frac{d\phi(t)}{dt} \qquad (17\text{-}2)$$

A sinusoidal wave of constant frequency is a special case of Eq. (17-2). Thus if in this instance the frequency is designated as f_c corresponding to the angular velocity $\omega_c = 2\pi f_c$, then

$$\phi(t) = \omega_c t + \theta \qquad (17\text{-}3)$$

where θ is the angular position at $t = 0$. Application of Eq. (17-2) yields the result

$$\omega_i = \frac{d\phi(t)}{dt} = \omega_c \qquad (17\text{-}4)$$

The instantaneous frequency corresponding to Eq. (17-4) is $\omega_c/2\pi = f_c$, which checks the original postulation.

A frequency-modulated wave with sinusoidal modulation is by definition a wave in which the instantaneous angular velocity is varied according to the relation[1]

$$\omega_i = \omega_c + 2\pi \, \Delta f \cos \omega_m t \qquad (17\text{-}5)$$

where ω_i = instantaneous angular velocity

ω_c = angular velocity of carrier wave (i.e., of unmodulated wave)

= average angular velocity

ω_m = 2π times the modulating frequency f_m

Δf = maximum deviation of instantaneous frequency from average

A fundamental characteristic of a frequency-modulated wave is that the frequency deviation Δf is proportional to the peak amplitude of the modulating signal, and is independent of the modulating frequency.

The equation of the frequency-modulated wave is now obtained by combining Eqs. (17-2) and (17-5) to give a value of $\phi(t)$ that can be substituted into Eq. (17-1). This operation results in the relation[2,3]

---

[1] This implies that the instantaneous value of the modulating voltage varies in accordance with $\cos \omega_m t$.

[2] The steps involved are as follows:

$$\omega_i = d\phi(t)/dt = \omega_c + 2\pi \, \Delta f \cos \omega_m t$$

Integrating gives

$$\phi(t) = \omega_c t + (2\pi \, \Delta f/\omega_m) \sin \omega_m t + \theta \qquad (17\text{-}7)$$

The constant of integration θ in Eq. (17-7) defines the angular position at time $t = 0$. Equation (17-6) is then obtained by substituting Eq. (17-7) into Eq. (17-1), and assuming $\theta = 0$ for the sake of simplicity.

[3] It is to be noted that the oscillations represented by Eq. (17-6) occur most rapidly

$$e = A \sin \left(\omega_c t + \frac{2\pi \, \Delta f}{\omega_m} \sin \omega_m t \right) \tag{17-6}$$

This is commonly written in the form

$$e = A \sin (\omega_c t + m_f \sin \omega_m t) \tag{17-8}$$

where m_f is termed the *modulation index* of the frequency-modulated wave and has the definition

$$m_f = \text{modulation index} = \frac{\text{frequency deviation}}{\text{modulating frequency}} = \frac{\Delta f}{f_m} \tag{17-9}$$

It will be noted that, for a given frequency deviation, the modulation index m_f varies inversely as the modulating frequency.

Frequency Spectrum of Frequency-modulated Waves. A superficial examination of Eq. (17-8) might lead one to believe

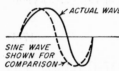

FIG. 17-2. Large-scale reproduction of a single cycle of a frequency-modulated wave for an instant when the frequency is increasing, showing in an exaggerated way how the wave shapes are not sinusoidal.

that intelligence could be transmitted by frequency modulation with an extremely narrow frequency band. Thus, in the case cited at the beginning of this section, it might appear that only 20 cycles bandwidth is required to transmit the 500-cycle signal. This is an incorrect conclusion drawn from Eq. (17-8) because the variations in the instantaneous frequency prevent the individual cycles from being exactly sinusoidal in shape, so one cannot treat these oscillations as though they were sine waves. This is illustrated in Fig. 17-2 where it is apparent that, since the changing frequency causes the time required to complete one quarter of a cycle to differ from the time required to complete the next quarter cycle, the actual wave is a distorted sinusoidal oscillation.

The frequency components actually contained in the wave represented by Eq. (17-8) can be determined by expanding the right-hand side by the trigonometric formula for the sum of two angles and evaluating the resulting expression. This gives[1]

---

when $\sin \omega_m t = 0$ rather than when $\sin \omega_m t = 1$. This is consistent with Eq. (17-5) which states that the highest instantaneous frequency occurs when $\cos \omega_m t = 1$.

[1] The transformation is carried out as follows: Equation (17-8) can be written

$$e = A[\sin \omega_c t \cos (m_f \sin \omega_m t) + \cos \omega_c t \sin (m_f \sin \omega_m t)] \tag{17-11}$$

But one has (see, for example, Woods, "Advanced Calculus," p. 281)

$$\cos (m_f \sin \omega_m t) = J_0(m_f) + 2J_2(m_f) \cos 2\omega_m t + 2J_4(m_f) \cos 4\omega_m t + \cdots \tag{17-12a}$$

$$\sin (m_f \sin \omega_m t) = 2J_1(m_f) \sin \omega_m t + 2J_3(m_f) \sin 3\omega_m t + \cdots \tag{17-12b}$$

Substituting Eqs. (17-12) into (17-11) and expanding the resulting trigonometric terms into the sum and difference angles gives Eq. (17-10).

$$e = A\{J_0(m_f) \sin \omega_c t$$
$$+ J_1(m_f)[\sin (\omega_c + \omega_m)t - \sin (\omega_c - \omega_m)t]$$
$$+ J_2(m_f)[\sin (\omega_c + 2\omega_m)t + \sin (\omega_c - 2\omega_m)t]$$
$$+ J_3(m_f)[\sin (\omega_c + 3\omega_m)t - \sin (\omega_c - 3\omega_m)t]$$
$$+ \cdots\} \tag{17-10}$$

where $J_n(m_f)$ means the Bessel function of the first kind and nth order, with argument m_f.

The analysis leading to Eq. (17-10) shows that the distorted oscillation corresponding to a wave with sinusoidal frequency modulation is made up of frequency components spaced by the modulating frequency. Thus, in the case of 500-cycle modulation, there would be, in addition to the carrier wave, a pair of first-order sidebands differing from the carrier frequency by 500 cycles and having an amplitude proportional to $J_1(m_f)$, a pair of second-order sidebands located $2 \times 500 = 1000$ cycles on either side of the carrier frequency and having amplitudes proportional to $J_2(m_f)$, etc. A frequency-modulated wave accordingly not only has the same frequency components as does an amplitude-modulated wave transmitting the same intelligence, but in addition has higher-order sidebands as well.

The amplitude of the different frequency components for the case of sinusoidal modulation depends upon the modulation index m_f, and can be either calculated with the aid of a table of Bessel's functions or obtained from Fig. 17-3. The character of the frequency spectra obtained under different conditions with frequency modulation is illustrated in Fig. 17-4. When the modulation index is less than 0.5, i.e., when the frequency deviation is less than half the modulating frequency, the second- and higher-order sideband components are relatively small, and the frequency band required to accommodate the essential part of the signal is the same as in amplitude modulation.[1] Also the amplitude of the first-order sidebands is then almost exactly proportional to the modulation index. On the other hand, when the modulation index m_f exceeds unity, i.e., when the frequency deviation is greater than the modulating frequency, there are important higher-order sideband components contained in the wave.

A useful rule is that a frequency-modulated wave contains sideband components of importance on either side of the carrier wave over a frequency interval approximating the sum of the frequency deviation and the modulating frequency. The total bandwidth in which most of the energy of the wave is contained is then twice this value. The various frequencies within this band will be spaced at frequency intervals that are

[1] Under these conditions the only difference between a frequency- and an amplitude-modulated wave is that the phase of the carrier relative to the sidebands differs by 90°, as explained in Sec. 17-3.

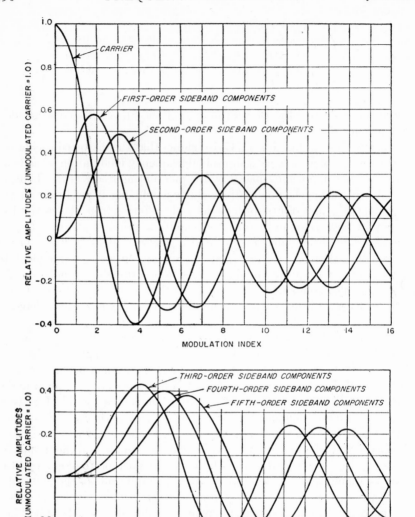

Fig. 17-3. Amplitude of frequency components of a frequency- or phase-modulated wave. In the case of the sidebands, the amplitude shown is the amplitude of the individual sideband component, and not of the pair of companion sidebands taken together.

equal to the modulating frequency, and so will be closer together the lower the modulating frequency.   It will be noted that, when the modulation index m_f is appreciably greater than unity, the bandwidth occupied by the two sidebands will be approximately twice the frequency deviation and will be only slightly affected by the modulating frequency.

Examination of Eq. (17-10) or Fig. 17-3 shows that, unlike the amplitude-modulated case, the amplitude of the carrier component of a frequency-modulated wave depends upon the intensity of the modulation. In fact, for certain values of the modulation index, the carrier amplitude is zero, and the entire frequency-modulated wave consists of sideband components of various orders.

When the instantaneous frequency of a frequency-modulated wave is varied in a more complex manner than that corresponding to sinusoidal modulation, the frequency spectrum becomes very complicated. The

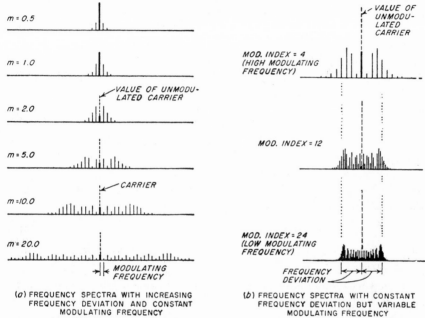

(a) FREQUENCY SPECTRA WITH INCREASING FREQUENCY DEVIATION AND CONSTANT MODULATING FREQUENCY

(b) FREQUENCY SPECTRA WITH CONSTANT FREQUENCY DEVIATION BUT VARIABLE MODULATING FREQUENCY

FIG. 17-4. Frequency spectra of frequency-modulated waves under various conditions.

sideband frequencies present include not only those that would be obtained with each modulation frequency acting separately, but likewise include various combination frequencies. However, although complex modulation greatly increases the number of frequency components present in a frequency-modulated wave, it does not widen the frequency band occupied by the energy of the wave. To a first approximation, this band is still approximately twice the sum of the maximum frequency deviation at the peak of the modulation cycle plus the highest modulating frequency involved.

Effect of Frequency Multiplication, Frequency Division, and Frequency Translation upon Frequency-modulated Waves. When a frequency-modulated wave is passed through a harmonic generator, the effect is to increase the modulation index by a factor equal to the frequency multiplication involved. Similarly, if the frequency-modulated wave is passed through a frequency divider, the effect is to reduce the modulation index by the factor of frequency division. Thus, the frequency components contained in the wave, and consequently the bandwidth of the wave, will be increased or decreased, respectively, by frequency multiplication or frequency division. No distortion in the nature of the modulation is introduced by the frequency change, however.

When a frequency-modulated wave is translated in the frequency spectrum by heterodyne action (see Sec. 16-10), the modulation index, and hence the relative positions of the sideband frequencies and also the bandwidths occupied by them, remain unchanged.

17-2. Phase Modulation. A phase-modulated wave is a sine wave such as represented by Eq. (17-3) in which the value of the reference phase θ is varied so that its magnitude is proportional to the instantaneous amplitude of the modulating signal. Thus for sinusoidal phase modulation at a frequency $f_m = \omega_m/2\pi$ one would have[1]

$$\theta = \theta_0 + m_p \sin \omega_m t \qquad (17\text{-}13)$$

where θ_0 is the phase in the absence of modulation, while m_p is the maximum value of the phase change introduced by modulation, and is called the *modulation index for phase modulation*. Substituting this expression for θ in Eq. (17-3) and in turn substituting the result in Eq. (17-1) give the equation of the phase-modulated wave as

$$e = A \sin (\omega_c t + m_p \sin \omega_m t) \qquad (17\text{-}14)$$

where A is the amplitude of the wave, and for the sake of simplicity, it is assumed that $\theta_0 = 0$. A comparison of Eqs. (17-8) and (17-14) shows that the phase-modulated wave contains the same sideband components as does the frequency-modulated wave, and if the modulation indexes in the two cases are the same, the relative amplitudes of these different components will also be the same. Thus the only difference between phase modulation and frequency modulation is the process by which a definition of the modulation index m is arrived at.

Further understanding of phase modulation can be gained by studying the factors that determine the instantaneous frequency of the phase-modulated wave. Applying the definition of instantaneous angular velocity given by Eq. (17-2) to the phase-modulated wave given by Eq. (17-14) results in

$$\left.\begin{array}{l}\text{Instantaneous angular velocity}\\ \text{of phase-modulated wave}\end{array}\right\} = \omega_c + \omega_m m_p \cos \omega_m t \qquad (17\text{-}15)$$

[1] This implies that the instantaneous value of the modulating voltage varies in accordance with sin $\omega_m t$. It will be noted that this is 90° different from the case of Eq. (17-5); thus to produce a phase-modulated wave that is identical in phase with the oscillations of a frequency-modulated wave, the modulating voltages must differ in phase by 90° in the two cases.

Comparison of this relation with Eq. (17-5) shows that the maximum frequency deviation $(\Delta f)_p$ produced by phase modulation is $\omega_m m_p/2\pi$, or

$$(\Delta f)_p = f_m m_p \tag{17-16}$$

Since the modulation index m_p for phase modulation is proportional to the modulating signal and independent of its frequency, it follows that the frequency deviation in a phase-modulated wave is proportional both to the amplitude and to the frequency of the modulating signal. In contrast, the frequency deviation of a frequency-modulated wave is independent of the modulating frequency. *Thus it can be said that modulation of phase is merely a way of obtaining a frequency-modulated wave in which the frequency deviation will be proportional to the modulating frequency.*

The phase-modulation process can therefore be used to generate a true frequency-modulated wave by arranging so that the amplitude of the voltage actually used to produce the phase variation is the signal modified by passage through a network in which the transmission is inversely proportional to frequency,[1] instead of being the actual modulating signal. If the voltage appearing at the output of such a network is then used to control the instantaneous phase, the result is exactly the same as if the original signal were employed to control the instantaneous frequency.

The relation that exists between phase-modulated and frequency-modulated waves can now be explained in simple physical terms. Thus a wave in which the instantaneous frequency is higher than the average or carrier frequency can be thought of as *changing*, i.e., advancing, in phase with respect to the carrier, since it completes each cycle of 2π radians faster than does the lower-frequency wave. This is illustrated in Fig. 17-5. Here, if the lower-frequency or solid-line wave is taken as the reference, then the higher-frequency wave, shown dotted, advances in phase by $\Delta\theta$ radians per cycle. Conversely, a wave that is advancing in phase has a higher instantaneous frequency than if its phase is not changing. Thus there is a direct relation between the *deviation* Δf of the instantaneous frequency and the *rate of change of phase*. A consequence of this situation is that when the phase is varied through a given range (i.e., phase modulation), then since the rate of change of phase is necessarily proportional to the modulating frequency, the frequency deviation of this phase-modulated wave will be proportional to the modulating frequency.

Since a wave that is varying in instantaneous frequency (frequency modulation) is alternatively advancing and retarding in phase position, such a wave can also be regarded as modulated in phase. A comparison

---

[1] A suitable network consists of a resistance-capacitance series circuit in which the resistance is much higher than the capacitive reactance. The voltage developed across the capacitor of such a circuit will be inversely proportional to the frequency of the voltage applied to the combination.

of Eq. (17-8) with Eq. (17-14) shows that the maximum phase shift in radians that a frequency-modulated wave experiences during the modulation cycle is m_f, the modulation index for frequency modulation. This phase shift will be directly proportional to the deviation Δf of the instantaneous frequency, since the phase change $\Delta\theta$ per radio-frequency cycle is proportional to Δf (see Fig. 17-5). It will also be inversely proportional to the modulating frequency, since the length of time, and hence the number of radio-frequency cycles, during which the instantaneous frequency is continuously higher than the average value and thus advancing in phase are inversely proportional to the modulating frequency. It is to be noted that this interpretation is consistent with Eq. (17-14).

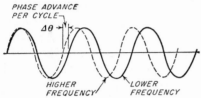

PHASE ADVANCE PER CYCLE

$\Delta\theta$

HIGHER FREQUENCY   LOWER FREQUENCY

Fig. 17-5. Comparison of waves of slightly different frequencies, showing how the higher-frequency wave may be regarded as advancing steadily in phase with respect to the lower-frequency wave.

Combinations of Amplitude Modulation with Phase and Frequency Modulation. Amplitude-modulated waves often possess frequency or phase modulation as incidental by-products. Thus in the plate-modulated oscillator, the plate-supply voltage of the oscillator tube is varied in accordance with the modulating signal and since the generated frequency ordinarily depends to some extent upon the plate voltage, the oscillations actually generated will therefore possess both frequency and amplitude modulation. For this reason, modulated oscillators are practically never used in radio communication.

Combined phase and amplitude modulation can occur in a number of ways. For example, if the tank circuit of a modulated amplifier or linear amplifier is not tuned exactly to resonance, a phase shift is introduced that varies with the amplitude of the wave. Another cause of simultaneous amplitude and phase modulation is energy transfer between the carrier wave after modulation and the unmodulated exciting frequency. The combination in this way of modulated and unmodulated waves can result in a phase shift that varies with the modulation, as discussed below in connection with Fig. 17-10.

The frequency spectrum of a wave having combined amplitude and frequency (or phase) modulation is quite complicated. Thus each frequency component associated with the frequency modulation can be considered as a separate carrier that is individually amplitude-modulated. The exact behavior for sinusoidal modulation can be obtained by substituting for A in Eq. (17-6) the value $A_m(1 + m_a \sin \omega_s t)$, where m_a is the degree of modulation for amplitude modulation and A_m is the average amplitude. However, the resulting mathematics becomes quite messy. It is sufficient to say that, in addition to the added complexity of the frequency spectrum that results when frequency (or phase) modulation is combined with amplitude modulation, the corresponding sideband frequencies on the opposite sides of the carrier do not necessarily have the same amplitude any more.

17-3. Relation of Frequency- and Phase-modulated Waves to Amplitude-modulated Waves. When the modulation index of a frequency- or phase-modulated wave is small compared with unity, the wave

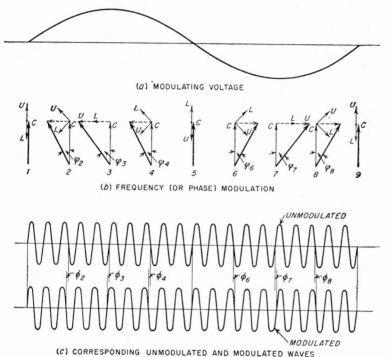

(a) MODULATING VOLTAGE

(b) FREQUENCY (OR PHASE) MODULATION

(c) CORRESPONDING UNMODULATED AND MODULATED WAVES

Fig. 17-6. Rotating vector representation of a frequency-modulated wave with small modulation index. Comparison with Fig. 16-11 shows that the difference with respect to the corresponding amplitude-modulated wave with the same sidebands is in the phase relation between the carrier and the sidebands.

contains exactly the same frequency components as does an amplitude-modulated wave having the same modulating frequency. The question then arises as to what is the difference between an amplitude-modulated wave and a frequency-modulated wave with small modulation index. The answer is obtained by comparing Eq. (1-3) with the first three terms in Eq. (17-10). The difference is that in the frequency-modulated case the sideband frequencies are shifted 90° in phase with respect to the phase relations that exist in amplitude modulation of the same carrier.[1]

The way in which the sideband frequencies introduce a phase shift, and

[1] Alternatively, it can be said that the difference between the two cases is a 90° phase shift of the carrier wave with respect to the sidebands.

hence a frequency deviation, in the frequency-modulated wave with small modulation index can be shown with the aid of rotating vectors as in Fig. 17-6. Here the sideband vectors L and U differ 90° in phase from the corresponding amplitude-modulated case of Fig. 16-11. This causes the resultant voltage of the wave (shown by the heavy vectors) to oscillate in relative phase position but to change little in magnitude.[1] This is in contrast with the corresponding amplitude-modulated case of Fig. 16-11, where the resultant voltage oscillates in magnitude, but does not change in phase.

17-4. Response of Networks to Frequency-modulated Waves. When the modulation index is less than unity, the effect of a network on a frequency-modulated (or phase-modulated) wave can be readily obtained by expressing the applied voltage in terms of its carrier and sideband components. The effect of the network on each of these frequency components is then calculated separately, and the network output obtained as the sum of the component waves.[2] This method is practical, however, only when sinusoidal modulation is used and the modulation index is small; otherwise, there are so many frequency components that the amount of labor involved is prohibitive.

An alternative procedure is to assume that the response of the network to a frequency-modulated voltage at any instant is the same as the steady-state sine-wave behavior that would be calculated on the basis of a sinusoidal applied voltage having a frequency equal to the instantaneous frequency of the frequency-modulated wave at that instant. This method can be referred to as the *quasi-steady-state* method of analysis, and leads to an equation of the form

$$I_{qss} = E(\omega_i) Y(\omega_i) \qquad (17\text{-}17)$$

where ω_i = instantaneous angular velocity as defined by Eq. (17-2)

$E(\omega_i)$ = applied voltage having an instantaneous angular velocity ω_i that may vary with time

$Y(\omega_i)$ = admittance (or transfer admittance) at the angular velocity ω_i of the circuit to which the voltage $E(\omega_i)$ is applied

I_{qss} = current produced by $E(\omega_i)$ as calculated on the quasi-steady-state basis

The quasi-steady-state approach assumes that the instantaneous frequency that exists at the moment has been present for some time; it thus ignores the transient effects that arise from the fact that the frequency is

---

[1] What small change does occur is a result of the failure to take into account the relatively small second-order sidebands by means of additional vectors that rotate at twice the rate of L and U for second-order sidebands and still other vectors with appropriate amplitudes and rotational rates for the higher-order cases.

[2] The rotating vector method of Sec. 16-7 is often found useful in obtaining this sum, and in interpreting its practical significance.

continually varying. Under most conditions the resulting error is small; when this is the case Eq. (17-17) provides a simple and direct method of determining the response of a network to an applied frequency-modulated wave. Thus to obtain the network response in this way, one merely needs a curve of admittance (or transfer admittance) $Y(\omega_i)$ as a function of frequency over the range of instantaneous frequencies through which the applied voltage varies, together with a curve of the instantaneous frequency of the applied voltage wave $E(\omega_i)$ as a function of time. The applied voltage wave $E(\omega_i)$ at each instant is then multiplied by the

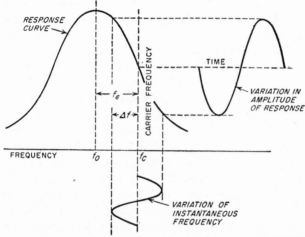

Fig. 17-7. Quasi-steady-state response of a resonant circuit to a frequency-modulated wave when the resonant circuit is detuned from the carrier frequency of the wave.

admittance $Y(\omega_i)$ applying to the instantaneous frequency possessed by the voltage wave at that instant. The resulting product gives the output wave, both in magnitude and phase, as a function of time. An example of this process is illustrated in Fig. 17-7, which shows the quasi-steady-state response of a resonant circuit to a frequency-modulated wave when the carrier (or average) frequency of the modulated wave lies on the side of the resonance curve.

The error in the quasi-steady-state analysis is to a first approximation taken into account by adding a correction term $Y_c(\omega_i,t)$ to $Y(\omega_i)$ in Eq. (17-17) to give an equivalent admittance $Y_{eq}(\omega_i,t)$ that is a function of time as well as of instantaneous frequency. When the modulation index appreciably exceeds unity, this equivalent admittance becomes[1]

$$Y_{eq}(\omega_i,t) = Y(\omega_i) + Y_c = Y(\omega_i) - \frac{j}{2}\frac{d\omega_i}{dt}\frac{d^2Y(\omega_i)}{d\omega_i{}^2} \qquad (17\text{-}18)$$

[1] See J. R. Carson and T. C. Fry, Variable Electric Circuit Theory with Application to the Theory of Frequency Modulation, *Bell System Tech. J.*, vol. 16, p. 513, October, 1937.

In the case of sinusoidal modulation, it follows from Eq. (17-5) that

$$\frac{d\omega_i}{dt} = -\omega_m \times 2\pi\Delta f \sin \omega_m t \tag{17-19}$$

Since the first term on the right-hand side of Eq. (17-18) is the quasi-steady-state admittance, the ratio $|Y_c(\omega_i,t)/Y(\omega_i)|$ is to a first approximation a measure of the error involved in the quasi-steady-state method of calculating behavior. Hence when the magnitude of the second term $Y_c(\omega_i,t)$ is relatively small compared with $Y(\omega_i)$, the quasi-steady-state method may be safely used. It therefore follows from Eq. (17-18) that the quasi-steady-state analysis applies quite accurately when (1) the maximum rate of change of instantaneous frequency is small [corresponding to sinusoidal modulation in which the product of frequency deviation and modulating frequency as given by Eq. (17-19) is not too large], or

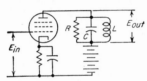

Fig. 17-8. Amplifier with resonant load impedance, used in illustrating application of quasi-steady-state method of determining the response of a circuit to a frequency-modulated wave.

(2) the curves giving magnitude and phase of the admittance $Y(\omega_i)$ as a function of frequency are both substantially linear over the range of instantaneous frequency involved. If condition 1 is fully met, i.e., if the instantaneous frequency changes only very slowly, then linearity of the admittance is unimportant. Similarly if condition 2 is satisfied, then results calculated by the quasi-steady-state analysis accurately give the circuit behavior irrespective of the rate of change of instantaneous frequency with time. To the extent that one of these requirements is only partially met, then the other must be more nearly satisfied if the quasi-steady-state results are to approximate the actual behavior.

The application of Eq. (17-18) to a practical situation can be illustrated by considering the response of the tuned amplifier of Fig. 17-8 to an input voltage consisting of a frequency-modulated wave with sinusoidal modulation as given by Eq. (17-5). Then

$$\text{Amplification} = \frac{g_m}{Y_{\text{eq}}} \tag{17-20}$$

where g_m is the transconductance of the tube, and Y_{eq} is the equivalent admittance of the parallel resonant circuit RLC, as given by Eq. (17-18). To evaluate Y_{eq} one notes that

$$Y(\omega_i) = \frac{1}{R} + j\left(\omega_i C - \frac{1}{\omega_i L}\right) \tag{17-21}$$

Then

$$\frac{d^2 Y(\omega_i)}{d\omega_i^2} = -j\frac{2}{\omega_i^3 L} \tag{17-22}$$

Substituting Eqs. (17-19), (17-21), and (17-22) into (17-18) gives

$$Y_{eq} = \left[\frac{1}{R} + j\left(\omega_i C - \frac{1}{\omega_i L}\right)\right] + \frac{1}{\omega_i L}\frac{\omega_m}{\omega_i}\frac{2\pi\,\Delta f}{\omega_i}\sin\,\omega_m t \quad (17\text{-}23)$$

The ratio of the magnitude of the second term to the magnitude of the first term gives the fractional error that results from assuming that the response is correctly given by the quasi-steady-state method. This ratio can be written

$$\left.\begin{array}{l}\text{Fractional} \\ \text{error}\end{array}\right\} = \frac{\text{2d term in } (17\text{-}23)}{Y(\omega_i)} = \left|\frac{\dfrac{\omega_m}{\omega_i}\dfrac{2\pi\,\Delta f}{\omega_i}\sin\,\omega_m t}{\dfrac{1}{Q_i} + j\left[\left(\dfrac{\omega_i}{\omega_0}\right)^2 - 1\right]}\right| \quad (17\text{-}24)$$

Here $Q_i = R/\omega_i L$ is the Q of the resonant system RLC at the instantaneous frequency,[1] while ω_0 is 2π times the resonant frequency $f_0 = 1/2\pi\sqrt{LC}$ of the resonant circuit.

Study of Eqs. (17-24) shows that the fractional error is less the lower the rate of change $d\omega_i/dt = \omega_m 2\pi\,\Delta f\sin\,\omega_m t$ of the instantaneous angular velocity. Such behavior is to be anticipated because the more slowly the instantaneous frequency $f_i = \omega_i/2\pi$ changes, the less the error that results from neglecting the fact that it changes at all. The error is also seen to vary during the modulation cycle in accordance with $\sin\,\omega_m t$. This is to be expected, since at $t = 0$, Eq. (17-19) shows that the instantaneous frequency is not changing at all, and there should then be no error in the quasi-steady-state analysis, as is indeed indicated by Eqs. (17-23) and (17-24). On the other hand, at $\omega_m t = 90°$, the instantaneous frequency is varying most rapidly, and the error as given by Eq. (17-24) is at a maximum. Study of the denominator of Eq. (17-24) also shows that the error will be less the lower the Q of the resonant system. This is because the lower the Q the less is the curvature of the admittance characteristic; i.e., the smaller will be $d^2 Y/d\omega^2$.

When the carrier frequency f_c of the applied wave does not differ greatly percentage-wise from the resonant frequency f_0, and if at the same time $\Delta f/f_c$ is small, as is true in all practical cases, Eq. (17-24) simplifies to[2]

$$\text{Maximum fractional error} = \frac{f_m}{f_c}\frac{\Delta f}{B + j2f_\delta} \quad (17\text{-}25)$$

[1] This definition of Q_i applies because R is here a shunt and not a series resistance.

[2] The steps involved are as follows: From Eq. (17-5) and Fig. 17-7 one can write

$$f_i = f_c + \Delta f\cos\,\omega_m t \quad (17\text{-}26)$$
$$f_c = f_0 + f_\delta \quad (17\text{-}27)$$

Substituting Eq. (17-26) in the numerator of Eq. (17-24) for $\omega_i/2\pi$, and noting that

Here B is the half-power bandwidth of the resonant circuit RLC as given by Eq. (12-4) and $f_\delta = f_c - f_0$ is the amount by which the carrier frequency exceeds the resonant frequency of the circuit (see Fig. 17-7).

Examination of Eq. (17-25) reveals that in the usual case where the modulating frequency is small compared with the carrier frequency, the error in the quasi-steady-state method of analysis will always be quite small when resonant circuits are involved, unless the frequency deviation Δf is very large compared with both the half-power bandwidth B of the system and the detuning f_δ of the resonant circuit from the carrier frequency.

17-5. Production of Frequency- and Phase-modulated Waves. There are a great many methods by which frequency modulation can be carried out. This section will describe a few of these, with particular emphasis on those methods that have had considerable commercial use. Although the discussion is from the point of view of frequency modulation, this involves no loss in generality because it has already been pointed out that frequency- and phase-modulated waves are essentially similar. In fact, some of the widely used methods of generating frequency-modulated waves are based upon phase-modulation processes.

Frequency-modulated Oscillator Using Reactance-tube Modulator. A simple and direct method of generating a frequency-modulated wave is

---

$\Delta f/f_c << 1$, so that $f_i \approx f_c$, gives

$$\text{Fractional error} = \frac{f_m}{f_c} \frac{\Delta f \sin \omega_m t}{(f_c/Q_i) + jf_c[(f_i/f_0)^2 - 1]} \tag{17-28}$$

To the extent that $f_c \approx f_0 \approx f_i$, one has

$$\text{Half-power bandwidth} = B \approx f_c/Q_i \tag{17-29}$$

The second term in the denominator can likewise be simplified by use of Eqs. (17-26) and (17-27):

$$
\begin{aligned}
f_c\left[\left(\frac{f_i}{f_0}\right)^2 - 1\right] &= f_c\left[\frac{(f_0 + f_\delta + \Delta f \cos \omega_m t)^2}{f_0^2} - 1\right] \\
&= f_c\left[\frac{2f_0(f_\delta + \Delta f \cos \omega_m t) + (f_\delta + \Delta f \cos \omega_m t)^2}{f_0^2}\right] \\
&= \frac{f_c}{f_0}\left[2(f_\delta + \Delta f \cos \omega_m t) + \frac{(f_\delta + \Delta f \cos \omega_m t)^2}{f_0}\right]
\end{aligned}
$$

Since $f_c \approx f_0$, while it has been assumed $(f_\delta + \Delta f \cos \omega_m t) << f_0$, then

$$f_c[(f_i/f_0)^2 - 1] \approx 2(f_\delta + \Delta f \cos \omega_m t) \tag{17-30}$$

Substitution of Eqs. (17-29) and (17-30) into Eq. (17-28) then leads to

$$\text{Fractional error} = \frac{f_m}{f_c} \frac{\Delta f \sin \omega_m t}{B + j2(f_\delta + \Delta f \cos \omega_m t)} \tag{17-31}$$

This expression is maximum when $\omega_m t = 90°$, for which condition it has the value given by Eq. (17-25).

to control the frequency of an oscillator by the modulating voltage.   The commonest method of doing this is with the aid of a reactance tube in a system such as illustrated in Fig. 17-9.   Here the tank circuit of an ordinary oscillator, shown as the Hartley oscillator of Fig. 14-2, is shunted by the plate-cathode circuit of a pentode, called a *reactance tube*, which is so arranged as to draw a reactive current that is varied in accordance with the modulating voltage.   This reactive current has an effect equivalent to shunting a reactance across the oscillator tank circuit, and so affects the generated frequency.

The reactance tube is an ordinary pentode, so arranged that when an alternating voltage is applied between plate and cathode, the resulting

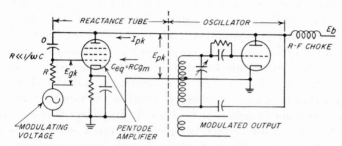

Fig. 17-9. Frequency modulation of an oscillator using a reactance tube.

plate current that flows is in quadrature with the plate-cathode voltage. Under these circumstances the tube behaves like a reactance to voltages applied between its plate and cathode.

A typical reactance-tube arrangement is shown in Fig. 17-9.   Here a voltage E_{gk} that is 90° out of phase with respect to the plate-cathode voltage E_{pk} is obtained by means of the resistance-capacitance phase splitter RC, in which R is made much smaller than the reactance of C.   Such an arrangement applies a voltage E_{gk} to the control grid that is 90° out of phase with the voltage E_{pk} and so causes the tube to draw an alternating plate current I_{pk} that leads E_{pk} by 90°.   Thus the action of the reactance tube is equivalent to shunting a capacitive reactance between the plate and ground of the oscillator tank circuit.   Frequency modulation is then obtained by applying the modulating voltage to the control grid of the reactance tube, superimposed upon the radio-frequency voltage.   This varies the transconductance of the reactance tube in accordance with the modulating voltage, and so varies the equivalent reactance offered to E_{pk} and hence the instantaneous frequency of the oscillator.[1]   If the

[1] The analysis of the reactance tube behavior can be carried out as follows: The oscillator frequency voltage E_{gk} applied between grid and cathode in Fig. 17-9 is $E_{pk} \dfrac{R}{R - j(1/\omega C)}$, where E_{pk} is the oscillator frequency plate-cathode voltage applied to

applied modulating voltage is not too large the variations in instantaneous frequency will be almost exactly proportional to the instantaneous amplitude of the modulating voltage.

Reactance-tube modulator systems are ordinarily operated at low power level, such as a few watts or less. The power is then raised to the desired level by means of Class C amplifiers and harmonic generators.

The output of a reactance-tube modulated oscillator ordinarily shows some amplitude modulation. This arises from the fact that the alternating current I_{pk} drawn by the plate of the reactance tube normally has a slight resistive component because it is an approximation to assume that $R - j(1/\omega C)$ in Eq. (17-32a) can be replaced by $-j(1/\omega C)$, and also because there is always some capacitance in shunt with R. This resistive current corresponds to a load on the oscillator tank circuit that varies in accordance with the modulation, and will hence vary the amplitude of the generated oscillation at the same time the frequency is being varied.

Such residual amplitude modulation can be removed by passing the frequency-modulated wave through a *limiter*, i.e., a device that develops an output that is substantially independent of the input voltage. Such limiting is commonly achieved by Class C amplifiers that are operated with sufficient exciting voltage to be well saturated (see Fig. 13-9).

Phase Modulators. Phase modulators are important in frequency-modulation work, because, as pointed out above, a frequency-modulated wave is obtained when the modulating voltage applied to a phase modulator is inversely proportional to the modulating frequency.

Many systems for producing phase modulation have been devised, each of which can be used to produce either phase or frequency-modulated waves. Several of the more frequently used and representative of these will now be described.[1]

---

the network RC. The resulting current I_{pk} flowing into the plate is

$$I_{pk} = g_m \frac{R}{R - j(1/\omega C)} E_{pk} \qquad (17\text{-}32a)$$

where g_m is the transconductance of the tube. Where $R << 1/\omega C$, this reduces to

$$I_{pk} = j[Rg_m/(1/\omega C)]E_{pk} \qquad (17\text{-}32b)$$

It will be noted that, in so far as E_{pk} is concerned, I_{pk} is a capacitive current and that the capacitive reactance offered by the plate-cathode circuit of the reactance tube to E_{pk} is

$$\left.\begin{array}{l}\text{Equivalent capacitive} \\ \text{reactance}\end{array}\right\} = E_{pk}/I_{pk} = Z_{eq} = -j[(1/\omega C)/Rg_m] \qquad (17\text{-}32c)$$

$$\text{Equivalent capacitance} = C_{eq} = CRg_m \qquad (17\text{-}32d)$$

[1] Space limitations prevent all of the types of phase modulators in common use from being described in these pages. An additional system of importance generates a phase shift by varying the instant during the cycle when a pulse is generated. Phase modulators of this type are capable of producing a modulation index approaching 2.0;

A very elementary form of phase modulator is illustrated in Fig. 17-10. Here an unmodulated wave E_A is combined with a somewhat smaller amplitude-modulated wave E_B having a carrier derived from the same source as E_A, but differing in phase from E_A by 90°. The phase of the resultant voltage then varies with the modulation as shown by vectors a, b, and c. It is possible in this way to obtain a substantially linear

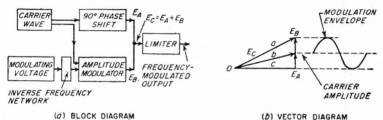

(a) BLOCK DIAGRAM   (b) VECTOR DIAGRAM

FIG. 17-10. Simple method of producing a phase-modulated wave. The inverse-frequency network is used if a frequency-modulated behavior is desired.

relationship between phase and modulating voltage up to a modulation index of about 0.25 (phase shift of $\pm 14°$). The slight variation in the amplitude of the resultant vector is eliminated by the limiter indicated in the block diagram. A simple circuit arrangement for carrying out the necessary operations (except limiting) is illustrated in Fig. 17-11. This is a grid-modulated amplifier (either Class A or Class C) in which the plate tank circuit has a very low Q and such low resonant impedance that the stage amplification is insufficient to give oscillation trouble from feedback through the grid-plate capacitance of the tube. In this circuit unmodulated carrier energy is delivered directly to the plate tank circuit with 90° phase shift through the grid-plate tube capacitance C_{gp}. At the same time, amplitude-modulated energy is present in the plate tank

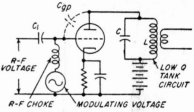

FIG. 17-11. Simple circuit arrangement for carrying out the operation indicated in Fig. 17-10.

circuit by normal grid-modulated amplifier action. Capacitor C_1 must be small enough to be an open circuit to the modulating voltage, and large enough to by-pass the radio frequency.

A second method of generating a phase-modulated or frequency-modulated wave, sometimes referred to as the Armstrong system, is shown

an example of such a system is given by James F. Gordon, A New Angular Velocity Modulation System Employing Pulse Techniques, *Proc. IRE*, vol. 34, p. 328, June, 1946. Again a special tube called the phasitron has been devised which varies the phase angle by control of an electron stream. This tube, which is capable of producing a modulation index of 6.0, is described by Robert Adler, A New System of Phase Modulation, *Proc. IRE*, vol. 35, p. 25, January, 1947.

schematically in Fig. 17-12. Here the output of a balanced modulator, consisting of the two sidebands with carrier suppressed, is combined with a somewhat larger unmodulated carrier wave that differs in phase by 90° from the carrier associated with the balanced modulator. This results in a frequency-modulated wave, as explained in connection with Fig. 17-6, since when the modulation index is small, the only difference

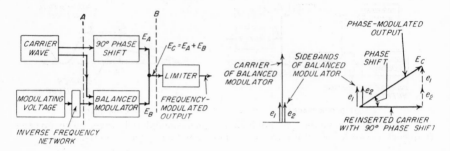

(a) BLOCK DIAGRAM   (b) VECTOR RELATIONS

FIG. 17-12. Armstrong type of phase modulator.

between an amplitude and a phase- or frequency-modulated wave is a 90° phase shift of the carrier with respect to the sidebands. It is possible with this arrangement to obtain a substantially linear relationship between the modulating voltage and phase shift up to a modulation index of approximately 0.5.

A particularly attractive method of obtaining phase modulation consists of employing a phase shifter that is controlled by the modulating

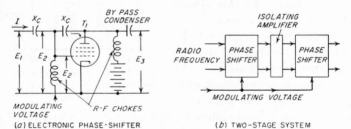

(a) ELECTRONIC PHASE-SHIFTER   (b) TWO-STAGE SYSTEM

FIG. 17-13. Phase-shifter type of phase modulator, together with two similar phase-shifter stages connected in cascade in order to increase the total phase shift.

voltage. The simplest and perhaps the most satisfactory arrangement of this type is illustrated in Fig. 17-13a.[1] It can be shown that in this circuit, variation of the transconductance g_m of tube T_1 has no effect on the magnitude of the output voltage, but will cause the phase of this voltage to vary over a total range of 180° as the transconductance varies

[1] This system is described in detail by S. M. Belaskas, Phase-modulation Circuit, *Proc. Natl. Electronics Conf.*, vol. 3, p. 654, 1947.

from zero to infinity.[1] Although the relationship between the phase shift and the transconductance is not linear, neither is the relationship between the modulating voltage applied to the control grid and the resulting transconductance of the tube. By properly balancing these nonlinearities against each other, it is easily possible to obtain a relationship between phase shift and modulating voltage that is reasonably linear up to phase shifts of the order of ± 1.0 radian.

In phase-shifter modulators, the maximum modulation index obtainable can be readily increased by connecting several modulators in cascade. A two-stage system of this type is illustrated schematically in Fig. 17-13b and gives twice as large a modulation index as does a single-stage arrangement; it is possible, morever, to employ as many stages as desired.

Systems of frequency modulation based on phase modulators have the advantage that the carrier frequency can be obtained directly from a crystal oscillator. They have the disadvantage, however, that the largest modulation index that can be obtained is smaller than in the case of a frequency-modulated oscillator. In order to obtain the relatively large values of modulation index required when a large frequency deviation is desired at a low modulation frequency, it thus becomes necessary to depend upon frequency multiplication in order to increase m_p to the value called for by Eq. (17-16). The amount of multiplication required will depend upon the modulation index that is initially produced. It will, for example, be much less with a cascaded system using a number of phase shifters of the type illustrated in Fig. 17-13 than with a one-stage system of the type illustrated in Fig. 17-11, which gives a maximum value of m_p of the order of 0.25.

17-6. Detection of Frequency- and Phase-modulated Waves. Detection of a frequency- or phase-modulated wave is ordinarily carried out by modifying the frequency spectrum of the wave in such a manner that its envelope fluctuates in accordance with the intelligence involved. The resulting amplitude-modulated wave is then applied to an ordinary

---

[1] This is demonstrated as follows: Referring to Fig. 17-13a, one can write:

$$I = E_2 g_m \qquad (17\text{-}33a)$$
$$E_2 = (E_1 + E_3)/2 \qquad (17\text{-}33b)$$
$$E_1 - E_3 = -j2X_cI = -j2X_cE_2 g_m \qquad (17\text{-}33c)$$

Substituting Eq. (17-33b) into Eq. (17-33c) to eliminate E_2 and reducing the result give

$$\frac{E_3}{E_1} = \frac{\text{output}}{\text{input}} = \frac{1 + jX_c g_m}{1 - jX_c g_m} \qquad (17\text{-}34)$$

Since $(1 + jX_c g_m)$ and $(1 - jX_c g_m)$ are conjugate quantities, the right-hand side of Eq. (17-34) is equal to unity irrespective of the value of g_m; however, the phase varies from 0 to 180° as g_m changes from zero to infinity.

amplitude-modulation detector.[1]   The circuit arrangement that transforms the frequency-modulated signal into a wave possessing amplitude modulation is termed a *discriminator*.

The detuned resonant circuit illustrated in Fig. 17-7 represents a simple form of discriminator.   Here variations in the instantaneous frequency of the applied wave produce corresponding variations in the amplitude of the response of the resonant circuit.   Such an arrangement has the disadvantage, however, that the side of a resonance curve cannot be regarded as particularly linear except over a very limited frequency range; also the characteristics of such a discriminator depend rather critically on the amount of detuning of the resonant circuit.[2]

The Phase-shift Discriminator.   The most widely used form of discriminator is the arrangement shown in Fig. 17-14a, in which the two tuned circuits P and S are resonant at the same frequency and are inductively coupled.   This arrangement depends upon phase shift for its operation and so is commonly called a *phase-shift discriminator*.[3]

The action of the discriminator of Fig. 17-14a can be explained as follows: The center of the secondary is connected to the top (high-potential) side of the primary P by the capacitor C that blocks the d-c plate voltage from the secondary system; C serves as a by-pass to signal frequency but need be no larger than required to do this.   Associated with C is radio-frequency choke L that provides a return path for the d-c component of the rectified current flowing through diodes T_1 and T_2. The inductance of L is effectively in shunt with inductance of P and is preferably considerably larger than L.

The radio-frequency voltages E_{a1} and E_{a2} applied to the two diodes are $E_3 + E_1$ and $E_3 - E_2$, respectively, where E_3 is the voltage across P and E_1 ($= E_2$) is the vector voltage across half the secondary coil as indicated in Fig. 17-14.

The phase relations existing in the discriminator are shown in Fig. 17-14b.   At the resonant frequency of the tuned secondary circuit, the

---

[1] Other methods of detecting a frequency-modulated wave are possible and find some use.   In particular, when a very linear relation is required between the detector output and the variations in the instantaneous frequency, as in measurement work, a cycle-counting type of frequency meter as in Fig. 18-47 is used.   Such an instrument will at any instant develop an output current exactly proportional to the instantaneous frequency; for further details see S. W. Seeley, C. N. Kimball, and A. Barco, Generation and Detection of Frequency-modulated Waves, *RCA Rev.*, vol. 6, p. 269, January, 1942; F. E. Terman and J. M. Pettit, "Electronic Measurements," p. 223, McGraw-Hill Book Company, Inc., New York, 1952.

[2] An analysis of this type of discriminator is given by A. R. Vallarino and Marilyn Buyer, Harmonic Distortion in Frequency-Modulation Off-resonance Discriminator, *Elec. Commun.*, vol. 26, p. 167, June, 1949.

[3] The phase-shift discriminator was originally developed as a means of obtaining automatic frequency control; see D. E. Foster and S. W. Seeley, Automatic Tuning, Simplified Circuits and Design Practice, *Proc. IRE*, vol. 25, p. 289, March, 1937.

secondary voltages E_1 and E_2 are in quadrature with the voltage E_3 existing across the primary inductance.[1]   However when the applied frequency is either higher or lower than the resonant frequency of the secondary, the phase position of E_1 and E_2 relative to E_3 will differ from 90°.

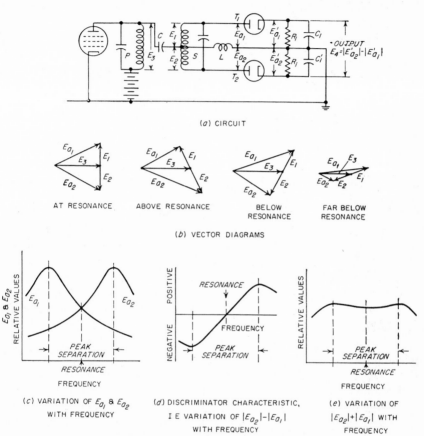

FIG. 17-14. Frequency-modulation detector employing phase-shift discriminator.

Thus when the instantaneous frequency differs from the resonant frequency f_0 by $f_0/2Q_s$ cycles, the phase shift will be 45° (or 135°).   The result of this situation is that at resonance the two resultant voltages E_{a1}

[1] This assumes that the impedance $(\omega M)^2/R_s$ that the secondary couples into the primary at resonance is small compared with the inductive reactance of the primary, which will always be true in practice.   With this simplification a voltage E_3 across the primary inductance induces a voltage in series with the secondary circuit that is in phase with E_3.   However, when the secondary is tuned to resonance, the voltage developed across the secondary inductance (or capacitance) is 90° out of phase with the voltage induced in series with the secondary circuit.   Thus the secondary voltage $E_1 + E_2$ is 90° out of phase with the primary voltage E_3 when the applied frequency coincides with the secondary resonant frequency.

and E_{a2} are equal in amplitude, but at frequencies slightly below resonance the amplitude of one of these voltages is decreased while that of the other becomes larger. Above resonance the situation is reversed. This is illustrated by the vector diagrams in Fig. 17-14b. The amplitudes of the voltages E_{a1} and E_{a2} will vary with instantaneous frequency in the general manner[1] shown in Fig. 17-14c.

Frequency-modulation Detectors Using the Phase-shift Discriminator. The two voltages E_{a1} and E_{a2} developed by the discriminator in Fig. 17-14a are separately rectified by the diodes T_1 and T_2 to produce output voltages E'_{a1} and E'_{a2} that reproduce the amplitudes of voltages E_{a1} and E_{a2} applied to the respective anodes. The individual diodes are, moreover, so arranged that the detector output voltage E_4 is the arithmetic difference $|E'_{a2}| - |E'_{a1}|$ between the rectified voltages developed by the individual diodes. The output voltage E_4 will therefore vary with instantaneous frequency in accordance with the difference $|E_{a2}| - |E_{a1}|$ between the two curves of Fig. 17-14c. Deviations in the instantaneous frequency away from the carrier frequency hence cause the rectified output voltage E_4 to vary in accordance with the curve of Fig. 17-14d, which is often called the *discriminator characteristic*. The result is that the rectified output voltage $E_4 = |E'_{a2}| - |E'_{a1}|$ will accurately reproduce the variations of the instantaneous frequency as long as operation is confined to the region between the peaks of E_{a1} and E_{a2}. The system of Fig. 17-14a thus acts as an excellent detector of frequency-modulated waves when the carrier frequency is at or near the center frequency of the discriminator characteristic.

The exact shape of the characteristic of Fig. 17-14d is a rather complicated function of the coupling between primary and secondary circuits, the absolute and relative Q's of these circuits, and the relative primary and secondary inductances.[2] Best results are obtained when the secondary inductance is equal to, or slightly greater than, the primary inductance, and when the effective Q's of the circuits are approximately equal

---

[1] The exact details are complicated by the fact that the voltages E_3 and $E_1 + E_2$ change in magnitude as well as relative phase as the frequency varies. Thus when the two resonant circuits are overcoupled, as is customary, E_3 and $E_1 + E_2$ have a double-peaked characteristic (See Sec. 3-5). Under these circumstances, increasing deviation of the signal frequency first causes these voltages to become larger until the frequency of the resonant peak is reached, after which both voltages rapidly diminish in amplitude. This is shown in Fig. 17-14b, where the second and third vector diagrams are for instantaneous frequencies closer to resonance than the coupling peak, whereas the final diagram applies to an instantaneous frequency somewhat below the low-frequency coupling peak.

[2] Quantitative analyses of discriminator behavior are given by K. R. Sturley, The Phase Discriminator, *Wireless Eng.*, vol. 21, p. 72, February, 1944; W. G. Tuller and T. P. Cheatham, Jr., Adjustable Bandwidth FM Discriminator, *Electronics*, vol. 20, p. 117, September, 1947.

when the loading of the diodes is taken into account.[1]   The coupling should simultaneously be of the order of twice the critical value.

When properly designed, the phase-shift discriminator will give a very linear relation over a range of instantaneous frequencies only slightly less than the frequency separation of the peaks of the individual curves of Fig. 17-14c.   This peak separation, which therefore must exceed twice the peak deviation Δf, is determined primarily by the Q's of the resonant circuits of the discriminator, but is affected somewhat by the coefficient of coupling.   When the coefficient of coupling is twice the critical value, the peak separation approximates $2f_0/Q$, and will be proportionately greater if the coefficient of coupling is higher.   Here f_0 is the resonant frequency of the secondary, and it is assumed that the Q's of the primary and secondary circuits are equal.   In proportioning the discriminator circuits, the Q that should be used is hence determined by the peak deviation Δf of the instantaneous frequency; for twice critical coupling, the proper value of Q is slightly less than $f_0/\Delta f$.

Many detailed variations are possible in frequency-modulation detectors using the phase-shift discriminator.   The circuit shown in Fig. 17-14a is particularly suitable for explaining the principles of operation.   Practical arrangements are, however, more likely to resemble the form illustrated in Fig. 17-15.   Here the ground connection is made to one of the output terminals, which causes capacitor C to perform the same function of capacitor C_1' in Fig. 17-14a.   In Fig. 17-15 it is necessary that C be small enough to offer a high impedance to modulation frequencies and yet large enough to serve as a by-pass to the radio-frequency signal.   By now rearranging the capacitor C_1 of Fig. 17-14a as shown in Fig. 17-15, the choke L of Fig. 17-14a is no longer necessary.   The circuit of Fig. 17-15 functions in exactly the same way as does the circuit of Fig. 17-14a, but has one output terminal grounded, and requires one less capacitor and no radio-frequency choke.   As an aid in tracing out the correspondence between these two circuits, the rectified voltages E_{a1}' and E_{a2}' appearing in different parts of the respective output systems are indicated in each circuit.

In practical arrangements, it is also customary to obtain the output through a resistance-capacitance combination $R_c C_c$, as shown dotted in Fig. 17-15.   In this way, there is no d-c voltage transmitted to the out-

---

[1] The input resistance of each diode in Fig. 17-14a is $R_1/2\eta$, where η is the efficiency of rectification.   With respect to the voltage $E_1 + E_2$ existing between the terminals of the secondary, the input resistances of the individual diodes are in series so that the diodes place a load R_1/η across the full secondary.   However, to the voltage E_3 developed across the primary circuit P the diode inputs are in parallel.   The equivalent load resistance that the diodes place on the primary is hence $R_1/4\eta$, a much lower value than the load on the secondary.   To achieve equality of Q's, it is therefore often found necessary to shunt the secondary with an additional resistance.

put terminals when the average or carrier frequency of the signal differs from the center frequency of the discriminator.

Frequency-modulation detectors based on the circuit of Fig. 17-14a (or Fig. 17-15) have the disadvantage that variations in the amplitude of the applied voltage produce a proportional change in the amplitude of the discriminator characteristic; this is shown in Fig. 17-16. Thus when

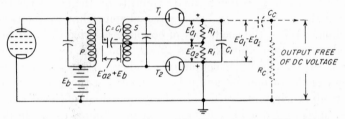

FIG. 17-15. Practical form of phase-shift discriminator of Fig. 17-14a.

the applied signal consists of a frequency-modulated wave that also varies in amplitude, the detector output will contain undesired components corresponding to the amplitude variations as well as the output representing the frequency modulation. This situation is generally to be avoided, since amplitude variations are commonly the result of interfering

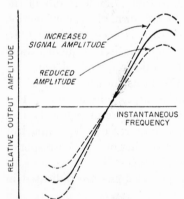

FIG. 17-16. Effect produced on the discriminator characteristic of Fig. 17-14d by changes in the amplitude of the applied frequency-modulated signal.

effects, such as noise. This limitation of detectors of the type shown in Figs. 17-14a and 17-15 is overcome in a modification known as the ratio detector.

17-7. The Ratio Detector.[1] The ratio detector is a modification of the phase-shift discriminator detector of Fig. 17-14a, which can be so designed as to be unresponsive to amplitude modulation while behaving toward frequency modulation in the same way as the detector of Fig. 17-14a.

The circuit of a simple form of the ratio detector is shown in Fig. 17-17a. Neglecting the capacitor C_2 for the moment, this arrangement is seen to differ from the detector of Fig. 17-14a only in that (1) diode T_2 has been reversed in polarity, and (2) the output voltage is obtained between ground and the center tap on the high resistance R_2 that shunts the load impedance of the two diodes.[2]

[1] For further discussion of this subject see S. W. Seeley and J. Avins, The Ratio Detector, *RCA Rev.*, vol. 8, p. 201, June, 1947.

[2] The radio-frequency choke and the capacitor C in Fig. 17-17a must meet the same requirements as in Fig. 17-14a.

It will now be shown that the output voltage in Fig. 17-17a varies with instantaneous frequency in exactly the same way as it does in the circuit of Fig. 17-14a, but is only half as great. To do this, it is to be noted first that the individual output voltages E'_{a1} and E'_{a2} developed by diodes T_1 and T_2 have the same magnitude as before. However, E'_{a2} is now reversed in polarity, so that the voltage E_4, instead of being $|E'_{a2}| - |E'_{a1}|$, as in Fig. 17-14a, is now $|E'_{a1}| + |E'_{a2}|$. The output voltage in Fig. 17-17a is the potential between the midpoint of R_2 and ground; its value is the potential E'_{a2} at the lower end of R_2, minus half the total voltage E_4 developed across R_2. Thus

$$\left.\begin{array}{l}\text{Output voltage}\\ \text{in Fig. 17-17}a\end{array}\right\} = |E'_{a2}| - \frac{|E'_{a1}| + |E'_{a2}|}{2} = \frac{|E'_{a2}| - |E'_{a1}|}{2} \quad (17\text{-}35)$$

This is exactly half the magnitude of the output obtained from the system of Fig. 17-14a. Thus, the ratio detector responds to variations in instantaneous frequency in exactly the same way as does the system of Fig. 17-14a.

Suppression of Response to Amplitude Modulation Occurring Simultaneously with Frequency Modulation.[1] Amplitude modulation simultaneously present with frequency modulation will not appear at the output of the ratio detector if the resistance R_2 is shunted by a capacitor C_2, and suitable resistors R'_2 are added to the circuit. It is necessary that C_2 be large enough to have a reactance at the lowest modulation frequency of importance that is small compared with the resistance R_2 in parallel with $2R_1$.

The effect of C_2 is to reduce greatly amplitude fluctuation in the voltage $E_4 = |E'_{a1}| + |E'_{a2}|$ appearing across R_2. This comes about through the fact that when C_2 is large, it acts as a low impedance load to any change in amplitude that might otherwise occur. For example, a momentary increase in amplitude of E_4 causes a large charging current to flow through the diodes into C_2. This represents power absorbed by the diodes from the resonant circuits P and S, and so causes the voltages that these circuits apply to the diodes to be reduced in magnitude. Conversely, if the amplitude of the incoming signal attempts momentarily to drop below the average amplitude, then C_2 attempts to prevent the voltage E_4 from dropping by supplying current that flows from C_2 into R_2 and R_1. This relieves the diode tubes of the necessity of supplying as much rectified current as before, thereby increasing their input impedance and reducing the loading on the resonant circuits P and S, with corresponding increase in the voltages they apply to the diodes. It is thus seen that the presence of C_2 reduces (but does not entirely eliminate) the amplitude variations that

[1] A quantitative analysis of amplitude-modulation rejection in the ratio detector is given by B. D. Loughlin, The Theory of Amplitude-modulation Rejection in the Ratio Detector, *Proc. IRE*, vol. 40, p. 289, March, 1952.

would otherwise occur in the voltage E_4, and likewise in voltages E_1, E_2, and E_3. It will also be noted that these variations in input impedance with amplitude modulation that are present also produce corresponding variations in the Q of the primary and secondary circuits P and S. Specifically, the effective Q's of the circuits will be reduced during the periods when the amplitude is greater than the carrier value, and will be increased when it is less.

Consider now the situation that exists when the incoming signal is a pure frequency-modulated wave. When C_2 is disconnected, the voltage

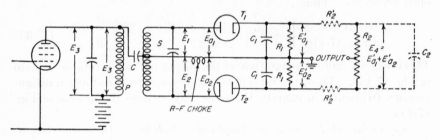

(a) BASIC CIRCUIT

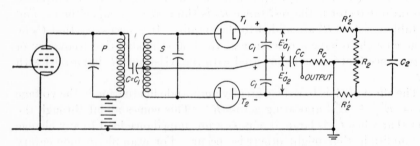

(b) PRACTICAL FORM OF RATIO DETECTOR CIRCUIT

FIG. 17-17. Ratio-detector circuits.

$|E'_{a1}| + |E'_{a2}|$ across resistance R_2 is proportional to $|E_{a1}| + |E_{a2}|$. This voltage varies with instantaneous frequency in the manner illustrated in Fig. 17-14e, and is seen to be substantially constant in the range of frequencies between the peaks of E_{a1} and E_{a2}. When C_2 is connected, it tends to make $|E'_{a1}| + |E'_{a2}|$ even more nearly constant than in Fig. 17-14c. This modifies the output voltage slightly in a way that is equivalent to increasing the discriminator output for instantaneous frequencies near the center frequency of the discriminator characteristic of Fig. 17-14d, and decreasing it slightly for instantaneous frequencies near the peaks. These effects are trivial in magnitude, however, and for all practical purposes the presence of C_2 can be regarded as having negligible influence on the detection of a wave possessing pure frequency modulation.

Next examine what happens when the amplitude of the frequency-modulated signal varies. The voltages E_1, E_2, and E_3 developed across the discriminator in Fig. 17-17a show corresponding but lesser variations in magnitude, as discussed above. At the same time, the effective Q of the resonant circuit S is altered in such a manner that Q becomes less when the amplitude increases above the average, and vice versa, as explained above. This change in secondary Q affects the phase relations between voltages E_3 and $E_1 + E_2$ in Fig. 17-14b. The consequences of these two actions have opposite effects on each other, because an increase in the amplitude of $E_1 + E_2$ and E_3 tends to make the detector output greater, while the reduction in Q and hence of phase shift that goes with increased amplitude of the signal tends to make the detector output less.

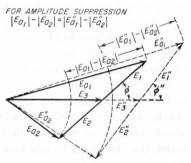

Thus by properly controlling the relative magnitudes of these two effects, they can be balanced against each other. When this is done, the output will be determined only by the variations in instantaneous frequency and the average amplitude of the incoming signal, and will be unaffected by amplitude variations at any modulation frequency for which C_2 is an effective by-pass.[1]

A vector diagram illustrating this behavior is shown in Fig. 17-18. Here the solid vectors correspond to the voltages E_1, E_2, and E_3 in the ab-

FIG. 17-18. Vector diagrams applying to a ratio detector, showing how a change in the amplitude of the applied voltages E_1, E_2, and E_3 is prevented from changing the discriminator voltage $|E_{a2}| - |E_{a1}|$ by the fact that as the vectors change in length, the angle ϕ simultaneously changes in magnitude.

sence of amplitude modulation when the instantaneous frequency is such as to cause the secondary circuit to shift the phase of the secondary voltages E_1 and E_2 by an amount ϕ. The dotted vectors illustrate what happens when the amplitude of the incoming waves is momentarily increased while maintaining the same frequency deviation. The corresponding vectors E_1'', E_2'', and E_3'' are now longer than before, but the phase shift ϕ'' produced by the same frequency deviation is less. With the conditions shown in Fig. 17-18, this change in phase angle is just enough to compensate for the increased length of the vectors, and results in the difference $|E_{a1}''| - |E_{a2}''|$ being the same for the dotted system as for the difference $|E_{a1}| - |E_{a2}|$ of the solid-line system.

The relative magnitudes of the effects that are thus to be balanced against each other can be controlled practically by means of the resistances R_2' shown in Fig. 17-17a. Increasing these resistances will decrease the variations in diode input resistance caused by a given amount of amplitude modulation; this causes the voltages E_1, E_2, and E_3 that actu-

---

[1] The name *ratio detector* arises from the fact that the variations in detector output that occur as the instantaneous frequency changes arise as a result of variations in the ratio $|E_{a1}'/E_{a2}'|$, while the sum $|E_{a1}'| + |E|_{a2}'$ remains substantially constant.

ally get applied to the diode to have their magnitude changed more and their phase position changed less by the amplitude modulation. Decreasing R_2' will have the opposite effect, accentuating shifts in the phase ϕ of $E_1 + E_2$ relative to E_3, while minimizing amplitude change in these voltages. Thus there is some particular value of R_2' for which amplitude modulation of the incoming signal will not affect the output of the ratio detector.

Practical Ratio-detector Circuits. Many variations in the circuit details of the ratio detector are possible. While the circuit of Fig. 17-17a is the arrangement best adapted to explain the principles involved, more practical forms are usually employed. An example is illustrated in Fig. 17-17b. Here, moving the ground to the center of R_2 makes it possible to omit the radio-frequency choke. Since this places the radio-frequency by-pass capacitor C effectively in shunt with the output terminals, it is now necessary, rather than being merely permissible, for this condenser to have a high impedance to modulation frequencies. A further simplification is made possible by omitting the two resistances R_1 of Fig. 17-17a, which were never really needed anyway, since R_2 provides a means by which the charge on C_1 can leak off in the circuits of both (a) and (b).

PROBLEMS AND EXERCISES

17-1. In Eq. (17-8) explain how the mathematics shows that the time required by an oscillation to go through one cycle is greatest when $m_f \sin \omega_m t$ is zero going negative.

17-2. Complete the detailed steps whereby Eq. (17-10) is obtained from Eqs. (17-11) and (17-12).

17-3. *a.* The following mathematical relation can be shown to be true for all values of x:

$$J_0{}^2(x) + 2 \sum_{n=1}^{n=\infty} J_n{}^2(x) = 1$$

Demonstrate that this relation proves that the energy contained in a sinusoidally modulated frequency-modulated wave is constant, irrespective of the frequency deviation or modulating frequency.

b. Explain how this relation shows that the sideband energy in a frequency-modulated wave is exactly the difference between the carrier energy of the unmodulated wave and the carrier energy of the modulated wave.

c. Verify the above equation by numerical values taken from Fig. 17-3 for a modulation index of 2.

17-4. A carrier wave is frequency modulated at 3000 cycles. What is the lowest value of frequency deviation for which all of the energy of the wave will be in the sidebands?

17-5. A carrier wave, having a crest amplitude of 10 volts and a frequency of 60 Mc, is modulated at 5000 cycles with a frequency deviation of 15 kc. From this information determine the amplitude of the carrier, and of the first-, second-, third-, fourth-, and fifth-order sideband components.

17-6. *a.* A frequency-modulated wave having a frequency deviation of 20 kc at a modulating frequency of 4 kc is passed through two harmonic generators connected in cascade. If the first generator doubles the frequency and the second triples the frequency, determine the frequency deviation and the modulation index of the ouput of the final harmonic generator.

b. What is the frequency separation of the adjacent sideband frequencies in the output of the final harmonic generator?

17-7. Follow through the detailed steps of deriving Eq. (17-14) from Eq. (17-13).

17-8. In a phase-modulation system, the phase shift at the peak of the modulating voltage is $\pm 75°$. What will be the modulation index, the frequency deviation, and the bandwidth in which most of the energy of a single sideband is concentrated, when the modulating frequency is (*a*) 100 cycles, and (*b*) 10,000 cycles?

17-9. A phase-modulated wave in which the peak phase shift is $\pm 75°$ is passed through a harmonic generator that triples the frequency. What effect (if any) does this have on (*a*) the maximum phase shift of the wave, and (*b*) the frequency difference between adjacent sidebands?

17-10. In a frequency-modulated wave, the frequency deviation is 25,000 cycles. What maximum phase deviation does this represent when the modulating frequency is (*a*) 100 cycles, and (*b*) 10,000 cycles?

17-11. Explain on a physical basis why the maximum deviation of the instantaneous frequency of a wave away from the carrier frequency, and the maximum deviation of the phase of this same wave away from the average phase, are 90° out of phase with respect to each other, assuming sinusoidal modulation.

17-12. In an amplitude-modulated wave generated by a modulated oscillator the degree of amplitude modulation is 0.8, and the modulating frequency is 5000 cycles. During the modulation process, the instantaneous frequency that is generated varies ± 2500 cycles about its mean value, according to a sinusoidal law.

a. Write the equation of this wave.

b. From this equation determine the relative amplitudes and phases of the upper and lower sideband frequencies with respect to the amplitudes and phases of these sidebands in the absence of frequency wobble, neglecting second- and higher-order sidebands (but not the first-order sidebands) arising from frequency modulation.

17-13. In a wave that was initially completely amplitude modulated (amplitude of individual sideband 0.5 times the carrier amplitude) the phase relations are so distorted that when the sidebands are in phase opposition to each other, they are 45° (or 135°) out of phase with respect to the carrier, instead of 90° as in Fig. 16-11. With the aid of rotating vectors show (*a*) that this phase displacement of the sidebands causes the resulting wave to possess both amplitude and phase modulation, (*b*) that the degree of amplitude modulation is reduced to less than 1.0, and (*c*) that the peak positive and peak negative phase shifts of the resultant wave are unequal.

17-14. Referring to Fig. 17-7, sketch the way in which the envelope of the response will vary with time when the deviation of the instantaneous frequency is three times as great as shown.

17-15. In a particular circuit carrying a frequency-modulated wave having sinusoidal modulation, conditions are such that the response can be accurately calculated by the quasi-steady-state method. However, when the sine-wave modulation is replaced by square-wave modulation of the same modulating frequency and producing the same frequency deviation, the quasi-steady-state analysis will no longer give correct results. Explain.

17-16. Demonstrate with the aid of Eq. (17-18) that the quasi-steady-state method of analysis will always give correct results in a circuit consisting of a capacitance C shunted by a conductance G, irrespective of the rate of change of instantaneous frequency.

17-17. Carry out the detailed substitutions and steps by which Eq. (17-24) is derived from Eq. (17-18).

17-18. Derive a relation analogous to Eq. (17-24) but representing the fractional error in the quasi-steady-state method of obtaining the current flowing in a circuit consisting of a resistance R in series with a capacitor C.

17-19. In Fig. 17-8 the input voltage is a frequency-modulated wave having a peak deviation of 75 kc and a carrier frequency of 8 Mc. The resonant circuit has a half-power bandwidth of 150 kc and is resonant at the carrier frequency of the wave.

a. What will be the maximum value of the fractional error in the quasi-steady-state response at a modulation frequency of 15 kc?

b. What is the narrowest half-power bandwidth that the circuit may have if the maximum error is not to exceed 5.0 per cent?

17-20. The reactance-tube system of Fig. 17-9 is modified by interchanging R and C. Assuming the reactance of C is now much less than R, derive an equation for the equivalent plate-cathode reactance that is produced by this modified arrangement, and state the kind of reactance that results.

17-21. Modify the analysis in the footnote on page 601 so that it gives the equivalent resistance as well as the reactance component of the impedance produced between plate and cathode of the reactance tube for the case where it is not assumed that R is negligible compared with $1/\omega C$. Consider the impedance of the reactance tube to be in the form of an equivalent capacitive reactance and an equivalent resistance in series.

17-22. In a particular reactance-tube-modulated oscillator of the type shown in Fig. 17-9, a capacitance variation of ± 1 $\mu\mu f$ will produce the desired frequency deviation. If $C = 3$ $\mu\mu f$ and $R = 500$ ohms, over what range must the transconductance of the tube be varied by the modulating voltage?

17-23. Discuss the factors that can cause lack of proportionality between the instantaneous amplitude of the modulating voltage and the instantaneous frequency in Fig. 17-9.

17-24. A method commonly used to determine experimentally the relationship between the modulating voltage in a frequency-modulated system, such as that of Fig. 17-9, and the frequency deviation that results consists in gradually increasing the amplitude of a sinusoidal modulating voltage, and observing the values of modulating voltage at which the carrier amplitude (irrespective of the presence of sidebands) becomes zero. Explain how this information enables one to determine frequency deviation, and give the values of modulation index corresponding to the first four times the carrier becomes zero as the modulating voltage increases.

17-25. Explain how the arrangement of Fig. 17-9 could be modified so that a modulating voltage would generate a phase-modulated wave instead of a frequency-modulated wave.

17-26. In the phase modulator of Fig. 17-10b the carrier amplitude of E_B is $0.5B_A$.

a. If the degree of amplitude modulation of E_B is 0.8, calculate the phase deviation that is produced at the positive and negative peaks of the modulating cycle.

b. Demonstrate that if E_B can be fully modulated, then the phase shift will be a linear function of the modulation envelope only to the extent that one can assume that $\tan E_B O E_A$ is equal to the angle $E_B O E_A$ expressed in radians.

17-27. Explain with the aid of Fig. 17-3 why the system of generating frequency-modulated waves shown in Fig. 17-12 gives a linear relationship between the amplitude of the modulating voltage and the modulation index only when the modulation index is less than approximately 0.5.

17-28. In a frequency-modulation broadcast system it is desired to obtain a frequency deviation of ± 75 kc at a carrier of 101.2 Mc. Modulation frequencies from 80 cycles to 12,000 cycles are expected to be encountered. The modulating system consists of five phase-shift stages of the type illustrated in Fig. 17-13 operated in cascade. Assuming that the maximum modulation index that can be obtained per stage is 1.0:

a. How much frequency multiplication must be employed if a frequency deviation of ± 75 kc is to be obtained at all modulating frequencies?

b. At what carrier frequency must the phase-shifting stages operate?

c. What is the relative value of modulating voltage that must be applied to the phase-shifting stages at modulating frequencies of 80 and 12,000 cycles to give a frequency deviation of 75 kc?

17-29. What is the effect on the discriminator characteristic of Fig. 17-14*d* of very considerably detuning the primary circuit P of Fig. 17-14*a*? Only qualitative answer with justifying explanation is required.

17-30. Discuss in a qualitative way how the magnitude of the individual voltages $E_1 + E_2$ and E_3 in Fig. 17-14 can be expected to vary with frequency, assuming that the coupling between circuits is appreciably greater than the critical value.

17-31. If the diode T_1 in Fig. 17-14*a* is removed from the circuit the system still functions as a detector of frequency-modulated waves, with modulation-frequency output appearing at E_4. Explain how this can be the case, and if it is true why two diodes are used in practice.

17-32. Explain why the quasi-steady-state method of analysis can be used to obtain accurately the behavior of a discriminator even at unusually high modulation frequencies, provided the instantaneous frequency always lies well between the peaks of the discriminator characteristic.

17-33. How would the behavior of the circuit of Fig. 17-15 be affected if C were large enough to be an effective by-pass to the modulation frequency?

17-34. The elimination of the radio-frequency choke inductance in Fig. 17-15 has the effect of requiring a smaller tuning capacitance for the primary circuit in Fig. 17-15 than in Fig. 17-14*a*, when the same primary and secondary inductance coils are used in the two circuits. Explain.

17-35. Referring to Fig. 17-15, draw oscillograms showing how the rectified voltage E'_{a2} combines with the radio-frequency voltage E_{a2} to produce a voltage between the cathode and anode of T_2.

17-36. What effect would be produced on the linearity of the discriminator characteristic of the ratio detector if the coupling between the primary and secondary circuits of the discriminator were so adjusted as to cause the voltage $|E_{a1}| + |E_{a2}|$ in Fig. 17-14*b* to be relatively rounded off on top? Assume a pure frequency-modulated wave.

17-37. What would be the effect in the circuit of Fig. 17-17*b* of making C so large as to be an effective by-pass to modulation frequencies?

17-38. Sketch a discriminator characteristic applicable to Fig. 17-17*a* on the assumption that the incoming signal is a pure frequency-modulated wave possessing no amplitude variations in its envelope. Next, superimpose upon the same axes the discriminator characteristic that would result when the amplitude of the incoming signal is increased and the resistances R'_2 are so large that the increase in signal amplitude produces negligible change in the input impedance of the diodes. Finally, sketch the discriminator characteristic that would result when the amplitude of the incoming signal is increased, and the resistances R'_2 are zero, so that the increase in amplitude of the incoming signal produces very little change in amplitude of the radio-frequency voltages developed by the discriminator, but does alter very considerably the phase relations of the voltages $E_1 + E_2$ and E_3 by making them closer to 90°.

17-39. Redraw the vector diagram of Fig. 17-18 for the case where the increase in magnitude of the voltages corresponding to the dotted vectors is twice as great as in the text, but with ϕ'' so chosen as to prevent the increased amplitude from affecting the output.

17-40. Discuss the extent to which there is a difference in the amount of rectified voltage appearing across capacitor C in Fig. 17-17*a* and 17-17*b*.

CHAPTER 18

WAVE SHAPING, NONLINEAR WAVES, AND PULSE TECHNIQUES[1]

18-1. Nonsinusoidal Wave Shapes. In electronics work extensive use is made of various types of nonsinusoidal waves, such as square and saw-tooth waves, and pulses. One method of generating a desired waveform consists in starting with some other type of wave, for example, a sine wave, and shaping it by the use of vacuum tubes and circuits to obtain the desired characteristics. The processes most commonly used in this connection are clipping, integration, differentiation, and clamping.

An alternative approach consists in employing a vacuum-tube arrangement that directly generates the desired waveform. The multivibrator, blocking oscillator, and saw-tooth wave generators are typical examples.

18-2. Clipping. In clipping, a portion of a wave is flattened off or *limited* to some arbitrary level, irrespective of the amplitude of the original signal. Clippers may be conveniently classified as peak clippers, base clippers, and slicers, according to the way in which they operate on a wave.

A *peak clipper*, also called a *peak limiter*, operates in such a manner as to prevent the positive (or negative) amplitude of the wave from ever exceeding a value set by the clipper. A simple example of such a clipper is illustrated in Fig. 18-1.

Here, when the instantaneous value of the input voltage wave lies between E_c and $-E_c'$, neither of the diodes conducts, and the input wave is transmitted directly to the output terminals without change. On the other hand, when the input voltage is more positive than E_c, diode T_1 will conduct and thus prevent the output voltage from rising appreciably

---

[1] A very large body of literature has grown up during the last ten years on this subject. The reader who desires to go into some aspect of the subject more deeply than the survey given in this chapter will find the following references useful: F. E. Terman and J. M. Pettit, "Electronic Measurements," McGraw-Hill Book Company, Inc., New York, 1952; Samuel Seely, "Electron-tube Circuits," McGraw-Hill Book Company, Inc., New York, 1950; J. F. Reintjes and G. T. Coate, "Principles of Radar," McGraw-Hill Book Company, Inc., New York, 1952; "Radar System Engineering" (vol. 1, Radiation Laboratory Series), McGraw-Hill Book Company, Inc., New York, 1947; "Waveforms" (vol. 19, Radiation Laboratory Series), McGraw-Hill Book Company, Inc., New York, 1949; "Pulse Generators" (vol. 5, Radiation Laboratory Series), McGraw-Hill Book Company, Inc., New York, 1948.

above E_c. Similarly, when the input voltage becomes more negative than $-E'_c$, diode T_2 will conduct and clip the negative peaks of the output voltage at a level approximating $-E'_c$. For the diode clippers T_1 and T_2 to be effective, the series resistance R_s must be considerably greater than the dynamic plate-cathode resistance of the tubes.

A clipping circuit employing a triode tube is shown in Fig. 18-2. Here the control grid and cathode function similarly to diode T_1 in Fig. 18-1, and in conjunction with bias E_c and series resistance R_s clip the positive peaks of the applied voltage at a level E_c, as shown; this is termed *grid*

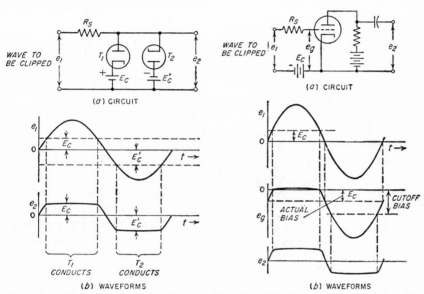

FIG. 18-1. Diode clipping circuit, together with waveforms involved when clipping a sine wave.

FIG. 18-2. Triode clipping circuit, together with waveforms illustrating the clipping of a sine wave.

limiting. In addition, if the instantaneous grid potential is driven more negative than the value corresponding to plate-current cutoff, then the output waveform will be clipped at an amplitude corresponding to cutoff; this is called *cutoff limiting.* The triode clipper of Fig. 18-2 can be regarded as being roughly the equivalent of the diode-clipping system of Fig. 18-1, plus one stage of amplification.

Still another limiting technique is illustrated in Fig. 18-3. Here, the load resistance R_L and the electrode voltages are so chosen that a virtual cathode forms in the tube when the instantaneous potential of the control grid approaches zero potential. This causes the output current, and hence output voltage, to be limited at the positive peaks of the applied voltage as shown; this limiting, moreover, occurs without input voltage e_1 being called upon to supply any current. The tube in such a system is said to *bottom* when the limiting takes place because of the formation of a virtual cathode.

Circumstances sometimes arise when it is desired to reduce to zero all

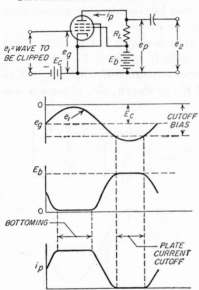

amplitudes of a wave that are less than some minimum value. *Base clipping* of this type can be obtained with circuit arrangements such as illustrated in Fig. 18-4. In Fig. 18-4a the diode tube is biased to a voltage E_c corresponding to the level of base clipping desired, so that no output current flows until the applied voltage exceeds this value. In Fig. 18-4b, base clipping is accomplished by biasing the control grid of the amplifier tube to a value that is more negative than cutoff by an amount equal to the desired level of base clipping.

Clippers may be combined in various ways. A particularly important combination is illustrated in Fig. 18-5. Here the combination of

Fig. 18-3. Clipping of positive peaks by "bottoming."

diode T_1, resistance R_s, and bias E_c serves as a peak clipper, while diode T_2 in association with bias E'_c simultaneously functions as a base clipper. The result is that all input voltages in excess of E_c are clipped in such a

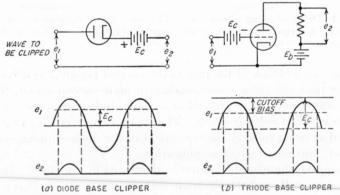

(a) DIODE BASE CLIPPER   (b) TRIODE BASE CLIPPER

Fig. 18-4. Diode and triode base clippers, together with waveforms illustrating the base clipping of a sine wave.

manner as to produce an output voltage having a value $E_c - E'_c$, while all values of input voltage that are less than E_c are reduced to zero amplitude in the output.   An arrangement of this type is termed a *slicer*, since the output wave can be regarded as consisting of a slice of the input waveform.

18-3. Integration and Differentiation of Waveforms.   A wave is said to be integrated when it is used to develop another wave having an amplitude that is proportional to the time integral $\int E\,dt$ of the original wave E. A simple integrating circuit consists of a large capacitance C in series with a high resistance R, as shown in Fig. 18-6a.   The application of a voltage

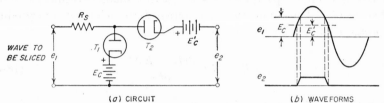

(a) CIRCUIT   (b) WAVEFORMS

Fig. 18-5. A slicer circuit, together with waveforms showing the behavior in the case of a sine-wave input.

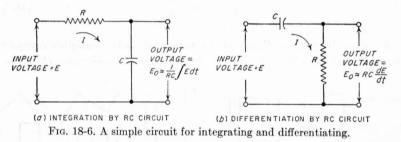

(a) INTEGRATION BY RC CIRCUIT   (b) DIFFERENTIATION BY RC CIRCUIT

Fig. 18-6. A simple circuit for integrating and differentiating.

E to such a circuit produces a voltage across the capacitor which by ordinary transient circuit theory has a value E_0 that is[1]

$$E_0 = \frac{1}{RC} \int (E - E_0)\,dt \tag{18-1a}$$

The integral is taken from time $t = 0$ to the value of time for which E_0 is desired.   When $E_0 << E$, then to good accuracy one has

$$E_0 = \frac{1}{RC} \int E\,dt \tag{18-1b}$$

[1] The differential equations applying to Fig. 18-6a are

$$E = IR + (1/C)\int I\,dt \tag{18-2}$$
$$E_0 = (1/C)\int I\,dt \tag{18-3}$$
$$I = C\,(dE_0/dt) \tag{18-4}$$

Eq. (18-1a) is obtained by substituting E_0 for the final term of Eq. (18-2), and Eq. (18-4) for I in the first term to the right of the equal sign.

In order for the voltage E_0 across the capacitor to be negligible compared with the applied voltage E, it is necessary that the resistance R be large compared with the reactance $1/2\pi f_1 C$ of C at the lowest frequency f_1 of any component of importance contained in the wave to be integrated; this means that the time constant RC must be large compared with $1/f_1$.

A wave is said to be differentiated when it is used to develop another wave having a shape that is proportional to the time derivative dE/dt of the original wave. A simple circuit for producing such a differentiation consists of a small capacitance in series with a small resistance, as shown in Fig. 18-6b. The application of a voltage E to such a network produces a voltage E_0 across the resistance that is[1]

$$E_0 = RC \frac{d(E - E_0)}{dt} \qquad (18\text{-}5a)$$

When $E_0 << E$, then to good accuracy one has

$$E_0 = RC \frac{dE}{dt} \qquad (18\text{-}5b)$$

In order for the voltage E_0 across the resistance to be negligible compared with the applied voltage E, it is necessary that the resistance R be small

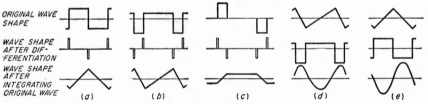

FIG. 18-7. Consequences of differentiating and integrating typical idealized wave shapes.

compared with the reactance $1/2\pi f_2 C$ of C at the highest frequency f_2 of any component of importance contained in the wave to be differentiated; this means that the time constant RC must now be small compared with $1/f_2$.

Differentiation and integration provide a straightforward means of converting from one type of wave shape to another type. This is illustrated in Fig. 18-7, which shows the effect produced by differentiation and integration of some typical standard waves. Thus differentiation of a square wave produces a succession of alternately positive and negative pulses of relatively short duration; in contrast, integration of a square wave results in a triangular wave. Conversely, a square wave can be

[1] This follows from the fact that now $E_0 = IR$, and $I = C[d(E - E_0)/dt]$.

produced by the integration of a succession of alternately positive and negative pulses that are of very brief duration, or by differentiation of a triangular wave.

Integration and Differentiation with the Aid of Operational Amplifiers. As noted above, the circuits of Fig. 18-6 give satisfactory integration and differentiation only when so proportioned that the output voltage E_0 is at all times a negligibly small fraction of the input voltage E. Thus, to obtain integrated or differentiated waves of reasonable amplitude it is necessary to employ some form of vacuum-tube amplifier.

A particularly desirable method of obtaining such amplification is illustrated in Fig. 18-8. Here, the amplifier A not only produces the desired gain, but at the same time through the action of the feedback impedance C_{fb} (or R_{fb}) it develops an input impedance that supplies one element of the integrating (or differentiating) network. The advantage of this

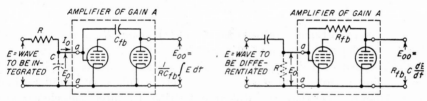

(a) OPERATIONAL INTEGRATOR   (b) OPERATIONAL DIFFERENTIATOR

Fig. 18-8. Operational amplifiers for integrating and differentiating.

arrangement is the fact, demonstrated below, that the amplified output voltage is not significantly affected by ordinary variations in the gain of the amplifier.

To obtain an understanding of such a system, consider first the integrating circuit of Fig. 18-8a, and assume that the magnitude of the amplifier gain is A, and that the phase shift is constant and equal to 180° for all frequency components of importance in the wave to be integrated.[1] The input admittance of such an amplifier, i.e., the impedance between terminals aa looking toward the amplifier, consists of a capacitance C which corresponds to the integrating capacitance C of Fig. 18-6a, and

---

[1] This requires that the amplifier have an odd number of plate-coupled stages, since each such stage produces a phase reversal; a cathode-coupled output stage may be added additionally, if desired, as such a stage does not introduce a phase reversal. The phase shift of the amplification can be made to approximate 180° almost exactly by employing a large amount of negative feedback that is resistive at all frequencies of importance.

It is also possible to obtain integration by employing an amplifier with zero phase shift, i.e., an even number of plate-coupled stages. In this case, the equivalent input capacitance developed between the terminals aa in Fig. 18-6a is a negative capacitance, i.e., an inductive (or positive) reactance inversely proportional to frequency. Integration still occurs when such a capacitance is substituted for C in Fig. 13-6a; the only effect is to reverse the polarity of voltage E_0.

which has the value[1,2]

$$C = C_{fb}(1 + A) + C_{gk} \tag{18-6}$$

Here, C_{fb} is a capacitance connected between amplifier input and output as shown in Fig. 18-8a, and C_{gk} is the control-grid-to-ground capacitance of the amplifier input tube.   By substituting Eq. (18-6) into Eq. (18-1b), and assuming $C_{gk} << C_{fb}(1 + A)$, one obtains

$$E_{00} = AE_0 = \frac{A}{RC_{fb}(1 + A)} \int E \, dt \tag{18-7a}$$

To the extent that the voltage gain A of the amplifier is very large compared with unity, then $A/(1 + A) \approx 1$, and Eq. (18-7a) can be written

$$E_{00} = \frac{1}{RC_{fb}} \int E \, dt \tag{18-7b}$$

It is seen from Eq. (18-7b) that the amplified output E_{00} of the integrating system depends only upon the circuit constants RC_{fb}, *and is substantially independent of the gain A of the amplifier*, and hence of supply voltages, aging of tubes, tube replacements, etc.   This very useful result arises from the fact that when the amplification A is large, any change in amplification alters the equivalent integrating capacitance C just sufficiently to offset the effect of the change in amplification.   It will be further noted that in the circuit of Fig. 18-8a the equivalent time constant of the integrating system is $RC_{fb}(1 + A)$.   The actual capacitance C_{fb} that need be provided is hence much less than the equivalent capacitance $C_{fb}(1 + A)$; this means that large time constants are easily obtained with condensers of convenient size.

The differentiating system of Fig. 18-8b can be analyzed in the same manner as Fig. 18-8a.   When the amplifier has a phase shift that is 180° for all the frequency components of importance in the wave to be differentiated, the input admittance of the amplifier system is a resistance R

---

[1] This relation is derived in the same manner as Eq. (12-28).   Thus the input admittance of the amplifier is I/E_0, where I_0 is the current indicated in Fig. 18-6a. Now

$$I = j\omega C_{fb}(E_0 + AE_0) + j\omega C_{gk}E_0$$

or

$$I/E_0 = j\omega C_{fb}(1 + A) + j\omega C_{gk}$$

This is the admittance of the capacitance given by Eq. (18-6).

[2] In the special case where the amplifier A consists of a single stage, the equivalent capacitance C of the integrating circuit is the input capacitance of the one-stage system due to the grid-plate tube capacitance augmented by whatever shunting capacitance may be added to achieve the circuit properties desired.   Such a one-stage system is commonly termed a *Miller integrator*, because it makes use of the Miller effect discussed in connection with Eq. (12-28).

having the value

$$R = \frac{R_{fb}}{1 + A} \qquad (18\text{-}8)$$

Here, R_{fb} is a resistance connected between the amplifier input and output as shown in Fig. 18-8b.[1]   Substituting Eq. (18-8) into Eq. (18-5b), and assuming that $A >> 1$, one finds that the amplified output voltage E_{00} of the differentiating system has the value

$$E_{00} = A E_0 = R_{fb}C \frac{dE}{dt} \qquad (18\text{-}9)$$

In analogy with Eq. (18-7b), it is seen that the amplified output E_{00} of the differentiating system depends only on the circuit constants $R_{fb}C$ and is substantially independent of the gain A of the amplifier; it is thus not affected by aging of the tubes, tube replacements, supply voltages, etc., as before.

The amplifiers used in systems such as illustrated in Fig. 18-8 are often termed *operational amplifiers*, because they participate in carrying out a mathematical operation.   Operational amplifiers are important components of analogue computers.

18-4. The Multivibrator.[2]   The multivibrator can be thought of as a two-stage resistance-coupled amplifier in which the voltage developed by the output of the second tube is applied to the input of the first tube.   A schematic diagram of the plate-coupled form of multivibrator is shown in Fig. 18-9a.[3]   Such an arrangement will oscillate because each tube produces a phase shift of 180°, thereby causing the output of the second tube to supply to the first tube an input voltage that has exactly the right phase to sustain oscillations.   The usefulness of the multivibrator arises because (1) the multivibrator can be used as a generator of square waves, pulses, or time intervals; (2) the frequency of oscillation is readily controlled by an injected voltage; and (3) the wave that is generated is very rich in harmonics.

[1] It is important that the amplifier have a phase shift of 180° rather than zero degrees.   This is because a phase shift of zero degrees will cause the equivalent input resistance R to have a negative value of relatively small magnitude.   This is to be avoided, because it represents a situation that offers the possibility of supporting parasitic oscillations.

[2] The multivibrator is an example of a class of oscillators (other examples include the blocking oscillator and saw-tooth-wave generators) which make use of the transient represented by the charge or discharge of a capacitance or inductance through a resistance.   Such systems are often called *relaxation oscillators*.

[3] The multivibrator circuit is often drawn as shown in Fig. 18-9b, with points of fixed potential, such as E_b, designated and so arranged that the more positive points are nearer the top of the schematic diagram.   Electrode voltages then rise or fall in accordance with current flow through load resistors, and waveforms can readily be visualized.

The operation of the multivibrator can be understood by reference to the oscillograms shown in Fig. 18-10. Oscillations are started (prior to $t = 0$) by a very small voltage at the grid of one of the tubes, say a posi-

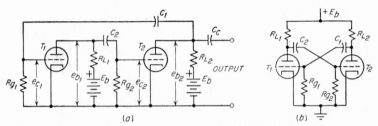

FIG. 18-9. Typical multivibrator circuit. The schematic diagram at a is drawn in such a way as to emphasize the similarity of a multivibrator to a two-stage amplifier. In b the same circuit is presented in a form that is particularly convenient for tracing instantaneous voltage changes.

tive random noise voltage on the grid of tube T_1. This voltage is amplified by the two tubes, and reappears at the grid of the first tube to be reamplified. This action takes place almost instantly and is repeated over and over, so that the grid potential e_{c1} of tube T_1 rises suddenly to a value that is zero,[1] while the grid potential e_{c2} of tube T_2 just as suddenly drops to a value that is much more negative than cutoff. The immediate result is that amplification ceases, and for the time being tube T_1 draws a heavy plate current while tube T_2 takes no plate current. This condition, depicted in Fig. 18-10 for $0 < t < t_1$, is not permanent, however, because the current through the grid-leak resistance R_{g2} of tube T_2 gradually brings the grid potential e_{c2} back toward zero. At the time t_1 that the grid potential e_{c2} reaches the cutoff level, tube T_2 begins to amplify the rising voltage e_{c2}. Since the resulting amplified output of T_2 is negative, it causes a sudden fall in voltage e_{c1}, which when amplified by T_1 causes e_{c2} to rise more, which causes e_{c1} to fall farther, and so on. The end result is

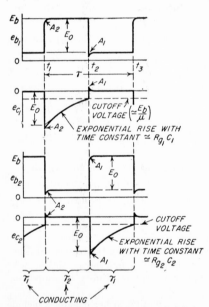

FIG. 18-10. Waveforms in the multivibrator of Fig. 18-9 for the symmetrical case where $R_{L1} = R_{L2}$, $R_{g1} = R_{g2}$, and $C_1 = C_2$.

[1] The speed of rise is determined by the 3-db bandwidth of the system considered as a two-stage amplifier, as discussed in Secs. 9-1 and 18-15.

hence to cause tube T_2 to become conducting and tube T_1 to be cut off. This action, which is shown in the oscillograms at t_1, takes place almost instantly and makes the situation similar to that existing prior to $t = 0$ except that the relative functions of the two tubes have been interchanged. Next the negative potential e_{c1} on the grid of tube T_1 gradually dies away as the result of leakage through resistance R_{g1} just as before, and finally the cycle repeats at time t_3.

The output voltage is usually taken from the plate of one of the tubes through a coupling capacitor (C_c in Fig. 18-9a). The output waveform is therefore that of e_{b1} or e_{b2} in Fig. 18-10. The amplitude E_0 is readily determined by a graphical "load-line" construction, as depicted in Fig. 18-11, where a straight line of slope $-1/R_L$ is superimposed upon the

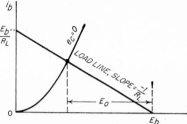

ACTUAL VOLTAGE e_b APPLIED TO PLATE ⟶

Fig. 18-11. Graphical load-line construction for determination of E_0 in Fig. 18-10.

static plate-voltage–plate-current characteristic curve for the tube.[1] The intersection with the tube curve for zero grid voltage is the operating point for whichever tube is conducting. The voltage E_0 that represents the difference between the plate voltage when the tube is conducting and when it is cut off is the peak-to-peak amplitude of the output voltage wave.

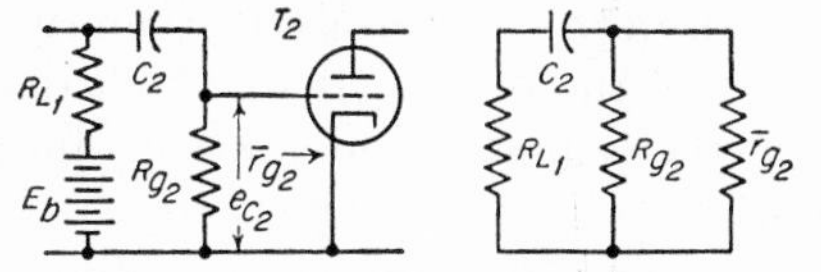

(a) EQUIVALENT CIRCUIT   (b) SIMPLIFIED CIRCUIT

Fig. 18-12. Equivalent and simplified circuits involved in the generation of the transient voltage A_2 on the grid of T_2 of Figs. 18-9 and 18-10.

The oscillograms of Fig. 18-10 are for the *symmetrical* case, i.e., where the circuits associated with the two tubes have the same constants. Except for the minor imperfections indicated by A_1 and A_2, the waveforms at e_{b1} and e_{b2} are then square waves. When the circuits are not symmetrical, and in particular when the time constants $R_{g2}C_2$ and $R_{g1}C_1$ of the two grid leak–capacitor combinations differ greatly, the length of successive half cycles will differ correspondingly.

Switching Transients in the Multivibrator. The switching of the plate current from one tube to the other in the multivibrator is always accompanied by brief transients indicated by A_1 and A_2 in Fig. 18-10. Thus at time t_1, the voltage e_{c2} at the grid of T_2 momentarily rises to a moderately positive value, and then quickly dies away to zero in accordance with

---

[1] This construction implies that the grid-leak resistance is high compared with R_L. If this is not the case, then the load line should be drawn on the basis of an equivalent load resistance corresponding to R_g in parallel with R_L.

the equivalent circuit of Fig. 18-12a, in which tube T_1 is omitted since at the moment it is nonconducting. Further simplification is shown at b where the grid-cathode circuit of the conducting tube T_2 is replaced by its d-c grid resistance $\bar{r}_{g2}$, where $\bar{r}_{g2}$ is the ratio of d-c voltage applied to the grid to the grid current.

The time constant of this transient A_2 associated with the grid of T_2 is then seen from Fig. 18-12b to be $R_{eq}C_2$ where R_{eq} is the total series resistance $R_{L1} + R_{g2}\bar{r}_{g2}/(R_{g2} + \bar{r}_{g2})$ of the circuit. Ordinarily $\bar{r}_{g2} << R_{g2}$, $R_{L_1} << R_{g_2}$, so that this time constant is very much less than the time constant $R_{g2}C_2$ determining the time $t_2 - t_1$ of the half cycle (see below) during which tube T_2 is conducting; as a result transient A usually lasts only a very small fraction of the half period of the multivibrator.

The effect of this transient in e_{c2} is to introduce at time t_1 a short negative spike in e_{b2}, and a slight rounding off of e_{b1}. At the same time the peak negative value of e_{c1} momentarily exceeds E_0. These effects are indicated by A_2 in the various oscillograms of Fig. 18-10. The corresponding transient associated with tube T_1 is designated as A_1 in Fig. 18-10, and occurs at time t_2 when tube T_1 starts to conduct.

Frequency of Multivibrator Oscillation. A multivibrator oscillating as above at a frequency determined solely by the characteristics of the multivibrator system is commonly termed a *free-running* multivibrator. This is in contrast to the situation that exists when the frequency is controlled by an injected voltage as described below in connection with Fig. 18-15.

The frequency of a free-running multivibrator is determined primarily by the time constants $R_{g1}C_1$ and $R_{g2}C_2$, and the potentials to which the grid return leads are brought, although the remaining circuit constants and electrode voltages have a slight effect.

The total period τ (Fig. 18-10) of a cycle of multivibrator operation is the sum of the two intervals $\tau_1 = t_2 - t_1$ and $\tau_2 = t_3 - t_2$. In the symmetrical case these two intervals are equal, but in any case if the grid-leak resistances are returned to the cathode as in Fig. 18-10, the total period τ is given with good accuracy by the approximate relation[1]

$$\tau = \tau_1 + \tau_2 = (R_{g1}C_1 + R_{g2}C_2) \log_\epsilon \frac{\mu E_0}{E_b} \qquad (18\text{-}10)$$

---

[1] This relation is derived as follows: Consider first the interval $t_3 - t_2$. Neglecting the short transient A_1 at time t_2, the duration of this interval is the time $t_3 - t_2$ required for e_{c2} (Fig. 18-10) to rise exponentially from $-E_0$ to the cutoff level $-E_b/\mu$. During this time interval, tube T_2 carries no plate current, so that Fig. 18-10 reduces to the circuit shown in Fig. 18-13. Likewise, to the extent that transient A_1 can be neglected, the voltage across R_{g2} then has the value $-E_0$ at t_2 after e_{b1} drops from E_b to $E_b - E_0$. Replacing tube T_1 by the d-c plate resistance $\bar{r}_{p1}$ (that is, $\bar{r}_{p1}$ is the ratio of d-c voltage e_b applied to the plate to the d-c plate current i_{b1}) gives the equivalent circuit of Fig. 18-13b, which by Thévenin's theorem can be simplified as shown at Fig. 18-13c

where R_{g1}, C_1, R_{g2}, C_2 are as designated in Fig. 18-9

  μ = amplification factor of T_1 and T_2 (assumed the same for both tubes)

  E_0 = plate-voltage drop as illustrated in Figs. 18-10 and 18-11

  E_b = plate-supply voltage

The frequency f of the multivibrator is simply the reciprocal of the period, i.e.,

$$f = \frac{1}{\tau} \qquad (18\text{-}12)$$

The frequency of the free-running multivibrator can be controlled by returning the grid circuits to an adjustable positive potential, as illustrated in Fig. 18-14. Such a positive bias shortens the time of each half cycle by causing the instantaneous grid potential to reach the cutoff value earlier in the discharge period than would otherwise be the case, as

where

$$E' = E_b \frac{\bar{r}_{p1}}{\bar{r}_{p1} + R_{L1}} \qquad R' = \frac{\bar{r}_{p1} R_{L1}}{\bar{r}_{p1} + R_{L1}}$$

In this final circuit one ordinarily finds that $R' << R_{g2}$, so that the time constant of the circuit can generally be taken to be $R_{g2} C_2$, although the true value is $(R_{g2} + R') C_2$.

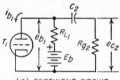

(a) PERTINENT CIRCUIT   (b) EQUIVALENT CIRCUIT   (c) FINAL EQUIVALENT CIRCUIT

FIG. 18-13. Equivalent circuits for determining the period $t_3 - t_2$ in Fig. 18-10. During this time interval tube T_2 is nonconducting and so acts as an open circuit.

Assuming therefore that the exponential voltage rise across R_{g2} has the time constant $R_{g2} C_2$, then since this voltage can be assumed to start with an amplitude $-E_0$ at t_2 and has an amplitude $-E_b/\mu$ at t_3, one can write

$$\frac{E_b}{\mu} = E_0 \epsilon^{-\frac{t_3 - t_2}{R_{g2} C_2}}$$

The interval $t_3 - t_2$ is obtained by rearranging, and taking the natural logarithm of both sides.

$$\epsilon^{\frac{t_3 - t_2}{R_{g2} C_2}} = \frac{\mu E_0}{E_b}$$

$$\frac{t_3 - t_2}{R_{g2} C_2} = \log_\epsilon \frac{\mu E_0}{E_b}$$

$$t_3 - t_2 = R_{g2} C_2 \log_\epsilon \frac{\mu E_0}{E_b} \qquad (18\text{-}11)$$

The value of $t_2 - t_1$ is obtained similarly.

seen by comparing b and c of Fig. 18-14.[1]   As a result adjusting the bias causes the frequency to change. The frequency range that can thereby be covered in this way using any one set of circuit components is quite large, of the order of 10 to 1.

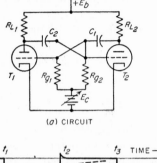

(a) CIRCUIT

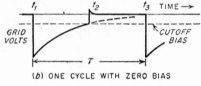

(b) ONE CYCLE WITH ZERO BIAS

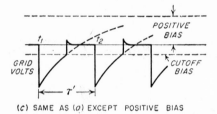

(c) SAME AS (a) EXCEPT POSITIVE BIAS

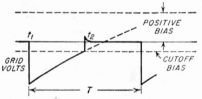

(d) POSITIVE BIAS WITH GRID LEAK-CONDENSER TIME-CONSTANT INCREASED SO τ IS SAME AS (b)

FIG. 18-14. Multivibrator with positive grid bias, together with oscillograms showing how this bias affects the frequency of oscillation.

The period τ of successive cycles of a free-running multivibrator can be expected to exhibit small random fluctuations as a result of noise voltages that necessarily exist in the system. Thus, in Fig. 18-10, when T_1 is conducting, the resistance noise from R_{L1} and R_{g2} and the tube noise from T_1 combine to superimpose a noise voltage on e_{c2} that will affect slightly the time t_3 at which tube T_2 starts conducting. This phenomenon, termed *jitter*, has an effect on the time of a half cycle that can be calculated from Eq. (18-13) by noting that the noise voltage producing the jitter is equivalent to a bias voltage. The effect of a given noise voltage is less the larger the positive bias.

Synchronizing the Multivibrator. When a pulsed or alternating voltage from an outside source is introduced into the circuits of a multivibrator, the multivibrator oscillations tend to adjust themselves in frequency so that the ratio of the injected to multivibrator frequency is exactly a ratio of

---

[1] With positive-bias voltage E_c instead of zero bias, the interval $t_3 - t_2$ previously given in Eq. (18-11) now becomes

$$t_3 - t_2 = R_{g2}C_2 \log_\epsilon \frac{E_c + E_0}{E_c + (E_b/\mu)} \qquad (18\text{-}13)$$

If both grids are returned to the same positive-bias voltage E, then the total period τ becomes

$$\tau = (R_{g1}C_1 + R_{g2}C_2) \log_\epsilon \frac{E_c + E_0}{E_c + (E_b/\mu)} \qquad (18\text{-}14)$$

integers.   This ratio may be unity, or greater or less than unity.   The
mechanism by which such synchro-
nization occurs is illustrated in Fig.
18-15a, which shows a symmetrical
multivibrator arranged to generate a
frequency that is exactly one-seventh
the frequency possessed by the injected voltage e_s.   Here the injected
voltage is applied to the grids of both
tubes, but with opposite polarity;
this causes the waveforms of both
e_{c1} and e_{c2} to have the character
shown in the figure (contrast this
with Fig. 18-10).   The ratio of one
to seven comes from the fact that
$3\frac{1}{2}$ cycles of the sine wave occur
during the interval t_2 to t_3, which is
a half period of the wave generated
by the multivibrator.

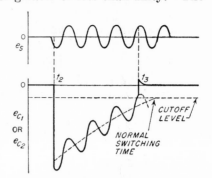

(a) SYNCHRONIZING WITH A SINE WAVE
IN RATIO OF 7 TO 1

In a like manner the multivibrator
can be synchronized with pulses, as
in the example illustrated in Fig.
18-15c.   Here there are four pulses
during the half period of the multivibrator, so the division ratio is 1:8.

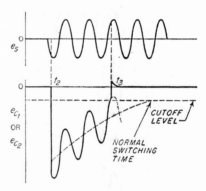

(b) SAME AS (a) EXCEPT AMPLITUDE OF
SYNCHRONIZING VOLTAGE INCREASED
TO GIVE SYNCHRONIZATION RATIO OF
5 TO 1

In both of these cases it will be
observed that the injected voltage
superimposed upon the grid potential determines the instant at which
the instantaneous grid voltage of the
multivibrator reaches the cutoff
value.   In this way, the length of
the multivibrator half period $t_3 - t_2$
is controlled by the injected voltage,
thus achieving synchronization.   If
the amplitude of the injected oscillation is increased, the multivibrator
oscillation will synchronize at a
lower ratio; i.e., the multivibrator
frequency is "drawn" toward the
frequency of the injected voltage, as
shown in Fig. 18-15b.   The stability

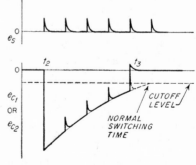

(c) SYNCHRONIZING WITH A PULSED VOLTAGE

Fig. 18-15. Synchronizing the multivibrator.

of control at a particular frequency ratio can be increased by the use
of a positive grid bias, as this increases the change in amplitude of

synchronizing voltage required to cause the frequency to jump to a new ratio.

The waveform of the multivibrator oscillations is rich in harmonics as a result of the sudden changes in amplitude that occur during the cycle of operation. Thus, a multivibrator operating at 10 kc can typically produce all harmonics up to at least the two hundredth with an amplitude sufficient to be detected by a radio receiver of only moderate sensitivity.

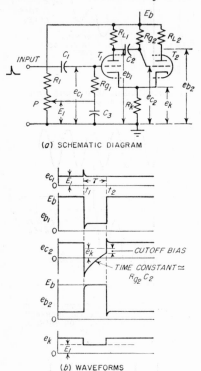

(a) SCHEMATIC DIAGRAM

(b) WAVEFORMS

FIG. 18-16. Cathode-coupled one-shot multivibrator, together with oscillograms showing operation.

The amplitude of the higher harmonics is greatest when the resistance-coupled stages of which the multivibrator is composed maintain their amplification up to frequencies that are much higher than the frequency of oscillation, since in this way the changes in wave shape are more abrupt.

"One-shot" (*Monostable*) *Multivibrators.* In certain applications, it is required that the multivibrator be quiescent until its action is initiated by a pulse of voltage from an external source. The multivibrator then goes through one cycle of operation, after which it reverts to the original quiescent condition provided the initiating pulse is no longer present. Such an arrangement is called a *one-shot* (*monostable*) *multivibrator*, and can be realized by biasing the grid of one of the multivibrator tubes to a voltage more negative than cutoff for the plate-supply potential employed.

A widely used form of one-shot multivibrator is shown in Fig. 18-16a, which differs from the multivibrator of Fig. 18-9 in that cathode coupling replaces grid leak–capacitor coupling in one of the amplifier stages. One-shot operation is achieved by returning the grid of tube T_2 to the plate-supply voltage through a grid-leak resistance R_{g2} while the grid of tube T_1 is returned to an adjustable positive-bias voltage E_1 through grid-leak resistance R_{g1}. Under quiescent conditions, tube T_2 carries a large plate current which causes the cathodes of both tubes to be enough positive with respect to ground to cause the plate current of tube T_1 to be cut off. However, when a large positive pulse is applied to the grid of tube T_1 multivibrator action is initiated, causing the plate current to be trans-

ferred to tube T_1, while the grid of tube T_2 is simultaneously driven negative, as shown in Fig. 18-16b, so that the plate current of tube T_2 is cut off.
This condition persists until the charge on capacitor C_2 is able to leak off
through resistance R_{g2} sufficiently to reduce the negative voltage on the
grid of tube T_2 to the point where this tube can again amplify.   The
plate current then switches back to tube T_2, and the original quiescent
condition is restored.

The length of the time interval $t_2 - t_1$ in Fig. 16b is readily adjustable
by means of the potentiometer P in Fig. 18-16a.   This adjustment controls the d-c bias voltage on T_1, and hence the plate current in T_1 during
the interval between t_1 and t_2 (Fig. 18-16b).   This plate current sets the
cathode potential during this interval, and consequently determines the
level to which e_{c2} must rise before T_2 can again conduct, and hence the
time at which conduction starts.   It can be shown that the relation
between time duration τ and time-interval $t_2 - t_1$ is closely linear with
respect to the bias voltage E_1.

18-5. The Flip-Flop (Eccles-
Jordan) Circuit.   The Eccles-
Jordan circuit, shown in Fig. 18-17-
is a two-stage direct-coupled ampli,
fier in which the output of the
second stage is connected to the

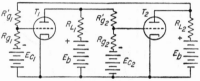

Fig. 18-17. Eccles-Jordan circuit.

input of the first stage.   The Eccles-Jordan circuit is thus similar to a
multivibrator, except that direct (or d-c) coupling is used instead of
resistance-capacitance coupling.

The Eccles-Jordan circuit has two stable conditions: In the first, the
first tube carries a large plate current and the second tube no current; in
the second, which is similar to the first, the second tube carries the large
current, and the first tube no current.   These correspond to the conditions that exist in a multivibrator on the alternate half cycles.   Unlike
the multivibrator, however, these conditions are stable in the Eccles-
Jordan circuit, since there is no capacitor being discharged which ultimately changes the operating condition.

The current in the Eccles-Jordan circuit can be switched from one tube
to the other by applying a positive pulse to the grid of the nonconducting
tube of sufficient amplitude to cause the instantaneous grid potential to
be momentarily less than cutoff.   Alternatively, one may employ a negative pulse applied to the control grid of the conducting tube, and having
sufficient amplitude to drive the grid potential of this tube momentarily
more negative than cutoff.   In either case, the system jumps almost
instantly from one stable state to the other, resulting in what is commonly called a *trigger* or *flip-flop* action, or *bistable* characteristic.

After a triggering pulse has caused the Eccles-Jordan circuit to flip in
this manner, a subsequent pulse of the same character applied to the same

tube will have no effect.   However, if triggering pulses are simultaneously applied to both grids, then each time either a positive or negative pulse arrives, the circuit flips to the alternate stable condition, irrespective of which tube was carrying the current just before the arrival of the pulse.   Thus a second pulse brings the system back to the condition that existed just before the arrival of the first of the two pulses.

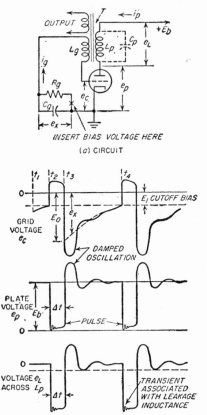

(a) CIRCUIT

(b) OSCILLOGRAMS

Fig. 18-18. Blocking oscillator circuit, together with typical oscillograms.

18-6. The Blocking Oscillator.

The arrangement shown in Fig. 18-18a, termed a *blocking oscillator*, finds wide use as a generator of short pulses of large amplitude.

The blocking oscillator can be looked upon as a tuned-plate oscillator circuit of the type shown in Fig. 14-1d that is so proportioned as to provide an extreme case of intermittent oscillations (see page 491).   This result is achieved by (1) making the plate inductance L_p large, and using only the tube and transformer distributed capacitance for tuning so that the ratio L_p/C_p is extremely high, (2) using a turn ratio between the plate and grid coils of the transformer T such that the peak driving voltage applied to the grid is of the same order of magnitude as the plate-supply voltage, (3) using a grid capacitor C_g that is not too large, and (4) employing a grid leak of sufficient resistance to make the time constant R_gC_g large.

Under these conditions the waveforms that are generated have the character illustrated in Fig. 18-18b.   A single half cycle of oscillation, representing the time interval $t_3 - t_2$, will build up sufficient charge on the grid leak–capacitor combination to provide a bias E_0 that is much greater than the cutoff voltage for the tube.   Thus at t_3 the tube becomes inactive, and the energy stored in the resonant system is dissipated in a damped oscillation[1] that is superimposed upon the bias voltage e_x existing

---

[1] In order that this oscillation may be damped out by the time t_4 when the next cycle of operation begins, the Q of the coil system is intentionally made quite low.

across the grid leak–capacitor combination, as shown. This bias voltage decays exponentially according to the time constant $R_g C_g$; when it has reached the cutoff value of the tube, amplification again occurs, and the cycle then repeats.[1] The result of this sequence of events is to produce an output voltage having the character shown in the bottom oscillogram of Fig. 19-18b.

Pulse Length and Shape. The voltage wave generated across L_p (and hence at the output terminals in Fig. 18-18a) by the blocking oscillator is seen to be periodic repetition of a short pulse, approximately rectangular in shape, that is followed by an oscillation that dies out rapidly. The most important single factor determining the *length* of the rectangular pulse produced is the transformer T. The second most important factor is the grid capacitor C_g. Reduction in the capacitance of this capacitor increases the rate at which bias voltage is built up by the grid current that flows during the pulse; as a result, decreasing the capacitance tends to terminate the pulse sooner and thus shorten its length.

The *shape* of the pulse generated by a blocking oscillator is determined primarily by the transformer. When the transformer is properly designed, the high value of L_p/C_p, the saturation of the transformer core, and the nonlinear behavior of the grid current, all combine in such a manner as to produce a pulse that is approximately flat-topped, as shown.[2] The steepness of the leading and lagging edges of the pulse is determined mainly by the leakage inductance, and will be greater the less the leakage.

The transformer T in Fig. 18-18a is seen to be the basic element determining the properties of a given blocking oscillator. This transformer is normally wound on a magnetic core in such a manner as to give minimum possible leakage inductance between the plate and grid windings consistent with small distributed and interwinding capacitances. Also, a careful balance must exist between the transformer and tube characteristics if a sharply defined pulse having a flat top, steep sides, and a specified length is to be achieved. Moreover, a given transformer used with a particular tube is relatively inflexible, in that any attempt to generate pulses having a length substantially different from the design value will usually result in marked deterioration in the shape of the pulse (except that the pulse may be terminated early by the use of a delay line as discussed in connection with Fig. 18-27). The situation is sufficiently complicated so that a considerable amount of development time is ordinarily involved in arriving at transformer proportions that will produce a well-shaped pulse.

[1] Noise will cause slight fluctuations (i.e., jitter) in the time of successive cycles, just as in the multivibrator.

[2] The initial portion of the flat top of the pulse ordinarily has superimposed upon it a small very high-frequency, highly damped, transient oscillation as shown in Fig. 18-18b. This oscillation is produced by shock excitation of the resonant system formed by the leakage inductance and the distributed capacitance C_p of the transformer.

Therefore, unless pulse shape is not important, it is desirable wherever possible to purchase a transformer intended for a blocking oscillator of the pulse duration desired, and then to use this transformer with the tube and under the conditions for which it was designed.

Repetition Frequency of Pulses and Synchronization with External Voltages. The repetition frequency of the free-running blocking oscillator, i.e., the number of cycles of operation per second, is given by the following relation, which is analogous to Eq. (18-14):

$$\text{Repetition frequency} = \frac{1}{\Delta t + R_g C_g \log_\epsilon \dfrac{E + E_0}{E + (E_b/\mu)}} \qquad (18\text{-}15)$$

where Δt = length of pulse, sec
$\quad E_0$ = voltage on C_g at end of pulse
$\quad E_b$ = plate-supply voltage
$\quad \mu$ = amplification factor of tube
$\quad E$ = positive bias voltage applied to control grid at point x in Fig. 18-18a (E is assumed zero in the oscillograms of Fig. 18-18b)
$\quad R_g$ = grid-leak resistance
$\quad C_g$ = grid-capacitor capacitance

This notation is illustrated in Fig. 18-18. The quantity E_0 is a complex function of transformer and tube characteristics, pulse length, grid-capacitor capacitance, and plate-supply voltage.

The repetition frequency can be controlled satisfactorily over a very wide range of values without change in pulse shape or length by varying the grid-leak resistance R_g. For any given value of R_g, continuous control over a substantial range can be achieved readily by means of an adjustable positive-bias voltage applied at point x in Fig. 18-18a, which in analogy with the positive-bias multivibrator increases the repetition frequency. Although Eq. (18-15) indicates that the repetition frequency depends upon C_g as well as R_g, this fact is seldom made use of to control the repetition frequency, as any substantial change in C_g will change the pulse length, and also may adversely alter the pulse shape.

The repetition frequency of a blocking oscillator will readily synchronize in harmonic relation with the frequency of an injected voltage, just as in the case of the multivibrator. The mechanism involved in such synchronization is essentially the same as that discussed in connection with Fig. 18-15; i.e., the injected voltage controls the instant t_4 at which the pulse is initiated.

One-shot Operation of the Blocking Oscillator. When a fixed negative bias somewhat greater than cutoff is inserted in the circuit of a blocking oscillator at point x in Fig. 18-18a, operation analogous to that of the one-shot multivibrator results. Such a system is inactive until an incoming positive trigger pulse is superimposed on the bias and momentarily reduces the grid potential of the tube to a value that is less negative than cutoff. The blocking oscillator then generates one pulse followed by a damped oscillation. After this oscillation dies out, the blocking oscillator again becomes inactive and remains quiescent with a grid bias greater than cutoff until the next positive pulse arrives. Operated in this manner, the blocking oscillator produces pulses that are accurately controlled by the incoming pulses, irrespective of whether these pulses arrive regularly or irregularly.

Practical Applications of the Blocking Oscillator.   The principal use of the blocking oscillator is as a generator of short pulses of large amplitude.

By the use of a suitably designed transformer, a pulse width anywhere in the range 0.1 to 25 μsec can be readily generated. The pulses have relatively steep leading and lagging edges, and a fairly rectangular shape, which can be made even more truly rectangular by the use of a slicer that selects a section of the pulse, such as the part between *a* and *b* indicated in the bottom line of Fig. 18-18*b*. The peak energy of the pulses obtainable from the blocking oscillator is relatively large. This arises from the fact that the tube carries current only during a small fraction of the time, so that very large peak plate and grid currents are permissible without overheating the tube. Finally, the blocking oscillator has the merit that the pulse repetition frequency can be readily controlled by an external voltage.

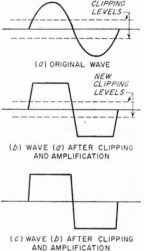

(a) ORIGINAL WAVE

(b) WAVE (a) AFTER CLIPPING AND AMPLIFICATION

(c) WAVE (b) AFTER CLIPPING AND AMPLIFICATION

FIG. 18-19. Generation of square wave by repeated clipping and amplification, starting with a sine wave.

18-7. Square-wave Generation.   There are two main ways of generating a square wave of voltage.   In the first, one produces the square wave directly by means of the multivibrator circuit of Fig. 18-9*a*.   As can be seen by the oscillograms of Fig. 18-10, the plate-voltage waveform of either tube very closely approximates a square wave except for transients such as indicated by A_1 and A_2; these imperfections can be removed by passing the waveform through a clipping circuit.

The second method used to obtain a square wave is to convert a sine wave into a square wave by alternately clipping, amplifying, clipping, etc.   The effect of clipping a sine wave, amplifying the clipped wave, clipping again, further amplifying, etc., is shown by the sequence of oscillograms given in Fig. 18–19.

18-8. Pulse Generators.   Two types of pulses, as shown in Fig. 18-20, are to be distinguished.   The rectangular pulse can be thought of as an unsymmetrical square wave, in which the positive (or negative) portion is of very short duration, and the remaining portion is of relatively long duration; its waveform in the ideal case consists of accurately horizontal and vertical segments.[1] Alternatively, a trigger pulse is characterized by a steep rise and a short duration, with the exact waveform being not critical. Such a pulse is used to initiate an action in other circuits.

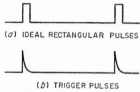

(a) IDEAL RECTANGULAR PULSES

(b) TRIGGER PULSES

Fig. 18-20. Rectangular and trigger pulses.

The trigger-type pulse is usually generated by differentiating either a square wave or a steeply rising (or falling) portion of some other waveform. Generation of a rectangular pulse calls for more refinement, however, and as in the case of square waves can be accomplished either by shaping operations performed upon another waveform, or by direct generation. Common methods used to obtain pulses will now be described.

Pulse Generation by Differentiation. Differentiation of a square wave will produce trigger pulses, as illustrated in Fig. 18-21, which have a length determined by the steepness of the vertical sides of the square wave. The trigger pulses can in turn be converted to short pulses that are very nearly rectangular by clipping, or slicing, and then amplifying, as illustrated in the final three lines of Fig. 18-21. When desired, a series diode rectifier can be used to permit pulses of only one polarity to be transmitted to the output.

A short trigger pulse can be derived from a longer pulse by differentiating, as illustrated in Fig. 18-22. By amplifying and slicing (or clipping), this trigger pulse can be made into a much shorter rectangular pulse than the original. The use of differentiation to shorten a pulse in this way is a standard technique.

Pulse Generation by Use of the Multivibrator.

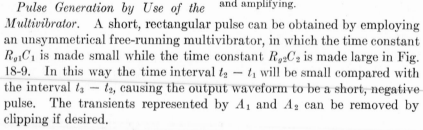

Fig. 18-21. Generation of a trigger pulse by differentiation of a square wave, together with conversion of the trigger pulse to a rectangular pulse by clipping and amplifying.

A short, rectangular pulse can be obtained by employing an unsymmetrical free-running multivibrator, in which the time constant $R_{g1}C_1$ is made small while the time constant $R_{g2}C_2$ is made large in Fig. 18-9. In this way the time interval $t_2 - t_1$ will be small compared with the interval $t_3 - t_2$, causing the output waveform to be a short, negative pulse. The transients represented by A_1 and A_2 can be removed by clipping if desired.

---

[1] The steepness of the vertical portions of a pulse (and also of a square wave) is ordinarily determined by the bandwidths of the circuits used in the generation and transmission of the pulse, as discussed in Secs. 9-1 and 18-15.

The pulse length is determined by the time constant $R_{g1}C_1$ (when the period between t_1 and t_2 in Fig. 18-10 is to be the pulse) and by the bias voltage to which R_{g1} is connected. If the pulses are to be of very short duration, it is best to connect the grid-leak resistor to a positive-bias voltage such as the plate-supply voltage. If it is desired that the pulse duration be adjustable, the resistor can be returned to a variable positive voltage.

The interval between pulses, i.e., their recurrence frequency, is determined by the other time constant $R_{g2}C_2$, and the voltage to which R_{g2} is connected. If the period between pulses is to be varied, this can be accomplished by adjusting the time constant $R_{g2}C_2$, or the bias voltage to which grid-leak resistor R_{g2} is returned. To the extent that the pulse duration is very small compared with the interval between pulses these two quantities are accordingly independently controllable.

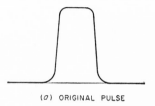

(a) ORIGINAL PULSE

The arrangement just described is of the free-running variety, in that it oscillates continuously and will provide a steady succession of pulses. On the other hand, the one-shot form of the multivibrator described on page 632 will provide one rectangular pulse for each trigger pulse received. The duration of this pulse is determined by the leak-capacitor time constant and the positive bias of the tube that conducts current in the intervals between pulses. This pulse length can be readily adjusted by varying the positive bias (or the bias potentiometer P of Fig. 18-16a when the multivibrator is cathode coupled).

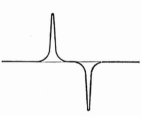

(b) PULSE AFTER DIFFERENTIATION

FIG. 18-22. Generation of a short pulse by differentiation of a longer pulse.

The multivibrator pulse generator has the advantage that the duration and repetition rate of the pulses can be easily and independently adjusted. It has the disadvantage, however, that one of the tubes must carry current during the period between pulses and so must be able to handle almost continuously an amount of power corresponding to the peak power of the pulse. Thus when appreciable pulse power is required advantage cannot be taken of the ability of small tubes to handle large amounts of power for relatively short intervals. In addition, the duration of the pulse is dependent somewhat upon the supply voltages and tube characteristics; however, this can be remedied by incorporating a delay line as part of the multivibrator circuit as will be discussed below.

Pulse Generation by Use of the Blocking Oscillator. It was pointed out above, in Sec. 18-6, that the blocking oscillator forms a useful pulse generator. Its great advantage is the ability to develop pulses of large voltage (or large power) with small tubes and minimum power-supply requirements; its disadvantage is its relative inflexibility as to pulse length which tends to be fixed at a specific value for any particular transformer unless a delay line (see page 643) is employed to control the length. The blocking-oscillator type of pulse generator can be arranged for either free-running or one-shot operation, as discussed in Sec. 18-6.

Pulse Generation Using a Tuned Circuit. Another method of gener-

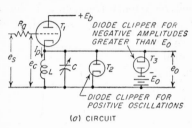

(a) CIRCUIT

ating pulses is illustrated in Fig. 18-23. Here a resonant circuit LC is placed between ground and the cathode of tube T_1. In the absence of an applied signal the grid of T_1 is at cathode potential, and plate current I_p flows through L. Assume now that a control voltage e_s of large amplitude is applied to the grid of T_1. When this signal goes negative, the plate current of T_1 is suddenly cut off. In the absence of diode clippers T_2 and T_3, the current originally flowing through L would set up a damped oscillation, as shown in Fig. 18-23b. The frequency of this oscillation is the resonant frequency of the circuit LC, and the peak amplitude of the voltage developed across LC is $I_p \sqrt{L/C}$. However, the diode clipper tube T_2 prevents the output voltage e_0 from becoming positive, thus causing the damped oscillation to be stopped after the first half cycle, as shown. Under these con-

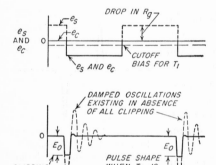

(b) WAVEFORMS

FIG. 18-23. The generation of a short pulse by the use of a clipped transient of a resonant circuit.

ditions the output voltage e consists of a pulse shaped like a half cycle of a sine wave, and having a length corresponding to a half cycle of the resonant frequency of the circuit LC. The repetition frequency of the pulses generated is equal to the frequency of the control voltage e_s.

Rectangular pulses can be obtained by clipping the sine-wave pulse at a level such as E_0 in Fig. 18-23b that is considerably less than the peak amplitude. This can be accomplished by adding a second clipping diode T_3 to the system, as shown in Fig. 18-23b. Further improvement in pulse shape can be achieved by amplification, followed by further clipping, in analogy with Fig. 18-19.

The control voltage e_s in Fig. 18-23 must change from zero amplitude to a value equal to the cutoff bias of T_1 in a time that does not exceed half of the length of the pulse to be generated. When very short pulses of low or moderate repetition frequency are desired, e_s must be a square wave with appropriately steep sides, and an amplitude preferably considerably greater than cutoff, as shown in Fig. 23b. However, in many cases it is permissible to employ a sine wave of large amplitude. Thus if a sine wave has an amplitude 32 times the cutoff bias, the time interval between zero and cutoff amplitude is $\sin^{-1} \frac{1}{32} = 1.8°$, which corresponds to a pulse that lasts not less than 3.6°. For a 2000-cycle sinusoidal control wave, this means that the shortest pulse that can be generated under these conditions is about 5 μsec.

The high resistance R_g in series with the grid in Fig. 18-29a is for the purpose of producing a clipping action such that on the positive half cycles of the control voltage e_s (whether it be sinusoidal or square) the grid will remain at very close to cathode potential.

The circuit of Fig. 18-23a provides a very simple means of generating pulses. The pulse length can moreover be easily controlled simply by varying the resonant frequency of the tuned circuit with variable capacitor C, and it is readily possible to obtain pulse lengths less than 1 μsec.

18-9. Lines and Pulse-forming Networks in Pulse Generation. *Line Pulsers.* An important technique for generating short pulses consists in

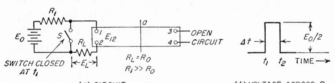

(a) CIRCUIT   (b) VOLTAGE ACROSS R_L

Fig. 18-24. Schematic diagram of a line pulser.

discharging through a load resistance the energy stored in a transmission line. Such a pulse generator is illustrated schematically in Fig. 18-24a. During the period between pulses the line is charged to a voltage E_0 through a high resistance R_1.* The pulse is then initiated by closing switch S which disconnects charging resistance R_1 from the line, and simultaneously connects across the line a load resistance R_L that equals the characteristic resistance R_0 of the transmission line.

When S is closed at t_1 the charged line starts supplying current to load resistance R_L, causing the voltage across terminals 1-2 to drop from the value E_0 that existed before switching to $E_0/2$. This voltage $E_0/2$ is maintained across R_L for a period equal to the time that it takes a transient wave on the line to travel from terminals 1-2 to the end of line 3-4 and back to 1-2. At the end of this period, time t_2, all of the energy originally stored in the line has been delivered to R_L, and the voltage

---

* In situations where power efficiency is important R_1 can be replaced by a high inductance, thus eliminating the power loss in R_1 during the changing period.

across the latter suddenly drops to zero. The result is the rectangular pulse of voltage across R_L that is shown in Fig. 18-24, which has an amplitude $E_0/2$ and a length $\Delta t = t_2 - t_1$, where $\Delta t/2$ is the length of time it takes a transient wave to travel the length of the line.

The process by which the line discharges its energy into the load resistance R_L can be explained in terms of waves that act as illustrated in Fig. 18-25.[1] Closing switch S in Fig. 18-24a causes a wave to be initiated at 1-2 that travels towards 3-4 with the line velocity.[2] This wave consists of a voltage having an amplitude $E_0/2$ everywhere accompanied by a current equal to $E_0/2R_0 = E_0/2R_L$, where R_0 is the characteristic impedance of the line. The wave voltage is negative, and so wipes out half of the original line voltage as it travels, as shown in the second section of Fig. 18-25. When the wave reaches the open end 3-4 of the line it is then reflected in such a manner that the voltage of the reflected wave has the same polarity as that of the incident wave, while the current of the reflected wave has the opposite polarity from the current of the incident wave. Thus as the reflected wave travels towards 1-2 it wipes out the remaining voltage on the line, while the current of the reflected wave cancels the current of the incident wave where the two waves superimpose. The result is that when the reflected wave reaches the terminals 1-2, no voltage and no current are present anywhere on the line. However, during the entire interval $t_2 - t_1 = \Delta t$, there is a voltage $E_0/2$ across the load resistance and a current $E_0/2R_0$ (corresponding to the current of the wave) flowing through R_L.

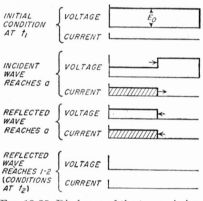

Fig. 18-25. Discharge of the transmission line in Fig. 18-24a after switch S is closed.

Lines and Switches. The transmission indicated in Fig. 18-24 is commonly termed a *delay line,* or a *pulse-forming line* (or network). It is normally an artificial line; actual lines are avoided because of the excessive length required even when the pulses are short. A variety of types of artificial lines are suitable.[3] A simple form is illustrated in Fig. 18-26a, where an appropriate amount of mutual inductance preferably exists

[1] A good introductory discussion of the properties of such waves is given by H. H. Skilling, "Electric Transmission Lines," chap. 14, McGraw-Hill Book Company, Inc., New York, 1951.

[2] In the case of an actual transmission line with air dielectric, this is the velocity of light. In the case of a cable it will be less than the velocity of light by a factor equal to the square root of the dielectric constant.

[3] For further information, see "Pulse Generators," *op. cit.,* pp. 175–224.

between the coils as shown. A ladder network composed of series inductances and shunt capacitances as in Fig. 18-26a is often converted into the
alternative but equivalent form shown in Fig. 18-26b.

Another type of artificial line, suitable for low power operation, consists of a coaxial cable in which the inner conductor is a continuous
coil of small wire wound on an insulating cylindrical core. This greatly
increases the inductance per unit length of line, with corresponding reduction of the velocity and increase in the time delay per unit length. It is
possible with such a line to obtain a round-trip transit time of as much as
1 μsec in a length as short as 2 ft.

The switch shown in Fig. 18-24 can take various forms according to the
requirements imposed by voltage,
switching rate, etc. A mechanical
commutator, or rotating contactor,
is occasionally employed. Alternatively, a rotary spark gap finds use
in high-voltage applications, in which
case a low-resistance spark discharge
takes the place of the mechanical
contact. Finally, extensive use is
made of electronic switching that is
provided either by a gas triode
(thyratron) or a high-vacuum triode
or pentode.[1]

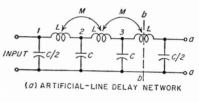

(a) ARTIFICIAL-LINE DELAY NETWORK

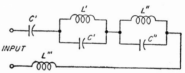

(b) PULSE-FORMING NETWORK

FIG. 18-26. Lumped-element networks
equivalent to the open-circuited transmission line of Fig. 18-24.

*Delay-line Control of Pulse Length
in the Multivibrator and Blocking
Oscillator.* The length of the pulse generated by a multivibrator or
blocking oscillator can be controlled by the use of a transmission line.
The basic idea as applied to the blocking oscillator of Fig. 18-18 is illustrated in Fig. 18-27.[2] Here the grid capacitor C_g in Fig. 18-18a is replaced
by the input terminals 1-2 of the delay line as shown. At the time t_2 in
Fig. 18-18 when the tube begins to conduct, the line terminals 1-2 act as a
resistance having a value equal to the characteristic impedance R_0 of the
line. Thus the grid current that starts to flow at time t_2 encounters an
impedance across the line terminals 1-2 corresponding to R_0 shunted by
R_g. The resulting voltage drop developed across 1-2 causes a wave of like
voltage to start traveling down the line. This wave has a polarity such
that terminal 1 is negative with respect to terminal 2. Upon reaching

---

[1] In high-power applications which use a gas triode the tube is commonly of the
hydrogen-filled type because of the shorter deionization time thus obtained as compared with the mercury-filled thyratron.

[2] This is only one of many ways in which a delay line can be employed to control the
length of the pulse generated by a blocking oscillator or multivibrator; for additional
examples see Terman and Pettit, *op. cit.*, pp. 571–574.

open-circuited terminals 3-4 of the line this negative wave is reflected without change in polarity, and so doubles the negative voltage on the parts of the line it has reached. Hence at the instant the reflected wave reaches input terminals 1-2 of the line, the voltage of terminal 1 will suddenly become twice as negative with respect to terminal 2 as had been the case since t_2. If the blocking oscillator circuits are appropriately designed in relation to the characteristic impedance R_0 of the line, this

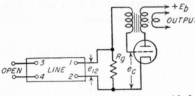

sudden reduction in grid potential will be sufficient to trigger off a cumulative action that will bring about termination of the conducting period of the tube. The charge on the line capacitance then leaks off through R_g until the voltage across 1-2 reaches cutoff, at which time the cycle repeats.

Fig. 18-27. Blocking oscillator provided with a delay line for controlling the pulse length.

The end result of this process is that the length of the pulse generated by the blocking oscillator is precisely determined by the length of the delay line, and is largely independent of the circuit details of the rest of the blocking oscillator, of the tube constants, and of the supply voltages, while the repetition frequency is determined by the line capacitance discharging through the grid-leak resistance R_g.

An analogous behavior can be achieved in a multivibrator by the use of a delay line.

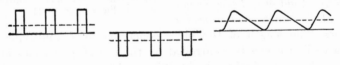

(a) WAVES WITH D-C COMPONENT (SHOWN DOTTED)

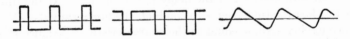

(b) WAVES WITH D-C COMPONENT REMOVED

Fig. 18-28. Unsymmetrical waveforms with and without a d-c component.

18-10. Clamping Circuits—D-C Restoration. Many unsymmetrical waveforms possess a d-c component; examples are illustrated in Fig. 18-28a. When one of these waveforms is passed through a transformer or a capacitor, the d-c component is not transmitted, and the output waves thus have the character illustrated in Fig. 18-28b. To regain the original waveform it then becomes necessary to reinsert a d-c component of appropriate amplitude. This process is termed *d-c restoration*.

Such d-c restoration is a special example of a more general process known as *clamping*, in which a reference level is introduced that has some desired relationship to the wave. Thus consider the pulsed waveform of Fig. 18-29a, which possesses no d-c component. If circuits are used that insert a d-c component of such amplitude and polarity that the negative peaks of the original wave are at zero level, as shown in Fig. 18-29b, then it is said that the negative peaks of this wave are clamped to zero. The same wave with its positive peaks clamped to zero potential, and to E volts positive, is shown in Fig. 18-29c and d, respectively.

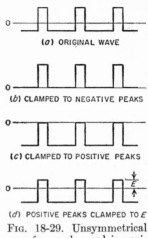

FIG. 18-29. Unsymmetrical waveforms clamped in various ways.

In some cases the reference level to which the wave is to be clamped is included as part of the waveform being transmitted. Thus a reference level may be transmitted in the form of flat steps in the waveform that occur at regular intervals t_1, t_2, t_3, etc., as shown in Fig. 18-30. The clamping circuit is then required to introduce a d-c level equal to the amplitude E_0 of these steps. This requires that the clamping system be keyed in such a manner that the reinserted d-c level is responsive to the amplitude of the wave shape only during the intervals t_1, t_2, etc., when the reference level is being transmitted.

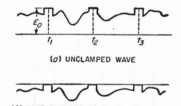

(a) UNCLAMPED WAVE

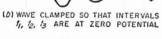

(b) WAVE CLAMPED SO THAT INTERVALS t_1, t_2, t_3 ARE AT ZERO POTENTIAL

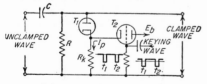

(c) KEYED CLAMPED CIRCUIT

FIG. 18-30. Example of keyed clamping.

Diode and Grid Clamps. The simplest form of clamping circuit consists of a diode associated with a resistance-capacitance network, as illustrated in Fig. 18-31. The resistance R in these circuits is quite large, so that the time constant RC is considerably greater than the time of one cycle of the applied wave.

The detailed action of the diode clamp of Fig. 18-31b can be understood by considering Fig. 18-32. If RC is so large that it can be considered as infinite, then the diode acts as a rectifier that charges capacitance C to a voltage E'_0 that just barely prevents the voltage at x from going positive; thus E'_0 is the reinserted d-c voltage. However, if RC is high but not infinite, then some of the charge on the capacitor leaks off during the time interval $t_3 - t_2$. This causes the output wave at x to decay with a time constant RC during the time interval $t_3 - t_2$; however, if RC is very much greater than the time $t_3 - t_2$, the change ΔE_0 in the amplitude of the output voltage will be small.   At t_3 the voltage at the

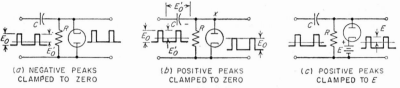

(a) NEGATIVE PEAKS
CLAMPED TO ZERO

(b) POSITIVE PEAKS
CLAMPED TO ZERO

(c) POSITIVE PEAKS
CLAMPED TO E

Fig. 18-31. Diode clamping arrangement.

output terminals increases suddenly in amplitude by the peak-to-peak amplitude E_0 of the applied wave, and makes the output voltage go ΔE_0

volts positive at time t_3.   This causes current to flow into the capacitor to replace the charge that leaked off during the previous period, as shown.   The time constant associated with this current flow corresponds to C being charged through the diode plate resistance, and is quite small because of the low resistance of the tube.

The proper value for the time constant RC is a compromise between two conflicting requirements. The larger this time constant, the less will be the variation ΔE of the clamping voltage during the cycle, and hence the smaller will be the positive spike at t_1 and t_3.   On the other hand, the larger the value RC, the more slowly is the clamping voltage able to adjust itself to reductions in amplitude of the wave that is to be clamped.

The positive peaks of a wave applied to the control grid of a vacuum tube may be conveniently clamped to zero by introducing a resistance-capacitor combination RC in the grid circuit, as shown in Fig. 18-33.   This grid clamping arrangement is equivalent to the diode clamper of Fig. 18-31b, since the combination of grid and cathode acts as a diode rectifier.

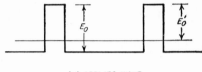

(a) APPLIED WAVE

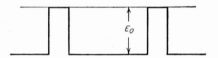

(b) OUTPUT WAVE – RC INFINITE

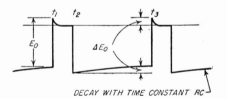

(c) OUTPUT WAVE—MODERATE RC

(d) CURRENT THROUGH DIODE
CORRESPONDING TO (c)

Fig. 18-32. Behavior of diode clamping circuit of Fig. 18-31, taking into account the time constant RC.

Keyed Clamps.   A simple form of keyed clamp applied to the waveform of Fig. 18-30a is shown in Fig. 18-30c.[1]   Here tube T_2 acts as a switch that turns the clamping action of diode T_1 on at times t_1, t_2, t_3, etc., and keeps it inactive the rest of the time.   This result is achieved by so proportioning the system that when the grid potential of T_2 is zero, the plate current I_p flowing through resistance R_k causes the potential above ground of cathode T_1 to be greater than the positive peaks of the applied wave; this makes the diode inactive. However, when T_2 is driven to cutoff, $I_p = 0$, and clamping action occurs; the effective diode plate resistance is then the actual resistance plus the series resistance R_k.   The clamping illustrated in Fig. 18-30b is hence obtained by applying to the grid of T_2 a voltage wave consisting of narrow negative pulses that are synchronized with the intervals t_1, t_2, etc., and

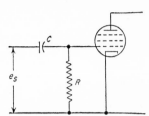

FIG. 18-33.   A triode circuit arranged so that the applied voltage e_s has its positive peak clamped to zero potential.

clamped so their positive peaks are at zero level.   This arrangement will cause the capacitor C to be charged to the voltage E_0 that corresponds to the amplitude of the applied wave at t_1, t_2, etc.; the wave amplitude at other times has no effect on the voltage across C.   Thus the reinserted d-c voltage has exactly the value needed to give the desired clamping action.

18-11. Saw-tooth-wave Generators.   A saw-tooth waveform is charac-

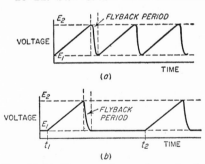

FIG. 18-34. Common types of saw-tooth waveforms.

terized by intervals during which the voltage rises (or falls) linearly with time.   Two basic types of saw-tooth waveforms are to be distinguished.   In the first, illustrated in Fig. 18-34a, the successive linear portions (shown rising) are separated by relatively short intervals during which the wave returns to the starting value; this return is often called the *flyback* period.   The second type of waveform, illustrated in Fig. 18-34b, involves a quiescent period before each linear section.   The starting, or triggering, times t_1, t_2, etc., of the linear portions of such a wave can then occur either at regular or irregular intervals, as the occasion may require.

Saw-tooth waveforms find many practical applications.   The most important of these are as sweep voltages of cathode-ray oscillographs, and for the deflection of the electron beam in television picture tubes.

---

[1] More elaborate keyed clamps having a performance superior to that of this simple arrangement are described by K. R. Wendt, Television D-c Component, *RCA Rev.*, vol. 9, p. 85, March, 1948.

Desirable characteristics in a saw-tooth wave are linearity of the rising portion of the wave, a flyback time that is a reasonably small fraction of the time of one cycle, uniformity of the waveform from cycle to cycle,[1] and ability to synchronize with other waveforms.

Saw-tooth waves may be generated in many ways. One possibility is to integrate a wave consisting of regularly recurring pulses, as illustrated in the second column of Fig. 18-7. A more frequently used approach is to generate the wave directly.

Thyratron Saw-tooth-wave Generator. A widely used form of saw-tooth-wave generator is illustrated in Fig. 18-35a, in which a voltage E_b is

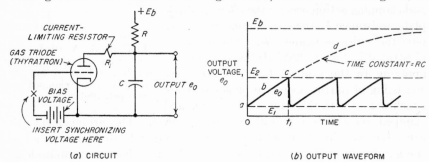

(a) CIRCUIT   (b) OUTPUT WAVEFORM

FIG. 18-35. Gas-triode (thyratron) type of saw-tooth-wave generator, together with typical waveforms.

applied to a circuit consisting of a resistance R and a capacitance C in series. The plate-cathode circuit of a gas triode (thyratron) is then shunted across C as illustrated, and biased so that the tube ionizes at a voltage E_2 that is a moderately small fraction of E_b.

When E_b is first applied to the system the voltage across C rises exponentially according to the time constant RC as indicated by abc in Fig. 18-35b. However, when the voltage across C reaches the value E_2 the thyratron ionizes, and C discharges quickly through the tube,[2] causing the voltage across C to drop to the extinction voltage E_1, at which ionization can no longer be maintained. The tube then becomes nonconducting, voltage again starts to build up across C, and the cycle repeats. The result is a saw-tooth wave, as illustrated.

Since the rising portion of the saw-tooth waveform is the first part of an exponential curve $abcd$, the linearity of the wave will be greater the smaller the ratio $E_2/(E_b - E_1)$. Thus the linearity will be poorer when the bias of the thyratron tube is adjusted to cause the ionization potential E_2 to be a large fraction of the supply-voltage E_b.

[1] Lack of uniformity is called jitter because it causes the pattern on a cathode-ray oscilloscope to jitter about when the time axis is provided by a saw-tooth generator that does not repeat exactly.

[2] A current limiting resistance R_1 is commonly employed in order to prevent the capacitor from discharging through the tube so rapidly as to make the plate current great enough to damage the tube.

The frequency of the saw-tooth wave oscillations in Fig. 18-35b can be readily adjusted without altering the amplitude of the waveform by changing either R or C.   The highest frequency that can be obtained with a thyratron saw-tooth-wave generator is determined by the deionization time of the tube.   This is typically of the order of 50 kc for tubes employing the lighter gases and below 10 kc for mercury-vapor thyratron tubes.

The thyratron saw-tooth generator, like the multivibrator, will readily synchronize with another waveform.   The synchronizing voltage is applied in series with the control grid as indicated in Fig. 18-35a.   This causes the ionizing voltage of the thyratron to be reduced when the synchronizing voltage is positive and increased when it is negative, as shown in Fig. 18-36.   As a result, the frequency of the saw-tooth oscilla-

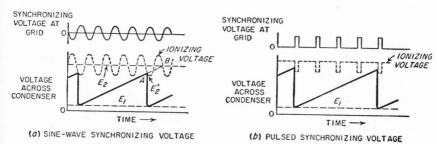

Fig. 18-36. Oscillograms illustrating synchronization of thyratron saw-tooth generator with sinusoidal and pulsed waveforms.

tion takes on a value that is in exact harmonic relationship with the synchronizing frequency, as shown in Fig. 18-36.   It is possible to maintain synchronization fairly satisfactorily when the frequency ratio is as great as 10:1.

Saw-tooth Generators Using High-vacuum Tubes.   The gas triode in the circuit of Fig. 18-35a can be replaced by a high-vacuum tube, as in Fig. 18-37a.   Here tube T_1 is alternately switched between conducting and nonconducting conditions by applying to its control grid a pulsed wave in which the positive peaks are clamped so that the grid voltage of T_1 alternates between zero and a negative value sufficient to cut off the plate current.   During the interval when the plate current is cut off, the output voltage e_0 across capacitor C rises exponentially in exactly the same way as does the voltage e_0 in the thyratron circuit of Fig. 18-35a when the thyratron tube is nonconducting.   During the interval when the voltage at the grid is zero, capacitor C then discharges rapidly through the tube.   When the pulse length is so short that the capacitor is still delivering current to the plate circuit of the tube at the end of the discharge period, the waveform has the character illustrated in Fig. 18-37b.   In contrast, when the pulse length is great enough to permit the capacitor to discharge as completely as it can, the waveform of Fig. 18-37c results.

Free-running action can be obtained by arrangements such as shown in Fig. 18-37d,[1] e, and f.   In each of these cases tube T_1 draws a large plate current for a small fraction of each oscillator cycle, and is then non-conducting the rest of the time just as in the case of tube T_1 in Fig. 18-37a.

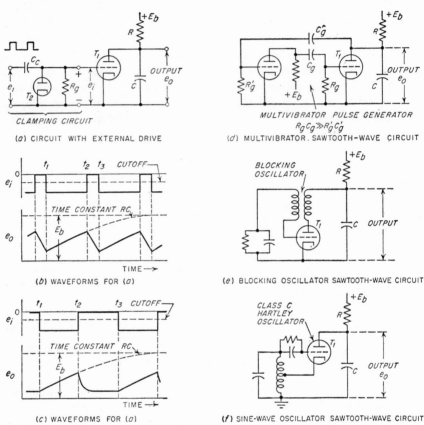

FIG. 18-37. Saw-tooth-wave generators employing high-vacuum triodes, together with typical waveforms.

By properly proportioning R and C, the voltage across C in these circuits will have the same saw-tooth shape that is shown at Fig. 18-37b or c.

18-12. Linearization Refinements in Saw-tooth-wave Generators. The saw-tooth waveforms generated by the circuits in Figs. 18-35 and 18-37 are not sufficiently linear for certain applications, such as radar or precision oscillographic work.   There exists a great variety of refinements whereby the linearity can be improved.

Constant-current Capacitor Charging by Use of a Pentode.   A straight

---

[1] In this circuit the return time is made less than the forward time by proportioning the multivibrator so that it acts as a pulse generator (see p. 638) in which $R_g C_g$ is large compared with $R_g' C_g'$.

forward approach to improving the linearity of a saw-tooth-wave generator consists in substituting the plate-cathode circuit of a pentode tube in place of the resistance R in Figs. 18-35a and 18-37; a typical arrangement of this type is illustrated in Fig. 18-38.   To the extent that the pentode tube is operated under conditions where the plate current is independent of the plate voltage, the pentode will deliver a constant current

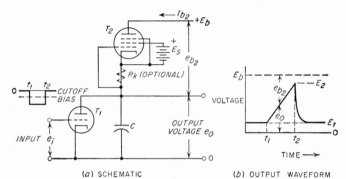

| (a) SCHEMATIC | (b) OUTPUT WAVEFORM |

FIG. 18-38. Saw-tooth-wave generator of Fig. 18-37a modified by use of a pentode to obtain constant-current charging.

to the capacitor C.   As a result, the output voltage e_0 across the capacitor will rise linearly with time, instead of exponentially as in Fig. 18-35b. The slope of the rise is I_{b2}/C volts per sec, where I_{b2} is the pentode plate current in amperes, and C is in farads.

Bootstrap Circuit.   Another means of obtaining a constant current for the charging of a capacitor is provided by the so-called *bootstrap circuit,* one form of which is schematically illustrated in Fig. 18-39.[1]   Here the

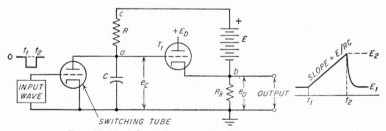

FIG. 18-39. A bootstrap saw-tooth-wave generator.

capacitor C is charged through the resistor R by a voltage consisting of E plus the output voltage e_0 of the cathode-follower stage T_1.   The cathode resistor R_k is made large, so that the amplification of T_1 approaches unity, that is, $e_0 \approx e_c$.   The voltage across the terminals ca of R hence approximates E at all times, corresponding to a current E/R.   The result is con-

---

[1] In practical bootstrap saw-tooth-wave generators, modifications are usually introduced that make it possible to obtain the voltage E from the same source of power that supplies the plate potential of T_1; see Terman and Pettit, *op, cit.,* p. 585.

stant-current charging of C that is substantially equivalent to that obtained by the use of the pentode in Fig. 18-38a. Saw-tooth waves are then generated by shunting C with a switching system consisting of a gas triode or a high-vacuum triode with pulsed-wave control voltage. The output voltage e_0 is the voltage e_c developed across the capacitor C, as amplified by the cathode-follower stage T_1; this provides the incidental benefit of the low output impedance typical of a cathode-follower circuit.

The name "bootstrap" comes from the fact that the potentials at points a and b in Fig. 18-39 rise simultaneously with respect to ground as

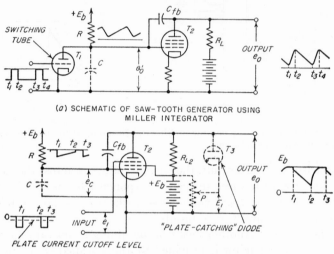

(a) SCHEMATIC OF SAW-TOOTH GENERATOR USING MILLER INTEGRATOR

(b) PRACTICAL FORM OF SAW-TOOTH-WAVE GENERATOR UTILIZING MILLER INTEGRATOR

FIG. 18-40. A saw-tooth-wave generator utilizing Miller integrator.

the capacitor C charges. These potentials are thus "raised by their own bootstraps."

Saw-tooth-wave Generators Based on the Miller Integrator. Saw-tooth-wave generators such as those of Fig. 18-35a and 18-37, which operate by charging a capacitance through a resistance, will develop an output that is almost ideally linear provided the amplitude is restricted to a value that is only a few per cent of the supply voltage E_b. Amplification can then be used to obtain an output wave of reasonable size.

The most desirable amplifier arrangement for this purpose is the Miller integrator shown schematically in Fig. 18-40a. This is a one-stage integrating operational amplifier of the type discussed in Fig. 18-8a, the input capacitance of which, as given by Eq. (18-6), supplies the capacitance used in the generation of the saw-tooth wave.

The Miller integrator arrangement has certain uniquely desirable properties that can be understood by examination of the factors that control the slope of the output waveform e_0. Assuming that in Fig. 18-40 the maximum voltage developed across C is small compared with E_b, the slope of the saw-tooth waveform e_0' across C will be[1]

$$\text{Slope of } e_0' \text{ waveform } = \frac{E_b}{RC} \tag{18-16}$$

The slope of the output waveform e_0 is $-A$ times as great, where A is the amplification (assumed to take place with no phase shift other than a reversal of polarity).   Hence

$$\text{Slope of } e_0 \text{ waveform } = -A\frac{E_b}{RC} \tag{18-17}$$

Substituting Eq. (18-6) into Eq. (18-17) and making the assumptions $A >> 1$, and $AC_{fb} >> C_{gk}$ give

$$\text{Slope of } e_0 \text{ waveform } = -\frac{E_b}{RC_{fb}} \tag{18-18}$$

This equation shows that the slope of the output wave is independent of the tube characteristics.   In particular, *it will be noted that amplitude distortion in the amplifier does not introduce nonlinearity in the amplified wave* when the Miller integrator is employed; hence the output wave can have a peak-to-peak amplitude only slightly less than the supply voltage E_b.

In practical Miller integrator systems the switching function of tube T_1 of Fig. 18-40a is usually obtained by applying a switching voltage to the suppressor grid of amplifier tube T_2 as shown in Fig. 18-40b.   Here, the switching is accomplished by negative pulses that have sufficient amplitude to turn the plate current of T_2 off when the positive part of the pulse is clamped to zero potential.   The resulting waveforms then have the character shown in Fig. 18-41.   Just prior to the time t_1, the plate current of T_2 is zero, and hence the output voltage is equal to E_b.   The control-grid voltage e_c is approximately zero, although very slightly positive by virtue of the grid being connected to the positive voltage E_b through the resistance R.   The control grid cannot go appreciably positive, because the resistance R is large compared with the plate resistance of the equivalent diode comprising the grid-cathode portion of the tube.

At time t_1 plate current is permitted to flow.   This results in a slight readjustment of the circuit voltages, since the initial flow of plate current causes the plate voltage to drop by small amount E_0.   This is accompanied by a simultaneous drop E_0 in the control-grid voltage, since the plate and grid are coupled by capacitance C_{fb}.   The tube is now in an amplifying condition, and has an input capacitance C as given by Eq. (18-6) which starts to charge up from voltage E as shown in Fig. 18-41.

[1] This results from the fact that when the voltage across C is small compared with E_b, the current I flowing into C is very nearly E_b/R.   The resulting rate of change of voltage across C, that is, the slope of e_0', is hence I/C.

The resulting amplified voltage is given in the final part of Fig. 18-41, and as indicated above will have a slope that is very closely $-E_b/RC_{fb}$.

The time interval τ during which the output voltage falls linearly with time is terminated in Fig. 18-41 when the plate voltage drops to a value $E_{\min}$ such that a virtual cathode forms between the suppressor and screen grids. When this happens, the tube ceases to amplify, and the effective input capacitance changes suddenly from AC_{fb} to C_{fb}. This causes the voltage at the grid to rise A times as fast as previously, and since A is

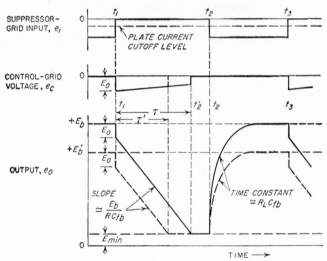

FIG. 18-41. Waveforms showing the behavior of the Miller integrator type of saw-tooth-wave circuit of Fig. 18-40b.

large, the result is that the grid voltage returns almost immediately to zero. In Fig. 18-40b, the linear slope interval is terminated by the switching voltage before $E_{\min}$ is reached. Again, the grid voltage rises immediately to zero, but now this is because the plate voltage rises at the same time. In both cases, the plate voltage rises to E_b when the switching voltage causes the plate current to be cut off; this is at t_2 in both Fig. 18-40 and Fig. 18-41. The rise of plate voltage follows a time constant represented by C_{fb} charging through R_L and the quite small grid-cathode resistance that the tube has when the grid of the tube is slightly positive.

Control of the amplitude and duration of the linear voltage slope can be conveniently obtained by connecting a diode clipper[1] T_3 across the output terminals, as shown dotted in Fig. 18-40b. This diode limits the positive excursion of the voltage e_0 at the tube plate to the value E_1. The result

---

[1] A diode connected like T_3 in Fig. 18-40b is usually referred to as a "plate-catching diode" because of the way it "catches," or arrests, the positive excursion of the plate voltage. Diodes can also be used to advantage in this way to set quiescent plate-voltage levels in various other circuits such as multivibrators.

is that the length of time required for the output voltage to drop to the minimum level can be adjusted by the setting of P; this is illustrated by the lower oscillogram in Fig. 18-41, in which the dotted curve corresponds to a setting of P that biases the cathode of T_3 to the potential $E_1 = +E_b'$.

A variety of other forms of saw-tooth-wave generators based on the Miller integrator circuit have also been devised. A particularly useful arrangement, termed the *phantastron*,[1] is a variation of Fig. 18-40b arranged to provide for one-shot operation. In the phantastron, the system is quiescent until the application of the triggering pulse, after which one cycle of operation of the type illustrated in Fig. 18-41 is executed. The system then becomes quiescent until the arrival of another triggering pulse. The phantastron thus provides a saw-tooth wave having the highly linear slope of the Miller integrator, a duration of this slope that is adjustable by means of the bias applied to a "plate-catching" diode, together with the feature that the exact time at which each linear slope is initiated is determined by a trigger pulse.

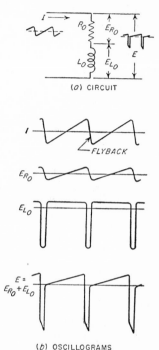

(a) CIRCUIT

(b) OSCILLOGRAMS

FIG. 18-42. Waveforms involved when a saw-tooth current wave flows through a resistance-inductance circuit.

18-13. Production of Saw-tooth Wave of Current in an Inductance-resistance Circuit. Sections 18-11 and 18-12 were concerned with the generation of saw-tooth voltage waves. However, it is sometimes necessary to pass a saw-tooth wave of current through an inductance. The most important example occurs when the electron beam of a cathode-ray beam is deflected magnetically, as is the case in television picture tubes.

The simplest method of passing a saw-tooth wave of current through an inductance is to place the inductor in the plate circuit of a pentode or beam tube and apply a saw-tooth voltage wave to the control grid. Since the plate current of a pentode varies in accordance with the voltage applied to the control grid, and is substantially independent of the voltage developed across the load impedance in the plate circuit, the current wave in the inductance is forced to have the same shape as the saw-tooth voltage wave applied to the control grid.

The waveform of the voltage developed across an inductor carrying a saw-tooth-wave current can be worked out as shown in Fig. 18-42. The

[1] For details of the phantastron see Terman and Pettit, *op. cit.*, pp. 593–597, or any one of the general references listed on p. 618.

resistance component of the inductor impedance produces a voltage drop having the same shape as the current wave. The saw-tooth wave of current flowing through the inductance component of the inductor impedance develops the pulsed waveform of the third oscillogram. The total voltage drop across the inductor accordingly has the shape given at the bottom of the figure; conversely, if a voltage wave of this shape is applied to the inductor, then a saw-tooth wave of current flows. Such a trapezoidal wave can be generated by modifying the circuit of Fig. 18-37a by adding the resistor R_2 as shown in Fig. 18-43, which generates waveforms as indicated. The trapezoidal shape of the voltage across terminals aa (and bb) is a result of the fact that during flyback the discharge of current from

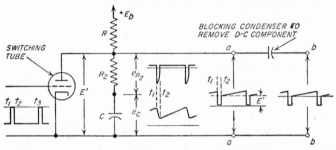

Fig. 18-43. Generation of trapezoidal wave shape by modifying the saw-tooth-wave generator of Fig. 18-37a.

C causes a large negative pulse of voltage to be developed across R_2. The slope of the wave at aa can be adjusted by varying either C or R, while the level E' of the plateau upon which the sloping wave rests can be controlled by varying R_2.

18-14. Time-delay Circuits. In many of the more sophisticated electronic systems it is necessary that two events occur in a definite time relationship to each other. The times involved are generally marked by short pulses (or sudden changes in amplitude), so the problem of generating a time delay commonly consists in obtaining two pulses (or edges of a rectangular wave) having a definite time difference between them.

One method of producing a time delay consists in employing a one-shot multivibrator such as illustrated in Fig. 18-16a in which the circuit elements are so proportioned that the time interval $\tau = t_2 - t_1$ is the desired time delay.[1] The multivibrator is then triggered into action by application of the reference pulse that marks the beginning of the interval in question (top oscillogram in Fig. 18-16b). A pulse corresponding to the end of the interval can then be obtained by differentiating the voltage e_{b1} (or e_{b2} or e_{c2}), thereby obtaining a pulse at time t_2. The delay time in such an arrangement can be adjusted by varying the potentiometer P.

---

[1] The phantastron circuit mentioned on p. 655 is the saw-tooth-wave equivalent of the one-shot multivibrator, and likewise can be employed to generate an adjustable time delay.

Another method of generating a time delay is illustrated in Fig. 18-44. Here the output from any convenient type of saw-tooth-wave generator is connected to a circuit called a *comparator*, which is actuated when the rising (or falling) saw-tooth wave reaches a specific level. Assume that the saw-tooth wave is of the type developed by a Miller integrator (see Fig. 18-40b). The comparator develops no output immediately after the time t_1 when the wave is first initiated, because the saw-tooth-wave voltage is then greater than the diode bias E_1, and the diode cathode is positive with respect to its anode. However, at the instant t_2 when the amplitude of the saw-tooth wave has dropped to the value E_1, current starts flowing through the diode. This develops a voltage across R_1 that when differentiated gives a sharp voltage drop as shown at t_2 in the wave applied to T_2, and which is delayed with respect to t_1 by the time interval

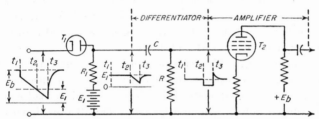

FIG. 18-44. Comparator circuit for utilizing a saw-tooth wave to obtain a time delay.

$\tau = t_2 - t_1$. This time delay can be adjusted by (1) varying the bias E_1 of the comparator diode, (2) controlling the slope of the saw-tooth wave by means of R in Fig. 18-40b, or (3) varying the initial amplitude E_b of the saw-tooth wave by adjusting the bias on a plate-catching "diode," as discussed in connection with Fig. 18-41.

A time delay may also be obtained by producing between two sine waves a phase difference corresponding to the desired time difference. Pulses marking the beginning and end of the time interval can then be obtained by separately clipping the sine waves to produce two square waves, and then differentiating these square waves to produce pulses as each wave passes through zero.

18-15. Circuit Requirements Imposed by Nonlinear Waveforms— Pulse Transformers. Wave shapes characterized by steep sides, sharp corners, absolutely linear slopes, and perfectly flat tops contain components extending over an extremely wide frequency range, and so impose severe requirements on associated circuits. If the circuits involved in either generating or *transmitting* such waveforms do not reproduce all of the frequency components of significance in correct amplitude and in correct *relative phase*, the waveform will be degraded. Thus restriction of the frequency range will cause steep sides to become sloping, will round off sharp corners, and in some cases will give rise to overshoot and to spurious oscillations. This deterioration of a pulse shape resulting from various circuit deficiencies is discussed in Sec. 9-1.

The maximum speed of rise obtainable in a circuit is in general determined by the bandwidth, as discussed in connection with Eq. (9-1). Low-frequency deficiencies in the circuit introduce sag in otherwise flat tops. Restriction of the high-frequency range rounds off sharp corners, may put wiggles in otherwise flat tops, and can cause variations in the slope of otherwise linear saw-tooth waves.

The bandwidth required to give good reproduction is considerable. For example, in order to reproduce a square or saw-tooth wave that is reasonably close to the ideal shape, it is necessary that harmonics up to the tenth or twentieth of the repetition frequency be preserved with substantially unchanged amplitude, and without phase distortion. In the case of pulses (or the steep portions of a square wave), a good wave shape requires that the top frequency transmitted be related to the desired rise time in accordance with Eq. (9-1); thus for a rise time 0.1 μsec, the 3-db bandwidth must be of the order of 4 Mc.

Pulse Transformers.[1] Transformers are sometimes called upon to handle nonlinear waveforms; a particularly important case occurs when a transformer is employed as in Fig. 10-12a to couple a load resistance to a source of pulsed power. Such a transformer will slow down the steepness of rise, cause the flat top of the pulse to sag, and may also introduce overshoot (and in some cases oscillation), as illustrated in Fig. 9-1.

Factors involved in the performance of a pulse transformer can be understood by considering the approximate equivalent circuit of Fig. 10-12c, where r_p corresponds to the internal resistance of the source of pulse power with which the transformer is associated, and the voltage E_s of this power source corresponds to $-\mu e_g$. During the intervals when E_s is rising (or falling) rapidly, the equivalent circuit takes the form shown in Fig. 10-12f, and the maximum possible speed of rise (or fall) is then determined primarily by the time constant $(r_p' + R_L')/L'$; the 10 to 90 per cent rise time is approximately twice this time constant. During the flat top of the pulse the first-order equivalent circuit takes the form shown in Fig. 10-12e. In order to minimize sag the time constant R_{eq}/L_p, where $R_{eq} = R_L'r_p'/(R_L' + r_p')$, must be of the order of ten to twenty times the pulse length. The capacitances in the exact equivalent circuit of Fig. 12-12b give rise to overshoot, and in exaggerated cases to oscillations.

It is apparent that the characteristics desired in a pulse transformer are very low leakage inductance and a primary inductance with a value that is proportional to the desired pulse length (and in any case as high as possible), together with small distributed capacitance. The ratio of leakage to primary inductance is kept small in practical transformers by

---

[1] For further information on this subject, see "Pulse Generators," *op. cit.*, chaps. 12–15.

coupling the primary and secondary windings as closely as voltage insulation requirements will permit, and employing a magnetic core of special high-permeability material, preferably arranged in the form of very thin laminations in order to minimize eddy currents during rapid changes of flux. The capacitance is minimized by proper arrangement of windings.

18-16. Miscellaneous Types of Special Circuit Arrangements. *Electronic Switches.* An electronic switch is an arrangement that utilizes an appropriate waveform to turn an amplifier tube on and off as desired.[1] Thus in Fig. 18-45, when a switching voltage of the wave shape shown is applied to the suppressor grid of the pentode tube, the plate current will

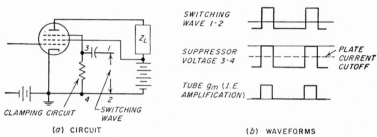

FIG. 18-45. Coincidence circuit.

be turned on when the wave is at its positive maximum, and off when the wave is negative.   In this way the time intervals during which the tube is able to amplify are controlled by the switching wave.

Switching voltages must always be arranged so that their amplitude is constant during the "on" interval.   This can be achieved by employing an appropriate clipping circuit.   Variations in switching voltage amplitude during the "off" interval are, of course, unimportant.   It is also desirable that the switching wave applied to an amplifier have a definite level during the "on" interval; this can be achieved by clamping the switching wave appropriately during the active period, as in Fig. 18-45b.

Coincidence Amplifier.   An amplifier in which the control grid is biased more negative than cutoff becomes a coincidence device when there is applied to the suppressor a switching voltage consisting of a short positive pulse clamped to zero voltage at its positive peaks.   Pulses applied to the control grid of such a system will then appear at the amplifier output only when they coincide in time with the "on" period of the switching pulse.

Counting and Scaling Circuits.   A large number of electronic circuits have been devised for counting pulses or cycles of an oscillating wave.

---

[1] An electronic switch applied in this way to an amplifier is often referred to as a *gate,* and the amplifier so controlled is termed a *gated amplifier.*   The gate is said to be open when the amplifier functions in the normal manner, and closed when the switch makes the amplifier inoperative.

These often take the form of scaling arrangements, i.e., systems that will produce one output pulse for each n input pulses.

The Eccles-Jordan (flip-flop) circuit of Sec. 18-5 can be used as a scaler by simultaneously applying the pulses to be counted to the control grids of both tubes of the flip-flop system. Each time a pulse arrives the system flips to the alternate quiescent condition, irrespective of which quiescent condition existed just before the arrival of the pulse. Thus after the arrival of two pulses the conditions are exactly as they were just before the arrival of the first pulse. One new pulse of *positive* polarity can now be derived for each such cycle of operation by differentiating the plate current of the tube that was initially conducting (or the plate voltage of the tube initially nonconducting). The result is a "scale-of-two" counter. If these new pulses are then applied to a second scale-of-two counter ($n = 2$) it will require two of these derived pulses, or four original pulses, to bring conditions back to their initial conditions; the result is a scale-of-four system ($n = 4$), etc.[1] The total count up to any time t is then $nm + p$, where m is the number of output pulses up to time t, n is the scale of counting, and p is an integer less than n that is determined by which tubes are conducting at time t. To understand how p is interpreted, assume in a scale-of-four system that a count of zero corresponds to tubes 2 and 4 conducting, where tubes 1 and 2 make up the first flip-flop system, and tubes 3 and 4 the second. Then the situation corresponding to various values for the total count[2] is as given in Table 18-1.

A quite different type of electronic counting circuit is shown in Fig. 18-46a. Here the pulses to be counted are applied with negative polarity to the control grid of amplifier T_1, which in the absence of pulses operates at zero bias. The peak amplitude of the applied pulses is made sufficiently great to cut off the plate current of T_1; hence each incoming pulse

---

[1] Scaling at ratios other than $n = 2$ can also be achieved by arranging $(n - 1)$ groups of bistable units (such as flip-flop circuits) in a ring so that they meet the following conditions: (1) the output pulse produced by one unit is applied to the second unit, the output pulse of which is applied to the third unit, and so on; (2) the pulses to be counted are applied simultaneously to all units; (3) the units are so interrelated that an incoming pulse will turn on (i.e., flip) a unit only if the immediately preceding unit is already on; i.e., only one unit can be flipped on at a time, so that when a new pulse arrives it turns on the unit immediately following the unit that was previously on (and which then goes off); and (4) the nth incoming pulse in addition to restoring all units to their initial condition, also puts out a special pulse to indicate n counts.

[2] This scale-of-four counting can be converted to a decimal system by using Table 18-1 to interpret the conditions of the various tubes in numbers from 0 to 9, and then providing an auxiliary circuit that functions in such a manner that (1) the next count after 9 is prevented from making tube 3 conducting; (2) the first flip-flop system is flipped so that tube 2 conducts and tube 1 becomes nonconducting; and (3) a special output pulse is developed. This forced recycling restores the indicated count to zero, and through the special pulse indicates 10 counts.

TABLE 18-1

Count	Tubes that conduct	Number of output pulses	Count	Tubes that conduct	Number of output pulses
0	2, 4	0	6	2, 3	1
1	1, 4	0	7	1, 3	1
2	2, 3	0	8	2, 4	2
3	1, 3	0	9	1, 4	2
4	2, 4	1	10	2, 3	2
5	1, 4	1	11	1, 3	2

makes the voltage at a rise momentarily to the value E_b. At this instant, capacitors C_1 and C_2 charge up through diode T_3 so that the sum of the voltages across them equals E_b. The charge thus received by C_1 is removed in the interval between pulses when T_1 draws plate current and the voltage at a drops. Discharge of capacitor C_2 during the period between pulses is prevented by T_3. By making C_2 very much larger than

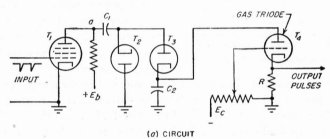

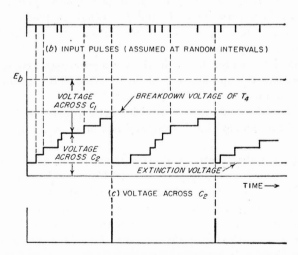

Fig. 18-46. System for counting pulses.

C_1, capacitor C_2 will receive an additional charge each time a negative pulse is applied to T_1, causing the voltage across C_2 to build up stepwise as shown.   When this voltage reaches a value that causes gas triode tube T_4 to start conducting (this is at the seventh pulse in Fig. 18-46b), the gas triode quickly discharges C_2.   This causes a pulse of current to pass through R that develops an output pulse, as shown in Fig. 18-46d.   The initial conditions are thereby restored, and the voltage across C_2 starts again to build up stepwise starting with the extinction voltage of T_4. The result of this process is the production of one output pulse for each group of n negative pulses applied to the system ($n = 7$ in Fig. 18-46).

This system of counting can be given a high degree of immunity against supply-voltage variations by deriving both the plate-supply voltage E_b and the gas-triode bias voltage E_c from the same source, so that these two potentials are proportional to each other.   When this is the case, the ratio n of the number of input to output pulses depends almost exclusively upon the circuit adjustment and constants, and only secondarily upon the tube characteristics and supply voltages.

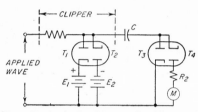

FIG. 18-47. A simple counting arrangement used to indicate frequency and as a frequency-modulation detector.

A form of counting circuit that finds use in the measurement of frequency, and as a frequency-modulation detector, is indicated in Fig. 18-47.   Here capacitor C is charged through diode T_3 on the positive half cycles of the applied wave, and discharged through diode T_4 and meter M (having internal resistance R_2) on the negative half cycles.   By clipping the input wave with diodes T_1 and T_2 so that the positive and negative peaks always have a definite value irrespective of the unclipped amplitude or the frequency of the wave, then the average or d-c current flowing through the meter M (or the d-c voltage across a load impedance) is proportional to the number of times per second that C is charged, and hence to the frequency.

Frequency Division.   Frequency division is the process of deriving from a frequency f a frequency that is exactly f/n, where n is an integer greater than one.

The use of the multivibrator to give frequency division has already been discussed above in connection with Fig. 18-15.   The blocking oscillator and the thyratron saw-tooth-wave generator can also be synchronized in such a manner as to give frequency division.   Frequency dividers of this type have the disadvantage, however, that the ratio of division depends to some extent upon the electrode voltages, the tube characteristics, and amplitude of the synchronizing voltage.

A counting system can be regarded as a frequency divider since it can be arranged to give one output pulse for every n input pulses or cycles. To the extent that the system counts correctly, the ratio of frequency division will be exactly n, irrespective of the amplitude of the incoming pulses, or of changes in tube conditions or supply voltages.

Another arrangement that is used extensively to divide frequencies, shown schematically in Fig. 18-48, is termed a *regenerative frequency divider*. Its method of operation can be understood by assuming that the system is functioning and developing an output frequency f/n. The $(n-1)$ harmonic of this output frequency is generated by means of a harmonic generator employing a suitable selective output circuit, and combined in the modulator with the input frequency f to generate the difference frequency

$$f - \frac{(n-1)f}{n} = \frac{f}{n} \quad (18\text{-}19)$$

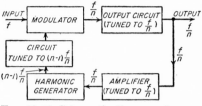

FIG. 18-48. Schematic diagram of regenerative frequency divider.

A typical practical regenerative frequency divider employs a pentagrid mixer as a modulator, and a diode-rectifier harmonic generator.[1]

The regenerative frequency divider differs from the multivibrator and related types of frequency divider in developing no output at all in the absence of an input voltage. Should the input voltage fail, or should some part of the system drop out of proper adjustment, the output will normally be zero. Off-frequency operation therefore cannot occur, whereas relaxation oscillators will become free-running if the synchronizing voltage is lost, or may operate at the wrong value of n if improperly adjusted.

Summing Amplifier. It is sometimes desired to obtain a wave that is the sum of two or more individual waves. One method of achieving this result consists in applying each wave to the control grid of a separate pentode amplifier tube, while connecting in parallel the plates of all the tubes involved, and providing a single plate load impedance for the combination.

An alternative type of adding circuit is illustrated in Fig. 18-49. This uses an operational amplifier identical with that of Fig. 18-8b. By so arranging that $A \gg 1$ and $R \gg R_{fb}/A$, where A is voltage gain, it can be shown by an analysis analogous to that used in deriving Eq. (18-6) that the output voltage of this arrangement will have the value

$$\left. \begin{array}{r} \text{Output} \\ \text{voltage} \end{array} \right\} = E_0 = \frac{E_1 + E_2 + E_3 + \cdots}{R/R_{fb}} \quad (18\text{-}20)$$

[1] For the system to be self-starting, the harmonic generator must be of a type that gives some output with very small inputs, i.e., Class C operation is to be avoided.

The amplifier output E_0 is thus seen to be proportional to the sum of the input voltage E_1, E_2, etc., and at the same time independent of the tube characteristics or supply voltages. Adders of this type find use in analogue computers, where a d-c amplifier is often used so that d-c as well as alternating waveforms can be added.

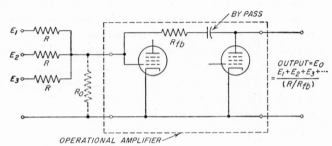

FIG. 18-49. Adding circuit employing operational amplifier.

PROBLEMS AND EXERCISES

18-1. In Fig. 18-1, what would be the effect on the clipped waveforms of using a very low value of resistance for R_s?

18-2. Show a circuit analogous to that of Fig. 18-4a, but giving base clipping of the negative part of the input wave.

18-3. Show a circuit arrangement analogous to that of Fig. 18-5, which develops an output that is a slice of a negative portion of the applied wave.

18-4. In the integrating circuit of Fig. 18-6a, it is desired that $E_0/E < 0.01$ for all frequencies in excess of 10 cycles. What is the minimum permissible value of R if C equals 1 μf?

18-5. Go through the detailed steps of deriving Eq. (18-5a).

18-6. Prove that power loss in C of Fig. 18-6a has the effect of reducing the time constant of the integrating circuit. Hint: Represent the power loss by its equivalent shunt resistance, and then apply Thévenin's theorem.

18-7. Sketch the wave shape that would result if the waveform in the bottom line of Fig. 18-7c were applied to (a) a differentiator, and (b) an integrator.

18-8. Go through the steps involved in deriving Eqs. (18-8) and (18-9).

18-9. In the operational integrator of Fig. 18-8a, show that when R and C_{fb} have assigned values, the lowest frequency that can be used without causing E_0/E to exceed an assigned value will be inversely proportional to the amplifier gain A.

18-10. Draw oscillograms analogous to those of Fig. 18-10, but applying to the case where the circuits of the two tubes are made unsymmetrical by arranging so that $C_2 = 2C_1$.

18-11. In Fig. 18-10 explain the mechanism whereby the transient A_2 in e_{c2} produces the effects on the waveforms of e_{b1}, e_{c1}, and e_{b2} that are designated as A_2.

18-12. The tube of Figs. 6-9 and 6-10 is used in the multivibrator of Fig. 18-9. What will be the amplitude E_0 of the square wave in Fig. 18-10 if $E_b = 250$ volts, $R_{L1} = 10,000$ ohms, and $R_{g2} = 250,000$ ohms?

18-13. Determine the frequency for the multivibrator of Prob. 18-12 if

$$R_{g1} = R_{g2} = 250,000 \text{ ohms} \quad \text{and} \quad C_1 = C_2 = 0.001 \ \mu\text{f}$$

18-14. Derive Eq. (18-13).

18-15. What would be the effect on the frequency generated by a multivibrator of returning the grid-leak resistance to a negative bias moderately less than cutoff? Illustrate the answer by oscillograms analogous to those of Fig. 18-14.

18-16. In a multivibrator for which $E_b = 250$ volts, $E_0 = 180$ volts, $\mu = 20$, what percentage change in time for a half cycle results when the noise voltage producing jitter is 10 μv, and (a) $E_c = 0$, and (b) $E_c = +250$ volts?

18-17. Explain how a reversal of polarity of the synchronizing voltage in Fig. 18-15a will not prevent synchronization from occurring at the same ratio, whereas in the case of pulses, as in Fig. 18-15c, it is necessary that the pulses superimposed upon the control-grid potential be positive if dependable synchronization is to be achieved.

18-18. Demonstrate that if a sine-wave synchronizing voltage is applied in the same polarity to the grids of the two tubes of a multivibrator, synchronization tends to occur at a ratio of frequencies represented by an even number, whereas if the voltages are of opposite polarity, then synchronization is at an odd ratio, as in Fig. 18-15a.

18-19. Draw oscillograms corresponding to Fig. 18-16, but applying to the multivibrator of Fig. 18-9, in which the grid-leak resistance R_{g1} is returned to a negative bias greater than cutoff.

18-20. In an Eccles-Jordan circuit, it is desired that negative trigger pulses make tube T_2 in Fig. 18-17 conducting and that positive pulses make it nonconducting. Explain how the sources of positive and negative pulses should be connected to the circuit to achieve this result.

18-21. Repeat the first oscillogram of Fig. 18-18b, and then below it draw oscillograms of grid current i_g and plate current i_p.

18-22. Derive Eq. (18-15).

18-23. Sketch oscillograms analogous to those of Fig. 18-18, but showing how a positive bias on the grid will increase the repetition frequency of a blocking oscillator.

18-24. Show how a large positive pulse superimposed upon the control grid of a blocking oscillator will always cause the repetition frequency of the blocking oscillator to be the same as the pulse repetition frequency, irrespective of the free-running frequency or the pulse repetition frequency provided only that the free-running frequency is less than the repetition frequency of the synchronizing pulses.

18-25. Sketch oscillograms analogous to those of Fig. 18-18b, except applying to the one-shot blocking oscillator.

18-26. In Fig. 18-19 the voltage amplification in each case is 20, and the clipping level is 5 per cent of the peak amplitude. Calculate the length of time in microseconds it takes the wave of Fig. 18-19c to rise from zero to maximum amplitude when the frequency of the wave is 1000 cycles.

18-27. Show oscillograms analogous to those of Fig. 18-10, but applying to the case where the output voltage of the circuit of Fig. 18-9 consists of short positive pulses about one-fifth as long as the space between pulses.

18-28. Draw a circuit showing a blocking oscillator, differentiator, amplifier, and clipper that are so combined as to give a positive rectangular pulse of very short duration.

18-29. It is desired to employ the arrangement of Fig. 18-23 to generate a pulse having a length of 1 μsec long with sides having a duration of 0.1 μsec. Specify the resonant frequency of the tuned circuit LC, the required clipping level of T_3 expressed as a percentage of the negative peak amplitude of the unclipped wave, and the maximum time that the control voltage has available to change from zero to cutoff.

18-30. In Fig. 18-25, draw waves of voltage and current at the mid-point of the line as a function of time, using a time axis on which $t = 0$ is the instant the switch S is closed.

18-31. Sketch oscillograms showing the voltages e_c and e_{1-2} as a function of time in the delay-line-controlled blocking oscillator of Fig. 18-27.

18-32. Modify the multivibrator circuit of Fig. 18-9 to give one-shot operation that develops a positive output pulse. Then show how a transmission line can be introduced into the multivibrator to control the length of the generated pulse, and explain the operation of this arrangement.

18-33. Devise a clamping circuit that will cause the negative peaks of a wave to be clamped to a voltage $+E$.

18-34. What effect, if any, will be produced on the positive spikes in Fig. 18-32c if one increases the ratio R/C while keeping the time constant RC unchanged?

18-35. Devise a modification of the keyed clamping circuit of Fig. 18-30c such that at times t_1, t_2, etc., the wave of a will be clamped, not to zero level, but rather to $+E$, where $E < E_0$.

18-36. What would be the effect of inserting a very well by-passed resistor in the cathode of the tube of Fig. 18-33?

18-37. *a.* Derive an equation giving the ratio of the slope of the exponential curve $abcd$ in Fig. 18-35 at time t_1 to the slope at time zero.

b. From the result of *a* determine the maximum value the ratio $(E_2 - E_1)/(E_b - E_1)$ can have if the variation in slope of the saw-tooth wave is not to exceed 5 per cent.

18-38. In Fig. 18-36a and *b*, show oscillograms for the case in which the peak amplitude of the synchronizing voltage is twice that in these figures, and specify the frequency ratio that will be obtained under these conditions.

18-39. Show the effect in Fig. 18-37a and *b* of making the time interval $t_3 - t_2$ of the input wave e_i half as great as shown while leaving everything else unchanged, including circuit constants.

18-40. In Fig. 13-38, discuss the factors that determine the peak amplitude E_2 that can be obtained and still preserve constant-current charging; likewise explain what determines the amplitude of E_1.

18-41. Draw a series of oscillograms applying to Fig. 18-39 showing input wave, voltage between a and ground, voltage between c and ground, and output voltage.

18-42. *a.* Run through the steps involved in obtaining Eq. (18-18) from Eq. (18-17).

b. Justify the statement that the slope of the e_0 waveform is independent of the tube characteristics only if the amplification A is large.

18-43. Verify the correctness of the information indicated in Fig. 18-41 to the effect that the time constant with which the output voltage returns to E_b at time t_2 approximates $R_L C$.

18-44. Reproduce the dotted curve in the final oscillogram of Fig. 18-41; then immediately below this curve and aligned with it, draw a curve showing the waveform of the current flowing through the plate-catching diode.

18-45. Redraw the oscillograms of Fig. 18-42 for (*a*) inductor resistance R_0 negligible, and (*b*) inductor resistance R_0 very high.

18-46. In the trapezoidal-wave generator of Fig. 18-43, discuss the effect on the wave shapes that is produced by (*a*) an appreciable increase in the resistance R_2, and (*b*) an increase in the plate resistance of the tube existing during the time interval t_1 to t_2.

18-47. Devise a comparator circuit analogous to that of Fig. 18-44, which operates on a rising waveform that starts with an amplitude slightly greater than zero and then rises.

18-48. Show the complete circuits of a time-delay system based on the saw-tooth-wave generator of Fig. 18-37a and the comparator of Fig. 18-44, and so arranged that the initiating time t_1 and the terminating time t_2 are both denoted by short pulses.

18-49. In reproducing a square wave, it is desired that the rise time of the sides from the negative to the positive peaks be less than 1 per cent of the length of time of a half cycle. If the repetition frequency of the wave is 10,000 cycles, calculate the maximum allowable peak-to-peak rise time, and from this determine the bandwidth that the circuit must handle.

18-50. Devise an "anticoincidence" amplifier arrangement such that pulses will always be amplified except when they coincide in time with a short pulse from a second source.

18-51. Construct a table analogous to Table 18-1 but for a scale-of-eight counter formed by applying the output pulses of a scale-of-four counter to a third Eccles-Jordan circuit. Assume that the tubes in the third unit are numbered 5 and 6, with tube 6 conducting when the count is zero.

18-52. In the oscillograms of Fig. 18-46, show the effect of (a) increasing the value of C_2 appreciably, and (b) decreasing the value of C_2 appreciably. Assume that C_1 remains unchanged, and that in all cases $C_2 > > C_1$.

18-53. In the counting circuit of Fig. 18-47, state the effect on the reading of the meter M of: (a) decreasing R_2, (b) increasing C, and (c) decreasing E_1 but leaving E_2 unchanged (assume $E_1 = E_2$ before change).

18-54. Devise circuits for a frequency-dividing system, which involve nothing more than modulators, harmonic generators, and resonant circuits, that will develop an output frequency that is $\frac{3}{5}$ times the frequency of the applied wave.

18-55. Go through the detailed steps required to derive Eq. (18-20).

18-56. Derive a modification of Eq. (18-20) that takes into account the effect of making the three resistors R indicated in Fig. 18-49 have different resistance values R_1, R_2, and R_3, all of which are much larger than R_{fb}/A.

CHAPTER 19

MICROWAVE TUBES

19-1. Microwave Tubes.[1] The limitations of triode, pentode, and similar tubes that arise at very high frequencies as a result of transit-time effects can be avoided by employing types of tubes which make use of transit time in achieving their normal operation. The most important tubes in this category are the multicavity and reflex klystrons, the traveling-wave tube, the backward-wave oscillator,[2] and the magnetron. Such tubes are particularly suitable for use in the microwave frequency range, and have made possible the practical development of these higher frequencies.

19-2. Multicavity Klystron Amplifier.[3] A two-cavity klystron amplifier is illustrated schematically in Fig. 19-1a. Here a high-velocity electron beam is successively passed through an input cavity resonator, called the *buncher*, a field-free *drift space*, and an output cavity resonator (the *catcher*), after which it goes to a collector electrode. The electron beam is normally produced with the aid of a Pierce gun (see Sec. 7-3); in some cases a magnetic field is employed, as shown in Fig. 7-12a or b, to prevent the beam from spreading as it traverses the distance ABC. The gaps A and C that represent the distance that the electron beam must travel in passing through the cavities are kept short by the use of reentrant cavities. The combination of anode voltage and gap length must be such that the transit time of the electrons in passing through each gap does not exceed a quarter of a cycle.

Mechanism of Klystron Operation—Velocity Modulation and Current Modulation. The signal to be amplified excites the input cavity, thereby developing an alternating voltage of signal frequency across gap A. Consider now the effect that this gap voltage has on the electron stream passing A. When the alternating voltage is zero going positive, an electron

---

[1] An excellent summary of recent developments is given by J. R. Pierce, Some Recent Advances in Microwave Tubes, *Proc. IRE*, vol. 42, p. 1735, December, 1954.

[2] The backward-wave oscillator is also called a carcinotron.

[3] The klystron tube was invented at Stanford University by Russell H. Varian. The literature describing its properties has become very extensive. A very readable account of the multicavity klystron is R. H. and S. F. Varian, A High-frequency Oscillator and Amplifier, *J. Appl. Phys.*, vol. 10, p. 321, May, 1939. A more detailed treatment is given by A. E. Harrison, "Klystron Tubes," pp. 201-310, McGraw-Hill Book Company, Inc., New York, 1947.

passing through gap A travels on toward gap C with unchanged velocity; this can be termed the reference electron.   However, an electron that passes through gap A slightly later than this reference electron is accelerated by the positive alternating field that it encounters at the gap, and so travels from A toward C with increased velocity; this electron therefore tends to overtake the reference electron.   Similarly, an electron that passes through C slightly before the reference electron, encounters a negative field at gap A, and so is slowed down.   This earlier electron hence tends to drop back and to be overtaken by the reference electron.

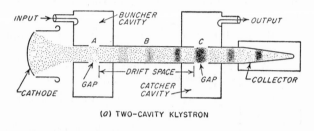

(*a*) TWO–CAVITY KLYSTRON

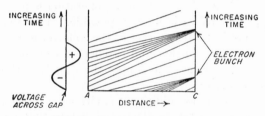

(*b*) DISTANCE–TIME DIAGRAM SHOWING
BUNCHING OF ELECTRON STREAM

Fig. 19-1. Two-cavity klystron amplifier, together with diagram showing the distance-time history of individual electrons.

As a result of these actions, the electrons gradually bunch together as they travel down the drift-tube space ABC, as illustrated in Fig. 19-1*a*. The result is that a pulsating stream of electrons passes through the gap C, and excites oscillations in the output cavity in the same way that the pulses of plate current in a Class C amplifier excite the plate tank circuit. The voltage developed across C is the alternating component of the bunched beam flowing through the shunt impedance (see Sec. 5-10) that the cavity develops across C.   When the system is properly designed and adjusted, the power delivered to the output cavity is much greater than the power in the input cavity, and amplification is achieved.

The bunching action that occurs in the klystron tube can be represented in the manner shown in Fig. 19-1*b* which is sometimes termed an Applegate diagram.   Here each line represents the distance-time history of an individual electron, the slope of each line being inversely proportional to the velocity of the electron being represented.   Electrons which pass gap A at uniform time intervals have their velocities (and hence slopes) varied in accordance with the gap voltage at the moment. As a result, after the electrons have traveled the distance AC they tend to be bunched about the electron that crossed A when the gap voltage at A was zero going positive, as shown by Fig. 19-1b.

It will be noted that although the electrons pass A at a uniform rate, they emerge from gap A with velocities that are a function of time. Such an electron beam is said to be *velocity modulated*. However, after the electrons have traveled sufficient distance down the drift-tube space to permit bunching to develop, the density of the electrons in the stream passing a given point, such as gap C, varies cyclically with time. Under these latter conditions the electron beam contains an a-c component, and

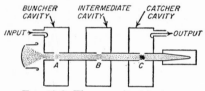

FIG. 19-2. Three-cavity klystron.

is said to be *current modulated*. Thus the effect of the drift space is to convert what was originally velocity modulation into current modulation.

This description of the klystron and its operation is presented only in general terms, and many variations are possible. Thus in some cases the catcher cavity simultaneously serves as the collector electrode. It is also possible to couple the buncher and catcher cavities so that a small part of the output power is used to supply the signal; in this way one obtains a klystron oscillator.

Very frequently one or more additional cavities are inserted between the catcher and buncher cavities as illustrated in Fig. 19-2, which shows a three-cavity system. Here oscillations are excited in the middle cavity by the partially bunched electron stream passing gap B; in this way a voltage is produced across B that also acts on the electron stream. By detuning the additional cavity so that its gap offers an impedance having an inductive component (i.e., resonant frequency slightly above the signal frequency) the phase of the voltage across B is related to the electron stream at B in such a manner as to cause further velocity modulation. This very considerably increases the voltage amplification of the tube, and likewise raises the efficiency that can be obtained. It is also possible to increase the bandwidth of a klystron amplifier by employing one or more intermediate cavities that are appropriately detuned; this expedient is used in all power klystrons designed for television service.

Performance and Applications of Multicavity Klystron Amplifier. The multicavity klystron finds its principal use as a power amplifier at frequencies of the order of 500 Mc and higher. By properly coordinating d-c anode voltage, the drift-space distance, and the signal amplitude in such a way as to achieve maximum bunching at the catcher position, efficiencies of the order of 40 per cent can be achieved. Continuous wave powers of the order of 15 kw have been developed in commercial tubes designed for television service at frequencies of the order of 900 Mc. Pulsed powers of 30,000 kw have been obtained from klystron tubes operating at 3000 Mc; this represents the highest power that has ever been obtained from a vacuum tube.[1]

The power gain of klystron power amplifiers is considerable, values of 30 db being easily possible in tubes of the three-cavity type. The bandwidth obtainable in klystron tubes is adequate for television applications. The output voltage is also very nearly proportional to the input voltage up to about 80 per cent of full output power,[2] so that the klystron is a fairly linear power amplifier.

Klystron amplifiers do not, however, find important use as amplifiers of relatively weak microwave signals. This is because the noise figure of the klystron tubes that are available exceeds 25 db. As a result, traveling-wave tubes (see Sec. 19-4) are much superior for the amplification of small microwave signals.

19-3. The Reflex Klystron Oscillator.[3]   The *reflex klystron,* or *reflex oscillator* as it is sometimes called, is a form of klystron oscillator that requires only a single resonant cavity. Since it has an efficiency of only a few per cent the reflex klystron is essentially a low-power device, typically being used to generate 10 to 500 mw. The reflex klystron is particularly satisfactory for use in the frequency range 1000 to 25,000 Mc.

The structure of the reflex klystron is illustrated in Fig. 19-3. The tube consists of a cathode, a focusing electrode at cathode potential, a coaxial line or reentrant cavity resonator that also serves as an anode, and a repeller electrode that is at a moderate negative voltage with respect to the cathode. The cathode is so shaped in relation to the focusing electrode and anode that an electron beam is formed that passes through a gap in the resonator as shown, and travels toward the repeller. Because the repeller has a negative potential with respect to the cathode, it turns these electrons back toward the anode when they have reached some

---

[1] High-power klystrons are described by Marvin Chodorow, E. L. Ginzton, I. R. Neilsen, and S. Sonkin, Development of 10 CM High-power Pulsed Klystron, *Proc. IRE*, vol. 41, p. 1584, November, 1953; D. H. Priest, C. E. Murdock, and J. J. Woerner, High-power Klystrons at VHF, *Proc. IRE*, vol. 41, p. 20, January, 1953.

[2] The output voltage is proportional to $J_1(aE_s)$, where J_1 denotes a Bessel function of the first kind and first order, E_s is the signal voltage, and a is a bunching parameter determined by the tube construction and the electrode voltages. Linearity between output and input voltages will thus exist to the extent that $J_1(aE_s) \approx aE_s$, an approximation that holds rather closely until aE_s approaches the value corresponding to the first maximum of the function (see Fig. 17-3).

[3] The theory of the reflex klystron is given by J. R. Pierce, Reflex Oscillators, *Proc. IRE*, vol. 33, p. 112, February, 1945. A very complete discussion of tubes of this type is presented by J. R. Pierce and W. G. Shepherd, Reflex Oscillators, *Bell System Tech. J.*, vol. 26, pp. 460–681, July, 1947.

point such as a in the repeller space; these returning electrons then pass through the gap a second time.

Mechanism of Operation. A qualitative understanding of the operation of the reflex klystron oscillator can be understood by assuming that oscillations already exist in the resonant cavity, and then examining the mechanism whereby the action of the electron beam sustains these oscillations.

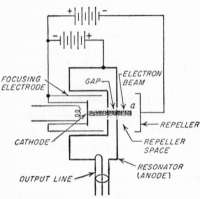

FOCUSING ELECTRODE

GAP

ELECTRON BEAM

CATHODE

REPELLER

REPELLER SPACE

RESONATOR (ANODE)

OUTPUT LINE

FIG. 19-3. Schematic representation of a reflex-klystron oscillator.

The radio-frequency voltage produced across the gap by the cavity oscillation acts on the electrons traveling toward the repeller, causing the velocity of the electrons that emerge from the gap into the repeller space to vary with time in accordance with the radio-frequency voltage. That is, the electron stream entering the repeller space is velocity modulated. This causes the electrons passing through the gap at different parts of the radio-frequency cycle to take different lengths of time to return to the gap. The result is that when the electrons return through the gap they tend to do so in bunches.

The variation of position with time for some typical electrons in the anode-repeller space is shown in Fig. 19-4. Here a corresponds to an electron that passes through the gap at the instant when the gap voltage

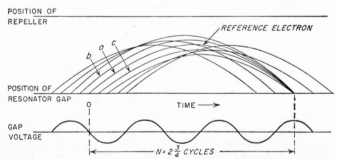

POSITION OF REPELLER

REFERENCE ELECTRON

a c

b

POSITION OF RESONATOR GAP

TIME ⟶

GAP VOLTAGE

$N = 2\frac{3}{4}$ CYCLES

FIG. 19-4. Position-time curves of electrons in anode-repeller space of reflex klystron, showing the tendency for the electrons to bunch around the electron passing through the anode at the time when the alternating gap voltage is zero and becoming negative.

is zero and just becoming negative. In the distance-time coordinate system shown, this electron follows a parabolic path, corresponding to the height-time curve of a ball thrown upward and returned to earth by the force of gravity. This is to be expected, since the electric field in the anode-repeller space acts like a gravitational field. A second electron b

that passes through the gap just before electron a is accelerated by the voltage across the gap, and enters the repeller space with greater velocity than did the first, or reference electron a.   Electron b accordingly penetrates farther toward the repeller against the retarding field, and as a result takes a longer time to return to the anode, just as a ball thrown upward with greater velocity takes longer to return to earth.   As a result, this second electron follows path b shown in Fig. 19-4 and tends to arrive at the anode on its return path at the same time as the reference electron because its earlier start is more or less compensated for by increased transit time.

In a similar manner, an electron passing through the anode gap slightly later than the reference electron will encounter a negative or retarding field across the gap, and so will emerge from the anode with less velocity than reference electron a.   This third electron will then follow trajectory c, and will return to the anode more quickly than electron a, just as a ball thrown upward with less velocity returns to earth more quickly.   Electron c hence tends to return to the anode at about the same time as electron a, since the later start of electron c is more or less compensated for by the fact that its transit time is less.

The end result of this action is that the returning electrons pass through the gap in bunches that occur once per cycle centered on a reference electron such as a in Fig. 19-4.   If these bunches return at such a time during the radio-frequency cycle that the returning electrons are slowed down by the alternating gap voltage, then energy is delivered to the gap voltage and hence to the oscillations in the cavity.   Examination of Fig. 19-4, plus a little reflection, will show that this condition occurs when the transit time N in the repeller space in cycles is

$$N = n + \frac{3}{4} \qquad (19\text{-}1)$$

Here n can be any integer, including zero; in Fig. 19-4 one has $N = 2\frac{3}{4}$.

Thus to generate oscillations, the frequency of the resonant system is tuned to the desired value, and then the negative voltage on the repeller electrode is adjusted to give a transit time N that approximates the value called for by Eq. (19-1).   It will be noted that the more negative the repeller voltage the more quickly will the electrons passing into the repeller space be returned to the gap, and hence the less will be the value N of the transit time.

Electronic Admittance of the Gap.   The interaction that takes place between the returning electrons and the alternating voltage across the gap is equivalent, as far as the resonant cavity is concerned, to shunting an admittance across the gap.   This is illustrated schematically in Fig. 19-5, where this admittance Y_e, commonly called the *electronic admittance*, is represented as a conductance G_e shunted by a susceptance B_e.   The magnitude of the electronic admittance Y_e with increasing repeller-space transit time N can be represented by a spiral starting from the origin for $N = 0$, and expanding outward with increasing N (that is, with less negative repeller voltage), as illustrated in Fig. 19-6. The size of the spiral, i.e., the magnitude of the admittance Y_e for any given tube and beam current, depends upon the amplitude of the voltage across the gap, being

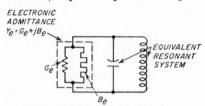

FIG. 19-5. Schematic representation of the resonant system of a reflex-klystron oscillator, showing the relationship of the electronic admittance to the resonant system.

maximum when the gap voltage is zero, and shrinking with increasing voltage. The phase angle of the admittance Y_e is, however, determined only by the transit time N, and is independent of the gap voltage; since $N = 0$ is vertically upward, the phase angle of Y_e is $360° \times (\frac{1}{4} - N)$.

Thus a position on the electronic admittance spiral such as p or p_1 has

a radial direction from the origin in Fig. 19-6 (including number of turns from the origin) that is determined by N. The position on the spiral is hence controlled by varying the repeller voltage. On the other hand, the absolute magnitude of the admittance corresponding to a point on the spiral such as p or p_1, that is, the distance $p0$ or p_10 from the origin to the

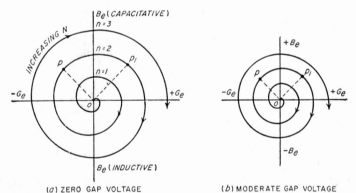

(a) ZERO GAP VOLTAGE   (b) MODERATE GAP VOLTAGE

FIG. 19-6. Polar diagram showing variation of the electronic admittance of the gap of a reflex klystron as the repeller-space transit time N is increased.

point in question (see Fig. 19-6), is determined both by the amplitude of the oscillations in the resonator, and by the number of turns N of p (or p_1) from the beginning of the spiral.[1]   When plotted in rectangular coordi-

[1] Thus for p in Fig. 19-6, $N = 1\frac{7}{8}$, and Y_e has a phase angle of 135°. If now the repeller voltage is made less negative by an amount that increases N by one-quarter of a cycle, the operating point moves from p to p_1. This increases the magnitude of Y_e slightly, since p_10 is greater than $p0$; it likewise causes the phase angle of Y_e to decrease by 90°, from 135 to 45°.

nates, the conductance and susceptance components of the electronic admittance have the character illustrated in Fig. 19-7; here the dotted curves correspond to a larger gap voltage than do the solid curves.

Oscillations will be generated in a reflex klystron whenever the electronic conductance G_e is negative and has an absolute magnitude for zero gap voltage that is more than the shunt conductance developed by the cavity across the gap.[1]   When this is the case oscillations will build up in amplitude until the magnitude of the negative electronic conductance is reduced to the point where it just equals the conductance of the cavity.

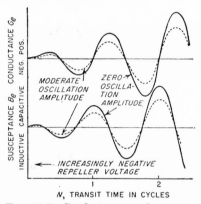

Fig. 19-7. Conductance and susceptance components of the electronic admittance of a reflex klystron for two amplitudes of gap voltage.

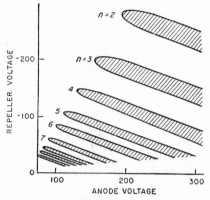

Fig. 19-8. Repeller mode pattern of a reflex klystron oscillator. The shaded areas correspond to those combinations of voltages for which oscillations occur.

Operating Characteristics of Reflex Klystron Oscillators.   Oscillations are obtained from a reflex klystron only for combinations of anode voltage and repeller voltage that give a favorable transit time.   The situation existing in a typical klystron at a given frequency is illustrated in Fig. 19-8.   Each shaded area corresponds to oscillations at a particular transit-time mode n.   If the frequency of the oscillations is changed appreciably, the pattern still has the same general character shown in Fig. 19-8, but the locations of the regions of oscillation are shifted.   This is because with a new frequency, a different transit time in seconds is required to give the same transit time in cycles.

When the resonant frequency of the cavity, and the anode voltage at which the tube is operated, are both kept constant, then the amplitude of the oscillations obtained from a reflex klystron varies with the repeller voltage as shown in Fig. 19-9.   The different oscillating regions correspond to different values of n in Fig. 19-8, i.e., to different transit-time modes.   Oscillations have the maximum amplitude when the transit time

[1] The conductance of the cavity gap is the reciprocal of the corresponding shunt resistance of the cavity as defined in Sec. 5-10.

is exactly $n + \frac{3}{4}$ cycles, corresponding to maximum possible negative conductance at a given oscillation amplitude. As the transit time departs from this optimum condition, the negative conductance tends to be less and the oscillations have progressively smaller amplitude. When the negative conductance for zero gap voltage is less than the shunt conductance of the cavity, oscillations cease.

Frequency—Electronic Tuning. The frequency of the oscillations obtained from a reflex klystron is determined primarily by the resonant

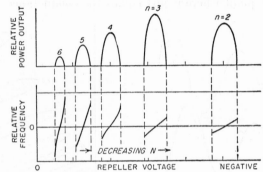

Fig. 19-9. Variation of output power and frequency of reflex oscillator as a function of repeller voltage for the tube of Fig. 19-8.

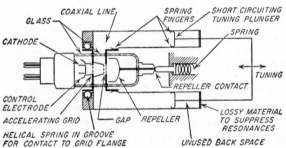

Fig. 19-10. Schematic representation of a reflex-klystron oscillator with external resonant system supplied by a coaxial line.

frequency of the cavity. When the resonant cavity is included in the evacuated portion of the tube, tuning can be accomplished over a moderate frequency range by mechanically flexing the walls of the cavity and/or simultaneously varying the gap spacing. Reflex klystrons are, however, often constructed so that the resonant system is external to the tube, as illustrated in Fig. 19-10. Under these conditions the frequency can be adjusted by means of a tuning plunger, and tuning ranges as great as 2 to 1 may be obtained provided the repeller voltage is simultaneously varied so that the repeller space transit time measured in cycles is kept approximately constant as the frequency is varied.[1]

[1] Reflex-klystron systems that are intended to operate over such wide frequency ranges must, however, be designed with special care in order to avoid holes or dis-

The electronic susceptance B_e also has an effect on the frequency as a result of the fact that it is a part of the equivalent resonant system (see Fig. 19-5).   This electronic susceptance depends upon the repeller-space transit time, as shown in Fig. 19-7.   Since the transit time depends on both the anode and repeller voltages, these voltages affect the generated

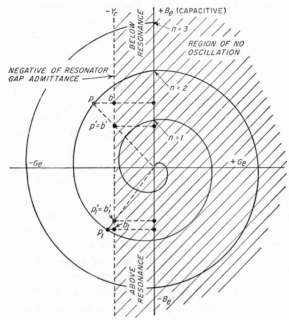

FIG. 19-11. Relationship of electronic admittance spiral to the admittance of the resonator gap.

frequency.   This is known as *electronic tuning* and is illustrated in Fig. 19-9; it provides a means for making slight corrections in the frequency and for achieving frequency modulation.

The mechanism whereby electronic tuning operates can be correlated with Fig. 19-6 by drawing on the admittance spiral for zero gap voltage the line corresponding to the *negative* of the resonator gap admittance Y_r, as shown[1] in Fig. 19-11.   Any repeller voltage that places the oper-

---

continuities in the tuning curve, and also to prevent the possibility of mode interference, i.e., simultaneous oscillation at two frequencies.   These problems are discussed further by F. E. Terman and J. M. Pettit, "Electronic Measurements," pp. 526–528, McGraw-Hill Book Company, Inc., New York, 1952.

[1] The admittance curve Y_r of the resonator gap is a straight line in Fig. 19-11 because in the very limited frequency range around resonance represented in Fig. 19-11, the shunt admittance of the resonator at the gap can be represented by a fixed resistance shunted by a susceptance that is zero at resonance and proportional to the frequency deviation from resonance when the frequency differs from resonance.   It follows that different positions along a given Y_r line correspond to different frequencies, with cycles off resonance proportional to distance from the horizontal axis.

ating point on a part of the spiral to the left of this line is a possible oscillatory condition. For example, consider point p corresponding to $N = 1.9$. Here oscillations start up at a frequency corresponding to the point b on the resonant-circuit line. As the oscillations increase in amplitude, the point p moves toward the origin along a radial line since the electronic admittance spiral diminishes in amplitude with increasing amplitude of oscillations. As this happens, point b moves downward and the frequency increases, until finally equilibrium is established at an amplitude and frequency such that p and b have both moved to $p' = b'$ as shown.

Electronic tuning obtained in this way by varying the repeller voltage is a very important feature of the reflex klystron. It provides a means of obtaining fine tuning, and also a means of introducing frequency modulation. For example, varying the repeller voltage between values corresponding to transit times represented by p and p_1 in Fig. 19-11 will cause the frequency to vary between values indicated by b' and b'_1. A total frequency variation of the order of 1 per cent can be obtained by electronic tuning in a typical case.

19-4. The Traveling-wave Tube.[1]   The traveling-wave tube is an amplifier that makes use of a distributed interaction between an electron beam and a traveling wave. It is particularly suitable for amplification of very high frequencies, such as 3000 Mc and higher.

The physical construction of a typical traveling-wave tube is shown in Fig. 19-12. Here an electron gun, normally of the Pierce type (Fig. 7-10), produces a pencillike beam of electrons having a velocity that typically corresponds to an accelerating voltage of the order of 1500 volts. This beam is shot through a long, loosely wound helix, and is collected by an electrode at anode potential, as shown. An axial magnetic focusing field, arranged as illustrated in either Fig. 7-12a or b, is provided to prevent the beam from spreading, and to guide it through the center of the helix.

The signal to be amplified is applied to the end of the helix adjacent to the electron gun. Under appropriate operating conditions an amplified signal then appears at the other end of the helix. Simple coaxial input and output couplings are illustrated in Fig. 19-12; other arrangements, for example, waveguide coupling, may be employed if desired.

Mechanism of Operation.   The applied signal propagates around the turns of the helix and produces an electric field at the center of the helix

[1] The literature on traveling-wave tubes has grown rapidly since this tube was first announced in 1946. References suggested as useful are J. R. Pierce and L. M. Field, Traveling-wave Tubes, *Proc. IRE*, vol. 35, p. 108, February, 1947; J. R. Pierce, "Traveling-wave Tubes," D. Van Nostrand Company, Inc., New York, 1950; R. Kompfner, Traveling-wave Tubes, "Reports of Progress in Physics," vol. 15, p. 275, Physical Society, London, 1952. This last reference gives a bibliography of over 70 titles.

that is directed along the helix axis.   Since the velocity with which the signal propagates along the helix wire approximates the velocity of light if the frequency is not too low, the axial electric field due to the signal advances with a velocity that is very closely the velocity of light multiplied by the ratio of helix pitch to helix circumference.[1]   When the velocity of the electrons traveling through the helix approximates the rate of advance of the axial field, an interaction takes place between this moving axial electric field and the moving electrons, which is of such a

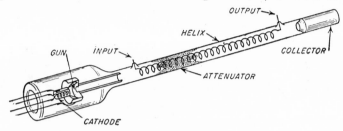

(*a*) TRAVELING WAVE TUBE

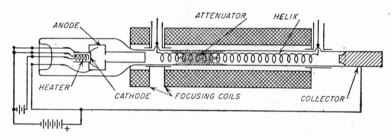

(*b*) TUBE MOUNTED IN MAGNETIC FOCUSING FIELD
FIG. 19-12. Schematic diagram of traveling-wave tube.

character that on the average the electrons deliver energy to the wave on the helix.   This causes the signal wave on the helix to become larger as the output end of the helix is approached; i.e., amplification is then obtained.

The mechanism of energy conversion by which the electrons deliver energy to the signal can be understood by reference to Fig. 19-13.   Here the solid line in Fig. 19-13a shows the distribution of the electric field strength along the helix axis produced by the signal in the absence of an electron beam.   This distribution assumes that the polarities are so chosen that a positive field accelerates the electrons, and the entire distribution can be regarded as traveling toward the right.[2]   Consider now

[1] At low frequencies the axial velocity varies with frequency, being higher the lower the frequency.

[2] As a result of this motion the axial field at position 1 in Fig. 19-13a is zero going positive with increasing time at the instant shown.

the group of electrons near the input end of the helix in the vicinity of e (see 1 of Fig. 19-13c) and assume that the axial electric field is zero at this point and is negative in the direction of the output end of the tube. An electron located exactly at e is then unaffected by the signal on the helix, as this electron encounters zero axial electric field. However, electron e' just to the left of e encounters a positive axial field and so is accelerated slightly thus tending to catch up with electron e. Similarly, electron e'' that was originally just to the right of e encounters a negative or decelerating field, and so slows down and tends to be overtaken by electron e. The electrons centered about e are thus velocity modulated. This action

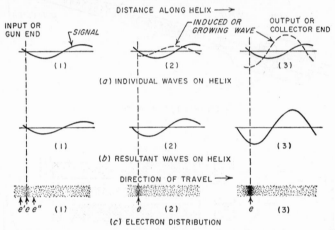

Fig. 19-13. Schematic diagram showing how the electrons bunch in a traveling-wave tube in a manner that causes the electron bunches to deliver energy to the wave.

is similar to that occurring about the reference electron in a klystron tube, except that the velocity modulation continues to take place as the electrons travel with the wave toward the collector, instead of being produced at only one localized position.

After the electrons centered around e have traveled some distance down the tube, they begin to be bunched about electron e as shown at 2 of Fig. 19-13c. If the velocity of the electrons at the input to the helix is the same as the velocity corresponding to the solid curve in Fig. 19-13a, then e in 2 is still located at the zero of the solid wave, as shown. However, the presence of the bunch of electrons centered on e induces a second wave on the helix which produces an axial electric field that lags the solid curve of Fig. 19-13a by a quarter wavelength as shown.[1] The resultant electric

---

[1] The following reasoning shows that the position of the induced wave lags that of the solid wave. Electrons such as e' that are to the left of e are accelerated and so absorb energy from the wave on the wire, weakening it to the left of e. Similarly, electrons such as e'' to the right of e are slowed down and so deliver energy to the wave that increases the wave amplitude to the right of e. This resultant effect is equivalent, as far as the axial electric field, to the original wave (i.e., solid curve of Fig. 19-13a)

field that is produced along the helix axis by the combined action of the
two waves on the helix, shown in Fig. 19-13b, is located a small fraction of
a wavelength closer to the gun end of the tube than is the solid curve of
Fig. 19-13a because the negative maximum of the induced wave is
opposite the center of the electron bunch.   The electrons in the bunch
therefore encounter a negative or retarding field and as a result deliver
energy to the wave on the helix, which therefore becomes larger than at
the input, as shown in Fig. 19-13b.   Bunching action continues to take
place in 2 in Fig. 19-13c in spite of the fact that electron e is no longer at
the zero of the resultant wave on the helix.   This is because although all
the electrons near e in 2 are slowed down, those to the left of e are slowed
down less than are the electrons to the right of e.

As the electrons travel further along the helix, the situation at 2 in
Fig. 19-13c changes to that at 3.   Here the bunching is more complete
and the induced wave grows in amplitude.   The shift in phase of the
resultant wave relative to the electron bunch is also increased because of
the fact that the induced wave is larger.[1]   Each electron in the bunch
now encounters a stronger retarding field, and furthermore, there are
more electrons in the bunch.   A large and increasing amount of energy is
thereby delivered by the electron bunch to the wave on the helix, which is
now much larger than the original signal.

Analysis shows that the amplitude of the resultant wave traveling
down the helix increases exponentially.   The total interchange of energy
between the electrons and the helix wave is such that large amounts of
power amplification can be achieved, typically from 20 to 40 db in a single
tube.

Suppression of Oscillations—Helix Attenuator.   In order to prevent
oscillations from being spontaneously generated in a traveling-wave tube,
it is necessary to prevent internal feedback arising from reflections due to
slight impedance mismatches at the terminals.   Thus energy reflected at
the output terminals will travel back to the gun end of the tube, and upon
reflection there provides a spurious or feedback signal that is further
amplified along with the desired signal.   It may also be necessary to prevent backward-wave oscillations from being generated (see p. 683).

This situation is controlled by introducing an attenuator some place
moderately near the input end of the tube, as shown in Fig. 19-12, that
absorbs any wave propagated along the helix.   This attenuator can take
a number of forms; a common arrangement is a conducting coating of
Aquadag painted on the glass wall of the tube.   The attenuator absorbs

---

plus an added or induced wave, the dotted curve of Fig. 19-13a, that lags by a quarter
wavelength.

[1] A complicating factor is that as the electrons slow down the center of the bunch
begins to lag slightly behind the zero of the solid wave of Fig. 19-13a, which in turn
modifies the retarding forces.

not only the undesired backward or feedback wave; it likewise absorbs the desired forward or growing wave that is present on the helix. However, the bunching of the electrons is to a first approximation unaffected by the presence of the attenuator. Hence as the bunches of electrons emerge from the attenuating region, they induce a new forward traveling wave on the helix on the output side of the attenuator. This wave then travels along the helix toward the output nearly synchronously with the electron bunches.

For proper operation the attenuator should introduce a loss roughly equal to the forward gain of the tube. The attenuator should also be so designed as to absorb the helix waves without introducing appreciable reflection.

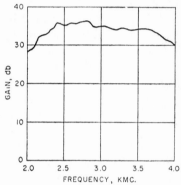

Fig. 19-14. Typical curve of amplification of a traveling-wave tube as a function of frequency.

Bandwidth. The traveling-wave tube is inherently a nonresonant device. As a result it can be made to have bandwidths that are enormous compared with those obtainable from amplifiers involving resonant circuits. The amplification characteristic of a typical helix traveling-wave tube is shown in Fig. 19-14; in this case the amplification is constant to within ±3 db from 2000 to 4000 Mc.

The principal factors causing the gain of a traveling-wave tube to vary with frequency are (1) variation in the velocity of the electric field along the axis of the tube (this causes the velocity of this wave and the electron velocity to be favorably related only over a limited range of frequencies), (2) variation of length of the tube in wavelengths, (3) variation in the strength of the axial electric field as a function of frequency, and (4) failure to match the terminal impedance of the tube accurately at all frequencies.

The helix form of the traveling-wave tube is particularly suitable for achieving wideband operation. Over a wide frequency range the velocity of the axial field produced by the helix is substantially independent of frequency. Also the strength of the axial field in a helix increases at low frequencies in approximately the correct amount to take into account the fact that the length of the tube measured in wavelengths becomes less as the frequency is reduced; thus factors 2 and 3 above tend to balance in the helix. It is also possible to obtain an impedance match to a helix over a very large frequency range.

Alternative Structures. Any arrangement that provides an axial component of electric field that advances with a velocity that is a small fraction of the velocity of light has the possibility of being used in a traveling-wave tube.   The helix is only one of many "slow-wave" structures that meet this requirement.   Two other possibilities are illustrated in Fig. 19-15.   Both of these happen to be dispersive structures, i.e., they have a wave velocity that varies with frequency, and so have less bandwidth than the helix.   However, their power dissipating ability is much greater. The folded line of Fig. 19-16 can also be used as a dispersive structure for a traveling-wave tube.

Operating Properties of Traveling-wave Tubes.   Power gains of the order of 20 to 40 db combined with a bandwidth approaching 2 to 1 are readily realized when using a properly designed helix stucture. Noise figures as low as 6 db at 3000 Mc and 11 db at 10,000 Mc have

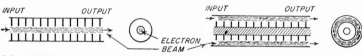

(*a*) WAVEGUIDE WITH APERTURED DISCS   (*b*) DISC - ON - ROD

Fig. 19-15. Examples of slow-wave structures that can be used in traveling-wave tubes.

been achieved.   Large amounts of continous wave power can be generated in traveling-wave tubes, values of 1000 watts at range 500 to 1000 Mc and 100 watts at 3000 Mc having been realized in early experimental tubes.   Pulsed powers of tens to hundreds of kilowatts have also been achieved in the laboratory.   Efficiencies are from 10 to 40 per cent.

Traveling-wave tubes are best adapted for operation in the frequency range 500 to 10,000 Mc.   They can, however, be constructed for still higher frequencies at the expense of extremely small helices; likewise, frequencies as low as 100 Mc can be realized by allowing the physical size of the tube to be relatively large.

19-5. Backward-wave Oscillators (the Carcinotron).[1]   The backward wave oscillator, or the O carcinotron, as it is sometimes called, is a development that has grown out of the traveling-wave idea.   However, in contrast with the traveling-wave tube it is inherently an oscillator.

A typical backward-wave oscillator is illustrated in Fig. 19-16.   The body of this tube consists of a folded transmission line, or alternately can be regarded as a waveguide operating in the TE_{10} mode, such that a wave traveling along the line winds itself back and forth, and in the process produces an axial component of electric field.   The total path length from one end of the structure to the other is typically of the order of a dozen wavelengths under the usual operating conditions, and in a typical structure the line might cross the axis about fifty times.

An electron beam is directed along the axis through holes in the struc-

[1] For more detailed information on this subject see R. Kompfner and N. T. Williams, *Backward-wave Tubes, Proc. IRE,* vol. 41, p. 1602, November, 1953; G. E. Helmke, A Hairpin Tube Backward-wave Oscillator, *Bell Lab. Record,* vol. 31, p. 286, August, 1953.

ture as shown. When this beam has a suitable velocity, there is an interaction between the electron stream and a wave traveling from right to
left, i.e., a *backward* wave, such that on the average energy is delivered to
this wave by the electron beam. The collector end of the folded line is
terminated with a matched load impedance for the purpose of absorbing
any power that might be reflected at the output or gun end of the structure as a result of an impedance mismatch at that point.

Mechanism of Operation. The principles involved in the operation of
the backward-wave oscillator can be understood by assuming that a wave
traveling from right to left in Fig. 19-16 (i.e., a backward wave) already

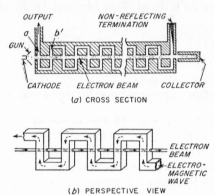

FIG. 19-16. Schematic diagram of backward-wave oscillator employing a folded-line
structure.

exists on the folded-line structure, and then examining the interaction
that results between this wave and the electron stream. First consider
the situation existing at gap a. Here electrons enter from the cathode
side at a uniform rate and are subjected to an alternating axial field that
varies with time, as shown in Fig. 19-17c. This situation is the same as
that existing in the gap of the buncher of a multicavity klystron since the
fact that the field happens to be produced by a backward wave instead of
by a cavity does not make any difference to the electrons. The electrons
passing through a thus experience velocity modulation, with a tendency
for a bunch of electrons to be formed about the electron that passes
through the gap when the alternating field at a is zero just turning decelerating[1] (see Fig. 19-17a and c). This reference electron also corresponds
to the reference electron in the traveling-wave tube of Fig. 19-13.

The reference electron passes through gap b at a time T_e seconds after it

[1] The arrows in Fig. 19-17 show the direction of the flux as one goes from a positive
to a negative charge. Hence when the arrow is directed *against* the direction in
which the electron is moving, the electron is accelerated. Thus just before the
reference electron crosses gap a, the position of zero field is below the beam, and the
field at the gap corresponds to an arrow directed toward the right; i.e., the electrons
are slowed down.

passed through gap a, where T_e is the time it takes the electron to travel
from a to b.   This delay corresponds to $N_e = T_e f$ cycles, where f is the
frequency.   Now the field at a lags $N_w = T_w f$ cycles behind the field at b
because of the time T_w it takes the wave to travel from gap b to a along the
folded line.   Thus when the electron crosses gap b the field it encounters
is $N_e + N_w$ cycles behind the phase of the field it encountered at a.   The
geometry of the folded line is such, however, that a given flux line is
directed oppositely at b from the direction of the same flux line when it

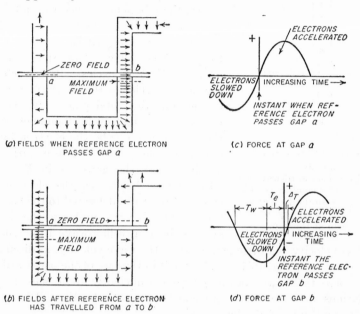

(a) FIELDS WHEN REFERENCE ELECTRON
PASSES GAP a

(c) FORCE AT GAP a

(b) FIELDS AFTER REFERENCE ELECTRON
HAS TRAVELLED FROM a TO b

(d) FORCE AT GAP b

Fig. 19-17. Relationship of fields and electrons in the folded-line backward-wave tube
of Fig. 19-16.

reaches a (see Fig. 19-17).   Therefore, if the electrons are given a velocity
such that $N_w + N_e$ is just less than a half cycle, then the field that the
reference electron encounters at gap b will be as shown in Fig. 19-17b.
This field at b will vary with time in the manner indicated by Fig. 19-17d,
where ΔT is a time such that $\Delta T \times f = N_\Delta$ is the fraction of a cycle by
which $N_e + N_w$ fails to be exactly a half cycle.   This field is substantially
the same as that encountered at gap a.   In fact, if $N_e + N_w$ is exactly a
half cycle ($N_\Delta = 0$), then fields of identical phase are seen by the reference
electron at gaps a and b.   Thus the electrons passing through b experience
further velocity modulation.

This situation is repeated over and over again as the electrons centered
about the reference electron pass one gap after another, since the wave on
the folded line always moves just far enough to the left during the transit
time of the electrons from the last gap to the next gap to cause the field at

the new gap to be of just the correct character to produce still further velocity modulation. Thus as the electrons travel toward the collector, the interaction with the backward wave on the folded line causes them gradually to group together in bunches, exactly as do the electrons in the

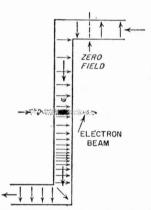

traveling-wave tube. However, since the velocity of the electrons is so chosen that the quantity $N_e + N_w = f(T_e + T_w)$ is less than a half cycle by a small amount N_Δ cycles, these bunches of electrons advance in time with respect to the time of zero electric field at the gap. After passing n gaps the electron bunch has thus advanced $nN_\Delta = n\,\Delta T \times f$ cycles. By so choosing the electron velocity that at the collector end of the tube this total phase advance is approximately a half cycle, then over much of the length of the tube the electron bunches encounter relatively strong decelerating fields as they cross the gaps, as in Fig. 19-18. These fields slow down the electrons and cause energy to be delivered to the backward wave. This is very similar to the situation existing in a traveling-wave tube when the electron velocity is a little greater than the wave velocity, as discussed in connection with Fig. 19-13. The result in the case of the backward-wave oscillator is that if the beam current is sufficiently great, self-sustaining oscillations are generated at a frequency such that $nN_\Delta \approx 0.5$.

FIG. 19-18. Electron bunches passing through a gap in folded-line backward-wave oscillator under conditions such that the bunched electron beam delivers energy to the electric field at the gap.

The amplitude of the backward wave on the line builds up as shown in Fig. 19-19; this wave becomes larger as it progresses toward the gun end of the tube and passes more and more bunches of electrons from which it receives energy. At the same time, the alternating component of the beam current, i.e., the bunching, becomes greater as the electrons progress toward the collector, as indicated in Fig. 19-19.

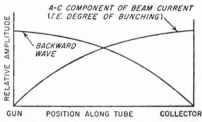

FIG. 19-19. Variation of amplitudes of the backward wave and of the a-c component of beam current, as a function of position along a backward-wave oscillator.

It is seen that the backward-wave oscillator is a special kind of traveling-wave tube that possesses a built-in feedback mechanism whereby the power generated by a traveling-wave tube type of interaction is used to supply the signal required at the gun end of the tube to produce bunching of the electron stream.

Helix Form of Backward-wave Oscillator. The folded line of Fig. 19-16 is not the only arrangement that will support backward-wave operation. In particular, a helix structure forms the basis of an excellent backward-wave oscillator when the frequency is such that the circumference of a single helix turn lies between a quarter and a half wavelength. Under these conditions the electric fields between successive turns have a phase difference similar to that existing between gaps a and b in Fig. 19-17. If now an electron beam of appropriate velocity travels along paths adjacent to the helix turns as shown in Fig. 19-20, it will encounter fields in gaps a and b qualitatively similar to those in gaps a and b of Fig. 19-17 when a backward wave is present on the helix. Although the exact details of the operation are a little more complicated than in the folded-line structure, the end result is the same. In a helix backward-wave oscillator it is desirable to employ a hollow cylindrical electron beam, since only the electrons that pass adjacent to the wires are fully effective in delivering energy to the wave.

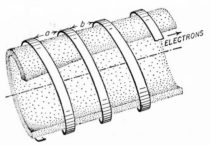

FIG. 19-20. Section of tape helix producing backward-wave action analogous to that existing in gaps a and b in Fig. 19-16.

In particular, electrons near the middle of the beam consume anode power but contribute little or nothing to the energy interchange that produces the backward-wave oscillations.

It is apparent that a given helix structure is able to function either as a traveling-wave amplifier in one frequency range, or as a backward-wave oscillator that operates at a somewhat higher frequency when using the same anode voltage. One may then wonder how a given tube knows whether it is supposed to be operating as a traveling-wave amplifier, or as a backward-wave oscillator. The answer is determined at least in part by whether or not an attenuator is present that absorbs a wave traveling along the helix. With an attenuator such as is shown in Fig. 19-12, the backward wave cannot reach the gun end of the tube and produce the velocity modulation that is necessary to sustain the backward wave; if the electron velocity has a suitable value, traveling-wave action may then occur. However, if the attenuator is removed, or if it is not adequate, then backward-wave oscillations may be generated spontaneously.[1]

Frequency of Oscillation. In the above discussion it was brought out

[1] It will be noted that the folded line structure of Fig. 19-15 can also be made to function as a traveling wave amplifier by (1) adjusting the velocity of the electron beam so that T_e approximately equals a half period plus the time T_w that it takes a forward wave to travel from gap a to gap b, and (2) providing an attenuator to suppress backward-traveling waves in a manner analogous to the action of the attenuator associated with the helix of Fig. 19-12.

that in order to generate oscillations the electron velocity must have a value such that $nN_\Delta = n\,\Delta T f$ approximates one-half cycle, where n is the number of gaps and $N_\Delta = \Delta T \times f$ represents the fraction of a cycle by which the field that the reference electron encounters at gap b differs in phase from a field passing through zero at this instant. Also $N_e + N_w$ is less than a half cycle by N_Δ (see page 685). Hence

$$N_e + N_w + N_\Delta = T_e f + T_w f + N_\Delta = 0.5$$

and

$$N_\Delta \approx \frac{0.5}{n}$$

Hence

$$f \approx \frac{0.5[1 - (1/n)]}{T_e + T_w} \tag{19-2}$$

Here T_e, T_w, and f are defined as above.

Since T_w in Eq. (19-2) is determined by the geometry of the tube and so is nearly constant for any given tube, the frequency generated by the backward-wave tube is controlled by the transit time T_e, that is, by the velocity of the electron stream. The frequency hence depends upon the anode voltage, and is almost completely independent of the load impedance associated with the output terminals of the backward-wave oscillator, and the beam current. *Thus the backward-wave oscillator has the unique property of being voltage tuned.* Under practical conditions it is possible to achieve a 2-to-1 frequency range in a given tube by a voltage variation that is of the order of 10 to 1 or less.

Backward-wave oscillators are particularly suitable for use at microwave frequencies. Frequencies as great as 100,000 Mc have been achieved in structures that are physically large enough to be fabricated without undue difficulty. At the other extreme, frequencies below 200 Mc have been obtained from experimental tubes less than 2 ft long. In general, the maximum frequency that can be generated by backward-wave-oscillator action in a given structure is somewhat greater than the maximum frequency at which the same structure will amplify satisfactorily when used as a traveling-wave amplifier.

Power and Efficiency. Powers of the order of milliwatts are readily achieved in backward-wave oscillators at frequencies as great as 100,000 Mc. At lower frequencies relatively large powers can be developed, 100 watts at 3000 Mc having been reported in an experimental tube using a folded-line structure such as shown in Fig. 19-16.

Efficiencies obtainable in backward-wave oscillators are of the same order of magnitude as those realized with traveling-wave tubes. When powers are low the efficiencies will be of the order of a few per cent or less. With higher powers, efficiencies exceeding 10 per cent have been realized experimentally, and higher values appear to be possible.

19-6. Magnetron Oscillators.[1]   The magnetron oscillator was the first device developed that was capable of generating large powers at microwave frequencies.   It was the basis of the microwave radar transmitters of World War II.

The essential elements of a typical magnetron oscillator are shown in Fig. 19-21.[2]   This consists of a cylindrical cathode surrounded by an anode structure that possesses cavities opening into the cathode-anode or *interaction* space by means of slots, as shown.   Output power is withdrawn by means of a coupling loop, as illustrated, or alternatively a tapered waveguide can be employed.

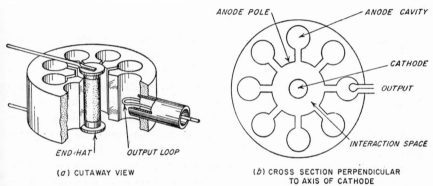

(*a*) CUTAWAY VIEW   (*b*) CROSS SECTION PERPENDICULAR
                                           TO AXIS OF CATHODE

FIG. 19-21. Diagrams showing principal physical features of the cavity magnetron oscillator.

The magnetron requires an external magnetic field with flux lines parallel to the axis of the cathode.   This field is usually provided by a permanent magnet, although an electromagnet can be employed.

Resonant Modes in Magnetrons and Their Separation.   The anode cavities, together with the spaces at the top and bottom of the anode block, represent the resonant system of the oscillator.   The fields associated with the cavities are of such a nature that the alternating magnetic flux lines pass through the cavities parallel to the cathode axis, while the alternating electric fields are confined largely to the slot and the region where the cavities open into the interaction space, and lie in planes perpendicular to the axis of the cathode (see Fig. 19-26).

The resonant system of a magnetron possesses a series of resonant fre-

---

[1] The literature on magnetrons is very extensive.   An excellent summary of basic principles is given by H. D. Hagstrum, The Generation of Centimeter Waves, *Proc. IRE*, vol. 35, p. 548, June, 1947; for a more detailed treatment see J. B. Fisk, H. D. Hagstrum, and P. L. Hartman, The Magnetron as a Generator of Centimeter Waves, *Bell System Tech. J.*, vol. 25, pp. 1–188, April, 1946; "Microwave Magnetrons" (vol. 6, Radiation Laboratory Series), McGraw-Hill Book Company, Inc., New York, 1948.

[2] The discussion given here will be limited to magnetrons of the cavity type.   Other forms of magnetrons have been devised, but have found only limited usefulness.

quencies, or *modes* as they are commonly called, equal in number to the number of cavities. This is because the resonant system can be regarded as consisting of a number of individual resonators, one for each cavity, which are all coupled together. It was shown in connection with Fig. 3-11 that when two resonant circuits are coupled together the result is to produce two resonant frequencies; similarly when n resonant cavities are coupled together, the result is n resonant frequencies or modes.

The mode employed in normal magnetron operation is that in which the phase difference between the adjacent anode poles is π radians; this is called the "π mode." The other modes are characterized by some other value of phase difference between adjacent poles, but with the limitation that the total phase shift around the periphery of the interaction space must always be some multiple of 2π. Thus for the eight-cavity magnetron of Fig. 19-21, the π mode corresponds to a total phase shift of $\pm 8\pi$ radians around the periphery, while other modes correspond to total phase shifts of $\pm 6\pi$, $\pm 4\pi$, and $\pm 2\pi$ radians, corresponding to progressive phase differences between adjacent poles of ± 180, ± 135, ± 90, and $\pm 45°$, respectively.

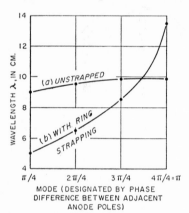

FIG. 19-22. Mode separation as observed experimentally in a particular magnetron oscillator when unstrapped, and with ring strapping.

It will be noted that the electric fields existing in the interaction space of the magnetron correspond to the rotating fields in the air gap of a polyphase electrical machine. The π mode corresponds to a single-phase system, while the other modes correspond to various polyphase arrangements. The phase differences that are characteristic of the various modes arise from the fact that each mode corresponds to a different frequency, and so is detuned differently from the resonant frequency of the cavities.

The relationship between the frequencies of the different modes in a typical magnetron is illustrated by the curve labeled "unstrapped" in Fig. 19-22. It will be noted that the desired mode differs very little in wavelength (or frequency) from the other modes. This situation intro-duces practical difficulties which make it important to separate the π mode from the other modes.

A method commonly used to achieve this result is called *strapping*, a typical example of which is shown schematically in Fig. 19-23. Here two rings are arranged in the end space as shown, with one ring connected to the even-numbered anode poles and the other ring connected to the odd-numbered anode poles. For the π mode all parts of each ring are at the same potential, but the two rings have opposite potential, as indicated by the + and − signs. The capacitance between the rings thus adds capacitive loading to the resonant cavities, thereby lowering the frequency of the π mode. For the other modes there is, however, a phase difference between the successive poles connected to a given ring. This causes current to flow along the straps. Since the straps have inductance, this action places an inductive shunt in parallel with the equivalent resonant circuit of the cavity, thus raising the frequency for these modes. The net result is accordingly a separation in frequency of the π mode from other modes as illustrated by the curve in Fig. 19-22 labeled "ring strapping."

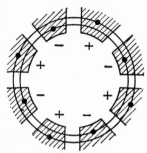

Fig. 19-23. Schematic representation of ring strapping. The rings touch the anode poles only at the points indicated by the dots.

The frequency of the oscillations generated by a magnetron can be changed only by varying the resonant frequency of the magnetron circuits in some manner. One method of doing this consists in employing a "C ring" as illustrated in Fig. 19-24, which adds capacitance between the straps of a ring-strapped magnetron and thereby lowers the resonant frequency of the π mode by an amount depending upon the position of the C ring. The mechanism for adjusting the position of such a ring must transmit its effect through the vacuum-tight envelope of the magnetron by means of a flexible diaphragm or bellows.

Another method of controlling the resonant frequency of the anode system involves closely coupling a tunable high-Q resonant cavity to one of the anode cavities. It is possible in this way to couple sufficient reactance into the magnetron cavity system to modify the resonant frequency by a moderate amount.

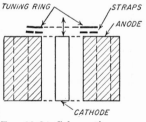

Fig. 19-24. Schematic representation of C-ring tuning of a magnetron.

Mechanism by Which Oscillations Are Generated. The first step in understanding the mechanism by which oscillations are generated in a magnetron consists in examining the behavior of the electrons emitted from the cathode when acted upon simultaneously by the d-c anode voltage and the axial magnetic field in the absence of radio-frequency oscillations. An electron emitted from the cathode under these conditions is accelerated toward the anode system by the radial electric field produced by the d-c anode voltage. If there were no magnetic field present, the electron would be drawn directly toward the anode in accordance with path *a* as shown in Fig. 19-25. However, as the electron gains velocity the axial magnetic field exerts a force on it for reasons explained in connection with Fig. 6-1. When the magnetic field is weak the electron path is deflected as shown by b in Fig. 19-25. However, when the intensity of the magnetic field is sufficiently great, the electrons are turned back toward the cathode without ever reaching the anode, as illustrated by paths c and d. The magnetic field which is just able to turn the electrons back to the cathode before reaching the anode is termed the *cutoff field;* when the magnetic field exceeds the cutoff value,

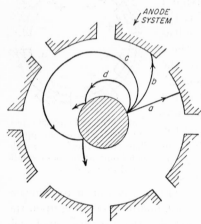

then in the absence of oscillations all the emitted electrons return to the cathode and the plate current is zero.

It will now be shown that if one postulates the existence of oscillations in the resonant structure, then when the magnetic field strength exceeds the cutoff there is an interaction between the electrons and the electric field that under favorable conditions causes the oscillations to receive energy from the electrons in the interaction space. Consider oscillations corresponding to the π mode; they produce radio-frequency fringing fields that extend into the interaction space in the manner illustrated in Fig. 19-26. If no radio-frequency field were present then

Fig. 19-25. Electron paths under the influence of a d-c anode voltage for different values of axial magnetic field. The paths shown are those followed when the magnetron is not oscillating.

electrons a and b would traverse paths shown by dotted lines a and b. However, the radio-frequency fields associated with the oscillations act on the electrons and modify the orbits. Thus electron a is so located with respect to these fields that its tangential velocity is opposed by the field. This electron is thus slowed down by the oscillations, and so delivers energy to the oscillations. Moreover, since electron a thereby loses velocity, the deflecting force that the magnetic field exerts on it is reduced; as a consequence this electron moves toward the anode, as shown by the solid path, instead of being turned back toward the cathode.

If the relationship between the d-c anode voltage and the magnetic field is now such that the tangential velocity of the electron makes the time required by electron a to travel from position 1 to 2 in Fig. 19-26 approximate a half cycle of the radio-frequency oscillations, then when electron a reaches point 2 in Fig. 19-26, it finds that the electric field has reversed its polarity from that shown.[1] The result is that electron a con-

[1] In this connection it is sometimes helpful to note that the radio-frequency fields in the interaction space can be regarded as being composed of components that rotate circumferentially about the cathode. Thus the π mode fields can to a first approxima-

tinues to be slowed down, and continues to drift toward the anode. However, the velocity that electron a possesses does not change appreciably as it approaches the anode since the energy that this electron acquires from falling through the d-c anode-cathode voltage is in large measure delivered to the oscillations rather than being used to increase the velocity of the electron.   Ultimately this working electron strikes the anode surface, after having delivered to the oscillations a large part of the energy represented by its fall through the d-c cathode-anode potential.

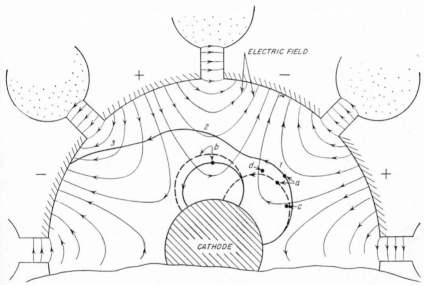

Fig. 19-26. Paths traversed by various electrons in a magnetron under oscillating conditions.

In contrast with this situation, consider next electron b in Fig. 19-26, which is emitted under circumstances such that it is accelerated by the radio-frequency field.   Instead of being slowed down, this electron gains velocity and is therefore deflected more sharply by the magnetic field than if there were no oscillations present.   As a result, this electron follows the solid line path b in Fig. 19-26; it is thus turned back toward the cathode even more quickly than indicated by the dotted path that would be followed in the absence of oscillations.   This electron is harmful

tion be regarded as being made up of two waves of equal amplitude rotating in opposite directions and progressing one pole distance per radio-frequency half cycle.   Such waves are often referred to as *traveling waves* or *space waves*.   They correspond to the rotating fields of a polyphase system.   To generate oscillations it is then necessary that the tangential velocity of the electrons approximate the speed of rotation of one or the other of these rotating space waves.

since it abstracts energy from the oscillations, but it is quickly removed from the scene of action and so does not have time to absorb very much energy. It does, however, bombard the cathode on its return with a velocity corresponding to whatever energy it has gained from the oscillating field; this causes "back heating" of the cathode analogous to that discussed on page 214. Typically about 5 per cent of the anode power of an operating magnetron is used in this way in heating the cathode.

Associated with the action described above, there is also a focusing mechanism that tends to keep the working electrons in step with the fields in the interaction space in such a way that the working electrons deliver the maximum possible energy to the oscillations. For example,

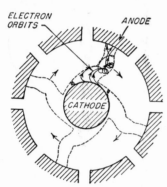

FIG. 19-27. Rotating space charge under oscillatory conditions, and paths followed by electrons working their way through the space charge toward the anode.

consider electron c in Fig. 19-26, which delivers some energy to the oscillations but was emitted a little too late to be in the correct position to make the maximum contribution. This electron is acted upon by a radial component of field from the oscillations as well as the tangential component. This radial field is in such a direction that it aids the d-c anode voltage. This increases the velocity with which electron c moves, and therefore assists it in catching up with electron a that is in the optimum position. Similarly, an electron d that is advanced beyond the optimum position encounters a radial field that opposes the anode voltage acting on it, and so is attracted less strongly toward the anode.

This causes electron d to be slowed down in its motion and thereby to fall back toward the optimum position. *This focusing action is equivalent to a velocity modulation that causes electrons such as c and d to form a bunch centered about electron a.*

The end result of these various actions that take place is to cause the orbit of the electrons to be confined to spokes, one for each two anodes, as illustrated in Fig. 19-27.[1] In the case of the π mode these spokes rotate at an angular velocity corresponding to two poles per cycle, and a certain fraction of the electrons emitted from the cathode travel out through the spokes, continuously delivering energy to the oscillations until these electrons reach the anode and disappear. Electrons emitted in the portions of the cathode between spokes are, however, returned very quickly to the cathode. Although these harmful electrons absorb some energy from the oscillations, this absorption is small in comparison with the energy that is

[1] The direction of rotation in Fig. 19-27 is opposite that in Figs. 19-25 and 19-26; this merely denotes that the polarity of the magnetic field is here reversed.

delivered by the electrons in the spoke.   The net result is that the oscillations receive a substantial net energy from the electrons.[1]

Performance of Magnetrons.   Magnetrons of the type described above are particularly suitable for generating relatively high powers at frequencies in the range 1000 to 25,000 Mc.   Peak powers exceeding 1000 kw can be obtained in magnetrons designed for pulsed operation at 3000 Mc, while 1 kw continuous-wave power can be achieved at the same

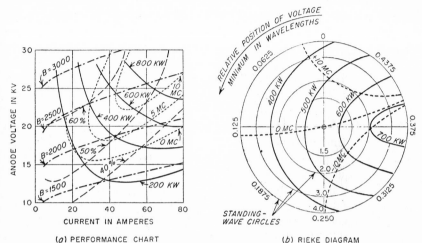

(*a*) PERFORMANCE CHART   (*b*) RIEKE DIAGRAM

FIG. 19-28. Diagrams showing performance of a magnetron oscillator.   The values of frequency indicated in the diagrams denote difference in frequency from an arbitrarily chosen reference value.

frequency.   Efficiencies are typically 30 to 60 per cent, and in some cases may run even higher.

The performance of a magnetron is relatively sensitive to the strength of the magnetic field, the anode voltage, and the load impedance.   Variations in any of these quantities will affect the output power, the efficiency, and the frequency to a marked extent.   The two methods shown in Fig. 19-28 are in common use for portraying the relations involved.   The first is the *performance chart* which presents the magnetron performance for a given load impedance.   The second is termed the *Rieke diagram* and gives the magnetron performance as a function of load conditions for a given anode voltage and magnetic field strength.   The Rieke diagram is a Smith chart (see Fig. 4-12), on which standing-wave circles and radial

[1] While this discussion has been carried out for the case of the π mode, it also applies to oscillations on other modes.   To excite one of these modes it is merely necessary to employ a combination of d-c anode voltage and magnetic field strength, such that the tangential velocity of the electrons at a position such as *a* approximates the circumferential velocity of the electric fields in the interaction space corresponding to the mode in question.

lines are drawn, but with the curvilinear impedance (or admittance) coordinates of the usual Smith chart are omitted.

It will be observed from Fig. 19-28b that the frequency of the magnetron oscillations is quite sensitive to changes in load impedance. This effect, termed "pulling," is a source of considerable difficulty in many magnetron applications. It is similarly shown in Fig. 19-28a that for a given load impedance and magnetic field, the frequency also changes with variation of the d-c anode voltage; this effect is termed "pushing."

19-7. Automatic Frequency Control of Microwave Oscillators. A system for stabilizing the frequency of a microwave oscillator is shown schematically in Fig. 19-29.[1] Here the two magic T's 1234 and $1'2'3'4'$, together with a resonant cavity, and crystal detectors A and B, form a phase-shift discriminator capable of developing a d-c output voltage having a magnitude and polarity depending on the extent and direction that the input frequency deviates from the resonant frequency of the cavity. This d-c voltage, after amplification, can be used to correct the frequency of the microwave oscillator supplying the input power, in such a manner as to reduce the deviation of the oscillator frequency from the resonant frequency of the cavity.

The action of the phase-shift discriminator of Fig. 19-29a can be explained as follows. A TE_{10} input wave fed into arm 3 divides equally between branches 1 and 2. The portion going down 2 is absorbed by the attenuator, while the wave in 1 enters $3'$ of the second magic T, and then divides again, this time between $1'$ and $2'$. Branch $1'$ is terminated in a short circuit and is $\lambda/8$ longer than branch $2'$ that is terminated (but not matched in impedance) by a high Q resonant cavity. When the waves reflected from the ends of $1'$ and $2'$ reach the junction of $3'$ and $4'$, each divides between arms $3'$ and $4'$. Thus crystal detector B is subjected to the vector sum of the two reflected waves that enter $4'$. Similarly crystal detector A is subjected to the vector sum of the two reflected waves entering $3'$, since these latter waves travel down $3'$ and $1'$, and divide between 2 and 3 and 4 when reaching the junction of 3 and 4.

It will now be shown that the voltages (i.e., electric fields) at detectors A and B vary with frequency in much the same manner as do the voltages of the phase-shift discriminator of Fig. 17-14. Thus at the resonant frequency of the cavity, the reflection at the end of $2'$ is either in phase (or in phase opposition) with the incident wave; the two reflected waves reaching B are then 90° out of phase as the round-trip length of $1'$ is a quarter of a guide wavelength greater than that of $2'$. This leads to the vector diagram shown at 1 of Fig. 19-29b, which corresponds to the first vector diagram of Fig. 17-14b. However, if the frequency differs from the resonant frequency of the cavity, then a phase shift occurs in the

[1] For further information see R. V. Pound, Frequency Stabilization of Microwave Oscillators, *Proc. IRE*, vol. 35, p. 1405, December, 1947.

reflection at 2′, causing a departure from the quadrature relation of the two electric fields at B, as shown at 2.   The resultant field at B and hence the d-c output voltage of detector B therefore depend upon the frequency of the oscillations relative to the resonant frequency of the cavity, being greater on one side of resonance (2 in Fig. 19-29b) and less on the other side of resonance.

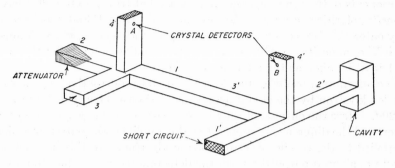

(a) MICROWAVE DISCRIMINATOR

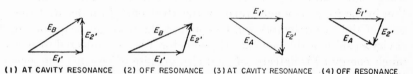

(1) AT CAVITY RESONANCE   (2) OFF RESONANCE   (3) AT CAVITY RESONANCE   (4) OFF RESONANCE
VOLTAGES AT B VOLTAGES AT A
(b) VECTOR DIAGRAMS OF VOLTAGES AT DETECTORS A AND B

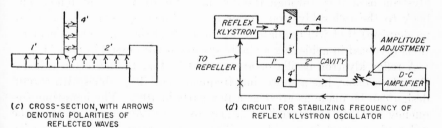

(c) CROSS-SECTION, WITH ARROWS   (d) CIRCUIT FOR STABILIZING FREQUENCY OF
DENOTING POLARITIES OF   REFLEX KLYSTRON OSCILLATOR
REFLECTED WAVES

Fig. 19-29. Microwave phase-shift discriminator, and application to automatic frequency control of a reflex-klystron oscillator.

A similar situation exists at detector A except that here the electric field of the wave reflected from the cavity is now reversed in phase relative to the wave reflected from the short circuit 1′.   The vector diagrams therefore differ from 1 and 2 in that E_2' is reversed, leading to diagrams 3 and 4, respectively.   Thus the same frequency deviation that causes the resultant field at B to increase likewise causes the resultant field at A to decrease, just as in the case of the voltages E_{a1} and E_{a2} in Fig. 17-14.

The reason that the two reflected waves E_2' have opposite polarity relative to E_1' at A and B arises from the action taking place at the junction of 3' and 4'. If the waves reflected from 1' and 2' both have a polarity that can be represented by upward arrows, as in Fig. 19-29c, then their components that travel down 3' toward I and A are likewise *both* represented by upward arrows. However, as shown in Fig. 19-29c, the components of the same two reflected waves that travel up branch 4 have *opposite* polarities because of the way the waves from 1' and 2' behave as they enter 4'. Hence the vector diagrams for the electric field at B must have E_2' of opposite polarity from the corresponding diagram for the field at A if E_1' is taken as the reference in both cases.

The discriminator of Fig. 19-29a can be used to control the frequency of a reflex klystron by the circuit arrangement shown schematically in Fig. 19-29d. Here the outputs of the two detectors are balanced against each other, and the difference is applied to a d-c amplifier, the output of which is applied to the repeller electrode of the klystron. In this way a very small unbalanced output between the detectors (corresponding to only a small frequency deviation from the resonant frequency of the cavity) will produce sufficient change in repeller voltage to make a large correction in the frequency generated by the klystron. In order that the outputs of the two detectors will be equal at the resonant frequency of the cavity in spite of the fact that the detector A is not subjected to nearly so much energy as is detector B, and also in spite of possible differences in the sensitivity of the two crystals, means are provided for adjusting the output voltage of detector B.

It will be noted that the loop circuit in Fig. 19-29d from the reflex klystron oscillator, through the discriminator to the d-c amplifier, and back to the reflex klystron, forms a closed-loop system (i.e., a servomechanism) that will oscillate if not carefully designed. The considerations involved in achieving a stable system are discussed in Sec. 11-3.

A reflex klystron oscillator arranged as in Fig. 19-29d, often called a *Pound oscillator*, has a short-time frequency stability which with careful design can be made as great as a few parts in 10^{10}. The long-time frequency stability is determined largely by the cavity, and can be of the order of one part in a million. These values compare favorably with those obtainable from quartz crystal oscillators.

PROBLEMS AND EXERCISES

19-1. Redraw Fig. 19-1b for (a) an increased amplitude of voltage across the gap A, and (b) increased d-c voltage between anode and cathode.

19-2. Explain why increasing the drift tube distance ABC will increase the small signal-voltage gain of the klystron amplifier of Fig. 19-1a.

19-3. Explain why the time it takes the electrons to pass across the gaps A and C

in Fig. 19-1a should not be too large compared with a cycle. In particular, explain what would happen if the transit time at gap A approximated a half cycle.

19-4. In Fig. 19-2 justify the statement on page 670 that the impedance of the middle cavity should have an inductive component, and explain what would happen if the cavity were resonant at the frequency of the applied signal.

19-5. A multicavity klystron is operated under conditions that cause it to function as a linear power amplifier. Discuss the variation of efficiency with amplitude of the input voltage.

19-6. Demonstrate, with the aid of distance-time curves of the type shown in Fig. 19-4, that the amplitude of the gap voltage does not change the time at which the bunch of electrons returns through the gap, but merely changes the current modulation of the returning electron beam.

19-7. Show curves analogous to those of Fig. 19-4 but for (a) increased anode voltage, and (b) less negative repeller voltage.

19-8. a. Show that if Fig. 19-4 is modified so that $N = 2 + \frac{1}{4}$, then the electrons returning through the gap will absorb energy from the oscillations, i.e., produce a positive electronic conductance.

b. Show similarly that when $N = 2 + \frac{1}{2}$, the bunches of returning electrons will react with the gap voltage in a way that causes the interchange of energy to be reactive.

19-9. In a reflex klystron, increasing the coupling of the load to the resonant cavity reduces the amplitude of oscillation. Explain the mechanism involved with the aid of the admittance spiral, assuming that the repeller voltage is such as to make the electronic admittance of the gap exactly a pure negative conductance.

19-10. Two hypothetical reflex klystrons have the same electronic admittance spiral, and the same resonator resonant impedance at the gap. The two systems differ, however, in that in one case the Q of the resonator is much higher than in the other case. It is found that the system with the high-Q resonator has a higher frequency stability; in particular, the frequency will vary less with a given change in repeller voltage than in the low-Q system. Explain how this behavior could have been predicted from the behavior of the electronic and resonator admittances at the gap.

19-11. In Fig. 19-9 it will be noted that the range through which the frequency can be varied by means of the repeller voltage is greater the higher the repeller mode. Show that this result could have been predicted from the admittance spiral of Fig. 19-11.

19-12. It is observed experimentally that the lowest value of repeller mode n at which oscillations will start is larger the greater the coupling of the load resistance to the resonator of a reflex klystron. Explain how this is consistent with the admittance spiral of Fig. 19-11.

19-13. The helix of a particular traveling-wave tube has 56 turns per in. and a mean diameter of 0.10 in. Determine approximately the value of anode voltage that is required.

19-14. In analogy with Fig. 19-13, discuss the behavior of the group of electrons that enters the gun end of the helix at about the time the axial electric field is zero going negative with increasing time.

19-15. Draw diagrams analogous to those of Fig. 19-13, but for the case where the electron velocity is slightly greater than the velocity with which the applied signal (the solid curve in Fig. 19-13a) would progress down the helix. Does amplification still occur?

19-16. Will the amplitude of the applied signal have any effect on the location of the center of the bunch in 3 of Fig. 19-13c relative to the zero point in the solid curve of Fig. 19-13a?

19-17. Discuss in a qualitative way the consequences of locating the attenuator in a traveling-wave tube (a) very close to the output end of the tube, and (b) very close to the gun end of the tube.

19-18. What would be the effect in a traveling-wave tube of employing an attenuator that introduced a very large reflection?

19-19. Describe means that could be used to couple to the input and output ends of the slow-wave structures of Fig. 19-15.

19-20. The corners in the folded line in Fig. 19-16 introduce discontinuity capacitances. How does this affect the velocity of the wave in the line as compared with the velocity of light?

19-21. Extend Fig. 19-17a to show the field at the next two gaps c and d to the immediate right of gap b, and likewise present oscillograms analogous to that of Fig. 19-17d, showing the variation of field with time at each of these gaps.

19-22. In Fig. 19-19, explain why the rate of increase of amplitude of the backward wave levels off as the wave approaches the gun end of the tube.

19-23. Explain the mechanism that causes oscillations in a backward-wave oscillator to take place at a frequency such that $nN_\Delta = 0.5$, as compared with nN_Δ appreciably smaller such as 0.1, or appreciably larger such as 0.9.

19-24. Show fields and oscillograms analogous to those of Fig. 19-17 but applicable to the top of the helix structure of Fig. 19-20. In order to simplify the discussion, assume that a tape helix is employed in which the width of the tape is a large fraction of the spacing between adjacent turns, so that the gap between turns is small. Likewise assume that at the frequency of operation it takes a wave one-quarter of a cycle to travel around one turn of the helix.

19-25. Transform Eq. (19-2) so that it expresses the frequency in terms of the phase constant β of the transmission line, the anode voltage E, the distance d between the centers of adjacent gaps, and the distance l that the wave must travel along the line with the velocity of light to go from one gap to the next gap, and the number of gaps n.

19-26. Assuming T_w in Eq. (19-2) is independent of frequency, show that when the anode voltage is very low, that the frequency of the oscillations is very nearly proportional to the square root of the anode voltage.

19-27. A particular backward-wave oscillator is so operated that $T_e = T_w$ at the high-frequency end of the tuning range. Determine the ratio of maximum to minimum anode voltage required to tune over a 2 to 1 frequency range, assuming T_w is independent of frequency.

19-28. In Fig. 19-24, assume that the diameter and positioning of the tuning ring is changed so that it partially obstructs the open end of the anode slots instead of acting as a capacitive shunt between the straps. Indicate whether the frequency will now be raised or lowered by bringing the ring closer to the anode, and explain the mechanism that causes the frequency to depend on the position of the ring.

19-29. How would the path indicated by the solid line in Fig. 19-26 be modified if the strength of the radio-frequency field were substantially increased as a result of reducing the loading on the resonant cavities of the magnetron?

19-30. Describe the forces acting on electron a in Fig. 19-26 when it reaches position 3, and discuss the effect of these forces upon the motion of the electron and the energy relations associated with it.

19-31. If the mode of operation in Fig. 19-26 were one in which the phase difference between adjacent poles was 90° instead of 180°, it would then be necessary for an electron to travel a distance corresponding to two poles in a half cycle. Explain from this fact why this particular mode requires a higher anode voltage for excitation than does the π mode for a given strength of magnetic field.

19-32. What would be the effect, if any, on the paths of the various electrons in Fig. 19-26 of reversing the polarity of the magnetic field?

19-33. Magnetron tubes frequently can be made to oscillate when the strength of the magnetic field is only slightly greater than the value corresponding to plate-current cutoff under nonoscillatory conditions. Such operation is, however, always associated with low efficiency, whereas high efficiency corresponds to a magnetic field strength much greater than cutoff. Explain this difference on the basis of the mechanism of operation that takes place in the magnetron.

19-34. The anode voltage of the magnetron of Fig. 19-28a is varied from 20 to 22.5 kv while maintaining the magnetic field at a strength of 2300 gauss. Determine the maximum and minimum power output over this voltage range, and the variation in magnetron frequency that can be expected.

19-35. A magnetron having the characteristics given in Fig. 19-28b is operated in an experimental setup in which the length of the transmission line connecting the magnetron to the load impedance can be varied. Determine the maximum variation that can occur in pulse power output, and in the generated frequency, as the length of this transmission line is varied, when the load impedance is such that the standing-wave ratio has values of 1.5 and 2.0.

19-36. The performance chart of Fig. 19-28a shows that for a given anode voltage the efficiency of operation is greater the stronger the magnetic field. Explain why this is consistent with the mechanism of operation of the magnetron discussed in connection with Fig. 19-26.

19-37. Will the frequency-control system of Fig. 19-29d still provide frequency stabilization if the difference between the lengths of arms 1' and 2' (a) departs slightly from $\lambda/8$, and (b) is exactly $\lambda/4$?

19-38. What is the effect on the vector diagrams of Fig. 19-29b, and the ability of the system of Fig. 19-29d to stabilize frequency, if the resonant cavity provides a matched-impedance termination for arm 2'?

19-39. Discuss the effects on the long-time stability of the oscillator in Fig. 19-29d of unequal aging of the two crystal detectors.

19-40. What would be the effect on the oscillator output in Fig. 19-29d of inserting an audio-frequency voltage at $\times$?

CHAPTER 20

POWER FOR OPERATING VACUUM TUBES

20-1. A-C Hum from Cathode-heating Power. When a-c power is used to heat the cathode of a tube, there is always the possibility that alternating components will thereby be introduced in the plate current, or that signals being amplified will be modulated by the alternating currents used to heat the cathode. The resulting effects are commonly referred to as *a-c hum*, since with the usual 60-cycle power source the result after amplification is a low-pitched hum when observed on a loudspeaker.

A-C Hum in Filament-type Tubes. Alternating-current hum is minimized in filament-type tubes by bringing the plate and grid return leads to a point that is at substantially the same potential as the mid-point of the filament. This may be done by one of the methods illustrated in Fig. 20-1. Under these conditions, the hum is primarily at the second harmonic of the power frequency, and is a result of (1) the action on the plate current of the magnetic field associated with the filament current, and (2) the effect of the voltage drop along the filament.[1]

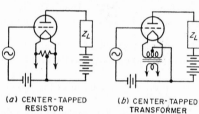

(a) CENTER-TAPPED RESISTOR   (b) CENTER-TAPPED TRANSFORMER

FIG. 20-1. Methods of connecting the grid- and plate-return leads of filament tubes when alternating filament current is used.

The magnetic field produced by the filament current deflects the electrons flowing to the plate according to the principles discussed in Sec. 6-2. As a result, the plate current tends to *decrease* slightly when filament current flows in either direction, as compared with the plate current that is obtained when the filament current is zero. Voltage drop in the filament causes the negative half of the filament to supply more electrons to the plate than does the positive half; moreover, since the number of electrons drawn from any portion of the filament is proportional to the three-halves power of the electrostatic field, the extra current from the negative end of the filament is greater than the reduction in current from

[1] It might be thought that the cyclical variation of filament temperature resulting from the use of alternating filament current would also be important. However, the heat capacity of filaments used in vacuum tubes is so high that the variation in filament temperature with 60-cycle filament current is too small to produce a significant amount of hum when a full space charge exists in the vicinity of the filament.

the positive end.   This action tends to cause the space current to increase when current is flowing through the filament.

Since these two principal causes of hum produce effects that are 180° out of phase with each other, they tend to cancel.   By designing the filament to take full advantage of this situation, it is possible to minimize the amount of residual hum that is present.   Doing so involves the proper choice of filament voltage, and an appropriate filament geometry usually involving a V or W configuration.   In large tubes having a multistrand filament, it is common practice to excite different strands from different phases of a polyphase source; this further reduces the residual hum.

It is permissible to use alternating current to heat filament cathodes only when the tubes involved carry large signal currents, for example, in the power stage of a public-address system, in radio transmitters, etc. Under such conditions the signal currents being amplified will be large compared with the residual hum normally present.   Filament tubes operating from alternating current are never used in low-level audio-frequency amplifiers, and are not considered very satisfactory in low-level radio-frequency amplifiers.

A-C Hum in Heater-type Tubes.   In heater-type tubes the a-c hum is much less than for the corresponding filament-type tubes.   Nevertheless, some residual hum will always be present as a result of such factors as magnetic field produced by the heater current, leakage resistances from the heater to other electrodes, etc.   However, these effects are normally so small that a-c power can be used to operate heater cathodes in nearly all applications.

20-2. Rectifiers for Supplying Anode Power.   Power for operating the anode (i.e., plate, screen-grid, etc.) electrodes of vacuum tubes is usually obtained from a rectifier-filter system that converts alternating power into d-c power of the appropriate voltage.

The rectifier in such an arrangement is usually either a high-vacuum diode, or a hot-cathode gas diode.[1]   Such tubes are discussed in Secs. 6-5 and 6-17, respectively.   They are rectifiers because when the plate is positive with respect to the cathode, electrons flow to it, while when the plate is negative the tube becomes nonconducting.   The important characteristics of a diode rectifier tube are the maximum allowable peak plate current, the maximum allowable average plate current, the maximum allowable peak inverse voltage, and the voltage drop in the tube.

The maximum allowable peak plate current represents the maximum electron emission that the cathode can be counted upon to supply during the useful life of the tube and still maintain a full space charge at all times; it is therefore determined by the cathode.   Since the rectifier

---

[1] In recent years, selenium rectifiers have also begun to compete with diode tubes in the generation of anode power.   As far as the associated circuits are concerned, they are the equivalent of a tube rectifier.

never allows current to flow for more than half the time, the average plate current, i.e., the d-c output current, will never exceed one-half the peak plate current and may be less. The maximum allowable value that the average current can have is determined by the plate dissipation that the tube is designed to handle, and is often less than half the allowable peak current.

The maximum allowable inverse plate voltage is the largest negative voltage that may be applied to the plate with safety; it determines the d-c voltage that can be obtained from the rectifier tube. The exact relationship between d-c output voltage and the allowable inverse voltage depends upon the rectifier circuit employed, but except for voltage-multiplying circuits (see below) the inverse voltage will be at least as great as the d-c voltage; in certain rectifier connections, it will be π times as great.

The voltage drop in the tube when carrying the allowable currents fixes the amount of plate dissipation that must be provided in the tube design, and is an important factor in determining the regulation of the d-c output voltage.

High-vacuum Rectifier Tubes. High-vacuum rectifier tubes find their principal use in supplying anode power for radio receivers, small radio transmitters, public-address systems, etc., at anode voltages of the order of 500 volts or less at currents up to several hundred milliamperes. Diode rectifier tubes for this service are often built with two plates and two cathodes in a common envelope, and are provided with very small spacing between anode and cathode to minimize the voltage drop in the tube.

High-vacuum thermionic rectifiers also find use in applications requiring a very high voltage with an extremely small current. An example is a cathode-ray tube requiring very high beam voltage. Rectifier tubes for such applications require very little cathode heating power; but must be designed to withstand a very high peak inverse voltage.

Characteristics of a few representative high-vacuum rectifier tubes are given in Table 20-1.

Hot-cathode Mercury-vapor Rectifier Tubes. The gas diodes used as rectifiers ordinarily employ mercury vapor in equilibrium with liquid mercury, although occasionally an inert gas is employed. The cathodes are invariably of the oxide-coated type, and both heater and filament cathodes are employed.

The cathode of a gas diode must be brought to normal operating temperature *before* the plate voltage is applied. Otherwise, the voltage drop in the tube during the warming-up period before the electron emission has reached its full value will exceed the cathode disintegration value (see Sec. 6-17) and the cathode will be permanently damaged. It is also necessary that the plate circuit be carefully protected from even momentary short circuits or overloads, since, if the peak current rating is exceeded for even a few seconds, the cathode of the tube may be permanently damaged.

A hot-cathode mercury-vapor rectifier tube will operate satisfactorily only when the temperature of the condensed mercury, i.e., the lowest temperature of any part of the tube envelope ("cold-spot" temperature), is maintained between definite limits. This is because it is the cold-spot temperature that determines the pressure of the mercury vapor within

TABLE 20-1
CHARACTERISTICS OF TYPICAL RECTIFIER TUBES

Type	Maximum inverse volts	Maximum peak amp	Maximum rated average amp	Filament Volts	Amp	Notes
High-vacuum types						
5Y3-GT	1,400	0.400[a]	0.075[a,b]	5	2	a
5U4-G	1,550	0.675[a]	0.135[a,b]	5	3	a
5R4-GY	2,800	0.650[a]	0.125[a]	5	2	a
6W4-GT	3,500	0.600	0.125	6.3	1.2	c
1V2	7,500	0.010	0.0005	0.62	0.3	d
1X2	18,000	0.010	0.001	1.25	0.2	d
1B3	30,000	0.017	0.002	1.25	0.2	d
Hot-cathode mercury-vapor types						
3B25	4,500	2.0	0.5	2.5	5.0	c,e
866-A	10,000[f]	1.0	0.25	2.5	5.0	c
872-A	10,000[f]	5	1.25	5	7.5	c
869-B	20,000[f]	10	2.5	5	18	c
857-B	22,000[f]	40	10	5	30	c

[a] These tubes have two plates and two cathodes in one envelope. Plate currents are given for one plate, but filament data are for both filaments.

[b] The maximum d-c current that is permissible in these tubes depends somewhat upon the d-c voltage. Values given cannot be obtained without lowering tube life if d-c voltage has highest value permitted by inverse voltage rating.

[c] Half-wave type, i.e., only one plate.

[d] For high-voltage low-current (cathode-ray) applications.

[e] Gas diode using inert gas rather than mercury vapor.

[f] Approximate; exact value depends on temperature of the condensed mercury.

the tube. If the pressure is too low (low cold-spot temperature), the intensity of ionization is reduced to the point where the space-charge neutralization action does not occur. The voltage drop in the tube is then excessive, and cathode disintegration occurs. On the other hand, when the pressure of the mercury is high (high cold-spot temperature), the inverse voltage at which an arcback will occur inside the tube becomes abnormally low. These effects of temperature are shown in Fig. 20-2 and are seen to limit the operating range to conditions that may not always be realizable in practice.

Compared with the high-vacuum rectifier, the hot-cathode mercury-vapor rectifier has the advantage of lower anode-to-cathode voltage drop, lower filament power, and lower first cost, provided the anode potential is of the order of 1000 volts or more and the current required is appreciable. At the same time, the mercury-vapor tube displays a tendency toward arcback, produces radio-frequency transients as the tube ionizes, and will suffer damage to the cathode from momentary overloads. As a result of this situation, the high-vacuum rectifier is used in home receivers and in similar applications where the voltages required are not large and the power is only moderate, while the hot-cathode mercury-vapor tube finds its chief use when the anode potential is of the order of 1000 volts or more and the required power is considerable.

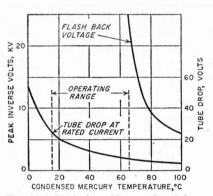

Fig. 20-2. Variation of inverse breakdown voltage, and of forward voltage drop, with condensed-mercury temperature of a hot-cathode mercury-vapor rectifier tube.

Characteristics of typical hot-cathode mercury-vapor rectifier tubes are given in Table 20-1.

20-3. Rectifier Circuits. Circuits in which rectifiers are used can be conveniently classified according to whether the power source is single phase or polyphase. Single-phase rectifier circuits are used to develop anode power for radio receivers, public-address systems, small radio transmitters, etc., wherever the power required is small, i.e., does not exceed a kilowatt or so. Polyphase rectifiers are used for higher powers; they have the advantage of utilizing more completely the possibilities of the transformers and rectifier tubes, and of delivering an output that requires less filtering.

Single-phase Rectifier Circuits. The various types of rectifier connections that may be employed with a single-phase source of power are shown in Figs. 20-3 and 20-4, together with the waveforms of the voltage that are developed across a resistance load.

The circuit shown at Fig. 20-3a, in which a single rectifier is placed in series with the source of alternating voltage and the load impedance, is called a *half-wave* rectifier circuit. It has the very great disadvantages of delivering an output voltage that is far from being a continuous d-c potential, and of producing a d-c magnetization in the core of the power-supply transformer as a result of the rectified current that flows through the secondary. This circuit is therefore seldom used.

The rectifier circuit most commonly employed with a single-phase power source is shown in Fig. 20-3b, and consists of two rectifier units operating in conjunction with a center-tapped transformer in such a way that the two tubes alternately supply rectified current to the load.   Such a *full-wave* rectifier produces an output voltage that is more nearly constant than that produced by the half-wave rectifier.   It also avoids d-c saturation in the core of the supply transformer.   This is because the d-c magnetizations in the two halves of the transformer secondary are opposed to each other and so give zero resultant magnetization.

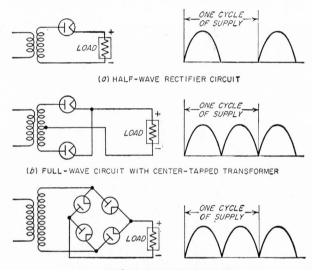

(*a*) HALF-WAVE RECTIFIER CIRCUIT

(*b*) FULL-WAVE CIRCUIT WITH CENTER-TAPPED TRANSFORMER

(*c*) FULL-WAVE BRIDGE CIRCUIT

FIG. 20-3. Rectifier circuits for operation with single-phase power sources, together with waveforms of voltage developed across a resistance load.

The bridge type of full-wave rectifier shown at Fig. 20-3c requires four rectifier units instead of the two called for by the center-tapped transformer arrangement, but has the advantage of requiring only one secondary winding instead of two.   This circuit is widely used with selenium and copper oxide rectifiers, but is seldom employed with tube rectifiers since the different cathodes are not at the same potential and so cannot be connected in parallel and supplied from a single filament transformer secondary.

Voltage-multiplying Circuits.   The single-phase rectifier circuits shown in Fig. 20-4 are known as *voltage-multiplying* systems and are capable of delivering a d-c voltage that is two or more times the peak amplitude of the alternating voltage which is available to be applied to the rectifier tubes.   In the voltage-doubling circuit of Fig. 20-4a, this is accomplished as a result of the fact that the capacitors C_1 and C_2 are each charged to the peak voltage of the transformer secondary on alternate half cycles, but with polarities such that the d-c voltages developed across the capacitors add, in so far as the output is concerned.

The cascade voltage doubler of Fig. 20-4b produces a result equivalent to that of the voltage-doubling circuit, but has the advantages that no transformer is required, and that there is a common terminal between the supply and the output so that both may be grounded simultaneously. The operation of this circuit can be explained as follows: If tube T_2 is disconnected, then capacitor C_1 will charge to the peak supply voltage E, and the instantaneous potential at point a will fluctuate between 0 and $2E$. If tube T_2 is now connected, the voltage between a and ground will tend

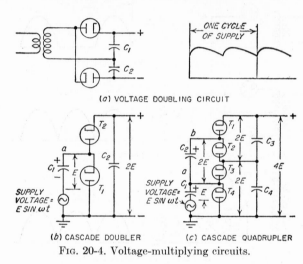

Fig. 20-4. Voltage-multiplying circuits.

to charge capacitor C_2 to the peak voltage existing at a, or $2E$. Such a cascading arrangement can be extended indefinitely. A four-stage system that on open-circuit load develops a d-c output potential approaching four times the peak supply voltage is shown in Fig. 20-4c.

The output voltage developed across a load impedance by a voltage-multiplying system depends upon the voltage drop in the rectifier tubes caused by the d-c current drawn by the load connected to the output. In general, it can be stated that the full extent of the voltage-multiplying action is present only with very small load currents, and that, as the load current is increased to a moderate value, the output voltage will drop off rapidly. That is, the voltage regulation in these systems is poor.

Polyphase Circuits. When a polyphase source of alternating power is employed, the number of possible rectifier connections is almost unlimited, although only a relatively few of these are of much practical importance in electronics. The polyphase rectifier circuits most commonly used with three-phase power sources are shown in Fig. 20-5, together with the corresponding waveforms of voltage developed across a resistance load.

The three-phase half-wave circuit of Fig. 20-5a is essentially three half-wave rectifiers of the type shown in Fig. 20-3a, with each leg of the secondary Y providing one phase.   In such an arrangement, each rectifier tube carries current one-third of the time, and the output wave ripples at three times the frequency of the alternating-current supply.   In order to avoid d-c saturation in the transformer, it is necessary to employ a three-phase transformer rather than three single-phase transformers.

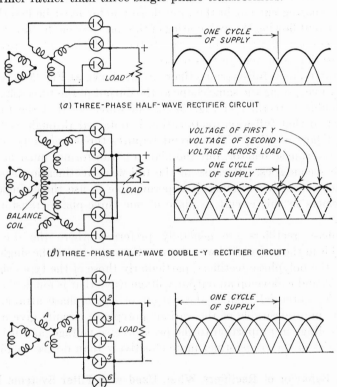

(a) THREE-PHASE HALF-WAVE RECTIFIER CIRCUIT

(b) THREE-PHASE HALF-WAVE DOUBLE-Y RECTIFIER CIRCUIT

(c) THREE-PHASE FULL-WAVE RECTIFIER CIRCUIT

FIG. 20-5. Rectifier circuits for operation with three-phase power source, together with waveforms of voltage developed across a resistance load.

The circuit of Fig. 20-5b consists of two three-phase half-wave circuits of Fig. 20-5a connected in parallel through an interphase reactor (also called balance coil).   The polarities of the corresponding secondary windings in the two parallel systems are reversed with respect to each other, so that the rectifier output voltage of one three-phase unit is at a minimum when the rectifier output voltage of the other unit is at a maximum, as shown.   The action of the balance coil is to cause the actual voltage at the output terminals to be the average of the rectified voltages developed by the individual three-phase systems.   The output voltage of the combination is therefore more nearly constant than that of a three-phase half-wave system, and moreover, the ripple frequency of the output wave is now six times that of the supply frequency, instead of three times. In order that the individual three-phase half-wave systems may operate independently with current flowing through each tube one third of the time, the interphase reactor must have sufficient inductance so that the alternating current flowing in it as a result of the voltage existing across the coil[1] has a peak value less than one half the d-c load current. That is, the peak alternating current in the interphase reactor must be less than the direct current flowing through one leg of the coil. Since the direct current flows in opposite directions in the two halves of the interphase reactor, no d-c saturation is present in this reactor.

The three-phase full-wave rectifier circuit shown at Fig. 20-5c gives an output wave having the same shape as the output of the three-phase half-wave double-Y rectifier of Fig. 20-5b, but differs in that the tubes are arranged so that full-wave rectification is obtained through each leg of the secondary winding. This circuit requires three secondary windings and no interphase reactor, but the filament transformer must have four separate secondaries. Because of the full-wave rectification associated with each secondary winding, it is permissible to use three single-phase transformers in this circuit in place of one three-phase transformer, if desired.

Polyphase rectifiers are generally preferred where the d-c power required is in the order of 1 kw or more. Compared with the single-phase circuits, the polyphase rectifiers, particularly those of the types shown in Fig. 20-5b and c, develop an output voltage wave that is much closer to a steady d-c potential than is the output of single-phase arrangements. Also, the more desirable of the various polyphase circuits give a higher output voltage in proportion to the peak inverse voltage, and utilize the possibilities of the transformer more effectively than do the single-phase circuits.

20-4. Behavior of Rectifiers When Used with Filter Systems Having Series-inductance (Choke) Input. The pulsating voltge developed by the rectifier output is smoothed into a steady d-c voltage suitable for applying to the plate circuit of a vacuum tube by passage through an appropriate electrical network consisting of series inductances or resistances, and shunt capacitors. Such networks, or *filters* as they are commonly called, can be divided into two types: those which present a series inductance to the rectifier output, and those which present a shunt capacitor. These are commonly referred to as *choke input* and *capacitor input*, respectively. Either arrangement can be used with any of the rectifier circuits of Figs. 20-3 and 20-5; however, the voltage multiplying circuits of Fig. 20-4 require capacitor input.

---

[1] This voltage is the difference between the output voltages of the individual three-phase systems.

Voltage and Current Relations in Rectifier Tubes with Choke-input Filters.
The voltage and current relations existing in rectifier systems having a
series-inductance or choke-input filter are illustrated by the oscillograms
of Fig. 20-6. While these apply to specific rectifier circuits, the same
general behavior occurs in all rectifier systems of the choke-input type.

When the input inductance in Fig. 20-6 is infinite, the current through
the inductance is constant and is carried at any moment by the rectifier

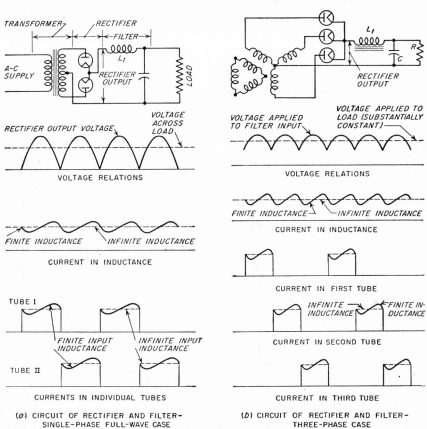

(*a*) CIRCUIT OF RECTIFIER AND FILTER—
    SINGLE-PHASE FULL-WAVE CASE

(*b*) CIRCUIT OF RECTIFIER AND FILTER—
    THREE-PHASE CASE

Fig. 20-6. Voltage and current waveforms existing in rectifier systems operating with
choke-input filters, assuming an idealized transformer with zero leakage reactance.

plate that has a positive voltage (or the most positive voltage) applied to
it at that instant. As the alternating voltage being rectified passes
through zero (or when another plate becomes most positive), the current
suddenly transfers from one plate to another, giving square current waves
through the individual rectifier tubes, as shown by the dotted lines in
Fig. 20-6.[1] When the input inductance is finite and not too small, the

---

[1] These oscillograms are idealized by assuming that the transformer leakage inductance is zero.   The effect of leakage inductance is considered below in connection with
Fig. 20-8.

situation is as shown by the solid lines in Fig. 20-6. The current through the input choke then tends to increase when the output voltage of the rectifier exceeds the average or d-c value, and to decrease when the rectifier output voltage is less than the d-c value. This causes the current to the individual plates to be modified as shown. If the input inductance is too small, the current decreases to zero during a portion of the time between the peaks of the rectifier output voltage, and the conditions then correspond to a capacitor-input filter system, as discussed in Sec. 20-5.

The voltage that the rectifier system applies to the input of a filter having a choke input can for nearly all practical purposes be considered as being given by the idealized curves of Figs. 20-3 and 20-5 (or Fig. 20-6). showing the shape of the output voltage produced by an ideal rectifier system across a resistance load. The only important exception is in the calculation of voltage regulation.

The output voltage wave of the rectifier can be considered as consisting of a d-c component upon which are superimposed a-c voltages, termed *ripple* voltages. In the case of the idealized full-wave single-phase rectifier, Fourier analysis shows that the output wave has the equation[1]

$$\left.\begin{array}{l}\text{Output voltage of}\\\text{single-phase full-wave rectifier}\end{array}\right\} = \frac{2E}{\pi}\left(1 - \frac{2}{3}\cos 2\omega t\right.$$

$$\left. - \frac{2}{15}\cos 4\omega t - \frac{2}{35}\cos 6\omega t - \cdots\right) \quad (20\text{-}1)$$

where E represents the peak value of the a-c voltage applied to the rectifier tube and ω is the angular velocity $(2\pi f)$ of the supply frequency. In this case the d-c component of the output wave is $2/\pi$ times the crest value of the a-c wave. The lowest frequency component of ripple in the output is twice the supply frequency and has a magnitude that is two-thirds the d-c component of the output voltage. The remaining ripple components are harmonics of this lowest frequency component and diminish in amplitude with the order of the harmonic involved in accordance with Eq. (20-1). (Also see Table 20-2.)

Table 20-2 gives the analyses for the output waves delivered by the

---

[1] This result is obtained as follows:

$$\text{D-c component} = \frac{E}{\pi}\int_{\omega t=0}^{\omega t=\pi}\sin \omega t\, d(\omega t) = \frac{2E}{\pi} \quad (20\text{-}2)$$

$$\left.\begin{array}{l}\text{Ripple component of}\\\text{frequency } n\omega/2\pi\end{array}\right\} = \frac{2E}{\pi}\int_{\omega t=0}^{\omega t=\pi}\cos n\omega t \sin \omega t\, d(\omega t)$$

$$= \frac{2E}{\pi}\left[\frac{\cos (n-1)\omega t}{2(n-1)} - \frac{\cos (n+1)\omega t}{2(n+1)}\right]_{\omega t=0}^{\omega t=\pi}$$

$$= \frac{2E}{\pi}\frac{-2}{n^2-1} \quad (20\text{-}3)$$

In these equations n may have values 2, 4, etc.

polyphase rectifier connections of Fig. 20-5. The ripple voltages are much less for the three-phase half-wave rectifier than for the single-phase connection, and are still less for the six-phase arrangements of Fig. 20-5b and c. In all cases, the amplitude of the ripple components diminishes rapidly as the order of the harmonics is increased.

The peak inverse voltage of a rectifier system operating in conjunction with a series-inductance input depends upon the connections. It ranges from as high as π times the d-c component of the output voltage, in the case of the single-phase center-tapped connection,[1] to barely more than the d-c voltage in the three-phase full-wave system. Results in typical cases are given in Table 20-2.

The ratio of peak current per individual plate to the d-c current developed by the over-all rectifier system depends upon the rectifier connection and upon the size of the input inductance. When the input inductance is infinite, then the plate of each rectifier tube must at some time during the cycle carry the entire load current, except in the case of the three-phase half-wave double-Y system, where each plate is called upon to carry only half of the load current. These and other useful current relations for different rectifier connections are tabulated in Table 20-2. When the input inductance is not infinite, the current through the input inductance will vary about the value for the infinite inductance case, as illustrated in Fig. 20-6. In the least favorable case, corresponding to an input inductance barely sufficient to obtain choke-input type of operation, the peak value of plate current is twice the value corresponding to infinite input inductance.

Input-inductance Requirements. To achieve normal choke-input operation, it is necessary that there be a continuous flow of current through the input inductance. The peak value of the alternating current flowing through the input inductance must, hence, be less than the d-c output current of the rectifier. This condition is realized by satisfying the approximate relation[2]

$$\omega L_1 \gg R_{\text{eff}} \frac{E_1}{E_0} \qquad (20\text{-}4a)$$

[1] This is determined as follows: The peak inverse voltage occurs when the voltage applied to the plate is at its negative peak value $-E$. At this instant, the cathode is at the positive peak voltage $+E$. Thus, the peak inverse voltage for the single-phase full-wave center-tapped circuit is $2E$, while the d-c voltage is $2E/\pi$. The ratio of the two is π.

[2] This is derived as follows: The average or d-c current is E_0/R_{eff}. The peak alternating current is very nearly the peak value $E_1/\omega L_1$ of the fundamental-frequency component, since the higher-frequency components of the ripple current are relatively small, being proportionately considerably smaller than the corresponding components of ripple voltage. The ratio of peak-to-average current hence approximates $(E_1/E_0)/\omega L_1 R_{\text{eff}}$, and this must not be less than unity. Solving for ωL_1 gives Eq. (20-4a).

TABLE 20-2
CHARACTERISTICS OF TYPICAL RECTIFIERS OPERATED WITH
INDUCTANCE-INPUT FILTER SYSTEMS

	Rectifier circuit				
	Single-phase, full-wave, center-tapped connection	Single-phase, full-wave bridge (Fig. 20-3c)	Three-phase, half-wave (Fig. 20-5a)	Double three-phase, half-wave (Fig. 20-5b)	Three-phase, full-wave (Fig. 20-5c)
Voltage relations (d-c component of output voltage taken as 1.0):					
a. Rms value of transformer secondary voltage (per leg).................	1.11*	1.11	0.855	0.855	0.428
b. Maximum inverse voltage.........	3.14	1.57	2.09	2.09	1.05
c. Lowest frequency in rectifier output (F = frequency of power supply)....	2F	2F	3F	6F	6F
d. Peak value of first three a-c components of rectifier output:					
Ripple frequency (fundamental)..	0.667	0.667	0.250	0.057†	0.057
Second harmonic of ripple frequency......................	0.133	0.133	0.057	0.014	0.014
Third harmonic of ripple frequency	0.057	0.057	0.025	0.006	0.006
e. Ripple peaks with reference to d-c axis:					
Positive peak..................	0.363	0.363	0.209	0.0472	0.0472
Negative peak.................	0.637	0.637	0.395	0.0930	0.0930
Current relations:					
f. $\dfrac{\text{Average current per plate}}{\text{Peak plate current}}$	0.500‡	0.500‡	0.333‡	0.333‡	0.333‡
g. $\dfrac{\text{Average current per plate}}{\text{Direct current in load}}$	0.500	0.500	0.333	0.167	0.333
h. $\dfrac{\text{Peak current per plate}}{\text{Direct current in load}}$	1.000‡	1.000‡	1.000‡	0.500‡	1.000‡
Transformer requirements (d-c output power taken as 1.0):					
i. Primary kva...................	1.11	1.11	1.21	1.05	1.05
j. Secondary kva.................	1.57	1.11	1.48	1.48	1.05
k. Average of primary and secondary kva...........................	1.34	1.11	1.35	1.26	1.05

NOTE: This table assumes that the input inductance is sufficiently large to maintain the output current of the rectifier substantially constant, and neglects the effects of voltage drop in the rectifier and the transformers.

* Secondary voltage on one side of center tap.

† The principal component of voltage across the balance coil has a frequency of 3F and a peak amplitude of 0.500. The peak balance coil voltage, including the smaller higher harmonics, is 0.605.

‡ Assumes infinite input inductance.

where E_1/E_0 is the ratio of lowest frequency ripple component to the d-c voltage in the rectifier output, as given by Table 20-2, R_{eff} is the effective load resistance (actual load resistance plus filter resistance plus equivalent tube and transformer resistance), and ωL_1 is the reactance of the incremental value of the input inductance at the *lowest ripple frequency*. In the important practical case of a 60-cycle single-phase full-wave circuit, Eq. (20-4a) becomes

$$L_1 > \frac{R_{\text{eff}}}{1130} \qquad (20\text{-}4b)$$

In polyphase systems, the required value of L_1 is very much less.

The higher the load resistance, i.e., the lower the d-c load current, the more difficult it is to maintain a continuous flow of current.   Also, with a given L_1, Eqs. (20-4) will not be satisfied when the load resistance exceeds a critical value.

The minimum allowable input inductance as given by Eqs. (20-4) is termed the *critical inductance*.   When the inductance is less than the critical value, the system acts as a capacitor-input system (see below). When the direct current drawn from the rectifier system varies from time to time, it is necessary to satisfy Eqs. (20-4) at all times if proper operation, and in particular if good voltage regulation, are to be maintained. In order that this requirement may be satisfied at very small load currents without excessive inductance, it is necessary to place a resistance (commonly termed a "bleeder" resistance) across the output of the rectifier-filter system in order to limit R_{eff} in Eqs. (20-4) to a value corresponding to a reasonable value of L_1.

It is important to keep in mind that the inductance L_1 effective in Eq. (20-4) is the *incremental inductance*, i.e., the inductance to the alternating current superimposed upon the d-c magnetization.   It was noted in connection with Fig. 2-4 that the incremental inductance always increases as the d-c magnetization decreases.   This fact is of assistance in satisfying Eqs. (20-4) at low load currents where R_{eff} is large.

Transformer Considerations.   The wave shapes of the currents that flow through the windings of the transformer in the idealized case of a rectifier system operating with an infinite input inductance are shown in Fig. 20-7 for two typical cases.   It will be noted that these waves are not sinusoidal.   As a result, the heating of the transformer windings is greater for a given d-c power output from the rectifier than would be the case if the same amount of a-c power were delivered by the transformer to a resistance load.   It is accordingly necessary to design the transformer windings more generously for rectifier applications than for cases where sinusoidal currents are involved.

The ratio of the actual d-c rectified power output to the kilovolt-ampere power capacity of the windings on the basis of sinusoidal waves, for the same heat loss due to winding resistance, is termed the transformer *utilization factor*, or *utility factor*. Its value depends upon the rectifier connections and is, in general, not the same for the primary and secondary windings, since the wave shapes in these windings will generally be different. Table 20-2 gives the reciprocal of the utility factor of the primary and secondary windings for some of the more commonly used rectifier connections.

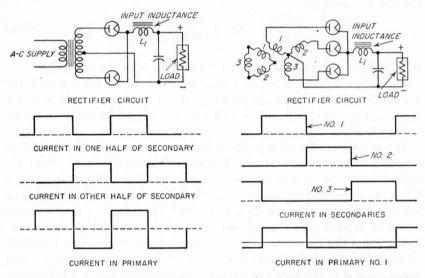

Fig. 20-7. Typical current waves in primary and secondary windings of transformer for ideal choke-input systems.

Voltage Regulation in Input-inductance Systems. The output voltage of a rectifier-filter system employing an input inductance that satisfies Eq. (20-4) falls off with increasing load as a result of resistances in the tubes, filter, and transformer, and as a result of the leakage reactance of the supply transformer. The various resistances in the circuit reduce the output voltage without affecting the wave shapes in the system. The leakage reactance of the transformer, however, distorts the wave shape of the output voltage by preventing the current from shifting instantly from one transformer winding to another, as in the ideal cases of Fig. 20-6. The situation in a typical case is shown in Fig. 20-8, where μ represents the time interval required to transfer the current. During this transition period, the output voltage assumes a value intermediate between the open-circuit voltages of the two windings that are simultaneously carrying current, as shown, instead of following the open-circuit potential of the more positive plate as is the case in an ideal system. This causes the average voltage of the output to be less than if there were no leakage inductance by the amount indicated by the shaded areas in Fig. 20-8.

The quantitative relations, which are quite complicated, depend upon both the rectifier and the transformer connections.

When the input inductance fails to satisfy Eq. (20-4), the output voltage rises, and when the effective load resistance R_{eff} is very large, the output voltage will approach the peak value of the rectifier output waveform. Failure to satisfy Eq. (20-4) causes the system to have poor voltage regulation; this is further discussed below in connection with Fig. 20-11.

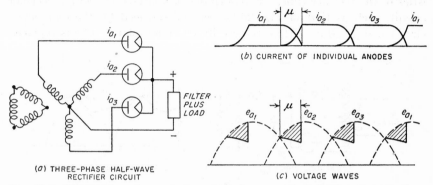

Fig. 20-8. Effect of transformer leakage inductance on the behavior of a polyphase rectifier.

20-5. Behavior of Rectifiers When Used With Filter Systems Having Shunt-capacitor Input.

The rectifier-filter system illustrated in Fig. 20-9 differs from that of Fig. 20-6a in that a shunt capacitor is presented to the rectifier output instead of a series inductance. This causes the behavior to be quite different from that illustrated in Fig. 20-6a. Each time the positive peak alternating voltage of the transformer is applied to one of the rectifier plates, the input capacitor charges up to just slightly less than this peak voltage. The rectifier then ceases to deliver current to the filter until another plate approaches its peak positive potential, when the capacitor is charged again. During the interval when the voltage across the input capacitor is greater than the potential of any of the plates, the voltage across the input capacitor drops off nearly linearly with time because the first filter inductance draws a substantially constant current from the input capacitor. A typical set of voltage and current waves is shown in Fig. 20-9c and d.

It is apparent from Fig. 20-9 that the use of an input capacitor increases the average voltage across the output terminal aa of the rectifier. This is because during those time intervals when no current flows through a rectifier tube, the voltage across the capacitor is greater than the most positive voltage applied to a rectifier plate; the output current during these intervals is supplied from the charge stored in the input capacitor. It is also to be observed that the use of an input capacitor reduces the amplitude of the ripple in the voltage across the rectifier output aa.

High-vacuum rectifier tubes are generally used in capacitor-input systems because the high-vacuum tube is not so critical with respect to large peak currents as is the hot-cathode mercury-vapor rectifier tube.

Analysis of Capacitor-input Systems.   The detailed action that takes place in a capacitor-input system depends in a relatively complicated way upon the load resistance in the rectifier output, the input capacitance, the leakage reactance and resistance of the transformer, and the characteristics of the rectifier tube.   For purposes of analysis, the actual rectifier circuit, such as that of Fig. 20-9a, can be replaced by the equivalent circuit of Fig. 20-9b.   Here the rectifying action of the tube is replaced

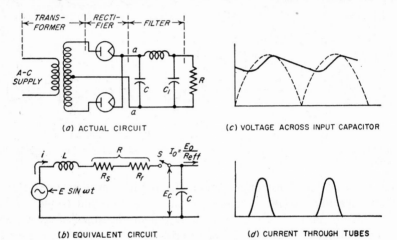

(a) ACTUAL CIRCUIT

(c) VOLTAGE ACROSS INPUT CAPACITOR

(b) EQUIVALENT CIRCUIT

(d) CURRENT THROUGH TUBES

Fig. 20-9. Actual and equivalent circuits of capacitor- input rectifier system, together with oscillograms of voltage and current for a typical operating condition.

by a suitable switch S, which is assumed to be closed whenever one of the rectifier plates is conducting current, and which is open the remainder of the time.   The transformer is replaced by an equivalent generator having a voltage equal to the open-circuit secondary voltage $E \sin \omega t$ measured to the center tap, and having equivalent internal impedance elements L and R_s.   The inductance L of the equivalent circuit is the leakage inductance of the transformer, measured in Fig. 20-9a across one-half the secondary winding with the primary short-circuited, and the equivalent resistance R is the corresponding transformer resistance R_s, measured in the same way, plus a fixed resistance R_r that takes into account the voltage drop in the rectifier tube.[1]   The input capacitor of the filter system is C, and the first inductance L_1 is assumed to draw a constant current I_0 equal to the d-c voltage E_0 developed across the input capacitor divided by an effective load resistance R_{eff} equal to the sum of the actual load resistance R plus the resistance of the filter inductance.

[1] In the case of hot-cathode gas rectifier tubes, R_r is preferably replaced by a bucking battery having a voltage equal to the voltage drop of the tube.

It is possible to utilize this equivalent circuit of the capacitor-input system to deduce the effects that result from changes in circuit proportions. Thus a decrease in the load resistance, i.e., an increase in the d-c output current, reduces the average or d-c output voltage, increases the ripple voltage, and increases the length of time during which the tube is conducting, as illustrated in Fig. 20-10a. Increasing the input capacitance of the filter has as its principal effect a decrease in the ripple voltage

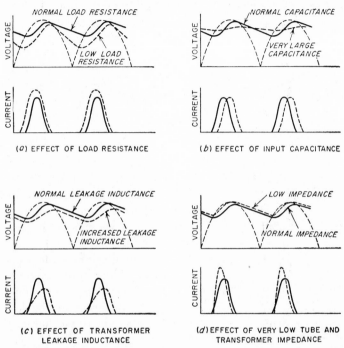

(a) EFFECT OF LOAD RESISTANCE

(b) EFFECT OF INPUT CAPACITANCE

(c) EFFECT OF TRANSFORMER LEAKAGE INDUCTANCE

(d) EFFECT OF VERY LOW TUBE AND TRANSFORMER IMPEDANCE

Fig. 20-10. Effect of circuit parameters and operating conditions on behavior of rectifier operated with capacitor-input filter.

developed across the capacitor, and to a lesser extent causes the average voltage developed across the capacitor to be increased slightly; these effects are shown in Fig. 20-10b. Increase in the leakage inductance (and resistance) of the transformer, i.e., an increase in the impedance of the source of power exciting the system, reduces the average output voltage as illustrated in Fig. 20-10c, and likewise decreases the ratio of peak-to-average current flowing through the rectifier tube. In the idealized case of a source having zero impedance, then if the tube resistance is very low the situation is as illustrated in Fig. 20-10d, and the peak plate current becomes quite high.

The variation of output voltage with load current in a typical capacitor-input system is illustrated in Fig. 20-11 for a typical power transformer and rectifier tube in a full-wave single-phase center-tapped circuit. The corresponding characteristic obtained with the same transformer and rectifier when used with choke input is also shown for purposes of comparison. In both arrangements the voltage drops off because of transformer impedance and tube resistance. However, with the capacitor-input system, the output additionally falls off because of the more rapid discharge of the input capacitor with increasing load current; this effect is not present in inductance-input operation.

Comparison of Capacitor-input and Inductance-input Systems. The basis for distinguishing between inductance-input and capacitor-input systems is that in the former the current flows continuously from the rectifier output into the filter system, while in the latter the current flows intermittently from rectifier into the filter. Intermittent action is present when the input inductance is less than the value called for by Eq. (20-4). When this is the case, the system is classified as a capacitor-input arrangement even though it possesses a series inductance.

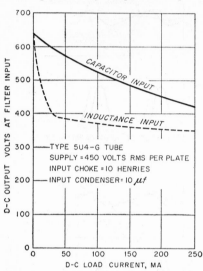

Fig. 20-11. Variation of d-c output voltage with increasing d-c load current in typical capacitor-input and inductance-input systems employing the same tube and transformer in a center-tapped full-wave circuit.

A comparison of the performance of inductance-input and capacitor-input systems shows that in the latter arrangement the d-c voltage is higher, the ripple voltage less, and the voltage regulation poorer, than when inductance input is used with the same tube, transformer, and load resistance. Also, with capacitor input the ripple voltage increases with increasing load current, unlike the inductance-input system where the ripple voltage is independent of load current. The utilization factor of the power transformer is much poorer with the capacitor-input system because of the higher ratio of peak-to-average current flowing through the rectifier tube, and likewise the tube is less efficiently utilized for the same reason.

Shunt-capacitor-input arrangements are generally employed in radio receivers, small public-address systems, etc., when the amount of d-c power required is small. In contrast, inductance-input arrangements are used when the amount of power required is large, since then the higher utilization factor and lower peak currents result in important savings in tube and transformer costs. Inductance input is also always employed when good regulation of the d-c voltage is important, as in supplying plate voltage to Class B amplifiers. Inductance-input systems are always employed in polyphase rectifier systems.

20-6. Filters. Figure 20-12 gives typical examples of filters that are placed between the rectifier output and the load impedance for the purpose of making the current delivered to the load substantially pure direct current in spite of the alternating components contained in the voltage applied by the rectifier to the filter input. These filters are made up of series impedances (either inductances or resistances) that oppose the flow of alternating current from the rectifier output to the load, and shunt

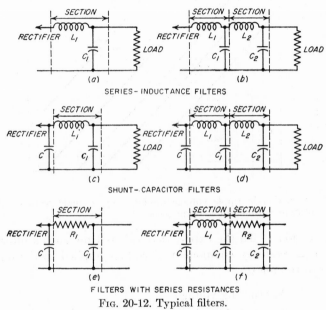

SERIES-INDUCTANCE FILTERS

SHUNT-CAPACITOR FILTERS

FILTERS WITH SERIES RESISTANCES

Fig. 20-12. Typical filters.

capacitors that by-pass the alternating currents that succeed in flowing through the series impedances.

For purposes of discussion and analysis, filters are ordinarily divided into sections, each of which consists of a series impedance followed by a shunt capacitor, as indicated in Fig. 20-12. It will be noted that in this classification the inductance in an inductance-input system is considered to be part of the first section of the filter. However, a shunt capacitance across the rectifier output is not included as part of a filter section, but rather is considered to be part of the rectifier system, which delivers to the first filter section a voltage corresponding to the voltage developed by the rectifier across the input capacitor.

Voltage and Current Relations in Filters. The input voltage to the filter is whatever output voltage is developed by the rectifier connection in the case of inductance-input systems, or is the voltage developed across the shunt capacitor in the case of capacitor-input systems. The ripple voltage in the output of the rectifier-filter system is then the alternating component of this input voltage reduced by the action of the filter sections.

Most filter sections are composed of a series inductance and a shunt capacitance. In practical filters of this type, the reactance of the shunt capacitance at the lowest ripple frequency is much smaller than the resistance of the load (or the reactance of the series inductance of the

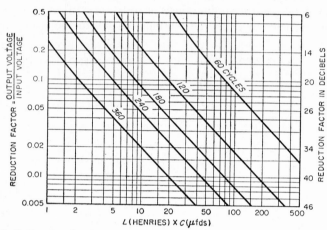

Fig. 20-13. Reduction in ripple voltage produced by a single section inductance-capacitance filter at various ripple frequencies.

following section). To the extent that this is true, such a filter section reduces each frequency component of voltage applied to the input side according to the relation[1]

$$\frac{\text{Alternating voltage across output of section}}{\text{Alternating voltage applied to input of section}} = \frac{1}{\omega^2 LC - 1} \qquad (20\text{-}5)$$

where L = series inductance of filter section
   C = shunt capacitance of section
   $\omega/2\pi$ = frequency of ripple voltage involved
Results of Eq. (20-5) are given in Fig. 20-13 for the usual case where the ripple components are harmonics of 60 cycles.

[1] This relationship can be derived as follows: To the extent that the reactance of the capacitor of the filter section is small compared with the load resistance or other impedance on the output side of the section, then substantially all ripple current entering the inductance L of the section flows through the capacitance C of the filter section. The current in the section is then $E_i/(\omega L - 1/\omega C)$, where E_i is the alternating voltage applied across the input to the filter section. The voltage that this current develops in flowing through the capacitor C is $E_i/(\omega L - 1/\omega C)\omega C = E_i/(\omega^2 LC - 1)$. Dividing by E_i results in Eq. (20-5).

When the current drawn by the load impedance is small, the series inductance of the filter section may be replaced by a series resistance as shown in Fig. 20-12e and f. This arrangement is widely used in resistance-coupled amplifiers, tuned radio-frequency amplifiers, etc., and has the advantage that a resistance is much less expensive than an inductance of corresponding effectiveness. The disadvantage is the d-c voltage drop that occurs in the resistance, and this limits the resistance-capacitance type of filter to cases where the current is small and where a moderate d-c voltage drop is permissible.

In practical resistance-capacitance filters, the reactance of the shunting capacitor is always made small compared with the series resistance of the filter and with the impedance to which the output of the filter section is delivered. Under these conditions, a section of resistance-capacitance filter reduces each frequency component of voltage applied to the input side according to the approximate relation[1]

$$\left. \begin{array}{l} \text{Alternating voltage} \\ \text{across output of section} \\ \hline \text{Alternating voltage applied} \\ \text{to input of section} \end{array} \right\} = \frac{1}{R\omega C} \qquad (20\text{-}6)$$

where R is the series resistance and C is the shunt capacitance (see Fig. 20-12e).

When a filter consists of more than one section, the total reduction in ripple voltage produced by the several sections is very nearly the product of the voltage-reduction factors of the individual sections (or the sum of the corresponding decibels). The effectiveness of the filtering accordingly increases rapidly with the number of sections. For many applications, a single section is entirely adequate, particularly with polyphase rectifiers. Only in special cases, such as audio-frequency amplifiers with very high gain, will the number of sections required exceed two, and then only for those parts of the amplifier that operate at very low signal-power levels.

Graded Filters. When the output of a rectifier-filter system is called upon to supply anode voltages for several stages of an amplifier system, the circumstances are ordinarily such that the amount of ripple or hum voltage that can be tolerated is different for the different stages, being least for those stages that operate at the lowest signal-power levels. This makes it desirable to arrange the filter system so that the voltages applied

---

[1] This follows from the fact that the ripple current flowing in R is

$$\frac{E_i}{\sqrt{R^2 + (1/\omega C)^2}} \approx \frac{E_i}{R}$$

where E_i is the ripple voltage applied to the section. The ripple output voltage of the section results from the current E_i/R flowing through the reactance $1/\omega C$ of the capacitance C of the section, and hence is $E_i/R\omega C$.

to different tubes operated from the rectifier-filter system undergo different amounts of filtering.

An example of such a *graded filter* is shown in Fig. 20-14. Here the output stage of the audio amplifier obtains its anode voltage directly from the input capacitor, which is permissible because of the high power level at which the output stage operates, combined with the hum-suppressing action of the push-pull connection (see Sec. 10-7). Progressively increased filtering is provided for the lower level stages, care being taken to design the system so that the reduction in ripple voltage introduced by the filter between *a* and *b*, and between *b* and *c*, is at least as great as the

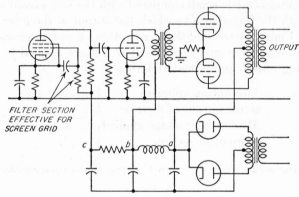

Fig. 20-14. Example of graded filter in which the amplifier stages operating at lower power levels are provided with progressively increased filtering.

amplification of the stages between these points for hum frequencies. In addition, it will be noted that the screen voltage of the first amplifier tube is obtained through a voltage-dropping resistance followed by a by-pass capacitor to the cathode. This also serves as a resistance-capacitance filter section, so that the screen voltage undergoes one more stage of filtering than does the plate voltage of the same tube.

A graded filter reduces to the lowest possible value the magnitude of the currents that must be carried by the series impedance arms of the filter.[1] This results in substantial economy in cost, weight, and size, compared to an arrangement in which the entire rectifier output is subjected to the maximum amount of filtering. A graded filter also provides isolation or decoupling between stages, thereby reducing regeneration, as discussed in Sec. 10-10 in connection with Fig. 10-26.

Filter Inductances and Capacitances. The inductance coils used in a filter must have laminated iron cores with an air gap that is sufficient to prevent the d-c magnetization from saturating the core. The inductance that is effective in the filter is the *incremental inductance*, and depends

[1] This often makes it practical to use resistance-capacitance filter stages in parts of the system, as illustrated in Fig. 20-14.

both upon the d-c and the a-c magnetizations of the core, as discussed in Sec. 2-1. In estimating the a-c magnetization that can be expected, it is normally permissible to assume for purposes of design that the alternating current flowing in the inductance is equal to the voltage of the lowest ripple frequency applied across the input of the filter section, divided by the reactance at this frequency of the inductance of the section. The alternating magnetization in the inductance of the first section may be relatively large, whereas the alternating magnetization for the inductances of the other filter sections will be very small if the filter is at all effective.

The capacitors used in filters must be capable of continuously withstanding a d-c voltage equal to the peak voltage applied to the rectifier. Electrolytic capacitors are ordinarily used where the peak voltages do not exceed 400 to 500 volts. Such capacitors have very low cost in proportion to capacitance, but they possess the disadvantage of a limited life. Paper capacitors are used at higher voltages and also find use at lower voltages where long life is more important than low cost.

20-7. Example of Rectifier-filter Calculations. The use of Table 20-2 and Fig. 20-13 is illustrated by the following example:

Example. It is desired to design a three-phase half-wave rectifier-filter system to operate from a 60-cycle power supply and to deliver a d-c output of 2500 volts and 0.4 amp with a ripple that must not exceed 2 per cent.

If the d-c resistance of the filter inductances is neglected, the rectifier must deliver a d-c output voltage of 2500 volts, and Table 20-2 shows that the rms voltage that each secondary leg must develop is $2500 \times 0.855 = 2135$ volts. Since the utilization factors of the primary and secondary, as given by Table 10-2, are $1/1.21 = 0.827$ and $1/1.48 = 0.675$, respectively, each of the three legs of the primary must have a rating of $1.21 \times 2500 \times 0.4/3 = 403$ watts, and each leg of the secondary requires a rating of $1.48 \times 2500 \times 0.4/3 = 493$ watts. Tentative calculation based on Fig. 20-13 shows that the filter of Fig. 20-12a with $C_1 = 1.0$ μf and $L_1 = 9.8$ henrys will keep the ripple voltage down to 2 per cent and will generally satisfactory. Reference to Table 20-2 shows that the peak plate current would be 0.4 amp for infinite input inductance, and the average current per plate is $0.4/3 = 0.133$. The maximum inverse voltage that each rectifier must stand is $2500 \times 2.09 = 5225$ volts. Table 20-1 shows that type 866A mercury-vapor tubes will easily meet these requirements. In actual practice, the secondary voltage of the transformer would be made greater than 2135 volts by perhaps 10 per cent to compensate for the loss of voltage caused by the resistance of the filter inductance, the voltage drop in the rectifier tube, the leakage reactance of the transformer, and the transformer resistance.

20-8. Voltage-regulated Power-supply Systems. In many circumstances it is desired to obtain an output voltage that will be substantially constant at some arbitrarily chosen value, irrespective of changes in a-c supply voltage or in the d-c load current. The method ordinarily employed to achieve this result is shown schematically in Fig. 20-15.

This is a feedback-control system of the type discussed in Sec. 11-6. Here a reference voltage E_R is compared with a fraction γE_0 of the output voltage obtained from an adjustable potentiometer P that is set at a point such that $\gamma E_0 \approx E_R$ when the output voltage has the desired value E_0. The difference $\gamma E_0 - E_R$ represents an error signal that is amplified by A and applied to the control grid of regulator tube T_1. The polarity of this error signal is made such that when the output voltage across aa is higher than the desired value E_0 (that is, when $\gamma E_0 > E_R$), the grid of T_1 becomes more negative, increasing the voltage drop in this tube and reducing the output voltage toward the desired

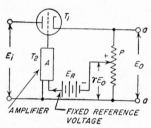

value. Conversely, when the output voltage E_0 is less than the desired value ($\gamma E_0 < E_R$), the amplified error signal is such as to make the grid of T_1 less negative, thus reducing the voltage drop in this tube and increasing the output voltage toward the desired value. If the amplification of T_2 is large, the output voltage E_0 will maintain a very nearly constant value, irrespective of changes in the load current or the supply voltage. The particular

Fig. 20-15. Schematic diagram of a voltage-regulated power-supply system.

value of the output voltage E_0 at which the stabilization occurs is controlled by the setting of the potentiometer P.

The circuit arrangement of a typical voltage-regulated system of this type is shown in Fig. 20-16a. Here the reference voltage E_R is provided by cold-cathode gas diode T_3 of a type that develops a substantially con-

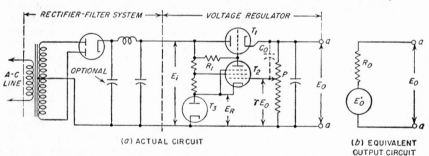

(a) ACTUAL CIRCUIT

(b) EQUIVALENT OUTPUT CIRCUIT

Fig. 20-16. Schematic circuit of an actual voltage-regulated power-supply system, together with equivalent output circuit.

stant voltage drop over a relatively wide range of current.[1] This voltage is balanced against γE_0 by applying E_R to the cathode and γE_0 to the control grid of the sharp-cutoff pentode tube T_2; thus the difference between these voltages can be regarded as an error signal acting between the control grid and cathode of T_2. Tube T_2 is a d-c amplifier, the output of which controls the grid potential and hence the voltage drop of T_1.

---

[1] The voltage drop in such a gas tube will, however, vary slightly with current, and hence with the supply voltage E_i applied to the system. When the very highest stability is required, the reference voltage is therefore preferably supplied by a battery.

In a practical system the circuit proportions are so chosen that when equilibrium is established the cathode of T_2 is always slightly more positive than the control grid; thus T_2 operates with the grid negative.[1]

A simple voltage-regulated power supply of the type illustrated in Fig. 20-16a will give an excellent performance. The variation of output voltage E_0 with changes in a-c line voltage will typically be only a few per cent as great as in the absence of a regulation system, and corresponding improvements result in the constancy of the output voltage with changes in load current.

The voltage-regulating system will also reduce the ripple voltage by the same amount that it reduces the effect of variations in the supply-line voltage. This is because the variations in voltage E_i in Figs. 20-15 and 20-16a due to ripple are treated in the same way as are the variations in E_i caused by line voltage changes. The ripple suppression is improved at high output voltages by the addition of by-pass capacitor C_0 (see Prob. 20-33).

The output voltage of the regulated system acts as though it were derived from a generator having the equivalent circuit of Fig. 20-16b, in which E_0' is the open-circuit voltage developed across terminals aa when the load current is zero, and R_0 is an equivalent internal impedance of the regulated system. The action of the voltage regulation is to make the actual output voltage E_0 only very slightly less than the open-circuit voltage E_0' even with large load currents. This means that the equivalent internal resistance R_0 of a well-regulated system is necessarily quite small; under typical conditions, values for R_0 of only a few ohms or even less are readily realized. This low equivalent output resistance is a very important feature of a voltage-regulated power supply. Not only does it mean that the output voltage is substantially independent of the load current, but it also minimizes the common coupling introduced when several amplifier stages are fed from a common source of power. This is particularly important in the control of the low-frequency regeneration that tends to trouble multistage audio and video amplifiers (see Sec. 10-10).

20-9. Anode Power for High-voltage Cathode-ray Tubes. Special problems are involved in providing anode power for a high-voltage cathode-ray tube. Anode voltages ranging from 5 to 100 kv may be required, while the current is small, typically on the order of 1 ma or less. At the same time, matters must be so arranged as to avoid all danger to the life of human beings in spite of the very high voltage. This requires that the system have a relatively low short-circuit current, and that the

---

[1] Analysis and design procedures for voltage-stabilized arrangements of this type are given by A. B. Bereskin, Voltage-regulated Power Supplies, *Proc. IRE*, vol. 31, p. 47, February, 1943; A. Abate, Basic Theory and Design of Electronically Regulated Power Supplies, *Proc. IRE*, vol. 33, p. 478, July, 1945; and W. R. Hill, Jr., Analysis of Voltage Regulator Operation, *Proc. IRE*, vol. 33, p. 38, January, 1945.

total amount of stored energy in the filter system available to be discharged quickly be small.

These requirements can be met in several ways. One common approach is to start with an oscillator operating at a plate potential of the order of 500 volts, and generating a few watts of power at a frequency that is typically several hundred kilocycles. A resonant load circuit having a high Q is then coupled to the oscillator tank circuit, as shown by LC in Fig. 20-17a. By proportioning this load circuit so that it possesses a high L/C ratio, and at the same time keeping circuit losses low so that the circuit Q is high, it is possible to obtain a high radio-frequency voltage by resonance. This can then be rectified, usually by a half-wave or by a

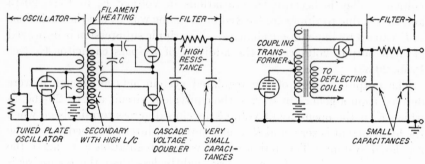

Fig. 20-17. Typical circuit arrangements for obtaining the high d-c anode voltage required by a cathode-ray tube.

voltage-multiplying circuit, to give a very high d-c potential. Such an arrangement[1] is illustrated in Fig. 20-17a.

In television receivers another convenient possibility is available for obtaining anode voltage for the cathode-ray tube. The cathode-ray beam in such equipment is ordinarily deflected by a saw-tooth wave of current that is passed through a magnetic deflecting coil. During the flyback interval, the current through this coil is changing rapidly, resulting in the development of a high voltage. This is particularly true in the case of the coil giving the horizontal deflection; here the frequency is 15,750 cycles, so that the flyback time is short, and the induced voltage is relatively high. This voltage can be stepped up by means of a transformer, and rectified to produce anode power in an arrangement such as illustrated schematically in Fig. 20-17b.[2]

[1] A comprehensive discussion of the design considerations involved is given by R. S. Mautner and O. H. Schade, Television High-voltage R-F Supplies, *RCA Rev.*, vol. 8, p. 43, March, 1947.

[2] The design considerations involved in power-supply systems of this type are treated exhaustively by O. H. Schade, Characteristics of High-efficiency Deflection and High-voltage Supply Systems for Kinescopes, *RCA Rev.*, vol. 11, p. 5, March, 1950.

Filament power for the rectifier tubes is commonly obtained from a secondary coupled to the same coil that develops the high voltage. This is illustrated in both a and b of Fig. 20-17, and is possible because rectifier tubes designed for this low current service consume very little filament power (see Table 20-1).

The filters required in the systems of Fig. 20-17 to smooth out the rectified output can be quite simple. The series element is conveniently a high resistance, since the d-c current is very small. Likewise the filter capacitances can be quite small because of the fact that the ripple frequency is very high.

The power-supply systems of Fig. 20-17 present no hazard to life in spite of the high voltage. This is because the total power capacity of either of the systems generating power in Fig. 20-17 is less than the power required to produce serious danger, combined with the fact that the very small filter capacitances store very little energy, and so do not produce a serious shock even when discharged through the human body.

20-10. Plate Power from Low-voltage D-C Sources. In automobiles, airplanes, etc., the only source of primary power is often a storage battery

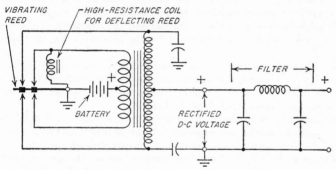

Fig. 20-18. Fundamental circuit of a vibrator power-supply system for obtaining d-c anode power from a low-voltage storage battery.

developing a voltage ranging from 6 to 32 volts. Direct-current power at voltages suitable for applying to the plate of a vacuum tube can be obtained in several ways under such circumstances.

One method is to employ a dynamotor, also called a rotary transformer. This is a d-c machine having two sets of brushes and two armature windings which functions as the equivalent of a motor generator. The motor section is designed to operate at the storage-battery voltage, while the generator section develops the desired plate voltage.

A second arrangement for obtaining plate power from a low-voltage storage battery consists in employing a vibrating contact to change the direct current from the battery into alternating current, which can be stepped up in voltage by a transformer and rectified to produce high-voltage d-c power. A typical arrangement of this type is shown in Fig. 20-18. Here the vibrating element is actuated in the same manner as an ordinary buzzer. By means of appropriate contacts, its vibration causes battery current to flow alternately through first one and then the other half of the primary winding in such a manner as to give the equivalent of an alternating primary current that is stepped up in voltage, and then rectified by a second set of contacts mounted on the same vibrating reed. In some cases a vacuum tube replaces the rectifying contacts. A capacitor-input filter must be used if sparking is to be avoided when the contacts break the circuit.

The vibrator provides an inexpensive means of obtaining small to medium quantities of anode power from a storage battery. It is widely used in automobile and aircraft radio receivers, and for small radio transmitters. Compared with a dynamotor, a vibrator power supply is less expensive, but has a shorter life and lower efficiency.

PROBLEMS AND EXERCISES

20-1. Explain why a-c hum from a-c filament current is a much more serious problem in audio-frequency amplifiers than in radio-frequency amplifiers.

20-2. What is the effect on the magnitude and the frequency of the a-c hum of returning the grid and plate leads to one end of the filament in Fig. 20-1 instead of to a center tap?

20-3. A filament triode tube is so designed and operated that the hum caused by voltage drop in the filament very nearly cancels the hum produced by the magnetic field from the filament current. Will increasing the plate voltage while leaving the grid bias unchanged affect this balance? Explain.

20-4. Explain why is it customary to design rectifier tubes so that the maximum permissible plate dissipation never exceeds half the plate dissipation that would result if the rated d-c plate current were drawn continuously through the tube.

20-5. Compare the effect of ambient temperature on the gas pressure in hot-cathode gas diodes which employ (a) mercury vapor, and (b) an inert gas such as argon or neon.

20-6. What would be the principal disadvantage of replacing the single transformer with a center-tapped secondary in Fig. 20-3b by two separate transformers?

20-7. Explain how the cascade quadrupler of Fig. 20-4c operates.

20-8. In Fig. 20-5b, the balance coil is replaced by a short circuit. What effect does this change in the circuit have upon (a) the shape of the output wave; (b) the magnitude of the average or d-c component of the output voltage, assuming the transformer secondary voltages are unchanged; and (c) the fraction of the cycle during which each plate carries current? Qualitative answers are satisfactory for (a) and (b).

20-9. In the rectifier system of Fig. 20-5c draw on three separate axes the voltage waves developed by windings A, B, C, respectively. Then indicate on each voltage wave the portions of the cycle during which that winding carries current, and also designate by number the particular tubes that carry the current.

20-10. With the aid of Eq. (20-1), verify the values presented in Table 20-2 for the maximum inverse voltage and the transformer secondary voltage in the single-phase full-wave bridge circuit of Fig. 20-3c.

20-11. Sketch current waves corresponding to those of Fig. 20-7a but representing the primary and secondary currents of the transformer supplying a full-wave bridge rectifier (Fig. 20-3b) with input inductance.

20-12. Sketch waves analogous to those of Fig. 20-7b except applying to the three-phase full-wave rectifier circuit of Fig. 20-5c. These curves should show the current in each secondary winding and its associated primary coil.

20-13. Calculate and tabulate the d-c output voltage, current, and power that result when type 872A hot-cathode mercury-vapor tubes are used in the (a) single-phase full-wave center-tap, (b) three-phase half-wave, and (c) three-phase full-wave systems, assuming that in each instance the transformer voltage and the load current are so adjusted as to utilize the tubes to the maximum possible inverse voltage, and to the maximum allowable average plate current. Discuss the relative effectiveness with which the three different circuits utilize the tube possibilities by showing in the table the d-c output power obtainable per tube in the different arrangements. Choke input is used in all cases.

20-14. Sketch current waves similar to those in the last three lines of Fig. 20-6a, except for the case where the input inductance approximates the critical value.

20-15. Verify the correctness of the numerical constant in Eq. (20-4b).

20-16. Derive an equation analogous to Eq. (20-4b), but applicable to a 60-cycle three-phase half-wave system.

20-17. A certain Class B amplifier operating at a plate potential of 1000 volts draws a plate current of 100 ma when developing maximum possible output, but only 12 ma when there is no applied signal. Determine the minimum permissible input inductance with no output and full output on the assumption of a 60-cycle single-phase full-wave rectifier system with inductance-input filter, and then repeat the calculation when a 50,000-ohm resistance is shunted across the rectifier output in addition to the load presented by the tube.

20-18. On the assumption that the current variation through the tube in Fig. 20-6a is composed entirely of 120-cycle current (for a 60-cycle supply), derive a formula giving the ratio of the peak tube current to the d-c current in terms of the effective load resistance R_{eff} and the input inductance L_1.

20-19. Verify the correctness of the value of primary kva called for in line i of Table 20-2 for the single-phase full-wave center-tapped connection.

20-20. Draw oscillograms analogous to Fig. 20-10a, showing normal load current, and very much less than normal load current. Give the reason that the smaller load current causes the d-c voltage to be greater and the ripple voltage to be less.

20-21. Explain in a qualitative way the mechanism whereby leakage inductance in the power transformer reduces the ratio of peak-to-average plate current in a capacitor-input system.

20-22. Draw oscillograms analogous to those of Fig. 20-9c and d, except for the case of an inductance-input system in which Eq. (20-4b) just fails to be satisfied.

20-23. In a capacitor-input system, what is the effect on the utilization factor of the transformer of (a) increasing the transformer leakage inductance, and (b) decreasing the load resistance (increasing the load current)?

20-24. Verify the fact that the curve for inductance input in Fig. 20-11 is consistent with Eq. (20-4b).

20-25. Draw oscillograms analogous to those of Fig. 20-10b for very large input capacitance, but for two values of d-c load current.

20-26. Assume one has available 8 μf of capacitance and 12 henrys of inductance for filtering the output of a single-phase center-tap rectifier with an inductance input. Should all of the capacitance and inductance be concentrated in a single filter section, or is it better to divide the capacitance and inductance to give two similar sections, each having 4 μf and 6 henrys, and how many decibels of difference in attenuation of the 120-cycle hum component are there in the two cases?

20-27. Under what circumstances could 60-cycle voltage appear in the output of a single-phase full-wave center-tap system operating from a 60-cycle power system?

20-28. A graded filter of the type shown in Fig. 20-14 is used to supply a three-stage tuned amplifier instead of a three-stage audio-frequency amplifier. Discuss in a general way the effect that this substitution of tuned stages for audio-frequency stages has on the amount of attenuation to the hum frequencies that filter section bc must have in order to ensure that the first amplifier stage will contribute negligible hum.

20-29. Design a rectifier-filter system to meet the requirements of the example of Sec. 20-7, but using type 866A mercury-vapor tubes in a single-phase center-tap transformer connection. Tabulate results for peak inverse voltage, required primary and secondary transformer ratings, and filter inductance and capacitance, alongside of the corresponding values given in Sec. 20-7 for the three-phase half-wave system. Discuss the significant differences.

20-30. In the example of Sec. 20-7, calculate the magnitude of the 180- and 360-cycle currents flowing through the input inductance.

20-31. The power supply for the final power amplifier of a high-power radio transmitter employs six type 869B hot-cathode mercury-vapor tubes in a three-phase full-wave circuit operating from 60 cycles. The power supply is rated at 18,000 volts and 5 amp, and has a single-section inductance-input filter consisting of 0.5 henry and 3.0 μf. Neglecting the resistance of the filter inductance, and the leakage reactance and resistance of the power transformer, calculate (a) the peak current through the rectifier tubes (assuming infinite input inductance) and the average plate current per tube, (b) the peak inverse voltage, (c) the secondary voltage of the power transformer, (d) the required kva ratings of transformer primary and secondary windings, and (e) the amount of 360-cycle and 720-cycle ripple voltage appearing in the output.

20-32. The value of output voltage that is maintained in the system of Fig. 20-16a is determined by the setting of the potentiometer P. However, it is found that there is a minimum output voltage that can be obtained, it being impossible in Fig. 20-16a to adjust the output voltage to values approaching zero. Explain why this is true.

20-33. In a voltage-regulated power supply of the type in Fig. 20-16a, a capacitor is often connected between the positive output lead and the control grid of T_2, as shown by dotted C_0. This decreases the hum output of the system when the output voltage is large, but gives no hum reduction when the output voltage has its minimum value. Explain.

20-34. Discuss the considerations affecting the stability of the circuit of Fig. 20-16a viewed as a negative feedback system. In particular, explain why with a single-stage amplifier T_2 no trouble is ordinarily encountered from self-oscillation, whereas if this stage is replaced by a three-stage direct-coupled amplifier trouble from oscillation is much more likely to occur.

20-35. In Fig. 20-17a, if the unloaded Q of LC has a fixed value Q_u irrespective of the ratio L/C, prove that the higher the ratio L/C the less power it then takes to produce a given d-c output power (i.e., d-c current at a specified voltage), and that the radio-frequency power required is not affected by the frequency of operation of the oscillator.

20-36. Discuss the relative merits, from the point of view of hazard to human life, of obtaining a given amount of filtering in the circuits of Fig. 20-17 by employing (a) a large series resistance and small capacitances, and (b) a small series resistance and large capacitances.

20-37. In a vibrator supply system such as shown in Fig. 20-18 sketch oscillograms showing (a) voltage across each half of the primary, (b) voltage across the secondary winding, and (c) current flowing in each half of the primary.

CHAPTER 21

TRANSISTORS AND RELATED SEMICONDUCTOR DEVICES[1]

21-1. Semiconductors.[2] The term *semiconductor* denotes solid material having a conductivity considerably more than that of a good insulator and yet much less than that of a metal. In recent years, a number of devices based on semiconductors have been developed that are of great practical usefulness in electronics. Most important of these is the transistor, which is an amplifier having properties similar to those of a vacuum tube, but which requires no cathode power, and at the same time offers the hope of practically unlimited life. Additionally, new types of rectifiers, improved photoconductive materials, etc., have also been developed.

The discussion of semiconductors that is to follow emphasizes germanium and silicon. While many other semiconducting materials are known, they find much less practical use in electronics. Furthermore, the principles determining the electrical behavior of germanium and silicon also apply with little or no change to these other materials.

21-2. Conductivity of Pure (Intrinsic) Semiconductors.[3] *Crystal Structure of Germanium—Covalent Bonds.* Germanium is a tetravalent

---

[1] The literature on semiconductors, with particular reference to transistors, is mostly of such recent origin, and is growing so rapidly, that no attempt is made to annotate this chapter beyond indicating the origin of some of the viewpoints and relations that are presented.

The purpose of this treatment is to introduce the basic phenomena of semiconductors, and particularly of transistors, in simple words that give a clear and accurate semiquantitative understanding of these devices.

[2] The reader who desires to do some supplementary reading on the properties of semiconductors and transistor fundamentals can profitably start with the paper by W. Shockley, Transistor Electronics: Imperfections, Unipolar and Analog Transistors, *Proc. IRE*, vol. 40, p. 1289, November, 1952. This entire issue of *Proceedings of the IRE* is devoted to transistors, and contains much useful and readable information on the subject.

[3] For convenience, this discussion is largely developed in terms of germanium; however, it also applies with little change to silicon. This is because, like germanium, silicon is a tetravalent atom that crystallizes in the manner illustrated in Fig. 21-1, which is from the *Bell System Tech. J.*, vol. 28, p. 338, July, 1949. The principal difference between silicon and germanium in so far as electrical properties are concerned is that it takes more energy to break the covalent bonds in the crystallized

atom; i.e., its outer shell contains four electrons that are available to react with electrons of other atoms. When molten germanium solidifies it does so by forming a crystalline structure in which each atom is equidistant from four neighboring atoms, as illustrated in Fig. 21-1. There are 4.52×10^{22} germanium atoms per cu cm in such a crystal.

In the crystalline germanium, each atom shares its valence electrons with the adjacent atoms. That is, each of the four electrons of a particular atom is also associated with a different one of the four nearest atoms, each of which in turn shares an electron with the first atom. The resulting electron pairs, termed *covalent bonds*, provide forces that bind

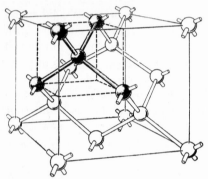

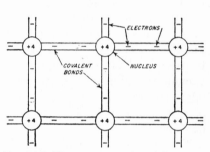

FIG. 21-1. Germanium (or silicon) crystal, showing arrangement of nuclei and the covalent bonds.

FIG. 21-2. Flat representation of the covalent bonds illustrated in Fig. 21-1.

the adjacent atoms of the crystal together. They can be disrupted only by the expenditure of a considerable amount of energy. The covalent bonds are illustrated schematically in Fig. 21-1 by the rods connecting the adjacent atoms; a flat version of the same situation is given in Fig. 21-2.

Production of Free Electrons by Thermal Processes. A crystal of pure germanium in which every electron is part of a covalent bond is a nonconductor of electricity; this is because no mobile carriers of electric current are present. The pure germanium crystal of Fig. 21-1 will possess conductivity only if some of the electrons break away from their covalent bonds. This takes energy, which in the case of germanium and silicon is, respectively, 0.75 and 1.12 electron volts.

At ordinary temperatures the crystal lattice is in continuous random agitation because of thermal energy. As a result, an individual electron of a covalent bond occasionally acquires sufficient energy when at room temperature to break the bond and become free.[1] Electrons that have

---

silicon; as a result, the intrinsic conductivity of silicon is less than that of germanium. The effect of impurities on the conductivity is also slightly different in detail, although not in character.

[1] When this occurs, only one electron of the pair is broken loose. The other electron remains behind, and seeks an opportunity to acquire a new mate, as discussed below.

thus escaped are able to move freely through the crystal lattice. The free electrons are neither attracted to nor repelled by the electrons and nuclei of the crystal; this is because the electrical effects that these charged bodies are capable of producing are completely engaged maintaining the covalent bonds. In the absence of an applied field, the free electrons therefore move about the crystal in a random way like the molecules of a gas. When an external electric field is applied, there is superimposed upon this random motion a steady *drift* toward the positive electrode that represents a flow of current carried by electrons.

Holes. The empty place left behind in the crystal structure when an electron breaks away from the covalent bond and becomes free is termed a *hole*. Since the electrons in the germanium crystal always seek to arrange themselves in covalent pairs, the single electron remaining with the atom attempts to pair off with a new electron. It does so by "stealing" an electron from an adjacent pair when the thermal agitation of the crystal lattice fortuitously brings one of the adjacent electrons into a situation favorable for making such a transfer. This does not, however, destroy the hole, but rather merely causes its location to be shifted to the place from which the electron was taken. This process then immediately repeats itself again, thus moving the hole to still another location, and so on. Thus when a hole is once created, it moves about in the crystal in a random way, in the same manner as do the free electrons. In fact, the hole acts much as though it were an electron with a charge that was positive instead of negative. Thus in the presence of an electric field, there is superimposed upon the random thermal motion a steady *drift* of the holes toward the negative electrode. This drift represents a current flow which is transported by the absence of electrons, and which is in addition to the current carried by the electrons.

Recombination of Holes and Electrons—Hole and Electron Density. When a free electron moves randomly about in the crystal, there is always the possibility that it will encounter a hole. This doesn't happen very frequently, but when it does, the electron reestablishes the missing covalent bond, thus destroying the hole and simultaneously eliminating the free electron.[1] The resulting *recombination* rate of electrons and holes is proportional to the product of the concentrations of electrons and holes.[2] The *lifetime* of an individual carrier is thus limited. It will typically range from less than 1 μsec to more than 1 msec, according to the circumstances.

The concentration of the electrons and holes in a pure semiconductor

---

[1] The energy required to create the electron-hole pair when the covalent bond was originally broken is given up in the form of heat when recombination takes place.

[2] The recombination rate is also increased by imperfections in the crystal lattice, and by chemical impurities other than the donors and acceptors discussed below. It also tends to be higher at the surface than in the body of the material.

builds up to a level such that the rate of recombination of holes and electrons equals their rate of production. An increase in the rate of production, such as occurs when the temperature is raised, therefore produces an increase in the concentration.

Conductivity and Carrier Density of Pure Germanium. It is now clear that the current flowing through a pure semiconductor is carried by *two* kinds of carriers, namely, electrons and holes. The resulting conductivity σ to an applied voltage, sometimes called the *drift* conductivity to distinguish it from diffusion effects discussed below, is given by the relation

$$\text{Conductivity} = \sigma = e(n\mu_n + p\mu_p) \qquad (21\text{-}1)$$

where σ = conductivity, mhos per cm

e = charge of electron (or hole)

p, n = concentration of holes and free electrons, respectively, carriers per cu cm

μ_n, μ_p = mobility of free electrons and holes, respectively, cm per sec per volt per cm

It is important to note that Eq. (21-1) shows that the *conductivity of a semiconductor is a measure of the concentration of current carriers present in the semiconducting material.*

The conductivity of an absolutely pure semiconductor is called the *intrinsic conductivity*, and is designated as σ_i. All of the carriers then arise from the electron-hole pairs that are generated when thermal energy breaks the covalent bonds. Electrons and holes are thus always present in equal concentrations in an intrinsic semiconductor, and Eq. (21-1) becomes

$$\sigma_i = en_i(\mu_n + \mu_p) \qquad (21\text{-}2)$$

Here $n_i = n = p$, and is called the *intrinsic concentration*.

The intrinsic concentration is very sensitive to temperature because of the effect of temperature on the rate of production of electron-hole pairs. Theory shows that for any intrinsic semiconductor the intrinsic concentration n_i, and hence the conductivity, follow the relation[1]

$$\text{Intrinsic concentration} = n_i = AT^{3/2}\epsilon^{-eE/2kT} \qquad (21\text{-}3)$$

Here E is the energy in volts required to break the covalent bond and is called the *ionization energy*, T is the absolute temperature, k is Boltzmann's constant ($= 1.374 \times 10^{-23}$), e is the charge on an electron ($= 1.59 \times 10^{-19}$ coulomb), and A is a constant that depends on the semiconducting material.

---

[1] It will be noted that Eq. (21-3) is very similar in form to Eq. (6-8), which gives the electrons emitted from a hot cathode as a function of temperature. This similarity is not entirely accidental, since the production of electron-hole pairs, and the thermionic emission of electrons, both result from electrons in a solid surmounting an energy barrier by means of thermal effects.

In pure germanium $E = 0.75$ volt, and $A \approx 9.64 \times 10^{15}$, so that Eq. (21-3) becomes

$$n_i \text{ (for germanium)} \approx 9.64 \times 10^{15} T^{3/2} \epsilon^{-4350/T} \qquad (21\text{-}4)$$

At a room temperature of $T = 300°$, substitution in Eq. (21-4) shows that

$$n_i \approx 2.5 \times 10^{13} \text{ electrons (or holes) per cu cm} \qquad (21\text{-}5)$$

The mobilities of holes and free electrons in germanium are 1700 and 3600 cm per sec per volt per cm, respectively.[1] Substitution of numbers into Eq. (21-2) then leads to an intrinsic conductivity for germanium of 0.0213 mho per cm (i.e., a resistivity[2] of 47 ohm-cm). Although the concentration of holes in an intrinsic semiconductor equals that of the free electrons, about two-thirds of the current that flows under intrinsic conditions is carried by the free electrons. This is because of the higher mobility of the free electrons.

21-3. Impurity Semiconductors. *Donor or n-type Semiconductors.* A very small amount of certain types of impurities will alter tremendously the relative and absolute concentrations of the electron and hole current carriers. An example of this is when the impurity is an atom, such as phosphorus, antimony, or arsenic, that is pentavalent, i.e., has five electrons in its outer shell available for interaction with other atoms. Assume that the amount of such impurity is very small, such as one impurity atom per million atoms of germanium.

Such impurity atoms are comparable in size to germanium atoms; they can, therefore, take positions normally occupied by germanium atoms. Because the impurity atoms are proportionately so few in number, each will ordinarily be entirely surrounded by germanium atoms. The four nearest germanium atoms then form covalent bonds with four of the five valence electrons of the impurity atom. This ties these four electrons into the crystal structure with forces that require a considerable amount of energy to disrupt. However, no such binding force holds the fifth valence electron. It can therefore be removed from the parent impurity atom by the expenditure of very little energy, only 0.01 electron volt for germanium and 0.05 electron volt for silicon. In contrast, it takes 0.75 electron volt to break a covalent germanium bond and 1.12 electron volts a covalent silicon bond. When freed from its parent impurity atom, this fifth valence electron moves randomly through the crystal in the same manner as do the free electrons present in an intrinsic semiconductor.[3]

---

[1] The corresponding values for silicon are 250 and 1200, respectively.

[2] The corresponding resistivity of silicon is 63,600 ohm-cm, the difference resulting from the higher value of E required to break the covalent bonds of silicon, with resulting production of fewer intrinsic electron-hole pairs.

[3] The crystal remains electrically neutral in spite of these electrons. This is because the crystal contains as many positive ions left behind by the electrons as it contains electrons in excess of holes.

When an electric field is applied there is superimposed upon this random motion a steady drift toward the positive electrode that represents a flow of current.

When the impurity atom loses an electron, it becomes a positively charged ion. The ion is immobile, however, since it is held in place by the four covalent bonds to the adjacent germanium atoms, and so cannot contribute to the conduction of electricity.

Impurity atoms that contribute free electrons as described above are called *donors*, because they donate free electrons. Semiconductors containing donors are called *n-type semiconductors* because the current carriers that the impurity supplies are negative charges. The free electrons supplied in this way are often called *excess* electrons.

Acceptor or p-type Semiconductors. Consider next the effect of a trivalent impurity such as boron, gallium, indium, or aluminum. As in the pentavalent case, such impurity atoms enter into the crystal structure and take places normally occupied by germanium atoms, and when few in number each is surrounded by germanium atoms. Three of these neighboring germanium atoms form covalent bonds with the three valence electrons of the trivalent impurity. Although there is a natural tendency for each atom in the crystalline structure to form four covalent bonds, the trivalent impurity atom is short one electron. As a result, it seeks to acquire a fourth electron, and it does this by taking advantage of any thermal motion that fortuitously brings an electron from a neighboring germanium atom into a favorable condition to be captured.[1] When this happens, the impurity atom establishes covalent bonds to the four nearest germanium atoms; it then becomes an immobile negative ion embedded in the crystalline structure.

However, the act of stealing an electron from an adjacent atom produces a hole that is similar to the holes arising from the breaking of covalent bonds. This hole moves about in a random way due to thermal effects, and when an electric field is applied, it tends to drift toward the negative electrode and thus contributes to the flow of current.

Impurity atoms that contribute holes in this manner are termed *acceptors*, because they accept, i.e., acquire, electrons from the germanium atoms. Semiconductors containing acceptors are called *p-type semiconductors* because the current carriers (holes) that this type of impurity supplies are equivalent to the negative of an electron, i.e., to a positive charge. Holes created in this way are often called *excess* holes.

Conductivity and Carrier Concentrations in Impurity Semiconductors. The conductivity of a semiconductor containing impurities is given by Eq. (21-1) provided that n and p are the actual electron and hole concentrations, respectively. These concentrations are determined by the

---

[1] The energy involved in consummating such a capture is small, 0.01 electron volt for germanium, and 0.08 electron volt in the case of silicon.

number of electrons contributed by donors, the number of holes supplied by acceptors, the rate of generation of electron-hole pairs arising from the breaking of covalent bonds, and the rate of recombination of holes and electrons.

The relative proportion of holes and electrons in a semiconductor is of considerable importance. In intrinsic (pure) semiconductors, holes and electrons are always present in equal concentrations, as discussed above; i.e.,

$$n = p = n_i \tag{21-6}$$

where n_i is given by Eq. (21-3) or Eq. (21-4).

If one now adds a few donor atoms[1] to the intrinsic material, the concentration of free electrons is increased. This makes it more likely that the holes present will encounter electrons and thus be destroyed by recombination; as a result, the hole concentration is reduced below the intrinsic value. Similarly, if acceptors are added instead of donors, the probability of recombination is also increased, and the concentration of free electrons is reduced below the intrinsic value. Quantitatively it is found that to a good approximation one can write

$$np = n_i^2 \tag{21-7}$$

where p and n are the actual hole and free-electron concentrations, respectively, and n_i is the free-electron (or hole) concentration in the semiconductor in the absence of impurities, as given by Eq. (21-3) or Eq. (21-4).

Thus if the concentration of donor atoms appreciably exceeds the intrinsic concentration n_i, then the conductivity of the resulting n-type semiconductor takes place almost entirely by means of free electrons, and the concentration of holes becomes so small as to have very little effect. The free electrons are then *majority* carriers and the holes *minority* carriers. The concentration of the majority carriers in the n-type semiconductor approximates the concentration N_D of the donor atoms, because the energy required to ionize a donor atom is so small that practically every such atom has contributed a free electron and has thus become ionized. As a consequence, the conductivity σ_n of the n-type semiconductor is

$$\sigma_n \approx eN_D\mu_n \tag{21-8}$$

This relation follows from Eq. (21-1) by noting that $n = N_D >> p$.

When the impurity is an acceptor, the concentration of the free electrons is by Eq. (21-7) reduced to less than the intrinsic value, and conduction then takes place primarily by holes. Thus for the p-type

---

[1] The addition of donor or acceptor atoms to a semiconductor is often referred to as "doping."

semiconductor the holes are the majority carriers and the free electrons the minority carriers. As in the case of donors, the energy required to ionize an acceptor atom and produce a hole is so small that practically all acceptors are ionized. Hence if N_A is the concentration of acceptor atoms, then in Eq. (21-1) one has $p = N_A >> n$, and

$$\sigma_p \approx eN_A\mu_p \qquad (21-9)$$

where σ_p is the conductivity of the p-type semiconductor.

When a mixture of donor and acceptor atoms is present, a cancellation takes place in which the more numerous carriers almost completely suppress the less numerous type of carrier, in accordance with Eq. (21-7). Thus if the acceptor atoms are 10 per cent as numerous as the donor atoms, then almost exactly 10 per cent of the free electrons supplied by the latter are used up combining with the holes contributed by the acceptor atoms. The end result is that the concentration of holes still remains negligible, while the concentration of free electrons is 10 per cent less than if no acceptor atoms were present. The conductivity is thus reduced 10 per cent by the presence of the acceptor impurity.

When both donors and acceptors are present simultaneously, the semiconductor is classified as being either n type or p type according to whether the free electrons or the holes carry the largest part of the current, i.e., according to whether $n\mu_e$ or $p\mu_p$ in Eq. (21-1) is the larger. It will be noted that for an intrinsic semiconductor, although free electrons and holes are present in equal numbers, the electrons have higher mobility and carry more of the current.

An extremely small amount of impurity is sufficient to be the controlling factor in determining the electrical behavior of an impurity semiconductor. Thus thermal agitation at room temperature will result in less than one covalent bond being broken at any one time per 10^9 atoms of germanium (and even fewer broken bonds in silicon). As a consequence, one acceptor or impurity atom per million germanium atoms will produce roughly a thousand times as many current carriers as are generated by the breaking of the covalent bonds of germanium by thermal action.

21-4. Mechanisms Involved in Current Flow—Drift and Diffusion. Detailed examination will now be made of some of the mechanisms involved when current flows in an impurity semiconductor.

In the absence of an electric field, the carriers of a semiconductor move about randomly, as illustrated schematically in Fig. 21-3a. Here each change in direction represents a collision with a nucleus that deflects the carrier in a new direction. This *diffusive motion* can be characterized by an average path length l and an average elapsed time t between collisions, corresponding to an average velocity of motion $v = l/t$. Diffusive motion is the result of thermal energy possessed by the carrier.

If now the carrier is placed in an electric field, it is subject to a force that produces a steady sidewise *drift* that is superimposed upon the diffusive motion. This is illustrated in Fig. 21-3b, which corresponds to the same motions as at *a* except for a drift to the right that represents current flow.

Current Flow Produced in n-type Material by an Applied Voltage. Consider first an *n*-type semiconductor placed between electrodes, as shown in Fig. 21-4a. Such a semiconductor contains a high concentration of free electrons that are in random motion, an equal concentration of

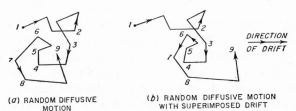

(*a*) RANDOM DIFFUSIVE   (*b*) RANDOM DIFFUSIVE MOTION
        MOTION   WITH SUPERIMPOSED DRIFT

Fig. 21-3. Random or diffusive motion without and with superimposed drift.

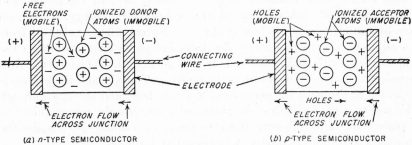

(*a*) *n*-TYPE SEMICONDUCTOR   (*b*) *p*-TYPE SEMICONDUCTOR

Fig. 21-4. Schematic representation of impurity semiconductors and their terminals.

immobile positive ions, and a negligible number of holes. Application of an external voltage to the electrodes produces a field that superimposes on the random motion of the electrons a *drift* toward the positive electrode. With suitably designed terminal connections (see below), the electrons that reach the positive terminal enter the metal of the electrode. At the same time, the immobile positive charges near the negative electrode that are left unneutralized by the drift away of free electrons attract replacement electrons from the metal of the negative electrode.

The result is that electrons at the terminals flow in the directions indicated in Fig. 21-4a, and do so at exactly the correct rate to account for the current flow expected because of the semiconductor conductivity. During this process, the concentration of free electrons in the semiconductor is everywhere just sufficient to equal the concentration of donor ions, so that the semiconductor is electrically neutral at all times. There is, however, a voltage gradient which produces the electron drift and which represents the voltage drop.

Current Flow Produced in p-type Material by an Applied Voltage. Next examine the case where the semiconductor is of the p type (Fig. 21-4b). Such a semiconductor contains a high concentration of holes that are in random motion, an equal concentration of immobile acceptor ions, and a very negligible number of free electrons. Application of an external voltage to the electrodes superimposes a *drift* on the random motion that causes the holes to move toward the negative electrode. As these holes reach the negative electrode, they combine with free electrons that they attract out of the metal of the negative electrode, and so disappear.

Concurrently, replacement holes are being generated in the vicinity of the positive electrode. This comes about because as holes drift away from the positive electrode they no longer neutralize the negative charges of the immobile acceptor ions. An electric field is thus set up between the positive electrode and the nearby unneutralized negative acceptor ions which detaches the ionizing electrons from the acceptor atoms and draws them to the positive electrode. This is possible because the electrons that ionize the acceptor atoms are only very loosely held by the atoms, and can be detached with the expenditure of very little energy. When an acceptor atom loses an electron in this way, it steals another electron from an adjacent valence bond in order to complete its own position in the valence structure, and a new hole is thus generated. The electron thus acquired is, however, soon lost to the positive electrode, and the process is repeated again, with the generation of a new hole, and so on. Through this mechanism, new holes are generated at exactly the rate required to replace those that drift away from the positive terminal, which is also the rate at which they disappear at the negative terminal.

During the conduction process, the concentration of the holes is everywhere exactly equal to the concentration of the immobile negative ions. The material therefore remains electrically neutral during conduction, although there is a voltage gradient that causes the hole drift.

It is to be noted that the flow of current in the actual p-type material is the result of hole motion, even though the current flow in the connecting wires and electrodes is still a movement of electrons.

Terminal-electrode Effects. The conducting mechanisms discussed above in connection with Fig. 21-4 require that electrons be able to pass freely between the semiconductor and the terminal electrodes.

The factors determining the electrical behavior of a transition between an electrode and a semiconductor are complicated, and to some extent obscure. In certain situations including transistors, electrons will pass freely in both directions between semiconductor and terminal with the expenditure of little or no energy; when this happens the transition is said to be *ohmic* or *nonrectifying*. In other cases electrons will pass freely from the semiconductor to the metal, but must expend considerable

energy in order to pass from the metal to the semiconductor.[1] In still
other circumstances, the functions of the metal and semiconductor are
interchanged, the direction of easy movement being from metal to semiconductor, with flow in the opposite direction being difficult. Transitions of these last two types are *rectifying*.

Metal-semiconductor transitions will be ohmic or rectifying depending
upon the way they are formed, and in some cases upon the relative values
of work function of the two mate-
rials involved. Thus a chemical
bond made after the surfaces have
been cleaned by etching behaves
differently from a connection between sand-blasted surfaces held
together by mechanical pressure.
In some circumstances the relative
work functions of the semiconductor and metal are important;
in other cases the work functions
have no significance.

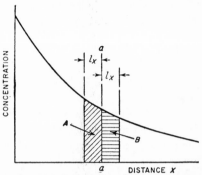

Fig. 21-5. Diagram used to explain current flow by diffusion.

Current Flow by Diffusion. When
mobile charges (either holes or free
electrons) are not uniformly distributed in a semiconductor, a current
will flow even in the absence of an electric field. Thus in Fig. 21-5,
diffusive motion will cause the carriers near a transverse plane such as
aa to cross back and forth across this plane. However, since each individual carrier is just as likely to move to the right as to the left, and there
are more carriers to the left of *aa*, then on the average there will be more
crossings from left to right than from right to left. This results in a net
flow of mobile carriers toward the right, corresponding to a current flow.
This *diffusion current* is just as real as that resulting from the drift of
mobile charges caused by an applied voltage. It is to be noted that
diffusive motion is *not* the same phenomenon as motion due to space-
charge repulsion.

The magnitude of the diffusion current crossing a plane *aa* transverse to
the concentration gradient is[2]

---

[1] This situation is analogous to thermionic emission (p. 172), where the metal
represents the cathode that emits the electrons, the semiconductor corresponds to the
space (i.e., vacuum) that receives them, and the energy involved is the equivalent
of the work function, i.e., the work that an electron must perform to escape.

[2] Equation (21-10a) can be derived as follows: Referring to Fig. 21-5, assume that
the random motion of each electron causes it *on the average* to travel *horizontally* a
distance l_x cm in the time t_x between successive collisions. Then half of the electrons
contained in volumes *A* and *B* of Fig. 21-5 will have crossed plane *aa* within a time t_x
(the other half will go the other way). The number of electrons crossing to the right
per unit area minus the number crossing to the left in time t_x is hence $0.5(l_x \, dn/dx) \times l_x$;

$$i_n = eD_n \frac{dn}{dx} \quad \text{for electrons} \tag{21-10a}$$

$$i_p = eD_p \frac{dp}{dx} \quad \text{for holes} \tag{21-10b}$$

Here subscripts n and p denote free electrons and holes, respectively, and

i = diffusion current per sq cm of cross section

e = charge of electron

D = diffusion constant, sq cm per sec

$\frac{dn}{dx}$ = concentration gradient of electrons

$\frac{dp}{dx}$ = concentration gradient of holes

For germanium at room temperature, $D_n = 93$ sq cm per sec, and $D_p = 44$ sq cm per sec.* It is to be noted that diffusion always acts in such a way as to cause current to flow from a high concentration to a lower concentration of mobile carriers.

Diffusion of minority carriers in the presence of majority carriers is discussed below on page 753.

The diffusion of charges takes place relatively slowly, so that effects associated with diffusion currents have a low velocity of propagation. In contrast, the electric fields that cause drift current propagate with the velocity of light.

21-5. Conductivity of Insulators, Metals, and Semiconductors in Terms of Energy Bands. The quantum-mechanics concept of energy bands in solids provides viewpoints that are useful in considering the conductivity of a solid.

In an isolated atom, each electron associated with the nucleus must lie in one of a number of orbits defined by quantum mechanics. Each of

---

the corresponding diffusion current i_n is

$$i_n = \frac{el_x{}^2}{2t_x} \frac{dn}{dx} = \frac{1}{2} el_x v_x \frac{dn}{dx}$$

Here $v_x = l_x/t_x$ is the average *horizontal* component of velocity of the electron motion. The diffusion constant D_n is then

$$D_n = \frac{l_x{}^2}{2t_x} = \frac{1}{2} l_x v_x \tag{21-11}$$

---

* The diffusion constant D and the mobility μ of the mobile carriers are related by the Einstein equation

$$\mu = \frac{e}{kT} D \tag{21-12}$$

where e is the electron charge, k is Boltzmann's constant, and T is the absolute temperature in degrees Kelvin.

these orbits corresponds to a different level of potential energy, since it takes energy to move an electron from an inner orbit to one that is more remote from the nucleus.   The electrons of an atom accordingly prefer the inner orbits; however, it is a fundamental law of nature that no more than two electrons in an atom may occupy the same energy level, and then only if they have opposite spins.[1]   Thus in a normal atom, the electrons occupy all the lower energy levels, while the higher energy levels remain unoccupied.

When two similar atoms are brought very close together, there is an interaction or coupling between the orbits of their electrons that causes each individual energy level to be split into two slightly different levels. This is analogous to the two resonant frequencies that result when two resonant circuits tuned to the same frequency are closely coupled together (see Fig. 3-11).   Similarly, when N identical atoms are brought close to each other, each energy level divides into N slightly different energy levels.   When N is very large, as when the atoms form a solid body, the N energy levels produced are so numerous and so close together as to form a band that can be regarded as essentially continuous.

Conduction of electricity is possible only when there is present an energy band that contains some electrons, but not as many as the maximum it is permitted to accommodate by the Pauli exclusion principle. Thus in quantum-mechanics language, a completely filled band simply means that there are no free electrons (or holes), whereas a band that is partially filled denotes that free electrons are present.   A situation such as illustrated in Fig. 21-1, where every valence electron is held in place, corresponds to a completely filled band, and so represents a nonconductor.

Since the electrons always fill the lower energy bands first, the conductivity of a solid is determined by the situation existing in the highest-level energy band that contains electrons, and the relationship of this band to the next higher, or unoccupied, band.   The various conditions that can exist are illustrated in Figs. 21-6 and 21-7.

Conductivity of Insulators and Semiconductors.   In Fig. 21-6a and b, the lower band is completely filled with electrons, while the upper band is normally entirely empty.   The gap between these energy levels is termed the *forbidden region*, and represents an energy difference of ΔE volts. An electron in the filled band will jump to the unfilled band if it acquires energy ΔE from thermal vibrations, incident light, or in some other manner.   When this happens, the electron is free to move about, and it hence contributes to the conduction of electricity because it is now in an unfilled band.   At the same time, the fact that the lower band has lost an electron means that this band is no longer completely filled; the electron deficit or hole in this band can and does move about and also contributes to the conduction of electricity.   This is seen to be another way to

---

[1] This is known as the Pauli exclusion principle.

describe the covalent bond relationship, and the conductivity that results from the production of an electron-hole pair when such a bond is broken.

When the energy gap ΔE in Fig. 21-6a and b is large, for example, 5 or 10 volts, corresponding to very strong valence or other bonds, it is only very rarely that an electron will acquire sufficient energy from thermal effects at room temperature to jump to the unfilled band. The solid material is then a good insulator. However, if the energy gap ΔE is of the order of 1 volt or less, corresponding to bonds of only moderate strength, enough electrons are able to acquire the energy necessary to

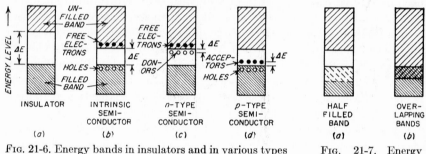

Fig. 21-6. Energy bands in insulators and in various types of semiconductors.

Fig. 21-7. Energy bands in metals.

jump the gap to result in appreciable conductivity. This is the situation that exists in semiconductors, where for germanium and silicon, the energy gaps are 0.75 and 1.12 volts, respectively.

Semiconductors containing impurities are illustrated in Fig. 21-6c and d. Donors represent isolated energy levels located so close to the unfilled band that very little energy is required to lift an electron from the donor level into the unfilled band, where it is available for the conduction of electricity. Similarly, acceptors represent isolated energy levels located so close to the filled band that it requires very little energy to lift an electron from the filled band to the acceptor. Since the individual donor (or acceptor) atoms are isolated from each other, the energy levels that they represent are shown as isolated dots rather than as a band.

Conductivity of Metals. The arrangements of energy bands encountered in metals are illustrated in Fig. 21-7. At a, typified by the alkali metals, the highest energy band containing electrons is only half filled because there are enough electrons for only one of the two spin states. The electrons within this band are therefore able to move about freely because the band is not filled, and the material is a good conductor. In case b the filled and unfilled bands overlap, so electrons from the filled band are able to enter the unfilled band without the expenditure of energy. This means that again electrons are able to move about freely in the material, resulting in high conductivity.

21-6. The Junction Diode. An electronic device having the rectifying characteristics of a diode vacuum tube can be made by utilization of the properties of a junction between p-type and n-type material. Such a device is called a *junction diode*, and can be constructed in several ways. Two principal techniques of fabrication are shown in Fig. 21-8. In the *grown junction*, a single crystal is grown from a melt which at the start contains impurities of one kind. However, in the middle of the process impurities of the opposite kind are added to the melt in sufficient quantity to change the type of the material grown thereafter.

The *fused-junction* diode is shown in Fig. 21-8b. It is prepared by placing a small sphere or "dot" of indium on a wafer of n-type germa-

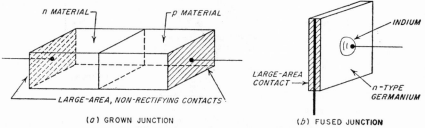

(a) GROWN JUNCTION   (b) FUSED JUNCTION
FIG. 21-8. Two types of junction diodes.

nium. When this combination is inserted in an oven for several minutes at a temperature that is suitably high, the indium fuses to the surface of the germanium, and produces p-type germanium immediately below the surface. Thus a p-n junction is formed between this p region and the main body of the n-type germanium wafer.

In both types of junction diodes the important rectifying action takes place at the boundary between the p-type and n-type materials. The area of this boundary is usually much greater than is the transverse depth of the transition region. Thus the analysis problem is essentially one dimensional, the important dimension being transverse to the boundary.

The Energy Barrier at the p-n Junction. In Fig. 21-9a is shown a schematic sketch of the p-n material itself, in which the circled charges represent the immobile ionized acceptor and donor ions. The variation in the concentration of these ions in the region of the boundary is shown schematically in Fig. 21-9b. The exact nature of the transition from donors to acceptors differs between the grown junction and the fused junction, being much more abrupt in the case of fused junctions; however, the essential behavior is much the same in both cases.

When there are no external connections, and no external applied voltage, there is a dearth of holes and free electrons in the vicinity of the junction (see Fig. 21-9c); this leaves the immobile ions in the region unneutralized. The positive and negative ions on opposite sides of the junction that are thus "uncovered" produce an electric field across the junction, as shown.   This *barrier field* as it is termed, is the result of an unstable situation initiated by the fact that when electrons and holes in the junction area combine, the resulting uncovered ions produce a field that drives the remaining electrons and holes away from the junction, which in turn uncovers more ions, etc.

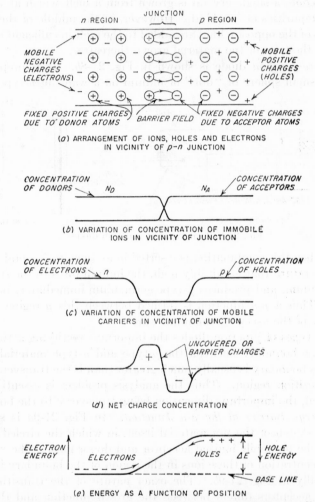

(*a*) ARRANGEMENT OF IONS, HOLES AND ELECTRONS
IN VICINITY OF *p-n* JUNCTION

(*b*) VARIATION OF CONCENTRATION OF IMMOBILE
IONS IN VICINITY OF JUNCTION

(*c*) VARIATION OF CONCENTRATION OF MOBILE
CARRIERS IN VICINITY OF JUNCTION

(*d*) NET CHARGE CONCENTRATION

(*e*) ENERGY AS A FUNCTION OF POSITION

Fig. 21-9. Conditions existing in a junction diode under equilibrium conditions, where the net flow of current across the junction is zero.

The net charge concentration in the region of the junction is the difference between the distributions of Fig. 21-9*b* and *c*, and so varies in the manner shown in Fig. 21-9*d*.   The actual details, particularly the length of the "uncovered" region transverse to the junction, are determined by an equilibrium condition established between the *n* and *p* regions by mobile charges that are able occasionally to cross the junction, as discussed below. The entire transition in Fig. 21-9d takes place within a space of a small fraction of a millimeter.

The energy required to move an electron from the n region toward the p region varies with position as shown in Fig. 21-9e. Transfer of the electron all the way across the junction requires the expenditure of ΔE electron volts of energy; this is termed the *barrier energy* or barrier height. An equal amount of energy is involved when a hole is moved from the p region to the n region. The magnitude of the energy hill or barrier ΔE is determined by the thickness of the uncovered region in Fig. 21-9a. The greater its thickness the more extended and stronger are the fields at the junction, and the greater the value of ΔE.

Carrier Movement and Current Flow across Unbiased Junction. Even with no external connection to the p-n junction in Fig. 21-9, there is a continuing though small flow of holes and free electrons across the junction. Thus holes produced in the n region by the breaking of covalent bonds through thermal effects flow freely across the junction into the p region, since the barrier field at the junction aids rather than opposes such flow. Free electrons similarly generated in the p region flow freely into the n region for the same reason. In the unbiased junction the current flow I_s of these "intrinsic" minority carriers is exactly counterbalanced by an equal and opposite flow of majority carriers that acquire from thermal sources the energy ΔE that is required for a carrier to travel across the junction *against* the barrier field.

The mechanism by which this equilibrium is established is based on the fact that the number of carriers that are hoisted over the barrier with the aid of thermal energy is determined by the height ΔE of the barrier. The width of the uncovered region accordingly adjusts itself so that the resulting value of ΔE makes the number of carriers crossing against the barrier field exactly equal to the number of carriers of intrinsic origin that cross the junction with the aid of the barrier field. If ΔE were lower than this, an excessive number of thermally aided carriers would cross against the field, making the n region more positive and the p region more negative, which would increase ΔE and reduce the number of thermally aided crossings. If ΔE is too large, the opposite sequence of events takes place. Thus equilibrium is automatically maintained.

Carrier Movement and Current Flow across a Biased Junction. If the p material in Fig. 21-9a is biased positively with respect to the n material, the bias potential exerts a force on the holes and free electrons in the p and n material, respectively, that opposes the restraining force of the barrier field, and causes these carriers to crowd closer to the junction. This reduces the thickness of the region in which the immobile charges are uncovered, and thereby lowers the height of the energy barrier, as seen by comparing a with b in Fig. 21-10. For a given temperature, more of the majority carriers can now surmount this barrier $\Delta E'$ than the higher barrier ΔE. At the same time the number of intrinsic carriers that conduct electricity in the opposite direction is unchanged because the rate at which intrinsic carriers are produced is determined by the breaking of covalent bonds, and is not affected by the voltages that are applied. A large current thus flows. An applied voltage of this kind is called a *forward bias*.

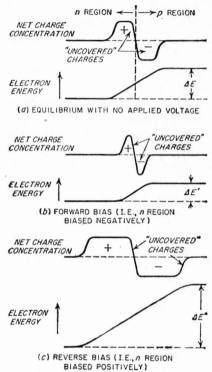

(a) EQUILIBRIUM WITH NO APPLIED VOLTAGE

(b) FORWARD BIAS (I.E., n REGION BIASED NEGATIVELY)

(c) REVERSE BIAS (I.E., n REGION BIASED POSITIVELY)

Fig. 21-10. Effect of forward and reverse bias on the "uncovered" region, and on the energy barrier at the junction, of a junction diode.

Application of a voltage of the opposite polarity, termed *reverse bias*, subjects the mobile majority carriers in the n and p regions to forces that tend to draw them away from the junction. This leads to the situation shown in Fig. 21-10c, in which the region where the fixed donor and acceptor ions are exposed is widened. A greater energy barrier $\Delta E''$ must, therefore, be surmounted. This reduces the number of carriers that are able to cross the junction *against* the barrier field to a negligible value. However, the flow of intrinsic carriers is largely unaffected by the change in barrier level; so there remains a small reverse current I_s termed the *reverse saturation current*.

The total net current flowing across a junction as a result of the application of a voltage V is[1,2]

$$I = I_s(\epsilon^{eV/kT} - 1) \qquad \text{amps per sq cm} \qquad (21\text{-}13)$$

[1] Strictly speaking the voltage across the junction is the actual voltage applied to the terminals of the junction diode, minus the voltage drop of the current flowing through the resistance of the n and p material. However, under most conditions this ohmic drop is negligible.

[2] Equation (21-13), which applies to both symmetrical and unsymmetrical junctions, results from the following line of reasoning: It can be shown that the effect of V on the barrier energy is such that the current due to the carriers crossing the junction *against* the barrier is $A\epsilon^{eV/kT}$, where A is a constant. At the same time, the reverse current due to intrinsic carriers equals the reverse saturation current I_s, irrespective of V up to values of V that are not more positive than about 0.1 volt. Hence

$$I = A\epsilon^{eV/kT} - I_s$$

Since $I = 0$ when $V = 0$, it follows that $A = I_s$.

where I_s = reverse saturation current (see below), amps per sq cm

    e = electron charge (= 1.59×10^{-19} coulomb)

    k = Boltzmann's constant (= 1.374×10^{-23})

    T = absolute temperature, °K

The applied voltage V is positive when it is a forward voltage. At "room temperature," for example, $T \approx 300°K$,

$$I = I_s(\epsilon^{39V} - 1) \tag{21-14}$$

When the forward bias V exceeds about 0.1 volt, Eq. (21-14) can be written

$$I \approx I_s\epsilon^{39V} \tag{21-15}$$

On the other hand, for a reverse bias of more than 0.1 volt (that is, $V \lessgtr -0.10$), Eq. (21-13) becomes

$$I \approx I_s \tag{21-16}$$

A graphical plot of Eq. (21-14) is shown in Fig. 21-11. Experimental results for typical junctions conform remarkably well to the form of the curve in Fig. 21-11.

If the reverse voltage is sufficiently great, the gradient of the electric field at the junction will be high enough to disrupt covalent bonds. This produces large numbers of electron-hole pairs in the vicinity of the junction, and thereby causes the reverse current to increase suddenly as indicated by the region marked "breakdown" in Fig. 21-11. This behavior is reproducible in that when the excessive reverse bias is removed, conditions return to normal, provided thermal heating has not damaged the crystal structure.

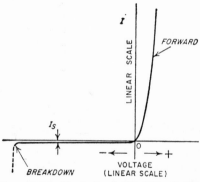

FIG. 21-11. Typical relationship of applied voltage to current in a junction diode. For the sake of clarity, the magnitude of the reverse current has been greatly exaggerated.

Junction Capacitance. Examination of Fig. 21-9a and d shows that on opposite sides of the p-n junction, there are regions containing immobile charges of opposite sign in close proximity to each other. This is the situation that exists in any capacitor. Since the capacitance of a capacitor depends on the spacing of the charges, and is greater if the charges are closer together, the capacitance of the p-n junction will change with applied voltage. It diminishes with increased voltage in the reverse-bias direction, because, as seen from Fig. 21-10, the average separation of the uncovered charges is greater in c than in a.   The fact that there is more total charge in c is of no consequence, for the capacitance of a condenser depends only upon the geometry of the situation, and not upon the charge actually present.

The junction capacitance can be directly measured with an a-c impedance bridge.   Theory verified by measurements shows that the capacitance varies inversely with the square root of the applied voltage when the transition from n-type to p-type material is a gradual one, as tends to occur with grown junctions.   However, if the transition is abrupt, as in

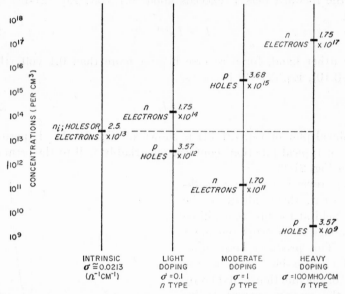

Fig. 21-12. Concentrations of mobile carriers in several germanium samples.   The degree of "doping" is here expressed in terms of the ratio of donor (or acceptor) atoms to germanium atoms, there being 4.52×10^{22} germanium atoms per cu cm.   Note that for every sample $np = n_i^2$.

the case of the fused junction, the capacitance turns out to vary inversely as the cube root of the applied voltage.

Unsymmetrical Junctions.   It was implied in Figs. 21-9 and 21-10 that the concentrations of donors and acceptors were the same in the n and p material, respectively; when this is true the junction is said to be *symmetrical*.   However, in the general case such symmetry will not exist, and indeed, in the case of the transistor it is essential that one of the junctions be highly unsymmetrical.

The concentrations of holes and free electrons in n and p materials for representative amounts of "doping" by donor and acceptor atoms, together with the concentrations for pure germanium, i.e., the intrinsic concentrations, are shown in Fig. 21-12.   In general, the greater the concentration of the majority carriers, the smaller will be the concentration of the minority carriers in accordance with Eq. (21-7). The degree of doping is commonly expressed in terms of the conductivity (or resistivity) of the resulting material in accordance with Eq. (21-8) or Eq. (21-9). This is convenient because conductivity can be easily measured in the laboratory on samples of material.

21-7. Further Consideration of Carrier Drift and Diffusion in Biased p-n Junctions. *Carrier Drift and Diffusion with Forward Bias.* While Eq. (21-13) gives the current that flows in a biased junction diode irrespective of the degree of symmetry, it says little about the way the electrons and holes transport this current by drift and diffusion. Such details are considered in this section for the case of an unsymmetrical junction in which the n and p materials correspond, respectively, to "heavy" and "moderate" doping as designated in Fig. 21-12.

When a forward bias is applied to such a junction, the resulting situation is as pictured in Fig. 21-13.[1] Free electrons from the n region drift toward the junction as a result of a slight voltage gradient in the n material, and enter the p region, where they represent minority carriers.[2,3] These minority carriers (electrons) diffuse away from the junction, and as they do, their concentration diminishes steadily because of recombination with holes. This produces a gradient in the concentration as shown in Fig. 21-13b, which controls the rate of diffusion and hence the diffusion current. At an appreciable distance from the junction, virtually all of the electrons emitted into the p material will have disappeared due to recombination, as shown.

Concurrently with the above action of the electrons, holes from the p region drift toward the junction as a result of a slight voltage gradient in the p material, traverse the junction, and then diffuse away from the junction into the n material as a result of the gradient that results from the recombination of these minority carriers (holes) with the majority carriers (electrons) of the n region. The only significant difference between the behavior of the holes and electrons in Fig. 21-13 is that since there are more electrons in the n region than there are holes in the p region, more electrons than holes cross the junction.

The current across any transverse plane is the sum of the current due to the diffusion of the minority carriers and the current due to the majority carriers. The total current must everywhere be the same, so

---

[1] This figure and also Figs. 21-14 and 21-16 were devised by R. D. Middlebrook during the course of his doctoral research at Stanford University under Dr. J. M. Pettit.

[2] Mobile carriers which cross a junction in this manner and are injected into a region where they become minority carriers are said to be *emitted* by the junction.

[3] It is to be noted that in Fig. 21-13b, the increase in concentration of minority carriers in the p region resulting from the addition of the emitted carriers still leaves the total concentration of electrons in this region much lower than the concentration of the holes (i.e., the majority carriers). This situation is typical of all practical cases.

(a) CIRCUIT

n REGION (σ_n =100)   p REGION (σ_p= 1)

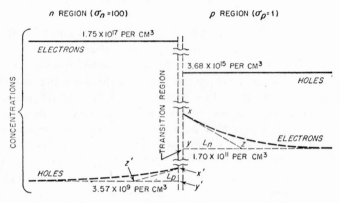

(b) CONCENTRATIONS OF CARRIERS AS A FUNCTION
OF DISTANCE FROM JUNCTION

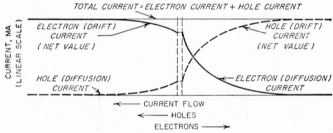

(c) CURRENT COMPONENTS AS A FUNCTION OF DISTANCE FROM JUNCTION

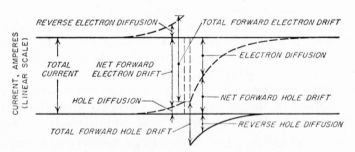

(d) CURRENT COMPONENTS, SHOWING REVERSE DIFFUSION EFFECTS

Fig. 21-13. Carrier concentrations and current components in a forward-biased
unsymmetrical p-n junction.

that these two components of current are complementary, as illustrated in Fig. 21-13c.

The current represented by the minority carriers, diffusing away from the junction, will be greatest adjacent to the junction, and also will be greater in the material having the lower conductivity, i.e., the p material in Fig. 21-13. These characteristics result from the fact that the diffusion current is proportional to the slope of the curve giving the concentration of the minority carriers.

If the carriers crossing the junction were simply added to the minority carriers already present in the region into which they are emitted, there would be unneutralized space charges on each side of the junction. This does not happen because these emitted carriers attract additional mobile carriers of unlike charge (i.e., majority carriers) to their general vicinity in exactly the correct number to make the material electrically neutral. Thus in Fig. 21-13, the extent to which the electron concentration in the p material exceeds the level determined by the doping is matched by a corresponding hole distribution,[1] with the additional holes required to accomplish this neutralization being generated in the p material adjacent to the electrode in the manner explained on page 742. As a result, there is a concentration gradient of majority carriers adjacent to the junction that produces a diffusion current of majority carriers that flows in the opposite direction from the flow of total current, and which would have the same magnitude as the diffusion current of the minority carriers except for the difference in the value of the diffusion constant. Thus the net value of the majority carrier current, which is the drift current in Fig. 21-13c, is the difference between a forward flowing component representing drift of the majority carriers toward the junction, and a backward flowing current caused by diffusion of the majority carriers away from the junction. This is shown in Fig. 21-13d.

Carrier Drift and Diffusion with Reverse Bias. When a reverse voltage is applied to a junction diode, the electrons and holes behave in the manner illustrated in Fig. 21-14.[2] Minority holes in the n material that reach the junction by diffusion are transported into the p region by the barrier field. As a result of this steady removal of holes from the n side of the junction, the concentration of holes in the n material varies as shown, which creates a concentration gradient that encourages the few holes present as minority carriers to diffuse toward the junction. After entering the p material, the holes from the n region join with the holes in the p material and drift (not diffuse) away from the junction.

---

[1] These additional holes do not show in the curve of Fig. 21-13b that gives the hole concentration in the p material. This is because the percentage charge in hole concentration is too small to be detectable on the scale used in the diagram.

[2] It is to be noted that the barrier is shown thicker in Fig. 21-14 than in Fig. 21-13. This is because an inverse voltage increases the number of ions that are uncovered, whereas a forward bias decreases the number.

Minority electrons in the p material behave in an analogous manner. The electrons that get near the junction are transported into the n region by the barrier field, causing a dearth of electrons in the p material near the junction and a resulting concentration gradient in the p material as shown. After entering the n material, the electrons from the p region

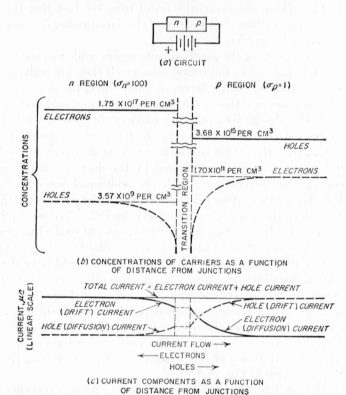

(a) CIRCUIT

(b) CONCENTRATIONS OF CARRIERS AS A FUNCTION
OF DISTANCE FROM JUNCTIONS

(c) CURRENT COMPONENTS AS A FUNCTION
OF DISTANCE FROM JUNCTIONS

Fig. 21-14. Carrier concentrations and current components in a reverse-biased unsymmetrical p-n junction. For the sake of clarity the magnitudes of the currents in c are greatly exaggerated compared with Fig. 21-13c.

merge with the electrons of the n material and drift away from the junction.

The currents that flow in the case of reverse bias, shown in Fig. 21-14c, are similar in character to those of Fig. 21-13c. The descriptive explanation is so similar that it need not be repeated; the principal difference is that the corresponding carriers move in the opposite directions in Figs. 21-13c and 21-14c, and that the currents are very much smaller in the reverse-bias case.

Diffusion Length. The distance L over which the concentration of the minority carriers is reduced by the factor $1/\epsilon = 0.37$ is termed the *diffusion length.* It is related to the diffusion constant D and the average lifetime τ of the minority carriers by the equation

$$L = \sqrt{D\tau} \tag{21-17}$$

Since the lifetime τ of the minority carriers is less the greater the concentration of the majority carriers,[1] the diffusion length will become less the greater the conductivity of the material. The diffusion length for germanium may range from a few mils to more than 100 mils, corresponding to values of lifetime from less than 1 μsec to more than 1 msec.

The diffusion length is useful in expressing the concentration *gradient*. Thus referring to the triangle xyz in the lower right-hand part of Fig. 21-13b, the fact that the concentration distribution is an exponential curve enables one to write

$$\left. \begin{array}{l} \text{Concentration gradient} \\ \text{of minority carriers} \\ \text{at point } x \end{array} \right\} = \frac{xy}{yz} = \frac{\left\{ \begin{array}{l} \text{minority concentration} \\ \text{at point } x \end{array} \right.}{L} \tag{21-18}$$

Thus for a given concentration of the minority carriers, the concentration gradient will be higher the smaller the diffusion length L.

Ratio of Electron to Hole Current at the Junction. The relative importance of electrons and holes in transporting current across the junction depends only upon the donor and acceptor concentrations (i.e., upon the relative conductivities) of the n and p materials, respectively, and is independent of the magnitude or sign of the voltage applied to the junction.

The magnitude of the ratio can be determined by noting that the electron and hole diffusion currents at x and x', respectively, in Fig. 21-13b, are likewise equal, respectively, to the electron and hole currents crossing the junction. Hence from Eq. (21-10)

$$\frac{\text{Electron current}}{\text{Hole current}} = \frac{D_n \times \left\{ \begin{array}{l} \text{concentration gradient} \\ \text{of electrons at } x \end{array} \right.}{D_p \times \left\{ \begin{array}{l} \text{concentration gradient} \\ \text{of holes at } x' \end{array} \right.} \tag{21-19}$$

However, from the discussion above on diffusion length one can, by reference to Fig. 21-13b, write

$$\frac{\left. \begin{array}{l} \text{Concentration gradient} \\ \text{of electrons at } x \end{array} \right|}{\left. \begin{array}{l} \text{Concentration gradient} \\ \text{of holes at } x' \end{array} \right|} = \frac{\text{slope of } xz}{\text{slope of } x'z'} = \frac{xy}{yz} \frac{y'z'}{x'y'} \tag{21-20}$$

---

[1] The lifetime is also affected by imperfections in the crystal lattice and by chemical impurities other than donors and acceptors, and by surface contamination that affects the rate of recombination at the surface.

But the lengths xy and $x'y'$ are proportional, respectively, to the concentrations $n = N_D$ and $p = N_A$ of electrons and holes in the n and p regions, while yz and $y'z'$ are, respectively, the diffusion lengths L_n and L_p of the electrons and holes. Hence[1]

$$\frac{\text{Electron current}}{\text{Hole current}} = \frac{N_D D_n L_p}{N_A D_p L_n} = \frac{\sigma_n L_p}{\sigma_p L_n} \qquad (21\text{-}21)$$

where N_D, N_A = donor and acceptor concentrations, respectively

D_n, D_p = diffusion constants for electrons and holes, respectively

L_n, L_p = diffusion lengths for electron and holes, in p and n regions, respectively

σ_n, σ_p = conductivities of n and p materials, respectively

It follows from Eq. (21-21) that the electron-to-hole ratio is controlled by the *relative* conductivities of the n and p materials, respectively, i.e., upon the relative doping of the n and p materials. This is true not only because of the ratio σ_n/σ_p appearing in Eq. (21-21), but also as a result of the fact that L_p/L_n also depends on the ratio of conductivities.

Distribution of Voltage Drop. In a forward-biased junction diode, practically the entire applied voltage is consumed in controlling the thickness of the barrier region.[2] While some voltage drop must exist in the n and p material to produce the necessary drift of the majority carriers in these regions, this drop is generally negligible in comparison with the drop at the junction.[3] What small voltage drop is present in the n and p material during forward-bias conditions distributes itself in such a manner as to equal the total drift current (as shown in Fig. 21-13d) multiplied by the resistivity of the material.

With reverse bias, virtually the full applied voltage is consumed as voltage drop at the junction. The ohmic drop in the material caused by the drift current is negligible because the currents involved are so small.

21-8. Circuit Properties of the p-n Junction. The circuit properties of the junction diode can now be briefly summarized. A large current

---

[1] The last form of the ratio in Eq. (21-21) arises from the fact that $N_D/N_A = n/p$, while from Eq. (21-12), $D_n/D_p = \mu_n/\mu_p$.

[2] It is to be noted that this does not mean that the applied voltage equals the height ΔE, $\Delta E'$, etc., of the energy barrier in Fig. 21-10. Rather, the applied voltage produces a force that alters the energy barrier, and so is a measure of the *change* in barrier height. The relationship is not a direct one, however, so that it is not correct to assume that the change in barrier height is equal to the applied voltage.

[3] It might be thought that the same voltage drop that causes the drift of the electrons (majority carriers) in the n material toward the junction in Fig. 21-13b would affect the movement of the holes emitted into the n region. However, a voltage drop that will cause enough drift of the very numerous majority carriers to produce the required majority-carrier drift current will produce negligible minority-carrier drift current because the minority carriers are so much fewer in number. As a result, the movement of the minority carriers due to drift is negligible compared with their movement caused by diffusion.

will flow in the forward direction with a low applied voltage [see Eq. (21-15)]. The *dynamic* resistance,[1] i.e., the *resistance to a small incremental voltage dV superimposed on the forward bias*, is obtained by differentiating Eq. (21-15) with respect to voltage, and so for germanium is

$$r = \frac{1}{A}\frac{dV}{dI} = \frac{1}{A}\frac{1}{dI/dV} = \frac{1}{39I_t} \qquad (21\text{-}22)$$

Here r is the dynamic resistance of the junction, and $I_t = AI$ is the total forward current for the cross section A. For a typical small diode such as might be used in a radio receiver, the dynamic resistance r will be of the order 25 ohms for a forward current of 1 ma, and still less for larger currents; this is far lower than for a small vacuum diode.

The reverse saturation current is small; commonly only a few microamperes for a small diode. The *dynamic* resistance with reverse bias is extremely high because the reverse current is essentially independent of reverse bias (see Fig. 21-11). This resistance is not, however, as high as in the vacuum diode, where it is essentially infinite, but is much higher than in crystal diodes with point contacts.

The junction capacitance under reverse-bias conditions is typically of the order of 5 to 50 $\mu\mu f$ for small diodes. This is large enough to be an important circuit element under many conditions. The junction capacitance is somewhat larger with forward bias, but is then unimportant because the forward dynamic resistance is so low.

Although at the present writing junction diodes are being used most extensively in the smaller sizes, they also show promise as high-power devices. Thus experimental germanium diodes have been made which have a voltage drop of less than 1 volt at 1000 amp in the forward direction, and less than 10 ma of reverse current for a reverse bias of 100 volts, for 1 sq cm cross section.

Charge-storage Phenomenon. Complications arise when it is desired to switch a diode as rapidly as possible from full conduction in the forward direction to full voltage (with small current) in the reverse direction. Looking at Fig. 21-13b for the forward-biased diode, it is seen from the numbers labeled on the curves that the concentration of minority carriers near the junction is high compared to the concentration in Fig. 21-14b for the reverse-biased diode. Thus during a transition from forward to reverse conditions, the charge concentration in the vicinity of the junction must be substantially reduced. Since these charge carriers can disappear only as a result of recombination with majority carriers moving into the junction area, or by diffusion of the minority carriers away from the junction, an appreciable time is required to establish a new set of equi-

---

[1] The dynamic resistance is to be distinguished from the static resistance, which is the ratio of the *total* applied voltage to the *total* resulting current.

librium conditions. The circuit result of this is that a spurious current flows for as much as several microseconds after the applied voltage is reversed. This phenomenon is usually given the name "charge storage."

Silicon versus Germanium. Junction diodes can be made conveniently from either germanium or silicon, with each material having certain advantages. With silicon, the reverse saturation current is substantially smaller than for a comparable germanium diode. This results from the fact that the higher ionization energy of silicon yields fewer thermally generated intrinsic electron-hole pairs at a given temperature. On the other hand, the rate of increase of reverse current with temperature is higher in silicon than in germanium. The lower reverse saturation current in silicon also results in a lower forward current for a given forward voltage, i.e., in a higher forward static resistance, than obtained with germanium.

21-9. The Junction Triode Transistor. The junction triode transistor is a logical extension of the junction diode, and in most respects is analo-

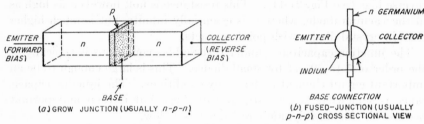

(a) GROW JUNCTION (USUALLY n-p-n)

(b) FUSED–JUNCTION (USUALLY p-n-p) CROSS SECTIONAL VIEW

Fig. 21-15. Two types of junction triode transistors.

gous to the triode tube. The junction triode transistor is illustrated schematically in Fig. 21-15a. It can be regarded as a sandwich of n, p, and n (or of p-n-p) material as shown. The center section is termed the *base*, while the outer sections are referred to as the *collector* and the *emitter*, as indicated. The combination of emitter and base can be regarded as one junction diode, while the base and collector form a second junction diode. For the proper operation of the transistor it is necessary that the two junctions be in close proximity to each other.

Types of Construction. Two common methods of manufacturing a junction transistor are illustrated in Fig. 21-15. In the grown-junction transistor, a junction is first made as described in Sec. 21-6. The crystal is then withdrawn from the melt a very slight distance, and an impurity is again added to the melt in sufficient quantity to reverse the type of dominant impurity, thus making a second junction. The cross-sectional area of such a transistor is typically of the order of 0.25 sq mm, and the thickness of the base layer between the junctions 0.1 mm.

The fused-junction transistor is illustrated in Fig. 21-15b. It is fabricated in much the same manner as the fused-junction diode described in Sec. 21-6, except that a small indium dot is placed on each side of the thin n-type germanium wafer instead of only on one side.   Control of the temperature and duration of firing governs the penetration of the indium into the germanium and hence the base thickness.

Current Flow—General Character.   In a transistor the emitter is biased in the forward direction and the collector in the reverse direction.   For the n-p-n transistor of Fig. 21-15a, this means that the emitter is negative with respect to the base, while the collector is positive.   For a p-n-p transistor, these polarities would be reversed.   Typical electrode voltages for a small transistor such as would be used in an audio-frequency voltage amplifier are $|V_e| = 0.1$ volt and $|V_c| = 6$ volts.   The emitter and collector currents under these conditions would commonly be several milliamperes.

Junction transistors are so designed that the conductivity of the base is always less by several orders of magnitude than the conductivity of the emitter material.   With the grown junction the collector conductivity is usually still lower than that of the base; however, with fused junctions the method of fabrication results in emitter and collector conductivities that are the same.

The behavior of the mobile charges in the junction transistor is shown in Fig. 21-16b.   Consider first the emitter-base junction (commonly called simply the *emitter junction*).   This is a forward-biased n-p junction similar in every respect to that discussed in Fig. 21-13.   Since $N_D >> N_A$ (that is, $\sigma_n >> \sigma_p$), the carriers crossing the emitter junction are predominantly electrons, which then become minority carriers in the p section.   It is correct to consider that the emitter material "emits" these minority carriers into the base.

These minority carriers diffuse through the base to the base-collector junction (commonly termed simply the *collector junction*).   Here the strong electric field existing at the collector junction as a result of the reverse bias between collector and base quickly sweeps the minority carriers across the collector junction into the collector material, where they then move toward the collector electrode.

The small distance between the emitter and collector junctions, and the low concentration of majority carriers produced by the base material because of its low conductivity, cause nearly all of the electrons emitted into the base to reach the collector before they have an opportunity to combine with the holes of the base, or to be drawn to the base terminal. As a result, the collector current will be almost as large as the emitter current.   This is true even though the collector voltage is a reverse bias such that in the absence of the emitter current, the collector current would be only the reverse-saturation diode current, and so would be almost zero.   It is further to be noted that the collector current is determined primarily by the emitter current rather than by the collector voltage.

Conventions on Polarities and Graphical Symbols.   Triode transistors

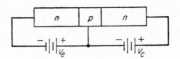

(a) CIRCUIT ARRANGEMENT, SHOWING APPLIED VOLTAGES

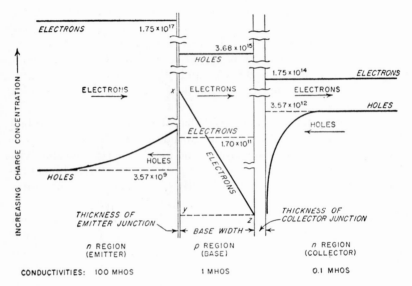

(b) AVERAGE CONCENTRATIONS

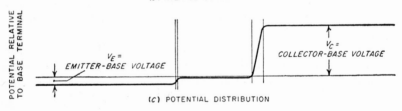

(c) POTENTIAL DISTRIBUTION

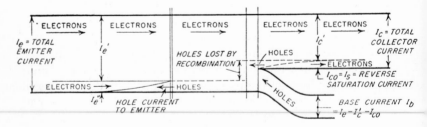

(d) FLOW DIAGRAM OF CURRENT AND ITS COMPONENTS

Fig. 21-16. Carrier concentrations and current components in junction triode transistor.

that are part of a circuit diagram are commonly symbolized in the manner shown in Fig. 21-17a. Here the emitter is distinguished from the collector by the arrow, which can be regarded as denoting carriers (either electrons or holes as the case may be) being emitted into the base region. The direction of the arrow indicates the direction of current flow with

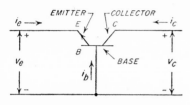

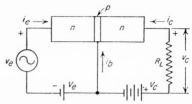

(a) STANDARD DIRECTIONS, POLARITIES, AND SYMBOLS

(b) SIMPLE TRANSISTOR AMPLIFIER

FIG. 21-17. Symbolic representation of a transistor, showing conventions as to polarities and positive directions of current flow, together with elementary transistor amplifier circuit.

forward bias; thus the arrow in Fig. 21-17a corresponds to an n-p-n junction. Letter symbols E, B, and C are also added sometimes, as shown, to further designate "emitter," "base," and "collector."

It is standard practice to consider that positive polarities for the applied voltages, and positive directions of current flow, are as designated in Fig. 21-17a. That is, the positive direction for current flow is *into* the transistor, irrespective of the particular electrode involved, while a positive voltage applied to either collector or emitter is always positive with respect to the base. For an n-p-n transistor the emitter voltage and current are hence negative, while the collector voltage and current are positive. In this connection it must be kept in mind that, as in vacuum tubes, a positive current flows in the opposite direction from the flow of electrons.

Voltages in transistor circuits are typically denoted by V instead of

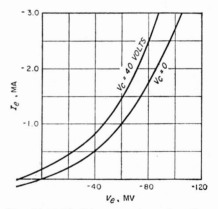

FIG. 21-18. Emitter current as a function of emitter-to-base voltage for an n-p-n junction transistor in the common-base connection.

the usual E; this is to avoid confusion with E as representing emitter or electric fields. Subscripts e, b, and c are used to denote voltages (or currents) associated with emitter, base, and collector, respectively.

Static Characteristics and Power Amplification. The voltage and current relations of a typical junction triode transistor are shown in Figs. 21-18 and 21-19. The emitter current varies with the emitter voltage as shown in Fig. 21-18; this relationship follows Eq. (21-13), and superficially appears to have the same general shape as the relation between the space current and the anode voltage of a vacuum diode. The emitter current is nearly independent of the collector voltage; there is, however, a second-order interaction effect, as shown, that will be discussed later. It is important to note at this point that a very small emitter voltage is sufficient to produce a relatively large emitter current. As a result, the dynamic resistance of the emitter circuit is very low to a small signal voltage superimposed on this electrode.

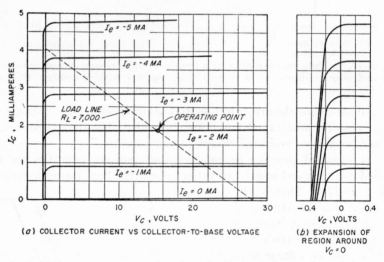

(a) COLLECTOR CURRENT VS COLLECTOR-TO-BASE VOLTAGE   (b) EXPANSION OF REGION AROUND $V_C = 0$

Fig. 21-19. Collector current as a function of collector-to-base voltage for an n-p-n junction transistor in the common-base connection.

The collector current I_c depends on the collector voltage and emitter current in the manner shown in Fig. 21-19. As long as the collector voltage is sufficient to collect all of the minority carriers in the base that diffuse over to the collector junction, the collector current is virtually independent of the collector voltage, and has a value almost, but not quite, equal to the emitter current. The characteristic curves of Fig. 21-19 are seen to be very similar to those of Fig. 6-17, applying to a pentode tube. The only significant difference is that in the case of the transistor the collector current, rather than the combination of control-grid and screen-grid voltages, provides the running parameter for the different curves.

A transistor having the characteristics given in Figs. 21-18 and 21-19 is capable of power amplification. This can be understood with the aid of the circuit of Fig. 21-17b. Here a small signal voltage v_e superimposed on the emitter bias develops a current i_e in the low-resistance emitter circuit that controls a similar current $i_c \approx - i_e$ in the high-resistance collector circuit.   Since the load resistance R_L connected in the collector can easily be made high compared with the dynamic resistance of the emitter circuit, more power is developed in R_L by v_e than is represented by the input (emitter) current i_e; thus power amplification is achieved.

21-10. Details of Actions Taking Place in the Junction Triode Transistor.   *Carrier Movement and Current Flow.*   The general picture of carrier behavior and the resulting current flow in the junction triode transistor is given in Fig. 21-16.[1]   Conditions in the emitter region of an *n-p-n* junction transistor are shown in Fig. 21-16*b*.   These are exactly the same as in the corresponding forward-biased junction diode (see Fig. 21-13), and so need no further discussion.

In the base, the concentration of the minority carriers (electrons) adjacent to the emitter junction is the same as in the corresponding diode.   However, adjacent to the collector junction the concentration of minority carriers is very low because of the rapid withdrawal of the electrons from this region by the collector barrier field.   Since the base width w of the junction transistor is small compared with the diffusion length of the minority carriers in the base material, the concentration of the minority carriers in the base varies almost linearly, as indicated diagrammatically in Fig. 21-16*b*.   The concentration gradient of the minority carriers is hence roughly constant throughout the base at the value.

$$\begin{Bmatrix} \text{Concentration} \\ \text{gradient} \end{Bmatrix} = \frac{\begin{Bmatrix} \text{minority carrier concentration} \\ \text{at emitter junction} \end{Bmatrix}}{\text{width of base}} \qquad (21\text{-}23)$$

This gradient is high because the base is always made quite narrow.   As a result the minority carrier currents that flow in the base are primarily diffusion currents.

The important carriers in the collector region are the carriers (i.e., electrons in Fig. 21-16) received from the base, which by a combination of diffusion and drift travel through the collector material to the collector terminal.   The minority carriers (holes) behave the same as in the corresponding reverse-biased diode of Fig. 21-14.   However, the holes in the collector are of only secondary importance in the transistor operation.

The charge distributions shown in Fig. 21-16*b* cause the potential within the junction triode transistor to vary from emitter to collector terminals in the manner illustrated in Fig. 21-16*c*.   Nearly all of the voltages applied to the emitter and collector are consumed as voltage drops in the emitter and collector junctions, respectively, just as in the forward- and reverse-biased diodes, respectively, of Figs. 21-13 and 21-14.   The entire base is seen from Fig. 21-16*c* to be at about the same potential as

[1] In this figure it is to be noted that the emitter junction is shown as being very thin compared with the collector junction.   This is intentional, and is done to emphasize the difference in the thickness of the barrier region with forward and reverse bias.

the connection to the base; actually it is very slightly negative with respect to the base terminal because of the slight ohmic voltage drop associated with the drift of holes away from the base terminal.

Flow Diagram of Currents. The interrelations of the various currents in a junction transistor are pictured visually in the flow diagram of Fig. 21-16d. Here the conditions in the emitter are the same as in the n side of the forward-biased junction diode of Fig. 21-13. Remote from the emitter junction, the current is due entirely to the flow of electrons, whereas close to the junction a part I_e'' of the current is carried by the holes originating in the base, so that the electron current I_e' at the junction is less than the total emitter current.[1]

The current crossing the collector junction consists of one component I_c' which results from electrons that originate in the emitter and succeed in passing through the base to the collector, and of a second component (usually very small) consisting of the reverse saturation current I_s of the collector junction, which in the case of transistors is commonly called I_{co} (meaning collector current with zero emitter current). The first of these components represents the useful current flow in the transistor.

The current flowing in the lead to the base involves holes generated in the base material adjacent to the base lead in accordance with the mechanism described on page 742. The rate at which holes are thus generated, and hence the magnitude of the base current, equals the net loss of holes in the base material; this consists of the holes lost by recombination with electrons in the base, plus the holes lost by passage across the emitter junction, minus the holes obtained from the collector.[2] In practical situations the base current of the junction transistor will be very small[3] compared with the emitter and collector currents because (1) practically all of the current crossing the emitter junction is carried by majority carriers from the emitter, and (2) the base is so thin that only a very small fraction of these carriers are lost in the base by recombination.

Effect of Collector Voltage on the Properties of the Junction Triode Transistor.[4] Although the emitter and collector currents are largely independent of the collector voltage, they are not entirely so. This comes about from the fact that the thickness of the collector junction increases with collector voltage. Since any change in this thickness alters the effective

---

[1] The reverse saturation component of emitter current is ignored in Fig. 21-16d as being negligible compared with I_e.

[2] It might be thought that electrons from the emitter would be attracted directly to the base electrode. This effect is not much of a factor, however, since the narrowness of the base causes the base connection to be much more remote from most of the electrons in the base than is the collector junction.

[3] In Fig. 21-16d the current components I_e'' and I_{co} are both greatly exaggerated in order to make the figure legible.

[4] This treatment follows J. M. Early, Effects of Space-charge Layer Widening in Junction Transistors, *Proc. IRE*, vol. 40, p. 1401, November, 1952.

width of the base, the base width decreases slightly as the collector volt-age increases.   This in turn increases the gradient of the minority carriers in the base in accordance with Eq. (21-23), and so reduces the time required for diffusion across the base.   Thus, when the collector voltage is increased, the minority carriers in the base are less likely to be lost through recombination, and the collector current increases slightly.   For the same reason, the spacing between collector current curves for different emitter currents in Fig. 21-19 varies slightly with collector voltage.

The collector voltage also affects the emitter current, as indicated in Fig. 21-18.   This comes about from the fact that the increase in the base width associated with a larger absolute magnitude of the collector voltage increases the gradient of the electron concentration in the base.   This in turn increases the rate at which electrons diffuse toward the collector junction, and so decreases the number of electrons that diffuse from the edge of the base back into the emitter.   The result is therefore an increase in the emitter current.

Ratio of Collector to Emitter Current—Transistor Alpha.   For reasons that will become clear later, it is desirable that the ratio of collector to emitter current in a junction transistor be very close to unity.   Four factors cause the total collector current to differ from the emitter current.   First, only the part I'_e of the emitter current in Fig. 21-16d that is carried across the emitter junction by majority carriers of the emitter can con-tribute to the collector current.   This ratio I'_e/I_e is termed the *emitter efficiency*,[1] and can be made to approach unity by doping the emitter material much more heavily than the base material, as indicated by the conductivities given at the bottom of Fig. 21-16b.   A typical value of emitter efficiency is 0.99; in a given transistor the exact value varies slowly with collector voltage, but is independent of the emitter current.

The second factor affecting the ratio of collector to emitter current is loss of minority carriers in the base by recombination.   The fraction of the minority carriers that cross the base without recombining is termed the *transport factor*, and might be about 0.99 in a typical case.   The exact value will depend upon the width base, but in general the thinner the base and the lower the base conductivity, the closer will the value of the transport factor approach unity.

The third factor affecting the ratio of collector to emitter current arises from the fact that electrons crossing the collector junction modify the hole concentration in the collector region in such a manner as to increase the hole concentration gradient, and hence the hole current to the base.

---

[1] The emitter efficiency for the n-p-n transistor can be calculated with the aid of Eq. (21-21) provided that L_n in this equation is replaced by the base width w, in order to take into account the fact that the concentration gradient of minority carriers in the base in Fig. 21-16b is xy/w, whereas the corresponding gradient next to the junc-tion in Fig. 21-13b is xy/L_n.

The resulting *current multiplication factor* has a value that departs from unity by an amount that increases with the concentration of the minority carriers in the collector region. A typical value for a junction transistor is 1.003.

The fourth factor affecting the ratio of collector to emitter current is the reverse saturation current $I_{co} = I_s$. However, this component is usually so small as to be unimportant.

In transistor systems in which a small signal voltage is superimposed on the bias voltages as in Fig. 21-17b, a very important transistor characteristic is the so-called *alpha*, defined as[1]

$$\text{Alpha} = \alpha = -\left.\frac{\partial I_c}{\partial I_e}\right|_{V_c\text{ constant}} = -\left.\frac{i_c}{i_e}\right|_{\substack{V_c\text{ constant}\\(\text{that is, }v_c = 0)}} \qquad (21\text{-}24)$$

Here i_c is the *change* in collector current produced by a change i_e in emitter current when the collector voltage is held constant. It follows from the above discussion that α will approach closer to unity the higher the emitter efficiency, the thinner the base, and the lower the conductivity of the base material. The alpha will also increase slightly with increase in collector voltage as a result of the fact that the effective width of the base is slightly affected by collector voltage.

21-11. Small-signal Equations and Equivalent Circuits of the Transistor. *Voltage and Current Equations.* In many transistor applications a signal voltage (or current) of small amplitude is applied between two of the terminals, and it is desired to determine the currents and voltages that flow in the system in response to this signal. It is convenient to think of the signal and its resulting effects as being small alternating voltages and currents that are superimposed upon the d-c voltages and currents present in the transistor in the absence of the signal.

The small-signal theory of the transistor begins by regarding the transistor as a "black box" with two input and two output terminals, as illustrated in Fig. 21-20. One of the transistor terminals, the base in Fig. 21-20, is necessarily common to both input and output. Without knowing anything as to what is inside the black box of Fig. 21-20 except that it functions linearly with respect to small superimposed (or incremental) voltages and currents, one can from the principles of network theory write the following general functional relations:[2]

$$v_e = h_{11}i_e + h_{12}v_c \qquad (21\text{-}25a)$$
$$i_c = h_{21}i_e + h_{22}v_c \qquad (21\text{-}25b)$$

---

[1] The subscript $_0$ is commonly used to denote the value of α ($= \alpha_0$) at low and moderate frequencies where it is independent of frequency.

[2] The discussion given here is for low and moderate frequencies. Under these conditions the h coefficients are real quantities (i.e., they have no phase angle), and their magnitudes are independent of frequency. At higher frequencies the coefficients become frequency-dependent both with respect to magnitude and to phase; this is discussed below in Sec. 21-12.

Here v_e, v_c, i_e, and i_c are the superimposed or incremental voltages and currents associated with the emitter and collector electrodes, as illustrated in Fig. 21-20.   The h's are parameters that define the characteristics of the transistor to small voltages and currents superimposed upon the conditions established by the emitter and collector bias voltages; these coefficients have the following definitions:

$$h_{11} = \frac{\partial V_e}{\partial I_e}\bigg|_{V_c \text{ constant}} = \frac{v_e}{i_e}\bigg|_{v_c=0} \tag{21-26}$$

$$h_{22} = \frac{\partial I_c}{\partial V_c}\bigg|_{I_e \text{ constant}} = \frac{i_c}{v_c}\bigg|_{i_e=0} \tag{21-27}$$

$$h_{12} = \frac{\partial V_e}{\partial V_c}\bigg|_{I_e \text{ constant}} = \frac{v_e}{v_c}\bigg|_{i_e=0} \tag{21-28}$$

$$h_{21} = \frac{\partial I_c}{\partial I_e}\bigg|_{V_c \text{ constant}} = \frac{i_c}{i_e}\bigg|_{v_c=0} = -\alpha_0 \tag{21-29}$$

Here the V's and I's represent *total* voltages and currents, respectively, in accordance with Fig. 21-17a, whereas the lower-case letters denote superimposed (or incremental) values.

It follows from Eq. (21-26) that h_{11} is the dynamic resistance[1] of the emitter-base circuit when the collector voltage is constant; it is typically less than 100 ohms.   Similarly, Eq. (21-27) shows that h_{22} is the dynamic conductance (reciprocal of dynamic

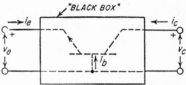

FIG. 21-20. The transistor regarded as the four-terminal "black box."

resistance) of the collector-base circuit for constant emitter current. Thus h_{22} is analogous to the reciprocal of the plate resistance of the vacuum tube.   The value of h_{22} is typically 0.5 to 5 μmhos, corresponding to a resistance of 2 to 0.2 megohm.

The coefficient h_{21} is the negative of the coefficient α_0 defined in Eq. (21-24), which is identical with Eq. (21-29).   Its absolute magnitude is nearly always just slightly less than unity in a junction transistor, and its sign is always negative.

The coefficient h_{12} accounts for the effect of the collector voltage on the emitter current.   It represents the relative effectiveness of the emitter and collector voltages in influencing the emitter current.

Values of the h parameters for a typical small junction transistor, such as would be used in a radio receiver or audio-frequency amplifier, are given in Table 21-1.

Small-signal Equivalent Circuits.[2]   The voltage and current relations

---

[1] The term dynamic resistance as applied to a transistor has the same meaning as in the case of vacuum tubes; i.e., it is the resistance to a small increment of applied voltage.

[2] Equivalent circuits all stem from the basic paper by L. C. Peterson, Equivalent

of Eqs. (21-25) can be represented by the equivalent input and output circuits of Fig. 21-21.

The circuit configuration of Fig. 21-21 is, however, not the only arrangement that will represent the voltage and current relation of Eqs. (21-25).

TABLE 21-1
CHARACTERISTICS OF A TYPICAL JUNCTION TRANSISTOR
$\alpha_0 = 0.98$ $f_\alpha = 1 \text{ M}_c$ $C_c = 10 \ \mu\mu\text{f}$

Coefficients for Eqs. (21-25) and Fig. 21-21	Coefficients for Eqs. (21-30) and Fig. 21-22	Coefficients for Eqs. (21-32) and Fig. 21-23	Coefficients for common-emitter circuit of Fig. 21-31b
$h_{11} = 30 \text{ ohms}$	$r_e = 20 \text{ ohms}$	$r'_e = 24 \text{ ohms}$	$r_e = 20 \text{ ohms}$
$h_{22} = 10^{-6} \text{ mho}^*$	$r_c = 10^6 \text{ ohms}^*$	$r'_c = 10^6 \text{ ohms}^*$	$r_c(1 - \alpha_0) = 20{,}000 \text{ ohms}$
$h_{12} = 5 \times 10^{-4}$	$r_b = 500 \text{ ohms}$	$r'_b = 300 \text{ ohms}$	$r_b = 500 \text{ ohms}$
$h_{21} = -0.98$	$a = 0.98$	$a = 0.98$	$a = 0.98$
		$m_0 = 2 \times 10^{-4}$	$\left.\begin{array}{l}\text{Current}\\ \text{gain}\end{array}\right\} = 49$

* Includes leakage over collector surface which is assumed to be directly in shunt with and hence a part of g'_c in Fig. 21-23b.

NOTE: The above are low-frequency values.

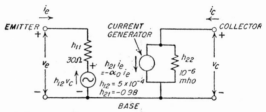

FIG. 21-21. A small-signal equivalent circuit of the transistor, showing typical circuit constants.

An alternative arrangement that finds considerable use is shown in Fig. 21-22a. Here r_e, r_b, and r_c are resistances, while ai_e is a current generator. As far as the terminals are concerned, this circuit is exactly equivalent to Fig. 21-21, and is an alternative way of representing Eq. (21-25), provided that the coefficients in Fig. 21-22a have the values

$$r_e = h_{11} - (1 + h_{21}) \frac{h_{12}}{h_{22}} \tag{21-30a}$$

$$r_b = \frac{h_{12}}{h_{22}} \tag{21-30b}$$

$$r_c = \frac{1 - h_{12}}{h_{22}} \approx \frac{1}{h_{22}} \tag{21-30c}$$

$$a = -\frac{h_{21} - h_{12}}{1 - h_{12}} \approx -h_{21} \approx \alpha_0 \tag{21-30d}$$

Numerical values of these parameters for a typical small junction triode transistor are given in Table 21-1, and are also indicated in Fig. 21-22a.

Current generators such as $h_{21}i_e$ in Fig. 21-21 and ai_e in Fig. 21-22a are imaginary devices that inject into the system a current having a value that is constant irrespective of changes in the constants of the associated circuits; they are also characterized by having infinite internal impedance. The combination of a current generator i shunted by a resistance r ($= 1/g$) can always, if desired, be replaced by the combination of a voltage generator ir in series with the resistance r, as explained in connection with Fig. 3-19c. This is done in Fig. 21-22, where the circuit at b is equivalent, in so far as the terminals are concerned, to the circuit at a. In this book the constant-current generator forms of the transistor equivalent circuit will be employed; however, the constant-voltage forms are equally satisfactory and are used in many articles on transistors.

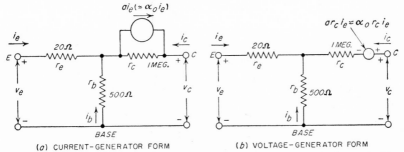

FIG. 21-22. Small-signal equivalent circuit of a transistor shown in the form of a T network, together with circuit values for the junction transistor of Table 21-1.

Equivalent Circuit Derived from Physical Processes of Transistor Operation. The equivalent circuits of Figs. 21-21 and 21-22 are derived from the general functional relation represented by Eqs. (21-25) and so are not directly correlated with the physical processes of the transistor. It is therefore instructive to see how an equivalent circuit can emerge from a consideration of the internal physics of the transistor.

A crude approximate circuit[1] is shown in Fig. 21-23a; this assumes that i_e is independent of the collector voltage, and that the collector current i_c has the value $-\alpha_0 i_e$ independently of the collector voltage or load impedance. The resistance r'_e in this figure is the dynamic resistance for the equivalent diode given by Eq. (21-22).

In Fig. 21-23b several refinements are introduced. The effect of the

---

[1] The voltages v_e and v'_c in Fig. 21-23a and b are the voltage drops developed internally across the emitter and collector junctions, respectively. These voltages *are not the same as the terminal voltages* v_e and v_c, because of the voltage $m_0 v'_c$ and the voltage drop in the base resistance r'_b.

collector voltage on the emitter current is taken into account by means of the voltage generator $m_0 v_c'$. Here v_c' is the voltage drop across the collector-base barrier, and differs only negligibly from the collector-base voltage v_c, while m_0 is a constant that depends on the base width and decreases slowly with increase in collector bias. A second refinement consists in placing a conductance g_c' (that is, resistance r_c') in shunt with

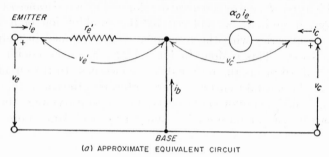

(a) APPROXIMATE EQUIVALENT CIRCUIT

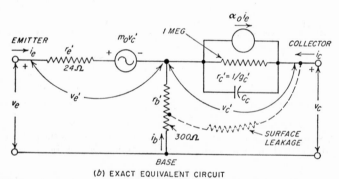

(b) EXACT EQUIVALENT CIRCUIT

FIG. 21-23. Small-signal equivalent circuit of a transistor derived from consideration of the physical processes taking place within the transistor, showing circuit constants for the junction transistor of Table 21-1.

the constant-current generator $\alpha_0 i_e$. This circuit element takes into account the fact, noted on page 764 in connection with Fig. 21-19, that with constant emitter current, the conductance that the collector-base circuit offers to an incremental applied voltage superimposed on the collector bias is low, but is not zero. This collector conductance[1] is defined as follows:

$$g_c' = \frac{\partial I_c}{\partial V_c}\bigg|_{I_e \text{ constant}} = -\frac{\partial(\alpha_0 I_e)}{\partial V_c} \approx -I_e \frac{\partial \alpha_0}{\partial V_c}\bigg|_{I_e \text{ constant}} \qquad (21\text{-}31)$$

[1] The conductance g_c' in Fig. 21-23b is the body conductance and does not include the surface leakage. The latter is always present to some degree, and places a high resistance from the collector terminal to some point on r_b', as shown dotted in Fig. 21-23b. The proper point of termination on r_b' may be anywhere from top to bottom, depending on where the leakage occurs. Because of surface leakage, measured values of collector conductance will generally be higher than theory would indicate.

Here α_0 is the transistor alpha as defined in Eq. (21-24). It follows from Eq. (21-31) that g_c' is proportional to the emitter current I_e, and to the rate of change of α_0 with collector voltage. Finally, Fig. 21-23b also shows a resistance r_b' in series with the base connection; this resistance takes into account the voltage drop occurring in the base as a result of the current flowing through the base material to the base terminal.

The circuit of Fig. 21-23b will be exactly equivalent to the circuits of Figs. 21-21a and 21-22 in so far as the voltage and current relations at the terminals are concerned, provided the following relations exist.

$$g_c' \approx h_{22} \tag{21-32a}$$
$$\alpha_0 \approx - h_{21} \tag{21-32b}$$
$$m_0 \approx h_{12} - g_c'r_b' = h_{12} - h_{22}r_b' \tag{21-32c}$$
$$r_e' \approx h_{11} - r_b'(1 - \alpha_0) = h_{11} - (1 - h_{21})r_b' \tag{21-32d}$$

The resistance r_b' is a fundamental parameter of the transistor, and can be measured directly in the manner described below in connection with Fig. 21-34f. Typical values for the circuit coefficients in Fig. 21-23b are given in Table 21-1, page 770.

The only difference in *form* between Figs. 21-22 and 21-23b is that the equivalent voltage generator m_0v_c' is absent in the former. This has been brought about by suitably modifying the coefficients r_e', r_b', g_c', and α_0 appearing in Fig. 21-23b so that their new values r_e, r_b, $r_c(= 1/g_c)$, and a in Fig. 21-22 take into account the effects produced by m_0v_c' in Fig. 21-23b. In this connection it is to be noted that since $g_c = g_c'$ and $a \approx \alpha_0$, only r_e and r_b are significantly affected by m_0v_c'.

21-12. High-frequency Effects in Junction Transistors.[1] In the above discussion, and also in the associated equivalent circuits of Figs. 21-21 to 21-23, it was assumed that conditions within the transistor responded instantly to changes in terminal voltages or currents; in addition the capacitances of the barriers were ignored. These approximations are permissible for d-c effects, at audio frequencies, and for the lower radio frequencies. However, as the frequency increases a point is finally reached where the capacitance of the collector junction must be taken into account, and where the time delay associated with the diffusion of current carriers is important. Transistors thus possess high-frequency limitations just as do vacuum tubes, and their equivalent circuits must be modified for high frequencies.

The capacitance of the collector barrier can be regarded as a shunt across the collector conductance g_c', as shown by C_c in Fig. 21-23b. For a small transistor this capacitance is of the order of 5 to 10 $\mu\mu f$ for a grown

[1] The treatment given here is based primarily on J. M. Early, Design Theory of Junction Transistors, *Bell System Tech. J.*, vol. 32, p. 1271, November, 1953; L. C. Giacoletto, Study of P-N-P Alloy Junction Transistor from D-C through Medium Frequencies, *RCA Rev.*, vol. **15,** p. 506, December, 1954.

junction, and 20 $\mu\mu f$ for a fused junction; the exact value will, however, decrease slowly with increase in collector voltage, as explained on page 751. Although a corresponding barrier capacitance is associated with the emitter junction, this can be ignored, because it is in shunt with a very low resistance.

Alpha Cutoff Frequency and Related Transit-time Effects. Because it takes time for minority carriers to diffuse across the base, the conditions inside the transistor are unable to follow the variations of a very high-frequency signal in the manner they would follow the variations of a low-frequency signal of the same amplitude. In particular, at very high frequencies a substantial fraction of the current carriers emitted into the base

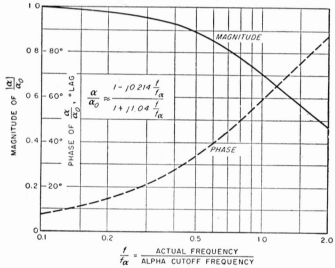

Fig. 21-24. Variation of transistor alpha as a function of frequency.

fail to reach the collector junction before the polarity of the applied signal reverses. As a result numerous carriers get trapped in the base material, and take an abnormally long time to reach the collector junction, with consequent increase in loss from recombination. This causes the alpha of the transistor to decrease in magnitude and to acquire a phase shift. At the same time and for the same reasons the coefficients m_0 and g_c' in Fig. 21-23b also fall off in magnitude and acquire a phase shift at high frequencies. The situation is analogous to that occurring in a vacuum tube under conditions where the transit time of the electrons is not negligible when compared with the time of a cycle, as discussed in Sec. 6-15.

Theory verified by experiment shows that the transistor alpha varies with frequency in the manner shown in Fig. 21-24; a mathematical law that is reliable until α/α_0 drops to about 0.4 is given in the figure. The frequency at which the magnitude of the alpha is 70.7 per cent of the value

α_0 applicable at low frequencies is termed the *alpha cutoff frequency*, and is designated as f_α. At the alpha cutoff frequency, the phase angle approximates 58°. It is to be noted that up to frequencies several times f_α the value of alpha varies with frequency in much the same manner as does the high-frequency response of a resistance-coupled amplifier, as presented in Fig. 8-9, with f_α corresponding to the 70.7 per cent (3 db) point. The value of the alpha cutoff frequency increases with decrease in the width of the base, and is independent of emitter and collector bias

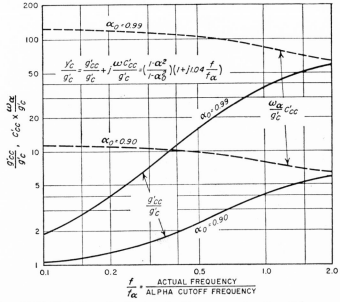

FIG. 21-25. Variation of collector admittance as a function of frequency.

voltages. Typical values of f_α for a small junction transistor are in the range 0.5 to 3 Mc.

The m_0 coefficient in Fig. 21-23 that takes into account the effect of the collector voltage upon the emitter current is affected by frequency in exactly the same way as is the transistor alpha, and is hence also given by Fig. 21-24.

At high frequencies, conductance g_c' in Fig. 21-23b becomes an admittance y_c' having a magnitude and phase angle that depend on the ratio f/f_α of actual frequency to alpha cutoff frequency in the manner shown in Fig. 21-25. This admittance y_c' can be regarded as a conductance g_{cc}' shunted by a capacitance C_{cc}'. The values of g_{cc}' and C_{cc}' are not constant, however, but vary with frequency as shown in Fig. 21-25, which shows that g_{cc}' is particularly sensitive to frequency and has increased by a large factor at $f = f_\alpha$.

Equivalent Transistor Circuits for High Frequencies. When the above effects are taken into account, the low-frequency equivalent circuit of Fig. 21-23b takes the form shown in Fig. 21-26 when the applied signal is a high frequency. Here α and m denote the high-frequency values of the coefficients α_0 and m_0, respectively, that appear in the low-frequency circuit of Fig. 21-23b, and the high-frequency collector admittance y_c' is a

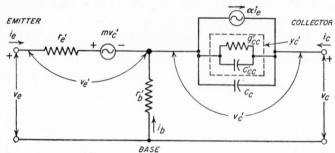

Fig. 21-26. Equivalent transistor circuit of Fig. 21-23b modified to take into account frequency effects.

conductance-capacitance[1] combination as discussed above. The collector barrier capacity C_c shunts the collector admittance y_c' as shown in Fig. 21-26; its value is independent of frequency, as are likewise the resistances r_e' and r_b' of Fig. 21-26.

While Fig. 21-26 is the high-frequency equivalent of Fig. 21-23, it is also possible by appropriate transformations of Fig. 21-26 to derive high-frequency forms of Figs. 21-21 and 21-22.

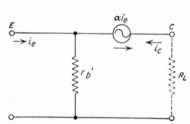

Fig. 21-27. Simple small-signal equivalent circuit of transistor applicable when the input terminal E is associated with a high-impedance source and the load resistance R_L is small compared with the collector resistance r_c' ($= 1/g_c'$).

The equivalent circuit of Fig. 21-26 can be simplified in certain situations. For example, if the source resistance from which the emitter current is derived is high then r_e' and $m_0 v_c'$ can be omitted. If in addition, the collector load resistance R_L is small compared with r_c' ($= 1/g_c'$) then the collector admittance y_c' and the barrier capacitance C_c can also be omitted, and the resulting equivalent circuit reduces to Fig. 21-27.

A different type of simplification is possible when the load resistance is high enough so that the parallel resistance $R_L r_c'/(R_L + r_c')$ formed by the load resistance R_L and the low-frequency collector resistance r_c' ($= 1/g_c'$) is much greater than the reactance $1/2\pi f_a C_c$ of the barrier capacitance at

---

[1] This capacitance is different from, and in addition to, the barrier capacitance C_c and it is usually very much smaller. Also, unlike the barrier capacitance, its magnitude is frequency-dependent, as shown in Fig. 21-25.

the alpha cutoff frequency.   The principal effect of frequency up to about $f = 0.5f_\alpha$ is then produced by the barrier capacitance, and the equivalent circuit simplifies to that shown in Fig. 21-28a.   The capacitance C_c in this circuit reduces the current through the load resistance R_L, because some of the current from the generator $\alpha_0 i_e$ that would go through the load resistance R_L at lower frequencies is now by-passed through the capacitance C_c.   When the equivalent circuit of Fig. 21-28a is transformed into a circuit of the type represented by Fig. 21-22, the result is as shown[1] in Fig. 21-28b.   This arrangement is more useful than Fig. 21-28a for studying the behavior of the transistor as viewed from the terminals,

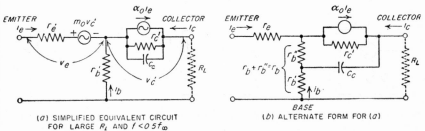

(a) SIMPLIFIED EQUIVALENT CIRCUIT FOR LARGE R_L AND $f < 0.5f_\infty$

(b) ALTERNATE FORM FOR (a)

FIG. 21-28. Simplification of the equivalent circuit of Fig. 21-23, applicable when the load resistance R_L in parallel with r_c' $(=1/g_c')$ forms a resistance that is much greater than the reactance of the barrier capacitance C_c at the alpha cutoff frequency.

since it avoids the generator $m_0 v_c'$ in the emitter circuit.   This circuit shows that for high load resistances at frequencies somewhat below the alpha cutoff frequency, the barrier capacitance C_c not only provides a path that shunts the collector resistance, but likewise causes the effective base resistance to have the value r_b' at the higher frequencies, and the value $r_b = r_b' + r_b''$ at low frequencies, where r_b and r_b' are as discussed above.

21-13. Common-emitter and Common-collector Connections for Transistors.   The discussion of transistors up to this point has assumed that the base terminal was common to both input (emitter) and output (collector) circuits; this is termed the *grounded-base* or *common-base* connection.   It is possible, however, for either the emitter or the collector to be the common electrode, leading to the *grounded-emitter* and *grounded-collector* circuits (or *common-emitter* and *common-collector* circuits), respectively, shown in Fig. 21-29b and c.   These circuits correspond to the grounded-cathode and grounded-plate (cathode-follower) connections of a triode tube, as shown at e and f, respectively, whereas the common-base transistor arrangement is analogous to a grounded-grid triode.

Common-emitter Circuit.   The transistor of Fig. 21-19 has the voltage-current characteristics given in Fig. 21-30 when operated in the common

[1] Note that this circuit still assumes that the frequency is appreciably below f_α but is still high enough so that the reactance of C_c cannot be neglected in comparison with $R_L r_c'/(R_L + r_c')$.

emitter circuit. Here the base current I_b is chosen as the running parameter, since the base is now the input electrode. Comparison of Figs. 21-19 and 21-30 shows that the collector voltage-current characteristic for constant input current has higher slope than in the common-emitter

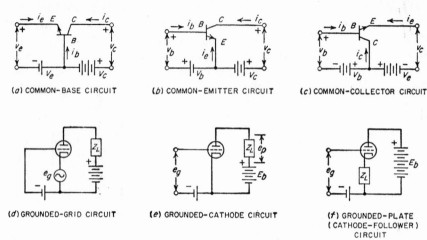

(a) COMMON-BASE CIRCUIT (b) COMMON-EMITTER CIRCUIT (c) COMMON-COLLECTOR CIRCUIT

(d) GROUNDED-GRID CIRCUIT (e) GROUNDED-CATHODE CIRCUIT (f) GROUNDED-PLATE
(CATHODE-FOLLOWER)
CIRCUIT

Fig. 21-29. Common-emitter and common-collector transistor circuits, together with the analogous vacuum-tube circuits. The battery polarities shown are appropriate for an n-p-n transistor.

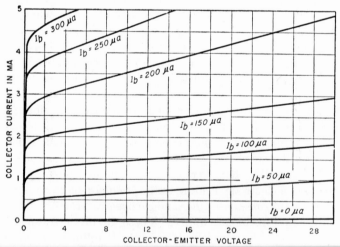

Fig. 21-30. Collector voltage-current curves of the junction transistor of Fig. 21-19 when the emitter is the common electrode.

case, denoting significantly lower output resistance. Also it is to be noted that output current I_c is considerably greater than the input current I_b; this is to be expected because the base current is the difference between the emitter and collector currents, and the latter two currents are almost equal.

Small-signal equivalent circuits for the common-emitter connection are obtained by rearranging the common-base circuits. Thus when the emitter is common to both input and output, Fig. 21-22 takes the form shown in Fig. 21-31a. The usefulness of this circuit can be increased by expressing the current generator in terms of the input current i_b instead of the emitter current i_e; this leads to the equivalent circuit of Fig.

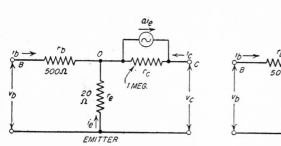

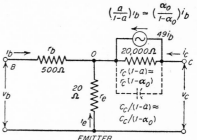

(a) COMMON-EMITTER EQUIVALENT
CIRCUIT BASED ON FIG 21-22

(b) MODIFIED FORM OF (a), IN WHICH
CURRENT GENERATOR IS IN TERMS OF i_b

(c) STEPS IN TRANSFORMATION OF OC IN (a) TO OC IN (b)

FIG. 21-31. Equivalent circuits for the common-emitter connection analogous to the common-base equivalent circuit of Fig. 21-22, showing circuit constants for the junction transistor of Table 21-1.

21-31b. The arm OC in Fig. 21-31a is transformed to the arm OC in Fig. 21-31b by the series of steps indicated in Fig. 21-31c wherein the current generator is converted into a voltage generator at 2, and then, after a series of steps in which voltage generator $-r_c a i_b$ opposing current i_c is replaced by resistance $a r_c$, is converted back to a current generator at 5.

Comparison of Figs. 21-31b and 21-22 shows that since a ($\approx \alpha_0$ at low frequencies) is only slightly less than unity, the current of the current generator is considerably greater than i_b. This *current gain* is

$$\text{Current gain} = \left| \frac{a i_e}{i_b} \right| = \frac{a}{1-a} \approx \frac{\alpha}{1-\alpha} \qquad (21\text{-}33)$$

When α is close to 1.0 the current gain will be very high. At the same time, the equivalent collector resistance (i.e., the resistance in arm OC of Fig. 21-31b) is corresponding by less than in the common-base case, the relation being

$$\left. \begin{array}{l} \text{Equivalent collector resistance} \\ \text{for common-emitter case} \\ \hline \text{Collector resistance for} \\ \text{common-base case} \end{array} \right\} = \frac{r_c(1-a)}{r_c} = 1 - a \approx 1 - \alpha \qquad (21\text{-}34)$$

Numerical data for a typical junction transistor are given in Table 21-1 and Fig. 21-31b.

An important consequence of Eqs. (21-33) and (21-34) is that the current gain, the effective collector resistance, and indeed the static characteristics of Fig. 21-30 are all quite sensitive to changes in the value of α because $1 - \alpha$ is very small. Since it is impossible at the present time to manufacture transistors in quantity which have exactly the same value of α_0, the effective terminal characteristics of transistors tend to be much more variable among transistors of the same type when the common-emitter connection is employed, as compared with the common-base connection.

The sensitivity of the common-emitter circuit to the value of α also causes frequency to have a considerable effect even at frequencies far below the alpha cutoff frequency. Thus for the transistor in Table 21-1, the current gain will drop to 70 per cent of the value at low frequencies when the frequency[1] is $0.016 f_\alpha$, and at $f = f_\alpha$ will be $0.83\underline{/-101°}$ instead of the low-frequency value of 49, and so has fallen nearly to the common-base value for $f = f_\alpha$. However, by way of partial compensation, the collector impedance is much less sensitive to frequency in the common-emitter case. With the transistor of Table 21-1 in the common-emitter connection the collector impedance at the alpha cutoff frequency f_α is $0.92\underline{/-23°}$ times the low-frequency value $r_c(1 - \alpha_0)$, whereas for the common-base case the corresponding factor is $0.0217\underline{/-66°}$.

When the load resistance connected between collector and emitter is very high, the barrier capacitance is of importance at frequencies well below the alpha cutoff value. This effect is taken into account by assuming that a capacitance $C_c/(1 - a) \approx C_c/(1 - \alpha)$, where C_c is the collector barrier capacitance, is shunted across the collector resistance, as shown dotted in Fig. 21-31b.

In spite of these frequency effects, the common-emitter connection is very widely used in practical transistor circuits. This is because of its high current gain, and the smaller disparity between impedance levels of the input and output circuits as compared with the common-base circuit. These features greatly simplify the design of the circuits associated with the transistor.

The close relationship between the grounded-emitter transistor circuit and the grounded-cathode circuit of a triode tube is brought out by converting the T circuit of Fig. 21-31b to the π circuit of Fig. 21-32. This is a straightforward mathematical transformation, with the necessary relations shown in the figure, which also gives numerical values for the transistor of Table 21-1. It will be noted the resistance r_{bc} in this circuit is so high that it can be regarded as an open circuit without introducing

---

[1] This result is obtained by substituting the expression for α given in Fig. 21-24 for α in Eq. (21-33).

appreciable error. When this simplification is introduced, the system becomes analogous to the grounded-cathode triode circuit of Fig. 21-29e when the tube is operated with a positive grid bias so that the grid-cathode resistance (corresponding to r_{be} in Fig. 21-32) has a finite value. Notable is the fact that g_m in Fig. 21-32 is considerably higher than the corresponding g_m of a typical small triode or pentode.

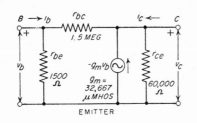

$$r_{be} = \frac{\Delta}{r_c(1-a)} \approx \frac{\Delta}{r_c(1-\alpha)}$$

$$r_{bc} = \frac{\Delta}{r_e} \qquad r_{ce} = \frac{\Delta}{r_b}$$

$$g_m = \frac{\alpha r_c}{\Delta} \approx \frac{\alpha r_c}{\Delta}$$

$$\Delta = r_e r_b + r_e r_c + r_b r_c(1-a)$$
$$\approx r_e r_b + r_e r_c + r_b r_c(1-\alpha)$$
$$\approx r_c[r_e + r_b(1-\alpha)] \dots \text{FOR JUNCTION TYPE}$$

(a) π EQUIVALENT OF FIG. 21-31(b)

(b) EQUATIONS FOR CONVERTING FROM FIG. 21-31(b) TO (a)

FIG. 21-32. Equivalent π form of the common-emitter equivalent circuit of Fig. 21-31b, showing circuit constants for the junction transistor of Table 21-1.

Common-collector Connection. When the common-emitter circuit of Fig. 21-31b is rearranged to give a common-collector connection, the resulting equivalent circuit is that shown in Fig. 21-33. Numerical values for the transistor of Table 21-1 are indicated on the figure. It is seen that the common-collector circuit is notable for the very low impedance level that it presents at its output (emitter) terminals. In this respect the common-collector transistor circuit resembles the triode cathode-follower circuit.

The effect of frequency on the behavior of the common-collector connection is accounted for almost entirely by the variation of $(1 - \alpha)$ with frequency. The common-collector circuit is most useful at low frequencies, where it can combine the unique function of power amplification with simultaneous impedance transformation between a moderate input-impedance level and a very low output-impedance level.

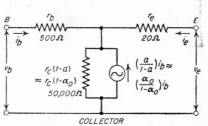

FIG. 21-33. Equivalent circuit for the common-collector connection, showing circuit constants for the junction transistor of Table 21-1.

21-14. Measurement of Transistor Characteristics.[1] The h parameters appearing in Eq. (21-25), and giving the small-signal behavior of the

[1] The argument for measuring the h parameters of Fig. 21-21 instead of the r parameters of Fig. 21-22 is presented by G. Knight, R. A. Johnson, and R. B. Holt, Measurement of the Small Signal Parameters of Transistors, *Proc. IRE*, vol. 41, p. 983, August, 1953.

transistor, can be readily measured by direct use of Eqs. (21-26) to (21-29). The necessary circuit arrangements are given in Fig. 21-34. In all of these circuits, the emitter bias is supplied by an adjustable voltage through impedance RL that is high at the test-oscillator frequency

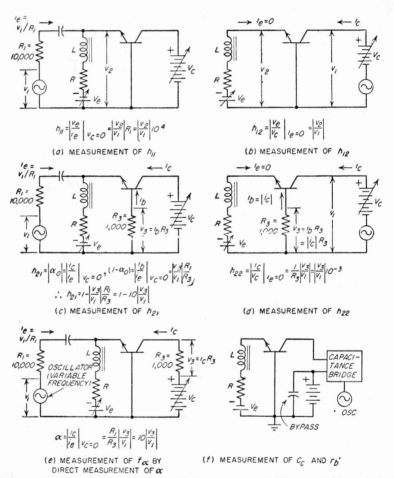

Fig. 21-34. Circuit arrangements suitable for measuring the fundamental small-signal equivalent-circuit parameters of a transistor.

compared with the input resistance of the emitter electrode, while the collector bias voltage is obtained from an adjustable voltage having an internal impedance low compared with the collector resistance.[1] Known values of a-c emitter current i_e are produced by applying a known voltage

---

[1] It is also convenient for the d-c resistances of emitter and collector bias supplies to be high and low, respectively, in order that there be no interaction in the adjustments of I_e and V_e.

v_1 from the test oscillator[1] to the emitter through a resistance R_1 that is high compared with the emitter resistance. Under these conditions $i_e = v_1/R_1$, where R_1 is typically 10,000 ohms. Currents flowing to a particular electrode are measured as the drop v_3 across a series resistance R_3 that is low enough not to affect the voltages or currents involved in the measurement; in Fig. 21-34c and d, R_3 must be small compared with the collector resistance, and can conveniently be 1000 ohms.

The alpha cutoff frequency f_α can be measured by the circuit arrangement shown in Fig. 21-34e; one simply increases the frequency of the test oscillator while keeping v_1 constant, until v_3 diminishes to 70.7 per cent of its low-frequency value. This circuit could also be used instead of Fig. 21-34c to measure $h_{21} = -\alpha_0$ directly, but has much less accuracy when α_0 is nearly unity.

The barrier capacitance C_c of the collector junction can be determined by taking advantage of the fact, shown in Fig. 21-22, that if the emitter is open-circuited $(i_e = 0)$, the output impedance on the collector side consists of C_c in parallel[2] with the high resistance r_c. The problem is thus one of determining the capacitance component of a parallel resistance-capacitance circuit, a task which can be accomplished with a standard commercial capacitance bridge arranged as shown in Fig. 21-34f, and operating at a frequency such as 1000 cycles.

The base resistance r_b' of Figs. 21-23 and 21-28b, which is essential to numerical calculations using Eqs. (21-32), can be measured with the apparatus arrangement shown in Fig. 21-34f, using a frequency as high as possible, such as 100 kc to 1 Mc, so that $\omega C_c >> g_c'$. Under this condition g_c' can be neglected, and the impedance Z_c'' observed by the bridge is seen from Figs. 21-23 and 21-28b to be due to r_b' in series with C_c, that is,

$$Z_c'' = r_b' + 1/j\omega C_c$$

Hence r_b' is the real part of the experimentally observed value of Z_c''.

The static voltage-current characteristics of the transistor are preferably obtained by "sweeping" techniques, using a cathode-ray tube display. This is because some of the transistor characteristics depend critically upon temperature, which makes it unwise to obtain point-by-point static characteristics in the higher-current regions.

21-15. Improved Junction Transistors for High Frequencies. The high-frequency limitations of the junction transistor result from a combination of three causes: (1) the barrier capacitance of the collector junction, (2) alpha cutoff; and (3) premature alpha cutoff due to r_b' in Fig. 21-23.

---

[1] The test oscillator preferably operates at a frequency of the order of 1000 cycles, except in the measurement of r_b', as discussed below.

[2] The combination is in series with r_b, but at a test frequency such as 1000 cycles the reactance of C_c is so large that r_b can be ignored.

When high-frequency considerations are important, the base resistance r_b in Fig. 21-22 should be as low as possible. This is because it can be shown that in an amplifier circuit such as Fig. 21-17b (or Fig. 21-40) the amplification will fall off more rapidly with frequency if r_b is increased while leaving all other circuit constants unchanged.[1]

The collector capacitance can be reduced by decreasing the junction area, but fabrication difficulties limit how far one may go in this direction.

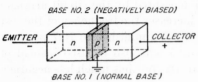

BASE NO. 2 (NEGATIVELY BIASED)

EMITTER

COLLECTOR

BASE NO. 1 (NORMAL BASE)

Fig. 21-35. Junction-tetrode transistor.

The collector capacitance can also be reduced by reducing the conductivity of the base and collector regions. However, reducing the base conductivity has the disadvantage that it increases the base resistance r_b in Fig. 21-22 (or r_b' in Fig. 21-23b), which is a step in the wrong direction; also reducing the collector conductivity is possible only in the grown junction type of transistor.

The alpha cutoff frequency f_α can be raised by reducing the base thickness. This, however, also increases the base resistance r_b' by decreasing the cross-sectional area through which the base current flows.

It is thus apparent that the obvious steps that will reduce the collector capacitance or increase the alpha cutoff frequency also increase the undesirable effects due to r_b'. Conversely, steps taken to reduce r_b', such as increasing the conductivity of the base material, or increasing the base thickness, have an unfavorable result on both C_c and f_α.

Junction Tetrode.[2] The conflict between the various factors that contribute to the high-frequency performance of a junction transistor is greatly reduced in the transistor structure illustrated in Fig. 21-35. This is called a *junction tetrode*, and is essentially a junction triode in which there are terminal connections to the opposite sides of the base, as illustrated. One of these connections serves as the normal base electrode, while a d-c bias is supplied to the second base terminal with such polarity as to force the emitter-to-collector current down into a very small region in the immediate vicinity (typically less than 1 mil) of connection 1. This is equivalent to converting a transistor large enough to be fabricated into a transistor having a very much smaller effective cross section. The principal advantage that results is that the base resistance r_b' in Fig. 21-23b

---

[1] Thus in Eq. (21-35) below, if frequency is taken into account by replacing α_0 by α, and r_c by $1/g_c'$, then it is apparent that the increase in the denominator with increasing frequency is larger the greater r_b, whereas if $r_b = 0$ the denominator is most nearly independent of frequency. Thus the tendency for the amplification in the common-emitter circuit to fall off with increasing frequency is greater the higher the value of r_b. It can be demonstrated that the common-base amplifier of Fig. 21-17 behaves similarly with respect to r_b.

[2] See R. L. Wallace, L. G. Schimpf, and E. Deckten, A Junction Transistor Tetrode for High-frequency Use, *Proc. IRE*, vol. 40, p. 1395, November, 1952.

can be kept low even though a very thin lightly doped base giving a high f_α is used. It is possible in this way to improve the useful frequency range by a factor of the order of 10 times.

The p-n-i-p Junction Triode Transistor.[1] A transistor structure offering great possibilities for improved high-frequency performance is the *p-n-i-p* arrangement shown in Fig. 21-36 (or its counterpart the *n-p-i-n* structure). The principal features here are a base region which is very thin and which has high conductivity[2] (heavily doped), but which is separated from the collector by a relatively thick layer of intrinsic material. The effect of the intrinsic layer is equivalent to increasing greatly the thickness of the base-collector transition region. This reduces the effective base-collector barrier capacitance C_c, while making it possible simultaneously to increase the base conductivity to the point where the base resistance r_b' is very low even when the base is made very thin in order to achieve a

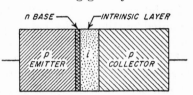

FIG. 21-36. The *p-n-i-p* triode-transistor structure.

high alpha cutoff frequency. An additional advantage of this arrangement is that it reduces the variation of base thickness with collector voltage; hence the output admittance y_c' and the voltage mv_c' in Fig. 21-26 can become almost negligible.

The low conductivity of the intrinsic material in Fig. 21-36 produces a large voltage drop across this layer and a substantial electric field within it. This is no particular disadvantage, however, since it can be compensated for by increasing the collector bias voltage correspondingly. Although the intrinsic material has low conductivity, the carriers from the base still cross it as a result of drift action induced by the electric field. Very few carriers are lost in the intrinsic material due to recombination because of the low concentration there of carriers of the opposite type.

21-16. Point-contact Diodes. A diode comprising a semiconductor crystal and a small-area metal contact was previously introduced in Sec. 16-14. The discussion here will correlate the behavior of such a point-contact diode with that of the *p-n* junction diode.

The physical structure of the point-contact diode is illustrated in Fig. 16-23a, and a typical voltage-current curve is shown in Fig. 16-23c.[3] The

---

[1] J. M. Early, P-N-I-P and N-P-I-N Junction Transistor Triodes, *Bell System Tech. J.*, vol. 33, p. 517, May, 1954.

[2] The emitter efficiency is still kept high by doping the emitter even more heavily than the base.

[3] This characteristic corresponds to that obtained with a polycrystalline silicon crystal. If a single-crystal semiconductor is used, it is possible to obtain a much lower reverse current. The basic action of the polycrystal and single-crystal point-contact diode is believed to be essentially the same, however.

reverse current characteristic is not as good as for the junction diode, but on the other hand, the junction capacitance is very much smaller.

The behavior of the point-contact diode can be interpreted as though it were a junction diode with special geometry. This comes about because it appears that the electrical "forming" process used in manufacture, in which a surge of current is pulsed through the diode, produces a small p region directly under the metal point when an n-type semiconductor is used. According to this hypothesis, one thus obtains a p-n junction of extremely small area associated with the metal point.

When the applied voltage is in the forward direction, the combination of point contact and associated p-n junction represents a low resistance shunted by the barrier capacitance, which correspond, respectively, to R and C in Fig. 16-23b. In addition, there is a spreading resistance R which takes into account the resistance of the base region to the majority carriers. This latter is negligible in the p-n junction diode, but must be shown here since the small area of the junction causes the current to be constricted into a region of extremely small cross-sectional area.

When a reverse voltage is applied to the point-contact diode only a very small current flows, and the resistance r in Fig. 16-23b is quite large. The most important circuit element then becomes the barrier capacitance C. This capacitance is much smaller than in the junction diode because of the very small junction area, which is a great advantage in high-frequency circuits.

The reverse current of a point-contact diode is not independent of reverse voltage to the same degree as in the junction diode. This results from a combination of circumstances: (1) Rather intense electric fields are developed in the immediate vicinity of the very sharp contact point; (2) the ohmic drop is of importance in the reverse direction because of the small cross section, so that carriers tend to travel by drift rather than by diffusion; and (3) the concentration of minority carriers is not necessarily always small compared with that of the majority carriers in the immediate vicinity of the point, where the cross-sectional area is very small.

Point-contact diodes can employ either silicon or germanium. The silicon diode finds extensive use at microwave frequencies as detectors and mixers, where its higher resistance more readily matches that of the associated circuit. The germanium point-contact diode is, however, desirable where very low forward resistance and very small reverse current are important, and finds use as second detectors, as diode clampers, in switching circuits, etc. In contrast, the principal use of the germanium junction diode is as a power rectifier.

21-17. The Point-contact Transistor.[1] The point-contact transistor is a logical extension of the point-contact diode, and can be thought of as

[1] Although the point-contact transistor was originated before the junction transistor, it is being superseded by the latter in most applications. As a result, and also because

a sort of junction transistor with special geometry which leads to very significant differences in the electrical behavior.

In the point-contact transistor two sharply pointed tungsten electrodes are placed very close together on the surface of a small wafer of single crystal germanium, usually n type, as shown in Fig. 21-37a. In order to make a good transistor it is found necessary to form the transistor by passing a current through the electrodes in the manufacturing process.

A very qualitative understanding of the way in which a point-contact transistor operates can be obtained by assuming that there exists a small p region underneath each of the points, as illustrated in Fig. 21-37b. This results in a sort of p-n-p system, analogous to that of the junction triode,

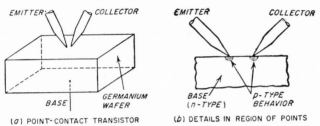

(a) POINT-CONTACT TRANSISTOR   (b) DETAILS IN REGION OF POINTS

FIG. 21-37. The point-contact transistor, showing the general character of the structure, together with details of conditions existing in the immediate vicinity of the points.

but differing in that the geometry converges down to a point. As a result, there are both similarities and differences between point-contact and junction transistors.

Emphasizing first the similarities rather than the differences, it is to be noted that one of the point contacts serves as the emitter electrode, while the other serves as the collector electrode, and the main body of semiconducting material represents the base. As in the junction type, the emitter and the collector are biased, respectively, in the forward and the reverse directions. The conventions as to symbols, polarities, etc., are the same for both types of transistors.

Typical curves giving collector current as a function of collector voltage are shown in Fig. 21-38. These are seen to be generally similar to the corresponding curves of Fig. 21-19 for the junction case, except that the collector current with zero emitter current is now greater, and the curves have a greater slope, corresponding to a lower output resistance. The small-signal equivalent circuit of Fig. 21-22 gives the low-frequency behavior of the point-contact transistor equally as well as it does for the junction transistor. The characteristics of a typical small point-contact

the theory of the junction transistor is clean-cut, whereas there is less understanding as to the details involved in the internal operation of the point-contact transistor, emphasis in this chapter is placed on the junction type. At the same time, the point-contact transistor has certain unique characteristics, notably an alpha greater than unity, and as a result can be expected to have a continued though limited use.

transistor are given in Table 21-2, together with the characteristics of a comparable junction type.

Several additional differences between the point-contact and junction transistors are brought out in Table 21-2. First, it will be noted the r_e is larger for the point-contact transistor; this is another manifestation of the higher forward resistance of the point-contact diode compared with

TABLE 21-2
COMPARISON OF COEFFICIENTS OF TYPICAL POINT-CONTACT
AND JUNCTION TRANSISTORS FOR EQUIVALENT CIRCUIT OF FIG. 21-22

	Junction*	Point-contact
r_e	20 ohms	150 ohms
r_c	10^6 ohms	15,000 ohms
r_b	500 ohms	120 ohms
$a\ (\approx \alpha_0)$	0.98	2.5

* From Table 21-1.

that of the junction diode. Second, the base resistance r_b is much lower for the point-contact transistor, a result principally of the geometry which permits the base current to spread into a large volume of material in the point-contact case, as contrasted to the junction case, where the base is uniformly thin. Thirdly, the collector resistance r_c is much lower in the case of the point-contact transistor, as represented by the greater slope of the static characteristic curves of Fig. 21-38. This is related to the failure of the reverse current to remain constant in the point-contact diode.

Finally, and quite importantly, it is to be noted that the alpha of the point-contact transistor is greater than unity; typical values lie in the range 1 to 5. This means that for each milliampere increase in the emitter current, the collector current will increase by more than 1 ma, as is apparent from a close examination of the spacings of the curves in Fig. 21-38. A search for a simple explanation of this collector multiplication action is an elusive one, and it will be sufficient for this treatment to acknowledge that the high concentrations of minority carriers and the high electric fields existing in the immediate vicinity of the points introduce differences such that the simple junction transistor theory that limits alpha to unity or slightly less no longer applies.

From the circuit standpoint, the fact that alpha is greater than unity is sometimes an advantage and sometimes a disadvantage. For example, when $\alpha_0 > 1$, a negative resistance can appear between any pair of transistor terminals, as for example between emitter and base in the common-base connection. This introduces the possibility of self-oscillation, which can be utilized as will be seen later to provide simple sine-wave oscillators.   On the other hand, the possibility of oscillation frequently proves to be a disadvantage in the design of stable amplifiers.

So far as the operation at high frequencies is concerned, the point-contact transistor possesses certain advantages over the junction type. First, because of the smaller junction area, the internal capacitance C_c tends to be smaller; second, the alpha cutoff frequency tends to be higher; finally, as mentioned above, the base resistance r_b is lower.   Point-contact transistors have been made to amplify at frequencies up to 100 Mc, which is far beyond the range of the junction triode.   However,

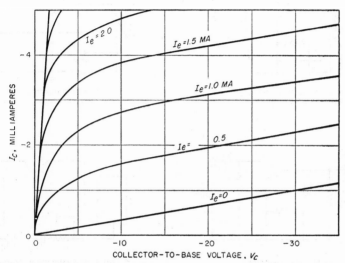

FIG. 21-38. A typical collector voltage-current characteristic of a point-contact transistor in the common-base connection.   These curves are to be compared with those of Fig. 21-19 for the junction transistor.

the advent of the junction tetrode and the p-n-i-p triode will probably enable junction devices to take over the high-frequency field as well.

21-18. Transistor Applications.   *Small-signal Amplifiers.*   Transistors are particularly suitable for the amplification of small signals because of their small size, low power requirements, and particularly the absence of cathode heating power.   Already many more amplifier arrangements have been devised than can be described here.   Accordingly the attention will be centered on a few simple examples of transistor amplifiers that illustrate certain considerations important in the design of all transistor amplifier circuits.   These examples are shown in Fig. 21-39, and include transformer and resistance-capacitance coupled audio-frequency amplifiers employing a common emitter, and a tuned amplifier in a common-base circuit.

The method of obtaining bias voltages and currents is of considerable practical importance.   In particular, the bias arrangement should recognize that the small-signal behavior depends upon the collector bias *voltage* and the emitter bias *current*. The collector voltage supply should therefore have a low internal resistance, so that the collector voltage is relatively independent of the collector current. Correspondingly, the emitter current supply should have a high internal resistance so that the emitter bias current is relatively independent of the exact value of the emitter resistance.

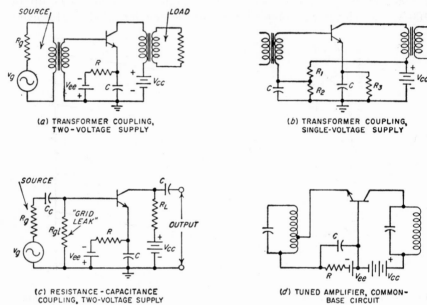

(a) TRANSFORMER COUPLING, TWO-VOLTAGE SUPPLY

(b) TRANSFORMER COUPLING, SINGLE-VOLTAGE SUPPLY

(c) RESISTANCE-CAPACITANCE COUPLING, TWO-VOLTAGE SUPPLY

(d) TUNED AMPLIFIER, COMMON-BASE CIRCUIT

FIG. 21-39. Typical audio-frequency and transistor amplifier circuits, showing different methods of applying bias voltages.

A straightforward biasing arrangement is shown in Fig. 21-39a, where the collector supply V_{cc} is connected as directly as possible between collector and base, while the emitter supply V_{ee} has a series resistance R that is large compared with the input resistance of the base-emitter circuit. The capacitor C provides a by-pass for the audio frequencies. Analogous arrangements for resistance-capacitance and tuned amplifiers are shown in Fig. 21-39c and d.

Means for obtaining the necessary biases from a single power source are shown in Fig. 21-39b. Here R_1 and R_2 form a resistance divider; since R_1 is in series between the supply voltage and the base, it should be made comparatively small. The large series resistance needed to stabilize the emitter current is provided by resistor R_3. Capacitors by-pass the audio frequencies.

The by-pass capacitors C in Fig. 21-39 must be large enough so that at the lowest frequencies of importance their capacitive reactances will be low compared with the associated resistances, including the dynamic electrode resistance. Because the impedance levels that go with the base and emitter electrodes of the transistor are low, the by-pass capacitors need to have relatively high capacitances. On the other hand, the voltage levels are low, and recent innovations in capacitor manufacture make it possible for the units to be physically small.

The d-c bias conditions determine a set of small-signal parameters for the transistor. These in turn provide the data required to set up an

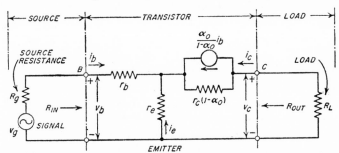

FIG. 21-40. Small-signal equivalent circuit for the common-emitter amplifiers of Fig. 21-39a, b, and c, incorporating the transistor representation of Fig. 21-31b.

equivalent transistor circuit from which various aspects of the small-signal a-c behavior can be calculated. An example is shown in Fig. 21-40, where R_g and R_L represent the source and load resistances, respectively, as observed from the base and collector terminals of the transistor.[1,2] The voltage amplification v_c/v_b is given by the relation[3]

$$\text{Voltage amplification} = \frac{v_c}{v_b} \approx \frac{-\alpha_0 r_c R_L}{r_b[R_L + r_c(1 - \alpha_0)] + r_e(R_L + r_c)} \quad (21\text{-}35)$$

The minus sign denotes a phase reversal.

Transistors make satisfactory tuned amplifiers provided the frequency of operation does not exceed the alpha cutoff value. A common-base tuned amplifier circuit is shown in Fig. 21-39d; this can be analyzed by

---

[1] The equations to follow could have been written as readily in terms of the h parameters of Fig. 21-21 or the π parameters of Fig. 21-32. The T equivalent circuit of Figs. 21-22 and 21-40 is widely used, however, and serves here to illustrate one method of calculating the amplifier behavior.

[2] The relation between v_b and v_g is

$$v_b = v_g \frac{R_{\text{in}}}{R_{\text{in}} + R_g} \quad (21\text{-}35a)$$

where R_{in} is the input resistance as given by Eq. (21-37).

[3] The approximations involved in Eq. (21-35) are

$$r_e << r_c(1 - \alpha_0) \quad (21\text{-}36a)$$
$$r_b << r_c \quad (21\text{-}36b)$$

These requirements are easily satisfied by typical junction transistors.

the common-base form of the equivalent T circuit (see Fig. 21-22). It is also possible to substitute tuned circuits for R_g and R_L in Fig. 21-40, thereby giving a common-emitter tuned amplifier. In either case some thought must be given to matching the impedance of the low-resistance input circuit of the transistor to the input resonant circuit in such a manner as to obtain a good transfer of energy, and at the same time not to lower the effective Q of the tuned input circuit excessively. One means of doing this is shown in Fig. 21-39d. Neutralization is normally not required in transistor tuned amplifiers because the coupling through the transistor between input and output circuits is resistive, instead of capacitive as in tubes, and because the input impedance of the transistor is so low.

Input and Output Resistances and Power Gain of Transistor Amplifiers. The input of the transistor amplifier, i.e., the base in *a*, *b*, and *c* of Fig. 21-39, and the emitter in *d*, presents a relatively low resistance to the signal source, and hence takes power from the signal. This is in contrast with the usual vacuum-tube amplifier, where by employing negative control-grid bias, the input resistance can be regarded as infinite. Thus power considerations enter importantly into a transistor amplifier, even when the purpose of such an amplifier is only to deliver an amplified voltage. Attention must therefore be given to the values of input and output resistances of the amplifier stage, and to suitable definitions of the power gain.

The following equations give the input and output resistances of the amplifier circuit of Fig. 21-40:[1]

$$\text{Input resistance} = R_{\text{in}} \approx r_b + r_e \frac{r_c + R_L}{r_c(1 - \alpha_0) + R_L} \tag{21-37}$$

$$\text{Output resistance} = R_{\text{out}} \approx r_c(1 - \alpha_0) + r_e \frac{\alpha_0 r_c + R_g}{r_e + r_b + R_g} \tag{21-38}$$

There are three standard definitions of power gain in common use. The first of these is called the *insertion power gain*. It is the power delivered to the load resistance R_L when the amplifier is connected in the circuit as in Fig. 21-40, compared with the power that would be delivered to R_L if the generator v_g with its internal resistance R_g were connected directly to the load R_L. The square root of this gain is called the insertion voltage gain. For the circuit of Fig. 21-40, the insertion power gain is

$$\left.\begin{array}{l}\text{Insertion} \\ \text{power gain}\end{array}\right\} = \left(\frac{v_c}{v_c'}\right)^2$$

$$\approx \left\{\frac{\alpha r_c(R_g + R_L)}{(R_g + r_b)[R_L + r_c(1 - \alpha_0)] + r_e(R_L + r_c)}\right\}^2 \tag{21-39}$$

[1] The approximations involved in these relations are the same as indicated by Eqs. (21-36).

Here v_c' is the voltage across load resistor R_L when the generator (that is, v_g in series with R_g) is connected directly to R_L; that is,

$$v_c' = v_g \frac{R_L}{R_L + R_g} \tag{21-40}$$

The second definition of power gain is called the *transducer power gain*. Mathematically, it is the ratio of the actual load power divided by the power available from the generator (i.e., the power delivered by the generator to a load resistance equal to R_g). In terms of the amplifier circuit of Fig. 21-40, one has

$$\left.\begin{matrix}\text{Transducer power}\\ \text{gain}\end{matrix}\right\} = \frac{v_c{}^2/R_L}{v_g{}^2/4R_g}$$

$$\approx \frac{4(\alpha_0 r_c)^2 R_g R_L}{\{(R_g + r_b)[R_L + r_c(1 - \alpha_0)] + r_e(R_L + r_c)\}^2} \tag{21-41}$$

For a given R_L, the transducer power gain will be maximum when the source impedance is matched to the input resistance of the transistor.

Finally, where noise calculations must be made in a cascade of amplifier stages, the important kind of gain is the so-called *available power gain*. This is the ratio of the available power from the output terminals of the transistor to the available power from the generator, where the available power is $v_g{}^2/4R_g$, as defined on page 7. The following equations apply to Fig. 21-40, where v_c'' is the open-circuit output voltage:

$$\left.\begin{matrix}\text{Available power}\\ \text{gain}\end{matrix}\right\} = \frac{v_c''{}^2/4R_{\text{out}}}{v_g{}^2/4R_g}$$

$$\approx \frac{(\alpha_0 r_c)^2 R_g}{(R_g + r_e + r_b)[(R_g + r_b)r_c(1 - \alpha_0) + r_e(R_g + r_c)]} \tag{21-42}$$

Audio-frequency Power Amplifiers. Transistors can be used as Class A or Class B power amplifiers, and will convert d-c collector input power to a-c amplified output power with efficiencies approaching closely the theoretical values of 50 and 78.5 per cent, respectively.

Analysis of the behavior of the Class A transistor power amplifier can be made with the aid of a load line analogous to that shown in Fig. 10-5 for a vacuum-tube power amplifier. Such a load line is drawn in Fig. 21-19 for bias values of $I_e = -2$ ma, $V_c = 15$ volts at the operating point, and a load resistance of 7000 ohms. The distortion of the output voltage v_c developed across the load resistance R_L relative to the emitter *current* wave is then obtainable from minimum, maximum, etc., values of collector voltage, using the relations applicable to the vacuum tube (page 326). To the extent that operation is limited to regions where the transistor characteristic consists of parallel straight lines with uniform spacing, the output wave will faithfully follow the input (base) *current* wave. Comparison of Fig. 21-19 with the corresponding curves for a vacuum tube, such as given in Fig. 10-5b shows that the transistor is considerably better in terms of the lines being straight, parallel, and uniformly spaced with regard to increments of emitter current. In fact, if the operating point and load resistance are properly chosen, the output of the transistor Class A power amplifier will follow the input current wave with very low distortion until the minimum instantaneous output current approaches zero, and the efficiency then approaches 50 per cent.

The principal distortion problem in Class A transistor power amplifiers arises because of the curvature of the emitter voltage-current curve (see Fig. 21-18), or the similar curvature of the base voltage-current characteristic. Because of this curvature, a sine wave of *voltage* applied to the transistor input circuit results in a distorted input current wave, and hence in a distorted output (collector) current. To obtain a sinusoidal collector current, it is necessary not only that the output reproduce the input current wave faithfully, but also that this current wave faithfully reproduce the signal to be amplified. This can be achieved if the signal has a high source impedance such that the waveform of the current is essentially independent of the input resistance of the transistor. The harmonic distortion of a typical Class A transistor amplifier will vary with generator resistance in the general manner indicated in Fig. 21-41, which applies to both common-grid and common-emitter circuits. Here the distortion for low values of R_g is primarily in the waveform of the input current, while for large values of R_g it is from the collector circuit as determined by a load line such as that shown in Fig. 21-19.

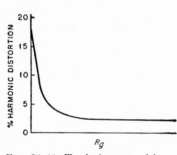

FIG. 21-41. Typical curve of harmonic distortion in the output of a transistor power-amplifier stage as a function of internal resistance R_g of the source of driving power.

As in the case of vacuum-tube power amplifiers, distortion can be reduced and power output increased for transistors of a given power rating if two of them are used in a push-pull Class A circuit (see Sec. 10-7). Class B transistor amplifiers are also possible by biasing the emitters to cutoff (i.e., $V_e 0$), and will give output efficiencies that approach very closely the theoretical maximum possible value of 78.5 per cent. A unique feature of push-pull transistor amplifiers, which is not possible with vacuum tubes, is that a complementary pair of n-p-n and p-n-p transistors can be used to give push-pull operation without the need of transformers or phase inserters (Fig. 21-42). In push-pull transistor amplifiers (either Class A or Class B), the distortion is remarkably low even when the collector circuit efficiencies approach very close to the maximum values theoretically possible (50 and 78.5 per cent, respectively).

Transistor Oscillators. The ability of the transistor to provide amplification also make possible its use in oscillator circuits. In fact, as in the case of the vacuum tube, self-oscillation can usually be achieved at higher frequencies than can useful amplification.

There are broadly two classes of oscillator circuits, one in which external feedback is applied and the other in which the internal feedback

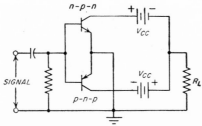

FIG. 21-42. Push-pull Class B operation made possible without transformers or phase inverters by using complementary n-p-n and p-n-p transistors.

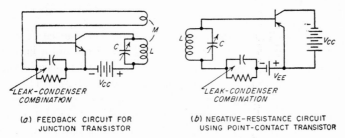

(a) FEEDBACK CIRCUIT FOR JUNCTION TRANSISTOR

(b) NEGATIVE-RESISTANCE CIRCUIT USING POINT-CONTACT TRANSISTOR

FIG. 21-43. Typical transistor oscillator circuits.

of the transistor itself is exploited. The circuit of Fig. 21-43a uses external feedback, and can be considered as a modification of the circuit of Fig. 21-39a.

The fact that the point-contact transistor can possess a negative input resistance because it has $\alpha_0 > 1$ is exploited in Fig. 21-43b. It is apparent from Eq. (21-37) that the input (i.e., base-emitter) resistance will be negative if r_b is not too large and if simultaneously $\alpha_0 > 1$ and $R_L = 0$. Since such a negative resistance shunts the tuned circuit in Fig. 12-43b, oscillations result if the magnitude of the negative resistance is less than the parallel resonant impedance of the tuned circuit.

Pulse Circuits. The junction transistor can be adapted to the various vacuum-tube circuits discussed in Chap. 18, with only slight modifications of the operating voltages and circuit parameters. For example, the circuit of Fig. 21-44 is a direct adaptation of the cathode-coupled multi-vibrator of Fig. 18-16, in which transistors replace the vacuum tubes. It can be expected that the application of transistors to pulse or switching circuits will become very important, especially in large-scale computers where power consumption and size are important factors.

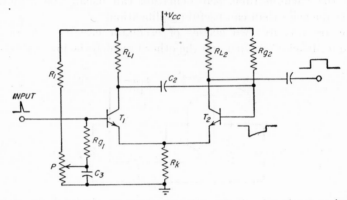

Fig. 21-44. "One-shot" multivibrator circuit employing junction transistors and analogous to the cathode-coupled multivibrator circuit of Fig. 18-16. To assist in tracing the similarity, corresponding circuit elements are labeled the same in both figures.

21-19. Noise in Transistors.
The transistor is a source of noise just as is a vacuum tube or a resistance. The transistor noise is, however, greater than can be accounted for by the actual resistances in the transistor equivalent circuit, such as shown in Fig. 21-22. This "excess noise" arises from random variations in the currents crossing the emitter and collector junctions, together with a partition effect due to random division of the emitter current between collector and base. Although the details of the excess noise in transistors are not as well understood as in a triode, the external behavior is as though there were noise generators in series with the emitter and collector terminals, with the collector noise generator being much the greater.

The noisiness of a transistor can be expressed in terms of a noise figure that has the same meaning as defined in Sec. 12-14. That is, the noise figure of the transistor amplifier is the ratio of the actual noise power, delivered to the load impedance of the transistor amplifier, to the noise power that would be delivered to the same load impedance if the only noise present was due to the resistances of the equivalent circuit. It can be shown that this noise figure is entirely independent of the load impedance, and in the case of transistors is affected only slightly by the source impedance associated with the transistor input.

At any given frequency, the transistor noise generators vary in magnitude with the d-c bias conditions. The behavior in a typical case is

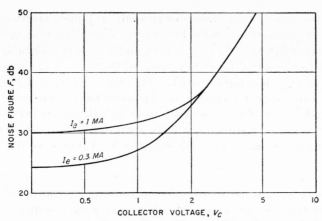

FIG. 21-45. Variation of noise figure with d-c-bias conditions for a particular junction transistor.

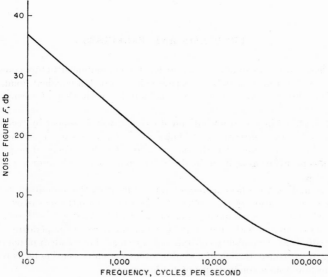

FIG. 21-46. Typical measured noise-figure curve of a junction transistor, showing inverse-frequency relationship of the transistor over the useful frequency range (i.e., below alpha cutoff).

shown in Fig. 21-45, where it is seen that the noise figure in a given circuit is lower for smaller emitter currents and for smaller collector voltages. At small collector voltages, the noise figure appears to depend primarily upon the emitter current, suggesting that the noise of the emitter junction then predominates.   At high collector voltages the noise figure is essentially independent of emitter current, suggesting that in this case the noise originates primarily in the collector junction.

The excess noise that a transistor generates is found experimentally to be inversely proportional to the frequency. Thus the noise figure varies in the manner illustrated in Fig. 21-46, and will be considerably greater than 0 db in the useful frequency range of the transistor, corresponding to frequencies below alpha cutoff. The noise figure, and the general behavior with respect to noise, are the same for the grounded-emitter and grounded-base circuits, so that there is little choice between these in so far as noise considerations are involved. However, the point-contact transistor has a much higher noise level than does the junction type.

Since the excess noise varies with frequency, it is necessary in comparing different circuits to specify the operating frequency. Where this cannot be done, it has become the custom to make comparisons at an arbitrary frequency of 1000 cycles. Typical noise figures at this frequency are from 20 to 30 db for junction transistors, and from 40 to 50 db for point-contact transistors.

PROBLEMS AND EXERCISES

21-1. Diamond is a form of carbon that has the crystalline structure shown in Fig. 21-1, and requires approximately 7 electron volts to break a covalent bond. On the basis of this information, compare its conductivity with that of germanium and silicon.

21-2. The probability that an individual electron will disappear by recombination is proportional to the concentration of holes, but independent of the concentration of electrons. From this, show that the rate at which free electrons must be produced to maintain a concentration n_i in an intrinsic (i.e., pure) semiconductor is proportional to n_i^2.

21-3. Calculate n_i for silicon at room temperature from the data given in Sec. 21-2.

21-4. The temperature of pure silicon is raised until its intrinsic carrier concentration n_i equals that of germanium at room temperature. What will be the conductivity of the silicon compared with that of the germanium at room temperature? Assume hypothetically that the mobility constants of silicon are independent of temperature.

21-5. *a.* What concentration of acceptor atoms per cubic centimeter is required in germanium to obtain a conductivity of 1 mho per cm?

b. What is the corresponding ratio of acceptor to germanium atoms?

c. What would be the conductivity if the impurity consisted of donor atoms in the same proportion?

21-6. Compute the concentration of free electrons and holes, and also the conductivity, for a semiconductor containing 1 μg of boron and 1 μg of antimony per 100 g of germanium. (Note: The atomic weights of boron, antimony, and germanium are 10.8, 121.8, and 72.6, respectively.)

21-7. Explain why the concentration of impurity atoms required to cause significant departure from intrinsic behavior is greater in germanium than in silicon.

21-8. Donors are added to an intrinsic semiconductor so that $n = xn_i$. Then show that $p = n_i/x$, thus proving Eq. (21-7).

21-9. It is observed experimentally that the conductivity of an impurity semiconductor depends on temperature in the general manner shown in the accompanying figure. Explain the shape of the curve, with particular reference to the significance of the knee at B, and the distinction between region AB and BC.

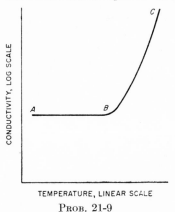

PROB. 21-9

21-10. Compare qualitatively the average lifetime of an electron in intrinsic, n, and p semiconductors.

21-11. Make a sketch corresponding to Fig. 21-3b, but for the case where the drift is to the left.

21-12. Discuss the current flow in pure (intrinsic) semiconductor material arranged between electrodes as in Fig. 21-1. In particular, explain the fact that for small or moderate applied voltages the current is proportional to the voltage, whereas for large applied voltages the current tends to be independent of voltage.

21-13. Verify that the values of diffusion constant given for germanium on page 744 are consistent with the values of mobility given on page 737.

21-14. In what way would the energy-band representation in Fig. 21-6b differ for germanium and silicon?

21-15. Discuss the conductivity of germanium containing as its only impurity one that introduces isolated energy levels at a level in the forbidden region that is one-third up from the bottom of the region.

21-16. When a sine wave of voltage is applied to a junction diode, a distorted wave of current flows. Derive an approximate formula for the ratio of second-harmonic to fundamental component of the current by expanding the exponential term in Eq. (21-13) into a series, and dropping all except the first three terms.

21-17. Describe qualitatively (with reasons) the changes that could be expected in Fig. 21-13 from increasing both donor and acceptor concentrations. Assume a symmetrical diode.

21-18. Discuss in a qualitative way the effect of temperature upon the reverse saturation current in a germanium junction diode.

21-19. *a.* Verify that the electron and hole concentrations for the cases of doping shown in Fig. 21-12 are consistent with n_i and the specified conductivities.

b. Compute the data applicable to Fig. 21-12, but for $\sigma = 20$ mhos, with (1) p material, (2) n material.

21-20. Redraw Fig. 21-13 to show how it would be modified if the doping of the p region were increased until $\sigma_p = 100$ mhos per cm. Be sure to take into account the fact that the lifetime of the minority carriers in the p region, and hence the associated diffusion length, is affected by this change in doping.

21-21. Same as Prob. 21-20 but applicable to Fig. 21-14.

21-22. Redraw Fig. 21-13 to show how it would be changed by the presence of a chemical impurity in the p region that reduced the lifetime of the minority carriers to one-fourth of the value in Fig. 21-13, but had no other effect.

21-23. Discuss in a qualitative way the effect on the reverse saturation current of the degree of "doping" in a germanium junction diode. Consider the two cases (a) where the doping of both n and p material is increased simultaneously, and (b) where the doping of only one of these materials is increased.

21-24. Show the effect on the curves of Fig. 21-14 of decreasing the diffusion length L_n for the electrons.

21-25. Explain why the diffusion length for minority carriers is normally less the higher the conductivity.

21-26. In Fig. 21-13, explain why appreciably less than 1 per cent of the current is carried across the emitter junction by holes even though p/n is approximately 0.01.

21-27. Prove that, when a forward-biased junction diode is carrying a given current, placing a second, similar junction diode in parallel will not change the dynamic resistance, but will lower the static resistance.

21-28. Compare the dynamic resistance of forward-biased silicon and germanium junction diodes carrying the same current. In order to obtain a quantitative answer, derive a formula analogous to Eq. (21-22) but applicable to silicon.

21-29. A grown junction n-p-n transistor having the conductivities shown in Fig. 21-16 is to be produced using boron and antimony as impurities. What amounts of impurity (in micrograms) must be added to the melt at various stages per 100 g of germanium? (Necessary atomic weights are given in Prob. 21-6.)

21-30. Describe a mechanism that would account for the fact, shown in Fig. 21-19b, that a large current flows to the collector even when $V_c = 0$.

21-31. In Fig. 21-16b calculate the concentration of minority carriers (electrons) in the base adjacent to the emitter junction for an emitter current of 3 ma. Assume that emitter efficiency = 0.99, $w = 0.1$ mm, and junction area = 0.25 sq mm, and that the electron concentration adjacent to the collector junction is negligible.

21-32. What significant changes (if any) would occur in Fig. 21-16 if the conductivity of the collector region were increased to 100 mhos per cm?

21-33. Redraw Fig. 21-16 to apply to a p-n-p transistor. Assume that the emitter, base, and collector conductivities are the same as in Fig. 21-16.

21-34. Discuss in qualitative terms the influence of base thickness on the extent to which the transistor alpha is affected by the collector voltage.

21-35. Explain the mechanism whereby the alpha of a transistor is affected by a change in the base conductivity, even when the emitter efficiency is kept constant by simultaneously changing the emitter conductivity.

21-36. Discuss the effect on emitter efficiency and transport factor of increasing the base conductivity while (a) changing the emitter conductivity in proportion, and (b) keeping the emitter conductivity unchanged.

21-37. Is it to be expected that the value of alpha for a junction transistor will be relatively sensitive or relatively insensitive to a change in temperature?

21-38. What would be the effect on the curves of Fig. 21-19a if the alpha of the transistor were considerably less than the value for the case illustrated?

21-39. For a transistor one can write $i_e = Cv_c + Di_c$. Define C and D in terms of the h's of Eq. (21-25).

21-40. How would the curves in Fig. 21-18 differ if $h_{12} = 0$?

21-41. Show that the numerical values in the second column of Table 21-1 are consistent with those for the h coefficients in the first column.

21-42. How would Fig. 21-22 have to be modified if the collector voltage had no effect whatsoever on the emitter current, but only affected the collector current?

21-43. Show that the numerical values given in the third column of Table 21-1 are consistent with those listed in the first column.

21-44. A resistance is connected in series with the base of a transistor, increasing the effective value of r_b. Which of the h coefficients are changed in value? And are they made greater or smaller as a result of the increase in base resistance?

21-45. Express each of the h constants in terms of a and the r coefficients of Fig. 21-22.

21-46. Determine the frequency at which $|\alpha| = 0.9$ for the transistor of Table 21-1.

21-47. In the equivalent circuit of Fig. 21-26, assign numerical values to the circuit constants applicable to the transistor of Table 21-1 when (a) the frequency is very low, (b) $f = 0.5 f_\alpha$, (c) $f = f_\alpha$.

21-48. Sketch simplified forms of Fig. 21-26 applicable to the transistor of Table 21-1 at higher frequencies under the following conditions: (a) generator resistance $R_g = 2000$, and load resistance $R_L = 20{,}000$; (b) $R_g = 2000$, $R_L = 200{,}000$; (c) $R_g = 200$, $R_L = 200{,}000$; (d) $R_g = 200$, $R_L = 1{,}000{,}000$.

21-49. By means of qualitative reasoning involving Figs. 21-24 to 21-26, show that the collector current i_c at the alpha cutoff frequency will differ more from the low-frequency value when the load resistance in series with the collector is very high than when it is very low.

21-50. Mark numerical values on the equivalent circuit of Fig. 21-31b that are applicable to a transistor identical with that in the first column of Table 21-1, except that $h_{21} = -0.90$.

21-51. Verify the numerical values given on page 780 for the effect of frequency on current gain and collector impedance for $f = f_\alpha$.

21-52. In Fig. 21-32, convert the current generator and its shunt resistance r_{ce} into a resistance in series with a voltage generator $-\mu v_b$, and derive a formula giving μ in terms of the transistor constants employed in Fig. 21-32.

21-53. Derive the circuit of Fig. 21-33 from Fig. 21-22.

21-54. a. Explain how the h coefficient of the transistor can be obtained directly from Figs. 21-18 and 21-19 by graphical means.

b. Derive the numerical values of the h coefficients from these figures for the operating condition $V_c = 20$ volts and $I_e = -2$ ma.

21-55. Devise a series of tests that would directly measure the r coefficients and also a in Fig. 21-22 without making use of the h coefficients.

21-56. It is observed experimentally that, as base 2 of the junction tetrode is made more negative, the low-frequency alpha of the transistor decreases. Suggest a cause for this behavior.

21-57. Suggest a method by which a p-n-i-p junction triode transistor could be fabricated.

21-58. In a point-contact diode in which the base is n material, deduce the polarity that the point must have to give forward bias.

21-59. a. Determine the numerical values of the h coefficients applicable to the point-contact transistor of Table 21-2.

b. From the result of (a) discuss the relative sensitivity of emitter current to changes in collector voltage for the particular point-contact and junction transistors of Table 21-2.

21-60. Determine numerical values applicable to the equivalent circuits of Figs. 21-31b and 21-32 for the point-contact transistor of Table 21-2.

21-61. In Fig. 21-39a suggest suitable values for R and C, assuming that the transistor has the characteristics shown in Table 21-1, and is to operate down to 60 cycles.

21-62. Derive Eq. (21-35).

21-63. Derive a formula analogous to Eq. (21-35) but differing in that the transistor is used in the common-base instead of common-emitter connection.

21-64. Discuss the factors that determine appropriate numerical values for C.

and R_{gl} in Fig. 21-39c when response at low frequencies is considered. Do the load resistance R_L and the source resistance R_g affect the considerations?

21-65. Calculate (a) the voltage amplification, (b) input resistance, (c) output resistance, and (d) insertion, transducer, and available power gain for the circuit of Fig. 21-40 when $R_g = 1000$, $R_L = 50,000$, and the transistor has the characteristics given in Table 21-1.

21-66. a. Derive (1) Eq. (21-37); (2) Eq. (21-38).

b. Derive analogous equations but applicable to the common-base transistor.

21-67. a. Derive (1) Eq. (21-39); (2) Eq. (21-41); (3) Eq. (21-42).

b. Derive similar equations but applicable to the common-base transistor.

21-68. a. When the transistor of Table 21-1 is used in the common-emitter circuit, through what range does the input resistance vary as the load resistance goes from zero to infinity?

b. Through what range does the output resistance vary when the input resistance goes from zero to infinity?

21-69. Repeat Prob. 21-68 for the point-contact transistor of Table 21-2.

21-70. Experiment shows that the effective Q of the output resonance system in the tuned amplifier of Fig. 21-39d differs from the actual Q of the resonant circuit. Explain.

21-71. Calculate the output power, the second-harmonic distortion, and the efficiency with which collector power is converted into audio output for the load line of Fig. 21-19 when the input current is a sinusoidal wave with a peak amplitude of 2 ma.

21-72. Propose suitable values of I_e and V_c at the operating point in Fig. 21-19 for $R_L = 3000$ ohms, when the signal current is a sine wave with a peak amplitude of 3 ma.

21-73. Using Table 10-1, calculate the second-harmonic component of the emitter current when sinusoidal signal waves having peak amplitudes of 1.5 and 0.75 ma are applied directly to the emitter of the transistor of Fig. 21-18 superimposed upon an emitter bias potential of -60 mv. Assume that R_L is sufficiently low so that the collector potential can be considered constant at 40 volts.

21-74. a. Suggest a suitable value of R_L in Fig. 21-42 when $V_{cc} = 40$ volts, the desired peak collector current $= 5$ ma, and the n-p-n and p-n-p transistors both have characteristics similar to those of the transistor of Fig. 21-19.

b. Calculate power output and the efficiency with which d-c collector input power is converted into amplified output power.

21-75. Experience shows that the circuit of Fig. 21-43b will oscillate more vigorously if an un-by-passed resistance is placed in series with either the collector or the base. Explain.

21-76. Sketch a Colpitts oscillator circuit employing a common-base transistor in place of a vacuum tube.

21-77. Sketch the transistor equivalent of the multivibrator circuit of Fig. 18-9, and review the details of operation. Assume a junction triode transistor.

21-78. Show a transistorized version of the bootstrap circuit of Fig. 18-39.

CHAPTER 22

PROPAGATION OF RADIO WAVES

22-1. Factors Involved in the Propagation of Radio Waves. There are a number of mechanisms by which radio waves may travel from a transmitting to a receiving antenna. The more important of these are designated by the terms *ground waves*, *sky waves*, and *space* or *tropospheric waves*.

The *ground wave* (also sometimes called surface wave) can exist when the transmitting and receiving antennas are close to the surface of the earth and are vertically polarized. This wave, supported at its lower edge by the presence of the ground, is of practical importance at broadcast and lower frequencies. Thus all broadcast signals received in the daytime are ground waves.

The *sky wave* represents energy that reaches the receiving antenna as a result of a bending of the wave path introduced by the ionization in the upper atmosphere. This ionized region, termed the *ionosphere*, which begins about 80 km above the earth's surface, accounts for practically all very long-distance radio communication.

The *space wave* represents energy that travels from the transmitting to the receiving antenna in the earth's *troposphere*, i.e., the portion of the earth's atmosphere in the first 10 miles adjacent to the earth's surface. The space wave commonly consists of at least two components. One of these is a ray that travels directly from transmitter to receiver, while the other is a ray that reaches the receiver as a result of reflection from the surface of the earth. Space-wave energy may also reach the receiver as a result of reflection or refraction produced by variations in the electrical characteristics of the troposphere, and by diffraction around the curvature of the earth, hills, etc. Radio transmission at frequencies above about 30 Mc, i.e., at the frequencies used for television, frequency modulation, radar, etc., is normally space-wave propagation.

22-2. The Ground Wave. The ground wave glides over the surface of the earth in the manner shown in Fig. 22-1. The ground wave is vertically polarized, because any horizontal component of electric field in contact with the earth is short circuited by the earth. The ground wave induces charges in the earth, as indicated in Fig. 22-1, which travel with the wave and so constitute a current.

In carrying this induced current, the earth behaves like a leaky capacitance, and so can be represented by a resistance (or conductance) shunted by a capacitive reactance as illustrated in Fig. 2-11c. The characteristics of the earth as a conductor can therefore be described in terms of conductivity σ and dielectric constant ϵ.

As the ground wave passes over the surface of the earth, it is weakened as a result of energy absorbed by the earth in order to supply the power loss resulting from the induced current flowing through the earth's resistance. Energy lost in this way is replenished, at least in part, by diffraction of additional energy downward from the portions of the wave present somewhat above the immediate surface of the earth.

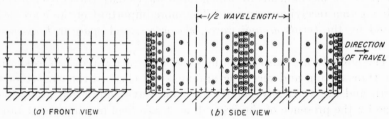

(a) FRONT VIEW   (b) SIDE VIEW

FIG. 22-1. Front and side views of a vertically polarized wave traveling over the surface of the earth. The solid lines represent electric field while the dotted lines and circles indicate magnetic flux.

Sommerfeld Analysis of Ground-wave Propagation. The solution of the relations involved in ground-wave propagation,[1] first given by Sommerfeld, can for an earth assumed flat be expressed in the form

$$\left.\begin{array}{l}\text{Ground-wave}\\ \text{field strength}\end{array}\right\} = A\,\frac{E_0}{d} \qquad (22\text{-}1)$$

where E_0 = field strength of wave at the surface of the earth at a unit distance from the transmitting antenna, neglecting earth's losses

d = distance to transmitting antenna

A = factor taking into account the ground losses

The field strength E_0 at unit distance in Eq. (22-1) depends upon the power radiated by the transmitting antenna, and the directivity of this antenna in the vertical and horizontal planes. When the antenna is nondirectional in the horizontal plane, and produces a radiated field that is proportional to the cosine of the angle of elevation (short vertical antenna), then for a radiated power of 1 kw, E_0 is 186 mv per m at a distance of 1 mile, or 300 mv per m at a distance of 1 km. For other values

[1] Much literature is available on this subject. Perhaps the most useful are the papers by K. A. Norton: The Propagation of Radio Waves over the Surface of the Earth and in the Upper Atmosphere, *Proc. IRE*, vol. 24, p. 1367, October, 1936, and The Calculation of Ground-wave Field Intensity over a Finitely Conducting Spherical Earth, *Proc. IRE*, vol. 29, p. 623, December, 1941.

of radiated power the value E_0 will be proportional to the square root of the power and will likewise be modified in accordance with the directivity in the horizontal plane, as well as for any added directivity that results when the radiated field is not proportional to the cosine of the angle of elevation. Thus with a 50-kw broadcast transmitter employing an antenna with vertical directivity that increases the field strength along the horizon by a factor of 1.41 times the field strength obtained with the assumed cosine law, one has $E_0 = 1.86 \times 1.41 \sqrt{50} = 1860$ mv per m at one mile.

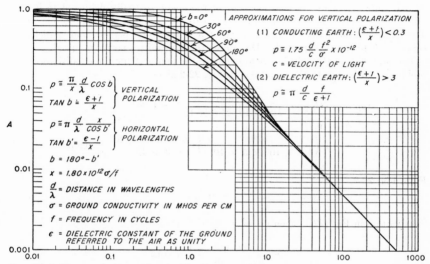

Fig. 22-2. Factor A, appearing in Eq. (22-1), which takes into account the effect of ground losses on the ground wave, neglecting earth curvature.

The factor A in Eq. (22-1) takes into account the effect of ground loss and depends in a relatively complicated way upon the conductivity and dielectric constant of the earth, the frequency, and the distance to the transmitter in wavelengths. The relationships involved are presented in graphical form in Fig. 22-2 where the reduction factor A is expressed in terms of two auxiliary variables, the numerical distance p, and the phase constant b. These auxiliary constants p and b are determined by the frequency, distance, and characteristics of the earth considered as a conductor of radio-frequency currents according to the formulas given in Fig. 22-2.

Examination of Fig. 22-2 shows that the reduction factor A depends primarily upon the numerical distance p. When p is less than unity, the factor A differs only slightly from unity. The losses in the earth then have little effect on the strength of the ground wave, which is accordingly nearly inversely proportional to distance. However, as the numerical distance p becomes greater than unity, the factor A decreases rapidly, and for $p > 10$ is almost exactly inversely proportional to actual physical distance. The field strength of the ground wave is hence inversely proportional to the *square* of the distance when the distance is great enough to make $p > 10$.

The use of Fig. 22-2 in practical radio problems is illustrated by the following example:

Example. A police radio transmitter operating at a frequency of 1690 kc is required to provide a ground wave having a strength of at least 0.5 mv per m at a distance of 10 miles (16 km). The transmitting antenna is expected to have an efficiency of 50 per cent; i.e., it radiates 50 per cent of the energy actually delivered to it, and produces a radiated field that is proportional to the cosine of the angle of elevation. The ground is such that a conductivity of 5×10^{-5} mho per cm and a dielectric constant of 15 can be expected. Determine the transmitter power required.

The first step in the solution is to evaluate the factor A for the conditions of the problem. Reference to the equations in Fig. 22-2 gives

$$\tan b = (15 + 1) \frac{1690}{1.8 \times 10^9 \times 5 \times 10^{-5}} = 0.301$$

$$b = 16.7°$$

$$p = \pi \left(\frac{1690}{1.8 \times 10^9 \times 5 \times 10^{-5}} \right) \frac{16 \times 1690 \times 10^3}{3 \times 10^5} \times 0.957$$

$$= 5.1$$

From Fig. 22-2,

$$A = 0.15$$

Substitution in Eq. (22-1) then gives

$$0.5 = \frac{300 \sqrt{P} \times 1}{16} \times 0.15$$

from which

$$P = 0.0315 \text{ kw}$$

With an antenna efficiency of 50 per cent, the transmitter must deliver 63 watts to the antenna.

Curves showing the way in which the ground-wave field strength varies with distance under representative conditions are given in Fig. 22-3. For purposes of comparison, an inverse-distance curve is shown. This corresponds to $A = 1$ in Eq. (22-1), i.e., to infinite ground conductivity and a flat earth. It is apparent that the ground losses can seriously reduce the strength of the ground wave below the inverse-distance value, with the effect being greater the lower the conductivity, the higher the frequency, and the greater the distance.

The curves of Fig. 22-3 have been corrected to take into account the curvature of the earth, which Eq. (22-1) and Fig. 22-2 neglect. The effect of earth curvature is entirely negligible up to a distance of $50/\sqrt[3]{f_{mc}}$ miles, where f_{mc} is the frequency in megacycles, and does not introduce a serious error in Eq. (22-1) until the distance exceeds twice this value.

However, at greater distances than this the reduction in field strength below the free-space value that occurs tends to be caused more by earth curvature than by ground losses.

Earth Constants. The conductivity and dielectric constants of the earth vary greatly with conditions. Typical values are given in Table 22-1.

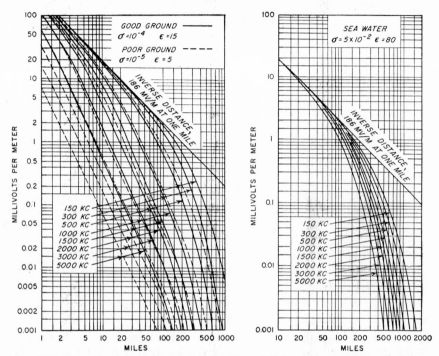

FIG. 22-3. Strength of ground wave as a function of distance, frequency, and soil conductivity, for 1 kw of radiated power from an antenna producing a radiated field proportional to the cosine of the vertical angle. For other powers the field strength will be proportional to the square root of the power. These curves take into account the curvature of the earth.

At broadcast and lower frequencies the ratio of capacitive reactance of the earth to the earth resistivity $1/\sigma$ is considerably greater than unity, so to a first approximation the earth can be regarded as purely resistive. Under these conditions the reduction factor A in Eq. (22-1) (i.e., the numerical distance) for a given physical distance is determined by the quantity f^2/σ, as shown in Fig. 22-2. Conversely, at frequencies of the order of 10 Mc and greater, the impedance represented by ground (but not sea water) is primarily capacitive, and ground-wave attenuation at a given physical distance is determined by the factor $f/(\epsilon + 1)$.

The values of earth conductivity and dielectric constant that are effective in determining the attenuation of a ground wave are a suitably weighted average value of these quantities for a distance below the earth's surface determined by the depth to which there are ground currents of appreciable amplitude. This depth of penetration depends upon the frequency, dielectric constant, and conductivity. It ranges from a few feet at the highest frequencies used in short-wave communication to tens and hundreds of feet at broadcast and lower frequencies.[1] As a result, the earth's constants are not particularly sensitive to conditions existing at the actual surface of the ground, as for example recent rainfall.

TABLE 22-1
TYPICAL GROUND CONSTANTS

Type of terrain	Dielectric constant	Conductivity, σ, mhos per cm*
Sea water†	81	$45{,}000 \times 10^{-6}$
Fresh water†	80	100
Pastoral, low hills, rich soil	20	100
Pastoral, medium hills, forestation	13	50
Rocky soil, flat sandy	10	20
Cities, industrial areas	5	10

* To convert to emu, multiply by 10^{-9}.
† Conductivity of water varies greatly with temperature and salt content.

22-3. Reflection of Radio Waves by the Surface of the Earth. When a *plane* wave strikes the surface of the earth it is reflected with an angle of reflection equal to the angle of incidence. The vector ratio of the reflected to incident wave is termed the *reflection coefficient*. It is designated as $R = r\underline{/\gamma}$, where r is the ratio of magnitudes of reflected to incident wave, and γ is their phase relation. The strength of the fields just above the earth is the vector sum of the incident and reflected waves, taking into account both time phase and space orientation.

The value of the reflection coefficient depends in a complex way upon the dielectric constant and conductivity of the earth, the frequency, the plane of polarization, and the angle of incidence with which the wave strikes the surface of the earth. In the case of a perfectly reflecting earth (i.e., earth having infinite conductivity), the reflected wave has the same magnitude as the incident wave, and therefore $r = 1$. Under these conditions the phases of the incident and reflected waves will be related in the manner illustrated in Fig. 22-4a or b, according to whether the incident wave is polarized vertically or horizontally, respectively. Examination of these vector diagrams shows that with a *perfect reflector* the horizontal components of electric field will exactly cancel each other at the

---

[1] At broadcast and lower frequencies, where the earth may be assumed resistive, the current penetrates the earth in accordance with the skin-effect laws discussed in Sec. 2-4.

surface of the perfect reflector.   In contrast, the vertical components of the electric field of the incident and reflected waves do not cancel, but rather add at the reflector surface with small values of ψ_2.

In the case of an actual earth with finite conductivity and dielectric constant, the magnitude of the reflection coefficient is less than unity and the angle γ of the reflected wave will in general differ from zero. The values of r and γ will now, moreover, vary with the angle of incidence.

A typical example showing the effect of the angle of incidence on the reflection coefficient of the ground is illustrated in Fig. 22-4c, which is for earth of high conductivity at a frequency of 20 Mc. With horizontally polarized waves it is seen that the reflection coefficient of the actual earth at grazing-incidence ($\psi_2 = 0$) has the same value $1/\underline{0^\circ}$ that applies to a perfect reflector.   However, as the angle of incidence increases, the magnitude of the reflection coefficient for horizontally polarized waves drops off moderately, and there is a small but increasing lagging phase shift introduced by the reflection with respect to the phase that would exist for a perfect reflector.

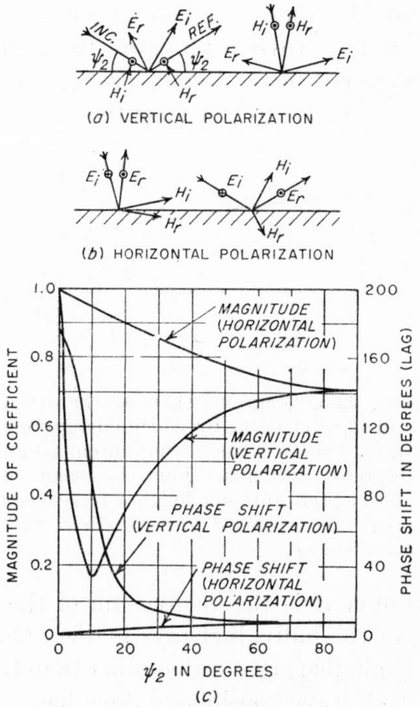

The effect of angle of incidence on the reflection coefficient is much more complicated in the case of a vertically polarized wave.   At grazing incidence the reflection coefficient is now $1/\underline{180^\circ}$ (i.e., the reflected wave has the same amplitude as the incident wave), but the phase now differs 180° from the phase that would exist if the reflecting surface had infinite conductivity.   At vertical incidence ($\psi_2 = 90^\circ$) the reflection coefficient of a vertically polarized wave has the same magnitude and phase shift as for a horizontally polarized wave; thus with vertical incidence the magnitude of the reflection coefficient is moderately less than unity and the phase shift is quite small.   Between these extremes in ψ_2, the magnitude of the reflection coefficient goes through a minimum at a small vertical

(a) VERTICAL POLARIZATION

(b) HORIZONTAL POLARIZATION

ψ_2 IN DEGREES

(c)

FIG. 22-4. Diagram showing polarities for reflections at a perfect earth, together with curves showing reflection coefficient as a function of angle of incidence for a typical case of imperfect earth.   (E and H denote electric and magnetic flux, respectively; subscripts i and r denote incident and reflected components.)

angle that corresponds to the Brewster angle in optics. At this particular angle of incidence the reflection coefficient for vertically polarized waves will be much smaller than unity and the phase of the reflected wave will differ 90° from the phase of a vertically polarized wave reflected from a surface of infinite conductivity.

22-4. Space-wave Propagation.[1] At radio frequencies above about 30 Mc, the ionosphere is not able to refract energy to earth, while the ground wave attenuates to negligible amplitude in a relatively few hundred feet. Useful propagation can, however, be achieved at these frequencies by means of the space wave traveling between elevated transmitting and receiving antennas.

Space-wave Propagation over Ideal Flat Earth. When the earth curvature can be neglected, space-wave propagation takes place in the manner illustrated in Fig. 22-5. Here energy reaches the receiver in two ways: (1) by a ray traveling directly between transmitting and receiving antennas over path TR, and (2) by a ray traveling over path TOR that involves a reflection from the surface of the ground. The field strength at the receiving antenna R is the vector sum of the fields represented by these two rays.

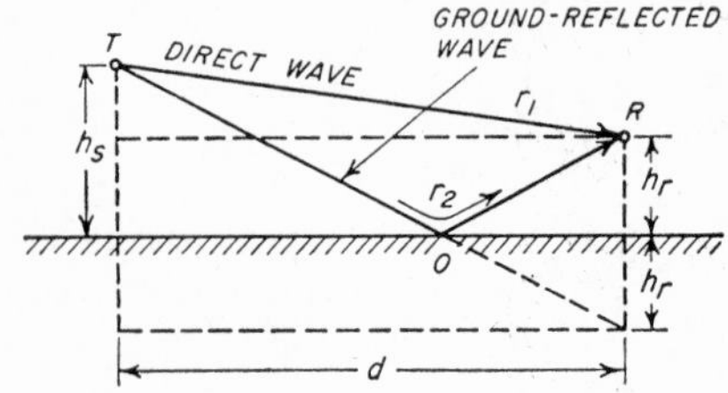

Fig. 22-5. Diagrams showing the direct and indirect paths by which energy may travel from a transmitting antenna to a receiving antenna. For the sake of clarity, the antenna heights have been greatly exaggerated in comparison with the distance.

As the individual rays in Fig. 22-5 travel through space, they undergo negligible attenuation other than that caused by spreading.[2] As a result, each wave considered alone has a strength that is inversely proportional to the distance from the transmitter.

When the distance between transmitting and receiving antennas is considerably greater than the antenna heights, the angle of incidence of the

---

[1] The literature on this subject is very extensive, and is growing rapidly. The following are references of a general character that will be helpful to the reader who wishes to pursue this subject more deeply: Kenneth Bullington, Radio Propagation at Frequencies Above 30 Megacycles, *Proc. IRE (Waves and Elec. Sec.)*, vol. 35, p. 1122, October, 1947, and Radio Propagation Variations at VHF and UHF, *Proc. IRE*, vol. 38, p. 27, January, 1950; Donald E. Kerr, Propagation of Very Short Waves, *Electronics*, vol. 21, p. 124, January, 1948, and p. 118, February, 1948; Kerr, "Radio Wave Propagation," Academic Press, Inc., New York, 1949; Kerr, "Propagation of Short Radio Waves" (vol. 13, Radiation Laboratory Series), McGraw-Hill Book Company, Inc., New York, 1951; also Tropospheric Propagation: A Selected Guide to the Literature, *Proc. IRE*, vol. 41, p. 588, May, 1953.

[2] An exception is that rain attenuates very high-frequency waves. At $\lambda = 3$ cm, this is less than 1 db per mile with heavy rain (not cloudburst), but increases to about 5 db per mile at $\lambda = 1$ cm. Also waves having lengths of 1 cm and less suffer attenuation owing to absorption lines associated with the gases composing the atmosphere.

ray TO at the surface of the earth will be small. The reflection at O can then be assumed to take place with no change in magnitude and with reversal of phase irrespective of polarization (see Fig. 22-4). Under these circumstances the two waves at the receiving point R have equal amplitude, but will, in general, differ in phase. The field strength at the receiving antenna R then is[1]

$$\left. \begin{array}{l} \text{Field strength at} \\ \text{receiver} \end{array} \right\} = \frac{2E_0}{d} \sin \frac{2\pi h_s h_r}{\lambda d} \qquad (22\text{-}2)$$

Here E_0 = field intensity produced at unit distance by the transmitting
    antenna in the desired direction when the earth is absent
    (= strength of direct ray at unit distance)
  d = distance from transmitter to receiver
  λ = wavelength, same units as d
h_s, h_r = heights of transmitting and receiving antennas, same units as d
E_0 will depend upon the directivity of the transmitting antenna and the transmitter power. When the transmitter is a half-wave antenna some distance from the ground, then

$$E_0 = 137.6 \sqrt{P_{kw}} \qquad \text{mv per m at one mile} \qquad (22\text{-}4)$$

where P_{kw} is the power in kilowatts.

Typical curves showing the variation of field strength with distance as calculated from Eq. (22-2) are given in Fig. 22-6. It will be noted that for distances less than the value d' that makes the angle $(2\pi h_s h_r/\lambda d)$ in Eq. (22-2) greater than $\pi/6$, the field strength oscillates about the value

---

[1] Equation (22-2) can be derived as follows. Referring to Fig. 22-5, it is seen from the dotted construction that $r_1{}^2 = (h_s - h_r)^2 + d^2$, and $r_2{}^2 = (h_s + h_r)^2 + d^2$. For $d > > (h_s + h_r)$, one can then write

$$r_1 = d + \frac{(h_s - h_r)^2}{2d} \qquad r_2 = d + \frac{(h_s + h_r)^2}{2d}$$

Consequently, the difference in path lengths is

$$r_2 - r_1 = \frac{(h_s + h_r)^2 - (h_s - h_r)^2}{2d} = \frac{2h_s h_r}{d}$$

The phase difference corresponding to this path difference is $2\pi \cdot 2h_s h_r/\lambda d = 4\pi h_s h_r/\lambda d$ radians. It is because of this angle that the direct and indirect rays fail to cancel, so that the resultant of the two waves is $2 \sin (2\pi h_s h_r/\lambda d)$ times the amplitude of one of the waves.

This derivation [and also Eq. (22-2)] assumes that the distance d is enough greater than the heights involved so that the wavefronts of the direct and ground-reflected waves can be assumed to coincide. When $2\pi h_s h_r/\lambda d$ is less than 0.5 (i.e., when the distance d is large), the sine of the angle can be replaced by the angle, and Eq. (22-2) becomes

$$\left. \begin{array}{l} \text{Field strength} \\ \text{at receiver} \end{array} \right\} = \frac{4\pi h_s h_r}{\lambda d^2} E_0 \qquad (22\text{-}3)$$

E_0/d that corresponds to the strength of the direct ray TR in Fig. 22-5 (often called the *free-space wave*). For a perfectly conducting earth the maximum amplitude of these oscillations is twice the free-space value, and occurs at distances so related to the antenna heights that the direct and ground-reflected waves add in phase. The minima (or nulls) have zero amplitude in the case of a perfectly reflecting earth, and occur at distances such that the direct and ground-reflected waves cancel each other.

At distances greater than the value d' as defined above, the path lengths of the direct and the ground-reflected rays always differ by less than $\lambda/6$, and the angle of incidence at the ground is so small that the

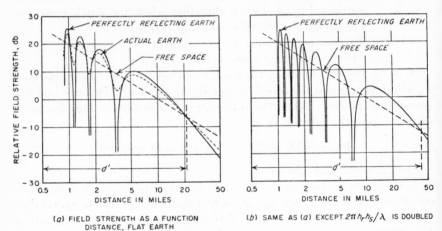

(a) FIELD STRENGTH AS A FUNCTION   (b) SAME AS (a) EXCEPT $2\pi h_r h_S/\lambda$ IS DOUBLED
      DISTANCE, FLAT EARTH

FIG. 22-6. Variation of field strength as a function of distance for hypothetical but nevertheless typical conditions of space-wave propagation. These curves assume a flat earth and horizontally polarized waves.

ground reflection takes place with reversal of polarity and unchanged amplitude, irrespective of polarization. The two rays are then largely out of phase, and the field strength at the receiving antenna is less than the free-space value, as shown in Fig. 22-6a. At distances appreciably greater than d', Eq. (22-3) applies, and the field strength for an ideal flat earth becomes *inversely proportional to the square of the distance*, and so drops off relatively rapidly.

Increasing the quantity $h_s h_r/\lambda$, either by increasing the antenna heights, or the frequency, produces the result shown in Fig. 22-6b. The oscillations in the amplitude now occur more rapidly with increasing distance, and furthermore, the distance d' at which the field strength is always less than the free space is greater than the value for the previous case. The result is an increase in the field strength at large distances.

Effect of Curvature of an Ideal Earth. It is to be noted that the discussion given above assumes that the earth is flat. However, when the distance between transmitting and receiving antennas is considerable, it is necessary to take into account the fact that the surface of the earth is curved.

When the receiving antenna is above the horizon of the curved earth, the geometry of Fig. 22-5 is modified as illustrated in Fig. 22-7. The field strength at the receiving antenna is still the vector sum of a direct and a ground-reflected wave. However, because of earth curvature, the antenna heights to be used in Eq. (22-2) are the effective values h'_s and h'_r above the tangent line tt, as shown. Since these effective heights are less than the actual values, one effect of earth curvature is to change the location and number of the maxima and minima of the flat-earth field-strength curve of Fig. 22-6a, and to reduce the distance d' beyond which the two rays tend to be out of phase.

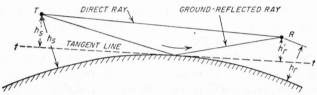

FIG. 22-7. Curved-earth geometry involving direct and ground-reflected rays.

The curvature of the earth also causes the ground-reflected ray to be a diverging rather than plane wave. As a result, the reflected ray at the receiving antenna is weaker than if the reflection were from a flat surface. While this effect is negligible when the angle of incidence at the surface of the earth is moderate to large, it increases as the angle of incidence becomes less. Thus, near glancing incidence the strength of the reflected wave is reduced significantly at the receiving point by the divergence effect. At large distances, where the angle of incidence is small, and the incident and ground-reflected waves are nearly in phase opposition, the resultant field strength at the receiving antenna is accordingly appreciably greater than it would be with a flat earth corresponding to the tangent line in Fig. 22-7.

Since these two effects of earth curvature tend to neutralize each other, the result is that Eq. (22-3) applies with reasonable accuracy as long as the direct path clears the surface of the curved earth (i.e., the radio horizon) by a nominal amount.

A third consequence of earth curvature arises from the fact that when a receiving antenna of moderate height is at a great distance from the transmitter, it is below the radio horizon and so cannot be reached either by a direct or a ground-reflected ray. This situation is illustrated in Fig. 22-8 where the shaded area is termed *the diffraction or shadow zone*.[1]

---

[1] The region outside the shadow zone where line-of-sight propagation is possible is commonly termed the interference region, because in it there are two waves that combine or interfere to give the resultant field.

There are, however, several mechanisms whereby at least some energy from the transmitter can reach a receiving antenna located in the shadow zone even in the absence of direct-ray transmission; these are discussed below on page 823.

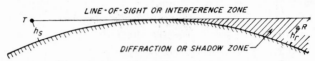

FIG. 22-8. Diagram indicating location of interference and shadow zones.

22-5. Miscellaneous Considerations in Space-wave Propagation.

Effect of Earth Imperfections and Roughness on Field Strength in the Interference Zone. The discussion of space-wave propagation up to this point has assumed that the reflection at the ground takes place with no change in amplitude and with reversal of phase. This assumption is very closely realized for both horizontally and vertically polarized waves provided that the angle of incidence of the rays is very nearly glancing. In all other situations, the finite conductivity and dielectric constant of the earth cause the magnitude of the reflection coefficient to be less than unity, and likewise cause the phase shift upon reflection to differ from 180°, as discussed in Sec. 22-3. The field strength at a receiving point such as R in Fig. 22-5 is still the vector sum of the direct and the ground-reflected waves, but the fact that the ground-reflected ray now has a smaller amplitude than the direct ray causes the field strength to behave in the manner shown by the dotted curves of Fig. 22-6a. The nulls are filled in to a considerable extent, while the field strength at large distances is increased.[1] These effects of earth imperfections are much less pronounced with horizontally polarized waves than with vertical polarization; with vertical polarization the magnitude of the reflection coefficient is commonly quite small at moderately small angles of incidence. (See Fig. 22-4.)

Shadowing Effects of Hills and Buildings. Hills, buildings, trees, etc., will both scatter and absorb energy. The result is a reduction in the strength of the ground-reflected ray that is equivalent to a reduction in the coefficient of reflection. This effect will be quite large in the case of forests, cities, or really rough ground. The criterion of roughness in such cases is the difference $r_1 - r_1'$ of the path lengths of the ground-reflected ray to the receiving antenna without and with the irregularity (see Fig. 22-9). If this difference does not exceed a quarter of a wavelength, the surface can be regarded as electrically smooth. Thus, with glancing

---

[1] For convenience, this dotted curve is drawn on the assumption that the reflection coefficient is independent of the angle of incidence, and that the phase is reversed by the reflection. As an actual matter, both the magnitude and phase of the reflection coefficient will change as increasing distance causes the angle of incidence to vary (see Fig. 22-4); this will affect the distances at which the minima and maxima occur.

incidence, the physical size of an irregularity can be relatively large without destroying the electrical smoothness of the reflecting surface, as compared with the permissible size of the irregularity when the angle of incidence is relatively great.

An irregularity in the terrain, such as a hill or valley, may result in the receiving antenna being located in a local shadow zone, as illustrated in Fig. 22-10. The field strength at the receiving antenna in this case can be determined by replacing the obstacle by an absorbing knife edge, as illustrated, and calculating the strength of the resulting field that is diffracted into the shadow zone.[1] The strength of this received field will be less than the free-space field for the same distance from the transmitter, but is often found to be

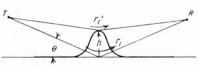

Fig. 22-9. Ground-reflected rays with and without an obstacle at the reflecting point. For the sake of clarity the heights of the obstacle and the antennas are greatly exaggerated.

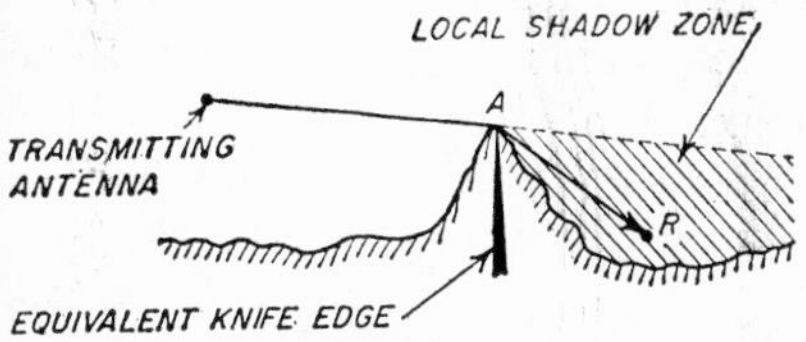

greater than if the obstacle were removed and replaced by a smooth perfectly reflecting earth. This *obstacle gain* results from the fact that the obstacle eliminates the ground-reflected wave. The strength of the field in the shadow zone is less the deeper the receiving antenna is in the shadow as measured in wavelengths. Thus, for a given situation the loss of field strength from a localized shadow will increase the higher the frequency.

Variation of Field Strength with Height. To the extent that Eq. (22-2) applies, then in the case of a flat earth the field strength will vary with height in the manner illustrated in Fig. 22-11. This pattern is characterized by nulls that go clear to zero, and maxima that are twice the free-space field strength. The location of the nulls and maxima will depend upon the height of the transmitting antenna, the frequency, and the distance.

LOCAL SHADOW ZONE

TRANSMITTING ANTENNA

EQUIVALENT KNIFE EDGE

Fig. 22-10. Schematic diagram illustrating local shadow zone produced by a hill.

In an actual case, the fact that the ground is not perfectly reflecting at angles of incidence other than zero prevents the nulls from going to zero, and also causes the maxima to be slightly less than twice the free-space field strength, as shown by the dotted curves in Fig. 22-11.[2] This effect

---

[1] An excellent discussion of the behavior of a wave passing over a knife edge is to be found in "Radio Wave Propagation," *op. cit.*, pp. 81–87.

[2] The imperfections of an actual ground will likewise cause some shifting of the phase of the reflected wave, which will also alter the exact position of the nulls and maxima in Fig. 22-11. For convenience in representation this effect is neglected in Fig. 22-11.

of earth imperfection is much more pronounced with vertically polarized waves than it is with horizontal polarization, since, as shown in Fig. 22-4, the magnitude of the reflection coefficient for vertical polarization departs

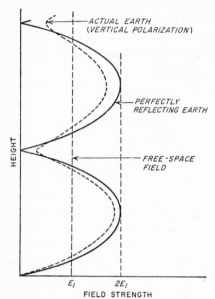

rather rapidly from unity as the angle of incidence deviates even slightly from grazing.

The relation between the field strength, height, and distance is often shown by a diagram of the type illustrated in Fig. 22-12, which consists of contours of constant field strength on a distance-height coordinate system. Such a representation is particularly useful in problems connected with maintaining continuous communication between an airplane and ground. For example, in Fig. 22-12, an airplane that approaches a receiving point at a constant elevation of 30,000 ft will have no difficulty communicating with the ground station when at a distance of 150 miles (point A) which is in a lobe maximum. However, when the

Fig. 22-11. Field strength as a function of height for a hypothetical case assuming a flat earth.

airplane comes in closer so it is 106 miles away (point B), it is in a null in the field-strength pattern. The signals will then be weak, and communication can be maintained only with great difficulty. Still closer to the ground station, for example, at 80 miles (point C), the field strength will again be strong. The actual details in Fig. 22-12, such as location of maxima and minima, depth of the nulls, etc., depend upon the frequency, height of the transmitting antenna, characteristics of the ground, and polarization.

When continuous communication between an airplane and ground is to be maintained, vertical polarization is preferable to horizontal polarization. This is because the behavior of the reflection coefficient with angles of incidence that depart slightly from grazing is such that the nulls in Fig. 22-12 are much less deep with vertical than they are with horizontal polarization.[1]

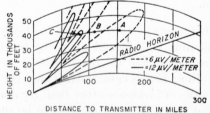

Fig. 22-12. Field-strength contours produced by a particular ground transmitter radiating vertically polarized waves.

[1] The problem of maintaining uninterrupted communication between an airplane

Transition between Ground and Space Waves.   When the transmitting antenna is located near the surface of the earth, a ground (or surface) wave is excited.   The concept of ray transmission then no longer applies in the space immediately adjacent to the earth, and the field strength in this region becomes independent of exact height of the transmitting and receiving antenna.

The antenna height above earth at which ray action in the form of direct and ground-reflected rays predominates over the ground wave depends on the frequency, the polarization, and the electrical constants of the earth.   With vertically polarized waves and earth having good conductivity, the height at which ground-wave action ceases to dominate and ray action begins to be most important is of the order of one or two wavelengths; with earth having very low conductivity this transition height is moderately less, while over sea water it is considerably greater.   This means that when the transmitting antenna is vertically polarized the strength of the ground wave is substantially independent of the height of the antenna above ground as long as this height is less than about one wavelength.   Likewise the strength of the resulting field does not vary significantly with height above ground until the height of the receiving point exceeds about one wavelength.   However, with appreciably greater heights the field strength will vary with height in accordance with the laws of space-wave propagation.

With horizontally polarized waves the critical height below which ground-wave action predominates and above which space-wave action takes over is less than a tenth of a wavelength for a very poorly conducting earth, and even less for good earth and sea water.   Thus the ground wave is normally a negligible factor when dealing with horizontally polarized waves, especially at frequencies above 30 Mc.

It is apparent from these considerations that at the lower frequencies, such as the standard broadcast frequencies (535 to 1605 Mc), the highest antennas that it is practical to use at the transmitter and receiver are such that the *direct* propagation of vertically polarized energy between transmitting and receiving antennas (i.e., not including ionosphere propagation) is necessarily by the ground wave.   The only practical exception to this is when an unusually high elevation is involved, for example, an airplane.   However, at very high frequencies, such as used in television and radar, the critical height at which ray propagation predominates is so small, measured in feet, that ground-wave propagation is of negligible practical importance under practically all conditions.

Comparison of Vertical and Horizontal Polarization in Space-wave

---

and ground is discussed further by Kenneth A. Norton, Gapless Coverage in Air-to-ground Communication at Frequencies above 50 Mc, *Proc. IRE*, vol. 52, p. 470, August, 1952; also see the book by Henry R. Reed and Carl M. Russell, "Ultra High Frequency Communication," John Wiley & Sons, Inc., New York, 1953, which discusses problems of this type very exhaustively.

Propagation. Most of the differences between vertical and horizontal polarization in space-wave propagation have been mentioned above. Briefly, the type of polarization affects the propagation in two principal ways: First, for any angle other than grazing incidence or vertical incidence, the magnitude of the reflected wave will be less with vertical polarization than with horizontal polarization, as discussed in Sec. 22-3. This reduces the amplitude of the ground-reflected wave, and thus modifies the resultant field strength in such a manner that the nulls in the field-strength-versus-distance, and field-strength-versus-height, curves tend to be less deep when the polarization is vertical than when it is horizontal. Second, the height below which ground-wave action must be taken into account is much less with horizontal polarization than with vertical polarization; this is of practical importance at broadcast and lower frequencies, and results in horizontal polarization being avoided at these frequencies.

Another difference between vertical and horizontal polarization that is of importance in practical radio communication is that man-made interference, such as that generated by automobile ignition systems and other electrical equipment, tends to be predominantly vertically polarized when observed close to the earth. Thus by employing horizontal polarization it is possible to achieve some discrimination against these disturbances in applications such as television and frequency-modulation broadcasting.

22-6. Atmospheric Effects in Space-wave Propagation. The atmosphere through which the space wave travels is able to influence the propagation to a significant degree. This arises from the fact that the presence of gas molecules, particularly of water vapor (which has a high dielectric constant), causes the air of the troposphere to have a dielectric constant slightly greater than unity. Now the density of the air, and also the distribution of water vapor, will vary with height. Therefore one can expect that the dielectric constant, and hence the refractive index, of air will also depend upon the height, and in general will decrease with increasing height. This variation of refractive index with height gives rise to a variety of phenomena such as refraction, reflection, scattering, duct transmission, and fading of signals.

Refractive Index of Air. The behavior of a ray traveling in the atmosphere is determined by the refractive index n of the air, which by definition is the square root of the dielectric constant. For reasons that will become obvious later, it has become customary in radio propagation work to express the actual refractive index in terms of a modified refractive index M defined by the relation

$$M = \left(n - 1 + \frac{h}{a}\right) \times 10^6 \qquad (22\text{-}5)$$

where n = refractive index

　　h = height above ground

　　a = radius of earth = 6.37×10^6 m

The aspect of M that is of importance in radio propagation is the variation dM/dh of M with height. When the dielectric constant, and hence n, are independent of height, as is always the case at quite high altitudes, then M, as defined above, increases 0.048 units per ft. However, *near the surface* of the earth the dielectric constant *over land* usually decreases linearly with increasing height. The value of M *near the earth's surface* then increases linearly at a constant rate that is less than 0.048 units per

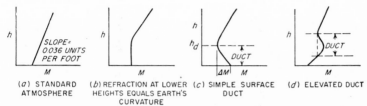

(a) STANDARD	(b) REFRACTION AT LOWER	(c) SIMPLE SURFACE	(d) ELEVATED DUCT
ATMOSPHERE	HEIGHTS EQUALS EARTH'S	DUCT	
	CURVATURE		

Fig. 22-13. Variation of modified refractive index M with height for typical cases. The examples shown are for conditions near the surface of the earth; at great heights the M curve always assumes a slope of 0.048 units per ft, corresponding to a constant refractive index.

ft. For typical conditions of this type, the value of dM/dh approximates 0.036 units per ft; this condition is termed *the standard atmosphere* and results in the M curve shown in Fig. 22-13a.

When air masses that differ in temperature and moisture content overlay each other, the M curve will no longer vary linearly with height. Various types of situations that may then result are illustrated in Fig. 22-13c and d. However, at heights much greater than in Fig. 22-13, the M curve will settle down in all cases (including a) to a steady increase of $0.048M$ units per ft.

Refraction of Rays, and the Radio Horizon. A change in the refractive index with height causes a ray traveling in the atmosphere to bend away from regions of low dielectric constant toward regions of high dielectric constant in accordance with Snell's law, as discussed in Sec. 22-9. Thus when conditions correspond to the standard atmosphere, the wave path will be bent, i.e., refracted, slightly, as illustrated by b in Fig. 22-14, in contrast with the straight-line path a which corresponds to a dielectric constant that does not change with height. When the decrease of dielectric constant with height is at such a rate that M remains *unchanged with height* (Fig. 22-13b), then the curvature of the ray is the same as that of the earth,[1] giving the result shown by c in Fig. 22-14. On the other

---

[1] It is now seen that the definition of the modified refractive index M is so chosen as to lead to this result.

hand, if the dielectric constant of the atmosphere increases with height, the ray path will be bent away from the earth as shown by d.

In studying the behavior of the space wave under conditions illustrated in Fig. 22-14, it is often convenient to change the coordinates in such a manner that the particular ray path of interest is a straight line instead of a curve. This requires that the radius of curvature of the earth be simultaneously readjusted to preserve the correct relative relations. The amount of change in the earth's radius required to achieve this result is given by the relation

$$k = \frac{\text{equivalent radius}}{\text{actual radius}} = \frac{0.048}{dM/dh} \tag{22-6}$$

where dM/dh is the change in M units per ft (assumed positive). For the standard atmosphere, where $dM/dh = 0.036$, the equivalent radius is

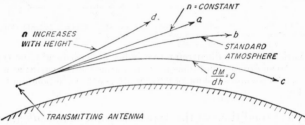

Fig. 22-14. Effect of different rates of variation of refractive index n with height on rays all initially directed horizontally, but subjected to different refractive gradients.

$\frac{4}{3} = 1.33$ times the actual radius of the earth. For Fig. 22-13b, where $dM/dh = 0$, the equivalent radius of the earth is infinite; i.e., the rays behave as though they traveled in a straight line over a flat earth.

The curvature of the ray paths by the atmosphere causes the *radio* horizon to differ from the *optical* horizon. The distance in miles from an antenna to the radio horizon is

$$\text{Radio horizon distance in miles} = \sqrt{1.5kh} \tag{22-7a}$$

where h is the antenna height in feet. In the special case of the standard atmosphere, $k = 1.33$ and the horizon distance becomes

$$\text{Radio horizon distance in miles} = \sqrt{2h} \tag{22-7b}$$

Again, h is in feet. The maximum possible distance at which direct-ray transmission is possible between transmitting and receiving antennas of given heights, the so-called "line-of-sight" distance, is equal to the sum of the horizon distances calculated separately for the individual antenna heights. When the distance involved is less than this line-of-sight value, the path is often referred to as being *optical;* this is in the sense that a ray can pass directly from the transmitting to the receiving antenna.[1]

[1] However, a *good* optical path requires that the ground, including any obstructions, be outside the first Fresnel zone surrounding the direct path. The first Fresnel zone

Duct Propagation.[1]   An M curve of the type illustrated in Fig. 22-13c occurs when the moisture content of the air at the surface of the ground is very high, but decreases rapidly with increasing height.   In the region where dM/dh is negative in Fig. 22-13c, the curvature of the rays passing through the atmosphere is greater than that of the earth.   As a result, energy originating in this region, and initially directed approximately parallel to the earth's surface, tends to be trapped and to propagate

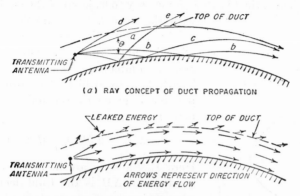

(*a*) RAY CONCEPT OF DUCT PROPAGATION

(*b*) WAVEGUIDE CONCEPT OF DUCT PROPAGATION

Fig. 22-15. Diagram illustrating duct propagation.   For the sake of clarity the duct height is greatly exaggerated in relation to the earth radius; also the angle θ is likewise exaggerated for the same reason.

around the curved surface of the earth in a series of hops involving successive earth reflections, as illustrated by rays a, b, and c in Fig. 22-15. This phenomenon is termed *duct propagation*.[2]

When duct propagation exists, the line-of-sight and diffraction-zone concepts no longer apply, and energy will travel great distances around the curvature of the earth with relative low attenuation.   A quantitative analysis of the situation involved is quite complex.   However, a qualitative understanding can be gained by means of ray concepts as illustrated in Fig. 22-15.   Here the energy represented by rays a, b, and c lying within the angular range θ about the horizontal is trapped within the duct, while rays such as d and e that are outside of this angular range

may be defined as a cylindrical surface of revolution having the direct path as its axis, and possessing a contour such that the distance from the transmitting antenna to a point on the surface plus the distance from this point to the receiving antenna is one-half wavelength greater than the direct path between transmitter and receiver.

[1] The reader desiring further information on this subject will find it helpful to consult "Radio Wave Propagation," *op. cit.*

[2] Duct propagation is also sometimes referred to by the terms *superrefraction*, and *anomalous propagation*.   The term "anomalous" is, however, hardly appropriate since over the open ocean, duct propagation is often the normal, rather than the abnormal, condition.

ultimately pass out of the duct to the space above.   The angle θ within which energy trapping occurs is typically of the order of 1° or less.

It is also possible to view a duct as a waveguide in which the top, represented by the height of the minimum in the M curve, is leaky and allows a part of the energy within the guide (or duct) to escape to the space above the guide, as illustrated in Fig. 22-15b. From the waveguide point of view, one might expect a cutoff phenomenon to exist, and this is indeed the case.   Thus, the tendency for energy to leak out of the guide increases

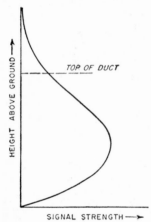

with the ratio λ/h_d of wavelength to duct height, and if this ratio is above a certain critical value the duct effect disappears almost completely.   The maximum wavelength λ_{max} for which duct propagation is possible is given by the following approximate formula

$$\lambda_{max} = 2.5h_d \sqrt{\Delta M \times 10^{-6}} \qquad (22\text{-}8)$$

Here λ_{max} and h_d are in the same units of length, and ΔM is the total decrease in M when going from the bottom to the top of the duct, as illustrated in Fig. 22-13c.

SIGNAL STRENGTH ⟶

Fig. 22-16. Schematic diagram illustrating variation of signal strength with height above earth for a surface duct of the type illustrated in Fig. 22-13c.

Duct heights typically range from tens to hundreds of feet; while ΔM will seldom exceed 50 units.   When these numbers are substituted into Eq. (22-8), it is found that duct propagation is ordinarily limited to ultra-high frequencies and microwaves.

Duct propagation can occur only when the transmitter antenna height is less than the height of the duct, i.e., less than the height of the minimum in the M curve.   When the transmitting antenna lies appreciably above the duct, the presence of the duct has relatively little effect on the signal strength either above or in the duct.   However, if the transmitter is within the duct, then the signal strength at a sufficient distance from the transmitter to be well below the line of sight will vary with height, as illustrated in Fig. 22-16, and at moderate heights will be enormously greater than in the absence of a well-defined duct.   This increase in field strength resulting from a duct extends some distance above the top of the duct as shown in Fig. 22-16; however, at heights that are considerably above the top of the duct the field strength is not significantly affected by the presence of a duct near the surface of the earth even when the transmitter lies within this duct.

Ground-based ducts such as discussed above and illustrated in Figs. 22-13c and 22-15 occur most commonly over water.   In fact, it is believed that such ducts are nearly always present over the ocean, particularly in the trade-wind belts. Ground-based ducts can also occur over land, but this happens less frequently; when it occurs it is always a temporary rather than a continuing condition.

Under certain meteorological conditions the M curve will have the character illustrated in Fig. 22-13*d*. This results in the formation of an elevated duct, as indicated. When the height of the transmitting antenna is such as to place it within such a duct, energy will propagate in the duct to points well beyond the normal radio horizon with surprisingly low attenuation. By locating a receiving antenna within the duct, it is then possible to obtain a strong received signal at distances such that the received field would be extremely weak in the absence of the duct.

Extended-range Propagation Resulting from Tropospheric Scattering[1] and Reflection. When duct propagation occurs, energy readily travels around the curvature of the earth, and greatly increases the signal strength in the part of the shadow zone that lies in the duct. However, even when no duct action whatsoever is present, the strength of a very high-frequency or micro-wave signal at locations very far

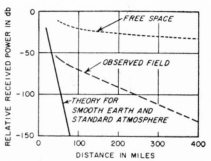

FIG. 22-17. Variation of field strength with distance, showing how the observed field in the shadow zone dies off only slowly with increasing distance.

from the transmitter and deep in the shadow zone is always much greater than would be expected on the basis of diffraction around a smooth earth.[2] The situation that exists is illustrated schematically in Fig. 22-17; the field strength at large distances normally falls off at a rate of only 0.1 to 0.2 db per mile.

Several factors appear to contribute to this result. In the first place, the waves may diffract (i.e., bend) around the curved surface of the earth in the same way that sound waves bend around a corner. The strength of the diffracted field in the shadow zone depends on the roughness of the earth's surface; over most land paths the roughness is great enough to cause the field in the shadow region to be very much greater than would be the case if the earth were perfectly smooth.[3] Second, turbulence in the troposphere gives rise to small irregularities in the refractive index

[1] The knowledge available on this subject is well summarized in an issue of *Proceedings of the IRE* that is to appear early in 1956, and is devoted exclusively to forward-scatter phenomena occurring in the troposphere and the ionosphere.

[2] A good summary of what can be expected is given by Kenneth Bullington, Radio Transmission beyond the Horizon in the 40 to 4000 Mc Band, *Proc. IRE*, vol. 41, p. 132, January, 1953.

[3] Kenneth Bullington, Propagation of UHF and SHF Waves beyond the Horizon, *Proc. IRE*, vol. 38, p. 1221, October, 1950.

which cause energy from rays passing through the troposphere above the intersection of the horizon lines to be scattered to points in the shadow zone, as illustrated in Fig. 22-18.[1] Finally, a gradual but continuous variation of the refractive index in a nonturbulent atmosphere, such as occurs in the standard atmosphere, will produce small reflections that scatter energy into the shadow zone in much the same manner as does turbulence.[2]

The relative contributions that these various mechanisms make to the signal strength observed in the shadow zone depend on circumstances and are not entirely clear; however, in any case the signal behavior in the

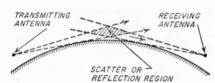

absence of ducts is as shown in Fig. 22-17, and at very great distances diminishes only very slowly with increasing distance. This phenomenon is sometimes referred to as *extended-range propagation*. When the transmitting power is very large and the receiving antenna is able to abstract energy from a large section of wavefront,

Fig. 22-18. Diagram illustrating region in the troposphere where reflections caused by turbulence will scatter energy in such a manner as to reach a receiving antenna located in the shadow zone.

then extended-range propagation makes it possible to obtain usable signals for at least several hundred miles into the shadow zone.[3]

The strength of a signal under extended-range conditions tends to be insensitive to antenna height, at least up to several hundred feet. The extended-range phenomenon is roughly independent of frequency.

Fading of Space-wave Signals. Space-wave signals received at a considerable distance from a transmitter will often fade, i.e., vary in intensity with time. This is a consequence of changing tropospheric conditions, and several different mechanisms can be involved. Thus near the radio horizon, or in a null such as illustrated by the solid lines in Fig. 22-6a, a very slight change in the behavior of the refractive index of the troposphere will produce a large change in signal strength. Again, when the signal at the receiving point is due in part or entirely to duct transmission, changes in the duct condition such as can be produced by local wind eddies will affect the signal strength. In the shadow region, the received

[1] See H. G. Booker and W. E. Gordon, A Theory of Radio Scattering in the Troposphere, *Proc. IRE*, vol. 38, p. 401, April, 1950.

[2] J. Feinstein, Tropospheric Propagation beyond the Horizon, *J. Appl. Phys.*, vol. 22, p. 1292, October, 1951; and Gradient Reflections from the Troposphere, *Trans. IRE (Professional Group on Antennas and Propagation)*, no. 4, p. 2, December, 1952; Thomas J. Carroll, Tropospheric Propagation Well beyond the Horizon, *Trans. IRE (Professional Group on Antennas and Propagation)*, no. 3, p. 84, August, 1952.

[3] Another type of extended-range propagation that is effective for very high frequencies over even greater distances arises from scattering in the ionosphere. This is discussed on p. 848.

signal is commonly the vector sum of several components that travel over different paths to reach the receiving point. Under these conditions the resultant field strength is sensitive to changes in the relative phases of the components, such as are produced by tropospheric turbulence or by small variations in the refractive index along the various paths.

Fading is most pronounced when the received signal is much weaker than the free-space value for the distance involved. Thus fading is usually greatest near the radio horizon and in the shadow zone, and tends to be small when a "good" optical path is present.

The extent and character of the fading on any given path will vary greatly from time to time. Thus the fades may be very deep on some occasions and very minor on others; likewise fading is sometimes rapid and sometimes relatively slow. The behavior in these respects is determined by the meterological conditions in the troposphere, and so will depend upon time of day, season, wind and temperature conditions, humidity, air masses, etc.

When fading is present the signal intensity at any instant is sensitive to frequency, just as is the fading of a short-wave signal, as discussed in connection with Fig. 22-33.

22-7. General Picture of the Ionosphere and Its Effect on Radio Waves.[1] Energy radiated in directions above the horizon will travel through space until it reaches the ionized region in the upper atmosphere. There, if conditions are favorable, the path of the wave will be bent earthward. Such a *sky wave* may return to earth at very great distances from the transmitter, and is the means by which long-distance radio communication is achieved.

The Ionosphere and Its Layers. The upper parts of the earth's atmosphere absorb large quantities of radiant energy from the sun, which not only heats the atmosphere but also produces some ionization in the form of free electrons and positive and negative ions.[2] The part of the upper atmosphere where the ionization is appreciable is called the *ionosphere*.

The ionization in the ionosphere tends to be stratified as a result of differences in the physical properties of the atmosphere at different heights, and because various kinds of radiation are involved. The levels at which the electron density reaches a maximum are termed layers. The three principal daytime maxima, called the E, F1, and F2 layers, are illustrated in Fig. 22-19a. In addition to these regular layers, there is a region below the E layer which is responsible for much of the daytime attenuation of high-frequency radio waves. Called the D region, it lies

---

[1] The literature on the ionosphere and its effects on radio waves is very extensive. The best summary available is "Ionospheric Radio Propagation," circular 462, National Bureau of Standards, 1948.

[2] Other ionizing agents, such as meteors, and possibly thunderstorms, contribute additional amounts of ionization.

between heights of about 50 and 90 km. Its detailed structure is not known with certainty. The heights of the maximum density of the regular E layer and of the F1 layer are relatively constant at about 110 km and 220 km, respectively, with little diurnal or seasonal variation. The F2 layer is more variable, with typical heights lying within the range 250 to 350 km. These are the true heights which are less subject to variation than are the virtual heights discussed below.

At night the F1 layer and F2 layer coalesce to form a single nighttime F2 layer, as shown in Fig. 22-19b. The regular E layer is governed closely by the amount of ultraviolet light from the sun, and at night tends to decay uniformly with time. The D-region ionization is largely absent at night.

An anomalous ionization, termed *sporadic E*, is often present in the E region in addition to the regular E ionization. Sporadic-E ionization usually exhibits the characteristics of a very thin layer which may appear anywhere in the height range of 90 to 130 km. It often occurs in the form of clouds varying in size from roughly 1 km to several hundred kilometers across. The occurrence of sporadic E is quite unpredictable; it may be observed both day and night. The cause of sporadic-E ionization is still uncertain.

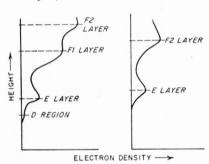

ELECTRON DENSITY ⟶

(*a*) DAY   (*b*) NIGHT

Fig. 22-19. Schematic diagrams illustrating the variation of electron density with height above the earth under typical conditions.

Layer Characteristics. The behavior of the ionospheric layers is usually described in terms of their *virtual heights* and *critical frequencies* because these quantities can be readily measured directly. The virtual height is the height that would be reached by a short pulse of energy showing the same time delay as does the actual pulse reflected from the layer, but traveling with the velocity of light. The virtual height is always greater than the true height of reflection because the interchange of energy that takes place between the wave and the electrons of the ionosphere causes the velocity of propagation to be reduced.[1] The amount of this difference is influenced by the electron distributions in the regions below the level of reflection; it is usually quite small but may on occasions be as large as 100 km, or more.

The critical frequency is the highest frequency that is returned by a

---

[1] Methods of computing the true height from virtual height measurements are given by L. A. Manning, The Determination of Ionospheric Electron Distribution, *Proc. IRE*, vol. 35, p. 1203, November, 1947, and The Reliability of Ionospheric Height Determinations, *Proc. IRE*, vol. 37, p. 599, June, 1949.

layer at vertical incidence.   For the regular layers it is proportional to the square root of the maximum electron density in the layer.

Typical ionosphere behavior is illustrated in Fig. 22-20, which shows the monthly median diurnal variation of virtual heights[1] and critical frequencies of the E, F1, and F2 layers and the sporadic-E (E_s) layer for the months of December, 1952, and June, 1953.   These data, taken at Stanford University, are typical of what can be expected in temperate latitudes near the minimum of the 11-year sunspot cycle.   The critical frequencies of the E and F1 layers depend primarily on the zenith angle of

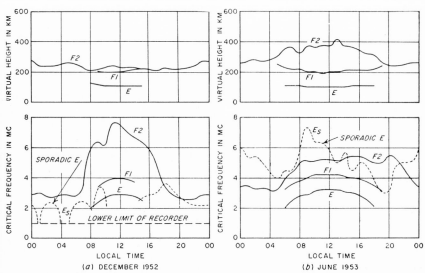

FIG. 22-20. Curves taken at Stanford University illustrating typical variation of virtual height and critical frequency of the various ionosphere layers with time of day during summer and winter.

the sun, and hence follow a regular diurnal cycle, being maximum at noon and tapering off on either side as shown.   The critical frequency of the F2 layer, on the other hand, shows a much larger seasonal variation, and also changes more from day to day.   It will be noted that the critical frequencies of the regular layers decrease greatly during the night as a result of recombination in the absence of solar radiation.   However, the sporadic-E critical frequency shows irregular variation throughout the day and night, a fact which suggests that sporadic E is affected strongly by factors other than solar radiation.

There is a long-term variation in all ionosphere characteristics closely associated with the 11-year sunspot cycle.   This is illustrated in Fig. 22-21, which shows the yearly averages of the twelve-month running-

[1] These values of virtual height are the minimum values observed for the respective layers in measurements of the type illustrated in Fig. 22-29.

mean sunspot number and the twelve-month running-mean F2 noon critical frequencies at Washington, D.C., throughout two cycles. From minimum to maximum of the cycle the F2-layer critical frequencies vary from about 6 to 11 Mc, or in a ratio of 1.8. On the other hand, the E-layer critical frequencies (not shown) vary from 3.1 to 3.8 Mc, a ratio of only 1.2. Long-term predictions of ionosphere characteristics are based on predictions of the sunspot number.[1] Reliable estimates can be made for as much as a year in advance.

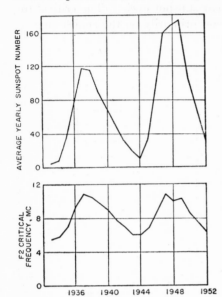

22-8. Mechanism by Which the Ionosphere Affects Radio-wave Propagation. When a radio wave passes through the ionosphere, the electric field of the wave exerts a force on the electrons of the ionosphere. To the extent that the earth's magnetic field does not complicate the situation, the electrons vibrate sinusoidally along paths parallel with the electric flux lines of the wave. These vibrating electrons represent an alternating current proportional to the velocity of vibration. Moreover, the maximum velocity of the electrons lags 90° behind the electric field; i.e., the electron current is inductive.

Fig. 22-21. Curves showing correlation of observed F2 layer critical frequency with sunspot numbers over 11-year sunspot cycles. The qualities plotted are the yearly averages for noon in Washington, D.C., of the 12-month running mean.

The actual current flowing through a volume of space in the ionosphere accordingly consists of two components: the usual capacitive current that leads the voltage by 90°, and the electron current that lags the voltage by 90° and therefore subtracts from the capacitive current. The effect of free electrons in space is therefore to decrease the current, which is equivalent to reducing the dielectric constant of the space below the value that would apply in the absence of electrons.[2] This

[1] Thus see "Ionospheric Radio Propagation," *op. cit.*, p. 76.

[2] The quantitative relations can be developed by imagining a cubic meter of space across which an electric field of $E = E_m \sin \omega t$ volts per m is acting. The capacitance of this unit volume is $k_0 = 8.854 \times 10^{-12}$ farads, and the capacitive current i_c through it is

$$i_c = \omega k_0 E_m \cos \omega t \qquad (22\text{-}9a)$$

Assume now that the space contains free electrons of charge e coulombs and mass m kg. Each electron is then acted upon by a force eE newtons, and assuming no

reduction in the effective dielectric constant introduced by the presence of the electrons in the ionosphere causes the path of a wave traveling through the ionosphere to be bent away from the regions of high electron density toward regions of lower electron density, as discussed below.

The magnitude of the electron current is greater the lower the frequency, as the average velocity of the vibrating electrons is inversely proportional to frequency. When the frequency is low enough so that the electron current is equal in magnitude to the capacitive (or displacement) current, the net current produced in space by the radio wave is zero. The dielectric constant of the ionosphere under these conditions is likewise zero.

An alternative but equivalent method of interpreting the effect that the electrons in the ionosphere have on a radio wave is to consider that each vibrating electron acts as a small radio antenna that abstracts energy from the passing radio wave, and then reradiates this energy. Since the electron current lags the electric field of the radio wave by 90°, these vibrating electrons act as parasitic antennas tuned to offer an inductive reactance (see page 905). The net effect is then to alter the direction in which the resultant energy flows.

Ions in the path of a radio wave behave in the same way as electrons. However, because of their heavier mass, ions move much more slowly than electrons when under the influence of the same electric field, and so in comparison have negligible effect.

Effect of the Earth's Magnetic Field.[1] The effect that electrons in the atmosphere have on radio waves is influenced by the fact that these electrons are in the presence of the earth's magnetic field, which exerts a

---

collisions, will move in accordance with the relation

$$-Ee = m \, dv/dt \tag{22-9b}$$

where v is the instantaneous velocity of the electron in meters per second *in the direction of the electric field*. Integrating, and setting the constant of integration equal to zero gives

$$v = (e/m\omega)E_m \cos \omega t \tag{22-9c}$$

Since current is equal to the product of velocity and charge, N negative electrons per cu m moving with velocity v will produce current which is

$$i_e = -(Ne^2/m\omega)E_m \cos \omega t \tag{22-9d}$$

The total current i flowing in 1 cu m is hence

$$i = i_c + i_e = \omega[k_0 - (Ne^2/m\omega^2)]E_m \cos \omega t \tag{22-9e}$$

The quantity $[k_0 - (Ne^2/m\omega^2)]$ is the effective dielectric constant of the ionized space, and is seen to be less than the value k_0 of space in the absence of ionization.

[1] An excellent tutorial discussion of this subject is given by G. W. O. Howe, The Effect of the Earth's Magnetic Field in the Ionosphere, *Wireless Eng.*, vol. 21, p. 1, January, 1944.

deflecting force on the moving electrons, as explained in Sec. 6-2. The force on each has a magnitude proportional to the product of instantaneous velocity of the electron and the component of the earth's magnetic field that is at right angles to the velocity of the electron. The direction of the force is at right angles to the velocity of the electron and also at right angles to the component of the magnetic field giving rise to the force.

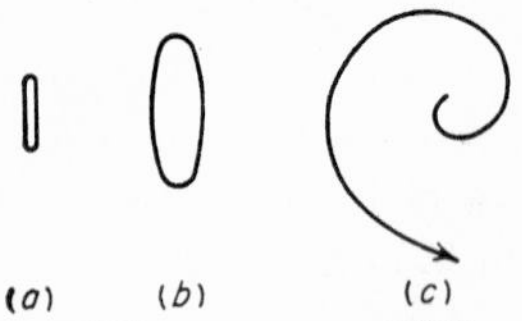

At the higher radio frequencies a component of magnetic field at right angles to the electric field of the incident radio wave causes the vibrating electrons to follow elliptical paths as illustrated in Fig. 22-22a and b. Since certain portions of such paths have components at right angles to the electric field of the wave, some of the energy absorbed by the electrons from the wave is reradiated with a polarization that is

(a)   (b)   (c)
HIGH   GYRO
FREQUENCIES   FREQUENCY

Fig. 22-22. The paths followed by an electron in the earth's magnetic field vibrating under the influence of a radio wave.

rotated 90° in space with respect to the polarization of the incident wave. This reradiated cross-polarized component also generally differs in time phase from the field of the incident wave. Hence the earth's magnetic field will normally cause a radio wave that was originally plane polarized to become elliptically polarized[1] after it has traveled some distance in the ionosphere.

The effect of the earth's magnetic field on the paths of the vibrating electrons is greater the lower the frequency. This is because the average velocity of the electrons is inversely proportional to frequency. Thus at very high frequencies the electrons vibrate in paths that are very narrow ellipses, but as the frequency is lowered the amplitude of the vibration increases and the minor axis of the ellipse becomes at the same time pro-

[1] Elliptical polarization results whenever there are vertical and horizontal components having different phase. Elliptical polarization is characterized by the fact that the resultant magnetic (or electric) fields produced by an alternating wave never at any instant pass through zero; rather, the resultant fields rotate in the plane of the wavefront at a rate corresponding to the frequency of the wave, while at the same time pulsating in amplitude. The resultant field produced by elliptical polarization can, therefore, be represented by a rotating vector of varying length as illustrated in Fig. 22-23. The field can never be zero because the vertical and horizontal components do not pass through zero at the same instant.

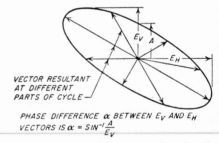

VECTOR RESULTANT
AT DIFFERENT
PARTS OF CYCLE

PHASE DIFFERENCE α BETWEEN E_V AND E_H
VECTORS IS $\alpha = SIN^{-1} \dfrac{A}{E_V}$

Fig. 22-23. Diagram illustrating electric fields of an elliptically polarized wave when the wavefront is in the plane of the paper.

The sense of the polarization depends upon the direction of the earth's magnetic field, and is accordingly different in the Northern and Southern Hemispheres.

portionately larger, as shown in Fig. 22-22*b*. This tendency continues until the frequency is lowered to a point where cyclotron resonance occurs, and the electrons then follow a spiral path of steadily increasing radius, as shown in Fig. 22-22*c*, along which the velocity also progressively increases. This resonance occurs at approximately 1400 kc, which is termed the *gyro frequency*. At still lower frequencies the electrons follow relatively complicated paths having components of motion that are both parallel and at right angles to the plane of polarization of the radio wave.

The effect of the earth's magnetic field upon a radio wave in any particular case will depend very greatly upon the relative orientation of the magnetic flux line with respect to the plane of polarization of the wave. For example, when the earth's magnetic field is in the same direction as the electric field of the radio wave, then the magnetic field has no effect whatsoever.

A quantitative analysis of the propagation of a radio wave through an ionized medium in the presence of a magnetic field shows that in addition to affecting the polarization, the magnetic field also causes the wave to be split into two components.[1] These are termed the *ordinary* and *extraordinary* rays, and they have elliptical polarizations that rotate in opposite directions. These two rays are bent different amounts by the ionized medium and hence travel through it along slightly different paths, and with rates of energy absorption and velocities that differ. This action is termed *magneto-ionic splitting;* its extent, i.e., the relative amplitude of the extraordinary ray, depends on the magnitude of the magnetic effects.

Energy Losses in the Ionosphere. Even though the gas pressure in the ionosphere is very low, the electrons set in vibration by a passing wave will from time to time collide with gas molecules. When such a collision occurs the kinetic energy that the electron has acquired from the radio wave is lost in so far as the radio wave is concerned. The amount of energy absorbed from a passing radio wave in this manner depends upon the gas pressure (i.e., upon the likelihood of a vibrating electron colliding with a gas molecule) and upon the velocity that the electron acquires in its vibration (i.e., upon the energy lost per collision), as well as upon the number of electrons. As a consequence, most of the absorption suffered by a wave passing through the ionosphere usually takes place at the lower edge of the ionized region where the atmospheric pressure is greatest, i.e., in the D region and the lower part of the E layer; very little loss normally occurs higher in the ionosphere because of the very low atmospheric pressure at the greater heights. Other things being equal, the absorption will also be less the higher the frequency; this is because the average velocity of the vibrating electrons, and hence the energy lost

[1] In some situations three components are produced; see O. E. H. Rydbeck, Magneto-ionic Triple Splitting of Atmospheric Waves, *J. Appl. Phys.*, vol. 21, p. 1205, December, 1950.

per collision, are inversely proportional to frequency. The absorption is also influenced by the earth's magnetic field, tending to be high at frequencies near the gyro frequency.

This energy absorption can be taken into account mathematically by assuming that the ionosphere has conductivity. Thus to a radio wave, the ionosphere behaves like a dielectric having a dielectric constant less than unity and possessing some conductivity. The proper values to assign to the dielectric constant and conductivity are affected by the presence and orientation of the earth's magnetic field, and are different for the ordinary and the extraordinary rays.

22-9. Refraction and Reflection of Sky Waves by the Ionosphere. *Refraction.* The bending of the radio-wave path introduced by the ionosphere can be readily expressed in terms of the refractive index of the ionized region, i.e., the square root of its dielectric constant. To the extent that one can neglect the effect of the earth's magnetic field and the effect of energy loss, the refractive index of the ionosphere is given by the expression[1]

$$n = \sqrt{k} = \sqrt{1 - \frac{81N}{f^2}} \qquad (22\text{-}10)$$

where n = refractive index

k = equivalent dielectric constant relative to that of free space

N = number of electrons per cc

f = frequency, kc

Examination of Eq. (22-10) shows that real values of the refractive index will always be less than unity, as is to be expected from the qualitative discussion in Sec. 22-8 regarding the effect of the electrons on the dielectric constant of the ionosphere. It will be noted further that the deviation of the refractive index from unity becomes greater the lower the frequency and the higher the electron density.

When $f^2 < 81N$, the refractive index is imaginary. The ionized region is not able to transmit a wave freely at such a frequency; instead an attenuation takes place that is analogous to the action of a waveguide operating beyond cutoff (see Sec. 5-8).

The phase velocity of a wave traveling through the ionosphere behaves the same as does the phase velocity of a wave on a transmission line; i.e., the velocity is inversely proportional to the square root of the dielectric constant. One can hence write

$$\text{Phase velocity} = \frac{\text{velocity of light}}{n} \qquad (22\text{-}11)$$

Since $n < 1$ for an ionized medium, the phase velocity in the ionosphere

[1] The value given for k is obtained from Eq. (22-9e) when appropriate numbers are substituted.

is always greater than the velocity of light by an amount that is greater[1] the larger the quantity N/f^2. As a result, when a wave enters the ionosphere, the edge of the wavefront in the region of highest electron density will advance faster than the part of the wavefront encountering regions of lower electron density. The wave path in the ionosphere is accordingly bent as in Fig. 22-24.

This bending of a wave produced by the ionosphere follows ordinary optical laws. Thus the direction in which a wave travels at a point P in the ionosphere is given by Snell's law, which for this case is

$$n \sin \phi = \sin \phi_0 \qquad (22\text{-}12)$$

where n = refractive index at point P

ϕ = angle of refraction at point P (see Fig. 22-24)

ϕ_0 = angle of incidence at lower edge of the ionosphere (see Fig. 22-24)

Equation (22-12) assumes that below the ionosphere, where the direction of travel is given by ϕ_0, the refractive index is unity.

The top P_m of the path in Fig. 22-24 corresponds to $\phi = 90°$, and so occurs at a point in the ionosphere where the refractive index n satisfies the relation

$$n = \sin \phi_0 \qquad (22\text{-}13)$$

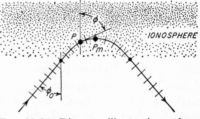

Fig. 22-24. Diagram illustrating refraction of a radio wave in the ionosphere, and showing notation used in Eq. (22-12).

The point P_m is commonly referred to as the point of reflection, although it is actually the point of refraction. Equation (22-13) shows that the smaller the angle of incidence ϕ_0, the smaller the refractive index (and hence the higher the electron density) required to return the wave toward the earth.

With vertical incidence ($\phi_0 = 0$), the refractive index must be reduced to zero for reflection to take place. The wave then penetrates the ionized region until it reaches a point where the electron density N and the frequency f_v of the vertically incident wave are so related that

$$f_v^2 = 81N \qquad (22\text{-}14)$$

---

[1] This behavior is analogous to that occurring in a waveguide, where the phase velocity is likewise always greater than the velocity of light. The group velocity in the ionosphere, i.e., the velocity with which energy actually travels, is less than the velocity of light, as discussed below in Sec. 22-11. An extraordinarily fine tutorial discussion of phase and group velocity in the ionosphere is given by G. W. O. Howe, Phase and Group Velocity in the Ionosphere, *Wireless Eng.*, vol. 20, p. 577, December, 1953.

The Critical Frequency. When N in Eq. (22-14) corresponds to the maximum electron density of an ionospheric layer, the frequency specified by Eq. (22-14) is termed the *critical frequency* of that layer, and is commonly designated as f_c. Waves of the critical frequency and lower will be reflected from the layer in question irrespective of angle of incidence. Waves having a frequency greater than the critical value will be returned to earth only when the angle of incidence ϕ_0 is sufficiently glancing to enable Eq. (22-13) to be satisfied at the frequency involved; otherwise, the wave will pass on through the layer. This is discussed further in Sec. 22-10.

Reflection. Equation (22-12) gives the path of a ray only when the change of refractive index n with height is small in a distance corresponding to one wavelength in the medium. Otherwise there is an appreciable reflection as well as refraction of the wave energy, and the propagation can no longer be described in terms of a simple ray path such as shown in Fig. 22-24. In the extreme case, where the change in refractive index is very large in the space of a wavelength, one has a true reflection from a well-defined boundary. For the intermediate situations a mixture of reflection and refraction takes place. Under these conditions the computation of propagation becomes a relatively difficult problem.[1]

At very low frequencies the distance corresponding to a wavelength is large, and reflection processes tend to predominate over refraction. Again in the case of sporadic-E layers, the assumption of a slowly varying medium does not hold; the observed behavior then corresponds to a partial reflection at a sharply defined boundary. At broadcast and shortwave frequencies, the characteristics of the normal ionospheric ionization are such that refraction theory is quite accurate.

22-10. Ray Paths, Skip Distance, and Maximum Usable Frequency. When the frequency of a wave exceeds the critical value, the effect of the ionosphere depends upon the angle of incidence at the ionosphere, as illustrated in Fig. 22-25. When the angle of incidence ϕ_0 is relatively large (ray 1), Eq. (22-13) is satisfied when the refractive index n drops to a value only slightly less than unity; under these conditions the wave is returned to the earth after only slight penetration of the ionized region. However, as the angle of incidence is decreased (rays 2, 3, and 4) the refractive index must be progressively smaller in order to return the wave, and the penetration into the layer is deeper. Finally, if the angle of incidence is small enough so that Eq. (22-13) cannot be satisfied even by the maximum electron density of the layer, the wave penetrates the layer (paths 5 and 6).

Study of Fig. 22-25 brings to light an interesting and important phenomenon. It will be noted that as the angle of incidence at the iono-

---

[1] Thus, for example, C. H. Bremmer, "Terrestrial Radio Waves," p. 214, Elsevier Press, Inc., Houston, Tex., 1949.

sphere decreases, the distance from the transmitter at which the ray
returns to ground first decreases (rays 1 and 2).   This behavior continues until eventually an angle of incidence is reached at which the distance is a minimum; this is called the *skip distance* (ray 3).   With further
decrease in the angle of incidence, the distance to the point of return first
increases (ray 4)[1] and then with still smaller (i.e., less grazing) angles the
wave will penetrate the layer (rays 5 and 6).

The skip distance represents the minimum distance from the transmitter at which a sky wave of a given frequency will be returned to earth

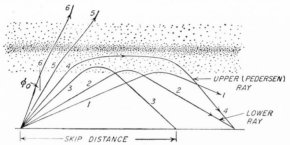

FIG. 22-25. Ray paths for different angles of incidence ϕ_0 at the ionosphere.

by the ionosphere.   Conversely, the frequency which makes a given
receiving point correspond to a distance from the transmitter equal to the
skip distance for that frequency is termed the *maximum usable frequency*
(often abbreviated MUF) for communication to the receiving point.   An
ionospheric layer will not return a sky wave to a given receiving point
when the frequency of transmission exceeds the maximum usable frequency for that receiving point.

At distances from the transmitter greater than the skip distance it is
apparent from Fig. 22-25 that two rays can reach a given receiving point;
these are termed the lower ray and the upper, or Pedersen, ray.   The
upper ray is usually not of great practical importance because it tends to
be much weaker than the lower ray.   This is because the upper-ray
energy that passes through a given solid angle from the transmitter is
spread over a much larger area over the ground than will be the case with
the lower ray.   However, the upper ray becomes of practical importance
when circumstances prevent the lower ray from reaching the receiver, as
for example when the curvature of the earth prevents one-hop lower-ray
transmission, and the critical frequency is such as to prevent two-hop
lower-ray transmission.

Two or even three separate layers may contribute to the propagation of

---

[1] This increase results from the fact that near the region of maximum electron
density, the change of electron density with height is relatively small.   Ray 4 in
Fig. 22-25 must therefore travel a long distance in this region before its path is bent
back to earth.

energy to a receiving point.   Such a situation is illustrated in Fig. 22-26.
Here the frequency of the wave is assumed to lie between the critical
frequencies of the E and F2 layers, and the receiving point is beyond the
skip distance for the E layer.   There is no skip distance for the F2 layer
in this case, since the frequency of the wave is less than the critical frequency of this layer.   In this situation there are two rays that reach the
receiver via the E layer, an upper ray (shown dotted) and a lower ray.
At a somewhat smaller value of angle ϕ_0 such that the refractive index for
the E-layer maximum electron density is greater than $\sin \phi_0$, the ray
penetrates the E layer and is reflected in the F2 layer, as shown by the

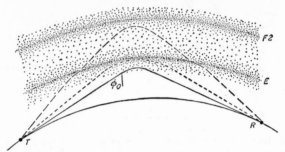

FIG. 22-26. Typical ray paths when two layers are present.

dashed path.   It will be noted that although the E layer is penetrated it
may still cause appreciable bending of the ray path.   In this case no
upper ray exists in the F2 layer; however, if the wave frequency were
greater than the F2 layer critical frequency an upper ray would exist.

Multiple-hop Transmission.   When the skip distance is less than half
of the distance to the receiving point, it is possible for energy to reach
the receiver simultaneously along several paths, corresponding to different
numbers of hops, as illustrated in Fig. 22-27a.   Under these circumstances it is generally found, however, that the rays will be weaker the
greater the number of hops (see Sec. 22-13).

The longest single-hop distance possible for lower-ray transmission corresponds to a ray that leaves the transmitter tangent to the earth's surface (see Fig. 22-27b).   The earth curvature is such that for typical
virtual heights of the ionosphere layers, these maximum one-hop distances are of the order of 2000 and 4000 km for E-layer and F2-layer
propagation, respectively.   At greater distances, lower-ray transmission
is possible only by means of two or more hops, depending on the total
distance, as shown in Fig. 22-27b.   Propagation will then be affected by
conditions in the ionosphere at *each* reflection point along the path.
These conditions will in general be different over east-west paths because
of time differences, and also in the case of paths which pass through or
near the auroral zone.

An example of multiple-hop propagation involving both the E and F2

layers is shown in Fig. 22-28.   An east-west transmission path is assumed
which crosses the line between day and night.   Only the lower ray is
shown for simplicity.   The frequency is chosen greater than both the E
and F2 critical frequencies, but low enough so that reflection from the E
layer can occur at low take-off angles.   On the daylight side of the path
the electron density of the E layer is sufficient to cause reflection of ray a.

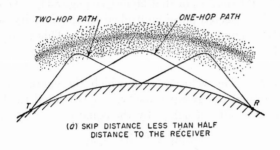

(a) SKIP DISTANCE LESS THAN HALF
DISTANCE TO THE RECEIVER

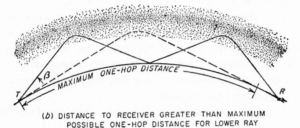

(b) DISTANCE TO RECEIVER GREATER THAN MAXIMUM
POSSIBLE ONE-HOP DISTANCE FOR LOWER RAY

FIG. 22-27. Typical examples of two-hop transmission.

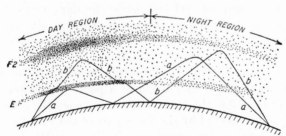

FIG. 22-28. Multiple-hop transmission involving both E and F2 layers.

However, on the second hop the E-layer critical frequency is enough
lower so that the ray passes through the E layer even though the angle
of incidence is the same as that on the first hop.   When the second-hop
ray reaches the F2 layer it is reflected because this layer has a greater
electron density.   Ray b, which takes off at a higher angle than a, penetrates the E layer and is reflected from the F2 layer.   On the second hop
it is likewise reflected from the F2 layer, but at a somewhat greater height,
since the ionization density of the night region of the F2 layer is less

22-11. Vertical-incidence Measurements of the Ionosphere—Group Velocity and Group Delay. The properties of the ionosphere are normally determined by transmitting vertically a short pulse of radio-frequency energy of about 50 μsec duration. If conditions are right, the pulse will be reflected by the ionosphere and returned to earth. The maximum frequency at which a reflection is obtained from a particular layer is the *critical frequency* of that layer (see page 834). One-half of the time delay of the reflected pulse multiplied by the velocity of light gives the apparent or *virtual height* of the reflection. This is always greater than the height actually reached since the pulse travels more slowly in the ionosphere than it does in free space.

Group Velocity. The velocity with which the energy travels in the ionosphere is termed the group velocity. It is related to the refractive index n and the velocity of light c by the equation

$$\text{Group velocity} = nc \qquad (22\text{-}15)$$

Since n is always less than unity in an ionized region, the ionosphere causes a slowing down in the speed with which information such as a pulse of energy travels; this is called *group delay*. The group delay is especially great when the apex of the ray path lies near the region of maximum electron density of a layer; thus the group delay (and hence the virtual height) with vertically incident signals is relatively large in the vicinity of the critical frequency.

Interpretation of Vertical-incidence Records. An actual record of virtual height as a function of frequency obtained using vertically transmitted pulses is reproduced in Fig. 22-29.[1] The horizontal lines represent virtual-height intervals of 100 km, while the dark vertical lines mark various points on the frequency scale. Starting at the low end of the frequency scale (about 1600 kc), there is seen an E-layer echo at a virtual height of 105 km. At 2.2 Mc this echo fades out,[2] reappearing at 2.3 Mc at a height of 115 km. The virtual height increases (primarily because of increased group delay) to 140 km at a point just below the E-layer critical frequency of 3.0 Mc. Above this frequency the pulse penetrates the E layer and is reflected by the lower part of the F1 layer. However, because of the large group retardation in the vicinity of the E critical frequency, the virtual height of the F1 echo is large (260 km in this case). With further increase in frequency the virtual height first drops because of the rapid decrease in E-layer retardation, and then as the F1 critical

---

[1] A summary discussion of such measurements is given by F. E. Terman and J. M. Pettit, "Electronic Measurements," pp. 470–478, McGraw-Hill Book Company, Inc., New York, 1952.

[2] This fadeout represents the region of a critical frequency due to a minor maximum in the electron density in the lower part of the normal E layer. The signal disappears near this critical frequency because there is then a large group delay and hence large time for energy absorption to take place in this energy-absorbing region.

frequency is approached begins to rise because of increasing F1 retardation. The virtual height reaches a maximum at the critical frequency (poorly defined on this record) at 4.3 Mc. This process is repeated in the F2 layer, whose critical frequency is 7.4 Mc. These rays, denoted by *o* in Fig. 22-29, are the *ordinary* rays.

Magneto-ionic separation of the incident pulse into two components with different time delays is clearly evident in the F1 and F2 traces of Fig. 22-29. The extraordinary trace, designated by *x*, is similar in

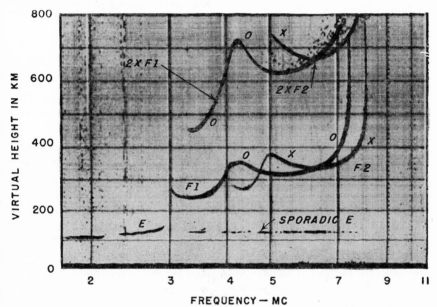

Fig. 22-29. Actual recording of virtual height as a function of frequency, taken at Stanford, California, in October, 1952, at 2:15 P.M.

shape, but is displaced to the right in frequency and upwards in height. The separation of the ordinary and extraordinary critical frequencies depends on the strength of the earth's magnetic field and in this case is about 0.7 Mc. The extraordinary echoes from the E layer do not appear because they are highly absorbed.

Two-hop echoes of $F1^o$, $F2^o$, and $F2^x$ appear at twice the heights of the first-hop echoes. Weak sporadic-E reflections appear between 3.3 and about 7.5 Mc at a height of 125 km. Note that these echoes appear simultaneously with those from the F1 and F2 layers, indicating that the sporadic-E layer produces only partial but not complete reflection.

22-12. Relations between Oblique- and Vertical-incidence Transmission. Since the basic information on the properties of the ionosphere is normally obtained by measurements made at vertical incidence, whereas propagation of radio waves to distant points involves oblique incidence at the ionosphere, it is necessary to know the relation between oblique- and vertical-incidence propagation.

Consider the situation illustrated in Fig. 22-30. An actual sky wave of frequency f traveling from T to R will follow a path such as TBR. The apex B of the path corresponds to a point in the ionosphere where the electron density is such as to make the refractive index satisfy Eq. (22-13). If f_v is the frequency that a wave must have to be reflected from the same point B in the ionosphere when vertically incident on the ionosphere (path GB), then by com-

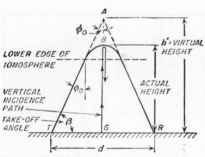

FIG. 22-30. Diagram showing actual wave path in the ionosphere, together with the equivalent triangular path that gives the virtual height.

bining[1] Eqs. (22-10), (22-13), and (22-14), and assuming a *flat* ionosphere,[2] one has

$$f = f_v \sec \phi_0 \qquad (22\text{-}16)$$

The relation expressed by Eq. (22-16) is commonly called the *secant law.*

Consider now the triangular path TAR defined in Fig. 22-30 by extending the straight-line portions of the actual path TBR. The time required for a signal to travel at the group velocity over the actual path TBR is then the same as that required for a signal traveling at the velocity of light to travel over the equivalent path TAR.[3] Thus the ionosphere could be replaced by a perfect reflector located at the height of point A (the virtual height) without affecting the conditions of propagation, to the extent that the spherical curvature of the ionosphere (but not of the earth) can be neglected.

It can also be shown that the height AG of the equivalent triangular

---

[1] This is done by substituting the value of n from Eq. (22-10) into Eq. (22-13), and then using Eq. (22-14) to eliminate N.

[2] When the distance of transmission is very great and the frequency is close to the maximum usable value, the wave travels sufficient distance horizontally in the ionosphere to make it necessary to take into account ionosphere curvature. This is done by multiplying sec ϕ_0 in Eq. (22-16) by a factor that depends on the distribution of electron density with height, and which increases with distance. For frequencies near the maximum usable frequency this factor is of the order of 1.2 for typical paths returning to earth at a distance of 4000 km, and drops to nearly unity for paths of the order of 1000 km and less; for frequencies well below the maximum usable frequency the factor tends to be closer to unity. Further details are given in "Ionospheric Radio Propagation," *op. cit.*, p. 72.

[3] This may be proved by noting that the horizontal component of the group velocity is $cn \sin \phi = c \sin \phi_0$, which means that the horizontal component of velocity is independent of the refractive index n. The signal therefore arrives at a point B of the actual path at the same instant as a signal traveling at the velocity of light would arrive at point A of the equivalent triangular path.

path with its apex at A in Fig. 22-30 is the same as the virtual height measured at the equivalent vertical incidence frequency f_v; this frequency f_v is related to the equivalent oblique incidence frequency f by the secant law of Eq. (22-16). This relation, called the *equivalence theorem*, is the basis for relating vertical-incidence data to oblique-incidence conditions.[1]

Transmission Curves and Their Use to Obtain Skip Distance and Maximum Usable Frequency. The angle ϕ_0 in Eq. (22-16) and Fig. 22-30 can be expressed in terms of distance d and the virtual height $h' = AG$ for the ionosphere conditions at the apex B of the actual path. Thus for the flat-earth geometry of Fig. 22-30 one has

$$\sec \phi_0 = \frac{\sqrt{h'^2 + (d^2/4)}}{h'} \tag{22-17}$$

When the distance is so great that the earth curvature must be taken into account, then the value of ϕ_0 in Eq. (22-16) is given by the relation

$$\tan \phi_0 = \frac{\sin (d/2R)}{1 + (h'/R) - \cos (d/2R)} \tag{22-18}$$

where R ($= 6367$ km) is the radius of the earth. It is necessary to use Eq. (22-18) in place of Eq. (22-17) only when the distance d is greater than about $100\sqrt{h'}$ km; for smaller distances the assumption of a flat earth is permissible. The maximum permissible value of d that can be used in Eq. (22-18) corresponds to the one-hop distance with zero take-off angle (see page 843).

Equation (22-17) or (22-18) in conjunction with Eq. (22-16) gives the relationship that must exist between distance d, frequency f, virtual height h', and the vertical incidence frequency f_v corresponding to this virtual height, in order for a ray path to be possible between the transmitter and the receiver. A relation of this type, calculated for a given value of distance d and frequency f, is called a *transmission curve;* examples are shown in Fig. 22-31a for a given d.

Ionospheric vertical-incidence measurements such as illustrated in Fig. 22-29 give the experimentally observed relationship between virtual height and f_v. A typical set of such data is also plotted in Fig. 22-31a. The points at which this experimental curve intersects the transmission curve for a specified frequency f correspond to virtual heights of paths by which energy at this frequency f may travel between a transmitter and a receiver separated by the specified distance d, when the ionosphere has the characteristics given by the experimental curve. One of these intersections corresponds to the lower ray, and the other to the upper ray, as illustrated schematically in Fig. 22-31b for $f = 10$ Mc. If either the frequency or the distance is changed, the transmission curve determining

---

[1] For proof, see S. K. Mitra, "The Upper Atmosphere," 2d ed., p. 237, The Asiatic Society, Calcutta, 1952.

the intersections is changed; i.e., the depth of penetration into the ionosphere is altered.

If a series of transmission curves is plotted for the same distance but different frequencies, as in Fig. 22-31a, then the particular curve that is tangent to the experimentally observed curve corresponds to the *maximum usable frequency* as defined on page 835. In Fig. 22-31a this frequency is about 11.5 Mc.

If a series of transmission curves for the same frequency but different distances are calculated and plotted, there will again be one particular curve that is tangent to the experimentally observed curve of virtual

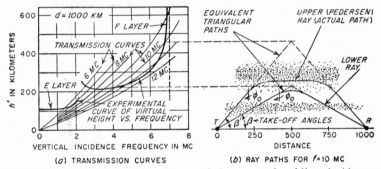

(a) TRANSMISSION CURVES   (b) RAY PATHS FOR f=10 MC

Fig. 22-31. Diagram illustrating use of transmission curves for oblique incidence, with data giving the virtual height as a function of frequency for vertical incidence, together with the actual and the equivalent triangular paths for a typical case.

height versus vertical incidence frequency. The distance corresponding to this condition is the *skip distance* for that frequency as defined on page 835. For it there is only one possible transmission path between transmitter and receiver; i.e., the upper and lower rays merge together.

The secant law, and the transmission curves derived from it, are based on Eq. (22-10), and so neglect the effect of the earth's magnetic field on the ray paths. In spite of this, values of maximum usable frequency and skip distance that are sufficiently accurate for most purposes can be obtained by calculating the transmission curves for zero magnetic field, i.e., by Eqs. (22-16) to (22-18), and then ignoring the extraordinary ray. The justification for this is that the ordinary ray is affected very little by the magnetic field, whereas for oblique incidence at the ionosphere the actual h'-f_v curve for the extraordinary ray is shifted sufficiently upward and to the right in Fig. 22-31a to cause the maximum usable frequency and the skip distance for this ray to be about the same as for the ordinary ray.

In actual practice, each individual layer of the ionosphere has its own skip distance and its own maximum usable frequency. The true maximum usable frequency that is effective in transmission to a given receiving point is then the highest of these several values. Similarly, the true skip distance governing the transmission at a given frequency is the smallest of the various skip distances applying to the individual layers.

Approximate Lower-ray Behavior at Oblique Incidence. At frequencies below, and not too extremely close to, the maximum usable frequency, the oblique-incidence behavior of the lower ray in Fig. 22-31 can be obtained with an accuracy satisfactory for most purposes by assuming that the ionosphere reflection takes place at a mirrorlike surface at a height corresponding to the minimum virtual height of the layer as determined by pulse measurements (see Figs. 22-20 and 22-29). The justification for this procedure is that unless the frequency is very close to the maximum usable frequency, an obliquely incident lower ray penetrates only slightly into the layer. Thus in Fig. 22-31, the apex of the equivalent triangular path for the 10-Mc lower ray is only about 20 km greater than the minimum virtual height of the layer.

On the basis of this assumption that the virtual height of the layer can be taken as its minimum value irrespective of frequency, the maximum usable frequency for a given distance of transmission is to a first approximation the frequency f given by Eq. (22-16), where f_v is the critical frequency of the layer, and ϕ_0 is the angle of incidence at the ionosphere corresponding to the distance and virtual height involved. Similarly, the skip distance for any frequency f is approximately the distance that makes ϕ_0 satisfy Eq. (22-16) when f_v is the critical frequency of the layer involved.

The results obtained in this way, while approximate, are sufficiently accurate for making preliminary estimates of a situation, and for other circumstances where very precise answers are not necessary.

Take-off Angles and Maximum Possible One-hop Distances. The take-off angle β in Figs. 22-27b and 22-30 is given by the relation

$$\beta = 90 - \phi_0 - 57.3\,\frac{d}{2R} \qquad (22\text{-}19)$$

where d is the distance from the transmitter to the point where the ray returns to earth, and R is the earth's radius ($= 6367$ km). Another curved-earth relation useful in estimating skip distances and maximum usable frequencies by the approximate method is

$$\sin\,\phi_0 = \frac{\cos\,\beta}{1 + (h'/R)} \qquad (22\text{-}20)$$

where h' is the virtual height of the ionosphere.

The maximum value that ϕ_0 can have occurs when $\beta = 0$. The distance corresponding to this largest possible ϕ_0, as calculated by Eq. (22-17) or Eq. (22-18), approximates the maximum possible distance of a single hop for a given value of virtual height h'.

Sporadic-E Reflections at Oblique Incidence. As indicated on page 826, sporadic-E ionization usually appears to be in the form of a very thin layer. As a result, a radio wave striking a sporadic-E layer at oblique incidence tends to behave in the manner illustrated in Fig. 22-32. Part of the energy of the wave is reflected toward the earth as though from a mirrorlike surface, while the remainder passes through the layer. There is no well-defined critical frequency, and the intensity of the reflected signal (i.e., the reflection coefficient) drops off continuously with increasing frequency. In spite of this behavior, it is found that for sporadic E at high frequencies the secant law of Eq. (22-16) leads to a useful first approximation in which f is the maximum usable frequency for a distance corresponding to ϕ_0, while f_v is the critical or apparent penetration frequency. However, since the apparent penetration frequency is power-dependent, this approximation is best when the oblique signal has a strength of the same order of magnitude as that of the equipment used to determine the critical (penetration) frequency.

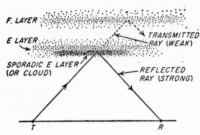

Fig. 22-32. Diagram illustrating partial transparency of sporadic-E layer.

Oblique-incidence Behavior at Low Frequencies. At very low frequencies the ionosphere is so effective as a refracting medium that its action approximates that of a mirrorlike reflecting surface. In the daytime, the level of the reflection is commonly about 70 km, corresponding to the D layer. At night after the D layer has disappeared, reflection occurs at the lower edge of the E layer, which is about 90 km high. In each case the penetration of the wave into the reflecting layer is very slight.

22-13. Sky-wave Signal Strength. The signal strength of a sky wave diminishes with distance as a result of two effects.[1] The first is spreading of the rays as they leave the transmitter, causing the signal strength to be inversely proportional to distance. The second effect causing reduction of the signal strength is loss of energy in the ionized regions as a result of collisions between the vibrating electrons and gas molecules, as explained on page 831.

At high frequencies the energy loss due to collisions occurs principally just below the E layer in the so-called D region, because it is here that the product of the collisional frequency and electron density is a maximum. This type of loss is called *nondeviative* absorption, since the ray passes through the absorbing region rather than being bent to earth by it.[2]

---

[1] A third effect occasionally of importance is focusing and defocusing associated with reflections from the ionosphere and the surface of the earth, respectively, which tend to behave like spherical mirrors.

[2] Energy absorption also occurs in the region where the wave is bent to earth. This is called *deviative* absorption, and tends to increase with the amount of retardation

Since the electron density of the D region depends primarily on solar radiation, the absorption tends to be a maximum at noon and relatively low at night. At frequencies high enough so that the electrons in the D region will execute a number of cycles of vibration before colliding with a gas molecule (above 2 or 3 Mc), the attenuation in decibels per unit distance is proportional to the product of electron density and gas pressure in the part of the D region through which the signal passes and is inversely proportional to the square of the wave frequency. Since maximum electron density in the D layer is approximately proportional to that in the E region, the D-region attenuation in decibels is therefore approximately proportional to the square of the E-layer critical frequency. This is a useful relation because values of E-layer critical frequency are readily available, whereas D-region ionization density is not ordinarily measured directly. These relations can be expressed by

$$\alpha = K \left(\frac{f_E}{f}\right)^2 \tag{22-21}$$

where α = attenuation constant for nondeviative absorption in D (or E) region, db per unit length of path

f_E = critical frequency of the E layer

f = wave frequency

K = constant which depends on the collisional frequency

It follows from Eq. (22-21) that high-frequency sky-wave signals will be stronger the closer the frequency is to the maximum usable frequency. Thus if the absorption is 40 db at 10 Mc, it will be about 10 db at 20 Mc.

Sky-wave absorption also increases as the distance from the transmitter to receiver increases. Several factors lead to this result. First, as the length of each hop increases, the portion of the path that lies in the D region increases in length. Second, as the number of hops increases, as it must over very long paths, the number of passages through the D region increases correspondingly, thereby increasing the total absorption. Finally, over long paths involving multiple hops there can be an appreciable loss associated with the ground reflections.

Daytime absorption increases down to frequencies of the order of 1 Mc. Below this frequency the height of maximum penetration drops sufficiently to reduce substantially the length of that portion of the path which lies in the absorbing region. The total attenuation over the path then becomes less as the frequency is further reduced, becoming relatively small at frequencies of the order of 20 kc.

At night ionospheric absorption tends to become small at all frequencies because of the almost complete disappearance of the ionization in the D

of the wave. However, deviative absorption is usually of less importance than D-region nondeviative absorption, because it occurs higher in the ionosphere where the collisional frequency is relatively low.

region. What energy loss that does occur is then either nondeviative absorption in the lower edge of the E layer, or deviative absorption along paths such as ray 4 in Fig. 22-25, in which the wave spends considerable time in the ionosphere because of the long path in the ionized region that is traversed with low group velocity.

22-14. Miscellaneous Aspects of Ionospheric Propagation. *Fading.* The strength of a sky-wave signal varies with time because of fluctuations in the properties of the ionosphere. The relatively short-period varia-tions which have durations of the order of a minute and less are generally called *fading.* Fading of a single sky wave can be explained by the fact that the ionospheric reflecting surface is not perfectly smooth, but instead exhibits irregular variations in ionization density. The effect is like a large number of separate moving reflectors, each of which contributes a small component to the total signal. Hence, at any given instant the total signal will be the vector sum of the separate com-ponents, which have random relative phases. Since the locations of the reflectors change with time, the relative phases of the components will likewise change, causing the total signal to vary in strength from mo-ment to moment. In a similar way, sky waves arriv-ing by different numbers of hops or by reflections from different layers will interfere with each other and give rise to fading. Again, the combination of a ground wave and one or more sky waves results in particularly bad fading effects. Fading tends to be more rapid the higher the frequency, because a given amount of move-ment of the irregularities in the reflecting layer, or a given movement of the reflecting layer, produces a greater phase shift the shorter the wavelength.

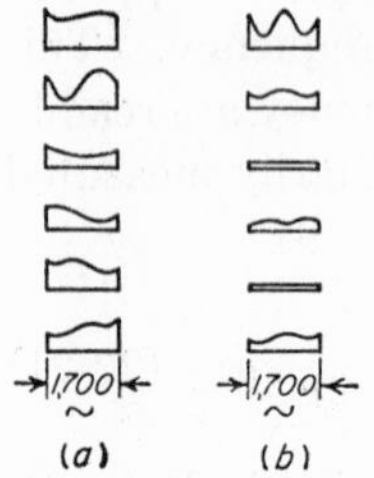

FIG. 22-33. Typi-cal fading patterns observed in short-wave transatlantic communication. The different fig-ures in each col-umn show trans-mission conditions in successive mo-ments over a 1700-cycle band of mod-ulation frequencies.

The fact that fading depends on frequency causes different frequency components in the sidebands of a modulated wave to fade differently. This gives rise to distortion of the modulation envelope, which is called *selective fading.* In multihop transmission, frequencies differing by as little as 100 cycles may fade quite independently, as shown in Fig. 22-33.

Back-scatter Measurements (*Scatter Sounding*). When a wave strikes the ground at R in Fig. 22-30, irregularities in the ground surface cause some of the energy to be scattered back along path RBT toward the transmitter. This phenomenon provides a means of directly measuring the skip distance. The idea is to transmit a pulse from T and observe with a suitable receiver located at T the length of time that elapses until energy is returned by the scatter echo from R. It can be shown that when the distance d is considerably greater than the virtual height of the ionosphere, the delay time of the back-scatter signal corresponds very closely to a wave traveling with the velocity of light over a distance equal to twice the skip distance.[1]

An example of an actual back-scatter record is shown in Fig. 22-34. Here distance in a radial direction is proportional to time delay, i.e., skip distance, while the direction from the center of the display gives the compass direction. The scales are so chosen in Fig. 22-34 that each ring represents a distance of 250 km to the point of ionospheric reflection. Accordingly the actual distance to a reflecting point in the bright area is then twice the distance shown in the display. Thus in the example, sporadic-E ionization is present in the southeast, filling up the region from 350 to 700 km, corresponding to a reflection returned from the earth at distances of 700 to 1400 km. Again reflections from the F2 layer can be seen in all directions except northeast, beginning at a range of about 800 km, corresponding to a skip distance of 1600 km. Two-hop F2 echoes are also seen in the western half of the display. The use of back scatter in this way

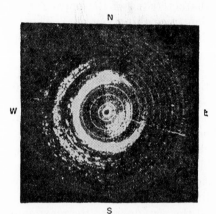

FIG. 22-34. Typical back-scatter record, showing sporadic-E patch to southeast and F2 echoes in all directions except northeast. Range circles represent 250-km intervals with respect to reflecting point in ionosphere.

to determine ionosphere conditions is termed *scatter sounding*, and gives directly the effect that the ionosphere will have on actual radio communication at the frequency used to make the sounding.[2]

Meteor Ionization. Meteors entering the earth's upper atmosphere produce trails of ionization that are located in the E region, and that are capable of reflecting detectable amounts of energy from transmitters radiating powers of the order of several kilowatts. When the trail is being formed, the frequency of the wave reflected from the moving head of the ionization column is shifted slightly as a result of the Doppler effect. When the signal thus reflected is combined with the original or unshifted frequency the result is therefore a beat note or "whistle."

When the ionization produced by the many minute meteors is taken

---

[1] The theory of back-scatter measurements is given by A. M. Peterson, The Mechanism of F-layer Propagated Back Scatter Echoes, *J. Geophys. Research*, vol. 56, p. 221, June, 1951.

[2] O. G. Villard, Jr., and A. M. Peterson, Scatter-sounding; a Technique for Study of the Ionosphere at a Distance, *Trans. IRE (Professional Group on Antennas and Propagation)*, PGAP-3, p. 186, August, 1952.

into account, along with the ionization of the larger visual meteors, it appears that the meteors are an important source of nighttime E-region ionization. Meteoric ionization is also a factor in extended-range propagation, as discussed below.

Reflections of radio waves from meteoric trails constitute a tool of unique value in the study of such properties of meteors as velocities, frequencies of occurrence, etc. They are also useful for investigating such characteristics of the upper atmosphere as rate of ion production, diffusion, recombination, etc. The Doppler shift in frequency imparted to the reflected signal by the drift of a fully formed meteor trail is a direct measure of the wind speed at E-region heights.[1]

Extended-range Propagation by Forward Scatter from the Ionosphere. Experiments have shown that up to distances of about 2000 km, it is possible to receive signals when the frequency is above the maximum usable frequency for the particular distance involved, provided sufficient power and directivity are used at the transmitter. Although the signal obtained under these conditions is relatively weak and fluctuates greatly in amplitude from moment to moment, it is nevertheless a dependable signal. This phenomenon was first observed at 50 Mc,[*] but since that time has been found to exist to an even greater degree at lower frequencies all the way down to the maximum usable frequency.[2]

These extended-range signals arise from energy that is scattered by the E layer of the ionosphere in the forward direction, i.e., away from the transmitter. The action involved is analogous to the troposphere scatter phenomenon discussed in connection with Fig. 22-18 except that the scatter region is now the E layer of the ionosphere, and so is much higher above the earth than in the troposphere case. Possible causes of scattering are (1) ionization trails left by meteors, the effects of which overlap in time as a result of the continuous rain of small meteors that bombard the upper atmosphere; (2) turbulence in the ionosphere arising from winds, auroral effects, etc. As more is learned about the characteristics of the small meteors, it appears that under many and probably most circumstances, the meteors account for most of the received signal, including particularly the fact that it is continuously present.[3] Other factors

---

[1] L. A. Manning, O. G. Villard, Jr., and A. M. Peterson, Meteoric Echo Study of Upper Atmosphere Winds, *Proc. IRE*, vol. 38, p. 877, August, 1950.

[*] D. K. Bailey, R. Bateman, L. V. Berkner, H. J. Booker, G. F. Montgomery, E. M. Purcell, W. W. Salisbury, and J. B. Weisner, A New Kind of Radio Propagation at Very High Frequencies Observable at Long Distances, *Phys. Rev.*, p. 86, vol. 141, April 15, 1952 (also *Electronics*, vol. 25, p. 102, June, 1952).

[2] O. G. Villard, Jr., A. M. Peterson, L. A. Manning, and Von R. Eshleman, Extended-range Radio Transmission by Oblique Reflection from Meteoric Ionization, *J. Geophys. Research.* vol. 58, p. 83, March, 1953.

[3] The understanding of the contributions made by meteors to forward scatter from the E layer is based largely on the researches of O. G. Villard, Jr., L. A. Manning, and

undoubtedly contribute at least somewhat to the situation, however, and are perhaps important under some circumstances.

The intensity of the energy scattered by the ionosphere drops off very rapidly with increasing frequency. As a result, the upper frequency limit for the practical use of forward scatter from the ionosphere is of the order of 100 Mc when one considers the maximum transmitter power and transmitting-antenna directive gain that it is feasible to use. The maximum range at which these forward-scatter signals are received corresponds to a single hop from the E layer, i.e., about 2000 km. This limit is set by the fact that the amount of energy that is scattered is not sufficient to give a useful signal over a path requiring a second hop. Even with these restrictions, the forward-scatter phenomena have important possibilities in practical radio communication, since they open up for moderate-distance communication additional frequencies that would otherwise be useful only for line-of-sight and tropospheric scatter propagation over much shorter distances.

22-15. Propagation Characteristics of Radio Waves of Different Frequencies in Relation to the Problems of Practical Radio Communication. Since radio waves of different frequencies have different propagation characteristics, the various parts of the frequency spectrum are used for different types of applications. The following paragraphs discuss the propagation characteristics of radio waves from the point of view of the practical problems involved in their use.

Propagation Characteristics of Radio Waves in the Frequency Range 20 to 100 Kc. The propagation of low-frequency waves is characterized by relatively low ground-wave attenuation and by the fact that the sky wave is reflected back to earth after only a very slight penetration into the ionosphere, and with little absorption.

Most of the energy at these frequencies that reaches receiving points up to 1000 km travels by way of the ground wave. Under such conditions the received signal shows very little diurnal, seasonal, or yearly variation. At much greater distances from the transmitter, most of the received energy has been reflected from the ionosphere. Since the energy loss in the ionosphere varies with the conditions at the lower edge of the ionized region, the signal intensity at great distances has a diurnal and seasonal variation, with the signals being stronger at night and in winter.

Although low-frequency radio signals that have traveled great distances behave in a fairly regular manner, neither the daily nor yearly cycles repeat exactly. The average yearly intensity correlates fairly closely with the 11-year sunspot cycle.

Von R. Eshleman at Stanford University. Their work, and that of others, is well summarized in an issue of *Proceedings of the IRE* to appear early in 1956, which is devoted exclusively to forward-scatter phenomena in the ionosphere and troposphere.

The strength of low-frequency signals changes only very gradually; thus fading in the normal sense does not occur at these frequencies.

Propagation Characteristics of Radio Waves in the Frequency Range 100 *to* 535 *Kc.* As the frequency is increased above 100 kc, the ground wave attenuates more rapidly and the ionospheric losses tend to be high in the daytime, though they remain low at night. The range of the ground wave is thus reduced as the frequency is increased, and it becomes necessary to depend upon the sky wave for communication to moderately distant points. However, because of the relatively high sky-wave absorption in the daytime, it is in general not possible to maintain dependable long-distance communication at the higher of these frequencies in the daytime, particularly in the summer, although nighttime transmission to distant points is normally possible.

Propagation Characteristics at Broadcast Frequencies (535 *to* 1600 *Kc*). Frequencies in this range are used primarily for broadcast purposes. Daytime broadcasting depends entirely upon ground-wave propagation, since sky waves at these frequencies are completely absorbed in the daytime. The daytime signal strength accordingly decreases more rapidly with distance the lower the earth's conductivity and the higher the frequency of the signal, as discussed in Sec. 22-2.

The region about a broadcast transmitting station in which the signal strength in the daytime is adequate to override ordinary interference is termed the daytime *primary service area*. Primary coverage depends on the transmitter power, the directivity of the transmitting antenna, and the ground-wave attenuation (i.e., the earth's conductivity and the frequency). With high-powered transmitters operating at the lower broadcast frequencies, the primary coverage will typically not exceed 50 to 100 miles even when the earth conductivity is high. At the higher broadcast frequencies, or with low earth conductivity, the range over which primary coverage is obtainable is much less (see Fig. 22-35a).

Outside of the primary coverage area is a region where the signal strength is often sufficient to be useful, but is still not sufficient to override interference fully. This region of daytime *secondary coverage* is determined by the same factors as the primary coverage, but with high powers, high earth conductivity, and the lower broadcast frequencies it may extend to a distance of several hundred miles at receiving locations where the noise level is low.

At night a sky wave of considerable intensity is returned to earth by the E layer. The resulting situation is illustrated in detail in Fig. 22-35a, where it is seen that there are three distinctive zones. Near the transmitter, the sky wave is relatively weak compared with the ground wave and the latter predominates. As the distance from the transmitter increases, the ground wave becomes attenuated, whereas the sky wave becomes stronger, thus making the ground and sky waves of approximately equal strength. At still greater distances, the sky wave tends to become still stronger and to maintain a relatively high and constant signal strength up to considerable distances.

The reason for this behavior of the sky wave lies in the fact that, as the distance from the transmitter is increased, the sky wave that reaches the receiver represents energy radiated from increasingly lower vertical angles, and the characteristics of broadcast antennas are such that the radiated energy is greater the lower the angle above the horizon. Furthermore, in view of the fact that the sky wave commonly reaches a

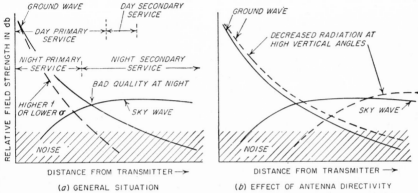

FIG. 22-35. Diagrams illustrating the behavior of broadcast signals under different conditions.

height of about 100 km at broadcast frequencies, the sky wave must travel nearly as far to reach receivers near the transmitter as it does to reach receivers several hundred kilometers away; thus locations near the transmitter do not have much advantage in distance as far as the sky wave is concerned.

The sky-wave attenuation and path at broadcast frequencies are to a first approximation independent of frequency, so that the distant night-time reception, which depends upon the sky wave, is about equally satisfactory for all frequencies. This is in contrast with the daytime (or ground-wave) coverage, for which the low frequencies are the most effective.

The region in Fig. 22-35 where the ground and sky waves have approximately equal intensity is of special importance. Here the resultant signal is the vector sum of two waves of approximately the same amplitude that have traveled along different paths. Since the difference in path lengths, when measured in wavelengths, changes greatly with variation in frequency, different sideband frequencies will combine differently, with some adding and others subtracting. The result is frequency distortion and received signals of poor quality. Furthermore, slight changes in the ionosphere, such as continually take place, will cause the phase of the sky wave to change.   This causes selective fading (see page 846) to occur.   As a result of this situation, the signals received in the region where the intensities of the ground and sky waves are approximately equal will have relatively poor quality.

When the transmitter power is adequate to give a strong nighttime signal at considerable distances, a usable nighttime secondary coverage of very considerable extent is obtained by means of sky-wave propagation.   This distant sky-wave signal ordinarily suffers a certain amount of fading and quality distortion due to time variations in the ionosphere.   The extent of the fading and distortion under such conditions is, however, much less severe than when there is interference between ground and sky waves of approximately equal intensity.

Increased transmitter power gives better daytime coverage and better night signals to distant listeners.   It does not, however, remove the region of high distortion, because both the ground and sky waves are strengthened equally.   When the transmitter power is large, the region of high distortion is commonly within the primary service area; certain listeners who then receive satisfactory signals in the daytime find that the signals have unsatisfactory quality at night, even though the night signal strength is quite satisfactory.

Because of this situation there is a considerable advantage in employing a broadcast transmitting antenna that concentrates the radiated energy at low angles above the horizon, and radiates relatively little energy at angles more than about 50° above the horizon.   In this way, the ground wave and the distant sky wave are made slightly stronger and at the same time a great reduction in strength is produced in the sky wave returned to earth at moderate distances from the transmitter.   This increases the primary service area during the day, gives better night coverage to distant listeners, and moves the region of high distortion farther from the transmitter, as shown in Fig. 22-35b.   The benefits obtained in this way by antenna directivity are especially large when the transmitter power is great enough to produce a usable ground-wave signal in the high distortion region.

Propagation Characteristics at Short Waves (1600 *Kc to* 30 *Mc*).   At frequencies above 1600 kc, the ground wave attenuates so rapidly as to be of no importance except for transmission over very short distances.   As a result practically all long-distance short-wave communications take place by means of ionospheric reflections.   For any given set of conditions there is generally a particular range of frequencies which can be used for such communications.   The upper limit is the maximum usable frequency (MUF), which depends on the distance of transmission and the heights and electron densities at the point or points of reflection in the ionosphere, as discussed on page 841.   The lower-frequency limit depends on the ionospheric absorption over the path, the radiated power, and the noise level at the receiver, since the losses in the ionosphere increase with wavelength.   In general, the frequency which gives the best signal is the maximum usable frequency.   In practice, the optimum frequency is taken 15 per cent below the maximum usable frequency to allow for short-time fluctuations in the maximum usable frequency.

Optimum frequencies tend to be high during the day and for long paths, while at night and for short paths lower frequencies are optimum. Typical values are 10 to 20 Mc during the day and 5 to 10 Mc during the night for transoceanic communication.   The optimum frequencies are not only greater in the day than at night, but are usually (but not always) greater in summer than winter.[1]   Optimum frequencies generally increase with sunspot activity (see page 828), and tend to be higher the lower the latitude of the path.   Other things being equal, the signal is better over north-south paths than over east-west paths because of the larger variation in the amount of sunlight, and hence ionization, over an east-west path.

In long-distance communication, the optimum frequency is usually determined by the F2 layer, although under some circumstances the E and F1 layers may control the situation at noon.   However, at intermediate distances, such as 200 to 1000 km, where the lower height of the E layer causes the angle of incidence of the wave at the layer to be much more glancing than for the F2 layer, then during the daytime the E layer nearly always determines the maximum usable frequency.   At relatively unpredictable times sporadic E causes the highest usable frequency to exceed the maximum usable frequency determined by the regular layers. Sporadic-E maximum usable frequencies as high as 80 to 100 Mc have been reported, although values of the order of 20 to 40 Mc are much more common.   Sporadic E is more prevalent in summer than winter and may control medium length (up to 2000 km) paths much of the time on frequencies as high as 15 Mc.   However, its occurrence is highly unpredictable and hence cannot be relied upon for regular transmission.

The optimum frequency increases with path distance up to the maximum distance for one-hop transmission, which averages 4000 km for the F2 layer and 2000 km for the E layer.   At short distances the optimum frequency is essentially the critical frequency since the value of sec ϕ_0 in Eq. (22-16) is then near unity.   For long distances the value of the F2 layer maximum usable frequency is typically about three times the critical frequency.

In point-to-point communication using high-frequency waves, it is desirable to employ a directive transmitting antenna.   The energy should normally be directed over the great circle path and at a vertical take-off angle β corresponding to the fewest number of hops possible

---

[1] Thus in Fig. 22-20, the F2 critical frequency is higher in winter during the sunlight hours, whereas at night and for the E and F1 layers it is higher in summer.

between transmitter and receiver.[1,2] The value of β corresponding to a given value of virtual height and a specified one-hop distance can be calculated by means of Eq. (22-19) and either Eq. (22-18) or Eq. (22-17). When the transmission distance is comparable with the ionosphere height, the optimum value of β is large. However, for long distances, low angles such as 5 to 15° are usually the most desirable. At angles below about 3.5°, the energy leaving the transmitter tends to be absorbed by the earth near the transmitting antenna and so is wasted.

The major variations of transmission conditions can be predicted at least three months in advance, and include the diurnal, month-to-month, and yearly variation components.[3] Although the day-to-day variations cannot be anticipated as accurately, a direct measurement of propagation conditions at the time of interest can be made using the technique of scatter sounding, as discussed in connection with Fig. 22-34.

Propagation of Frequencies above 30 *Mc.* Frequencies above 30 Mc are seldom reflected back to earth by the ionosphere, and only intermittent sporadic-E reflections occur in the range 30 to 60 Mc.

The practical usefulness of frequencies above about 30 Mc therefore depends largely upon space-wave propagation and is affected by the possibilities and limitations of this type of propagation. In general, one can state that radio communication with reasonable power is not possible to points appreciably beyond the line-of-sight distance, and that the elevations of the transmitting and receiving antennas are the factors that determine this distance.[4] These very high frequencies find extensive use for such applications as television and frequency-modulation broadcasting; radar; aircraft-to-ground radio communication; radio navigation; radio-relay systems; and short-distance radio communications of all types, including point-to-point, moving-vehicle, walkie-talkie, etc.

22-16. Relation of Solar Activity to the Propagation of Radio Waves. The fact that the propagation of all except the very shortest radio waves depends to a marked extent upon the conditions in the ionosphere implies that some relation exists between solar activity on the one hand and wave propagation on the other, and this is indeed the case. One type of relation is illustrated in Fig. 22-21, while two others are discussed below.

----

[1] Energy at a larger take-off angle β will not be reflected in the layer if the frequency is close to the maximum usable frequency.

[2] A simple graphical method for computing vertical angles, as well as other parameters, is given by R. A. Helliwell, Graphical Solution of Sky Wave Problems, *Electronics*, vol. 26, p. 150, February, 1953.

[3] "Ionospheric Radio Propagation," *op. cit.*, chap. 6.

[4] However, when sufficient power is employed, useful signals up to several hundred miles may be obtained by means of tropospheric scattering, as discussed on p. 823, while E-layer scattering will give useful signals up to about 2000 km at frequencies not too much greater than 30 Mc (see p. 848).

Ionospheric Storms. Ionospheric storms are disturbances in the ionosphere that are correlated with the rapid and excessive fluctuations, termed magnetic storms, that occur in the earth's magnetic field. Ionospheric storms tend to develop rather suddenly, with recovery to normal conditions often requiring three or four days. They show a tendency to recur in intervals of 27.3 days, which is the period of rotation of the sun, and are associated with sunspots in some manner not fully understood.

An ionospheric storm causes an abnormal decrease in the critical frequency and a corresponding increase in the virtual height of the F2 layer. In addition, D-region ionization, and hence absorption, is usually increased. The effects on the E and F1 layers are usually less pronounced. The effect of an ionospheric storm on short-wave radio transmission is to narrow the range of frequencies that are useful for communication over a given circuit; if the storm is unusually severe, all high frequencies may become unusable. At frequencies of the order of 100 kc and less, ionospheric storms have relatively little effect; in fact, propagation conditions for low frequencies are often improved during ionospheric disturbances.

The effect of ionospheric storms tends to be more severe when the transmission path passes near the earth's magnetic pole. Thus ionospheric storms have relatively little effect on short-wave transmission between North and South America, or between North America and North Africa, but have a very great effect on those transmission paths, such as New York to Northern Europe, which pass through the polar regions.

Sudden Ionospheric Disturbances. High-frequency sky-wave transmission is sometimes completely cut off for a period of 15 to 60 min by what is known as a sudden ionospheric disturbance. These temporary fadeouts occur most frequently when the sunspot cycle is at a maximum and are observed only on the daylight side of the globe. The effect is caused by a solar burst of ultraviolet light which is not absorbed in the normal F2, F1, and E regions but which produces intense ionization in the D region where the air density is relatively high. This results in almost complete absorption of waves passing through the D region, although the signal strength of low-frequency waves which are normally reflected from the lower edge of the ionosphere may be actually improved during a sudden ionospheric disturbance. Since absorption of waves passing through the D region (i.e., broadcast and higher frequencies) is inversely proportional to the square of the frequency, the effect of the fadeout is less the higher the frequency. Thus, during a mild fadeout it is sometimes possible to maintain communication by going to a higher frequency, if by doing so one does not exceed the maximum usable frequency.

22-17. Noise and Static. The output of a sensitive radio receiver nearly always contains a background of rumbles, crashes, rattles, etc., which disappears when the antenna is disconnected. This noise is the result of voltages induced in the antenna by either natural or man-made sources of interference and is often of sufficient magnitude to be the practical factor determining the minimum usable signal. It is not to be confused with the circuit and tube noise (see page 434) that establishes an ultimate limit to the weakest signal that can be detected.

Man-made noise arises from electrical devices and so is especially strong in cities, particularly in industrial areas, and near the ignition systems of internal-combustion engines.

Radio waves generated by natural causes are referred to as *static* and produce the familiar clicks, rumblings, crashes, etc., sometimes heard in all radio receivers. Static normally has its origin in thunderstorms and similar natural electrical disturbances and is in the form of impulses, the energy of which is distributed throughout the range of useful radio frequencies. The field strength of static from nearby thunderstorms is on the average observed to be approximately inversely proportional to frequency.

Since static is fundamentally a radio signal containing frequency components distributed over a wide range of frequencies, the static within any frequency range is propagated over the earth in the same way as ordinary radio signals of the same frequency. Thus the static received at any given location is the sum of nearby static and static of distant origin. Hence in the absence of local thunderstorms, the received static will depend on the propagation conditions, and will tend to possess diurnal and seasonal variations in intensity as a result of corresponding variations in wave propagation. For example, at broadcast frequencies only static of local origin is observed in the daytime; however, at night the static level will increase greatly as a result of static of distant origin being received. The same situation exists in the short-wave frequency band; the static intensity follows propagation conditions, being high when the conditions are favorable for long-distance propagation, and low when the propagation is such that the only static able to reach the receiver is that generated locally.

Very little static is observed at frequencies too high to be reflected from the ionosphere. This is largely due to the limited range of such high frequencies, combined with the fact that natural electrical discharges generate relatively little static energy on such very high frequencies.

Cosmic (Galactic) and Solar Noise.[1] It has been found that the earth receives radio-frequency radiation from the Milky Way, from other galaxies, and from the sun. This radiation is in the form of noise such as that produced by circuits and tubes.

The sources of cosmic (galactic) noise are continuously distributed

---

[1] A useful article is given by Charles R. Burrows, Radio Astronomy, *Electronics*, vol. 22, p. 75, February, 1949.

throughout our galaxy; in addition, a few point sources of noise having very high intrinsic intensity have been discovered embedded in this general background. It is interesting that in some cases these latter do not correlate with anything observable through an astronomical telescope. Some of these point sources are believed to lie outside our own galaxy.

Two components of solar noise are to be distinguished. Under "quiet" conditions there is a roughly constant radiation considerably more intense at some radio frequencies than would be expected on the basis of black-body radiation from an object at the temperature of the sun. However, solar disturbances such as sunspots, solar flares, etc., produce additional noise which sometimes reaches a very high intensity compared with the "quiet" noise; such additional noise appears to come from limited parts of the sun's disk.

The intensity at the earth's surface of these radiations of extraterrestrial origin varies with frequency, and in general, is greater the lower the frequency up to the point where the ionosphere prevents penetration of the earth's atmosphere. The reduction in the noise intensity with increasing frequency presumably arises from mechanisms present where the noise is generated. Most of the investigations of solar and cosmic noise have been made in the frequency range of 40 to 200 Mc, although the noise has been observed at both higher and lower frequencies.

While galactic and solar noise will under certain conditions set a limit to the weakest signal usable for radio communication, its principal importance arises from the fact that it provides a new tool for scientific research. Galactic noise extends the ability of the astronomers to see into outer space. Solar-noise studies hold the promise of leading to an increased understanding of the sun, and of the sun's effect on the ionosphere and hence on radio communication.

The study of these extraterrestrial radio-frequency radiations, commonly called radio astronomy, has in recent years become a very active and exciting subject for research.

Precipitation Static.[1] The term *precipitation static* denotes a type of interference frequently observed in an airplane passing through snow or rain. Under such circumstances, the airplane may become electrically charged to such a high potential with respect to the surrounding space that a corona discharge breaks out at some sharp point on the plane. The interference that this corona discharge produces with radio reception, termed *precipitation static*, is particularly serious at short-wave and lower frequencies.

Precipitation static can be minimized by the use of antennas that are either insulated wires or shielded loops, by equipping the plane with dischargers that provide a noninterfering means of getting rid of the charge

---

[1] For further information on this subject, see the series of articles entitled Army-Navy Precipitation Static Project, *Proc. IRE*. vol. 34, April and May, 1946.

being acquired by the plane, and by locating receiving antennas as far as possible from the corona discharges.

22-18. Rayleigh-Carson Reciprocity Theorem. There are various reciprocal relations that relate the properties of waves traveling in one direction to the properties of waves traveling in the opposite direction, and similarly connect the properties possessed by an antenna when transmitting with the properties possessed in reception. These relations are incorporated in reciprocal theorems, the most important of which was formulated by Rayleigh and extended to include radio communication by John R. Carson. It is to the effect that, *if an electromotive force E inserted in antenna 1 causes a current I to flow at a certain point in a second antenna 2, then the voltage E applied at this point in the second antenna will produce the same current I (both in magnitude and phase) in a short circuit at the point in antenna 1 where the voltage E was originally applied.*

The Rayleigh-Carson theorem fails to be true only when the propagation of the radio waves is appreciably affected by the presence of the earth's magnetic field. It thus holds for all practical radio work except for long-distance communication involving the ionosphere. Even then it can be expected to apply to results averaged over a reasonable interval of time, even though it cannot be depended upon to be exactly correct at every given moment.

The Rayleigh-Carson theorem shows that in radio communication between two fixed points, the same behavior as to signal strength, optimum frequency, etc., is to be expected, irrespective of which end of the circuit is the transmitting end and which is the receiving end. The theorem also provides a means of relating the transmitting and receiving properties of antennas, as discussed in Sec. 23-21.

PROBLEMS AND EXERCISES

22-1. In the example on page 806, what transmitter power would be required if the frequency were: (a) 2500 kc, and (b) 1000 kc?

22-2. A broadcast station delivers 50 kw to an antenna that radiates 80 per cent of this power and has a directional characteristic such that the field radiated along the horizontal is 1.28 times as great as when the antenna radiates a field proportional to the cosine of the angle of elevation. Using Eq. (22-1), determine the strength of the ground wave at a distance of 100 km (62.5 miles) under the following conditions, and tabulate all results:

   a. Frequency of 550 kc with: (1) sea-water earth, (2) $\sigma = 10^{-4}$ mho per cm, $\epsilon = 20$ ("good" soil), and (3) $\sigma = 0.2 \times 10^{-4}$ mho per cm, $\epsilon = 10$ ("poor" soil).

   b. Same earth conditions as (a) but for a frequency of 1500 kc.

22-3. A series of field-strength measurements about a broadcast station operating at 900 kc shows that at a distance of 20 miles the strength of the ground wave is 0.25 of the value calculated on the basis of zero ground losses. Deduce the earth conductivity for this case, assuming a reasonable value for the dielectric constant.

22-4. Calculate skin depth for the earth conditions designated in Table 22-1 as sea water, pastoral (rich soil), and rocky soil, for frequencies of 25, 600, and 1500 kc. The effect of the dielectric constant can be neglected because of the low frequencies involved.   Tabulate all results.

22-5. Calculate the magnitude and phase of the impedance represented by a conductor 1 cm square and 1 cm long, composed of types of grounds designated in Table 22-1 as: (a) sea water, (b) pastoral (rich soil), and (c) rocky soil.   Make each calculation for frequencies of 600 kc, 1500 kc, and 10 Mc, and tabulate all results.

22-6. Show that when a wave is reflected from the ground with vertical incidence, the strength of the resultant electric field near the surface of the ground is very sensitive to the magnitude and phase of the reflection coefficient, whereas the strength of the resultant magnetic field is not.

22-7. A system of communication to moving vehicles is to be established using 50 Mc, a transmitter power of 100 watts, and a directive transmitting antenna for which the field strength in the desired direction is three times that of a half-wave antenna.   The transmitting antenna has a height of 150 ft, and the receiver antenna height can be taken as 6 ft.   It is estimated that a field strength of 100 μv per m is required to give satisfactory signals at the receiving point.   Calculate the range of the system, assuming a perfectly reflecting flat earth.

22-8. A television transmitter having a power of 10 kw operates with an antenna located on the top of a hill 1600 ft high, and having directivity such that the field strength in the desired direction is four times that of a half-wave antenna.   Assuming a perfectly reflecting flat earth, calculate and plot field strength as a function of distance on a logarithmic scale from 0.5 to 40 miles for a receiving antenna height of 30 ft for frequencies of 67.25 and 211.25 Mc.

22-9. Check the solid curve of Fig. 22-6a by recalculating it.

22-10. Discuss the character of the changes that would occur in Fig. 22-6a if the frequency of the waves were decreased to a value about half as great.

22-11. Earth curvature shifts the location of the maxima and minima in Fig. 22-6a.   Does this changed situation represent maxima and minima that are closer together, farther apart, or merely shifted in position without affecting the distance between them?   Explain.

22-12. Draw a vector diagram showing schematically the phase relation of the direct and ground-reflected rays at a given distance that is appreciably greater than d' in Fig. 22-6 for (a) flat earth, and (b) curved earth.   Assume a perfectly reflecting ground in both cases.

22-13. In a particular experiment, the transmitting and receiving antennas are 400 m apart and are each 30 m above the earth.   If the wavelength is 4.5 m, calculate the strength of the field at the receiving antenna relative to the free-space field for (a) perfectly reflecting earth, (b) earth as in Fig. 22-4c, vertically polarized antennas, and (c) earth as in Fig. 22-4c, horizontally polarized antennas.   In each case draw a vector diagram showing how the direct and ground-reflected rays add to produce the received field.

22-14. Explain the mechanism whereby an imperfect ground causes the field strength at large distances in Fig. 22-6a to be greater than in the case of a perfectly reflecting ground, and discuss the effect of polarization on the magnitude of the effect.

22-15. Derive a formula analogous to Eq. (22-2), but assuming that the reflection coefficient is $r/\underline{\gamma}$ instead of the value $1/\underline{0^\circ}$ applicable to a perfect earth.   Assume horizontal polarization.

22-16. In Fig. 22-9, derive a formula giving the maximum height h_{max} the irregularity may have in terms of wavelength λ and angle of incidence θ, without destroying the electrical smoothness, and then calculate h_{max}/λ for $\theta = 0.1$, 1.0, and 10°.   Assume that the distance r_1 is very very much greater than h.

22-17. For the system of Prob. 22-8, calculate and plot the field strength as a function of receiving antenna height at a distance of 10 miles, for 67.25 and 211.25 Mc, carrying the curves up to a height of 1000 ft.   Assume a flat perfectly conducting earth.

22-18. Explain qualitatively how Fig. 22-12 and the dotted curve of Fig. 22-11 would be modified if the waves were horizontally polarized.

22-19. Sketch in a qualitative way the variation of field strength with distance an airplane in Fig. 22-12 would experience when approaching to within 25 miles of the transmitter at an altitude of 30,000 ft, starting from a distance of 200 miles.

22-20. Explain why vertical polarization is superior to horizontal polarization for communication between transmitting and receiving antennas that are both very close to the ground as measured in wavelengths (such as 0.1λ or less) at (a) broadcast frequencies (550 to 1600 Mc), and (b) very high frequencies.

22-21. A vertically polarized transmitting antenna is located three-quarters of a wavelength above the earth.   The distance to the receiving point is such that for the wavelength employed the ground wave is significant.   What will be the qualitative effect of decreasing the ground conductivity on the strength of the received wave at (a) the surface of the ground, and (b) five wavelengths above the ground?   Explain.

22-22. Explain on the basis of space-wave propagation why when very high-frequency interfering waves are generated by automobile ignition systems or other electrical equipment located close to the ground, that at receiving locations such as used in the reception of television signals, the horizontally polarized component of the interference is weaker than the vertically polarized component.

22-23. The distance between a transmitting and receiving antenna is small enough so that a flat earth can be assumed; at the same time the antenna heights are such that the actual distance d is greater than the distance d' at which the field strength is less than the free-space value.   Under these conditions how will the field strength as calculated by Eq. (22-3) compare with the actual field strength when the refractive index of the air corresponds to paths a, b, c, and d, respectively, in Fig. 22-14?

22-24. Show in a qualitative way the changes produced in Fig. 22-14 when the coordinates are so changed that path b can be considered as a straight line.   Show the original paths and earth surface in dotted lines.

22-25. The antenna of a television transmitter is located at a height of 500 ft. Calculate and plot, as a function of distance to the transmitter, the height that the receiving antenna must have in order to be above the radio horizon.   Assume a standard atmosphere.

22-26. a. On the assumption of a flat earth and equal transmitting and receiving antenna heights, derive a formula giving required antennna heights in terms of wavelength λ and distance d if the surface of the earth is to lie outside of the first Fresnel zone.

b. Calculate the resulting heights for λ = 1 m and (1) d = 1 km, and (2) d = 10 km.

22-27. Show ray paths analogous to those of Fig. 22-15a, but applying to the case where the transmitting antenna is appreciably above the duct.

22-28. Calculate the maximum wavelength at which propagation is possible by means of a ground-based duct 100 ft high when $\Delta M = 25$.

22-29. Draw ray paths analogous to those of Fig. 22-15a and b, but applying to the case of an elevated duct (Fig. 22-13d), when the transmitting antenna lies within the duct.

22-30. Draw a curve analogous to Fig. 22-16, but illustrating the type of behavior to be expected in the case of an elevated duct centered at the height of the transmitting antenna.

22-31. In the situation illustrated in Fig. 22-18, it is often found that some of the energy reaching the receiving antenna appears to come from azimuth directions differing slightly from the exact direction of the transmitting antenna.   Explain how this result could occur.

22-32. At locations near the radio horizon, explain why considerable variation in signal strength (i.e., considerable fading) results when the meteorological conditions cause ΔM to change only slightly, whereas the change in signal strength is very little at locations well above the radio horizon.

22-33. State the time to the nearest year when the critical frequencies of the ionosphere can next be expected to go through a maximum.

22-34. Go through the steps of obtaining Eq. (22-9c) from Eq. (22-9b).

22-35. Give the orientation of the plane in which the electron vibrations of Fig. 22-22a and b take place, in terms of the wavefront and the direction of polarization of the wave, when the magnetic field is at right angles to the direction of polarization and (a) lies in the plane representing the wavefront, and (b) is perpendicular to the plane of the wavefront.

22-36. Explain why the earth's magnetic field has no effect upon a wave passing through the ionosphere when the wave is so oriented that the electrostatic lines of force of the wave are parallel with the magnetic flux lines of the earth's magnetic field.

22-37. Sketch a curve analogous to that of Fig. 22-23, but for an elliptically polarized wave in which the horizontally polarized component is half as great as the vertically polarized component, and lags the vertical component by 45°.

22-38. Explain why the losses in the ionosphere tend to be high at the gyro frequency.

22-39. Justify the assertion that the energy loss in a particular cubic meter of ionosphere in the absence of magnetic field effects is proportional to the product of electron density, atmospheric pressure, and square of the wavelength of the radio wave.

22-40. Derive Eq. (22-10) from Eq. (22-9e).

22-41. Calculate and plot, as a function of frequency, the refractive index and dielectric constant at the point of maximum electron density in the F2 layer for conditions corresponding to those in Fig. 22-20a at noon in December, 1952. Carry the calculations over the range of frequencies for which the refractive index varies from 0.95 to 0.

22-42. A wave having a frequency of 8 Mc enters the E layer at an angle $\phi_0 = 45°$ when the ionosphere conditions correspond to those given in Fig. 22-20a for noon in December, 1952.

a. What will be the angle ϕ at the point of maximum electron density in the E layer?

b. Which layers, if any, will the wave fail to penetrate?

22-43. Determine the maximum electron densities of the E, F1, and F2 layers at noon in December, 1952, on the basis of the ionosphere characteristics given in Fig. 22-20a.

22-44. Sketch a reproduction of Fig. 22-25, and then show qualitatively by dotted red lines how the paths in the ionosphere would be modified if the frequency of the wave were increased appreciably. Discuss the differences for each ray and the change in skip distance.

22-45. In Fig. 22-27a the single-hop path is shown as penetrating less deeply into the ionosphere than do the two-hop paths. Why is this the case?

22-46. In Fig. 22-27b sketch an upper ray that reaches the receiving point R by means of a single hop.

22-47. Redraw Fig. 22-28 for a time of day such that sunrise is occurring near the middle of the path, so that the left hand (western) end is in darkness, whereas the right hand (or eastern) end is in daylight.

22-48. Discuss the relative group delays experienced by paths 2, 4, and 6 in Fig. 22-25 in passing through the ionosphere.

22-49. In a vertical-incidence record such as shown in Fig. 22-29, the echoes tend to be weak or to disappear in the vicinity of the critical frequency of the E layer, or of a lower layer, but never behave in this way for the critical frequencies of the F1 and F2 regions. Explain why the behavior for the F1 and F2 layers differs from that for lower layers.

22-50. Go through the steps involved in deriving Eq. (22-16).

22-51. Derive Eq. (22-18).

22-52. Sketch the general character of the actual and equivalent paths in Fig. 22-31b when the frequency is (a) 9 Mc, and (b) critical value.

22-53. What is the highest frequency that will be returned to earth 1000 km from the transmitter by the E layer when the ionosphere conditions are as in Fig. 22-31a?

22-54. Superimpose the ionosphere characteristics of Fig. 22-29 upon a set of transmission curves for $d = 1000$ km (see Fig. 22-31a) and from the result determine the maximum usable frequency.

22-55. By means of transmission curves, determine the skip distance at 9 Mc when the ionosphere has the characteristics given in Fig. 22-29. Assume a flat earth.

22-56. Determine the maximum usable frequency for the ionosphere in Fig. 22-31a, using the approximate method on page 843, and compare with the actual value.

22-57. Determine the take-off angles β and β' for the two rays in Fig. 22-31b. Assume a flat earth.

22-58. Calculate the maximum distance that a single-hop lower-ray reflection from each layer can reach for ionosphere virtual heights that are as shown in Fig. 22-20 at noon in (a) winter, and (b) summer. Assume that the transmitted wave takes off in the direction of the horizon ($\beta = 0$ in Fig. 22-27b).

22-59. Give a physical justification for the fact that the nondeviative energy loss in the D region is inversely proportional to the *square* of the frequency.

22-60. When the ionosphere conditions correspond to those for June, 1953, as given in Fig. 22-20b, what frequency undergoes the same nondeviative D-layer attenuation at 6 A.M. as does 15 Mc at noon?

22-61. Determine a relationship between ϕ_0 and the nondeviative D-layer absorption, under conditions where it can be assumed that the group velocity in the D region does not differ significantly from the velocity of light.

22-62. The most serious distortion resulting from selective fading occurs when the carrier frequency of the wave fades out completely while the sidebands are of nearly normal strength. Explain why under these conditions none of the sideband frequencies contained in the modulated wave are correctly reproduced by the detector output, whereas with other conditions of selective fading there will be at least some sidebands that will not be seriously distorted in the detector output.

22-63. Show with the aid of sketches how the F2 layer reflection in Fig. 22-34 would be modified by reducing the frequency.

22-64. Explain why the Doppler shift in frequency produced by the moving head of an ionization column created by a particular meteor can be different for observing stations at different locations on the earth's surface.

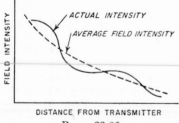

DISTANCE FROM TRANSMITTER

PROB. 22-66

22-65. Explain why it is unreasonable to expect that extended-range or forward-scatter signals will be observed at distances such as 3000 km corresponding to a single hop from the F layer.

22-66. The signal strength observed at the ground at a moderate distance, such as several hundred kilometers, from a low-frequency radio transmitter is often observed to vary with increasing distance from the transmitter in the manner illustrated in the accompanying figure. Suggest a possible explanation for this behavior.

22-67. It is found by observation that the location of the high-distortion region about a broadcast transmitter changes somewhat during the course of a single night and also varies from night to night and season to season. Explain.

22-68. Calculate and plot, as a function of frequency over the range 500 to 2000 kc, the distance at which the ground-wave field strength is 1 mv per m, when the transmitter power is 50 kw, the antenna directivity corresponds to a field strength along the horizontal 1.28 times as great as for a short vertical antenna, and the earth's conductivity is (a) 0.045 (sea water), (b) 10^{-4} (good earth), and (c) 0.2×10^{-4} (poor earth) mho per cm. From these results discuss the importance of the earth's conductivity and the frequency in obtaining a large primary coverage from a broadcast station.

22-69. Explain why the ratio of lower frequency limit to maximum usable frequency for carrying on radio communication at short-wave frequencies is generally smaller at night than in the daytime.

22-70. Explain why it is reasonable to expect that the optimum short-wave frequency will be higher at lower latitudes.

22-71. Radio communication is to be maintained to a very distant receiving point. The ionosphere conditions along the entire path are assumed to be as shown in Fig. 22-20, and the F2 layer can be assumed to control the propagation. If the time of communication is at noon, will the optimum frequency be highest in summer or in winter? During which season will the minimum number of hops required for the signal to reach the receiver be greatest? Assume that the minimum practical value of take-off angle is 5°.

22-72. It is desired to carry on continuous communication between two points only a moderate distance apart (such as 200 miles) without using more than two frequencies to cover the 24-hour period. If the ionosphere conditions correspond to those shown in Fig. 22-20, suggest a suitable pair of frequencies for summer and winter.

22-73. When an ionospheric storm makes direct communication between New York and London impossible, it is found that messages can still reach their destination if they are transmitted to North Africa and then relayed. Explain why this indirect routing gives satisfactory communication when the direct route does not function.

22-74. Give *two* reasons why in the daytime the static level at broadcast frequencies is less the higher the frequency.

22-75. Discuss the relationship of the time of day, season, and direction from transmitter to receiver, on the possibility of solar noise being the factor that determines the weakest signal that can be received, assuming (a) that highly directional receiving antennas are used, and (b) that the receiving antennas involved have very low directivity.

22-76. It is found experimentally that, when precipitation static is serious, its intensity can be reduced by lowering the speed of the airplane. Give a possible explanation for this observation.

CHAPTER 23

ANTENNAS[1]

23-1. Radiation from a Doublet Antenna. Radio waves represent electrical energy that has escaped into free space; they are described in detail in Sec. 1-1. Radio waves are produced to some extent whenever a wire in open space carries a high-frequency current. The laws governing such radiation are obtained by using Maxwell's equations to express the fields associated with the wire; when this is done there is found to be a component, termed the *radiated field*, having a strength that varies inversely with distance.

The simplest wire radiator or antenna is the elementary doublet shown in Fig. 23-1a. This consists of a conductor of length δl that is short compared with the wavelength λ, and which is assumed to have such large capacitance areas associated with each end that the current throughout the length of the doublet everywhere has the same value I. The strength $\mathcal{E}$ of the field radiated from such an elementary antenna in volts per unit length by a current $I \cos (\omega t + 90°)$ is given by the formula

$$\mathcal{E} = \frac{60\pi}{d} \frac{l}{\lambda} I \cos \theta \cos \omega \left(t - \frac{d}{c} \right) \tag{23-1}$$

Here d is the distance from the doublet to a distant observing point P, and θ is the direction of P with respect to a plane perpendicular to the axis of the doublet while c is the velocity of light. The strength of the radiated field is distributed in space in accordance with the doughnut pattern with a figure-of-eight cross section shown in Fig. 23-1b.

The phase of the field $\mathcal{E}$ at distance d is determined by the phase of the

---

[1] There have been so many developments during recent years in the theory and practice of radio antennas that this chapter is necessarily confined to a consideration of general principles illustrated by a few examples. For further information on the subject, including references to the literature, the reader is referred to the books, S. A. Schelkunoff and H. T. Friis, "Antennas," John Wiley & Sons, Inc., New York, 1952; John D. Kraus, "Antennas," McGraw-Hill Book Company, Inc., New York, 1950; "Microwave Antenna Theory and Design" (vol. 12, Radiation Laboratory Series), McGraw-Hill Book Company, Inc., New York, 1949; "Very High Frequency Techniques," chaps. 1–8, McGraw-Hill Book Company, Inc., New York, 1947; F. E. Terman, "Radio Engineers' Handbook," sec. 11, McGraw-Hill Book Company, Inc., New York, 1943; Keith Henney, "Radio Engineering Handbook," 4th ed., chap. 14, McGraw-Hill Book Company, Inc., New York, 1950; E. A. Laport, "Radio Antenna Engineering," McGraw-Hill Book Company, Inc., New York, 1952.

current I in the doublet, retarded by the time it takes the wave to reach P when traveling with the velocity of light.   This lag of d/c seconds due to retardation can be expressed as

$$\text{Phase lag in radians} = 2\pi\frac{d}{\lambda} \qquad (23\text{-}2)$$

The intensity B of the magnetic field of the radio wave is everywhere proportional to the strength ε of the electric field.   The relation between the two is

$$\varepsilon = 300B \qquad (23\text{-}3)$$

Here B is in lines per square centimeter and ε is in volts per centimeter.

The wavefront of the radiated wave lies in a plane perpendicular to the line drawn toward the doublet, and the waves are polarized in the same

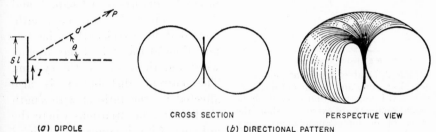

CROSS SECTION

PERSPECTIVE VIEW

(*a*) DIPOLE   (*b*) DIRECTIONAL PATTERN

Fig. 23-1. Elementary doublet antenna consisting of a length of wire carrying a current I, together with directional patterns.

direction as the axis of the doublet.   Thus a plane can be passed through the antenna and an electric flux line of the radiated wave.   The magnetic flux lines are perpendicular to such a plane.

Induction Fields.   The electric and magnetic fields in the immediate vicinity of a doublet antenna are greater in magnitude and different in phase from the radiation field calculated with the aid of Eq. (23-1). The electric and magnetic fields that must be added to this *radiation field* in order to give the fields actually present are termed *induction fields.* These induction fields diminish in strength more rapidly than in inverse proportion to distance, and at distances of a few wavelengths they become negligible in comparison with the radiation fields.   However, at distances from the doublet that are small compared with a wavelength (or small compared with the antenna dimensions if the antenna is large), the induction electric and magnetic fields will be much stronger than the radiation field of the antenna.

23-2. Characteristics of Wire Radiators Remote from Ground.   The doublet is a special case of a wire antenna in which the length is very small.   When the antenna length is not small the antenna wire with its current distribution can be considered as being composed of a large number of doublets properly located in space and carrying appropriate currents; thus the antenna with the current distribution shown in Fig. 23-2a can be broken down into a succession of doublets carrying suitably chosen currents, as shown in Fig. 23-2b. In such a situation the field radiated in any particular direction is then the vector sum of the fields radiated from the individual doublets, taking into account the magnitude, phase, and space orientation of the component fields produced at a distant observing point by each doublet.

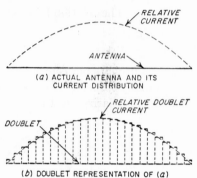

(a) ACTUAL ANTENNA AND ITS CURRENT DISTRIBUTION

(b) DOUBLET REPRESENTATION OF (a)

Fig. 23-2. Doublet representation of an actual antenna and its current distribution. It is apparent that when the individual doublets are extremely short the array of doublets approximates very closely the actual antenna.

Current Distribution in Wire Antennas. A wire antenna is a circuit with distributed constants; hence the current distribution in a wire antenna that results from the application of a localized voltage follows the principles discussed in Chap. 4, and depends upon the antenna length, measured in wavelengths; the terminations at the ends of the antenna wire; and the losses in the system. The current distribution is also affected by the ratio of wire length to diameter in situations where the antenna wire is unusually thick.[1]

Under most circumstances, the losses are sufficiently low and the ratio of wire length to diameter sufficiently great so that to a first approximation the current distribution can be taken as that for a line with zero losses; it then has the characteristics discussed in Sec. 4-5.[2]

Radiation Characteristics of a Resonant Wire Remote from Ground. A resonant wire corresponds to a transmission line that is an exact number of half wavelengths long, and is open at both ends.[3] The current distribution as observed in such a resonant wire serving as an antenna ordinarily approximates very closely the distribution that would be obtained on the assumption of zero losses, provided the wire length does not exceed

[1] The behavior of thick antenna is discussed in Kraus, *op. cit.*, chap. 9; and Schelkunoff and Friis, *op. cit.*, pp. 436–454.

[2] It is obviously an approximation to neglect losses, because if the antenna radiates it consumes energy and so must behave as though it possessed loss. However, under most circumstances, the distribution of radiated fields about the antenna, as determined by postulating a current distribution corresponding to zero losses, differs only negligibly from the distribution of the radiated fields produced by the current distribution that actually exists.

[3] For resonance, the *electrical* length must be an exact number of half wavelengths long. Because of end effects, an isolated wire acts electrically as though it were slightly longer than it actually is; as a result, the physical length required to give resonance with a thin wire is of the order of 0.025λ less than the electrical length in wavelengths.

8 to 10 wavelengths.   The current distribution, accordingly, has the character illustrated in Fig. 23-3.[1]

The distribution of the radiation about a resonant wire depends upon the length of the wire.   The relative field strength as a function of direction[2] for a number of representative cases is shown in Fig. 23-4.   These patterns can be regarded as cross sections of figures of revolution about an axis coinciding with the wire.   The directional characteristic is seen to consist of a number of lobes, the largest of which is the one making the

LENGTH=$\frac{\lambda}{2}$ LENGTH=λ LENGTH=$\frac{3\lambda}{2}$

FIG. 23-3. Typical current distributions in resonant lines.   The distributions shown have been idealized by assuming zero losses.

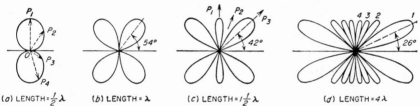

(a) LENGTH=$\frac{1}{2}\lambda$ (b) LENGTH=λ (c) LENGTH=$1\frac{1}{2}\lambda$ (d) LENGTH=4λ

FIG. 23-4. Polar diagrams showing strength of field radiated in various directions from antennas consisting of resonant wires remote from ground.

smallest angle with respect to the wire axis.   Increasing the wire length, as measured in wavelengths, reduces the angle that this major lobe makes with the axis, and also increases the number of minor lobes.   The relation between wire length and the first few lobes and nulls is given in Fig. 23-5.

The directional characteristic of a resonant wire differs from that of an elementary doublet because the distance from a remote point to various parts of the wire will differ by an appreciable fraction of a wavelength, and also because, when the wire is more than a half wavelength long, the currents in different parts of the wire may differ in phase.   The result is that the fields radiated from different elementary sections of a long wire add vectorially to give a sum that depends upon direction.   Thus, in Fig. 23-6, an observer in the direction P_1 receives no radiation because he is equidistant from the two halves of the antenna, and these halves carry currents of opposite phase.   An observer in the direction P_3 likewise receives no radiation, because each elementary length of antenna radiates zero field in the direction of its axis.   On the other hand, the field in the direction P_2 is relatively strong because, although the radiations from the

---

[1] These current distributions are those that would be obtained by applying the exciting voltage in series with the wire at a current loop, or to one end of the wire.

[2] In diagrams of this type the radial distances OP_1, OP_2, etc., represent the relative strength of the field radiated in the directions of lines OP_1, OP_2, etc., as indicated in Fig. 23-4a.

two halves of the antenna start toward P_2 in opposite phase, the distance from P_2 to the two halves of the antenna is different.   Hence cancellation does not take place in direction P_2 as it does toward P_1.   The result is a

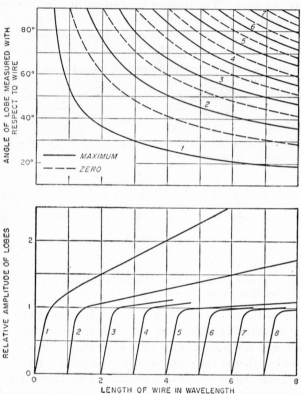

Fig. 23-5. Characteristics of the lobes in the radiation pattern of a resonant wire remote from ground.   The lobes are numbered so that lobe 1 makes the smallest angle with the wire axis, as in Fig. 23-4d.

directional pattern in which the maximum of radiation occurs at an angle with respect to the wire axis,[1] which for the case shown in Fig. 23-6 is approximately 54° (see Fig. 23-4a).

[1] The equation of the patterns in Fig. 23-4 can be obtained by considering the wire to consist of a number of elementary lengths as in Fig. 23-2b, each of which radiates independently.   The resultant field produced at a distant point is then the vector sum of these component fields.   Thus, consider the case where the wire is an even number of half wavelengths long, as in Fig. 23-6.   If the reference point is the mid-point of the antenna ($x = 0$ at mid-point), and if I_0 is the maximum current, then assuming zero losses the current distribution can be written as

$$i = I_0 \sin (2\pi x/\lambda) \cos (\omega t + 90°) \qquad (23\text{-}4)$$

Radiation from element dx at a distance x from the mid-point reaches distant point P_2 sooner than radiation from the reference point because the distance is less by $x \cos \theta$, which corresponds to $(2\pi x/\lambda) \cos \theta$ radians advance in phase.   By combining Eqs. (23-1) and (23-4), the field $\Delta \varepsilon$ produced at P_2 by an elementary length of the

Radiation Characteristics of a Nonresonant Wire Remote from Ground.
When power is applied to one end of an antenna wire, and the other end is
terminated so that there is no re-
flected wave, the antenna then acts
as a nonresonant transmission line.
The current distribution under these
circumstances has the character
discussed in connection with Fig.
4-4c, and also shown in Fig. 23-7a,
being constant everywhere if the
attenuation is zero, and decaying
exponentially when there are losses.
In either case the phase of the current drops back progressively at a

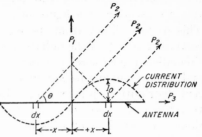

FIG. 23-6. Diagram used to illustrate
factors controlling the directional characteristic of a resonant antenna.

rate of 2π radians per wavelength as one recedes from the end of the
antenna to which power is applied.

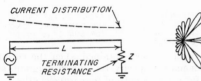
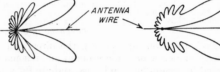

(*a*) NONRESONANT ANTENNA   (*b*) DIRECTIONAL PATTERN   (*c*) DIRECTIONAL PATTERN
                                 FOR $L=4\lambda$ AND   FOR $L=4\lambda$ AND TOTAL
                            NEGLIGIBLE ATTENUATION   ATTENUATION $\alpha L=0.8$

FIG. 23-7. Nonresonant antenna, together with typical directional patterns.

The relative field strength as a function of direction about such a nonresonant wire depends upon the length of the wire and the attenuation.

---

antenna is

$$\Delta\mathcal{E} = \frac{60\pi}{d_0\lambda} I_0 \sin\frac{2\pi x}{\lambda} \cos\left[\omega\left(t - \frac{d_0}{c}\right) + \frac{2\pi x}{\lambda}\cos\theta\right]\sin\theta\,dx \qquad (23\text{-}5)$$

where θ = angle of elevation measured with respect to the wire axis
      c = velocity of light
      d_0 = distance from the wire center to P_2
The total radiation from the entire length L of the antenna is

$$\mathcal{E} = \frac{60\pi}{d_0 x} I_0 \sin\theta \int_{x=\frac{-L}{2}}^{x=\frac{L}{2}} \sin\frac{2\pi x}{\lambda}\cos\left(\omega t - \frac{\omega d_0}{c} + \frac{2\pi x}{\lambda}\cos\theta\right)dx \qquad (23\text{-}6)$$

After carrying out the indicated integration, and then simplifying by taking advantage of the fact that L is a whole number of wavelengths, one obtains

$$\mathcal{E} = \frac{60}{d_0} I_0 \frac{\sin\left[(\pi L/\lambda)\cos\theta\right]}{\sin\theta}(-1)^n \sin\omega\left(t - \frac{d_0}{c}\right) \qquad (23\text{-}7)$$

where n is the number of wavelengths contained in L.

An analogous procedure is followed when the antenna length is an odd number of
half wavelengths, except that the current distribution is now

$$i = I_0 \cos\left(2\pi x/\lambda\right)\cos\left(\omega t + 90°\right)$$

When the attenuation is assumed to be zero, an approximation permissible
when the wire is not over a few wavelengths long, the directional characteristic has the character[1] shown in Fig. 23-7b, which can be considered as
the cross section of a figure of revolution having the wire as the axis.
This pattern differs from the corresponding pattern of Fig. 23-4 for a
resonant line in that the radiation is strongly unidirectional. At the same
time, there is a close relation between the directional pattern of a resonant
and a nonresonant wire antenna. This arises from the fact that the current distribution on a resonant wire can be expressed as the sum of two
traveling waves, as discussed in connection with Fig. 4-2. Thus the directional characteristic of a resonant system is the vector sum of the directional patterns of two similar nonresonant patterns pointed in opposite

(a) RADIATION PATTERN OF
WAVE TRAVELING TOWARD
RIGHT (FROM FIG. 23-7b)

(b) RADIATION PATTERN OF
WAVE TRAVELING TOWARD
LEFT (SAME AS (a) BUT
REVERSED IN DIRECTION)

(c) RADIATION PATTERN OF
RESONANT WIRE, I.E. VEC-
TOR SUM OF (a) AND (b)

FIG. 23-8. Relationship between the directional pattern obtained when the current
distribution on a wire is nonresonant and resonant, respectively. These diagrams are
idealized by assuming zero losses, and are for a wire length of four wavelengths.

directions, as illustrated in Fig. 23-8. One consequence of this situation
is that the major lobe makes almost the same angle with the wire axis in
both resonant and nonresonant antennas of the same length. The minor
lobes that are immediately adjacent to the major lobes also have substantially the same directions in the two cases.

Losses in a nonresonant antenna wire modify the directional characteristic of the radiation in the manner shown in Fig. 23-7c, which is drawn
for about as much attenuation as is ever likely to be encountered in
practice. Even with this high attenuation, the field pattern is seen to
have the same general character as with zero losses. The chief differences
are a slight distortion of the major lobe, and a filling in of the minima
between the minor lobes.

23-3. Directive Gain of Antennas. Examination of Figs. 23-1b, 23-4,
and 23-7 shows that an antenna concentrates its radiated energy to a
greater or lesser extent in certain preferred directions. The extent of such
concentration relative to that of some standard antenna, termed the
directive gain, is defined[2] quantitatively as the *ratio of power that must be*

---

[1] The formulas for the radiation patterns of Fig. 23-7b and c are derived in "Radio
Engineering," 3d ed., p. 669.

[2] Directive gain depends entirely on the distribution in space of the *radiated* power.
The power input to the antenna, the antenna losses, or the power consumed in a terminating resistance have nothing to do with *directive* gain. Such factors are taken

radiated by the comparison antenna to develop a particular field strength in the direction of maximum radiation to the power that must be radiated by the directional antenna system to obtain the same field strength in the same direction. Unless otherwise specified, the comparison antenna is an isotropic radiator.[1] Thus the directive gain can also be defined as the ratio of the power intensity that is radiated in the preferred direction to the radiation power intensity averaged over all directions.

TABLE 23-1
DIRECTIVE GAIN OF SIMPLE ANTENNAS RELATIVE
TO ISOTROPIC RADIATOR

Wire length, λ	Directive gain	
	Resonant wire (Fig. 23-3)	Nonresonant wire (Fig. 23-7a)
0.5	1.64	3.2
1.0	1.8	4.3
1.5	2.0	5.5
2	2.3	6.5
3	2.8	8.6
4	3.5	10.5
8	7.1	17.4

Directive gain of elementary doublet = 1.5

The directive gain can be expressed either as a power ratio, or in terms of the equivalent number of decibels. Thus a gain of 4 (or 6 db) means that the power intensity in the direction of maximum radiation is 4 times as great (field intensity twice as great) as would be the case if the radiator in question were an isotropic antenna radiating the same total power.

Methods of calculating directive gain of an antenna are outlined in Sec. 23-11. For the present it is sufficient to understand that directive gain is a quantitative measure of the extent to which the total radiated power is concentrated in one direction. The directive gains for a number of simple antennas are given in Table 23-1. It will be noted that the gain of an

---

into account in terms of the *power* gain of the antenna which is defined as the ratio of the power *input* to the comparison antenna required to develop a particular field strength in the direction of maximum radiation, to the power *input* that must be delivered to the directional antenna to obtain the same field strength in the same direction. Unless otherwise specified the comparison antenna is a *lossless* isotropic radiator.

[1] An isotropic antenna produces waves that are of equal strength in all directions. Although an isotropic radiator of coherent waves does not exist because it cannot satisfy Maxwell's equations, the properties of such an imaginary antenna are easily visualized, and the concept of an isotropic radiator is often found useful in the analysis of antenna systems.

elementary dipole is 1.5, whereas patterns such as those of Figs. 23-4d and 23-7b, which are obviously more directional have much higher gains.

23-4. Arrays of Antennas. A radiating system that is composed of several spaced radiators is termed an antenna *array*. The total field developed by an array at a distant point is the vector sum of the fields produced by the individual antennas of the array. The relative phases of these component fields is determined by the relative distances to the various radiators of the array, and so will depend upon the direction. As a result, the component fields tend to add in some directions and to cancel in others. By properly exploiting this property of spaced antennas, it is

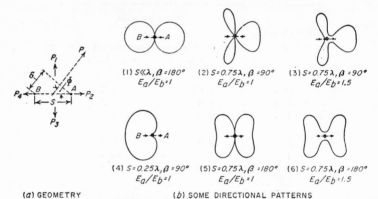

(*a*) GEOMETRY   (*b*) SOME DIRECTIONAL PATTERNS

Fig. 23-9. Pair of spaced antennas, together with directional patterns in the plane of the paper obtained in typical cases when the antennas radiate uniformly in this plane.

possible to concentrate the radiated energy very strongly in a desired direction. This is illustrated by the following examples.

Radiation Characteristic of a Pair of Spaced Antennas. The simplest possible antenna array consists of two spaced antennas, as illustrated schematically in Fig. 23-9a. The field produced by such an arrangement at a distant point P is the vector sum of the fields produced by each radiator considered as acting independently. In determining this vector sum it is to be noted that at P the phase difference of the individual radiations is affected by the difference in distance from P to the individual antennas, as well as by the difference in phases of the currents in the two antennas.

The mathematical expression for the resultant field is[1]

$$\text{Total field at } P = \sqrt{E_a{}^2 + E_b{}^2 + 2E_aE_b \cos\left(\beta + 2\pi\frac{S}{\lambda}\cos\phi\right)} \qquad (23\text{-}8a)$$

[1] This can be derived as follows: If P is a great distance from A and B, it is $\delta = (S/\lambda) \cos \phi$ wavelengths farther from B than A. This corresponds to $2\pi (S/\lambda) \cos \phi$ radians lag in phase of the radiation from B due to its more distant position. Thus, radiation arriving at P from B lags $\beta + 2\pi(S/\lambda) \cos \phi$ radians behind that arriving from A. The total radiation at P is hence the sum of two vectors of magnitude

where E_a and E_b = magnitudes of fields produced at P by individual
radiators A and B, respectively

S = spacing of antennas

β = phase angle by which current in B lags current in A

ϕ = angular direction of P with respect to line joining A
and B (see Fig. 23-9a)

The directional pattern represented by Eq. (23-8a) can take a great
variety of shapes according to the particular values of E_b/E_a, β, and S/λ
that apply. A few typical examples are illustrated in Fig. 23-9 for the
case of antennas that radiate uniformly in all directions in the plane of the
paper. The effect of antenna directivity in the plane of the paper can be
taken into account by multiplying the patterns shown in Fig. 23-9 by the
actual directional pattern of the radiating antennas (assumed the same
for the two antennas).

A special case of particular interest occurs when the antennas are
spaced a quarter of a wavelength apart and carry equal currents 90° out
of phase. Assuming $\beta = \pi/2$, $S/\lambda = 0.25$, and $E_a = E_b$, then for an
isotropic radiator (E_a independent of direction) Eq. (23-8a) becomes

$$\text{Radiated field} = 2E_a \cos\left[\frac{\pi}{4}(1 + \cos\phi)\right] \qquad (23\text{-}8b)$$

The resulting radiation pattern has the unidirectional cardioid-shaped
character given by 4 of Fig. 23-9b. Here zero field is produced in direction P_2 because the radiation from antenna B starts out in this direction
90° behind the radiation from A, and then loses another 90° while traveling the quarter wavelength spacing S; hence the radiation from B that
reaches P_2 is exactly 180° out of phase with the radiation reaching P_2 from
A. In contrast, the radiation reaching P_4 from A starts out a quarter of a
cycle ahead of the radiation from B, but takes exactly a quarter of a cycle
to reach B because of the quarter-wavelength spacing between the
antennas. The radiations from A and B thus add in phase in direction
P_4 and the total field strength is $2E_a$. In the side directions P_1 and P_3, a
remote receiving point is equidistant from the two antennas; the radiations from the two antennas in these directions are thus in time quadrature, and the field strength at P_1 and P_3 is $\sqrt{2}E_a$.

The Broadside Array. A broadside array consists of a number of radiators equally spaced along a line, and carrying currents of the same phase
in all radiators. Such an arrangement has the ability to concentrate the
radiation in a plane at right angles to the line of the array, while producing
relatively little radiation in other directions, as illustrated in Fig. 23-10.

E_a and E_b, differing in phase by the above amount. Equation (23-7) is then obtained
by employing the formula for the third side of a triangle, given two sides and the
included angle.

The mechanism by which the broadside array achieves this result can be understood by noting that a distant point in a plane perpendicular to the line of the array, i.e., in direction P_1 or P'_1, is substantially the same distance from all parts of the array. The component radiations from each individual antenna accordingly add in phase in directions P_1 and P'_1, since these radiations start out with the same phase and all have the same distance to travel. However, waves traveling toward P_2 from the various antennas arrive with different phase relations as a result of the fact that the various antennas are at different distances from P_2. If the array is at

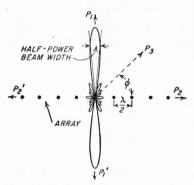

FIG. 23-10. Broadside array consisting of radiators assumed to radiate uniformly in all directions in the plane of the paper, together with directional pattern in this plane. The same antenna configuration becomes an end-fire array if the radiators are phased for end-fire instead of broadside action.

least several wavelengths long, the resultant radiation in the direction P_2 will be small or zero. A similar situation will occur in the direction P_3, provided the array is sufficiently long and the angle ϕ is enough less than 90° so that the difference in distance from P_3 to the two ends of the array will approach or exceed a wavelength; the component fields produced in direction P_3 by the different antennas of the array then differ sufficiently in phase so that their vector sum is small; i.e., the radiations from the different antennas will largely cancel in direction P_3.

The width of the major lobe of the broadside array is less the longer the array, as shown in Fig. 23-11a. This is because the longer the array, the smaller the deviation in direction from P_1 in Fig. 23-10, for which the difference in distance to the two ends of the array will be of the order of a wavelength. For array lengths exceeding two wavelengths, the width of the major lobe is almost exactly inversely proportional to the array length. The directive gain under these conditions will be proportional to array length.

The spacing of the individual antennas in a broadside array has only a secondary effect upon the directional characteristics of the array provided the spacing is not too great. Thus, when the individual antennas are isotropic radiators, varying the spacing from very small values up to $3\lambda/4$ affects only the minor lobe structure, as shown in Fig. 23-11b. With spacing greater than $3\lambda/4$, large secondary lobes appear, however, and may even be more prominent than the lobe in the broadside direction. These secondary or parasitic lobes arise from the fact that, with large spacings, there are certain directions other than P_1 in Fig. 23-10 for which the component fields produced by the various radiators are also all in phase. This occurs for any direction ϕ' such that the difference in distance Δ from a distant point to adjacent antennas is an integral multiple of a whole number of wavelengths, that is, when

$$\Delta = S \cos \phi' = n\lambda \qquad (23\text{-}9)$$

where n can be 1,2, etc., and S is the spacing between adjacent antennas. Thus if $S = \lambda$, then a major secondary lobe will occur at $\phi = 0°$, i.e., in direction P_2. This is to be expected, because for one-wavelength spacing, a wave traveling in the direction P_2 takes exactly one cycle to traverse the

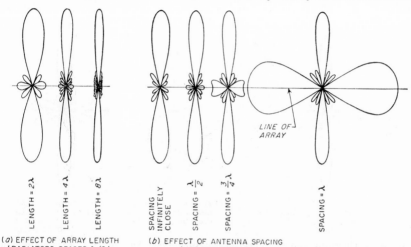

LINE OF ARRAY

(a) EFFECT OF ARRAY LENGTH
(RADIATORS SPACED λ/2)

LENGTH = 2λ
LENGTH = 4λ
LENGTH = 8λ

(b) EFFECT OF ANTENNA SPACING
(ARRAY LENTH=3λ)

SPACING INFINITELY CLOSE
SPACING = λ/2
SPACING = 3λ/4
SPACING = λ

Fig. 23-11. Effect of array length and element spacing on the directional pattern of a broadside array in which the individual antennas are assumed to be isotropic radiators.

distance from one antenna to the next and so adds in phase with the radiation starting out from this next antenna in the direction P_2.

When the individual radiators of a broadside array are directive instead of isotropic, the array pattern is then the pattern for isotropic radiators multiplied by the directional pattern of the actual antennas that are used. Thus, if the individual radiators are short doublets with their axes coinciding with the line of the array as illustrated in Fig. 23-12a, then the actual pattern (Fig. 23-12c) corresponds to that given in Fig. 23-12b for the individual radiators, multiplied by Fig. 23-12a, the pattern of the array in the isotropic case. Under these conditions it is seen that the individual radiators can be spaced a full wavelength apart without large

[1] If the individual radiators have greater broadside directivity than a doublet, then still greater spacing is permissible between the adjacent radiators of the broadside array. Specifically, large parasitic lobes will always be avoided as long as the spacing S between adjacent radiators is small enough so that $S \cos \phi' \leqslant \lambda$ when

$$\phi' = 90° - \delta/2$$

where δ is the beam width between nulls of the individual radiators. That is,

parasitic side lobes being developed.[1]   This is because the individual half-wave antennas radiate little energy in the general direction of these unwanted side lobes.   As long as the spacing between the centers of the adjacent collinear doublets does not exceed one wavelength, the broadside pattern in three-dimensional space as represented by the major lobes is then pancake-shaped, with the plane of the pancake being at right angles to the line of the array.   Next consider the case of a broadside array in which the individual radiators are spaced $\lambda/2$ apart and are short doublets oriented at right angles to the line of the array.   The field strength in a plane perpendicular to the line of the array will then be

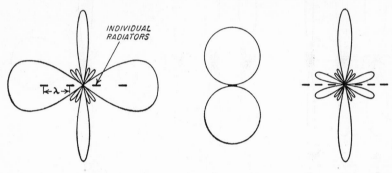

(a) DIRECTIONAL PATTERN OF BROAD-   (b) ACTUAL DIRECTIONAL   (c) DIRECTIONAL CHARAC-
SIDE ARRAY WITH ISOTROPIC RAD-   CHARACTERISTIC OF   TERISTIC OF BROAD-
IATORS SPACED ONE WAVELENGTH   INDIVIDUAL RADIATOR   SIDE ARRAY — THE
APART   PRODUCT OF (a) AND(b)

FIG. 23-12. Diagrams showing effect of the directional characteristic of the individual radiators on the directional characteristic of a broadside array.

proportional to cos θ, where θ is the angle in this plane measured perpendicular to the axis of the doublets as in Fig. 23-1a.   The resulting pattern in space consists of two thin circular fans or ears pointing in opposite directions.

Quantitative relations giving the width of the major lobe, and the directive gain, of idealized broadside arrays are given in Table 23-2.[1]

Broadside Array with Tapered Current Distribution to Minimize Side Lobes.   In the above discussion of broadside arrays, it was assumed that the individual radiators carried equal currents.   The antenna patterns corresponding to such an array are characterized by side lobes, which although much smaller than the main lobe when the antenna spacing is

parasitic lobes will be avoided if

$$S \leqslant \frac{\lambda}{\sin\ (\delta/2)} \qquad (23\text{-}10)$$

[1] These relations are obtained from Kraus, *op. cit.*, chap. 4, and Schelkunoff and Friis, *op. cit.*, chaps. 5 and 6; this reference should be consulted for derivations, and for additional quantitative information on broadside and end-fire arrays.

not excessive, are nevertheless of significant amplitude as is apparent from Fig. 23-11.

In many applications it is highly desirable that the side lobes be either eliminated altogether, or at least reduced in amplitude relative to the main lobe. This can be accomplished by so arranging matters that the antennas near the center of the broadside array radiate more strongly than do the antennas near the edge.

Side lobes will be entirely eliminated in a broadside array provided (1) the spacing between adjacent antennas does not exceed $\lambda/2$, and

TABLE 23-2
WIDTH OF MAJOR LOBE AND DIRECTIVE GAIN IN
BROADSIDE AND END-FIRE ARRAYS IN FREE SPACE

Broadside array:

Width of major lobe between nulls................................... $\dfrac{115°}{L/\lambda}$

Width of major lobe between half-power points....................... $\dfrac{51°}{L/\lambda}$

Directive gain (isotropic radiators or antennas up to $\lambda/2$ long with axes

parallel to array axis).. $\dfrac{2L}{\lambda}$

Directive gain (elementary doublets at right angles to array axis)........ $\dfrac{4L}{\lambda}$

End-fire array:

Width of major lobe between nulls................................... $\dfrac{115°}{\sqrt{L/2\lambda}}$

Directive gain (isotropic radiators, or radiators not over $\lambda/2$ long at right

angles to array axis).. $\dfrac{4L}{\lambda}$

NOTES: L = length of array between centers of end antennas. Number of individual radiators assumed large. Arrays assumed to be in free space.

(2) the currents of the various radiating antennas, starting from the outer edge and going toward the center, are proportional to the coefficients of the successive terms in the binomial series

$$(a + b)^{n-1} = a^{n-1} + (n - 1)a^{n-2}b + \frac{(n - 1)(n - 2)}{2!} a^{n-3}b^2 + \cdots$$

$$(23\text{-}11)$$

where n is the number of radiators. Thus for $n = 5$ the currents in the individual radiators should have the relative amplitudes[1] 1, 4, 6, 4, 1. The directional pattern for such an array is shown in Fig. 23-13b, which is to be compared with the pattern of Fig. 23-13a that is obtained for the same broadside array carrying equal currents in all five radiating antennas. It will be noted that in eliminating the side lobes, the width of the main lobe has been widened. Stated another way, if a main lobe

---

[1] When the radiators are so closely spaced that the current distribution can be regarded as continuous, this binomial distribution becomes the Gaussian error curve.

of specified width is to be obtained free of side lobes, then the antenna required must be longer than if side lobes are tolerated.

In many practical situations it is merely necessary that the side-lobe amplitude be reduced to a point where the side lobes are less than a specified small percentage of the main lobe. This result can be achieved by suitably tapering the current distribution, and will result in a width of the main lobe intermediate between that for a uniform current distribution with its large side lobes, and that given by the binomial distribution and its freedom from side lobes. For example, if the relative amplitudes of the currents in the five antennas referred to above are 1, 1.6, 1.9, 1.6, and 1, the side-lobe amplitude will be 10 per cent, and the main lobe will have a width intermediate between that for the binomial and for the uniform distributions; the resulting pattern is shown in Fig. 23-13c.[1]

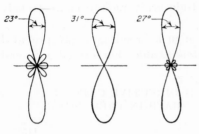

(a) UNIFORM   *(b)* BINOMIAL   *(c)* DOLPH-TCHEBYSCHEFF

Fig. 23-13. Reduction of side-lobe amplitude by tapering current distribution in broadside array consisting of five elements spaced $\lambda/2$ apart. The beam widths shown are values between half-power points (70.7 per cent amplitude).

The End-fire Array. The end-fire array consists of a number of identical equally spaced antennas arranged along a line and carrying currents of equal amplitude, just as with the usual broadside array. However, in the end-fire array the individual antennas are so excited that there is a

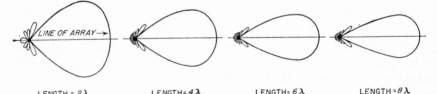

LENGTH = 2λ   LENGTH = 4λ   LENGTH = 6λ   LENGTH = 8λ

Fig. 23-14. The effect of array length on the directional characteristics of an end-fire array in which the individual radiators are spaced $\lambda/4$ and radiate uniformly in the plane of the paper.

progressive phase difference between adjacent antennas equal in cycles to the spacing between the antennas expressed in wavelengths.

Typical directional patterns of an end-fire array are illustrated in Fig. 23-14. These can be regarded as cross sections of figures of revolution that give the three-dimensional radiation pattern when the individual

[1] A current distribution, such as this, that gives the minimum lobe width for a given maximum permissible amplitude of the side lobes is termed a Dolph-Tchebyscheff distribution. For further information see C. L. Dolph, A Current Distribution for Broadside Arrays Which Optimizes the Relation between Beam Width and Side-lobe Level, *Proc. IRE*, vol. 34, p. 335, June, 1946; also Kraus, *op. cit.*, pp. 93–110.

antennas are isotropic radiators. The radiation pattern is seen to be unidirectional; it points along the array axis in the direction in which the antenna currents become more lagging. When viewed in three-dimensional space, the end-fire pattern is cigar-shaped. The width of the major lobe decreases as the array length increases just as in the broadside array, except that the lobe width is now inversely proportional to the square root of the array length. In addition, for a given array length the major lobe with end-fire action has a greater width than when the phasing of the same antennas is such as to give broadside operation. The quantitative relations are given in Table 23-2.

These directional characteristics of the end-fire array result from the fact that although a distant point in the direction in which the radiation concentrates (direction P_2 in Fig. 23-10) is at different distances from the individual antennas, the phases of the more distant antennas are just enough leading to compensate for the greater distance. Thus, the radiations from all antennas add in phase this direction. In directions that are appreciably different, including the opposite direction, the radiations from the individual antennas will not be in phase at a distant point, and as a consequence will more or less cancel each other.

An important and very simple case of end-fire action consists of two antennas spaced an odd number of quarter wavelengths apart, and excited with currents that differ in phase by the same odd multiple of 90°. Such an antenna system has already been discussed in connection with 4 of Fig. 23-9b.

The directional pattern of the end-fire array, like that of the broadside array, is substantially independent of the spacing of the antenna radiators, provided this spacing does not exceed a critical value. When the individual antenna radiators are isotropic, this critical spacing is approximately $3\lambda/8$. However, if the individual antennas possess directivity that aids the concentration of radiation along the axis of the array, then greater spacing is permissible for reasons analogous to those discussed in connection with Fig. 23-12.

Directivity of the individual antennas of an end-fire array is taken into account by multiplying the array pattern obtained by postulating isotropic radiators by the actual directional characteristic of the antennas used. In the common case where the individual radiators are half-wave antennas oriented at right angles to the line of the array, then the over-all pattern is practically the same as for isotropic radiators provided the array is at least moderately long. This is because under these conditions the array pattern has appreciable amplitude only in those directions in which the radiation from the half-wave antennas is at or near a maximum.

The directive gain of an end-fire array that has appreciable length is almost exactly twice the gain of a broadside array of the same length when both are composed of isotropic radiators (see Table 23-2). This arises because although the major lobe of the end-fire array is broader than in the corresponding broadside case, this is more than balanced by its unidirectional character. The directive gain is proportional to array length. The minor lobes in the end-fire pattern may be reduced in amplitude, or even eliminated entirely, by appropriately tapering the current distribution along the array, and also in some cases by likewise making the phase difference in cycles between adjacent antennas differ from the spacing in wavelengths. This is analogous to the behavior of the broadside array with tapered current distribution discussed above. However,

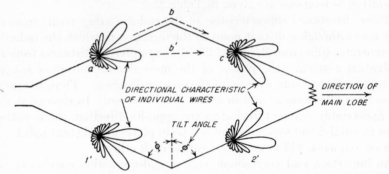

FIG. 23-15. Rhombic antenna, together with radiation patterns of the individual legs.

by simultaneously controlling *both* the current distribution and the phase difference between adjacent antennas, it is possible to reduce or eliminate the side lobes of an end-fire array and at the same time to reduce the width of the main lobe.[1]

Rhombic Antenna.[2] A different type of spaced antenna array that finds extensive use is illustrated in Fig. 23-15. Here four lengths of wire (called legs) are arranged in the form of a diamond or rhombus. A non-resonant current distribution is then obtained by making the terminating resistance approximate the characteristic impedance of the system in which the two sides of the rhombus are regarded as the conductors of a two-wire transmission line. When the system is properly proportioned there is a strong concentration of radiation in the direction indicated, combined with negligible radiation in the backward direction. The directional pattern of a typical rhombic antenna is shown in Fig. 23-16.

The tilt angle Φ in Fig. 23-15 must be chosen in relationship to the

---

[1] For further details see R. H. DuHamel, Optimum Patterns for End-fire Arrays, *Proc. IRE*, vol. 41, p. 652, May, 1953; D. R. Rhodes, The Optimum Linear Array for a Single Main Beam, *Proc. IRE*, vol. 41, p. 793, June, 1953.

[2] For further information, including equations and design procedures, see Schelkunoff and Friis, *op. cit.*, chap. 14; Kraus, *op. cit.*, pp. 408–412; E. A. Laport, Design Data for Horizontal Rhombic Antennas, *RCA Rev.*, vol. 13, p. 71, March, 1952; A. E. Harper, "Rhombic Antenna Design," D. Van Nostrand, Company, Inc., New York, 1941.

lengths of the legs in such a manner as simultaneously to meet as nearly
as possible the two requirements that (1) the main lobe of the radiation
pattern of an individual leg of the antenna considered as an isolated
nonresonant wire will have an angle[1] 90° − Φ with respect to the wire and

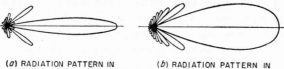

(*a*) RADIATION PATTERN IN   (*b*) RADIATION PATTERN IN
HORIZONTAL PLANE   VERTICAL PLANE

FIG. 23-16. Directional characteristic of a horizontal rhombic antenna in free space for
which the leg length is 6λ and Φ = 67.9°.

(2) the distance *abc* between mid-points of adjacent legs via the wire is a
half wavelength greater than the direct distance *ab'c* in Fig. 23-15.   To
the extent that the first requirement is met, each leg produces a lobe that
points in the direction of the axis of the rhombic antenna.   To the extent
that the second requirement is met,
the radiation from these four lobes
adds in phase in the direction of the
axis.[2]   The tilt angles required to
meet these two requirements are
given in Fig. 23-17 as a function of
leg length.   The optimum tilt angle
is a compromise value intermediate
between these curves.[3]

When the leg length exceeds
about two wavelengths, the optimum value of Φ does not vary appreciably with change in length.

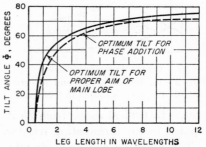

FIG. 23-17. Optimum tilt angles for
rhombic antennas in free space (assuming zero attenuation).

Under these conditions, the rhombic antenna will operate satisfactorily
from the frequency for which the tilt angle is optimum to a considerably
lower frequency.   As the frequency is reduced below the value for which
the design is optimum, the angle that the major lobes make with the wire

---

[1] As indicated on p. 870, this angle is very nearly equal to the angle of the major
lobe given in Fig. 23-5.

[2] This is because the extra half wavelength of distance that the current on the wire
must travel along path *abc*, as compared with the distance the radio wave in space
must travel (path *ab'c*), exactly compensates for the fact that the *lower* lobe of the
left-hand wire has opposite polarity from the *upper* lobe of the right-hand wire.

[3] This discussion is concerned with concentrating the radiation along the axis of
the antenna when the antenna is remote from ground.   When the antenna is parallel
to the ground, and the radiation is to be concentrated at an angle above the horizon,
the tilt angle Φ must be increased slightly to obtain optimum results.   However,
when the angle of elevation is of the order of 15° or less, and the leg lengths do not
exceed about 6λ, the increase in Φ involved does not exceed a few degrees.   For full
details see Schelkunoff and Friis, *op. cit.*, p. 466.

axis increases, and the lobes of the forward and rear legs no longer add in phase. These actions cause the main lobe to be somewhat broader than in an optimum design for a leg of the same length operating at the lower frequency. However, the deterioration of performance is not serious until the frequency is less than 40 to 50 per cent of the value for which the design is optimum. At frequencies appreciably greater than the value for which the design is optimum, the main lobe will split into two parts. Therefore, a rhombic antenna that is required to operate over a considerable range of frequencies is always designed so the tilt angle is optimum near the high-frequency end of the range.

Some of the power delivered to a rhombic antenna is radiated, and some is dissipated in the terminating resistor. The fraction of the total power lost in this latter way depends primarily upon the characteristic impedance of the two-wire transmission line represented by the two sides of the rhombic. It is therefore advantageous to use multiple-wire conductors, as this gives lower characteristic impedance and hence lower terminating power loss for a given antenna current.

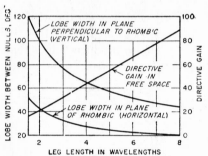

FIG. 23–18. Beam widths and directive gain of optimum rhombics in free space.

In typical cases, from 35 to 50 per cent of the input power is dissipated in the terminating resistor.

The directive gain of a rhombic antenna is a relatively complicated function of leg length and tilt angle. Values for optimum rhombics[1] in free space are given in Fig. 23-18. The *power* gain, as defined in the footnote on page 870, will be reduced to something like 50 to 65 per cent of the *directive* gain as a result of the loss in the terminating resistor.

Figure 23-18 also gives the free-space width of the major lobe for the optimum rhombus in the plane of the rhombus, and in the plane at right angles to the rhombus. It will be noted that the pattern is considerably narrower in the plane of the rhombus than it is at right angles to this plane.

23-5. Effect of Ground on the Directional Pattern of Ungrounded Antennas—Image Antennas.

In the discussion of antennas up to this point it has been assumed that the antenna was remote from ground. When this is not the case, the directional characteristic of the antenna is modified, since energy radiated toward the earth is reflected as shown in Fig. 23-19.[2] The total field in any direction then represents the vector sum of a direct wave plus a reflected wave.

[1] The curves of Fig. 23-18 are calculated from Eqs. (4), (7), (8), and (21) of Schelkunoff and Friis, *op. cit.*, chap. 14.

[2] This reflection by the earth is exactly the same as though plane waves were

For purposes of calculation, it is convenient to consider that the reflected wave is generated, not by reflection, but rather by an "image" antenna located below the surface of the ground.   The image antenna is so chosen that the joint action of the actual antenna and its image produces the same conditions in the space above the earth as exists with the actual antenna in the presence of the earth.   This result requires that the image antenna have a physical configuration that is the mirror image of the actual antenna, as illustrated in Fig. 23-20.

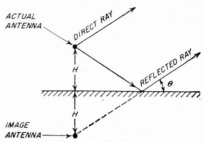

When the earth can be considered as having a reflection coefficient approximating unity, an assumption that is very commonly made, the currents in the corresponding

Fig. 23-19. Diagram illustrating how the wave reflected from the earth can be considered to have been produced by an image antenna.

parts of the actual and image antennas (i.e., in parts lying on the same vertical line and at the same distance from the earth's surface) are of the same magnitude.   The direction of current flow is such that the vertical component of the current in the image is in the same direction as the

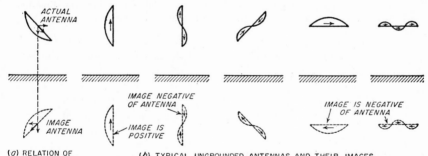

Fig. 23-20. Relation of vertical and horizontal components of current flowing in an antenna and its image, together with image antennas and image-antenna current distributions for typical cases of ungrounded antennas and a perfect earth.

vertical component of the current in the corresponding part of the actual antenna, while the horizontal components of the currents are in opposite directions, as illustrated in Fig. 23-20a.   Images for a number of typical cases are given in Fig. 23-20b in the ideal case of a perfectly reflecting earth.

involved instead of the spherical waves actually present.   This follows from the reciprocity theorem, which in effect states that the action in the case when the antenna is transmitting is the same as when the antenna is receiving (i.e., when the arrows in Fig. 23-19 are reversed); in the receiving case, the transmitter is so distant that the waves can be considered as plane.

Examination of Fig. 23-20 shows that a negative image will be present when the antenna wire is horizontal with respect to the earth, and also in the case of a resonant vertical antenna that is an even number of half wavelengths long. Under these conditions, the effect of the presence of the earth on the directional pattern is given by multiplying the actual directional characteristics of the antenna by the directional characteristic of a two-element array of isotropic radiators carrying equal currents of opposite phase, and spaced a distance twice the height of the antenna

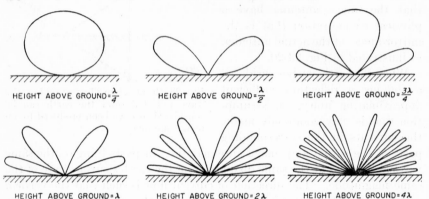

HEIGHT ABOVE GROUND=$\frac{\lambda}{4}$ HEIGHT ABOVE GROUND=$\frac{\lambda}{2}$ HEIGHT ABOVE GROUND=$\frac{3\lambda}{4}$

HEIGHT ABOVE GROUND=λ HEIGHT ABOVE GROUND=2λ HEIGHT ABOVE GROUND=4λ

FIG. 23-21. Polar diagrams for the negative image factor $|2 \sin [(2\pi H/\lambda) \sin \theta]|$ for various values of H/λ, showing how the height above the earth affects the directional characteristics of the antenna when the earth is a perfect reflector.

center above the surface of the ground. By substituting $E_a = E_b$, $\beta = 180°$, $\phi = 90° - \theta$, and $S = 2H$ in Eq. (23-8a) one has for the negative-image case

$$\left.\begin{array}{l}\text{Actual radiation in} \\ \text{presence of ground}\end{array}\right\} = 2 \sin\left(2\pi \frac{H}{\lambda} \sin \theta\right) \left\{\begin{array}{l}\text{radiation from} \\ \text{antenna when} \\ \text{in free space}\end{array}\right. \qquad (23\text{-}12)$$

Here H/λ is the height in wavelengths of the antenna center above earth, and θ is the angle of elevation above the horizon, as indicated in Fig. 23-19.

In a similar manner, a positive image is obtained in Fig. 23-19 with a vertical resonant antenna that is an odd number of half wavelengths long. In analogy with Eq. (23-12) one has for the positive image

$$\left.\begin{array}{l}\text{Actual radiation in} \\ \text{presence of ground}\end{array}\right\} = 2 \cos\left(2\pi \frac{H}{\lambda} \sin \theta\right) \left\{\begin{array}{l}\text{radiation from} \\ \text{antenna when} \\ \text{in free space}\end{array}\right. \qquad (23\text{-}13)$$

The nature of the factors in Eqs. (23-12) and (23-13) is indicated in Figs. 23-21 and 23-22. It is seen that with a negative image, and hence in the important case of horizontal polarization, the ground reflection causes cancellation of radiation along the ground and also at certain vertical angles, thus giving rise to nulls in the radiation pattern. In between these nulls are maxima corresponding to angles at which the reflected waves reinforce the direct wave to give lobe maxima having an amplitude twice that of the waves directly radiated in the same direction. The angle of elevation of the first lobe above the horizontal decreases as the height of the antenna above earth is increased. Consequently, to obtain strong radiation in directions approaching the horizontal using a horizontally polarized radiating system, it is necessary

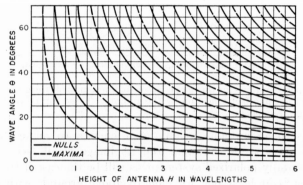

Fig. 23-22. Curves showing the vertical angles at which the negative image factor $|2 \sin [(2\pi H/\lambda) \sin \theta]|$ is maximum and zero. These curves give the vertical angles at which the reflections from the ground cause complete reinforcement and complete cancellation of the radiation. With a positive image the positions of the nulls and maxima are interchanged.

that the height of the antenna above earth be of the order of one wavelength or more. With a positive image, the positions of the lobes and nulls are interchanged from the conditions shown in Figs. 23-21 and 23-22, and there is a maximum of radiation along the ground.

When the ground cannot be assumed perfectly reflecting, the quantitative relations that exist can be calculated by regarding the antenna and its image as a two-element array in which the magnitude and phase of the currents in the image antenna are related to the currents in the actual antenna in accordance with the magnitude and phase of the reflection coefficient of the ground for the particular angle θ and polarization involved. The principal effects of an imperfectly conducting earth are to reduce slightly the magnitude of the maxima of the pattern, and to fill in the minima somewhat, as shown in Fig. 23-23. In the case of horizontal polarization the effect of an imperfect ground is seen to be quite small, especially at low vertical angles. With vertical polarization the ground imperfections have greater effect; in particular, the filling in of the nulls at moderately low vertical angles is very pronounced,[1]

---

[1] This same effect is discussed from a slightly different viewpoint on p. 816.

because of the low reflection coefficient near the Brewster angle (see Fig. 22-4).

Effect of Ground on Directive Gain of Ungrounded Antennas. Consider an antenna that is far enough from ground so that the total power radiated by a given set of antenna currents is independent of the presence or absence of the ground. Then a ground reflection that reinforces the main lobe will double the field strength of the main lobe, and so will increase directive gain of the antenna system by a factor of 4.* This condition

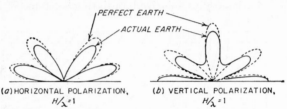

(*a*) HORIZONTAL POLARIZATION,   (*b*) VERTICAL POLARIZATION,
$H/\lambda = 1$ $H/\lambda = 1$

FIG. 23-23. Polar diagrams for the image factor that accounts for the ground reflection, showing effect of imperfect reflection by the ground. These curves are for a typical earth at a high frequency.

corresponds to an antenna height great enough to make the mutual impedance between the antenna and its image small (see page 894). With horizontally polarized systems this will be the case if the center of the antenna is at least one wavelength above ground; with vertically polarized systems it is true even at lower heights.

However, when the antenna is sufficiently close to the ground the effect of the ground reflection is to cause the directive gain to differ from 4. Thus, for a vertical doublet close to the ground, the directive gain is twice the free-space value, since the presence of the ground does not alter the directional pattern and there is no energy radiated in the direction of the hemisphere occupied by the ground. In contrast, the directive gain of a horizontal antenna very close to the ground can be more than 4 as compared with the same antenna in free space, as discussed below in connection with Fig. 23-35.

23-6. Grounded Antennas. Typical examples of grounded antennas are shown in Fig. 23-24. Such antennas can be considered as low-loss transmission lines that have as their sending end the junction between antenna and ground, and are open-circuited at the far end. The current is accordingly sinusoidally distributed in the manner discussed in Sec. 4-4 where the length is the total length along the antenna wire, irrespective of whether the antenna wire is straight or whether a portion of it is folded over to form a horizontal flat top.[1] The image antenna, taking

---

* This assumes that the free-space directional pattern of the transmitting antenna has a maximum in the direction in which the ground reflected wave reinforces the direct radiation.

[1] In the T antenna, the two halves of the top can be considered as being in parallel as far as currents and impedance are concerned.

into account the effect of the earth, is determined by the rules discussed in connection with Fig. 23-19 and, accordingly, possesses a mirror-image type of current distribution with continuity at the surface of the ground where the actual antenna and its image join, as shown in Fig. 23-24.

The directional characteristic of a simple vertical grounded conductor depends upon the height of the conductor as shown in Fig. 23-25, in

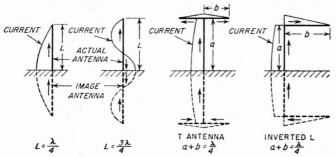

FIG. 23-24. Examples of grounded antennas and their images, together with typical current distributions.

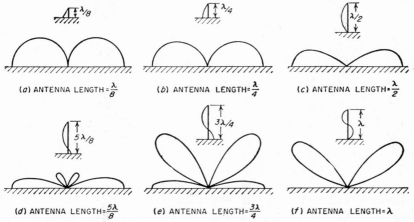

FIG. 23-25. Directional characteristics in a vertical plane of the fields radiated by grounded vertical antennas of varying lengths.

which the patterns shown can be considered as cross sections of figures of revolution having the antennas as the axes. When the antenna height is appreciably less than a quarter of a wavelength, the radiated field is proportional to the cosine of the angle of elevation. As the antenna height increases, the radiation is first concentrated increasingly along the horizontal until the antenna length is between $\lambda/2$ and $5\lambda/8$, after which high-angle lobes appear, as shown. This behavior can be explained by the fact that, as the antenna length increases up to slightly over a half wavelength, the antenna and its image act at least qualitatively as a two-element broadside array, thus giving directivity in the broadside (horizontal) direction which increases with increasing array length (i.e., increased height). However, when the length is of the order of three-quarters of a wavelength or more, the current in some parts of the antenna flows in a negative direction; this reduces the radiation along the horizontal and tends to favor an angle above the horizontal.

At long wavelengths, the far end of the grounded antenna is commonly folded over parallel to the earth as in the T and inverted L antennas in Fig. 23-24. In this way, the current in the vertical section can be made substantially constant, thus increasing the effectiveness with which the available height is used. The total radiated field produced by such a system can be determined by calculating the vertically polarized field due to the vertical portions of the antenna and its image and combining this

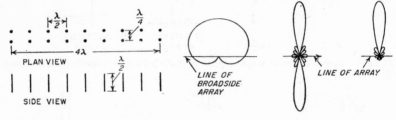

(*a*) ACTUAL ARRAY CONSISTING OF TWO BROADSIDE ARRAYS ARRANGED TO FORM A TWO-ELEMENT END-FIRE ARRAY   (*b*) PATTERN OF TWO-ELEMENT END-FIRE ARRAY   (*c*) PATTERN OF BROADSIDE ARRAY   (*d*) ACTUAL PATTERN (PRODUCT OF *b* AND *c*)

Fig. 23-26. An array of arrays that can be regarded as a broadside array in which each elementary radiator is a two-element end-fire array.

with the horizontally polarized field produced by the current in the horizontal portions of the antenna and of the image. Under conditions where the physical height of the antenna is a small fraction of a wavelength, the flat top contributes relatively little to the radiation because of the small distance in wavelengths to its negative image; practically all the radiation then arises from the vertical portion of the antenna.

23-7. Arrays of Arrays. A desired directional pattern may often be most easily obtained by assembling a number of individual antennas into an array, and then combining two or more such arrays in an *array of arrays* to give the desired over-all result. A simple example is illustrated in Fig. 23-26*a*, which can be regarded as consisting of a two-element end-fire array corresponding to case 4 of Fig. 23-9*b*,[1] in which each element is a broadside array. The resulting directional characteristic then is the product of the cardioid characteristic *b* given by case 4 of Fig. 23-9*b* and the broadside characteristic of Fig. 23-10.

A desired directional characteristic can be systematically built up in this way from antennas having simpler directional characteristics by using the following principles as a guide:

[1] Alternatively, one may regard the antenna of Fig. 23-26*a* as consisting of a broadside array in which each element is a two-element end-fire array.

1. Concentration of the radiation in azimuth can be obtained by arranging radiators (or arrays) to form a broadside array in which the line of the array is horizontal. The direction of concentration will then be at right angles to the line of the array.

2. Concentration of radiation in the vertical plane can be obtained by arranging radiators (or arrays) to form a broadside array in which the line of the array is vertical.

3. A unidirectional characteristic can be obtained by arranging two radiators (or two arrays) so that they are an odd number of quarter wavelengths apart and are excited an odd number of quarter cycles out of phase.

4. In systems radiating horizontally polarized waves, the angle of elevation above the ground of the major lobe is determined in large measure by the height above ground of the center of the antenna system.

5. The directional characteristics of the individual radiators may have a significant effect upon the over-all directional pattern.

The antenna system of Fig. 23-27[1] is an example of how a highly directional radiation pattern may be achieved in this way. Here horizontal antennas are arranged broadside in the horizontal plane to obtain horizontal directivity, and are stacked vertically to give vertical directivity. Two such curtains are then arranged in a simple end-fire system to give a unidirectional effect. The array is finally placed so that the height of its center above ground has the value required by Eq. (23-12) to concentrate the radiation at the desired angle above the horizon. The resulting directional characteristic in three-dimensional space then has the general character

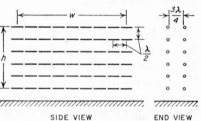

FIG. 23-27. Antenna array composed of resonant half-wave radiators arranged to produce a unidirectional beam that is sharply defined in both the vertical and horizontal planes.

shown in Fig. 23-28, when the mattress is vertical with its lower edge close to the ground as shown in Fig. 23-27.

The directional pattern of an array such as that of Fig. 23-27 can be expressed by the formula

$$\text{Relative field strength} = F_a F_h F_v F_e F_g \qquad (23\text{-}14)$$

Here F_a is the directional characteristic of the individual antenna used in the system, when this antenna is remote from ground. F_h is a factor representing the directional characteristic of a horizontal broadside array employing isotropic radiators equal in number to the number of actual

---

[1] This type of array when designed for use at very high frequencies is often called a "mattress" antenna.

radiators in the horizontal direction in Fig. 23-27 (or Fig. 23-12). Similarly F_v is the corresponding factor that takes into account the vertical stacking of these horizontal broadside arrays, and is the directional characteristic that would be obtained from a broadside array composed of isotropic radiators equal in number to the tiers of radiators in Fig. 23-27. The factor F_e is the directional pattern of a two-element end-fire array composed of isotropic radiators having the same spacing and phasing as the curtains in Fig. 23-27. The factor F_g takes into account the effect of the earth reflection, and in this case is given by Eq. (23-12) or Eq. (23-13), as the case may be. The quantities F_h, F_v, and F_e in Eq. (23-14) are sometimes called *array factors*.

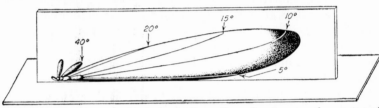

Fig. 23-28. Directional characteristics in three-dimensional space of an array of the type shown in Fig. 23-27.

The directional pattern of the mattress array of Fig. 23-27 depends on the effective value of height h and width w of the array as defined in Fig. 23-27, and upon the current distribution among the individual radiators. When the current is the same in each antenna, the width of the main lobe between nulls and between half-power points in the vertical and horizontal planes is given by the formulas listed in Table 23-2 as applicable to a broadside array; it is merely necessary to replace L by h and w, respectively. On the other hand, when the current is greatest in the antennas at the center of the array, and decreases progressively as the edges of the array are approached, the main lobe is broader than for a uniform distribution, but the side lobes are reduced in amplitude.

The directive gain of a mattress antenna depends upon the effective area wh of the array, and upon the current distribution. The quantitative relation is given by Eq. (23-28), below.

23-8. Radiation Resistance and Radiated Power. The relation between the total energy radiated from a transmitting antenna and the current flowing in the antenna can be conveniently expressed in terms of a *radiation resistance*. This is the resistance that, when inserted in series with the antenna, will consume the same amount of power as is actually radiated. The magnitude of the radiation resistance depends upon the antenna configuration and upon the point in the antenna system at which the resistance is considered as being inserted. Unless specifically stated to the contrary, it is customary to refer the radiation resistance to a current maximum in the case of an ungrounded antenna, and to the current at the base of the antenna when the antenna is grounded.

Calculation of Radiated Power and Radiation Resistance. The total power radiated from an antenna system can be determined by imagining that the antenna is at the center of a very large sphere. The rate at which energy passes through each square meter of surface of such a sphere is the average energy density per cubic meter of volume at the surface of the sphere multiplied by the velocity with which the wave is traveling, i.e., the velocity of light. As a consequence, the power passing through each square meter of such a spherical surface is $\mathcal{E}^2/120\pi$ watts,* where $\mathcal{E}$ is the field strength in root mean square volts per meter. The total power radiated from the antenna is then found by summation over the portion of the spherical surface that is above ground. The effect of the earth is taken into account through the contribution to the field made by an appropriate image antenna. The radiation resistance is then this total radiated power divided by the square of the antenna current at the point in the antenna to which the resistance is referred.

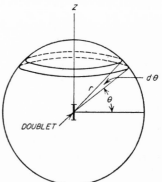

Fig. 23–29. Geometry involved in deriving Eq. (23-18).

The details involved in carrying out a determination of radiated power in this way, which is called the Poynting vector method, can be understood by analyzing the case of a doublet antenna remote from ground. The geometry involved is shown in Fig. 23-29, and the field strength radiated is given by Eq. (23-1). It will be assumed that the axis of the doublet is vertical (*Z* direction in Fig. 23-29). The area dA of any ring in the spherical surface of elevation θ and width $d\theta$, formed by revolving about the vertical axis Z, is

$$dA = 2\pi r \cos \theta \times r \, d\theta \qquad (23\text{-}15)$$

where r is radius of the sphere (i.e., distance to the antenna). The rate at which energy is radiated through this area is then from Eq. (23-1)

$$\text{Power} = \frac{\mathcal{E}^2}{120\pi} \, dA = 60\pi^2 \left(\frac{\delta l}{\lambda} I\right)^2 \cos^3 \theta \, d\theta \qquad (23\text{-}16)$$

* This can be shown as follows: The capacitance of a 1-m cube is

$$C = (1/0.9 \times 4\pi) \times 10^{-10} \; \mu\mu\mathrm{f}$$

The average energy stored in C by the electrostatic field of the wave is $\frac{1}{2}C\mathcal{E}^2$, and this is half of the total energy. The rate at which energy traverses an area of 1 sq m is hence $(1/0.9 \times 4\pi)10^{-10} \times 3 \times 10^8 \mathcal{E}^2 = \mathcal{E}^2/120\pi$.

The total power over the entire spherical surface is, hence,

$$\text{Total radiated} \atop \text{power} \Big\} = 60\pi^2 \left(\frac{\delta l}{\lambda} I\right)^2 \int_{\theta=-\frac{\pi}{2}}^{\theta=+\frac{\pi}{2}} \cos^3 \theta \, d\theta = 80\pi^2 \left(\frac{\delta l}{\lambda}\right)^2 I^2 \quad (23\text{-}17)$$

Dividing by I^2 gives the radiation resistance, which is

$$\text{Radiation resistance of} \atop \text{doublet antenna} \Big\} = 80\pi^2 \left(\frac{\delta l}{\lambda}\right)^2 \quad (23\text{-}18)$$

The radiation resistance of other types of antennas is obtained by following exactly the same procedure as employed for the doublet antenna; the only difference is in the mathematical expression that is substituted in Eq. (23-16) for the field strength $\mathcal{E}$. However, in most cases, the integration over the spherical surface is quite difficult mathematically, and numerical or graphical[1] integration must often be resorted to. When the analysis is carried out for a resonant half-wave antenna remote from earth, the radiation resistance is found to be 73.13 ohms.

Another method of evaluating the energy radiated from a transmitting antenna consists in assuming an appropriate current distribution, and then determining the power that must be supplied to the antenna system to sustain these currents. This power is

$$\text{Power} = \int E_x I_x \, dx \quad (23\text{-}19)$$

where I_x is the current in an elementary length dx of the antenna system, and E_x is the total component of the electric field parallel to dx and in phase with I_x, as produced by the entire antenna system including any image antennas that must be postulated to take into account the effect of the ground reflections on the fields (and hence on E_x). The integration indicated by Eq. (23-19) is carried out over the entire actual antenna system, but not over the image antennas.[2]

23-9. Impedance and Mutual Impedance of Antennas. *Antenna Resistance and Efficiency.* In addition to the radiated energy, energy may also be consumed by an antenna system as a result of (1) wire and ground resistance; (2) corona; (3) eddy currents induced in neighboring masts, guy wires, and other conductors; and (4) dielectric losses arising from imperfect dielectrics, such as trees and insulators, located in the

---

[1] A systematic procedure for carrying out such integrations graphically is given by F. E. Terman and J. M. Pettit, "Electronic Measurements," p. 434, McGraw-Hill Book Company, Inc., New York, 1952.

[2] The application of this method to antenna calculations is described by P. S. Carter, Circuit Relations in Radiating Systems and Applications to Antenna Problems, *Proc. IRE*, vol. 20, p. 1004, June, 1932; also see R. E. Burgess, Aerial Characteristics, *Wireless Eng.*, vol. 21, p. 154, April, 1944, for a discussion giving the justification of this method.

field of the antenna.   These losses can be represented in the same way as
the radiated energy, i.e., by a lumped resistance of a value such that when
inserted in series with the antenna, it will consume the same total power
as is actually dissipated in these various ways.   The total resistance component of antenna impedance is then the sum $R_r + R_l$ of the radiation
resistance R_r and the loss resistance R_l.   This total resistance determines
the amount of energy that must be supplied to the antenna to produce a
given current at the point to which the resistance is referred.

The efficiency of the antenna as a radiator is the ratio $R_r/(R_r + R_l)$ of
radiation to total resistance.   This represents the fraction of the total
energy supplied to the antenna
which is converted into radio
waves.[1]

The antenna efficiencies achieved
in practice depend upon the wavelength.   At broadcast and higher
frequencies, where the antenna
dimensions can be of the order of a
quarter wavelength or more, efficiencies ranging from 75 to over 95
per cent are typical.   At lower frequencies, the efficiency becomes
small; at the very lowest fre-
quencies used in radio, it may be only a few per cent.

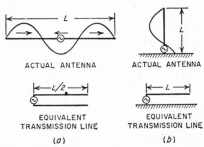

Fig. 23-30.   Two typical resonant antennas, together with transmission lines
that are equivalent in so far as impedance
characteristics are concerned.

Antenna Impedance.   The antenna impedance as observed at any particular reference point normally possesses a reactive as well as a resistive
component.   This is to be expected since the magnetic and electric induction fields necessarily associated with an antenna represent stored reactive
energy.   An antenna can therefore be regarded as a resonant system with
distributed constants.   As a result, the impedance of an antenna behaves
in much the same manner as does the impedance of a transmission line
(see Sec. 4-7).

The equivalent transmission line representing the impedance at the
mid-point of an ungrounded antenna is as shown in Fig. 23-30a, while the
impedance at the base of a grounded antenna behaves in the same way as
the equivalent transmission line of Fig. 23-30b.   In these representations
of antennas, the antenna resistance (including radiation resistance) may
be considered either as being lumped at the generator or some other
point, or alternatively, one may postulate a distributed resistance of such
value per unit length as to give the same total energy loss as is actually
present.

It is apparent from Fig. 23-30 that in resonant antennas the impedance

[1] This relation must, however, be modified for the special case of a nonresonant
antenna with terminating resistance.

is low and resistive when the length of the equivalent transmission line is an odd number of quarter wavelengths, and is high and resistive when it is an even number of quarter wavelengths. At in-between lengths, the impedance will have either an inductive or capacitive component, depending upon the length.

Mutual Impedance. An antenna carrying current will induce a voltage in another antenna in the vicinity; i.e., two nearby antennas act as though they were coupled. One can accordingly postulate a mutual impedance Z_{12} between the antennas that has the same significance as $j\omega M$ in the

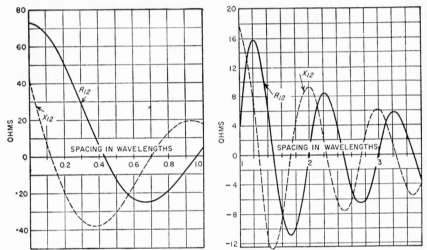

FIG. 23-31. Mutual impedance between parallel half-wave radiators (not staggered) as a function of spacing.

ordinary coupled circuits of Secs. 3-3 to 3-5. The mutual impedance Z_{12} between antennas 1 and 2 is thus defined by the relation[1]

$$Z_{12} = \frac{E_2}{I_1} \tag{23-20}$$

Here I_1 is the current flowing at the reference point in antenna 1 (the excited or primary antenna), and E_2 is the voltage that would have to be applied to the reference point in antenna 2 (the secondary or coupled antenna), with antenna 1 removed, to produce the current I_2 that actually flows in antenna 2. Thus E_2 is the equivalent voltage induced by antenna 1 in antenna 2 when this induced voltage is referred to the reference point in the second antenna.

The magnitude and phase angle of the mutual impedance that can be expected between two antennas will depend upon their spacing and the

[1] Discussions of the details involved in calculating the mutual impedance, together with a number of examples, are given by P. S. Carter, *loc. cit.*; Kraus, *op. cit.*, pp. 262–271. Also see Terman, "Radio Engineers' Handbook," sec. 11, for data on mutual impedance under different conditions.

geometrical configurations involved. The magnitude will be smaller the greater the spacing and will be greater the larger the antenna size, where spacing and size are measured in wavelengths. The phase angle will vary from 0 to 360° depending upon the spacing and geometry. The situation for two parallel half-wave resonant antennas remote from earth[1] is shown in Fig. 23-31. Data on other cases are found in the references listed on page 894.

23-10. Voltage and Current Relations in Systems Involving Coupled Antennas. In a system of coupled antennas, the voltage that must be applied to produce a given current in a particular antenna is the voltage that would be required to produce this current in the absence of other antennas, plus a voltage required to overcome the back voltages induced in this antenna as a result of the currents flowing in the coupled antennas. Accordingly, one can write a series of simultaneous equations as follows:

$$E_1 = I_1 Z_{11} + I_2 Z_{12} + \cdots + I_n Z_{1n}$$
$$E_2 = I_1 Z_{21} + I_2 Z_{22} + \cdots + I_n Z_{2n}$$
$$\cdots\cdots\cdots\cdots\cdots\cdots\cdots\cdots$$
$$E_n = I_1 Z_{n1} + I_2 Z_{n2} + \cdots + I_n Z_{nn}$$

(23-21)

where E_1, E_2, etc. = voltages applied to antennas 1, 2, etc.

I_1, I_2, etc. = currents flowing in antennas 1, 2, etc.

Z_{11}, Z_{22}, etc. = self-impedances of antennas 1, 2, etc.

Z_{12}, Z_{2n}, etc. = mutual impedances between antennas denoted by subscripts (note $Z_{12} = Z_{21}$, etc.)

This system of equations can be solved simultaneously to obtain the voltage and current relations that exist in any particular part of the system of coupled antennas. In applying Eqs. (23-21) it is to be noted that, if some of the individual radiators involved are not excited, then the corresponding applied voltages are zero, whereas if certain of the antennas are open-circuited so that they carry no current, then the currents in these antennas are assigned the value zero in the equations.

Measurement of Mutual Impedance. The mutual impedance Z_{12} between two antennas 1 and 2 can be obtained experimentally by measuring the impedance offered at the terminals of antenna 1 when antenna 2 is open-circuited ($I_2 = 0$), the impedance at the terminals of 2 when 1 is open-circuited ($I_1 = 0$), and finally the impedance of 1 when 2 is short-circuited and excited only by coupling from antenna 1 ($E_2 = 0$). For the first two conditions, the impedances observed are the self-impedances Z_{11} and Z_{22} of antennas 1 and 2, respectively. For the third condition, one has from Eq. (23-21)

$$E_1 = I_1 Z_{11} + I_2 Z_{12}$$
$$0 = I_1 Z_{12} + I_2 Z_{22}$$

(23-22)

[1] The mutual impedance between two quarter-wave grounded vertical antennas is half of the value given in Fig. 23-31.

An expression for the observed impedance E_1/I_1 for this case is obtained by simultaneous solution of Eqs. (23-22) and leads to

$$\text{Observed impedance} = \frac{E_1}{I_1} = Z_{11} - \frac{Z_{12}^2}{Z_{22}} \tag{23-23}$$

Knowing Z_{11}, Z_{22}, and the observed impedance, one can calculate Z_{12}.

23-11. Calculation of Directive Gain. The obvious method of calculating directive gain consists in using the radiated fields to determine directly the powers radiated by the actual and the comparison antennas entering into the definition of directive gain given in Sec. 23-3. The procedure involved can be made clear by using this method to obtain the directive gain of a doublet antenna. A current I in the doublet antenna produces the radiated field given by Eq. (23-1), and this represents the amount of radiated power given by Eq. (23-17). In comparison, an isotropic radiator producing a field strength $\mathcal{E} = (60\pi\ \delta l/r\lambda)I$ in all directions would correspond to a radiated power of

$$\left.\begin{array}{l}\text{Power radiated by} \\ \text{isotropic radiator}\end{array}\right\} = (\text{area of sphere})\ (\mathcal{E}^2/120\pi)$$

$$= 4\pi r^2\ \frac{1}{120\pi}\ \left(\frac{60\pi}{r}\right)^2\left(\frac{\delta l}{\lambda}\right)^2 I^2$$

$$= 120\pi^2\left(\frac{\delta l}{\lambda}\ I\right)^2 \tag{23-24}$$

Dividing this by Eq. (23-17) gives

$$\left.\begin{array}{l}\text{Directive gain of doublet} \\ \text{relative to isotropic} \\ \text{antenna}\end{array}\right\} = 1.5 \tag{23-25}$$

By a similar procedure, it can be shown that the power gain of an isolated half-wave antenna is 1.64 compared with an isotropic antenna.

Radiated Power and Directive Gain in Terms of Self- and Mutual Impedance. A second method of determining directive gain consists in assuming currents in the actual and comparison antennas, and then using the self- and mutual impedances of the antenna system to calculate the power required to sustain these currents. Thus the power radiated by a current I in a comparison antenna of radiation resistance R is I^2R, while the power radiated by an individual radiator of an array (designated as 1) is

$$\left.\begin{array}{l}\text{Power radiated} \\ \text{by antenna 1}\end{array}\right\} = I_1^2 R_{11} + I_1(\overline{I_2 Z_{12}}^* + \overline{I_3 Z_{13}}^* + \cdots) \tag{23-26}$$

where
I_1 = current in designated radiator
R_{11} = radiation resistance of designated radiator
I_2, I_3, etc. = currents in radiators 2, 3, etc. (vectors)
Z_{12}, Z_{13}, etc. = mutual impedances between radiators denoted by subscripts (vectors)

The notation $\overline{I_1 Z}^*$ means component of $I_1 Z$ in phase with I_1. The parentheses must contain terms involving the mutual impedance between the designated radiator 1 and each other radiator of the system. When the designated antenna is not remote from ground, the parentheses must also include terms that take into account the mutual impedance between radiator 1 and every image antenna.

The total power radiated by an antenna array is the sum of the powers of the individual radiators that compose the antenna array. This summation does not include image antennas, since the effect of the ground is taken into account by the mutual-impedance terms in Eq. (23-26) that involve the image antennas.

The use of self- and mutual impedances in problems involving directive gain is made clear by the following examples:

Example 1. Two half-wave radiators remote from earth are arranged broadside (same currents with same phase), and it is desired to determine the spacing for maximum directive gain and to determine what this gain will be.

The solution is obtained by noting that for a given value of current the field produced in the desired direction is independent of spacing, so that the optimum spacing is that for which the radiated power is lowest.   From Eq. (23-26), and noting that the $I_2 = I_1$, one has

$$\text{Total radiated power } = 2I_1{}^2(R_{11} + R_{12}) \tag{23-27}$$

where R_{12} is the resistance component of Z_{12}.   For a half-wave antenna,

$$R_{11} = 73.1 \text{ ohms}$$

while R_{12} is given by Fig. 23-31 as a function of spacing. The minimum, (i.e., most negative) value of R_{12} occurs at a spacing of 0.67λ, corresponding to $R_{12} = 25$ ohms. For this spacing the effective radiation resistance of each antenna is

$$73.1 - 25 = 48.1 \text{ ohms}$$

and the total radiated power from Eq. (23-27) is $2I^2 \times 48.1$ watts. The corresponding power for a half-wave antenna is $I^2 \times 73.1$ watts. The directive gain of the array with this optimum spacing is obtained by noting that the two-antenna array radiates twice as much field and hence four times the power in the desired direction as does a single half-wave antenna carrying the same current, whereas the input power is $2(48.1/73.1) = 1.32$ as great. The directive gain is accordingly $4/1.32 = 3.03$ times compared with a half-wave antenna, or $1.64 \times 3.03 = 4.97$ compared with an isotropic radiator.

Example 2. It is desired to determine the gain of a broadside array consisting of six parallel half-wave vertical radiators remote from earth, and spaced a half-wavelength apart.

Solution. Since all the currents are equal and in phase, the power P_1 radiated by the first radiator is from, Eq. (23-26).

$$P_1 = I^2(R_1 + R_{12} + R_{13} + R_{14} + R_{15} + R_{16})$$

Here R_{12}, R_{13}, etc, represent the resistance components of the mutual impedances between the various antennas denoted by the subscripts. These values of mutual resistance can be obtained from Fig. 23-31. If radiator 1 is the end wire, then

$$P_1 = I^2(73.1 - 12.5 + 4.0 - 1.8 + 1.0 - 1.0) = 62.8I^2$$

Similarly for the next to end wires

$$P_2 = I^2(73.1 - 2 \times 12.5 + 4.0 - 1.8 + 1.0) = 51.3I^2$$

Again

$$P_3 = I^2(73.1 - 2 \times 12.5 + 2 \times 4.0 - 1.8) = 54.3I^2$$

The total power P is hence

$$P = 2(P_1 + P_2 + P_3) = 336.8I^2$$

In comparison, a half-wave radiator radiates a power of $73.1I^2$ watts, and produces a field strength in the desired direction that is only one-sixth as great, corresponding to $P/36$. Thus if the array and the comparison antennas have the same current in each radiating element, then the array consumes $336.8/73.1 = 4.61$ times as much power as the comparison antenna and radiates 36 times as much power in the desired direction. Its directive gain is therefore $36/4.61 = 7.81$ times that of a half-wave antenna, or $7.81 \times 1.64 = 12.8$, compared with an isotropic radiator.

Example 3. A half-wave resonant antenna remote from ground is converted into a two-element end-fire array by the addition of a second half-wave radiator as in case 4, Fig. 23-9b. What increase in gain is thereby achieved?

Solution. From Fig. 23-31, $Z_{AB} = 41 - j28 = 49.6\underline{/-34.8°}$. Since $I_A = |I_B|\underline{/90°}$, one has $I_A Z_{AB} = |I_B| \times 49.6\underline{/90° - 34.8°}$, and

$$\begin{aligned} \text{Power radiated by } B &= |I_B|^2(73.1 + 49.6 \cos 55.2°) \\ &= |I_B|^2 \times 101.3 \end{aligned}$$

Similarly

$$\begin{aligned} \text{Power radiated by } A &= |I_A|^2[73.1 + 49.6 \cos(-90° - 34.8°)] \\ &= |I_B|^2 \times 44.9 \end{aligned}$$

The total radiated power of the end-fire arrangement is hence

$$(101.3 + 44.9)|I_B|^2 = 146.2|I_B|^2 \text{ watts}$$

and this produces twice as great a field strength, and hence four times as much power, in the favored direction as does a current $|I_B|$ radiating $|I_B|^2R = 73.1|I_B|^2$ watts. Hence the power gain of the end-fire arrangement relative to a half-wave comparison antenna is $4 \times (73.1/146.2) = 2$.

Attention is called to the fact that the two antennas of the end-fire do not radiate equal powers.

When the individual radiators composing an antenna array have low mutual impedance, either as a result of the geometrical relation of the radiators to each other, or because of large spacing, the directive gain can ordinarily be determined quite simply. For example, consider an array consisting of n identical radiators so arranged that the field produced by the system in the desired direction is n times as great as the field of an individual radiator. If the coupling between the individual radiators is then small so that the mutual impedances can be neglected compared with their radiation resistance, the directive gain of the system will be n times the gain of the individual radiators. This result is arrived at from the fact that the n antennas radiate n times as much power as a single radiator, but produce a field in the desired direction that is n times as great, corresponding to power in this direction n^2 times as great. Thus, the ratio of power radiated in the desired direction to total power radiated by the antenna system is increased by the factor n.

Antenna Gain in Terms of Antenna Area. The mattress antenna of Fig. 23-27, as well as the horn, parabolic, and lens antennas discussed below, are characterized by the fact that they produce a planar distribution of field immediately adjacent to the antenna provided the antenna extends several wavelengths in all directions. It is shown below, in connection with Eq. (23-44), that the directive gain of such an antenna system in free space can be defined by the relation

$$\text{Directive gain} = 4\pi \frac{A}{\lambda^2} = 4\pi \frac{A_0 k}{\lambda^2} \qquad (23\text{-}28)$$

Here A_0 is the actual area of the antenna aperture, defined as the area bounded by the centers of the perimeter radiators; thus in Fig. 23-27, one has $A_0 = wh$.

The constant k in Eq. (23-28) takes into account the uniformity of the amplitude and phase of the fields distributed over the aperture, and also whether or not the antenna pattern is unidirectional. When the fields are uniform and of constant phase, and the pattern is unidirectional, as is the case with the mattress antenna in Fig. 23-27, then $k \approx 1$. However, if the field distribution is tapered across the aperture so that it is zero at the edges and maximum at the middle, then k lies between 0.5 and 0.6. If the antenna is bidirectional instead of unidirectional, as would be the case if the reflecting curtain in Fig. 23-27 were omitted, the value of k will be exactly half as great as would otherwise be the case.

Approximate Calculation of Directive Gain from Lobe Dimension. When most of the radiated power is concentrated in a relatively narrow lobe, it is possible to estimate the directive gain by the following simple procedure: Let B be defined as the area over which the power density in the lobe is at least half of the power density on the lobe axis, and arbitrarily assume that all of the power radiated from the directional antenna is concentrated within this area. The resulting directive gain for this hypothetical situation is the quotient of the surface represented by a complete sphere divided by the beam area B. That is,

$$\text{Directive gain} = \frac{4\pi r^2}{B} \qquad (23\text{-}29)$$

where r is the radius of the spherical surface in which B is located. The area B may now be conveniently expressed in "square degrees"; thus, in a mattress antenna, if the half-power lobe widths in the vertical and horizontal planes are W_v and W_h degrees, respectively, the major lobe can be considered to possess an area $B = W_v \times W_h$ square degrees. The total number of square degrees in the surface of a sphere is

$$(57.3)^2 \times 4\pi = 41,253$$

so that

$$\text{Directive gain} = \frac{41,253}{B} \tag{23-30}$$

Values of gain calculated with the aid of Eq. (23-30) are not exact, as they fail to take into account the precise shape of the lobe sides and the details of the minor lobes. However, in the case of antennas producing a pencillike major lobe with relatively small minor lobes, results accurate to within ±3 db can be expected.

23-12. Impedance Matching and Phasing Systems. Power can be conveyed from the radio transmitter to a transmitting antenna by means of a transmission system consisting of a two-wire line, a concentric line, or a waveguide. Nonresonant operation is ordinarily desired in these arrangements to minimize power losses and, in the case of high power, to keep the voltage maxima small. This introduces the necessity of matching the antenna impedance to the transmission system in a manner that will avoid reflected waves.[1] Such matching can be achieved by the use of impedance-matching networks, stub lines, quarter-wave matching sections, etc., as discussed in Secs. 4-11, 4-12, and 5-7.

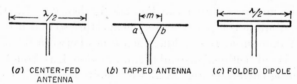

(a) CENTER-FED   (b) TAPPED ANTENNA   (c) FOLDED DIPOLE
ANTENNA

FIG. 23-32. Methods of matching a resonant half-wave antenna to a two-wire transmission line.

A number of special means have been devised for matching a half-wave antenna to a two-wire transmission line. The obvious arrangement of Fig. 23-32a is not particularly satisfactory since the load impedance of 73.1 ohms that the resonant antenna presents to the line is lower than the characteristic impedance of a typical two-wire line. Two simple solutions are possible. One consists in tapping the line across a substantial portion m of the antenna, as in Fig. 23-32b, such that the antenna impedance between a and b equals the characteristic impedance at the end ab of the tapered line. Another arrangement is the *folded dipole* of Fig. 23-32c. Here the antenna consists of two identical conductors in parallel, which serve as a transformer. Thus, in Fig. 23-32c, the current of each conductor, and hence the line current, is one-half as great as in Fig. 23-32a. This makes the load impedance presented to the line ($2^2 \times 73.1 = 292.4$ ohms), a value readily realized by the character-

---

[1] The radiation resistance, antenna efficiency, directional pattern, and directive gain are not affected by failure to match impedance. Matching merely makes it easier to get the available power into the antenna, reduces the transmission loss, and lowers the maximum voltage stress in the transmission system.

istic impedance of a two-wire line. Other values of impedance may be achieved by making the diameters of the two conductors unequal so they carry different currents, or by using more than two conductors.

Phasing of Radiators in Antenna Arrays. The phase relations desired in an antenna array are ordinarily obtained with the aid of transmission lines (or waveguides).[1] A nonresonant transmission line in open air shifts the phase at a uniform rate of 360° per wavelength, so that any desired phase difference can be obtained by the use of a nonresonant transmission line of suitable length. Thus, in Fig. 23-27, the phase

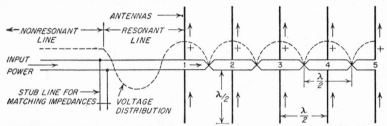

Fig. 23-33. Broadside array phased by a resonant transmission line that is then matched to a nonresonant line by means of a stub line.

difference of 270° required between the two curtains to obtain a unidirectional characteristic can be obtained by connecting them together by a nonresonant transmission line three-quarters of a wavelength long.

Another method of using a transmission line for phasing is to take advantage of the fact that the phase always shifts exactly 180° every half wavelength along a transmission line (or waveguide), even when resonances prevent the phase from changing uniformly with distance. The use of this principle to obtain proper phasing of the radiators of a broadside antenna is illustrated in Fig. 23-33, which also incorporates impedance matching by means of a stub line. Here the individual half-wave radiators are connected to the resonant feeder line at voltage loops, and are spaced a half wavelength apart.[2] By connecting successive radiators to alternate sides of the line as shown, all of the radiators are then excited in the same phase.

23-13. Balance-to-unbalance Transformation. It is sometimes desirable to be able to deliver power to a grounded antenna through a two-wire transmission line, or, conversely, to use a coaxial transmission line to deliver power to an ungrounded antenna system that is symmetrical with

---

[1] An exception is in antenna arrays operating at standard broadcast frequencies, where impedance matching and phasing is ordinarily accomplished simultaneously by suitably designed lumped-element networks of the type discussed in Sec. 4-12.

[2] Under these conditions the half-wave transformer action discussed in connection with Eq. (4-32) causes the impedance at point 1 of the transmission-line system to equal an impedance that corresponds to all of the antenna pairs that place loads on the line acting as though they were all in parallel at 1.

respect to ground.   In either case, it is necessary to convert between a balanced system that is symmetrical with respect to ground, and an unbalanced system in which one side is grounded.

An obvious method of effecting such a transformation is to use a transformer, as illustrated in Fig. 23-34a.   Here the winding associated with the balanced system is symmetrically arranged with respect to a grounded electrostatic shield so that the stray capacitances inevitably present will not introduce unbalances.

At frequencies high enough for resonant lines to be practical, arrangements of the type shown in Fig. 23-34b are employed; they are termed

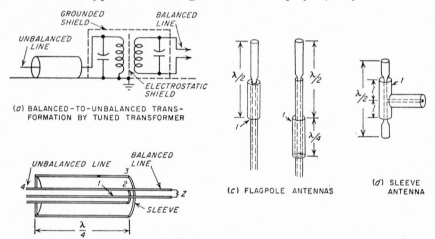

(a) BALANCED-TO-UNBALANCED TRANS-
FORMATION BY TUNED TRANSFORMER

(b) BALANCING UNIT (BALUN)

(c) FLAGPOLE ANTENNAS

(d) SLEEVE ANTENNA

FIG. 23-34. Examples of arrangements for transforming a system that is balanced with respect to ground to a system that has one side grounded.

baluns (short for *bal*ancing *un*it).   Their operation may be understood by considering the situation that exists when a voltage is applied to the balun from the balanced side.   Since this voltage is applied across the conductors 1-2 of the coaxial line, it is transferred to the coaxial system without change.   At the same time, the fact that 2 is an extension of the outer conductor 4 of the coaxial system does not introduce an unbalance in the balanced system at 2 because when the sleeve is exactly a quarter wavelength long the impedance across 2-3 approaches infinity.   That is, sleeve 3 acts as an extension of 4 and remains at ground potential, whereas point 2 is free to assume any potential the balanced system desires it to have.

A half-wave antenna may be excited from a coaxial transmission line by arrangements of the type shown in Fig. 23-34c and d, known as flagpole and sleeve antennas, respectively.   By proper choice of the characteristic impedance of the coaxial line such arrangements match impedance as well as giving transformation from a balanced load to an unbalanced feed.

In the flagpole antenna the high impedance at 1 isolates the antenna from the lower part of the flagpole, and prevents the latter from becoming a part of the antenna.

23-14. Miscellaneous Antenna Systems. This section describes a number of antenna types that illustrate important principles, but which are not considered elsewhere in this chapter.

Half-wave Antenna with Reflector. When a reflector such as a copper screen is placed close to a half-wave antenna, as in Fig. 23-35, a unidirectional radiation pattern is obtained as shown. To analyze this situation the reflector is replaced by a *negative* image antenna A' and Eq. (23-8a) is

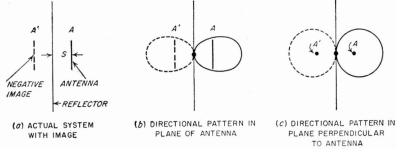

(*a*) ACTUAL SYSTEM
WITH IMAGE

(*b*) DIRECTIONAL PATTERN IN
PLANE OF ANTENNA

(*c*) DIRECTIONAL PATTERN IN
PLANE PERPENDICULAR
TO ANTENNA

FIG. 23-35. Half-wave antenna close to and parallel with a plane reflector.

then used to determine the directional pattern of the resulting two-element array consisting of antennas A and A' carrying equal and opposite currents, and spaced $2S$. When S is a small fraction of a wavelength the radiated field is distributed as in b and c of Fig. 23-35, and is moderately directive.

The directive gain can be readily determined by the method of self- and mutual impedances. Let

$\mathcal{E}_0$ = field radiated by half-wave antenna at right angle to reflector in absence of reflector, when carrying current I_0

$\mathcal{E}$ = actual field radiated by I_0 in direction at right angles to reflector in presence of reflector

Now the field $\mathcal{E}$ is the difference of two vectors of magnitude $\mathcal{E}_0$ and differing in phase by $2\pi \times 2S/\lambda$ radians. Hence

$$\mathcal{E} = 2\mathcal{E}_0 \sin\left(2\pi \frac{S}{\lambda}\right) \qquad (23\text{-}31a)$$

The input powers corresponding to I_0 are

Power in absence of reflector $= P_0 = I_0{}^2 R_1$ $\qquad$ (23-31b)

Power in presence of reflector $= P = I_0{}^2(R_1 - R_{12})$ $\qquad$ (23-31c)

Here R_1 is the radiation resistance of the radiating half-wave antenna, and R_{12} is the resistance component of the mutual impedance between it and a like antenna a distance $2S$ away, as given in Fig. 23-31. The negative sign in Eq. (23-31c) arises from the fact that the effect of the reflector is equivalent to a negative image. The directive gain of the half-wave antenna parallel to the reflector is hence

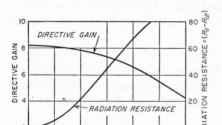

FIG. 23-36. Characteristics of antenna-reflector system of Fig. 23-35, for $\lambda/2$ antennas.

$$\text{Directive gain} = 1.64 \frac{(\mathcal{E}/\mathcal{E}_0)^2}{P/P_0}$$

$$(23\text{-}32)$$

Values obtained from Eq. (23-32) with the aid of Fig. 23-31 are plotted in Fig. 23-36, together with the equivalent radiation resistance R_{11}-R_{12} of the half-wave antenna when near the reflector. It is seen that with very close spacing the gain is about 8, but that at the same time the antenna radiation resistance becomes very low when the spacing is very small. In order to prevent incidental loss resistances from making the antenna efficiency very low, the spacing S should accordingly be at least 0.05λ, and preferably 0.1λ.

Corner Reflector.[1] The directivity of an antenna-reflector combination can be increased by bending the reflector to form a corner as shown in Fig. 23-37a. Here the corner angle α must be $180°/n$, where n is an integer. Such an arrangement concentrates the radiation in the direction shown by the arrow, with the beam being narrower in the horizontal than the vertical plane. A directive gain of approximately 16 is obtained with a 90° corner and $S = 0.25\lambda$, and about 28 for $\alpha = 60°$. Since the maximum dimensions of the reflector need not exceed a wavelength, this arrangement gives a substantial amount of directivity rather compactly.

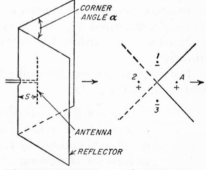

(a) CORNER REFLECTOR (b) IMAGES FOR 90° CORNER

FIG. 23-37. Corner reflector antenna in perspective, together with image system for a 90° corner.

The directional pattern of a corner reflector can be calculated by replacing the reflecting surfaces by a system of images. In the case of a 90° corner two negative images and one positive image are required, as illustrated in Fig. 23-37b. The greater gain of the corner reflector as com-

---

[1] For further details see Kraus, *op. cit.*, pp. 328–336; E. F. Harris, An Experimental Investigation of the Corner Reflector Antenna, *Proc. IRE*, vol. 41, p. 645, May, 1953.

pared with a flat reflector results from the fact that the multiplicity of images involved makes the system equivalent to an antenna array involving a considerable number of radiators.

Directional Systems Involving Parasitic Antennas—Yagi Antennas. A secondary antenna coupled to a driven antenna will affect the directional pattern as a result of the currents that are induced in it. A secondary antenna used in this way is termed a *parasitic* antenna.

The exact effect on the directional pattern that is produced depends upon the magnitude and phase of the induced current, i.e., upon the spacing of the antennas and upon the tuning of the parasitic antenna. For example, if the driven and parasitic antennas are relatively close together and parallel, then the current induced in the parasitic antenna will be such as to reduce the strength of the radiation in the direction of the parasitic antenna when the latter is resonant at a lower frequency than that being transmitted. If resonant at a higher frequency than is being transmitted, the parasitic antenna acts as a "director" and tends to concentrate the radiated field in its direction. This is shown in Fig. 23-38.

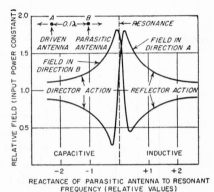

REACTANCE OF PARASITIC ANTENNA TO RESONANT FREQUENCY (RELATIVE VALUES)

Fig. 23-38. Curve showing effect of the tuning of a parasitic antenna on the relative field strength in a typical case. One unit of detuning corresponds to $\frac{1}{2}Q$ off resonance (i.e., 70.7 per cent point on resonance curve).

The quantitative relations existing in systems involving parasitic antennas can be calculated by the system of equations given in Eqs. (23-21). Thus, considering the simple case of Fig. 23-38 and designating the driven antenna by the subscript 1 and the parasitic antenna by the subscript 2, one then has

$$E_1 = I_1 Z_{11} + I_2 Z_{12}$$
$$0 = I_1 Z_{12} + I_2 Z_{22}$$

Simultaneous solution of these two equations yields

$$I_1 = \frac{E_1}{Z_{11} - (Z_{12}^2/Z_{22})}$$

$$I_2 = -I_1 \frac{Z_{12}}{Z_{22}} = \frac{E_1}{Z_{12} - (Z_{11}Z_{22}/Z_{12})} \tag{23-33}$$

The field distribution of the system is then obtained by assuming a convenient current in the driven antenna and calculating the magnitude and phase of the current in the parasitic antenna. The directional pattern for this two-element array corresponding to the driven and parasitic antennas can then be obtained from Eq. (23-8). As indicated in Fig. 23-38, this pattern will be affected by the impedance of the parasitic antenna. This is because Eq. (23-33) shows that the tuning of the parasitic antenna (that is, Z_{22}) affects both the magnitude and phase of the current in the parasitic antenna.

The fact that a parasitic antenna placed close to a radiating antenna can be used either to reflect or to direct the radiated energy can be taken advantage of to obtain a compact directional antenna system. A simple example is shown in Fig. 23-39, where the reflector length is such that it is resonant at a lower frequency than that being transmitted, while the director length is chosen so that it is resonant at a higher frequency than that being radiated.

SIDE VIEW

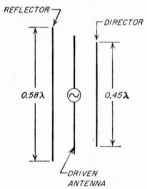

PLAN VIEW

FIG. 23–39. A typical Yagi array.

Antennas of this type, consisting of a radiating antenna, and one or more directors and reflectors arranged along a line, are often called *Yagi* antennas, after their originator. They are capable of achieving moderate directive gains in a very small space; thus the antenna of Fig. 23-39 will give a gain of the order of 6 when adjusted for maximum radiation in the indicated direction.

Close-spaced Arrays—Super-gain Antennas. A review of the behavior of broadside and end-fire arrays might make it appear that in order to achieve high gain it is necessary that the antenna system be distributed over a considerable space. However, the antennas of Figs. 23-35 and 23-39 obtain enhanced directivity by employing antennas that are closely spaced. Moreover, it can be shown that an end-fire type of array that is short compared with a wavelength can theoretically achieve any desired directive gain provided enough radiators are employed and they are suitably phased. Such antennas which give great gain using small over-all dimensions are referred to as super-gain antennas.[1]

A characteristic of all close-spaced arrays is that as the ratio of size to antenna gain is reduced, the radiation resistance also goes down; this is illustrated by Fig. 23-36. The result is a practical limit to the amount of gain that can be achieved in a compact antenna system, since as the

---

[1] A consideration of such antennas is given by H. J. Riblet, Note on the Maximum Directivity of an Antenna, *Proc. IRE*, vol. 36, p. 620, May, 1948, and in discussion by T. T. Taylor, *Proc. IRE*, vol. 36, p. 1135, September, 1948; see also L. J. Chu, Physical Limitations of Directive Radiating Systems, *J. Appl. Phys.*, vol. 19, p. 1163, December, 1948.

radiation resistance goes down the fraction of the total power dissipated in the antenna loss resistance goes up.   The Yagi antenna of Fig. 23-39, and the corner reflector, represent about the best that can be achieved in a practical way with respect to directive gain in a compact antenna array.

Loop Antennas.   The loop antenna (see Fig. 23-40a) can be thought of as a coil carrying a radio-frequency current.[1]   The loop may have one or more turns according to the frequency employed.   Under ordinary circumstances the loop dimensions are small compared with a wavelength, and the current in the wires of the loop is everywhere substantially the same in both magnitude and phase.

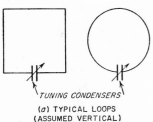 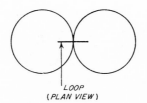 

LOOP
(PLAN VIEW)

(*a*) TYPICAL LOOPS   (*b*) DIRECTIONAL CHARACTERISTIC   (*c*) DIRECTIONAL CHARAC-
(ASSUMED VERTICAL)   IN HORIZONTAL PLANE   TERISTIC IN PERSPECTIVE

Fig. 23-40. Typical loops, shown as one turn for simplicity, together with directional characteristic that applies to all loops that are small compared with a wavelength.

The field distribution about a loop remote from ground and small compared with a wavelength is proportional to $\cos \theta$, where θ is the angle with respect to the plane of the loop (see Fig. 23-40c).   This doughnut-shaped pattern can be explained as follows.   The opposite sides of the loop act as a pair of spaced antennas carrying currents of opposite polarity as in case 1 of Fig. 23-9b.   No energy is radiated in a direction perpendicular to the plane of the loop because the radiation in this direction from any section of the loop is always canceled by radiation from a corresponding section on the diametrically opposite side of the loop carrying current in the opposite direction.   On the other hand, the radiation will be maximum in the plane of the loop because here the two sides of the loop carrying currents in opposite directions are farthest apart, so their radiations have the maximum possible (although often still small) phase difference. The directional pattern is independent of the exact shape of the loop, provided the loop is small compared with a wavelength.

The directional pattern of a small loop is identical with that of an elementary doublet.   The only difference is that the electric and magnetic fields are interchanged.   For this reason a small loop is often referred to as a *magnetic doublet.*

The radiation resistance of a loop antenna is less the smaller the loop area.   For the radiation resistance to be large enough to give good

---

[1] Loops are sometimes provided with magnetic cores.   This increases the equivalent diameter of the loop, and is a useful expedient when size is important, as in airplane applications or in portable broadcast receivers.

antenna efficiency, it is necessary that the loop perimeter be of the order of a wavelength. This introduces a difficulty, since when the perimeter approaches or exceeds a half wavelength, then the loop current in Fig. 23-40 will not be constant, nor will its phase necessarily be the same in different parts of the loop. The practical solution is to build up the loop in such a way that the perimeter consists of sections of resonant antennas so arranged that the current everywhere in the loop perimeter flows in the same direction around the loop. A variety of practical physical arrangements for achieving this result have been devised, three examples of which are illustrated in Fig. 23-41.

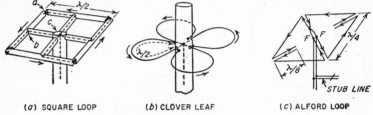

(a) SQUARE LOOP   (b) CLOVER LEAF   (c) ALFORD LOOP
Fig. 23-41. Ultra-high-frequency loops.

In all of these arrangements, the radiation comes almost entirely from the perimeter; the members leading from the center of the loop to the periphery are either coaxial conductors or closely spaced two-wire lines, and so do not radiate appreciable energy. Loop antennas of this type find extensive use at very high frequencies for obtaining a radiation pattern in the horizontal plane that is circular and at the same time horizontally polarized.

The Turnstile Antenna. In the turnstile antenna, two half-wave resonant wire radiators are placed at right angles to each other in the same plane and excited 90° out of phase with each other. The directional patterns of the individual antennas, and of the combination, in the plane of the system are illustrated in Fig. 23-42. Since the individual radiations are in time quadrature, the total radiation in any direction from the system is the square root of the sum of the squares of the radiations from the individual antennas in that particular direction. As a result, the pattern is very nearly circular in the plane of the turnstile, as shown.[1] It will be noted that the field radiated in a direction at right angles to the plane of the turnstile array is elliptically polarized.

Dielectric-rod (Polyrod) Antennas.[2] A tapered dielectric rod (typically

[1] If the individual antennas are short doublets instead of half-wave antennas the directional pattern of the turnstile will be exactly circular in the horizontal plane, and the radiation in the vertical plane will be circularly polarized.

[2] See G. E. Mueller and W. A. Tyrrel, Polyrod Antennas, *Bell System Tech. J.*, vol. 26, p. 837, October, 1947. A good concise summary of the basic quantitative relations applicable to such antennas is given in Kraus, *op. cit.*, pp. 404–407.

of polystyrene) arranged as illustrated in Fig. 23-43 will act as a directional antenna. This is because the waves in the guide tend to follow the dielectric even after the termination of the metal walls, but because of the rod taper the energy of these waves is gradually transferred to the adjacent air. The result is that a wave gets launched in an end-fire manner. Proportions of a typical dielectric-rod antenna composed of polystyrene ($\epsilon = 2.5$) are shown in Fig. 23-43, together with the corresponding directional pattern. The directive gain for the proportions illustrated in Fig. 23-43 is approximately 40.

Helical Antenna.[1] A loosely wound helix will serve as an effective directional antenna. The characteristics obtained depend upon the helix proportions, but if the circumference approximates a wavelength, then a traveling (nonresonant) wave progressing around the turns of the helix will radiate energy in a lobe that is directed along the axis of the helix (end-fire action), and is

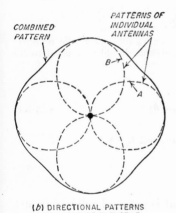

(*a*) TURNSTILE ARRAY

(*b*) DIRECTIONAL PATTERNS IN PLANE OF TURNSTILE

FIG. 23-42. Turnstile antenna system together with directional pattern in the plane of the turnstile.

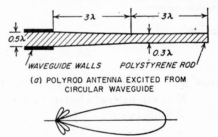

(*a*) POLYROD ANTENNA EXCITED FROM CIRCULAR WAVEGUIDE

(*b*) DIRECTIONAL CHARACTERISTIC

FIG. 23-43. Cylindrical polyrod antenna, together with directional pattern.

circularly polarized. The directive gain is appreciable, a six-turn helix having a diameter of 0.30λ with a spacing of 0.30λ between turns developing a gain of 45 when provided with a reflecting screen at the input end that is normal to helix axis. A helical antenna is relatively broadband in its characteristics.

23-15. Antenna Systems Employing Parabolic Reflectors.[2] A parabolic reflector can be used to concentrate the radiation from an antenna

---

[1] See Kraus, *op. cit.*, chap. 7.

[2] In addition to the references listed on p. 864, the reader desiring supplementary information on this subject will find it helpful to consult C. C. Cutler, Parabolic

located at the focus in the same way that a searchlight reflector produces a sharply defined beam of light. The parabolic reflector does this by converting the spherical waves originated by the radiator at the focus of the parabola into a plane wave of uniform phase across the mouth or aperture of the parabola,[1] as illustrated in Fig. 23-44a.[2] By Huygens' principle, the field in each elementary area ΔA of a wavefront can be regarded as an independent radiator producing a field given by the

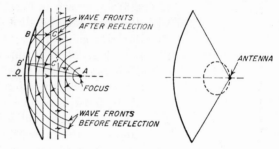

(a) WAVEFRONTS IN PARABOLIC
REFLECTOR SYSTEM

(b) RELATION OF PARABOLIC
SURFACE TO DIRECTIONAL
PATTERN OF ANTENNA

Fig. 23-44. Conversion of spherical waves to plane waves by a parabolic reflector, together with diagram showing how a directional antenna should be related to the parabolic surface.

relation[3]

$$\Delta \mathcal{E} = \frac{E}{2d\lambda} \Delta A (1 + \cos \theta) \qquad (23\text{-}34)$$

where $\Delta \mathcal{E}$ = magnitude of radiated field generated by ΔA
E = strength of electric field at ΔA
d = distance to ΔA
λ = wavelength
θ = angle with respect to an axis that is perpendicular to mouth of parabola

The total field radiated by the parabola is the vector sum of the fields generated by the elementary areas making up the aperture (or mouth) of the parabola.

Antenna Design for Microwaves, *Proc. IRE*, vol. 35, p. 1284, November, 1947; H. T. Friis and W. D. Lewis, Radar Antennas, *Bell System Tech. J.*, vol. 26, p. 219, April, 1947.

[1] The terms "mouth" and "aperture" are synonymous as applied to parabolic, horn, and lens antenna systems.

[2] This results from the fact that by definition the parabola is a surface so shaped that all paths of the type $AB'C'$ and ABC in Fig. 23-44a have the same length, where AB and AB' are rays originating at the focus A, while BC and $B'C'$ are these same rays after reflection from the parabola, and CC' is a plane surface perpendicular to the axis AO.

[3] It is to be noted that $\Delta \mathcal{E}$ varies with θ in such a manner as to give a cardioid type of pattern similar to (but not exactly identical with) that of case 4 of Fig. 23-9b.

In the ideal case where the field across the mouth of the parabola is everywhere of the same phase, the parabola is equivalent to a broadside antenna with reflector such as shown in Fig. 23-26. The result is a sharply unidirectional beam.

The width and shape of the major lobe of the radiation pattern of a parabola depend upon the size and shape of the mouth of the parabola, and the variation of field intensity over the aperture defined by the mouth. Quantitative relations for typical cases are summarized in Table 23-3. When the mouth of the parabola has the same shape as a mattress

TABLE 23-3

BEAM WIDTHS OF PARABOLIC ANTENNAS

Shape of mouth	Field distribution across mouth	Width of major lobe	
		Between nulls	Between half-power points
Rectangular......	Uniform	$\dfrac{115°}{L/\lambda}$	$\dfrac{51°}{L/\lambda}$
	Sinusoidal along L	$\dfrac{182.5°}{L/\lambda}$	$\dfrac{68°}{L/\lambda}$
Circular.........	Uniform	$\dfrac{140°}{L/\lambda}$	$\dfrac{58°}{L/\lambda}$

NOTE: L = length of rectangular mouth in direction of interest, or diameter of circular mouth.

antenna, and the field intensity is distributed in the same way as are the antenna currents in the mattress array, then the major lobe will be almost exactly the same for the parabola and the corresponding mattress.

The field pattern of a parabolic antenna ordinarily possesses minor lobes, just as do other types of broadside arrays. These minor lobes can be minimized or even eliminated by tapering the field distribution across the aperture of the parabola so that the field intensity is maximum at the center and minimum at the edges. The principles involved are exactly the same as those discussed in connection with broadside and mattress arrays (see pages 877 and 890); i.e., by suitably tapering the field distribution, the minor lobes can be reduced to any desired extent. This result is achieved at the expense of a broadening of the major lobe, however. For example, a sinusoidal distribution of field intensity across the mouth of a rectangular parabola will reduce the amplitude of the first minor lobe to 7 per cent, which is one-third the amplitude with uniform field distribution; at the same time the half-power width of the major lobe is increased 34 per cent.

The directive gain of an antenna system using a parabolic reflector is given by Eq. (23-28), where the constant k takes into account any non-uniformity of magnitude and phase in the field distribution across the aperture of the parabola, and also any failure of the illuminating antenna to radiate all of its energy against the reflecting surface. In the ideal case of a system in which the field across the mouth has constant intensity and uniform phase, and in which no energy fails to strike the reflecting surface, one has $k = 1.0$. Under practical conditions, where the field is somewhat weaker near the edges of the aperture, and some of the energy is wasted by failing to strike the reflector, the value of k will be typically of the order of 0.5 to 0.7.

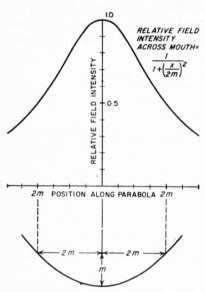

At very short wavelengths, a parabola of reasonable physical size will be a number of wavelengths across. The power gain and beam sharpness obtained by the use of a parabola are then very great. Thus at a wavelength of 10 cm a paraboloid of revolution having a mouth diameter of 3 m (approximately 10 ft) will have a power gain of about 4500, and a half-power beam width that is less than 3°.

Feed Systems for Parabolic Reflectors, and Representative Examples of Parabolic Antenna Systems. The radiator that illuminates the parabolic reflector, commonly called the feed system, should direct substantially all of its radiated energy

Fig. 23-45. Field distribution across the mouth of a paraboloid of revolution produced when the antenna at the focus is an isotropic radiator.

against the reflecting surface, since this is the only energy that contributes to the directivity of the parabola. Thus, in Fig. 23-44a it is apparent that if antenna A radiates equally in all directions, less than half of the radiated energy will be intercepted by the parabola. The power gain will then be less than half as great as when all of the energy is directed against the parabola. Such loss of gain is ordinarily prevented by shaping the parabolic reflector so that the focus lies somewhat outside of the mouth, as illustrated in Fig. 23-44, and then giving radiator A a simple directional pattern such that substantially all the radiated energy is directed against the parabolic surface, as in Fig. 23-44b. At the same time the directivity of antenna A must not be so great that only the center part of the parabola receives appreciable illumination, since then the outer edges of the parabola could just as well be removed and the lobe width will be unnecessarily large. The situation is complicated by the fact that the geometry is such that even when the feed antenna radiates equally strongly toward all parts of the reflecting surface, the field inten-

sity across the aperture will not be uniform, as shown in Fig. 23-45.[1]
Thus the radiator that illuminates the parabolic surface must have its
directional characteristics carefully proportioned so that on the one hand
a minimum of energy is wasted, and on the other hand the energy is so
directed as to produce the desired distribution of field intensity across
the mouth of the parabola.

The feed system may take a great
variety of forms. Typical arrangements that find common use to
illuminate a paraboloid of revolution are shown in Fig. 23-46.

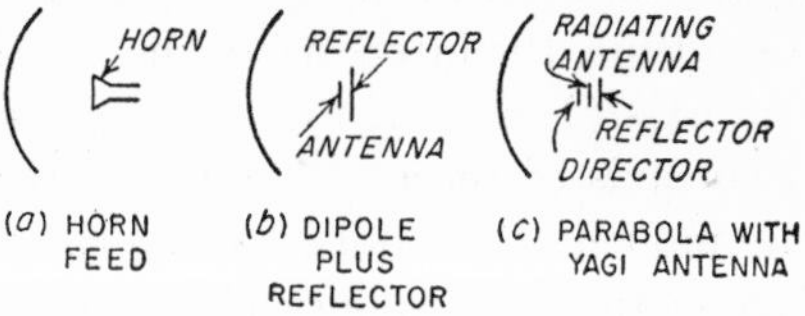

A considerable choice in parabolic
reflectors is available, according to

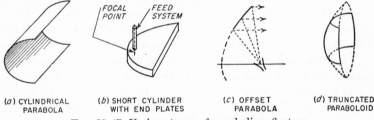

(*a*) HORN   (*b*) DIPOLE   (*c*) PARABOLA WITH
    FEED   PLUS   YAGI ANTENNA
           REFLECTOR

Fig. 23-46. Methods of illuminating a
parabolic antenna.

the requirements to be met. A circular mouth is obtained by using a
paraboloid of revolution, as already seen. The cylindrical parabola of
Fig. 23-47a provides a rectangular mouth. In this case the focus is a line
instead of a point, so that the radiator that illuminates the parabolic
surface must be a line source, such as a line of unidirectional couplets
arranged in broadside and directing their radiation toward the cylindrical
surface, or a broadside array of slots as in Fig. 23-54, below. A fan-
shaped beam can be obtained by employing a cylinder that is short in the
axial direction, and provided with conducting end plates, as illustrated in

(*a*) CYLINDRICAL   (*b*) SHORT CYLINDER   (*c*) OFFSET   (*d*) TRUNCATED
   PARABOLA   WITH END PLATES   PARABOLA   PARABOLOID

Fig. 23-47. Various types of parabolic reflectors.

Fig. 23-47b. Here the usual method of illuminating the reflecting surface
is to extend the inner conductor of a coaxial line through the space
between the plates as shown; the current flowing in this conductor produces radiation that is reflected by the cylindrical surface, and gives rise
to a field distribution across the mouth. It is also possible to employ
reflectors that are unsymmetrical sections cut from a parabolic surface;
the offset and truncated parabolas of Fig. 23-47c and d, respectively, are
examples.

23-16. Horn Antennas. A typical horn antenna is illustrated in Fig.
23-48. It consists of a waveguide flared so the wave inside the guide
expands in an orderly manner. The result is a field distribution across

---

[1] This curve was supplied by F. W. Terman.

the mouth of the horn that serves as a source of radiation in accordance with Eq. (23-34). Relative to the parabolic reflector, the horn is thus an alternative means of producing a field distribution across an aperture.

The amplitude and phase of the fields in the plane of the horn mouth depend upon the type of wave fed into the horn from the waveguide, and upon the horn proportions. In the usual case where this wave is of the TE_{10} type, the intensity of the electric field at the mouth is constant along one axis (Y axis in Fig. 23-48) and is sinusoidally distributed along the other axis of the horn (Z axis in Fig. 23-48). However, the field across the mouth of the horn, unlike the field across the mouth of the parabola, is a section of a spherical wavefront having its center at the apex of the

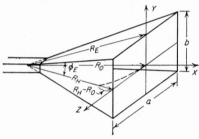

horn. Accordingly the field near the rim of the horn lags in phase behind the field at the center because the distances R_H and R_E from the equivalent apex of the horn to the corresponding edges are greater than the distance R_0 to the center of the plane defined by the mouth. The extent of the resulting variation in phase across the plane of the mouth depends upon the flare angles of the horn, and the horn length in wavelengths.

Fig. 23-48. Pyramidal horn excited from a waveguide carrying a TE_{10} wave.

When the relation of flare angle and horn length is such that $R_H - R_0$ (and also $R_E - R_0$) is a small fraction of a wavelength (i.e., less than about 0.15λ), then the field distribution across the horn mouth has everywhere nearly the same phase, and the action of the horn is almost exactly the same as that of a parabola having the same shape of mouth and the same field distribution across this mouth. Under these conditions Table 23-3 and the associated discussions of beam width and directive gain apply to the horn as well as to the parabola. However, if the flare angles of the horn are too large, i.e., if the horn length is too small in proportion to the mouth dimensions, then the distance that the wave must travel to reach the rim of the mouth is enough greater than the distance it must travel to reach the center so that the field across the mouth can no longer be considered to be an equiphase field. This increases the beam width and reduces the power gain. In addition, if the difference in distance is appreciably more than a half wavelength, large minor lobes develop and ultimately the major lobe splits into two lobes.

From the above discussion, it is apparent that very small flare angles give the sharpest beam and highest power gain for a given mouth size. However, small flare angles correspond to a horn of excessive length. Since the length is the largest dimension of the horn, the usual practical problem is to obtain the desired directional pattern with the shortest possible horn.   Proportions that achieve this result are said to result in an optimum horn.   Referring to Fig. 23-48, they correspond to a flare angle Φ_H in the XZ plane (often called H plane) such that $R_H - R_0 = 0.4\lambda$, and a flare angle Φ_E in the XY or E plane that makes[1] $R_E - R_0 = 0.25\lambda$.

TABLE 23-4
FORMULAS FOR OPTIMUM HORNS

Case	Horn and notation	Property that is optimized for given length	Optimum proportions	Half-power beam widths in degrees		Value of k for calculating directive gain from Eq. (23-28)
				H (or YZ) plane	E (or XY) plane	
1	Pyramidal (Fig. 23-48)	Gain*	$a \approx \sqrt{3l\lambda}$ $b \approx 0.81a$ $\text{Gain} \approx 15.3\dfrac{l}{\lambda}$	$\dfrac{80}{(a/\lambda)}$	$\dfrac{53}{(b/\lambda)}$	0.50
2	Sectoral (H plane) (Fig. 23-49b)	Beam width in H (or XZ) plane	$a \approx \sqrt{3l\lambda}$	$\dfrac{80}{(a/\lambda)}$	$\dfrac{51}{(b/\lambda)}$	0.63
3	Sectoral (E plane) (Fig. 23-49c)	Beam width in E (or XY) plane	$b \approx \sqrt{2l\lambda}$	$\dfrac{68}{(a/\lambda)}$	$\dfrac{53}{(b/\lambda)}$	0.65
4	Conical (Fig. 23-49a) (TE_{11} mode)	Gain	$d \approx \sqrt{2.8l\lambda}$	$\dfrac{70}{(d/\lambda)}$	$\dfrac{60}{(d/\lambda)}$	0.52

Notation:

a = mouth dimension in Z direction (as in Fig. 23-48)
b = mouth dimension in Y direction (as in Fig. 23-48)
d = mouth diameter in Fig. 23-49a
l = horn length from mouth to apex ($= R_0$ in Fig. 23-48)

* A pyramidal horn required to have an assigned beam shape that differs from the shape of (1) is optimized for minimum length by using (2) and (3) to determine the mouth dimensions, and then employing whichever value length l comes out greatest in the two calculations.

NOTE: These formulas all assume that both a and b are at least several wavelengths in magnitude.   If either a or b is one wavelength, then the beam width controlled by this dimension is roughly 20 per cent greater than indicated in the table, and k is 20 per cent less.

Formulas for beam widths and power gain applicable to optimum horns of various types are given in Table 23-4.[2]

[1] The difference in the E- and H-plane behavior arises from the fact that the fields across the mouth are of constant intensity in the XY plane, but are sinusoidally distributed in the XZ plane.

[2] These formulas are from Schelkunoff and Friis, *op. cit.*, p. 601.

The pyramidal horn of Fig. 23-48 and the conical horn of Fig. 23-49a give pencillike beams that have pronounced directivity in both vertical and horizontal planes. Fan-shaped beams result when one dimension of the horn mouth is much smaller than the other; the sectoral horns of Fig. 23-49b and c, formed by flaring in only one dimension, have this behavior. The biconical horn of Fig. 23-49b produces a pancake-shaped beam, thin in the vertical direction but uniform in the horizontal plane. It is commonly excited by means of a coaxial transmission line as shown, instead of a waveguide.

(a) CONICAL (ASSUMING TE_{11} WAVEGUIDE MODE)   (b) SECTORAL HORN (FLARED IN H PLANE)   (c) SECTORAL HORN (FLARED IN E PLANE)   (d) BICONICAL HORN (TEM MODE)

FIG. 23-49. Various forms of horn antennas.

Horns find extensive use at microwave frequencies under conditions where the power gain required is only moderate. However, to realize high gains the horn must be so long that for such service it is at a disadvantage compared with the corresponding parabola or lens antenna.

23-17. Lens Antennas.[1] The directivity of parabolic and horn antennas results from a field distribution corresponding to a plane wave across an aperture. The same result can be achieved by employing a point source of radiation in conjunction with a lens. Such an arrangement is termed a *lens antenna*.

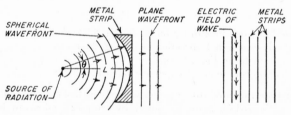

(a) SIDE VIEW OF LENS AND WAVEFRONTS   (b) END VIEW OF LENS

FIG. 23-50. Metallic conducting-strip lens.

Several types of lens antennas are to be distinguished. In Fig. 23-50 the lens consists of conducting strips that are placed parallel to the electric field of the wave that approaches the lens, and are spaced slightly in excess of a half wavelength. To the incident wave, such a structure behaves like a large number of waveguides in parallel, with each hypothetical waveguide having a dimension in a direction perpendicular to

---

[1] For further information see W. E. Krock, Metal Lens Antennas, *Proc. IRE*, vol. 34, p. 828, November, 1946, and Metallic Delay Lenses, *Bell System Tech. J.*, vol. 27, p. 58, January, 1948.

the electric field (i.e., dimension a in Fig. 5-1) corresponding to the spacing between the parallel strips.

Reference to Eq. (5-5) shows that the velocity of phase propagation of a wave traveling in a waveguide is greater than the velocity in free space. Accordingly, by suitably shaping the plates of the lens so that those parts of the spherical wavefront farthest from the axis travel a suitably greater distance when passing through the lens than does the wavefront at the axis, the increased velocity of propagation through the lens will cause the spherical wave that enters the lens to emerge as a plane wave.

The focusing action of the lens of Fig. 23-50 is sensitive to frequency because the phase velocity in the lens depends upon frequency. This limitation can be overcome by employing a dielectric lens (see Fig. 23-51) that delays the wave because of its dielectric constant (or refractive index) and thus converts a spherical wavefront into a plane wave. The optical analogue is a lens that produces parallel rays from a point source. While the lens can be composed of ordinary dielectric, it has been found possible to employ an artificial dielectric consisting of conducting elements such as rods or spheres that are small compared with a

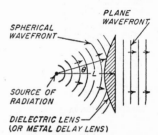

Fig. 23-51. Schematic diagram of dielectric lens.

wavelength and arranged in a three-dimensional lattice structure. Such an arrangement, termed a *metallic delay lens*, has less weight than a solid dielectric, along with an effective dielectric constant and index of refraction that are constant over wide frequency bands.

In a lens antenna the exit side of the lens can be regarded as an aperture across which there is a field distribution. This field distribution then acts as a source of radiation just as do the fields across the mouth of a parabola or horn. The fact that a properly designed lens produces an accurately plane wavefront even when the focal distance is relatively short gives it a distinct advantage in length over a high-gain horn of comparable aperture. In addition, when the aperture is large, the tolerances required in a plate lens of the type shown in Fig. 23-50 are easier to achieve and maintain than in a parabola of similar gain.[1]

23-18. Slot Antennas.[2] The slot antenna makes use of the fact that energy is radiated when a radio-frequency field exists across a narrow slot

---

[1] The lens antenna is also superior to the parabola when it is necessary to minimize backward radiation. This is because in the parabola radiated energy that fails to strike the parabolic surface will "spill over" the edge of the parabola, representing radiation actually directed in the backward direction.

[2] In addition to consulting the general references listed on p. 864, the reader desiring to pursue this subject further will do well to read H. G. Booker, Slot Aerials and Their

in a conducting plane. A typical slot antenna is illustrated in Fig. 23-52a; here the fields are excited by a two-wire transmission line. The electric field across the slot is maximum at the center and tapers off toward the edges as indicated, while at the same time currents flow in the conducting plane in the general manner indicated. When the slot is exactly a half wavelength long, the electric field distribution is sinusoidal and the impedance offered by the slot to the two-wire line is a resistance of 363 ohms.

It can be shown that the radiation produced by a narrow slot in a conducting plane has exactly the same directional pattern as the radiation from a thin, flat, wire-type antenna having a shape corresponding to the

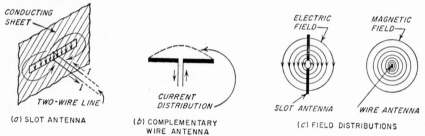

FIG. 23-52. Slot antenna and its complementary wire antenna.

slot, and a current distribution that is the same as the distribution of electric field across the slot. This relation is illustrated in Fig. 23-52b. The only differences between the slot and its complementary antenna are that (1) the polarizations are different since the electric fields associated with the slot are identical with the magnetic field of the complementary wire antenna; and (2) the radiation from the back side of the conducting plane has the opposite polarity from that of the complementary antenna because of the way in which the fields are directed (see arrows in Fig. 23-52c).

A narrow slot may be excited in a variety of ways in addition to the two-wire line arrangement of Fig. 23-52a. Some of the possibilities are illustrated in Fig. 23-53. The arrangement a is similar to Fig. 23-52a except that coaxial feed is employed; when one side of the slot is closed by a cavity (shown dotted) then radiation occurs in only one direction. The antenna at b differs from a only in that the conducting sheet is of limited size. The "fishtail" or "batwing" configuration shown has been found empirically to have a good impedance characteristic over a wide frequency band. In practice the sheet is simulated by a grid of tubular members as indicated; in this way wind resistance is largely eliminated. The slots in the waveguide of c radiate because as discussed in connection with Fig.

Relation to Complementary Wire Aerials (Babinet's Principle), *J. IEE*, vol. 93 (pt. III A), p. 620, 1946.

5-5, slots located anywhere on the top or bottom except along the center line, or anywhere on the sides except with vertical orientation, will be excited by the fields of the TE_{10} mode.

A longitudinal slot in a cylinder, as shown in Fig. 23-53d, has a radiation pattern that is practically circular[1] in a plane perpendicular to the axis provided the cylinder diameter is a small fraction of a wavelength, such as 0.1λ. When the cylinder is larger the pattern is unsymmetrical if

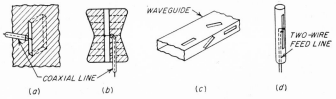

FIG. 23-53. Various slot-antenna arrangements.

there is only a single slot, but a circular pattern can still be achieved if two or more slots are arranged around the circumference. When the cylinder is small the slot may be excited by a two-wire line, as shown in Fig. 23-53d. When the diameter is great enough to be larger than cutoff for waveguide propagation, then the system can be arranged to function as a slotted cylindrical waveguide. In either case the length of the slot required for half-wave resonance is greater than a half wavelength in free space because of the effect of the cylinder on the fields both inside and outside.

A broadside array of slots is illustrated in Fig. 23-54. Here the centers of successive slots are spaced a half guide wavelength apart, and placed on opposite sides of the center line as shown. In this way all slots radiate in the same phase, since the reversal of polarity of the field inside the guide at half-wavelength intervals is compensated by the fact that alternate slots are on

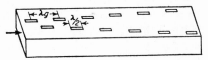

FIG. 23–54. Slotted waveguide antenna designed to act as a broadside array of slots.

opposite sides of the center line. The radiation from all the slots can be made the same in spite of the fact that the fields inside the guide become weaker as they progress down the guide, by the expedient of placing the slots progressively farther from the center line, as shown.

An annular slot having fields everywhere in the same phase is illustrated in Fig. 23-55. Its complementary antenna is a loop with a constant current distribution, as shown. When the diameter of the slot is appreciably less than a half wavelength, the directional distribution and the polarization of the resulting radiation are identical with that produced by the short, vertical, grounded antenna of Fig. 23-55c.

[1] See George Sinclair, The Patterns of Slotted-cylinder Antennas, *Proc. IRE*, vol. 36, p. 1487, December, 1948.

Slots provide a particularly desirable form of high-frequency antenna for high-speed aircraft. By closing the aperture with insulating material, such an antenna does not affect the streamlining of the plane. Slots are, however, limited to use at relatively high frequencies because to radiate efficiently the slot length must be of the order of a half wavelength or more, and this is a reasonable dimension only at very high frequencies.

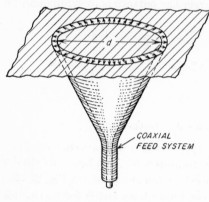

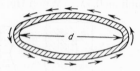

(b) COMPLEMENTARY ANTENNA

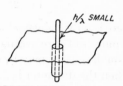

COAXIAL FEED SYSTEM

h/λ SMALL

(a) ANTENNA CONSISTING OF ANNULAR SLOT

(c) EQUIVALENT ANTENNA SYSTEM WHEN h/λ IS SMALL

Fig. 23-55. Antenna consisting of an annular slot, together with complementary and equivalent antennas.

23-19. Broad-band Considerations in Transmitting Antennas.[1] In many circumstances it is necessary for a transmitting antenna and its impedance-matching system to operate over a wide band of frequencies. Thus, television transmitters must transmit a sideband 5 Mc or more in width with almost complete absence of reflected waves in the antenna and associated transmission lines. In other circumstances, it is desired to be able to transmit different frequencies satisfactorily over the same antenna system, for example, in long-distance short-wave communication systems, where different frequencies must be used in the daytime and at night.

Systems for broad-band operation must meet two requirements: (1) The general character of the directional pattern of the antenna must be maintained over the range of frequencies involved; although it is to be expected that the directivity will increase with frequency, the main lobe should not change materially in direction nor should it split into two lobes within the frequency range involved. (2) The load impedance that the antenna offers to the transmission line supplying it with power must behave in such a manner as not to cause the standing-wave ratio to become excessive at any frequency in the band of interest.

[1] Special attention to broad-band antennas is given in "Very High Frequency Techniques," pp. 1–25 and 53–191, McGraw-Hill Book Company, Inc., New York, 1947.

There are three general methods for achieving broad-band characteristics in an antenna.   The first possibility is to employ a nonresonant system such as a rhombic or horn antenna, or a dielectric-lens arrangement.   A parabolic or corner reflector is likewise nonresonant, and if excited by a nonresonant system, for example, a horn, will likewise have a broad-band characteristic.   Nonresonant systems are capable of covering very wide frequency ranges, sometimes as great as 2 to 1.

The second possible way to achieve broad-band characteristics consists in starting with a resonant antenna, but so proportioning this antenna as to minimize resonance effects.   Thus a resonant antenna employing a thin wire is equivalent to a moderately high Q system and so has a relatively narrow frequency band.   However, if the diameter of the antenna wire is made large, the effective Q is very substantially reduced with resulting increase in the bandwidth.[1]   This behavior of a thick antenna arises from the fact that whereas the energy radiated from the antenna for a given current distribution is substantially independent of the antenna diameter, the reactive energy stored in the electric and magnetic fields adjacent to the antenna is less with the thick conductor.   Thus, the thick antenna corresponds to a resonant circuit having a low L/C ratio but with the same resistance as the thin antenna possessing high L/C.

The energy stored in the electric field adjacent to the thick antenna is less than with a thin antenna because by making the antenna conductor thick, one increases the capacitance in the space surrounding the antenna through which the charge represented by the wire current must pass. This results in less stored energy for a given charge.   Similarly, the use of a large-diameter conductor reduces the energy stored in the magnetic field adjacent to the antenna, since the inductance of a wire is less the larger its diameter.

A particularly effective manner of utilizing the thick antenna principle to obtain a wideband is to employ a cone antenna.   Excitation at the apex starts a spherical wave, as illustrated in Fig. 23-56, which spreads out along the cone and in the adjacent space without reflection until reaching the end of the cone.   The variation of the cone impedance with frequency depends on the fraction of this wave that is reflected from the end of the cone, and will in general be less the larger the angle θ of the cone, and the longer the cone.   When $\theta > 100°$, then if the length of the cone is appreciably more than a quarter wavelength, the cone antenna tends to become a nonresonant system.   This is because under these conditions the cone antenna becomes a biconical horn of the type illustrated in Fig. 23-49d.

The third method of broadening the bandwidth of an antenna consists

---

[1] The effect of a thick antenna is also achieved by spaced wires connected in parallel. Thus the folded dipole antenna of Fig. 23-32c is a wideband antenna, a property that makes it particularly desirable for many applications.

in employing a network of reactances designed to transform the actual antenna impedance to a value that over the frequency range of interest is as nearly as possible a constant resistance. The ideal of a resistance that is actually constant with frequency can be approximated more closely the more complex the compensating network. However, the bandwidth obtainable in this way with practical networks is in a general way proportional to the bandwidth before compensation. Hence, although a properly designed compensating network will always improve a system, it cannot be used to convert a very narrow-band system into a very wideband system, but only into a system having a less narrow bandwidth.[1]

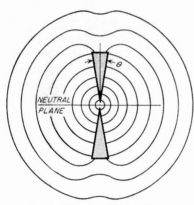

23-20. Practical Transmitting Antennas. An antenna employed for transmitting should have good efficiency; i.e., it should radiate a large fraction of the power supplied to it. In many cases, the antenna is also required to possess a substantial amount of directivity.

Fig. 23-56. Diagram illustrating schematically how a spherical wave originating at the apex of a cone spreads out along the cone and is transferred to space with a minimum of disturbance of the wave as a result of the conical shape.

Transmitting antennas for frequencies below 535 kc are ordinarily of the grounded type with a flat top, as illustrated in Fig. 23-24. It is impractical to use directivity at these frequencies.

For the standard broadcast band (535 to 1605 kc), it is customary to employ a grounded antenna consisting of a vertical tower. When the transmitting power is high, there is an advantage in making the height of the tower slightly greater than a half wavelength (about 0.53λ) in order to reduce the radiation at high vertical angles, as discussed on pages 852 and 887. Simple arrays of vertical antennas are frequently employed in broadcast work to give a desired directional characteristic.

In grounded antennas such as used at broadcast and lower frequencies the ground carries considerable current, and being a poor conductor, it tends to be an important cause of energy loss. As a result, considerable effort is usually made to reduce the ground losses. This takes the form of an extensive system of buried wires radiating out from the antenna, or a

---

[1] The design of such networks in the general case is a very complicated and specialized subject. However, compensating arrangements involving only one or two reactances will make a great improvement, and are commonly sufficient. The design of simple compensating systems of this type is discussed in "Very High Frequency Techniques," *op. cit.*, pp. 52–85.

network of wires arranged above ground, or some combination.   In any case, such wires are arranged to carry a substantial part of the current that would otherwise be required to flow through the ground.

In the high-frequency range an ungrounded half-wave antenna is customary when directivity is not important.   Moderate directivity can be realized by a simple array, which is often of close-spaced type such as a Yagi.   When considerable directivity is important, a horizontal rhombic antenna is generally employed, supported at an appropriate height above earth by telephone poles at the four corners.   The rhombic has the merit of simplicity and wide frequency range.

At very high and ultra-high frequencies, many types of antennas find practical use, including half-wave antennas, corner reflectors, high-frequency loops, horns, parabolas, slot antennas, Yagi arrays, mattress antennas, etc.   The choice in any particular case depends upon the characteristics desired, economic and space considerations, etc.

A situation of particular importance at these higher frequencies occurs in connection with television and frequency-modulation broadcasting. Here horizontal polarization is used and it is generally desired to radiate a circular pattern in the horizontal plane.   Methods of achieving this result include the turnstile antenna (including turnstiles based on the fishtail antenna of Fig. 23-53b), the high-frequency loop, and the slotted cylinder.   When a high degree of directivity is required in the vertical plane, several such antennas can be stacked one above the other with half-wavelength spacing to give broadside action in the vertical plane. The result is then a pancake pattern.

At microwave frequencies the horn antenna finds widest use when moderate directivities are desired, the parabola is generally preferred for high directivities, while the lens antenna is best when extremely high directivities are required.   In addition, other arrangements find occasional use at microwave frequencies to meet particular requirements.

23-21. Behavior of Antennas When Receiving Radio Signals.   A wire antenna is able to abstract energy from a passing radio wave as a result of the voltages that the magnetic flux of the wave induces in the antenna. These induced voltages are distributed along the entire length of the antenna and have a value which per meter of antenna length is $\varepsilon \cos \psi \cos \theta$, where ε is the field strength of the wave in volts per meter, ψ is the angle between the plane of polarization and the wire in which the voltage is induced, and θ is the angle between the wavefront and the direction of the antenna wire.   It will be observed that the quantity $\varepsilon \cos \psi \cos \theta$ is the component of the field strength which has a wavefront parallel to the antenna and is polarized in the same plane as the antenna.

The distributed voltages induced in a receiving antenna cause currents to flow,[1] so that if a load impedance is inserted in series with the antenna,

[1] The current distribution in a receiving antenna will not in general be of the type

energy that has been abstracted from the passing radio wave will be delivered to this load. The antenna, in so far as such a load impedance is concerned, can by Thévenin's theorem be considered as a generator having an equivalent voltage E and an internal impedance Z_a, as illustrated schematically in Fig. 23-57. Here Z_a is the impedance one would measure between the antenna terminals, considering it as a transmitting antenna, and corresponds to Z_{11} in Eq. (23-21). The current that flows in this equivalent circuit is exactly the same as the current that flows in the antenna at the point where the load is inserted.

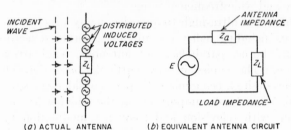

(a) ACTUAL ANTENNA   (b) EQUIVALENT ANTENNA CIRCUIT

Fig. 23-57. Actual receiving antenna with load impedance Z_L and distributed induced voltages, together with equivalent antenna circuit.

The energy represented by the induced current flowing through the resistance component of $Z_a + Z_L$ in Fig. 23-57b is the energy abstracted by the receiving antenna from the passing radio wave. The part of this energy consumed in the resistance component of Z_L is the useful part of the abstracted energy. The portion of the abstracted energy that is consumed in the radiation resistance is reradiated. Thus an antenna excited by a passing wave acts like a parasitic antenna such as discussed on page 905 and modifies the resultant field distribution in its vicinity.

Reciprocal Relations between Receiving and Radiating Properties of Antenna Systems. The receiving properties of an antenna can be expressed in terms of the transmitting properties by the use of the reciprocity theorem (see Sec. 22-18). These relations can be developed in terms of the properties of the system shown in Fig. 23-58. The field strength $\mathcal{E}_a$ of the radio wave produced at antenna B by the power P_a delivered to terminals aa of antenna A and radiated with *power* gain G'_a is

$$\mathcal{E}_a = K \sqrt{P_a G'_a} \qquad (23\text{-}35)$$

where K is an appropriate constant. For P_a one can write

$$P_a = \left(\frac{e_a}{z_{aa}}\right)^2 R_a \qquad (23\text{-}36)$$

shown in Fig. 23-3. This is because Fig. 23-3 gives the current produced when the exciting voltage is applied at a single point, whereas in the receiving antenna exciting voltages are distributed continuously along the antenna.

where e_a is the exciting voltage which when applied to antenna A at terminals aa will produce field $\mathcal{E}_a$, while R_a is the radiation resistance of antenna A, and z_{aa} is the *magnitude* of the impedance offered to e_a by antenna system A at terminals aa. Combining Eqs. (23-35) and (23-36) to eliminate P_a gives

$$e_a = \frac{\mathcal{E}_a z_{aa}}{K \sqrt{R_a G_a'}} \qquad (23\text{-}37a)$$

In a similar manner the field $\mathcal{E}_b$ in the vicinity of antenna A produced by applying an exciting voltage e_b to terminals bb of antenna B is related to

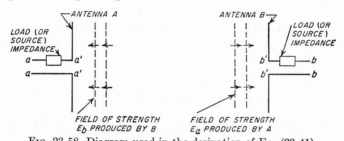

FIG. 23-58. Diagram used in the derivation of Eq. (23-41).

the properties of antenna B by the relation

$$e_b = \frac{\mathcal{E}_b z_{bb}}{K \sqrt{R_b G_b'}} \qquad (23\text{-}37b)$$

Now, according to the reciprocity theorem, the magnitude of the current i_a, induced in antenna A by the field $\mathcal{E}_b$ when terminals aa are shorted, and of the current i_b induced in antenna B by field $\mathcal{E}_a$ when terminals bb are shorted, are related by the equation

$$\frac{e_a}{i_b} = \frac{e_b}{i_a} \qquad (23\text{-}38)$$

Substituting Eqs. (23-37a) and (23-37b) for e_a and e_b, respectively, and rearranging terms gives

$$\frac{i_a z_{aa}}{\mathcal{E}_b \sqrt{R_a G_a'}} = \frac{i_b z_{bb}}{\mathcal{E}_a \sqrt{R_b G_b'}} \qquad (23\text{-}39)$$

All of the quantities on the right-hand side are properties of antenna B and the field $\mathcal{E}_a$ adjacent to it, while all of those on the left-hand side are properties of antenna A and adjacent field $\mathcal{E}_b$. However, no restriction has been made as to the nature of these antennas, so that antenna B can be any antenna; i.e., the right-hand side (and also the left-hand side) in Eq. (23-39) must be a constant that is the same for all antennas and conditions. The value of this constant can be determined by substituting appropriate values for the simplest possible antenna under the simplest possible conditions, i.e., a doublet antenna of Fig. 23-1 with zero losses, the incident wave arriving from a direction perpendicular to the axis of δl, the load impedance in Fig. 23-58 a reactance that tunes out the antenna reactance and makes $Z_{bb} = R_b$, and zero loss resistance so that the power gain G' equals the directive gain G. For the doublet antenna under these conditions, the equivalent voltage E in Fig. 23-57 is $(\mathcal{E}_a \cos \psi) \, \delta l$, so that $i_b = (\mathcal{E}_a \cos \psi) \, \delta l / R_b$. Making use of this fact, and also of Eqs. (23-17) and (23-18), gives

$$\frac{i_b z_{bb}}{\mathcal{E}_a \sqrt{R_b G_b}} = \frac{\lambda \cos \psi}{\pi \sqrt{120}} \tag{23-40}$$

Here ψ is the angle between the planes of polarization of the wave and of the receiving antenna. Substituting this result into Eq. (23-39) and rearranging leads to

$$i_a = \frac{\sqrt{R_a G_a} \, \lambda \cos \psi}{z_{aa} \pi \sqrt{120}} \mathcal{E}_b \tag{23-41}$$

Here R_a, G_a, and z_{aa} are, respectively, the radiation resistance, the directive gain, and the *magnitude* of the impedance of the equivalent antenna circuit including load impedance (see Fig. 23-58).

Fundamental Equation of the Receiving Antenna. Equation (23-41) is the fundamental equation of the receiving antenna. It gives the relationship between the magnitude of the induced current i_a, the field strength $\mathcal{E}_b$ of the field in the vicinity of the antenna, and the properties that the receiving antenna A has when operated as a transmitting antenna.[1]

Examination of Eq. (23-41) shows that the current i_a induced in antenna A is the same current that a voltage

$$E_a = \frac{\sqrt{R_a G_a} \, \lambda \cos \psi}{\pi \sqrt{120}} \mathcal{E}_b$$

would produce when applied to an impedance z_{aa}. This proves the validity of the equivalent circuit of Fig. 23-57. Moreover, since in the notation of this circuit $Z_{aa} = Z_a + Z_L$, it is seen that the antenna impedance is the same for reception as it is when a voltage is applied either to terminals aa or $a'a'$ in Fig. 23-58 to achieve transmission.

Another important consequence of Eq. (23-41) is that the directional characteristic of antenna A for reception is identical with its directional characteristic for transmission.

The ratio of the equivalent lumped induced voltage E_a to the field strength $\mathcal{E}_b$ is termed the *effective height* of the receiving antenna. Hence

---

[1] Note that in Eq. (23-41) the effect of the ground is taken into account through the effect of the ground on directive gain and radiation resistance.

the effective height is given by the equation

$$\left.\begin{array}{l}\text{Effective height of}\\\text{receiving antenna}\end{array}\right\} = \frac{\sqrt{R_a G_a}\,\lambda\,\cos\psi}{\pi\,\sqrt{120}} \tag{23-42}$$

The power delivered by the receiving antenna to a load impedance in the system shown in Fig. 23-57b (and in Fig. 23-58 with terminals aa and bb shorted) will be maximum if simultaneously (1) the antenna loss resistance is zero, (2) the resistance of the load equals the radiation resistance R_a, (3) $\psi = 0$, and (4) the reactance of the load is equal in magnitude but opposite in sign to the reactive component of the equivalent antenna impedance.[1] This situation corresponds to $z_{aa} = 2R_a$ in Eq. (23-41). The power delivered to the load under these conditions is $i_a{}^2 R_a$, or from Eq. (23-41)

$$\left.\begin{array}{l}\text{Maximum possible power deliv-}\\\text{ered to load by antenna } A\end{array}\right\} = \frac{G_a\lambda^2}{480\pi^2}\,\mathcal{E}_b{}^2 \tag{23-43}$$

It is instructive to compare this maximum possible power that a receiving antenna can abstract from a passing wave of strength $\mathcal{E}_b$ with the power $\mathcal{E}_b{}^2/120\pi$ that passes through a unit area of the wavefront. Dividing the right-hand side of Eq. (23-43) by this factor, the maximum possible energy that an antenna of directive gain G can abstract from a wave is seen to correspond to the energy contained in a portion of the wavefront having an area A given by

$$A = \frac{G}{4\pi}\lambda^2 \tag{23-44}$$

The quantity A is variously termed the *capture area, intercept area,* and *cross section* of antenna A, and is in the same units of length as the wavelength λ. The value of A for an elementary doublet ($G = 1.5$) is $0.12\lambda^2$. In the case of a unidirectional mattress antenna with uniform current distribution (Fig. 23-27), A will approximate the cross section of the antenna. Likewise, for a parabolic reflector arranged with a feed system such that in transmitting the mouth is uniformly illuminated and no energy fails to strike the reflecting surface, then A equals the area of the mouth. In other cases, A will be less than the actual mouth area as discussed on pages 899 and 911;[2] with receiving antennas this means that some of the energy in the incident wavefront is reflected after entering the mouth instead of all being absorbed as is the case when A equals the actual area.

[1] This assumes zero loss resistance. With a loss resistance R_l then the power delivered to the load will be maximum when the resistance component of the load impedance is $R_l + R_a$, and the maximum realizable load power will be $R_a/(R_a + R_l)$ as great as for an ideal antenna with zero loss resistance.

[2] With horns, the relation between capture and mouth area is given by Table 23-4 (p. 915) for typical cases.

It is apparent from Eq. (23-44) that *the maximum energy that an antenna can abstract from a passing wave depends only on the directive gain of the antenna and the square of the wavelength; the particular kind of antenna involved is unimportant except as it may affect the gain.* It is apparent that a large amount of energy can be abstracted at the lower frequencies using a simple antenna with minimum directivity. For example, at $\lambda = 300$ m (frequency $= 1$ Mc) the capture area of a simple doublet is 10,750 sq m. On the other hand, at very high frequencies it is difficult to abstract very much energy even with highly directional antennas. Thus at $\lambda = 10$ cm (3000 Mc) the capture area of a doublet is 0.0012 sq m, and even when the gain is 10,000 the capture area is only 8.0 sq m.

Practical Considerations in Receiving Antennas. Factors of practical importance in receiving antennas are the ability to abstract energy from passing radio waves, the directional characteristic including the extent to which minor lobes are present, and the susceptibility to locally generated noise fields.

An ideal receiving antenna has sufficient capture area so that the noise energy picked up by the antenna from static and other sources of noise is comparable with the noise generated by the tubes and circuits of the input portion of the receiving system. At the lower radio frequencies, this ideal can be readily approximated with simple antenna systems, since the intercept area of low-frequency antennas is large even without the aid of directivity; in addition, the static noise level tends to be higher, the lower the frequency. As the frequency becomes higher, however, it becomes increasingly desirable to resort to directivity to increase the intercept area, and at microwave frequencies it becomes necessary to employ extremely great directivity to obtain even a moderate intercept area. At these higher frequencies, the static noise level is also low. As a result of this situation, the sensitivity of very high-frequency radio receivers is always limited by the ability of the antenna to abstract energy from the passing signal.

Directivity in a receiving antenna system has three principal functions: (1) It increases the intercept area (at least in the favored direction); (2) it reduces the noise energy picked up by the receiving antenna from the static and other noise fields provided that not all the noise sources are in exactly the same direction as the desired signal; and (3) it provides a means of discriminating against undesired signals originating in directions other than that in which the desired transmitter lies. At broadcast and lower frequencies, the second and third considerations are the most important, but as the frequency becomes higher, the effect of directivity upon the intercept area of the antenna becomes an increasingly important consideration, until at frequencies higher than about 30 Mc this consideration usually dominates the situation.

The presence of minor lobes of significant amplitude, even though quite narrow, introduces the possibility that an interfering signal, or disturbances from a localized source such as a thunderstorm, will be received with an effectiveness almost as great as is the desired signal, even when originating in a different direction (i.e., the direction of a minor lobe). The susceptibility of antennas to locally generated noise varies. In particular, a loop antenna responds much less to the electric induction field than does a simple wire antenna of comparable intercept area. This is of importance because electric induction fields predominate in the man-made noise that causes disturbances in radio receivers, and this explains in part the popularity of loop antennas in broadcast receivers.

Receiving antennas for the higher radio frequencies are ordinarily connected to the receiver through a transmission line that is preferably terminated by the receiver in such a manner as to minimize resonances. The impedance match between the antenna and the sending end of the transmission line does not affect the standing-wave ratio on this line, but only the extent to which the available energy that the antenna is capable of abstracting from passing radio waves is actually delivered to the transmission line. In general, the loss in energy resulting from failure to match the antenna to the transmission line is not serious until the mismatch is so great that it results in a standing-wave ratio that would be much larger than acceptable for the transmitter case.

PROBLEMS AND EXERCISES

23-1. A vertical wire 1 m long carries a current of 5 amp of frequency 2 Mc. Assuming that the wire is in free space, calculate the strength of the radiated field produced at distances of 1, 25, and 200 km in a direction at right angles to the axis of the wire.

23-2. Sketch the current distribution on a resonant wire antenna two wavelengths long, and also sketch the general character of the radiation pattern applicable to this wire when remote from ground.

23-3. Give a discussion analogous to that on page 867, but applying to a resonant antenna 1.5λ long (Fig. 23-4c) instead of to a one-wavelength antenna. In particular, explain qualitatively why in Fig. 23-4c there is now a lobe in direction P_1 as well as P_3, and why a null can be present between P_1 and P_3.

23-4. Carry out the integration indicated in Eq. (23-6), and then transform the result to give Eq. (23-7).

23-5. Set up a differential equation analogous to Eq. (23-5), but applicable to the case where the antenna length is an odd number of half wavelengths.

23-6. Calculate the directional pattern of a resonant wire 2.0λ long. Minimize the number of points that must be calculated by noting that an individual lobe may be accurately defined by only a few properly chosen points, and by taking advantage of the fact that the pattern is symmetrical in the four quadrants.

23-7. On the basis of the analogy between resonant and nonresonant wires, sketch the main lobes in the directional pattern of a nonresonant wire that is three wavelengths long (showing direction of these lobes and their widths between nulls), and likewise show the first minor lobes in the correct direction.

23-8. Draw a directional pattern analogous to that of Fig. 23-8c, but applying to the case where the wire is so terminated that the wave reflected at the right-hand end of the antenna is half as large as the wave traveling toward the right.

23-9. How much greater in decibels is the directive gain of a resonant wire eight wavelengths long than the directive gain of a half-wave resonant antenna?

23-10. Explain why the directive gain of a nonresonant antenna would be expected to be at least twice as great as that of a resonant antenna of the same length, whereas the *power* gain of the two can be expected to be of the same order of magnitude.

23-11. Sketch the way the pattern for case 4 of Fig. 23-9b would look if antennas A and B were short doublets oriented with axes coinciding with line AB.

23-12. Derive a formula for the directional characteristic of the two spaced antennas in Fig. 23-9a as a function of the azimuth angle ϕ in the plane of the paper, and vertical angle θ above the plane of the paper, assuming that radiators A and B are isotropic and carry currents having the same magnitude and phase.

23-13. Derive a formula for the directional characteristic in the horizontal plane of three vertical antennas spaced along a line a distance d between adjacent antennas, with phases of $-\alpha$, 0, and α, respectively, and carrying currents of the same magnitude.

23-14. Sketch the directional pattern of a broadside array in a plane perpendicular to the axis of the array, when the individual radiators are vertical resonant wires one wavelength long.

23-15. A broadside array composed of half-wave radiators arranged coaxially along a line with centers spaced $\lambda/2$ is required to develop a major lobe that is 10° wide between half-power points. Determine the length of the array, the width of the major lobe between nulls, and the directive gain, assuming free-space conditions.

23-16. Justify the assertion made in the footnote on page 875 that large parasitic lobes will not be developed if $\phi' \lessgtr (90° - \delta/2)$, and then proceed to go through the detailed steps involved in deriving Eq. (23-10).

23-17. Determine the relative currents required in the various antennas of a binomial broadside array having eight radiators.

23-18. In a linear array such as illustrated in Fig. 23-10, the phase difference between adjacent antennas is made k times that for end-fire action, where $k < 1$. Prove that the radiation is then maximum at an angle of α with respect to the lagging end of the line of the array such that $\cos \alpha = k$.

23-19. Show by sketches the effect on the directional pattern for $L = 2\lambda$ in Fig. 23-14 of using short doublet radiators coaxial with the line of the array in place of the isotropic radiators of Fig. 23-14.

23-20. An end-fire array composed of $\lambda/2$ radiators with axes at right angles to the line of the array is required to have a power gain of 30. Determine the array length and the width of the major lobe between nulls. Assume free-space conditions.

23-21. Derive a formula analogous to Eq. (23-10), but giving a relation between the beam width δ between nulls of the individual radiators composing an end-fire array, and a spacing between adjacent radiators which if not exceeded will ensure the avoidance of large parasitic lobes.

23-22. The legs of a rhombic antenna are limited to a length of 90 m. If the performance is to be optimum at a wavelength of 20 m, determine the tile angle, and estimate the free-space directive gain, and the principal dimensions of the major lobe at this wavelength.

23-23. Show by sketch the general character of the directional pattern that would be obtained in a rhombic antenna if the terminating resistor were replaced by an open circuit. Assume that because of radiation, the effective amplitude of the reflected wave is half the amplitude of the incident wave. Concentrate attention only on the major lobes.

23-24. A particular rhombic antenna is designed to give optimum performance at a frequency that makes the legs four wavelengths long. Show by sketches why doubling the frequency will cause the main lobe to be split into two parts.

23-25. Two resonant wires arranged in a V and excited in opposite phase, as in the attached illustration, form a directional antenna system if the apex angle 2α is properly chosen.   State the value that 2α must have if the wire length is 6λ, explain why this

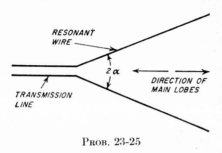

RESONANT
WIRE

2α

DIRECTION OF
MAIN LOBES

TRANSMISSION
LINE

PROB. 23-25

angle is required to concentrate the radiation along the axis, and explain why the two wires must be excited in opposite phase.

23-26. Derive Eq. (23-12) from Eq. (23-7).

23-27. Assume that case 4 of Fig. 23-9b is the directional pattern in the vertical plane of a pair of spaced antennas in free space.   Make a sketch showing qualitatively the nature of the directional pattern obtained when the axis AB is parallel to and $3\lambda/4$ above a perfect ground.   Assume horizontal polarization.

23-28. A rhombic antenna is placed with its plane parallel to the ground.   It is desired that the radiation be concentrated at a height of 20° above ground.   With the aid of the data in Table 23-2 show that it would not be permissible for the legs to have a length as great as 6λ.

23-29. Calculate points on the solid and dotted curves of Fig. 23-23b for vertical angles of 15, 30, 60, and 90°, assuming that the reflection coefficient of the ground is given by Fig. 22-4.

23-30. Prove that the directional pattern for $L = \lambda/2$ of Fig. 23-25 is the same as that of a two-element broadside array in which the individual radiators are spaced with centers a half wavelength apart and are half-wave resonant wires.

23-31. Two identical rhombic arrays with $L = 4\lambda$ are placed in broadside so that they lie in a common plane.   Assuming optimum design of the rhombics, how far apart should the centers of the individual rhombics be to make the width of the main lobe of the two-element array between nulls half the lobe width between nulls of the lobes of the individual rhombics?

23-32. Show a geometrical arrangement in which four resonant wires each 6λ long and carrying equal currents of the same phase will form a broadside array that concentrates radiation in an assigned direction.   Make an estimate of the proper spacing between adjacent radiators.

23-33. *a.* Calculate the vertical and horizontal width between nulls for the array of Fig. 23-27, and also the directive gain.   Assume that all radiators carry the same current, and that the antenna is in free space.

b. At what angle above the horizontal will the radiation be concentrated if the lowest line of antennas is $\lambda/2$ above the earth?   Likewise, what will the directive gain be when the earth is taken into account?

23-34. Starting from Eq. (23-18) calculate the radiation resistance at the base of a T antenna, such as illustrated in Fig. 23-24, in which $a = 0.1\lambda$.   Assume that the current in the vertical section is constant, and neglect the radiation from the flat top.   Take into account the effect of the ground by using an appropriate image, but note that actual radiation takes place only over the upper hemisphere.

23-35. The radiation resistance of a half-wave resonant wire remote from ground is

73.13 ohms referred to a current maximum.   What is the radiation resistance referred to a point 0.125 wavelengths from the end of the wire?   Neglect end effects.

23-36. Explain the mechanism whereby the resistance of nearby ground causes an antenna to possess a loss resistance even when the antenna is ungrounded.

23-37. Will the antenna impedance in Fig. 23-30b be inductive or capacitive? Explain.

23-38. Explain why the mutual impedance between two quarter-wave grounded vertical antennas is exactly one-half of the value between two parallel half-wave antennas remote from ground, and spaced the same distance.

23-39. Derive a formula analogous to Eq. (23-23), but giving the observed impedance of antenna 1 when in the presence of antennas 2 and 3, which have coupling to 1 and also coupling between each other.

23-40. Three half-wave antennas are arranged at the corners of an equilateral triangle with their axes vertical.   Assuming that the antennas are remote from the earth and that the sides of the triangle are $\lambda/2$, calculate the resistance component of the impedance of each antenna, assuming that all three antennas carry currents of the same magnitude and phase.

23-41. Calculate and plot the resistance component of the impedance of a half-wave horizontal antenna as a function of height above a perfect earth (up to height = 2λ), using Fig. 23-31 to obtain the resistance component of the impedance which the *negative* image antenna couples into the actual antenna.

23-42. Three vertical half-wave radiators equally spaced and remote from ground are arranged to operate in broadside (i.e., same currents with same phase).   Determine the spacing for maximum directive gain, and determine the value of this directive gain compared with an isotropic radiator.

23-43. Calculate the directive gain of a broadside array differing from that in Example 2, page 987, only in that there are 11 radiators spaced 0.25 wavelength apart. Compare the results with those of Example 2 and discuss the relationship.

23-44. Prove that when two identical antennas carry currents of the same magnitude but 90° out of phase, the total power radiated with a given current is independent of both the magnitude and phase angle of the mutual impedance between the antennas.

23-45. Determine the directive gain of an array consisting of three parallel half-wave radiators in free space that are $\lambda/4$ apart along a line and carrying currents of equal magnitudes with relative phases of 90, 0, and $-90°$, respectively.

23-46. Calculate the directive gain of the array of Fig. 23-27 by both Eqs. (23-28) and (23-30), assuming all antennas carry the same current, and determine the error in decibels arising from the use of the approximate relation represented by Eq. (23-29).

23-47. A mattress antenna carrying uniform currents is required to have a directive gain of 100 in free space, and to develop a major lobe that is twice as high as it is wide. Determine the number of $\lambda/2$ radiators required in the vertical and horizontal directions and the dimensions of the major lobe between half-power points in the vertical and horizontal planes.

23-48. In Fig. 23-32b, explain why the value of m required to match the transmission line will depend upon the height of the antenna above ground.

23-49. Explain how the arrangement illustrated in the accompanying figure results in a broadside array.

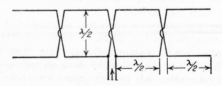

PROB. 23-49

23-50. The balancing unit shown in Fig. 23-34b will be balanced on the two-wire line side only when the frequency is such as to make the sleeve exactly a quarter wavelength long. Explain the mechanism whereby an unbalance to ground is introduced at any other frequency.

23-51. Verify the correctness of Fig. 23-36 for $S/\lambda = 0.1$ and 0.2.

23-52. In the corner reflector antenna of Fig. 23-37b, $S = 0.25\lambda$, and the radiating antenna is a half wavelength long.

a. Determine the increase in field strength in the direction of the arrow that is produced by a given antenna current by the presence of a 90° corner reflector.

b. Calculate the radiation resistance of antenna A in the presence of the 90° corner reflector.

c. From the results of *a* and *b* calculate the directive gain of the 90° corner reflector antenna system compared with an isotropic radiator.

23-53. *a.* A parasitic antenna is 0.2 wavelength distant from a radiating half-wave antenna. Calculate the magnitude and phase of the current in the parasitic antenna when it is resonant at a lower frequency than that being radiated such that the impedance of the parasitic antenna is $Z_{22} = 73.1 + j73.1$ at the radiating frequency.

b. Show that the radiation from the parasitic antenna will increase the field produced in the direction away from the parasitic antenna and will reduce the field radiated in the direction of the parasitic antenna, as compared with field produced by the same current in the radiating antenna, in the absence of the parasitic antenna.

23-54. Prove that detuning a parasitic radiator so that it is resonant at a higher frequency than that being radiated will cause it to act as a director.

23-55. *a.* Explain why the radiation pattern of the square loop of Fig. 23-40a in a horizontal plane perpendicular to the plane of the loop is determined only by the vertical sides of the loop, and is not affected by the horizontal sides.

b. With the aid of Eq. (23-8a) show that when the spacing of these sides is a small fraction of a wavelength, the pattern is proportional to cos θ, where θ is the angle with respect to the plane of the loop.

23-56. In Fig. 23-41a, determine the load impedance placed across the end c of the vertical coaxial feed line by the four branching transmission lines acting in parallel at c, if at gaps such as a the antennas present a load resistance of 1600 ohms, while the values of characteristic impedance of the quarter wave lines ab and bc are 100 ohms and 50 ohms, respectively.

23-57. Prove that, if the individual antennas of a turnstile array are short doublet antennas, then the combined pattern is exactly circular in the plane of the turnstile.

23-58. Describe in a qualitative way how the reflected wavefront of Fig. 23-44a would appear if the radiating antenna were located considerably closer to the parabola than the focus.

23-59. *a.* Calculate the lobe width between half-power points in the vertical and horizontal planes for wavelengths of 3 and 10 cm for a parabola having a mouth 3 ft long and 2 ft high. Assume that the field is sinusoidally distributed across the mouth along both the horizontal and vertical.

b. Estimate the directive gain in decibels by means of Eqs. (23-28) and (23-30).

23-60. A paraboloid of revolution is to have a power gain of 1000 at $\lambda = 10$ cm. Estimate the diameter required.

23-61. Specify the aperture dimensions that the mouth of a cylindrical parabola must have to produce a beam 2° $\times$ 10° between nulls at a wavelength of 3 cm. Assume uniform distribution of the field across the mouth in the long dimension, and sinusoidal distribution across the smaller dimension of the mouth.

23-62. Explain the mechanism whereby the antenna of Fig. 23-47b produces a fan-shaped beam, describe the orientation of the fan with respect to the antenna aperture, and explain the effect on the shape of the fan of increasing the height of the aperture.

23-63. The pyramidal horn of Fig. 23-48 is required to have a half-power width of

10° in both the vertical and horizontal planes. Determine the dimensions of the horn mouth and the length of the horn in wavelengths, and the directive gain.

23-64. Why will the pyramidal horn of Prob. 23-63 have smaller side lobes in the horizontal plane than the vertical?

23-65. Explain why the thickness of the fan-shaped beam developed by the horn of Fig. 23-49b will be less than that given by the horn of Fig. 23-49c, assuming that the long dimension of the mouth is the same in both cases.

23-66. Explain why it is that when a horn has a length greater in proportion to mouth size than the value called for in Table 23-4 for an optimum horn, the proper value of k to use in calculating gain is greater than the value given in the table.

23-67. Discuss the effect of strip spacing in Fig. 23-50 upon the phase velocity in the lens, and hence the phase shift per unit distance of travel through the lens. Do this on the basis that the adjacent strips represent the vertical sides of a waveguide such as illustrated in Fig. 5-2. Include in this discussion the considerations that determine the minimum permissible spacing between strips.

23-68. What impedance will the slot of Fig. 23-53a present to the coaxial line when the slot length approximates a half wavelength? Note that only one side of the slot radiates.

23-69. When a circular waveguide carries the TE_{11} mode (see Fig. 5-15), how should a long, narrow slot be cut in the walls so that this slot will act as an antenna?

23-70. In Fig. 23-54 what would be the disadvantage of omitting all of the slots on one side of the center line?

23-71. Explain the considerations that determine the highest and lowest frequencies for which the horn antenna of Fig. 23-48 will operate satisfactorily as a directive antenna.

23-72. Discuss in general terms whether or not the width of the slot in Fig. 23-51a might be expected to have an effect on the bandwidth of the slot antenna.

23-73. With the aid of Fig. 23-25c and d, explain why one would expect that a vertical radiator 0.53λ high would be superior as a broadcast transmitting antenna to vertical radiators having lengths of either 0.5λ or 0.625λ.

23-74. A lossless receiving antenna is tuned to resonance so that Z_a in Fig. 23-57 equals the radiation resistance. Assume Z_L is changed from $Z_L = Z_a$ to $Z_L = 0.5Z_a$. By what factor does this action alter (a) the power delivered to Z_L, (b) the total power abstracted by the antenna from a passing radio wave, and (c) the power reradiated by the antenna?

23-75. Carry out the actual substitutions and rearrangements necessary to obtain Eqs. (23-40) and (23-41).

23-76. With the aid of Eq. (23-41) show that when an antenna is used for reception the pattern giving the way in which the induced current varies with the direction of the passing radio wave is exactly the same as the radiation pattern of the same antenna when used for transmission.

23-77. Determine the ratio of the effective height to actual length of a half-wave resonant antenna.

23-78. Calculate the maximum power that a half-wavelength receiving antenna in free space can be expected to deliver to a load impedance when receiving a signal having a wavelength of 20 m and a field strength of 5 μv per m.

23-79. Determine the intercept area of the antenna of Example 2 on page 897, and compare it with the area 2.5λ × 0.5λ = 1.25λ² occupied by this bidirectional antenna structure.

23-80. A resonant receiving antenna delivers its power to a transmission line that is terminated by a receiver that provides a load equal to the characteristic impedance. Calculate and plot the power loss in decibels resulting from mismatch between the antenna and the transmission line for ratios of antenna resistance to transmission line characteristic impedance in the range 0.2 to 5.0.

CHAPTER 24

RADIO TRANSMITTERS, RECEIVERS, AND COMMUNICATION SYSTEMS

24-1. Amplitude-modulated Transmitters. A radio transmitter is essentially a device for producing radio-frequency energy that is controlled by the intelligence to be transmitted. A block diagram of a typical transmitter in which the energy control is by amplitude modulation is shown in Fig. 24-1. Here the desired frequency is generated at a low power level by a stable oscillator, ordinarily a crystal oscillator. This is followed by a chain of Class C amplifiers that simultaneously increase the power level and isolate the oscillator from the modulator.

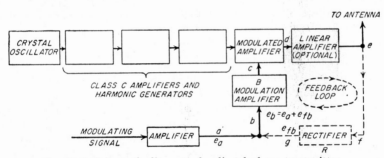

FIG. 24-1. Schematic diagram of radio-telephone transmitter.

When the frequency to be radiated is higher than can be obtained directly from a crystal oscillator, harmonic generators are included in the Class C chain. In this case the crystal operates at a subharmonic of the frequency that is radiated. The final Class C amplifier is modulated; plate modulation is most frequently employed, but control-grid and suppressor-grid modulation find use when the power being handled is not too high. In some cases the modulated amplifier is followed by one or more linear amplifiers, as shown in Fig. 24-1.

Transmitters in which the power output is generated directly by the modulated amplifier are described as possessing high-level modulation. In contrast, arrangements in which the modulation takes place at a power level less than the transmitter output are referred to as low-level modulation systems.

Negative Feedback in Amplitude-modulated Transmitters. The performance of an amplitude-modulated transmitter can be improved in

935

many respects by introducing negative feedback, as indicated schematically in Fig. 24-1. Here the rectifier R generates a modulation-frequency wave that reproduces the variations in the modulation envelope of the transmitter output. This output e_{fb} of the rectifier is then superimposed on the input to the modulation-frequency amplifier B in such a manner as to oppose the modulation-signal input e_a to B. The result is equivalent to negative feedback of the type discussed in Chap. 11. The fact that the modulation-frequency wave with which the feedback is concerned is transformed into an envelope by the modulator, and then reconverted from an envelope back to a modulation-frequency wave by means of the rectifier, merely alters the situation in detail but not in principle.

To the extent that the rectifier R develops an output wave that is an exact reproduction of the modulation envelope of the transmitter output, the effect of the feedback action in Fig. 24-1 is to make the modulation envelope of the transmitter output at point e more nearly reproduce the modulating signal voltage at a than would otherwise be the case. The result is to reduce amplitude, frequency, and phase distortion in the modulation envelope generated in the section $bcde$ of the transmitter, and likewise to reduce noise and hum modulation of the output, just as in the case of the feedback systems discussed in Chap. 11.

The quantitative relations affecting the modulation envelope at e in Fig. 24-1 are the same as given in Eqs. (11-1) to (11-4) provided $A\beta$ in these equations is defined as the ratio of the modulation-frequency voltage e_{fb} fed back at point b to the magnitude $e_b = e_a + e_{fb}$ of the net resultant voltage actually applied to amplifier B. It is assumed further that polarities are so defined that $A\beta$ is negative when the feedback voltage e_{fb} is in exact phase opposition to the modulating input signal e_a. Thus in Fig. 24-1 $A\beta$ represents the effective amplification of the modulation-frequency voltage around the feedback loop $bcdefgb$.

In accordance with the equations in Sec. 11-1, the effect of negative feedback on the radio transmitter of Fig. 24-1 is to reduce the hum modulation, and also the amplitude and frequency distortion,[1] of the output envelope by the factor $1/(1 - A\beta)$. At the same time, the gain of the amplifier B must be increased by the factor $(1 - A\beta)$ in order to compensate for the loss of amplification caused by the negative feedback. The amount of feedback employed in a radio transmitter is normally specified in terms of this increase in amplification that must be used in order to compensate for the presence of negative feedback.

Negative feedback in transmitters introduces the possibility of oscillation, exactly as does feedback in corresponding audio-frequency systems.

[1] This assumes that the rectifier present in the feedback loop introduces negligible distortion. The rectifier is normally a diode and so must be designed with considerable care to avoid peak clipping and to have a very good response characteristic at high frequencies.

The criterion for avoiding oscillations is the same in both cases, namely, that for the system to be unconditionally stable it is necessary that at frequencies where the phase of $A\beta$ has shifted 180° from normal and so transformed negative feedback to positive feedback, the magnitude of $A\beta$ must have dropped to less than unity.

The variation in magnitude and phase of $A\beta$ with frequency includes not only the effects of the audio-frequency amplifier in the feedback loop $bcdefgb$ in Fig. 24-1, but also the phase changes in the modulation envelope produced by the radio-frequency circuits involved.   Thus, as explained in connection with Eq. (12-14), a symmetrical phase shift of the sidebands with respect to the carrier of α degrees arising in the tuned circuits produces the same phase shift α of the modulation envelope.   Accordingly, a simple tuned circuit, carrying a wave modulated at a frequency such that the sidebands suffer a symmetrical phase shift of 45°, will cause the modulation envelope to be likewise shifted 45° at the modulation frequency.   As a consequence of this behavior, each simple resonant circuit in the radio-frequency system can produce phase shifts up to 90° at high modulation frequencies.   At low modulation frequencies the radio-frequency circuits will introduce negligible phase shift of the modulation envelope.

The transmitter circuits must accordingly be designed with considerable care if a large amount of feedback is to be employed.   The fundamental principles involved in this design are discussed in Sec. 11-3 and can be summarized by saying that the transmission $A\beta$ around the feedback loop must not fall off too rapidly at the low and at the high modulation frequencies; in particular the falling off should not exceed 10 db per octave until $|A\beta| < 1$.   These requirements are usually more difficult to meet at the high-frequency end of the modulation range, because here the radio-frequency circuits contribute to the phase shift as well as the audio-frequency circuits in the feedback loop.   The practical procedure for designing a system involving feedback is to make the radio-frequency stages as broad-band as convenient, and at least sufficiently broad-band so that the sideband trimming in the important range of frequencies is negligible.   The audio-frequency amplifier in the section bc in Fig. 24-1 is then equalized in such a way as to make $|A\beta|$ have the desired over-all transmission characteristic around the feedback loop.

Negative feedback makes it possible to achieve lower distortion and less hum modulation than would otherwise be possible in a practical transmitter.   Alternatively, negative feedback reduces the cost of obtaining a very high quality characteristic, since it enables the designer to sacrifice linearity of modulation and of amplification to obtain increased plate efficiency, to use less well filtered power supplies, and to employ alternating currents for heating filaments, and then to rely upon negative feedback to raise the quality of performance to an acceptable level.   At the same time, negative feedback is not a cure-all for all transmitter troubles, and in particular should not be relied upon to compensate for poor design or improper operation. For example, negative feedback will not prevent distortion that arises from overmodulation. Also, when resonant circuits in the transmitter are sufficiently selective to discriminate significantly against the high modulation frequencies, the benefits of negative feedback will be effective only if the degree of modulation is less than unity. This is because if the wave is initially fully modulated at a high modulation frequency, then negative feedback will result in an attempt to modulate the transmitter more than 100 per cent to correct for the falling off in output, and this will introduce additional distortion.

Special Considerations Relating to the Modulation Systems of Amplitude-modulated Transmitters. The modulation system, including both the modulator and the associated amplifiers, is often provided with such features as peak limiters, automatic volume control, and volume compressors.

Peak limiters that provide volume compression on occasional high intensity negative peaks of the modulating voltage prevent the envelope of the transmitter output wave from suddenly going to zero amplitude. This prevents the generation of high-frequency sideband components that lie outside the channel assigned to the station, and which would cause *adjacent channel interference.*

Automatic volume control (see Fig. 10-28) can be used to maintain the average percentage of modulation at a relatively high value irrespective of the average level of the incoming modulating signal. It is particularly helpful to do this in radio extensions of wire-telephone systems, in police radios, etc, where the average voice power that is encountered will vary over a wide range from speaker to speaker.

Volume compressers are used to raise the *average* degree of modulation that can be maintained, without overmodulating during the periods of high intensity. They improve the signal-to-noise ratio, particularly during weaker passages, but do so at the expense of lower volume range.

24-2. Frequency-modulated Transmitters. Transmitters that are frequency-modulated find extensive use at frequencies above 40 Mc for such purposes as frequency-modulated broadcasting, television sound, mobile radio, radio-relay systems, etc.

Frequency-modulated Transmitters for Very High- and Ultra-high-frequency Bands. Two types of frequency-modulated transmitters are in common use for these frequency bands—those using oscillators frequency-modulated by a reactance tube and those employing phase modulation. Block diagrams for typical transmitters of these types are shown in Fig. 24-2. In both cases the modulated wave is generated at a low power level, and a chain of Class C amplifiers and harmonic generators is used to develop the required transmitter power and frequency. In such a system, the Class C stages do not in any way distort the frequency variations of the frequency-modulated wave, so that in contrast with amplitude-modulated systems Class C amplification *after* modulation is permissible. It is generally desirable that the Class C amplifiers after the modulator operate well "saturated" (see page 466) in order to provide a limiting action that will remove any incidental amplitude modulation that may be present. It is to be noted that passing the frequency-modulated wave through harmonic generators increases the frequency deviation, and this

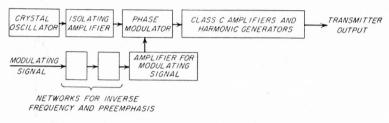

(*a*) PHASE MODULATED TYPE OF FREQUENCY MODULATION TRANSMITTER

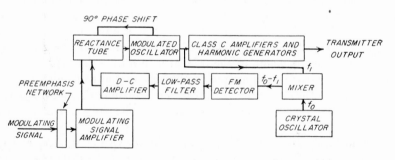

(*b*) REACTANCE-TUBE MODULATED OSCILLATOR WITH MIXER—FM DETECTOR
SYSTEM FOR STABILIZING THE CARRIER FREQUENCY

FIG. 24-2. Schematic diagrams of two types of frequency-modulation transmitters, together with reactance-tube arrangement for stabilizing the carrier frequency when reactance-tube modulation is employed.

fact must be taken into account in the design of the system. In most frequency-modulated transmitters means are provided that cause the frequency deviation produced by a given modulating voltage to be greater at high than at the medium and low modulating frequencies. Termed *preemphasis*, this makes it possible to reduce the background noise of the received signal, as discussed in Sec. 24-10.

The phase-modulated type of transmitter has the advantage that the carrier frequency is derived directly from a crystal oscillator, and so is inherently very stable in frequency. The disadvantage of phase modulation is that the maximum frequency deviation obtainable from the modulator, particularly at low modulation frequencies, is small. As a result, a considerable number of harmonic-generator stages must be employed to obtain a reasonable deviation.

The reactance-tube type of transmitter can be readily arranged to generate large frequency deviations. However, it has the disadvantage that the average (i.e. carrier) frequency is not obtained from a stable oscillator. It is therefore necessary to provide some auxiliary means by which a very stable frequency generated by a crystal will be able to control the average frequency of the oscillator tube. One method of effecting this control is illustrated in Fig. 24-2b. Here the output of a crystal oscillator is applied to a mixer tube along with the output derived from the frequency-modulated oscillator. The crystal frequency f_0 is so selected that when the transmitter is operating at its assigned frequency f_i the difference-frequency output $f_d = f_0 - f_i$ of the mixer will have a predetermined, relatively low value. The output of the mixer is applied to a phase-shift discriminator (see Sec. 17-6) in which the center frequency is f_d. When the transmitter has exactly the correct carrier frequency, the discriminator will develop zero d-c output. Frequency deviations of the transmitter from its assigned value will, however, cause the discriminator to develop a d-c output voltage having a polarity determined by the sense of the transmitter drift. This d-c output voltage, after suitable d-c amplification, is applied to the control grid of the reactance tube in such a way as to modify the frequency of the oscillator in a direction that tends to correct for the error in the average frequency of the transmitter. The low-pass filter in the discriminator output prevents modulation-frequency variations from being transmitted to the reactance tube along with the d-c component.

A second method by which a crystal oscillator can be used to control the carrier frequency of the modulated oscillator is illustrated schematically in Fig. 24-3.[1] Here a portion of the modulated oscillator output is passed through a chain of frequency dividers and reduced to an audio frequency of the order of 5000 cycles, which possesses practically no frequency modulation because of the large demultiplication. The output of the monitoring crystal oscillator is also passed through another chain of frequency dividers. The crystal frequency and the amount of frequency division used in the two sets of dividers are so chosen that, when the transmitter has the correct frequency, the two systems of frequency dividers develop identical output frequencies. These two outputs are then applied to two balanced modulators, with a 90° phase shift being inserted in one of the leads as shown. Each balanced modulator accordingly develops a difference-frequency output that has a frequency propor-

[1] For further details of systems of this type, see J. F. Morrison, A New Broadcast-circuit Design for Frequency Modulation, *Proc. IRE*, vol. 28, p. 444, October, 1940; N. J. Ornan, An Exciter Unit for Frequency-modulated Transmitters, *RCA Rev.*, vol. 7, p. 118, March, 1946.

tional to the deviation in frequency of the transmitter from the desired value.   Furthermore, because of the 90° phase shift referred to above, the outputs of the two modulators are in quadrature and therefore comprise a two-phase system, with the sense of rotation depending upon whether the transmitter frequency is above or below the desired value.   This two-phase output, after amplification, is applied to the stator windings of a two-phase induction motor, the rotor of which is geared to the tuning control on the oscillator, as indicated.   Hence, when the output frequency deviates from the value corresponding to that set by the crystal monitor, the rotor turns in a direction depending on the sense of the

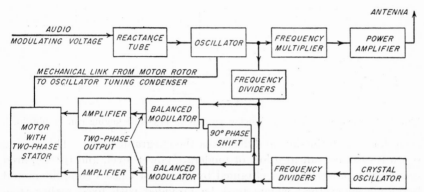

FIG. 24-3. Schematic diagram illustrating method by which the mean frequency of a frequency-modulated transmitter can be made to have an exact relation to a crystal monitor, irrespective of all other factors.

deviation, and this rotation continues until the tuning of the oscillator has been readjusted to eliminate the frequency deviation.   When this has been achieved, there is no difference in frequency between the outputs of the two systems of frequency dividers; also no voltage is applied to the two-phase motor and the control system comes to rest.

Frequency-modulated Transmitters for Microwave Frequencies.   The usual method of generating a frequency-modulated wave at microwave frequencies consists in employing a reflex klystron oscillator, and applying the modulating voltage to the repeller electrode.   This takes advantage of the fact, shown in Fig. 19-9, that the frequency of oscillation is a linear function of repeller voltage in a limited range of repeller voltages about the voltage that is most favorable for generating oscillations.

Negative Feedback in Frequency-modulated Transmitters.   The advantages of negative feedback can be readily realized in frequency-modulated transmitters.   This is done by applying a sample of the transmitter output to a frequency-modulation detector that is carefully designed to have low amplitude and frequency distortion.   The resulting modulation-frequency output of the detector is then introduced into the modulation-frequency amplifier of the transmitter in a negative polarity, thus reducing the modulation-frequency amplification. The benefits obtained are then exactly the same as those obtained from feedback in an amplitude-modulated system, i.e., reduction of distortion, noise, hum, etc., generated within the transmitter. The problem of avoiding oscillation is also the same and so need not be discussed again.

24-3. Radio-telegraph Transmitters. *Amplitude (On-off) Keying.* An amplitude-keyed radio telegraph transmitter differs from the corresponding amplitude-modulated transmitter in that instead of being modulated in accordance with a continuously varying signal, such as an audio-frequency signal, the transmitter output is turned on and off in

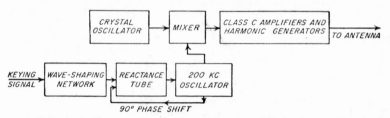

Fig. 24-4. Schematic diagram showing how frequency-shift keying can be obtained.

accordance with the dots and dashes of the telegraph code.[1]   This keying is always carried out at a low or moderate power level, and the required transmitter power is then obtained by means of Class C amplifiers and harmonic generators, which must be provided with fixed rather than grid-leak bias, because when the key is off these amplifiers receive no excitation.

Frequency-shift Keying.[2]   An alternative to on-off keying is to use one frequency for the mark intervals and another for the spacing intervals. Such *frequency-shift keying* can be obtained in many ways. The most common method is illustrated schematically in Fig. 24-4. Here the frequency used is the sum (or difference) frequency obtained by combining the output of a crystal oscillator with the output of a 200-kc oscillator associated with a reactance tube that is controlled by the keying signal. Frequency shifts of the radiated wave used in practice are usually in the range 500 to 2000 cycles; if frequency multiplication is used the actual frequency shift of the 200-kc oscillator will be correspondingly less.

Frequency-shift keying is used in all radio-telegraph systems employing automatic printing equipment.   Its advantage over on-off keying for such applications arises from the fact that being a frequency-modulation system it possesses inherent discrimination against noise that is weaker

---

[1] In some cases the output is simultaneously modulated (either by amplitude or frequency) at an audio rate while being keyed in order to reduce fading, as discussed on p. 959.

[2] A very comprehensive discussion of this topic is given by J. R. Davey and A. L. Matte, Frequency-shift Telegraphy—Radio Wire Application, *Bell System Tech. J.*, vol. 27, p. 265, April, 1948.

than the signal (see page 961), a characteristic that is very helpful in reducing errors when operating automatic printing equipment.

Key Clicks. In amplitude keying, the dots and dashes should have rounded edges, as shown in Fig. 24-5*b*. If the energy rises and falls very rapidly, as in Fig. 24-5*c*, the abrupt changes in amplitude will introduce high-order sidebands. These represent energy at frequencies differing appreciably from the carrier frequency; although weak, they are capable of introducing disturbances in neighboring receivers in the forms of clicks or thumps even when these receivers are tuned to carrier frequencies differing appreciably from the carrier frequency of the keyed signal.

The problem of key clicks is the same with frequency-shift keying as with on-off keying. In order to minimize this type of trouble the frequency must not be shifted too abruptly from one value to the other, i.e., the code characters must have rounded, rather than abrupt, edges. The desired result can be easily obtained by the use of a network be-

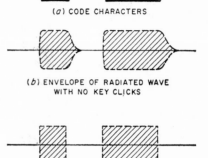

(*a*) CODE CHARACTERS

(*b*) ENVELOPE OF RADIATED WAVE WITH NO KEY CLICKS

(*c*) ENVELOPE OF RADIATED WAVE PRODUCING KEY CLICKS

FIG. 24-5. Envelope of radiated wave under conditions favorable and unfavorable for reduction of key clicks with on-off modulation.

tween the key and the reactance tube (see Fig. 24-4) which does not transmit the very high-frequency components of the dot-dash characters.

24-4. Radio Receivers—General Considerations. All radio receivers except a few designed to meet specialized needs are of the superheterodyne type. Such receivers can be represented schematically as shown in Fig. 24-6; they consist of a radio-frequency section, a mixer (or first detector)

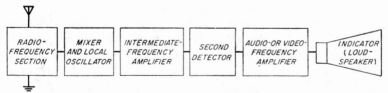

FIG. 24-6. Schematic diagram of superheterodyne receiver.

and local oscillator, an intermediate-frequency amplifier, a second detector, an audio-frequency amplifier, and a loudspeaker or other indicating device.

The radio-frequency section provides coupling from the antenna input terminals of the receiver to the grid of the first tube, and also includes any stages of tuned radio-frequency amplification that amplify the incoming signal before its frequency is changed. The chief purposes of the radio-frequency section are (1) to provide an efficient coupling between the antenna and first tube that utilizes as effectively as possible the energy abstracted from the radio wave, and (2) to provide discrimination or selectivity against image and intermediate-frequency signals, as discussed on page 951.   Selectivity obtained in this way is commonly termed *preselection* because it precedes the mixer.

The local-oscillator-and-first-detector section provides a frequency-conversion system of the type discussed in Sec. 16-10 that converts the incoming signal to a predetermined fixed *intermediate frequency*, usually lower than the signal frequency.   The intermediate-frequency section consists of one or more stages of tuned amplification having a bandwidth corresponding to that required for the particular type of signal that the receiver is intended to handle.   This section provides most of the receiver amplification and selectivity.

The second detector is normally a diode detector in the case of amplitude-modulated signals, or a phase-shift discriminator or ratio detector in the case of frequency-modulated signals.   It is followed by a modulation-frequency amplifier (audio or video according to the type of signal involved) to provide additional amplification, and finally an indicating device such as a loudspeaker.

Specification of Receiver Characteristics.[1]   The receiver characteristics of greatest importance are the *sensitivity, selectivity, fidelity*, and *noise figure*.   Other characteristics, such as power capacity, distortion, response to spurious frequencies, and cross-modulation effects, also frequently must be given consideration.

The sensitivity of a radio receiver is expressed in terms of the voltage (or power) that must be applied to the receiver input to give a standard output.   In the case of amplitude-modulation broadcast receivers, the definition of sensitivity has been standardized as the amplitude of carrier voltage modulated 30 per cent at 400 cycles, which when applied to the receiver input terminals through a standard "artificial antenna"[2] will develop an output of 0.5 watt in a resistance load of appropriate value substituted for the loudspeaker.   The sensitivity under these conditions is accordingly expressed in microvolts, or decibels below 1 volt.   A typical sensitivity curve of a relatively high-grade broadcast receiver is shown in Fig. 24-7.   The most important factor determining the sensitivity of a radio receiver is the gain of the intermediate-frequency amplifier.

The selectivity of a radio receiver is the characteristic that determines the extent to which the receiver is capable of distinguishing between the desired signal and signals of other frequencies.   Selectivity is expressed as a curve that gives the strength of the carrier (modulated in some

[1] For further information on the specification and measurement of receiver characteristics see F. E. Terman and J. M. Pettit, "Electronic Measurements," chap. 9, McGraw-Hill Book Company, Inc., New York, 1952.

[2] In the standard broadcast band the artificial antenna for simulating a wire antenna can be represented by an inductance of 20 μh, in series with a capacitance of 200 $\mu\mu$f.

standard way) required to produce a given receiver output, as a function of the cycles off resonance of the carrier, with the input at resonance taken as the reference. A typical selectivity curve is shown in Fig. 24-8. The selectivity of most receivers is determined largely by the characteristics of the intermediate-frequency system.

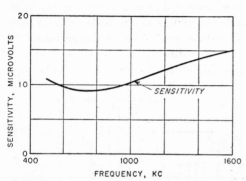

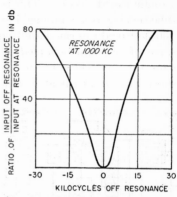

Fig. 24-7. Typical sensitivity curve of a standard broadcast receiver.

Fig. 24-8. Typical selectivity curve of a standard broadcast receiver.

The fidelity of a receiver represents the variation of the output with modulation frequency when the output load impedance is a resistance. Fidelity is expressed in the form of a curve such as shown in Fig. 24-9; in this particular case the output at 400 cycles is taken as the reference value. Fidelity at the lower modulation frequencies is determined primarily by the low-frequency characteristic of the audio- (or video-) frequency amplifier. At the higher modulation frequencies the fidelity is affected by the high-frequency characteristics of the audio-frequency amplifier, and likewise by the discrimination against the corresponding sideband frequencies in the intermediate-frequency system and in some instances in the radio-frequency section as well.

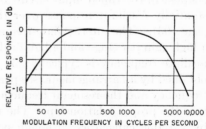

Fig. 24-9. Typical fidelity curve of a standard broadcast receiver.

The noise figure of a receiver is a measure of the extent to which the noise appearing in the receiver output in the absence of a signal is greater than the noise that would be present if the receiver were a perfect receiver from the point of view of generating the minimum possible noise. The noise figure determines the smallest power that may be received without being drowned out by the noise. It represents one of the most important characteristics of receivers for the higher frequencies; it is discussed in detail in Sec. 24-9.

24-5. Receivers for Particular Applications. Radio receivers have been developed for a great many different applications. Some of the more commonly used types are dicussed in this section.

Receivers for Standard Broadcast Band. In receivers for the standard broadcast band (535 to 1605 kc) the radio-frequency section is ordinarily a single tuned circuit. This is followed in order by a multigrid converter tube serving as a combined local oscillator and mixer, one or two stages of double-tuned intermediate-frequency amplification, a diode detector, one stage of resistance-coupled amplification, and a beam power tube. A loop antenna contained in the case is ordinarily employed, although a short wire, resonant at a somewhat higher frequency than 1605 kc, can

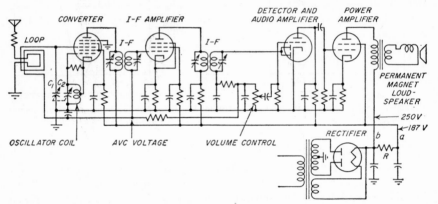

Fig. 24-10. Simplified circuit diagram of a typical broadcast receiver for the frequency range 535 to 1605 kc.

also be used if more sensitivity is required. In any case, the antenna is coupled to the tuned input circuit in such a manner as to provide a substantially constant response over the tuning range of the receiver (see page 403). The intermediate-frequency amplifier is designed to provide a high gain per stage and a bandwidth slightly less than 10 kc; the intermediate frequency is typically 455 kc. Single-dial control of tuning is obtained by an arrangement (see page 949) that causes the local oscillator frequency and the resonant frequency of the tuned input circuit to maintain the proper relationship. The resonant circuits are typically tuned by variable capacitors, although permeability tuning finds use in auto radios. Anode power for the receiver is usually obtained from the 60-cycle power line using a capacitor-input rectifier-filter system. However, some receivers are designed so that they can be operated directly from 110-volt d-c power systems, while equipment to operate in an automobile ordinarily employs a vibrator power supply. Portable receivers employ dry batteries. A simplified circuit diagram of a typical broadcast receiver is shown in Fig. 24-10.

Receivers for Amplitude-modulated Signals at Short-wave and Higher Fre-

quencies. Receivers of this class are similar to standard broadcast receivers except for certain details. Thus the radio-frequency section normally contains one or two stages of tuned radio-frequency amplification; this is in order to improve the noise figure (see page 959) and the ability to reject signals of image frequency (see below). The mixer is likewise often a type producing less noise than a multigrid converter. The intermediate frequency is often higher than the value used in broadcast receivers in order to improve the rejection of image signals.

The maximum frequency range that can be covered in a single tuning band at the higher frequencies is of the order of 2 to 1. Coverage of more than a single band is obtained in the case of a capacitor-tuned system by switching the coils associated with various sections of the capacitor, while using the same capacitor for every band. When tuning is accomplished by varying the position of a magnetic core (permeability tuning), the entire tuning assembly is switched to change bands. By

TO ANTENNA

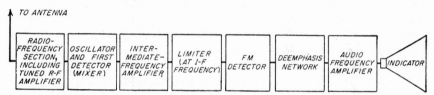

Fig. 24-11. Block diagram of frequency-modulation broadcast receiver.

proper circuit proportions it is of course also possible to arrange so that a narrow frequency band will be spread out over a full tuning range. This is done when signals of interest are allocated a small section of the frequency spectrum; examples are short-wave broadcast signals and amateur signals.

Frequency-modulation Receivers for Very High and Ultra-high Frequencies. Frequency modulation is used extensively in the frequency range 40 to 1000 Mc for broadcasting, television sound, police radio, military systems, etc. A typical receiver for such applications is shown schematically in Fig. 24-11.

In Fig. 24-11 the radio-frequency section always has at least one stage of tuned amplification in order to give effective image rejection. This stage of amplification, in combination with a low-noise type of mixer, serves to give a good noise figure.

The intermediate-frequency amplifier typically operates at a relatively high frequency in order to ensure good image rejection; thus 10.7 Mc is standard for frequency-modulation broadcast receivers. The receiver bandwidth varies with the type of service for which the receiver is intended. In frequency-modulation broadcasting the standards provide for a maximum frequency deviation of 75 kc, corresponding to a total bandwidth of 150 kc. On the other hand, in types of service where the primary objective is to obtain intelligible communication, as in police radio, frequency deviations as low as 15 kc are often employed.

The noise output of a frequency-modulation receiver will be minimized when the receiver does not respond to amplitude variations of the incoming signal (see Sec. 24-10). This result can be achieved by arranging so that the output of the intermediate-frequency amplifier undergoes limiting, or by employing a ratio detector, or by a combination of both. Limiting action can be introduced by means of a crystal diode, or alternatively by grid limiting (Figs. 18-1 and 18-2) in the final intermediate-frequency amplifier stage.

The audio circuits of a frequency-modulation receiver must be so proportioned as to reduce the higher audio frequencies in direct proportion to the amount of preemphasis employed at the transmitter. This is termed *deemphasis*.

Special Considerations Involved in Reception of Radio-telegraph Signals. Reception of radio-telegraph signals is normally accomplished by employing an ordinary amplitude-modulation receiver provided with a fixed-frequency oscillator that injects oscillations into the intermediate-frequency system that differ from the center of the intermediate-frequency band by 1000 to 2000 cycles.

Heterodyne action between the incoming signal and this "beating" oscillator causes the second detector output of the receiver to be in the form of an audio tone. In the case of on-off keying this tone is of constant pitch, and reproduces dots and dashes of constant pitch.

In frequency-shift keying, the beating oscillations injected into the intermediate-frequency system cause the output of the second detector to be an audio tone that possesses the same frequency-shift characteristics that were introduced at the transmitter. In a typical case, one might have a center frequency of 2000 cycles, with a frequency deviation of ± 800 cycles; i.e., the mark intervals might appear as 2800 cycles while the space intervals would be denoted by 1200 cycles. This frequency-modulated tone is then amplified, limited, and applied to a discriminator having a center frequency corresponding to the center frequency of the frequency-shift signal.[1] The discriminator output accordingly develops a d-c voltage of one polarity for the mark indication, and of the opposite polarity for space indication.

24-6. Miscellaneous Techniques and Considerations of Importance in Radio Receivers. *Automatic Volume Control.* Practically all receivers for amplitude-modulated signals are provided with an automatic-volume-control system (abbreviated AVC) to maintain the carrier voltage at the second detector approximately constant. This is accomplished by biasing the grids of the radio-frequency, intermediate-frequency, and mixer

[1] Discriminators for frequency-modulation detection in which the center frequency is in the audio band are described in Davey and Matte, *op. cit.*

tubes[1] negative with a d-c voltage derived by rectifying the carrier, as shown in Fig. 24-10. An increase in the signal hence increases the bias, which tends to counteract the increased signal by reducing the amplification, and vice versa. A receiver with AVC may be tuned from strong to weak signals without the necessity of resetting the manual volume control; AVC likewise smooths out variations in signal strength due to fading.

Automatic-volume-control action is normally obtained by deriving from the usual diode detector a d-c voltage proportional to the amplitude of the carrier at the diode input terminals, and free of modulation. A typical circuit arrangement to accomplish this, shown in Figs. 16-2 and 24-10, causes the voltage applied to the detector to vary with signal strength in the manner shown by curve b of Fig. 24-12. This characteristic is not ideal, however, because the output voltage is reduced by AVC action even when the output is less than the desired value. As a result, circuit modifications involving a second diode are sometimes introduced that cause the AVC system to be inoperative until the signal at the second detector reaches the desired level. Such an AVC

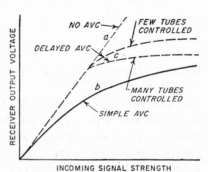

Fig. 24-12. Characteristics of different automatic-volume-control arrangements.

system is said to possess *delay*, and results in performances of the type shown at c in Fig. 24-12. In this case the characteristic will tend to approach the ideal more closely the greater the number of amplifier tubes that have their gain controlled.

Tracking and Alignment of Circuits for Single-dial Tuning. Satisfactory single-dial tuning of a receiver requires that all resonant circuits in the radio-frequency section of the receiver be tuned together, and that their resonant frequencies correspond to a predetermined standard printed scale. This can be accomplished by making the inductance and capacitance of each resonant circuit as nearly alike as possible, and then resorting to individual adjustment of circuit elements to correct for residual errors. Thus when capacitance tuning is employed, exact alignment of the radio-frequency circuits is obtained at the high-frequency end of the tuning range by the use of an adjustable trimmer capacitor in shunt with the coil, as shown in Fig. 24-13a. Exact alignment at the low-frequency end of the tuning range is commonly achieved by adjusting the inductance of each coil by shifting the position of an end turn until exact alignment is obtained.

---

[1] The tubes controlled in this way are always variable-mu types; this is to minimize cross-talk, as discussed on p. 410.

Single-dial operation also requires that the local oscillator frequency differ from the resonant frequency of the radio-frequency section by a fixed amount that always equals the intermediate frequency, irrespective of the frequency to which the receiver is tuned. When capacitor tuning is employed this result is usually achieved by using a gang capacitor in which the different sections are made as nearly identical as possible. Tracking is then obtained by using a coil of somewhat less inductance for

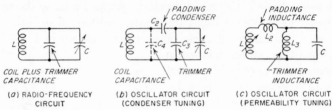

COIL PLUS TRIMMER   COIL   TRIMMER   *TRIMMER*
CAPACITANCE   CAPACITANCE   INDUCTANCE

(*a*) RADIO-FREQUENCY   (*b*) OSCILLATOR CIRCUIT   (*c*) OSCILLATOR CIRCUIT
CIRCUIT   (CONDENSER TUNING)   (PERMEABILITY TUNING)

Fig. 24-13. Alignment and tracking systems for radio-frequency and oscillator circuits of a superheterodyne receiver.

the oscillator than for the radio-frequency section, and associating the oscillator coil with series and shunt capacitors as illustrated in Fig. 24-13*b*.[1] By properly proportioning such an arrangement, it is possible to obtain exactly correct tracking at three frequencies in any tuning range, as shown in Fig. 24-14.   The best average tracking is obtained when the frequencies of exact tracking (commonly termed *crossover* frequencies) are so chosen that the maximum errors of the tracking curve within the desired tuning range all have the same value (solid curve in Fig. 24-14).   The maximum error in tracking that results will then be so small as to be of no consequence.

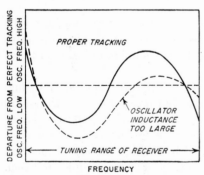

Fig. 24-14. Tracking curves of super-heterodyne oscillator.

It is customary to adjust the oscillator trimming and padding capacitors experimentally.   When doing so, it is to be kept in mind that with a given coil, adjustment of the shunt trimmer capacitor determines to a first approximation the high-frequency crossover point, while the series padding capacitor is the principal factor controlling the low-frequency crossover.   The middle-frequency crossover is then determined by the inductance of the oscillator section, with too much inductance causing the crossover to occur at a frequency that is high, as shown by the dotted curve in Fig. 24-14.

[1] It is possible, however, to obtain tracking by making the oscillator section of the gang capacitor differ in maximum capacitance and in plate shape from the sections used to tune the radio-frequency circuits.

In receivers tuned by varying the position of a magnetic core (permeability tuning), the tracking and alignment problems involved are analogous to those encountered where tuning is by means of a variable condenser. The only difference is that the roles of capacitance and inductance are interchanged; thus variation in the capacitance of a permeability-tuned circuit corresponds to change in the coil size with capacitor tuning. Tracking of the oscillator of a superheterodyne receiver employing permeability tuning can accordingly be accomplished by means of auxiliary fixed inductances, as illustrated in Fig. 24-13c, where L_2 has a small reactance, and L_3 a high reactance, compared with the reactance of L_1. These circuit elements correspond to C_2 and C_3, respectively, in the capacitively tuned case of Fig. 24-13b.

Spurious Responses in Superheterodyne Receivers—Image Signals. In superheterodyne receivers, there is the possibility of obtaining a variety of spurious responses. Some of these appear in the form of whistles having a pitch dependent upon the tuning of the receiver; others cause an interfering program to be heard at unexpected places on the dial. The principal sources of spurious responses are (1) image-frequency signals, (2) signals of intermediate frequency, (3) harmonics of the intermediate frequency generated by the second detector, and (4) harmonics of the incoming signal generated in the converter tube.

In a superheterodyne receiver the mixer will develop an intermediate-frequency output when the signal frequency is both greater and less than the local oscillator frequency by an amount equal to the intermediate frequency. This introduces the possibility of simultaneous reception of two signals differing in frequency by twice the intermediate frequency. As a result it is necessary to employ selective circuits in the radio-frequency section (i.e., between the antenna and the mixer) in order to favor the desired signal while discriminating against the undesired or *image* signal. The suppression of the unwanted image will be more effective the greater the number of tuned circuits involved, and also the higher the ratio of intermediate to signal frequency. For broadcast receivers operating in the 535- to 1605-kc band the standard intermediate frequency is 455 kc. Frequency-modulation receivers operating in the 88- to 108-Mc band normally employ an intermediate frequency of 10.7 Mc, while television sets (which operate at still higher frequencies) employ an intermediate frequency for the picture carrier that is sometimes about 26 Mc, and sometimes about 46 Mc.

Radio signals of intermediate frequency will be heard in the output of a radio receiver if such signals are able to reach the input of the mixer tube in appreciable amplitude. This can be prevented by providing selectivity in the radio-frequency section that is adequate to discriminate against intermediate-frequency signals.

When the harmonics of the intermediate frequency that are present at the output of the second detectors get coupled back into the radio-frequency section, whistles appear in the receiver output that vary with the tuning. Thus, if the incoming signal has a carrier frequency of 910 kc and the receiver is so tuned that the local-oscillator frequency is 1365.6 kc, then the difference frequency that results from the mixer operation is 455.5 kc. Now if the second harmonic of this frequency that appears in the output of the second detector gets coupled back to the input of the mixer, this second-harmonic component of $2 \times 455.5 = 911$ kc will combine with the local oscillator frequency to produce an intermediate frequency of $1365.5 - 911 = 454.5$ kc. These two intermediate frequencies then combine in the second detector to produce a 1-kc whistle. The remedy for this situation is to provide filters at the output of the second detector that will confine the harmonics of the intermediate frequency, and also to arrange the wiring so that the coupling between the radio-frequency and second-detector circuits is a minimum.

When very strong signals are being received at a frequency f_s that is approximately twice the intermediate frequency f_i, it is possible for high-order modulation action in the mixer to produce a mixer output having a frequency $2f_s - f_o$, where f_o is the local-oscillator frequency; this is in addition to the normal output $f_o - f_s = f_i$. When $f_s = 2f_i$, the mixer output will then include a second or spurious component $2f_s - f_o$ that approximates the intermediate frequency. This component beats with the normal intermediate-frequency output to produce a whistle having a pitch that varies with the tuning of the receiver. Since this type of spurious response originates from action from within the converter, it cannot be eliminated by selectivity in the radio-frequency section; instead the amplitude of the troublesome signal at the mixer input must be reduced.

The spurious responses discussed above represent the types that are most troublesome in superheterodyne receivers.[1] Other types of combination frequencies are possible, however, and are occasionally encountered.

Triple-detection Receivers. A triple-detection receiver is shown schematically in Fig. 24-15. Here the incoming signal is first transformed to a relatively high intermediate frequency in the usual manner. After one or two stages of amplification at this frequency, the signal is then transformed to a second and lower intermediate frequency by means of a second mixer in association with a second local oscillator of appropriate fixed frequency.

Such an arrangement effectively suppresses image signals, since the high value of the first intermediate frequency causes the desired and

---

[1] At one time, cross-talk (see p. 410) was an important source of spurious responses. The introduction of the variable-mu tube has largely eliminated this problem for reasons discussed on pp. 194 and 411.

image signals to differ greatly in frequency. At the same time, the relatively low value of second intermediate frequency makes it possible to obtain high amplification per stage as well as sharp discrimination against signals differing only slightly in frequency from the desired signal. The result is that triple-detection receivers provide a combination of greater image suppression and higher adjacent channel selectivity (i.e., better bandwidth ratio) than can be realized in a simple superheterodyne receiver. Because of this, the best grade receivers used for short-wave

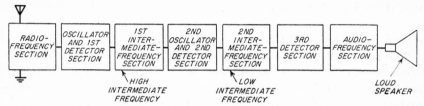

Fig. 24-15. Block diagram of triple-detection receiver.

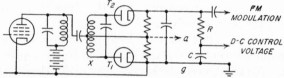

Fig. 24-16. Circuit for producing a control voltage in an automatic-frequency-control system.

and higher-frequency service normally employ the triple-detection principal.

Receivers with Automatic Frequency Control. The term *automatic frequency control*, abbreviated AFC, as applied to a receiving system, denotes an arrangement for automatically keeping the frequency of the local oscillator of the superheterodyne receiver at the value required to produce the desired intermediate frequency, even in spite of the normal tendency of the local-oscillator frequency to drift with temperature, line voltage changes, etc.

Features that must be included in the detector of a frequency-modulation receiver to achieve automatic frequency control are illustrated schematically in Fig. 24-16. Here any deviation of the average value of intermediate frequency from the center frequency of the phase-shift discriminator[1] will cause the detector output to develop a d-c voltage having a polarity determined by the sense of the frequency deviation. This d-c voltage is separated from the modulation frequency component of the detector output by low-pass resistance-capacitance filter RC as shown. It is then applied to the control grid of a reactance tube associated with the local oscillator in such a way that the local-oscillator fre-.

[1] An alternative form of discriminator that is suitable for use at microwave frequencies is described in Sec. 19-7.

quency is changed in a direction that tends to correct for the error in the average intermediate frequency. It is thereby possible to reduce the tuning errors resulting from frequency drift of the local oscillator (or transmitter) to a value that is a very small fraction of the value they would otherwise have.

The circuit arrangement in Fig. 24-16 can also be used as an amplitude modulation detector while simultaneously generating an automatic-frequency-control voltage. This is done by taking advantage of the fact that the voltage between points a and g corresponds to the output of T_1 acting as a diode detector for the envelope variations of the radio-frequency voltage applied between x and ground.

The arrangements shown in Figs. 24-2b and 24-3 for stabilizing the carrier frequency of frequency-modulation transmitters are also forms of automatic-frequency-control systems, and may be applied to a receiver to make the intermediate frequency coincide in frequency with a local oscillation. Thus when the system of Fig. 24-2b is applied to a receiver, f_i becomes the intermediate frequency, and the "modulated oscillator" is the local oscillator of the receiver.

In receivers where reflex klystron local oscillators are employed the automatic-frequency-control voltage is applied to the repeller voltage of the klystron. No reactance tube is necessary under these circumstances.

Automatic frequency control finds extensive practical use at frequencies that are so high that a small percentage drift of the local-oscillator frequency would prevent the receiver from functioning satisfactorily. It is thus a feature of the better frequency-modulation broadcast receivers, and is often found in military equipment.

Modified forms of automatic frequency control in systems involving pulses are also encountered in television receivers (p. 997) and in radar (page 1028).

Receivers with Crystal-controlled Local Oscillators. When a receiver is required to receive only one predetermined frequency, or at most only a small number, there is an advantage in replacing the ordinary tunable local oscillator by a crystal oscillator of suitable frequency. A push button can be used to change the crystal connected in the circuit if it is necessary to select among several frequencies. In this way, it is possible to obtain crystal-oscillator frequency stability in receiver operation, with the resulting assurance that the receiver will always be correctly tuned to the desired frequency.

Crystal-controlled receivers find extensive use in police, aircraft, mobile, and military equipment, where it is necessary to guard a channel and always be in correct adjustment to receive any call that may come over it.

Squelch (Quieting) Systems. When AVC is employed with a receiver having considerable sensitivity, a disagreeable amount of noise will be heard in the receiver output when no carrier is present, either while waiting for a station to come on the air or when tuning from one station to another. Arrangements for suppressing this noise have been given such names as *squelch, muting,* and *quieting systems, tuning silencers,* and *interchannel noise suppressors.* Such devices are also sometimes referred to as *codans,* from the first letters of the words in the phrase "carrier operated device antinoise."

Various ways can be employed to obtain squelch action. One arrangement makes use of an auxiliary tube arranged to bias the grid of the first audio tube beyond cutoff unless the grid bias of the auxiliary tube approaches or exceeds cutoff. By using the AVC system to bias the auxiliary tube, it is then possible to make the receiver inoperative until a carrier of predetermined amplitude is present.

Squelch arrangements find their principal use in systems, such as police radio, where transmission is not continuous but receivers must always be ready for a signal.

Adjustable Selectivity. In crowded frequency bands, such as those used by amateurs, there is an advantage in employing an intermediate-frequency system in which the width of the acceptance band is controllable, and which in addition provides the opportunity to reject a signal differing only very slightly in frequency from the desired signal.

The method most frequently used to achieve this result consists in employing a quartz crystal as a circuit element that couples together two resonant circuits in the intermediate-frequency system, as illustrated in Fig. 24-17a.[1,2] The equivalent electrical circuit of this arrangement is shown at *b,* and the corresponding transmission characteristic is given at *c.* The transmission characteristic is characterized by a relatively narrow response band corresponding to the series resonant frequency of the crystal (as determined by LC). The width of this band depends on the series resistance R of the crystal as augmented by the resistances that the parallel resonant circuits place in series with the crystal, and can accordingly be controlled by a variable resistance R_s in series with L_sC_s. Bandwidths of the order of 200 cycles for R_s zero to about 5000 cycles with R_s large can be obtained in this way.

Examination of Fig. 24-17c shows that there is a frequency of extremely low response very close to the response band. This corresponds to the

---

[1] It is also possible to combine ordinary circuit elements in a feedback system to give a result equivalent to that obtained with this crystal filter; see O. G. Villard, Jr., and W. L. Rorden, Flexible Selectivity for Communications Receivers, *Electronics,* vol. 25, p. 138, April, 1952.

[2] An alternative is to provide two or more bandpass filters of different bandwidths, such as 300 cycles and 6000 cycles, which the user can choose between at will. These filters normally consist of a chain of mechanical resonators (such as crystals or coupled metal resonators with magnetostriction drive and take-off), and can be made to have uniform response in the passband and extremely great discrimination against frequencies even just slightly outside of the passband.

frequency at which the crystal network LCC_1 is in parallel resonance. The exact location of this rejected frequency can be controlled without changing the frequency of maximum response by adjusting the capacitor C_n which neutralizes a portion of the crystal capacitance and hence controls the effective value of the shunt capacitance C_1 of the equivalent crystal circuit.

Tuning Indicator. A tuning indicator gives a visual means of determining when the carrier is at the center of the response band of the receiver. Tuning indicators are useful for receivers provided with AVC, since the AVC system tends to maintain the loudness of the output substantially unchanged, even when the receiver is so badly mistuned as to

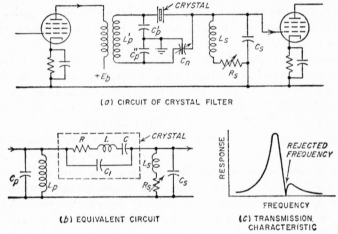

(a) CIRCUIT OF CRYSTAL FILTER

(b) EQUIVALENT CIRCUIT   (c) TRANSMISSION CHARACTERISTIC

Fig. 24-17. Typical crystal filter in a radio receiver.

distort the reproduced signal because of unequal transmission of the various sideband components. Tuning indicators are also useful in frequency-modulation receivers, since the limiter action in such receivers makes it difficult to tune the signals to the center of the discriminator characteristic by ear alone.

Two types of tuning indicators are in common use. The first is a d-c milliammeter connected to indicate the plate current of the tubes controlled by the AVC system; minimum current then corresponds to maximum signal strength. The second type consists of a form of cathode-ray tube which produces a sector-shaped fluorescent pattern in which the angle of the sector is variable between 90 and 0° according to the voltage applied to a control electrode. When used as a tuning indicator, the control voltage is obtained from the AVC system of the receiver.

24-7. Single-sideband Systems. The transmission of radio-telephone signals by a single sideband has the advantage that all of the transmitted power is in the intelligence carrying sideband, and that the total bandwidth required is only half as great as with a double-sideband system. As a result, a single-sideband system has a signal-to-noise power ratio that is eight times as great as that of a fully modulated double-sideband system for the same peak power.

A typical single-sideband transmitter is shown schematically in Fig. 24-18a. Here the single sideband is produced by modulating a 100-kc carrier using a balanced modulator, and then separating one of the sidebands by means of a crystal filter. The resulting 100-kc single sideband

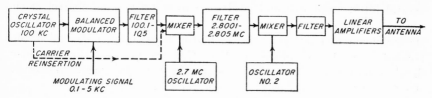

(*a*) SCHEMATIC DIAGRAM OF TRANSMITTER

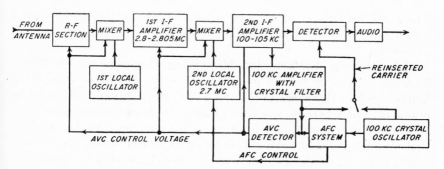

(*b*).SCHEMATIC DIAGRAM OF RECEIVER

Fig. 24-18. Schematic diagram of single-sideband transmitter and receiver.

is shown as being transformed first to 2.7 Mc by heterodyne action, and then to a still higher frequency by a second heterodyne action. This is all done at low power level, after which the power is increased to the desired value by a chain of linear amplifiers.[1]

Single-sideband signals are received by reinserting the carrier at the receiver before detection. When the amplitude of the reinserted carrier is large compared with the amplitude of the single sideband, the envelope of the combined wave varies in accordance with the original modulation, which is then recovered by a conventional diode detector.

The reinserted carrier must be within 10 cycles of the correct value if

---

[1] An alternative possibility is to produce a single sideband directly at higher power level by the method described in connection with Fig. 15-14. This has the advantage of simplicity, but does not give as effective suppression of the second sideband as does the system of Fig. 24-18a, and so is most appropriate where the requirements are not too severe, as, for example, in amateur work.

speech is to sound natural.   While manual adjustment of a tunable oscillator will meet these requirements for short time intervals, it is customary in single-sideband systems to transmit a carrier of reduced amplitude along with the single-sideband signal to give continuous indication of the carrier frequency.   A method of doing this is indicated in Fig. 24-18a.

A receiver for utilizing such a pilot carrier is shown in Fig. 24-18b. Here the reduced carrier in the final intermediate-frequency amplifier is approximately 100 kc; this carrier is separated by a highly selective crystal filter, amplified, and used for automatic volume control of the receiver.   The frequency of this reduced carrier is likewise compared with the frequency of a 100-kc crystal oscillator in a frequency-control system analogous to that employed in Fig. 24-3 (except that the frequency dividers may be omitted).   This operates in such a manner as to readjust the second local oscillator in the receiver as required to make the frequency of the reduced carrier in the final intermediate-frequency amplifier have a value that is exactly the crystal-oscillator frequency, thus aligning this intermediate frequency accurately with its 100-kc crystal filter. The reinserted carrier can then be supplied either by the 100-kc crystal oscillator of the receiver, or by the amplified and "reconditioned" carrier, as shown.

24-8. Diversity Systems for Minimizing Consequences of Signal Fading.   Automatic volume control is obviously helpful in minimizing fading effects.   However, AVC is not a complete solution to the problem of fading signals, because when the signal fades down into the noise level, all an AVC system can do is to bring up the noise level to the intensity that the signal should have.   This difficulty can be solved almost perfectly, however, by the use of a diversity receiving system, of which two types are in common use, namely, space diversity and frequency diversity.

Space Diversity.   Space diversity takes advantage of the fact that signals received at different locations do not fade together.   Thus in the short-wave range of frequencies (2 to 30 Mc) tests show that signals received on antennas spaced of the order of 3 to 10 wavelengths will fade more or less independently.   Again, at ultra-high and microwave frequencies, it is found that though the signal received on any one antenna will occasionally fade to negligible amplitude, the signal will never fade out simultaneously on two antennas at different heights provided that these heights are properly related to each other.

The several antennas of a space-diversity system are each provided with a separate receiver.   These receivers then go to a common output, so that a satisfactory received signal is obtained as long as the signal intensity from at least one of the antennas is acceptable.   The several receivers are preferably operated from a common AVC system derived from the sum of the AVC output voltages of the various receivers.   In this way the channel that receives the loudest signal at the moment dominates the situation, and the other channels contribute little or nothing to the output at that instant either in the way of noise or signal.

Frequency Diversity. In frequency diversity, advantage is taken of the fact that signals of slightly different frequencies do not fade synchronously. This possibility is commonly utilized to minimize fading in radio-telegraph circuits. Thus if the keyed carrier wave is modulated at an audio frequency, the dots and dashes will be simultaneously transmitted on carrier and sideband frequencies, irrespective of whether the keying is of the on-off or frequency-shift type. While either amplitude or frequency modulation can be employed, there is some advantage in using frequency modulation since if the frequency deviation is made great enough so that m $\geqslant$ 1.4 then the sidebands will always be at least as large as the carrier, a result that can never be achieved in amplitude modulation. Modulating frequencies of the order of 500 cycles are usually used; in the case of frequency modulation a deviation of 800 cycles is typical. When frequency-shift keying is employed it is necessary to relate the modulating frequencies and the frequency shift produced by the keying so that the sideband components for the mark and space intervals do not overlap.

24-9. Receiver Noise. The minimum usable signal is determined by noise in the receiver output. This noise can be (1) noise picked up by the antenna from passing noise or "static" radio fields (such noise is not chargeable to the receiver or the receiving system), (2) thermal noise generated by the resistance that the antenna system presents to the input terminals of the receiver, and (3) noise generated within the receiver consisting of circuit (thermal) and tube noise.

Noise Figure. As far as noise is concerned, the part of a radio receiver between the antenna and the output of the intermediate-frequency amplifier can be regarded as an amplifier. The fact that the mixer of the receiver shifts the frequency of the noise does not change the situation in any significant manner; it merely causes the output noise to lie in a different place in the frequency spectrum from the input noise.[1]

The relationship between the signal-to-noise ratio at the output of the intermediate-frequency amplifier of an actual radio receiver and the signal-to-noise ratio at the output of an ideal receiver that generates no tube or circuit noise, but is otherwise the same as the actual receiver (e.g., same bandwidth, amplification, etc.), is expressed in terms of a *noise figure*, just as in the case of an amplifier.[2] Thus from Eq. (12-43) one has

---

[1] The only exception is when the receiver has no image rejection. In this case the noise figure of the receiver is 3 db worse than it would be for the same receiver with good image rejection. This is because the image noise appears in the receiver output along with the noise associated with the desired frequency band, thus doubling the noise power reaching the output of the intermediate-frequency system.

[2] The noise figure is always defined at the input of the final detector, since the noise output of a detector (but not of a mixer) is affected by the presence of a signal; for

$$\text{Noise figure of receiver} = F = \frac{\begin{cases} \text{signal-to-noise-power} \\ \text{ratio of ideal receiver} \end{cases}}{\begin{cases} \text{actual signal-to-noise-} \\ \text{power ratio of receiver} \\ \text{output} \end{cases}} \quad (24\text{-}1)$$

As with the corresponding amplifier, the ideal system is one in which the only source of noise is the resistance component of the impedance that supplies the input power to the receiver. This implies that the internal impedance of the antenna or other signal source connected to the receiver input terminals is considerably less than the input impedance of the receiver, just as in the amplifier case. The noise figure of a receiver is determined experimentally in the same way as for an amplifier (see Sec. 12-14).[1]

The proper value to assign to T when using Eq. (12-41) to determine the signal-to-noise ratio of an ideal system presents an interesting question because at least a part of the resistance of the system supplying signal power to the receiver is antenna radiation resistance. The proper temperature to associate with the radiation resistance is the effective temperature of the surroundings with which the antenna can exchange energy by radiation; this normally approximates the ambient temperature.

Receiver Noise and Its Minimization. The principal source of the noise generated in a receiver is usually the first tube.[2] This is because the noise generated in the first tube experiences more amplification than does the noise of the second and later tubes. Only when the amplification of the first tube is very low, or when the second tube has unusually high noise, is it necessary to take into account the possibility that a significant part of the total noise might come from other than the first tube.

When it is desired to achieve the lowest possible noise figure at frequencies below about 1000 Mc, a triode amplifier should be employed in the radio-frequency section of the receiver, because triodes (either neutralized or in a grounded-grid circuit) have lower noise than any other tube arrangement.[3] A pentode amplifier designed to have low screen-grid

---

example, a frequency-modulation signal will suppress weak noise but will be suppressed itself by strong noise (see Sec. 24-10). The effect of the detector and the audio system on the signal-to-noise ratio of amplitude-modulated receivers is given by E. G. Fubini and D. C. Johnson, Signal-to-noise Ratio in AM Receivers, *Proc. IRE*, vol. 36, p. 1461, December, 1948.

[1] Also see F. E. Terman and J. M. Pettit, *op. cit.*, p. 408.

[2] This assumes that the input impedance of the receiver is appreciably greater than the source resistance associated with the receiver input, as noted above.

[3] A single stage of tuned radio-frequency amplification is usually sufficient to achieve low noise. However, two stages may be required at the higher frequencies where the amplification per stage is low, or at lower frequencies when a very noisy mixer, such as one of the multigrid types, is used.

current gives nearly as low noise as does a triode, while a triode mixer is somewhat less desirable as the first tube in a receiver than a pentode amplifier, but is better than a pentode mixer.   Multigrid mixers are very noisy, in comparison with pentode mixers, and should never be used as the *first* tube in a receiver when low noise figure is important, although they are still permissible if preceded by one or two stages of radio-frequency amplification.

At frequencies above about 1000 to 1500 Mc, a good crystal mixer has a noise figure (see Eq. 16-18) that is less than the noise figure of the best amplifier available for microwave frequencies.   Accordingly, microwave receivers do not use amplification in the radio-frequency section.[1]

Noise Considerations in Practical Receivers.   At broadcast and lower frequencies the noise figure of the receiver is usually not important.   This is because static noise fields of significant magnitude are usually present at the lower radio frequencies (see Sec. 22-17), and because even small antennas have a large capture area at these frequencies.   As a result the noise energy that is picked up by the antenna under these circumstances is usually not only much greater than the thermal noise generated in the resistance of the antenna, but is likewise greater than the noise generated in a receiver of relatively large noise factor.   Hence receivers for broadcast and lower frequencies normally use multigrid mixers, and do not need to employ amplification in the radio-frequency section.

As the frequency is increased from 2 to 30 Mc the static energy becomes progressively less.   As a result, in this frequency range there is an advantage to be gained by keeping the noise figure of the receiver reasonably low; therefore, amplification is always provided in the radio-frequency section, usually from a pentode.

At frequencies above about 30 Mc, the incoming signal is almost entirely free of static most of the time.   The smallest signal power available at the receiver input terminals that will produce a useful signal is then determined by the noise figure of the receiver.   In turn, the available signal power developed at the input terminals of the receiver by a radio wave of given field strength is determined by the capture area of the receiving antenna.   Since this capture area is seen from Eq. (23-44) to be proportional to (directive gain)/(frequency)^2, a favorable ratio of desired signal to interfering noise in a very high-frequency receiving system requires a receiver with low noise figure associated with an antenna having high directive gain.

24-10. Noise and Interference Reduction in Frequency-modulation Systems.   One of the most important features of frequency-modulation systems is that they can be so designed and operated as to reduce greatly the effects of noise and interference.

---

[1] However, it is now possible to build traveling-wave amplifiers that have nearly as low noise as the best crystal mixers.

Suppression of Tube and Circuit Noise Weaker than the Signal. Noise superimposed on a frequency-modulated wave that is stronger than the noise causes the envelope of the resulting wave to fluctuate in amplitude and will likewise produce phase variations. Thus if E_s in Fig. 24-19 represents a frequency-modulated wave,[1] a superimposed noise voltage of magnitude E_n can cause the magnitude of the resultant voltage to vary between $E_s + E_n$ and $E_s - E_n$, while the phase of the resultant voltage relative to E_s oscillates between the limits $\phi = \pm \sin^{-1}(E_n/E_s)$, as the noise E_n varies in phase relative to the signal E_s. Thus the combined wave is modulated by the noise both in amplitude and phase, and the

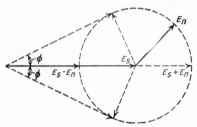

situation is analogous to that illustrated in Fig. 16-16 except that now the noise replaces the weaker oscillation.

The noise contained in the wave represented by Fig. 24-19 can be prevented from producing appreciable noise in the output of a receiver by (1) employing a limiter or a ratio detector or both in the receiver so that amplitude fluctuations of the incoming signal produce no receiver output, and (2) using a frequency deviation at the transmitter so great that for full modulation the frequency deviation m_s is large compared with unity. When the response to amplitude fluctuations is eliminated, the only way noise can appear in the receiver output is through its effect on the phase. However, if $E_n < E_s$, then the modulation index m_n produced by the noise will always be less than unity and so is much smaller than m_s when the frequency deviation is large. For example, if a particular 500-cycle signal produces a 50,000-cycle deviation, then the signal modulation index $m_s = 50,000/500 = 100$. In comparison, a noise voltage half as large as the signal ($m_n = 0.5$) produces a phase deviation only 0.005 times as great as the deviation produced by the signal. Thus, noise only slightly weaker than the signal is almost completely suppressed.

The extent to which noise is suppressed in this way is greater the larger the frequency deviation of the signal. Thus the signal-to-noise ratio of a wideband frequency-modulation system is superior to that of a narrow-band system, *provided that the signal is larger than the noise.*

It will be noted that the higher the modulating frequency, the less complete is the suppression of the noise. This is because the modulation index m_s corresponding to a given frequency deviation produced by the signal is less the higher the modulating frequency [see Eq. (17-9)]. Fur-

FIG. 24-19. Vector diagram useful in explaining noise suppression in frequency-modulation systems.

---

[1] This vector will of course rotate forward and backward during modulation in accordance with the instantaneous phase position of the wave.

thermore, in ordinary speech, the higher frequencies are relatively weak, and so produce only small frequency deviation. This still further reduces the modulation index of the signal at high modulation frequencies.

As a result, it is desirable to increase the amplitude of the higher modulation frequencies before modulation at the transmitter. Termed *preemphasis*, this improves the noise suppression at the receiver by making the modulation index at high modulation frequencies greater than would otherwise be the case. The receiver circuits following the detector are then so proportioned as to restore these higher frequencies to their proper relative amplitude, a process termed *deemphasis*. The result of the preemphasis-deemphasis operation is to improve the signal-to-noise ratio at the higher modulation frequencies.

The amount and character of preemphasis used varies with circumstances. In frequency-modulated broadcasting it is standard to emphasize the higher frequencies in accordance with an inductance-resistance circuit having a time constant of 75 μs. In police radio and similar systems, phase modulation is often used without the inverse-frequency network at the transmitter; this gives preemphasis in proportion to the modulating frequency.

When a noise voltage is momentarily larger than the desired signal, then the noise suppresses the desired signal, just as a strong signal will suppress a weaker noise. Accordingly, when noise of the continuous type such as produced by tubes and circuits has an amplitude great enough to cause the noise peaks to exceed the amplitude of the desired signal an appreciable fraction of the time, then the desired signal will be intermittently replaced by noise. This introduces a "sputter" that causes the output of the frequency-modulation system to be completely unusable unless the signal level is significantly greater than the average value of the tube and circuit noise.

Minimization of Noise Pulses. Consider the situation that exists when the frequency-modulation signal has sufficient amplitude to suppress the tube and circuit noise, but is less in amplitude than the disturbances produced by lightning, ignition systems, etc., which consist of relatively infrequent pulses of extremely high amplitude, and of duration less than the rise time of the receiver circuits. When such pulses are passed through the circuits of a receiver, they are distorted because of the finite bandwidth of the receiver. In particular, the width of the pulses is increased, and becomes approximately equal to the reciprocal of the receiver bandwidth (see page 414). At the same time the peak amplitude of the noise pulse is reduced and assumes a value that is directly proportional to the receiver bandwidth.

A frequency-modulation receiver provided with amplitude limiting and possessing wideband radio-frequency and intermediate-frequency circuits will then respond only slightly to such an interfering noise pulse, irrespective of the initial amplitude of the noise pulse.   This is because the wide-band minimizes pulse duration and hence the time during which the noise is greater than the signal, i.e., minimizes the capture time during which the instantaneous frequency changes from that corresponding to the signal to that of the noise transient.   At the same time, limiting prevents the noise that reaches the detector from ever being larger than the signal.[1] It is also helpful to design the frequency-modulation system so that deemphasis is used in the receiver, since most of the pulse noise is at the higher frequencies and so is further reduced when deemphasis is used. Likewise, it is important that the receiver be tuned so that the inter-mediate-frequency carrier is accurately aligned with the center frequency of the intermediate-frequency amplifier.   This is because the transient produced by the noise pulse is at this center frequency, and the frequency shift and associated phase disturbance produced when the noise "cap-tures" the system will on the average be less the smaller the difference between the instantaneous frequency of the signal and the frequency of the noise transient (i.e., the center frequency).

Common-channel Interference.[2]   When two frequency-modulated trans-mitters located within range of a receiver are operated on the same fre-quency, the signal that is the stronger tends to suppress the weaker signal almost entirely and prevent its modulation from appearing in the receiver output.   This *capture effect* is similar to the noise-suppressing action just discussed, with the weaker signal playing the role of the noise that is weaker than the desired signal.   This ability to suppress co-channel interference is one of the important and useful features of a frequency-modulation system.

Wideband versus Narrow-band Frequency Modulation.   The proper bandwidth to employ in a frequency-modulation system depends upon the circumstances.   With large frequency deviation (wideband system), thermal and circuit noise that is weaker than the desired signal will be more completely suppressed than in a narrow-band system.   Likewise, pulse noise will be less when the bandwidth is great, as discussed above. At the same time, the amount of thermal and circuit noise energy accepted by the receiver is proportional to the bandwidth, so that a wideband system must have a greater signal strength in order for the signal to be larger than the noise.

These considerations cause wide bands to be used where high quality signals are to be transmitted; thus in frequency-modulation broadcasting the standard deviation is 75 kc.   On the other hand, where the purpose is

---

[1] A thorough discussion of the interfering effects of pulsed noise is given by D. B. Smith and W. E. Bradley, The Theory of Impulse Noise in Ideal Frequency-modula-tion Receivers, *Proc. IRE*, vol. 34, p. 743, October, 1946.

[2] For further information see M. S. Corrington, Frequency Modulation Distortion Caused by Common and Adjacent Channel Interference, *RCA Rev.*, vol. 7, p. 522, December, 1946.

to transmit intelligible signals, rather than to entertain, as in military and police communications, deviations of the order of 15 kc are typical.

24-11. Minimization of Noise in Amplitude-modulated Systems. In amplitude-modulated receivers, thermal and circuit noise produce amplitude variations in the envelope of the received signal that are rectified by the final detector and inevitably appear as background noise in the receiver output. There is no suppression of noise by a stronger carrier, as is present in a frequency-modulation system.

Pulse noise can, however, be discriminated against in amplitude-modulated receivers just as in frequency-modulation receivers. It is merely necessary to employ a clipper (i.e., limiter) that eliminates all amplitudes in excess of twice the carrier amplitude.[1] The maximum disturbance introduced by a noise pulse can then not exceed that corresponding to 100 per cent modulation of the desired carrier, irrespective of the original amplitude of the noise. The bandwidth of the receiver up to the point where the limiting occurs should be wider than required to accommodate the desired signal with its sidebands. This is because the greater the receiver bandwidth, the shorter will be the duration of the noise pulse in the receiver circuits, and hence the less the interfering effect of the pulse that remains after clipping.

It might be thought that trouble would arise from the fact that the widened band accepts interfering signals that a narrow-band receiver would reject. However, when the desired signal is considerably stronger than the interfering signals that are accepted as a result of the added bandwidth, then the interfering signal is suppressed by the amplitude-modulated detector, as discussed in Sec. 16-8.

Comparison of Amplitude- and Frequency-modulation Systems with Respect to Noise and Interference. It is now possible to draw some interesting comparisons between amplitude- and frequency-modulation systems. First, it is to be noted that with frequency modulation a desired signal that is moderately stronger than circuit and tube noise will suppress the latter almost completely, and thus give an extremely high signal-to-noise ratio in the receiver output even when the actual signal-to-noise ratio at the input to the final detector is quite low. No such characteristic is possessed by amplitude-modulated receivers. However, when the desired signal is only slightly stronger than the average noise level, then amplitude modulation is superior to frequency modulation because of the sputter effect referred to on page 963.

---

[1] For a detailed discussion of limiters that automatically set the clipping level at twice the carrier level, see Emerick Toth, Noise and Output Limiters, *Electronics*, vol. 19, p. 114, November, 1946, and p. 120, December, 1946. A general discussion of pulse interference in amplitude-modulation receivers is given by D. Weighton, Impulsive Interference in Amplitude-modulation Receivers, *J. IEE (Radio Sec.)*, vol. 95, pt. III, p. 69, March, 1948.

Second, amplitude- and frequency-modulation systems are equally able to suppress disturbances introduced by noise pulses provided the receiver bandwidths are the same. However, the ability of a frequency-modulation receiver to suppress pulse noise is reduced seriously if the receiver is mistuned slightly (see page 964), whereas no such need for exact tuning exists in the amplitude-modulated case.

Third, a frequency-modulated receiver has the ability to suppress almost completely an interfering signal that is only slightly weaker, irrespective of whether this signal is in the same channel or on an adjacent channel, whereas an amplitude-modulated receiver will only suppress such an interfering signal when the difference in frequency between the desired and undesired carriers is greater than the highest modulation frequency contained in the desired signal.

Last, but by no means least, amplitude-modulation stations can be assigned channels differing in carrier frequency by twice the highest modulation frequency, even though wideband receivers are employed; thus a number of amplitude-modulated channels may be assigned to the same frequency band that would be occupied by a single wideband frequency-modulation transmitter.

When these considerations are all taken into account, it is found that the difference between amplitude and frequency modulation is not as great as is often believed. In general, for high-quality service where effective suppression of even weak background noise is desired, as in broadcasting, wideband frequency modulation is superior to amplitude modulation. However, where a higher background noise level can be tolerated, as when intelligible but not entertaining speech is to be transmitted, the relative merits of frequency modulation versus amplitude modulation *employing a wideband receiver with limiter* are not greatly different.[1] Hence although frequency modulation is employed in most very high-frequency and ultra-high-frequency radio-telephone systems, amplitude modulation is sometimes chosen instead.

24-12. Pulse Systems of Communication.[2] Pulse communication is based on the fact that a complex waveform representing a signal can be reproduced by taking samples of this wave at regular intervals, and then transmitting these samples with the aid of pulses that are modulated upon the carrier. A simple example of this sampling procedure is illustrated in Fig. 24-20b, in which the amplitudes of the successive pulses are propor-

---

[1] A stimulating discussion of this subject is given by M. G. Nicholson, Comparison of Amplitude and Frequency Modulation, *Wireless Eng.*, vol. 24, p. 197, July, 1947. Also see David Middleton, On Theoretical Signal-to-noise Ratios in F-M Receivers. A Comparison with Amplitude Modulation, *J. Appl. Phys.*, vol. 20, p. 334, April, 1949.

[2] A useful survey of this subject is given by E. M. Deloraine, Pulse Modulation, *Proc. IRE*, vol. 37, p. 702, June, 1949.

tional to the corresponding amplitudes of the signal wave; this arrangement is known as pulse-amplitude modulation.

It is apparent that the successive pulses in Fig. 24-20b will rather faithfully reproduce the signal wave. In fact, it can be shown that if the number of samples per second exceeds twice the highest frequency contained in the signal wave, the original signal wave can be reconstructed from the succession of pulses.

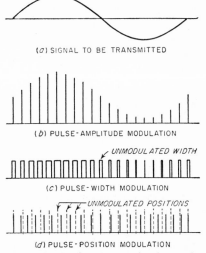

(a) SIGNAL TO BE TRANSMITTED

Instead of pulse-amplitude modulation, one may alternatively employ pulses of constant amplitude, and transmit the magnitude of the sample of signal wave by varying the width of the pulse (pulse-width modulation), by varying the position of the pulse (pulse-position or pulse-time modulation), by a code of pulses (pulse-code modulation), etc. The first two of these types of modulation are illustrated in Fig. 24-20c and d, respectively.

(b) PULSE-AMPLITUDE MODULATION

(c) PULSE-WIDTH MODULATION

(d) PULSE-POSITION MODULATION

Fig. 24-20. Various types of pulse modulation.

Pulse-width modulation can be achieved in many ways. One possibility is illustrated in Fig. 24-21. Here trigger pulses from A occurring at the sampling rate are applied to a one-shot multivibrator similar to that in Fig. 18-16, except that the signal wave E_s to be sampled is superimposed upon the bias voltage E_1, as shown schematically. Each trigger pulse

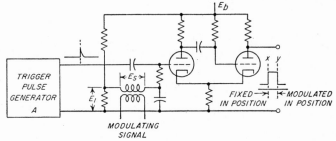

Fig. 24-21. Circuit for producing a width-modulated pulse.

from A initiates a cycle of multivibrator operation, which terminates after a time interval that varies linearly with the voltage E_s, as discussed on page 633. Thus the pulses of plate voltage produced by the multivibrator have a trailing edge y that varies in position in accordance with signal voltage E_s, while the leading edge x is fixed in position. The length xy of the pulse is hence width modulated.

Pulse-position modulation can now be achieved by differentiating these width-modulated pulses, and then using a rectifier to separate the pulses having the polarity corresponding to the differentiated trailing edge of the width-modulated pulses, as illustrated in Fig. 24-22.

In a pulse system of radio communication the pulses obtained from the sampling action are modulated upon a radio-frequency carrier and then transmitted in the same manner as any other radio signal. The receiver is typically a superheterodyne having a bandwidth appropriate for the pulses involved; its second detector then produces an output corresponding to the pulses originally modulated on the carrier.

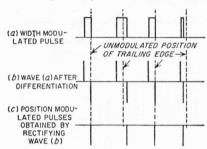

(a) WIDTH MODU-LATED PULSE

UNMODULATED POSITION OF TRAILING EDGE→

(b) WAVE (a) AFTER DIFFERENTIATION

(c) POSITION MODU-LATED PULSES OBTAINED BY RECTIFYING WAVE (b)

Fig. 24-22. Derivation of position-modulated pulses by differentiation of width-modulated pulses.

The process of obtaining the original signal wave from the received pulses depends upon the type of modulation. In the case of pulse-amplitude modulation or pulse-width modulation, it is merely necessary that the train of pulses developed in the output of the second detector be applied to the input of a low-pass filter having a cutoff frequency equaling the highest frequency contained in the original signal.

In the case of pulse-position modulation it is customary to convert the received pulses that vary in position to pulses that vary in length. One way to achieve this is to employ a flip-flop circuit (Sec. 18-5) so arranged that the plate current of tube 1 is turned on when the position-modulated pulse arrives, and is then turned off by locally generated trigger pulses so synchronized as to occur at a definite time[1] after the position corresponding to the unmodulated position of the incoming pulses. The result is that the plate current of flip-flop tube 1 flows in the form of width-modulated pulses, as shown in Fig. 24-23.

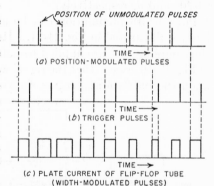

POSITION OF UNMODULATED PULSES

TIME→

(a) POSITION-MODULATED PULSES

TIME→

(b) TRIGGER PULSES

TIME→

(c) PLATE CURRENT OF FLIP-FLOP TUBE (WIDTH-MODULATED PULSES)

Fig. 24-23. Conversion of position-modulated pulses to width-modulated pulses.

Time Multiplex. When very short pulses are used there is a considerable amount of unallocated time between pulses. Thus consider pulse-

---

[1] Such synchronism is achieved in practice by periodically sending a special synchronizing pulse from the transmitting station to maintain the receiver trigger pulses in the proper time relationship to the incoming pulses.

position modulation in which each pulse is 1 μsec long, and the maximum time deviation corresponding to peak modulation is ±4.5 μsec. Each pulse must then be allocated approximately 10 μsec, whereas if the sampling rate is 10,000 times per second there are 100 μsec available per pulse. The remaining 90 μsec can be used by other pulses transmitting other signals.

This introduces the possibility of time multiplexing, in which successive intervals of time are assigned to different channels. Thus, in the case cited above, one could simultaneously transmit eight signals assigned successive 12-μsec time intervals (10 μsec for the pulse, plus an additional 2 μsec to provide protection against adjacent channels), and send an extra-long synchronizing pulse during the remaining 4 μsec of each 100-μsec period. Such a time-multiplexed signal can be obtained by generating the pulses for each individual channel just as though this channel were acting alone, except that the pulses for the successive channels have a progressive time difference, which in the case indicated above would be 12 μsec. The mixture of pulses obtained in this way from the various channels is then modulated on the transmitter carrier. At the receiving end of the system, the receiver output will deliver pulses that are identical with those that were modulated on the transmitter.

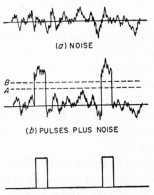

(a) NOISE

(b) PULSES PLUS NOISE

(c) OUTPUT RESULTING FROM SELECTING AMPLITUDE RANGE AB AND AMPLIFYING

FIG. 24-24. Oscillograms showing noise-suppressing action in pulse system.

This output is then applied to a system consisting of a series of gates, one for each channel, with inputs connected in parallel. These gates are controlled by the synchronizing pulse, which can be distinguished from the other pulses by its greater width. The control is such that the gate associated with a given channel is open during the particular 12-μsec part of the 100-μsec period in which the pulses of that channel are transmitted.

Signal-to-noise Ratio. When pulse-width or pulse-position modulation is used, it is possible to derive pulses from the receiver output that are almost entirely free of superimposed noise provided only that the signal is moderately stronger than the noise peaks. The mechanism by which this result is obtained can be understood by considering the ideal case of a pulse having vertical sides and an amplitude moderately greater than the noise, as illustrated in Fig. 24-24b. If such a wave is passed through a slicer that develops an output corresponding to the portion of this wave lying in the region AB, the output thus obtained is free of noise, as shown.

In an actual system the sides of the pulses will slope somewhat instead of being vertical.   The superimposed noise will then change the position of the leading and trailing edges of the portion of the pulse that is selected by the slicer.   This effect of the noise will depend upon the steepness of the sides of the pulse, which in turn depends upon the bandwidth of the system.   Thus in a pulse-modulated system employing pulses of constant amplitude, noise that is appreciably weaker than the pulses will be more completely suppressed the wider the bandwidth of the system.   This behavior is analogous to that of a wideband frequency-modulation system (page 962).

Practical Pulse Communication Systems.   Because they require a very wide frequency band, pulse communication systems normally operate at ultra-high or microwave frequencies.   They have found considerable use where multichannel voice communication is desired and wire communication is not practical, for example, in military applications where mobility is important, or over difficult terrain.   Pulse-position modulation is used[1] in the systems now in field use.

Distances greatly in excess of the line-of-sight range can be covered by relaying.   Here the signal, as received over a path short enough to give line-of-sight conditions, is retransmitted over a second line-of-sight path, and so on.

24-13. Pulse-code Modulation.[2]   Pulse-code modulation is a sophisticated form of pulse transmission.   In pulse-code transmission the peak-to-peak amplitude range available for the signal to be transmitted is divided into a number of standard values,[3] as shown in Fig. 24-25a.   The sample of signal is then transmitted, not as its actual amplitude, but rather as the nearest standard amplitude.   Thus actual amplitude a in Fig. 24-25b is transmitted as standard amplitude 3, whereas actual amplitude b would be transmitted as standard amplitude 4.   This process, which is termed *quantizing* the information, introduces a certain amount of error in the transmitted signal, as shown by comparing the solid and dotted curves of Fig. 23-25b, but this error is small if a large number of standard amplitudes are available to choose between.

The selected standard amplitude is not transmitted directly in pulse-code modulation, but rather is indicated by a code of pulses.[4]   Thus each

[1] Practical pulse communication equipment is described by H. S. Black, J. W. Beyer, T. J. Greiser, and F. A. Polkinghorn, A Multichannel Microwave Radio Relay System, *Trans. AIEE*, vol. 65, p. 798, December, 1946.

[2] An excellent discussion of the general principles involved in pulse-code modulation is given by B. M. Oliver, J. R. Pierce, and C. E. Shannon, The Philosophy of PCM, *Proc. IRE*, vol. 36, p. 1324, November, 1948.

[3] Although the standard values shown in Fig. 24-25a increase in amplitude in increments of fixed size, it is possible to taper the successive increments.

[4] Circuit arrangements for coding and decoding, and equipment for a complete pulse-code modulation system, are described by L. A. Meacham and E. Peterson, An Experimental Pulse-code Modulation System of Toll Quality, *Bell System Tech. J.*, vol. 27, p. 1, January, 1948.

of the eight standard amplitudes in Fig. 24-25a can be specified by a different combination of pulses in a three-place code in which a pulse may be either present or absent in each place, as indicated in Fig. 24-25a. Such a code corresponds to a system of numbers having base 2 (binary system), instead of the usual system of numbers having base 10. The total count or number is indicated in Fig. 24-25a, where pulses in positions going from right to left have values 1, 2, 4, etc., while the absence of a pulse denotes zero. It is seen that a seven-digit code is capable of transmitting $2^7 = 128$ standard amplitudes.

At the receiver the code of pulses is translated back to the corresponding standard amplitude. The simplest way to do this is to transmit the

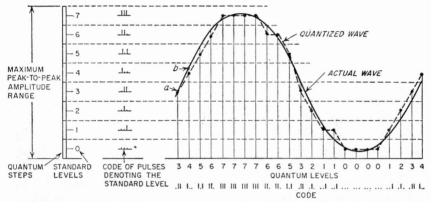

(a) QUANTIZING OF AMPLITUDE LEVEL AND LEVEL DESIGNATION BY A CODE OF PULSES

(b) REPRESENTATION OF A WAVE BY A SUCCESSION OF CODED PULSE GROUPS

Fig. 24-25. Basic concepts involved in pulse-code modulation.

code group in "reverse order," i.e., with units in the left-hand or first place, and with the pulse having the highest value in the right-hand or last place. Each received pulse is then caused to deliver a given charge to a capacitor. This capacitor is shunted by a resistor of such value that the charge on the capacitor leaks off to half amplitude in the time corresponding to the interval between pulses. At the end of the pulse group the voltage present on the capacitor then gives the standard amplitude that is represented by the code. This results from the fact that the full charge of the final pulse contributes to the voltage existing across the capacitor at the end of the pulse code, whereas the next-to-final pulse has decayed to half its original amplitude, and the second-from-final pulse contributes only one-fourth of its original amplitude, etc. Thus each pulse of the code makes a contribution to the total voltage in proportion to its numerical value in the binary system of numbers.

The receiving equipment will reproduce the correct standard amplitude provided it is able to recognize correctly the code of pulses. *Thus noise will not introduce any error whatsoever, provided only that the signal-to-noise ratio is such that the largest noise peaks will not be mistaken for pulses.* When the noise present is of the random type (circuit and tube noise) it is possible to determine mathematically for any given ratio of signal-to-average-noise power the probability that a noise peak of amplitude comparable with the pulse will occur. When this is done for 10^5 pulses per second, one obtains Table 24-1.

TABLE 24-1
ERROR RATE AS A FUNCTION OF SIGNAL-TO-NOISE RATIO

$\dfrac{\text{Signal power}}{\text{Average noise power}}$	Error rate (approx)
17 db	1 error in 0.1 sec
20 db	1 error in 20 min
22 db	1 error in 3 months

It is seen that there is a threshold signal-to-noise ratio of about 20 db, above which the noise produces virtually no errors. This is in contrast with other methods of transmitting information, where with signal-to-noise ratios even as great as 60 db the noise will still introduce some effect. Moreover, the error-free signal obtained with pulse-code modulation can be retransmitted, i.e., relayed, as many times as desired without the introduction of additional noise effects. In other systems, including frequency modulation, additional noise is introduced each time the signal is repeated.

The price paid to achieve this result is that each signal sample is transmitted as the nearest standard amplitude rather than as its actual level. The resulting error has a maximum value that is half the quantizing interval. Since all values of error up to this maximum are equally likely, the result is a fluctuating error component in the receiver output that has many of the characteristics of random noise. This error component is accordingly termed *quantizing noise*. The magnitude of the quantizing noise can be reduced to any desired extent by making the standard amplitude levels sufficiently close together. The relationship of the quantizing noise to the number of digits n in the binary code, assuming uniform quantum increments, is given approximately by the relation

$$\frac{\text{Peak signal power}}{\text{Average power of quantizing noise}} = (10.8 + 6n) \quad \text{db} \quad (24\text{-}2)$$

Thus with a seven-digit code, the quantizing noise will be approximately 53 db weaker than the peak signal that can be accommodated by the channel.

It follows from Eq. (24-2) that the signal-to-noise ratio in decibels will vary linearly with the number of digits in the code group. If now the entire code group is to be transmitted in a given length of time, then the pulses must be shorter and the bandwidth correspondingly greater, the larger the number of digits. Hence in a pulse-code modulation system operating with a signal strength that is above the threshold value, the signal-to-noise ratio in decibels at the receiver output will be directly proportional to the bandwidth of the system. This again is analogous to frequency modulation, and to pulse-width and pulse-position modulation. The principal application that has been made up to this time of pulse-code modulation is in multichannel telephone communciation over wire circuits, although the pulse-code groups could, of course, be modulated on a carrier wave and then transmitted as a radio signal. Pulse-code modulation has the advantage over other methods of modulation in that if the signal is kept above the threshold value, the signal can be repeated even hundreds of times and still remain free of tube and circuit noise. The noise in the output will therefore always be just the quantizing noise as given by Eq. (24-2), irrespective of circuit length.

PROBLEMS AND EXERCISES

24-1. List the principal advantages and disadvantages of high-level modulation as compared with low-level modulation in a radio transmitter.

24-2. Go through the mathematical steps required to show that the presence of the feedback loop $bcdefgh$ of Fig. 24-1 causes the degree of modulation at e produced by a given audio voltage e_a to be reduced by the factor $1/(1 - A\beta)$.

24-3. *a.* The feedback arrangement shown in Fig. 24-1 will largely prevent the hum modulation produced in the Class C amplifiers and harmonic generators by an incompletely filtered power supply from appearing in the envelope of the modulated wave delivered to the antenna. Explain the physical process by which this hum reduction is accomplished.

b. Will there be a similar reduction of hum modulation originating in the modulated and linear amplifiers?

24-4. Sketch the way the modulated wave delivered to the antenna in Fig. 24-1 will be distorted if the negative peaks of the rectifier output are clipped.

24-5. Draw a circuit diagram of a peak limiter that will compress peaks of negative polarity that exceed a given amplitude, while not affecting smaller amplitudes.

24-6. In a frequency-modulation transmitter, discuss the effect that the modulating frequency, the frequency deviation, and the carrier frequency have on the highest tank-circuit Q that is permissible in the final Class C amplifier. Assume that the frequency deviation is considerably greater than the modulating frequency.

24-7. A frequency-modulation broadcast station operating at 96.5 Mc employs a three-stage phase-shift modulator of the type illustrated in Fig. 17-13. If the modulating frequencies employed cover the range 60 to 12,000 cycles, and a maximum deviation of 75 kc is desired, specify the frequency of the crystal oscillator and an appropriate combination of harmonic generators in Fig. 24-2a.

25-8. The system shown for monitoring the frequency in Fig. 24-2b is observed to oscillate if the amplification of the d-c amplifier drops off too sharply as the frequency increases, whereas oscillations do not occur if the amplification falls off only slowly with the increasing frequency. Explain.

24-9. Is it possible for the frequency-control system of Fig. 24-3 to oscillate? Explain.

24-10. A radio-telegraph transmitter is keyed at a low power level by on-off keying in such a manner as to produce rounded dots and dashes. It is observed, however, that the key clicks will be more serious if the Class C stages following the keyed stage are operated highly saturated than if they are not saturated.   Explain.

24-11. Is it possible to achieve frequency-shift keying by the use of a phase-shift modulator?

24-12. Explain why one stage of intermediate-frequency amplification ordinarily contributes more to the sensitivity of a receiver than one stage of tuned-radio-frequency amplification employing the same amplifier tube type.

24-13. *a.* Which of the following sections of a receiver can affect the selectivity: radio-frequency section, mixer section, second detector, audio-frequency amplifier?

b. Which sections can affect the fidelity?

24-14. If a broadcast receiver is designed so that it discriminates very effectively against unwanted carrier frequencies only slightly different from the desired carrier, it is found that the fidelity at high audio frequencies is poor.   Explain.

24-15. In Fig. 24-10, the voltage applied to the plate of the beam tube by lead *b* contains a large hum component because it has been subjected only to partial filtering. Explain why the resulting hum appearing in the loudspeaker is relatively small when a beam power tube is used, but would be high if this tube were replaced by a triode.

24-16. Sketch a circuit analogous to Fig. 24-10, but for the reception of frequency-modulation signals.   Include one stage of tuned radio-frequency amplification; three intermediate-frequency stages, the last of which also serves as a limiter; and a ratio detector.

24-17. Explain why the intermediate-frequency amplification per stage is less in a frequency-modulation broadcast receiver than in an amplitude-modulation receiver using the same amplifier tubes.

24-18. Modify the schematic diagram of Fig. 24-6 to include provision for receiving on-off type of radio-telegraph signals.

24-19. Show by a sketch the effect on curve *b* in Fig. 24-12 of increasing the number of tubes controlled by the AVC system.

24-20. In Fig. 24-13*a* explain why the trimmer capacitance C_3 is much more important in determining the alignment at the high-frequency end of the tuning range than at the low-frequency end.

24-21. In Fig. 24-13*b* explain why the padding capacitor C_2 is proportionally more important in determining the alignment at the low-frequency end of the tuning range than at the high-frequency end.

24-22. Explain why the suppression of image signals will be more effective the higher the ratio of intermediate to signal frequencies.

24-23. *a.* In the whistle example on page 952, calculate and plot the frequency of the whistle as a function of the detuning of the local oscillator from its normal value of $910 + 455 = 1365$ kc, up to a whistle frequency of 10 kc.

b. Repeat for the case where the signal frequency is $3 \times 455 = 1365$ kc, and the normal value of oscillator frequency is $1365 + 455 = 1820$ kc.

24-24. It is desired to apply automatic frequency control to a triple-detection receiver.   Which of the two oscillators should have its frequency controlled, and why?

24-25. Modify the circuits of the receiver of Fig. 24-10 to incorporate automatic frequency control based on the circuit of Fig. 24-16.

24-26. Modify Fig. 24-6 in such a manner as to incorporate the schematic diagram of an automatic-frequency-control system analogous to that of Fig. 24-2*b*, which acts in such a way as to tend to make the intermediate frequency coincide rather closely with the frequency of a crystal oscillator.

24-27. Show a circuit diagram that will give squelch action in accordance with the method mentioned on page 955?

24-28. Justify the statement on page 955 that the bandwidth of the circuit of Fig.

27-17 depends in part upon the parallel resonant impedances of the circuits L_pC_p and L_sC_s.

24-29. Explain where in the circuit of Fig. 24-10 one would insert a meter-type tuning indicator.

24-30. On the assumption that noise power is proportional to bandwidth, demonstrate the correctness of the statement on page 957 that the signal-to-noise-power ratio of a single-sideband system is eight times that of a fully modulated double-sideband system for the same peak power.

24-31. In Fig. 24-18 discuss the advantages and disadvantages of using the crystal oscillator to provide the reinserted carrier instead of the reconditioned carrier. Be sure to include effects of fading signals in this assessment.

24-32. In receiving an amplitude-modulated signal, the most serious consequence of selective fading is associated with the fading out of the carrier. Does space diversity at the receiving point reduce the possibility of this situation arising?

24-33. In a particular radio-telegraph transmitter, frequency diversity is obtained by frequency-modulating the transmitter at 500 cycles. Determine the frequency deviation that is required to make the carrier and the two first-order sideband components of the wave have equal amplitudes, so that most of the transmitted power is divided relatively equally among three frequencies.

24-34. A particular receiver possessing no image rejection is found experimentally to have a noise figure of 9 db. The receiver is then modified so that the response to image signals is reduced by 3 db. What is the noise figure of the modified receiver?

24-35. A particular amplitude-modulated receiver operating at 100 Mc has a band width of 10 kc and a noise figure of 6 db. If a half-wave receiving antenna is used, calculate the field strength required at the receiving antenna to produce a signal-to-noise ratio in the receiver output of 20 db. Ignore the effect of the ground.

24-36. A microwave receiver employs a parabolic receiving antenna having a diameter of 2 m. The associated receiver has a noise figure of 16 db and a bandwidth of 1.5 Mc. Calculate the strength of the field that must be present at the receiving point in order to make the ratio of signal to noise in the receiver equal 20 db. Note that the results are independent of wavelength.

24-37. In a receiver using a stage of pentode radio-frequency amplification, why is the noise figure improved if the screen-grid current is low?

24-38. A radio receiver possesses equal bandwidths in the radio- and intermediate-frequency sections, and has a noise figure of 12 db. To what value would the noise figure be changed if the bandwidth of the intermediate-frequency amplifier were doubled while leaving the bandwidth of the radio-frequency section unchanged and (*a*) all the set noise came from the first detector, and (*b*) half the set noise came from the first detector, the remaining half coming from the radio-frequency section?

24-39. *a.* A 6SA7 mixer operated under the conditions given in Table 12-3 (page 438) has applied to it a signal voltage developed across a circuit having a parallel resonant impedance of 50,000 ohms. Calculate the signal voltage that must be developed across this circuit in order to achieve a 20-db signal-to-noise ratio for a bandwidth of 10 kc. Assume that the room temperature is 291°K.

b. Repeat the calculations when a 6AC7 pentode mixer is used.

c. Would there be any substantial further improvement in the behavior if a triode mixer were used in place of the pentode mixer?

24-40. In a particular frequency-modulation broadcast situation, the signal-to-noise ratio at the limiter input of the receiver is 10 db. What is the signal-to-noise ratio in decibels at the receiver output for modulation frequencies of 100 and 10,000 cycles, when the frequency deviation is (*a*) 75 kc and (*b*) 15 kc?

24-41. In frequency modulation, it is found that if preemphasis is employed, then for a fixed maximum frequency deviation, the frequency deviation at the lower audio frequencies will be less than for the same maximum deviation in the absence of pre-emphasis. Explain.

24-42. What will be the effect of designing a frequency-modulation receiver to handle a maximum frequency deviation that is substantially greater than the frequency deviation of the signals to be observed? Consider both circuit noise that is weaker than the signal and pulse noise that is stronger than the signal.

24-43. How much greater must the transmitter power be in a 75-kc deviation system than in a 15-kc deviation system in order to achieve the same degree of freedom from sputter arising from the intermittent capture of the system by noise peaks of unusually high amplitude?

24-44. In a frequency-modulation system, it is found that with a given transmitter power the maximum range at which a usable signal can be received will be greater the narrower the bandwidth of the system. Explain.

24-45. In receiving amplitude-modulated signals from a given transmitter, does changing from a wideband receiver to one having a bandwidth barely able to accommodate the sidebands affect the maximum range at which the signal is usable?

24 46. Is there any difference between the maximum range at which amplitude- and frequency-modulation signals will be usable when the carrier power is the same, and the same bandwidth is used in the receivers?

24-47. It is sometimes claimed that frequency-modulation broadcasting has higher intrinsic fidelity than amplitude-modulation broadcasting. Discuss whether or not this is necessarily true, assuming that the amplitude-modulation system uses the same power, carrier frequency, and range of modulation frequencies.

24-48. What advantage, if any, does frequency-shift keying have over on-off keying in the presence of (a) noise that is weaker than the signal, and (b) pulse noise much stronger than the signal.

24-49. Devise a method of producing pulse-width modulation that differs from the method shown in Fig. 24-21.

24-50. Devise a method of producing position-modulation pulses which consists in starting with a phase-modulated sinusoidal wave and deriving the pulses from this.

24-51. Note that if the position-modulated pulses of Fig. 24-20d are applied to a bandpass filter having a passband centered on the pulse repetition frequency, one obtains a phase-modulated wave in which the carrier frequency is the pulse repetition frequency. How can this fact be utilized to provide a system of reception for position-modulated pulses?

24-52. In pulse-position modulation, the *average* transmitter power required in order to make the pulses stronger than the noise is independent of the bandwidth of the system, even though the amount of noise power present is proportional to the bandwidth. Explain how this can be so.

24-53. Draw a diagram similar to Fig. 24-25, but applicable to a pulse code employing four digits.

24-54. In a seven-digit pulse code, show the combination of pulses that represents the following numbers: 6, 23, 58, 84, 125.

24-55. Is it desirable to introduce a slicer, or a peak or base limiter, in the receiver of pulse-code modulation signals?

24-56. In pulse-code modulation is it possible by any combination of limiting and/or slicing, and large bandwidth, to prevent errors arising from noise pulses having greater intensity than the pulses of the code group?

24-57. Sketch as a function of time the voltage across the decoding capacitor discussed on page 971, when the pulse group being received is a three-digit code representing a value of 7. Repeat for values of 5 and 2.

CHAPTER 25

TELEVISION

25-1. Elements of a System of Television.[1] Television is accomplished by successively exploring different portions of the scene to be reproduced, using a "camera" tube that at each instant develops a voltage proportional to the light intensity of the portion of the scene under examination. The varying voltage that results from this *scanning* process is amplified and then modulated upon a radio-frequency carrier wave that is radiated. The television receiver synthesizes the original scene on the fluorescent screen of a cathode-ray tube[2] by causing the cathode-ray spot to trace over successive portions of the reproduced scene in accordance with the scanning of the original scene, while at the same time varying the brightness of the spot in accordance with the envelope amplitude of the received signal. When the scanning process is carried out with sufficient rapidity, the illusion of continuous motion is achieved.

In television broadcasting it is necessary that all transmitters employ the same picture shape, the same procedure in scanning the scene to be transmitted, the same means for synchronizing the receivers, etc. Otherwise, it would not be possible for a given receiver to reproduce satisfactory pictures from different transmitters. The government therefore establishes standards to which all television broadcast transmitters are required to conform.

Scanning Sequence—Interlacing. The standard television picture employed in the United States has a ratio of width to height of 4:3. The scanning sequence when looking at the picture tube is shown in Fig. 25-1. The scanning spot starts in the upper left-hand corner and travels at a uniform rate from left to right along lines that lie at a constant distance below each other, as shown by the solid lines in Fig. 25-1*a*. When the end of a line such as *ab* is reached, the scanning spot quickly returns to

---

[1] For a more extensive treatment of the subject of television see Glenn M. Glasford, "Fundamentals of Television Engineering," McGraw-Hill Book Company, Inc., New York, 1955; H. A. Chinn, "Television Broadcasting," McGraw-Hill Book Company, Inc., New York, 1953; K. Fowler and H. B. Lippert, "Television Fundamentals," McGraw-Hill Book Company, Inc., New York, 1953; D. G. Fink, "Television Engineering," McGraw-Hill Book Company, Inc., New York, 1952; V. K. Zworykin and G. A. Morton, "Television," 2d ed., John Wiley & Sons, Inc., New York, 1954.

[2] The cathode-ray tube used in a television receiver is often called a picture tube.

the left, i.e., from *b* to *c*, to start a new line *cd*; during this return interval
the spot is blanked out and so is not shown in the figure. As the scanning
spot travels back and forth across the tube, the spot also moves downward
at a constant rate; the lines in Fig. 25-1*a* are hence slightly sloped, and
each line begins at a level that is a little below the end of the previous line.
When the bottom of the picture is reached (point *f* in Fig. 25-1*a*), the spot
quickly returns to point *g* at the top of the picture while maintaining the
back and forth horizontal line motion uninterrupted. Since the time
required to travel from *f* to *g* corresponds to the passage of a number of
lines, the spot traverses a path of the character shown in Fig. 25-1*b* as it

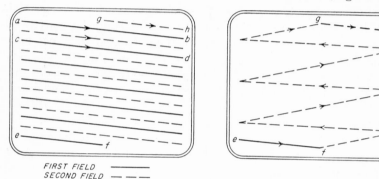

FIRST FIELD ————
SECOND FIELD — — —

(*a*) SCANNING RASTER

(*b*) PATH OF SPOT DURING
VERTICAL RETURN (SCHEMATIC)

FIG. 25-1. The scanning sequence for interlaced scanning. For the sake of clarity,
the spacing between the lines in the vertical direction is enormously exaggerated.

goes from *f* to *g*. This return pattern is not seen by the eye, however, as
the spot is blanked out during the return.

The standard television picture takes $\frac{1}{60}$ sec to go from the top to the
bottom of the picture and return to the top. During this time, which is
called one *field*, 262.5 lines are transmitted. Because each field contains
a half line, the next field lies between the lines of the first field as shown
by the dotted lines in Fig. 25-1*a*; thus successive fields are *interlaced*. The
complete picture, called a *frame*, therefore consists of 525 lines, and is
transmitted in $\frac{1}{30}$ sec.* The pattern shown at Fig. 25-1*a* is what is
observed on a television receiver in the absence of a picture, and is termed
the *raster*.

Interlacing makes it possible to avoid flicker while using the lowest

* In scanning motion-picture film, a complication arises from the fact that the
standard frame rate for film is 24 per second, while the standard television frame rate
corresponding to two interlaced fields is 30 per second. This problem is solved by
arranging so that successive film frames are scanned two and three times, respectively,
at the 60-cycle television field rate. This causes the *average* frame rate of the film to
be 24 per second, and results in a reproduced picture that appears to the eye to be
essentially the same as though the frame rates of the film and of the television system
were the same.

repetition frequency for the picture that will satisfactorily portray motion. Thus, while a picture repetition rate of 30 times per second is adequate to give the illusion of continuous motion under nearly all circumstances, large bright areas repeated 30 times per second will have a noticeable flicker. By interlacing as in Fig. 25-1, a flicker rate of 60 cycles is achieved, which is too high to be perceptible; at the same time the picture is repeated only 30 times a second.

Blanking Pulses. During the horizontal- and vertical-return intervals, the picture tube is made inoperative by means of *blanking* pulses. These pulses are generated at the transmitting station, and are modulated on the transmitter carrier for use by the television receivers tuned to the transmitter.

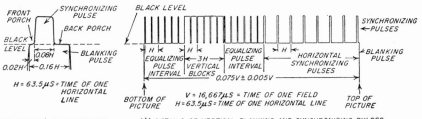

(*a*) DETAILS OF HORIZONTAL BLANKING AND SYNCHRONIZING PULSES

(*b*) DETAILS OF VERTICAL BLANKING AND SYNCHRONIZING PULSES

FIG. 25-2. Details of blanking, synchronizing, and equalizing pulses.

In the television standards of the United States, the blanking pulses for the horizontal retrace are allocated 16 per cent of the time available for scanning one line, or about 10 μsec (see Fig. 25-2a). This means the spot moves across the picture from left to right in 53.5 μsec. Similarly, the vertical blanking pulses occupy between 7 and 8 per cent of the total time, and so have a length of about 1250 μsec (see Fig. 25-2a). The number of active lines in the picture is therefore approximately 485.

Synchronization. Synchronization between the scanning operations at the transmitter and at the receiver is accomplished by means of special pulses that are generated at the transmitting station and modulated on the radiated carrier wave. These synchronizing pulses are transmitted during the blanking periods; they therefore do not show on the reproduced picture.

The pulses used for horizontal or line synchronization in the United States standards are 5 μsec long, and are superimposed on the horizontal blanking pulses in the manner shown in Fig. 25-2a.[1] The leading vertical edges of the line synchronizing pulses must be very accurately timed, and for best results should be very steep.

[1] The short interval between the beginning of the blanking pulse and the beginning of the synchronizing pulse is commonly called the *front porch*, while the corresponding interval after the end of the synchronizing pulse is termed the *back porch*, as indicated in Fig. 25-2a.

In the standard United States television signal, the vertical synchronizing pulses are distinguished from the horizontal synchronizing pulses by being given a length equal to the time required by three lines. This is approximately 19 times the length of the horizontal synchronizing pulses. Horizontal synchronization is maintained during the presence of the vertical synchronizing pulses by serrations that break up the vertical synchronizing pulse into six "blocks," as illustrated in Fig. 25-2b. These serrations have twice the line frequency, and are so timed that the rise of every other serration occurs at the instant the horizontal synchronizing pulse would have risen in amplitude if it had been present.

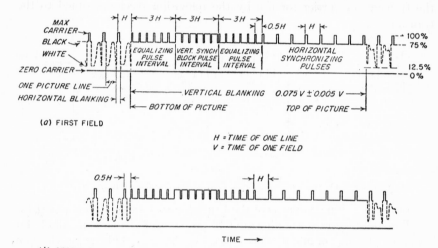

(a) FIRST FIELD

H = TIME OF ONE LINE
V = TIME OF ONE FIELD

(b) SECOND FIELD

Fig. 25-3. Standard envelope for a modulated carrier, according to United States television standards.

Field-frequency irregularities due to the interlacing are minimized, as explained on page 996, by introducing six so-called *equalizing pulses* just before and just after the vertical blocks in place of three horizontal synchronizing pulses, as shown in Fig. 25-2b. These equalizing pulses have twice the repetition frequency of the horizontal synchronizing pulses, and are half as long. They maintain horizontal synchronization just as do the serrations in the vertical blocks, and simultaneously provide brief time intervals just before and just after the vertical synchronizing blocks that are identical for both fields of the interlaced scanning pattern, as shown in Fig. 25-3.

Standard Signal for Television Transmitters. The television standards of the United States specify that the signal modulated on the transmitter carrier have the character shown in Fig. 25-3. Here black is represented by an amplitude that is 75 per cent of the maximum envelope amplitude, while white corresponds to an amplitude normally about 12.5 per cent of the maximum. The blanking pulses correspond to black, while the synchronizing and equalizing pulses occupy the range between 75 and 100 per cent of maximum envelope amplitude, and so are transmitted as "blacker than black."

The synchronizing, blanking, and equalizing pulses of the standard signal are produced by a combination of oscillators, pulse generators, frequency dividers, clippers, gates, etc., termed the *synchronizing generator*. All of the individual operations performed by the synchronizing generator are described in Chap. 18 or elsewhere in this volume. However, the details are quite involved, because of the variety of different operations to be performed, and because of the precise time relations that are required between different parts of the standard signal.[1]

25-2. Television Camera Tubes— the Image Orthicon. At the television transmitter, a special tube called a camera or pickup tube scans an optical image of the scene to be transmitted, and develops an output voltage that varies in accordance with the light intensity of successive elements of this image. Although many types of camera tubes have been devised, nearly all television with live pickup is now accomplished with the aid of either the image-orthicon or the vidicon camera tube. When a slide or motion picture film is to be reproduced, the iconoscope[2] and the flying-spot scanner also find use.

The structure of the image-orthicon camera tube[3] is shown schematically in Fig. 25-4a. Referring first to the image section, this includes a photosensitive surface operated at a very negative potential, a target plate of thin glass of low resistivity, and a screen having about 1000 meshes per inch and located only a few thousandths of an inch from the target. The photosensitive film is so thin that when an optical image is focused on its left-hand side, photoelectrons are emitted from the right-hand side in proportion to the light intensity. These electrons are attracted toward the screen but most of them pass through the meshes and strike the target. Focusing means, described below, cause all of the electrons originating from a given point on the photosensitive surface to focus at a common point on the target. As these primary electrons strike the target they produce secondary electrons that are drawn to the screen, leaving positive charges on the target having an intensity distribu-

---

[1] For further information on this subject, the reader is referred to Glenn M. Glasford, *op. cit.*

[2] The iconoscope was for a number of years the best television camera tube available. It is now obsolescent, however, having been displaced by the image orthicon. This has come about because the latter is able to produce a usable picture at much lower levels of illumination. Since the iconoscope is now on its way out, it is not described in this edition. Information on it can be found in "Radio Engineering," 3d ed., and in the references listed on p. 977.

[3] For further details see R. B. Janes, R. E. Johnson, and R. S. Moore, Development and Performance of Television Camera Tubes, *RCA Rev.*, vol. 10. p. 191, June, 1949.

tion that reproduces the light distribution of the optical image projected on the photocathode.

The back of the target plate (the right-hand side in Fig. 25-4) is then scanned in accordance with the standard scanning sequence by an electron beam produced by a cathode that is at zero (ground) potential. This beam deposits just enough electrons at each point on the back of the target to neutralize the positive charge on the image side; the remaining electrons in the scanning beam are returned toward the gun. The target

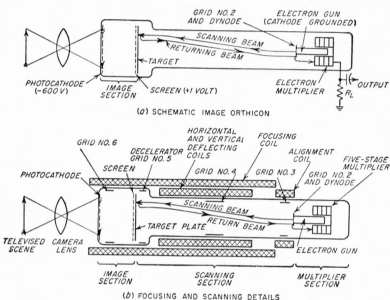

(a) SCHEMATIC IMAGE ORTHICON

(b) FOCUSING AND SCANNING DETAILS

Fig. 25-4. Schematic diagram of an image-orthicon camera tube.

plate is made of glass having a conductance such that the electrons deposited on the target by the scanning beam will leak through the target plate and neutralize the positive charge on the opposite side of in the $\frac{1}{30}$ sec that elapses between successive scans.[1] Accordingly, as the electron beam scans the target it deposits electrons in proportion to the light intensity during the previous $\frac{1}{30}$ sec of the successive portions of the optical image. The current in the returning electron beam therefore varies in amplitude in accordance with the variations of the light intensity of the successive portions of the optical image being scanned.

Most of the electrons in the return beam strike the aperture of the electron gun (i.e., grid 2), the surface of which is treated to be a good emitter of secondary electrons.[2] The secondary electrons thus produced

---

[1] Making the target very thin leaves little opportunity for the charges to leak parallel to the surface of the target and so destroy the fine detail.

[2] An electrode designed in this way to serve as an emitter of secondary electrons is often called a *dynode*, meaning dynatron electrode.

are deflected into an electron-multiplier system consisting of a succession of surfaces at progressively higher positive potentials, treated to give relatively high secondary-electron emission, and so arranged that the secondary electrons produced at one surface are focused upon the next. In this way the secondary electrons produced by the returning beam when striking grid 2 will produce still more secondary electrons upon striking the next surface, and so on. Since the number of secondary electrons is always exactly proportional to the number of incident electrons, the output of the electron multiplier is an amplified reproduction of the current in the returning beam.

The output of the electron multiplier accordingly varies in the general manner shown in Fig. 25-5. The maximum possible output current represents the full beam current after passage through the electron multiplier, and corresponds to black. Output currents less than this maximum represent increasing lighter shades of gray. The minimum possible output current is obtained when the positive potential of the target

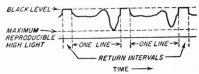

FIG. 25-5. Typical variation with time of the output current of an image-orthicon tube.

plate equals the screen potential, so that secondary electrons produced at the target in the image section cease to be drawn to the screen. Light intensities greater than the value required to bring this about obviously have no additional effect on the output. In between these limits, the output current of the image orthicon varies linearly with light intensity.

Blanking pulses are applied to the target screen with negative polarity during the horizontal- and vertical-return portions of the scanning sequence. This prevents the electrons in the scanning beam from reaching the target plate, with the result that during the retrace period the output of the image orthicon corresponds to black, as indicated in Fig. 25-5.

In the image-orthicon tube of Fig. 25-4a, some of the focusing electrodes, as well as arrangements for producing the magnetic fields used in focusing and scanning the beam, were omitted to avoid confusing the explanation. These details are shown schematically in Fig. 25-4b. The focusing coil produces magnetic-flux lines parallel to the axis of the tube, and in conjunction with grid 4 brings the scanning beam into focus at the target. Grid 3 serves to control the motion of the secondary electrons produced by the returning beam in such a manner as to guide them into the electron multiplier. Grid 5, adjacent to the target, decelerates the scanning beam so that it strikes the target at a low velocity, yet still remains in proper focus at all times during the scanning operation. The electron beam is caused to scan the target by means of saw-tooth waves of current that are passed through two sets of deflecting coils arranged to produce horizontal and vertical transverse magnetic fields. The alignment coil produces a magnetic field that aligns the beam as it leaves the electron gun.

In the image section, the electrons emitted by the photocathode are focused on the target by the combined action of the electrostatic field set up by the ringlike accelerator grid 6 and the axial magnetic field of the focusing coil. By proper adjustment of the voltage between cathode and target in relationship to the strength of the magnetic field and the potential on grid 6, it is possible through the mechanism discussed in connection with Fig. 7-8 to focus at a single spot on the target all of the electrons originating at a given spot on the cathode.

The lowest level of illumination that can be employed with an image-orthicon camera tube is less than required for fast motion-picture film. This minimum level is determined by the shot noise in the output current of the electron multiplier, rather than by thermal noise in the output load resistance R_L or by the noise of the subsequent amplifier tube.

The finest detail that a typical image orthicon will reproduce under ordinary operating conditions approximates the full detail possible in a picture having about 500 lines. If special care is used in adjusting the tube, even better resolution is obtainable.

25-3. The Vidicon.[1] The vidicon camera tube makes use of semiconducting material such as amorphous selenium, which is characterized by a resistance that decreases upon exposure to light.[2] The method of using such photoconductivity in a camera tube can be explained with the aid of Fig. 25-6. Here the signal plate is a conducting metallic film so thin that it is transparent. One side of this plate is coated with a very thin layer (0.0002 in.) of the photoconductive material. The optical image is focused on the other side of the signal plate, and the photoconductive material is scanned with an electron beam originating at a cathode that is at a potential of about -30 volts with respect to the signal plate.

The scanning beam deposits just enough electrons on each spot that it touches to reduce the potential of that side of the photoconductive material to cathode potential. Thus immediately after being scanned, the potential difference across a given spot on the photoconductive material approximates 30 volts. However, during the $\frac{1}{30}$-sec interval between

---

[1] For further information see B. H. Vine, R. B. Janes, and F. S. Veith, Performance of the Vidicon, a Small Developmental Television Camera Tube, *RCA Rev.*, vol. 13, p. 3, March, 1952.

[2] The conductivity of a semiconductor is affected by light because light provides energy that aids in the production of free carriers from the breaking of covalent bonds or from donor or acceptor action (thus see page 745). The effect of light will be important when the energy-band relations in the semiconductor are such that the number of additional current carriers resulting from the presence of the light is appreciable compared with the number of carriers produced by thermal effects in the absence of light, i.e., in the dark.

successive scans, charge leaks through the photoconducting material at a
rate determined by the intensity of the illumination to which this part of
the photoconducting material is subjected.[1]   Hence the charge deposited
on any particular part of the photoconducting material the next time it is
scanned will be sufficient to replace those electrons that have been lost by
leakage since the last passage of the electron beam.   The result is that

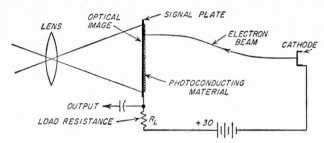

Fig. 25-6. Schematic diagram useful in explaining operation of the vidicon camera tube.

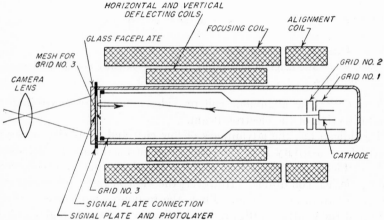

Fig. 25-7. Schematic diagram of a complete vidicon tube, together with associated
coils for focusing, deflecting, and aligning the electron beam.

as the electron beam scans the surface of the photoconductive material,
the charge it deposits varies with time in accordance with the variations in
the illumination of the successive elements of the photoconductive film.
The current through the load resistance R_L, and hence the output voltage,
therefore reproduces the variations in the light intensity of the successive
portions of the optical image being scanned.

The details of a practical vidicon camera tube are shown in Fig. 25-7.
Here the signal plate is deposited directly on the flat glass end of the tube.
The scanning beam is formed by the combination of the cathode, control
grid 1, accelerating grid 2, and anode grid 3.   The beam velocity inside of

[1] The leakage conductance is made low enough so that only a part of the total
charge leaks off during $\frac{1}{30}$ sec.

grid 3 is approximately 300 volts.   The beam emerges from grid 3 through a fine mesh screen having 500 to 1000 meshes per inch, which provides a uniform decelerating field adjacent to the photoconductive layer that slows down the electrons as they approach the layer.   The focusing coil provides an axial magnetic field of such strength in relationship to the length of the tube and the velocity of the electrons as to cause all electrons emitted from the aperture in grid 2 to focus at a common point on the photoconductive surface in accordance with the principles discussed in connection with Fig. 7-8.   Vertical and horizontal deflection of the beam is achieved by passing saw-tooth current waves through deflecting coils that produce transverse horizontal and vertical magnetic fields,

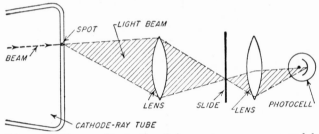

FIG. 25-8. Schematic diagram illustrating flying-spot scanner arranged for use with transparent slides.

respectively.   The alignment coil provides a means of controlling the initial direction of the electron beam.

The vidicon has the advantages of low cost and simplicity of adjustment.   Its sensitivity is of the same order of magnitude as that of the image orthicon, and resolutions of the order of 350 lines can be achieved under practical conditions.   However, the vidicon tubes presently available have two disadvantages.   First, the response characteristic is nonlinear and the contrast with bright illumination is less than given by the image orthicon.   Second, the resistance of the photoconductive film does not vary instantaneously with changes in light intensity, but rather takes time to adjust itself to a new level of illumination; as a result very rapid motion is not reproduced entirely satisfactorily.   It is reasonable to expect, however, that within a few years improved photoconductive materials will be developed that will largely eliminate these disadvantages of the vidicon tube.   When this occurs, photoconductive camera tubes may well make the image orthicon obsolete.

25-4. Flying-spot Scanner.   The flying-spot scanner is used for reproducing slides, and also with motion-picture film.   The essential features of a flying-spot scanning system for transparent slides are shown in Fig. 25-8.   Here a light spot produced by a cathode-ray tube with very short persistence is focused on the slide as shown.   The light transmitted through the slide is then projected on a photocell, often of the electron-multiplier type, the output of which is the output of the flying-spot scanner. Scanning of the slide is achieved by deflecting the spot of the cathode-ray tube in accordance with the standard scanning sequence.

Flying-spot scanning of motion-picture film is accomplished by moving the film continuously past the scanning area. Compensating motion of the spot is then introduced by a system of rotating mirrors such that during the scanning interval of a single frame of the film, the action is equivalent to a stationary film.[1]

25-5. Frequency Band and Resolution. The detail of a television picture in the vertical direction is determined by the number of scanning lines, since gradations in the light intensity of the image in the vertical direction that take place in a distance less than the width of a line obviously cannot be reproduced. Resolution in the horizontal direction is similarly determined by the rapidity with which the television system is able to respond to abrupt changes, i.e., by the frequency band that the television system transmits.

The frequency band required by a television signal conforming to United States standards can be estimated as follows: Assume first that in scanning a horizontal line the transition from black to white is to be accomplished in a distance along the line equal to the spacing between adjacent lines. With 485 active lines in a picture, and a width-to-height ratio of 4:3, this distance is $1/(485 \times 1.33) = 0.00155$ of the active length of one line, and corresponds to a time interval of $0.00155 \times 53.5 = 0.08$ μsec. From Eq. (9-1) it follows that a video system which will permit the response to rise from a minimum to a maximum in this length of time without overshoot must have a bandwidth of not less than $0.35/0.08 = 4.375$ Mc. A larger bandwidth than this will give greater horizontal resolution; a reduction in the bandwidth degrades the horizontal resolution. It will be noted that these bandwidths in all cases are easily adequate to transmit the synchronizing, equalizing, and blanking pulses.

25-6. Television Transmitters. *Standard Television Channel.* Television broadcasting stations in the United States are assigned channels 6 Mc wide, arranged as shown in Fig. 25-9a. Vestigial sideband transmission is used (see page 543), with the picture carrier 1.25 Mc above the low-frequency end of the band. A frequency band slightly over 4.25 Mc wide is available for the upper sideband.

The sound accompanying the television picture signal is obtained by use of a separate frequency-modulation transmitter having a maximum frequency deviation of 25 kc, and a carrier frequency 4.5 Mc greater than the picture carrier.

Television stations are assigned channels in the frequency range from

---

[1] A good description of the principal features involved in such a system is given by R. E. Graham, Continuous Scanner for Televising Film, *Bell Lab. Record*, vol. 32, p. 25, July, 1954.

54 to 88 Mc (omitting 72 to 76 Mc), 174 to 216 Mc, and 470 to 890 Mc. The first two of these ranges lie in the very high-frequency (VHF) range, while the third is in the ultra-high-frequency (UHF) band.

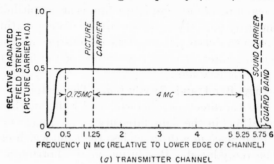

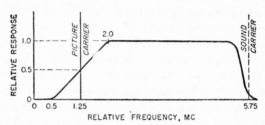

Fig. 25-9. Standard vestigial-sideband channel used in television transmitters, together with response characteristics of receiver for use with such transmitters.

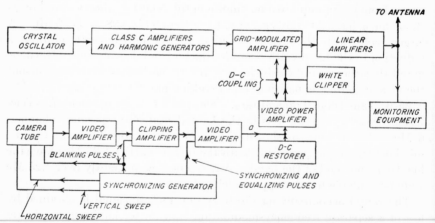

Fig. 25-10. Simplified block-circuit diagram of television transmitter.

Radio-frequency System of Television Transmitter. Figure 25-10 gives a schematic block diagram of a typical television transmitter. It indicates the principal features of such equipment, but for the sake of simplicity omits many of the details that are necessarily included in a system that is to be used in practice.

The radio-frequency system consists of a crystal oscillator, buffer amplifier and harmonic generators, grid-modulated Class C amplifier, and generally one or more linear amplifiers. Grid modulation is always employed because video modulating power is difficult to obtain; low-level modulation followed by linear amplification is likewise commonly used for the same reason. The vestigial-sideband characteristic of Fig. 25-9a is obtained by tuning the tank circuits of the linear amplifiers to one side of the carrier frequency in such a way as to discriminate against the lower sideband in the manner specified for the standard channel.[1]

In television transmitters for the very high-frequency band, the final power amplifier is typically an especially designed triode employed in a grounded-grid push-pull circuit. For the ultra-high-frequency band, the final power tube is normally a high-power klystron, such as illustrated in Fig. 19-2.

Video System and the Composite Video Signal. The video output of the camera tube is first amplified to a moderate level, at which point the blanking pulses are inserted. The clipper amplifier cuts off the tops of the blanking pulses at a level just beyond the black level. This makes the tops of the blanking pulses flat irrespective of noise or hum, and simultaneously makes certain that the receiver will be blanked out during the return periods. The synchronizing and equalizing pulses are then inserted into the system as shown.

The resulting composite video signal containing the synchronizing, equalizing, and blanking pulses, and the amplified camera tube output, then undergoes further video amplification to bring it up to the power level required to modulate the transmitter. The final video amplifier is direct coupled to the modulated amplifier in such a manner as to amplify d-c voltages as well as video-frequency voltages applied to the grid of the amplifier. A clamping circuit providing d-c restoration is then associated with the grid circuit of the final video amplifier; this is arranged to apply a d-c voltage to the grid of the video amplifier tube of such amplitude that the positive peaks of the synchronizing pulses always drive the grid of the modulated amplifier to the same positive peak voltage with respect to the cathode,[2] irrespective of the brightness of the picture being transmitted.

The effect of d-c restoration is to line up the tips of the synchronizing

---

[1] In the case of high-level modulation, where the modulated stage develops the final output power, the required vestigial-sideband characteristic is obtained by means of a suitable filter placed between the tank circuit of the modulated stage and the antenna.

[2] In some cases, a keyed clamping circuit is employed, in which the keying is so timed as to clamp the back porch of the blanking pulses at a level that is 75 per cent of the peak voltage that the synchronizing pulses should have. This arrangement has the advantage that it sets the black level at a value that is independent of any variations in the amplitude of successive synchronizing pulses.

pulses (and hence the blanking level), as shown in Fig. 25-11*b*, irrespective of the picture brightness.   Before d-c restoration the video signal for this case is as shown in Fig. 25-11*a*, and if modulated on the transmitted carrier would obviously not produce an envelope in which all of the blanking pulses were at the same level, as required in the standard signal.

The "white clipper" associated with final video stage in Fig. 25-10 is a negative peak clipper that prevents the negative peaks of the composite signal voltage after d-c restoration from ever dropping to less than 12.5 per cent of the peak amplitude of the synchronizing pulses.

The entire video system, from camera tube to the grid of the modulated amplifier, must have a 3-db bandwidth of about 4.4 Mc, as explained in

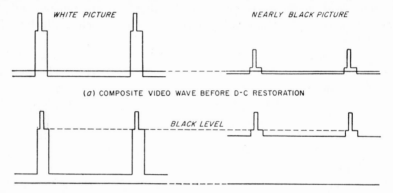

(*a*) COMPOSITE VIDEO WAVE BEFORE D-C RESTORATION

(*b*) COMPOSITE -VIDEO WAVE AFTER D-C RESTORATION

Fig. 25-11. Composite video waves before and after d-c restoration, showing how d-c restoration causes the blanking level to be independent of the average brightness of the picture.

Sec. 25-5.   The individual stages should also be designed for low overshoot.   The sag of the over-all system must likewise be limited to a maximum value that will not produce visible effects in the reproduced picture, which means something of the order of 10 to 20 per cent.

The Transmitting Antenna.   The antenna used with a television transmitter is normally arranged to have directivity in the vertical plane that concentrates the radiated energy along the horizon.   The antenna must be of the wideband type; also the antenna impedance must match that of the associated transmission line very closely over the entire 6-Mc band of the standard television channel.   Otherwise, weak delayed images or "ghosts" are produced as a result of waves reflected from the antenna back to the transmitter, where they are again reflected and finally radiated with a time delay corresponding to twice the electrical length of the antenna transmission line.

Horizontal polarization is standard for television broadcasting in the United States.   A horizontally polarized radiation pattern that is circular in the horizontal plane can be obtained with a turnstile, a horizontal loop, or a slotted cylinder (see page 923); vertical directivity can be achieved by stacking such antennas vertically and exciting the different units in the same phase to give a vertical broadside array.

The same antenna is often used for both the picture and sound transmitters. This is done by a bridge arrangement, termed a *diplexer*, that makes it possible for the two transmitters to feed their power into a single radiating structure without interacting upon each other in any manner. A diplexer for a turnstile antenna is shown in Fig. 25-12. Here two of the bridge arms are provided by the two sets of antennas that make up the turnstile,[1] while the remaining two arms are reactances provided by appropriate capacitances (or inductances). When the bridge is balanced, none of the output of one transmitter can reach the other transmitter, yet all of the power generated by each transmitter is delivered to the antenna system.

25-7. Television Receivers. The block diagram of a representative television receiver is shown in Fig. 25-13. Up to the output of the second detector this is similar to any other amplitude-modulated superheterodyne receiver for the same frequency range (see Fig.

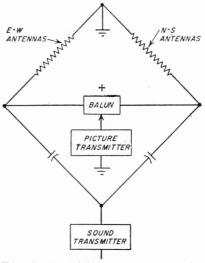

Fig. 25-12. Diplexer arrangement for permitting sound and picture transmitters to use a common antenna

24-6), except for the wideband required to accommodate the television signal. The radio-frequency section of the receiver typically contains one or two stages of tuned radio-frequency amplification; these stages aid in achieving a good noise figure (Sec. 24-9), provide image rejection, and prevent radiation of local oscillator energy. A low-noise converter system is also employed, commonly a triode with separate oscillator.

The intermediate-frequency amplifier typically consists of three or four stagger-tuned stages of appropriate bandwidth. The intermediate frequency in television receivers designed exclusively for the very high-frequency band is usually about 26 Mc for the picture carrier; however, in receivers intended to handle signals in the ultra-high-frequency band, intermediate frequencies in the range of 41 to 46 Mc are often used in order to improve image rejection.

The frequency-response characteristic of the intermediate-frequency

---

[1] Provision for the 90° phase shift required by the turnstile arrangement is not shown separately, but is a part of the antennas indicated in Fig. 25-12.

amplifier as observed at the input to the second detector should vary with frequency over the channel as indicated in Fig. 25-9b. When the vestigial-sideband signal of Fig. 25-9a is applied to a receiver with this response, the frequency-response characteristic of the over-all transmitter-receiver combination will be constant for video-modulation frequencies from zero up to over 4 Mc. The required shape of receiver response is typically obtained by making the 3-db bandwidth of the intermediate-frequency system about 5.5 Mc, and then coupling a broadly resonant circuit to the first intermediate-frequency tuned circuit in such a way as to reduce the response at the carrier frequency to 50 per cent of

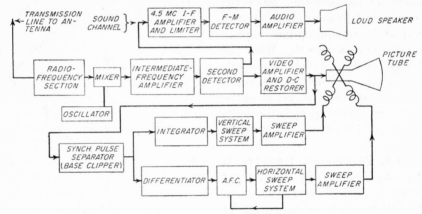

FIG. 25-13. Simplified block diagram of a television receiver.

the value that would otherwise be obtained. In order to permit the use of the intercarrier sound system (see below) the response characteristic of the intermediate-frequency system should be so shaped that the response to the sound carrier is about 10 per cent of the maximum response.

The second detector is always either a vacuum or germanium diode, with low load resistance and small shunting capacitance in order to achieve the required bandwidth.

Separation and Reproduction of Sound—Intercarrier-sound System. In the receiver shown in Fig. 25-13, the picture signal applied to the second detector acts as a local oscillator that beats against the frequency-modulated sound carrier to produce a component in the output of the second detector representing a new intermediate frequency of 4.5 Mc that is frequency modulated by the sound. This second intermediate frequency is selected by a tuned circuit that is relatively sharply resonant at 4.5 Mc, and is then fed into a standard frequency-modulation receiving system consisting of a 4.5-Mc intermediate-frequency amplifier having a bandwidth of 50 kc, a limiter, a frequency-modulation detector, an audio amplifier, and a loudspeaker. This arrangement, known as the *inter-*

carrier sound system, is used in most television receivers.   It has the very desirable feature that the 4.5-Mc carrier frequency supplied to the sound channel is determined only by the difference in the crystal-controlled carrier frequencies of the sound and picture transmitters, and is independent of any drift in the frequency of the local oscillator of the receiver.

In order for the intercarrier system to be satisfactory, it is necessary (1) that the transmitter picture carrier be free of frequency or phase modulation, and (2) that the picture signal at the second-detector input always be at least as large as the sound signal.   Frequency or phase modulation of the picture carrier is to be avoided since such modulation will appear as sound in the 4.5-Mc sound channel.   The picture signal at the second detector should be at least as large as the sound carrier, since then the amplitude variations of the 4.5-Mc sound signal produced by the amplitude modulation of the picture signal will be small enough to be easily removed by a limiter.   The required relation of picture and sound signals is achieved by the "white clipper" of Fig. 25-10, which limits the minimum envelope amplitude of the transmitter picture signal, and by using an intermediate-frequency amplifier having a response to the sound carrier that is only about 10 per cent of the maximum response (see Fig. 25-9b).

Video Amplification and D-C Restoration.   The output of the second detector is amplified and applied to the cathode-ray picture tube in such a manner as to control the beam current of the tube.   Normally one stage of pentode amplification, or two stages of triode amplification, are sufficient.   High-frequency compensation of some type is normally used, but an adequate low-frequency-response characteristic can generally be obtained by employing grid leak–capacitor combinations having large time constants together with adequate by-passing of any bias or dropping resistors that are necessary.   The combination of the number of video stages, the type of second-detector circuit, and the method of coupling to the cathode-ray tube must be such that an increase in the amplitude of the envelope of the signal wave being applied to the second detector will reduce the beam current of the cathode-ray tube.   An example of a suitable arrangement is shown in Fig. 25-14.

The voltage applied to the cathode-ray tube must have its d-c component restored in order that the blanking pulses will always just cut off the electron beam of the tube irrespective of the white content of the picture.   In Fig. 25-14 this result is achieved by returning the grid leak of the second video stage directly to the cathode, and suitably choosing the time constant of the resistance-capacitance combination R_2C_2 to provide grid clamping, as discussed in connection with Fig. 18-33.[1]   This

---

[1] If a single video stage is employed, the clamp is normally of the diode type and is placed in the plate circuit in order to have sufficient voltage for the clamp to operate effectively.

causes the tips of the synchronizing pulses to be clamped to zero grid-cathode voltage at V_2 irrespective of the picture brightness. This stage of video amplification is then d-c coupled to the picture tube, the cathode potential of which is adjusted manually by the "brightness control" to a value such that the blanking pulses just barely turn off the cathode-ray beam. If the adjustment is such that the blanking pulses do not turn off the beam, then the scanning spot is visible on the picture tube during its return trace. On the other hand, if the cathode-ray beam is turned off before the amplitude of the applied signal reaches the black

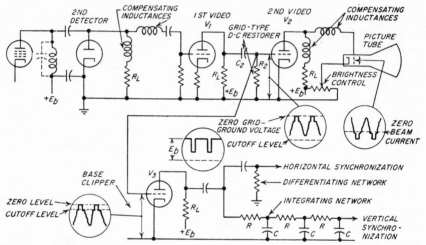

Fig. 25-14. A typical video system of a television receiver, showing method of separating the vertical and horizontal synchronizing pulses.

level, then the darker grays in the scene are reproduced as black, and the lighter grays are darker than they should be. The picture is then darker than it should be, and likewise has reduced contrast.

Contrast Control. All television receivers are provided with a so-called contrast control. This is a manually operated gain (volume) control that varies the sensitivity of the receiver by adjusting the bias voltage of the intermediate-frequency amplifier tubes. The contrast control thus provides a means by which the video signal applied to the picture tube can be adjusted to the optimum amplitude irrespective of the actual strength of the received signal.

25-8. Receiver Sweep Circuits and Their Synchronization. *Separation of Synchronizing Signals.* Synchronizing signals free of picture information are obtained at the receiver by applying the composite video signal, after d-c restoration, to a base clipper adjusted to transmit only those amplitudes that are appreciably greater than the blanking pulses. One way to achieve this result is shown in Fig. 25-14, where the base clipper is of the triode type discussed in connection with Fig. 18-4b, in which tube

V_3 has an amplification factor that is appropriately higher than the amplification factor of V_2.

The horizontal and vertical synchronizing information is separated by networks that respectively differentiate and integrate the signal (see Fig. 25-14). The differentiating network is typically of the resistance-capacitance type, as shown, and converts the front or rising edge of each horizontal and equalizing pulse, and of each vertical block, into a positive voltage pulse which is used to control the line synchronization. This action is depicted in Fig. 25-15b.

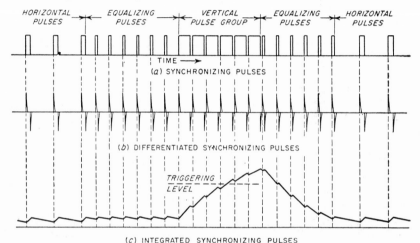

FIG. 25-15. Outputs obtained by differentiating and integrating the synchronizing pulses.

The integrating network consists of a chain of resistance-capacitance integrators, as shown in Fig. 25-14. Its action can be understood by noting that when the time constants of the individual resistance-capacitance combinations are suitably chosen, the amplitude of the integrator output voltage tends toward a small value when the spacings between the applied pulses are greater than the widths of these pulses, but grows steadily in amplitude when the spacings between the pulses are less than their widths. The result is that each group of blocks representing a vertical synchronizing signal produces a pulse, as illustrated in Fig. 25-15c.[1] The return period of the vertical sweep oscillator is then triggered into action when the amplitude of the integrator output pulse reaches some particular value, such as indicated by the dotted line in Fig. 25-15c.

Equalizing pulses cause the integrator output to reach this triggering level at a time in the vertical synchronizing period that is the same for

[1] For the sake of simplicity the waveforms in this figure are for a one-section capacitance integrator; the multisection system will behave similarly except that the amplitude fluctuations will be more rounded.

successive fields. In contrast, the triggering of successive fields would occur at slightly different times if the regular line synchronizing pulses replaced the system of equalizing pulses. Such a situation, shown in Fig. 25-16, leads to poor interlacing because it means that successive fields do not lie midway between each other.

Sweep Circuits. Magnetic deflection is used in television picture tubes because it enables the cathode-ray beam to be deflected over a wide angle with a minimum of deflection defocusing (see page 243). Saw-tooth current waves for the deflection coils are typically obtained by coupling

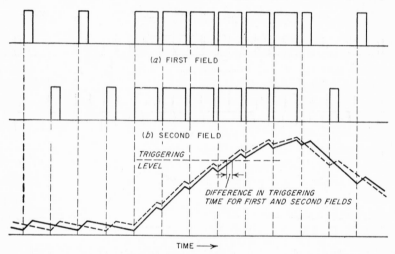

(a) FIRST FIELD

(b) SECOND FIELD

TRIGGERING LEVEL

DIFFERENCE IN TRIGGERING
TIME FOR FIRST AND SECOND FIELDS

TIME ⟶

(c) INTEGRATED OUTPUT

Fig. 25-16. The integrated outputs of the synchronizing pulses for successive fields for the case in which equalizing pulses are not employed.

these coils through a transformer to the plate circuit of a pentode or beam amplifier tube that is driven by a saw-tooth-wave generator. In such arrangements it is customary to balance nonlinearities arising from curvature of the tube characteristic, the saturation in the magnetic yokes of the deflecting coils, and the nonlinearity of the saw-tooth wave against each other in such a manner as to obtain a linear over-all result.

The saw-tooth-wave generator for the vertical sweep circuit is commonly of the type illustrated in Fig. 18-37d or e, with the free-running frequency of the blocking oscillator or multivibrator adjusted to be slightly lower than the required field frequency. Synchronization is then achieved by injecting pulses from the integrator output into the sweep generator.

The horizontal sweep system is one of the most critical elements in determining the quality of a television picture. The usual arrangement employs a free-running saw-tooth-wave generator, such as d, e, or f of Fig. 18-37, associated with an automatic-frequency-control system that compares the frequency of the saw-tooth wave with the horizontal synchronizing pulses, and corrects the free-running frequency as required to achieve synchronization.

The operation of the horizontal deflecting system is complicated by the fact that the horizontal deflection coils with their distributed capacitance form a tuned circuit that is typically resonant at a frequency for which the time of one-half cycle approximates the horizontal return time. As a result, the pulse of voltage developed across the coil during the return period (see Fig. 18-42) will excite an oscillatory transient in the deflecting coil which must be suppressed at the end of its first half cycle. This can be done by means of a so-called *damping diode* connected as shown in Fig. 25-17. Here the polarities are so chosen that on the second half cycle of the oscillatory transient the diode becomes conducting, and so stops the oscillatory transient that would otherwise continue for a number of cycles. At the same time, the bias voltage E_0 developed across C by the rectified current passing through the diode prevents the rel-atively small scanning voltage that is applied to the deflecting coils during the period of forward scan from being affected by the presence of the diode.[1]

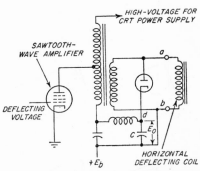

Fig. 25-17. Circuit arrangement asso-ciated with horizontal deflecting coil, showing damping diode, and also trans-former arrangement for producing high voltage for the cathode-ray-tube power supply.

No damping diode is required in the vertical deflection system because the vertical retrace time is many times as great as the time of a half cycle of the transient oscillation. As a result, the transient that is excited has only a small amplitude, and it furthermore has ample time to die away before the end of the vertical flyback period.

Automatic Frequency Control for Horizontal-sweep Generators. A num-ber of automatic-frequency-control systems have been devised for tele-vision receivers; one that is in common use is shown in Fig. 25-18a. Here synchronizing pulses applied in the absence of a saw-tooth wave cause equal currents to flow through diodes T_1 and T_2, and so charge capacitors C_1 and C_2 equally. Because of the symmetry of the circuit no charge is then delivered to C_0 and hence the output voltage E_0 is zero. Assume now that a saw-tooth voltage wave derived from the sweep system and much smaller than the pulses is applied between the center tap on the secondary coil L_s and ground, as shown. Because the synchronizing

---

[1] This bias voltage can simultaneously provide part of the plate voltage of the saw-tooth-wave amplifier as shown in Fig. 25-17.

pulses are larger than this saw-tooth wave, no current passes through either diode except when a synchronizing pulse is present. If the phase relations are such that the synchronizing pulses come at the instant when the return trace passes through zero, as in Fig. 25-18b, the situation is essentially the same as though no saw-tooth wave were present; under these conditions the d-c output voltage E_0 is zero. However, if the relative phase of the saw-tooth wave and the synchronizing pulses is changed, as in Fig. 25-18c, then the voltage E_1 developed between a and ground is greater than voltage E_2 between b and ground, and capacitor C_1 is charged to a higher voltage than capacitor C_2. The result is that more charge flows through C_1 than through C_2, causing C_0 to receive a charge that makes the output voltage E_0 positive. Conversely, if the saw-tooth wave has the phase position shown in Fig. 25-18d, more current flows through C_2 than C_1 and capacitor C_0 develops a negative output voltage.

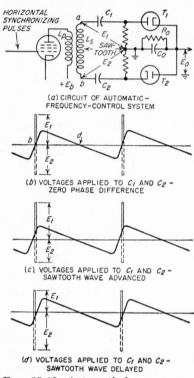

(a) CIRCUIT OF AUTOMATIC- FREQUENCY-CONTROL SYSTEM

(b) VOLTAGES APPLIED TO C_1 AND C_2 - ZERO PHASE DIFFERENCE

(c) VOLTAGES APPLIED TO C_1 AND C_2 - SAWTOOTH WAVE ADVANCED

(d) VOLTAGES APPLIED TO C_1 AND C_2 - SAWTOOTH WAVE DELAYED

FIG. 25-18. Automatic-frequency-control system, together with oscillograms showing how it operates.

The output voltage E_0 thus has an amplitude and polarity that are determined by the magnitude and sign, respectively, of the phase difference between the saw-tooth wave and the synchronizing pulses. Automatic frequency control is then obtained by using the voltage E_0 to control the frequency of the saw-tooth-wave generator. In the case of the circuits of Fig. 18-37d and c this is done by using E_0 to vary the grid bias of T_1; with the sine-wave oscillator of Fig. 18-37f, E_0 acts on the control grid of a reactance tube that determines the oscillator frequency.

By means of automatic frequency control, the horizontal line synchronization can be made relatively immune from the effect of noise pulses. In Fig. 25-18a this is accomplished by making the capacitance C_0 very large compared with C_1 and C_2, so that the change in E_0 produced by a single synchronizing pulse is small compared with E_0, and then making the time constant C_0R_0 very large. As a result E_0 depends on the average effect of a large number of pulses, and so is only very slightly affected by the instant at which an individual noise pulse occurs.

25-9. Brightness Distortion and Gamma. The relation between the brightness of an element of the reproduced image and the brightness of the corresponding element of the original scene, termed the *transfer characteristic* of the television system, is normally plotted on log-log paper as illustrated in Fig. 25-19. The slope of the transfer characteristic is called the *gamma* of the system and is denoted by the symbol γ.

A straight line with $\gamma = 1$ corresponds to a linear system completely free of brightness or amplitude distortion. A straight line for which $\gamma \neq 1$ is said to have uniform brightness distortion, since the distortion then appears to the eye to be independent of the brightness. When the transfer characteristic is curved the apparent brightness distortion will depend upon the brightness of the area under observation.

Brightness distortion is introduced by such factors as (1) the fact that the brightness of the spot of the cathode-ray picture tube is not a linear function of the voltage applied to the control electrode of the tube, (2) incorrect setting of the d-c level in the transmitter or the

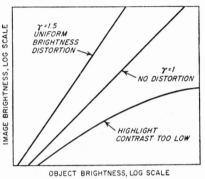

Fig. 25-19. Different types of image-object brightness relationships.

receiver, (3) room light superimposed on the picture tube, and (4) lack of linearity in the camera tube arising from such factors as saturation at high levels of light, the fact that the minimum usable light level is finite, etc.

25-10. Color Television[1,2]—Fundamental Concepts of a Three-color System. It is well known that a color picture can be obtained by appropriately combining three primary colors—red, green, and blue.[3] Thus a simple-minded system of color television would consist of a separate television transmitter and receiver for each of the primary colors, and some means of optically superimposing the three receiver outputs to obtain a color picture. Alternatively, one might transmit the red, green, and blue components of the picture in such rapid succession that to the eye they would merge into a single color. However, both of these arrangements have the disadvantage that they are extravagant with

---

[1] For further information on this subject the reader should refer to *Proc. IRE*, vol. 42, January, 1954, which is devoted exclusively to the subject of color television, and covers all aspects of the subject, as well as containing references to all of the pertinent earlier literature.

[2] The color system described here conforms to the United States standards.

[3] These are the additive primaries. In the subtractive process of producing colors, which is used in kodachrome film, the primaries are bluish red (magenta), bluish green (cyan), and lemon yellow.

bandwidth, and furthermore do not give a picture that can be viewed on a conventional black-and-white (monochrome) television receiver.

A more sophisticated method of transmitting a color picture that overcomes these limitations begins from the observation that the three signals transmitted need not be the actual red, green, and blue components E_R, E_G, and E_B, respectively, but rather can be any three independent combinations of them. That is, if E_Y, E_I, and E_Q are the three signals that are transmitted, then the general form of these signals is

$$E_Y = aE_G + a_1E_R + a_2E_B \qquad (25\text{-}1a)$$
$$E_I = bE_G + b_1E_R + b_2E_B \qquad (25\text{-}1b)$$
$$E_Q = cE_G + c_1E_R + c_2E_B \qquad (25\text{-}1c)$$

Here the a's, b's, and c's are numerical constants that can be arbitrarily chosen.

In the standard color-television system, the a's in Eq. (25-1a) are so chosen as to weight each of the three primary colors in proportion to its contribution to the brightness of the scene. This is accomplished by choosing the a coefficients so that Eq. (25-1a) becomes

$$E_Y = 0.59E_G + 0.30E_R + 0.11E_B \qquad (25\text{-}2)$$

The signal E_Y when defined in this way is called the luminance signal and is identical with the video signal of a conventional monochrome television system. *When received on a conventional monochrome television receiver, the luminance signal hence produces a black-and-white version of the color picture.* To a color television receiver, the luminance signal provides the brightness information.

The signals E_I and E_Q indicate the way the color of the picture departs from shades of gray, and so are called *chrominance signals*, or color-difference signals. *These chrominance signals carry no information regarding the brightness of the picture.* Although the b and c coefficients of the chrominance signals can be chosen arbitrarily, it is found for reasons given below that the most desirable result for television is obtained when

$$E_I = 0.74(E_R - E_Y) - 0.27(E_B - E_Y)$$
$$= 0.60E_R - 0.28E_G - 0.32E_B \qquad (25\text{-}3)$$
$$E_Q = 0.48(E_R - E_Y) + 0.41(E_B - E_Y)$$
$$= 0.21E_R - 0.52E_G + 0.31E_B \qquad (25\text{-}4)$$

When E_Y, E_I, and E_Q are defined as above, then by simultaneous solution

$$E_G = E_Y - 0.28E_I - 0.64E_Q \qquad (25\text{-}5a)$$
$$E_R = E_Y - 0.96E_I + 0.62E_Q \qquad (25\text{-}5b)$$
$$E_B = E_Y - 1.10E_I + 1.70E_Q \qquad (25\text{-}5c)$$

The two chrominance signals E_I and E_Q taken together can be represented by a single vector on a complex plane, as shown in Fig. 25-20a. Here the direction of the resultant color vector $E_C = E_Q + jE_I$ denotes the color (or hue) that the luminance signal should have, while the length of the vector indicates the intensity of this color.   Thus for an unsaturated (pastel) red, which is a mixture of red and white light, the color vector E_C will have smaller amplitude, but the same direction, as the color vector (see Fig. 25-20a) for a saturated red of the same brightness.

The relation between the direction of the resultant color vector $E_C = E_Q + jE_I$ and the color is shown in Fig. 25-20b; the vector lengths indicated correspond to saturated colors.   It will be noted that plus and minus values along the I axis range from saturated orange through unsaturated oranges to white ($E_I = 0$, $E_Q = 0$) and then through unsaturated

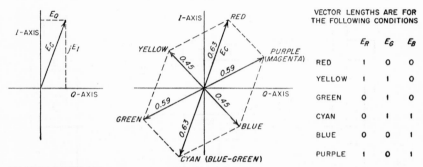

(*a*) COLOR VECTOR FOR SATURATED RED

(*b*) COLOR VECTORS FOR VARIOUS SATURATED COLORS

	E_R	E_G	E_B
RED	I	0	0
YELLOW	I	I	0
GREEN	0	I	0
CYAN	0	I	I
BLUE	0	0	I
PURPLE	I	0	I

Fig. 25-20. Vector diagram showing the color vectors that represent the subcarrier amplitudes and phases corresponding to six saturated colors.

bluish cyan to saturated bluish cyan.   Similarly, along the Q axis the color ranges from saturated bluish purple to white to yellow-green.

The three signals of the color system do not all require the same bandwidth.   This is because the eye is able to see fine detail represented by differences in brightness, but does not observe fine detail represented by different colors of substantially the same brightness.   Specifically, in the standard 525-line television signal, a bandwidth of 1.6 Mc will convey all the color detail that the eye is able to utilize for colors along the I axis of Fig. 25-20b, while 0.6 Mc is adequate for colors along the Q axis.[1]

25-11. Color-television Transmitter.   The schematic diagram of a color-television transmitter is shown in Fig. 25-21.   The color camera typically consists of three separate pickup tubes having appropriate color responses, in conjunction with an image-dividing optical system.   The adjustments are such as to make the three color outputs have equal intensity when viewing white light.[2]

---

[1] These values approximate the maximum and minimum resolutions that are obtained with different color at constant brightness.   The definitions of E_I and E_Q given by Eqs. (25-3) and (25-4) were intentionally selected to achieve this result.

[2] In the color cameras used in practice a nonlinear element giving a response proportional to $E^{1/\gamma}$ is introduced at point x in order to compensate for the gamma of a typical receiver.   This is disregarded here in order to simplify the discussion.

The three signals E_Y, E_I, and E_Q required in the color system are obtained by adding the outputs of the three color cameras in the proportions given by Eqs. (25-2), (25-3), and (25-4), respectively. The adders (or matrices as they are often called) can be of the type illustrated in Fig. 18-49; negative quantities can be obtained with the aid of a phase inverter consisting of a one-stage amplifier having unity gain. Filters are incorporated in the I and Q channels in order to restrict their bandwidths to the appropriate values.

The Q signal is then modulated on a subcarrier having a frequency of $455\frac{1}{2}$ times the line frequency, or approximately 3.6 Mc. A balanced

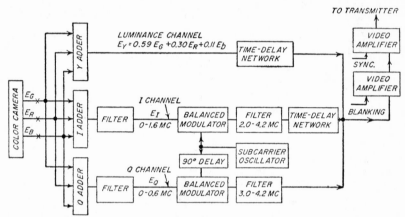

Fig. 25-21. Simplified schematic diagram of color-television transmitter.

modulator is used (see Fig. 15-13), thus giving a pair of sidebands extending from 3.0 to 4.2 Mc, and free of carrier. The I channel is likewise modulated upon a subcarrier that is identical except for a 90° phase difference. This causes the sidebands of the I channel to differ by 90° with respect to the phase of the sideband components of the Q channel. A filter at the output of the I modulator limits the frequency range to 2.0 to 4.2 Mc; the result is a vestigial-sideband signal possessing double sidebands for modulation frequencies up to 0.6 Mc, and a single sideband for modulation frequencies between 0.6 and 1.6 Mc.

The sidebands from the I and Q channels are then superimposed on the luminance channel, to give a combined video signal covering the frequency range 60 cycles to 4.2 Mc, and to which standard blanking and synchronizing pulses are added.[1] In addition, a "burst" of at least eight cycles of the subcarrier frequency at a standard phase is superimposed on the back porch of each horizontal synchronizing pulse, as shown in Fig.

---

[1] Time-delay networks are inserted in the Y and I channels as shown to compensate for the greater time delay in the Q channel (due to its narrower bandwidth) and thus ensure that the currents from all three channels are transmitted in time coincidence.

25-22.[1,2]   These color bursts tell the color television receiver the correct frequency and exact phase of the color subcarrier.   The resulting combined video signal is then amplified and modulated on the transmitter in the usual manner.

25-12. Reception of Color Signal on Monochrome Receiver.

When a conventional monochrome receiver is tuned to the signal radiated by the transmitter of Fig. 25-21, the luminance component of the incoming signal produces a conventional black-and-white picture, while the I and Q sidebands that are also contained in the received signal produce little or no visible effect on the picture tube.   This color system is therefore *compatible* with the standard monochrome system.

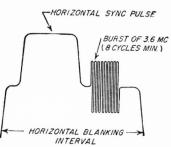

FIG. 25-22. Horizontal blanking and synchronizing pulse, together with color-synchronizing burst.

The invisibility of the I and Q sideband components arises from the fact that their subcarrier frequency is an *odd* multiple of *half* the line frequency.   This causes the phase of the I and Q sideband components to reverse on successive frames, since if the subcarrier oscillation is at the start of a cycle when a particular frame begins, it will end that frame after the completion of a full number of cycles *plus a half cycle*.   Now the successive half cycles of the chrominance sidebands produce a spurious pattern of alternate light and dark dots during a single frame of the monochrome picture.   However, the phase reversal of the chrominance sidebands on successive frames causes the light dots of one frame to be superimposed on the dark dots of the next frame, and vice versa, as shown in Fig. 25-23.

To the extent that the system is linear, the chrominance compo-

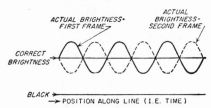

FIG. 25-23. Diagram illustrating frequency interlacing, showing how the brightness error of successive traces along the same line are of opposite polarity, and hence tend to average out.

nents therefore have no effect on the *average* brightness of the black-and-white picture, but merely cause a 15-cycle flicker in the very small areas.   Since a 15-cycle flicker of a very small area is imperceptible to the eye,[3]

---

[1] The bursts are omitted during the portion of the vertical synchronizing period in which the horizontal synchronizing pulses are replaced by the equalizing pulses and the vertical blocks.

[2] Means for producing and inserting the color bursts are omitted from Fig. 25-21 to avoid complicating the figure.

[3] In contrast, a 15-cycle flicker of a single large area is very visible if the area is at all bright.

the Q and I components are to a first approximation invisible on a black-and-white receiver.

This phenomenon, by which an effect is made invisible by proper choice of relative frequencies, is sometimes termed *frequency interlacing.*

25-13. Three-color Picture Tube. A practical color-television receiver requires a picture tube that is capable of producing any combination of

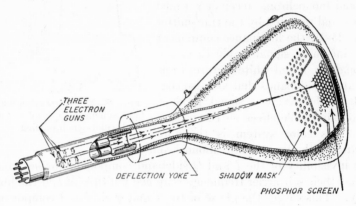

(*a*) SHADOW-MASK TUBE

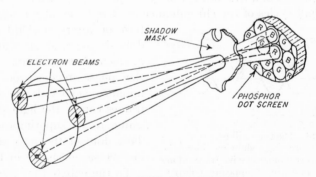

(*b*) DETAILS OF BEAMS, MASK, AND DOTS

FIG. 25-24. Schematic diagram of shadow-mask color tube.

red, green, and blue by application of appropriate voltages. Two types of tubes that successfully achieve this result are available in at least sample quantities at the time of this writing. These are the shadow-mask and the Chromatron (or Lawrence) tubes.

Shadow-mask Color Tube. The basic idea of the shadow-mask tube is illustrated in Fig. 25-24. Here three spaced electron guns in the neck of the cathode-ray tube provide three separately controllable beams, one for each primary color. These guns are so aligned that their beams cross at a moderate distance from the fluorescent screen. At the plane of the crossover is a thin metal sheet or *shadow mask* perforated with several hundred thousand very fine holes. The viewing screen is a glass plate upon which closely spaced groups of phosphor-dot trios are deposited. Each trio is associated with a particular hole in the shadow mask, and consists of three dots of phosphors that respectively emit red, green, and blue light when struck by electrons. The alignment and geometry are such that the electrons from the "red" gun can strike only red emitting dots, and are prevented by the shadow mask from striking the other dots. Similarly, the electrons from the "green" gun can strike only dots that emit green light, while electrons from the "blue" gun can strike only those dots that emit blue light.

By separately controlling the number of electrons produced by each gun, the proportions of red, green, and blue light originating with any trio can be varied at will. If the viewing distance is then great enough so that the separate dots of the trio cannot be resolved, the eye will perceive a color determined by the proportions of red, green, and blue light originating from the trio. By deflecting the three beams together, it is possible to scan the surface of the fluorescent screen and thus produce a colored scene.

The shadow-mask tube is capable of giving good-quality color, and at the time of this writing is available in moderate production quantities. The chief disadvantages of the shadow-mask tube are the facts that it is expensive to construct, and that the shadow mask intercepts a substantial fraction of the electrons in the beams so that a bright picture is obtained only with difficulty.

The Chromatron Color Tube. The Chromatron tube is illustrated schematically in Fig. 25-25.[1] Here the fluorescent screen consists of very narrow strips of color phosphors arranged in the sequence: red, green, blue, green, red, green, etc., as shown. Immediately in front of this fluorescent screen is a grid structure consisting of wires accurately aligned parallel with the red and blue strips. The grid wires associated with the red strips are connected together, while those associated with the blue phosphor strips are connected in parallel but are insulated from the red wires. A common d-c accelerating voltage is applied to the two sets of grids.

A single electron beam directed toward the grid can be made to strike a red, green, or blue phosphor strip as desired by controlling the voltage difference between the two sets of grids. Thus if no voltage difference exists between the grids, the d-c accelerating voltage common to both grids produces a focusing field that deflects all incoming electrons so that they hit green strips irrespective of their initial position in the vertical

---

[1] In order to make this illustration legible the spacing between grid wires and phosphor strips has been greatly exaggerated. Actually, there are typically of the order of 100 phosphor lines and 50 grid wires per inch.

plane, as shown in Fig. 25-25c. However, if a voltage difference is applied between the two sets of grids, then the electrons approaching the grid structure will be deflected toward the phosphor strips that are opposite the more positive set of grid wires, as in Fig. 25-25d. Such a tube can therefore be made to produce a color picture by switching the beam back and forth rapidly between the color strips (for example, at the

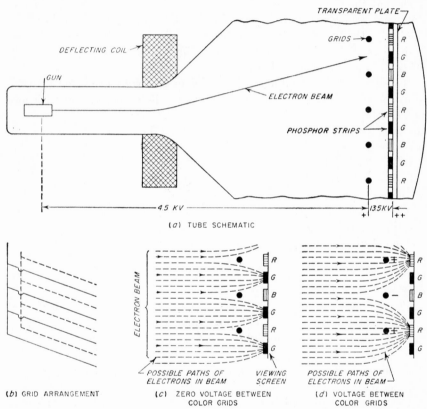

FIG. 25-25. Schematic diagram of Chromatron color tube. For the sake of clarity, the spacings between adjacent grid wires and phosphor strips are enormously exaggerated in part a (but not in parts c and d.)

subcarrier frequency of approximately 3.6 Mc), and then synchronously supplying the control electrode of the gun with voltages corresponding to the amount of each color desired.

The Chromatron tube is much simpler to construct than the shadow-mask tube. However, the presently available tubes of this type have the disadvantage that the line structure is definitely noticeable in the bright red areas. They have the further disadvantage that the switching frequency required for television is so high, namely, 3.6 Mc, that the reactive power that must be supplied to the grids is great enough to present a radiation problem within the receiver. At the present time samples of Chromatron tubes showing promise have been made, but these tubes are not available on a production basis.

25-14. Color-television Receiver. The schematic diagram of a color-television receiver is shown in Fig. 25-26. Here the radio-frequency section, mixer, intermediate-frequency amplifier, second detector, and intercarrier sound system are the same as in a monochrome receiver. The luminance or E_Y channel is also similar to the video channel of a monochrome receiver except for a sharply tuned trap resonant at 3.6 Mc that suppresses the subcarrier bursts and thus prevents them from unblanking the color tube.

The chrominance sidebands are selected by a bandpass filter as shown. Separate I and Q signals are derived from these sidebands by means of appropriately operated synchronous detectors, as explained below. The I channel contains an equalizer that develops an output twice as great above 0.6 Mc as it does below 0.6 Mc, in order to compensate for the fact that the I channel contains only a single sideband above 0.6 Mc.

Red, green, and blue signals corresponding to E_R, E_G, and E_B are then generated by adding[1] E_Y, E_Q, and E_I in the proportions given by Eqs. (25-5). After amplification, they are applied to the color tube, which is adjusted so that it will produce a white (or gray) picture when the color signals applied to the red, green, blue guns are equal in amplitude.

During the blanking periods the I and Q components are zero, and the red, green, and blue channels contain only the blanking and synchronizing signals. Direct-current restoration similar to that in a monochrome system is required for each color channel. The sweep circuits and their control by the synchronizing pulses are the same as in a monochrome receiver, and so are not shown.

Demodulation of Chrominance Sidebands. The Q and I components of the received signal are recovered from the chrominance sidebands by means of the so-called "synchronous detectors" shown in Fig. 25-26. Each of these consists of an ordinary amplitude-modulation detector, to the input of which is simultaneously applied the various chrominance sidebands superimposed upon a locally generated oscillation identical in frequency and phase with the transmitter subcarrier of the corresponding channel. The output of such a detector, after appropriate filtering, will then contain only the I or Q component, as the case may be.

The ability of a synchronous detector to respond only to the I or Q sidebands, but not to both, arises from the phase relations that exist between these sidebands. Thus in the case of the I detector, the I and Q sidebands are so phased relative to the reinserted carrier as to produce

---

[1] The adders, which are also often termed matrices, are conveniently of the resistance type illustrated in Fig. 18-49. Where negative I and Q signals are required, a phase inverter is inserted in series with the appropriate branch of the adder.

amplitude and frequency modulation, respectively. However, as the I detector does not respond to frequency modulation, its output is unaffected by the presence of the Q sidebands. The situation is analogous in the case of the Q detector up to 0.6 Mc, where the I component consists of double sidebands phased to correspond to frequency modulation. Above 0.6 Mc the single sideband of the I channel will produce an amplitude fluctuation that appears as output from the Q detector, but as this fluctuation is above 0.6 Mc it is removed by the filter in the output of the Q channel.

Elimination of Interference between Luminance and Chrominance Channels by Frequency Interlacing. In the above discussion the fact that the

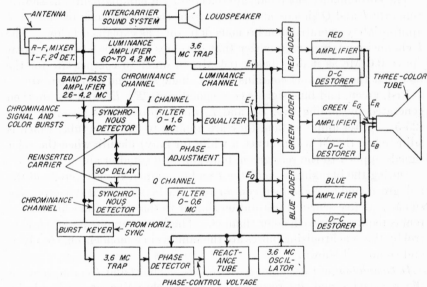

FIG. 25-26. Simplified schematic diagram of color-television receiver.

chrominance sidebands appear in the luminance channel has been ignored, as has likewise the fact that the components of the luminance signal lying in the frequency range 2.6 to 4.2 Mc pass through the chrominance filter and are applied to the synchronous detectors. This is permissible because these spurious components are to a first approximation invisible as a result of the frequency interlacing phenomenon discussed on page 1004. Thus the chrominance sidebands present in the luminance channel produce a 15-cycle small-area brightness flicker in a colored picture just as they do in a monochrome receiver. Similarly, the luminance components that find their way into the Q and I channels produce analogous 15-cycle color fluctuations about the correct color that are likewise not perceived by the eye, because they do not affect brightness, and are moreover usually small-area effects.

Reverse Compatibility. The color receiver of Fig. 25-26 will reproduce a black-and-white picture when receiving signals from a monochrome television transmitter. This is termed *reverse compatibility*, and results from the fact that the monochrome signal contains no chrominance sidebands, but only the luminance or E_Y component. Since it follows from Eqs. (25-5) that under these circumstances equal voltages are applied to the red, green, and blue guns of the color tube, the resulting picture is in shades of gray.

Synchronization of Receiver Subcarrier Oscillator. The receiver oscillator associated with the synchronous detectors must maintain a definite phase relation to the transmitter subcarrier oscillations as indicated to the receiver by the subcarrier bursts contained in the received signal. An arrangement for achieving this result is shown schematically in Fig. 25-26. It consists of a phase detector that compares the phases of the color bursts[1] and the receiver oscillator, and generates a d-c control voltage having a magnitude and polarity determined by the magnitude and direction, respectively, of the phase difference. The d-c voltage is then applied to a reactance tube that controls the frequency of the receiver oscillator. The polarities are so chosen that when the oscillator phase starts to lag the oscillator frequency is raised, and vice versa, thus achieving control action.

A suitable phase detector is shown schematically in Fig. 25-27a.[2] This is the same as Fig. 17-14a except that the E_3 in Fig. 17-14a is now supplied by voltage E_0 from the local oscillator, while the voltages across S in Fig. 17-14a become $\pm E_s$, and are derived from the synchronizing color bursts associated with the received signal. The d-c output E_{dc} is the difference between the rectified outputs of diodes T_1 and T_2, and so depends on the difference $e_1 - e_2$ between $e_1 = |E_0 + E_s|$ and $e_2 = |E_0 - E_s|$. The effect of the relative phases of E_0 and E_s on this difference is shown in the diagrams of Fig. 25-27c (analogous to Fig. 17-14b), and by the curve of b which gives the d-c output voltage as a function of phase and is analogous to Fig. 17-14d. It is apparent that whenever the phase difference between E_0 and E_s departs from 90°, the phase detector develops a d-c output voltage having a polarity determined by the sense of the phase deviation, and a magnitude proportional to the amount of the phase difference. No complications are introduced by the fact the E_s is intermittent; this is because in the absence of E_s the phase detector output is

---

[1] These color bursts are separated from the chrominance signal by a gate, termed a burst keyer, controlled from the horizontal synchronizing signal. This gate is open only during the part of the back-porch period of the horizontal synchronizing pulse when the color bursts are present, and is associated with a sharply tuned resonant trap circuit, as shown in Fig. 25-26.

[2] In practice, a modification of this circuit would be used that bears the same relation to Fig. 25-27a that Fig. 17-15 bears to Fig. 17-14a.

zero. It is merely necessary that the time constant RC be very large so that the control voltage E_{dc} will be substantially constant in amplitude in spite of the fact that the color-synchronizing signal arrives only intermittently in short bursts.

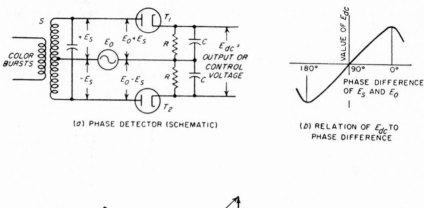

(a) PHASE DETECTOR (SCHEMATIC)   (b) RELATION OF E_{dc} TO PHASE DIFFERENCE

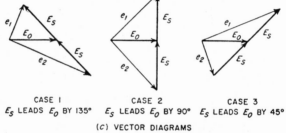

CASE I   CASE 2   CASE 3
E_S LEADS E_0 BY 135° E_S LEADS E_0 BY 90° E_S LEADS E_0 BY 45°

(c) VECTOR DIAGRAMS

Fig. 25-27. Circuit and operating details of phase detector.

25-15. Receiving Antennas. Receiving antennas used in television are always directional systems designed to cover the entire television band without requiring any adjustment. A typical arrangement consists of a folded dipole associated with reflector and/or director antennas to provide directivity. A wideband characteristic is obtained by taking advantage of the inherently wide bandwidth characteristics of a folded dipole, combined with the fact that an antenna so proportioned as to be suitable for the lower-frequency channels in the very high-frequency band when operating in the fundamental mode will likewise be suitable for the higher very high frequencies when operating in the third-harmonic mode (i.e., length approximately 1.5λ). A second antenna associated with the same transmission line can be used for signals from the ultra-high-frequency band when one desires to employ a common antenna system and transmission line for the ultra-high and very high-frequency bands.

Television receiving antennas are usually mounted as high as practical above the earth, because the strength of the high-frequency signals from a distant transmitter will be directly proportional to height (see Sec. 22-4). The minimum height necessary to obtain a usable signal will depend on the distance to the transmitter.

Directivity is required in the receiving antenna in order to increase the capture area, and to provide the possibility of discriminating against undesired transmission paths. When the signal strength is not great the receiving antenna should not only be as high as possible, but should be of a type having a relatively large directive gain.

25-16. Multiple-path Phenomena. When a large structure such as a building or tower is near the receiving antenna, it is then possible for a television signal to reach the receiver over two paths, as illustrated by the solid lines in Fig. 25-28. The reflected or indirect signal is delayed by a time interval corresponding to the additional distance it must travel, and is usually weaker than the direct signal. As a result, a normal picture is obtained from the direct signal, which also controls the synchronization and blanking, but superimposed on this is a weak or *ghost* image displaced

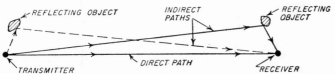

FIG. 25-28. Schematic diagram illustrating how reflecting objects near either the transmitter or receiver cause a signal to reach the receiver that is delayed slightly in time with respect to the signal that follows a direct path.

horizontally to the right by a distance corresponding to the time delay involved.[1]

Ghost images arising from reflections occurring near the receiver can be minimized by a receiving antenna location that gives a strong direct signal, combined with trial and error adjustment of the antenna orientation such that the directional pattern of the receiving antenna possesses a null in the direction of the indirect signal.

Ghost images can also arise as a result of reflections occurring near the transmitter, as illustrated by the dotted paths in Fig. 25-28. While television broadcasting transmitters are always located where there are no nearby reflecting objects, this is not necessarily the case with mobile transmitters that relay a program to the broadcasting station. As a result, programs originating in field pickups often exhibit ghosts.

Reflecting objects more or less midway between transmitting and receiving locations do not produce ghost images because the intensity of the reflected signal that reaches the receiver under these conditions is relatively weak compared with the direct signal.

[1] If the indirect signal is the stronger, it controls the synchronization, and a ghost displaced to the left is produced by the weaker direct signal.

PROBLEMS AND EXERCISES

25-1. Would it be possible to obtain interlacing if a picture frame contained an even number of lines?

25-2. Explain why interlacing would accomplish no useful result if the eye were as responsive to flicker in a small area as it is to flicker in a large area.

25-3. Explain why it would be undesirable to use an ordinary sine wave for scanning instead of the saw-tooth wave always employed, even if sine waves were employed at *both* transmitter and receiver and were carefully synchronized.

25-4. Synchronizing could be achieved by momentarily reducing the amplitude of the blanking pulse to zero. Is there any disadvantage to such an arrangement?

25-5. Show that if the vertical synchronizing blocks had a length of nearly one horizontal line and a repetition frequency equal to the line frequency, instead of half this length and twice this frequency, then the horizontal line synchronization would be interrupted during the vertical return of every other field.

25-6. In the image orthicon, what would be the consequences of making the leakage conductance of the target plate negligible?

25-7. In the image orthicon, would it be permissible to allow the beam to strike the target plate during the return period, and then subsequently blank out the signal obtained during the return time by means of a blanking pulse?

25-8. Sketch a diagram similar to Fig. 25-5, but applying to a scene consisting of two parallel, diagonal black bars sloping upward to the right and on a white background.

25-9. In the image orthicon, how is the return circuit completed to the cathode for the current represented by those electrons that are deposited on the back of the target plate?

25-10. In the image orthicon of Fig. 25-4, how is the d-c voltage across R_L related to the average brightness of the scene being scanned?

25-11. In the vidicon tube, is it necessary to prevent the scanning beam from reaching the photoconductive material during the return periods, or is it merely sufficient to blank out the output of a subsequent amplifier tube during the return periods by means of blanking pulses?

25-12. Would it be possible to use the current variations in the returning beam of the vidicon tube to develop the output of the tube in the same way as is done in the image orthicon?

25-13. In the vidicon tube what would be the consequence of employing photoconductive material having such high leakage when illuminated that practically all of the charge deposited by the beam would leak off in less than $\frac{1}{30}$ sec with only moderately bright illumination?

25-14. What is the order of magnitude of the maximum persistence permissible for a cathode-ray tube used in a flying-spot scanner?

25-15. Determine the frequency band required to obtain equal vertical and horizontal resolution in a television system employing 725 lines and reproducing a picture having a width-to-height ratio of 1:1. Assume that the vertical- and horizontal-return times are the same percentage as in the standard United States television signal.

25-16. Calculate the band width required to transmit the equalizing pulses with reasonable fidelity.

25-17. Draw a circuit diagram for the portion of the transmitter in Fig. 25-10 between point *a* and the grid electrode of the grid-modulated amplifier.

25-18. How could the d-c restorer be arranged in Fig. 25-10 so that it would be unnecessary to provide direct coupling between the video power amplifier and the grid-modulated amplifier? Show an actual circuit arrangement.

25-19. Is it necessary in Fig. 25-10 that the white clipper come after d-c restoration?

25-20. The antenna for a television transmitter consists of four horizontal loops stacked coaxially above each other in the vertical direction. Show a diplexer arrangement suitable for use with this antenna system.

25-21. Why is care taken to design a television receiver for low noise figure, while this is not done in a standard broadcast receiver?

25-22. A 60-cycle buzz will be heard on an intercarrier type of receiver when the white clipper at the transmitter is incorrectly adjusted so that the minimum envelope amplitude of the transmitted signal can become very small. Explain.

25-23. Sketch a circuit arrangement for a second-detector, one-stage video amplifier employing pentode tube, d-c restorer, and picture tube that will reproduce the standard television signal with correct polarity.

25-24. In a television receiver using the circuit arrangement of Fig. 25-14, what will be the effect on the contrast of the reproduced picture, and on the functioning of the blanking action, if the sensitivity (gain) of the receiver is (a) considerably greater than the value which gives the best picture, and (b) considerably less than this optimum?

25-25. In Fig. 25-14 what would be the effect, if any, on the separation of the synchronizing pulses from the remainder of the signal, if the sensitivity (gain) of the receiver is (a) much greater than that giving the best picture, and (b) much less than this optimum?

25-26. Sketch the way the raster of Fig. 25-1 would be modified if the vertical synchronization were obtained as in Fig. 25-16.

25-27. Sketch the complete circuit of a vertical sweep system, including a suitable sweep generator and sweep voltage amplifier to drive the deflecting system. Show means for injecting the synchronizing pulses.

25-28. Show oscillograms giving the voltage across the terminals ab of the horizontal deflecting coil in Fig. 25-17, the current in this coil, the current passing through the diode tube, and the voltage between d and b. Neglect the possibility of capacitance in the deflecting coil.

25-29. Assume the circuit of Fig. 25-18a is arranged so that it will correctly control the frequency of a saw-tooth-wave generator in the manner indicated. Is there then anything that prevents the system from synchronizing so that point d of the saw-tooth wave coincides with the synchronizing pulses instead of the desired point b in the oscillogram of Fig. 25-18b?

25-30. Why is it necessary in the automatic-frequency-control system of Fig. 25-18 that the pulses have a greater amplitude than the saw-tooth wave?

25-31. Show that if the actual transfer characteristic of a television system is a straight line, then superimposing a constant amount of light upon the reproduced picture will cause the transfer characteristic to be curved in such a manner as to reduce the gamma for the portions of the picture that are the least bright.

25-32. Two areas of a scene have equal brightness, but the first is green and the other is blue. Determine the relative values of the Q signals for these two areas.

25-33. Derive Eq. (25-5a) starting with Eqs. (25-2) to (25-4).

25-34. In Fig. 25-20, determine the magnitude of the E_I and E_Q components of the color vector for yellow ($E_R = E_G = 1$, $E_B = 0$), using Eqs. (25-3) and (25-4).

25-35. By means of rotating vectors show that each balanced modulator, such as used in the television transmitter of Fig. 25-21, will develop an output that can be represented by a vector of constant phase that oscillates in length between $\pm 2E_s$, where E_s is the amplitude of an individual sideband in the output.

25-36. When a color signal is received on a monochrome television receiver, is there any difference in the reproduced picture when the gamma of the transmitter-receiver combination is greater than unity, as compared with $\gamma = 1$?

25-37. In a shadow-mask color tube, calculate the number of holes required in the shadow mask if the resolution of the tube is to be limited by the line structure of the raster and not by the number of holes.

25-38. Draw electric field lines between the grids and the viewing screen for the situations existing in Fig. 25-25c and d, and explain how these fields cause the electrons to land on the green and red phosphor strips, respectively.

25-39. In Fig. 25-26, what would be the effect on the reproduced picture of drastically reducing the bandwidths of the filters in the I and Q channels to, say, 0.4 and 0.15 Mc, respectively.

25-40. In Fig. 25-26, what would be the effect on the reproduced picture if the box labeled "phase adjustment" were incorrectly adjusted?

25-41. Where in Fig. 25-26 could the synchronizing signals be separated from the video signal and the blanking pulses?

25-42. In a color-television system, what would the picture be like if the Q channel at the transmitter became inoperative so that the radiated signal contained no Q component?

25-43. Devise a phase detector based on the ratio detector of Fig. 17-17a in the same way that the phase detector of Fig. 27-27a is based on the phase-shift discriminator of Fig. 17-14a.

25-44. In a television picture that is 15 by 20 in., a ghost appears that is displaced $\frac{1}{16}$ in. What is the difference between the lengths of the direct and indirect paths?

CHAPTER 26

RADAR AND RADIO AIDS TO NAVIGATION

26-1. Radar.[1] The term *radar* is derived from the phrase *"radio detection and ranging."* Radar is essentially an echo-ranging system in which the radar transmitter sends out energy in the form of periodic pulses of very high power but very short duration. Objects such as aircraft, ships, mountains, buildings, etc., reflect some of this energy back to the transmitter. The time delay of a returned echo is a measure of the distance to the reflecting object, since, for a wave traveling with the velocity of light, each microsecond of delay corresponds to a round-trip time of travel over a path 492 ft long. The direction of the reflecting object can be obtained by the use of directional transmitting and receiving antennas.

Radar can be employed in various ways as a navigational aid, and it has numerous military uses. Since mountains, plains, cities, oceans, rivers, etc., differ in the extent to which they reflect high-frequency radio waves, radar equipment in an aircraft can provide information useful for navigation that is not affected by poor visibility or darkness. Similarly, radar equipment on a ship can give information as to the location of land masses, other ships, marker buoys, etc. In military operations, radar is used for such purposes as aiming guns at ships and aircraft, bombing ships or cities through overcast or at night, directing guided missiles, giving warning of approaching aircraft or ships, searching for submarines, aiding night-fighter aircraft in locating and attacking enemy aircraft, etc.[2] In

[1] Radar systems are based largely on the components and techniques considered in detail in the previous chapters describing high-frequency oscillators, receivers, pulse generators, directional antennas, wideband video and intermediate-frequency amplifiers, waveguides and transmission lines, cathode-ray tubes, servo systems, etc. Because of space considerations, this chapter attempts only to present a general picture of what is involved in radar systems. The most complete treatment of radar and related techniques is the 28-volume Radiation Laboratory Series on radar published by McGraw-Hill Book Company, Inc., New York, the first volumes appearing in 1947; a general survey is given in "Radar System Engineering," vol. 1. Other useful books include J. F. Reintjes and G. T. Coate, "Principles of Radar," 3d ed., McGraw-Hill Book Company, Inc., New York, 1952; Donald Fink, "Radar Engineering," McGraw-Hill Book Company, Inc., New York, 1947. Suggested summary articles are Edwin G. Schneider, Radar, *Proc. IRE*, vol. 34, p. 528, August, 1946; Lloyd V. Berkner, Naval Airborne Radar, *Proc. IRE*, vol. 34, p. 671, September, 1946.

[2] An excellent summary of the military uses of airborne radar in naval warfare is given in Berkner, *loc. cit.*

addition, radar finds important uses in aiding the landing of aircraft under conditions of poor visibility, in monitoring air traffic in the vicinity of airports, in enabling an aircraft to determine its height above ground, etc. Some microwave radars are particularly suitable for distinguishing dense cloud masses, and these find extensive use in locating highly turbulent storm centers that should be avoided in aircraft flight.

Elements of a Radar System.   A block diagram of a radar system is given in Fig. 26-1.   The transmitting system usually consists of a radio-frequency oscillator that is controlled by a modulator (pulser) in such a

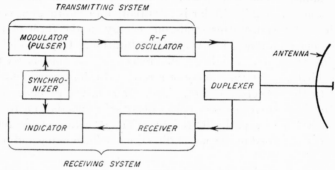

Fig. 26-1. Block diagram of a radar system.

manner as to generate periodic pulses of high power but of relatively short duration.

The antenna is highly directional and is ordinarily arranged so that it can be rotated to direct the beam as desired.   In most systems, a single antenna is used for both transmitting and receiving.   This necessitates the use of a switching arrangement, called a *duplexer*, which isolates the sensitive receiver from the damaging effects of the high-power transmitter pulses, and then switches the antenna to the receiver in the intervals between pulses during which the reflected energy is being received.

The radar receiver is an ordinary radio receiver having the lowest possible noise figure, high sensitivity, and a bandwidth appropriate for handling the pulses involved.   The receiver video output is usually displayed on a cathode-ray tube indicator in such a manner as to show the time difference between the outgoing pulses and the returning echoes. To achieve this result, the sweep voltage of the cathode-ray-tube display is synchronized with the transmitted pulses.

The Radar Equation.   The factors that determine the range of a radar set can be derived as follows:

Notations:

d = distance to target

S = equivalent cross-sectional area of target

P_T = transmitter power (peak)

P_R = echo power (peak) absorbed by receiving antenna

G_T = power gain of transmitter antenna relative to isotropic radiator

G_R = power gain of receiving antenna relative to isotropic radiator

λ = wavelength

A = capture area of receiving antenna

A_0 = aperture area of receiving antenna

k = A/A_0 = a constant having a value of about 0.65 for parabolic antennas, and 0.9 for mattress antennas

Consistent units of length and power must be used.

The equivalent power in the direction of the beam is P_TG_T, while the surface area of a sphere of radius d is $4\pi d^2$. Hence

$$\left.\begin{array}{l}\text{Power per unit}\\\text{area at target}\end{array}\right\} = \frac{P_TG_T}{4\pi d^2} \tag{26-1}$$

This energy strikes the target and is scattered in various directions, some being returned in the direction of the radar antenna. It is customary to describe the target in terms of an equivalent cross section S such that if the total power contained in a section of the incident wavefront having the area S were radiated by an isotropic radiator located at the target, the strength of the wave thereby reaching the receiving antenna would be the same as the strength of the actual echo produced by the target. The echo power per unit area of wavefront at the radar receiver is accordingly

$$\left.\begin{array}{l}\text{Echo power per unit}\\\text{area at receiver}\end{array}\right\} = \frac{P_TG_T}{4\pi d^2} S \frac{1}{4\pi d^2} \tag{26-2}$$

The power delivered to the receiving system is this power density multiplied by the capture area A_0 of the receiving antenna, or

$$\text{Received power} = P_R = \frac{P_TG_TS}{(4\pi)^2 d^4} A \tag{26-3}$$

The capture area A is related to the gain of the antenna according to Eq. (23-28):

$$G_R = 4\pi \frac{A}{\lambda^2} = \frac{4\pi k A_0}{\lambda^2} \tag{26-4}$$

When the same antenna is used for reception and transmission, $G_R = G_T$, and one has

$$P_R = \frac{P_TG_R{}^2\lambda^2 S}{(4\pi)^3 d^4} = \frac{P_TSk^2A_0{}^2}{4\pi\lambda^2 d^4} \tag{26-5}$$

If $P_{R_{\min}}$ is then the minimum value of available received power P_R that is detectable by the receiver as limited by receiver noise, then solving Eq. (26-5) for d gives the maximum range:

$$d_{\max} = \sqrt[4]{\frac{P_TG_R{}^2\lambda^2 S}{(4\pi)^3 P_{R_{\min}}}} = \sqrt[4]{\frac{P_Tk^2A_0{}^2 S}{4\pi\lambda^2 P_{R_{\min}}}} \tag{26-6}$$

Radar Performance Factors.   Examination of Eq. (26-5) shows that the received echo energy is inversely proportional to the fourth power of the range; a 16-fold increase in peak power is thus required to double the range.   In contrast, it follows from Eq. (26-6) that increasing the physical size of the antenna is a very effective means for increasing the range; this is because a larger antenna concentrates the transmitted power in a narrower beam and simultaneously has a larger capture area.[1]   Reducing the wavelength likewise increases the received power for a given transmitter power (neglecting variation of atmospheric absorption with frequency), because with an antenna of a given physical size, a shorter wavelength concentrates a given amount of radiated power into a narrower, and hence more intense, beam, while not affecting capture area.

The proper pulse length is a compromise.   A short pulse is necessary for resolving individual targets close together in range, or for seeing targets close to the radar.   On the other hand, the receiver bandwidth, and hence receiver noise power, are inversely proportional to the pulse length.   Thus for a given peak power, long pulses give greater range than short pulses.   In actual practice radar pulse lengths usually lie in the range 0.1 to 10 μsec.

The maximum allowable pulse-repetition frequency is limited by the need for allowing a sufficient time interval between successive pulses for the return of echoes from the maximum range desired for the radar.   On the other hand, the repetition frequency should not be lower than necessary, since the integration effect discussed below causes weak echoes to be more easily detected the greater the number of pulses received per second. Pulse-repetition frequencies normally lie in the range 200 to 10,000 cycles, although values as low as 60 cycles are sometimes employed.

The fact that long pulses give greater range than short pulses of the same peak power, plus the fact that a weak echo is more easily distinguished from the noise the higher the pulse-repetition frequency, leads to the important conclusion that *range* depends primarily upon the *average power* rather than upon the peak power.

The effective target area S is a function of the properties of the target rather than of radar design.   For a small propeller-driven fighter plane, S may on the average be 10 sq m, while for a large bomber S might be 150 sq m, although the exact values will vary greatly with the direction from which the aircraft is viewed.   Ships represent much larger values of S, while land masses, cities, etc., are even larger targets.

The noise figure of the radar receiver is a particularly important factor in determining the performance of a radar system.   It is apparent from Eq. (26-6) that decreasing $P_{R_{min}}$ by improving the noise figure of the

---

[1] The maximum amount of directivity that it is practical to use is limited, however, since if the beam is too sharp, the time it takes to scan a region thoroughly enough to locate a target becomes excessive.

receiver is equivalent to increasing the transmitter power. This improvement in the receiving system usually involves not only less cost but also less size and weight than does an equivalent improvement obtained by increased transmitter power.

The ability to observe a weak echo in the presence of receiver noise is increased by the fact that the echo reappears on each range sweep at a fixed range for successive radar pulses, whereas interfering noise is random in character. Thus any integration process that averages the response over a period of time emphasizes the echo in relationship to the noise. The eye is an effective integrator of this type, and there are likewise types of cathode-ray screens for which the full visual response is obtained only by a succession of pulses ("hits") at the same point on the fluorescent screen.

The maximum range of a radar set is ordinarily many miles for even a small aircraft. For example, if one assumes $P_T = 250$ kw, $G_R = 2000$, $S = 12.5$ sq m, $\lambda = 10$ cm, and $P_{R_{min}} = 1 \times 10^{-13}$ watt (corresponding to a receiver bandwidth of 1 Mc and a noise figure of 14 db for signal equal to noise), Eq. (26-6) gives the maximum range d_{max} as 158 km or 98 miles.

Powers and Frequencies Used in Radar. The output of a radar transmitter is expressed in terms of the *peak power*. This is the power that would be generated if the transmitter operated continuously at the power level represented by the pulses. Typical values of radar power lie within the range 100 to 500 kw, although values both lower and higher find use in particular cases.

The fraction of time the radar transmitter is generating pulse power is termed the *duty cycle*, and is given by the product of pulse repetition frequency and pulse width. Thus, in any one second, a radar producing 1-μsec pulses at a rate of 1000 per sec is "on" for

$$1 \times 10^{-6} \times 1000 = 0.001 \text{ sec}$$

The duty cycle is then 0.001, and the *average power* is given by the product of duty cycle and peak power; thus if the peak power were 500 kw, the average power would be 500 watts.

Most radar equipments operate in the frequency range 100 to 25,000 Mc, with concentrations in a few bands in the 1000- to 10,000-Mc range. These bands are commonly identified by letters—L, S, X, etc.—commonly applied to the broader frequency divisions listed in Table 26-1.

Long-range radars usually operate in the S and L bands, with P band also finding some use for this application. Most airborne radars, and practically all radars designed for high resolution in range and bearing, operate at frequencies above 2500 Mc and generally in the order of 10,000 Mc. This permits the generation of narrow, high-gain antenna patterns with antenna structures of reasonable size.

TABLE 26-1
BAND DESIGNATION

Band	Frequency range, Kmc*	Wavelength range, cm*	Center of active region, Mc
P	0.22–0.39	133–77	300
L	0.39–1.55	77–19	1,000
S	1.55–5.2	19–5.8	3,000
C†	3.9–6.2	7.7–4.8	5,500
X	5.2–10.9	5.8–2.7	9,000
K	10.9–36	2.7–0.83	25,000

* The limits given are approximate as no formal standards exist.
† The C band is composed of adjoining portions of the S and X bands.

26-2. Radar Transmitting Systems. As indicated in Fig. 26-1, a radar transmitter, when reduced to its simplest elements, consists of a source of radio-frequency power, a modulator and associated synchronizer for controlling this power in the form of pulses, an antenna, and a duplexer.

Radars operating at frequencies up to about 600 Mc commonly obtain their power from triode tubes in a resonant-line oscillator circuit. For higher frequencies, the cavity magnetron has until recently been the only tube capable of generating the high peak powers required in radar. However, the successful development of the high-power klystron now makes available an alternative to the magnetron.

Modulators.[1] The modulator, indicated in Fig. 26-1, generates a pulse of appropriate amplitude, length, and repetition rate, for application between the anode and cathode of the power tube of the radar transmitter. The power requirements involved may be considerable; thus a 1-megawatt radar operating at 50 per cent efficiency will require a modulator capable of supplying 2000 kw peak power to the power tube.

Two types of modulators are in common use: the line pulser, described in Sec. 18-9, and the hard-tube, or power-amplifier, pulser. A typical line pulser for operating a magnetron is shown in Fig. 26-2. Here an artificial line is employed which is designed to have a characteristic impedance equal to the load impedance represented by magnetron tube T_2, and an equivalent length such that a round trip corresponds to the desired pulse duration. During the interval between pulses the line is charged to the voltage E_b through inductance L and diode T_3; the diode is necessary to permit the passage of the line charging current because the magnetron does not conduct when its anode is negative. The synchronizer initiates output pulses by applying trigger pulses to T_1, which connects the line to its magnetron load during the short pulse interval;

---

[1] The reader desiring detailed information on modulator practices is referred to J. F. Reintjes and G. T. Coate, *op. cit.*, chap. 3, pp. 153–214.

the inductance L serves to isolate the power supply.   The line pulser is simple and efficient but inflexible in operation.

A typical hard-tube pulser is shown in Fig. 26-3a, where the load is again supplied by magnetron tube T_2.   Here triode tube T_1 is biased beyond cutoff and then excited by positive pulses of the desired length and repetition frequency.   Between these pulses tube T_1 carries no current and capacitor C is charged up to plate-supply voltage E_b through very high resistance R and series diode T_3.   However, during the pulse the grid of T_1 is driven moderately positive, causing the plate-cathode circuit of T_1 to change suddenly from an open circuit to a low resistance

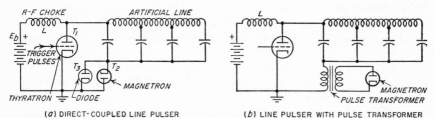

(a) DIRECT-COUPLED LINE PULSER   (b) LINE PULSER WITH PULSE TRANSFORMER

Fig. 26-2. Magnetron tube operated by a line pulser.

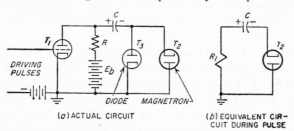

(a) ACTUAL CIRCUIT   (b) EQUIVALENT CIR-
                                      CUIT DURING PULSE

Fig. 26-3. Hard-tube pulser.

R_1.   The equivalent circuit of the system then takes the form shown in Fig. 26-3b, and a large positive voltage is applied to the magnetron anode. For proper operation, the capacitor C should be sufficiently large so that during the time it is discharging into the magnetron the change of voltage across C will not be sufficient to alter appreciably the frequency and power output of the magnetron.

As compared with the line pulser, the hard-tube pulser has the advantage that the pulse length can be easily adjusted by merely changing the length of the driving pulse; it is also more suitable for generating multiple or "coded" pulses.   The disadvantage of the hard-tube pulser is that it is bulkier and more expensive, since the total energy that must be stored in the capacitor is much greater than the energy of a single pulse; also the high-vacuum switching tube has a higher voltage drop and hence consumes more power than does the thyratron.   Both types of modulators find extensive use in radar systems.

A pulse transformer is often used to couple a modulator to the load

impedance. Such an arrangement applied to the line pulser of Fig.
26-2a is shown in Fig. 26-2b; a similar arrangement could also be used
with a hard-tube pulser. The pulse transformer must be designed to
preserve the shape of the pulse, as discussed on page 658, and must likewise be so proportioned that it can handle high power and high voltage
without core saturation or insulation breakdown. The use of a pulse
transformer provides flexibility in the design and use of a modulator.

26-3. Radar Antennas. *Pattern Types and Considerations.* The
character of the directive pattern desired in a radar antenna depends upon
the application. Thus, radars designed to locate targets by "searchlight" techniques use "pencil" beams of circular cross section. On the
other hand, ground-based air-search radars normally employ a beam with
maximum possible azimuth resolution, but with a vertical pattern shaped

FIG. 26-4. Typical antenna directional patterns used in a ground-based radar intended
to search for airborne targets, and used in airborne radar for observing ground
targets.

as shown in Fig. 26-4. Here some energy is radiated at high vertical
angles in order to detect the presence of planes at these angles (compare
with Fig. 26-8d), but since the planes at such vertical angles will be close
to the radar, the energy at high angles is made less than at low angles.[1,2]
Again, "height-finder" radars, i.e., radars which are to give an accurate
measure of elevation angle, will have a directivity in the vertical plane
that greatly exceeds that in the horizontal plane. Antenna directivity
and coverage is sufficiently important so that some complex radar systems employ multiple transmitters and antennas, which in combination
produce the desired pattern.

The type of antenna employed in a particular radar system depends on
the frequency and also on the application involved. Low-frequency
ground radars normally employ mattress antennas with reflectors. At
higher frequencies parabolic reflectors are standard for practically all
applications. Such reflectors are sometimes rotational paraboloids, and

[1] The strength of the echoes received from a particular target at a given altitude
will be independent of the distance over the range of vertical angles θ (measured with
respect to the horizontal) for which the antenna pattern possesses a field strength
proportional to csc θ. This corresponds to radiated power proportional to $\csc^2 \theta$,
and the antenna giving this result is commonly called a "cosecant-squared" antenna.
The antenna patterns of Fig. 26-4 possess a csc θ characteristic for values of θ from
$\theta_{\min}$ to $\theta \rightarrow 90°$.

[2] The same pattern is commonly used by an airborne radar that is to view ground
targets, as shown in Fig. 26-4.

sometimes cylindrical paraboloids; they also often have portions cut away or are deformed in order to modify the shape of the pattern.

The directive gain of a radar antenna depends upon the physical size of the antenna measured in wavelengths in accordance with Eq. (23-28). Thus even a large antenna will have only a moderate gain at the lower radar frequencies, whereas at the shorter microwaves beams of small diameter can be produced for tracking radars such that a target is difficult to find without the aid of a second radar having a less directive beam.

It is important that the directive pattern of a radar antenna be free from minor lobes of significant amplitude, particularly in the horizontal plane. Otherwise objects that are not too distant will produce detectable

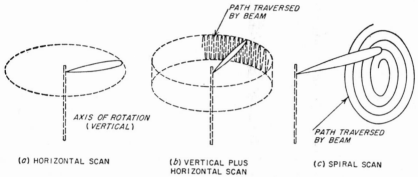

(a) HORIZONTAL SCAN   (b) VERTICAL PLUS   (c) SPIRAL SCAN
                             HORIZONTAL SCAN

Fig. 26-5. Representative scanning methods.

echoes when illuminated by a minor lobe. Such echoes will be displayed by the radar indicator as though they were returned from the direction in which the main lobe points, with the result that the radar indication is partially incorrect in a way that results in confusion. Thus the techniques mentioned on page 876 for minimizing or eliminating minor lobes find important applications in radar work.

Antenna Scanning. In nearly all types of radar it is necessary to be able to vary the direction in which the antenna beam points. Such *scanning* is ordinarily accomplished by an actual motion of the antenna; a few representative examples of scanning sequences are shown in Fig. 26-5. In radar equipment designed for general search or navigational purposes, scanning ordinarily involves rotating the antenna about a vertical axis (Fig. 26-5a). A typical scan for height-finder radars combines a rapid rocker motion in the vertical plane with a much slower azimuth scan about a vertical axis, as in Fig. 26-5b. The spiral scan of Fig. 26-5c provides an effective means of searching a limited solid angle. In all complex arrangements involving motion in both vertical and horizontal directions, it is necessary that the separation between adjacent sweeps of the beam not exceed half of the width of the beam. Otherwise some directions in space will not be searched.

Rotating Joint.   In systems where the antenna is mechanically scanned, it is necessary to transfer the transmitted and received power through some form of rotating joint.   Sliding contacts can be avoided by the use of *choke joints,* such as shown in Fig. 26-6.   Here gap *a* acts as a short circuit to current flowing axially in the wall of the outer conductor because it is a half wavelength distant from short circuit *c* (see page 121). At the same time, gap *b* does not adversely effect the behavior since it is located a quarter of a wavelength away from the short circuit, and so is in series with the line *abc* at a point where the line impedance looking toward *c* is extremely high.   A similar arrangement can be devised for the center conductor, as shown.   Thus the right-hand side of the coaxial line in Fig. 26-6 may be rotated freely with respect to the left-hand side without the necessity of providing an electrical contact.

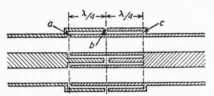

With circular waveguides, a rotating joint can be used that is similar to that of Fig. 26-6.   In the case of systems involving rectangu-

Fig. 26-6. A choke-type rotating joint for use with coaxial line.

lar guides, it is possible to use a tapered section to transform to a guide having a circular cross section that contains the rotating section, and then to taper back to a rectangular guide; alternatively one may transform from waveguide to coaxial line and back again.

Lobe Switching.   The accuracy with which the angular direction of a radar target can be determined is greatly increased by comparing the power received for two different orientations of the radiated beam.   This technique, termed *lobe switching,* is illustrated in Fig. 26-7a, where the directional pattern of the antenna is switched rapidly between A and B. A target in the direction α_0 will then give echo signals that have equal strength for the two lobe positions, while targets that are slightly off to one side, such as α_1 or α_2, will give return signals for the two lobe positions that are distinctly unequal in strength.   The direction α_0 in which equality in response is obtained for the two lobe positions is very sharply defined, so its angular position can be obtained with high precision.

With mattress antennas lobe switching can be obtained by a mechanical switch that connects the feed line alternately to one end and to the other end of the antenna system, as illustrated schematically in Fig. 26-7a.   Such an arrangement takes advantage of the fact that the attenuation and phase shift accompanying the transmission of power across the mattress can be made to cause the lobe maximum to deviate slightly from perpendicular to the array, toward the end away from the feed point.

A common method of obtaining lobe switching in parabolic antennas consists in placing the exciting antenna slightly off center with respect to the focal point, and then rotating it about the axis of the parabola at a rotation rate slow compared with the pulse-repetition frequency. This arrangement, termed *conical scanning*, is illustrated in Fig. 26-7*b*, and is especially convenient where it is necessary to make angle measurements in both vertical and horizontal planes.

Effect of Ground on Radar Antenna Characteristics.　　The ground has an important effect on the directional characteristics of the radar antenna in

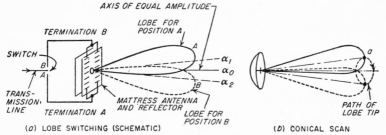

(a) LOBE SWITCHING (SCHEMATIC)　　　　　　(b) CONICAL SCAN

Fig. 26-7. Lobe switching with mattress antenna, and conical-scan type of lobe switching.

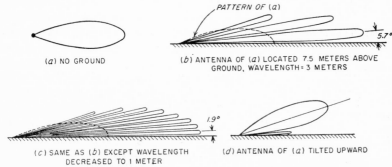

(a) NO GROUND　　　　　　(b) ANTENNA OF (a) LOCATED 7.5 METERS ABOVE GROUND, WAVELENGTH = 3 METERS

(c) SAME AS (b) EXCEPT WAVELENGTH DECREASED TO 1 METER　　　　　(d) ANTENNA OF (a) TILTED UPWARD

Fig. 26-8. Effect of ground on directional characteristics of antennas.

the vertical plane when the antenna is located near the ground. Thus if the directional characteristic of the particular radar antenna in the absence of the ground is as shown in Fig. 26-8*a*, then the directional pattern at 100 Mc with the antenna 7.5 m (25 ft) above the ground is as shown in Fig. 26-8*b*.[1] It will be noted that while the ground reflection can produce an important increase in the field strength at certain angles, it also produces blind spots resulting from the pattern nulls. When an aircraft flies through the lobes at a constant height, it will as a consequence alternately appear and disappear from the sight of the radar.

Increasing the frequency of the radar, while keeping the antenna height above the ground constant, lowers the angle above the horizon at which the first lobe appears (as shown in Fig. 26-8*c*), and thus improves the low-

[1] This assumes horizontal polarization, or in the case of vertical polarization, that the vertical angle is appreciably less than the Brewster angle.

angle coverage.[1] As the frequency increases, the lobe structure also becomes finer; as a result of the more numerous nulls in the pattern, an aircraft target is lost more frequently but for shorter time intervals.

Ground effects can be eliminated by orienting the transmitting antenna so that little energy strikes the ground.   This is illustrated in Fig. 26-8d. Under such conditions there is no fine-lobed structure, but the coverage is poorer at low vertical angles.

26-4. The Duplexer.   The *duplexer*, indicated in Fig. 26-1, enables the same antenna to be used for both transmission and reception.   It makes use of fast-acting radio-frequency switches known as "TR (transmit-receive) boxes" and "anti-TR (ATR) boxes" which are operated by

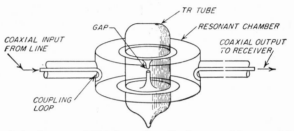

FIG. 26-9. Typical microwave TR tube and cavity for use with a coaxial transmission system.

energy from the transmitted pulse, and which protect the sensitive receiver from the damaging effect of the high energy of the transmitter.

A typical TR box arranged for use in coaxial circuits is shown in Fig. 26-9 and consists of a resonant cavity associated with a special cold-cathode tube.[2]   The tube contains gas at low pressure, and the presence of the high-energy transmitter pulse causes ionization across the narrow, internal gap.   This destroys the resonance in the TR box, which then acts essentially as a short circuit, and there is little transmission of energy from input to output line.   The discharge takes very little energy to maintain.   On the other hand, when the gas tube is inoperative, the cavity resonance enables energy to be transferred freely through the resonant cavity.   There are similar units for waveguide systems, the coupling loops being replaced by "windows" that match the cavity to the impedance of the guide.

An anti-TR box is a TR box with the output lead omitted.   Normally it serves as either a short-circuited or open-circuited load impedance.

---

[1] Low-angle coverage is very important to a long-range search radar, since the range for low-flying aircraft, which at best is severely limited by the earth curvature, is further reduced if there is little or no signal radiated close to the horizon.

[2] An extensive discussion of gas tubes suitable for TR and ATR service is given by A. L. Samuel, J. W. Clark, and W. W. Mumford, The Gas-discharge Transmit-receive Tube, *Bell System Tech. J.*, vol. 25, p. 48, January, 1946.

A typical duplexer, suitable for either a coaxial or two-wire line system, is shown in Fig. 26-10a. With the transmitter output power on, the TR and ATR boxes both ionize and approximate short circuits. The equivalent circuit of the system is then as shown in Fig. 26-10b. The branch lines cd and ab now have no effect upon the transmitter operation, because, being an odd number of quarter wavelengths long and short-circuited at the ends d and b, respectively, they represent an extremely high impedance shunting the transmission line. At the same time, since the TR box approximates a short circuit at b, it prevents what little energy does reach b from going on to the receiver, and so serves the highly important purpose of isolating the receiver.

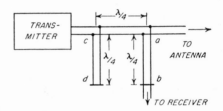

(a) LAYOUT OF DUPLEXER SYSTEM

Following the end of the pulse, the TR and ATR boxes deionize very rapidly and become open circuits, which leads to the equivalent circuit shown in Fig. 26-10c. The open circuit at d places a very low impedance across the line at c, which in turn causes the impedance looking toward the transmitter from a to be very high. As a consequence, substantially all of the echo energy coming in from the receiving antenna and reaching a travels toward the receiver, and the transmitter is effectively disconnected.

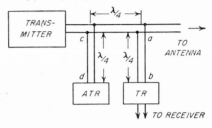

(b) EQUIVALENT CIRCUIT DURING TRANSMISSION OF PULSE

Duplexers analogous to that of Fig. 26-10 can be devised for use with waveguide systems.

26-5. Radar Receivers. Radar receivers are fundamentally ordinary ultra-high-frequency or micro-

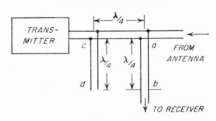

(c) EQUIVALENT CIRCUIT WHEN TRANSMITTER IS INOPERATIVE

FIG. 26-10. A duplexer system for enabling the same antenna to be used for both transmission and reception.

wave superheterodyne receivers (Sec. 24-4) having a low noise figure and possessing the intermediate-frequency and video bandwidths required to reproduce the radar pulse. The most commonly used intermediate frequencies are 30 and 60 Mc.

A low noise figure is important because at the frequencies used in radar, the weakest signal that can be detected is determined by noise generated within the receiver itself, as discussed on page 961. At frequencies in the L band and lower, a grounded-grid triode radio-frequency amplifier aids in achieving a low noise figure.   However, at higher frequencies a good crystal mixer will have a lower noise figure than an amplifier, which is therefore omitted.   In the S band, an over-all noise figure of the order of 8 to 10 db is about the best that can be obtained when duplexer and transmission-line losses are taken into account.   At lower frequencies the noise figure will generally be better than this, and at higher frequencies somewhat worse.

The proper receiver bandwidth is a compromise between the desire to preserve the form of the received echo pulses, and the desire not to admit an undue amount of noise.   If the pulse width is τ sec, the highest signal-to-noise ratio is obtained when the bandwidth of the intermediate-frequency system is approximately $1.2/\tau$.   The maximum is broad, and

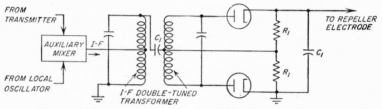

Fig. 26-11. Automatic-frequency-control system suitable for use in a microwave radar receiver to correct for slow drifts in the frequencies of transmitter and receiver oscillators.

bandwidths between $1/\tau$ and $2/\tau$ are acceptable in most radar applications.   However, in those systems in which it is necessary to preserve the sharpness of the leading edge of a pulse as an aid to accurate range determination, bandwidths up to $5/\tau$ are sometimes used at the expense of a poorer signal-to-noise ratio.   The bandwidth of the video system should be at least half that of the intermediate-frequency amplifier.

Automatic Frequency Control.   In microwave radar receivers, the intermediate frequency is such a small percentage of the transmitted frequency that it is desirable automatically to control the frequency of the local oscillator in such a manner as to ensure that the difference between the transmitted and local-oscillator frequencies will lie within the passband of the intermediate-frequency amplifier.

A typical automatic-frequency-control system that will prevent slow drifts in the intermediate frequency is shown in Fig. 26-11.   Here, a small amount of pulsed energy obtained directly from the transmitter is combined in a separate mixer with energy from a klystron local oscillator. The resulting difference-frequency output of the mixer is applied to a phase-shift discriminator such as that of Fig. 17-15, which is adjusted so that its center frequency corresponds to the desired intermediate frequency.   The discriminator will accordingly develop a d-c output having a magnitude and polarity determined by the magnitude and sense of the deviation of the local oscillator from the value required to produce the desired intermediate frequency. This control voltage is then applied to the repeller electrode of the reflex-klystron local oscillator, thus correcting its frequency.

The time constant of the output circuit of the discriminator in Fig. 26-11 must be great enough to maintain the output voltage sufficiently constant during the interval between transmitted pulses so that the frequency change in the reflex klystron between pulses will be appreciably less than the bandwidth of the intermediate-frequency amplifier. At the same time, the time constant of the circuit should be no greater than required to achieve this result, since otherwise the automatic-frequency-control system will be unnecessarily sluggish in responding to needed changes in frequency.

In radar transmitters operating at the higher microwave frequencies and powered by magnetron tubes, the transmitted frequency is affected by waves reflected back into the antenna from nearby reflecting objects. The transmitted frequency then varies as the radar beam is scanned past such an object; if this scanning is rapid it may be necessary to employ a fast-acting automatic-frequency-control system in the receiver. This requires that the output circuit of the discriminator have a small time constant, i.e., small by-pass capacitors. The resulting output is then in the form of pulses having a magnitude and sign which depend on the amount and direction of the deviation of the intermediate frequency from the assigned value. Since these pulses would pulse the klystron frequency if they were applied directly to its repeller electrode, they are instead used as a control for the magnitude of the d-c voltage that is actually applied to the repeller electrode. This control operates so that each pulse from the discriminator outputs corrects the d-c voltage in a way determined by the magnitude and polarity of the pulse.[1]

26-6. Indicators for Radar Receivers.   The output of a radar receiver is nearly always presented to the radar operator in the form of visual indications obtained with the aid of a cathode-ray tube.   Presentations are *deflection modulated,* or *intensity modulated,* depending on whether the trace is deflected or brightened by the presence of an echo.   Since radar is fundamentally a range-measuring device, one coordinate in practically all displays represents range.   Beyond this, the displays take a variety of forms in accordance with the nature and objective of the radar.

Deflection Modulation.   The most common form of deflection is the type A display, illustrated in Fig. 26-12.   Here horizontal deflection is obtained by the use of a linear saw-tooth voltage wave synchronized with the transmitted pulses, while vertical deflection is produced by the

---

[1] For further details see "Microwave Receivers" (vol. 23, Radiation Laboratory Series), pp. 56–74, McGraw-Hill Book Company, Inc., New York, 1948.

receiver output.   Direct-current restoration is employed in the receiver so that the vertical deflection will always be upward from the base line.

The type A presentation, such as illustrated in Fig. 26-12, will normally show numerous fixed echoes originating from objects in the vicinity of the transmitter and often called "ground clutter," as illustrated, together with additional more-distant permanent echoes arising from relatively large fixed objects further away.   In general, the sensitivity of radar receivers is always adjusted so that the receiver noise will produce visible deflections, termed "grass," above the base line.

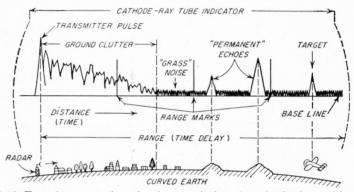

FIG. 26-12. Type A presentation, showing correlation of received echoes with ground and air targets.

Intensity Modulation.   The most widely used form of intensity modulation is the plan-position indicator (PPI) illustrated in Fig. 26-13.   Here a saw-tooth timing wave deflects the cathode-ray spot radially outward from the center, and is so synchronized with the transmitted pulse that distance outward from the center is proportional to the distance of the echo-producing target from the radar transmitter.   The angular direction in which the saw-tooth timing wave deflects the cathode-ray spot at any instant is made to correspond to the direction in which the antenna beam is directed at that moment.   The signals from the receiver output are applied to the control electrode of the cathode-ray tube after d-c restoration.   The bias on the control electrode is adjusted to be just slightly greater than cutoff.   Thus a signal of significant amplitude causes the spot to be turned on.   The result is that the echoes are presented to the radar operator as bright spots that give range and azimuth on a map in their true relation in polar coordinates.[1]   The usual method of obtaining

[1] In the case of a PPI picture of the ground obtained from an aircraft (or of aircraft as observed on a ground radar), the distance to the target is the *slant range*, and is significantly greater than the true horizontal distance for horizontal distances that are not considerably greater than the aircraft height.   Under these conditions the PPI pattern is distorted near the center.

the radial deflection required in the PPI indication is to employ magnetic deflecting coils[1] that are rotated synchronously with the antenna.

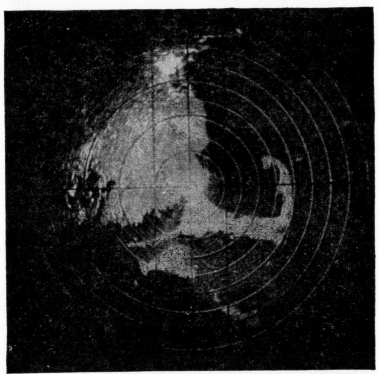

FIG. 26-13. PPI presentation showing Cape Cod as viewed by a radar in an aircraft.

Electrical Coordinates. Coordinates are often introduced electrically in such a manner as to be made part of the presentation. Thus range markers can be introduced on a type A presentation, as shown in Fig. 26-12, by superimposing on the vertical deflecting system very short pulses spaced in time according to the range intervals to be indicated, and appropriately synchronized with the transmitted pulses.

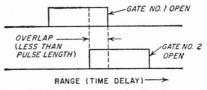

FIG. 26-14. Arrangement of gates used in range tracking.

Again, circles corresponding to particular range values may be added to the PPI display as shown in Fig. 26-13. These are produced by applying to the control electrode short positive pulses that are synchro-

[1] To obtain a deflection that starts from the center and travels outward linearly with time, it is necessary that the current through the magnetic deflecting coil be a saw-tooth wave, and include a d-c component such that the minimum amplitude of the wave is zero.

nized with the transmitted pulse, but delayed to correspond to the various ranges to be marked.

Cathode-ray-tube Characteristics.   Cathode-ray tubes used in PPI displays employ long-persistence phosphors which retain the pattern from antenna scan to antenna scan.   The build-up characteristics of such phosphors are such as to favor repetitive "hits" representing successive returns from a particular target; this improves the signal-to-noise discrimination, as discussed on page 1019.

On the other hand, short-persistence screens are normally used in deflection-modulation displays.   Here the same pattern is normally retraced many times per second, and the eye serves as an effective integrating device.

26-7. Automatic-tracking Radars.   A radar is sometimes arranged so that its antenna is continuously pointed in the direction of a target, while simultaneously a "range gate" follows the same target and provides continuous range information.   Such an automatic-tracking arrangement can be used to aim guns, provide continuous data for plotting, etc.

Tracking both in azimuth and elevation can be readily obtained by employing a conical scan.[1]   When the antenna does not point in exactly the proper direction, the return pulses will then be modulated in amplitude at the conical-scan rate, with the phase of the amplitude modulation indicating the error in direction.   This modulation envelope of the returning pulses is used as an error signal to actuate a servo system that readjusts the antenna position in both azimuth and elevation as required.

Tracking in range can be achieved by applying the receiver output to two gated amplifiers having their inputs connected in parallel.   The gates on these amplifiers are synchronized with the transmitted pulses in such a manner that each gate is open for only a moderate number of microseconds at a definite and adjustable time interval after each transmitted pulse.   The two gates are adjusted in timing to give an overlap slightly less than a pulse length, as illustrated in Fig. 26-14.   If the returning pulses lie entirely in one gate or in the other, the overlap portion corresponds to a range that is either slightly too small or slightly too large, as the case may be.   The difference in output of the gates thus represents an error signal that can be used to readjust the range of the pair of gates so that the overlap of the two gates corresponds to a time delay representing the exact range of the target.   When the gate system is thus correctly adjusted, the two gated amplifiers produce equal output signals, and the time delay of the gates corresponding to this condition gives the

---

[1] Automatic tracking in azimuth only is obtained by employing a simple lobe-switching arrangement that shifts the position of the beam slightly in the horizontal plane (see Fig. 26-7*a*).   The difference in strength of the returned signals for the two lobe positions is then used as an error signal that actuates a servomechanism which corrects the antenna position.

actual range.   As an aid to target discrimination, only energy common
to both range gates is fed to the angle-tracking circuits.

**26-8. Moving-target Indicators (MTI) and Suppression of Permanent
Echoes.**   It is difficult for an observer to distinguish a moving target
in the presence of permanent echoes of comparable appearance on a radar
presentation.   A further difficulty arises if the moving target has a range
and bearing such that its echo is actually superimposed on the ground
clutter.   This is a particularly troublesome situation in mountainous
regions and near cities.

The Doppler Effect Associated with Moving Targets.   The relationship
existing at the radar between the phase of the transmitted pulse and the
phase of the resulting echo from a fixed target is the same for successive
pulses.   In contrast, the relative phase of the echo signals received from a
moving target continually changes with respect to the phase of the transmitted pulse, because of the fact that the distance to the target is changing.   For example, movement of the target by a distance $\Delta d/\lambda$ wavelengths during the time interval Δt between pulses will cause the relative
phase of the returned echoes to shift by an amount $\Delta\phi$ radians, where

$$\Delta\phi = 2 \times 2\pi \frac{\Delta d}{\lambda} \qquad (26\text{-}7)$$

The fact that the relative phase of the echo varies when the target is
moving, and is constant when the target is fixed, provides a means of distinguishing between fixed and moving targets.

The continuous change in phase of the echoes from a radially moving
target causes the frequency of the echoes to differ from the frequency of
the outgoing pulses.   This Doppler shift Δf in frequency is given by the
relation

$$\Delta f = \frac{1}{2\pi} \frac{\Delta\phi}{\Delta t} = 2 \frac{V_r}{\lambda} \qquad (26\text{-}8)$$

where Δt is the time between pulses during which the phase shifts $\Delta\phi$
radians, and $V_r = \Delta d/\Delta t$ is the radial velocity of the target.

MTI Systems.   A means of utilizing the Doppler effect to eliminate
permanent echoes while preserving echoes from a moving target, illustrated in Figs. 26-15 and 26-16, is termed a *moving-target-indicator
(MTI) system.*   Here the phase of the echo signal existing in the intermediate-frequency amplifier system of a standard radar receiver is compared in a phase detector with the phase of a reference oscillator so
operated that its phase is related in a definite way to the phase of the
transmitted pulse.   In such a system, the permanent echoes have the
same relative phase from pulse to pulse, and so produce a phase-detector
output that is identical for successive pulses (see Fig. 26-15).   Consequently, by subtracting the phase-detector output for the first pulse from

that for the second, the second from the third, etc., the permanent echoes are canceled out, and so do not appear on the oscilloscope presentation of the radar receiver output.

In contrast, successive echoes from moving targets have different phases with respect to the reference oscillator. The phase detector will accordingly deliver an output from a moving target that varies in amplitude from pulse to pulse, as illustrated in Fig. 26-15. When the phase-detector outputs for successive pulses are subtracted from each other the moving targets therefore fail to cancel, and so are visible in the presentation,[1] free of fixed echoes.

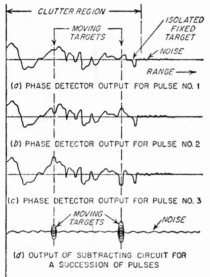

(a) PHASE DETECTOR OUTPUT FOR PULSE NO. 1

(b) PHASE DETECTOR OUTPUT FOR PULSE NO. 2

(c) PHASE DETECTOR OUTPUT FOR PULSE NO. 3

(d) OUTPUT OF SUBTRACTING CIRCUIT FOR A SUCCESSION OF PULSES

Fig. 26-15. MTI video waveforms.

The apparatus for carrying out the necessary MTI operations is illustrated schematically in Fig. 26-16. Here the receiver-channel components are identical with those of a standard radar receiver, except that the local oscillator is designed to have particularly good frequency stability,[2] and a limiter (i.e., clipper) is included in the intermediate-frequency amplifier so that the echo signals applied to the phase detector will always have the same amplitude. The oscillator providing the reference phase is termed a coherent or *coho* oscillator, and is a stable oscillator operating at a frequency that is very closely the difference between transmitter and stalo frequencies.

When a magnetron is employed in the radar transmitter, the phase of each transmitted pulse is randomly related to the phase of the previous pulses. It is hence necessary that the phase of the coho oscillator be matched anew with the phase of the transmitter for each transmitted pulse. This is accomplished by injecting power from each transmitted pulse into the "coho channel" of Fig. 26-16 by means of the coupling indicated. If the coho oscillator is stable in frequency, its phase in the time interval between pulses is then related to the phase of the oscillations of the last outgoing pulse in exactly the same way for successive pulses. The phase comparison between the coho oscillator and the amplitude-

[1] The only exceptions to this occur when (1) the radial velocity of the target is zero, or (2) when the velocity is such that the phase difference between successive returning pulses is exactly a multiple of 2π; this latter condition is termed a "blind" speed. However, in practice, neither of these conditions is likely to persist for more than a few seconds at a time.

[2] The term *stalo* is often used to designate such a *sta*ble *lo*cal oscillator.

limited intermediate-frequency echo signal can be made by means of a
phase detector of the type illustrated in Fig. 25-27.

The phase-detector outputs for successive pulses may be subtracted
from each other by employing a delay line in the manner illustrated.
This line typically consists of a mercury or quartz transmission line,
upon which are impressed mechanical vibrations lying in the frequency
range 10 to 20 Mc, modulated by the video signals.[1]   The line length is

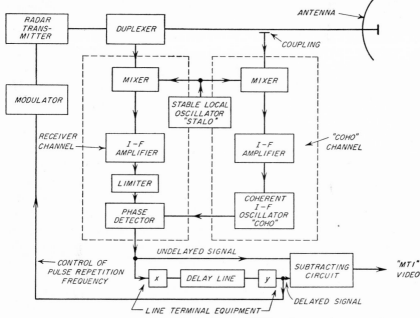

Fig. 26-16. Schematic diagram of MTI radar system.

such as to produce a delay corresponding exactly to the interval between
successive pulses; this can be ensured by using the delayed outgoing pulse
to trigger off the next outgoing pulse.   Thus at the same instant that an
echo is received from a particular target due to the last pulse transmitted,
the output of the delay line is delivering an echo from the same target
corresponding to the phase-detector output produced by the next-to-last
transmitted pulse.   The delayed and undelayed echoes are then subtracted by first reversing the polarity of one of them, and adding.

It will be noted that the phase comparison in Fig. 25-16 is carried out
at the intermediate frequency.   This is more convenient than doing it at
the much higher transmitted frequency, and is permissible because, as
explained on page 570, the relative phase relations between two signals are

---

[1] The electrical signals are converted into mechanical vibrations, and vice versa,
at the terminals of the line by means of piezoelectric or magnetostriction devices, in
association with suitable modulation and demodulation equipment.   This terminal
equipment is indicated by x and y in Fig. 26-16.

not altered by the mixing process provided the same local oscillator signal is employed in both channels.

Practical MTI systems following the general pattern illustrated in Fig. 26-16 are capable of canceling echoes from fixed targets having amplitudes of the order of 40 db or greater above visibility. At the same time, it is possible to observe moving targets which are superimposed on fixed targets and which are weaker than the fixed targets by as much as 25 db.

26-9. Continuous-wave (CW) and Frequency-modulation Radar.[1] Although most radar systems employ energy radiated in the form of pulses, it is possible to detect moving targets by radiating unmodulated continuous-wave energy. The idea is illustrated in Fig. 26-17. Here

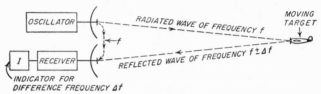

FIG. 26-17. Schematic diagram of a CW radar.

the energy reflected by the moving target is shifted in frequency in accordance with Eq. (26-8). At the receiver this reflected energy combines with energy of frequency f reaching the receiver directly from the transmitter to produce a difference frequency Δf that indicates the presence of the moving target, and simultaneously gives its radial velocity through Eq. (26-8).

Such a continuous-wave radar system provides a simple and accurate method of measuring the speed of automobiles, shells, guided missiles, etc. It is also able to detect the presence of moving objects such as people, motor vehicles, etc., and so is useful in military work as a sentry that functions in the dark, in bad weather, and in the presence of camouflage. A continuous-wave radar system is also able to detect the presence of aircraft and has the merit that unlike pulse radar, its ability to do so is not adversely affected by echoes from fixed objects. However, the practical usefulness of CW radar in this application is limited by the fact that multiple targets at a given bearing introduce confusion, and range discrimination can be added only at a severe cost in system complexity.

Frequency-modulation Radar (FM Altimeter). In frequency-modulation radar the schematic arrangement of equipment is the same as for CW radar as given in Fig. 26-17, except that the transmitted wave is frequency modulated in a manner such that the instantaneous frequency will on the average change many cycles per microsecond. The direct and reflected signals reaching the receiver will then have different instantaneous fre-

[1] An excellent discussion of this subject is to be found in "Radar System Engineering" (vol. 1, Radiation Laboratory Series), chap. 5, McGraw-Hill Book Company, Inc., New York, 1947.

quencies, because during the time it takes a wave to travel from the transmitter to the target and back to the receiver, the instantaneous frequency of the transmitter will have changed. The frequency difference between the two waves reaching the receiver hence indicates the time delay of the reflected wave, i.e., the distance to the reflecting point, which can be either a fixed or a moving target. With sinusoidal frequency modulation this difference frequency will vary during the modulation cycle; nevertheless its *average* value over a modulation cycle of the transmitter is still proportional to the distance from the transmitter to the target.[1,2]

The principal use of frequency-modulation radar is as an altimeter for enabling an aircraft to determine its height above the ground. Typical equipment developed for this purpose has a power of less than 1 watt, and operates at a carrier frequency of 440 Mc, with f_m = 120 cycles and Δf either 2 or 20 Mc. In such applications, the output of the receiver is applied to a frequency meter that develops a d-c output current proportional to the *average* frequency; this current is then passed through a d-c meter calibrated to read altitude in feet.

26-10. Radar Beacons. A radar beacon, sometimes called a *transponder*, includes a receiver, pulse transmitter, and antenna system. Beacon action is ordinarily initiated by the reception of a radar pulse. If this "interrogation" is in a form acceptable to the beacon (i.e., preselected frequency, pulse width, pulse-repetition frequency, etc.), the beacon replies by transmitting a pulse or a combination of pulses. The reply can be on the radar frequency, in which case the radar receiver handles both radar echoes and beacon replies simultaneously. Alternatively the reply may be on a widely different frequency, perhaps assigned to beacons alone; in this case a separate beacon receiver is required.

Since the beacon replies with full power even when the signal it receives is weak, long ranges are possible with only moderate beacon receiver sensitivities and beacon transmitter powers. The maximum range limitation is usually set by line-of-sight propagation to the horizon.

The response of a radar beacon can be so coded that it replies with a

---

[1] Radial motion of the target will also affect the difference frequency; however, in frequency-modulation radar the frequency differences produced by the frequency modulation are purposely made hundreds of times the frequency shift arising from target motion. As a result, the latter can be neglected.

[2] For sinusoidal frequency modulation it can be shown that if f_m denotes the modulating frequency and Δf the frequency deviation, then the target distance d and the *average* difference frequency at the receiver output have the relation

$$\left.\begin{array}{r}\text{Average frequency of}\\ \text{receiver output}\end{array}\right\} = \frac{8f_m\,\Delta f\,d}{c} \tag{26-9}$$

where c is the velocity of light.

distinctive combination of pulses that serve to identify the particular beacon. Beacons can also be arranged so that they will not respond to the usual radar signal, but will operate if, for example, the pulse length is increased, or if the pulse-repetition frequency is changed to some particular value.

Beacon Applications. Radar beacons have a variety of uses. They can be employed to extend the range of radar tracking by reinforcing the normal echo signal from a small target. Beacons are also used to identify landing fields, shore lines, mountains, ships, or other important locations as an aid to air or sea navigation. Coded beacon techniques can be used to add identification and other information to the beacon reply, and are used by the military to distinguish between friendly and unfriendly radars in so-called *IFF* systems (*i*dentification, *f*riend or *f*oe).

Radar beacons can be used by an aircraft to determine its position. Thus the response of a single beacon supplies information both on the distance and direction of the beacon with respect to the interrogating aircraft radar. The distance obtained in this way is very accurate, while the directional information has an accuracy determined by the beam width of the interrogating radar. Very precise location of position can be obtained by determining the distance from beacons located at two known positions.[1]

The ease with which distance may be measured by the radar beacon technique has led to the development of special *distance-measuring equipment* (commonly abbreviated DME) for use in commercial aircraft. This consists of a low-power radar transmitter with an omnidirectional transmitting antenna, which is used in conjunction with beacons located along air traffic lanes. Frequencies in the vicinity of 1000 Mc have been allocated for this application. Range at this frequency is limited to the line of sight. Accuracies of the order of 0.25 mile are possible up to maximum range. The range indication is typically presented on a clock-type meter driven by an automatic range-tracking circuit, such as discussed on page 1032. Choice of a particular beacon is made by transmitting the interrogating signal on the proper frequency and using the appropriate pulse-code combination.

26-11. Loran. In loran (short for *l*ong-*ra*nge *n*avigation), high-powered pulses are sent out from two transmitting stations. A constant known time difference is maintained between the instants of departure of these pulses, so that the time difference of arrival of the pulses from the two transmitters as observed at a receiving point becomes a measure of the difference in distance of this receiving point from the two transmitters. A particular difference in distance corresponds to a receiving point

---

[1] Equipment specially designed for determining position in this manner has been developed for military purposes and is referred to as *shoran* (for *sh*ort *ra*nge *n*avigation).

located somewhere on a particular hyperbola.[1] This is because a hyperbola is the locus of points that differ in distance from two fixed points by a constant amount. A station at a third location can now be used to determine a second hyperbola, the intersection of which with the first hyperbola gives the position of the receiver, as shown in Fig. 26-18.

Standard loran operates in the frequency range 1.8 to 2.0 Mc. The individual stations are typically 200 to 400 miles apart, and are synchronized by means of the ground wave, one station acting as the master and the others as the controlled or slave stations. Ranges of the order of 700 nautical miles are obtained over sea water for ground-wave propaga-

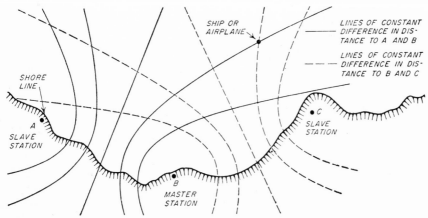

FIG. 26-18. Details pertaining to loran system.

tion, with an error of the order of 1 mile at this maximum range. With sky-wave propagation somewhat greater ranges can be obtained at night, but the error is appreciably greater in proportion to the distance.

A low-frequency version of loran operating at about 100 kc has also been developed. This increases the ground-wave range, and also gives more reliable sky-wave operation at higher latitudes since the lower frequencies are relatively unaffected by ionospheric storms and related disturbances that center about the polar regions.

Loran finds extensive use as a navigational aid for both ships and aircraft.

26-12. Radio Range. A navigation system that establishes a course through space along which aircraft can navigate from one location to another is termed a *radio range.*

Long-wave Radio Range. The long-wave or low-frequency radio range has been a standard airway navigational aid for many years. As ordinarily employed, it makes use of a special five-tower antenna system in association with two transmitters operating in the frequency range 200 to

---

[1] For this reason, navigation systems of this type are sometimes called hyperbolic navigation systems.

400 kc, and differing in frequency from each other by a convenient audio frequency that is commonly 1020 cycles.

The antenna system is shown in Fig. 26-19a. Here, tower pairs AA' and BB' each form a two-element antenna array, arranged to have figure-of-eight directional patterns in the horizontal plane, as shown in Fig. 26-19b. The unmodulated output of the first transmitter is switched back and forth between antenna systems AA' and BB' in a systematic manner, so that the radiation of one antenna pair corresponds to the code character for the letter A (– —), while the radiation from the other pair is the complementary code character corresponding to the letter N (— –).

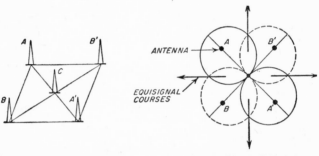

(a) ANTENNA ARRANGEMENT   (b) RADIATION PATTERNS IN HORIZONTAL PLANE

Fig. 26-19. Antenna system and lobe patterns for generating the equisignal courses of a long-wave radio range.

The central tower C continuously radiates energy from the second transmitter in an omnidirectional pattern.

When such signals are observed on an ordinary radio receiver, one hears an audio-frequency beat note of 1020 cycles, corresponding to the difference between the frequencies of the two transmitters. In the directions indicated by the arrows in Fig. 26-19b this note is of constant intensity because switching from AA' to BB' does not affect the strength of the signal received from the first transmitter. In contrast, any position either to the right or left of such an *equisignal* course will receive greater radiation from either AA' or BB' as the case may be, with the result that the code character A or N, respectively, will predominate.

The four courses of the radio range in Fig. 26-19 can be aligned to the actual routes used in air travel by such expedients as supplying unequal powers to the two antennas of a single pair, exciting one pair of antennas with less power than the other pair, etc.

The long-wave radio range has the disadvantage that it provides only a limited number of courses in preselected arbitrary directions; likewise, the aircraft has no simple means of determining which of the four possible courses it is following. In addition, the range signals are occasionally drowned out by precipitation static. The principal merit of the long-wave range is that since it operates at frequencies where the ground wave is strong, its signals reach aircraft flying well below the line of sight.

The Very High-frequency Omnirange.[1]   The very high-frequency (VHF) omnirange, or VOR (short for very high-frequency omnidirectional range), overcomes most of the limitations of the long-wave range, and has largely replaced it on the airways of the United States.

In the standard United States system the VOR transmitter operates in the frequency band 108 to 118 Mc, and is associated with an antenna system that at any instant has a directional pattern that is a limaçon, as

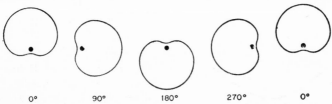

     0°   90°   180°   270°   0°

FIG. 26-20. Antenna patterns at successive 90° intervals of 30-cycle pattern rotation of VOR antenna.

shown in Fig. 26-20, which rotates at a rate of 30 revolutions per second.[2] The rotation of the unsymmetrical antenna pattern causes the signal at a particular receiving point to be amplitude modulated at a 30-cycle rate, with the phase of the 30-cycle modulation being determined by the bearing of the transmitting station relative to the receiver, as shown in Fig. 26-21.   A reference phase independent of bearing is supplied to the receiver by frequency modulating a 9960-cycle wave at a 30-cycle frequency in synchronism with the rotation of the antenna pattern, and then amplitude modulating this frequency-modulated subcarrier on the radiated carrier.[3]   The phase of this reference 30-cycle frequency modulation is such that it is in phase with the 30-cycle modulation due to antenna rotation when the receiving point is due north of the VOR.

The aircraft VOR receiver is typically a high-quality superheterodyne provided with means for recovering and separating the audio frequencies obtained from the complex signal radiated by the VOR.   The 30-cycle amplitude modulation due to pattern rotation is recovered directly.   The 9960-cycle subcarrier is selected by a suitable filter, and applied to a frequency-modulation detector to recover the 30-cycle reference signal. The phase difference between the two 30-cycle signals, which determines

[1] For a more detailed discussion, see H. C. Hurley, S. R. Anderson, and H. F. Keary, The Civil Aeronautics Administration VHF Omnirange, *Proc. IRE*, vol. 39, p. 1506, December, 1951.

[2] The rotation can be achieved in a variety of ways; the arrangement in the standard system is an electromechanical one that is described by Hurley, Anderson, and Keary, *op. cit.*

[3] The radiated carrier can be further amplitude modulated by voice or tone for communication or identification purposes.

the bearing from the VOR relative to north, is then determined by some form of phase meter, for example, the one shown in Fig. 25-27.

The carrier power of VOR stations ranges from 50 to 200 watts, and provides line-of-sight coverage for aircraft flying as high as 20,000 ft. Accuracy is typically within less than ±1.5°. Different VOR stations are identified by their frequencies, the same frequencies not being repeated for stations separated by less than about 500 miles.

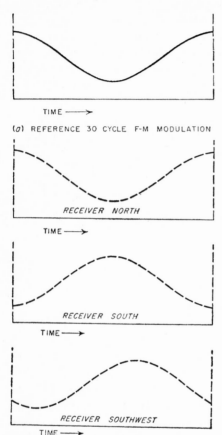

(a) REFERENCE 30 CYCLE F-M MODULATION

(b) AMPLITUDE MODULATION FROM PATTERN ROTATION FOR RECEIVER IN DIFFERENT DIRECTIONS FROM VOR

FIG. 26-21. Phase relations in VOR system, showing effects of azimuth on phase of received amplitude modulation produced by pattern rotation in Fig. 26-20.

Compared with the long-wave radio range, the VOR has the advantage that it supplies bearing information to all directions, and is therefore not restricted in the number of radial courses it provides. In addition, it operates in a frequency range where both natural static and precipitation static are largely absent. The chief disadvantage of the VOR is that since it operates in the very high-frequency range, the received signal will be dependable only under line-of-sight conditions. Hence the VOR does not serve aircraft that are flying very low unless they are close to the VOR transmitter.

26-13. Aircraft-landing Systems. The ability to land an aircraft under conditions of low or zero visibility and ceiling is one of the most important factors determining the reliability of air travel. Two electronic systems now in use provide at least a partial solution to this problem. These are the *ground-controlled approach* (GCA) and the *instrument landing system* (ILS). Although they can be used in emergencies to accomplish a true blind landing, both of these arrangements are fundamentally blind-approach systems, in which the final landing is normally carried out visually after the electronics system has brought the aircraft out of the overcast in the correct position to complete a landing.

Instrument Landing System.[1]   The essential elements of the instrument landing system, illustrated in Fig. 26-22, consist of a runway localizer, glide-path equipment, and marker beacons.

The runway localizer provides the lateral guidance that enables the airplane to approach the runway from the proper direction.   It consists of a special form of two-course horizontally polarized very high-frequency radio range, in which the equisignal course is defined by antenna patterns of the character shown in Fig. 26-23.   The runway localizer range differs from the long-wave radio range, however, in that the radiated wave con-

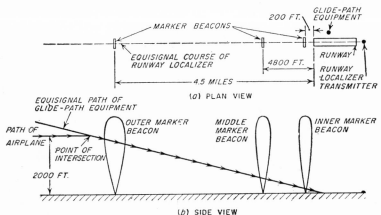

Fig. 26-22. Schematic diagram showing essential features of the instrument landing system.

sists of a single carrier wave which is simultaneously associated with two sets of continuously radiated amplitude-modulated sidebands representing modulation frequencies of 90 and 150 cycles, respectively.   The two patterns of Fig. 26-23 then correspond to the relative strengths of the 90- and 150-cycle sidebands, respectively, as a function of direction.   Thus the equisignal course directions are indicated by equality in the strengths of the two modulations, which are separated by suitable filters in the receiver output, separately rectified, and then applied with opposite polarity to a zero-center meter.   Equal tone amplitudes (i.e., the on-course condition) hence produce no meter deflection, while a preponderance of one or the other tone will deflect the pointer in a way that indicates the direction to be taken by the aircraft to "correct" its flight.

Marker beacons are used to indicate position along the localizer path as shown in Fig. 26-22.   They consist of low-power very high-frequency transmitters exciting antenna systems that produce fan-shaped beams so orientated that the broad dimension of the fan is at right angles to the

[1] For detailed information on this type of equipment, see Sidney Pickles, Army Air Forces Portable Instrument Landing System, *Elec. Commun.*, vol. 22, no. 4, p. 262, 1945.

localizer path.[1]   The different markers are identified by means of distinctive tone modulations, and by dot-and-dash keying.

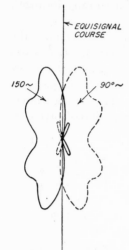

Fig. 26-23. Directional pattern used in runway localizer of instrument landing system.

The glide-path equipment, or "glide-path facility" as it is officially designated, provides an equisignal-path type of guidance in the vertical plane analogous to the guidance in azimuth provided by the equisignal path of the localizer. This result can be achieved by employing two horizontally polarized antennas one above the other at heights that give patterns such as those indicated by the solid and dotted lines in Fig. 26-24. In order to ensure that there will be only one equisignal glide path, the lower antenna is (1) so excited that its lobe maximum is larger than the maxima of the upper antenna, and (2) placed so close to the ground that its pattern in the vertical plane is broad and has a maximum that is at a relatively large angle above the horizon. Different sideband frequencies are radiated from these two antennas, in the same manner as in Fig. 26-23.

The proper glide angle is in the range 2 to 5°. Since the glide-path equipment must be placed to the side of the runway so that it will not present a hazard (see Fig. 26-22), the antenna patterns in the horizontal plane must be carefully controlled so that the glide path will have the correct slope along the azimuth course defined by the localizer. A frequency in the high end of the very high-frequency band such as 330 Mc is commonly used.

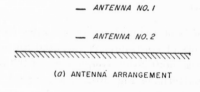

(a) ANTENNA ARRANGEMENT

The receiver for the glide path signals separates the two modulation tones, which are then rectified and applied with opposite polarity to a zero-center meter. This indication is normally combined with the localizer indication by housing the two meter movements in a common case

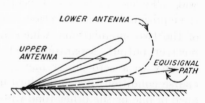

(b) ANTENNA PATTERNS

Fig. 26-24. Antenna patterns producing equisignal glide path for instrument landing system.

in such a manner that localizer and glide-path pointers are, respectively, vertical and horizontal when not deflected. Thus any flight corrections

[1] Thus the marker-beacon antenna patterns shown in Fig. 26-22 represent the thin dimension of the fan.

required to follow the prescribed courses in both vertical and horizontal planes can be obtained by a quick glance at one meter face.

It is extremely important that both the localizer and glide-path antenna systems of an ILS installation be completely free of even very weak spurious equisignal paths arising from side-lobe effects or reflections from hangars, etc. Otherwise there is always the possibility that an aircraft will sometime accidentally run across such a spurious equisignal path, assume it to be the desired path, and carry through with a landing that might well end in disaster. Therefore each ILS installation is always carefully checked for spurious courses by flight tests before it is released for general service.

The combination of runway localizer and glide-path equipment provides the pilot with sufficient information to approach the runway in the correct direction, and to bring the aircraft down to earth along a glide path that will provide a safe landing. The marker beacons keep the pilot informed as to his distance from the runway. When the final marker beacon is reached, the plane should be only a few feet above the ground, and unless there is absolutely zero visibility and zero ceiling the pilot should be able to carry out the remainder of the landing visually.

Ground-controlled Approach (*GCA*). The ground-controlled approach system employs two radars. The first is for general surveillance, and for control of the traffic pattern of aircraft in the vicinity of the landing field; it has a range of approximately 30 miles. The second is a high-resolution short-range set[1] that is used to conduct the actual landing. This second radar has two displays: one arranged to present elevation as a vertical displacement, and range as a horizontal displacement, while the other presents azimuth on a PPI indicator. An appropriate glide path is indicated on the first display in the form of an overlay, while the direction of approach that should be followed to make a proper landing is indicated by an overlay on the face of the second display.

An aircraft to be landed with this system is first brought into the proper position for starting its descent by means of the surveillance radar. A controller at the indicators of the high-resolution radar set then takes over, and from moment to moment issues instructions to the pilot as to what must be done to keep the plane on the desired glide path. Thus the aircraft is "talked" down a path corresponding to a proper landing, so that when it breaks through the overcast, it should be in the proper position to permit the landing to be completed visually. If for any reason the aircraft cannot be talked into the proper glide path, it is instructed to discontinue the landing and turn back for a second attempt.

The ground-controlled approach system has the advantage that no

---

[1] The GCA is a mobile equipment. For permanent installation, the two radars are designated the Airport Surveillance Radar (ASR) and the Precision Approach Radar (PAR).

equipment is required in the aircraft other than an ordinary radio receiver, and that the ground installation can be mobile. The disadvantages are that there are a number of human links in the chain, and that the chief responsibility for making a successful landing is taken away from the pilot.

26-14. Radio Direction Finding.[1] The fact that radio waves propagate away from the transmitter along a great-circle route makes radio direction finding a useful navigational aid. Thus a ship or aircraft can obtain its location by determining the directions of arrival of radio waves sent out by two transmitters at known locations. Similarly, it is possible to

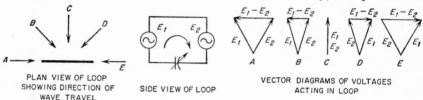

PLAN VIEW OF LOOP
SHOWING DIRECTION OF   SIDE VIEW OF LOOP
WAVE TRAVEL

VECTOR DIAGRAMS OF VOLTAGES
ACTING IN LOOP

Fig. 26-25. Vector diagrams showing how the voltages induced in the two sides of a loop by a passing radio wave combine to give a resultant voltage acting around the loop.

determine the location of a radio transmitter by simultaneously taking bearings on the radio waves at two receiving locations.

Loop Direction Finders. Direction finding at broadcast and lower frequencies is normally carried out with the aid of a loop antenna, utilizing the ground wave. The loop antenna is arranged with its plane vertical and is rotatable about a vertical axis. The directional pattern of such a loop, discussed on page 907, is characterized by sharp nulls in the horizontal plane in directions perpendicular to the plane of the loop.

The physical action involved in the loop receiving antenna can be understood with the aid of Fig. 26-25, which shows the effect that a vertically polarized wave produces on a vertical rectangular loop. When the plane of such a loop is perpendicular to the direction of travel of the wave, as shown by C in Fig. 26-25, the voltages induced in the two vertical sides are of equal magnitude and have the same phase. Being directed around the loop in opposite directions, however, these voltages cancel each other and result in zero loop current. On the other hand, when the plane of the loop is parallel to the direction of wave travel, as in cases A and E of Fig. 26-25, the wave reaches the two sides at slightly different times. This causes a phase difference that gives rise to a resultant voltage acting around the loop as shown.

The quantitative relationship between the voltage induced in such a

[1] An encyclopedic coverage of direction finding, as well as of various types of radio navigational systems, is given by R. Keen, "Wireless Direction Finding," 4th ed., Iliffe and Sons, Ltd., London, 1947; also see D. S. Bond, "Radio Direction Finders," McGraw-Hill Book Company, Inc., New York, 1944.

vertical loop by a vertically polarized wave and the field strength of the wave, assuming the loop is small compared with a wavelength, is[1]

$$\left.\begin{array}{l}\text{Resultant voltage } E_1 - E_2 \\ \text{acting around the loop}\end{array}\right\} = 2\pi\mathcal{E}N \left\{\dfrac{\begin{array}{c}\text{loop area}\\ \text{in sq m}\end{array}}{\lambda} \cos\theta \quad (26\text{-}10)$$

where $\mathcal{E}$ = strength of radio wave, volts per m
N = number of turns in loop
λ = wavelength of radio wave, m
θ = direction of travel of wave with respect to plane of loop

Equation (26-10) applies to loops of any shape, provided that the maximum dimension does not exceed about 0.15 wavelength.

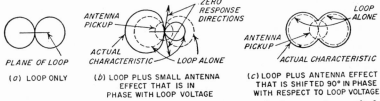

FIG. 26-26. Directional characteristics for vertically polarized wave of a vertical loop which possesses a small amount of vertical-antenna effect.

The direction in which a radio wave travels is determined by rotating the loop antenna until an associated radio receiver indicates zero response. The radio wave is then seen from Eq. (26-10) and Fig. 23-40 (or Fig. 26-26a) to be traveling in a direction that is perpendicular to the plane of the loop. It is customary to adjust the loop for minimum rather than maximum response because the minimum is sharper than the maximum.

The sense of the bearing can be determined by inducing in series with the loop a small voltage derived from a vertical antenna, but 90° out of phase with the voltage that the passing wave induces in the vertical antenna. The directional pattern of the combination of a loop and a vertical antenna arranged in this manner is shown in Fig. 26-26b, where one lobe of the loop pattern is seen to be enlarged while the other is reduced. This action is a consequence of the fact that, as shown in Fig. 26-25, the equivalent voltage acting around the loop as a result of loop

---

[1] This formula can be readily derived as follows for the case of a square loop with height l and width s. The voltage induced in each vertical side is $\mathcal{E}Nl$, while the phase difference between the voltages is $(2\pi s/\lambda) \cos\theta$ radians, since the wave must travel a distance $s \cos\theta$ to pass from one side to the other. Subtracting the voltages in the sides to get the resultant voltage acting around the loop (voltage $E_1 - E_2$ in Fig. 26-25) gives

$$E_1 - E_2 = 2\mathcal{E}Nl \sin\left(\frac{\pi s}{\lambda}\cos\theta\right)$$

When $(\pi s/\lambda)\cos\theta$ is small, this leads at once to Eq. (26-10).

pickup is 90° out of phase with the voltage induced in a vertical antenna located at the loop center, and has a polarity that depends upon the direction of arrival of the radio wave.   Hence, when the voltage induced in such a vertical is used to introduce a voltage into the loop with a 90° phase shift, this voltage will either add to or subtract from the loop pickup according to the direction from which the wave arrives.

The practical procedure for determining the direction of arrival of a radio wave[1] is accordingly first to adjust the loop for minimum response

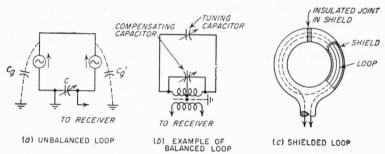

(a) UNBALANCED LOOP   (b) EXAMPLE OF   (c) SHIELDED LOOP
                              BALANCED LOOP

FIG. 26-27. Unbalanced, balanced, and shielded loop arrangements.

with the vertical antenna disconnected.   The loop is then rotated 90° and the vertical antenna is connected into the receiving system by means of a push button.   This causes the receiver output to decrease or increase, according to sense of the bearing.   By checking the arrangement against a wave of known sense at the time of installation, and thereafter always making the 90° rotation of the loop in the same direction, all uncertainty as to the sense of the bearing is removed.

Errors in Loop Bearing.   A loop antenna will give spurious bearings unless it is electrically balanced with respect to ground.   The reason for this can be understood by considering the action of the unbalanced loop of Fig. 26-27a.   When the loop is in the zero-signal position, the voltages induced in the vertical sides are of the same magnitude and phase, and, being directed around the loop in opposite directions, produce no resultant voltage around the loop circuit.   However, if one side of the tuning capacitor is grounded, the resulting dissymmetry causes capacitance currents to flow to ground through C_g' and tuning capacitance C, whereas the corresponding currents through C_g do not flow through C.   This behavior causes a signal to be delivered to the receiver even though the loop is in

---

[1] In direction-finding systems employed on aircraft, it is common practice to employ a motor-driven loop that automatically seeks a signal null.   The loop orientation is then displayed to the pilot by means of a pointer indicator.   Such *automatic direction finders* include a sense antenna as well as a loop, and employ a circuit arrangement such that there is no ambiguity in the sense of the bearing that is indicated.   For details of various apparatus arrangements that can be used to obtain this result, see Bond, *op. cit.*, chap. 6.

the position for zero response; the action is equivalent to coupling a small amount of vertical antenna pickup into the loop circuit with a 90° phase shift. Zero response then corresponds to a loop position other than perpendicular to the direction of travel of the radio wave, as is apparent from Fig. 26-26b. The presence of such antenna effect can be detected by rotating the loop 180° after the zero-response setting has been obtained. If there is no unbalance, the output will again be zero. However, if some antenna effect is present, a signal will appear upon reversal of the loop, because, as seen from Fig. 26-26b, the two zero directions are not exactly 180° with respect to each other in the presence of antenna effect.

Errors from unbalance can be minimized by using circuit arrangements that are symmetrical with respect to ground, such as shown in Fig. 26-27b. It is also helpful to enclose the loop in an electrostatic shield, such as a metal housing broken by an insulated bushing, as shown schematically in Fig. 26-27c. Such a shield ensures that all parts of the loop will always have the same capacitance to ground irrespective of the loop orientation in relation to neighboring objects. It is also customary in loop antennas to provide an adjustment such as shown in Fig. 26-27b to compensate for any residual unbalances that may be present. The proper adjustment of such a balancing arrangement is obtained experimentally by varying the compensation until a 180° rotation of the loop does not affect the null, as explained above.

The bearings obtained with a loop are influenced by the presence of wires and other conductors in the vicinity of the loop. This is because these metal objects abstract energy from the passing wave and then produce radiation and induction fields that induce spurious voltages in the nearby loop. It is accordingly always necessary experimentally to determine a correction curve for loop bearings unless the space near the loop is entirely free of metal objects, including those that are buried.

When the influence of nearby conductors is appreciable, it is commonly found that, in addition to the errors in bearing, there will be no position for which the loop output drops to zero. This arises when the spurious voltage induced in the loop contains a component 90° out of phase with the voltage acting around the loop. There is then no loop position for which the total voltage acting around the loop will be zero, and the minimum will be obscured, as in Fig. 26-26c.

A properly balanced, compensated, and calibrated loop antenna will give bearings accurate to better than 1° on radio signals from nearby transmitters operating at frequencies below 500 Kc. The error becomes greater the higher the frequency and the greater the transmission distance, as the result of "night effect." Greater errors may also occur when the bearings closely follow a coast line, or when the waves travel over mountainous land.

Night Effect. A loop antenna will give correct bearings only when no horizontally polarized downcoming waves are present. The reason for this is that such waves induce voltages in horizontal members of the loop that do not cancel out even when the plane of the loop is perpendicular to the bearing angle of the radio wave. The result is then either a false bearing, or an indistinct minimum, or both. This action is termed *night effect*, because at the frequencies ordinarily used in loop direction-finding work, i.e., below 2000 kc, the strength of the sky wave reflected to earth by the ionosphere, and hence the strength of the downcoming wave, are much greater at night than during the day. Night effect becomes more pronounced the higher the frequency and the greater the distance, because under these conditions the ratio of sky-wave strength to ground-wave strength is higher.

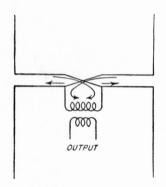

FIG. 26-28. Simple form of Adcock antenna.

Adcock Antenna. The errors in bearing caused by downcoming horizontally polarized sky waves can be eliminated by replacing the loop antenna with an Adcock antenna, which in its simplest form consists of two spaced vertical antennas, connected as shown in Fig. 26-28. The action of such an antenna, as far as vertically polarized waves are concerned, is identical with the loop. This is so because the resultant current in the output coil of the Adcock antenna is proportional to the vector difference of the voltages induced in the two vertical members, exactly as is the case with the loop. Horizontally polarized downcoming waves do not affect the Adcock antenna, however, since the voltages induced in the two horizontal members are the same in phase as well as magnitude and so cancel out as a result of the circuit arrangement.

By maintaining symmetry with respect to ground and by enclosure in an electrostatic shield, the Adcock antenna will give accurate bearings over distances up to 100 miles at frequencies in excess of 5000 kc under conditions where a loop antenna is utterly useless. The practical value of the Adcock antenna is, however, limited by the fact that the equivalent height is the same as that of a one-turn loop and so tends to be quite small. This causes the energy pickup to be quite small when loss resistances are taken into account.

Goniometer. When it is desirable to avoid the necessity of physically rotating a loop or Adcock antenna, as when their dimensions are very large, it is possible to obtain the effect of rotation by employing two such antennas at right angles to each other and combining their output in a goniometer, as illustrated in Fig. 26-29. The goniometer consists of two primary coils, one for each antenna, arranged at right angles to each other and coupled to a secondary as shown. The physical proportions are such that the mutual inductance between each primary coil and the secondary is proportional to the cosine of the angle that the axis of the secondary makes with the axis of the primary coil involved. For any position of the secondary, the relation between the secondary output and the direction from which the waves arrive will then be identical in charac-ter to the directional characteristics of a single loop or Adcock, provided that these individual antennas are small enough so that their response is given by Eq. (26-10). How-ever, the orientation of this pattern depends upon the position of the goniometer second-ary. Thus the rotation of the goniometer secondary is equivalent electrically to rotat-ing the loop (or Adcock) antenna.

Direction Finding by Lobe Switching. Instead of indicating bearings by means of a null, it is also possible to employ lobe switch-ing. The idea is illustrated in Fig. 26-30. Here the directional pattern of the receiving antenna is alternated between A and B by some switching device which simultaneously switches the receiver output to alternate cir-cuits. The receiver outputs corresponding to these two antenna positions are then com-pared, and the antenna orientation adjusted until the outputs are equal. The equisignal

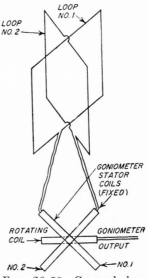

Fig. 26-29. Crossed loop antennas connected to goniometer.

direction thus obtained is very sharply defined,[1] and is a precise measure of the direction from which the received waves are arriving.

Lobe-switching systems of direction finding are particularly useful at the higher frequencies, where loop antennas are unsatisfactory both

Fig. 26-30. Receiving antenna patterns suitable for direction finding by the lobe-switching method.

because of polarization troubles arising from "night effect" and because of small capture area. It will be noted that the lobe-switching system permits the use of highly directional antennas, thus permitting large energy pickup at very high, ultra-high, and microwave frequencies, and simultaneously defines the equisignal direction with extreme sharpness.

---

[1] If minor lobes are present in the antenna pattern, there will, however, also be present spurious equisignal directions as indicated in Fig. 26-30.

PROBLEMS AND EXERCISES

26-1. Starting with Eq. (26-6), derive a relation giving d_{max} in terms of *average* power per pulse, receiver bandwidth, pulse-repetition frequency, signal-to-noise ratio, receiver noise figure, G_R, S, and λ. Assume that the intermediate-frequency bandwidth is 1.2/(pulse length).

26-2. Derive a formula giving the signal-to-noise ratio for a radar receiver, and involving the receiver noise figure and bandwidth and the available received power P_R, but not involving $P_{R_{min}}$.

26-3. Prove that the maximum range of a radar operating at a given frequency is proportional to the linear dimension of the antenna.

26-4. The difference in distance from a radar to two particular targets is 400 ft. Each target has a radial width of 100 ft. What is the longest pulse that will resolve these targets (i.e., the longest pulse that will not give overlapping echoes)?

26-5. Determine the maximum pulse-repetition frequency that can be used if it is desired to have a range of (a) 100 miles, and (b) 15 miles.

26-6. What is the total power reflected by the airplane in the example on page 1019?

26-7. If the radar described in the example on page 1019 is directed on a bomber having an effective area of 125 sq m and flying at an altitude of 30,000 ft over a point on the ground 50 miles distant from the radar, how many decibels above the receiver noise is the echo from the aircraft?

26-8. Discuss the advantages and disadvantages of employing wavelengths of less than 1 cm in radar, from the point of view of (a) propagation characteristics, (b) ability to obtain high angular resolution, and (c) range obtainable for given angular resolution, transmitter power, and minimum detectable received power.

26-9. In the example on page 1019, what is the minimum power that the radar transmitter could have and still detect the airplane at a range of 5 miles, assuming the receiver characteristics and antenna gain were unchanged?

26-10. In Figs. 26-2a and 26-3a, would it be permissible to replace diodes T_3 by a radio-frequency choke having a high parallel impedance at the magnetron frequency?

26-11. Calculate the fraction of the total energy stored in capacitance C of the hard-tube pulser of Fig. 26-3b that is delivered to the magnetron during a single pulse, when the anode voltage of the magnetron is maintained constant to within 1 per cent. Neglect the voltage drop in the resistance R_1.

26-12. Prove the csc θ law referred to in the first footnote on page 1022.

26-13. Derive a formula applicable to the scanning system in Fig. 26-5b which gives the maximum permissible horizontal scanning rate in revolutions per minute; in terms of the half-power beam width in the horizontal plane, and the rate at which the beam is rocked vertically in cycles per minute in the horizontal plane. Assume that every target in the area to be scanned is to be illuminated with pulses having a power that is at least half of the maximum beam power. From the results, discuss the relationship between horizontal scanning rate and wavelength when using an antenna of given physical size, rocked in the vertical plane at a fixed rate.

26-14. A rotating joint is introduced in a system employing a rectangular waveguide by tapering to a circular waveguide, as explained on page 1024. For such a system:

  a. Sketch the field configuration that will exist in the circular waveguide, assuming a TE_{10} mode in the rectangular guide.

  b. Calculate the minimum permissible radius of the circular waveguide in relationship to the dimension a (see Fig. 5-2) of the rectangular guide.

26-15. In a lobe-switching system, discuss the factors that determine the optimum angle through which the lobe should be switched. In particular, what are the disadvantages of making the switching angle too large, and too small?

26-16. A microwave radar operating at a wavelength of 10 cm is located close to the ground and employs a rotational parabola 2 m in diameter. What is the lowest vertical angle above the horizon for the center of the beam that will prevent the main lobe from being broken up into a fine lobe structure of the type shown in Fig. 26-8c? Assume uniform field intensity across the mouth of the parabola.

26-17. A radar antenna is located on the top of a 50-ft tower, and the main lobe is directed against the horizon. Calculate and plot as a function of frequency the angle above earth at which the first maximum of the radiation pattern occurs when taking into account the ground reflection. Cover the range 100 to 10,000 Mc, and discuss the significance of the results from the point of view of frequency affecting the ability to detect low-flying aircraft.

26-18. Sketch a possible TR box analogous to that of Fig. 26-9, but arranged for use with a waveguide instead of a coaxial transmission system.

26-19. Analyze the behavior of Fig. 26-10a when the ATR box and its associated transmission line cd are omitted. In particular, determine whether this modified arrangement will operate at all satisfactorily, and if so, what is the advantage gained by adding the ATR box and its associated line.

26-20. Determine the intermediate-frequency bandwidth B in terms of the pulse length τ, if B is such as to make the 10 to 90 per cent rise time one-half of the pulse length. How well do these results agree with the value of B given on page 1028?

26-21. Is it permissible to use a ratio detector in an automatic-frequency-control system, in place of the phase-shift discriminator of Fig. 26-11?

26-22. What would be the practical consequence of misaligning the automatic-frequency-control system of Fig. 26-11 so that the center frequency of the discriminator was several megacycles too high? Assume the receiver is designed for a pulse length of 0.5 μsec.

26-23. What would the type A display of Fig. 26-12 look like if no d-c restoration were employed?

26-24. In a PPI display, echoes from airplanes that are a considerable distance away appear as short segments of arcs that are concentric with the center of the pattern. What determines the radial thickness of these arcs and their length (expressed in terms of subtended angle)?

26-25. How would the PPI display of Fig. 26-13 be modified if the radar antenna possessed two pronounced minor lobes, one on each side of the major lobe?

26-26. In an automatic tracking system employing a conical scanning antenna, sketch the modulation envelope of the received pulses as a function of time for (a) correct azimuth but target above axis of antenna pattern, and (b) target to right and above the center axis of the antenna pattern as viewed from antenna. Assume that the lobe rotates in the direction shown in Fig. 26-7b, and that the reference for zero time corresponds to the center of the lobe passing point a in Fig. 26-7b.

26-27. An MTI radar operating at $\lambda = 10$ cm has a pulse-repetition frequency of 1000 cycles. Calculate the two lowest "blind" speeds.

26-28. Give the details of a subtracting circuit suitable for use in Fig. 26-17.

26-29. What adverse consequences would result in Fig. 26-16 if the limiter in the output of the intermediate-frequency amplifier were omitted?

26-30. Will the MTI system of Fig. 26-16 function correctly if the frequency of the stable local oscillator (stalo) drifts with time, provided that the drift in phase position in radians between the time the outgoing pulse leaves the transmitter and the time the echo from a particular target is received is *exactly* the same for successive pulses?

26-31. A CW radar operates at $\lambda = 3$ cm. What is the Doppler frequency produced (a) by an airplane flying at a speed of 200 miles per hr, and (b) by a man crawling at a rate of 1 in. per sec?

26-32. What determines the bandwidth that the receiver in a CW radar system must have?   Compare with the bandwidth required for a typical pulse-type radar, and from this explain why a CW radar will give satisfactory results with powers that are only a small fraction of the peak powers employed in pulse radar.

26-33. Derive Eq. (26-9).

26-34. Discuss the effect of time delay in a beacon transponder on the accuracy with which distance may be measured.   Could this error be eliminated by adjusting all beacons of the system so that they possessed a predetermined time delay?

26-35. A beacon is so coded that when interrogated it responds immediately with a short pulse followed by two additional short pulses delayed in time by 10 and 20 μsec, respectively.   What will the response of this beacon look like on a PPI display?

26-36. When using a loran navigation system, such as shown in Fig. 26-18, it is found that whereas the pulses radiated from the slave stations A and C lag 3000 μsec behind the pulses radiated from the master station, the pulses as received from A lag only 1900 μsec behind those from B while those received from C lag 4600 μsec behind those received from B.   From this data determine the difference in distances of the receiving point from A and B and from C and B, and indicate the general area on the map of Fig. 26-18 in which the receiving point is located.

26-37. Explain how, in a long-wave radio-range system, it would be possible for an airplane pilot, following a particular equisignal course, to determine whether he was approaching or receding from the radio-range transmitter.

26-38. Explain the experimentally observed fact that long-wave radio-range signals are more dependable over earth of good conductivity than over earth of poor conductivity.

26-39. Is there anything inherent in the very high-frequency omnidirectional range that limits the use of this principle to very high frequencies?

26-40. Show a detailed circuit arrangement that could be used in a VOR receiver for recovering and separating the various audio frequency components.

26-41. The ILS localizer antenna system is always horizontally polarized.   What considerations determine its optimum height above the earth?

26-42. It is observed experimentally that if a truck is parked close to either the localizer or the glide path antennas of an ILS installation, a distortion of the equisignal path will result, and in some cases false equisignal paths are created.   Explain.

26-43. Discuss the consequences of exciting the two antennas in Fig. 26-24 so that the maxima of the dotted and solid patterns have equal amplitudes.

26-44. Discuss the relative merits of GCA and ILS with respect to (a) the number and training level of operating personnel required, (b) the ease with which landing path can be modified in accordance with the characteristics of the individual plane and the wind conditions existing at the moment, and (c) the possibility of an accident resulting from failure to identify correctly on the surveillance radar the particular airplane that is coming in for a landing when many aircraft are in the vicinity.

26-45. a. Derive a formula for the effective height of a small loop antenna, starting from Eq. (26-10).

b. Calculate the effective height of a 20-turn rectangular loop in which the sides are 3 by 2 ft, when the wavelength is 1000 m, and the loop is oriented for maximum reception.

26-46. Discuss the factors that put a practical limit to how much the resultant voltage induced in a loop can be increased by increasing the number of turns.

26-47. Derive a formula for the directional characteristic of a system such as shown in Fig. 26-26b and c, when there is a certain amount of antenna effect associated with a loop.   In this derivation designate the magnitude of the antenna-effect voltage induced in the loop as E_A, and designate by E_B the magnitude of the resultant loop voltage acting around the loop when the loop response is maximum.   Derive formulas for cases (a) when E_A and E_B have the same (or opposite) phase, and (b) when they differ in phase by 90°.   Assume $E_A < E_B$.

26-48. Explain why the zero-signal position of a vertical loop is not affected by horizontally polarized waves traveling parallel to the ground, or by vertically polarized downcoming waves, but is affected by horizontally polarized downcoming waves.

26-49. The magnitude of the night-effect error in direction-finding work is greater when the waves travel over land than over sea.   Explain.

26-50. Show how the use of pulsed signals could entirely eliminate night-effect error as long as the ground wave at the receiver had usable intensity, even if much weaker than the sky wave.

26-51. Demonstrate by a mathematical analysis the correctness of the statement on page 1051 that rotation of the goniometer pickup coil is equivalent to rotating a single loop (or Adcock) antenna, as far as output as a function of wave direction is concerned.

26-52. *a.* Describe a lobe-switching system using loop antennas.

b. Will this lobe-switching arrangement be less susceptible to night-effect errors than a simple loop direction finder for the same frequency?   Why?

NAME INDEX

SUBJECT INDEX